Numbers

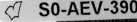
 Zero, 0 One, 1 Two, 2 Three, 3 Four, 4 Five, 5 Six, 6 Seven, 7 Eight, 8

 Nine, 9 Ten, 10 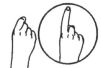 Eleven, 11 Twelve, 12 Thirteen, 13 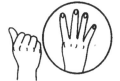 Fourteen, 14

 Fifteen, 15  Sixteen, 16  Seventeen, 17  Eighteen, 18

 Nineteen, 19  Twenty, 20 Twenty-one, 21 Twenty-two, 22

 Twenty-three, 23   Twenty-four, 24  Twenty-five, 25

 Twenty-six, 26  Twenty-seven, 27  Twenty-eight, 28  Twenty-nine, 29  Thirty, 30

RANDOM HOUSE WEBSTER'S

American Sign Language Dictionary

UNABRIDGED

ELAINE COSTELLO, PhD

RANDOM HOUSE REFERENCE

NEW YORK   TORONTO   LONDON   SYDNEY   AUCKLAND

Please address inquiries about electronic licensing of any products for use on a network, in software or on CD-ROM to the Subsidiary Rights Department, Random House Information Group, fax 212–572–6003.

This book is available at special discounts for bulk purchases for sales promotions or premiums. Special editions, including personalized covers, excerpts of existing books, and corporate imprints, can be created in large quantities for special needs. For more information, write to Random House, Inc., Special Markets/Premium Sales, 1745 Broadway, MD 6–2, New York, NY, 10019 or e-mail specialmarkets@randomhouse.com.

Visit the Random House Reference Web site: www.randomwords.com

Library of Congress Cataloging-in-Publication Data
Costello, Elaine.
    Random House American Sign Language dictionary / Elaine Costello
    p. cm.
    ISBN 978–0-375–42616–2
1. American Sign Language—Dictionaries.
HV2475.C66 1994 419/.03   95-105155

Printed in the United States of America

10 9 8 7 6 5 4 3

For Jennifer, Laura, Maria, and my special angel, Gabriel, who sustain me and for whom I feel enormous love.

Contents

Abbreviations Used in This Dictionary

adj.	adjective
adv.	adverb
conj.	conjunction
indef. article	indefinite article
interj.	interjection
n.	noun
n. phrase	noun phrase
pl. n.	plural noun
prep.	preposition
prep. phrase	prepositional phrase
pron.	pronoun
v.	verb
v. phrase	verb phrase

Acknowledgments

This dictionary is the result of considerable effort involving many people. The complex task of preparing a book of this nature involved suggestions and ideas from many sources. I appreciate all those individuals, particularly Deaf people, who throughout the years expanded not only my collection of signs but my knowledge, so that a volume of this magnitude, which would faithfully present signs from American Sign Language in printed form, could be produced.

Three Deaf artists skillfully reproduced the signs in this dictionary. The artists are to be highly commended for their ability to take live, three-dimensional models and movements and reduce them to flat drawings that realistically depict the performance of each sign. Most of these illustrations are the work of Lois Lenderman, whose talent I admire greatly and with whom I have worked in a successful team relationship for many years. Her outstanding skill in drawing signs at once detailed and uncluttered, as well as her organizational skills, contributed significantly to this book. Linda Tom and Paul Setzer used their considerable artistic talents to draw additional sign models for the book.

Special thanks are due to all of the special people at Random House, who persisted in a process that may at times have seemed endless. First my thanks go to LuAnn Walther, who initiated the project and gave me great support. And then I wish to express my highest regard to my soul-mate Enid Pearsons, editor and lexicographer, who worked with sensitivity and preciseness in making sure that the English citations reflected the linguistic properties of sign language as closely as possible. Her faithfulness and laborious attention in making this dictionary complete, accessible, and accurate are deeply appreciated. I also want to thank Laurie Calkhoven, Maria Padilla, Wanda Hernandez, and the many others who spent countless hours perfecting the entries. Likewise my thanks go to Jan Ewing of Ewing Systems for his fine design and production of the book.

More than 80 people served as models for the illustrations in this dictionary. Almost all of them are Deaf people who also served as sign informants and who helped ensure that accurate sign presentations were recorded together with appropriate English glosses. The input of the sign models during the modeling and proofing sessions was invaluable. With a heartfelt thank you, their names are listed below:

Mary Beth Aquilla	Julie Cantrell	Shannon Gilley-Fike
Jenifer Baker	Kristine Cantrell	Thomas Gilmore
James E. Ballard, Jr.	Donna Ann Carter	Elisabeth G. Godbey
Joseph K. Bath, II	Alan Cheifetz	Vickie Guerry
Gina Bearden	Hal Clapp	Larry Harrelson
Theresa M. Boney	Millie Colson	Debby Henderson
John S. Borum, Jr.	Linda G. Crosby	Leigh Higgins
Larry W. Bost	Thomas Coughlin	Ann Hyde
William L. Bowie	Elizabeth Dawson	Theodora Ing
Anna Maree Bright	D'Anne R. deBeck	Maureen Irons
Tracy Cross Broom	Robert J. deBeck	Gary M. Jackson
Deborah R. Bruce	Judith Dick	Vera Jackson
Clifford P. Bruffey	Deborah Dugger	Rayna A. Kozerka
Ruth A. Bruffey	Mary Beth Ethridge	Robert Lenderman
Dawn Adella Burke	Phil Gabany	Kelly McIntire Lee

Michael A. Lewis
Pamela D. Luhn
J. Charlie McKinney
Helen B. Maddox
Daisy Melby
Robert Millard
Gladys Z. Miller
Louise Gervais Miller
Mary Mirchandani
Ramesh H. Mirchandani
Corina S. Moore

Marcus R. Myers
Phyllis T. Petty
Barbara S. Porter
Frank W. Post
Katharine S. Preston
Pacifico Santiago
Anthony F. Schiffiano, III
Marlene Seaborn
Kathleen Russell Setzer
Kathleen A. Seymour
Martha F. Sigmon

Joel Silberstein
Darragh Simon
Jeffrey Simon
Ronald J. Siudzinski
Ruth Siudzinski
Melinda Smith
Dorothy Steffanic
Ronald Taylor
David W. Warner
Gladys Winstead

I respectfully acknowledge William C. Stokoe, Jr., who—many years ago, when I first began to study the structure of American Sign Language—generously shared his ideas and research, gave me license to study in his extensive personal library, and critically and lovingly reviewed my work. It is this great pioneer whose scientific investigation of the linguistics of American Sign Language set the standards for future research and whose work continues to inspire me.

To my family and friends I wish to extend sincere and loving gratitude for their patience and support through the many stages of preparation of this volume. Special thanks to my daughters Jennifer Ruane, Laura Grizzard, and Maria Costello, who helped by sharing in the work at various stages. Most especially, my thanks go to Gabriel J. Fontana for his moral support and unwavering enthusiasm during the long hours of work that it sometimes seemed would never come to fruition.

And finally, my deepest appreciation goes to Deaf people for their generosity in sharing their beautiful native language with me as I gathered signs and studied their use. I acknowledge that this volume is necessarily an incomplete documentation of the richness and dimensionality of American Sign Language, including its grammar, lexicon, and usage. I ask for tolerance from native users of American Sign Language and ask that they put this work into perspective by contemplating the wise words of Charlton Laird in his essay "Language and the Dictionary" in *Webster's New World Dictionary* (1970):

> A dictionary, at its best, is a mine of incomplete answers, but in a world where profound answers are vague and most answers are partly wrong, a collection of well-founded answers about man's most useful tool, language, can be a boon.

Thus this dictionary is merely a snapshot in time of the lexicon of a living language that is constantly changing. It cannot even begin to document the many regional variations or the new signs emerging throughout the country, for as quickly as signs are collected, new signs and new meanings come into existence. I encourage people to let me know of additional signs that may-be included in future editions.

It is my desire that this work may provide the impetus for more and more people to gain a greater knowledge of American Sign Language and, as a result, may foster greater communication and understanding.

Preface

WHY THIS DICTIONARY

This dictionary represents a commitment to American Sign Language, known familiarly as ASL—a commitment to its authenticity as a living, evolving, fully functional language and to its role as a cohesive force among the large numbers of its regular deaf and hearing users known as the Deaf community.

Numbering more than 16 million, people with hearing loss form the largest disability group in this country. Adding to this number are the 4,000 to 5,000 babies who are born deaf every year, countless numbers of people who suffer injuries or illnesses that cause deafness, and those whose hearing is deteriorating as a natural result of the aging process.

After a long and controversial history, American Sign Language has emerged in recent decades not only as the standard means of communication for deaf people and for their families, friends, and colleagues, but also as a symbol of cultural unity. Sign language is in fact the native language, i.e., the language learned before any other, of some 300,000 to 500,000 users in North America. At any given time there are roughly 100,000 people actively learning ASL, both in formal institutions of learning and in classes conducted by social agencies, churches, and other groups. It is estimated that 13 million people, including members of both the deaf and hearing populations, can now communicate to some extent in sign language. If we count all of them, this would make ASL the fourth most commonly used language in the United States.

American Sign Language is becoming even more important as federal law increasingly mandates acceptance and accommodation of deaf people in the workplace, the education system, and public accommodations. Most recently, the landmark Americans with Disabilities Act (ADA), which became law on July 26, 1990, has extended to deaf people what may be the world's strongest civil rights legislation for the disabled. Businesses and public entities of all kinds must now be prepared to communicate effectively—through sign language if necessary—with job applicants, employees, customers, and service users who are deaf.

Clearly, the need for reference materials in sign language is great. To help meet this need, the *Random House Webster's Unabridged American Sign Language Dictionary* offers a comprehensive and up-to-date treasury of signs, faithfully recording their formation and usage. In addition to the standard signs used in day-to-day communication throughout the nation, this book features signs from an expanding technical vocabulary and new signs for countries of the world reflecting the way natives of those countries refer to themselves. Thus, this dictionary is a broad reference work designed to be useful to a wide range of users, from novices seeking "survival signs" for rudimentary communication to sophisticated users already fluent in ASL and looking to enlarge their vocabularies. This compendium is drawn from an ever-growing collection, maintained by the author and continually augmented by contributions from members of the Deaf community.

This dictionary does not depend on simple one- or two-word translations to indicate the meanings of the signs. Since different meanings of the same English word may be represented by entirely different signs in ASL, the main entry for each sign in this book is expanded by one or more short definitions to clarify the exact meanings covered by the sign. The formation of each sign is depicted in relation to the entire upper torso, in illustrations prepared by Deaf artists using models from the Deaf community. And each illustration is accompanied by a complete verbal description of how the sign is made, and, often, by a "hint" to help the reader remember the sign.

As with any other living, growing language, American Sign Language can never be fully and finitely documented: it constantly evolves and changes; it has variant forms that shift according to individual, group, or regional usage; and most saliently, as a language transmitted not by writing but by gesture, it is in many respects a language to which no printed reference book can fully do justice. What this dictionary can do, however, is provide the fundamental building blocks of this language: a comprehensive vocabulary of ASL signs. Of course, language consists of more than just vocabulary; the words or signs are put into phrases and sentences according to grammatical principles, and they are used in a cultural context. These larger aspects of ASL are discussed in the "Introduction."

And so, welcome to the beautiful visual language called American Sign Language! Enjoy the physical character of each sign and the messages that its gestures convey. Through interaction with its community of users, add the nuances of the language that come so naturally to its native speakers. Above all, put aside inhibitions, physically and emotionally entering into the essential conceptual nature of the language.

Introduction

AMERICAN SIGN LANGUAGE IN CONTEXT

Deafness and the Deaf Community

What Is the Deaf Community?

A presentation of American Sign Language (ASL) would not be complete without some perspective on *deafness*, the medical condition, and *Deaf* people, the native users of ASL. The definition of deafness—the partial or total inability of a person to hear sound unaided—focuses purely on the medical aspects of deafness. However, Deaf people tend to find this view restrictive and limiting, in that it fails to describe the sociological implications of deafness. Terminology like "hearing impaired" is considered undesirable because it refers to a presumed disability.

ASL-users generally prefer to view deafness not as a handicap but as a shared experience underlying their sense of community. As a symbol of pride and identity within this community, the word *Deaf* is often capitalized when referring to this group. Thus, the Deaf community is a cultural group, sharing common experience, concerns, and language.

Since the primary binding force of this cultural group is its shared language, deaf people who do not use American Sign Language are not considered part of the Deaf community. Conversely, some hearing people do belong to the Deaf community, particularly the hearing children of Deaf parents, who acquire the language naturally from infancy.

The Deaf community now includes perhaps as many as half a million people throughout the United States. In part because of the presence of postsecondary schools with special programs to accommodate their needs, there are significant populations of Deaf people in the large metropolitan areas of the East and West Coasts; unlike members of many subcultures, however, they are not usually concentrated in particular neighborhoods. Deaf people are found in all walks of life, but because of common interests and ease of communication, they tend to gravitate toward one another and often travel great distances to take part in activities with other Deaf people.

In recent years, technical devices have opened up many aspects of the hearing world to deaf people. Captioned television provides real-time and prerecorded access to programming. Recent legislation requires that new televisions with 13-inch or larger screens have a built-in microchip to decode printed captions that are transmitted with the image.

Telecommunication devices for the deaf (TDDs), including teletypewriters (TTYs) and Text Telephones (TTs), have allowed deaf people to communicate by telephone since the early 70s, if each party has appropriate equipment. Relay services have been established to give deaf and hearing people easy telephone access to one another: the hearing person is connected by regular telephone to a human link, or "relay" who in turn is connected to the deaf person by a Text Telephone. Deaf people also use flashing lights to signal doorbells, a baby crying, and other sounds of everyday life. The improvements in and availability of desktop and portable computers have provided deaf people much improved access to information and needed services. More recently the development of an array of small wireless hand held devices has made communication services for deaf people even more accessible. These devices make audio, video, and text channels available. Additionally such technologies include easy and quick access to email and Internet services. One could apply the adage that each of the societal and technological advances noted here contribute to "leveling the playing field" for deaf and hard of hearing people. And yet, the primary, natural, and preferred means of communication among Deaf people themselves remains American Sign Language.

Types of Hearing Loss

The causes of hearing loss and deafness are diverse. The primary cause among children is heredity, although seldom is there a direct link from one generation to the next; in fact, about 90 percent of deaf children are born to hearing parents. Other causes of hearing loss include illness, medications, and trauma to the head. Many children have, over the years, become deaf from meningitis or, especially in the 1930s and 1940s, from drugs such as mycins used to treat meningitis. In the 1960s, a large number of infants were born deaf because their mothers had contracted rubella (German measles) during the first trimester of pregnancy. Prolonged exposure to noise in the workplace or to loud music can cause hearing loss. But among the 16,000,000 people with hearing loss, the most common cause is presbycusis, the loss of hearing through the aging process.

By and large, deafness is a permanent condition. For some whose hearing loss is a result of either a malformation or deterioration of the neural auditory structures in the cochlea of the inner ear, surgery has recently become an option. For more than two decades surgeons have been performing a type of microscopic surgery called a *cochlear implant* on select deaf patients. As technical knowledge and surgical skill has improved, the success of this type of surgery has increased. Many people, including young children, experience improved hearing following such surgery. The need remains however for these children, as well as others, to have access to a selection of assistive technical devices, special education strategies, and communication options.

Educational Impact of Hearing Loss

It is generally agreed that children pass through a critical period of time, usually before the age of four, that is optimal for language acquisition. During this period, they easily absorb the structure and vocabulary of their native language, and can even acquire several languages simultaneously. The impact of deafness on language development is felt most severely when a baby is born deaf and therefore does not have the opportunity to learn spoken language naturally by hearing and using it. Unless such prelingually deaf children are born into a household of sign language users, and so have natural access to a communicative system, they often spend their formative years with no language at all. They must then learn both sign language and English with great difficulty, much like learning a second language but without the advantages and understanding conferred by a native language. On the other hand, postlingually deaf people—those who acquired a spoken language prior to losing their hearing—have a much less difficult time in school, since they have a particular language on which to base their learning and, even more fundamentally, have a sense of the very concept of language as a means of communication. Similarly, those individuals who have only a slight hearing loss, commonly referred to as hard of hearing, also have an educational advantage over those who have a severe and profound hearing loss.

For all children with any degree of deafness, communication and educational choices must be made by others, usually by hearing parents and other caregivers who, more likely than not, have had no contact with Deaf people. Typically, a parent's desire to have the child function in a hearing society plays a large role in the choices that are made. On the surface, teaching the child to speak English and *speechread* (the older term was *lipread*) seems desirable. However, the paucity of language stimuli during the critical years of language acquisition takes its toll, and the barriers to learning spoken language are enormous. Spoken language must be learned by memorizing the physical movements of the speech organs that go together to make up a word or sound, and many of these movements are difficult or impossible to see, distinguish from one another, and replicate. Speechreading as the sole vehicle for reception is seldom successful, and a deaf child's own speech very often remains unintelligible. Therefore, language learning and usage on the part of these children is rarely up to age or grade level.

In the past, deaf children have generally attended segregated residential schools, going home only for holidays and summer vacations. Through the mandates of federal law, deaf children can now attend mainstream schools with their hearing peers and live at home with their families. Most often, however, deaf children remain in segregated classrooms in the public school, although, with the assistance of an educational interpreter, they sometimes attend integrated classes. Because deafness impacts language acquisition in such a dramatic way, deaf children usually begin special training very early.

Although the first teacher of the deaf in the United States was deaf himself, most such teachers today are hearing persons trained in special education. Because hearing parents and educators often have difficulty learning the structures of American Sign Language, and because English is the predominant language of the nation, various artificial sign systems, commonly referred to as Manually Coded English, have been invented for educational purposes. These systems, such as Seeing Exact English, Signed English, and Seeing Essential English, use the vocabulary of sign language (i.e., signs) to display English visually by putting the signs in English word order. In effect, they take the vocabulary of one language and use it with the grammar of another. Since there is not a one-to-one equivalency between ASL signs and English words, these artificial systems employ additional signs invented specifically to reflect English syntax.

Some of these systems are well-meaning and even useful, especially when they have as their goal assisting deaf children to learn English, thereby helping them to become literate in the language of the hearing world. On the other hand, some of their problematic features include real violations of the principles of sign formation in ASL. Signs are forced into configurations and combinations that obscure their conceptual references. Conventions relating to symmetry and point of contact are ignored. English (rather than ASL) word formation techniques are employed, such as the frequent use of prefixes and suffixes, commonly represented by an extra gesture added to the ASL sign. All of these violations occur because the underlying principle of all Manually Coded English is "one sign for one English word," regardless of consequent distortions of sign language structure. It should be noted that these invented systems are not natural languages, in that they do not have native users and do not have other requisites and characteristics of true languages. Over the years, however, some of the signs and structures of Manually Coded English have by a natural process been incorporated into American Sign Language.

The use of Manually Coded English systems to the virtual exclusion of ASL has been pervasive in the field of deaf education, to the dismay of concerned linguists and the Deaf community. However, as more Deaf teachers are being hired by schools, the use of American Sign Language is increasing in the classroom, becoming the preferred mode of communication through which English and all other subjects are taught.

The Nature of American Sign Language

Origins

As its name suggests, American Sign Language is a product of North America. Its use is heavily concentrated in the United States, but it has also spread to other parts of the world, notably Canada, Africa, and the Philippines. Note that there is no universal sign language, one single language of gesture used worldwide. Any country or other geographical region with a sizable population of deaf people is likely to have one or more sign languages of its own, and the list of such languages in current use is large indeed.

The first recorded instance of deafness in the United States occurred in the eighteenth century following the marriage of one Thomas Bolling to his first cousin, a common practice of that time. The Bollings had three deaf children and, subsequently, some deaf grandchildren. They founded a small school for the deaf, but it was short-lived. Other small schools were founded, but they, too, failed to survive.

The first permanent school for the deaf was founded in 1817 in Hartford, Connecticut, to serve the growing deaf population in the United States. Now known as the American School for the Deaf, this school was the first to receive state funding. It was established as a residential school to serve a wide geographical population. It is at this school that sign language was formally established in America through its first teacher, a deaf Frenchman named Laurent Clerc.

The fact that the Hartford school used sign language as its means of communication and instruction was somewhat a matter of happenstance. In 1815, a clergyman named Thomas Hopkins Gallaudet, challenged with teaching a neighbor's young deaf daughter, had traveled to Europe to learn techniques for educating deaf people. In order to learn the oral teaching techniques used in England, Gallaudet found that he would have been required to stay there as an apprentice for several years. Not willing to be away from home that long, and frustrated by philosophical differences he had with the teachers in England, Gallaudet went to a school in Paris where he was welcomed and initiated into the use of manual communication, or sign language, as a system for teaching deaf children. It was there that Gallaudet came to know Laurent Clerc, who agreed to return to the United States to teach sign language at the Hartford school. This accounts for the considerable component of French Sign Language in the fledgling system of gestures that has evolved into American Sign Language, and for the fact that, even today, American Sign language has much more in common with French Sign Language than it has with British Sign Language.

Is American Sign Language a Language?

All languages share common features. For example, they are composed of symbols that can be combined and manipulated in order to express meaning. The use of the symbols of any language is organized and governed by rules specific to that language. A *natural language* is a language with native users, who learn it from birth and for whom it fulfills the diverse communicative needs of daily life. No matter who else learns such a language as a second language, a natural language is defined by the existence of its native users.

Although American Sign Language may have originated as a consciously constructed system, adapted from the French system, the strong consensus among linguistics scholars is that ASL has long since become a natural language, exhibiting all of the defining features of language. For example, ASL has principles governing the formation of signs and their use in combination. Just like spoken languages, it has a native-speaker population for whom it provides all the needs of daily discourse. Indeed, infants who are exposed to ASL from birth go through all the sequential language-learning phases experienced by any group of babies learning their first language, including the hand-movement equivalents of the babbling engaged in by babies before they speak their first words. Moreover, American Sign Language is a growing language, one that continues to evolve as new terminology is developed and as older forms of signs are replaced with newer ones. And like living languages everywhere, ASL displays considerable regional variation, though with the growing cohesiveness of the Deaf community nationwide and increasing ease of travel, the degree of variation may be diminishing.

The Structure of American Sign Language

Phonology: The Parts of a Sign

In spoken language, *phonology* is the study of how basic units of sound combine to make up a language. Just as the words in a spoken language consist of specific combinations of individual sounds (the different vowel and consonant sounds), so each of the "words"—that is, the *signs*—in American Sign Language consists of a combination of gestures. These gestural components fall into certain clearly defined categories: the *location* in which a sign is produced in relation to the body; the *handshape(s)* used in the formation of the sign; the *movement* of the hands used in executing the sign; and finally, the *orientation* of the palms. These four units or features of signs have been used for descriptive purposes since linguists first began to describe and transcribe signs more than thirty years ago. More recently, linguists have added a fifth feature, *nonmanual* cues, which are discussed in more detail in a later section. Some linguists have also begun to describe sign formation in terms of a *movement* segment and a *hold* segment, the latter defined as a period of time during which the hands pause momentarily. Using all these phonological features of sign language, scholars have designed intricate notation systems to facilitate written transcription of American Sign Language for linguistic analysis and study.

Just as changing a single sound in a spoken word may change its meaning or render it meaningless, so changing any one of the phonological features of a sign may change the meaning of the sign or result in a meaningless gesture. The following examples show how changing one phonological feature can completely change the meaning of a sign:

Location

eleven
(in front of shoulder)

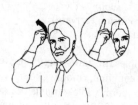

understand
(near the temple)

Handshape

principal
("P hand")

appointment
("A hand")

Movement

(I) lend
(forward toward another)

(I) borrow
(back toward the body)

Orientation

your
(palm facing forward)

my
(palm facing back)

As these examples illustrate, careful production of each phonological feature of a sign is essential to clear communication.

The number of permissible variants of location, handshape, movement, and orientation is limited. Fewer than fifty different handshapes exist, and there are at most twenty-five different locations relative to the body where signs can be made. These various handshapes and locations can be used in connection with some twelve movements and twelve orientations. However, every language operates according to phonetic rules that restrict the way its elements are combined. For example, although English has both *k*-sounds and *b*-sounds, the combination *kb* never occurs in a single syllable. In ASL, the possible ways in which the various phonological elements (handshape, movement, etc.) can be combined in signs are likewise limited; thus learning the patterns of signing is a more manageable task than it might at first appear.

Morphology: The Meaningful Units of a Sign

Morphology is the study of word formation, or how a language uses small meaningful linguistic units, called *morphemes*, to build larger ones. An example of such construction in English would be the addition of an *s*-sound (representing a morpheme for plurality) to *hat* (a morpheme representing a particular article of clothing) to form the word *hats*. The vocabulary of every language—including the signs of ASL—is built up of such units of meaning, which are classified as *free morphemes* if they can stand alone, like *hat* in English, and *bound morphemes* if, like the pluralizing morpheme in English, they exist only in combination with other morphemes. Of course, the morphemes in American Sign Language consist of signs or gestures rather than words or sounds.

One of the simplest examples of how words can be formed from smaller units is *compounding*, in which distinct words combine to form a single new word. This occurs very commonly both in English and in American Sign Language. Thus, just as English has compound words like *textbook* and *housewife*, so ASL often blends two or more signs together (usually with some streamlining of form) to create a new sign with its own particular meaning, as in *Jesus + book* (forming one of the signs for *Bible*) and *girl + hat + scarf* (forming the sign for *bonnet*).

Another close parallel between English and ASL morphology is in the formation of a particular kind of noun. Certain suffixes, such as *-er, -or,* and *-ist,* can be added to English words to mean "one who . . ."; e.g., *run + er = runner,* "a person who runs." American Sign Language has a morpheme, referred to in this dictionary as the person marker, which serves the same purpose:

person marker

As in English, this marker is added to the sign that expresses what the person does, as in the following examples:

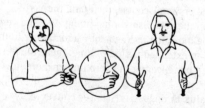

writer
(write + person marker)

teacher
(teach + person marker)

In general, however, morphological and grammatical processes in American Sign Language are quite different from those of English. ASL shares many such structures with a wide range of spoken languages other than English; in some structures, however, ASL utilizes three-dimensional space in ingenious ways that could be closely paralleled only in other sign languages. The fact that American Sign Language has evolved its own blend of linguistic features so distinct from English is one of the major reasons that linguists have come to regard ASL as an independent member of the world's family of mature natural languages.

The frequent lack of parallelism between English and American Sign Language may be illustrated by considering how ASL performs some of the functions served in English by affixation—the addition of prefixes and suffixes, either to convey grammatical information (like the pluralizing -s in *hats*) or to derive new words from old (like the -er in *runner*). Whereas affixation is an extremely common linguistic device in English, it is quite rare in American Sign Language, which employs a wide array of different techniques to achieve the same purposes.

For example, the concept of plurality in American Sign Language may be expressed in a number of ways. One of the most common is simply to sign a number or other quantifier before signing the noun. Thus, the term *cat* can be made plural by signing *three cat* or *horde cat* (i.e., a lot of cats). Note that, as in many of the world's spoken languages, there is no change in the form of the noun itself (the sign for *cat*) to make it plural: no bound morpheme analogous to the English -s is added to it. Another pluralizing strategy (and again, one that is also found in many other natural languages) is reduplication of the noun. For example, since the singular *cat* is formed with a single movement, the plural *cats* can be formed by repeating the sign one or more times. Not all nouns can be reduplicated, although many can. A third method of forming plurals is to reduplicate the verb, though often the result may be to express duration or repetitive action rather than plurality. An example of verb reduplication that works to show the plural of a noun is *wash-wash-wash dish,* which indicates that one has washed (many) dishes. In yet another technique, the signer can point or gesture toward several locations to indicate a plural noun, such as *there-there-there cat.* As can be seen, a wealth of strategies is available, and signers can be guided by both context and their own personal style.

English uses a complex system of suffixes, auxiliary verbs, and form changes to express various tenses and time aspects of verbs (-ed, -ing, -en, will, had, etc.). In American Sign Language, the basic concept of tense may be represented in relation to an imaginary time line running from behind the speaker's body (the past) through the torso and out away from the body (stretching into the future). Within this framework, specific signs can be used to signal that the action being discussed concerns the past (indicated by a wave back over the shoulder), the present (a sign directly in front of the body), or the future (a sign moving forward from the body). (See entries *ago, new,* and *will*[3,4,5] in this dictionary.) The more expansive the gesture along this line, the more remote the time being indicated ("long ago" vs. "recently," "in the distant future" vs. "soon"). In discourse, a signer generally establishes the time frame being discussed by using a time sign; the entire discourse, including the verbs, from that point until the time is changed, remains in the established time frame. When a verb refers to actions of a continuous nature (as might be indicated in English by adding -ing to the verb), or actions that take place repeatedly or over an extended period of time, these time-related aspects of the sentence can often be signified by repeating the verb one or more times, sometimes with certain additional movements.

In many cases, meanings communicated by an affix in English are simply conveyed by separate, independent signs in ASL, as with the English prefix *un-*:

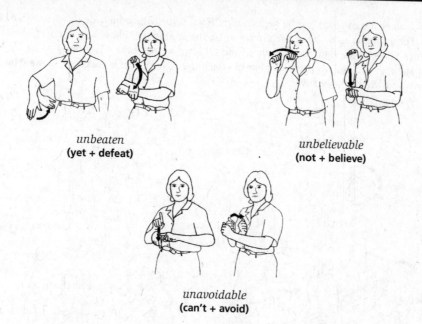

unbeaten
(yet + defeat)

unbelievable
(not + believe)

unavoidable
(can't + avoid)

Often, however, an English suffix such as *-ment, -tion,* or *-ful* simply has no corresponding structure in American Sign Language. For example, a single sign serves for both the verb *congratulate* and the noun *congratulations,* another sign for both the noun *beauty* and the adjective *beautiful.* At first glance this might seem confusing, but in fact it is no different from the use in English of a word like *spy* (which can be either a verb or a noun) or *red* (which can be either a noun or an adjective); in context, the particular grammatical function being served by the word is clear. Nevertheless, inventors of various types of Manually Coded English, in order to create a system that mimics the structure of English as closely as possible, have devised special gestures for such suffixes as these, some of which are now seen from time to time in ASL.

Functions of Space

We have just seen how American Sign Language uses space to divide time into past, present, and future. But space is used in ASL to convey a number of other grammatical features as well, including pronouns, location, and directionality.

English pronouns can be expressed in ASL with specific signs. Frequently, however, the functions performed by pronouns in English are carried out by establishing a location in space for the person or thing referred to and then *indexing*—that is, pointing, gesturing, or even just glancing—toward that location in lieu of signing the name of the referent. In this way, the location of a number of people or objects can be established around the speaker and pointed to throughout the conversation. The conversational partner is able to index these same locations to refer to the persons and objects under discussion.

Location can be directly incorporated into a sign through the use of space. Papers can be indicated as lying everywhere on one's desk or stacked neatly on the corner of the desk, as distinguished through appropriate spatial gestures. People can walk side by side, cars can pass one another, and a dog and cat can have a face-to-face encounter through clear spatial manipulation.

Yet another use of space can be seen in *directional verbs*, which indicate the direction of an action. For example, as we have already noted (in the section on "Phonology" above), the difference between the signs for *(I) borrow* and *(I) lend* is simply the direction in which the handshape moves. Similarly, the direction in which the sign for *give* is executed shows who is the giver and who is the receiver:

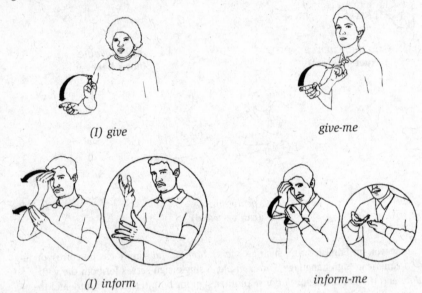

(I) give

give-me

(I) inform

inform-me

Classifiers

A noteworthy characteristic of American Sign Language is its use of *classifiers*—morphemes that can stand for any member of a large class of nouns and that have special grammatical functions. This is a linguistic feature common to many Asian, African, and Native American languages but largely unknown among English and European languages.

The classifiers in American Sign Language are handshapes (not complete signs) that serve to categorize the subject of a verb of motion or location. Such a handshape is a bound morpheme; that is, it is never used in isolation. Rather it combines with the movement, location, and orientation elements of the verb as a mandatory part of any complete expression describing the movement, existence, or location of a previously specified person or thing.

Classifiers often represent some common characteristic of a class of nouns, such as size, shape, or manner of use; their existence as part of the total verb sign makes it unnecessary for signers to keep making separate signs or gestures to refer to the subject, and so gives the language great fluidity and flexibility. In discussing a car, for example, the use of the classifier for "vehicle" permits the signer to show the car starting or stopping (either abruptly or smoothly), moving around, or even—through use of an additional classifier with the other hand—trailing along after, passing, crossing, or running into another vehicle, animal, or person.

Related Noun-Verb Pairs

We have already noted that in American Sign Language, as in English, it is common for nouns and verbs that are closely related in meaning to be similar or even identical in form. For example, in English, *fish* represents both the noun (a creature that swims) and the verb (to catch fish); similarly, a single sign in ASL represents both the verb *congratulate* and the noun *congratulations*. And in ASL, as in English, a noun like *teacher* is derived from the corresponding verb (*teach*) simply by the addition of a suffix: the person marker in ASL and *-er* in English.

Another important and very common derivational process in American Sign Language, however, has no parallel in English: verbs can often be turned into nouns by reduplication, that is, repeating the sign. Typically, the repeated movements of the noun are short, sharp, and quick, in contrast to the one long, smooth motion of the verb. This phonological difference—a change in the movement element of the sign, while the handshape and other elements remain unchanged—along with the reduplication, serves to distinguish the nouns from their related verbs in such pairs, as in the following examples:

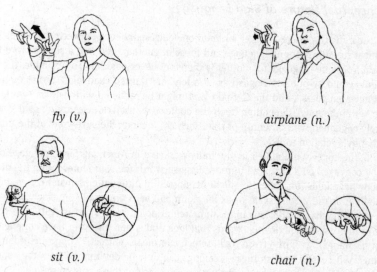

fly (v.) airplane (n.)

sit (v.) chair (n.)

The Role of Nonmanual Cues

Facial expression and body position play an important part in the grammar of American Sign Language. These nonmanual features are in many ways analogous to intonation in spoken language and punctuation in written language: they organize and add meaning to the words and signs. Such cues are not mere improvisations; rather, they are chosen from a repertoire of gestures that are understood among ASL users as serving specific purposes.

Perhaps the most basic role of nonmanual cues is in specifying sentence type. In English, intonation or punctuation can make the difference between a statement ("He's going.") and a question ("He's going?") or between a question ("Stop?") and a command ("Stop!"); in American Sign Language, this function is performed by nonmanual cues. Thus a simple declarative sentence typically carries a neutral facial expression, whereas a question may be signaled by raised eyebrows and a subtle tilt forward of the head or body, and an imperative sentence by a furrowed brow and intense eye contact.

Additional functions for nonmanual cues include intensification, modification of verbs, and indexing. For example, exaggerated movement combined with a furrowed brow and pinched lips can convert *beautiful* to *very beautiful*, while signing *ago* with a constrained movement accompanied by hunched shoulders and squinted eyes makes it *just a short while ago*. Adverbs of manner are often indicated nonmanually while signing a verb or sentence; thus, a slightly open mouth, head tilt, and the tongue pressed against the lower lip indicates that the activity described in the sentence was done carelessly or lackadaisically. And as noted above in the section on "Functions of Space," a glance or nod toward the location previously identified with a particular person or object under discussion suffices to refer to that person or object without the need for any sign at all.

Finally, it may be noted that some facial expressions seem to accompany certain signs quite naturally, without altering the meaning. The sign for *fatten*, for example, is usually accompanied by a puffing out of the cheeks, and *thick* is seldom signed without squinting the eyes as if to contemplate the measure of thickness being discussed.

Signs: The Vocabulary of American Sign Language

The Conceptual Nature of Sign Language

It is axiomatic that there is never a one-to-one correspondence between the words or grammatical structures of one language and those of another, and that a simple word-for-word translation from one language to another is therefore never possible. For example, the French *j'ai dix ans* would be put into English as "I'm ten" or "I'm ten years old," rather than the literal "I have ten years"; and the German *Welt* might be rendered variously as "world," "society," or "humanity" depending upon the context, while *Weltanschauung* could only be adequately explained with an entire phrase, such as "a comprehensive view of the universe and humanity's relation to it."

So, too, the concept embodied in any individual sign in American Sign Language often cannot be conveyed by a single all-purpose English word; the sign representing the dimming of automobile headlights, for example, might be glossed in different circumstances as the adjective *dim*, as the verb *darken*, or as the noun and verb *tint*. And conversely, a single English word may have variations in meaning requiring different signs in ASL. This is most obvious in the case of homonyms (words that look and sound alike but have completely different meanings), as in the word *right*, which can mean "correct," "opposite of left," or "a just claim." Whereas in English these meanings can only be determined from the context in which the word appears, ASL has a distinct sign for each of these concepts:

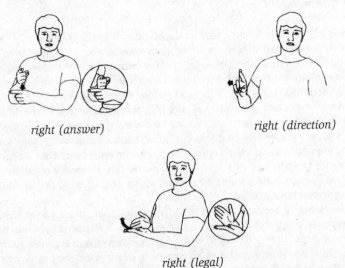

right (answer)   right (direction)

right (legal)

But the inevitable lack of symmetry between languages goes even further in American Sign Language. As a visual-gestural language, ASL exploits the medium of space and so is not confined to the strict linearity of spoken and written languages. In space, many things can be going on at the same time. We have seen, for example, how nonmanual cues can modify or intensify verbs and adjectives as they are being signed, how use of classifiers with both hands can describe simultaneously how two different subjects are situated or moving in relation to each other, how several different persons and objects under discussion can be assigned locations in space and then indexed nonmanually without interrupting the flow of signs. In these ways, concepts that require a whole sentence in English—"John drove recklessly"; "The car crashed into the tree"—may be conveyed in a single gesture in American Sign Language. Indeed, ASL even has a sign meaning "I love you"!

This incongruence between the structures of sign language and those of spoken language is perhaps what most stymies students learning ASL as a second language. Unlike the various systems of Manually Coded English, the signs of American Sign Language cannot be thought of as standing for English words and structures, and statements in one language cannot be mechanically rendered into the other word by word and sign by sign. Such a literal approach is tempting for the beginner but can lead to meaningless or ludicrous results even in situations where the structures of the two languages are sufficiently parallel to make such an attempt possible. (For example, the phrase *kick the bucket,* rendered literally into ASL, would not be understood to mean "die," because *kick the bucket* is an English idiom, not an idiom of American Sign Language.) Instead, in translating from English to ASL or vice versa, the interpreter must understand the concept being expressed in the first language and then render it in the words, signs, and structures appropriate to the second language.

Arbitrariness and Iconicity

All languages have both arbitrary and iconic forms. An arbitrary form of word or sign is simply an abstract symbol; an iconic word or sign is one that resembles or is somehow analogous to some aspect of the thing or activity it represents. In spoken language, iconicity takes the form of onomatopoeia, the imitative quality found in such words as *bang, boom, fizz, buzz,* and *hum.*

A widespread misconception about signing is that it is largely or entirely iconic—that it is simply the use of pantomime as a substitute for language. But in fact, just as with spoken languages, most signs in American Sign Language bear no evident relationship to the concepts they represent; either they were created as arbitrary symbols in the first place, or their original similarity to some referent has been lost through time.

It is nevertheless true that the medium in which sign language is expressed—space—invites a much broader range of iconicity than is possible in spoken languages. The wide variety of imaginative ways in which American Sign Language exploits this opportunity for iconism is one of the delights of the language, and certainly its most accessible feature for beginners. Here are a few examples:

What the Referent Looks Like

airplane
(shape of wings)

tree
(shape of trunk)

What the Referent Does

monkey
(scratches itself)

waiter
(serves)

What You Do with the Referent

car
(drive it)

flower
(smell it)

A Concrete Expression of an Abstract Referent

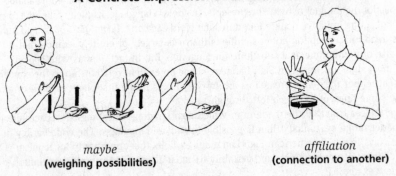

maybe
(weighing possibilities)

affiliation
(connection to another)

The actual history of many signs is not known; it is therefore often a matter of speculation whether a sign that appears to mime some aspect of its referent is truly iconic or whether the resemblance is coincidental. In either case, the similarity can be extremely helpful to the learner; accordingly, in this dictionary the apparent iconic significance of signs is pointed out in the form of "hints" as an aid in remembering the meaning of the sign and the way it is formed.

Fingerspelling

Just as English words can be spelled out orally by naming each of the letters in turn, they can also be *fingerspelled* in American Sign Language, using a set of 26 handshapes called the American Manual Alphabet, reproduced in full on the endpapers of this book. The sign languages of other countries have their own manual alphabets for the spoken and written languages prevailing in those countries.

A common misunderstanding about sign language is that it consists entirely of fingerspelling; and in fact some attempts have been made to educate deaf children solely through the medium of fingerspelling. But even for a hearing child who is a native English speaker, spelling is a skill that takes years to develop. And even for an adult with a complete mastery of English, spelling out every word in a speech or conversation would be extremely difficult and cumbersome, as can easily be appreciated simply by trying to carry on such a conversation for a few minutes, or by reciting out loud a familiar story or joke using letters instead of words. It is clear that fingerspelling is not a practical substitute for sign language.

Nevertheless, the manual alphabet is a useful tool in a number of situations. Fingerspelling provides an important bridge between English speakers who are just learning American Sign Language and signers competent in written English. Within the Deaf community the manual alphabet is commonly used to spell out proper names (in full or in shortened form), in borrowing English technical terms having no exact equivalent in sign, for emphasis (compare English "This means Y-O-U!"), and, often in a streamlined form, as the sign for certain concepts that can be expressed with very short English words or abbreviations such as *on*, *dog*, *TV*, or *a-p-t* for "apartment." Some words borrowed from English in full fingerspelled form have evolved into ASL signs employing only the first and last letters of the word, joined by a transitional movement. See, for example, the entry for *was*[2]. Linguists refer to words taken into one language from another as "loan words"; these signs from English are regarded as "loan signs."

In fingerspelling, the handshapes of the manual alphabet are typically formed comfortably in front of the right shoulder (left shoulder in the case of left-handed signers). But the handshapes found in the manual alphabet are also combined with a variety of movements, locations, and orientations to make other signs, the formation of which can then be described by reference to use of the "*A hand*," the "*P hand*," and the like. This is a particularly prominent feature of *initialized signs*, that is, signs intentionally designed to employ the handshape of a key letter of a corresponding English word, as in signs for days of the week.

Many initialized signs began as ASL signs with different handshapes, then were adapted for use in Manually Coded English by substitution of the handshape for the initial letter of a specific English word. For example, the traditional sign for *try* employs the S hand, but the same gesture may now be seen with the T hand (for *try*), the A hand (corresponding to English *attempt*), or the E hand (for English *effort*). Some variants of this sort may be in the process of being incorporated into ASL from Manually Coded English.

Numbers

Like letters, numbers are formed with one hand, held in front of the signing shoulder and moving smoothly from number to number. The chart on the endpapers shows handshapes for the numbers from *zero* to *twenty-nine*; the remaining two-digit numbers are made by signing the two digits in order (30 = *three-zero*, 31 = *three-one*, etc.), with a slight shift to the signer's right (to the left for left-handed signers) between the first and second digit. The numbers *eleven* through *fifteen* are always signed with the palm facing in toward the signer, and when counting discrete objects up to five the palm likewise faces in; in all other contexts and in all higher numbers the palm should face forward. In what is probably a carryover from French sign language, the concepts of *hundred*, *thousand*, and *million* are represented by the signed letters *C*, *M*, and *MM:*

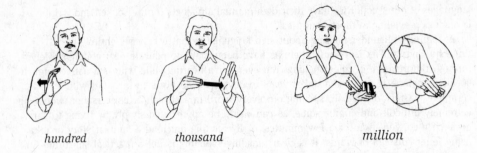

hundred   thousand   million

The general rule is to sign numbers just as they are spoken in English. Thus 15,671 is signed as *fifteen thousand six hundred seventy-one* (i.e., *fifteen M six C seven-one*), 3311 Russell Road as *thirty-three eleven,* the year 1994 as *nineteen ninety-four,* and the time 3:45 as *three forty-five.* The dollar amount $49.32 may be signed as *forty-nine dollars and thirty-two cents* (i.e., *four-nine dollar and three-two cent*).

Like the letter shapes, handshapes for the numbers up to *ten* are employed in many signs, which are described as using the *"3 hand,"* the *"5 hand,"* and so on. In most such signs these handshapes have no numerical significance. But indexing with a number hand can convey such concepts as *"you two," "we three,"* or *"the four of them"*; and number handshapes can be incorporated into certain other signs, such as those for *week* and *month,* specifically to add a numerical component:

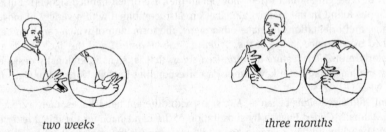

two weeks   three months

Ordinal numbers corresponding to the numerals *one* through *nine* are formed by the addition of a twisting motion, and these same signs can also be used to express dollar amounts up to nine:

first or one dollar

third or three dollars

Historical Change in Sign Language

Like all living languages, American Sign Language grows and changes continuously. In fact, within the twentieth century alone, some 20% of signs recorded early in the century have undergone formational changes. The process of linguistic change is never completely uniform and predictable; in ASL, for example, some signs formerly made with two hands have become one-handed at the same time that some signs made with one hand have become two-handed. However, linguists studying the history of American Sign Language have noted some general trends in the evolution of the language, including:

Centralization. Older signs involving wide-ranging gestures have generally become confined to a signing space within easy view of the listener—roughly from the waist to the top of the signer's head and extending about a foot out to each side of the signer. And even within this space there has been a tendency for one-handed signs to move toward the middle, where more detailed handshapes and movements can be utilized because they are near the center of the listener's visual field. At the same time, some signs that originally involved movement of both hands with different handshapes now employ the same handshape with both hands, again reducing the amount of detail that the listener must perceive through peripheral vision.

Assimilation. A compound sign, that is, one originally made up of two separate signs, may have changed in various ways to make the parts more alike, to smooth out the transition between them, and generally to make the compound simpler and more unified. For example, in the sign for *agree* (*think* + *same*), certain movements of the two component signs have disappeared and the resulting compound simply joins the final positions of both.

Abstraction. Perhaps the most pronounced overall trend has been for signs that originated through pantomime to lose their iconic quality. Unique handshapes and movements may evolve into more familiar, standard forms; broad gestures may become more restrained and centralized; facial expressions and other nonmanual features associated with the original mime may disappear, and dissimilar features may be smoothed out through assimilation, until the iconic origin of the sign is no longer apparent and the sign becomes purely an abstract manual symbol (see section on "Arbitrariness and Iconicity" on page xxiii). The cumulative effect of decades of such evolutionary changes has been to regularize sign formation and make the language more systematic.

In addition to changes in formation of existing signs, the vocabulary of American Sign Language, like that of every living language, is continually augmented through the appearance of new slang and idiom, borrowing of terminology of other languages, and creation of new signs to reflect the explosive growth of knowledge in all fields.

A notable example of change through the borrowing of signs from other languages may be seen in names of countries and nationalities. The traditional—and still most commonly used—American signs for other nationalities were often iconic. Although never intended to be insulting, some of these historical signs have been considered offensive by the people of the countries referred to; and within the Deaf community there is a growing awareness that their use is not in keeping with modern sensibilities and with the internationalization of community spirit among deaf people. In a recent trend, these traditional American signs are being replaced by the signs used by deaf people in each country to refer to themselves.

In Conclusion

There is something fascinating and compelling about sign language. People from the hearing world who have occasion to take it up find themselves caught up in this new way of communicating—intrigued by the shift from a language of sound to a language of gesture, delighted by the pantomimic quality of many of the signs. But as a person becomes more fluent in ASL, it is the more subtle aspects of the language, such as the charm of classifiers, the sophisticated use of space, and the role of nonmanual cues, that keep the learner challenged and stimulated. Although this dictionary provides a foundation in the vocabulary of American Sign Language, the nuances of the language can be absorbed only from its native speakers—Deaf people themselves. In the end, it is through interaction with the Deaf community that this marvelous language can be learned and made to come alive.

ELAINE R. COSTELLO

Guide

HOW TO USE THIS DICTIONARY

What This Dictionary Contains

Requirements of a Lexicon of Sign Language

Like any specialized dictionary, such as a legal or medical lexicon, this one contains a specialized vocabulary. Rather than embracing the full spectrum of terms—from common to technical—that one finds in a standard dictionary of English, this book focuses on the body of signs most responsive to the needs of users and students of American Sign Language (ASL).

This means that while a broad range of concepts is covered, many English words are not included. In some cases this is simply because their signs are used infrequently. Other terms do not have a corresponding sign; their meanings are communicated quite differently in sign language—e.g., as an integrated component of some other sign, as a nonmanual cue accompanying a sign, as a pointing (or "indexing") movement, or by fingerspelling.

Conversely, there are strings of words in this book—phrases and entire clauses—that would be out of place in a standard dictionary. Here they represent concepts expressed in one unified signing gesture in ASL. Examples are **sell to me, close the window, I love you, gain weight, not responsible,** and **Now I remember.**

Sources of Signs

For the most part, the signs in this dictionary are firmly established elements of American Sign Language. New signs for nations and nationalities (see "Introduction," p. xxvii), and some signs from systems of Manually Coded English (see "Introduction," p. xiii) such as the affixes **-ment** and **'s** (the possessive), have also been included, to reflect recent borrowings into ASL. In addition, the dictionary includes a few fingerspelled forms, like **ha ha,** which are considered to be ASL signs (see "Introduction," p. xxiv), although no attempt is made to give a comprehensive listing of these terms.

Although some regional variation is represented, the signs have been collected primarily from up and down the East Coast. The general tendency is for these signs to spread westward.

Usage Levels: The Social Appropriateness of Signs and Their English Translations

Like English and every other language, American Sign Language contains its share of terms that would be inappropriate in polite conversation. If a dictionary is to present an accurate picture of a language, it must include even vulgar or disparaging terms. In this dictionary, to prevent the novice from inadvertently insulting a conversational partner by unwittingly using a sign that would cause offense, cautionary notations or labels have been included for such signs. For example, a note at the end of the description of the sign might indicate that the sign is used disparagingly, or a cautionary usage label may be added to an English translation.

How to Find a Sign

Complete Entries

All entries—whether words or phrases, and whether common terms or proper nouns—are presented in large boldface type in a single alphabetical listing, following a strict letter-by-letter order that disregards spaces between words; e.g., **ever, everlasting, ever since.** An exception to this order is made for verb phrases, which are shown as a group; for example, **cast off** and **cast out** are grouped together after **cast,** and so precede **castle.**

Most signs can be found by looking them up under any of several English words or phrases, only one of which, however, will set forth a complete description of the sign. That complete entry usually includes one or more part-of-speech labels (*n.* for noun, *v.* for verb, etc.), and one or more short definitions and sample phrases or sentences, to make it clear exactly what meanings and uses of the main entry word are encompassed by the sign.

Additional words for concepts covered by that sign are often listed within the entry in small boldface type, although the list of words with equivalent or related meanings is by no means exhaustive. Typical examples may be seen at the entry for **confident,** which lists the related form **confidence** as another meaning for that sign, and the entry for **art,** which notes that the same sign is used for **drawing, illustration,** and **sketch.** Where appropriate, these additional words are given usage labels (e.g., informal, slang, vulgar, diminutive) to emphasize that the sign portrayed in that entry may be interpreted in those various ways depending upon the context and manner in which it is used, and that it should therefore be used with some caution.

Cross References

A cross-reference entry, at its own alphabetical listing, shows neither definitions nor signs. Such an entry simply sends the reader to one or more complete entries, where appropriate signs will be found. An example is the entry for **fatigue,** which states: See signs for TIRED, WEAK.

An additional type of cross reference, signaled by the instruction to "See also sign for . . . ," is found within complete entries. This occurs when the signs for two different words are interchangeable. For example, at **gold** there is an instruction to "See also sign for CALIFORNIA," while at **California** we find a matching instruction to "See also sign for GOLD." This means that either sign may be used to represent either concept.

Because the range of additional meanings for a sign may differ widely from the meanings of its closest English translation, the relationship between a main entry and its cross references—all of which share the same sign—is sometimes obscure to a person who is not fluent in ASL. Although a cross reference may be virtually synonymous with the main entry (**employment** refers to entries for **job** and **work**), it is more likely to be linked to the main entry in some more nebulous, conceptual fashion, without being directly substitutable for it in an English sentence (at **eat up** the reader is referred not only to the verb **consume,** but also to the noun **acid**). Occasionally, the dictionary suggests a connection, as at the entry for **alert**[2], which reads: "See sign for INSOMNIA. Shared idea of remaining awake."

Multiple Entries for the Same Word

Often there are two or more separate entries for the same word, each marked by a small identifying superscript number. These numerically sequenced groups of entries are of three sorts: (1) Entries that have different signs because they differ in meaning (**crown**[1] "royal headdress" and **crown**[2] "artificial covering for a tooth") or in part of speech (**end**[1] a noun and **end**[2] a verb). Each one is handled separately as a complete entry. (2) Separate entries for a word that, though not varying in meaning or part of speech, may be expressed by two or more interchangeable signs. In these cases each numbered entry includes a sign and sign description, but only the first entry in the group is defined; those that follow are simply labeled "alternate sign." See, for example, the two interchangeable signs at the entries **birth**[1] and **birth**[2]. (3) Entries with at least one of the terms in the group a cross reference to a different sign elsewhere in the alphabet—e.g., **ear**[1], a complete main entry, and **ear**[2], a cross reference to **hear.** Cross-reference entries are always shown last in any such sequence.

How to Make the Sign

Illustrations

Formation of the sign is illustrated at every complete entry and at every entry labeled "alternate sign," sometimes by a single picture but more often by a series of full-torso line drawings that take the reader step by step through a sequence of movements. Arrows show the direction in which the hands move, and the accompanying description gives any special instructions needed on how to execute the movement.

All the illustrations demonstrate how a right-handed signer would execute each sign as seen by the listener; the model's right hand is on the reader's left. A left-handed signer should transpose the illustrated hands as well as the arrows when forming the sign—in other words, treating the picture as if it were the reader's mirror image.

In a sequence of pictures, the illustrations in a circle focus on some significant portion of the movement, often the final position of the hands. The reader should execute the signs in the order shown, from left to right.

Descriptions

Each illustration is supplemented by a verbal description giving detailed instructions for making the sign. The formation of the sign is described in terms of the four component parts of a sign (see "Introduction," the section on "Phonology," p. xv). These four parts are: (1) handshape, (2) location in relation to the body, (3) movement of the hands, and (4) orientation of the palms. Occasionally a fifth component, a description of nonmanual cues, is added, as at the entry for **small**[2], where "while hunching the shoulders" signifies an intensification of the smallness, making the term mean "very small," "meager," or "tiny."

In cases where the rhythm of the movement is a critical component of the sign's formation, the description may state that, for example, the hands "move quickly" or the sign is "made with a deliberate movement." An indication is also given when a double movement is required or when a movement is to be "repeated"—that is, made two or more times.

Within the description, italicized terms such as *A hand* and *C hand* refer to handshapes shown in the chart of the Manual Alphabet on the endpapers. Terms such as *1 hand* or *10 hand* refer to handshapes for numbers on the endpapers. Other special handshapes, such as *bent hand, open hand,* and *flattened C hand,* are also shown on the endpapers.

Hints

Beginning most descriptions is a bracketed memory aid, or *hint.* These hints use a number of devices to help the reader understand the nature of the sign and better remember how it is made. For a *pantomimic sign,* for example, the reader may be instructed to perform an appropriate imitative action, as at **golf:** [Mime swinging a golf club]. The hint for an *iconic sign* might point out the sign's resemblance to the thing depicted or to some aspect of that thing, e.g.: [Shape of two stripes on a corporal's uniform] at **corporal** or, at **ear**[1]: [Location of an ear].

The hint for a *compound sign,* one formed by combining two or more independent signs, tells the reader which signs are to be combined, as at **omnipotent,** where the hint is: [**most + strong**]. Superscript numbers specify which of the multiple entries for the same word the reader may use in forming the compound. For example, the hint [**birth**[1,2] **+ day**] at **birthday**[1] reveals that one may form **birthday** using either of the two signs for **birth,** although both the description and the illustration refer only to **birth**[1]. The sign for a compound often involves some streamlining of the component signs, which is reflected in the description.

An *initialized sign* is formed with the handshape for the salient letter in the English term, taken from the American Manual Alphabet (see chart on the endpapers). The hint for **Dallas:** [Initialized sign], reminds the reader that the handshape required is the *D hand.* Similarly, the hint for **hum** is: [Initialized sign using **m** indicating the sound that is made when humming].

Fingerspelled signs use the Manual Alphabet to spell out a short word or abbreviation, as indicated by such hints as: [Fingerspell **n-o**] for **no** and, at **jack-o'-lantern:** [Abbreviation **j-o-l**].

Two special notations used in the hints need a word of explanation. First, an occasional reference is made to "the finger used for feelings." Signs made with the bent middle finger often refer to concepts of sensitivity, feelings, or personal contact; examples include the signs for **mercy, sick,** and **network.** Second, allusions to the "male" and "female" areas of the head relate to the fact that signs referring to men, such as **father** and **uncle,** begin at or are made near the forehead, whereas signs referring to women, such as **mother** and **aunt,** begin at or are made near the chin. A clear example of the importance of this distinction may be seen in the signs for **cousin,** made near the temple for a male cousin and near the lower cheek to refer to a female cousin.

a *indef. article.* Any or one (used to indicate one unspecified thing): *looking for a job.*

- [Initialized sign] Move the right *A hand,* palm facing forward, to the right in front of the right shoulder.

abandon[1] *v.* To give up with the intent of not reclaiming: *Abandon your wild ways.* Related form: **abandonment** *n.* Same sign used for: **cast off, desert, discard, drop, forsake.**

- [Natural gesture of casting something away] Beginning with both *S hands* in front of each side of the body, palms facing forward, quickly throw the hands downward and forward while opening into *5 hands,* ending with the palms facing down and fingers pointing forward.

abandon[2] *v.* (alternate sign) Related form: **abandonment** *n.* Same sign used for: **cast out, discard, evict, expel, get rid of, throw out.**

- [Natural gesture of giving up hope] Beginning with both *S hands* in front of the chest, both palms facing in and the right hand above the left hand, quickly throw the hands upward to the right while opening into *5 hands* in front of the right shoulder, ending with the palms facing back and the fingers pointing up.

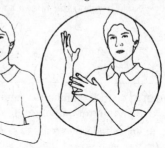

abandon[3] *v.* See sign for LEAVE[3].

abbreviate *v.* See sign for BRIEF[1].

abdomen[1] *n.* The mid-portion of the body, below the chest: *a pain in my abdomen.* Related form: **abdominal** *adj.* Same sign used for: **gut, stomach.**

- [Natural gesture indicating location] Pat the palm of the right *open hand,* fingers pointing left, against the body with a double movement.

abdomen[2] *n.* (alternate sign) Same sign used for:
gut, stomach.

- [Location of stomach] Tap the fingertips of the right *bent hand*, palm facing up, against the center of the body with a double movement.

abduct[1] *v.* To carry off by force: *to abduct a child.* Related form: **abduction** *n.* Same sign used for: **kidnap.**

- [Action of snatching something] Beginning with the right *5 hand,* palm facing in and fingers pointing left, under the palm of the left *open hand* held in front of the chest, palm facing down, pull the right hand quickly upward to the right, ending with the right *S hand* in front of the right shoulder, palm facing left.

abduct[2] *v.* (alternate sign) Same sign used for: **kidnap.**

- [Action of snatching something] Beginning with the right *V hand,* palm facing up, in front of the chest, pull the hand deliberately back toward the chest while bending the fingers in tightly.

abend *v.* To terminate (a computer program) early due to an error condition: *to abend the program.*

- [Initialized sign similar to sign for **end**[2]] Move the palm side of the right *A hand,* palm facing down, from the base to off the fingertips of the left *B hand,* palm facing in and fingers pointing right. Then move the right *open hand,* palm facing left and fingers pointing forward, straight down near the left fingertips.

abhor *v.* To hate very much: *to abhor violence.* Related form: **abhorrence** *n.* See also sign for DETEST[2]. Same sign used for: **avoid, loathe.**

- [Hands push away what is distasteful] Beginning with both *open hands* in front of each side of the chest, palms facing forward and fingers pointing up, push the hands forward while pulling the body back.

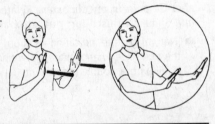

ability *n.* Same sign as for ABLE[1] but formed with a double movement. See also sign for SKILL.

ablaze *adj.* On fire: *The bush was ablaze.*

- [Flames leaping upward] Beginning with the palm sides of both *A hands* together in front of the body, bring the hands quickly upward while opening into *5 hands*, ending with the hands near each side of the head, palms facing back and fingers pointing up.

able[1] *adj.* Having the skill or power to do something: *able to swim.*

- [Initialized sign similar to sign for **can**[2]] Move both *A hands,* palms facing down, downward simultaneously in front of each side of the body.

able[2] *adj.* See sign for SKILL.

abnormal *adj.* Being not as it should be; not usual: *abnormal weather for this time of year.* Same sign used for: **unnatural.**

- [**not**[1] + **nation**] Bring the extended thumb of the right *10 hand* from under the chin, palm facing left, forward with a deliberate movement. Then move the right *N hand* in a circular movement and then downward, ending with the fingers of the right *N hand* on the back of the left *S hand,* both palms facing down.

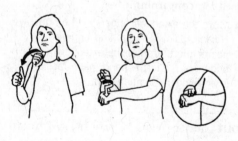

abolish[1] *v.* See sign for DAMAGE. Shared idea of destruction.

abolish[2] *v.* See signs for ELIMINATE[1,2], REMOVE[1].

abort *v.* See signs for ELIMINATE[1,2], REMOVE[1].

abortion[1] *n.* The removal or expulsion of a fetus prior to natural birth before it can survive: *to have an abortion before the fourth month of pregnancy.*

■ [Similar to sign for **remove**[1] but represents discarding the fetus] Bring the fingertips of the right *curved hand* against the body while changing into an *A hand.* Then thrust the right *A hand* forward while opening into a *5 hand,* ending with palm facing down and fingers pointing forward.

abortion[2] *n.* (alternate sign)

■ [Represents removing the fetus and throwing it away] Beginning with the palm of the left *open hand,* palm facing down, resting on the palm side of the right *A hand,* palm facing up, turn the right hand over and move it outward to the right while opening into a *5 hand* in front of the right side of the body, palm facing down.

about[1] *prep.* Having something to do with: *a movie about tropical rain forests.* Same sign used for: **concerning, regarding.**

■ [One thing moving about another] Move the extended right index finger, palm facing in and finger pointing left, around the fingertips of the left *flattened O hand,* palm facing in and fingers pointing right.

about[2] *prep.* (alternate sign) Same sign used for: **concerning.**

■ Move the extended fingers of the right *H hand,* palm facing in and fingers pointing left, around the extended fingers of the left *H hand,* palm facing in and fingers pointing right.

about[3] *adv.* See signs for ALMOST[1], APPROXIMATELY.

above[1] *prep.* **1.** At or to a higher place than: *The kite floated above the trees.* —*adv.* **2.** Higher or overhead: *the sky above.* See also sign for OVER[1].

■ [Indicates area above] Beginning with the right *open hand* on the back of the left *open hand,* both palms facing down, bring the right hand upward in an arc, ending several inches above the left hand.

above[2] *prep., adv.* (alternate sign) Same sign used for: **overhead.**

■ [Indicates area above] Move the right *5 hand*, palm facing down, in a flat circular movement above the right side of the head.

abrasive *adj.* See sign for ROUGH.

abrupt[1] *adj.* Sudden: *The road came to an abrupt end.* Related form: **abruptly** *adv.* Same sign used for: **accelerate, quick, quickly, snap.**

■ [A sudden action] Beginning with the right *D hand* in front of the right shoulder, palm facing in, snap the thumb off the middle finger as the hand moves downward.

abrupt[2] *adj.* (alternate sign) Same sign used for: **accelerate, quick, quickly.**

■ Beginning with the right *modified X hand*, flick the right thumb off the right bent index finger while moving the hand quickly downward from near the right side of the chest, palm facing left.

abscess *n.* A collection of pus around inflamed tissue: *an abscess in my gum.* Related form: **abscessed** *adj.*

■ [Location of swollen abscesses] Touch the fingertips of both *flattened O hands* against the right cheek. Then turn the hands slightly while opening the fingers and touch the fingertips of the *curved 5 hands* to the cheek again.

abscond *v.* See signs for DISAPPEAR[1], ESCAPE, ZOOM[1].

absent *adj.* **1.** Not present: *absent from class.* —*v.* **2.** To keep (oneself) away: *Do not absent yourself from class without a good excuse.* Related form: **absence** *n.* See also signs for DISAPPEAR[1], SKIP[1]. Same sign used for: **drain, extinct, gone, miss, missing.**

■ [Something seems to go down the drain] Pull the right *flattened C hand*, palm facing in, downward through the left *C hand*, palm facing right, while closing the fingers and thumb of the right hand together.

absent-minded *adj.* See sign for BLANK[1].

absolute *adj.* Free from restriction or doubt: *the absolute truth.* Related form: **absolutely** *adv.* Same sign used for: **certain, truly.**

- ■ [**true** + a gesture that is used when one gives a promise] Beginning with the thumb side of the extended right index finger against the chin, palm facing left and finger pointing up, move the hand forward while opening into a *5 hand,* palm facing forward and fingers pointing up.

absorb[1] *v.* To take in or suck up: *A sponge will absorb the liquid.* Related forms: **absorbent** *adj.*, **absorption** *n.* Same sign used for: **attract, magnetic.**

- ■ [The hands seem to be pulled together as if by a magnet] Beginning with both *5 hands* in front of each side of the body, palms facing down and fingers pointing forward, bring the hands back while forming *flattened O hands,* ending with the fingers of both hands touching in front of the chest.

absorb[2] *v.* See sign for RAPTURE.

abstain[1] *v.* To do without voluntarily: *to abstain from eating candy.* Related form: **abstinence** *n.* Same sign used for: **fast.**

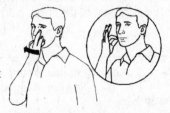

- ■ [Sealing the lips closed] Move the fingertips of the right *F hand,* palm facing in, from left to right across the mouth.

abstain[2] *v.* To voluntarily refrain from sexual relations: *to abstain from sex until after marriage.* Related form: **abstinence** *n.* Same sign used for: **celibate.**

- ■ [**sex** + **none**[1,2,3]] Touch the index-finger side of the right *X hand* first near the right eye and then to the right side of the chin. Then move both *flattened O hands* from in front of the chest outward to each side.

abstract *adj.* Not concrete: *abstract words like "beauty" and "justice."*

- ■ [Initialized sign similar to sign for **idea**] Move the right *A hand,* palm facing forward, from near the right side of the forehead upward and forward in a double arc.

absurd[1] *adj.* Ridiculous: *It is absurd to think that a broken mirror causes bad luck.* Same sign used for: **ridiculous.**

■ Beginning with the index finger of the right *4 hand* touching the right side of the forehead, palm facing left, bring the hand forward in a series of small arcs.

absurd[2] *adj.* See signs for SILLY[1,2].

abundant *adj.* See sign for PLENTIFUL.

abuse[1] *v.* See signs for BEAT[4], BEAT UP.

abuse[2] *n., v.* See sign for TORTURE.

accelerate *v.* See signs for ABRUPT[1,2].

accept *v.* To receive with favor: *to accept the invitation.* Related form: **acceptance** *n.* Same sign used for: **adopt, adoption, approval, approve.**

■ [Bring something that is accepted toward oneself] Beginning with both *5 hands* in front of the chest, fingers pointing forward, bring both hands back toward the chest while pulling the fingers and thumbs of each hand together.

access *n.* See signs for ANALYZE, ENTER.

access code See sign for PASSWORD.

accessible *adj.* Easily approached or entered: *The grocery store is accessible to customers in wheelchairs.*

■ [Represents movement of entering repeatedly] Move the back of the right *open hand* forward in a downward arc under the palm of the left *open hand*, both palms facing down, with a repeated movement.

accident[1] *n.* An unintended, damaging incident involving vehicles: *injured in a car accident.* Same sign used for: **collide, collision, crash.**

■ [Two things collide with each other] Move both *5 hands* toward each other from in front of each side of the chest, palms facing in and fingers pointing toward each other, while changing into *A hands*, ending with the knuckles of both *A hands* touching in front of the chest.

accident

accident[2] *n.* See signs for HAPPEN, MISTAKE[1].

accidentally *adv.* By chance: *spilled the milk accidentally.*
Alternate form: **by accident.** Related form: **accidental**
adj. Same sign used for: **amiss, by mistake.**

- [Similar to sign for **mistake**[1] except made with a twisting
movement] Twist the knuckles of the right *Y hand*, palm
facing in, on the chin from right to left.

acclaim *v.* See sign for ANNOUNCE.

acclamation *n.* See sign for PRAISE.

accompany[1] *v.* To go along with: *I'll accompany you to the store.* Related form:
accompaniment *n.*

- [**we**[3] + **go with**] Move the right
V hand, palm facing back, from
side to side with a repeated
movement near the shoulder by
bending the wrist. Then, with the
palm sides of both *A hands*
together, move the hands straight
forward in front of the chest.

accompany[2] *v.* (alternate sign)
Related form: **accompaniment** *n.*

- [**both** + **go with**] Bring the right
V hand, palm facing in,
downward in front of the chest
through the left *C hand*, palm
facing in and fingers pointing
right, closing the left hand around
the right fingers as they pass through, pulling them together. Then, with the palm side
of both *A hands* together in front of the chest, move the hands straight forward.

accompany[3] *v.* See sign for GO WITH.

accomplish *v.* See sign for SUCCESSFUL. Related form: **accomplishment** *n.*

according to[1] In agreement with: *Modify your
exercise routine according to your goals.* Same sign
used for: **proportion, ratio.**

- [Initialized sign similar to sign for **proportion**
showing two similar things] Move both *P hands*,
palms facing down, from in front of the left side
of the body to the right side of the body by
bringing the hands upward simultaneously in
large arcs.

according to² See sign for AS¹.

accordion *n.* A portable musical instrument with a keyboard and bellows: *play the accordion in a band.*

- [Mime movement of an accordion] Beginning with both *S hands* in front of each side of the chest, palms facing each other, pull the hands apart and upward, including the arms and elbows, with a repeated movement.

account *n.* **1.** A list of monetary transactions: *The bookkeeper kept an account of business expenses and income.* **2.** A business relationship involving an exchange of money, particularly on credit, for goods or services: *Charge this to my account.* Related form: **accounting** *n.*

- [Similar to sign for **count** except formed with a double movement] Move the fingertips of the right *F hand,* palm facing left, across the left palm, palm facing right, from the heel to the fingertips with a double movement.

accountant *n.* A person who is responsible for keeping or auditing financial records: *My accountant prepares my taxes for me.*

- [**account** + **person marker**] Move the fingertips of the right *F hand,* palm facing left, across the left palm, palm facing right, from the heel to the fingertips with a double movement. Then move both *open hands,* palms facing each other, down along the sides of the body.

accredit *v.* To give official acceptance to: *to accredit a college.* Related forms: **accreditation** *n.,* **accredited** *adj.* Same sign used for: **adopt, certify.**

- [Stamping something with a seal] Beginning with the right *S hand* in front of the right shoulder, palm facing down, twist the wrist to hit the upturned left *open hand* with the little-finger side of the right hand with a deliberate movement.

accrue *v.* See signs for ADD¹,².

accumulate

accumulate[1] *v.* To collect or pile up in increasing quantities: *Dust accumulated on the furniture.* Related form: **accumulation** *n.* Same sign used for: **amass.**

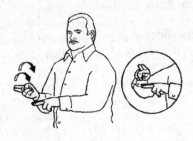

- [More and more of something being piled up on top of other things] Beginning with the right *U hand,* palm facing left, beside the left *U hand,* palm facing down, flip the right hand over with a double movement, tapping the right fingers across the left fingers each time.

accumulate[2] *v.* See signs for ADD[1], COLLECT[1,2].

accurate *adj.* See signs for PERFECT, PRECISE, RIGHT[3].

accusation *n.* See sign for FAULT[2].

accuse[1] *v.* To make an allegation against: *The landlord accused the tenant of not paying the rent on time.* Related form: **accusation** *n.* Same sign used for: **allegation, charge.**

- [Similar to sign for **blame**[1] except formed with a double movement] Push the little-finger side of the right *A hand,* palm facing left, forward with a double movement across the back of the left *A hand,* palm facing down.

accuse[2] *v.* See sign for BLAME[1].

accustomed to[1] In the habit of: *accustomed to coming home at 5 o'clock.*

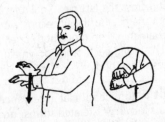

- [Similar to sign for **custom**] Beginning with the heel of the right *curved 5 hand* on the back of the left *open hand* in front of the chest, both palms facing down, bring the hands downward while closing into *S hands.*

accustomed to[2] (alternate sign)

- [Initialized sign] Beginning with the heel of the right *A hand,* palm facing forward, on the back of the left *A hand,* palm facing down, in front of the chest, bring the hands downward with a deliberate movement.

accustomed to[3] See sign for HABIT.

ache *v.*, *n.* See signs for HURT[1], PAIN[1,2].

achieve[1] *v.* To succeed in doing or getting by one's own efforts: *achieve one's purpose; achieve fame.* Related form: **achievement** *n.* See also sign for SUCCESSFUL. Same sign used for: **chalk up, success.**

- [An accumulation of something] Beginning with the left *bent hand* over the right *bent hand* in front of the chest, both palms facing down, move the hands with an alternating movement over each other to in front of the face.

achieve[2] *v.* See sign for PROCEDURE. Shared idea of accomplishing something.

acid *n.* See sign for CANCER. Shared idea of being capable of devouring a substance.

acquaint *v.* See sign for ASSOCIATE.

acquaintance *n.* A person you know, but usually not a close friend: *lunch with an old acquaintance.*

- Beginning with both *V hands* in front of the face, palms facing each other and fingers angled up, bring the hands in downward arcs to in front of each side of the body, ending with the palms facing down.

acquire *v.* See signs for GET, LEARN, TAKE[2].

acquit *v.* See sign for DISMISS.

acreage *n.* See sign for LAND[1].

acrobat *n.* A person who performs stunts by turning handsprings or performing other bodily feats: *an acrobat on a trapeze.*

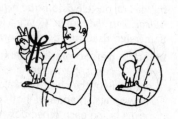

- [The movement of an acrobat] Move the right *V hand*, palm facing down, in a twisting circular movement, ending with the fingers of the right *V hand* pointing down on the upturned left *open hand* in front of the body.

across *prep.* **1.** From one side to another of: *to walk across the street.* **2.** On the other side of: *The mailbox is across the street.* —*adv.* **3.** From one side to another: *How can we get across?* Same sign used for: **after, afterward, cross, over.**

- [Movement across another thing] Push the little-finger side of the right *open hand*, palm facing left, across the back of the left *open hand*, palm facing down.

act¹ *v.* **1.** To perform an action: *to act quickly in an emergency.* —*n.* **2.** Anything done or being done: *an act of mercy.* Related forms: **action, activity** *n.* Same sign used for: **deed.**

■ [The hands seem to be actively doing something] Move both *C hands,* palms facing down, simultaneously back and forth in front of the body with a swinging movement.

act² *v.* To play a part: *to act in the school play.* Same sign used for: **drama, perform, play, show, theater.**

[Initialized sign] Bring the thumbs of both *A hands,* palms facing each other, down each side of the chest with alternating circular movements.

active¹ *adj.* Doing things or moving much of the time: *She is an active child.* Related forms: **action,** *n.,* **activity,** *n.* Same sign used for: **deed, labor, work.**

■ [The hands seem to be actively doing something] Move both *C hands,* palms facing down, back and forth in front of the body in opposite directions with a double swinging movement.

active² *adj.* See sign for AMBITIOUS¹.

actor¹ *n.* A person who performs in plays or movies or on television: *the actor who played Macbeth in the movie.* Related form: **actress** *n.* Same sign used for: **performer.**

■ [act² + person marker] Bring the thumbs of both *A hands,* palms facing each other, down each side of the chest with alternating circular movements. Then move both *open hands,* palms facing each other, down along the sides of the body.

actor² *n.* (alternate sign) Same sign used for: **performer.**

■ [act¹ + person marker] Move both *C hands,* palms facing down, simultaneously back and forth in front of the body with a swinging movement. Then move both *open hands,* palms facing each other, downward along each side of the body.

actual *adj.* See signs for REAL, TRUE.

actually[1] *adv.* In fact: *What actually happened?*

■ [**true** + **l-y**] Beginning with the right index finger pointing up near the mouth, palm facing left, bring the finger forward in a large arc while changing into an *L hand* and then a *Y hand*.

actually[2] *adv.* See signs for REALLY, TRUE.

adapt *v.* See signs for CHANGE[1], CONVERT[2].

add[1] or **add up** *v.* or *v. phrase.* To combine so as to find the sum: *to add 2 and 2; to add up the numbers.* Related forms: **addition** *n.*, **additional** *adj.* See also sign for PLUS. Same sign used for: **accrue, accumulate, amount, sum, total.**

■ [Hands bring two quantities together] Beginning with the right *5 hand* from above the right shoulder, palm facing down, and the left *5 hand* near the left side of the waist, palm facing up, bring the hands toward each other while changing into *flattened O hands,* ending with the fingertips touching each other in front of the chest.

add[2] or **add to** *v.* or *v. phrase.* To put together with something else: *to add sugar to tea.* Related forms: **addition** *n.*, **additional** *adj.* See also sign for PLUS. Same sign used for: **accrue, amend, bonus, extra, supplement.**

■ [One hand brings an additional amount to the other hand] Swing the right *5 hand* upward from the right side of the body while changing into a *flattened O hand,* ending with the right index finger touching the little-finger side of the left *flattened O hand* in front of the chest, both palms facing in.

addict *n.* A person who is physiologically or psychologically dependent on an addictive substance, such as alcohol or a narcotic: *The addict committed himself for treatment.*

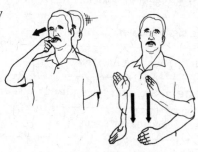

■ [**addicted**[1] + **person marker**] Hook the index finger of the right *X hand* in the right corner of the mouth and pull outward a short distance. Then move both *open hands,* palms facing each other, downward along the sides of the body.

addicted[1] *adj.* Being a slave to a habit: *addicted to drugs.* Related form: **addiction** *n.* Same sign used for: **hooked.**

■ [Gesture indicates that one is "hooked"] With the index finger of the right *X hand* hooked in the right corner of the mouth, pull the mouth outward to the right.

addicted[2] *adj.* (alternate sign)

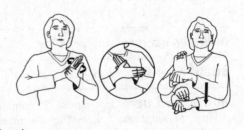

■ [**become** + **habit**] With the palms of both *open hands* together, right hand on top of left hand, twist the wrists in opposite directions in order to reverse positions. Then, with the heel of the right *C hand* across the wrist of the left *S hand*, move the hands down simultaneously in front of the chest while changing the right hand into an *S hand.*

addition *n.* See sign for PLUS.

address[1] *n.* **1.** The designation of a place where a person or business resides or may be reached: *Write the address on the envelope.* —*v.* **2.** To affix directions for delivery on: *to address the envelope.* Same sign used for: **residence.**

■ [Initialized sign similar to sign for **live**[2]] Move both *A hands*, palms facing in, upward on each side of the chest with a double movement.

address[2] *v.* See sign for SPEAK[2].

adept *adj.* See sign for ADROIT.

adequate *adj.* See sign for ENOUGH.

adhere *v.* See signs for APPLY[3], STICK[1].

adhesive *adj., n.* See sign for STICK[1].

adhesive tape *n.* See signs for BANDAGE[1], TAPE[2].

adjacent *prep.* See signs for BESIDE[1,2,3].

adjust *v.* See sign for CHANGE[1].

administer *v.* See sign for MANAGE. Alternate form: **administrate.**

administrator *n.* A person who manages the affairs of a business or other organization: *the administrator of the day-care program.* Same sign used for: **dictator, director, manager, ruler.**

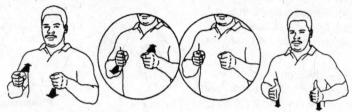

- [**manage + person marker**] Beginning with the palms of both *modified X hands* facing each other in front of each side of the chest, move the hands forward and back with an alternating movement. Then move both *open hands,* palms facing each other, downward along each side of the body.

admire *v.* See sign for LOOK UP[1].

admission *n.* The right to enter: *The university approved the applicant's request for admission.* Alternate form: **admittance.** Same sign used for: **entrance, entry.**

- [Similar to sign for **enter** except formed with a double movement] Move the back of the right *open hand* forward in a downward arc under the palm of the left *open hand,* both palms facing down, with a double movement.

admit[1] *v.* To acknowledge as true: *Admit that you made a mistake.* Related form: **admission** *n.* Same sign used for: **confess, confession, submit, willing.**

- [Hand seems to bring a confession from the chest] Move the right *open hand,* palm facing in, from the chest forward in an arc while turning the palm slightly outward.

admit[2] *v.* (alternate sign) Related form: **admission** *n.* Same sign used for: **confess, confession, submit, willing.**

- [Hands bring a confession from the chest] Beginning with the fingers of both *5 hands* on the chest, move the hands forward in an arc.

admit[3] *v.* See sign for ENTER.

admonish *v.* See signs for SCOLD, WARN.

adolescent *n.* A child growing up into adulthood; a teenager: *teaching a class of adolescents.* Related form: **adolescence** *n.* Same sign used for: **youth.**

■ [**young** + **children**[2]] Move the fingertips of both *bent hands,* palms facing in, upward with a double movement on each side of the chest. Then, beginning with the index-finger side of both *B hands* touching in front of the body, palms facing down and fingers pointing forward, move the hands outward to each side with a wavy movement.

adopt[1] *v.* To take (another's child) to bring up as one's own: *to adopt an orphan.* Related form: **adoption** *n.*

■ [**baby**[1] + **accept**] With the right bent arm cradled on the left bent arm, both palms facing up, swing the arms from left to right in front of the body with a double movement. Then, beginning with both *5 hands* in front of the chest, fingers pointing forward, bring the hands back toward the chest while pulling the fingers and thumbs of each hand together.

adopt[2] *v.* See signs for ACCEPT, ACCREDIT, TAKE[2]. Related form: **adoption** *n.*

adore *v.* See signs for FALL FOR, WORSHIP[1].

adorn *v.* To decorate: *adorn the dress with ribbons.*

■ [Similar to sign for **fix**[1]] With the fingertips of both *flattened O hands* touching in front of the chest, left palm facing in and right palm facing forward, twist the wrists in opposite directions and touch the fingertips again, repeating the movement as the hands move upward in front of the face.

adrift[1] *adj.* Floating without being fastened or guided: *The boat was adrift in the sea.*

■ [A boat moving aimlessly] Beginning with the palm side of the right *3 hand* touching the back of the left *open hand* near the chest, both palms facing in, move the right hand forward and to the right with a wavy movement.

adrift[2] *adj.* See signs for ROAM[1,2].

adroit *adj.* Skillful: *an adroit mountain climber.* Same sign used for: **adept, expert, good at, skillful, whiz** (*informal*).

- Beginning with the fingertips of the right *F hand* touching the chin, palm facing forward, twist the hand to turn the palm inward.

adult *n.* **1.** A fully grown person, animal, or plant: *Children must be accompanied by an adult.* —*adj.* **2.** Mature, as befitting adults: *an adult movie.* Same sign used for: **grown-up.**

- [Initialized sign formed in the traditional male and female positions; can be formed with an opposite movement] Move the thumb of the right *A hand,* palm facing forward, from the side of the forehead to the lower cheek.

adultery[1] *n.* Unfaithfulness of a husband or wife: *a wife guilty of adultery.*

- [Initialized sign indicating moving from one partner to another] Tap the heel of the right *A hand,* palm facing down, first on the index fingertip and then on the middle fingertip of the left *V hand,* palm facing up.

adultery[2] *n.* (alternate sign)

- [Represents slipping or sneaking around] Slide the palm of the right *open hand,* fingers pointing left, around the little-finger side of the left *open hand,* palm facing right and fingers pointing up.

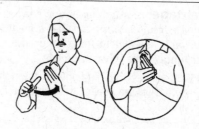

adultery[3] *n.* (alternate sign) Same sign used for: **sneak.**

- [Represents slipping or sneaking around] Slide the extended right index finger around the little-finger side of the left *open hand,* palm facing right and fingers pointing up.

adults *pl. n.* Same sign used for: **elders, grown-up.**

■ [Comparative form of **old** + indicating the height of adults] Move the right *C hand,* palm facing left, from in front of the chin to the right while closing into an *S hand.* Then move both *bent hands* upward one at a time with an alternating movement near each side of the head, palms facing each other.

advance *v.* **1.** To move forward or upward: *The army advanced a short distance.* **2.** To further the development or progress of: *to advance AIDS research.* Same sign used for: **exalt.**

■ [Moving to a more advanced position] Beginning with the back of the right *bent hand* touching the palm of the left *open hand,* both palms facing in, move the right hand upward and forward of the left hand.

advanced *adj.* Beyond a beginning level: *advanced algebra.* Same sign used for: **elevate, elevated, elevation, exalt, exalted, exaltation, higher, prominent, promote, promotion, supreme.**

■ [Moving to a more advanced position] Move both *bent hands,* palms facing each other, from near each side of the head upward a short distance in deliberate arcs.

advantage[1] *n.* Anything in one's favor: *Her knowledge of Spanish gave her a great advantage over me.* Same sign used for: **scrounge, take advantage of.**

■ Flick the bent middle finger of the right *5 hand* upward off the heel of the upturned left *open hand.*

advantage[2] *n.* See sign for BENEFIT.

Advent *n.* The season before Christmas: *the first Sunday in Advent.* Same sign used for: **Coming.**

■ [Indicates the Coming of Christ down to earth] Beginning with both extended index fingers pointing up in front of the head, palms facing back, bring both hands downward simultaneously, ending with the fingers pointing toward the chest.

adventure[1] *n.* An exciting experience: *an adventure traveling across the country.*

■ [Moving forward into the unknown] Beginning with the extended right index finger under the left *bent hand* held in front of the chest, move the right finger forward with a wavy movement.

adventure[2] *n., v.* See sign for TOUR[1].

advertise *v.* To announce or praise publicly in order to sell: *to advertise a new soap on television.* Related form: **advertisement** *n.* Same sign used for: **broadcast, commercial, propaganda, publicity, publicize.**

■ Beginning with the thumb side of the right *S hand,* palm facing left, against the little-finger side of the left *S hand,* palm facing right, move the right hand forward and back with a double movement.

advice *n.* Someone's opinion about what should be done: *He gave them good advice.* Same sign used for: **effect.**

■ [Sending information to another] Beginning with the fingertips of the right *flattened O hand* on the back of the left *open hand,* palm facing down, move the right hand forward while spreading the fingers into a *5 hand.*

advise[1] *v.* Same sign as for ADVICE but made with a double movement.

advise[2] *v.* See sign for COUNSEL.

advisor *n.* A person with the authority to give advice to another person: *The student met with her advisor.* Same sign used for: **consultant, counselor.**

■ [advice + person marker] Beginning with the fingertips of the *flattened O hand* on the back of the left *open hand,* palm facing down, move the right hand forward while spreading the fingers into a *5 hand.* Then move both *open hands,* palms facing each other, downward along each side of the body.

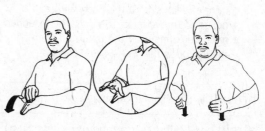

advocate *v.* See signs for SUPPORT[1,2].

aerial[1] *adj.* Occurring in or done from the air: *an aerial photograph*.

■ [**fly**[2] + **above**[2]] Move the right hand with the thumb, index finger, and little finger extended, palm facing down, forward in front of the right shoulder. Then move the right *5 hand*, palm facing down and fingers pointing forward, in a repeated circle above the right side of the head.

aerial[2] *n.* See sign for ANTENNA.

affect *v.* See signs for COUNSEL, INFLUENCE.

affection *n.* See sign for HUG[1]. Related form: **affectionate** *adj.*

affiliation *n.* See sign for COOPERATION.

affirm *v.* See sign for PROMISE[1]. Related form: **affirmation** *n.*

affix *v.* See sign for APPLY[3].

afford[1] *v.* To have money for: *We can't afford a new car*. Same sign used for: **debt, due, liability, owe, payable.**

■ [Indicates that money should be deposited in the palm] Tap the extended right index finger on the upturned palm of the left *open hand* with a double movement.

afford[2] *v.* (alternate sign)

■ [**can**[2] + **afford**[1]] Move both *S hands,* palms facing down, downward simultaneously in front of each side of the body with a deliberate movement. Then tap the extended right index finger on the upturned palm of the left *open hand.*

affront *v.* See signs for INSULT[1,2].

afraid *adj.* Feeling fear: *afraid of heights*. Same sign used for: **fright, frightened, panic, scare, scared, terrified, terrify, timid.**

■ [Hands put up a protective barrier] Beginning with both *A hands* in front of each side of the chest, spread the fingers open with a quick movement forming *5 hands,* palms facing in and fingers pointing toward each other.

Africa[1] *n.* A continent south of Europe: *living in Zaire in west central Africa.* Related form: **African** *adj., n.*

- [Initialized sign showing the shape of the African continent] Move the right *A hand,* palm facing forward, from in front of the right shoulder to the right and downward while opening into a *5 hand* and closing into an *A hand* again in front of the right side of the body.

Africa[2] *n.* (alternate sign, sometimes considered offensive) Related form: **African** *adj., n.*

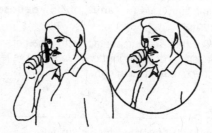

- [Initialized sign] Move the thumb of the right *A hand,* palm facing left, in a circle in front of the nose, ending with the thumb tip on the nose.

after[1] *prep.* **1.** Later in time than: *after dinner.* —*conj.* **2.** Subsequent to the time that: *The speaker arrived after you left.* —*adv.* **3.** Afterward: *the day after.* Same sign used for: **afterward, beyond, from now on, rest of.**

- [A time frame occurring after another thing] Beginning with the palm of the right *bent hand* touching the back of the fingers of the left *open hand,* both palms facing in, move the right hand forward a short distance.

after[2] *prep.* See sign for ACROSS.

after a while See signs for LATER[1,2].

afternoon *n.* The part of the day between noon and evening: *this afternoon.* Same sign used for: **matinee, P.M.**

- [The sun going down in the afternoon] With the bottom of the right forearm resting on the back of the left *open hand,* palm facing down, move the right *open hand* downward with a double movement.

afterward *adv.* See signs for ACROSS, AFTER[1], LATER[1,2].

again *adv.* Once more: *do it again.* Same sign used for: **encore, over, reiterate, repeat.**

■ Beginning with the right *bent hand* beside the left *curved hand,* both palms facing up, bring the right hand up while turning it over, ending with the fingertips of the right hand touching the palm of the left hand.

against *prep.* In opposition to: *I was against the idea.* Same sign used for: **anti-** [prefix], **opposed to, prejudice.**

■ [Demonstrates making contact with a barrier] Hit the fingertips of the right *bent hand* into the left *open hand,* palm facing right.

age *n.* Length of life or existence: *She left school at age sixteen.*

■ [An old man's beard] Move the right *O hand,* palm facing left, downward a short distance from the chin while changing into an *S hand.*

agency *n.* See sign for ASSOCIATION.

agenda *n.* A list of things to deal with: *on the agenda for the next meeting.*

■ [Initialized sign similar to sign for **list**[1]] Move the palm side of the right *A hand* from first touching the fingers and then the heel of the left *open hand,* palm facing right.

aggravate[1] *v.* **1.** To make worse or more severe: *By doing that, you're aggravating an already bad situation.* **2.** To annoy: *Stop aggravating me with your silly questions.* Related form: **aggravated** *adj.,* **aggravation** *n.*

■ [Stirring up emotions] Move the index-finger side of both *B hands,* palms facing each other and fingers angled up, in large alternating circles on each side of the chest.

aggravate[2] *v.* (alternate sign) Related form:
aggravated *adj.*, **aggravation** *n.*

- [Mixing up emotions] Move both *curved 5 hands,* palms facing in, in large alternating circles on each side of the chest.

---

aggravated *adj.* See sign for DISGUSTED[1].

---

aggressive *adj.* See sign for AMBITIOUS[1].

---

aghast *adj.* Being suddenly surprised and horrified: *aghast at the high bill.* Same sign used for: **horrified.**

- [Natural gesture] Beginning with both *5 hands* on the chest, both palms facing in and fingers pointing in opposite directions, stiffen the hands while spreading the fingers.

---

agile *adj.* See sign for SKILL.

---

agitate *v.* To excite or make anxious: *agitated by the news.*

- [**trouble**[1] + **mix**[1]] Beginning with both *B hands* near the sides of the head, move the hands in front of the face with alternating circular movements, palms facing each other and fingers pointing up. Then, beginning with the right *curved 5 hand* over the left *curved 5 hand* in front of the body, palms facing each other, move the hands in repeated alternate circles.

---

ago[1] *adj.* Past: *two weeks ago.* Same sign used for: **last, past, was, were.**

- [Indicates a time in the past] Move the right *bent hand* back over the right shoulder, palm facing back.

---

ago[2] *adv.* In the past: *long ago.* Same sign used for: **long ago; long time ago, a.**

- [Indicates a time in the past] Move the right *open hand,* palm facing left, over the right shoulder.

agony *n.* See sign for SUFFER[2].

agree[1] *v.* **1.** To have the same opinion: *I agree with the association rules.* **2.** To consent: *He agreed to finish the work for us.* **3.** To suit: *The climate doesn't agree with me.* Same sign used for: **all in favor, in accord, in agreement, compatible, compromise, concur, deal.**

■ [**think**[1] + **same**[1]] Move the extended right index finger from touching the right side of the forehead downward to beside the extended left index finger, ending with both fingers pointing forward in front of the body, palms facing down.

agree[2] *v.* To have the same opinion as the person one is conversing with or within view: *I agree with you.* Same sign used for: **me too.**

■ [Directional sign showing that two people share the same opinion] Move the right *Y hand,* palm facing left, from the right shoulder forward and back with a double movement.

agriculture *n.* See sign for FARM.

ahead[1] *adv.* In front: *Walk ahead of me.* Same sign used for: **forward, further.**

■ [The hand moves to a position ahead] Beginning with the palm sides of both *A hands* together, move the right hand forward in a small arc.

ahead[2] *adv.* (alternate sign) Same sign used for: **forward, further.**

■ [The hand moves to a position ahead] Beginning with the back of the right *bent hand,* fingers pointing left, touching the palm side of the left *open hand,* fingers pointing right, move the right hand up in an arc over the left hand.

aid *v., n.* See signs for HELP[1,2].

aide *n.* See signs for ASSISTANT[1,2].

ailment *n.* An illness: *stomachaches and other minor ailments.*

- [**sick**[2] + **pain**[2]] Touch the bent middle finger of the right *5 hand* to the forehead while touching the bent middle finger of the left *5 hand* to the chest, both palms facing in. Then, beginning with both extended index fingers pointing in opposite directions in front of the body, palms facing in, jab the fingers past each other.

aim[1] *v.* To direct at something: *aim at the target.*

- [Initialized sign similar to sign for **goal**[1]] Move the right extended index finger from near the right eye forward to point at the left *A hand* held in front of the face, palm facing forward.

aim[2] *v.* See sign for GOAL[1].

air *n.* See sign for BREEZE[1].

air conditioning *n.* A system for cooling air within a building or vehicle: *turn up the air conditioning.* Same sign used for: **air conditioner.**

- [Abbreviation **a-c** + a gesture showing air blowing at one's face] Form an *A* and then a *C* in front of the right shoulder. Then with both *open hands* near each side of the face, palms facing back and fingers pointing up, bend the fingers up and down with a double movement.

air force *n.* The unit of a country's military forces that is related to aviation: *He enlisted in the United States Air Force.*

- [**airplane** + **army**] Move the right hand with the thumb, index finger, and little finger extended, palm facing down, forward with a short repeated movement in front of the right shoulder. Then tap the palm sides of both *A hands* against the left side of the chest, right hand above the left hand, with a repeated movement.

airplane *n.* A vehicle for flying in the air: *fly in an airplane.* Same sign used for: **airport, jet, plane.**

■ [Shape and movement of an airplane] Move the right hand with the thumb, index finger, and little finger extended, palm facing down, forward with a short repeated movement in front of the right shoulder.

airtight *adj.* See sign for SEAL ONE'S LIPS[1].

ajar *adj.* Slightly open: *The door is ajar.*

■ [Door swinging open] Beginning with the fingertips of both *B hands* touching in front of the chest, palms angled in, swing the right hand forward, ending with the palm facing left and fingers pointing forward.

alarm *n.* A warning or a device to sound a warning: *a burglar alarm.* Same sign used for: **alert, drill.**

■ [Action of clapper on alarm bell] Tap the extended index finger of the right hand, palm facing forward, against the left *open hand,* palm facing right, with a repeated movement.

alas *interj.* Exclamation of grief or regret: *Alas, it was too late!* Same sign used for: **drat, shoot.**

■ [Natural gesture] Snap the middle finger off the thumb of the right *3 hand,* palm facing in, while swinging the right hand in toward the center of the chest.

Alaska[1] *n.* A state of the United States in the northwestern part of North America: *Alaska is the biggest state.*

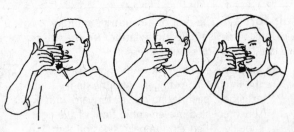

■ Beginning with the fingers of the right *bent hand* in front of the nose, palm facing in, bend the right fingers from side to side with a repeated movement, brushing the nose each time.

Alaska[2] *n.* (alternate sign)

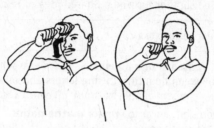

■ [Initialized sign] Beginning with the thumb of the right *A hand* touching the forehead, palm facing left, move the hand forward a short distance and then down, ending with the thumb touching the right side of the chin.

album[1] *n.* A book with blank pages for storing mementos: *a photo album.* Same sign used for: **scrapbook.**

■ [**picture + book**[1]] Move the right *C hand* from near the right side of the face, palm facing forward, downward, ending with the index-finger side of the right *C hand* against the palm of the left *open hand,* palm facing right. Then, beginning with the palms of both *open hands* together in front of the chest, fingers pointing forward, bring the hands apart at the top while keeping the little fingers together.

album[2] *n.* See sign for BOOK.

alcohol *n.* See signs for COCKTAIL, WHISKEY.

Alcoholics Anonymous *n.*

A self-help rehabilitation organization for alcoholics: *I belong to Alcoholics Anonymous.*

■ [Abbreviation **a-a**] Move the right *A hand,* palm facing forward, from in front of the right side of the body a short distance to the right.

alcove *n.* A small area off a larger room: *sit in the alcove.*

■ [The shape of an alcove around a thing] Beginning with the right *curved hand,* fingers pointing down, near the left *flattened O hand,* fingers pointing up, palms facing each other, move the right hand forward and around to in front of the right side of the chest, ending with the palm facing left and the fingers pointing down.

alert[1] *v.* See sign for WARN.

alert[2] *adj.* See sign for INSOMNIA. Shared idea of remaining awake.

alert[3] *n.* See sign for ALARM.

algebra[1] *n.* A branch of mathematics that deals with relations between quantities, using letters and other symbols to represent numbers: *study algebra.*

- ■ [Initialized sign similar to sign for **mathematics**] With a repeated movement, brush the palm side of the right *A hand* as it moves left in front of the chest, palm facing down, against the palm side of the left *A hand,* palm facing up, as it moves right.

algebra[2] *n.* (alternate sign)

- ■ As both *A hands* swing past each other in front of the chest with a double movement, brush the palm side of the right *A hand* on the back of the left *A hand,* both palms facing down.

algorithm *n.* A procedure for solving a mathematical problem in a series of finite steps, esp. in computer programming: *apply the algorithm to the problem.*

- ■ [Abbreviation **a-m**] Move the right *A hand* downward on the left *open hand,* palm facing right, while changing into an *M hand,* palm facing down.

align[1] *v.* To bring into a line: *align the tires.* Related form: **alignment** *n.*

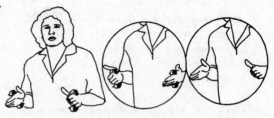

- ■ [Indicates lining up a thing] With both *open hands* in front of each side of the body, palms facing each other, turn the hands back and forth toward and away from each other with a repeated movement.

align[2] *v.* To arrange in a straight line: *align the chairs in a row.*

- ■ [Putting something into alignment with another thing] Move the little-finger side of the right *B hand,* palm facing left and fingers pointing forward, forward with a wavy movement along the extended left index finger, palm facing right and finger pointing forward.

align[3] *v.* See sign for LINE UP.

alike[1] *adj.* **1.** Similar (used for two people or things): *The twins are alike in many ways.* —*adv.* **2.** In the same manner (used for two people or things): *to treat them both alike.* See also signs for LOOK ALIKE, SAME[1]. Same sign used for: **identical, similar.**

- [Sign moves between two people or things that are similar] Move the right *Y hand,* palm facing down, from side to side with a short repeated movement in front of the body.

alike[2] *adj., adv.* (alternate sign) See also sign for SAME[1]. Same sign used for: **identical, similar.**

- [Sign shows that two people or things are similar] Move the right *Y hand,* palm facing down, from in front of the body to the right with a large arc.

alike[3] *adj.* **1.** Similar (used for more than two people or things): *They are all alike.* —*adv.* **2.** In the same manner (used for more than two people or things): *to treat them all alike.* See also sign for SAME[1]. Same sign used for: **similar, uniform.**

- [Sign moves between things that are similar] Move the right *Y hand,* palm facing down, in a flat circle in front of the body.

alimony *n.* Court-ordered allowance paid periodically following a divorce or separation: *She received alimony from her ex-husband on the first of every month.* Same sign used for: **maintenance, spousal support.**

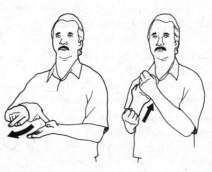

- [**pay**[1,2] + **support**] Beginning with the extended right index finger touching the palm of the left *open hand,* palms facing each other, move the right finger forward with a double movement off the left fingertips. Then push the knuckles of the right *S hand* upward under the little finger side of the left *S hand,* both palms in, pushing the left hand upward a short distance in front of the chest.

alive *adj.* See signs for LIVE[1,2].

all[1] *pron.* Everyone or everything: *All the hot dogs were eaten.* Same sign used for: **entire, total, whole.**

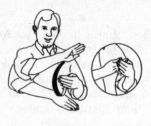

- ■ [The hand encompasses the whole thing] Move the right *open hand* from near the left shoulder in a large circle in front of the chest, ending with the back of the right hand in the left *open hand* held in front of the body, palms facing in.

all[2] *pron.* (alternate sign)

- ■ [Abbreviation **a-l**] Smoothly move the right *A hand*, palm facing forward, to the right in front of the chest while changing into an *L hand*.

all afternoon Through the whole afternoon: *worked all afternoon.*

- ■ [**afternoon** formed with a continuous movement indicating duration] With the right forearm on the back of the left *open hand*, palm facing down, move the right *B hand* smoothly downward from in front of the right shoulder.

all along See signs for GO ON[1], SINCE[1].

all day Through the whole day: *stayed all day.*

- ■ [Shows movement of the sun through the day] With the fingers of the left *open hand* in the crook of the right arm, move the right *B hand* smoothly from the right side of the body in a large arc in front of the body, ending with the right hand, palm facing down, on the back of the left arm near the elbow.

allegation *n.* See sign for ACCUSE[1].

allegiance *n.* See signs for SUPPORT[1,2].

allergy *n.* Unusual sensitivity to certain substances: *an allergy to ragweed.*

- ■ [**nose** + **opposite**] Move the extended right index finger from touching the nose downward to meet the extended left index finger held in front of the chest. Then, beginning with both index fingers touching, both palms facing in, bring the right hand forward and downward.

all gone See signs for NOTHING[5], RUN OUT OF[1,2].

alligator *n.* A large reptile with a broad head and powerful jaws: *the alligator's teeth.* Same sign used for: **jaws.**

[Mimes action of alligator's jaws] Beginning with the fingertips and heels of both *curved 5 hands* touching, right hand on top of the left hand and fingers forward, bring the hands apart and together again with a double movement.

all in favor See sign for AGREE[1].

all morning Through the whole morning: *worked all morning without a break.*

■ [**morning** formed with a continuous movement indicating duration] With the fingers of the left *open hand* in the crook of the right arm, move the right *B hand* smoothly upward from in front of the right side of the body to in front of the right shoulder, palm facing back.

all night Through the whole night: *to lie awake all night.* Same sign used for: **overnight.**

■ [**night** formed with a continuous movement indicating duration] With the fingers of the left *open hand* in the crook of the right arm, move the right *B hand* smoothly downward from in front of the right side of the chest, ending under the left arm, palm facing back.

allocate[1] *v.* To divide and set apart (a portion) for a particular purpose: *allocate some of the funds for the new program.* Related form: **allocation** *n.*

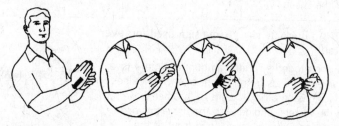

■ [**some-some**] Slide the little-finger side of the right *open hand,* palm facing left, with a double movement across the palm of the left *open hand,* palm facing up, moving to a different section of the left hand each time.

allocate[2] *v.* (alternate sign) Related form: **allocation** *n.* Same sign used for: **awards, donation, gift.**

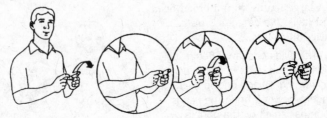

- **[contribution** formed in different directions] Move both *X hands* from in front of the left side of the body, palms facing each other, forward in simultaneous arcs. Repeat in front of the right side of the body.

all over Everywhere: *spread the paint all over.* Same sign used for: **overall.**

- [Surrounds entire thing] Move the right *5 hand* from in front of the right side of the body, palm facing forward, in a large arc in front of the face, ending in front of the left side of the body.

allow *v.* See signs for LET[1,2].

allowance *n.* See sign for PENSION.

all right See sign for RIGHT[2].

all the time[1] Continuously: *The baby cries all the time.* Same sign used for: **ever since.**

- [Hands bring together a total amount of time] Beginning with both *5 hands* in front of each side of the body, palms facing down and fingers pointing forward, move the hands outward and forward in a large, flat circular movement, ending with the fingertips of both *flattened O hands* touching in front of the chest.

all the time[2] (alternate sign) Same sign used for: **ever since, total.**

- [Hands bring together a total amount of time] Move both *curved 5 hands* from in front of each shoulder, palms facing each other, toward each other while closing the fingers, ending with the fingertips of both *flattened O hands* touching in front of the chest.

ally *n.* See sign for RELATIONSHIP.

almighty *adj.* Having unlimited power: *almighty God.*

- [**all**¹ + **power**²] Beginning near the left shoulder, move the right *open hand* in a large circle in front of the chest, ending with the back of the right hand in the upturned left *open hand.* Then move both *S hands,* palms facing in, forward with a short deliberate movement from in front of each shoulder.

almost¹ *adv.* A little less than; very nearly: *almost time to go.* Same sign used for: **about, barely, nearly.**

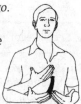

- Brush the fingertips of the right *open hand* upward off the back of the left fingers, both palms facing up.

almost² *adv.* See sign for CLOSE CALL.

alone¹ *adv.* **1.** Without company: *He played alone.* —*adj.* **2.** Separate or without help from others: *She alone knows how to open the safe.* Same sign used for: **isolated, lone, lonely, only, orphan, solely.**

- [Shows one thing alone] With the right index finger extended up, move the right hand, palm facing back, in a small repeated circle in front of the right shoulder.

alone² *adv.* (alternate sign) Same sign used for: **do it myself, isolated, lone, lonely, only, solely.**

- [Shows one] With the right index finger extended up, palm facing back in front of the right shoulder, move the finger back in an arc to the center of the chest.

alone³ *adv.* See sign for SINGLE¹.

aloof *adj.* Unfriendly or distant in manner: *a cold and aloof person.*

- [A gesture indicating being stuck up + **advanced**] Push the nose upward with the extended right index finger, palm facing left. Then move both *bent hands,* palms facing each other, from in front of each shoulder upward a short distance in a deliberate arc.

a lot[1] *adv.* A great many: *a lot of books.* Same sign used for: **lots.**

■ [The hands seem to hold a large quantity of something] Beginning with the fingertips of both *curved hands* touching in front of the body, palms facing each other, bring the hands outward, ending with one hand in front of each side of the chest.

a lot[2] *adv.* See signs for MANY, MUCH.

aloud *adv.* See sign for NOISE.

alphabet *n.* The letters of a language in sequential order: *26 letters in the English alphabet.*

■ [a-b-c + **fingerspell**] With the right hand, palm facing forward, sequentially form the first three manual alphabet letters in front of the right shoulder, moving the hand slightly to the right after each letter. Then move the right *5 hand,* palm facing down, to the right in front of the right shoulder while wiggling the fingers.

already *adv.* See signs for FINISH[1,2].

also *adv.* See signs for AS[1,2].

altar *n.* A table used for religious ceremonies: *worship at the altar.*

■ [Initialized sign showing the shape of an altar] Beginning with the thumbs of both *A hands* touching in front of the body, palms facing down, move the hands apart and then down in front of each side of the body.

alter *v.* See sign for CHANGE[1].

alternate *v.* See sign for TURN[2].

alternative *n.* See signs for EITHER[1,2].

although *conj.* See sign for BUT.

altitude *n.* See sign for HIGH[1].

alumnus *n.* A graduate of a specific school: *The alumni came together for a reunion.*

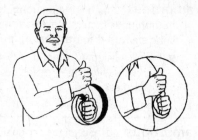

■ [Initialized sign similar to sign for **year**] Beginning with the right *A hand,* palm facing left, over the left *A hand,* palm facing right, move the right hand forward in a complete circle around the left hand, ending with the little-finger side of the right hand on the thumb side of the left hand.

always *adv.* Every time: *Night always follows day.* Same sign used for: **ever.**

■ [A continuous circle signifying duration] Move the extended right index finger, palm facing in and finger angled up, in a repeated circle in front of the right side of the chest.

am[1] *v.* First person singular present tense form of the verb *be: I am tired.*

■ [Initialized sign similar to sign for **be**[2]] Move thumbnail of right *A hand* from the lips, palm facing left, forward a short distance.

am[2] *v.* See sign for BE[2].

amass *v.* See signs for ACCUMULATE[1], COLLECT[1,2].

amaze *v.* See signs for SURPRISE, WONDERFUL[1,2]. Related form: **amazement** *n.*

amazed *adj.* See sign for INCREDIBLE[1].

ambassador *n.* A representative of high rank sent from one government to another: *the U.S. ambassador to Mexico.*

■ [Initialized sign similar to sign for **king**] Move the right *A hand,* palm facing in, from near the left shoulder downward to near the right hip.

ambiguous *adj.* See sign for VAGUE.

ambitious[1] *adj.* Having a strong desire for success: *an ambitious actress.* Related form: **ambition** *n.* Same sign used for: **active, aggressive.**

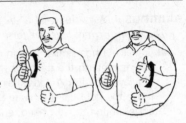

- [Initialized sign] Move both *A hands*, palms facing in, in large alternating circles upward on each side of the chest.

ambitious[2] *adj.* See signs for GOAL[1], ZEAL.

ambulance[1] *n.* A vehicle for carrying sick or injured people, usually to a hospital: *Call an ambulance!* Same sign used for: **siren.**

- [Represents flashing light on an ambulance] Move the right *flattened O hand* in a circular movement near the right side of the head by repeatedly twisting the wrist and opening the fingers into a *5 hand* each time.

ambulance[2] *n.* (alternate sign) Same sign used for: **siren.**

- [Represents the flashing light on an ambulance] Move the right *curved 5 hand* in a circular movement near the right side of the head by repeatedly twisting the wrist.

ambulance[3] *n.* (alternate sign)

- [Initialized sign similar to sign for **hospital**[1]] Move the thumbnail of the right *A hand* first down and then across from back to front on the upper left arm.

amen[1] *interj.* Expression of solemn agreement: *forever and ever, amen.* Same sign used for: **pray, prayer.**

- [Natural gesture for folding one's hands to pray] Bring the palms of both *open hands* together, fingers angled upward, while moving the hands down.

amen[2] *interj.* (alternate sign)

■ [Natural gesture showing piety or prayer] With the right fingers cupped over the left *A hand,* bring the hands down and in toward the chest.

---

amen[3] *n.* See sign for APPROVE[1].

---

amend *v.* See sign for ADD[2].

America *n.* **1.** The lands of the Western Hemisphere: *North and South America.* **2.** The United States: *The pilgrims came to America in 1620.* Related form: **American** *adj., n.*

■ With the fingers of both hands loosely entwined, palms facing in, move the hands in circle in front of the chest.

American Indian *n.* See sign for INDIAN.

American Sign Language[1] *n.* A visual-gestural language used by deaf people in the United States: *to communicate in American Sign Language.* See also sign for SIGN LANGUAGE. Same sign used for: **Ameslan** (no longer in use), **ASL.**

■ [Initialized sign + **language**] With both *A hands* in front of the chest, palms facing forward and right hand higher than the left, move the hands in an alternating circular movement toward the chest. Then move both *L hands* from together in front of the chest, palms facing down, simultaneously apart to each side of the chest.

American Sign Language[2] *n.* See also sign for SIGN LANGUAGE. Same sign used for: **ASL.**

■ [Abbreviation a-s-l] Form the fingerspelled letters **A, S, L** in front of the right side of the chest with the right hand, palm facing forward, while moving the hand slightly to the right as the letters are formed.

---

amid or **amidst** *prep.* See sign for AMONG.

---

amiss *adj.* See sign for ACCIDENTALLY[1].

ammunition *n.* Bullets or explosives: *Take ammunition for the guns.*

- [**bullet** + **line up**] Brush the fingertips of the right *G hand,* palm facing left, downward on the extended left index finger held up in front of the chest, palm facing right. Then, beginning with the little-finger sides of both *4 hands* touching in front of the chest, palms facing in, move the hands apart.

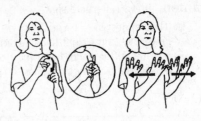

among *prep.* **1.** In the middle of or surrounded by: *You are among friends.* **2.** With a share for each of: *divided it among ourselves.* **3.** By the joint action of: *argued among ourselves.* Same sign used for: **amid, amidst, midst.**

- [Shows one moving among others] Move the extended right index finger in and out between the fingers of the left *5 hand,* both palms facing in.

amount[1] *n.* A quantity: *a small amount of money.* Same sign used for: **heap, lump, pile.**

- [Shows a small amount in a pile] Move the extended right index finger, palm facing down, in an arc from near the heel to the fingers of the upturned left *open hand,* ending with the right palm facing in toward the chest.

amount[2] *n.* (alternate sign) Same sign used for: **heap, lump, pile.**

- [Shows a small amount in a pile] Beginning with the index-finger side of the right *B hand,* palm angled forward, touching near the heel of the upturned left *open hand,* move the right hand in a small upward arc, ending with the little-finger side of the right hand, palm facing in, touching the left fingers.

amount[3] *n.* See sign for ADD[1].

ample *adj.* See signs for ENOUGH, PLENTIFUL.

amputate *v.* To cut off (all or part of a limb): *amputate the diseased leg.* Related form: **amputation** *n.*

- [Mime cutting off an arm and a leg] Move the right *B hand,* palm facing in, downward with a deliberate movement near the extended left arm, and then from left to right across the top of the right leg.

amuse *v.* **1.** To cause to laugh: *Your jokes don't amuse me.* **2.** To keep occupied in a pleasant manner: *to amuse the baby with toys.* Related forms: **amusement** *n.*, **amusing** *adj.*

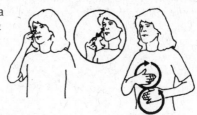

- [**funny** + **enjoy**] With a double movement, brush downward on the nose with the fingertips of the right *U hand,* palm facing down. Then rub the palms of both *open hands* on the chest, right hand above the left hand and fingers pointing in opposite directions, in repeated simultaneous circles moving in opposite directions.

amusing *v.* See sign for FUNNY.

an *indef. article.* Any or one (the form of **a** used before words beginning with a vowel sound): *eat an apple.*

- [Initialized sign with **n**] Beginning with the right *N hand* in front of the right shoulder, palm facing left, twist the hand forward.

analog *adj.* Denoting a device that measures changing conditions and converts them into quantities: *an analog computer.* Related forms: **analogical** *adj.,* **analogous** *adj.*

- [Initialized sign] Move both *A hands* from in front of the right side of the body, palms facing down, across to the left side of the body in arcs and then back to the right again.

analyze *v.* To examine carefully: *analyze the situation.* Related form: **analysis** *n.* Same sign used for: **access, diagnose, diagnosis, examine, evaluate, gauge, investigate.**

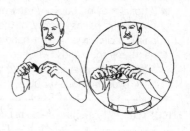

- [Taking something apart to analyze it] With both *bent V hands* near each other in front of the chest, palms facing down, move the fingers apart from each other with a downward double movement while bending the fingers.

anatomy[1] *n.* The structure of an animal or plant: *human anatomy.*

- [Initialized sign similar to sign for **body**] Move both *A hands,* palms facing in, downward from each side of the chest to each side of the waist.

anatomy[2] *n.* **1.** The science dealing with the structure of the human body: *to study anatomy in college.* **2.** The structure of the human body.

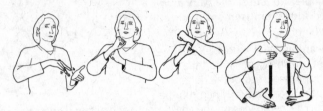

- ■ [**study + body + structure**] While wiggling the fingers, move the right *5 hand,* palm facing down, with a double movement toward the left *open hand* held in front of the body, palm facing up. Then pat the palm side of both *open hands* first on each side of the chest and then on each side of the abdomen. Then, beginning with the left *S hand* on the back of the right *S hand,* both palms facing down, move the right hand in a forward and upward arc to reverse positions. Repeat as the hands move upward in front of the chest.

ancestor[1] *n.* A person from whom one is descended: *My ancestors came from Germany.*

- ■ [**old + primitive**] Beginning with the index-finger side of the right *S hand* against the chin and the index-finger side of the left *S hand* against the little-finger side of the right hand, palms facing in opposite directions, move the hands downward with a wiggly movement. Then, beginning with both *5 hands* in front of the right shoulder, left hand somewhat forward of the right hand, palms facing in opposite directions and fingers pointing up, move the hands backward in alternating repeated arcs over the right shoulder.

ancestor[2] *n.* (alternate sign)

- ■ [Shows moving back into the past] Beginning with both *open hands* in front of the right shoulder, palms facing in and right hand above the left hand, roll the hands over each other with an alternating movement while moving the hands back over the right shoulder.

ancestor[3] *n.* See sign for PREDECESSOR.

anchor *n.* A piece of iron fastened by a chain or rope to a ship to hold it in place: *drop the anchor.*

- ■ [Represents unhooking an anchor and dropping it] Beginning with the thumb side of the right *X hand,* palm facing down, against the palm of the left *3 hand,* palm facing right and fingers pointing forward, bring the right hand downward in an arc, ending with the palm facing left.

ancient *adj.* See signs for LONG AGO[1,2].

and *conj.* As well as: *you and I.*
- Move the right *curved 5 hand,* palm facing left, to the right in front of the body while closing the fingers to the thumb, ending in a *flattened O hand.*

and so forth See sign for VARIETY[1].

angel *n.* A spiritual being serving God: *an angel from heaven.* Same sign used for: **wings.**
- [Shows movement of an angel's wings] Beginning with the fingertips of both *bent hands* touching each shoulder, palms facing down, twist the hands forward and outward and bend the fingers up and down with a repeated movement.

anger[1] *n.* A strong feeling of displeasure and hostility: *broke the vase in anger.* Related form: **angry** *adj.* Same sign used for: **cross, enrage, fury, mad, outrage, rage.**
- [Hands bring up feelings of anger in the body] Beginning with the fingertips of both *curved 5 hands* on the lower chest, bring the hands upward and apart, ending in front of each shoulder.

anger[2] *n.* (alternate sign) Related form: **angry** *adj.* Same sign used for: **cross, furious, grouchy, grumpy, mad, rage.**
- [Hand seems to pull the face down into a scowl] With the palm of the right *5 hand* in front of the face, fingers pointing up, bring the hand slightly forward while constricting the fingers into a *curved 5 hand.*

angle[1] *n.* The shape formed by two surfaces or lines meeting: *A right angle is an angle of 90°.*
- [Shape of an angle] With the extended right index finger, trace along the index finger and thumb of the left *L hand,* palm facing forward.

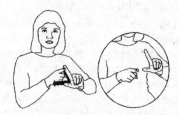

angle² *v.* See sign for DIVIDE¹.

angry *adj.* See signs for CROSS², FIERCE¹.

animal *n.* A living thing not a plant: *Dogs are my favorite animals.* Same sign used for: **beast.**

- Beginning with the fingertips of both *curved 5 hands* on the chest near each shoulder, roll the fingers toward each other on their knuckles with a double movement, while keeping the fingers in place.

ankle *n.* The joint between the foot and the leg: *She sprained her ankle while running.*

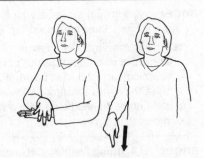

- [**wrist** + point to ankle] With the bent middle finger and thumb of the right *5 hand*, grasp each side of the wrist of the left *open hand*, palm facing down. Then point downward to the ankle with the extended right index finger.

annex *v.* See sign for BELONG¹.

anniversary¹ *n.* The yearly return of a special date: *celebrate our wedding anniversary.*

- [**annual** + **celebrate**] Beginning with the little-finger side of the right *S hand* on the thumb of the left *S hand,* flick the right index finger forward and back with a double movement. Then move both modified *X hands* in large simultaneous circles, palms facing back, near each side of the head.

anniversary² *n.* See sign for CELEBRATE.

announce *v.* To give public notice of: *announce the score.* Related form: **announcement** *n.* Same sign used for: **acclaim, declaration, declare, proclaim, proclamation, reveal, tell.**

- [**tell¹** with a movement that shows a general announcement] Beginning with the extended index fingers of both hands pointing to each side of the mouth, palms facing in, twist the wrists and move the fingers forward and apart from each other, ending with the palms facing forward and the index fingers pointing outward in opposite directions.

annoy[1] *v.* To disturb in a way that irritates: *annoy the teacher with constant interruptions.* Same sign used for: **bother, disturb, interfere, interrupt, intervene, irritate, nuisance.**

- ■ [A gesture showing something interfering with something else] Sharply tap the little-finger side of the right *open hand,* palm facing in at an angle, at the base of the thumb and index finger of the left *open hand,* with a double movement.

annoy[2] *v.* (alternate sign) Same sign used for: **bother, bug** (*informal*), **disturb, interfere, interrupt, irritate, pester.**

- ■ Bring the knuckles of the right *bent V hand,* palm facing in, with a double movement against the extended left index finger held up in front of the chest, palm facing forward.

annual *adj.* **1.** Once a year: *annual event.* **2.** Of or for one year: *annual salary.* Related form: **annually** *adv.* Same sign used for: **every year, per annum.**

- ■ [Formed like **year** as it moves into the future] Beginning with the little-finger side of the right *S hand* on the thumb side of the left *S hand,* palms facing in opposite directions, flick the right index finger forward and back with a double movement.

annul *v.* See sign for CANCEL.

annulment *n.* Court-ordered declaration that annuls a marriage: *The annulment allowed him to marry again.* Related form: **annul** *v.*

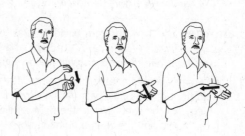

- ■ [**marry** + **cancel**] Bring the right *curved hand,* palm facing down, downward in front of the chest to clasp the left *curved hand,* palm facing up. Then, with the extended right index finger, draw a large *X* across the palm of the upturned left *open hand.*

anoint[1] *v.* To put oil on (a person), especially in a religious ceremony: *anoint the king.*

- ■ [Mime pouring oil on something] Move the extended thumb of the right *10 hand,* palm facing right and thumb pointing down, in a flat circle over the left *S hand,* palm facing down, with a double movement.

anoint[2] *v.* (alternate sign) Same sign used for: **Lent.**

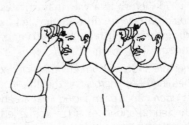

- [Initialized sign formed with the sign of the cross on the forehead] Move the thumbnail of the right *A hand,* palm facing left, first downward and then across from left to right to form a small cross on the forehead.

anoint[3] *v.* (alternate sign)

- [Mime pouring oil on something + anointing the cheek with oil] Move the extended thumb of the right *10 hand,* palm facing right and thumb pointing down, in a flat circle over the upturned left *open hand* held in front of the body. Then, with the thumb of the right *A hand* against the right cheek, twist the hand forward.

anonymous *adj.* Not named or identified: *The newspaper received an anonymous letter.*

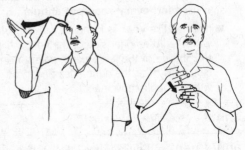

- [**don't know** + **name**[1]] Beginning with the fingers of the right *open hand* touching the right side of the forehead, swing the hand forward by twisting the wrist, ending with the fingers pointing forward in front of the right shoulder. Then tap the middle-finger side of the right *H hand* across the index-finger side of the left *H hand* with a double movement.

another *adj.* **1.** A different or additional (one): *another glass of water.* —*pron.* **2.** A different or additional one: *He went from one thing to another.* Same sign used for: **other.**

- [Points away to another] Beginning with the right *10 hand* in front of the body, palm facing down and thumb pointing left, flip the hand over to the right, ending with the palm facing up and the thumb pointing right.

answer *n.* **1.** A response to a question: *the right answer.* —*v.* **2.** To respond to a question: *Please answer the question.* Same sign used for: **react, reply, respond, response.**

- [Indicates directing words of response to another] Beginning with both extended index fingers pointing up in front of the mouth, right hand nearer the mouth than the left and both palms facing forward, bend the wrists down simultaneously, ending with the fingers pointing forward and the palms facing down.

ant *n.* A small insect that lives in large groups: *ants crawling all over the picnic table.*

■ [Initialized sign showing the movement of an ant's legs] With the heel of the left *A hand* on the back of the right *curved 5 hand,* palm facing down, move the right hand forward while wiggling the fingers.

---

antagonism *n.* See sign for STRUGGLE.

---

antagonistic *adj.* See sign for CONTRARY[1].

---

antenna *n.* A wire or rod for conducting radio or television signals: *adjust the antenna to get a better picture.* Same sign used for: **aerial.**

■ [Shape of an antenna] Place the palm of the right *3 hand* on the extended left index finger pointing up, palm facing right.

---

anti- *prefix.* See signs for AGAINST, RESIST.

---

anticipate *v.* See signs for HOPE[1,2]. Related form: **anticipation** *n.*

---

antsy *adj.* See signs for RESTLESS[1,2].

---

anus *n.* The posterior opening through which human wastes are excreted: *inserted the thermometer in the anus.*

■ [Shape and location] Point the extended right index finger first to the thumb side of the left *F hand,* palm facing forward, and then to the right hip.

---

anxiety *n.* See signs for CONCERN[2], NERVOUS.

---

anxious *adj.* See signs for EXCITE, NERVOUS, TROUBLE[1,2], ZEAL.

---

any *adj.* **1.** One or some, no matter which: *Choose any book you like.* —*pron.* **2.** An unspecified person or thing: *I don't want any.*

■ Beginning with the right *10 hand* in front of the chest, palm facing left, twist the wrist and move the hand down and to the right, ending with the palm facing down.

anybody[1] *pron.* Any person: *Anybody can make a mistake.*

- [**any** + **you**[2]] Beginning with the right *10 hand* in front of the chest, palm facing left, twist the wrist and move the hand down and to the right, ending with the palm facing down. Then move the extended right index finger, palm facing left and finger pointing forward, in an arc from left to right in front of the body.

anybody[2] *pron.* (alternate sign)

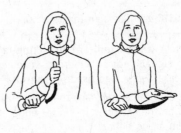

- [**any** + **them**[2]] Beginning with the right *10 hand* in front of the chest, palm facing left, twist the wrist and move the hand down and to the right, ending with the palm facing down. Then move the right *open hand*, palm facing up and fingers pointing forward, in an arc from left to right in front of the body.

anyone *pron.* Any person: *Is anyone home?*

- [**any** + **one**] Beginning with the right *10 hand* in front of the chest, palm facing left, twist the wrist and move the hand down and to the right, ending with the palm facing down. Then hold the extended right index finger up in front of the chest, palm facing in.

anything *pron.* A thing of any kind: *Do you want anything from the store?*

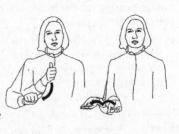

- [**any** + **thing**[1,2]] Beginning with the right *10 hand* in front of the chest, palm facing left, twist the wrist and move the hand down and to the right, ending with the palm facing down. Then move the right *curved hand* from the right side of the body, palm facing up, outward to the right in a double arc.

anyway *adv.* In any case: *I will do it anyway, whether you want me to or not.* Same sign used for: **despite, doesn't matter, even though, hardly, however, nevertheless, regardless, whatever.**

- [Flexible hands signify no firm position] Beginning with both *open hands* in front of the body, fingers pointing toward each other and palms facing in, move the hands forward and back from the body with a repeated alternating movement, striking and bending the fingers of each hand as they pass.

anywhere *adv.* In or to any place: *Put it anywhere.*

■ [**any** + **where**] Beginning with the right *10 hand* in front of the chest, palm facing left, twist the wrist and move the hand down and to the right, ending with the palm facing down. Then move the extended right index finger, pointing up in front of the chest and palm facing out, back and forth with a repeated movement.

apart *adv.* See signs for PART³, SEPARATE.

apathy *n.* Lack of interest or enthusiasm: *student apathy toward politics.* Same sign used for: **helpless, idle, impassive.**

■ [Demonstrates lack of energy] Drop both *5 hands*, palms facing down, downward from in front of each side of the chest.

ape *n.* See signs for GORILLA, MONKEY.

apologize *v.* See sign for SORRY. Related form: **apology** *n.*

apostrophe *n.* The mark ' used in contractions or with possessive nouns: *The word "don't" has an apostrophe.* Same sign used for: **comma.**

■ [Mime drawing an apostrophe in the air] Draw an apostrophe in the air with the extended right index finger, pointing forward, by twisting the wrist in front of the right shoulder.

apparel *n.* See sign for CLOTHES.

apparently *adv.* See sign for SEEM.

appeal¹ *v.* **1.** To request a review of (a matter) by a higher court: *appeal the case.* —*n.* **2.** An application for review by a higher court: *He lost the appeal in court.*

■ [Initialized sign similar to sign for **review**] Beginning with the palm side of the right *A hand* against the left open palm, twist the right hand back toward the chest.

appeal² *v.* See sign for SUGGEST.

appear *v.* See signs for SEEM, SHOW UP.

appearance[1] *n.* One's outward look: *He has a sinister appearance.*

- [Shows area of facial appearance] Move the right *5 hand,* palm facing in, in a large circle in front of the face.

appearance[2] *n.* One's outward looks: *He admired his appearance in a mirror.* Same sign used for: **good-looking, handsome, looks, resemblance.**

- [The location of a person's face] Move the extended right index finger in a circle in front of the face, palm facing in.

appease *v.* See sign for SATISFY[1].

appendix[1] *n.* A small tube attached to the intestine: *The doctor is going to remove your appendix.*

- [Shape and location of appendix] Bend the extended right index finger, palm facing back, forward and back with a double movement near the right side of the waist.

appendix[2] *n.* (alternate sign)

- [Shape of appendix] Beginning with the thumb side of the extended right index finger under the palm side of the left *A hand,* bend the right index finger up and down with a double movement.

appetite[1] *n.* A desire for food: *Teenagers have a big appetite.*

- [**hungry** + **food**] Beginning with the fingertips of the right *C hand* touching the chest, palm facing in, move the hand downward a short distance. Then bring the fingertips of the right *flattened O hand,* palm facing down, to the lips with a double movement.

appetite[2] *n.* (alternate sign)

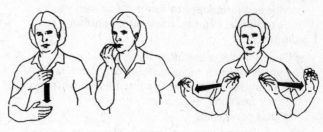

- [**hungry + food + none**[1,2]] Beginning with the fingertips of the right *C hand* touching the chest, palm facing in, move the hand downward a short distance. Then bring the fingertips of the right *flattened O hand*, palm facing down, to the lips with a double movement. Then, beginning with both *flattened O hands* in front of each side of the chest, move the hands forward and outward away from each other.

appetite[3] *n.* See sign for HUNGRY.

applaud *v.* To express approval by clapping the hands: *applaud your favorite candidate.* Related form: **applause** *n.* Same sign used for: **clap, commend, ovation, praise.**

- [Natural gesture for clapping] Pat the palm of the right *open hand* across the palm of the left *open hand* with a double movement.

apple[1] *n.* A rounded firm fruit with red, green, or yellow skin: *eat an apple.*

- With the knuckle of the right *X hand* near the right side of the mouth, twist the wrist downward with a double movement.

apple[2] *n.* (alternate sign)

- [Initialized sign] With the thumb of the right *A hand* near the right side of the mouth, twist the wrist downward with a double movement.

apply[1] *v.* To assign for a specific purpose: *apply the payment to the loan.* Related form: **applicable** *adj.* Same sign used for: **charge, file, implement, install, post, use.**

- [Put messages on a spindle] Move the fingers of the right *V hand*, palm facing forward, downward on each side of the extended left index finger, pointing up in front of the chest.

apply[2] *v.* To make a formal request: *to apply for a job*. Related form: **application** *n.* Same sign used for: **candidate, eligible, nominate, voluntary, volunteer.**

- ■ [Seems to pull oneself forward to apply for something] Pinch a small amount of clothing on the right side of the chest with the fingers of the right *F hand* and pull forward with a short double movement.

apply[3] *v.* To put on: *apply glue on an envelope's flap*. Same sign used for: **adhere, affix.**

- ■ [Mime applying tape or a label] Tap the fingers of the right *H hand*, palm facing left, first against the palm of the left *open hand*, palm facing right, and then against the heel of the left hand.

apply[4] *v.* See sign for LABEL.

appoint[1] *v.* To assign officially, as to an office or position: *appoint a committee to study the issue*. Same sign used for: **choose, elect, select.**

- ■ [Fingers seems to pick someone] Beginning with the thumb side of the right *G hand*, palm facing down and fingers pointing forward, against the left *open hand*, palm facing right and fingers pointing up, pull the right hand in toward the chest while pinching the index finger and thumb together.

appoint[2] *v.* To choose for a position: *to be appointed chairman*. Related form: **appointment** *n.* Same sign used for: **assign.**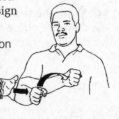

- ■ [Hand seems to grab someone and set that person aside] Beginning with the right *curved 5 hand* in front of the right side of the body, palm facing left, move the hand to the left while closing into an *S hand*. Then move the right *S hand* forward and to the left in a short arc.

appointment *n.* A meeting at an established time: *I have a doctor's appointment at 5:00*. Same sign used for: **assignment, book, engagement, reservation.**

- ■ Move the right *S hand*, palm facing down, in a small circle and then down to the back of the left *A hand*, palm facing down in front of the chest.

appraise *v.* To estimate the value of: *We wanted an expert to appraise the diamond ring.* Related form: **appraisal** *n.*

- [**evaluate** + **check**[1]] Move both *E hands,* palms facing forward, up and down with a repeated alternating movement in front of each side of the chest. Then move the extended right index finger from the nose down to strike sharply off the upturned left palm, and then upward again.

appreciate[1] *v.* To recognize and think highly of: *appreciate good music.* Related form: **appreciation** *n.*

- [Similar to sign for **enjoy**] Move the bent index finger of the right *5 hand* in a small circle on the chest.

appreciate[2] *v.* See sign for ENJOY. Related form: **appreciation** *n.*

appreciative *adj.* See sign for GRATEFUL.

apprehend *v.* See signs for CAPTURE[1,2,3], COMPREHEND[1], UNDERSTAND.

apprehensive *adj.* See sign for NERVOUS.

approach[1] *v.* **1.** To come near: *A storm is approaching.* —*n.* **2.** An act of coming nearer: *the approach of the train.* Same sign used for: **close to, near, pursue.**

- [One hand moves to approach the other] Move the back of the right *bent hand* from near the chest forward with a double movement toward the palm of the left *bent hand,* both palms facing in and fingers pointing in opposite directions.

approach[2] *v.* See signs for CLOSE[1,2], FACE[2].

appropriate *adj.* Particularly suitable: *wear appropriate clothes to church.* Related form: **appropriately** *adv.* Same sign used for: **proper, suitable.**

- [**right** formed with a double movement] With the index fingers of both hands extended forward at right angles, palms angled inward, and with the right hand above the left, hit the little-finger side of the right hand down across the thumb side of the left hand with a double movement.

approve[1] *v.* A statement of concurrence: *The committee approved the proposal.* Related form: **approval** *n.* Same sign used for: **amen, confirm, seal, stamp.**

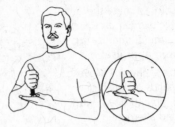

- [Signifies a stamp of approval] Hit the little-finger side of the right *A hand*, palm facing left, down into the left upturned palm.

approve[2] *v.* See signs for ACCEPT, CHECK[1]. Related form: **approval** *n.*

approximate *adj.* See sign for ROUGH.

approximately *adv.* Nearly: *approximately the correct amount.* Related form: **approximate** *adj.* Same sign used for: **about, around.**

- [Natural gesture of vagueness] Move the right *5 hand*, palm facing forward, in a circle in front of the right shoulder with a double movement.

apron *n.* A garment worn to protect the front of one's clothes: *I wear an apron when I cook.*

- [Mime tying an apron around the waist] Bring both modified *X hands* from in front of the waist, palms facing in, apart to each side of the body.

aquarium *n.* A glass container in which fish and water plants are kept: *fill the aquarium with fish.*

- [Initialized sign showing the movement of fish] Beginning with the little-finger side of the right *A hand*, palm facing left, on the back of the left *open hand*, palm facing down, twist the right hand back and forth with a double movement from the wrist.

arbitrate *v.* See sign for DEBATE. Related form: **arbitration** *n.*

arch *n.* A curved structure, usually over an opening: *Walk under the arch into the garden.* Same sign used for: **arc, curve.**

- [Shape of an arch] Beginning with the right *B hand* in front of the chin, palm facing forward and fingers pointing to the left, move the hand in a large arc in front of the face, ending in front of the right side of the body, palm facing left.

archbishop *n.* The highest ranked bishop over an archdiocese.

- ■ [**advanced** + **bishop**[2]] Move both *bent hands,* palms facing each other, from near each side of the head upward a short distance in deliberate arcs. Then bring the back of the right *A hand,* palm facing forward, against the lips as if kissing a ring on the ring finger.

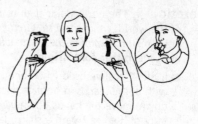

archery[1] *n.* Shooting with a bow and arrow: *practice archery.* Same sign used for: **arrow.**

- ■ [Mime shooting a bow] Beginning with the right *A hand* near the right ear, palm facing left, and the left *S hand* forward of the left side of the chest, move the right hand forward past the right side of the face and then back toward the right shoulder while moving the left hand forward.

archery[2] *n.* (alternate sign) Same sign used for: **arrow.**

- ■ [Represents pulling and releasing a bow string] Beginning with the fingertips of both *8 hands* touching in front of the chest, palms facing each other, pull the right hand back toward the right shoulder while moving the left hand forward and opening it into a *curved hand.*

architect *n.* A person who designs buildings: *the architect's plans for the new community center.*

- ■ [**architecture** + **person marker**] Beginning with the thumbs of both *A hands* touching in front of the face, palms facing forward, move the hands apart and down a short distance at an angle, and then straight down to in front of each side of the chest. Then move both *open hands,* palms facing each other, downward along each side of the body.

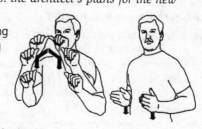

architecture *n.* **1.** The profession of designing buildings: *He majored in architecture in college.* **2.** The character or style of a building: *The cathedral is a fine example of Gothic architecture.* Related form: **architectural** *adj.*

- ■ [Initialized sign similar to sign for **house**] Beginning with the thumbs of both *A hands* touching in front of the face, palms facing forward, move the hands apart and down a short distance at an angle, and then straight down to in front of each side of the chest.

arctic *n.* **1.** The north polar region, the most northern part of the world: *traveled to the arctic.* —*adj.* **2.** Of the north polar region: *explored the arctic wilderness.* Same sign used for: **bitter cold, frigid.**

■ [Natural gesture used when one is very cold] Beginning with both *S hands* in front of each shoulder, palms facing down, move the hands downward toward each other in front of the chest with a sharp deliberate movement, ending with the palms facing in.

are[1] *v.* Plural and second person singular present form of the verb *be: Are you ready?*

■ [Initialized sign similar to sign for **be**[2]] Move the fingers of the right *R hand,* palm facing left, straight forward a short distance from in front of the chin.

are[2] *v.* See sign for BE[2].

area[1] *n.* **1.** A geographical region: *living in the New York area.* **2.** A place with a designated function: *the playground area.* Same sign used for: **place, region, space, vicinity.**

■ [Indicates an area] Beginning with both *5 hands* in front of the chest, palms facing down and fingers pointing forward, move the hands outward and apart in a circular movement to in front of each side of the body.

area[2] *n.* (alternate sign) Same sign used for: **place, region, space, vicinity.**

■ [Initialized sign indicating an area] Beginning with the thumbs of both *A hands* touching in front of the chest, palms facing down, move the hands apart in a backward circular movement until they touch again near the chest.

area[3] *n.* (alternate sign) Same sign used for: **place, region, space, vicinity.**

■ [Indicates an area] Beginning with both *open hands* in front of each side of the body, palms facing down and fingers pointing forward, move the right hand in a large flat arc in front of the body, ending over the left hand.

area[4] *n.* (alternate sign) Same sign used for: **place, region, space, vicinity.**

- [Indicates an area] Move the right *5 hand,* palm facing down and fingers pointing forward, in a flat forward arc in front of the right side of the body.

area[5] *n.* See sign for DISTRICT[1].

argue[1] *v.* To express disagreement in words: *argue about the bill in Congress.* Related form: **argument** *n.* Same sign used for: **controversy, debate, dispute, fight, quarrel, squabble.**

- [Represents opposing points of view] Beginning with both extended index fingers pointing toward each other in front of the chest, palms facing in, shake the hands up and down with a repeated movement by bending the wrists.

argue[2] *v.* (alternate sign) Related form: **argument** *n.* Same sign used for: **controversy, debate, dispute, fight, quarrel, squabble.**

- [Represents opposing points of view] Beginning with both extended index fingers pointing toward each other in front of the chest, one hand higher than the other and palms facing in, move the hands up and down in opposite directions with a repeated movement by bending the wrists.

argument *n.* See signs for DISCUSS[1,2].

arise *v.* To move upward: *arise from your seats.* Same sign used for: **ascend, ascension.**

- [Fingers represent legs rising] Beginning with the fingertips of the right *V hand* touching the upturned left *open hand,* raise the right hand upward a few inches.

aristocracy *n.* A class of people high in social class because of birth or rank: *a well-known member of the aristocracy.* Related form: **aristocrat** *n.*

- [**advanced** + **people**] Move both *bent hands,* palms facing down, from near each shoulder upward in deliberate arcs to the sides of the head. Then move both *P hands,* palms facing down, in alternating forward circles in front of each side of the body.

arithmetic *n.* The method or process of computing with numbers by addition, subtraction, multiplication, or division: *Your arithmetic is incorrect.* Same sign used for: **estimate, figure, figure out, multiplication.**

- Brush the back of the right *V hand* across the palm side of the left *V hand,* both palms facing up, as the hands cross with a double movement in front of the chest.

Arizona *n.* A state in the southwestern United States: *The Hopi live in Arizona.*

- [Initialized sign similar to sign for **dry**] Move the thumb of the right *A hand,* palm facing left, in an arc from the right side of the chin to the left side of the chin.

arm *n.* The limb between the wrist and the shoulder: *a broken arm.*

- [Location] Slide the palm of the right *curved hand* up the length of the extended left arm beginning at the wrist.

army *n.* A military organization for fighting on land: *join the army.* Same sign used for: **Armed Forces, military.**

- [Holding a gun while marching] Tap the palm sides of both *A hands* against the right side of the chest, right hand above the left hand, with a repeated movement.

around¹ *adv.* **1.** On all sides: *A crowd gathered around.* —*prep.* **2.** On all sides of: *build a fence around the yard.* Same sign used for: **orbit, revolve, rotary, surrounding.**

- [Demonstrates moving in a circle around something] Move the extended right index finger, pointing down, in a small circle around the extended left index finger, pointing up in front of the chest.

around[2] *adv.* (alternate sign) Same sign used for: **orbit, revolve, rotary, surrounding.**

■ [Demonstrates moving in a circle around something] Move the extended right index finger, pointing down, in a small circle around the fingertips of the left *flattened O hand,* pointing up in front of the chest.

around[3] *prep.* See sign for APPROXIMATELY.

arouse[1] *v.* To excite: *Their conversation aroused my interest.*

■ [Represents heart palpitations] Beginning with the thumb side of the right *flattened O hand* against the chest, palm facing down, open and close the fingers to the thumb.

arouse[2] *v.* (alternate sign)

■ [Represents heart palpitations] Beginning with the little-finger side of the right *flattened O hand* against the chest, palm facing up, open and close the fingers to the thumb.

arouse[3] *v.* See sign for AWAKE[1].

arrange *v.* See signs for PLAN[1,2], PREPARE. Related form: **arrangement** *n.*

array *n.* A series or display of related items: *an array of numbers.*

■ [Initialized sign showing shape of a column] Bring both *A hands,* palms facing down, up and down simultaneously in front of each side of the chest with a double movement.

arrest *v.* See signs for CAPTURE[1,2,3].

arrive *v.* To reach a destination: *arrive home.* Related form: **arrival** *n.* Same sign used for: **reach.**

■ [Hand moves to arrive in other hand] Move the right *bent hand* from in front of the right shoulder, palm facing left, downward, landing the back of the right hand in the upturned left *curved hand.*

arrogant *adj.* See signs for CONCEITED, HAUGHTY, PROUD.

arrow *n.* See signs for ARCHERY[1,2].

art *n.* **1.** The production of drawings, paintings, or sculpture: *study art.* **2.** The class of objects subject to aesthetic criteria, as drawings, paintings, or sculpture: *an exhibit of Mexican art.* Same sign used for: **drawing, illustration, sketch.**

- [Demonstrates drawing something] Move the extended right little finger with a wiggly movement down the palm of the left *open hand* from the fingers to the heel.

article *n.* A part of a newspaper, magazine, or book dealing with one subject: *read the article on rock climbing.* Same sign used for: **journal.**

- [Shape of a column of newspaper type] Move the right *modified C hand* down the palm of the left *open hand* from the fingers to the heel with a double movement.

artificial *adj.* See signs for FAKE[3,4].

artist *n.* A person who is proficient in one of the fine arts, especially drawing, painting, or sculpture: *The artist exhibited her paintings.* Same sign used for: **illustrator.**

- [art + person marker] Move the extended right little finger with a wiggly movement down the palm of the left *open hand* from the fingers to the heel. Then move both *open hands,* palms facing each other, downward along each side of the body.

as[1] *adv.* **1.** To the same degree: *not as tall.* —*conj.* **2.** In the same manner that: *Do as I say.* **3.** To the same degree that: *to grow as tall as a tree.* Same sign used for: **according to, also, too.**

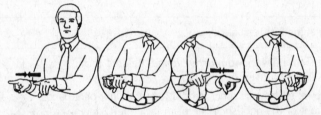

- [Shows two similar things side by side] Tap the sides of both extended index fingers, palms facing down, together, first in front of the right side of the body and then in front of the left side of the body.

as[2] *adv., conj.* (alternate sign) Same sign used for: **also, too.**

- [Shows two similar things side by side] Tap the sides of both extended index fingers, palms facing down, with a double movement in front of the body.

ascend[1] *v.* To go up or rise: *ascend the mountain.* Same sign used for: **ascent.**

- [Represents climbing upward] Beginning with both *H hands* in front of the chest, right palm up and left palm down, repeatedly flip the hands over to place the right *H hand* across the fingers of the left *H hand* as the hands move upward in front of the face.

ascend[2] *v.* See signs for ARISE, CLIMB[1,2,3,4].

ascension *n.* See sign for ARISE.

ashamed[1] *adj.* Feeling shame or disgrace: *ashamed of myself for losing my temper.* See also sign for BASHFUL[1]. Same sign used for: **embarrassed, embarrassment, shame, shameful, shy.**

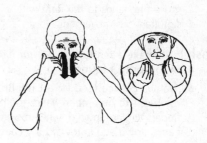

- [Blood rising in the cheeks when ashamed] Beginning with the back of the fingers of both *curved hands* against each cheek, palms facing down, twist the hands forward, ending with the palms facing back.

ashamed[2] *adj.* See sign for EMBARRASS.

ashtray *n.* A container for tobacco ashes: *Put out the cigar in the ashtray.*

- [Mime smoking and tapping off the cigarette ash] Beginning with the fingers of the right *V hand* touching the mouth, palm facing in, bring the right hand downward while changing into a *G hand.* Then rest the thumb of the right *G hand* on the thumb of the left *C hand,* palm facing right, and tap the right index finger up and down on the thumb with a double movement.

Asia *n.* The largest continent, located in the Eastern Hemisphere: *India is in southern Asia.* Related form: **Asian** *adj.*

- [Initialized sign similar to sign for **China**[2]] With the thumb of the right *A hand*, palm facing out, near the outside corner of the right eye, twist the hand forward with a double movement.

aside[1] *adv.* Away to the side: *Put your work aside.* Same sign used for: **put aside, put away.**

- [Natural gesture for pushing something aside] Beginning with both *open hands* in front of the body, both palms facing right and fingers pointing forward, push the hands deliberately to the right.

aside[2] *adv.* (alternate sign) Same sign used for: **put aside, put away.**

- [**put**[1] formed off to the side] Beginning with both *flattened O hands* in front of each side of the body, palms down, move the hands to the right with a simultaneous movement.

ask *v.* To make a request: *to ask for help.* Same sign used for: **pray, request.**

- [Natural gesture used for asking] Bring the palms of both *open hands* together, fingers angled upward, while moving the hands down and in toward the chest.

ASL *n.* See signs for AMERICAN SIGN LANGUAGE[1,2].

asleep *adv.* See signs for FALL ASLEEP[1,2].

aspire *v.* See signs for METHODIST, ZEAL. Related form: **aspiration** *n.*

ass *n. Vulgar.* See sign for BUTTOCKS.

assassin *n.* A person hired to kill a prominent person: *Lincoln's assassin.* Same sign used for: **killer, murderer.**

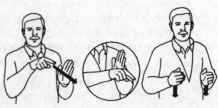

- [**kill**[1] + **person marker**] Move the thumb side of the right extended index finger, palm facing down, across the left *open hand*, palm facing right, with a deliberate movement. Then move both *open hands*, palms facing each other, downward along each side of the body.

assemble[1] *v.* To put together: *assemble the parts of a car.* Same sign used for: **put together.**

- [Mime putting parts together] Bring the fingertips of both *flattened O hands* together, palms facing down, with a double movement in front of the chest changing the angle of the hands each time.

assemble[2] *v.* (alternate sign) Same sign used for: **put together.**

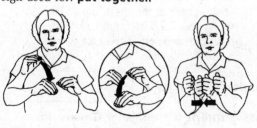

- [**pack**[1] + **with**] Beginning with both *flattened O hands* in front of the chest, palms facing down, move the hands downward with an alternating double movement. Then, beginning with both *A hands* in front of each side of the chest, bring the palms of the hands together in front of the chest.

assemble[3] *v.* To translate symbolic computer code into equivalent machine code: *assemble the program before it can be used.*

- [Initialized sign similar to sign for **interpret**] With the palm side of the right *T hand* on top of the palm side of the left *A hand* in front of the body, twist the wrists in opposite directions to reverse positions.

assemble[4] *v.* See signs for GATHER[1,2,3,4].

Assemblies of God *n.* A Pentecostal church body: *I attend an Assemblies of God church.*

- [Initialized sign + **God**] Move the thumb of the right *A hand*, palm facing left, downward on the forehead. Then move the right *B hand*, palm facing left, from above the head downward in an arc while tipping the fingertips back to point at the center of the forehead.

assembly[1] *n.* The process of putting together the parts of a machine or other products in a sequence of operations: *the assembly of an automobile's parts.*

- [Initialized sign] Tap the side of the right thumb of the *A hand* on the back of the left *open hand*, palm facing down, with a repeated movement.

assembly[2] *n.* See sign for MEETING.

assembly line *n.* An arrangement of
equipment and workers that
assembles a product, piece by piece,
in sequence: *The engines were put
together on an assembly line.* Same
sign used for: **mass-produce.**

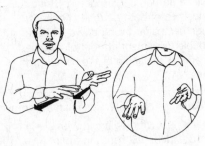

- [Pushing things along on an assembly
  line] With both *4 hands* near each
  other in front of the chest, right palm
  facing down and left palm facing up,
  push the hands off to the right with
  a double movement.

assign *v.* See signs for APPOINT[2], CHOOSE[1,2].

assignment *n.* See sign for APPOINTMENT.

assist *v.* See signs for HELP[1,2].

assistant[1] *n.* **1.** One who helps in a job: *the
teacher's assistant.* —*adj.* **2.** Assisting or
subordinate: *the assistant manager of the store.*
Same sign used for: **aide.**

- [One hand assists the other hand] Use the thumb
  of the right *L hand* under the little-finger side of
  the left *A hand* to push the left hand upward in
  front of the chest.

assistant[2] *n.* (alternate sign) Related form: **assist** *v.*
Same sign used for: **aide.**

- [Initialized sign showing giving a boost or aid to
  another] Use the thumb of the right *A hand* under
  the little-finger side of the left *A hand* to push the
  left hand upward in front of the chest.

associate *v.* **1.** To come together with others: *to associate with
criminals.* —*n.* **2.** A person who shares actively in an
enterprise: *a business associate.* Same sign used for:
**acquaint, brotherhood, each other, fellowship,
fraternity, interact, mingle, mutual, one another,
socialize.**

- [Represents mingling with each other] With the
  thumb of the left *A hand* pointing up and the thumb
  of the right *A hand* pointing down, circle the thumbs
  around each other while moving the hands from left
  to right in front of the chest.

association *n.* An organization of people with common interests: *a professional association*. Related form: **associate** *v.* Same sign used for: **agency, fellowship.**

■ [Initialized sign similar to sign for **class**] Beginning with the thumbs of both *A hands* touching in front of the chest, palms facing down, move the hands apart and forward in a circular movement by twisting the wrists until the little fingers touch and the palms face in.

assume *v.* See signs for GUESS, TAKE[2]. Related form: **assumption** *n.*

assure *v.* See sign for VOW[1]. Related form: **assurance** *n.*

asterisk *n.* See sign for STAR. Shared idea that a star and an asterisk have a similar shape.

asthma[1] *n.* A disease that makes breathing difficult: *an asthma attack*.

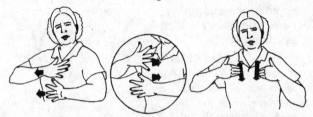

■ [**breath + lung**] With the right *5 hand* in front of the chest above the left *5 hand*, fingers pointing in opposite directions and palms facing in, move both hands forward and back toward the chest with a short double movement. Then rub the fingertips of both *bent hands* up and down on each side of the chest with a double movement.

asthma[2] *n.* (alternate sign)

■ [Initialized sign formed similar to **lung**] Rub the palm sides of both *A hands* up and down on each side of the chest with a double movement.

astonish[1] *v.* To surprise greatly: *astonished at the huge donation*. Related form: **astonishment** *n.*

■ [Represents jumping up with bent legs and falling over in astonishment] Beginning with the fingertips of the right *V hand*, palm facing in, on the palm of the left *open hand* held in front of the chest, palm facing up, bring the right hand upward in front of the chest while crooking the fingers and then down again, landing with the back of the *bent V hand* on the left palm.

astonish[2] *v.* See sign for SURPRISE. Related form: **astonishment** *n.*

astound *v.* See signs for FLABBERGAST[1,2], SURPRISE.

astounded *adj.* See sign for SHOCK[1].

astray *adv., adj.* Off the right path or course: *The letter went astray.* Same sign used for: **backslide, deviate, estranged, offshoot, off the point, off track, out of the way, sidetracked, stray.**

- [Shows one hand veering off the path] Beginning with both index fingers touching in front of the chest, palms facing down, slide the right index finger forward along the side of the left index finger, moving the right hand off to the right as it moves forward.

astrology *n.* The study of stars and planets and their influence on people and events: *My sign in astrology is Virgo.* Related form: **astrological** *adj.*

- [Initialized sign similar to sign for **star**] Beginning with the thumbs of both *A hands* together in front of the chest, palms facing forward, move the right hand upward while bringing the left hand downward, and then reverse the positions of the hands.

asylum *n.* A hospital for mentally ill people: *They put her in an asylum.*

- [**insane**[1] + **hospital**[1]] Move the fingers of the right *4 hand,* palm facing down and fingers pointing in, back and forth with a double movement in front of the face. Then bring the fingertips of the right *H hand,* palm facing in, from back to front on the upper left arm and then downward a short distance.

asynchronous *adj.* Denoting a mode of data communications that provides a variable time interval between characters: *asynchronous transmission of data.*

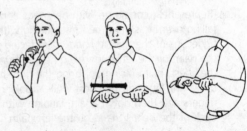

- [**not**[1] + **standard**[2]] Bring the extended thumb of the right *10 hand* from under the chin, palm facing left, forward with a deliberate movement. Then, beginning with both *Y hands* in front of the left side of the body, palms facing down, move the hands smoothly across to in front of the right side of the body.

at *prep.* **1.** Used to show location in space: *She's at home now.* **2.** Used for locations in time: *at night.*

- ■ [Fingertips arrive at back of other hand] Hit the fingertips of the right *bent hand* against the back of the left *open hand,* palm angled forward.

at fault *adj.* See sign for BLAME[1].

athletics *n.* See sign for RACE[1,2].

Atlanta *n.* The capital of Georgia: *Atlanta is the commercial center of the southeastern United States.*

- ■ [Initialized sign] Move the thumb of the right *A hand* in an arc from a position touching the left side of the chest, palm facing left, to touch the right side of the chest.

at last *adv. phrase.* See sign for FINALLY[1].

atmosphere *n.* **1.** The air that surrounds the earth or other planet: *the city's polluted atmosphere.* **2.** Pervading mood or environment: *the atmosphere of freedom.*

- ■ [Initialized sign similar to sign for **situation**] Beginning with the right *A hand,* palm facing left, near the extended left index finger held in front of the chest, palm facing right, move the right hand in a small circle forward and around the left index finger.

at odds *adj.* See sign for STRUGGLE.

atop *prep.* On top of: *atop the mountain.*

- ■ [Indicates location of something atop another thing] Place the fingertips of the right *curved 5 hand,* palm facing down, on the back of the left *S hand* held in front of the chest, palm facing down.

attach *v.* See sign for BELONG[1].

attack[1] *v.* **1.** To set upon with violence: *attack the enemy.* —*n.* **2.** The act of attacking: *set up a defense against an attack.*

- [**hit**[1] + forcing another down] Bring the knuckles of the right *S hand,* palm facing in, forward from in front of the right shoulder to hit against the extended left index finger, palm facing forward and finger pointing up, forcing the left finger downward in front of the body.

attack[2] *v.* **1.** To set upon with violence (used for more than one person or thing going after another): *The gang attacked the old man.* —*n.* **2.** The act of many attacking one: *to protect oneself from an attack by muggers.*

- [One hand attacks the other and pushes it down] Bring the palm of the right *curved 5 hand* forward to push the extended left index finger downward in front of the body.

attack[3] *v.* See sign for HIT[1].

attain *v.* See sign for GET.

attempt[1] *v.* **1.** To make an effort: *attempt an escape but fail.* —*n.* **2.** The effort made to accomplish something: *His attempt to win the election failed.* Same sign used for: **make an effort.**

- [Initialized sign similar to sign for **try**[1]] Move both *A hands* from in front of each side of the body, palms facing each other, downward and forward simultaneously in an arc.

attempt[2] *v.* See sign for TRY[1].

attend[1] *v.* To be present at: *attend church.* Same sign used for: **go to.**

- [Represents people moving toward an event] Beginning with both extended index fingers pointing up in front of the chest, right hand closer to the chest than the left and both palms facing forward, move both hands forward simultaneously while bending the wrists so the fingers point forward.

attend[2] *v.* See signs for GATHER[2,3].

attendance *n.* Same sign as for ATTEND[1] but formed with a double movement. Same sign used for: **go to regularly.**

attention *n.* Careful concentration on something: *Pay close attention to what I'm doing.* Related form: **attend** *v.* Same sign used for: **concentrate, concentration, focus on, pay attention, watch.**

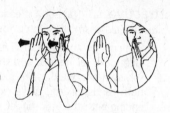

- [Forms blinkers to direct one's attention] Move both *open hands* from near each cheek, palms facing each other, straight forward simultaneously.

attic *n.* A space in a house just below the roof and above the other rooms: *to hide in the attic.*

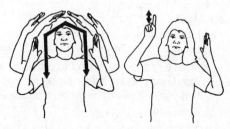

- [**house** formed higher than usual + **upstairs**] Beginning with the fingertips of both *open hands* touching at an angle above the head, palms angled toward each other, bring the hands downward at an angle outward to in front of each shoulder and then straight down, ending with the fingers pointing up and the palms facing each other. Then point the extended right index finger upward with a double movement near the right side of the head.

attitude *n.* A general way of feeling about something: *a bad attitude toward work.*

- [Initialized sign similar to sign for **personality**] Move the thumb of the right *A hand* in a circular movement around the heart, palm facing left, ending with the thumb against the chest.

attorney *n.* A person who represents another in a legal situation: *hire an attorney to defend him.* Same sign used for: **lawyer.**

- [**law** + **person marker**] Place the palm side of the right *L hand*, palm facing left, first on the fingers and then the heel of the left *open hand*, palm facing right. Then move both *open hands*, palms facing each other, downward along each side of the body.

attract[1] *v.* To draw by appeal: *attract a crowd of admirers.* Same sign used for: **draw.**

- [Hands pull something to oneself] Beginning with both *curved hands* in front of each side of the body, palms facing up, bring the hands back toward the body while closing into *A hands.*

attract[2] *v.* See sign for ABSORB[1].

attractive *adj.* Having a pleasant appearance: *an attractive smile.* Related form: **attracted to.**

■ Beginning with the right *C hand* in front of the face, palm facing left, and the left *C hand* somewhat forward, palm facing right, move both hands forward while closing into *S hands,* ending with the little-finger side of the right hand near the thumb side of the left hand.

auction *n.* **1.** A public sale of goods by bidding: *to sell a painting at an auction.* —*v.* **2.** to sell at auction: *to auction off your furniture.* Same sign used for: **bid.**

■ [Mime raising one's hand to bid at an auction] Move both *open hands,* palms facing forward, in an alternating upward movement beside each side of the head.

audience[1] *n.* **1.** A group assembled at a performance: *a large audience in the theater.* **2.** A regular public with interest in a book, a play, or the like: *The audience for this book is parents of chuldren with disabilities.* See also sign for HORDE. Same sign used for: **congregation, crowd.**

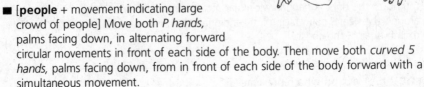

■ [**people** + movement indicating large crowd of people] Move both *P hands,* palms facing down, in alternating forward circular movements in front of each side of the body. Then move both *curved 5 hands,* palms facing down, from in front of each side of the body forward with a simultaneous movement.

audience[2] *n.* (alternate sign) See also sign for HORDE. Same sign used for: **congregation, crowd.**

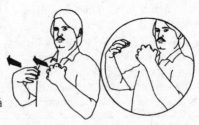

■ [Represents large crowd of people swelling forward] Move both *curved 5 hands,* palms facing in, from near each side of the chest forward with a simultaneous movement.

audience[3] *n.* (alternate sign) Same sign used for: **crowd.**

[Represents people standing in a circle around an attraction] Beginning with both *4 hands* in front of the chest, palms facing in and fingers pointing up, move the hands away from each other in arcs back toward the chest, ending with the hands in front of each shoulder, palms facing each other.

audiologist *n.* A person trained to measure hearing and hearing loss: *The audiologist tested my hearing.*

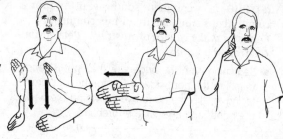

- **[person marker + specialty + hear]** Move both *open hands*, palms facing each other, downward along the sides of the body. Then slide the little-finger side of the right *B hand* along the index-finger side of the left *B hand* held in front of the chest. Then bring the extended right index finger to touch the right ear.

audiology *n.* The study of hearing and hearing measurement: *to study clinical audiology.* Related form: **audio** *adj.*

- [Initialized sign formed near the ear] Move the thumb of the right *A hand* in a circular movement, palm facing forward, around the right ear.

audit *n.* **1.** A formal examination of financial records: *The comptroller reviewed the audit of the company records.* —*v.* **2.** To make an audit of (accounts, records, etc.): *audit the company's books.*

- [Initialized sign similar to sign for **count**] Swing the palm side of the right *A hand* with a double movement from the fingers to the heel of the left *open hand* held in front of the body, palm facing up.

auditor *n.* A person who formally examines financial records: *The auditor examined the accounts.*

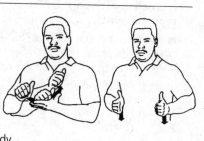

- **[audit + person marker]** Swing the palm side of the right *A hand* with a double movement from the fingers to the heel of the left *open hand* held in front of the body, palm facing up. Then move both *open hands*, palms facing each other, downward along the sides of the body.

auditory *adj.* See sign for HEAR.

aunt *n.* **1.** The sister of one's mother or father: *my aunt and uncle.* **2.** The wife of one's uncle: *Meet my new aunt.*

- [Initialized sign formed near the female area of the head] Move the right *A hand* in a circular movement, palm facing forward, near the right cheek.

Australia[1] *n.* A continent southeast of Asia, or a country consisting chiefly of this continent: *Canberra is the capital of Australia.* Related form: **Australian** *adj., n.*

- Beginning with the fingers of the right *B hand* touching the right side of the forehead, palm facing in, flip the hand over, bringing the back of the right hand against the forehead.

Australia[2] *n.* (alternate sign)

- [Mimics a kangaroo's jump] Beginning with both *F hands* in front of the body, palms facing down, move the hands forward in small arcs while opening both thumbs and index fingers.

Austria *n.* A republic in eastern Europe: *The capital of Austria is Vienna.* Related form: **Austrian** *adj., n.*

- [Design on the Austrian flag] With the wrists crossed, place the index-finger sides of both *X hands* on the chest near the opposite shoulder, palms facing in.

author *n.* A person who writes a book, story, article, or other work: *the author of this book.* Same sign used for: **journalist, playwright, recorder, reporter, writer.**

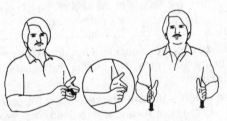

- [**write**[1] + **person marker**] Slide the palm side of the right *modified X hand* across the upturned left *open hand* with a double movement. Then move both *open hands*, palms facing each other, downward along each side of the body.

authority[1] *n.* A person with power or expertise: *My boss is the real authority in this office.*

- [Initialized sign similar to sign for **strong**[2]] Beginning with the extended thumb of the right *A hand*, palm facing left, near the left shoulder, move the hand down in an arc while twisting the right wrist, ending with the little-finger side of the right hand in the crook of the left arm, bent across the body.

authority[2] *n.* (alternate sign)

■ [**powerful** + **have**[1]] Touch the fingertips of the right *claw hand* to the left upper arm. Then bring in the fingertips of both *bent hands,* palms facing in, to touch each side of the chest.

automatic[1] *adj.* Having a self-acting mechanism: *an automatic starter in the new car.* Same sign used for: **automatic transmission.**

■ [Indicates repetitive movement of something operating automatically] Move the extended right curved index finger, palm facing in, back and forth on the back of the left *open hand,* palm facing in, with a repeated movement.

automatic[2] *adj.* (alternate sign) Same sign used for: **automatic transmission.**

■ Move the extended right curved index finger, palm facing in, back and forth on the side of the extended left index finger, palm facing down.

automatic[3] *adj.* See signs for FAST[1,2,3].

automobile *n.* See signs for CAR[1,2].

autopsy *n.* A medical examination of a dead body to find the cause of death: *The autopsy revealed cancer.*

■ [**die**[1] + **operate**[2] formed with a repeated movement] Beginning with both *open hands* in front of the body, right palm facing up and left palm facing down, flip the hands to the left, turning the right palm down and the left palm up. Then move the thumbs of both *10 hands* downward on each side of the chest, in short alternating movements.

autumn *n.* See sign for FALL[3].

available *adj.* See sign for EMPTY.

avenge *v.* See sign for REVENGE.

avenue *n.* See sign for ROAD[1].

average[1] *adj.* Approximately midway: *an average score.* Same sign used for: **mean, medium.**
- ■ [Shows split down the middle] Beginning with the little-finger side of the right *open hand* across the index-finger side of the left *open hand,* palms angled down, twist the wrists down, bringing the hands apart a short distance with a double movement, palms facing down.

average[2] *adj.* (alternate sign) Same sign used for: **mean, medium.**
- ■ [Indicates the middle ground] Brush the little-finger side of the right *open hand,* palm angled left, back and forth on the index finger of the left *open hand,* palm angled right, by twisting the right wrist.

aviator *n.* See sign for PILOT.

avoid[1] *v.* To keep away from: *avoid the cold.* Related form: **avoidable** *adj.* Same sign used for: **back out, elude, evade, fall behind, get away, shirk.**
- ■ [One hand moves away from the other to avoid it] Beginning with the knuckles of the right *A hand,* palm facing left, near the base of the thumb of the left *A hand,* palm facing right, bring the right hand back toward the body with a wiggly movement.

avoid[2] *v.* See sign for ABHOR.

awake[1] *v.* To cease sleeping: *awake in the morning.* Related form: **awaken** *v.* Same sign used for: **arouse, wake up.**
- ■ [Indicates eyes opening when becoming awake] Beginning with the *modified X hands* near each eye, palms facing each other, quickly flick the fingers apart while widening the eyes.

awake[2] *adj.* See sign for INSOMNIA.

award[1] *n.* Something given as a prize: *win the award for the best essay.*

- [**trophy**[1] + **gift**[1]] Tap the thumbs and little fingers of both *Y hands,* palms facing in, against each other with a double movement in front of the chest. Then, beginning with both *X hands* in front of the chest, palms facing each other, move the hands forward in simultaneous arcs.

award[2] *n.* See signs for GIFT[1,2], TROPHY[1].

award[3] *v.* See sign for GIVE[1].

awards *pl. n.* See sign for ALLOCATE[2].

aware[1] *adj.* Having knowledge: *was not aware of the fact.* Same sign used for: **conscious, familiar, knowledge.**

- [Shows location of awareness] Tap the fingertips of the right *bent hand,* palm facing in, against the right side of the forehead with a double movement.

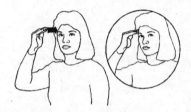

aware[2] *adj.* See sign for NOTICE[1].

away *adj., adv.* In or to another place: *She is away. Go away.* Same sign used for: **get away, go.**

- [Natural gesture as if shooing something away] Flip the fingers of the right *open hand* from pointing down near the right side of the body outward to the right by flicking the wrist upward with a quick movement.

awesome *adj.* See signs for FLABBERGAST[1,2].

awful *adj.* Disagreeable or dreadful: *an awful choice.* Same sign used for: **disastrous, dreadful, fierce, horrible, sordid, terrible.**

- [Natural gesture used when indicating something terrible] Beginning with both *8 hands* near each side of the head, palms facing each other, flip the fingers open to *5 hands* while twisting the palms forward.

a while ago See signs for RECENTLY[1]; WHILE AGO, A[1].

awkward *adj.* Not graceful: *awkward movements.* Same sign used for: **clumsy.**

- ■ [Represents walking awkwardly] Beginning with both *3 hands* in front of the body, right hand higher than the left and both palms facing down, raise the left and then the right hand in alternating movements.

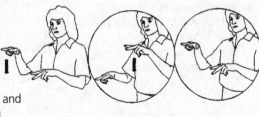

babble *v.* See signs for BLAB, PRATTLE.

baby[1] *n.* A very young child: *a six-month-old baby.*
Same sign used for: **infant.**

- [Action of rocking a baby in one's arms] With the bent
right arm cradled on the bent left arm, both palms
facing up, swing the arms to the right and the left in
front of the body with a double movement.

baby[2] or **babe** *n. Slang.* A flirting term of address:
Hey, baby!

- Beginning with the back of the left *curved hand* resting
in the palm of the right *curved hand,* both palms facing up
and fingers pointing in opposite directions in front of the
body, drop the hands slightly.

bachelor *n.* A man who has never married:
He's 45 years old and still a bachelor. Related
form: **bachelorette** *n.*

- [Initialized sign] Move the index finger of the
right *B hand* from touching the left side of the
chin, palm facing left, in an arc to touch the
right side of the chin.

back[1] *n.* The rear upper portion of the body below the neck:
Scratch my back. Same sign used for: **dorsal, lumbar, rear.**

- [Natural gesture indicating location] Pat the fingertips
of the right *open hand* behind the right shoulder with
a repeated movement.

back[2] *n.* **1.** The rear part or reverse side of
something: *the back of an envelope.* —*adv.* **2.** In
or toward a former place: *go back home.* **3.** In or
toward the past: *Back in my youth I could do a
somersault* —*adj.* **4.** Situated in the rear: *the back
staircase.* Same sign used for: **rear.**

- [Indicates a time or place in the past] Move the
thumb of the right *10 hand,* palm facing left,
with a deliberate movement back over the right shoulder.

back[3] *v.* See signs for SUPPORT[1,2].

backache *n.* A pain or ache in the back, usually in the lumbar region: *He does exercises to alleviate the pain of his backache.* Same sign used for: **lumbago.**

- [**pain**[1] formed near the back] Beginning with the extended index fingers of both *1 hands* pointing toward each other near the right side of the body, right palm facing down and left palm facing up, twist the wrists in opposite directions, ending with the right palm facing up and the left palm facing down.

back and forth See sign for COMMUTE.

backbone *n.* See sign for SPINE.

background *n.* **1.** Past experience, training, or family origins: *a background in journalism. She comes from a working-class background.* **2.** The part of a scene behind the main objects: *The volcano was far in the background behind the pastoral scene.* **3.** The circumstances leading up to or explaining an event or situation: *the background of the war.*

- [Abbreviation **b-g**] In quick succession tap the index-finger side of the right *B hand* and then *G hand*, palm facing forward, against the left *open hand*, palm facing right.

back out *v. phrase.* See signs for AVOID[1], RECOIL, RESIGN.

backpack *n.* **1.** A bag with straps designed to be carried on the back: *carried his books in a backpack.* —*v.* **2.** To go hiking with a bag of food and equipment on the back: *to go backpacking in the hills.*

- [Action of putting on a backpack] Move the thumbs of both *curved 3 hands,* palms facing forward, downward toward each shoulder with a double movement.

backslide *v.* See signs for ASTRAY, BEHIND.

backslash *n.* **1.** A keyboard key. **2.** A character (\) used to separate directory and file names in some operating systems: *Access the hard drive by typing "C" followed by a colon and backslash.*

- [**slash + backspace**] Bring the right *B hand,* palm facing left, from in front of the right shoulder downward to the left with a deliberate movement. Then, beginning with the right *10 hand* in front of the chest, palm down, twist the hands upward to the right, ending with the palm up and the extended thumb pointing right.

backspace *n.* **1.** A keyboard key. **2.** A keyboard operation that moves the cursor one position to the left, allowing modification of what has already been typed.

- [Indicates a location in the past] Beginning with the right *10 hand* in front of the chest, palm down, twist the hand upward to the right, ending with the palm up and the extended thumb pointing right.

backup[1] *n.* **1.** A duplicate copy of computer data or a software program for use if the original fails: *Keep a backup of your file.* —*adj.* **2.** Designating such a copy: *a backup copy to be kept in a safe place.* —*v.* **3. back up** To make such a copy: *Back up your program.*

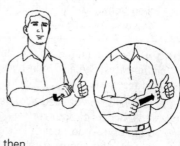

- [Hand moves to provide support for the other hand] Beginning with the right *10 hand,* palm facing down, beside the left *10 hand,* palm facing right, move the right hand clockwise in an arc and then forward to the heel of the left hand, ending with the right palm facing left.

backup[2] *n.* See signs for SUPPORT[1,2].

bacon *n.* Smoked meat from a hog, usually in thin slices: *bacon and eggs for breakfast.*

- [Hands indicate wavy shape of fried bacon] With the thumbs of both hands pointing up and fingers of both *U hands* touching in front of the chest, palms facing in, bring the hands apart while bending the fingers back into each palm with a double movement.

bad *adj.* **1.** Not good; harmful: *Sugar is bad for your teeth.* **2.** Inaccurate or invalid: *a bad idea.* **3.** Unpleasant or unfavorable: *to have a bad time at the party.* Related form: **badly** *adv.* Same sign used for: **evil, nasty, naughty, wicked.**

- [Gesture tosses away something that tastes bad] Move the fingers of the right *open hand* from the mouth, palm facing in, downward while flipping the palm quickly down as the hand moves.

badge[1] *n.* A small sign worn for identification: *wear a name badge.* Same sign used for: **button, emblem, get pinned.**

- [Putting on a badge] Bring the index-finger side of the right *F hand,* palm facing left, against the left side of the chest with a double movement.

badge[2] *n.* See signs for POLICE[1,2].

badminton *n.* A game played using light, slender rackets to hit a shuttlecock over a high net: *Let's play badminton instead of tennis.*

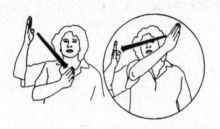

- [Initialized sign similar to sign for **tennis**] Bring the right *B hand*, palm facing left, first from above the right shoulder downward diagonally across the face, and then from above the left shoulder downward to the right.

bag *n.* A soft container that opens at the top: *a bag of potato chips.* See also sign for BASKET. Same sign used for: **sack.**

- [Shows shape of filled bag] Beginning with the little fingers of both *curved hands* touching in front of the body, palms facing up, bring the hands apart and upward in an arc while spreading the fingers, ending with both *curved 5 hands* in front of each side of the chest, palms facing each other.

baggage *n.* The containers one carries when traveling, as trunks and suitcases: *The airline misplaced my baggage when I changed planes.* Same sign used for: **luggage.**

- [Shows carrying a bag in each hand] Shake both *S hands*, palms facing in, up and down with a short movement near each side of the waist with the elbows bent.

bail *n.* Money used to guarantee a released prisoner's appearance in court: *He posted bail for his friend.*

- [jail[1,2] + **money** + **deposit**[2]] Bring the back of the right *5 hand* from near the chest, forward, while bringing the left *5 hand* in to meet the right hand, ending with the fingers crossed at angles, both palms facing in. Then tap the back of the right *flattened O hand*, palm facing up, with a double movement against the palm of the left *open hand*, palm facing up. Then, beginning with the thumb of the right *C hand* on the back of the left *open hand*, palm facing up, move the right hand forward in a short arc.

bait *n.* Something used on a hook as a lure in fishing: *to use worms as bait.*

- [**fish**[1,2] + **addicted** + **catch**[2,3]] Beginning with the extended left index finger pointing toward the wrist of the right *B hand,* palm facing left and fingers pointing forward, wave the fingers of the right hand from side to side with a double movement by bending the wrist. Then, with the index finger of the right *X hand* hooked in the right corner of the mouth, pull the mouth outward to the right. Then move the right *curved 5 hand* from in front of the right side of the chest, palm facing left, to the left to close around the extended left index finger held up in front of the chest, palm facing right.

bake[1] *v.* To cook by dry, indirect heat, especially in an oven: *bake a cake.*

- [Putting something in the oven] Move the fingers of the right *open hand,* palm facing up, forward under the left *open hand* held in front of the chest, palm facing down.

bake[2] *v.* See sign for COOK[1].

balance *v.* **1.** To be or hold steady: *to balance on one leg.* **2.** To be or make equivalent in weight, amount, or proportion: *to balance work and pleasure.* —*n.* **3.** Equal distribution of weight, amount, etc.: *An excess of goods destroyed the trade balance.* **4.** An instrument for weighing: *to weigh gold on a balance.*

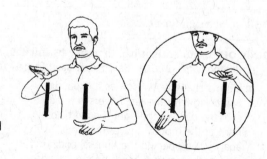

- [Action shows trying to balance something] With an alternating movement bring the right *open hand* and the left *open hand,* both palms facing down, up and down in front of each side of the chest, shifting the entire torso slightly with each movement.

balcony *n.* An outside platform with a door to an upper floor: *go out on the balcony.*

- [**outside**¹ + represents a porch affixed to the exterior] Beginning with the right *flattened O hand* inserted in the opening of the left *C hand*, move the right hand upward and forward in an arc. Then tap the fingertips of the right *C hand* against the back of the left *open hand*, both palms facing in.

bald *adj.* Without hair: *a bald head.* Related form: **baldness** *n.* Same sign used for: **bareheaded, halo, scalp.**

- [Indicates bare area of head] Move the bent middle finger of the right *5 hand*, palm facing down, in a circle around the top of the head.

ball¹ *n.* A round object used in games: *throw the ball.*

- [The shape of a ball] Touch the fingertips of both *curved 5 hands* together with a double movement in front of the chest, palms facing each other.

ball² *n.* Anything round: *a ball of string.* Same sign used for: **globe, sphere.**

- [The shape of a globe] Beginning with the index-finger side of both *curved 5 hands* together in front of the chest, palms facing down and fingers pointing forward, bring the hands downward and outward with a circular movement, coming back together in front of the body, ending with the little-finger sides of both hands together, palms facing up and fingers pointing forward.

ball³ *n.* See sign for DANCE.

balloon¹ *n.* An airtight bag that may be inflated, used as a toy or decoration: *blowing up balloons for a party.* Same sign used for: **expand.**

- [Shows shape of balloon as it expands] Beginning with the left fingers cupped over the back of the right *S hand* held in front of the mouth, move the hands apart while opening the fingers, ending with both *curved 5 hands* near each side of the face, palms facing each other.

balloon[2] *n.* (alternate sign) Same sign used for: **expand.**

- [Shows shape of balloon as it expands] Beginning with the thumb of the right *S hand* near the mouth and the index finger of the left *S hand* touching the right little finger, palms facing in opposite directions, move the hands apart while opening the fingers, ending with both *curved 5 hands* near each side of the face, palms facing each other.

balloon[3] *n.* (alternate sign)

- [Shows shape of balloon] Beginning with the thumbs of both *curved 5 hands* near each side of the mouth, palms facing each other, move the hands apart and forward in an arc until the little fingers touch, palms facing in.

ballot *n.* A piece of paper used in voting: *cast your ballot.*

- [**vote** + **paper**] Bring the thumb and forefinger of the right *F hand* downward with a double movement into the opening at the top of the left *S hand* held in front of the chest, palm facing right. Then brush the heel of the right *open hand*, palm facing down, on the heel of the left *open hand*, palm facing up, in front of the body with a double movement.

ballroom *n.* A large room for dancing: *Reserve the ballroom for the dance.*

- [**big**[1,2] + **dance** + **room**[1,2]] Move both *L hands* from in front of the waist, palms facing each other and index fingers pointing forward, apart to each side in large arcs. Then, swing the fingers of the right *V hand*, palms facing in and fingers pointing down, back and forth over the upturned left *open hand*. Then, beginning with both *open hands* in front of each side of the body, palms facing each other, turn the hands sharply in opposite directions, ending with both palms facing in.

Baltimore[1] *n.* A seaport city in Maryland: *They live in Baltimore.*

- [Initialized sign] Move the right *B hand*, palm facing left, downward with a short double movement and then to the right in an arc and down again.

Baltimore[2] *n.* (alternate sign)

- [Initialized sign] Move the right *B hand,* palm facing left and fingers pointing forward, up and down with a double movement in front of the right side of the body.

ban *v.* See signs for FORBID, PREVENT.

banana[1] *n.* A long, curved, yellow tropical fruit: *peel a banana.*

- [Mime peeling a banana] With the extended left index finger pointing up in front of the chest, palm facing forward, bring the fingertips of the right *curved 5 hand* downward, first on the back and then on the front of the index finger, while closing the right fingers to the thumb each time.

banana[2] *n.* (alternate sign)

- [Mime peeling a banana] With the extended left index finger pointing up in front of the chest, palm facing forward, bring the right *A hand,* palm facing down, downward, first on the back and then on the front of the left index finger.

band[1] *n.* A group of musicians: *plays drums in the band.* Same sign used for: **choir, orchestra.**

- [**music + class**] Swing the little-finger side of the right *open hand,* palm facing in, back and forth across the length of the bent left forearm. Then, beginning with the thumbs of both *C hands* near each other in front of the body, palms facing, bring the hands apart and outward in an arc, ending with the hands in front of the chest, palms facing in.

band[2] *n.* (alternate sign) Same sign used for: **choir, orchestra.**

- [**music + group**[1]] Swing the little-finger side of the right *open hand,* palm facing in, back and forth across the length of the bent left forearm. Then, beginning with the thumbs of both *G hands* near each other in front of the body, palms facing, bring the hands apart and outward in an arc, ending with the little fingers together in front of the chest, palms facing in.

bandage[1] *n.* **1.** A strip of material used in dressing a wound: *Put a bandage on the cut.* **2.** *v.* To apply a dressing to a wound: *The nurse bandaged the open sore.* Same sign used for: **adhesive tape, Band-Aid** (*trademark*), **tape.**

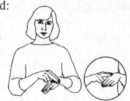

■ [Mime putting on a bandage] Pull the right H fingers, palm facing down, across the back of the left *open hand,* palm facing down.

bandage[3] *n., v.* (alternate sign)

■ [Putting tape around a wound] Beginning with the fingers of the right *H hand* touching the little-finger side of the left *open hand,* palm down, move the right hand in a circular movement completely around the left hand.

banded together See sign for RELATIONSHIP.

bandit *n.* See signs for ROBBER[1,2].

bang *n.* **1.** A sudden, loud noise: *I heard a loud bang on the door.* —*v.* **2.** To hit sharply or with a sudden, loud noise: *banging on the door with his fist.* **3.** To hit with a violent blow: *I banged my head on the door.* Same sign used for: **pound.**

■ [Action of striking something] Bring the little-finger side of the right *S hand* from in front of the right side of the chest, forward to hit against palm of the left *open hand* with a double movement.

bangs *pl. n.* A fringe of hair worn over the forehead: *I have curly bangs.*

■ [Shows location of bangs] Place the fingers of the left *4 hand* on the forehead, palm facing back and fingers pointing down.

bank *n.* **1.** A place of business for keeping money and executing other money transactions: *to deposit money in the bank.* —*v.* **2.** To put or keep money in a bank: *I bank at City National Bank.*

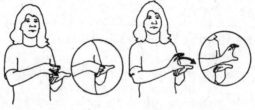

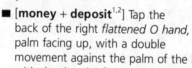

■ [**money** + **deposit**[1,2]] Tap the back of the right *flattened O hand,* palm facing up, with a double movement against the palm of the left *open hand,* palm facing up. Then, beginning with the thumb of the right *C hand* on the back of the left *open hand,* palm facing up, move the right hand forward in a short arc.

bankrupt *adj.* See sign for PENNILESS[3].

banquet *n.* A large meal prepared for a special occasion: *a wedding banquet.* Same sign used for: **feast, reception.**

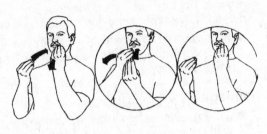

- [Indicates continuous eating] Bring the fingertips of both *flattened O hands,* palms facing down, to the mouth with repeated alternating movements.

banter *v., n.* See sign for STRUGGLE.

baptism[1] *n.* A Christian religious ceremony using water as a sign of washing away sin: *the child's baptism.* Related form: **Baptist, baptize** *v.*

- [Indicates dipping a person into water] Move both *A hands,* right palm facing up and left palm facing down, from in front of the right side of the body in a large arc to in front of the left side of the body and back again, flipping the hands over each time.

baptism[2] *n.* (alternate sign) Related form: **baptize** *v.* Same sign used for: **christen.**

- [**water** + sprinkling water on the head] Tap the index finger of the right *W hand* against the chin with a double movement. Then, beginning with the right *flattened O hand* above the right side of the head, palm facing down, flick the fingers open with a deliberate movement.

baptism[3] *n.* (alternate sign) Related form: **baptize** *v.*

- [**water** + pouring water on the head] Tap the index finger of the right *W hand* against the chin with a double movement. Then, beginning with the right *C hand* above the right side of the head, palm facing left, tip the hand backward as if pouring.

baptism[4] *n.* (alternate sign) Related form:
baptize *v.*

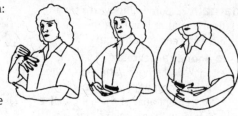

- [Sprinkling water + **baby**[1]] Beginning
  with the *flattened O hand*, palm
  facing down, above the left bent arm
  cradled across the front of the body,
  flick the fingers open with a deliberate
  movement. Then, with the bent right
  arm cradled on the bent left arm, both palms facing up, swing the arms to the left
  and then to the right in front of the body with a double movement.

Baptist *n.* See sign for BAPTISM[1].

bar *n.* See signs for DRINK, SALOON.

barbecue *n.* **1.** An outdoor meal where meat is roasted
over an open fire: *to have a barbecue in the back yard.*
—*v.* **2.** To roast meat over an open fire: *Let's barbecue
the steaks.*

- [Abbreviation **b-b-q**] Form the letters B, B, and Q in
  front of the right shoulder, palm facing forward, moving
  the hand slightly to the right with each letter.

barber *n.* A person in business to cut hair,
especially men's hair: *I go to the barber
regularly.*

- [Mime cutting hair + **person marker**] Move
  the right *V hand*, palm facing left, back along
  the side of the head while opening and closing
  the fingers. Then move both *open hands*,
  palms facing each other, down along the sides
  of the body.

bar code *n.* See sign for STRIPE.

bare[1] *adj.* Without covering: *bare shoulders.*

- [Indicates a bare area] Move the bent middle
  finger of the right *5 hand*, palm facing down,
  in a double circle on the back of the left *open
  hand*, palm facing down.

bare[2] *adj.* See signs for EMPTY, NUDE.

bareheaded *adj.* See sign for BALD.

barely *adv.* See signs for ALMOST[1], CLOSE CALL.

bargain *n.* Something worth buying that is sold at less than the usual cost: *to shop for a bargain.*

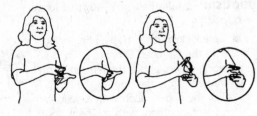

- **[money + decrease**[2,3]**]** Tap the back of the right *flattened O hand*, palm facing up, with a double movement against the palm of the left *open hand*, palm facing up. Then, with the thumb of the right *C hand* resting on the left *open hand*, palm facing down, lower the right fingers forming a *flattened C hand*.

bark[1] *n.* The outside covering of a tree: *strip the bark from the tree trunk.*

- **[tree** + a movement demonstrating peeling back a tree's bark] With the fingers of the left *open hand*, palm down, touching the elbow of the bent right arm, twist the right *5 hand* back and forth with a double movement. Then, beginning with the palm side of the left *A hand* near the bent right elbow, move the left hand forward in an arc with a double movement, turning the palm upward each time.

bark[2] *v.* To make the loud, sharp sound a dog makes: *The dog always barks at strangers.*

- [The movement of a dog's jaws when barking] Beginning with the fingertips of both *open hands* touching, palms facing each other and heels apart, bring the fingers apart and then together again with a repeated movement.

barn *n.* A storage building on a farm: *cows sheltered in the barn.*

- [Initialized sign similar to sign for **house**] Beginning with the fingertips of both *B hands* touching in front of the chest, palms facing forward, bring the hands apart and down at an angle to each side of the chest and then straight down to in front of each side of the waist.

barometer *n.* An instrument for measuring air pressure, used in forecasting the weather: *read the barometer.* Related form: **barometric** *adj.*

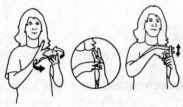

- **[weather**[1] + **temperature]** With the right *W hand* near the left *W hand*, palms facing each other, twist the hands in opposite directions with a double movement. Then, with the extended right index finger, palm facing down, near the top of the extended left index finger, palm facing right, move the right finger down the length of the left finger with a double movement.

barrel *n.* See sign for CYLINDER.

barrier *n.* See sign for PREVENT.

base[1] *n.* The bottom or supporting part: *the base of the statue.* Related forms: **basic** *adj.*, **basis** *n.*

- [Initialized sign] Move the right *B hand,* palm facing left, in a flat circle under the left *open hand,* palm facing down.

base[2] *n.* (alternate sign) Related form: **basic** *adj.* Same sign used for: **beneath.**

- [Initialized sign] Move the right *B hand,* palm facing down, in a flat circle under the left *open hand,* palm facing down.

base[3] *n.* See sign for BASEMENT.

baseball *n.* **1.** A game played with a ball and bat by two teams on a field with four bases: *Baseball is the most popular American sport.* **2.** The ball used in this game: *Throw the baseball to me.* Same sign used for: **softball.**

- [Natural gesture of swinging a baseball bat] With the little finger of the right *S hand* on the index finger of the left *S hand,* palms facing in opposite directions, move the hands from near the right shoulder downward in an arc across the front of the body with a double movement.

based on See sign for ESTABLISH.

base eight *n.* See sign for OCTAL.

basement *n.* The lowest story of a building, below ground: *a washing machine in the basement.* Same sign used for: **base, basic, basis, beneath, cellar, underlying.**

- [Indicates an area beneath a house] Move the right *10 hand,* palm facing in, in a flat circle under the left *open hand* held across the chest, palm facing down.

bashful[1] *adj.* Shy or easily embarrassed: *a bashful child.* See also sign for ASHAMED[1]. Same sign used for: **embarrassed.**

- [Shows a blush rising in the face] Move the palms of both *open hands* slowly upward from each side of the chin to each side of the forehead, palms facing in and fingers pointing up.

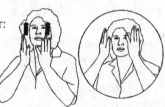

bashful² *adj.* (alternate sign) Same sign used for: **embarrassed.**

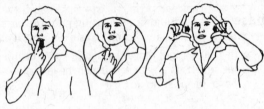

■ [**red**^1,2,3 + **face²**] Flick the extended right index finger, palm facing in, downward across the lips while bending the finger. Then tap the index-finger side of both *L hands* against each temple.

bashful³ *adj.* See sign for SHY¹.

basic *adj.* See sign for BASEMENT.

basis *n.* See sign for BASEMENT.

basket¹ *n.* A woven container: *a picnic basket.* See also sign for BAG. Same sign used for: **suitcase.**

■ [Initialized sign showing where a basket hangs from the arm] Move the index-finger side of the right *B hand* from the wrist to near the elbow of the bent left arm.

basket² *n.* See sign for BOWL.

basketball *n.* **1.** A game played by two teams that try to throw a large ball through a high hoop: *I'm too short to play basketball.* **2.** The ball used in the game of basketball: *She handles that basketball like a pro.*

■ [Mime tossing a basketball] Move the *curved 5 hands* from in front of the chest, palms facing each other, upward with a double movement by twisting the wrists upward.

bastard *n.* **1.** A mean, despicable person: *She considered him a bastard for the terrible way he treated her.* **2.** A child born to a woman who is not married to the child's father: *The son of the earl was a bastard.*

■ [Initialized sign in the male area of the head similar to sign for **bitch**] Strike the index-finger side of the right *B hand* sharply back against the center of the forehead.

baste¹ *v.* To sew with large, loose, temporary stitches: *basted the hem of the skirt.*

■ [Mime sewing] Move the fingertips of the right *F hand*, palm facing down, with a double movement in a large arc across the palm of the left *open hand*, palm facing up.

baste[2] *v.* To apply fat or liquid to meat while roasting or broiling: *Baste the turkey with orange juice.*

- ■ [Initialized sign miming the action of basting] Swing the fingertips of the right *B hand*, palm facing in and fingers pointing down, forward and back with a repeated movement over the palm of the left *open hand.*

bat[1] *n.* A small flying mammal: *Bats fly at night.*

- ■ [The crossed arms represent a bat hanging with folded pointed wings] With the arms crossed at the wrists on the chest, scratch the extended index fingers of both hands up and down near each shoulder with a repeated movement.

bat[2] *n.* **1.** A wooden stick used in baseball: *Hit the ball with the bat.* —*v.* **2.** To hit with a bat: *He batted the ball over the left-field fence.*

- ■ [Mime swinging a baseball bat] Beginning with the little finger of the right *A hand* on the index-finger side of the left *S hand* in front of the right shoulder, bring the hands down and forward with a short movement by bending the wrists.

batch *n.* See sign for PILE[1].

bath *n.* A washing of the whole body, especially by immersion in a tub: *take a hot bath.* Related form: **bathe** *v.*

- ■ [Washing oneself when bathing] Rub the knuckles of both *10 hands*, palms facing in, up and down on each side of the chest with a repeated movement.

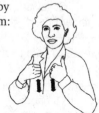

bathrobe *n.* See signs for COAT, ROBE.

bathroom[1] *n.* A room with a bathtub or shower and usually a sink and toilet: *a hotel room with a private bathroom.*

- ■ [**bath** + **room**[1,2]] Rub the knuckles of both *10 hands*, palms facing in, up and down on each side of the chest with a repeated movement. Then, beginning with both *R hands* in front of the body, palms facing in, turn the hands sharply in opposite directions, ending with the palms facing each other.

bathroom[2] *n.* See sign for TOILET.

bathtub *n.* A tub to bathe in: *The baby likes to take a bath in the little bathtub.*

■ [**bath** + **bury**[2]] Rub the knuckles of both *10 hands*, palms facing in, up and down on each side of the chest with a repeated movement. Then bring the fingers of the right *H hand*, palm facing down and fingers pointing forward, downward past the palm of the left *open hand*, palm facing right.

baton *n.* A stick used by the leader of an orchestra or other music group: *waving the baton to show the beat.*

■ [Mime waving a baton] Beginning with the right *S hand* in front of the right shoulder, move the hand in a wavy movement back and forth in front of the right shoulder by twisting the wrist.

batter *n.* See signs for BEAT[1,2].

battery *n.* See sign for ELECTRIC.

battle[1] *n.* **1.** A fight between opposing forces: *The army won the battle.* —*v.* **2.** To engage in a fight or struggle: *The opponents battled over first place.* Same sign used for: **war.**

■ [Indicates opponents in warlike maneuvers] Beginning with both *5 hands* in front of the right shoulder, fingers pointing toward each other, move the hands toward the left shoulder and then back toward the right shoulder.

battle[2] *n.* (alternate sign) Same sign used for: **war.**

■ [Indicates opponents in warlike maneuvers] Beginning with both *5 hands* in front of each shoulder, fingers pointing toward each other, move the hands toward each other and apart again with a double movement.

battlefield *n.* A place where a battle is or was fought: *a Civil War battlefield.* Related form: **battleground** *n.*

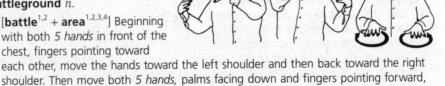

■ [**battle**[1,2] + **area**[1,2,3,4]] Beginning with both *5 hands* in front of the chest, fingers pointing toward each other, move the hands toward the left shoulder and then back toward the right shoulder. Then move both *5 hands*, palms facing down and fingers pointing forward, forward and outward in flat circular movements away from each other.

bawl out *v. phrase.* To scold severely: *bawled me out for breaking the dish.* Same sign used for: **burst, burst out, chew out, tell off, yell at.**

■ [Represents a sudden burst of words] Beginning with the little finger of the right *S hand* on the top of the index-finger side of the left *S hand,* flick the hands forward with a deliberate double movement while opening the fingers into *5 hands* each time.

be[1] *v.* To exist, occur, or have the specified quality, identity, or location: *Try to be good. She wants to be a doctor. I will be in London on Friday.*

■ [Initialized sign] Move the index-finger side of the right *B hand,* palm facing left, from the mouth straight forward a short distance.

be[2] *v.* (alternate sign) Same sign used for: **am, are, is, was, were.**

■ Move the extended right index finger, palm facing left, from the mouth straight forward a short distance.

beach *n.* See sign for WAVE[1].

beads *pl. n.* Small ornaments with holes through them for stringing: *a string of beads.* Same sign used for: **necklace.**

■ [Location and shape of a necklace of beads] Move the index finger side of the right *F hand,* palm facing left, from the left side of the neck smoothly around to the right side of the neck.

beak *n.* The hard, projecting part of a bird's mouth: *The sparrow picked up a seed in its beak.* Same sign used for: **bill.**

■ [**bird** + shape of bird's beak] Close the index finger and thumb of the right *G hand,* palm facing forward, with a repeated movement in front of the mouth. Then move the right *G hand* forward from in front of the mouth, closing the index finger and thumb.

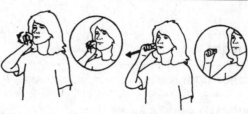

beam *v.* **1.** To smile brightly: *He beamed at his wife.* —*n.* **2.** A bright look or smile: *He had a beam of delight on his face.* Same sign used for: **glow, radiant, shiny.**

■ [The shine in a person's eyes] Beginning with the bent middle fingers of both *5 hands* pointing toward each eye, palms facing in, bring the hands forward with a wavy movement.

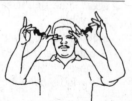

bean *n.* The long, smooth pod of a climbing plant, eaten as a vegetable: *Eat your green beans.*

- [Shape of a string bean] With a double movement, bring the fingers of the right *G hand* to grasp the extended left index finger, both palms facing down and fingers pointing toward each other, and pull the right hand outward to the right while pinching the thumb and index finger together.

bear[1] *n.* A large, heavy mammal with thick, rough fur: *a grizzly bear.*

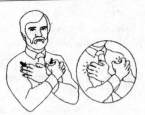

- [Action of a bear scratching itself] With the arms crossed at the wrist on the chest, scratch the fingers of both *curved 5 hands* up and down near each shoulder with a repeated movement.

bear[2] *v.* See signs for BURDEN, HURT[2], PATIENT[1].

beard[1] *n.* Hair covering a man's chin and cheeks: *He shaved off his beard.*

- [Location and shape of beard] Beginning with the right *C hand* around the chin, palm facing in, bring the hand downward while closing the fingers to the thumb with a double movement.

beard[2] *n.* (alternate sign)

- [Location and shape of beard] Move the fingertips of both *C hands* from near each ear down each cheek until the little fingers meet in front of the chin.

beard[3] *n.* See sign for SANTA CLAUS[1].

bear up *v. phrase.* See sign for ENCOURAGE.

beast *n.* See sign for ANIMAL.

beat[1] *v.* To mix by stirring rapidly: *beat the eggs.* Same sign used for: **batter, mix, stir, whip.**

- [Mime using a rotary mixer] Move the right *A hand* in a quick repeated circular movement near the index-finger side of the left *S hand*, both palms facing down.

beat[2] *v.* (alternate sign) Same sign used for: **batter, mix, stir, whip.**

- ■ [Mime beating using a spoon in a bowl] Move the right *A hand,* palm facing the chest, in a quick repeated circular movement near the palm side of the left *C hand,* palm facing right.

beat[3] *n.* The accent or rhythm of music: *dance to the beat.* Same sign used for: **vibrates, vibration.**

- ■ [Feeling the rhythm of music] Move both *5 hands,* palms facing down, from side to side with a short repeated alternating movement in front of each side of the body.

beat[4] *v.* To strike again and again: *He beat his hand against the wall.* Same sign used for: **abuse, hit, strike.**

- ■ [Indicates beating something] Hit the back of the right *S hand,* palm facing in, against the palm of the left *open hand,* palm facing right, with a double movement.

beat[5] *v.* See signs for DEFEAT[1,2,3].

beat up *v. phrase.* To strike repeatedly so as to injure: *The man constantly beat up his wife and children.* Same sign used for: **abuse, hit, strike.**

- ■ [Indicates beating something repeatedly] Swing the right *S hand,* palm facing in, in a large arc in front of the chest, repeatedly striking the extended left index finger, palm facing right, each time it passes and returns.

beau *n.* See sign for SWEETHEART.

beautiful[1] *adj.* Very pleasing, especially to the eye or other senses: *a beautiful view of the mountains.* Related form: **beauty** *n.* Same sign used for: **lovely, pretty.**

- ■ [Hand encircles a beautiful face] Move the right *5 hand* in a large circular movement in front of the face while closing the fingers to the thumb, forming a *flattened O hand.* Then move the hand forward while spreading the fingers quickly into a *5 hand.*

beautiful[2] *adj.* (alternate sign) Related form: **beauty** *n.* Same sign used for: **lovely, pretty.**

- ■ [The hand encircles the beauty of the face] Beginning with the right *5 hand* in front of the face, palm facing in, move it in a circular movement, closing the fingers to the thumb in front of the chin forming a *flattened O hand.*

beaver[1] *n.* A large rodent with a broad flat tail: *A beaver built the dam.*

- [The gnawing action of a beaver's teeth] Tap the fingers of the right *bent V hand* on the knuckles of the left *E hand,* palms facing each other, with a repeated movement while keeping the heels together.

beaver[2] *n.* (alternate sign)

- [The gnawing action of a beaver's teeth on a tree trunk] Pinch the fingertips of the right *curved 3 hand* together with a repeated movement near the elbow of the bent left arm held up in front of the left side of the body.

be careful See sign for CAREFUL.

because[1] *conj.* For the reason that: *They canceled the picnic because it was raining.* Same sign used for: **since.**

- Bring the index finger of the right *L hand* with a sweeping movement across the forehead from left to right, changing to a *10 hand* near the right side of the head.

because[2] *conj.* (alternate sign) Same sign used for: **since.**

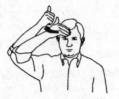

- Wipe the fingertips of the right *open hand* with a sweeping movement across the forehead from left to right, changing to a *10 hand* near the right side of the head.

beckon *v.* To signal by a gesture to come: *Beckon the child to come here.* Same sign used for: **come here.** Same sign used for: **recruit.**

- [Natural beckoning gesture] Beginning with the extended right index finger pointing forward in front of the chest, palm facing up, bend the index finger into an *X hand* while bringing the hand back toward the chest, with a double movement.

become *v.* To grow to be: *to become accustomed to the cold.* Same sign used for: **turn into.**

- [Hands reverse positions as if to change one thing into another] Beginning with the palm of the right *open hand* laying across the upturned palm of the left *open hand,* rotate the hands, exchanging positions while keeping the palms together.

become fat See sign for FAT[3].

become successful See signs for SHOOT UP, TOP.

---

bed[1] *n.* A piece of furniture used for
sleeping: *lying in bed.*

- [Mime laying the head against a pillow]
  Rest the right cheek at an angle on the
  palm of the right *open hand.*

---

bed[2] *n.* (alternate sign)

- [Mime laying the head against a pillow]
  With the palm of the left *open hand*
  on top of the palm of the right *open hand,*
  rest the right cheek at an angle on the
  back of the left hand.

---

bedroom *n.* A room to sleep in: *fast asleep in a bedroom.*

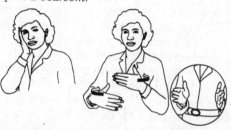

- [**bed**[1,2] + **room**[1,2]] Rest the right
  cheek at an angle on the palm
  of the right *open hand.* Then,
  beginning with both *open hands* in
  front of the body, palms facing in,
  turn the hands sharply in opposite
  directions, ending with the palms
  facing each other.

---

bee[1] *n.* A stinging insect with four wings that produces wax
and honey: *A bee stung me.* Same sign used for: **mosquito.**

- [The biting action of an insect and then a natural gesture of
  brushing it away] Press the index finger and thumb of the
  right *F hand* against the right cheek. Then brush the index-
  finger side of the right *B hand,* palm facing forward, from
  near the right ear forward by bending the wrist.

---

bee[2] *n.* (alternate sign) Same sign used
for: **mosquito.**

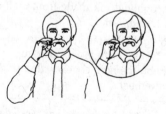

- [The biting action of an insect]
  Beginning with the fingertips of the
  right *G hand* on the right cheek, pinch
  the index finger to the thumb with a
  repeated movement.

---

bee[3] *n.* (alternate sign) Same sign used for:
mosquito.

- [The biting action of an insect] With the
  index finger and thumb of the right *F hand*
  against the right cheek, palm facing left,
  twist the hand downward with a double
  movement.

beef[1] *n.* Meat from a cow: *had roast beef for dinner.*

- [**cow**[1,2] + **meat**] With the thumbs of both *Y hands* on each side of the forehead, palms facing each other, twist the wrists forward and back again. Then grasp the flesh between the index finger and thumb of the left *open hand,* facing in, with the bent index finger and thumb of the right *5 hand,* and shake.

beef[2] *n.* See sign for MEAT.

beehive *n.* A house for bees: *bees in the beehive.*

- [**bee**[1,2,3] + the shape of a beehive] With the index finger and thumb of the right *F hand* against the right cheek, twist the hand downward with a double movement. Then, beginning with the index-finger side of both *curved hands* touching in front of the chest, palms facing down, move the hands in an arc away from each other and downward, ending with the palms facing each other in front of each side of the chest.

been *v.* See sign for SINCE[1].

been (there) (Sign indicates that one has visited or stayed at a place previously): *I've been to Hawaii.* Same sign used for: **finish.**

- [Similar to sign for **touch**[1], except made more quickly] With both palms facing down, bring the bent middle finger of the right *5 hand* downward to tap quickly on the back of the left *open hand* held across the chest.

beer *n.* An alcoholic drink made from malt and hops: *drink a cold beer.*

- [Initialized sign] Slide the index-finger side of the right *B hand,* palm facing forward, downward on the right cheek with a short double movement.

beet *n.* A red root vegetable: *to eat pickled beets.*

- [**red**[1,2,3] + slicing a beet] Brush the extended right index finger, palm facing down, downward on the lips. Then move the right *B hand,* palm facing left and fingers pointing up, forward past the left *C hand,* palm facing down.

before[1] *adv.* In the past: *I had never skied before.*
Same sign used for: **last, past, previous, prior to.**

- [Indicates a time or place in the past] Move the
fingertips of the right *open hand*, palm facing
back, from near the right cheek back and down to
touch the right shoulder.

before[2] *prep.* Earlier than: *a nap before dinner.* Same sign used for:
pre-, preceding, prior to.

- [Indicates a time or place experienced in the past] Beginning with
the back of the right *open hand*, palm facing in and fingers pointing
left, touching the back of the left *open hand*, palm facing forward
and fingers pointing up, move the right hand in toward the chest.

before[3] *prep.* (alternate sign) Same sign used for:
pre-, preceding, prior to.

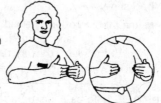

- [Indicates a time or place in the past] Beginning with
the back of the right *open hand*, palm facing in and
fingers pointing left, touching the palm of the left
open hand, palm facing in and fingers pointing right,
move the right hand in toward the chest.

before[4] *prep.* See sign for IN FRONT OF.

beg[1] *v.* To ask for urgently or as charity: *beg for
food.* Same sign used for: **implore, plead.**

- [Mime extending a hand while begging] While holding
the wrist of the upturned right *curved 5 hand* in the
left palm, constrict the right fingers with double
movement.

beg[2] *v.* (alternate sign) Same sign used for:
implore, plead.

- [Mime extending a hand while begging]
With the wrist of the upturned right *curved
5 hand* resting of the back of the left *open
hand*, palm facing down, constrict the right
fingers with a double movement.

beg[3] *v.* See sign for WORSHIP[1].

beggar *n.* A very poor person who lives by begging
for money or food: *Give money to the beggar.*

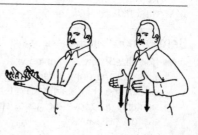

- [**beg**[1,2] + **person marker**] While holding the
wrist of the right *curved 5 hand* in the left palm,
both palms facing up, constrict the right fingers
with a double movement. Then move both *open
hands*, palms facing each other, downward along
each side of the body.

begin *v.* See sign for START[2].

beginning *n.* See sign for START[1].

behavior *n.* Way of acting: *praised the child's good behavior in the restaurant.* Related form: **behave** *v.* Same sign used for: **conduct.**

- [Initialized sign similar to sign for **act**] Move both *B hands,* palms facing forward, simultaneously from side to side in front of the body with a repeated swinging movement.

behind *prep.* At or to the rear of: *standing behind the chair.* Same sign used for: **backslide.**

- [Indicates a position behind another] Move the right *10 hand,* palm facing left, from in front of the left *10 hand,* palm facing right, back toward the chest in a large arc.

belch[1] *v.* **1.** To pass gas from the stomach through the mouth: *belched after dinner.* —*n.* **2.** An act or instance of belching: *Everyone around the table heard his belch.* Same sign used for: **burp.**

- [Indicates gas moving up from the stomach] Move the fingertips of the right *bent hand,* palm facing in, up and down on the chest with a double movement.

belch[2] *v.* (alternate sign) Same sign used for: **burp.**

- [Indicates gas moving up from the stomach] Beginning with the right *S hand* in front of the chest and palm facing in, flick the index finger upward.

Belgium[1] *n.* A country in northwestern Europe: *The capital of Belgium is Brussels.*

- [Initialized sign] Move the index-finger side of the right *B hand,* palm facing left, from the left shoulder downward to the right hip.

Belgium[2] *n.* (alternate sign)

- [Initialized sign] Beginning with the index finger of the right *B hand* touching the right side of the chin, palm facing left and fingers pointing up, move the hands straight forward a short distance.

believe *v.* To think something is true or real: *to believe in ghosts.* Related form: **belief** *n.*

■ [**mind**[1] + clasping one's beliefs close] Move the extended right index finger from touching the right side of the forehead downward while opening the hand, ending with the right hand clasping the left *open hand,* palm facing up, in front of the body.

belittle[1] *v.* To represent as less important: *belittle the athlete's accomplishments.*

■ [**feel** + indicates something becoming small] Move the bent middle finger of the right *5 hand,* palm facing in, upward on the chest with a double movement. Then, with the thumb of the right *L hand,* palm facing forward, resting on the back of the left *open hand,* palm facing down, close the right index finger down to the right thumb.

belittle[2] *v.* See sign for REDUCE[2].

bell[1] *n.* A hollow metal cup that rings when struck by a clapper: *ring the bell.* Same sign used for: **reverberate, reverberation, ring.**

■ [Indicates the striking of a bell's clapper and the sound reverberating] Hit the thumb side of the right *S hand,* palm facing down, against the palm of the left *open hand.* Then move the right hand to the right while opening the fingers into a *5 hand* wiggling the fingers as the hand moves.

bell[2] *n.* (alternate sign) Same sign used for: **ring.**

■ [Mime ringing a hand-held bell] Swing the fingertips of the right *F hand,* palm facing down, forward and back in front of the chest with a repeated movement by twisting the wrist.

bell[3] *n.* (alternate sign) Same sign used for: **ring.**

■ [Mime ringing a hand-held bell] Swing the fingertips of the right *flattened O hand,* palm facing down, forward and back in front of the chest with a repeated movement by twisting the wrist.

bell[4] *n.* A hollow metal cup that is rung by pulling a rope, causing it to tip so a clapper strikes it: *ring the church bell.* Same sign used for: **ring.**

- [Mime ringing a church bell by pulling a rope] With the little-finger side of the right *S hand* on the index-finger side of the left *S hand*, palms facing in opposite directions, move the hands up and down with a long repeated movement, from in front of the head to in front of the waist.

bell[5] *n.* An electronic device that makes a signaling sound when pressed: *the doorbell.* Same sign used for: **ring.**

- [Mime ringing a doorbell] Press the thumb of the right *10 hand*, palm facing in, with a deliberate movement into the palm of the left *open hand*, palm facing right and fingers pointing up.

belly *n.* An enlarged stomach: *a belly full of food.*

- [Shows location and shape of enlarged stomach] Beginning with the heel of the right *curved hand* in front of the body, palm facing down and fingers pointing forward, move the hand forward in a large arc and then back to touch the fingers against the lower abdomen, ending with the palm facing up and fingers pointing in.

belly button *n.* See sign for NAVEL.

bellydance *n.* **1.** A dance originating in the Middle East, performed by a woman, using exaggerated movements of the hips and pelvis: *The bellydance is popular in Algiers.* —*v.* **2.** To dance a bellydance: *We watched in fascination as the woman bellydanced.*

- [Indicates movement of a bellydancer's hips] With the left *S hand* in front of the chest, palm facing in, swing the right *C hand*, palm facing left, forward and back with a double movement under the little-finger side of the left hand.

belong[1] *v.* To be a member: *to belong to a church.* Same sign used for: **annex, attach, combine, connect, fasten, hook up, join, joint, link, on-line, unite.**

- [Two things coming together] Beginning with both *curved 5 hands* in front of each side of the body, palms facing each other, bring the hands together while touching the thumb and index fingertips of each hand and intersecting with each other.

belong[2] *v.* To be one's property: *Does this book belong to you?* Same sign used for: **entitle, truly yours.**

■ [**true** + **your**[1]] Move the extended right index finger, palm facing left, from in front of the mouth forward while changing into an *open hand,* palm facing forward.

below[1] *prep.* **1.** Lower than: *an apartment below ground level.* —*adv.* **2.** In a lower place: *a two-story house with a full basement below.* Same sign used for: **beneath, bottom.**

■ [Indicates a position below] Beginning with the left *open hand* on the back of the right *open hand,* both palms facing down, bring the right hand downward in an arc, ending several inches below the left hand.

below[2] *prep., adv.* (alternate sign) Same sign used for: **beneath.**

■ Move the right *open hand,* palm facing down, in a flat circle under the left *open hand,* palm facing down, in front of the chest.

below[3] *adv.* See signs for LESS, MINIMUM[1].

belt[1] *n.* A strip of leather or cloth fastened around the waist: *Wear a belt with these pants.*

■ [Location of a belt] Move both *H hands* from each side of the waist around toward each other until the fingers overlap in front of the waist.

belt[2] *n.* (alternate sign) Same sign used for: **sash, waistband.**

■ [Location of a belt] Beginning with both *modified C hands* touching near the waist, bring the hands apart along the waist to each side of the body.

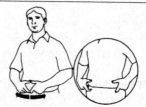

bench *n.* A long, hard seat: *sit on a bench in the park.*

■ [Legs dangling from sitting on a bench] Bring the curved finger of the right *H hand* downward on the base of the extended left *H hand* with a double movement, both palms facing down. Then, slide the curved fingers of the right *H hand* along the length of the left *H hand* to off the end.

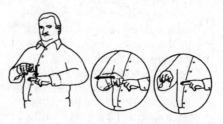

bend

bend[1] *v.* To move one's leg from a straight position to an angular one: *Bend your knees.* Related form: **bent** *adj.*

■ [A person's leg bending] Beginning with both extended index fingers side by side, pointing forward in front of the body, palms facing down, crook the right index finger, forming an *X hand.*

bend[2] *v.* To force into a curved or angular shape: *bend the pipe.* Related form: **bent** *adj.*

■ [Indicates the ability to bend] Grasp the fingers of the left *open hand,* palm facing right, with the fingers of the right *flattened O hand,* and then bend the left fingers downward until both palms are facing down and hands are bent.

bend[3] *v.* (alternate sign) Same sign used for: **warp.**

■ [Demonstrates direction of something bending] Beginning with the little-finger side of the right *open hand,* palm facing left, across the fingers of the left *open hand,* palm facing up, bend the right hand back toward the chest, ending with the palm facing in.

bend[4] *v.* To force something to curve: *bend the twig.* Related form: **bent** *adj.*

■ [Indicates the ability to bend] Beginning with the index fingers of both *S hands* touching in front of the chest, palms facing down, bend the elbows downward, ending with the knuckles of both hands close together and the palms facing in.

bend[5] *v.* See signs for BOW[1], DENT.

beneath *prep., adv.* See signs for BASE[2], BASEMENT, BELOW[1,2].

beneficiary *n.* A person designated to receive funds or property from an estate: *She was the beneficiary of her parents' will.* Same sign used for: **distributee.**

■ [**receive + person**] Beginning with both *curved 5 hands* in front of the body, right hand higher than the left hand and both palms facing back, bring the hands back toward the chest while closing into *S hands,* ending with the right little finger on the index-finger side of the left hand. Then move both *P hands,* palms facing each other, downward along the sides of the body.

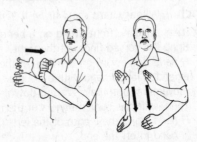

benefit *n.* Something useful or good; an advantage or aid: *for your personal benefit.* Same sign used for: **advantage.**

- [Pocketing a beneficial item] Push the thumb side of the right *F hand* downward on the right side of the chest, palm facing down, with a short double movement.

benevolent *adj.* See sign for GOOD.

bent *adj.* See sign for DENT.

bequeath *v.* See sign for GIFT².

Be quiet! See sign for QUIET².

berry¹ *n.* A small edible fruit: *to pick just one ripe berry from the bush.*

- [Twisting a berry to pick it from a vine] Grasp the extended little finger of the left hand, palm facing in, with the fingertips of the right *O hand* and twist the right hand outward with a double movement.

berry² *n.* (alternate sign) See also sign for CHERRY.

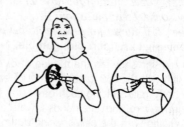

- [Picking a berry] While grasping the extended left index finger, palm facing in, with the fingertips of the right *flattened O hand,* twist the right hand forward and back with a double movement.

beside¹ *prep.* By the side of: *beside the door.* Same sign used for: **adjacent, next to.**

- [Indicates a location beside another] Beginning with the palm of the right *open hand,* palm facing in and fingers pointing left, touching the back of the left *open hand,* palm facing in and fingers pointing right, move the right hand forward in a small arc.

beside² *prep.* (alternate sign) Same sign used for: **adjacent, near, next to.**

- [Indicates a location beside another] Beginning with the right *open hand,* palm facing in and fingers pointing left, a short distance forward of the back of the left *open hand,* palm facing in and fingers pointing right, move the right hand toward the chest, ending with the right palm on the back of the left hand.

beside³ *prep.* (alternate sign) Same sign used for:
adjacent, next to.

- [Indicates a location beside another] Beginning
  with the little-finger side of the right *B* hand on
  the index-finger side of the left *B* hand, palms
  facing inward at an angle, move the right hand
  upward and then down to the right in an arc.

beside⁴ *prep.* See sign for SIDE¹.

best *adj.* **1.** Most excellent: *the best part.* —*adv.* **2.** To the
highest degree or in the most excellent way: *Who reads best?*

- [Modification of **good,** moving the sign upward to form the
  superlative degree] Bring the right *open hand,* palm facing in
  and fingers pointing left, from in front of the mouth upward
  in a large arc to the right side of the head, changing to a
  10 hand as the hand moves.

best friend See sign for FRIEND².

bet *n.* **1.** A promise to forfeit something if you prove
wrong in predicting the outcome of an activity;
wager: *make a bet on the fifth race.* **2.** an amount
of money so wagered: *place your bet.* —*v.* **3.** To
make a bet: *It is illegal for a player to bet on the
game.* Same sign used for: **bid, gamble, wager.**

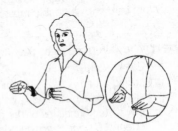

- [Initialized sign showing the turning of dice]
  Beginning with both *B hands* in front of each side
  of the body, palms facing each other and fingers
  pointing forward, turn the hands toward each
  other, ending with the palms facing down.

betray¹ *v.* To be unfaithful to: *betray a trust;
betray a friend.* Same sign used for: **con,
deceive, fib, fool, swindle.**

- Strike the knuckles of the right *A hand,* palm
  facing forward, against the extended left index
  finger, palm facing forward, with a double
  movement.

betray² *v.* (alternate sign)

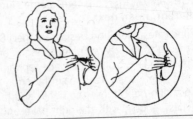

- [Initialized sign similar to sign for
  against] Hit the fingertips of the right
  B hand, palm facing left, against the left
  open hand, palm facing in with a double
  movement.

betray³ *v.* See signs for CHEAT¹,².

better *adj.* **1.** Superior, as in quality or excellence: *a better deal at the other store.* —*adv.* **2.** To a greater degree or in a more excellent manner: *a child trying to read better.*

- [Modification of **good,** moving the sign upward to form the comparative degree] Bring the right *open hand,* palm facing in and fingers pointing left, from in front of the mouth upward in an arc to the right side of the head, changing to a *10 hand* as the hand moves.

between *prep.* In the interval separating (two things): *Put the picture between the two windows.* Same sign used for: **gap, lapse.**

- [Indicates space between two things] Brush the little-finger side of the right *open hand,* palm facing left, back and forth with a short repeated movement on the index-finger side of the left *open hand,* palm angled right.

beverage *n.* See sign for DRINK¹.

beware *v.* See sign for WARN.

bewilder *v.* See sign for SURPRISE.

bewildered *adj.* See sign for PUZZLED.

bewitch *v.* To put under a magic spell: *The sorceress bewitched the prince and turned him into a frog.*

- [As if putting a spell on something] Wiggle the fingers of both *curved 5 hands* near each side of the face, palms facing down and fingers pointing in.

beyond¹ *prep.* Farther on than: *beyond the city limits.*

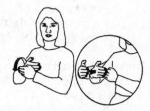

- [Shows moving beyond a given place] Beginning with the back of the right *open hand,* palm facing in and fingers pointing left, touching the palm of the left *open hand,* palm facing in and fingers pointing right, move the right hand in a small arc over the index-finger side of the left hand, and then forward a short distance.

beyond² *prep., adv.* See sign for AFTER¹.

beyond³ *n.* See sign for YONDER.

bi- *prefix.* Twice, two, or every two: *biannual meetings; bilingual teachers; bimonthly issues of the magazine.*

- Tap the heel of the right *bent V hand,* palm facing forward, with a double movement on the fingertips of the left *V hand,* palm facing in.

biannual *adj.* Happening two times each year: *The biannual convention is held in May and November.* Same sign used for: **semiannual.**

■ [**six** handshape used to sign **month**] Move the right *6 hand,* palm facing forward and fingers pointing up, downward with a double movement on the extended left index finger held in front of the chest, palm facing right and finger pointing up.

biannually *adv.* Same sign as for BIANNUAL but made with a double movement to indicate repetition. Same sign used for: **semiannually.**

bias *n.* See sign for PREJUDICE[1]. Related form: **biased** *adj.*

Bible[1] *n.* The book of sacred writings of the Christian religion; the Old Testament and the New Testament: *read the Bible.* Related form: **Biblical** *adj.*

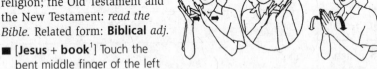

■ [**Jesus** + **book**[1]] Touch the bent middle finger of the left *5 hand* in the center of the palm of the right *open hand* in front of the right side of the body; touch the bent middle finger of the right *5 hand* in the center of the palm of the left *open hand* in front of the left side of the body. Then, beginning with the palms of both *open hands* together, fingers pointing forward at an angle, separate the palms while keeping the little-finger sides of the hands together.

Bible[2] *n.* The book of sacred writings of the Christian or Jewish religion; the Old Testament and the New Testament, or the Old Testament alone. Related form: **Biblical** *adj.*

■ [**God** + **book**[1]] Move the right *B hand,* palm facing left, from above the head in an arc downward in front of the face. Then, beginning with the palms of both *open hands* together, fingers pointing forward at an angle, separate the palms while keeping the little-finger sides of the hands together.

bicycle *n.* A lightweight vehicle with two wheels in tandem: *ride a bicycle.* Same sign used for: **bike, pedal, ride a bicycle.**

■ [Shows action of pedaling a bicycle] Move both *S hands* in alternating forward circles, palms facing down, in front of each side of the body.

bid *n., v.* See signs for AUCTION, BET, SUGGEST.

big[1] *adj.* (alternate sign) See also sign for LARGE.

■ [Shows big size] Move both *open hands* from in front of the body, palms facing each other and fingers pointing forward, apart to each side in large arcs.

big² *adj.* (alternate sign) Same sign used for: **enlarge, grow big.**

- [Initialized sign showing big size] Move both *B hands* from in front of the body, palms facing each other and fingers pointing forward, apart to each side.

big-headed *adj.* See sign for CONCEITED.

big shot *n.* See sign for CONCEITED.

big word A multisyllable word that may be difficult to spell or pronounce.

- Touch the thumb and little finger of the right *Y hand,* palm facing down, first to the wrist of the bent left arm, and then to the extended left index finger.

bike *n.* See sign for BICYCLE.

bill¹ *n.* **1.** A piece of paper money: *a dollar bill.* **2.** Money owed, or a statement of money owed, for goods or services: *I'll pay the bill next month.*

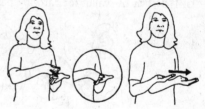

- [**money** + **give you**] Tap the back of the right *flattened O hand,* palm facing up, with a double movement against the palm of the left *open hand,* palm facing up. Then move the right *open hand,* palm facing up, forward a short distance.

bill² *n.* (alternate sign)

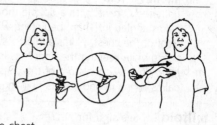

- [**money** + a directional form of **give you** toward oneself] Tap the back of the right *flattened O hand,* palm facing up, with a double movement against the palm of the left *open hand,* palm facing up. Then move the right *open hand,* palm facing up, toward the chest, ending with the fingers against the chest.

bill³ *n.* (alternate sign)

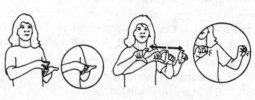

- [**money** + **card**¹] Tap the back of the right *flattened O hand,* palm facing up, with a double movement against the palm of the left *open hand,* palm facing up. Then, beginning with both *modified C hands* touching in front of the chest, palms facing forward, bring the hands apart to in front of each shoulder and pinch each thumb and index finger together.

bill[4] *n.* See sign for DOLLAR.

bill[5] *n.* See sign for BEAK.

billboard[1] *n.* A flat board, usually outdoors, for posting large advertisements or notices: *to advertise on billboards along the highway.*

■ [**outside**[1] + **advertise** + **square**[1]] With the fingers of the right *flattened O hand* by the opening of the left *C hand*, palms facing in, bring the right hand upward and outward in an arc. Then, beginning with the thumb of the right *S hand* touching the little finger of the left *S hand*, palms facing in opposite directions, move the right hand forward with a double movement. Then, beginning with both extended index fingers touching in front of the face, palms facing forward, bring the hands apart from each other to in front of each shoulder, then straight down, and then back together in front of the body.

billboard[2] *n.* See sign for SIGN[2].

billfold[1] *n.* A wallet for carrying paper money: *Put the large bills back in your billfold.*

■ [**money** + **fold** + a gesture putting money into a billfold] Tap the back of the right *flattened O hand* with a double movement on the palm of the left *open hand*, both palms angled in. Then, beginning with the fingertips of both *open hands* touching in front of the chest, palms angled toward each other, move the heels of the hands apart while keeping the fingertips in place. Then slide the back of the right *flattened hand* downward in front of the chest across the palm of the left *bent hand*, both palms facing in and fingers pointing in opposite directions.

billfold[2] *n.* See sign for WALLET.

billiards *n.* See sign for POOL[1].

billion *n.* **1.** One thousand millions: *The young woman is now worth several billion in her own right.* —*adj.* **2.** Having multiples of one thousand millions: *a billion dollars.*

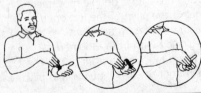

■ [Initialized sign similar to sign for **million**] Tap the fingertips of the right *B hand*, palm facing in, first on the heel of the left *open hand* and then on the fingers of the left *open hand*, palm facing up.

billionaire *n.* A person having assets valued at a billion dollars or more: *The billionaire made his wealth in real estate.*

- [**billion + person marker**] Tap the fingertips of the right *B hand*, palm facing in, first on the heel of the left *open hand* and then on the fingers of the left *open hand*, palm facing up. Then move both *open hands*, palms facing each other, downward along the sides of the body.

bimonthly *adj.* **1.** Happening once every two months: *The bimonthly newsletter is sent out six times a year.* —*adv.* **2.** Every two months: *The elevators are inspected bimonthly.* Same sign used for: **every two months, two months.**

- [**month** formed with a **two** handshape] Move the back of the right *2 hand*, palm facing in and fingers pointing left, downward with a double movement on the extended left index finger held in front of the body, palm facing right and finger pointing up.

binary *adj.* Having only two possible choices of elements or results, as "0" and "1" or "yes" and "no": *a binary code in computer machine language.*

- [Initialized sign] Move the right *B hand*, palm facing forward, under the left *open hand*, palm facing down and fingers pointing right, changing into a *2 hand* as it moves.

bind *v.* To fasten or tie in place: *bind the hostage to the chair.* Same sign used for: **bondage, bound, locked into, tie up.**

- [Shows wrists bound together] Beginning with the wrists of both *S hands* crossed in front of the chest, but slightly apart, palms facing in, bring the wrists against each other.

binoculars *pl. n.* A small, hand-held double telescope made for viewing with both eyes: *I can see the dancers' faces through the binoculars.*

- [Mime looking through binoculars] Beginning with both *C hands* near each side of the face, palms facing each other, twist the hands upward and toward each other in a double arc.

biology *n.* The scientific study of living matter, including plants and animals: *a course in biology.*

- [Initialized sign similar to sign for **science**] Move both *B hands*, palms facing forward, in large alternating circles toward each other in front of the chest.

bird *n.* An animal that lays eggs, is covered with feathers, and has wings: *Some birds can't fly.* Same sign used for: **chicken, coward, fowl.**

■ [Mime the action of a bird's beak] Close the index finger and thumb of the right *G hand*, palm facing forward, with a repeated movement in front of the mouth.

birth[1] *n.* A coming into life: *the birth of a baby.* Same sign used for: **born.**

■ [Indicates the birth of a baby] Bring the right *open hand*, palm facing in, from the chest forward and down, ending with the back of the right hand in the upturned palm of the left *open hand.*

birth[2] *n.* (alternate sign) Same sign used for: **born.**

■ [Indicates the birth of a baby] Beginning with the back of the right *open hand*, palm facing in and fingers pointing left, touching the palm of the left *open hand*, palm facing in and fingers pointing right, bring the right hand down under the little-finger side of the left hand, ending with the right palm facing down.

birthday[1] *n.* The day on which a person was born: *to celebrate my birthday.*

■ [**birth**[1,2] + **day**] Bring the right *open hand*, palm facing in, from the chest forward and down, ending with the back of the right hand in the upturned palm of the left *open hand*. Then, with the right elbow resting on the back of the left hand held across the body, palm down, bring the extended right index finger downward toward the left elbow in a large sweeping arc.

birthday[2] *n.* (alternate sign)

■ Touch the bent middle finger of the right *5 hand*, palm facing in, first to the chin and then to the center of the upper chest.

birthmark *n.* A spot on the skin that was there at birth: *She has a small birthmark on her face.*

■ [**birth**[1,2] + showing location and shape of a birthmark] Bring the right *open hand*, palm facing in, from the chest forward and down, ending with the back of the right hand in the upturned palm of the left *open hand*. Then bring the index-finger side of the right *F hand*, palm facing forward, against the right cheek.

biscuit *n.* See sign for COOKIE.

bishop[1] *n.* A high-ranking member of the clergy who supervises a number of local churches: *bishop of the diocese.*

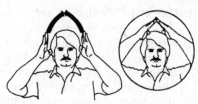

- [Shape of bishop's hat] Beginning with both *B hands* near each side of the head, palms facing in, move the hands upward and toward each other until the fingers touch above the head.

bishop[2] *n.* (alternate sign)

- [Kissing a bishop's ring] Bring the back of the right *A hand,* palm facing forward, against the lips as if kissing a ring on the ring finger.

bison *n.* A wild ox of North America: *hunt for bison.* See also sign for BUFFALO.

- [A bison's horns] Beginning with the index-finger sides of both *S hands* against each side of the head, palms facing forward, bring the hands forward in an arc, ending with the palms facing back near each side of the head.

bit[1] *n.* The smallest unit of information recognized by a computer: *a bit with a value of either "0" or "1."* ·

- [Initialized sign similar to sign for **law**] Beginning with the thumb side of the right *B hand,* palm angled forward, against the palm of the left *open hand,* palm facing right, move the right hand downward from the fingertips to the heel of the left hand.

bit[2] *n.* See signs for TINY[1,2].

bitch *n.* Slang. A nasty, spiteful woman: *She's a bitch when you don't go along with her ideas.*

- [Initialized sign in the female area of the head similar to sign for **bastard**] Strike the index-finger side of the right *B hand,* palm facing left, against the chin.

bite *v.* To seize with the teeth: *to bite an apple.*

- [Mime teeth biting into something] Bring the fingertips of the right *C hand,* palm facing down, down to close around the index-finger side of the left *open hand.*

bitter *adj.* See sign for SOUR.

bitter cold See sign for ARCTIC.

biweekly *adj.* **1.** Happening once every two weeks: *The music club has biweekly meetings, on the first and third Mondays of the month.* —*adv.* **2.** Every two weeks: *The music club meets biweekly, on the first and third Mondays of the month.* Same sign used for: **every two weeks, two weeks.**

■ [**week** formed with a **two** handshape] Move the palm side of the right *2 hand* with a double movement from the heel to the fingertips of the left *open hand* held in front of the body, palm facing up.

bizarre *adj.* See signs for FANTASY[2], STRANGE.

blab *v.* To talk too much or indiscreetly: *blabbed to his sister about the secret.* See also sign for PRATTLE. Same sign used for: **babble, chat, chatter, gab, gossip, talk, talkative.**

■ [Action of the mouth opening and closing] Beginning with both *flattened C hands* near each side of the face, palms facing each other, close the fingers and thumbs together simultaneously with a double movement.

black *adj.* **1.** Of the darkest color: *a simple black dress, appropriate anywhere.* —*n.* **2.** A dark-skinned person, especially one of African descent: *blacks and other minorities.*

■ Pull the side of the extended right index finger, palm facing down and finger pointing left, from left to right across the forehead.

blackboard *n.* See sign for BOARD[1].

blah *n. Slang.* See sign for NEVER MIND.

blame[1] *v.* To hold responsible: *They blamed me for the accident.* Same sign used for: **accuse, at fault, charge.**

■ [Shoves blame at someone] Push the little-finger side of the right *A hand*, palm facing left, forward across the back of the left *A hand*, palm facing down.

blame[2] *n.* See sign for FAULT[2].

blank[1] *adj.* Unable to think of or remember something: *My mind is blank.* Same sign used for: **absent-minded.**

- [Indicates a blank mind] Bring the bent middle finger of the right *5 hand,* palm facing in, from left to right across the forehead.

blank[2] *adj.* See sign for EMPTY.

blanket *n.* A large rectangular piece of soft fabric, used as a covering: *Cover the baby with a blanket.*

- [Initialized sign similar to sign for **cover**[2] miming pulling up a blanket to the chest] Move both *B hands* from in front of the body, palms facing down and fingers pointing toward each other, upward, ending with both index fingers against the upper chest.

blast *v.* See sign for EXPLODE[1].

blaze *n.* See signs for FIRE[1,2], FLAME[1].

bleed *v.* Same sign as for BLOOD but formed with a double movement.

blemish *n.* A flaw on the skin: *a facial blemish.* Related form: **blemished** *adj.*

- [red[1,2,3] + the location of a facial blemish] Bring the extended right index-finger, palm facing in, downward on the lips with a double movement. Then bring the index finger side of the right *F hand,* palm facing forward, against the right cheek.

blend *v.* See signs for CIRCULATE[1], COMBINE[1], MAINSTREAM[2], MESH, MIX[1].

bless[1] *v.* To make or pronounce holy: *to bless the sacramental wine.* Related form: **blessed** *adj.*

- [Taking a blessing from the lips and distributing it] Beginning with the thumbs of both *A hands* touching the lips, palms facing each other, move the hands down and forward while opening into *5 hands* in front of each side of the chest, ending with palms facing down and fingers pointing forward.

bless[2] *v.* (alternate sign) Related form: **blessed** *adj.*

- [Taking a blessing from the lips and distributing it] Beginning with the index fingers of both *bent hands* touching the lips, palms facing down and fingers pointing toward each other, move the hands down and apart while opening into *5 hands* in front of each side of the body, ending with palms facing down and fingers pointing forward.

blind *adj.* Not able to see: *a blind person listening to books on tape.*

- [Poking out the eyes] Jab the fingertips of the right *bent V hand* back toward the eyes with a short, deliberate movement.

blindfold[1] *n.* **1.** A piece of opaque cloth placed over the eyes to prevent seeing: *put a blindfold on the condemned prisoner.* —*v.* **2.** To cover the eyes of: *to blindfold the victim.*

- [Mime tying a blindfold over the eyes] Beginning with both *modified C hands* touching the face near the sides of each eye, palms facing in, bring the hands around to the back of the head. Then bring the hands apart from each other in large outward circles and mime tying a knot.

blindfold[2] *n., v.* (alternate sign)

- [Shows location and shape of blindfold] Beginning with the index fingers and thumbs of both *C hands* circling the eyes, palms facing each other, bring the hands apart to the sides of the head.

blinds *pl. n.* Something that keeps out light, especially a window covering: *Close the blinds before you leave the house.* Same sign used for: **venetian blinds.**

- [Represents opening the slats of venetian blinds] Beginning with the little fingers of both *B hands* touching in front of the chest, palms facing in and fingers pointing in opposite directions, move the left hand down to bring the hands slightly apart while spreading the fingers into *5 hands.*

blink *v.* See sign for WINK.

blizzard *n.* A fierce snowstorm with very high winds: *The blizzard left high snowdrifts along the street.*

- [**snow**[2] + **wind**[1] formed with vigor] Beginning with both *5 hands* in front of the face, palms facing out and fingers pointing upward, wiggle the fingers while moving the hands downward with a wavy movement. Then, beginning with both *5 hands* over the right shoulder, palms facing forward and fingers angled up, bring the hands downward to the left with a double movement.

bloat[1] *v.* To expand or swell, as with air or water: *The child's stomach was bloated from starvation.*

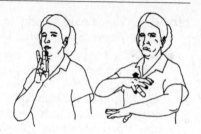

- [**water** + a swelling on an arm] Bring the index finger of the right *W hand*, palm facing left, against the chin with a double movement. Then, beginning with the fingers of the right *curved 5 hand* near the bent left arm, bring the right hand upward while puffing out the cheeks.

bloat[2] *v.* (alternate sign)

- [**water** + a swelling on the face] Bring the index-finger side of the right *W hand*, palm facing left, against the chin with a double movement. Then, beginning with the fingers of both *curved 5 hands* near each cheek, palms facing in and fingers pointing up, bring the hands outward while puffing out the cheeks.

block[1] *n.* A solid object, as of wood, with flat sides: *children playing with blocks.* Same sign used for: **cube.**

- [Shape of a cube or block] Beginning with both *B hands* in front of each side of the chest, palms facing each other and fingers pointing up, bend the hands sharply, ending with the left hand above the right hand, both palms facing down.

block[2] *v.* To obstruct, as an opponent in sports: *block the pass from the quarterback.*

- [Represents preventing the legs of the opponent from moving] Bring the middle finger side of the right *H hand*, palm facing up, against the index-finger side of the left *H hand*, palm facing in and fingers pointing down.

block[3] *v.* See sign for PREVENT. Related form: **blockage** *n.*

blockage *n.* See sign for CARBURETOR. Shared idea of the narrow opening located in a carburetor, used to regulate the flow of fuel and air.

blocked *adj.* See sign for STUCK.

blockhead *n.* See signs for MORON[1,2].

blond or **blonde** *adj.* Light in color: *blond hair.*

- [**yellow** + **hair**] Wiggle the right *Y hand*, palm facing left, near the right side of the head. Then grasp a small strand of hair with the thumb and index finger of the right *F hand*, palm facing left.

blood *n.* The red fluid flowing through veins and arteries: *donating blood for the accident victims*. Related form: **bloody** *adj*. Same sign used for: **shed**.

- [**red**[1,2,3] + a gesture representing the flow of blood from a wound] Brush the extended right index finger, palm facing in, downward on the lips. Then open the right hand into a *5 hand* and bring it downward while wiggling the fingers, palm facing in, past the left *open hand* held across the chest, palm facing in and fingers pointing right.

bloom *v.* **1.** To produce blossoms: *The daffodils bloom in spring.—n.* **2.** The flower of a plant: *Cut the blooms and put them in a vase*. Same sign used for: **blossom**.

- [Shows a bloom opening up] Beginning with the fingertips and heels of both *curved 5 hands* touching in front of the chest, palms facing each other, while keeping the heels together, move the fingers away from each other while opening slightly.

blossom *n.* See sign for BLOOM.

blouse *n.* A garment worn on the upper body: *wearing a silk blouse with a wool skirt*.

- [Location and shape of woman's blouse] Touch the bent middle fingers of both *5 hands* on each side of the upper chest, and then bring the hands down in an arc, ending with the little fingers of both hands touching the waist, palms facing up and fingers pointing toward each other.

blow[1] *v.* To force air through the nose, as to clear it: *Blow your nose*. Same sign used for: **fool**.

- [Mimes blowing one's nose] Squeeze the nose with the thumb and index finger of the right *A hand* while pulling the hand slightly forward.

blow[2] *v.* To force a current of air onto or into: *blowing out the candles; blowing up an air mattress*.

- [Indicates the flow of air through the mouth] Beginning with the back of the *flattened O hand* at the mouth, palm facing forward and fingers pointing forward, move the hand forward a short distance while opening the fingers into a *5 hand*.

blowup *n.* **1.** An outburst of temper or a violent quarrel: *They had a terrible blowup just before the wedding.* —*v.* **2. blow up** To become violently angry: *blew up at his mother for no reason.* Same sign used for: **blow one's top, burst, bust, erupt, temper.**

- ■ [Demonstrates the top blowing off of something] Beginning with the palm of the right *5 hand*, palm facing down, on the thumb side of the left *S hand*, palm facing right, bring the right hand upward and back down again.

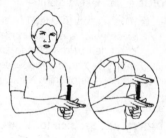

blue *adj.* Having the color of the sky: *a blue flower.* Same sign used for: **navy.**

- ■ [Initialized sign] Move the right *B hand*, fingers angled up, back and forth by twisting the wrist in front of the right side of the chest.

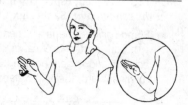

blueberry *n.* A small edible fruit: *pick blueberries.*

- ■ [**blue** + **berry**[1,2]] Move the right *B hand*, fingers angled up, back and forth by twisting the wrist in front of the right side of the chest. Then twist the fingertips of the right *flattened O hand* forward and back with a double movement on the extended left index fingertip.

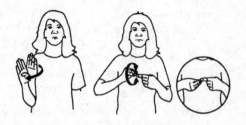

Bluetooth[1] or **Bluetooth technology** *n.* Refers to a short-range wireless radio frequency that enables the exchange of information between devices with transceiver microchips, such as mobile phones, PCs, laptops, digital cameras, and video game consoles: *He talked on a Bluetooth hands-free headset while driving.*

- ■ [**telephone**[1] + hooks around ear] Bring the knuckles of the right *Y hand*, palm facing in, against the cheek, holding the thumb near the ear and in front of the mouth. Then bring the index-finger side of the right *modified C hand*, palm facing forward, firmly down around the right ear.

Bluetooth[2] or **Bluetooth technology** (alternate sign)

- ■ [**earbuds** + shape of Bluetooth headset] Beginning with both *G hands* in front of the body, fingers pointing toward each other, bring the hands upward to each ear while pinching each thumb and index finger together. Then move the fingers of the right *G hand* along the right cheek from the ear to the side of the mouth.

bluff *v.* See sign for FLATTER. Shared idea of insincerity.

blur *v.* To make indistinct or cloudy: *Tears blurred my vision.*

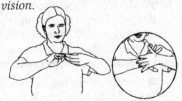

- [Obstructing the view] Beginning with the fingertips of both *flattened O hands* touching in front of the chest, left palm facing in and right palm facing out, move the hands in opposite directions across each other while opening into *5 hands*, palms facing each other.

blurry *adj.* See sign for VAGUE.

blush *v.* To redden, especially in the face: *She blushed at the compliment.* Same sign used for: **flush.**

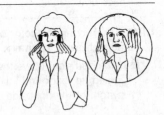

- [Blood rising in the face when blushing] Beginning with both *flattened O hands* near each cheek, palms facing in and fingers pointing up, spread the fingers slowly upward, forming *5 hands*.

boar *n.* A wild pig: *hunt boars.*

- [**pig** + the tusks of a boar] With the back of the right *bent hand* under the chin, palm facing down, wiggle the fingers. Then bring the right hand, with the little finger and index finger extended, up against the chin, palm facing in and fingers pointing up.

board[1] *n.* A hard smooth surface used for writing on with chalk: *write on the board.* Same sign used for: **blackboard, chalkboard, wall.**

- [Initialized sign showing the flatness of a chalkboard or a wall] Beginning with the index-finger sides of both *B hands* together in front of the chest, palms facing forward and fingers pointing up, move the hands apart to in front of each shoulder.

board[2] *n.* A group of people who supervise the management of an institution: *a school board.*

- [Initialized sign similar to sign for **member**] Touch the index-finger side of the right *B hand*, palm facing left, first to the left side of the chest and then to the right side of the chest.

board[3] *n.* A thin rectangular board, containing or imprinted with various electronic components and microchips, that can be inserted into a computer to enable additional functions, such as increased memory or graphics capabilities: *insert a new graphics board.* Same sign used for: **circuit board, expansion board, expansion card.**

- [Insertion of board in slot] Bring the little-finger side of the right *B hand*, palm left, sharply against the palm of the left *C hand* held in front of the chest, palm up.

board of directors *n. phrase.* An elected or appointed group that governs the affairs of a business or corporation: *The board of directors had an emergency meeting to replace the president of the company.*

- [Abbreviation **B-D** similar to sign for **member**] Touch the index-finger side of the right *B hand* to the right side of the chest, and then move the hand in an arc while changing to a *D hand* to touch again on the left side of the chest.

boast *v.* See signs for BRAG[1,2].

boat *n.* An open vessel for traveling on the water: *go fishing in a small boat.* Related form: **boating** *n.* Same sign used for: **cruise, sail, sailing, ship.**

- [Shows the shape of a boat's hull] With the little-finger sides of both *curved hands* together, palms facing up, move the hands forward in a bouncing double arc.

body *n.* The trunk or torso of a person or animal, excluding the head and limbs: *to wrap a blanket around my body.*

- [Location of the body] Touch the fingers of both *open hands,* palms facing in and fingers pointing toward each other, first on each side of the chest and then on each side of the waist.

boil *v.* To heat to 212° F.: *to boil some water for tea.* Same sign used for: **cook, heat.**

- [Action of flames under a boiling pot] Move the right *5 hand,* palm facing the chest, in a flat circle under the left *open hand,* palm facing down, while wiggling the right fingers.

boiling mad Extremely angry and upset; stirred up: *I was boiling mad when I saw the repair bill.* Same sign used for: **burning mad, flare up, fume, furious, resent, seethe, smolder.**

- [**boil** formed close to the body as if boiling inside] Wiggle the fingers of the right *5 hand,* palm facing the chest, in a flat circle under the left *open hand,* held close to the chest, palm facing down.

bold *adj.* See signs for BRAVE, CONFIDENT, STRICT, THICK[4,5], WELL[1].

bologna or **baloney** *n.* A large cooked and smoked sausage: *slices of bologna on the sandwich.*

- [The shape of sausage links] Beginning with the thumbs and index fingers of both *C hands* touching in front of the chest, palms facing down, move the hands apart while closing the fingers, ending with both *S hands* in front of each side of the chest.

bolt[1] *n.* A threaded rod intended to screw through a nut: *to fasten a gate to the fence with a bolt.*

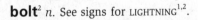

- [**square**[1] + turning a bolt in a nut] With both extended index fingers, palms facing down, draw a square in the air in front of the chest. Then, while grasping the extended left index finger with the fingertips of the right *O hand,* twist the right hand forward with a double movement.

bolt[2] *n.* See signs for LIGHTNING[1,2].

bomb *n.* See signs for BURST[1], CRASH[1], EXPLODE[1,2].

bond *n.* See sign for RELATIONSHIP.

bondage *n.* See sign for BIND.

bone[1] *n.* One of the structures forming the skeleton of a vertebrate animal: *I broke a bone in my arm.*

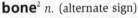

- [**rock**[1,2] + **skeleton**[1]] Tap the palm side of the right *A hand,* palm facing down, against the back of the wrist of the left *A hand.* Then, with the hands crossed at the wrists, tap the fingers of both *bent V hands* on the opposite side of the chest, palms facing in.

bone[2] *n.* (alternate sign)

- [Indicates the hardness of a bone] With a double movement, tap the back of the right *bent V hand,* palm facing up, on the back of the left *S hand,* palm facing down.

bone[3] *n.* See sign for SKELETON.

bonfire *n.* A large fire built outside in an open space: *building a bonfire to toast the marshmallows.*

- [**outside**[1] + **set up**[1] + **flame**[1]] Beginning with the fingertips of the right *flattened O hand* inside the palm side of the left *C hand,* palm facing right, bring the right hand upward in an arc to the right. Then beginning with the fingertips of both *curved hands* touching in front of the chest, palms facing down, bend the fingers upward ending with the fingers meshed with each other. Finally, beginning with both *5 hands* in front of the chest, one hand higher than the other, palms facing in and fingers pointing up, move the hands upward with an alternating circular movement in front of each side of the body while wiggling the fingers.

bonnet *n.* A women's or children's head covering that ties under the chin: *wearing an old-fashioned bonnet with a lace brim.*

- [**girl**[1] + **hat** + **scarf**] Move the thumb of the right *A hand*, palm facing left, downward on the right cheek to the right side of the chin. Then pat the top of the head with the fingers of the right *open hand* with a double movement, palm facing down. Then bring both *modified X hands* from each side of the head downward to under the chin, palms facing in.

bonus *n.* See signs for ADD[2], GIVE ME[2].

book[1] *n.* A long printed work on consecutive sheets of paper bound together between covers: *to read a book on the plane.* Same sign used for: **album, manual, textbook.**

- [Represents opening a book] Beginning with the palms of both *open hands* together in front of the chest, fingers angled forward, bring the hands apart at the top while keeping the little fingers together.

book[2] *v.* See sign for APPOINTMENT.

boom *v.* See signs for BURST[1], EXPLODE[1,2].

boost *n.* See signs for SUPPORT[1,2].

boot[1] *v.* **1.** To start or restart a computer by loading the operating system: *to boot the computer again after the program aborted.* —*n.* **2.** A starting-up of the computer: *A warm boot resets a computer that is already on.*

- [**kick** + **start**[2]] Bring the right *B hand* from in front of the right side of the body, palm facing left and fingers angled down, upward to strike against the little-finger side of the left *B hand* held in front of the body, palm facing in and fingers pointing right. Then, with the extended index finger of the right hand, palm facing down, at the base of the index and middle fingers of the left *open hand*, palm facing right, twist the right hand forward, ending with the palm facing in.

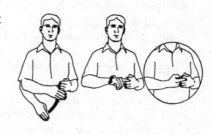

boot[2] *v.* See sign for KICK[2].

boots[1] *pl. n.* A pair of coverings for the foot and lower part of the leg, made of rubber, leather, etc.: *to wear boots in cold weather.* Same sign used for: **galoshes.**

■ [Mime pulling on boots] Beginning with both *A hands* in front of the left side of the waist, palms facing each other, bring the hands sharply back and upward toward the body by twisting the wrists. Repeat in front of the right side of the waist.

boots[2] *pl. n.* (alternate sign) Same sign used for: **galoshes.**

■ [**shoe** + showing the length of boots] Tap the index-finger sides of both *S hands*, palms facing down, together in front of the waist with a double movement. Then tap the little-finger side of the right *open hand*, palm facing in, inside the crook of the bent left arm, palm facing down.

border *n.* The outer edge of a surface or area: *wallpaper with a floral border.*

■ [Outlines the border] Bring the palm side of the right *open hand* from the wrist along the little-finger side of the left *open hand*, palm facing down, and then straight back toward the body along the left fingertips.

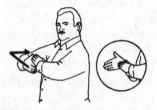

bore *v.* To make a hole by turning a tool: *bore a hole through the baseboard.*

■ [Mime boring a hole with a drill] With the extended right index finger at the base of the middle finger and ring finger of the left *open hand*, palm facing right, twist the right hand toward the body with a double movement.

bored *adj.* See sign for STALE. Related form: **boring** *adj.*

boring[1] *adj.* Uninteresting; tedious; tiresome: *a boring lecture.* Related forms: **bore** *v.*, **bored** *adj.* Same sign used for: **dull, monotonous, tedious.**

■ [Boring a hole on the side of the nose] With the tip of the extended right index finger touching the side of the nose, palm facing down, twist the hand forward.

boring[2] *adj.* (alternate sign) Related forms: **bore** *v.*, **bored** *adj.* Same sign used for: **dull.**

■ [Similar to sign for **dry**] Bring the thumb of the right *5 hand*, palm facing down and fingers pointing left, across the chin from left to right while closing into an *S hand*.

boring³ *adj.* See sign for DRY.

born *adj.* See signs for BIRTH[1,2].

born-again *adj.* See sign for REBIRTH.

borrow *v.* To get something from another with the understanding that it will be returned: *I'd like to borrow your sweater till tomorrow.* Same sign used for: **lend me.**

■ [Bring borrowed thing toward oneself; opposite of movement for **lend**] With the little-finger side of the right *V hand* across the index-finger side of the left *V hand,* bring the hands back, ending with the right index finger against the chest.

bosom *n.* See sign for BREAST.

boss *n.* See signs for CAPTAIN, CHIEF[1].

Boston¹ *n.* The capital of Massachusetts: *He lived in Boston for two years.*

■ [Initialized sign] Move the right *B hand,* palm facing forward, downward a short distance in front of the right side of the chest with a double movement.

Boston² *n.* (alternate sign)

■ [Initialized sign] Move the right *B hand,* palm facing forward, from in front of the center of the chest in an arc to the right and then downward in front of the right side of the body.

both *adj.* **1.** Being the two: *Both houses are mine.* —*pron.* **2.** The two together: *I like both, but I live in the smaller one.* Same sign used for: **pair.**

■ [Two things pulled together to form a pair] Bring the right *2 hand,* palm facing in, downward in front of the chest through the left *C hand,* palm facing in and fingers pointing right, closing the left hand around the right fingers as they pass through and pulling the right fingers together.

bother *v.* See signs for ANNOY[1,2].

both of them See sign for YOU³.

both of us See sign for WE³.

bottle[1] *n.* A glass or plastic container with a narrow neck: *a medicine bottle.* Same sign used for: **glass.**

■ [Shape of a bottle] Beginning with the little-finger side of the right *C hand*, palm facing left, on the upturned left *open hand*, raise the right hand.

bottle[2] *n.* (alternate sign).

■ [Cylindrical shape] Beginning with the little-finger side of the right *C hand*, palm facing left, on the upturned left *open hand* raise the right hand upward in front of the chest while closing into an *S hand*.

bottom[1] *n.* **1.** The lowest part: *the bottom of the barrel.* —*adj.* **2.** Lowest: *on the bottom branch.*

■ [Indicates a location at the bottom of something] Beginning with the right *open hand* under the palm of the left *open hand*, both palms facing down and fingers angled in opposite directions, move the right hand straight down in a double movement.

bottom[2] *n.* See sign for BELOW[1].

boulevard *n.* See sign for ROAD[1].

bounce[1] *v.* To spring back, as after striking a surface: *The ball bounced off the wall.* Same sign used for: **reflect.**

■ [Demonstrates something deflecting off a surface] Bring the fingertips of the right *B hand*, palm facing in, against the palm of the left *open hand*, palm facing right. Then bounce the right hand back to the right, ending with the palm facing left and fingers pointing forward.

bounce[2] *v.* To cause to spring into the air after striking a surface: *bounce a ball.* Same sign used for: **dribble.**

■ [Mime bouncing a ball] Move the right *open hand*, palm facing down, up and down in front of the right side of the body with a repeated movement.

bounce[3] *v.* See sign for RICOCHET.

bound *v.* See sign for BIND.

boundary *n.* The limiting line of an area or between two areas: *to put a fence on the boundary between their yard and ours.*

- [Demonstrates the boundary of something] Beginning with the little-finger side of the right *B hand,* palm facing left and fingers pointing forward, on the index-finger side of the left *B hand,* palm facing right and fingers pointing forward, tip the right hand from side to side with a double movement.

bouquet *n.* A bunch of flowers: *a bouquet of roses*

- [**flower** + **bowl**] Touch the fingertips of the right *flattened O hand,* palm facing in, first to the right side of the nose and then to the left side. Then, beginning with the little fingers of both *C hands* touching, palms facing up, bring the hands apart and upward, ending with the palms facing each other.

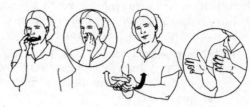

bout *n.* A period of time spent in a specified way; spell: *a bout of sickness.*

- [**sick**[1,2] + **hit**[1]] Touch the bent middle finger of the right *5 hand* to the forehead and the bent middle finger of the left *5 hand* to the chest. Then move the right *A hand,* palm facing left, against the extended left index finger held in front of the chest, palm facing right.

bountiful *adj.* See sign for PLENTIFUL.

bow[1] *v.* To bend the head or body: *to bow before the king.* Same sign used for: **bend, nod.**

- [Represents bowing one's head] Beginning with the forearm of the right *S hand,* palm facing forward, against the thumb side of the left *B hand,* palm facing down and fingers pointing right, bend the right arm downward while bending the body forward.

bow[2] *n.* A knotted ribbon with two large loops: *She likes to wear a bow in her hair.* Same sign used for: **ribbon.**

- [The shape of a hair bow] With both *S hands* crossed on the right side of the head, palms facing in, flip the index and middle fingers of both hands outward with a deliberate movement.

bow³ *v.* See sign for HAIL².

bowel movement *n.* See sign for FECES.

bowl *n.* **1.** A somewhat deep, rounded dish or basin: *using a large bowl for soup.* **2.** The contents of a bowl; bowlful: *a bowl of cereal.* Same sign used for: **basket, pot.**

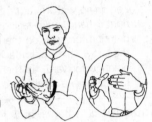

- ■ [The shape of a bowl] Beginning with the little fingers of both *C hands* touching, palms facing up, bring the hands apart and upward, ending with the palms facing each other.

bowling *n.* An indoor game in which players take turns rolling a large, heavy ball at a group of pins: *to go bowling.* Related form: **bowl** *v.*

- ■ [Mime throwing a bowling ball] Swing the right *curved 3 hand*, palm facing forward and fingers pointing down, from near the right hip forward and upward in an arc.

bow tie *n.* A small necktie tied in a bow: *wear a bow tie.*

- ■ [The shape of a bow tie] With both *S hands* crossed near the neck, palms facing in, flip the index and middle fingers of both hands outward with a deliberate movement.

box *n.* A container with four sides: *a box of toys.* Same sign used for: **package, present, room.**

- ■ [Shape of a box] Beginning with both *open hands* in front of each side of the chest, palms facing each other and fingers pointing forward, move the hands deliberately in opposite directions, ending with the left hand near the chest and the right hand several inches forward of the left hand, both palms facing in. (This sign may also be formed with the hands beginning in the final position and then changing to the first position.)

boxing *n.* **1.** The sport of fighting with the fists: *I like to watch boxing.* —*adj.* **2.** Of or used in the sport of boxing: *boxing gloves.* Related form: **box** *v.* Same sign used for: **fight.**

- ■ [Mime boxing] Move both *S hands* at an angle toward each other in alternating circular movements in front of the chest.

boy[1] *n.* A male child: *a little boy.* Same sign used for: **male.**

■ [Grasping the visor of a boy's cap] Beginning with the index-finger side of the right *flattened C hand* near the right side of the forehead, palm facing left, close the fingers to the thumb with a double movement.

boy[2] *n.* (alternate sign)

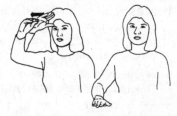

■ [**boy**[1] + **little**[2]] Beginning with the index-finger side of the right *flattened C hand* near the right side of the forehead, palm facing left, close the fingers to the thumb. Then lower the hand, placing the right *open hand*, palm facing down and fingers pointing forward, near the right side of the body.

boycott *v.* See sign for COMPLAIN.

boyhood *n.* The state or time of being a boy: *during my boyhood.*

■ [**boy**[1] + **raise**[1]] Beginning with the index-finger side of the right *flattened C hand* near the right side of the forehead, palm facing left, close the fingers to the thumb with a double movement. Then bring the right *open hand*, palm facing down, upward in front of the right side of the body.

Boy Scout *n.* A member of the Boy Scouts: *You can tell from his behavior that he was a Boy Scout.*

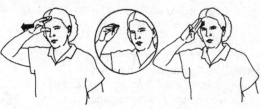

■ [**boy** + **Scout**[1]] Beginning with the index-finger side of the right *flattened C hand* against the forehead, palm facing left, close the fingers to the thumb with a double movement. Then, beginning with the index, middle, and ring fingers of the right hand held close together in front of the right side of the forehead, palm facing down and fingers angled left, tap the index finger against the right side of the forehead with a double movement.

brace *n.* **1.** Something that holds parts together or in place: *Use the stick as a brace for the plant.* —*v.* **2.** To give support to something: *Brace the wall with a pole.*

■ [**power**[1] + the location and shape of handcuffs] Bring both *S hands*, palms facing back, forward in front of each shoulder with a deliberate movement. Then grasp the wrist of the right *S hand*, palm facing in, with the left *C hand*, and move the right arm forward slightly.

bracelet *n*. An ornamental band for the wrist: *a gold bracelet.*

- [The location of a bracelet] With the right thumb and middle finger encircling the left wrist, twist the right hand forward with a double movement.

braces *pl. n*. An oral appliance consisting of wires and bands used to correct misalignment of the teeth and jaws: *The teenager's braces hurt her teeth.* Same sign used for: **retainer.**

- [Shows location of braces] Bring the fingertips of the right *bent V hand* from left to right in front of the teeth.

bracket *n*. See sign for CLASS.

brag[1] *v*. To praise oneself; speak with excess pride about one's appearance, accomplishments, possessions, etc.: *Please stop bragging about your new car.* Same sign used for: **boast, show off.**

- [Natural gesture while bragging] Tap the thumbs of both *10 hands,* palms facing down, against each side of the waist with a double movement.

brag[2] (alternate sign) Same sign used for: **boast, show off.**

- [Natural gesture while bragging] Tap first the thumb of the left *10 hand* and then the thumb of the right *10 hand,* palms facing down, against each side of the waist with an alternating movement.

braid[1] *n*. **1.** Strands of hair woven together: *to wear a braid.* —*v*. **2.** To weave strands of hair together: *braiding her hair.*

- [Represents hair being braided] Beginning with both *R hands* near the right side of the head, right hand above the left hand and palms facing each other, twist the right hand down and then the left hand down with an alternating movement as the hands move downward.

braid[2] *n., v*. (alternate sign)

- [Represents hair being braided] Beginning with both *X hands* near the left side of the head, palms facing each other, twist the wrists with a repeated alternating movement while moving the hands downward.

Braille *n.* A system of writing using combinations of raised dots to represent letters, numbers, etc., devised to allow blind people to read by touch: *a book written in Braille.*

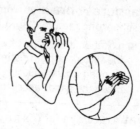

- [**blind** + mime reading Braille with the fingertips] Jab the fingertips of the right *bent V hand* back toward the eyes with a short deliberate movement. Then move the right *5 hand* back and forth across the upturned left *open hand* while wiggling the right fingers.

brain *n.* See sign for MIND.

brake[1] *n.* **1.** A device for stopping or slowing the movement of a vehicle or other mechanism: *Step on the brake.*
—*v.* **2.** To slow or stop by using a brake: *I brake for animals.*

- [Shows action of stepping on the brake] Push the right *A hand* downward in front of the right side of the body, palm facing forward, with a double movement.

brake[2] *n.* See sign for PEDAL[1].

branch[1] *n.* A limb growing from the main trunk of a tree: *to cut a branch from the top of the tree.*

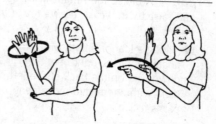

- [**tree** + indicating a branch shooting off the tree] With the bent right elbow resting on the palm of the left hand held across the body, twist the right *5 hand* forward and back near the right side of the head with a double movement. Then push the extended left index finger, palm facing in and finger pointed right, in an arc past the bent right forearm.

branch[2] *n.* (alternate sign)

- [**tree** + indicating the shape of branches on a tree] With the bent right elbow resting on the palm of the left hand held across the body, twist the right *5 hand* forward and back near the right side of the head with a double movement. Then, beginning with both *flattened O hands* together at the chest, palms facing in and fingers pointing down, move the hands down at an angle to near each side of the waist while opening into *5 hands.*

branch[3] *n.* See sign for LIMB.

branches *pl. n.* See sign for CHANNEL[3].

brand *n.* See signs for LABEL, STAMP[2].

brandy *n.* See sign for WHISKEY.

brassiere or **bra** *n.* A woman's undergarment for supporting the breasts: *to wear a brassiere*.

- [Location and shape of a brassiere] Beginning with the fingers of both *flattened C hands*, fingers pointing down, touching the center of the chest, move the hands apart to each side of the chest.

brat *n.* See sign for CONCEITED.

brave *adj.* Having the inner strength to confront danger: *a brave soldier*. Same sign used for: **bold, courage.**

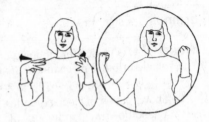

- [Hands seem to take strength from the body] Beginning with the fingertips of both *5 hands* on each shoulder, palms facing in and fingers pointing back, bring the hands deliberately forward while closing into *S hands*.

brawny *adj.* See sign for STRONG².

bread *n.* A baked food made with flour and raised with yeast: *eating bread and butter*.

- [Slicing a loaf of bread] Move the fingertips of the right *bent hand* downward on the back of the left *open hand* with a repeated movement, both palms facing in.

break¹ *v.* To force to come apart violently: *break a dish*. Same sign used for: **tear apart.**

- [Mime breaking something] Beginning with both *S hands* in front of the body, index fingers touching and palms facing down, move the hands away from each other while twisting the wrists with a deliberate movement, ending with the palms facing each other.

break² *n.* See signs for HALFTIME, INTERMISSION.

break³ *v., n.* See sign for FRACTURE. Related form: **broken** *adj.*

break down *v. phrase.* To cease to function; become inoperative: *The engine broke down*. Same sign used for: **cave in, collapse, crash, destruction, fall through, tear down.**

- [Indicates things crumbling down] Beginning with the fingertips of both *curved 5 hands* touching in front of the chest, palms facing each other, allow the fingers to loosely drop, ending with the palms facing down.

breakfast[1] *n.* The first meal of the day: *It's wise to eat breakfast.*

- [Initialized sign] Tap the index-finger side of the right *B hand,* palm facing left, against the chin with a double movement.

breakfast[2] *n.* (alternate sign)

- [**eat** + **morning**] Bring the fingertips of the right *flattened O hand* to the lips. Then, with the left *open hand* in the crook of the bent right arm, bring the right *open hand* upward, palm facing in.

break up *v. phrase.* To end a relationship: *break up with your sweetheart.*

- [**break** + **u-p**] Beginning with both *S hands* in front of the body, index fingers touching and palms facing down, move the hands away from each other while twisting the wrists. Then change the hands into *U hands,* palms facing forward, and drop the hands slightly while changing into *P hands,* ending with the palms facing each other in front of each side of the chest.

breast *n.* **1.** Either of the two mammary organs on the upper front part of the female body: *The baby fed from the mother's breast.* **2.** The female chest: *clutched the child to her breast.* Same sign used for: **bosom, bust.**

- [Location of breasts] Touch the fingertips of the right *bent hand* first on the right side of the chest and then on the left side of the chest.

breath *n.* **1.** The air inhaled and exhaled from the lungs: *I am all out of breath from running.* **2.** A single such inhalation: *Take a big breath.* Related form: **breathe** *v.* Same sign used for: **exhale, expel, inhale, pant, respiration.**

- [Indicates the movement of the lungs when breathing] With the right *5 hand* in front of the chest above the left *5 hand,* fingers pointing in opposite directions and palms in, move both hands forward and back toward the chest with a double movement.

breed *v.* See signs for CONFLICT[1], PREGNANT[2].

breeze[1] *n.* A light, gentle wind: *A breeze blew through the window.* Same sign used for: **air.**

- [Shows movement of the wind] Beginning with both *4 hands* in front of the body, palms in and fingertips facing each other, swing the hands from side to side then back in with a double movement by bending the wrists.

breeze[2] *n.* (alternate sign)

- [Shows movement of the wind] Beginning with both *5 hands* near the left shoulder, palms facing each other and fingers pointing forward, move the hands slowly in a wavy movement to in front of the right shoulder and back again to the left shoulder.

brew *v.* To make a beverage by boiling slowly: *Brew some coffee.*

- [Boiling something repeatedly or continuously] Move both *5 hands* upward with alternating movements in front of each side of the chest, palms facing up and fingers pointing up, while wiggling the fingers.

bribe *v.* **1.** To offer a reward to entice someone to do something: *bribed him to steal.* —*n.* **2.** Anything offered as an enticement: *offered him a bribe.* Related form: **bribery** *n.*

- [Slip money under the table] Move the right *flattened O hand*, palm facing up and fingers pointing left, from right to left under the left *open hand*, palm facing down.

brick *n.* A block of baked clay: *a house made of bricks.*

- [red[1,2,3] + card[1] + rock] Bring the extended right index finger, palm facing in, downward on the chin. Then, beginning with the fingertips of both *modified C hands* touching, palms facing forward, bring the hands apart to in front of each side of the chest and pinch each thumb and index finger together. Then tap the right *S hand* with a double movement, palm facing forward, on the back of the left *S hand*.

bride *n.* A newly-married woman or one about to be married: *the bride and groom.* Same sign used for: **bridesmaid.**

- [Mime walking with a bride's bouquet] With the little-finger side of the right *S hand* on the thumb-side of the left *S hand*, move the hands forward a short distance and then forward again in small arcs.

bridge[1] *n.* A structure built to provide a passage over a river or road: *to walk over the bridge.*

- [Shows the structure of supports for a bridge] Touch the fingertips of the right *V hand*, palm facing left, first to the bottom of the wrist and then near the elbow of the left arm held in front of the chest, palm facing down.

bridge[2] *n.* A partial denture attached to adjacent teeth: *The dentist says I'll need a bridge to replace the three pulled teeth.*

- [Pushing up dentures in the mouth] Beginning with both *10 hands* near each side of the chin, palms facing each other, push the extended thumbs upward against each side of the upper teeth.

brief[1] *adj.* Lasting for a short time or using few words: *a brief announcement.* Same sign used for: **abbreviate, condense, reduce, squeeze, summarize.**

- [Squeeze information together as if to condense] Beginning with both *5 hands* in front of the chest, right hand above the left hand and fingers pointing in opposite directions, bring the hands toward each other while squeezing the fingers together, ending with the little-finger side of the right *S hand* on top of the thumb side of the left *S hand.*

brief[2] *adj.* (alternate sign) See also sign for SHORT[1].

- [Measures off a short part of the finger] Slide the middle-finger side of the right *H hand* across the index-finger side of the left *H hand* with a short double movement, palms angled in.

bright *adj.* Very light or clear: *a room full of bright sunlight.* Same sign used for: **clarify, clear, light, radiant.**

- [Hands spread to reveal brightness] Beginning with the fingertips of both *flattened O hands* touching in front of the chest, palms facing each other, move the hands quickly upward in arcs to above each shoulder while opening to *5 hands.*

brilliant *adj.* See signs for INTELLIGENT[1], SMART[1,2,3].

brim *n.* The edge of a cup or bowl: *Fill it to the brim.* Same sign used for: **rim.**

- [Shows the top edge of a container] Move the fingers of the right *G hand*, palm facing down and fingers pointing down, in a circular movement around the opening made by the left *C hand* held in front of the body, palm facing right.

bring *v.* To carry something along: *You'd better bring your jacket to the picnic.* Same sign used for: **deliver, return, transport.**

- [Moving an object from one location to another] Move both *open hands*, palms facing up, from in front of the left side of the body in large arcs to the right side of the body. (This sign may be formed in the direction of the referent or its proposed new location.)

brisk *adj.* Quick and active; lively: *a brisk walk.*

- [**brief** + **walk**²] Slide the middle-finger side of the right *H hand* across the index-finger side of the left *H hand* with a short double movement, palms angled in. Then, beginning with both hands in front of each side of the body, left palm facing in and fingers pointing down and right palm facing down and fingers pointing forward, move the fingers of both hands upward and downward with an alternating movement by bending the wrists.

Britain *n.* See sign for ENGLAND.

British *n., adj.* See signs for ENGLAND, ENGLISH.

broad *adj.* See signs for GENERAL¹, WIDE.

broadcast *v., n.* See sign for ADVERTISE.

broad-minded *adj.* Free of prejudice: *The jury should remain broad-minded throughout the trial.* Same sign used for: **liberal, open-minded, tolerant.**

- Beginning with both *open hands* near each other in front of the forehead, palms angled toward each other, move the hands forward and outward away from each other.

Broadway *n.* A large street running through New York City, famous for its theaters: *to see a show on Broadway.*

- [Initialized sign similar to sign for **act**²] Bring the index-finger sides of both *B hands*, palms facing each other, down each side of the chest with alternating circular movements.

brochure *n.* See sign for MAGAZINE.

broil *v.* To cook directly over or under an open flame: *to broil the steaks.*

- ■ [Indicates fire above broiled food] Move the right *5 hand*, palm facing in and fingers pointing down, from side to side with a double movement while wiggling the fingers over the left *open hand*, palm facing up.

broke *adj. Informal.* See sign for PENNILESS[3].

bronchitis *n.* Inflammation in the bronchial tubes: *I have bronchitis.*

- ■ [Initialized sign similar to sign for **lung**] Bring the index-finger sides of both *B hands*, palms facing each other, straight down the center of the chest with a double movement.

broom[1] *n.* A brush with a long handle for sweeping: *to sweep the floor with a broom.* Same sign used for: **sweep.**

- ■ [Mime sweeping] Beginning with both *S hands* in front of the right side of the body, right hand above the left hand and palms facing in, move the hands to the right with a double swinging movement.

broom[2] *n.* (alternate sign)

- ■ [Shows action of sweeping] Brush the little-finger side of the right *open hand*, palm facing in, upward with a double movement on the upturned palm of the left *open hand*.

brother[1] *n.* A son of the same parents: *presents from my uncle for my brother and me.*

- ■ [**boy**[1] + **same**[1]] Beginning with the index-finger side of the right *flattened C hand* near the right side of the forehead, palm facing left, close the fingers to the thumb with a repeated movement. Then move the right hand smoothly down while changing to a *1 hand*, ending in front of the body side by side next to the left *1 hand*, both palms facing down and fingers pointing forward.

brother[2] *n.* (alternate sign)

- ■ Beginning with the thumb of the right *L hand* touching the right side of the forehead, palm facing left, move the right hand downward, landing across the thumb side of the left *L hand*, palm facing right.

brotherhood *n.* See sign for ASSOCIATE.

brother-in-law *n.* The brother of one's husband or wife or the husband of one's sister: *to visit my brother-in-law.*

■ [**brother**² + **law**] Beginning with the thumb of the right *L hand* touching the right side of the forehead, palm facing left, move the right hand downward, placing the palm side of the right *L hand* first on the fingers and then on the heel of the palm of the left *open hand*.

brown *adj.* Having the color of coffee: *a brown bear.*

■ [Initialized sign] Slide the index-finger side of the right *B hand*, palm facing left, down the right cheek.

Brownie *n.* A member of the junior division of the Girl Scouts: *join the Brownies.* Same sign used for: **brownie** (cookie), **Cub Scout.**

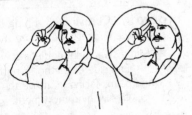

■ [Mime the Brownie salute] Bring the index-finger side of the right *H hand*, palm facing left, against the right side of the forehead with a double movement.

browse *v.* See signs for LOOK OVER², SCAN¹,²,³.

bruise *n.* A usually painful discolored spot on the skin resulting from a blow to the body: *a bruise on my arm from falling.* Same sign used for: **contusion.**

■ [**purple** + showing the area and shape of a bruise] Move the right *P hand*, fingers pointing up, down in an arc in front of the right side of the chest. Then bring the palm side of the right *modified C hand* to touch the left upper arm near the elbow.

brush¹ *n.* **1.** A tool with bristles used for grooming the hair: *a brush and comb.* —*v.* **2.** To use a brush to groom the hair: *brush my hair.* Same sign used for: **hairbrush.**

■ [Mime brushing one's hair] Move the palm of the right *A hand* down the right side of the head with a repeated movement.

brush² *n.* See signs for PAINT¹,².

brush³ *n.* See sign for WHISK BROOM.

bubble[1] *n.* A thin spherical film of liquid, usually forming an envelope filled with air: *covered with soap bubbles.*

- [Shows action of bubbles] Wiggle the fingers of both *curved 5 hands,* palms facing down, while moving them upward a short distance.

bubble[2] *n.* (alternate sign)

- [Shows shape of bubbles in suds] Beginning with both *F hands* in front of the chest, palms facing forward, move the right hand above the left hand and the left hand above the right hand as the hands move upward in front of the chest with an alternating movement.

bubble[3] *n.* A thin spherical film, filled with air, formed by blowing: *blew an enormous bubble with the new gum.*

- [Shows shape of bubble as it expands when being blown] Beginning with the right *curved 5 hand* in front of the lips, palm facing in, bring the hand forward a short distance while opening the fingers slightly.

bubble[4] *n.* (alternate sign)

- [Shows shape of bubble as it bursts on one's face] Beginning with the fingertips of the right *flattened O hand* near the lips, move the hand in while opening the fingers into a *5 hand.*

bucket *n.* A pail made of wood, plastic, or metal: *a bucket of coal.* Same sign used for: **pail, pot.**

- [Shape of a bucket + mime holding a bucket's handle] Move both *C hands* upward in front of each side of the chest, palms facing each other. Then move the right *S hand* upward a short distance in front of the right side of the body with a double movement.

buckle *n.* **1.** A clasp used to fasten two loose ends, as on a belt: *a gold buckle.*
—*v.* **2.** To fasten with a buckle: *Buckle your seat belt.* Same sign used for: **seat belt.**

- [Mime fastening a seat belt] Bring both *bent V hands* from in front of each side of the waist, palms facing each other, around to mesh the fingers together in front of the waist.

budget[1] *n.* **1.** A plan for spending money based on an estimate of expected income for a given period: *to make a monthly budget.* —*v.* **2.** To make a such a plan: *They carefully budgeted to save for a car.* Same sign used for: **exchange.**

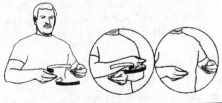

- [Shows moving money around] Beginning with both *flattened O hands* in front of each side of the body, palms facing each other, move the right hand in a circle back toward the body, over the left hand, forward to return to its original position.

budget[2] *n.* See signs for TRADE[1,2,3].

buffalo *n.* An American bison: *saw a buffalo at the zoo.* See also sign for BISON. Same sign used for: **Buffalo, NY.**

- [A bison's horns] Twist the knuckles of the right *Y hand,* palm facing in, back and forth on the right side of the head with a double movement.

buffer *n.* A temporary storage area for computer data: *The program keeps your active calculations in the buffer.*

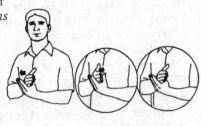

- [Symbolizes buffer area] Beginning with the little-finger side of the right *open hand,* palm angled left, at the base of the index finger and thumb of the left *flattened C hand,* palm facing up, rock the right hand from side to side with a double movement.

bug[1] *n.* **1.** An insect, especially one that crawls: *a bug under a rock.* **2.** A defect in a computer system or program that keeps it from working properly: *a bug in the program shut down the computer.* Same sign used for: **insect.**

- With the extended thumb of the right *3 hand* on the nose, palm facing left, bend the extended index and middle fingers with a repeated movement.

bug[2] *v.* See sign for ANNOY[2].

build[1] *v.* To construct by putting materials or parts together: *to build a boat.* Related form: **building** *n.* Same sign used for: **construct, construction.**

- [Shows putting one thing upon another to build something] Beginning with the fingers of the right *bent hand* overlapping the fingers of the left *bent hand* in front of the chest, palms facing down, reverse the position of the hands with a repeated movement as the hands move upward.

build[2] *v.* (alternate sign) Related form: **building** *n.* Same sign used for: **construct, construction, develop, increase.**

- [Shows putting one thing upon another to build something] Beginning with the fingers of the right *H hand* overlapping the fingers of the left *H hand* in front of the chest, both palms facing down and fingers pointing toward each other, bring the right fingers down to touch the left fingers, and then reverse the position of the hands with a repeated movement as the hands move upward.

building *n.* A built structure, especially one with walls and a roof: *A barn is a building.*

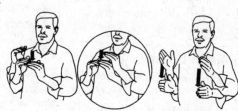

- [**build**[1,2] + the shape of a building's walls] Beginning with the fingers of the right *bent hand* overlapping the fingers of the left *bent hand* in front of the chest, palms facing down, reverse the position of the hands with a repeated movement as the hands move upward. Then move both *open hands,* palms facing each other, downward along each side of the chest.

Bulgaria *n.* A republic in southeast in Europe: *Sofia is the capital of Bulgaria.* Related form: **Bulgarian** *adj., n.*

- [The shape of a mustache characteristic of many Bulgarian men] Slide the index-finger side of the right *flattened C hand,* palm facing left, from under the nose to the right and downward to the right side of the mouth.

bulk *n.* See sign for PILE[1].

bull[1] *n.* A full-grown male cow: *a bull in the pasture.* Same sign used for: **nose ring.**

- [Ring through a bull's nose] Hold the nostrils with the thumb and index finger of the right *F hand* and wiggle it back and forth with a repeated movement.

bull[2] *n.* (alternate sign)

- [A bull's horns] Beginning with the thumbs of both *Y hands* touching each side of the forehead, palms facing forward, move the hands upward in short arcs.

bullet *n.* A small piece of metal shaped to be fired from a gun: *to remove a bullet from the victim's shoulder.*

- Brush the fingertips of the right *G hand*, palm facing left, past the left extended index finger, palm facing right, with a double movement.

bulletin board[1] *n.* A board on which notices are posted: *Put the rest of the announcements on the bulletin board.* Same sign used for: **post, post a notice, poster.**

- [Mime posting something on a wall] Push the thumbs of both *10 hands,* palms facing each other, forward with a short movement, first in front of each shoulder and then in front of each side of the body.

bulletin board[2] *n.* (alternate sign)

- [**board**[1] + **bulletin board**[1]] Beginning with the index-finger sides of both *B hands* together in front of the chest, palms facing forward and fingers pointing up, move the hands apart to in front of each shoulder. Then push the thumbs of both *10 hands,* palms facing each other, forward with a short movement, first in front of each shoulder and then in front of each side of the body.

bullheaded *adj.* See sign for CONTRARY[1].

bullshit[1] *n. Vulgar Slang.* Foolish and uninformed talk; nonsense: *That's bullshit.*

- Beginning with the thumb side of the right *S hand* on the nose, palm facing left, twist the hand deliberately downward.

bullshit[2] *n. Vulgar Slang.* (alternate sign)

- [Initialized sign] Move the right *B hand,* palm facing in, deliberately downward a short distance in front of the chest while changing into an *S hand.*

bullshit[3] *n. Vulgar Slang.* See sign for FECES.

bully[1] *n.* A person who threatens and intimidates weaker people: *bothered by the bully in the schoolyard.*

- Bring the knuckle side of the right *Y hand,* palm facing down, forward and upward on the extended left index finger, palm facing right, with a double movement.

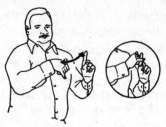

bully[2] *n.* See sign for CONCEITED.

bum *n. Informal.* See sign for FARM. Shared idea of a country bumpkin.

bump[1] *n.* A swelling, as one caused by a blow: *a large bump on his head.* Same sign used for: **lump, node.**

- [Shape of a bump on the head] Beginning with the fingertips of the right *curved 5 hand* on the right side of the head, palm facing in, move the hand upward a short distance.

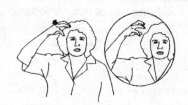

bump[2] *n.* (alternate sign) Same sign used for: **lump, node.**

- [Shape of a bump on the head] Beginning with the index-finger side of the right *B hand* touching the right side of the head, palm angled down, twist the wrist to bring the little-finger side against the right side of the forehead.

bump[3] *n.* (alternate sign) Same sign used for: **lump, node.**

- [Shape of small swelling] Beginning with the side of the extended right index finger, palm facing left, on the back of the left *open hand,* palm facing down, bring the right finger upward in a small arc, ending farther back on the back of the left hand.

bumper-to-bumper *adj.* Characterized by long lines of slow-moving cars: *bumper-to-bumper traffic.*

- [Demonstrates a vehicle very close behind another vehicle] Beginning with the right *open hand* near the base of the thumb of the left *open hand,* both palms facing down and fingers pointing forward, move the hands forward with a short double movement.

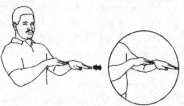

bunch *n.* See sign for CLASS.

bunk beds *pl. n.* Narrow beds stacked one above another: *to sleep in bunk beds.*

- [**bed**[1,2] + the location of one bunk bed above another] Rest the right cheek at an angle on the palm of the right *open hand.* Then place the left *H hand* above the right *H hand,* both palms facing down and fingers pointing forward.

bunny *n.* See signs for RABBIT[1,2].

burden *n.* A load, especially one that is carried with difficulty: *to carry the burden of supporting the family.* Same sign used for: **bear, fault, liability, obligation, responsibility, responsible.**

- [The weight of responsibility on the shoulder] With the fingertips of both *bent hands* on the right shoulder, push the shoulder down slightly.

bureau *n.* See sign for BUSINESS.

burglar *n.* See signs for ROBBER[1,2].

burglary *n.* See signs for ROB[1,2], SHOPLIFT, STEAL[1].

burial *n.* The act of putting a dead body in a grave: *A large crowd attended the burial of the senator.*

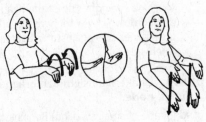

- [**bury**[1] + a gesture indicating inserting a body into a grave] Move both *curved hands,* palms facing down and fingers pointing down, back toward the body in double arcs. Then move both *open hands,* palms facing each other and fingers pointing down, straight down in front of the chest.

burn[1] *v.* **1.** To be on fire: *The house is burning.* **2.** To damage or destroy by fire: *The furniture was burned badly.* **3.** To produce by fire: *burned a hole in the rug.*

- [Flames leaping up from a fire] Wiggle the fingers of both *curved 5 hands* with a repeated movement in front of each side of the body, palms facing up.

burn[2] *v.* See sign for LASER.

burning mad *adj.* See sign for BOILING MAD.

burp *n., v.* See signs for BELCH[1,2].

burr or **bur** *n.* A rough, prickly cover around the seeds of certain plants: *burrs on my clothes.*

- [Burrs adhering to clothing] Touch the fingers of the right *curved hand* on the back of the left hand and then, moving up the left arm, on the wrist and on the forearm twice, both palms facing down.

burst[1] *v.* To break open suddenly: *The balloon burst.* Same sign used for: **bomb, boom, bust, explode.**

- [Demonstrates something expanding and bursting] Beginning with the palms of both *A hands* together in front of the chest, move the hands apart quickly while opening into *5 hands* in front of each side of the chest, palms facing each other.

burst[2] *v.* See signs for BAWL OUT, BLOWUP.

burst out *v. phrase.* See sign for BAWL OUT.

bury[1] *v.* To put a dead body in the earth: *to bury the dead bird.* Same sign used for: **grave.**

- [Shape of a mound of dirt on a grave] Move both *curved hands*, palms facing down and fingers pointing down, back toward the body in double arcs.

bury[2] *v.* (alternate sign) Same sign used for: **grave.**

- [Represents legs being laid beneath ground level] Bring the fingers of the right *H hand*, palm facing down and fingers pointing forward, downward past the palm of the left *open hand*, palm facing right.

bus[1] *n.* A large motor vehicle with seats to carry many passengers: *I took a bus to Chicago.*

- [Initialized sign] Beginning with the little-finger side of the right *B hand* touching the index-finger side of the left *B hand*, palms facing in opposite directions, move the right hand back toward the right shoulder.

bus[2] *n.* (alternate sign)

- [Initialized sign] Beginning with the little-finger side of the right *B hand* touching the index-finger side of the left *C hand*, palms facing in opposite directions, move the right hand back toward the right shoulder.

business *n.* A commercial enterprise: *in the bakery business.* Same sign used for: **bureau.**

- [Initialized sign similar to sign for **work**[1,2]] Tap the base of the right *B hand,* palm facing forward, with a repeated movement on the back of the left *open hand,* palm facing down.

bust[1] *n.* A statue of a person's head and upper part of the body: *a bust of Lincoln.*

- [**face**[1] + **sculpture**[1]] Move the extended right index finger in a circle around the face, palm facing in. Then move both *A hands* from in front of each side of the chest, palms facing out, with a wiggly movement down in front of the chest.

bust[2] *v.* **1.** To destroy or damage: *The farmer busted up the branches for firewood.* **2.** To make an arrest: *The warden busted the illegal betting game.* —*n.* **3.** A sudden economic loss: *boom and bust.* **4.** A police raid: *The gang was arrested in a bust of their headquarters.*

- Bring the right *curved 5 hand,* palm facing left, downward in front of the chest while closing into an *10 hand,* brushing the knuckles of the left *10 hand,* palm facing right, as it passes.

bust[3] *v.* See signs for BLOWUP, BURST[1].

bust[4] *v.* Same sign used for MEAN[1]. Shared idea of anger, violence, and destruction.

bust[5] *n.* See sign for BREAST.

busy[1] *adj.* **1.** Actively engaged in some occupation: *I'm too busy with work to relax.* **2.** Filled with activity: *a busy day.*

- [Initialized sign] Brush the base of the right *B hand,* palm facing forward, with a repeated rocking movement on the back of the left *open hand,* palm facing down.

busy[2] *adj.* (alternate sign) Same sign used for: **lots to do.**

- [Fingerspell **d-o** in a continuous pattern] With both *D hands* in front of the chest, palms facing up, pinch the index fingers and thumbs together repeatedly while moving the hands in repeated circles. [Note: the number of repetitions increases to reflect an increase in things to be done.]

but *conj.* On the other hand: *You may go, but come home early.*
Same sign used for: **although, different, however, unlike.**

- [Indicates opinions moving in opposite directions] Beginning with both extended index fingers crossed in front of the chest, palms facing forward, bring the hands apart with a deliberate movement.

butcher *n.* A person who prepares and deals in meat: *the butcher in the grocery store.*

- Tap the thumb of the right *Y hand,* palm facing left, against the right side of the neck with a double movement.

butt *n. Slang.* See sign for BUTTOCKS.

butter *n.* A yellowish fatty solid that separates from milk or cream when it is churned, used as a spread: *put butter on my bread.* Same sign used for: **margarine.**

- [Mime spreading butter] Wipe the extended fingers of the right *U hand,* palm facing down and thumb extended, across the palm of the left *open hand* with a repeated movement, drawing the right fingers back into the palm each time.

butterfly *n.* An insect with a slender body and large, colored wings: *a butterfly poised on the flower.*

- [Symbolizes shape of butterfly's wings] With the thumb of the right *open hand* hooked around the thumb of the left *open hand,* both palms facing the chest, bend the fingers of both hands in and out with a repeated movement.

butt in *v.* See sign for NOSY[2].

buttocks *pl. n.* The fleshy lower hind part of the body: *to sit on your buttocks.* Same sign used for: **ass** (vulgar), **butt** (slang).

- [Location of buttocks] Pat the right *open hand* on the right buttock with a double movement.

button[1] *n.* A small disk or knob that fastens one piece of cloth to another when passed through a buttonhole or loop: *a row of buttons on the sweater.*

- [Shape and location of buttons] Touch the index-finger side of the right *F hand,* palm facing left, first in the center of the chest and then lower on the chest.

button[2] *n.* See sign for BADGE[1].

buy *v.* To acquire by paying a price: *buy a toy.*
Same sign used for: **purchase.**

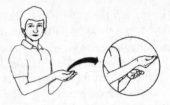

■ [**money** + **give you**] Beginning with the back of
the right *flattened O hand*, palm facing up, in
the upturned palm of left *open hand*, move the
right hand forward in an arc.

buzz *n.* **1.** A vibrating humming sound, as one made by flying
insects: *Listen to the buzz of that swarm of bees.* —*v.* **2.** To make
such a sound: *I hate it when flies buzz around my head.*

■ [Initialized sign changing from **b** to **z**] Move the right *B hand*
from in front of the upper chest, palm facing forward, to the
right while changing into a *1 hand*, moving the *1 hand* down
with a jagged movement in front of the right side of the body.

by *prep.* See sign for PASS[1].

bye *interj.* See sign for GOOD-BYE.

bylaw or **by-law** *n.* A standing rule governing the affairs
of a specified group or corporation: *A change in the
bylaws permitted her to add a deck to her beach house.*

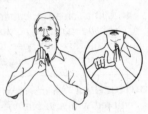

■ [Abbreviation **B-L** similar to sign for **law**] Place the index-
finger side of the right *B hand*, palm forward, on the
fingers of the left *open hand*, palm facing right and
fingers pointing up, and then, while changing to an
L hand, touch again on the heel of the left hand.

by mistake See sign for ACCIDENTALLY.

bypass *n.* A road used as an alternate to the main road, as to avoid
congestion or an obstruction: *Take the bypass around town.*

■ [Demonstrates going around another thing] Beginning with the
knuckles of the right *10 hand* on the wrist of the left *10 hand*,
palms facing in opposite directions and thumbs pointing up,
move the right hand forward in a large arc around the
left hand.

byte *n.* A group of adjacent binary digits, usually
eight, stored and processed by a computer as a
unit: *Eight bits equal a byte.*

■ [Initialized sign] Move the thumb side of the
right *B hand*, palm facing forward and fingers
pointing up, down the palm of the left *open
hand*, palm facing right, touching first on the
fingers and then on the heel.

by way of See sign for THROUGH.

cab *n.* A public passenger automobile that can be hired with its driver for individual trips: *to take a cab to the airport.* Same sign used for: **taxi.**
- [Represents the lighted dome on top of a taxi] Tap the fingertips of the right *C hand*, palm facing down, on the top of the head with a double movement.

cabbage *n.* A vegetable with thick leaves forming a round, compact head: *eat corned beef and cabbage.* Same sign used for: **lettuce.**
- [The head represents a head of cabbage] Tap the heel of the right *curved hand* against the right side of the head with a repeated movement.

cabinet *n.* A piece of furniture with shelves and drawers or doors: *Put the dishes in the cabinet.*
- [Demonstrates opening and closing of multiple cabinet doors] Beginning with the index-finger sides of both *B hands* together in front of the left side of the head, palms facing forward, bring the hands apart by twisting the wrists in opposite directions, ending with the palms facing back. Repeat in front of the right side of the head.

cabinetmaker *n.* See signs for CARPENTER[1,2].

cable *n.* A strong, thick rope or bundle of wires: *a bridge supported by cables.*
- [Shape of thick cable] Beginning with the index-finger side of both *C hands* touching in front of the body, palms facing down, bring the right hand outward to the right.

cable television or **CATV** *n.* Originally *Community Antenna Television.* A system for providing televison signals to consumers through optical fibers or coaxial cables as contrasted with satellite signals: *I subscribe to cable TV.*

■ [Shows shape of cable + **T-V**] Beginning with both *S hands* held in front of the chest, left hand nearer the chest than the right hand and both palms facing down, bring the right hand back toward the chest to hit on the little-finger side of the left hand. Then form a *T* and a *V* in front of the chest.

cafeteria *n.* A *restaurant* where people carry their own food to the tables: *to eat in the school cafeteria.* Alternate form: **café.**

■ [Initialized sign similar to sign for **restaurant**] Touch the index-finger side of the right *C hand,* palm facing left, first on the right side of the chin and then on the left side.

cage *n.* A place enclosed with wire or bars: *a bird cage.*

■ [Shape of a wire cage] Beginning with the fingertips of both *4 hands* touching in front of the chest, palms facing in, bring the hands away from each other in a circular movement back toward the chest, ending with the palms facing forward.

cake[1] *n.* A sweet baked food made of a batter containing flour, eggs, sugar, and other ingredients: *a chocolate cake.*

■ [Shape of slices of cake] Move the fingertips of the right *C hand,* palm facing down, across the upturned palm of the left *open hand,* first from the heel to the fingertips and then perpendicularly across the left palm.

cake[2] *n.* (alternate sign)

■ [Represents a cake rising] Beginning with the fingertips of the right *curved 5 hand* on the palm of the left *open hand,* raise the right hand upward in front of the chest.

calculator *n.* An electronic device used for mathematical calculations: *Add up the total on the calculator.*

■ [Mime using a calculator] Alternatingly tap each fingertip of the right *5 hand* while moving up and down the upturned left *open hand* held in front of the body.

calculus *n.* A system of calculation in advanced mathematics: *studying calculus in college.* Related form: **calculate** *v.*

- ■ [Initialized sign similar to sign for **mathematics**] Beginning with both *C hands* in front of each side of the chest, palms facing each other, move the hands past each other with a repeated movement.

calendar *n.* A table showing the days, weeks, and months of the year: *According to the calendar, next Friday is the 10th.*

- ■ [Initialized sign indicating turning pages on a calendar] Move the little-finger side of the right *C hand,* palm facing left, from the heel upward in an arc over the fingertips of the left *open hand,* palm facing in and fingers pointing up.

calf *n.* A young cow: *The calf is in the barn.*

- ■ [**baby**[1] + **cow**[1,2]] With the bent right arm cradled on the bent left arm, both palms facing up, swing the arms to the right and then to the left in front of the body. Then, with the thumb of the right *Y hand* on the right side of the forehead, palm facing forward, twist the hand forward with a repeated movement.

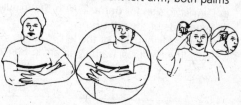

California *n.* A large state on the west coast of the United States: *to visit Hollywood in California.* See also sign for GOLD[1].

- ■ [Shows a gold earring, referring to the gold rush in California] Move the bent middle finger of the right *5 hand* from near the right ear, palm facing in, outward to the right with a wiggling movement.

call[1] *v.* To ask to come: *The boss called me into her office.* Same sign used for: **summon.**

- ■ [Tap on the hand to get one's attention] Slap the fingers of the right *open hand* on the back of the left *open hand,* palm facing down, dragging the right fingers upward and closing them into an *A hand* in front of the right shoulder.

call[2] *v.* To talk or try to talk to by telephone: *Call me when you get home.* Same sign used for: **phone.**

- ■ [Represents a telephone receiver] Bring the palm side of the right *Y hand* to the right side of the face, ending with the thumb near the ear and the little finger near the chin.

call[3] *v.* To communicate with on a
telecommunications device: *Call me on my TDD.*

- Bring the index finger of the modified *X hand*,
palm facing down, from the base forward
along the length of the extended left index
finger, palm facing right and finger pointing
forward.

call[4] or **call out** *v.* or *v. phrase.* To shout loudly: *Call out
the names during the ceremony.* Same sign used for: **cry,
holler, yell.**

- [Natural gesture of cupping the mouth when yelling] Place
the index-finger side of the right *C hand* against the right
side of the chin.

call[5] *v.* To give a name to: *called the baby
"John."* Same sign used for: **name.**

- [Similar to sign for **name**[1]] With the middle-
finger side of the right *H hand* across
the index-finger side of the left *H hand*,
move the hands forward in an arc in front
of the body.

call[6] *v.* See signs for TELEPHONE[1,2].

calligraphy *n.* Decorative handwriting: *Writing the
certificate in calligraphy was an excellent idea.*

- [Initialized sign similar to sign for **write**[2]] Beginning
with the thumb of the right *C hand*, palm facing
left, on the palm of the left *open hand*, palm
facing up, move the right thumb with a wavy
movement across the left palm and fingertips.

call out *v. phrase* See signs for SCREAM[1,2].

calm[1] or **calm down** *v.* or *v. phrase.* To make or
become quiet: *The teacher tried to calm the class
down.* Same sign used for: **relax.**

- [Natural gesture that seems to push down the noise
level, used in quieting a crowd] Beginning with both
5 hands in front of each side of the body, palms
facing down and fingers pointing forward, push the
hands downward with a double movement.

calm[2] *adj.* See signs for QUIET[1,2].

camcorder *n.* See sign for VIDEOTAPE[2].

camel *n.* A large, humped four-footed mammal living especially in desert regions: *Some camels have one hump and some have two.*

■ [Initialized sign showing the shape of a camel's humps] Move the right *C hand,* palm facing forward, from left to right in front of the chest in a double arc.

camera¹ *n.* An apparatus for taking photographs: *Take my picture with the new camera.*

■ [Mime taking a picture with a camera] Beginning with the *modified C hands* near the outside of each eye, palms facing each other, bend the right index finger up and down with a repeated movement.

camera² *n.* See sign for MOVIE CAMERA.

camp *n.* A place where people live for a short time in tents or similar temporary shelters: *sending the children to summer camp.* Same sign used for: **tent.**

■ [Shape of a tent] Beginning with the extended index fingers and little fingers of both hands touching at an angle in front of the chest, bring the hands downward and apart with a repeated movement. The same sign is used for the verb, as in *to camp on the beach for the weekend,* but the sign is made with a single movement.

camper *n.* A vehicle outfitted for camping: *We can sleep in the camper during the whole trip.*

■ [Represents a camper on top of a truck] Tap the fingertips of the right *flattened C hand* on the back of the left *open hand,* palm facing down, with a double movement.

can¹ *v.* To seal in an airtight container so as to preserve: *can peaches for the winter.*

■ [Represents sealing a canned jar] With the right *curved 5 hand,* palm facing down, over the thumb side of the left *S hand,* bring the right palm downward and twist to the right with a double movement.

can[2] *auxiliary v.* To be able to do something: *She can run fast.* Same sign used for: **may.**

- [Similar to sign for **able**[1]] Move both *S hands*, palms facing down, downward simultaneously with a short double movement in front of each side of the body.

can[3] *n.* See sign for CUP.

Canada *n.* A country in the northern part of North America: *English and French are spoken in Canada.* Related form: **Canadian** *adj.*, *n.*

- Tap the palm side of the right *A hand*, thumb pointing up, against the right side of the chest with a double movement.

cancel *v.* **1.** To decide or announce that something planned will not take place: *cancel an appointment.* **2.** To put a stop to or revoke: *cancel an order.* Same sign used for: **annul, condemn, correct, criticize, cross out, null, revoke, void.**

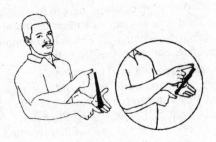

- [Finger crosses out something to cancel it] With the extended right index finger, draw a large X across the upturned left *open hand.*

cancer *n.* A malignant and invasive growth or tumor: *to have lung cancer.* Same sign used for: **acid, carcinoma, eat up, malignant, sarcoma.**

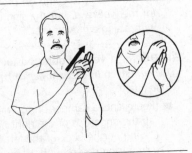

- [Shows devouring nature of cancer] Open and tightly close the finger of the right *curved 5 hand* as it moves with a crawling movement from the heel to the fingertips of the left *open hand*, palm facing right.

candidate *n.* See sign for APPLY[2].

candle *n.* A stick of wax with a wick for burning: *light a candle.* Same sign used for: **flame, glow.**

- [Represents the flame on a candle] With the extended right index finger touching the heel of the left *5 hand*, palm facing right, wiggle the left fingers.

candy *n.* A confection made with sugar and flavoring: *a box of chocolate candy.* Same sign used for: **sugar.**

- [Similar to sign for **sweet**] Bring the fingers of the right *U hand* downward on the chin with a repeated movement, bending the fingers each time.

cannibal *n.* A person who eats human flesh: *a book about cannibals who lived in the jungle.*

- [**people** + **eat** + **people**] Move both *P hands,* palms facing down, in alternating forward circles in front of each side of the body. Then bring the fingertips of the right *flattened O hand,* palm facing in, to the lips. Then, again move both *P hands,* palms facing down, in alternating forward circles in front of each side of the body.

canoe *v., n.* A light boat pointed on both ends: *to paddle a canoe down the river.* Related form: **canoeing** *n.* Same sign used for: **kayak, kayaking, oar, row, rowing.**

- [Mime paddling a canoe] With both *S hands* in front of the right side of the chest, right hand higher than the left hand, both palms facing in, bring both hands downward and back simultaneously with a repeated movement.

can't *contraction.* To be unable to do something: *I can't see through the fog.* Alternate form: **cannot.**

- Bring the extended right index finger downward in front of the chest, striking the extended left index finger as it moves, both palms facing down.

cantankerous *adj.* See sign for CONTRARY[1].

canteen *n.* A small container for carrying liquids: *carry a canteen of water during the hike.*

- [Mime taking a canteen from one's side and drinking from it] With the palm side of the left *flattened C hand* against the right side of the body, fingers pointing right, push the fingers of the right *flattened C hand* downward into the opening of the left hand. Then, with the index-finger side of both *flattened C hands* near each side of the mouth, palms facing each other, tip the hands back toward the face.

cap[1] *n.* A close-fitting covering for the head, often with a visor: *wearing a baseball cap*.

- ■ [Mime tipping a cap with a visor] Bring the right *modified X hand* from in front of the head, palm facing left, back to the top of the head.

cap[2] *n.* (alternate sign)

- ■ [Mime pulling on a stocking cap] Beginning with the palm sides of both *A hands* on top of the head, bring the hands downward on the sides of the head, keeping the palms close to the head.

cap[3] *n.* A covering for a tube or bottle: *Put the cap back on the bottle*.

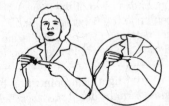

- ■ [Represents putting a cap on something] Push the fingertips of the right *flattened O hand* around the extended left index finger, both palms facing down.

cap[4] *n.* See signs for CROWN[2,3].

capable *adj.* See sign for SKILL.

capacity *n.* The amount that something can contain: *a computer disk with a storage capacity of two million bytes*.

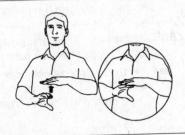

- ■ [Initialized sign showing filling something to capacity] Bring the right *C hand*, palm facing left, upward under the left *open hand*, palm facing down and fingers pointing right.

capital[1] *adj.* **1.** Designating a letter belonging to the series A, B, C, . . . Z, rather than a, b, c, . . . z: *a capital letter to start each sentence.* —*n.* **2.** A capital letter: *Start each sentence with a capital*.

- ■ [Shows size of capital letter] Hold the right *modified C hand*, palm facing forward, in front of the right side of the body.

capital[2] *n.* The city where the government of a country or state is located: *Harrisburg is the capital of Pennsylvania*.

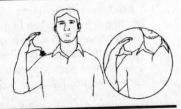

- ■ [Initialized sign] Tap the thumb of the right *C hand*, palm facing left, on the right shoulder with a short double movement.

capital punishment *n. phrase.* The killing of a person by the government as punishment for a crime: *He was sentenced to die by lethal injection as a capital punishment.* Same sign used for: **death penalty, execute, execution.**

- [**punish** + **die**] Strike the extended right index finger, palm facing left, downward across the elbow of the left bent arm. Then, beginning with both *open hands* in front of the body, right palm up and left palm down, flip the hands to the right, turning the right palm down and the left palm up.

capsule *n.* See signs for PILL[1,2,3].

captain *n.* **1.** A high-ranking military officer: *He is a captain in the army.* **2.** The head of a group: *captain of the basketball team.* See also sign for CHIEF[2]. Same sign used for: **boss, chairperson, general, officer.**

- [Location of epaulets on captain's uniform] Tap the fingertips of the right *curved 5 hand* on the right shoulder with a repeated movement.

caption *v.* To add subtitles to: *to caption the movie.* Related form: **captioned** *adj.* Same sign used for: **closed captions, subtitle.**

- [Similar to sign for **sentence**] Beginning with the fingertips of both *F hands* touching in front of the chest, palms facing each other, bring the hands apart with a repeated movement.

capture[1] *v.* To take prisoner: *to capture a rabbit in a trap.* See also sign for CATCH[3]. Same sign used for: **apprehend, arrest, claim, conquer, occupy, possess, repossess, seize, takeover.**

- [Mime grabbing at something to capture it] Beginning with both *curved 5 hands* in front of each shoulder, palms facing forward, move the hands downward while closing into *S hands.*

capture[2] *v.* (alternate sign) Same sign used for: **apprehend, arrest, convict, grip, nab, seize.**

- [Hand moves to "capture" the finger of the other hand] Move the right *C hand* from in front of the right shoulder, palm facing left, forward to meet the extended left index finger, palm facing right and finger pointing up, while changing into an *A hand.*

capture[3] *v.* (alternate sign) Same sign used for: **apprehend, arrest, convict, grip, nab, seize.**

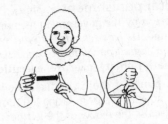

■ [Hand moves to "capture" the finger of the other hand] Move the right *C hand* from in front of the right side of the chest to the left, palm facing left, to close around the extended left index finger held up in front of the chest, palm facing right.

capture[4] *v.* (alternate sign, used to indicate others taking the speaker prisoner, especially by force) Related form: **captive** *n., adj.* See also sign for CATCH[3]. Same sign used for: **seize.**

■ [Directional sign made with movement toward oneself] Beginning with both *curved 5 hands* in front of each shoulder, palms facing in, bring the hands back against each side of the chest while closing into *A hands.*

capture[5] *v.* See sign for NAB[1].

car[1] *n.* A passenger vehicle for driving on an ordinary road or street: *The cars were bumper-to-bumper on the freeway.* Same sign used for: **automobile, drive, vehicle.**

■ [Mime driving] Beginning with both *S hands* in front of the chest, palms facing in and the left hand higher than the right hand, move the hands in an up-and-down arc with a repeated alternating movement.

car[2] *n.* A passenger vehicle typically with four wheels and an engine: *to drive a car to work.* Same sign used for: **automobile.**

■ [Initialized sign] Beginning with the little-finger side of the right *C hand* on the index-finger side of the left *C hand*, palms facing in opposite directions, bring the right hand back toward the right shoulder.

carat *n.* A unit of weight for precious stones: *The diamond is one carat.*

■ [Indicates location of a ring with a large stone on the hand] Touch the fingertips of the right *curved 5 hand* on the ring finger of the left *A hand.*

carburetor *n.* A mechanical device for mixing fuel with air in an internal-combustion engine: *We'll have to bring the car to the mechanic to fix the broken carburetor.* Same sign used for: **blockage, choke.**

■ [Mimes choking] Tap the fingertips of the right *flattened C hand* against the neck with a double movement.

carcinoma *n.* See sign for CANCER.

card[1] *n.* A stiff rectangular piece of paper: *to keep notes on index cards.* Same sign used for: **check, envelope.**

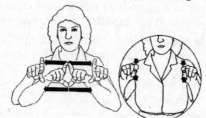

■ [Shows shape of a rectangular card] Beginning with the fingertips of both *L hands* touching in front of the chest, palms facing forward, bring the hands apart to in front of each shoulder, and then pinch each thumb and index finger together.

card[2] *n.* A credit card: *You can charge the dinner to my card.* See also sign for CREDIT CARD.

■ [Initialized sign showing shape of credit card] With the fingers of the right *C hand* curved around the left *open hand,* palm facing in and fingers pointing right, pull the right hand from the base of the left thumb to the fingertips with a double movement.

cardiac *adj.* See sign for HEART.

cardinal *n.* A crested songbird, the male of which has red feathers: *The cardinal in the tree was a striking sight.*

■ [red[1,2,3] + bird] Brush the extended right index finger downward on the lips. Then close the index finger and thumb of the right *G hand,* palm facing forward, with a repeated movement in front of the mouth.

cards *n.* Any of several games played with one or more sets of cards (playing cards) that typically are marked with numbers and symbols or pictures: *to win at cards.* Same sign used for: **play cards.**

■ [Mime dealing cards] Beginning with both *A hands* in front of the body, palms facing each other, flick the right hand to the right with a repeated movement off the left thumb.

card slot *n.* An opening in a computer, card reader, printer, or other device that accepts a media card for downloading or printing.

■ [card + insert] Beginning with the fingertips of both *modified C hands* touching in front of the chest, palms facing each other, bring the hands apart and then pinch each thumb and index finger together. Then slide the fingers of the right *open hand*, palm facing down, between the thumb and fingers of the left *flattened C hand*, palm facing right.

care[1] *n.* Serious attention: *to work on the project with care.* Same sign used for: **monitor, patrol, supervise, take care of.**

■ [Represents eyes watching out in different directions] With the little-finger side of the right *K hand* across the index-finger side of the left *K hand*, palms facing in opposite directions, move the hands in a repeated flat circle in front of the body.

care[2] *v.* See signs for TROUBLE[1,2].

carefree *adj.* See signs for NOT RESPONSIBLE[1,2].

careful *adj.* Taking care: *Be careful moving the painting.* Same sign used for: **be careful, cautious, take care, watch out.**

■ Tap the little-finger side of the right *K hand* with a double movement across the index-finger side of the left *K hand*, palms facing in opposite directions.

carefully *adv.* In a careful manner: *Walk carefully on the rough sidewalk.* Same sign used for: **cautiously.**

■ With the little-finger side of the right *K hand* across the index-finger side of the left *K hand*, palms facing in opposite directions, move the hands upward and forward in large double circles.

careless[1] *adj.* Showing lack of due care: *a careless mistake.* Related form: **carelessly** *adv.* Same sign used for: **reckless.**

■ [Misdirected eyes] Move the right *V hand* from near the right side of the head, palm facing left and fingers pointing up, down to the left in front of the eyes with a double movement.

careless[2] *adj.* (alternate sign) Related form: **carelessly** *adv.* Same sign used for: **reckless.**

- Beginning with both *V hands* near each side of the head, palms facing each other, move the right hand to the left in front of the eyes and the left hand to the right in front of the eyes with a double movement.

carnival[1] *n.* A place of amusement, as a special festival or a traveling fair with rides: *to take the children to the carnival.*

- [**fair**[3] + **partying**] Beginning with the right *bent V hand* in front of the right shoulder and the left *bent V hand* in front of the left side of the body, palms facing down, move the hands forward in large alternating circles. Then, beginning with both *open hands* near each side of the face, palms facing down and fingers pointing toward each other, swing the hands forward with a double movement while spreading the fingers into *5 hands.*

carnival[2] *n.* See signs for CRUSADE, FAIR[2].

carpenter[1] *n.* A person who builds or repairs wooden structures: *The carpenter built this house.* Same sign used for: **cabinetmaker.**

- [Action of sawing + **person marker**] Beginning with the right *S hand* near the right side of the chest and the left *S hand* forward of the body, both palms facing in opposite directions, swing the hands forward with a double movement. Then move both *open hands,* palms facing each other, downward along each side of the body.

carpenter[2] *n.* (alternate sign) Same sign used for: **cabinetmaker, woodworker.**

- [**carpentry** + **person marker**] Move the right *S hand,* palm facing left, across the length of the upturned left *open hand* with a double movement. Then move both *open hands,* palms facing each other, downward along each side of the body.

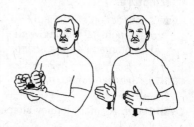

carpentry *n.* The trade of a carpenter: *good carpentry.*

- [Action of sanding wood] Move the right *S hand,* palm facing left, across the length of the upturned left *open hand* with a double movement.

carry *v.* To take from one place to another: *Carry the boxes inside.* Alternate forms: **carry on** or **onto.**

- [Having something in one's hands to transfer to another place] Beginning with both *curved hands* in front of the right side of the body, move the hands in a series of simultaneous arcs to the left, ending in front of the left side of the body.

cart *n.* A small vehicle on wheels, moved by hand: *push the grocery cart down the aisle.*

- [Mime pushing a cart] Beginning with both *S hands* in front of the body, palms facing down, push the hands forward.

carton *n.* A box made of cardboard: *a carton of cigarettes.*

- [Initialized sign showing shape of carton] Beginning with the fingertips of the index fingers and thumbs of both *C hands* touching in front of the chest, palms facing forward, bring the hands apart to in front of each side of the body.

cartoon *n.* A drawing or filmed sequence of drawings designed to entertain: *watch cartoons on television.*

- [Initialized sign similar to sign for **funny**] Move the right *C hand,* palm facing left, downward with a double movement from in front of the nose.

carve *v.* **1.** To cut into pieces or slices: *to carve the turkey.* **2.** To form by cutting: *to carve a statue out of marble.* Same sign used for: **engrave, sculpture.**

- [Mime action of carving] Flick the right thumb of the right *10 hand* upward off the heel of the upturned left *open hand.*

cash *n.* See sign for FORTUNE.

cashew *n.* A small, kidney-shaped nut: *eat a cashew.*

- [**peanut**[1] + shape of a cashew] Move the thumb of the right *10 hand* forward from behind the edge of the front teeth. Then, beginning with the fingers of both *G hands* pointing toward each other in front of the chest, move the hands away from each other in small downward arcs.

cashier *n.* A person whose primary function is handling money in exchange for goods or services: *The cashier overcharged me for the dress.* Same sign used for: **clerk.**

- [**cash register** + **person marker**] Move the right *5 hand,* palm facing down, from in front of the right shoulder downward with a repeated movement while wiggling the fingers. Then, move both *open hands,* palms facing each other, downward along the sides of the body.

cashmere *n.* A fine, soft wool used for making clothes: *a scarf made of cashmere.*

- [**sweater** + **soft** + feeling the softness of cashmere] Beginning with the palm side of both *A hands* on each side of the chest, move the hands downward to near the waist. Then, beginning with the right *flattened C hand* in front of the chest, palm facing up, bring the hand downward with a double movement to land on the back left *open hand* held across the body, palm facing down, while closing the fingers to the thumb each time. Then move the right *5 hand* above the bent left forearm in a flat circle.

cash register *n.* A business machine that records sales, totals receipts, and has a drawer for holding money: *Ring this sale up on the cash register.*

- [Mime action of using a cash register] Move the right *5 hand,* palm facing down, from in front of the right shoulder downward with a repeated movement while wiggling the fingers.

casket *n.* A container for burying a body: *They lowered the casket into the ground.* Same sign used for: **coffin.**

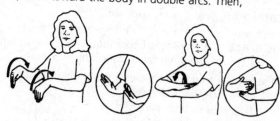

- [**bury**[1] + action of opening the lid of casket] Move both *curved hands,* palms facing down and fingers pointing down, back toward the body in double arcs. Then, beginning with the bent right arm resting on the bent left arm, palms facing down and fingers pointing in opposite directions, move the right *open hand* upward, ending with the palm facing in and fingers pointing left.

cassette tape *n.* See sign for RECORD[3].

cast *v.* See signs for THROW[1,2].

cast off *v. phrase.* See sign for ABANDON[1].

cast out *v. phrase.* See sign for ABANDON[2].

castle *n.* A large building with thick walls and defenses against attack: *the king's castle.*

- [**large** + **house** + the shape of a castle's turrets] Move both *L hands* from in front of each side of the chest, palms facing each other and index fingers pointing forward, apart to each side in large arcs. Then, beginning with the fingertips of both *open hands* touching, palms angled toward each other, bring the hands downward at an angle to in front of each shoulder and then straight down, ending with the fingers pointing up and the palms facing each other. Then move both *C hands,* palms facing each other, up and down with alternating movements in front of each shoulder.

casual *adj.* See signs for BUM, DAILY, FARM.

cat[1] *n.* A small, furry mammal with whiskers and sharp claws, bred in a number of varieties and often kept as a pet: *my pet cat.*

- [Cat's whiskers] Move the fingertips of both *F hands,* palms facing each other, from each side of the mouth outward with a repeated movement.

cat[2] *n.* (alternate sign)

- [Cat's whiskers] Beginning with the bent index finger and thumb of the right *5 hand* touching the right cheek, palm facing in, bring the hand outward to the right with a repeated movement while pinching the index finger and thumb together each time.

catalog *n.* See sign for MAGAZINE.

cataract *n.* An abnormal condition of the eye in which the lens becomes clouded: *to have an operation for cataracts in your eyes.*

- [**eye**[1] + **blur**] Point the extended right index finger, palm facing in, to the right eye. Then, beginning with the fingertips of both *flattened O hands* touching in front of the chest, palms facing in opposite directions, move the hands toward each other while opening into *5 hands,* palms facing each other.

catch[1] *v.* To take and hold, especially a moving object: *to catch a ball.*

- [Mime catching ball] Beginning with both *5 hands* in front of the body, palms facing each other, bring the hands back toward the body while constricting the hands into *curved 5 hands.*

catch[2] *v.* To take hold of a baseball or other ball that has been thrown or hit: *The outfielder tried to catch the fly ball.*

- [Mime a catcher's hand position] Beginning with the back of the left *C hand*, palm facing forward, against the palm of the right *open hand*, palm facing left, bring both hands back against the chest.

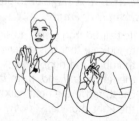

catch[3] *v.* To incur a disease: *catch a cold.* Same sign used for: **prone.**

- [One's fingers receive something and bring it to oneself] With an alternating movement, first move the right *curved 5 hand* and then the left *curved 5 hand* from in front of the chest, both palms facing down and fingers pointing forward, back to the chest while changing into *flattened O hands.*

catch[4] *v.* See signs for CAPTURE[1,2,3], NAB[1].

catcher *n.* A baseball player who stands behind the batter to catch the ball: *Throw the ball to the catcher to get the runner out at home plate.*

- [**catch**[2] + **person marker**] Beginning with the back of the left *C hand*, palm facing forward, against the palm of the right *open hand*, palm facing left, bring both hands back against the chest. Then move both *open hands*, palms facing each other, downward along each side of the body.

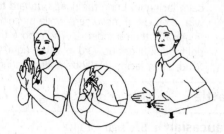

catch up *v. phrase.* To come from behind and be even: *to catch up with my work.*

- [One hand catches up with the other hand] Bring the right *A hand* from near the right side of the chest, palm facing left, forward to the heel of the left *A hand*, palm facing right, held in front of the body.

category *n.* See sign for CLASS.

caterpillar *n.* The wormlike larva of a butterfly or moth: *a fuzzy caterpillar.*

- [Action of caterpillar crawling] Beginning with the palm side of the right *X hand* on the bent left forearm, move the right hand up the left arm toward the elbow, bending the index finger up and down as it moves.

cathedral *n.* A large or important church: *to see the famous cathedrals of France.*

- [Initialized sign similar to sign for **church** but moving upward to indicate that it is larger than a church] Beginning with the thumb of the right *C hand,* palm facing left, on the back of the left *open hand,* palm facing down, held in front of the chest, move the right hand upward in an arc to in front of the right shoulder.

Catholic *adj.* Of the Christian church governed by the Pope: *a Catholic priest.*

- [Sign of the cross on the forehead] Bring the extended fingers of the right *H hand,* palm facing down, first down-ward on the forehead and then from left to right across the forehead.

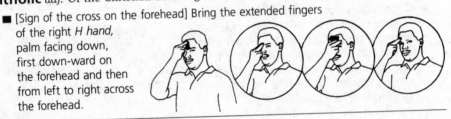

catsup *n.* A condiment made of a thick spiced tomato sauce: *to put catsup on my hamburger.* See also sign for KETCHUP.

- [**cat**[1] + **up**] Beginning with the bent index finger and thumb of the right *5 hand* touching the right cheek, palm facing in, bring the hand outward to the right with a repeated movement while pinching the index finger and thumb together. Then move the extended right index finger upward near the right side of the head, palm facing left and finger pointing up.

cattle *n.* See signs for COW[1,2].

Caucasian *n.* See sign for PALE.

caught *v.* See sign for STUCK.

caught in the act *v. phrase.* See sign for NAB[1].

cause *v.* To make happen: *caused a fire in the house by playing with matches.*

- Beginning with both *S hands* near the body, palms facing up and left hand nearer the body than the right hand, move both hands forward in an arc while opening into *5 hands.*

caution *v.* See sign for WARN.

cautious *adj.* See signs for CAREFUL, WARY.

cautiously *adv.* See sign for CAREFULLY.

cave in *v. phrase.* See sign for BREAK DOWN.

cease *v.* See sign for STOP[1].

cedar *n.* **1.** An evergreen tree: *a tall cedar growing on the hill.* **2.** The fragrant reddish wood of this tree: *a cedar closet.*

■ [**red**[1,2,3] + **wood**[1,2] + **smell**[1]] Brush the extended right index finger downward on the lips. Then slide the little-finger side of the right *open hand* back and forth across the index-finger side of the left *open hand* with a double movement. Then raise the palm side of the right *open hand* in front of the nose with an outward arc, palm facing in.

ceiling *n.* The overhead interior surface of a room: *Don't bump your head on the low ceiling.*

■ [Shape and location of the ceiling] Beginning with both *B hands* above the head, right in front of left, palms facing down and fingers pointing in opposite directions, move the right hand straight forward while keeping the left hand in place.

celebrate *v.* To observe a special time or event with planned activities: *to celebrate your birthday with a party.* Related form: **celebration** *n.* Same sign used for: **anniversary, festival, gala, holiday, rejoice, victory.**

■ With *modified X hands* in front of each shoulder, move both hands in large repeated outward movements, palms angled up.

celery *n.* A pale green vegetable with crisp stalks: *eating a stalk of celery.*

■ [**green** + action of eating celery stalk] Beginning with the right *G hand* in front of the right shoulder, palm facing in, twist the hand back and forth with a double movement. Then move the right *G hand* from near the right side of the mouth, palm facing up, in toward the mouth while moving the mouth as if eating.

celibate

celibate *adj.* See sign for ABSTAIN.

cellar *n.* See sign for BASEMENT.

cell phone or **cellular phone** *n.* Mobile telephone using a system of radio transmitters, each covering separate areas: *to call home on a cell phone.*

- [Holding a cell phone] Hold the right *curved hand* near the right ear.

cemetery *n.* A place for burying the dead: *She placed flowers on the grave at the cemetery.* Same sign used for: **graveyard.**

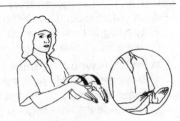

- [Shape of mounds of dirt on graves] Move both *curved hands*, palms facing down and fingers pointing forward, with a double movement back toward the body in double arcs.

cent *n.* A monetary unit or coin worth 1/100 of a dollar: *This newspaper still costs 30 cents.* Same sign used for: **penny.**

- With a double movement, move the extended right index finger forward at an outward angle from touching the right side of the forehead, palm facing down.

center *n.* The middle point of anything: *standing in the center of the room.* Related form: **central** *adj.* See also sign for MIDDLE.

- [Indicates location in center of something] Move the right *open hand*, palm facing down, in a circular movement over the upturned left *open hand*, bending the right fingers as the hand moves and ending with the fingertips of the right *bent hand* touching the middle of the left palm.

century *n.* A period of one hundred years: *the greatest novel of the twentieth century.*

- [one + hundred + year] Form a *1* and then a *C hand* with the right hand in front of the right shoulder, palm facing forward. Then move the right *S hand* in a circle around the left *S hand*, ending with the little-finger side of the right hand on the index-finger side of the left hand.

cereal *n.* Food made from grain: *eat cereal for breakfast.*

- [Action of scooping cereal from bowl to mouth] Move the right *curved hand,* palm facing up, from the palm of the left *open hand,* palm facing up, upward to the mouth with a double movement.

cerebral *adj.* See sign for HEAD.

certain *adj.* See signs for ABSOLUTE, SURE[1], TRUE.

certainly *adv.* See sign for TRUE.

certificate[1] *n.* An official document attesting to a fact: *a birth certificate.* Related forms: **certification** *n.,* **certify** *v.*

- [Initialized sign showing a stamp of approval] Move the right *C hand,* palm and fingers facing forward, in a circular movement over the upturned left *open hand,* turning the right palm in as it moves, ending with the little-finger side of the right hand in the left palm, right palm and fingers facing left.

certificate[2] *n.* (alternate sign) Related forms: **certification** *n.,* **certify** *v.*

- [Initialized sign showing shape of certificate] Tap the thumbs of both *C hands* together in front of the chest with a repeated movement, palms facing each other.

certify *v.* See sign for ACCREDIT.

Cesarean[1] *adj.* **1.** Designating a surgical operation for the delivery of a baby: *She had to have a Cesarean delivery.* —*n.* **2.** A Cesarean operation: *Their second baby was delivered by Cesarean.*

- [**pregnant**[1] + **operate**[2]] Beginning with the right *curved hand* on the stomach, palm facing in and fingers pointing down, bring the hand forward a short distance. Then draw the thumb of the right *10 hand,* palm facing in, across the lower abdomen from left to right.

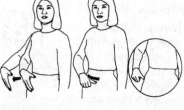

Cesarean[2] *adj., n.* (alternate sign)

- [Location of surgery for Cesarean section operation] Move the left *A hand,* palm facing in, across the lower abdomen from right to left.

---

chain *n.* A series of connected metal links: *tied to the roof of the car with a chain.* Same sign used for: **Olympics.**

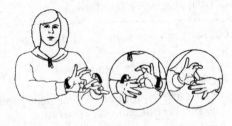

- [Shape of chain] Beginning with the index fingers and thumbs of both *F hands* intersecting in front of the left side of the chest, palms facing each other and the right hand above the left hand, release the fingers, flip the hands in reverse positions, and connect the fingers again with a repeated alternating movement as the hands move across the front of the body from left to right.

---

chair *n.* A seat with a back intended for one person: *sit in a chair.* Same sign used for: **seat.**

- [Fingers represent legs hanging down when sitting] With a double movement, tap the fingers of the right *curved U hand* across the fingers of the left *U hand,* both palms facing down.

---

chairperson[1] *n.* A person who is in charge of a meeting: *The chairperson called the meeting to order.*

- [**captain** + **person**] Tap the fingertips of the right *curved 5 hand* on the right shoulder with a double movement. Then move both *P hands,* palms facing down, downward along each side of the body.

---

chairperson[2] *n.* See signs for CAPTAIN, CHIEF. Related form: **chair** *n.*

---

chalk *n.* A soft white or colored stick used to write on a chalkboard: *Hand the teacher a piece of chalk.*

- [**white** + shape of chalk + mime writing on chalkboard] Beginning with the fingers of the right *curved 5 hand* against

---

the chest, palm facing in, bring the hand forward while changing into a *flattened O hand*. Then, beginning with the fingers of both *G hands* pointing toward each other in front of the chest, palms facing each other, bring the hands apart a short distance and pinch the index finger to the thumb of each hand. Then move the right *modified X hand,* palm facing forward in front of the right side of the head, to the right in a jagged up and down movement.

chalkboard *n.* See sign for BOARD[1].

chalk up *v. phrase.* See sign for ACHIEVE.

challenge *v.* **1.** To call or summon to a contest: *challenged me to a game of tennis.* —*n.* **2.** A call or summons to engage in a contest: *accepted our challenge to see which office would raise more money for charity.* Same sign used for: **dare, play against, versus.**

- [Hands seem to confront each other] Swing both *10 hands,* palms facing in, from in front of each side of the chest toward each other, ending with the knuckles touching in front of the chest, thumbs pointing up.

champagne *n.* See sign for COCKTAIL.

champion *n.* The winner in a contest: *the swimming champion in the ten meter race.* Same sign used for: **trophy.**

- [Symbolizes placing crown on head of winner] With the fingers of the right *curved 3 hand,* tap the right palm on the extended left index finger pointing up in front of the chest.

chance[1] *n.* A risk or gamble: *to take a chance.*

- [Grabbing dice] Bring the right *C hand,* palm facing left, toward the body from the fingers to the base of the upturned palm of the left *open hand,* while changing into an *S hand.*

chance[2] *n.* An opportunity: *a chance to earn some extra money.*

- [Initialized sign formed like turning over dice] Beginning with both *C hands* in front of each side of the body, palms facing up, flip the hands over, ending with the palms facing down.

change[1] *v.* To make or become different: *to change the color of the bedroom walls; plans that suddenly changed.* Same sign used for: **adapt, adjust, alter, justify, modify, shift, switch, turn.**

- [Hands seem to twist something as if to change it] With the palm side of both *A hands* together, right hand above left, twist the wrists in opposite directions in order to reverse positions.

change[2] *v.* See sign for SHARE. Shared idea of dividing an amount of money to be shared.

change[3] *v.* See sign for CONVERT[2].

change places See sign for TRADE PLACES.

change the subject To shift from the topic under discussion to another topic: *He changed the subject whenever someone mentioned his past.* Same sign used for: **change the topic.**

- [One hand moves away to another topic] Beginning with both *bent V hands* near each other in front of the chest, palms facing down, swing the right hand off to the right.

change the topic See sign for CHANGE THE SUBJECT.

channel[1] *n.* A band of frequencies that carries television or radio programs: *change the channel on the TV.*

- [t-v + mime turning dial to change TV channel] Form a *T* and then a *V* in front of the right shoulder with the right hand, palm facing forward. Then twist the right *curved 5 hand*, palm facing forward, with a double movement to the right in front of the right side of the body.

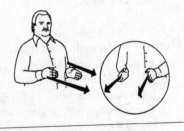

channel[2] *n.* A passage or groove through which something may pass: *The boat went through the narrow channel.* Same sign used for: **path.**

- [Shape of narrow channels] Beginning with both *open hands* in front of the body, palms facing each other and fingers angled toward the left, move the hands forward. Then angle the hands toward the right and repeat the movement.

channel[3] *n.* A transmission path that connects peripheral devices to a computer: *connecting the printer to the right channel.* Same sign used for: **branches.**

■ [Indicates various channels a transmission might take] Slide the thumb side of the right *1 hand,* palm facing down, from the heel to off the index finger of the left *5 hand,* palm facing right and fingers pointing forward. Repeat movement off the left ring finger.

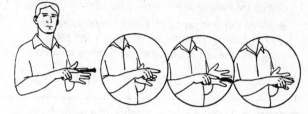

chant *n.* See sign for MUSIC.

Chanukah *n.* See signs for HANUKKAH[1,2].

chaos *n.* See sign for MESS[1], MESSY.

chap[1] *v.* To become rough and cracked: *My lips are chapped.*

■ [crack[1] + break] Move the little-finger side of the right *open hand,* palm facing left, down the palm of the left *open hand,* palm facing up, with a jagged movement. Then, beginning with both *S hands* in front of the body, index fingers touching and palms facing down, move the hands away from each other while twisting the wrists with a deliberate movement, ending with the palms facing each other.

chap[2] *n.* See sign for CRACK[1].

chapel *n.* See sign for CHURCH.

chapter[1] *n.* A main division of a book, usually having a number or a title: *to read a chapter before going to bed.*

■ [Initialized sign showing a column of text] Move the fingertips of the right *C hand* down the upturned left *open hand* with a repeated movement.

chapter[2] *n.* See sign for COURSE.

character[1] *n.* The quality and nature of someone or something: *a fine leader of sterling character.* Related form: **characteristic** *n.*

■ [Initialized sign similar to sign for **personality**] Move the right *C hand,* palm facing left, in a small circle and then back against the left side of the chest.

character[2] *n.* A person in a story, play, or film: *The court jester is my favorite character in the play.*

- [Initialized sign similar to sign for **role**] Move the right *C hand*, palm facing left, in a small circle against the left *open hand*, palm facing forward.

charge[1] *v.* To put down as a debt to be paid: *to charge the purchase to the corporate account.* See also sign for CREDIT CARD.

- [Represents getting impression of credit card charge] Rub the little-finger side of the right *S hand*, palm facing in, back and forth on the upturned left *open hand.*

charge[2] *v.* See signs for ACCUSE[1], APPLY[1], BLAME[1], COST[1].

charity *n.* **1.** Donating one's money or time to the poor or to organizations set up to help them: *a philanthropist noted for his charity.* **2.** An institution or fund set up to help those in need: *raising money for charity.* Same sign used for: **contribute, contribution, donate, donation.**

- [**gift**[1] formed repeatedly to indicate frequent contributions] With the right *X hand* closer to the chest than the left *X hand*, move each hand, palms facing each other, forward from the chest with a double alternating movement.

charley horse *n.* See sign for CRAMP[2].

chart[1] *n.* A sheet giving information in the form of a list or diagram: *kept track of the project's schedule on a chart.*

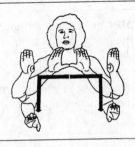

- [Initialized sign showing shape of chart] Beginning with the thumbs of both *C hands* touching in front of the chest, palms facing forward, move the hands apart to about shoulder width, and then move them straight down.

chart[2] *n.* See sign for SCHEDULE[1].

chase *v.* To run after to catch: *to chase a bus for a whole block.* Same sign used for: **pursue.**

- [One hand seems to pursue the other hand] Move the right *A hand*, palm facing left, in a spiraling movement from in front of the chest forward, to behind the left *A hand* held somewhat forward of the body.

chat[1] *v.* To talk in an easy, informal manner: *to chat about the weather.* Same sign used for: **talk.**

- [Represents **talk**[2] from two people] Move both *5 hands,* palms angled up, from in front of each shoulder downward at an angle toward each other with a repeated movement.

chat[2] *v.* See signs for BLAB, PRATTLE, TALK[4]. Related form: **chatter** *n.*

chatter *v.* See signs for BLAB, JABBER.

chauffeur *n.* See sign for DRIVER.

cheap *adj.* Costing relatively little; inexpensive: *It doesn't pay to buy cheap shoes.* Same sign used for: **inexpensive.**

- Brush the index-finger side of the right *B hand* downward on the palm of the left *open hand,* bending the right wrist as it moves down.

cheat[1] *v.* To behave in a manner that is not honest: *to cheat on the test.* Same sign used for: **betray, deceive, fraud.**

- Slide the right *3 hand* between the index and middle fingers, palm facing in, onto the index-finger side of the left *B hand,* palm facing down, with a double movement.

cheat[2] *v.* (alternate sign) Same sign used for: **betray, deceive, fraud.**

- Slide the right *3 hand* between the index and middle fingers, palm facing in, downward onto the index-finger side of the left *open hand,* palm facing right, with a double movement.

check[1] *v.* To inspect for accuracy: *Check your work before you hand it in.* Same sign used for: **approve, examine, inspect.**

- [Bringing one's attention to something to inspect it] Move the extended right index finger from the nose down to strike sharply off the upturned palm of the left *open hand,* and then upward again.

check[2] *n.* A mark used to show that something has been examined or is correct: *Put a check near the right answer.* Same sign used for: **check off, mark.**

- ■ [Shape of a check-mark] Move the extended right index finger sharply off the upturned palm of the left *open hand,* and then upward again.

check[3] *n.* A written order directing a bank to pay out money: *to pay for the clothing by check.*

- ■ [**write**[1,2] + **card**[2]] Move the fingertips of the right *modified X hand* from the heel to the fingertips of the upturned left *open hand.* Then, with the fingers of the right *C hand* curved around the left *open hand,* palm facing up and fingers pointing right, pull the right hand from the base of the left thumb to the fingertips with a double movement.

check[4] *n.* See sign for CARD[1].

checkers *n.* A board game played by two people, using red and black disks as playing pieces: *I haven't played a game of checkers since I was a child.*

- ■ [Action of moving a checker on a checkerboard] Move the fingers of the right *curved 3 hand,* palm facing down, in a small arc to the right and then to the left, in front of the right side of the body.

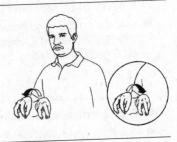

check for *v. phrase.* See signs for LOOK FOR[1,2,3].

check off *v. phrase.* See sign for CHECK[2].

cheek *n.* The side of the face below the eye: *a child with beautiful rosy cheeks.*

- ■ [Location of cheek] Touch the fingertips of the right *flattened C hand* against the right cheek.

cheer *n.* See sign for HAPPY. Related form: **cheerful** *adj.*

cheerful *adj.* See sign for FRIENDLY.

cheerleader *n.* A person who directs spectators in organized cheering at a sporting event: *The cheerleaders waved their pompoms and jumped into the air.*

- [Movement of cheerleader's pompoms + **person marker**] Beginning with both *S hands* in front of the chest, palms facing each other, move the hands forward in an arc with a double movement. Then move both *open hands,* palms facing each other, downward along each side of the body.

cheese *n.* A solid food made from the curds of milk: *some cheese in the sandwich.*

- With the heel of the right *open hand* pressed on the heel of the upturned left *open hand,* palms facing each other and perpendicular to each other, twist the right hand forward and back slightly with a repeated movement.

chemistry *n.* See sign for SCIENCE. Related form: **chemical** *adj.*

cherish *v.* See sign for PRECIOUS.

cherry *n.* A small, round, usually red fruit with a pit: *a bowl of beautiful ripe cherries.* See also sign for BERRY².

- [The stem of a cherry] Move the fingertips of the right *F hand,* palm facing left, from near the mouth forward and downward with a wavy movement.

chest¹ *n.* A box with a lid: *Put the toys in the chest.*

- [**room**² + opening the lid of a chest] Beginning with both *open hands* in front of each side of the body, palms facing each other, turn the hands sharply in opposite directions, ending with both palms facing in. Then, beginning with the right *open hand,* palm facing down, above the left *open hand,* palm facing in and fingers pointing right, move the right hand up, ending with the palm facing in and fingers pointing left.

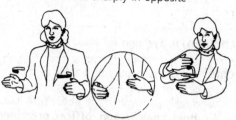

chest² *n.* The top, front part of the body: *a pain in my chest.*

- [Location of chest] Rub the fingertips of both *open hands,* palms facing in and fingers pointing toward each other, up and down on the chest with a repeated movement.

chew *v.* To crush or grind with the teeth: *Chew your food well before swallowing it.* Same sign used for: **grind.**

■ [Represents grinding motion of teeth when chewing] With the palm sides of both *A hands* together, right hand on top of the left hand, move the hands in small repeated circles in opposite directions, causing the knuckles of the two hands to rub together.

chewing gum *n.* A sweetened and flavored substance made of chicle for chewing: *a pack of chewing gum.* Same sign used for: **gum.**

■ [Action of jaw when chewing gum] With the fingertips of the right *V hand* against the right side of the chin, palm facing down, move the hand toward the face with a double movement by bending the fingers.

chewing tobacco *n.* See sign for TOBACCO.

chew out *v. phrase.* See sign for BAWL OUT.

Chicago *n.* A city in Illinois, on Lake Michigan: *Chicago is the third largest city in the U.S.*

■ [Initialized sign] Move the right *C hand*, palm facing left, from in front of the right side of the chest to the right a short distance and then straight down, ending with the palm facing down.

chicken[1] *n.* **1.** A domestic fowl raised for its eggs or for food: *to raise chickens.* **2.** The flesh of this fowl used for food: *having roast chicken for dinner.* Same sign used for: **hen.**

■ Tap the thumb of the right *3 hand*, palm facing left and fingers pointing up, against the chin with a repeated movement.

chicken[2] *n.* See sign for BIRD.

chief[1] *n.* **1.** The person of highest authority in an organized group: *the chief of police.* —*adj.* **2.** Highest in rank or authority: *the chief copyeditor in the publishing house.* Same sign used for: **boss, chairperson, officer, prominent, superior, VIP.**

■ [Shows higher location] Move the right *10 hand* upward from in front of the right side of the chest, palm facing in and thumb pointing up.

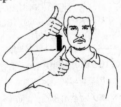

chief[2] *n.* See sign for CAPTAIN.

child *n.* A young boy or girl: *The child is lost.*

■ [Patting child on the head] Pat the right *bent hand* downward with a short repeated movement in front of the right side of the body, palm facing down.

children[1] *pl. n.* Young boys and/or girls: *games for children.*

■ [Patting a number of children on their heads] Pat the right *open hand,* palm facing down, in front of the right side of the body and then to the right with a double arc.

children[2] *pl. n.* (alternate sign)

■ [Shows height of a number of children] Beginning with the index-finger side of both *B hands* touching in front of the body, palms facing down and fingers pointing forward, move the hands outward to each side with a bouncy movement.

chilly *adj.* See sign for COLD[2].

chimney *n.* An upright structure used to carry smoke away from a fireplace or furnace: *a brick chimney.*

■ [Initialized sign showing shape of a chimney] Bring both *C hands* from in front of each side of the body, palms facing each other, straight upward to about shoulder height, and then at an angle toward each other and continuing upward in front of the face.

chimpanzee *n.* See sign for MONKEY.

chin *n.* The front of the lower jaw below the mouth: *He was knocked unconscious when he was hit on the chin.*

■ [Location of chin] Touch the extended right index finger on the chin, palm facing in.

China[1] *n.* A large country in eastern Asia:
*Beijing is the capital of the People's Republic
of China.* Related form: **Chinese** *adj., n.*

- [Shape of Chinese military uniforms] Move
  the extended right index finger, palm facing
  in, from the left to the right side of the chest
  and then straight down.

China[2] *n.* (alternate sign, sometimes considered
offensive) Related form: **Chinese** *n., adj.*
Same sign used for: **Oriental.**

- [Points to characteristic shape of an Asian person's
  eyes] With the extended right index finger touching
  near the corner of the right eye, palm facing down,
  twist the hand forward, ending with the palm facing back.

chip *n.* A small silicon wafer on which electronic components are deposited: *to replace
the memory chip in the computer.*

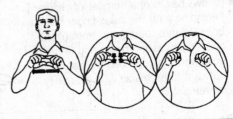

- [Shape of a computer chip]
  Beginning with the fingers of both
  G hands touching in front of the
  chest, palms facing forward, bring
  the hands apart a short distance
  and pinch each thumb and index
  finger together.

chip in *v. phrase.* To join others in giving money for
a common cause: *We all chipped in to buy her a
gift.* Same sign used for: **pool.**

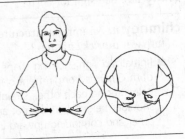

- Beginning with both *flattened O hands* in front
  of each side of the body, palms facing up and
  fingers pointing toward each other, bring the
  hands toward each other while sliding the
  fingers closed into *A hands.*

chisel *n.* **1.** A tool with a steel cutting edge: *to use a chisel
in sculpting the block of wood.* —*v.* **2.** To cut or shape with
a chisel: *to chisel the marble into shape.*

- [Action of using a chisel on wood] Slide the fingertips of
  the right *H hand*, palm facing in, across the palm of the
  left *open hand*, palm facing up, from the heel to the
  fingers with a short double movement.

chocolate[1] *n.* **1.** A brown food substance made from grinding
cacao seeds, often sweetened and flavored: *I like chocolate better
than vanilla.* —*adj.* **2.** Made with chocolate: *chocolate cake.*

- [Initialized sign] Brush the index-finger side of the right *C hand*,
  palm facing forward, downward on the right side of the chin
  with a repeated movement.

chocolate[2] *n., adj.* (alternate sign)

- ■ [Initialized sign] Move the thumb side of the right *C hand*, palm facing forward, in a repeated circle on the back of the left *open hand* held in front of the chest, palm facing down.

choice *n.* See signs for CRITICAL, EITHER[1,2], SAMPLE[1].

choir[1] *n.* A group of singers, especially one that performs at a church service: *She always wanted to sing in the choir.*

- ■ [Initialized sign similar to sign for **music**] Move the right *C hand*, palm facing down, with a swinging double movement above the extended left forearm.

choir[2] *n.* See signs for BAND[1,2].

choke[1] *v.* To have or cause to have the windpipe blocked: *Help her—she's choking on a bone.*

- ■ [Location of choking sensation] Touch the fingertips of the right *flattened C hand* against the neck.

choke[2] *n.* See sign for CARBURETOR.

choose[1] *v.* To select from a number of possibilities: *to choose a partner for the dance.* Related form: **choice** *n.* Same sign used for: **assign, draw, option, pick, select.**

- ■ [Hand picks from alternatives] Beginning with the bent thumb and index finger of the right *5 hand* touching the index finger of the left *5 hand*, palms facing each other, pull the right hand back toward the right shoulder while pinching the thumb and index finger together.

choose[2] *v.* (alternate sign) Related form: **choice** *n.* Same sign used for: **assign, draw, option, pick, select.**

- ■ [A directional sign demonstrating choosing something] Beginning with the bent thumb and index finger of the right *5 hand* pointing forward in front of the right shoulder, palm facing forward, bring the right hand back toward the right shoulder while pinching the thumb and index finger together.

choose[3] *v.* (alternate sign) Related form: **choice** *n.* Same sign used for: **either, option, pick, select.**

choose

- [Hand picks from alternatives] Beginning with the bent thumb and index finger of the right *5 hand* touching the index finger of the left *V hand,* palms facing each other, pull the right hand back toward the right shoulder while pinching the thumb and index finger together. Repeat from the middle finger of the left *V hand.*

choose[4] *v.* See sign for APPOINT[1].

chop[1] *v.* To cut (food) into small pieces by hitting with something sharp: *to chop onions.*

- [Mime chopping food] Sharply hit the little-finger side of the right *open hand,* palm facing left, on the upturned left *open hand* with a repeated movement.

chop[2] *v.* To cut (a tree) down with an ax or hatchet: *chop down a tree.*

- [Represents cutting a tree down at its base] Hit the little-finger side of the right *open hand,* palm facing up, with a double movement near the elbow of the bent left arm held up in front of the left side of the body, palm facing in.

chop[3] *v.* See sign for HARVEST[1].

Christ *n.* Jesus, the source of the Christian religion: *to believe in Christ.*

- [Initialized sign similar to sign for **king**] Move the right *C hand,* palm facing left, from the left shoulder diagonally down to the right side of the waist.

christen *v.* See sign for BAPTISM[2].

Christian[1] *n.* **1.** A person who believes in and adheres to the teachings of Christ: *a Christian who goes to church regularly.* —*adj.* **2.** Believing in the religion based on the teachings of Christ: *the Christian members of the interfaith council.*

- [**Christ + person marker**] Move the right *C hand,* palm facing left, from the left shoulder diagonally down to the right side of the waist. Then move both *open hands,* palms facing each other, downward along each side of the body.

Christian[2] *n.* (alternate sign)

■ **[Jesus + person marker]** Touch the bent middle finger of the left *5 hand* into the palm of the right *5 hand*, palms facing each other. Repeat with the other hand. Then move both *open hands*, palms facing each other, downward along each side of the body.

Christmas *n.* The annual Christian holiday celebrated on December 25, commemorating the birth of Jesus: *plans to go home for Christmas.*

■ [Initialized sign showing the shape of a wreath] Move the right *C hand*, palm facing forward, in a large arc from in front of the left shoulder to in front of the right shoulder.

chronic *adj.* Of or pertaining to long-term, continuing illnesses that are usually not curable, though their symptoms can be controlled.

■ **[disease** with a continuing movement] With elliptical repeated movements, bring the bent middle finger of the right *5 hand* in a circular movement toward the forehead while bringing the bent middle finger of the left *5 hand* in a circular movement toward the abdomen.

chubby *adj.* See signs for FAT[1,2].

chunk *n.* A thick piece: *a chunk of wood.*

■ **[large** + showing a lump of something] Move both *modified C hands* from in front of the chest, palms facing each other and index fingers pointing forward, apart to in front of each shoulder. Then bring the fingertips of the right *curved 5 hand* downward to land on the upturned left *open hand* in front of the chest.

church *n.* **1.** A building for public Christian worship: *raised funds to build a new church.* **2.** A religious service held in a church: *go to church every Sunday.* Same sign used for: **chapel.**

■ [Initialized sign similar to sign for **rock**] Tap the thumb of the right *C hand*, palm facing forward, on the back of the left *S hand*, palm facing down.

cigar *n.* A cylindrical roll of tobacco leaves for smoking: *likes to smoke a cigar after dinner.*

- [Location of a cigar in the mouth] Bring the back of the right *R hand,* palm facing down and fingers pointing forward, back against the chin with a double movement.

cigarette *n.* A small roll of finely cut tobacco for smoking, usually wrapped in thin paper: *You're allowed to smoke a cigarette at the tables along the wall.*

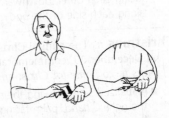

- [Tapping a cigarette to settle the tobacco] Tap the extended index finger and little finger of the right hand with a double movement on the extended left index finger, both palms facing down.

cinema *n.* See sign for FILM[1].

circle[1] *n.* A round line: *draw a circle.* Same sign used for: **cycle, round.**

- [Shape of circle] Draw a circle in the air in front of the right side of the chest with the extended right index finger, palm facing down and finger pointing forward.

circle[2] *n.* A circular or ringlike pattern: *Let's sit in a circle for the group discussion.*

- [Represents a number of people sitting in a circular pattern] Beginning with both *4 hands* in front of the chest, palms facing forward, bring the hands away from each other in outward arcs while turning the palms in, ending with the little fingers together.

circle[3] *n.* (alternate sign)

- [Represents bent legs of people sitting in a circle] Beginning with the knuckles of both *bent V hands* touching in front of the body, palms facing each other, bring the hand away from each other in outward arcs while turning the palms in, ending with the little fingers together.

circuit *n.* An electric or electronic link between points: *attaching a wire to complete the circuit.*

- [cord[1] formed in the shape of a circuit board] Beginning with the little fingers of both *I hands* touching in front of the chest, palms facing each other, bring the hands apart to in front of each side of the chest, straight down, and then together again to touch in front of the chest.

circuit board[1] *n.* A thin rectangular board containing or imprinted with various electronic components and microchips: *insert a circuit board in the computer.*

- ■ [Inserting a circuit board in a slot] Beginning with the left *flattened C hand* in front of the left side of the body, palm and fingers facing up, insert the right *B hand*, palm facing left and fingers pointing forward, between the left thumb and fingers.

circuit board[2] *n.* See sign for BOARD[3].

circulate[1] *v.* To go around or pass around: *blood circulating through the body; to circulate the paper.* Related form: **circulation** *n.* Same sign used for: **blend, merge, mix, random.**

- ■ [Movement of circulating similar to sign for **mix**] Beginning with the right *5 hand* hanging down in front of the chest, palm facing in and fingers pointing down, and the left *5 hand* below the right hand, palm facing up and fingers pointing up, move the hands in circles going in opposite directions.

circulate[2] *v.* (alternate sign) Related form: **circulation** *n.*

- ■ [Indicates something moving to replace another thing in order to circulate it] Beginning with both *curved hands* near the right side of the chest, right hand slightly above left, palms facing up and fingers pointing toward each other, move the hands in circular movements to exchange positions, ending with the left hand slightly higher than the right.

circumcise[1] *v.* To cut off the foreskin of: *The baby was circumcised.* Related form: **circumcision** *n.*

- ■ [**operate**[1] around a thumb representing a penis] Move the thumb of the right *10 hand* in a circle around the thumb of the left *10 hand,* both palms facing down.

circumcise[2] *v.* (alternate sign) Related form: **circumcision** *n.*

- ■ [**operate**[1] around an index finger representing a penis] Move the thumb of the right *A hand* in a circle around the extended left index finger, both palms facing down.

circumcise[3] *v.* (alternate sign) Related form:
circumcision *n.*

■ [**cut**[2] near the tip of an index finger representing a penis] Bring the index finger and middle finger of the right *V hand*, palm facing in, together at the tip of the extended left index finger, palm facing down and finger pointing right.

---

circumstance *n.* See sign for CONDITION.

---

circus[1] *n.* A traveling show of clowns, acrobats, and performing animals: *taking the children to the circus.*

■ [Shape of a circus tent] Beginning with the fingertips of both *V hands* touching in front of the chest, palms facing each other, bring the hands apart in a double arc outward and downward.

---

circus[2] *n.* See sign for CLOWN.

---

citation *n.* See sign for TICKET.

---

cite *v.* See sign for GET A TICKET.

---

city[1] *n.* A large or important town: *I'm going to meet friends in the city for lunch and some shopping.* Same sign used for: **community.**

■ [Multiple housetops] Tap the fingertips of both *open hands,* palms angled toward each other, first in front of the right shoulder and then in front of the left shoulder.

---

city[2] *n.* (alternate sign) Same sign used for: **community.**

■ [Multiple housetops] With the palms of both *bent hands* facing in opposite directions and the fingertips touching, separate the fingertips, twist the wrists, and touch the fingertips again.

---

civilization *n.* The ways of living of a society or nation: *studying the Aztec civilization.*

■ [Initialized sign similar to sign for **generation**] Beginning with both *C hands* in front of the chest, right palm facing left and left palm facing right, and the right hand held higher than the left, roll the hands over each other in a forward arc, ending with the little-finger side of the right *C hand* on the index-finger side of the left *C hand.*

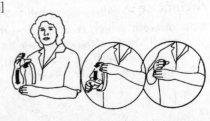

claim[1] *v.* To assert ownership of: *I claim that book.*

- [**my** + pointing to possession] Pat the palm of the right *open hand* on the chest with a double movement while pointing the extended index finger of the left hand downward.

claim[2] *v.* See sign for CAPTURE[1].

clam *n.* A mollusk with two hinged shells: *search along the beach for clams.*

- [Mime inserting a knife into a clam and opening its shell] With the fingers of the right *flattened O hand* in the opening formed by the left *flattened C hand*, both palms facing down, twist the right palm inward. Then, with both *curved hands* together, palms facing each other and right hand on top of left, open the fingers while keeping the heels together.

clamp *n.* **1.** A device used to hold two things together: *After applying the glue, hold the boards together with a clamp.* —*v.* **2.** To fasten with or place in a clamp: *Clamp the boards together.*

- [Action of clamping something and screwing the clamp tight] Close the fingers of the right *open hand* firmly around the index-finger side of the left *B hand,* both palms facing down. Then twist the right *S hand* backward with a double movement under the left *B hand.*

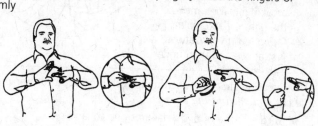

clap *v.* See sign for APPLAUD.

clarify *v.* See sign for BRIGHT.

class *n.* **1.** A group of people considered as belonging together by reason of common characteristics: *catering to the interests of writers as a class.* **2.** A group of students taught together: *Join our art class.* Same sign used for: **bracket, bunch, category, group, mass, section, series.**

- [Initialized sign showing an identifiable group] Beginning with both *C hands* in front of the chest, palms facing each other, bring the hands away from each other in outward arcs while turning the palms in, ending with the little fingers near each other.

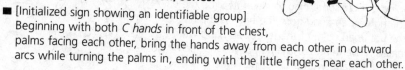

classical *adj.* See signs for FANCY[1,2].

classification *n.* See sign for MODULAR.

classified *adj.* See sign for SECRET.

classify *v.* See sign for MODULAR. Related form: **classification** *n.*

classy *adj.* See signs for FANCY[1,2].

claw[1] *n.* The usually split part of a hammer used for pulling nails: *Pull out the nails with the hammer's claw.*

- ■ [**hammer** + removing a nail] Bring the fingers of the right *S hand*, palm facing left, down with a double movement against the thumb side of the left *S hand*, palm facing right. Then, beginning with the right *curved 3 hand* over the palm of the left *open hand*, both palms facing up, pull the right hand upward toward the chest.

claw[2] *n.* The pincers of a lobster or crab: *eat a lobster claw.*

- ■ [**crab** + shape around a claw] Close the fingers of the left *C hand*, palm facing forward, with a double movement. Then move the right *C hand*, palm facing left, in an outward arc, first above and then under the left *C hand*.

claw[3] *n.* The sharp, hooked nail on the foot of a bird or other animal: *The cat scratched at the door with its claws.*

- ■ [**bird** + shape of bird's claw moving to land on a branch] Close the index finger and thumb of the right *G hand*, palm facing forward, with a repeated movement in front of the mouth. Then move both *3 hands* downward and forward to in front of each side of the body, constricting the fingers as the hands move.

clean or **clean up** *v.* or *v. phrase.* **1.** To remove dirt: *to clean the windows with a special cleaner.* **2.** Put in order: *You'd better clean up your room before your friend comes over.* Same sign used for: **neat, nice, pure, tidy.**

- ■ [Wiping dirt off something to clean it] Slide the palm of the right *open hand* from the heel to the fingers of the upturned palm of the left *open hand* with a repeated movement. For the adjective, the same sign is used, but made with a single movement.

cleaners *n.* A place for dry-cleaning clothing: *Take the soiled coat to the cleaners.* Same sign used for: **dry cleaners.**

■ [Action of a presser] Bring the palm of the right *open hand,* palm facing down and fingers pointing left, with a double movement down on the palm of the left *open hand,* palm facing up and fingers pointing right.

clear *adj.* See sign for BRIGHT.

clearly *adv.* See sign for OBVIOUS.

cleaver *n.* A tool with a heavy blade and short handle used for cutting up meat: *Cut the chicken into small pieces with a cleaver.*

■ [Mime chopping action of using a cleaver] Move the little-finger side of the right *B hand,* palm facing left, downward with a double movement, hitting the palm of the left *open hand* held in front of the body.

clerk *n.* See sign for CASHIER.

clever *adj.* See signs for NEAT[2], SMART[1,2,3].

click *v.* To quickly press and release the button on a computer mouse to place the cursor at a particular position in a document or to make a selection: *click on the mouse.*

■ [Action of pressing button on mouse] Beginning with the right index finger pointing forward in front of the chest, bend the finger deliberately downward.

client[1] *n.* A person seen in a clinical setting by a therapist: *a counseling session with the client.*

■ [Initialized sign similar to sign for **hospital**[1]] Move the index-finger side of the right *C hand,* palm facing left, first from back to front on the upper left arm and then downward a short distance, forming a cross.

client[2] *n.* (alternate sign) Same sign used for: **customer.**

■ [Initialized sign similar to sign for **person**] Move both *C hands,* palms facing each other, downward on each side of the chest.

climate[1] *n.* The prevailing weather conditions of a region: *They want to retire to a state with a warm climate.*

■ [**different**[2] + **weather**[1]] Beginning with both extended index fingers crossed in front of the chest, palms facing forward, bring the hands apart from each other with a double movement, first toward the right side of the chest and then toward the left. Then, with the little fingers and thumbs of both *W hands* touching each other in front of the chest, twist the hands with a double movement in opposite directions.

climate[2] *n.* See signs for WEATHER[1,2].

climax *n.* An orgasm: *to have a climax.* Same sign used for: **orgasm.**

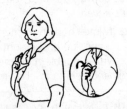

■ With the thumb of the right *curved 3 hand* on the chest, palm angled in, curl the extended index finger and middle finger downward toward the palm.

climb[1] *v.* To go up with the help of the hands: *to climb the ladder.* Same sign used for: **ascend, ladder.**

■ [Mime climbing a ladder] Beginning with both *curved 5 hands* in front of the chest, palms facing forward and right hand higher than the left, move the hands upward one at a time with an alternating movement.

climb[2] *v.* (alternate sign) Same sign used for: **ascend, ladder.**

■ [Mime climbing a ladder] Beginning with both *S hands* in front of the chest, palms facing forward and left hand higher than the right, move the hands upward one at a time with an alternating movement.

climb[3] *v.* (alternate sign) Same sign used for: **ascend, ladder.**

■ [Fingers represent legs climbing a ladder] Move the fingers of the right *V hand* with an alternating movement up the length of the extended left middle finger, pointing down in front of the chest.

climb[4] *v.* To go upward (used especially of animals): *Watch the monkey climb the tree.* Same sign used for: **ascend.**

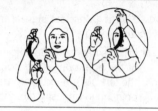

- Beginning with both *bent V hands* in front of the chest, left hand higher than the right and palms facing each other, raise the right hand above the left hand and then the left hand above the right hand with an alternating movement as the hands move in front of the face.

climb down[1] *v. phrase.* Same signs as for CLIMB[1,2] but formed with opposite movement.

climb down[2] *v. phrase.* See sign for DESCEND[3].

cling to *v. phrase.* See sign for DEPEND.

clip *n.* See signs for PAPER CLIP[1,2].

clippers[1] *pl. n.* A tool used for cutting fingernails: *cutting my nails with clippers.*

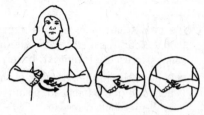

- [Mime using clippers] Move the thumb of the right *A hand*, palm facing in, up and down with a repeated movement as the right hand moves along the fingertips of the left *5 hand* held in front of the chest, palm facing down and fingers pointing right.

clippers[2] *pl. n.* See sign for SCISSORS.

clock[1] *n.* An instrument for measuring and showing time: *The clock says that it's ten past three.*

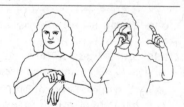

- [**time**[2] + round shape of a clock's face] Tap the curved right index finger on the back of the left wrist. Then hold both *modified C hands* in front of each side of the face, palms facing each other.

clock[2] *n.* (alternate sign)

- [**time**[2] + round shape of a clock's face] Tap the curved right index finger on the back of the left wrist. Then hold both *C hands* in front of each side of the face, palms facing each other.

close[1] *adv.* Separated by very little; near: *Sit close together.* Same sign used for: **approach, near.**

- [Moves one hand close to the other] Beginning with the right *open hand* somewhat forward of the chest and the left *open hand* near the chest, palms facing in and fingers pointing in opposite directions, move the right palm to the back of the left hand, pushing the left hand toward the chest.

close

close[2] *adv.* (alternate sign) Same sign used for: **approach, near.**

■ [Moves one hand close to the other] Bring the back of the right *open hand* from the chest forward toward the left *open hand,* both palms facing in and fingers pointing in opposite directions.

close[3] *v.* **1.** To obstruct an entrance or opening in: *close the box.* **2.** To put in a position to cover an opening: *close the door.* **3.** To make inaccessible: *closed his mind to new ideas.* Same sign used for: **shut.**

■ [Action of a door closing] Bring the index fingers of both *B hands* sharply together in front of the chest, palms facing forward.

close call A narrow escape, as from something dangerous: *Whew! That was a close call.* Alternate form: **close shave.** Same sign used for: **almost, barely.**

■ Beginning with the fingertips of the right *F hand* against the right side of the forehead, palm facing in, bring the hand forward a short distance.

closed captions *pl. n.* See sign for CAPTION.

close friend See sign for FRIEND[2].

close one's eyes To shut one's eyelids: *Close your eyes and go to sleep.* Same sign used for: **shut one's eyes.**

■ [Action of eyes closing] Pinch the index fingers and thumbs of both *G hands* together near the outside corners of the eyes while closing both eyes.

closet[1] *n.* A small room for storing clothes: *Hang your coat up on the long bar in the closet.*

■ [clothes + door] Brush the thumbs of both *5 hands* downward on each side of the chest with a double movement. Then, beginning with the index-finger side of both *B hands* touching in front of the chest, palms facing forward and fingers pointing up, swing the right hand back toward the right shoulder with a double movement by twisting the wrist.

closet[2] *n.* (alternate sign) Same sign used for: **locker.**

- [Represents hangers] Beginning with the fingers of both *H hands* crossed in front of the chest, twist the wrists to alternate positions.

close the door[1] To bring a door or parts of a door into position to obstruct an entrance: *Close the door and lock it.* Same sign used for: **shut the door, slam the door.**

- [Action of a door closing] Beginning with both *B hands* in front of each shoulder, palms facing back, twist the wrists and bring them sharply toward each other until the index fingers touch, ending with palms facing forward.

close the door[2] (alternate sign) Same sign used for: **shut the door, slam the door.**

- [Action of a door closing] Bring the right *B hand* from in front of the right side of the chest, palm facing left, in an arc back toward the chest to touch the index-finger side of the right *B hand* against the index-finger side of the left *B hand,* ending with both palms facing forward and fingers pointing up.

close the window To move the open part of a window down or up to cover an opening: *to close the window when it gets cold.* Same sign used for: **shut the window, slam the window.**

- [Action of a window closing] Bring the little-finger side of the right *open hand* down sharply to hit the index-finger side of the left *open hand,* both palms facing in and fingers pointing in opposite directions.

close to *adj.* See sign for APPROACH[1].

close up *adv.* At a near distance: *I saw it happen close up.*

- [Location of something close up to the face] Move the right *open hand,* palm facing in and fingers pointing up, back toward the face.

cloth *adj., n.* See signs for FABRIC, MATERIAL.

clothes *pl. n.* Wearing apparel: *It's time to put on my clothes and go to work.* Same sign used for: **apparel, costume, dress, fashion, garment, suit.**

- [Location of clothes on body] Brush the thumbs of both *5 hands* downward on each side of the chest with a double movement.

clothes dryer *n.* A machine using heated air for removing moisture from newly washed laundry: *The towels didn't get dry in the clothes dryer.* Same sign used for: **dryer.**

■ [**clothes** + **dry** + a gesture showing a dryer's tumbling action] Brush the thumbs of both *5 hands* downward on each side of the chest with a double movement. Then drag the index-finger side of the right *X hand*, palm facing down, from left to right across the chin. Then move the extended right index finger in a circle near the thumb side of the left *curved hand* held in front of the body, palm facing down.

clothes hanger *n.* See sign for HANGER.

clothespin[1] *n.* A clip used to hold clean laundry on a clothesline for drying: *Hang the shirts from the bottom with two clothespins.*

■ [**clothes** + clipping a clothespin on a clothesline] Brush the thumbs of both *5 hands* downward on each side of the chest with a double movement. Then pinch the right index and middle fingers and thumb together, palm and fingers pointing down, on both sides of the extended left index finger, palm facing in and finger pointing right.

clothespin[2] *n.* (alternate sign)

■ [Clipping a clothespin on a clothesline] Pinch the right index and middle fingers and thumb together, palm and fingers pointing down, on both sides of the extended left index finger, palm facing in and finger pointing right.

cloud *n.* A visible mass of water particles suspended in the air above the earth's surface: *dark clouds covering the sun.*

■ [Shape and location of clouds] Beginning with both *C hands* near the left side of the head, palms facing each other, bring the hands away from each other in outward arcs while turning the palms in, ending with the little fingers close together. Repeat the movement near the right side of the head.

clover *n.* A small plant with usually three small leaflets: *hunting for a four-leaf clover.*

- ■ **[green** + shape of a clover] Beginning with the right *G hand* in front of the right shoulder, palm facing left, twist the right hand forward and back with a double movement. Then, beginning with both extended index fingers pointing forward in front of the face, bring the hands downward while forming the shape of a clover.

clown *n.* A costumed comedy performer, as in a circus: *act like a clown.* Same sign used for: **circus.**

- ■ [Shape of clown's big nose] Put the fingertips of the right *curved 5 hand* on the nose.

clue *n.* Something that aids in solving a problem or mystery: *looking for clues to the identity of the murderer.*

- ■ [Initialized sign] Beginning with the right *C hand* in front of the right shoulder, palm facing left, twist the hand forward with a double movement.

clumsy[1] *adj.* Awkward in movement; lacking grace: *The clumsy girl bumped into the furniture.* Same sign used for: **inexperienced.**

- ■ While holding the thumb of the right *5 hand* tightly in the left *S hand,* twist the right hand forward and down.

clumsy[2] *adj.* See signs for AWKWARD, UNSKILLED.

clutch[1] *n.* A lever or mechanism used to connect or disconnect the engine of a car: *step on the clutch.*

- ■ **[drive**[1] + mime pushing up and down on the clutch] Beginning with both *S hands* in front of the chest, palms facing in and the right hand higher than the left hand, move the hands in an up-and-down arc with a repeated alternating movement.
Then, beginning with both *B hands* in front of the chest, the right hand forward of the left hand, both palms facing forward and fingers pointing up, push the hands forward and back with an alternating double movement.

clutch² *v.* **1.** To grasp tightly: *clutch the teddy bear.*
—*n.* **2.** A tight grasp: *held the ticket in his clutch before boarding the plane.*

■ [Mime grabbing at something] Beginning with both *3 hands* in front of each side of the chest, palms facing down and fingers pointing forward, bring the hands forward and down while constricting the fingers.

coach *n.* A person who trains athletic teams: *a football coach.*

■ [Initialized sign similar to sign for **captain**] Tap the thumb of the right *C hand*, palm facing left, against the right shoulder with a double movement.

coarse *adj.* See sign for ROUGH.

coat *n.* An outer garment with sleeves: *wearing a warm coat.* Same sign used for: **bathrobe, jacket, overcoat.**

■ [A coat's lapels] Bring the thumbs of both *A hands* from near each shoulder, palms facing in, downward and toward each other, ending near the waist.

coax *v.* See sign for ENCOURAGE.

cobbler *n.* See sign for SHOEMAKER.

cocaine or **coke** *n.* A bitter, addictive narcotic used as an illicit drug and also as a local anesthetic to deaden pain: *The addict used cocaine.* Same sign used for: **crack.**

■ [Shows method of ingesting cocaine] Place the extended thumb of the right *10 hand*, palm facing left, first on the right nostril and then on the left nostril.

cochlear implant *n.* A surgically implanted hearing device that converts sound reaching the cochlea into electrical impulses that are transmitted by wire to the auditory nerve.

■ [Shows location of cochlear implant device] Touch the fingertips of the right *bent V hand*, palm facing left, to behind the right ear.

cock *n.* See sign for ROOSTER.

cocktail *n.* A mixed alcoholic drink: *Would you like a cocktail while we're waiting for dinner?* Same sign used for: **alcoholic drink, champagne, drink, liquor.**

■ [Mime drinking from a small glass] Beginning with the thumb of the right *modified C hand* near the mouth, palm facing left, tip the index finger back toward the face with a double movement.

coconut *n.* The large, round, hard-shelled seed of the coconut palm tree, having white edible meat and containing a milky liquid: *pick coconuts.*

■ [Shake a coconut] With the palms of both *curved 5 hands* facing each other and held near the right side of the head, shake the hands with a repeated movement.

cocoon *n.* The silky case spun by a caterpillar or similar larva that serves as a protective covering while it develops into its adult form: *Out of that cocoon will come a beautiful butterfly.*

■ [Represents the thread used to make a cocoon + the shape of a cocoon] Move the right *I hand* from the lips upward and forward in a circular movement. Then, beginning with the index fingers of both *curved hands* touching in front of the chest, palms angled outward, bring the hands forward in an arc until the little fingers touch, palms facing in.

coffee *n.* **1.** A dark brown drink made from the ground seeds (coffee beans) of a tropical tree: *I drink three cups of hot coffee every morning.* **2.** The whole or ground seeds themselves: *buy a can of coffee.*

■ [Grind coffee beans] Move the little-finger side of the right *S hand* with a circular movement on the index-finger side of the left *S hand*, palms facing in opposite directions.

coffin *n.* See sign for CASKET.

cogitate *v.* See sign for MULL.

coin[1] *n.* A flat piece of metal with a designated value, issued by a government for use as money: *a pocketful of coins.*

■ [Shape of coin held in the hand] Move the extended right index finger, palm facing in and finger pointing down, in a double circular movement on the left *open hand*, palm facing up.

coin[2] *n.* (alternate sign)

■ [Shape of a coin] Place the curved fingers of the right *F hand,* palm facing left, in several places on the palm of the left *open hand* held in front of the body, palm facing up.

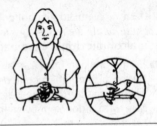

coincidence *n.* See sign for HAPPEN.

Coke *n. Trademark.* A carbonated soft drink containing an extract made from kola nuts, together with sweetener and other flavorings: *to order a Coke and a hamburger.* Alternate form: **Coca-Cola** (trademark).

■ [Mime injecting a drug] With the index finger of the right *L hand,* palm facing in, touching the upper left arm, move the right thumb up and down with a double movement.

cold[1] *n.* A common respiratory illness characterized by a runny nose and often a cough and sore throat: *to catch a cold when the weather changes.*

■ [Mime blowing one's nose] Grasp the nose with the thumb and index finger of the right *A hand,* palm facing in, and pull the hand forward off the nose with a double movement.

cold[2] *adj.* Lacking warmth: *cold hands.* Same sign used for: **chilly, frigid, shiver, winter.**

■ [Natural gesture when shivering from cold] Shake both *S hands* with a slight movement in front of each side of the chest, palms facing each other.

collapse *v.* See sign for BREAK DOWN.

collar *n.* The band around the neck of a garment, often folded down, rolled over, or standing up: *a pointed collar.*

■ [Shape and location of a collar] Move the fingertips of the right *G hand,* palm facing in, from the right side of the neck around to the front.

collate *v.* To arrange (pages) in proper order: *collate the copies of the annual report.*

■ [Shows filing things in order] Beginning with the palms of both *open hands* together in front of the chest, fingers pointing forward, move the right hand in a series of double arcs to the right.

collect[1] *v.* To receive payment of: *to collect dues from the membership*. Related form: **collection** *n.* Same sign used for: **accumulate, amass, deserve, gather, reap.**

■ [Pulling money to oneself] With a double movement, bring the little-finger side of the right *curved hand,* palm facing left, across the palm of the left *open hand,* palm facing up, from its fingertips to the heel while changing into an *S hand* each time.

collect[2] *v.* (alternate sign) Related form: **collection** *n.* Same sign used for: **accumulate, gather, reap.**

■ [Gathering money together] Beginning with the little-finger side of the right *curved hand,* palm facing left, on the fingers of the left *open hand,* palm facing up, twist the right wrist to slide the hand in an arc back toward the heel while turning the palm in.

college[1] *n.* A school beyond high school that provides a general education and grants degrees: *go away to college.*

■ [Similar to sign for **school** but moves upward to a higher level] Beginning with the palm of the right *open hand* across the palm of the left *open hand* in front of the chest, move the right hand upward in an arc, ending in front of the upper chest, palm angled forward.

college[2] *n.* (alternate sign)

■ [Initialized sign similar to sign for **school**] Beginning with the thumb side of the right *C hand* on the palm of the left *open hand,* move the right hand forward and upward in an arc, ending in front of the upper chest, palm angled forward.

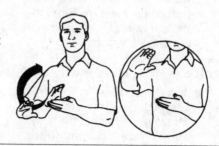

collide *v.* See sign for ACCIDENT[1]. Related form: **collision** *n.*

color[1] *n.* Any of the hues of the rainbow and their variations, as produced by the quality of the light reflected from an object: *My favorite color is purple.*

■ Wiggle the fingers of the right *5 hand* in front of the mouth, fingers pointing up and palm facing in.

color² *v.* **1.** To put color on: *to color the picture with crayons.* —*n.* **2.** Something used for coloring: *thick colors on an artist's canvas.* Same sign used for **crayon.**

- [Action of coloring with a crayon] Rub the extended right little finger, palm facing down, back and forth on the upturned left *open hand* with a repeated movement.

color³ *v., n.* (alternate sign) Same sign used for: **crayon.**

- [Action of coloring with a crayon] Rub the extended right index finger, palm facing in, back and forth on the upturned left *open hand* with a repeated wiggly movement.

color⁴ *v., n.* (alternate sign) Same sign used for: **crayon.**

- [Action of coloring with a crayon] Rub the fingertips of the right *modified X hand*, palm facing down, back and forth with a repeated movement on the upturned palm of the left *open hand*.

color⁵ *n.* See sign for RACE³.

colorful *adj.* Picturesque: *a colorful landscape.*

- Beginning with both *5 hands* in front of the face, right hand closer to the face than the left hand, palms facing in and fingers pointing up, move the hands to and from the face with an alternating movement while wiggling the fingers.

colt *n.* A young horse: *feed the colt.* See also sign for PONY.

- [baby¹ + horse] With the bent right arm cradled on the bent left arm, both palms facing up, swing the arms from left to right in front of the body with a double movement. Then, with the extended thumb of the right *U hand* on the right side of the head, palm facing forward, bend the fingers up and down with a repeated movement.

column¹ *n.* **1.** A slender, upright structure: *Greek temples supported by columns.* **2.** One of the sections of an arrangement into vertical divisions on a page: *a page divided into two columns.* **3.** A vertical arrangement of items: *a column of numbers.*

- [Shape of a column] Move the right *C hand* from in front of the right side of the chest, palm facing forward, downward a short distance.

column[2] *n.* The vertical members of one line in an array: *The addresses are listed in the second column.* Same sign used for: **field.**

■ [Shape of a column in an array] Move the right *G hand*, palm forward, from in front of the right shoulder downward.

column[3] *n.* See sign for PILLAR.

coma *n.* See sign for FAINT.

comb[1] *n.* A small device with a row of teeth used to arrange hair: *lost my comb.*

■ [Mime combing hair] Drag the fingertips of the right *curved 5 hand* through the hair on the right side of the head with a short double movement. The verb is the same sign as the noun but made with a longer double movement.

comb[2] *v.* Same sign as for COMB[1], but made with a double movement.

combat *n.* **1.** A fight or struggle, as between ideas or people: *to participate in a combat over leadership of the organization.* **2.** Battle, as in war: *soldiers engaged in combat.* Same sign used for: **fight.**

■ [Represents two people hitting each other] Beginning with both *S hands* in front of each shoulder, palms facing each other, move the hands toward each other with a double movement by bending the wrists.

combination *n.* A sequence of numbers used to set the locking mechanism of a combination lock: *figure out the combination to the padlock on my locker.*

■ [1-2-3 + mime twisting a combination on a lock] With the heel of the right hand on the left *open hand*, palm facing right, form a 1-2-3 with the right hand. Then move the right *curved 5 hand*, palm facing left, with a double movement by twisting the wrist forward near the palm of the left *open hand*, palm facing right.

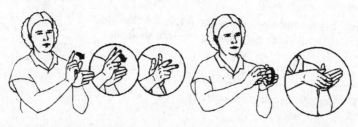

combine[1] *v.* To join or mix two or more things together to form a whole: *First we'll combine the dry ingredients in the mixing bowl.* Same sign used for: **blend.**

■ [**match**[1] + **mix**[1]] Beginning with both *curved 5 hands* in front of each side of the chest, palms facing in, bring the hands together, ending with the fingers meshed together. Then, with the right *curved 5 hand* over the left *curved 5 hand*, palms facing each other, move the hands in repeated circles going in opposite directions.

combine[2] *v.* See signs for BELONG[1], MATCH[1], MESH.

come[1] *v.* To move toward or reach the speaker or a particular place: *come home.*

■ [Indicates direction for another to come toward oneself] Beginning with both extended index fingers pointing up in front of the body, palms facing in, bring the fingers back to each side of the chest.

come[2] *v.* (alternate sign)

■ [Movement of something coming toward oneself] Beginning with both index fingers pointing toward each other in front of the chest, left hand closer to the body than the right hand and palms facing in, roll the hands over each other with a circular movement to exchange places until reaching the chest.

come back *v. phrase.* See sign for REFUND[1].

come here *v. phrase.* See sign for BECKON.

come on or **come in** *v. phrase.* To approach: *Come on—the door's open.*

■ [Natural gesture beckoning someone] Move the right *open hand*, palm angled up, back toward the right shoulder.

come up *v. phrase.* See sign for SHOW UP.

comfortable *adj.* Having or providing physical ease: *not comfortable standing outside in the cold; a comfortable chair.* Same sign used for: **convenient, cozy.**

■ [Stroking as a gesture of comfort] Wipe the palm of the right *curved hand* down the back of the left *curved hand,* and then repeat with the palm of the left *curved hand* on the back of the right *curved hand,* both palms facing down.

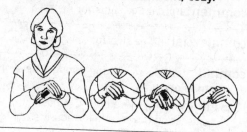

comical *adj.* See sign for HUMOROUS.

Coming *n.* See sign for ADVENT.

comma[1] *n.* A punctuation mark (,) used to separate numbers, words, or parts of a sentence: *Put a comma between those two adjectives in the sentence.*

■ [Mime drawing a comma] Make a small curved movement in the air in front of the right shoulder with the right *modified X hand,* by twisting the right wrist.

comma[2] *n.* See sign for APOSTROPHE.

command *n., v.* See signs for ORDER[1,2].

Commandment *n.* One of the biblical Ten Commandments: *broke a Commandment by stealing.* Same sign used for: **Constitution.**

■ [Initialized sign similar to sign for **law**] Move the right *C hand,* palm facing forward, from touching first the fingers and then the heel of the left *open hand,* fingers pointing up and palm facing right.

commence *v.* See sign for START[2].

commend *v.* See sign for APPLAUD.

comment[1] *n.* **1.** A remark, observation, or expression of opinion: *Write your comments in the margin of the paper.* —*v.* **2.** To make a comment: *Feel free to comment at any time.*

■ [**say**[2] + **write**[1,2]] Move the extended right index finger from in front of the mouth, palm facing in and finger pointing left, forward in a small arc. Then, slide the right *modified X hand,* palm facing left, from the base to the fingertips of the left *open hand,* palm facing right and fingers pointing forward.

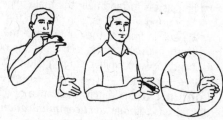

comment[2] *v.* See signs for SAY[1,2].

comments *pl. n.* See signs for SAY[1,2].

commercial *n.* See sign for ADVERTISE.

commit[1] *v.* To do something wrong: *The shoplifter committed a felony.* Related form: **commission** *n.*

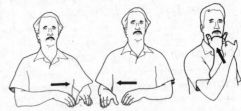

- [**do** + **wrong**] Move both *C hands*, palms facing down, simultaneously back and forth in front of the body with a swinging movement. Then bring the middle fingers of the right *Y hand*, palm in, back against the chin with a deliberate movement.

commit[2] *v.* See signs for DO, PROMISE[1], VOW[1]. Related form: **commitment** *n.*

committee *n.* A group of people selected to perform a special function: *appoint a committee of teachers to study the problem of cheating.*

- [Initialized sign similar to sign for **member**[2]] Touch the fingertips of the right *curved 5 hand* first to the left side of the chest and then to the right side of the chest, palm facing in.

common *n., adj.* See signs for STANDARD[1,2].

common-law *adj.* Of or designating a marriage that becomes recognized as legal without the benefit of an official wedding ceremony, based on the amount of time the couple has lived together: *a common-law wife.*

- [Initials **m-w** representing "man" and "woman"] Form an *M* in front of the right shoulder with the right hand, palm facing forward, changing to a *W* as the hand moves slightly to the right.

common sense *n.* Practical intelligence and sound judgment: *He never went to college, but he shows common sense in handling problems.*

- [Initials **c-s** formed near the brain for "common sense"] Beginning with the right *C hand* in front of the right side of the forehead, palm facing left, move the right hand forward while changing into an *S hand.*

communication *n.* The exchange of information, thoughts, or opinions: *important for friends to have good communication.* Related form: **communicate** *v.* Same sign used for: **conversation, converse.**

■ [Initialized sign indicating words moving both to and from a person] Move both *C hands*, palms facing each other, forward and back from the chin with an alternating movement.

communion *n.* A Christian sacrament commemorating the death of Jesus Christ: *to celebrate communion*.

■ [The sign of the cross in front of the lips] Move the fingertips of the right *F hand*, palm facing left, first down the lips and then across the lips from left to right.

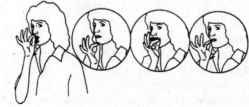

communism *n.* A system of social organization in which property is owned by the state and shared by the populace: *believe in communism*. Related form: **communist** *n.*

■ [Hands form the hammer and sickle insignia used to represent communism] Beginning with the left *C hand* in front of the left side of the chest, palm facing forward, move the extended right index finger, palm facing left, against the right thumb with a double movement to form a cross.

community *n.* See signs for CITY[1,2], TOWN.

commute *v.* To travel back and forth regularly: *commute to work.* Same sign used for: **back and forth.**

■ [Demonstrates movement to and from] Move the right *10 hand*, palm facing left, from in front of the right side of the body to in front of the left side of the body with a double movement.

companion *n.* See sign for STEADY[1].

company *n.* **1.** A group of people associated for business purposes: *to form a small company.* **2.** A guest or guests: *expecting company for dinner.* Same sign used for: **guests.**

■ [Initialized sign similar to sign for **class** except with a repeated movement] Beginning with both *curved hands* in front of each side of the chest, palms facing each other, bring the hands downward in small, repeated outward arcs while turning the palms in.

compare *v.* To examine to identify likenesses or differences: *compare ideas.* Related form: **comparison** *n.*

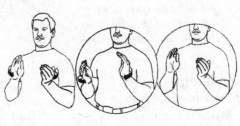

- [Holding something in one hand and comparing it with something in the other hand] With both *curved hands* in front of each side of the chest, alternately turn one hand and then the other toward the face while turning the other hand in the opposite direction, keeping the palms facing each other and the fingers pointing up.

compassion *n.* See signs for MERCY[1,2].

compatible[1] *adj.* Able to exist together or with another in harmony: *a compatible couple; a compatible friend.* Related form: **compatibility.**

- [Bringing something to combine with something else] Beginning with both *curved 5 hands* in front of each side of the chest, palms facing in, move the right hand to the left to mesh the fingers with the bent fingers of the left hand.

compatible[2] *adj.* See sign for AGREE[1].

compensate *v.* See signs for PAY[1,2,3,4]. Related form: **compensation** *n.*

competent *adj.* Possessing sufficient mental capacity to make rational decisions about legal matters.

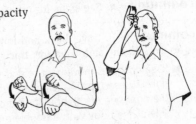

- [**can + understand**] Move both *S hands,* palms facing down, downward simultaneously in front of each side of the body. Then, beginning with the right *modified X hand* near the right side of the forehead, palm facing in, flick the index finger upward with a deliberate movement.

competition *n.* See sign for RACE[2].

compilation *n.* The translation of a computer program from the source code written by the programmer to object code that can be executed by a given computer: *perform compilation of the program.* Related form: **compile** *v.*

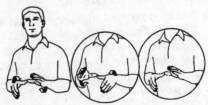

- [Initialized sign] Beginning with the thumbs of both *C hands* together in front of the body, palms facing each other, right fingers angled downward and left fingers angled upward, twist the hands in opposite directions.

complain *v.* To express dissatisfaction or pain: *The employee complained about the long hours with no overtime pay.* Same sign used for: **boycott, grievance, gripe, grumble, object, protest, riot, strike.**

- ■ Tap the fingertips of the right *curved 5 hand* against the center of the chest.

complaint *n.* See sign for PROTEST[1].

complete *v., adj.* See signs for CONCLUSION, END[2], FINISH[1,2], FULL[2].

complex[1] *adj.* Having many elements that are difficult to analyze: *a complex situation.* Same sign used for: **complicated.**

- ■ Beginning with both extended index fingers pointing toward each other in front of each side of the face, both palms facing down, continuously bend the fingers up and down as the hands move past each other in front of the face.

complex[2] *adj.* See sign for MIX[1].

complicate *v.* See sign for MIX[1].

compliment *v., n.* See sign for PRAISE.

comprehend[1] *v.* To understand: *She fully comprehends how vital the new information is.* Same sign used for: **apprehend.**

- ■ [Comprehension seems to pop into one's head] Beginning with the right *S hand* near the right side of the forehead, palm facing left, flick the right index finger upward with a sudden movement.

comprehend[2] *v.* See sign for UNDERSTAND.

compromise[1] *n.* The settlement of a disagreement by yielding on both sides: *They came to a compromise over wages and hours.*

- ■ [Initialized sign indicating two minds coming into agreement] Beginning with both *C hands* near each side of the head, palms facing each other, turn the hands downward, ending with the palms facing down.

compromise[2] *n.* See sign for AGREE[1].

computer[1] *n.* A programmable electronic machine for processing data at high speeds, including performing calculations, word processing, and database management: *using a computer to keep track of inventory and customers.*

- ■ [Initialized sign] Move the right *C hand,* palm facing left, from the right side of the forehead forward with a circular movement.

computer[2] *n.* (alternate sign)

- ■ [Initialized sign] Move the thumb side of the right *C hand,* palm facing left, from touching the lower part of the extended left arm upward to touch the upper arm.

computer[3] *n.* (alternate sign)

- ■ [Shows movement of computer tape drives] Beginning with both extended index fingers pointing forward in front of each side of the chest, palms facing down, move both fingers in simultaneous counterclockwise circles.

computer[4] *n.* (alternate sign)

- ■ [Initialized sign showing movement of computer tape drives] Beginning with both *C hands* in front of either side of the chest, palms facing forward, move both hands in simultaneous repeated circles going in opposite directions away from each other.

comrade *n.* See signs for FRIEND[1,2].

con *v., n.* See signs for BETRAY[1], TRICK.

con artist *n.* See sign for SWINDLER.

conceal *v.* See sign for HIDE.

conceited *adj.* Having excessive pride in oneself: *You can tell from his arrogant behavior how conceited he is.* Same sign used for: **arrogant, big-headed, big shot, brat, bully.**

- ■ [**big**[1] formed near the head, signifying a person with a "big head"] Beginning with both *L hands* in front of each side of the forehead, index fingers pointing toward each other and palms facing in, bring the hands outward away from each other a short distance.

conceive *v.* See sign for PREGNANT[2].

concentrate *v.* See sign for ATTENTION. Related form: **concentration** *n.*

concept *n.* A general idea: *The concept for the TV show is good, but the actors are terrible.* Same sign used for: **creative.**

- [Initialized sign similar to sign for **invent**] Move the right *C hand*, palm facing left, from the right side of the forehead forward and slightly upward in a double arc.

concern[1] *v.* **1.** To trouble, worry, or disturb: *concerned about my grades.* **2.** To be of interest to: *The environment is an issue that concerns me.* Same sign used for: **consider, think.**

- [Thoughts moving through the brain] Beginning with both extended index fingers in front of each side of the forehead, palms facing in and fingers angled up, move the fingers in repeated alternating circular movements toward each other in front of the face.

concern[2] *v.* (alternate sign) Same sign used for: **anxiety.**

- Beginning with the bent middle fingers of both *5 hands* pointing to each side of the chest, left hand closer to the chest than the right hand and palms facing in, bring the hands forward and back to the chest with a repeated alternating movement.

concerning *prep.* See signs for ABOUT[1,2].

concise *adj.* See sign for PRECISE.

conclude *v.* See sign for END[2].

conclusion *n.* The final result or end: *to bring the project to a conclusion at last.* Related form: **conclude** *v.* Same sign used for: **complete.**

- [Initialized sign similar to sign for **end**[2]] Slide the thumb of the right *C hand*, palm angled left, along the length of the left *B hand*, palm facing in, and then downward off the end of the left fingertips.

concur *v.* See sign for AGREE[1].

condemn *v.* See signs for CANCEL, CURSE[1,2,3].

condense *v.* See sign for BRIEF[1].

condition *n.* The existing state or situation of a person or thing: *a used car in good condition.* Same sign used for: **circumstance, culture.**

- [Initialized sign similar to sign for **environment**] Beginning with the right *C hand*, palm facing left, near the extended left index finger, palm facing right, move the right hand in a circle forward and around the left finger.

conduct[1] *v.* To direct the performance of a musical event.

- [Mime conducting an orchestra] Beginning with both extended index fingers angled forward in front of the chest, palms facing toward each other, swing the hands outward away from each other with a repeated movement.

conduct[2] *v.* See signs for DO, LEAD[1,2].

conductor *n.* See sign for ORCHESTRA.

conference[1] *n.* A meeting of interested persons to discuss a topic: *attend a conference on crime prevention.*

- [**gather**[2] + **meeting**] Beginning with both *5 hands* in front of each side of the chest, palms facing each other, bring the fingers together in front of the chest. Then, beginning with both *5 hands* in front of each shoulder, palms facing each other and fingers pointing up, close the fingers into *flattened O hands* while moving the hands together with a double movement.

conference[2] *n.* See sign for MEETING.

confess *v.* See signs for ADMIT[1,2]. Related form: **confession** *n.*

confession *n.* An acknowledgment and disclosure of one's mistakes in a criminal situation: *The police recorded the prisoner's confession.*

- [**admit**[2] + **jail**[1,2]] Beginning with the fingers of both *5 hands* on the chest, move the hands forward in an arc. Then move the back of the right *4 hand* against the palm side of the left *4 hand* held in front of the chest, both palms facing in.

confident *adj.* Being certain; sure of oneself, one's abilities, and one's future prospects: *I am confident that we will win the election.* Related form: **confidence** *n.* Same sign used for: **bold, trust.**

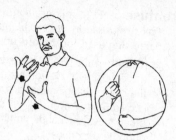

- [Holding firmly to one's beliefs] Beginning with both *curved hands* in front of the chest, right hand above the left and palms facing in, bring both hands downward a short distance with a deliberate movement while closing into *S hands.*

confidential *adj.* See sign for SECRET.

confined *adj.* See sign for STUCK.

confirm *v.* See sign for APPROVE[1]. Related form: **confirmation** *n.*

confirmation *n.* A ceremony in which a person is admitted into membership in a church: *We attended his confirmation last Sunday morning.* Related form: **confirm** *v.*

- [Gesture of confirmation + sign of the cross on the forehead] Pat the right cheek with the right *open hand.* Then move the thumbnail of the right *A hand,* palm facing left, first downward and then across from left to right to form a small cross on the forehead.

conflict[1] *n.* **1.** Active opposition: *The discussion ended in conflict.* —*v.* **2.** To clash or disagree: *Their stories conflicted as to what happened.* **3.** To differ: *Although their methods conflict, they are able to work together.* Same sign used for: **breed, contradict, cross-purposes, fertilize.**

- [Represents a crossing of opinions] Beginning with both extended index fingers in front of each side of the body, palms facing in and fingers angled toward each other, move the hands toward each other, ending with the fingers crossed.

conflict[2] *v., n.* See sign for STRUGGLE.

confront[1] *v.* To encounter someone or something in acknowledgment, defiance, or opposition: *The lawyer confronted the defendant with the evidence.* Related form: **confrontation** *n.*

- [Bringing two things to a face-to-face encounter] Beginning with both *open hands* in front of the lower chest, palms facing each other and fingers pointing up, move both hands upward toward the left in an arc with a deliberate movement.

confront[2] *v.* See sign for FACE[2]. Related form: **confrontation** *n.*

confuse[1] *v.* **1.** To mix up: *confuse the two packages.* **2.** To bewilder: *I was confused by your explanation.* Related form: **confusion** *n.* Same sign used for: **mixed up.**

- [**think**[1] + **mix**[1]] Bring the extended right index finger from touching the right side of the forehead, palm facing in, down to in front of the chest, changing into a *curved 5 hand.* Then, with the right *curved 5 hand* over the left *curved 5 hand,* palms facing each other, move the hands simultaneously in repeated circles going in opposite directions.

confuse[2] *v.* See sign for MIX[1].

congratulate *v.* To express pleasure at the good fortune of (another person): *congratulate the groom.* Related form: **congratulations** *pl. n., interj.*

- [Mime clasping hands to congratulate another] Clasp both *curved hands* together in front of the body and shake them with a repeated movement.

congregate *v.* See signs for GATHER[2,3].

congregation *n.* See signs for AUDIENCE[1,2].

Congress *n.* **1.** The national law-making body of the U.S., consisting of the Senate and the House of Representatives: *Congress passed the law.* **2. congress** An association of representatives from similar organizations: *a meeting of a congress of teachers.*

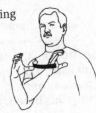

- [Initialized sign similar to sign for **committee**] Touch the thumb of the right *C hand,* palm facing left, first on the left side of the chest and then on the right.

connect *v.* See signs for BELONG[1], JOIN[1].

connection *n.* See sign for RELATIONSHIP.

conquer *v.* See signs for CAPTURE[1], DEFEAT[1].

conscious[1] *adj.* **1.** Able to think and feel; aware: *He is conscious of his errors.* **2.** Intentional; deliberate: *a conscious decision to go home.*

- [Initialized sign similar to sign for **think**[2]] Beginning with the right *C hand* in front of the right side of the forehead, palm facing left, move the hand in a circle.

conscious[2] *adj.* See sign for AWARE[1].

consequence *n.* See signs for RESULT[1,2].

Conservative *adj.* Being of a movement in Judaism that adheres to religious traditions and practices while permitting some adaptation to the modern world: *a Conservative Jew.*

■ [Initialized sign similar to sign for **clean**] Slide the thumb of the right *C hand,* palm facing left, from the heel to the fingertips of the palm of the left *open hand.*

---

consider *v.* See signs for CONCERN[1], WONDER.

---

consistent[1] *adj.* Staying constant in activity, principle, or course: *consistent in her philosophy toward life.* Related form: **consistently** *adv.* Same sign used for: **faithful, regular, regularly.**

■ [Similar to sign for **right**[2] formed with a continuous movement] With the little-finger side of the right *1 hand* across the index-finger side of the left *1 hand,* palms facing in opposite directions, move the hands downward in front of the chest.

---

consistent[2] *adj.* See signs for CONSTANT[1,3], RESULT[1,2].

---

console *n.* The part of a computer that allows user input, including the keyboard and the screen: *working at the console.*

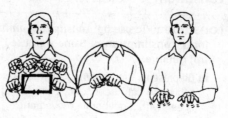

■ [**square**[1] + **type**] Beginning with both extended index fingers touching in front of the chest, palms facing forward, move the hands out-ward to each side of the chest and then down and back together in front of the chest. Then wiggle the fingers of both *5 hands* in front of the body, palms facing down.

---

constant[1] *adj.* Continuing without stopping: *The rain was constant.* Same sign used for: **consistent, continuous, momentum.**

■ [Similar to sign for **alike**[1] but indicating a continuous action] Beginning with both *Y hands* in front of each side of the chest, palms facing down, move the hands in simultaneous circles, moving inward in opposite directions.

---

constant[2] *adj.* **1.** Always the same; unchanging; steady: *Keep a constant temperature in the room.* **2.** Steadfast and loyal: *a constant friend.* Same sign used for: **even, steady.**

■ [Indicates a steady movement] Beginning with the right *open hand* in front of the right shoulder, palm facing down and fingers pointing forward, move the hand straight forward with a slow movement.

constant[3] *adj.* Recurring regularly: *the constant ringing of the telephone.* Same sign used for: **consistent, continual, persistent, steadfast, steady.**

- [Indicates continuing movement] Beginning with the thumb of the right *10 hand* on the thumbnail of the left *10 hand*, both palms facing down in front of the chest, move the hands downward and forward in a series of small arcs.

Constitution *n.* See sign for COMMANDMENT.

construct[1] *v.* To build or form from materials: *The children constructed a tower out of blocks.* Related form: **construction** *n.*

- [Initialized sign similar to sign for **build**[1]] Beginning with the thumb of the left *C hand*, palm facing right, on the fingers of the right *C hand*, palm facing left, reverse the position of the hands with a repeated alternating movement as the hands move upward.

construct[2] *v.* See signs for BUILD[1,2]. Related form: **construction** *n.*

consult *v.* See sign for COUNSEL. Related form: **consultation** *n.*

consultant *n.* See sign for ADVISOR.

consume *v.* To use up: *consumes too much time.* Related form: **consumption** *n.* Same sign used for: **devour, eat up, gullible.**

- [Represents food entering the mouth to be consumed] Move the right *bent hand*, palm facing in, past the right cheek with a deliberate movement.

consumer *n.* A person who purchases goods or services.

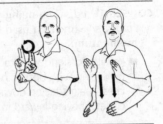

- [use + person] With the heel of the right *U hand* on the back of the left *S hand*, move the right hand in a small circle. Then move both *open hands*, palms facing each other, downward along the sides of the body.

contact[1] *n.* **1.** The state of touching or being in communication: *Stay in contact with me.* —*v.* **2.** To get in touch with: *Contact me later.* Same sign used for: **in touch with.**

- [Indicates two things coming into contact with each other] With the right hand above the left hand in front of the chest, touch the bent middle finger of the right *5 hand* to the bent middle finger of the left *5 hand* with a double movement, palms facing each other.

contact[2] *n., v.* (alternate sign) Same sign used for: **touch with.**

- [Indicates one thing coming into contact with another] Touch the bent middle finger of the right *5 hand*, palm facing down, with a double movement on the back of the left *open hand*, palm facing down.

contact lens *n.* A thin plastic disk designed to fit on the cornea to improve vision: *wear contact lenses instead of glasses.*

- [Action of putting in contact lenses] Bring the bent middle finger of the right *5 hand,* palm facing in, first toward the right eye and then toward the left eye.

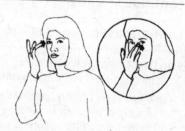

contained in See sign for INCLUDE.

contemplate *v.* See sign for WONDER.

contempt *n.* A feeling or expression of disdain for something or someone mean, vile, and low: *looked at him with contempt.* Same sign used for: **look down at** or **on, scorn.**

- [Represents eyes looking down on another] Beginning with both *V hands* in front of each side of the face, palms facing forward and fingers pointing up, twist the wrists downward to point the fingers forward with a slow movement.

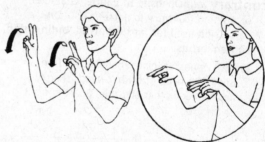

content[1] *adj.* See signs for RELIEF, SATISFY[1]. Related form: **contentment** *n.*

content[2] *n.* See sign for MEAT. Shared idea of substance.

contest *n.* See sign for RACE[2].

contingency *adj.* See sign for DEPENDABLE.

contingent *adj.* See sign for DEPEND.

continual *adj.* See sign for CONSTANT[3].

continuance *n.* See sign for POSTPONE.

continue[1] *v.* To go on or keep on: *to continue going to work.* Same sign used for: **endure, last, lasting, permanent, remain.**

■ [Indicates continuous movement] Beginning with the thumb of the right *10 hand* on the thumbnail of the left *10 hand,* both palms facing down in front of the chest, move the hands forward.

continue[2] *v.* See sign for GO ON[1].

continuous *adj.* See sign for CONSTANT[1].

contract *n.* A legal agreement: *a contract to buy a house.* Same sign used for: **endorsement, registration, signature.**

■ [Represents placing one's name on paper] Pat the extended fingers of the right *H hand,* palm facing down, with a double movement on the upturned palm of the left *open hand* held across the chest.

contraction *n.* See sign for CRAMP[2].

contradict *v.* See sign for CONFLICT[1]. Related form: **contradiction** *n.*

contrary *adj.* Opposite in nature, character, or opinion: *contrary to popular opinion.* Same sign used for: **antagonistic, bullheaded, cantankerous.**

■ [Two opposing things meeting head-on] Bump the heels of both *Y hands* sharply against each other and then apart in front of the chest.

contrast *v.* See signs for DISAGREE, OPPOSITE.

contribute *v.* See signs for CHARITY, GIVE[1].

contribution *n.* See signs for GIFT[1,3].

control[1] *v.* To restrain (one's feelings): *Control your temper.* Same sign used for: **restrain, suppress, tolerate.**

■ [The hands seem to suppress one's feelings] Beginning with the fingertips of both *curved 5 hands* against the chest, palms facing in, bring the hands downward while forming *S hands,* palms facing up.

control[2] *v.* See sign for MANAGE.

controlled substance *n.* See sign for DRUG[2].

controller *n.* See sign for MOTHERBOARD.

controversy *n.* See signs for ARGUE[1,2], STRUGGLE.

contusion *n.* See sign for BRUISE.

convenient *adj.* See signs for COMFORTABLE, EASY.

convent *n.* See sign for MONASTERY.

convention *n.* See sign for MEETING.

converse *v.* See sign for COMMUNICATION. Related form: **conversation** *n.*

conversion *n.* See sign for UPDATE.

convert[1] *v.* To change one's faith or purpose: *convert to Christianity.*

■ [Initialized sign similar to sign for **change**[1]] With both *C hands* in front of the chest, thumbs touching, palms facing each other, and right hand above the left hand, twist the wrists in opposite directions in order to reverse positions, and then back again to original position.

convert[2] *v.* To change to another form or use: *convert the dining room into a home office.* Related form: **conversion** *n.* Same sign used for: **adapt, change, modify.**

■ [Similar to sign for **change**[1]] Beginning with the palms of both *modified X hands* together, twist the hands in opposite directions to reverse positions, and then back again to original position.

convertible *n.* An automobile with a folding top: *to ride in a convertible with the top down.*

■ [Represents lowering and raising a convertible top] Beginning with both *X hands* in front of each shoulder, palms facing each other, bring the hands upward and backward, and then forward again, in a simultaneous double arc.

convey *v.* See sign for NARROW DOWN.

convict[1] *n.* A person incarcerated for a crime: *The convicts could have visitors on Sundays.* Same sign used for: **prisoner.**

- [**jail**[1,2] + **person marker**] Bring the back of the right *4 hand* from near the chest forward while bringing the left *4 hand* in to meet the right hand, ending with the fingers crossed at angles, both palms facing in. Then move both *open hands,* palms facing each other, downward along each side of the body.

convict[2] *v.* See signs for CAPTURE[2,3].

convince[1] *v.* To persuade by argument or evidence: *I remain convinced of his innocence.* Same sign used for: **persuade.**

- Beginning with both *open hands* in front of each shoulder, palms angled upward, bring the hands down sharply at an angle toward each other.

convince[2] *v.* (alternate sign, used especially when referring to convincing one other person) Same sign used for: **persuade.**

- [One hand hits the other hand to influence it] Move the little-finger side of the right *open hand,* palm facing up, sharply against the extended left index finger held up in front of the chest.

convince[3] (alternate sign, used especially when referring to being convinced by another or others) Same sign used for: **persuade.**

- [Represents being hit by other people's ideas] Hit the little-finger sides of both *open hands,* palms facing down and fingers pointing back, against each side of the neck with a sharp movement.

convocation *n.* See sign for MEETING.

cook[1] *v.* To prepare food by using heat: *to cook dinner.* Same sign used for: **bake, flip, fry, turn over.**

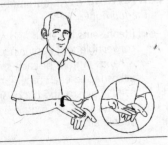

- [As if turning food in a frying pan] Beginning with the fingers of the right *open hand,* palm facing down, across the palm of the left *open hand,* flip the right hand over, ending with the back of the right hand on the left palm.

cook[2] *v.* See sign for BOIL.

cookie *n.* A small, flat cake: *chocolate chip cookies.* Same sign used for: **biscuit.**

- ■ [Mime using a cookie cutter] Touch the fingertips of the right *C hand,* palm facing down, on the upturned palm of the left *open hand.* Then twist the right hand and touch the left palm again.

cool *adj.* Lacking in warmth: *a cool day.* Same sign used for: **neat, pleasant, refresh.**

- ■ [As if fanning oneself] With both open hands above each shoulder, palms facing back and fingers pointing up, bend the fingers up and down with a repeated movement.

cooperate *v.* To put forth a united effort. *If we cooperate, we can finish the job faster.* Related form: **cooperation** *n.* Same sign used for: **affiliation, union, unity, universal.**

- ■ [Shows unity between two] With the thumbs and index fingers of both *F hands* intersecting, move the hands in a flat circle in front of the chest.

coordinate *v.* To arrange or combine so as to function harmoniously: *Coordinate your plans with the rest of the committee.* Same sign used for: **relate.**

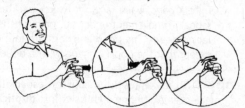

- ■ With the thumbs and index fingers of both *F hands* intersecting, move the hands forward and back with a double movement.

coordinator *n.* A person who coordinates: *Get in touch with the coordinator about the schedule.*

- ■ [**coordinate** + **person marker**] With the thumbs and index fingers of both *F hands* intersecting, move the hands forward and back with a double movement. Then move both *open hands,* palms facing each other, downward along each side of the body.

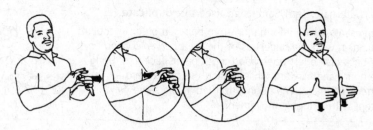

cop *n.* See signs for POLICE[1,2].

---

copy[1] *v.* **1.** To make a written copy of, especially from something distant: *Copy the homework assignment from the board.* **2.** To reproduce from another source; imitate: *To copy an author's style.* Same sign used for: **duplicate, imitate, parrot.**

■ [Represents taking information and recording it on paper] Move the right *curved hand* in front of the chest, palm facing forward, down to touch the palm of the left *open hand* while closing the right fingers and thumb into a *flattened O hand*. The noun is formed in the same way except with a double movement.

---

copy[2] *v.* **1.** To reproduce by photocopying: *Copy this report for everyone.* —*n.* **2.** A photocopy: *Make a copy for each person.* Same sign used for: **duplicate, photocopy, xerography, Xerox** (*trademark*).

■ [Represents the action of a photocopy machine] Move the fingers of the right *curved hand,* palm facing up, downward from touching the palm of the left *open hand* while closing the right fingers and thumb into a *flattened O hand.*

---

copy[3] *v., n.* (alternate sign) Same sign used for: **duplicate, photocopy, xerography, Xerox** (*trademark*).

■ [Initialized sign for xerography showing the movement of exposure on a copy machine] Move the bent index finger of the right *X hand,* palm facing forward, back and forth with a repeated movement under the palm of the left *open hand,* palm facing down. The noun and verb are formed in the same way except that the noun is made with a double movement.

---

copy[4] *v.* To make a written copy of, especially from something near you: *You can copy my class notes.* Same sign used for: **duplicate.**

■ [Represent taking information from paper in order to copy it] Move the fingers of the right *curved hand,* palm facing down, from touching the upturned palm of the left *open hand,* upward while closing the right fingers and thumb into a *flattened O hand.* The noun is formed in the same way except with a double movement.

---

copy[5] *v.* (alternate sign) Same sign used for: **duplicate.**

■ [Represents taking information from paper in order to copy it] Beginning with the fingertips of the right *curved 5 hand* on the back of the left *open hand,* both palms facing in, bring the right hand forward while closing the fingers into a *flattened O hand.* The noun is formed in the same way except with a double movement.

---

copy[6] *n., v.* See sign for EXCERPT.

cord[1] *n.* A small flexible cable or thin rope: *Tie the package with cord.* Same sign used for: **thread, wire.**

- [Shape of a coiled cord] Beginning with both extended little fingers pointing toward each other in front of the chest, palms facing in, move the fingers in opposite circular movements while moving the hands away from each other.

cord[2] *n.* The wire connecting a hearing-aid receiver to the earpiece: *My hearing-aid cord is broken.* Same sign used for: **wire.**

- [Location of wire from a hearing-aid earpiece to the receiver worn on the body] Move the extended right little finger, palm facing in, from touching the right ear down to the middle of the chest.

corn *n.* A cereal plant that bears small, usually yellow, kernels on large ears: *eating corn for dinner.*

- [Mime eating corn on the cob] With both *flattened C hands* held near each side of the face, palms facing each other, twist both hands forward simultaneously with a repeated movement.

corner[1] *n.* A place where two lines or surfaces meet: *standing in the corner of the room.*

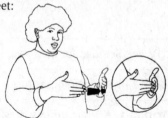

- [Hands form the shape of a corner] Move the fingertips of both *open hands,* palms angled toward each other, to touch each other at an angle with a repeated movement.

corner[2] *v.* See sign for NAB[1].

coronary *n.* See sign for HEART ATTACK.

corporal *n.* A low-ranking noncommissioned officer: *In the sergeant's absence, the corporal commanded the squad.*

- [Shape of two stripes on a corporal's uniform] Move the fingertips of the right *V hand,* palm facing right, first upward a short distance and then downward on the upper left arm, from back to front.

correct *v.* See signs for CANCEL, EDIT[1], RIGHT[3].

correspond *v.* To communicate by letter: *close friends who correspond every week.* Related form: **correspondence.**

- [Represents the sending and receiving of letters] Beginning with *modified X hands*, palms facing each other and the right hand closer to the chest than the left, flick the index fingers toward each other with a repeated alternating movement.

corridor *n.* See sign for HALL.

cosmetics *pl. n.* See signs for MAKE-UP[1,2].

cost[1] *n.* **1.** The price paid or charged for something: *The cost is $5.00 for each ticket.* —*v.* **2.** To have a price of: *The candy costs 50 cents.* Same sign used for: **charge, duty, fare, fee, fine, price, tax.**

- Strike the knuckle of the right *X hand*, palm facing in, down the palm of the left *open hand*, palm facing right and fingers pointing forward.

cost[2] *n.* (alternate sign) Same sign used for: **price, value, worth.**

- Tap the fingertips of both *F hands* together, palms facing each other, with a repeated movement.

costly *adj.* See sign for EXPENSIVE.

costume *n.* See sign for CLOTHES.

cotton *n.* **1.** A white fibrous substance attached to the seeds of a plant, used to make fabric: *picked cotton in the fields all day.* **2.** The fabric made from this substance: *loves to wear clothing made of soft cotton.* —*adj.* **3.** Made of cotton: *a cotton dress.*

- [Fingers seem to draw out strands from a cotton boll] Close the fingers of the right *flattened C hand* around the fingertips of the left *flattened O hand*, both palms facing each other. Then pull the right hand outward to the right while closing into a *flattened O hand* with a double movement.

couch *n.* A long upholstered piece of furniture for seating two to four people: *Sit over there, on the couch.* Same sign used for: **pew, sofa.**

- [sit + loaf[2] to indicate the elongated shape of a couch] Place the fingers of the right *curved U hand* across the fingers of the left *U hand,* both palms facing down. Then, beginning with the index-finger sides of both *C hands* touching, palms facing down, bring the hands apart to each side of the body.

cough[1] *v.* **1.** To force air from the lungs with a sharp noise: *I coughed all night.* —*n.* **2.** The act or sound of coughing: *The baby's cough woke me up.*

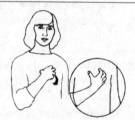

- [Location of the origin of a cough in the chest] With the fingertips of the right *curved 5 hand* on the chest, palm facing in, lower the wrist with a repeated movement while keeping the fingertips in place.

cough[2] *v., n.* (alternate sign)

- [Natural gesture one uses after a hacking cough] Bring the index-finger side of the right *S hand,* palm facing left, back against the chest with a double movement.

council *n.* See sign for MEETING.

counsel *v.* To give advice to: *to counsel the students.* Same sign used for: **advise, affect, consult, consultation.**

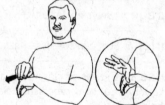

- [Represents the spreading of one's counsel to others] Beginning with the fingertips of the right *flattened O hand* on the back of the left hand, palm facing down, move the right hand forward with a double movement while spreading the fingers into a *5 hand* each time.

counselor *n.* See sign for ADVISOR.

count *v.* **1.** To name consecutive numbers: *See if the child can count to ten.* **2.** To find or determine the total number of: *count the chairs.* Same sign used for: **figure.**

- Move the fingertips of the right *F hand,* palm facing down, across the upturned palm of the left *open hand* from the heel to the fingers.

counter *adj.* See sign for OPPOSITE.

counterfeit *n.* See signs for FAKE[3,4].

count on *v. phrase.* See sign for DEPENDABLE.

country[1] *n.* A state or nation or its territory: *to live in a foreign country.* Same sign used for: **land.**

- Rub the bent fingers of the right *Y hand,* palm facing in, in a circle near the elbow of the bent left arm with a repeated movement.

country[2] *n.* **1.** (alternate sign) **2.** Rural areas, as opposed to cities and towns: *to spend a day in the country, away from the dirt and the crowds.*

- Rub the palm of the right *open hand* in a circle near the elbow of the bent left arm with a repeated movement.

couple[1] *n.* **1.** Two people paired together: *a newly married couple.* **2.** Two things thought of or used together: *a couple of diaper pins.* Same sign used for: **pair, partners.**

- [Pointing to two people making up a couple] Move the fingers of the right *V hand,* palm facing up and fingers pointing forward, from side to side in front of the right side of the body with a repeated movement.

couple[2] *n.* See sign for DOUBLE DATE.

courage *n.* See sign for BRAVE.

courier *n.* See sign for MESSENGER.

course *n.* A series of classes on a subject: *register for the course in word processing.* Same sign used for: **chapter, lesson.**

- [Initialized sign similar to sign for **list**] Move the little-finger side of the right *C hand,* palm facing in, in an arc, touching first on the fingers and then near the heel of the upturned left hand.

court *n.* See sign for JUDGE[1].

courteous *adj.* See signs for POLITE[1,2]. Related form: **courtesy** *n.*

courthouse *n.* A building in which courts of law are held: *The hearing for this case is in the old courthouse.*

■ [**judge**[1] + **house**] Move both *F hands,* palms facing each other, up and down in front of each side of the chest with an alternating movement. Then, beginning with the fingertips of both *B hands* touching in front of the neck, palms angled toward each other, bring the hands apart and down at an angle to about shoulder width, and then straight down.

cousin[1] *n.* A male child of one's uncle or aunt: *my cousin, John.*

■ [Initialized sign formed near the male area of the head] Move the right *C hand,* palm facing left, with a shaking movement near the right side of the forehead.

cousin[2] *n.* A female child of one's uncle or aunt: *my cousin, Mary.*

■ [Initialized sign formed near the female area of the head] Move the right *C hand,* palm facing left, with a shaking movement near the right side of the chin.

cover[1] *n.* **1.** Something placed over or upon, as to protect or conceal: *the cover of the book.* —*v.* **2.** To put something over or upon to protect or conceal it: *to cover your face with your hands.*

■ [Demonstrates pulling a cover over something] Move the right *open hand,* palm facing down, from in front of the right side of the body in a large circular movement over the bent left arm held across the body.

cover[2] *n., v.* (alternate sign)

■ [Represents pulling up the covers on a bed] Beginning with both *A hands* in front of each side of the lower chest, palms facing down, move them upward and inward to each side of the upper chest.

cover[3] *n., v.* (alternate sign)

■ [Represents the location of a cover on something] Bring the palm side of the right *open hand* toward the chest in an arc over the back of the left *open hand,* palm facing down.

cover[4] *n.* See signs for LID[1,2].

cover-up *n.* **1.** An action calculated to hide the truth or impede an investigation: *a high-level cover-up designed to avert scandal.* —*v. phrase.* **2. cover up** To conceal and prevent exposure of (a crime, scandal, etc.): *Everyone tried to cover up the judge's part in the crime.* Same sign used for: **fraud, hide.**

- [Hands seem to try to blur the truth] Beginning with both *5 hands* in front of the chest, palms facing each other, bring the right hand to the left in an arc past the left hand, ending with the wrists crossed.

cover one's mouth See sign for MUFFLE.

covetous *adj.* See sign for GREEDY[1].

cow[1] *n.* A full-grown female bovine animal: *Milk comes from a cow.* Same sign used for: **cattle.**

- [A cow's horns] With the thumbs of both *Y hands* on both sides of the forehead, palms facing forward, twist the hands forward.

cow[2] *n.* (alternate sign) Same sign used for: **cattle.**

- [A cow's horns] With the thumb of the right *Y hand* on the right side of the forehead, palm facing forward, twist the hand forward with a repeated movement.

coward[1] *n.* A person who lacks courage: *He is a coward who refuses to confront your anger.*

- [**bird** + **fear**[1]] Close the index finger and thumb of the right *G hand*, palm facing forward, with a repeated movement in front of the mouth. Then, beginning with both *5 hands* in front of each side of the chest, palms facing in and fingers pointing toward each other, move the hands toward each other with a double movement.

coward[2] *n.* See signs for BIRD, FEAR[1].

cozy *adj.* See sign for COMFORTABLE.

crab *n.* A broad, flat shellfish with two large claws: *to catch crabs along the shore.*

- ■ [A crab's claws] Beginning with both *C hands* in front of each side of the body, palms facing each other, close the fingers to the thumbs of each hand with a double movement.

crack[1] *n.* A narrow break: *a crack in the sidewalk.* Same sign used for: **chap, split.**

- ■ [Shape of a crack] Move the little-finger side of the right *open hand*, palm facing left, down the palm of the left *open hand*, palm facing up, with a jagged movement.

crack[2] *n.* See sign for RAGGED. Related form: **cracked** *adj.*

crack[3] or **crack cocaine** *n.* See sign for COCAINE.

cracker *n.* A dry, thin biscuit: *to eat crackers with the soup.* Same sign used for: **matzo, Passover.**

- ■ Strike the palm side of the right *A hand* near the elbow of the bent left arm with a repeated movement.

cradle *n.* A small bed for a baby, usually on rockers: *Rock the cradle gently.*

- ■ [**baby**[1] + the rocking movement of a cradle] With the bent right arm cradled on the bent left arm, both palms facing up, swing the arms back and forth in front of the body with a double movement. Then, beginning with both *curved hands* in front of each side of the body, swing the hands in an arc from side to side with a double movement.

cramp[1] *n.* **1.** An involuntary contraction or spasm: *I got a cramp in my leg.* —*v.* **2.** To have an involuntary contraction, usually painful: *My muscles cramped in the cold water.* Related form: **cramps** *pl. n.*

- ■ [A gesture indicating a cramp] Beginning with both *A hands* in front of each side of the body, right palm facing down and left palm facing up, twist the hands in opposite directions.

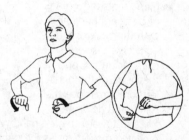

cramp[2] or **the cramps** *n.* (alternate sign) Related form: **cramps** *n.* Same sign used for: **charley horse, contraction, spasm.**

- [Shows twist of tight muscles] Beginning with the thumb side of the right *S hand*, palm facing right, and the thumb side of the left *S hand*, palm facing in, twist the right hand forward, ending with the palm facing in.

cramped *adj.* See signs for CROWDED[1,2].

crash[1] *n.* **1.** The violent and noisy striking of one solid thing against another: *There was a terrible crash when two cars ran into each other head-on.* —*v.* **2.** To strike against another thing or collide violently and noisily: *The car crashed into a tree.* Same sign used for: **bomb.**

- [Shows impact of a crash] Beginning with the right *5 hand* near the right side of the chest, palm facing down and fingers pointing forward, move the hand deliberately forward to hit against the palm of the left *open hand*, bending the right fingers as it hits.

crash[2] *n.* **1.** The violent striking of an airplane against another airplane, the ground, or another object: *The passengers survived the airplane crash.* —*v.* **2.** To fall to the earth or strike another object in such a way as to be destroyed or severely damaged: *The airplane crashed into a mountain.*

- [**airplane** + showing the impact of a crash] Move the right hand with the thumb, index finger, and little finger extended from in front of the right shoulder, palm facing down, in an arc across the chest, changing to an *S hand* as it strikes the open left palm.

crash[3] *n.* See signs for ACCIDENT[1], BREAK DOWN.

crave *v.* See signs for DROOL, HUNGRY.

crawl *v.* **1.** To move with the body near the ground, as on one's hands and knees: *The baby has learned to crawl across the floor.* **2.** To move slowly: *The traffic is crawling today.*

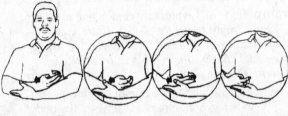

- [Represents movement of crawling] Beginning with the back of the right *bent V hand*, palm facing up, on the inside of the bent left forearm, move the right hand down the forearm toward the left hand while crooking the fingers of the *bent V hand* with a repeated movement as the right hand moves.

crayon *n.* See signs for COLOR[2,3,4].

crazy[1] *adj.* **1.** Mentally disordered: *behaving like a crazy person.* **2.** Wildly impractical: *crazy ideas.* **3.** Unusual; bizarre: *a crazy day.* Same sign used for: **wacky** (*slang*).

- [Natural gesture used when referring to a person who is confused or unstable] Move the extended right index finger, palm facing down, in a circle near the right side of the head.

crazy[2] *adj.* (alternate sign) Same sign used for: **wacky** (*slang*), **wild.**

- [Indicates that things are confused in one's head] Twist the right *curved 5 hand,* palm facing in, forward with a repeated movement near the right side of the head.

crazy[3] *adj.* See sign for RAVE.

cream[1] *n.* The yellowish part of whole milk containing butterfat, tending to rise to the surface in milk that is not homogenized: *a pint of cream.*

- [Initialized sign representing skimming cream from the top of milk] Bring the little-finger side of the right *C hand,* palm facing left, back toward the chest in a circular movement across the palm of the left *open hand.*

cream[2] *n.* A thick, soft medicinal or cosmetic preparation: *spread moisturizing cream on your face.*

- [Mime taking cold cream from a jar and putting it on one's face] Move the fingers of the right *curved hand* downward in an arc near the thumb side of the left *C hand,* palm facing right. Then wipe the fingers of the right *open hand* in a circular movement on the right cheek.

create[1] *v.* To cause to come into being: *to create a unique work of art.* Related form: **creation** *n.*

- [Initialized sign similar to sign for **make**[1]] Beginning with the little-finger side of the right *C hand* on the index-finger side of the left *C hand,* both palms facing in, separate the hands slightly and twist the wrists outward in opposite directions. Then touch the hands together again, ending with the palms facing outward in opposite directions.

create[2] *v.* See signs for INVENT, MAKE[1,2].

creative *adj.* See sign for CONCEPT.

credit card *n.* A card authorizing the holder to charge purchases: *We'll charge the lunch on my credit card.* See also signs for CARD², CHARGE¹.

■ [**charge**¹ + **card**¹] Rub the little-finger side of the right *S hand,* palm facing in, back and forth on the upturned palm of the left *open hand.* Then, beginning with the tips of the index fingers and thumbs of both *modified C hands* touching in front of the chest, palms facing forward, bring the hands apart to in front of each shoulder, and then pinch each thumb and index finger together.

creek *n.* See sign for RIVER².

crew cut *n.* A haircut in which all the hair is cropped very closely: *He got a crew cut when he joined the Army.*

■ [Length of hair with a crew cut] Move the thumb of the right *G hand,* palm facing left, from the center of the forehead back over the top of the head.

crime¹ *n.* An act that is contrary to laws established for the welfare of the public at large: *to commit the crime of robbery.* Same sign used for: **felony, illegal infraction, misdemeanor, offense, unlawful, violation.**

■ [**law** + **break**] Place the palm side of the right *L hand,* palm facing left, first on the fingers and then on the heel of the left *open hand,* palm facing right and fingers pointing up. Then, beginning with both *S hands* in front of the body, index fingers touching and palms down, move the hands away from each other while twisting the wrists with a deliberate movement, ending with the palms facing each other.

crime² *n.* (alternate sign) Same sign used for: **felony, illegal infraction, misdemeanor, offense, unlawful, violation.**

■ [**against** + **law**] Hit the fingertips of the right *bent hand* into the left *open hand,* palm facing right and fingers pointing forward. Then place the palm side of the right *L hand,* palm facing left, first on the fingers and then on the heel of the left *open hand,* palm facing right and fingers pointing up.

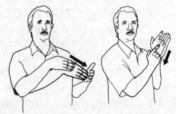

crime³ *n.* (alternate sign)

- ■ [**bad** + **happen**] Move the fingers of the right *open hand* from the mouth, palm facing in, downward while flipping the palm quickly down as the hand moves. Then, beginning with both extended index fingers in front of the body, palms facing in and fingers angled upward, flip the hands over toward each other with a double movement, ending with the palms down.

criminal *n.* A person who commits a crime: *The criminal was arrested for robbery.* Same sign used for: **offender.**

- ■ [**crime**¹ + **person marker**] Place the palm side of the right *L hand,* palm facing left, first on the fingers and then on the heel of the left *open hand,* palm facing right and fingers pointing up. Then, beginning with both *S hands* in front of the body, index fingers touching and palms down, move the hands away from each other while twisting the wrists with a deliberate movement, ending with the palms facing each other. Then move both *open hands,* palms facing each other, downward along the sides of the body.

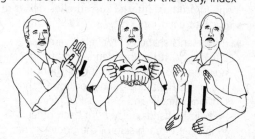

crippled *adj.* Being physically disabled, especially in a way that interferes with use of the legs: *a crippled animal.* Same sign used for: **lame, limp.**

- ■ [Represents the uneven steps of someone limping] Beginning with both extended index fingers pointing down in front of each side of the body, palms facing in, move the hands up and down with an alternating uneven movement.

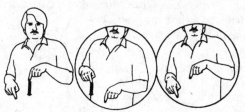

crisis *n.* **1.** A time of intense difficulty or danger. **2.** The turning point of a disease, when it becomes clear whether the patient will recover: *The patient's condition reached a crisis during the night.* Same sign used for: **critical point, turning point.**

- ■ [Initialized sign that represents moving up to a critical point] Bring both *C hands,* palms facing each other, upward from each side of the chest to meet in front of the neck.

critical *adj.* Important at a time of crisis or other turning point: *a critical decision.* Same sign used for: **choice.**

■ [Initialized sign similar to sign for **priority**] Touch the thumb of the right *C hand*, palm facing forward, first to the thumb, then to the index finger, and then to the middle finger of the left *5 hand*, palm facing right.

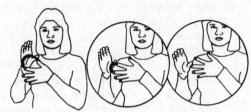

critical point See sign for CRISIS.

criticize *v.* See sign for CANCEL.

crochet *v.* To do needlework with a hooked needle made for drawing yarn through loops to produce interlocked stitches: *learn to crochet by making small doilies.* Same sign used for: **knit.**

■ [Represents shape of crocheted yarn] Beginning with both extended index fingers pointing in opposite directions in front of the chest, right index finger on top of the left index finger and both palms facing in, pull the hands away from each other to in front of each side of the body with a repeated movement, changing into *X hands* each time.

crook *n.* See signs for ROBBER[1,2].

cross[1] *n.* **1.** A structure made of an upright beam with a horizontal bar across it: *Jesus was nailed to a cross.* **2.** A representation of a cross used as a symbol of the Christian faith: *to wear a cross on a chain around the neck.* Same sign used for: **crucifix.**

■ [Shape of a cross] Bring the right *C hand*, palm facing forward, first downward in front of the right side of the body and then from left to right.

cross[2] *adj.* See sign for ANGER[1,2].

cross[3] *prep., adv.* See sign for ACROSS.

crossing *n.* See signs for INTERSECTION[1,2].

cross out *v. phrase.* See sign for CANCEL.

cross-purposes *n.* See sign for CONFLICT[1].

cross your heart See sign for SWEAR[1].

crowd *n.* See signs for AUDIENCE[1,2,3,4], HORDE.

crowded[1] *adj.* Having many people or things packed into a small space: *a crowded room.* Same sign used for: **cramped, crushed, small.**

- Beginning with the palms of both *A hands* together in front of the chest, twist the hands in opposite directions.

crowded[2] *adj.* (alternate sign) Same sign used for: **cramped, crushed.**

- [Represents people coming together into a crowded area] Beginning with both *curved 5 hands* in front of each shoulder, palms facing each other, bring the hands together while bending the fingers and pushing the knuckles together.

crowded[3] *adj.* See signs for JAM[1,2].

crown[1] *n.* A royal headdress, usually of precious metal and jewels, worn to symbolize a monarch's sovereignty: *The queen wears a crown on formal occasions.* •

- [Placing a crown on the head] Bring both *modified C hands,* palms facing each other, downward to each side of the head.

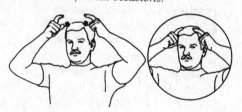

crown[2] *n.* An artificial covering for a tooth: *The dentist put a crown on the tooth.* Same sign used for: **cap.**

- [Hand seems to place a cap on something] Place the right *curved 5 hand* down over the extended left index finger, palm facing in and finger pointing up.

crown[3] *n.* (alternate sign) Same sign used for: **cap.**

- [Fingers seem to push a crown up on a tooth] Push the fingertips of the extended right index finger, middle finger, and thumb, palm facing in, upward on one of the upper front teeth.

crucial *adj.* See signs for IMPORTANT[1,2].

crucifix *n.* See sign for CROSS[1].

crucify *v.* To put to death by nailing or tying the hands and feet to a cross: *Jesus was crucified.*
- ■ [**pound** formed in each hand + holding up one's hands as if hanging on a cross] Strike the little-finger side of the left *S hand* into the upturned right *open hand*. Strike the little-finger side of the right *S hand* into the upturned left *open hand*. Then hold up both *open hands* in front of each shoulder, palms facing forward.

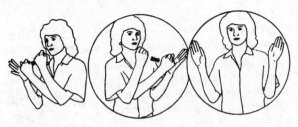

crude *adj.* See sign for ROUGH.

cruel *adj.* See signs for MEAN[1], MEANNESS[1,2], ROUGH.

cruise *n.* See signs for BOAT, SHIP[1].

crusade *n.* **1.** A vigorous movement on behalf of a cause: *participate in the crusade against drug abuse.* —*v.* **2.** To take part in a crusade: *crusaded for women's right to vote.* Same sign used for: **carnival.**
- ■ [Initialized sign similar to sign for **fair**[3]] Beginning with both *C hands* in front of each side of the chest, palms facing each other, move the hands in alternating circular movements.

crushed *adj.* See signs for CROWDED[1,2].

cry[1] *v.* To shed tears, as from grief or pain: *I cried for a long time when my grandmother died.* Same sign used for: **weep.**
- ■ [Represents tears pouring out of the eyes] Beginning with the index fingers of both *X hands* near each eye, palms facing in, turn the palms forward and bring the hands down in front of each side of the chest.

cry[2] *v.* (alternate sign) Same sign used for: **weep.**

- [Tears flowing down the cheeks] Bring both extended index fingers, palms facing in and fingers pointing up, downward from each eye with alternating movements.

cry[3] *v.* See signs for CALL[4], SCREAM[1,2].

cube *n.* See sign for BLOCK[1].

Cub Scout *n.* See sign for BROWNIE.

culture *n.* See sign for CONDITION.

cup *n.* An open drinking vessel: *drinking a cup of tea.* Same sign used for: **can, glass, jar.**

- [Shape of cup] Bring the little-finger side of the right *C hand,* palm facing left, down to the upturned left *open hand* with a double movement.

cure *n., v.* See signs for DISSOLVE, WELL[1].

curious *adj.* Eager to know: *curious about their Christmas presents.* Related form: **curiosity** *n.*

- With the fingertips of the right *F hand* against the neck, palm facing left, twist the hand downward with a double movement.

curler *n.* See sign for HAIR ROLLER[1].

curly[1] *adj.* Forming coils or ringlets: *curly hair.*

- [Shape of curly hair] Move both *curved 5 hands,* palms facing in, in alternating circles near each ear.

curly[2] *adj.* (alternate sign)

■ [Shape of curly hair] Move both *4 hands*, palms facing in, from near each ear downward with a wavy movement.

current *adj.* See signs for NOW[1,2].

curriculum *n.* A course of study or a group of such courses: *Teachers were asked to follow the curriculum more closely.*

■ [Abbreviation **c-m**] Move the index-finger side of the right *C hand*, facing forward, upward on the palm of the left *open hand* palm from the heel to the fingers, palm facing right and fingers pointing up. Then change the right hand to an *M hand* and move back down the left palm from the fingers to the heel.

curse[1] *n.* **1.** A word or phrase calling for evil and misfortune to fall upon someone or something: *yelled a curse at the driver of the car as it sped past, barely missing us.* —*v.* **2.** To ask that evil and misfortune be brought on: *cursed those who had stolen his inheritance.* **3.** To swear at, as from annoyance: *cursed the dog for tripping him on the stairs.* Same sign used for: **condemn, cuss** (*slang*), **swear, wrath.**

■ Beginning with the right *curved 5 hand* near the mouth, palm facing in, bring the hand downward with a deliberate movement while closing into an *S hand.*

curse[2] *n., v.* (alternate sign) Same sign used for: **condemn, cuss** (*slang*), **swear.**

■ Beginning with the right *curved 5 hand* near the mouth, palm facing in, bring the hand upward with a deliberate movement while closing into an *S hand.*

curse[3] *n., v.* (alternate sign) Same sign used for: **condemn.**

■ [Initialized sign similar to sign for **swear**[1]] Beginning with the thumb of the right *C hand* near the mouth, palm facing left, bring the right hand down and forward in a large arc, brushing the tip of the extended left index finger as it passes.

cursor *n.* A symbol on a computer screen that indicates where the next character will appear: *She needs to find a program that enlarges the blinking cursor.* Same sign used for: **prompt.**

■ [Movement of a computer cursor] Beginning with the right index finger and thumb pressed together in front of the right shoulder, palm angled forward, move the right hand upward and forward with a jagged movement.

curtains *pl. n.* A piece of cloth hung at a window: *to open the curtains.*

■ [Shape of curtains hanging on a window] Beginning with both *4 hands* in front of the face, palms facing forward, bring the hands downward in an arc to about shoulder width and then straight down, ending with the palms facing down.

curve[1] *n.* A line that has no straight part: *a curve in the road.*

■ [Shape of a curve] Move the right *B hand* from in front of the right shoulder, palm facing forward, downward in an arc, ending with the palm facing up and the fingers pointing forward.

curve[2] *n.* See sign for ARCH.

cushion *n.* See sign for PILLOW[1].

cuss *slang.* See signs for CURSE[1,2].

custodian *n.* See signs for JANITOR[1,2].

custom[1] *n.* A habitual practice: *It is our custom to open presents on Christmas Eve.*

■ [Initialized sign similar to sign for **habit**] Beginning with the thumb of the right *C hand*, palm facing forward, on the back of the left *S hand*, palm facing down, move both hands downward in front of the chest.

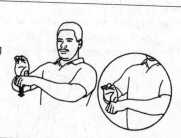

custom[2] *n.* See sign for HABIT.

customer[1] *n.* A person who buys: *The store was filled with customers.* Same sign used for: **buyer, consumer, shopper.**

- [**buy + person marker**] Beginning with the back of the right *flattened O hand*, palm facing up, in the upturned palm of the left *open hand*, move the right hand forward in an arc. Then move both *open hands*, palms facing each other, downward along each side of the body.

customer[2] *n.* See sign for CLIENT[2].

cut[1] *n.* An opening in the skin made by or as if by a sharp object: *a cut on my knee.* Same sign used for: **scratch.**

- [Location of a cut on the hand] Move the extended right index fingertip, palm facing left, across the back of the left *open hand* or other location of a cut.

cut[2] *v.* To shorten (hair): *I just cut my hair before the trip.* Same sign used for: **haircut.**

- [Mime cutting hair] Move both *V hands*, palms facing down, back over each shoulder while opening and closing the fingers of the *V hands* repeatedly as the hands move.

cut[3] *v.* To separate or remove with scissors: *to cut the wrapping paper the right size.*

- [Represents cutting across a piece of paper] Move the right *V hand*, fingers pointing left, across the fingertips of the left *open hand*, palm facing down, with a deliberate movement while closing the fingers together.

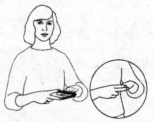

cut[4] or **cut out** *v., v. phrase* (alternate sign)

- [Represents cutting around a clipping] Move the right *V hand*, palm facing left, around the fingertips of the left *open hand*, palm facing up, while opening and closing the right index and middle fingers with a repeated movement as the hand moves.

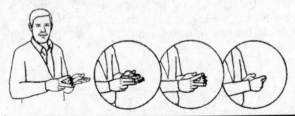

cut back *v. phrase.* See sign for LESS[1].

cut class See sign for SKIP[1].

cut down *v. phrase.* See sign for HARVEST[1].

cute *adj.* Pleasingly pretty or endearing: *a cute doll.*
- With the right thumb extended, brush the fingers of the right *U hand*, palm facing down, downward on the chin while changing into a *10 hand*.

cut off *v. phrase.* See signs for INTERCEPT[1], TRUNCATE.

cutthroat *adj.* See sign for RISK[1].

cycle[1] *n.* One complete series of changes or events: *The washing machine finished its cycle.*
- [Represents the circular or continuous nature of a cycle] Move the extended right index finger in a circle around the opening formed by the left *modified C hand* held in front of the left side of the body, palm facing down and fingers pointing down.

cycle[2] *n.* See signs for CIRCLE[1], YEAR-ROUND.

cylinder *n.* **1.** A shape with a circular top and bottom and long straight sides: *draw a cylinder in geometry.* **2.** A hollow object of this shape, with one or both ends open, for use as a container: *The flour is kept in the cylinder on the shelf.* Same sign used for: **barrel, drum.**
- [Shape of a cylinder] Move both *C hands,* palms facing each other, from in front of each side of the waist straight upward.

cylinders *pl. n.* See sign for ENGINE[1].

Czechoslovakia *n.* A former republic in central Europe: *a writer born in Czechoslovakia.* Related form: **Czech** *n., adj.*
- [Initialized sign] Move the right *C hand,* palm facing left, from the left shoulder diagonally down to the right side of the waist.

Czech Republic *n.* A republic in central Europe: *The capital of the Czech Republic is Prague.* Related form: **Czech** *n., adj.*

■ Move the fingers of the right *open hand,* palm facing in and fingers pointing up, from the mouth upward to in front of the right cheek. Then, beginning with both extended index fingers pointing to each side of the forehead, palms facing in, twist the hands forward and outward, ending with the palms facing forward.

dad *n.* See signs for FATHER[1,2]. Diminutive form: **daddy.**

daily *adj.* **1.** Of, done, or occurring every day: *Daily attendance at school is required.* **2.** Pertaining to the home, family, and other everyday matters: *to do one's daily chores.* —*adv.* **3.** Every day: *to exercise daily.* Same sign used for: **casual, domestic, everyday, every day, ordinary, routine, usual.**

- ■ [Similar to sign for **tomorrow,** only repeated to indicate recurrence] Move the palm side of the right *A hand* forward on the right side of the chin with a repeated movement.

dairy *adj.* Of or made with milk or milk products: *Go to the dairy section of the store for bulk cheese.*

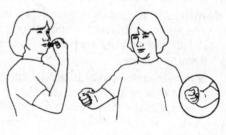

- ■ [**food** + **milk**[1]] Bring the fingertips of the right *flattened O hand* to the lips, palm facing down. Then, beginning with the right *C hand,* palm facing left, in front of the right side of the chest, squeeze the fingers together with a double movement forming an *S hand.*

Dallas *n.* A city in northeastern Texas: *to live in Dallas.*

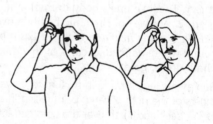

- ■ [Initialized sign] Tap the fingertips of the right *D hand,* palm facing in, on the right side of the forehead with a double movement.

dam[1] *n.* A wall built across a stream or river to hold back the flow of water: *When the dam broke, the town was flooded.*

- ■ [**water** + shape of dam's retaining wall] Tap the index-finger side of the right *W hand,* palm facing left, against the chin with a double movement. Then bring the little-finger side of the right *open hand,* palm facing in and fingers pointing left, downward in front of the face to land on the back of the left *open hand* held across the chest, palm facing in and fingers pointing right.

dam[2] *n.* (alternate sign)

- ■ [**water** + curved shape of dam] Tap the index-finger side of the right *W hand* against the chin with a double movement. Then, beginning with both *curved hands* in front of the chest, palms facing in, move the hands in an arc to each side of the body, ending with the palms facing each other in front of each shoulder.

damage *n.* **1.** Harm or injury that reduces something's value or usefulness: *The crash caused severe damage to the car.* —*v.* **2.** To cause such harm or injury: *Wet cups will damage the finish on the table.* Same sign used for: **abolish, demolish, destroy, ruin.**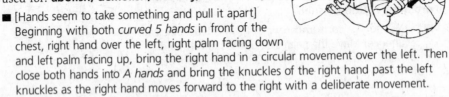

- ■ [Hands seem to take something and pull it apart] Beginning with both *curved 5 hands* in front of the chest, right hand over the left, right palm facing down and left palm facing up, bring the right hand in a circular movement over the left. Then close both hands into *A hands* and bring the knuckles of the right hand past the left knuckles as the right hand moves forward to the right with a deliberate movement.

damn *interj.* A condemning utterance, used to express anger, annoyance, etc.: *Damn! I slammed the car door on my finger!* Same sign used for: **darn.**

- ■ [Initialized sign similar to sign for **curse**[1]] Move the right *D hand,* palm facing left, from in front of the right shoulder forward with a deliberate movement.

damp *adj.* See signs for WET[1,2].

dance *v.* **1.** To move one's body in rhythm to music: *Dance with me.* —*n.* **2.** A series of rhythmic bodily movements performed to music: *an exciting new dance with a Latin beat.* **3.** A social gathering where dancing occurs: *go to a dance.* Same sign used for: **ball, disco, gala.**

- ■ [Represents legs moving in rhythm to dance music] Swing the fingers of the right *V hand,* palm facing in and fingers pointing down, back and forth over the upturned left *open hand* with a double movement.

Dane *n.* See signs for DENMARK[1,2].

danger *n.* Risk of injury or harm: *These days, there is danger in the city.* Related form: **dangerous** *adj.* Same sign used for: **endanger, harassment, harm, hazard, peril, risk, threat, unsafe.**

- ■ [Movement of hidden danger coming at a person] Move the thumb of the right *10 hand,* palm facing left, upward on the back of the left *A hand,* palm facing in, with a repeated movement.

Danish *adj.* See signs for DENMARK[1,2].

dare[1] *v.* To have the courage to try: *dare to cross the river.*
- Move the right *X hand,* palm facing left, from the chin forward.

dare[2] *v.* See signs for CHALLENGE, GANG[1].

dark *adj.* Being without light: *a dark room with the shutters drawn.* Related form: **darkness** *n.* Same sign used for: **dim, dusk, shadow.**
- [Hands shade the eyes from light] Beginning with both *open hands* in front of each shoulder, palms facing back and fingers pointing up, bring the hands past each other in front of the face, ending with the wrists crossed and the fingers pointing in opposite directions at an angle.

darken *v.* See signs for DIM[1,2].

darling *n.* **1.** A person who is dear to another: *She is my darling.* —*adj.* **2.** Very dear; cherished: *my darling wife.*
- [**my** + **embrace**[1]] Lay the palm side of the right *open hand* against the chest. Then, with the wrists of both *S hands* crossed in front of the chest, palms facing in, bring the arms back against the chest.

darn[1] *adj., adv., interj.* Damned: *That darn cat keeps eating the plants.* Same sign used for: **drat.**
- Forcibly insert the thumb of the right *5 hand,* palm facing forward, into the opening of the left *S hand* held in front of the chest.

darn[2] *adj., adv., interj.* See sign for DAMN.

dart *n.* A small, pointed weapon usually thrown by hand: *to throw a dart at the board.*
- [Mime throwing a dart] Beginning with the right *F hand* near the right side of the head, palm facing left, bring the hand forward while releasing the fingers into a *5 hand* in front of the right side of the body.

data *pl.n.* See sign for INFORMATION.

daughter[1] *n.* A female child in relation to her parents: *my oldest daughter.*

- [**girl**[1] + **baby**] Bring the thumb of the right *10 hand* downward on the right side of the chin. Then swing the right hand down while opening into an *open hand*, ending with the bent right arm cradled on the upturned bent left arm held across the body.

daughter[2] *n.* (alternate sign)

- [Begins at the female area of the head + **baby**[1]] Beginning with the index-finger side of the right *B hand*, palm facing left, touching the right side of the chin, swing the right hand downward, ending with the bent right arm cradled in the bent left arm held across the body.

daughter-in-law *n.* The wife of one's son: *My son and daughter-in-law came to dinner.*

- [**daughter**[1,2] + **law**] Beginning with the index-finger side of the right *B hand*, palm facing left, touching the right side of the chin, swing the right hand downward, ending with the bent right arm cradled in the bent left arm held across the body. Then place the palm side of the right *L hand*, palm facing left, first on the fingers and then near the heel of the left *open hand*, palm facing up.

daven *v.* To recite the Jewish prayers; pray: *He davens every morning.* Related form: **davening** *n.*

- [Mime bowing down while davening] With both *open hands* together in front of the chest, palms facing each other and fingers angled up, move the hands and body forward at the same time with a repeated movement.

day *n.* **1.** The period between sunrise and sunset: *a nice sunny day.* **2.** A period of 24 hours: *to complete the project in one day.*

- [Symbolizes the movement of the sun across the sky] Beginning with the bent right elbow resting on the back of the left hand held across the body, palm facing down, bring the extended right index finger from pointing up in front of the right shoulder, palm facing left, downward toward the left elbow.

daydream *v., n.* See sign for DREAM.

dazed *adj.* See sign for SHOCK².

deacon¹ *n.* An officer of the church: *the deacon's role.*

- [Initialized sign similar to sign for **king**] Move the fingertips of the right *D hand,* palm facing in, from touching first near the left shoulder downward to touch again near the right side of the waist.

deacon² *n.* (alternate sign)

- [Initialized sign similar to sign for **member**²] Move the fingertips of the right *D hand,* palm facing in, from touching first near the left shoulder across the chest to touch again near the right shoulder.

dead *adj.* See sign for DIE¹.

deadline *n.* The time by which something should be finished, accomplished, etc.: *He missed the deadline for applying to college.*

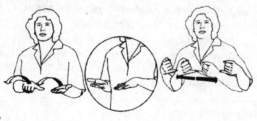

- [**die**¹ + **line**] Beginning with both *open hands* in front of the body, right palm facing down and left palm facing up, flip the hands to the right, turning the right palm up and the left palm down. Then, beginning with both extended little fingers pointing toward each other in front of the chest, palms facing in, move the hands away from each other.

deadlock *adj.* Same sign used for STUCK.

deaf¹ *adj.* Being partially or wholly unable to hear: *a deaf person.*

- [Points to the ear and mouth to indicate that a person cannot hear or talk] Touch the tip or side of the extended right index finger first to near the right ear and then to near the right side of the mouth.

deaf[2] *adj.* (alternate sign)

■ [Indicates that the ear is closed] Touch the extended right index finger to near the right ear. Then move the right hand down in front of the chest while changing into a *B hand*, ending with the index-finger side of both *B hands* together in front of the body, palms facing down.

deal[1] *v.* To be concerned (with); occupy oneself or itself (with): *Math deals with numbers.*

■ [Initialized sign similar to sign for **coordinate**] With the fingertips of both *D hands* together, palms facing each other and right hand closer to the chest than the left hand, move the hands forward and then back toward the chest.

deal[2] *v.* See signs for AGREE, PASS AROUND, PASS OUT[1,2].

dealer *n.* A person who makes a living by buying and selling: *to buy a new car from the dealer.* Same sign used for: **salesperson, seller.**

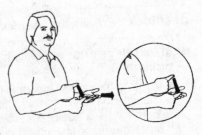

■ [**sell** + **person marker**] Beginning with both *flattened O hands* held in front of each side of the chest, palms facing down and fingers pointing down, swing the fingertips forward and back by twisting the wrists upward with a double movement. Then move both *open hands*, palms facing each other, downward along each side of the body.

dear *adj.* See sign for EMBRACE[1].

death *n.* See sign for DIE[1].

death penalty See sign for CAPITAL PUNISHMENT.

debate[1] *v.* **1.** To discuss opposing viewpoints: *to debate the issues during a campaign.* —*n.* **2.** A discussion involving opposing viewpoints: *Neither candidate won the debate.* Same sign used for: **arbitration.**

■ [**discuss** formed while moving toward another person] Tap the side of the right extended index finger, palm facing in and finger pointing left, across the upturned left *open hand*, first on the palm and then again on the fingers as the left hand moves forward slightly.

debate[2] *v.* See signs for ARGUE[1,2].

debt *n.* See sign for AFFORD[1].

decal *n.* See sign for LABEL.

decay *v.* See sign for WEAR OUT.

deceive[1] *v.* To mislead by a false appearance or statement: *They deceived the teacher.* Related forms: **deceit** *n.*, **deceitful** *adj.* Same sign used for: **betray, defraud, fraud.**

- With the index and little fingers of both hands extended, both palms facing down, slide the palm side of the right hand from the wrist forward on the back of the lift hand.

deceive[2] *v.* See signs for BETRAY[1], CHEAT[1,2], FRAUD. Related form: **deceit** *n.*

decide[1] *v.* To make up one's mind; come to a conclusion: *decide where to go.* Related form: **decision** *n.* Same sign used for: **determine, make up your mind, officially.**

- [**think** + laying one's thoughts down decisively] Move the extended right index finger from the right side of the forehead, palm facing left, down in front of the chest while changing into an *F hand,* ending with both *F hands* moving downward in front of the body, palms facing each other.

decide[2] *v.* (alternate sign) Related form: **decision** *n.* Same sign used for: **determine.**

- [**think**[1] + an initialized movement that represents laying one's thoughts down decisively] Move the extended right index finger from the right side of the forehead, palm facing left, down in front of the chest while changing into a *D hand,* ending with both *D hands* moving downward in front of the body, palms facing each other.

decimal *n.* A fraction based on the number 10, usually written with a dot (decimal point) before the numerator: *One half would be expressed in decimals as .5, or five tenths.*

- [**base**[1] + **ten**] Move the right *B hand,* palm facing out and fingers pointing up, to the right under the palm of the left *open hand* held across the chest, while changing into a *10 hand.*

decimal point *n.* See sign for PERIOD[1].

deck *n.* A pack of playing cards: *Cut and shuffle the deck so we can start the game.*

- ■ [Represents lifting a deck of cards and giving cards to another person] Beginning with the thumb of the right *flattened C hand,* palm angled left, on the palm of the left *open hand,* palm facing up, move both hands forward in a short arc.

declaration *n.* See sign for SENTENCE.

declare *v.* See sign for ANNOUNCE. Related form: **declaration** *n.*

decline[1] *v.* **1.** To lose or fail in power, strength, or value: *His health declined with age.* —*n.* **2.** A change to a lower or worse level: *a decline in prices.* Same sign used for: **deteriorate, diminish.**

- ■ [Hands move downward to indicate a decline] Beginning with both *10 hands* in front of each shoulder, palms facing in and thumbs pointing up, move both hands down in front of each side of the chest.

decline[2] *v., n.* (alternate sign)

- ■ [Shows a declining terrain] Move the right *bent hand* from near the right side of the head, fingers angled forward and palm facing out, downward and forward in an arc.

decline[3] *v., n.* (alternate sign) Same sign used for: **deteriorate.**

- ■ [Shows a movement downward] Touch the little-finger side of the right *open hand,* palm facing in, first near the shoulder, then near the elbow, and finally near the wrist of the extended left arm.

decline[4] *v.* To refuse politely: *to decline to attend the reception.* Same sign used for: **drop, refuse, turn down.**

- ■ [**true** + **excuse**] Move the extended right index finger from pointing up in front of the mouth, palm facing left, downward while opening the hand, ending with the fingers of the right *open hand* wiping forward across the length of the upturned left *open hand.*

246

decode *v.* To translate the meaning of: *to decode the hidden message.*

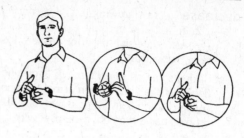

- [Initialized sign similar to sign for **translate**] Beginning with the fingertips of both *D hands* touching in front of the chest, right palm facing down and left palm facing up, twist the hands in opposite directions with a double movement.

decoder *n.* A device that decodes: *to turn on the decoder.*

- [Initialized sign similar to sign for **caption**] Beginning with the index-finger side of both *D hands* touching in front of the chest, palms facing forward, move the hands apart to in front of each side of the chest with a double movement.

decorate[1] *v.* To add something to in order to make more attractive; adorn; embellish: *to decorate the cake.* Related form: **decoration** *n.*

- [Hands seem to arrange ornamental items] Beginning with both *flattened O hands* in front of each side of the chest, palms facing forward, move them in alternating circles with a repeated movement.

decorate[2] *v.* (alternate sign) Related form: **decoration** *n.* Same sign used for: **elaborate, fancy, ornament.**

- [Hands seem to arrange ornamental items] Beginning with both *curved 5 hands* in front of each side of the head, palms facing forward, move them upward and toward each other with a double movement.

decorate[3] *v.* (alternate sign) Related form: **decoration** *n.*

- [Initialized sign showing hands arranging ornamental items] Beginning with the fingers of both *D hands* touching in front of the left side of the chest, palms facing each other, move the hands in an arc in front of the chest, twisting the wrists to trade positions of the hands several times as the hands move.

decrease[1] *n.* **1.** A growing less: *a decrease in spending.* —*v.* **2.** To make or become less: *I plan to decrease my use of salt.* Same sign used for: **lessen, lose, loss, reduce, reduction.**

■ [Taking some off to decrease it] Beginning with the fingers of the right *U hand* across the fingers of the left *U hand,* both palms facing down, take the right fingers off by flipping the right hand over with a double movement.

decrease[2] *n., v.* (alternate sign, used especially to indicate a total reduction or depletion) Same sign used for: **deflate, diminish, reduce, shrink.**

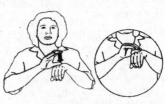

■ [Shows amount decreasing in size] Beginning with the thumb of the right *C hand,* palm angled forward, on the back of the left *curved hand,* palm facing down, close the right fingers to the thumb, forming a *flattened O hand.*

decrease[3] *n., v.* (alternate sign) Same sign used for: **lessen, reduce.**

■ [Shows decreasing size] Beginning with both extended index fingers pointing forward in front of the chest, right hand over the left hand and palms facing each other, bring the hands toward each other.

dedicate *v.* See sign for DEVOTED. Related form: **dedication** *n.*

deduct *v.* See sign for SUBTRACT.

deed *n.* See signs for ACT[1], ACTIVE[1], DO.

deep *adj.* **1.** Having a great distance from top to bottom: *deep water at one end of the pool.* **2.** Not superficial; profound: *a deep discussion of all aspects of the problem.* Same sign used for: **depth, detail, in depth.**

■ [Indicates direction of bottom of something deep] Move the extended right index finger, palm facing down, downward near the fingertips of the left *5 hand,* palm facing down.

deer *n.* A cud-chewing mammal that has hoofs and, in the male, antlers; known for its grace: *The deer bounded off into the woods.* Same sign used for: **reindeer.**

■ [A deer's antlers] Tap the thumbs of both *5 hands,* palms facing forward, against each side of the forehead with a repeated movement.

deface *v.* To spoil the appearance of: *to deface the wall with graffiti.*

- [Mime writing on a wall + **spoil**[1]] With the right *modified X hand,* palm facing forward, draw an imaginary jagged line in front of the face. Then, beginning with the right *X hand* resting on top of the left *X hand* near the chest, palms facing in opposite directions, move the right hand forward in an arc.

defeat[1] *v.* To overcome, as in a war or game: *to defeat the enemy in hand-to-hand combat.* Same sign used for: **beat, conquer, overcome, subdue, vanquish.**

- [Represents forcing another down in defeat] Move the right *S hand* from in front of the right shoulder, palm facing forward, downward and forward, ending with the right wrist across the wrist of the left *S hand,* both palms facing down.

defeat[2] *v.* (alternate sign) Same sign used for: **beat.**

- [Directing a single blow] Beginning with the right *S hand* in front of the right shoulder, palm facing left, move the hand quickly forward while opening the fingers to form an *H hand.*

defeat[3] *v.* (alternate sign, used when the speaker is defeated by someone or something) **1.** To conquer or overcome, as in a conflict: *Their team defeated our team with skillful maneuvers.* **2.** To overcome or overpower: *I was defeated by my fears.* Same sign used for: **beat, overcome.**

- [Directional sign for **defeat**[1] formed toward oneself] Beginning with the extended left index finger, palm facing in and finger pointing right, on the wrist of the right *S hand,* palm facing up, bring the right bent arm back toward the right side of the chest, pushing the index finger back against the chest as the hand moves.

defecation *n.* See sign for FECES.

defend[1] *v.* To guard from harm or attack: *She swore to defend him from slander.* Related forms: **defense** *n.,* **defensive** *adj.* See also sign for GUARD. Same sign used for: **protect, security, shield.**

- [Blocking oneself from harm] With the wrists of both *S hands* crossed in front of the chest, palms facing in opposite directions, move the hands forward with a short double movement.

defend

defend[2] *v.* (alternate sign) Related forms: **defense** *n.*, **defensive** *adj.* See also sign for GUARD.

- [Initialized sign blocking oneself from harm] With the wrists of both *D hands* crossed in front of the chest, palms facing in opposite directions, move the hands forward with a short double movement.

defensive *adj.* See sign for RESIST.

defer[1] *v.* To put off until a later time: *The committee deferred a decision until there was a quorum present.* Same sign used for **delay, procrastinate, put off.**

- [Represents taking something and putting it off several times] Beginning with both *F hands* in front of the body, palms facing each other and the left hand nearer to the body than the right hand, move both hands forward in a series of small arcs.

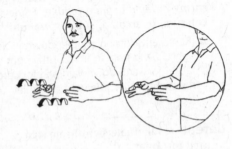

defer[2] *v.* See sign for POSTPONE.

deficiency *n.* The lack of something needed: *an iron deficiency in the blood.* Related form: **deficient** *adj.* Same sign used for: **inadequate, insufficient.**

- [**not**[1] + **enough**] Bring the extended thumb of the right *10 hand* from under the chin, palm facing left, forward with a deliberate movement. Then brush the palm side of the right *open hand*, palm facing down, across the index-finger side of the left *S hand*, palm facing right.

define *v.* See signs for DESCRIBE[1,2]. Related form: **definition** *n.*

deflate *v.* See sign for DECREASE[2].

deformed *adj.* Having the natural form changed or distorted; misshapen: *The boy's left arm is deformed.*

- [**wrong** + **grow**] Bring the bent fingers of the right *Y hand*, palm facing in, back against the chin with a deliberate movement. Then bring the right *flattened O hand*, palm facing in, up through the left *C hand*, palm facing right and fingers pointing right, while spreading the right fingers into a *5 hand*.

defraud *v.* See signs for DECEIVE[1], FRAUD[1].

degree[1] *n.* A unit for measuring temperature: *It's twenty-eight degrees outside.*

- [Initialized sign similar to sign for **temperature**] Move the fingers of the right *D hand,* palm facing left, up and down with a double movement on the extended left index finger, palm facing right.

degree[2] *n.* See signs for DIPLOMA[1,2,3].

dejected *adj.* See signs for DEPRESSED[1,2,3].

Delaware *n.* An eastern state: *to move to Delaware when you retire.*

- [Initialized sign showing that Delaware was the first state] Beginning with the right *D hand* in front of the right shoulder, palm facing forward and index finger pointing up, move the hand upward while twisting the palm forward.

delay *n., v.* See signs for DEFER[1], LATE, POSTPONE.

delegate[1] *n.* **1.** A person given authority to act for others: *a delegate to the political convention.* —*v.* **2.** To give (powers or functions) to another as one's agent: *He seems unable to delegate tasks to his subordinates.*

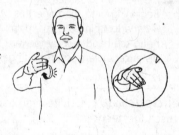

- [Initialized sign] Brush the fingers of the right *D hand,* palm facing in and index finger pointing left, downward on the right side of the chest with a double movement.

delegate[2] *n., v.* (alternate sign)

- [**gift**[1] + **responsibility**] Move both *X hands,* palms facing each other, from in front of the body forward in simultaneous arcs. Then tap the fingertips of both *R hands* on the right shoulder, with a double movement.

delete *v.* See signs for ELIMINATE[1,2].

deliberate *v.* See sign for MULL.

delicate *adj.* **1.** Requiring skill, caution, or tact: *a delicate situation.* **2.** Skillful, careful, and precise: *a delicate touch in painting miniatures.*

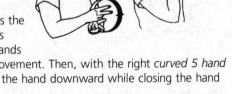

■ **[careful + precious]** Beginning with the little-finger side of the right *K hand* across the index-finger side of the left *K hand*, palms facing in opposite directions, move the hands upward and forward in a large circular movement. Then, with the right *curved 5 hand* in front of the chin, palm facing in, bring the hand downward while closing the hand into an *S hand.*

delicious[1] *adj.* Highly pleasing to the taste: *This sandwich is absolutely delicious.* Same sign used for: **tasty.**

■ Touch the bent middle finger of the right *5 hand* to the lips, palm facing in, and then twist the right hand quickly forward.

delicious[2] *adj.* (alternate sign) Same sign used for: **tasty.**

■ **[As if savoring something from the lips]** Beginning with the fingertips of the right *8 hand* touching the lips, palm facing in, bring the hand quickly forward a short distance while closing the fingers into an *A hand.*

delicious[3] *adj.* (alternate sign) Same sign used for: **tasty.**

■ **[As if savoring something from the lips]** Beginning with the fingertips of the left *8 hand* touching the lips and the right *8 hand* held somewhat forward of the face, both palms facing in, bring both hands quickly forward a short distance while closing the fingers into both *A hands.*

delighted *adj.* See sign for HAPPY.

deliver[1] *v.* To set free from danger or evil: *The rescuers delivered the hostages without harm.* Related form: **deliverance** *n.*

■ **[Initialized sign similar to sign for save**[1]**]** Beginning with both *D hands* crossed at the wrists in front of the chest, palms facing in opposite directions, twist the wrists and move the hands apart, ending with the hands in front of each shoulder, palms facing forward.

deliver[2] *v.* See sign for BRING.

deluxe *adj.* See signs for FANCY[1,2].

demand[1] *v.* To ask or ask for with authority; claim as a right: *I demand to see the supervisor.*

- [Initialized sign similar to sign for **require**[1]] With the fingertips of the right *D hand*, palm facing left, touching the palm of the left *open hand* bring both hands back toward the chest.

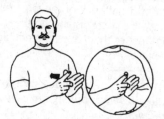

demand[2] *v.* (alternate sign) Same sign used for: **insist, require.**

- With the extended right index finger, palm facing in, touching the palm of the left *open hand* bring both hands back toward the chest.

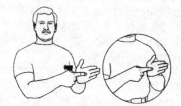

demise *n.* See sign for DIE[1].

Democrat *n.* A member of the Democratic party: *The polls predict that a Democrat will win the election.*

- [Initialized sign] Shake the right *D hand*, palm facing forward, from side to side in front of the right shoulder.

demolish *v.* See sign for DAMAGE.

demon *n.* See sign for DEVIL.

demonstrate *v.* See signs for DISPLAY[1,2], SHOW[1], SHOW ME. Related form: **demonstration** *n.*

demote *v.* See sign for LOW[2].

Denmark[1] *n.* A country in northern Europe: *Shakespeare's Hamlet takes place in Denmark.* Related forms: **Dane** *n.*, **Danish** *adj., n.*

- [Represents the ships for which the seafaring Danes are known] Move the right *3 hand*, palm facing in, from left to right in a wavy movement in front of the chest.

Denmark[2] *n.* (alternate sign) Related forms: **Dane** *n.*, **Danish** *adj.*

- [Initialized sign] Move the right *D hand,* palm facing left, from in front of the right side of the forehead downward a short distance to the left in front of the face with a double movement.

denomination *n.* A religious sect: *to study the differences among Protestant denominations.*

- [Initialized sign similar to sign for **religion**] Beginning with the palm side of the right *D hand* touching near the left shoulder, move the hand forward while twisting the palm down.

dent *v.* **1.** To form a depression in, as from a blow or pressure: *He dented the bumper on the new car.* —*n.* **2.** A depression caused by a blow or pressure: *a small dent in the fender.* Same sign used for: **bend, bent.**

- [Bending of a surface] Beginning with the fingertips of both *open hands* touching in front of the chest, palms facing in, bend the fingers toward the chest while keeping fingertips together.

dentist *n.* A doctor who treats diseases of and damage to the teeth and gums: *The dentist had to fill three cavities in my teeth.*

- [Initialized sign formed similar to **tooth**] Tap the fingers of the right *D hand,* palm facing in and index finger pointing up, against the right side of the teeth with a repeated movement.

dentures *pl. n.* See signs for FALSE TEETH[1,2].

deny[1] *v.* To declare not to be true: *to deny the rumor.*

- [**not**[1] with a repeated movement] Beginning with the thumb of the right *A hand* under the chin, palm facing left, and the left *A hand* held somewhat forward, palm facing right, move the right hand forward while moving the left hand back. Repeat the movement with the left hand.

deny[2] *v.* (alternate sign)

-  [Hand seems to hold oneself back or suppress oneself] Beginning with the fingertips of the right *C hand* on the upper chest, palm facing in, bring the hand straight down while quickly closing into an *S hand.*

deny[3] *v.* To withhold from (oneself) things one wants: *to deny myself sweets.*

-  [Pushing down of desire in oneself] Beginning with both *10 hands* near each other on the upper chest, palms facing forward and thumbs pointing down, move both hands downward simultaneously.

deodorant[1] *n.* A liquid preparation for inhibiting or masking unpleasant odors, applied by spraying: *to use an underarm deodorant.*

-  [Mime spraying on deodorant] With the left arm raised above the head, bend the extended right index finger up and down with a double movement near the left armpit.

deodorant[2] *n.* A liquid or solid preparation for inhibiting or masking unpleasant odors, applied by spreading from a hand-held container: *to put on a roll-on deodorant.*

-  [Mime using a roll-on or solid deodorant] With the left arm extended above the head, move the index-finger side of the right *S hand* in a short downward double movement near the left armpit.

depart *v.* See signs for FORSAKE, GO[2], LEAVE[1], PARTING. Related form: **departure** *n.*

department *n.* One of the official parts or branches of an organization, as a government or business: *the payroll department.* Same sign used for: **division.**

-  [Initialized sign similar to sign for **class**] Beginning with the fingertips of both *D hands* touching in front of the chest, palms facing each other, bring the hands away from each other in outward arcs while turning the palms in, ending with the little fingers together.

depend or **depend on** *v. or v. phrase.* To rely for help: *I can always depend on my mother.* Related form: **dependency** *n.,* **dependent** *adj.* Same sign used for: **cling to, contingent, rely.**

- [Represents resting on another] With the extended right index finger across the extended left index finger, palms facing down, move both fingers down slightly.

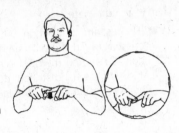

dependable *adj.* Capable of being relied on: *I need a dependable babysitter.* Same sign used for: **contingency, count on, reliable, rely on.**

- [**depend** formed with a double movement] With the extended right index finger across the extended left index finger, palms facing down, move both fingers down slightly with a double movement.

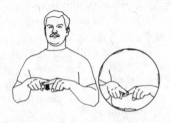

dependent *n.* An individual who depends upon another for financial support: *The single mother has three dependents.*

- [**dependable** + **person marker**] With the extended right index finger across the extended left index finger, palms facing down, move both fingers down slightly with a double movement. Then move both *open hands*, palms facing each other, downward along the sides of the body.

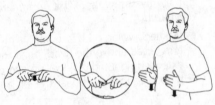

deplete *v.* See signs for RUN OUT OF[1,2].

deposit[1] *v.* **1.** To put (money) in the bank: *I'd better deposit my check before the bank closes.* —*n.* **2.** Money put in the bank for safekeeping: *My bank deposit was small this week.*

- [Sealing a deposit envelope with the thumbs] Beginning with the thumbs of both *10 hands* touching in front of the chest, both palms facing down, bring the hands downward and apart by twisting the wrists.

deposit[2] *v.* (alternate sign)

- [Giving a sum of money to a bank teller] Move the right *C hand,* palm facing forward, from in front of the right shoulder forward by turning the wrist down.

deposit[3] *v.* See sign for INVEST[1].

depreciation *n.* The gradual decrease in the value of tangible property that occurs because of wear and tear: *claim the depreciation of the rental property as a deduction on your taxes.* Related form: **depreciate** *v.*

- [**cost²** + **decline¹**] Tap the fingertips of both *F hands* together, palms facing each other, with a repeated movement. Then, beginning with the thumbs of both *10 hands* pointing up in front of the chest, palms facing each other, move both hands down in wavy movements in front of the body.

depressed¹ *adj.* Being low-spirited: *She feels depressed about losing her job.* Related forms: **depressing** *adj.,* **depression** *n.* Same sign used for: **dejected, despair, discouraged.**

- [Initialized sign showing emotions moving downward in the body] Beginning with the fingertips of both *D hands* on each side of the chest, palms facing in and index fingers pointing toward each other, move the hands downward with a simultaneous movement.

depressed² *adj.* (alternate sign) Related forms: **depressing** *adj.,* **depression** *n.* Same sign used for: **dejected, despair, discouraged.**

- [Emotions moving downward in the body] Beginning with the fingertips of both *5 hands* on each side of the chest, palms facing in and fingers pointing toward each other, move the hands downward with a simultaneous movement.

depressed³ *adj.* (alternate sign) Related forms: **depressing** *adj.,* **depression** *n.* Same sign used for: **dejected, despair, discouraged.**

- [Feelings moving downward in the body] Beginning with the bent middle fingers of both *5 hands* on each side of the chest, palms facing in and fingers pointing toward each other, move the hands downward with a simultaneous movement.

depth *n.* See sign for DEEP.

descend¹ *v.* To move from a higher to a lower place; go down: *descend the stairs.*

- [Movement of someone or something to a lower place] Move the extended right index finger, palm facing down, downward with a wavy movement from near the right side of the head to in front of the body.

descend[2] *v.* (alternate sign, used only for people)

- [Represents a person's legs moving to a lower place] Beginning with the fingertips of the right *V hand*, palm facing in, pointing down on the upturned left *open hand*, move the right hand downward in an arc off the left fingertips.

descend[3] *v.* To descend by grasping with the hands: *descend the ladder.* Same sign used for: **climb down.**

- [Mime climbing down a ladder] Beginning with both *S hands* in front of the shoulders, palms facing forward and right hand higher than the left, move the hands downward with an alternating movement.

describe[1] *v.* To tell about in words: *to describe the event in detail.* Related form: **description** *n.* Same sign used for: **define, definition, direct, direction, explain, explanation, instruct, instruction.**

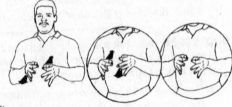

- Beginning with both *F hands* in front of the chest, palms facing each other and fingers pointing forward, move the hands forward and back with an alternating movement.

describe[2] *v.* (alternate sign) Related form: **description** *n.* Same sign used for: **define, definition, direct, direction.**

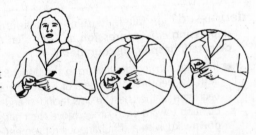

- Beginning with both *D hands* in front of the chest, palms facing each other and index fingers pointing forward, move the hands forward and back with an alternating movement.

desert[1] *n.* A dry, barren, sandy region: *The Sahara is a vast desert in northern Africa.*

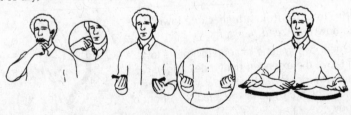

- [**dry + dirt + area**[1,2,3,4]] Pull the side of the index finger of the right *X hand*, palm facing down, from left to right across the chin. Then, beginning with both *flattened*

O hands in front of each side of the body, palms facing up, with a double movement move the thumb of each hand smoothly across each fingertip, starting with the little fingers and ending as *A hands.* Then, beginning with the fingers of both *open hands* pointing toward each other at an angle, move the hands apart in large arcs to each side of the body.

desert[2] *v.* See signs for ABANDON[1], LEAVE[1].

deserve *v.* See signs for COLLECT[1,2], EARN.

design *v.* **1.** To conceive and make preliminary drawings or plans for: *to design a new apartment building.* —*n.* **2.** An outline or plan showing features to be executed: *The artist sketched the design for the brochure.* **3.** The pattern of or on something: *The design of the fabric had bold flowers.* Same sign used for: **draw, drawing, draft.**

- [Initialized sign similar to sign for **art**] Move the fingertips of the right *D hand,* palm facing left, down the palm of the left *open hand* with a wavy movement. The sign may be repeated for the noun form.

desire *v.* See signs for WANT, WISH.

desist *v.* To stop: *ordered to desist from smuggling across the border.* Same sign used for: **stop.**

- [Natural gesture used when asking another to stop doing something] Beginning with the fingers of both *5 hands* in front of each side of the chest, palms facing in, twist the wrists to flip the hands in a quick movement, ending with the palms facing down.

desk[1] *n.* A piece of furniture with a flat top for writing and often drawers or compartments: *to study at my desk.*

- [Initialized sign similar to sign for **table**[1]] With the elbow of the bent right arm resting on the left *open hand* held across the chest, palm facing down, tap the heel of the upturned right *D hand* on top of the left arm with a repeated movement.

desk[2] *n.* (alternate sign) Same sign used for: **table.**

- [**table**[2] + shape of a desk] Pat the forearm of the bent right arm with a double movement on the bent left arm held across the chest. Then, beginning with the fingers of both *open hands* together in front of the chest, palms facing down, move the hands apart to in front of each shoulder and then straight down, ending with the palms facing each other.

desk[3] *n.* See sign for TABLE.

despair *n., v.* See signs for DEPRESSED[1,2,3].

desperate *adj.* Nearly hopeless and driven to take any risk: *The day after he quit smoking, he became desperate for a cigarette.*

■ [**must** + **have**[1,2]] Move the bent index finger of the right *X hand*, palm facing forward, downward with a deliberate movement in front of the right side of the body while bending the wrist down. Then bring the fingertips of both *bent hands*, palms facing in, back to touch each side of the chest.

despise *v.* See signs for DETEST[1,2], HATE.

despite *prep.* See sign for ANYWAY.

dessert *n.* A course of sweet food served at the end of a meal: *Let's have ice cream for dessert.*

■ [Initialized sign] Tap the fingertips of both *D hands*, palms facing each other, together with a repeated movement in front of the chest.

destiny *n.* One's fate: *It was her destiny to become famous.*

■ [**your**[1] + **future**[1,2]] Push the palm of the right *open hand*, palm facing forward and fingers pointing up, forward in front of the chest. Then move the right *open hand* palm facing left and fingers pointing up, forward in an arc near the right side of the head.

destitute *adj.* See sign for POOR[1].

destroy *v.* See sign for DAMAGE.

destruction *n.* See sign for BREAK DOWN.

detach *v.* See sign for DISCONNECT.

detail *n.* See sign for DEEP. Shared idea of careful attention to important matters.

detain *v.* To keep from leaving or proceeding: *The police detained the suspect for questioning.*

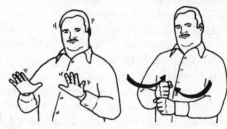

■ [**settle** + **hold**[1]] Beginning with both *5 hands* in front of each side of the chest, palms facing forward and fingers pointing up, shake the hands back and forth slightly. Then bring the hands together to place the little-finger side of the right *S hand* on the index-finger side of the left *S hand,* both palms facing in, in front of the chest.

detect *v.* To discover or notice: *to detect the smell of gas in the room.*

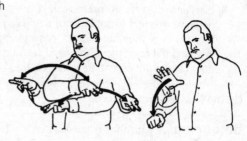

■ [**observe**[1] + **capture**[1]] Beginning with the right *V hand* in front of the right shoulder, palm facing down, and the left *V hand* in front of the left side of the chest, palm facing down, move both hands from side to side with a double movement. Then, beginning with the right *5 hand* in front of the right shoulder, palm facing forward, move the hand suddenly forward while closing into an *S hand.*

detective *n.* A person whose business is to obtain information and evidence, as of criminal activity: *They plan to hire a detective to find the missing jewels.* Same sign used for: **private eye** (*informal*).

■ [Initialized sign similar to sign for **police**[1,2]] Move the right *D hand,* palm facing left, in a circular movement near the left side of the chest.

detergent *n.* A substance used for cleaning: *a box of laundry detergent.*

■ [**soap** + **washing machine**] Beginning with finger-tips of the right *open hand,* palm facing down, on the upturned left *open hand,* move the right fingertips back across the heel of the left hand, changing the right hand to an *A hand.* Then, with the right *curved 5 hand* over the left *curved 5 hand,* palms facing each other in front of the chest, twist the hands in a double movement in opposite directions.

deteriorate *v.* See signs for DECLINE[1,2].

determine *v.* See signs for DECIDE[1,2].

determined *adj.* See sign for STUBBORN.

detest[1] *v.* To dislike intensely; hate: *Why do so many children detest spinach?* Same sign used for: **despise, loathe.**

■ [Similar to sign for **vomit**] Beginning with the right *5 hand* near the chin, palm facing left, and the left *5 hand* somewhat forward, palm facing right, move both hands forward with a deliberate movement.

detest[2] *v.* (alternate sign) See also sign for ABHOR. Same sign used for: **despise, loathe.**

■ [Similar to sign for **vomit** indicating a strong negative reaction to something] Beginning with the thumb of the right *5 hand,* palm facing left, touching the chin, move the hand forward and downward with a deliberate movement.

detest[3] *v.* See sign for HATE.

detour *n.* **1.** A path that is used when a direct path cannot be traveled: *to take a detour around the construction.* —*v.* **2.** To go another way because of an obstruction: *to detour through back streets.*

■ [Shows changing the course of movement] Beginning with the right *B hand* in front of the right shoulder, palm facing in and fingers pointing left, move the fingers toward the extended left index finger, palm facing right, and then twist the wrist to bring the right hand back outward to the right, ending with the palm facing forward.

Detroit *n.* A city in Michigan: *Detroit is the center of the automobile industry in the U.S.* Same sign used for: **Denver.**

■ [Initialized sign] Move the right *D hand,* palm facing left, from in front of the right shoulder outward a short distance and then straight down.

devastated *adj.* Overwhelmed by shock and hurt: *devastated by the news of his death.*

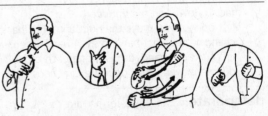

■ [**feel** + **damage**] Move the bent middle finger of the right *5 hand,* palm facing in and fingers pointing left, upward on the chest with a short outward movement. Then, beginning with both *curved 5 hands* in front of the chest, right hand over the left hand, right palm facing down and left palm facing up, bring the right hand in a circular movement over the left. Then close both hands into *A hands* and bring the knuckles past each other as they move in opposite directions.

develop[1] *v.* To make or become bigger, more advanced, or more useful: *develop a new interest.*

- ■ [Initialized sign moving upward to represent growth or development] Move the fingertips of the right *D hand,* palm facing left, upward from the heel to the fingers of the left *open hand,* fingers pointing up and palm facing right.

develop[2] *v.* See sign for BUILD[2].

development *n.* The process of growth: *keeping track of the child's development.*

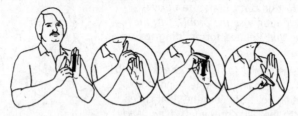

- ■ [**develop**[1] + the suffix **-ment**] Move the fingertips of the right *D hand,* palm facing left, upward from the heel to the fingers of the left *open hand,* fingers pointing up and palm facing right. Then move the index-finger side of the right *M hand* down the left *open hand* from the fingers to the heel.

deviate *v.* See sign for ASTRAY.

device *n.* See signs for EQUIPMENT[1,2].

devil *n.* **1.** (*cap.*) The supreme evil being: *Such crimes are the work of the Devil.* **2.** An evil, cruel, or mischievous person: *The little devil broke the television set on purpose.* Related form: **devilish** *adj.* Same sign used for: **demon, evil, mischief, mischievous, naughty, rascal, Satan, wicked.**

- ■ [Represents a devil's horns] With thumbs of both *3 hands* on each side of the forehead, palms facing forward, bend the index and middle fingers of both hands downward with a double movement. [This sign can be formed with one hand.]

devoted *adj.* Very loyal: *a devoted friend.* Related form: **devotion** *n.* Same sign used for: **dedicate, dedication.**

- ■ [Initialized sign similar to sign for **suggest**] Beginning with both *D hands* near each side of the chest, left hand a bit forward of right, palms facing each other and index fingers angled up, move both hands forward in arcs.

devour[1] *v.* To eat greedily: *devour the food*.

- ■ [**eat** + a gesture showing grabbing food greedily] Bring the fingertips of the right *flattened O hand*, palm facing down, to the lips with a double movement. Then, beginning with both *curved 5 hands* in front of each side of the chest, with a double movement alternatingly move each hand forward, closing them into *S hands* each time.

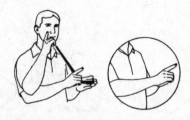

devour[2] *v.* See sign for CONSUME.

dew *n.* See signs for WET[1,2].

diagnose[1] *v.* To find out the nature of by examination: *to diagnose the problem in the computer program*. Related forms: **diagnosis** *n.*, **diagnostic** *adj.*

- ■ [Initialized sign similar to sign for **check**[1]] Bring the right *D hand*, palm facing left and index finger pointing up, from near the right cheek, downward to the palm of the left *open hand* and then across the left palm off the fingertips.

diagnose[2] *v.* See sign for ANALYZE. Related form: **diagnosis** *n.*

diagonal *n.* **1.** A straight line that cuts across in a slanting direction: *to walk across the diagonal*. —*adj.* **2.** Having the direction of a diagonal; oblique: *a diagonal line*.

- ■ [Shows diagonal angle] Move the right *open hand*, palm facing left and fingertips angled upward, from near the right side of the head downward at a slant to in front of the chest with a double movement.

dial *v.* To call by means of a rotary telephone dial: *to dial the wrong number*.

- ■ [Mime dialing a rotary phone] Move the extended right index finger, palm facing down, with a double circular movement near the thumb side of the left *C hand* held in front of the left shoulder, fingers pointing forward. To indicate touch-tone dialing, tap the extended right index finger downward with a short repeated movement.

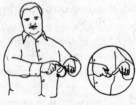

dialect *n.* See sign for LANGUAGE.

dialogue[1] *n.* **1.** A conversation between two people: *This couple should have a dialogue to resolve their problems in communicating.* **2.** Conversation among characters, as in a play or novel: *She's a new author who writes realistic dialogue.*

- [Initialized sign, similar to sign for **talk**[1]] Beginning with the extended index finger of the right *D hand* near the right side of the chin, palm facing left, and the left *D hand* somewhat forward of the left shoulder, palm facing right, move the hands forward and back with an alternating movement.

dialogue[2] *n.* See sign for TALK[1].

diamond[1] *n.* A very hard transparent precious stone: *a diamond ring.*

- [Initialized sign showing locating and glitter of a diamond ring] Move the right *D hand*, palm facing down, from touching the base of the ring finger of the left *open hand*, palm facing down, upward to the right with a wavy movement.

diamond[2] *n.* (alternate sign)

- [Initialized sign showing location of a diamond ring] Tap the right *D hand*, palm facing down, with a double movement on the base of the ring finger of the left *5 hand*, palm facing down.

diaper *n.* An absorbent undergarment for a baby: *to pin the diaper.*

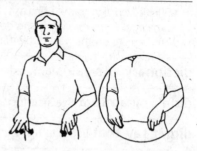

- [**pin**[1,3] formed at location of diaper pins] Beginning with the thumbs of both *3 hands* on each side of the waist, palms and fingers pointing down, bring the index and middle fingers of both hands back toward the thumbs with a double movement.

diarrhea *n.* A condition of abnormally frequent and usually watery bowel movements: *sick with diarrhea during the whole trip.*

- [**disgusted**[1] + **feces**] Move the fingertips of the right *curved 5 hand* in a repeated circle on the stomach. Then, beginning with the thumb of the right *5 hand*, palm facing left and fingers pointing forward, inserted up the little-finger side of the left *10 hand*, palm facing right, bring the right hand deliberately downward.

diary *n.* A written daily record of events or feelings: *to keep a diary of my vacation.* Same sign used for: **journal, scribble.**

- [**write**[1,2] repeated to indicate frequency] Bring the right *modified X hand*, palm facing down, with a repeated movement from the heel to the fingers of the upturned palm of the left *open hand* held in front of the body.

dice *pl. n.* See sign for GAMBLE[1].

dictate *v.* To say something aloud for another person to write down or type out: *to dictate a letter for her secretary to send out.* Related form: **dictation** *n.*

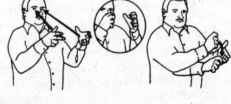

- [**excerpt** + **write**[1,2]] Beginning with both *3 hands* held in front of each side of the chest, palms facing each other and fingers pointing forward, bring the hands back toward the face while constricting the fingers. Then move the right *modified X hand*, palm facing left, with a double movement from the heel to off the fingers of the palm of the left *open hand*, palm facing up.

dictator *n.* See sign for ADMINISTRATOR[1].

dictionary[1] *n.* A reference book listing words and their definitions, often including pronunciations, inflections, and other information, and usually arranged in alphabetical order: *to look up difficult words in the dictionary.* Same sign used for: **directory, folder.**

- [Initialized sign formed similar to **page**[1,2]] Move the fingertips of the right *D hand*, palm facing down, upward with a double movement on the heel of the upturned left *open hand*.

dictionary[2] *n.* See sign for PAGE[2].

didn't mean that See sign for: SHUT UP[2].

didn't say that See sign for: SHUT UP[2].

die[1] *v.* To stop living: *The flowers died.* Same sign used for: **dead, death, demise, perish.**

- [Represents a body turning over in death] Beginning with both *open hands* in front of the body, right palm facing down and left palm facing up, flip the hands to the right, turning the right palm up and the left palm down.

die[2] *v.* (alternate sign) Same sign used for: **kick the bucket** (*slang*).

- [Represents a dead bug lying on its back with its legs up] With both *bent V hands* in front of the chest, palms facing up, twist the wrist from side to side with a shaking movement.

diet *n.* A special selection of foods eaten, as to lose weight: *on a diet to control his weight.* Same sign used for: **lean, shrink, slim, thin.**

- [Shows slimmer body] Beginning with both *L hands* in front of each side of the chest, palms facing in, swing the hands downward by twisting the wrists, ending with the hands in front of each side of the waist, both palms facing down.

different *adj.* See signs for BUT, VARIABLE, VARIETY[2]. Related form: **difference** *n.*

difficult *adj.* Hard to do, understand, solve, or deal with: *faced with a difficult problem.* Related form: **difficulty** *n.* Same sign used for: **hard, problem, trouble.**

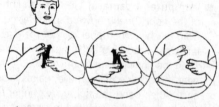

- Beginning with both *bent V hands* in front of the chest, right hand higher than the left hand, palms facing in, move the right hand down and the left hand upward with an alternating movement, brushing the knuckles of each hand as the hands move in the opposite direction.

dig[1] *v.* To use a shovel or other tool to make a hole or turn over ground: *to dig a hole in the back yard.* Same sign used for: **shovel.**

- [Mime using a shovel to dig] Beginning with both *modified X hands* in front of each side of the waist, left hand lower than right, palms facing each other, move the hands downward with a deliberate movement and then upward in a large arc over the right shoulder.

dig[2] *v.* See sign for SPATULA.

digit *n.* See sign for NUMBER.

digital *adj.* Relating to technology wherein all information is encoded numerically: *to use a digital camera.* Related form: **digitize.**

- [**to + number**] Move the extended right index finger, palm down and finger pointing forward, a short distance forward to meet the extended left index finger held up in front of the chest, palm in. Then, beginning with the fingertips of both *flattened hands* touching, palms facing in opposite directions, bring the hands apart slightly while twisting the wrists in opposite directions, and touch the fingertips again.

---

digital audio player (DAP) *n.* A portable, handheld digital music player that stores, organizes, and plays audio files: *She listened to her digital audio player while working out.* Same sign used for: **iPod, MP3 player.**

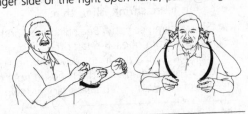

■ [**music + earbuds**] Swing the little-finger side of the right *open hand*, palm facing in, back and forth with a double movement across the length of the bent left forearm held in front of the chest. Then, beginning with both *G hands* in front of the body, fingers pointing toward each other, bring the hands upward to each ear.

---

digital camera *n.* A camera that can record and store photographs that are represented in numerical form: *She used a digital camera on her vacation.*

■ [**computer + camera**] Move the thumb side of the right *C hand* upward, palm facing left, from touching the upper part of the extended left arm to touching again near the wrist. Then, beginning with both *modified C hands* near the outside of each eye, palms facing each other, bend the right index finger up and down with a repeated movement.

---

dignity *n.* Conduct or manner showing self-respect and seriousness: *She maintained her dignity in the face of hostile questions.*

■ [Holding one's head up with dignity] Place the extended right index finger, palm facing left, against the bottom of the raised chin.

---

digress *v.* To depart or wander from the main topic being discussed: *The speaker digressed for a moment to tell a joke.* Same sign used for: **distracted, off the point, off the subject, off track.**

■ [Begins similarly to sign for **goal** and then veers off to the side] Move the extended right index finger forward from in front of the right shoulder, palm facing left, toward the extended left index finger held up in front of the chest, turning sharply to the left near the left index finger.

---

dim[1] *adj.* **1.** Less bright; lacking intense light: *a dim light seen across the road.* —*v.* **2.** To make less bright: *Dim your headlights on the city streets.* Same sign used for: **darken, tint, turn down the lights.**

■ [**light**[1] + gesture showing headlights going down] Beginning with the fingertips of the right *8 hand* near the chin, palm facing in, flick the middle finger upward and

---

forward while opening into a *5 hand.* Then, beginning with both *5 hands* near the chest, palms facing forward and fingers pointing up, bring the fingers down to form *flattened O hands.*

dim² *adj., v.* (alternate sign) Same sign used for: **darken, tint.**

- [Represents headlight beams going down to dim] Beginning with both *5 hands* in front of each shoulder, palms facing forward, bring the hands downward while constricting the fingers into *curved 5 hands.*

dim³ *adj.* See sign for DARK.

dime *n.* A coin of the U.S. and Canada worth 10 cents: *Do you have two dimes and a nickel as change for my quarter?* Same sign used for: **ten cents.**

- [**cent + ten**] Beginning with the extended right index finger touching the right side of the forehead, palm facing down, bring the right hand forward while changing into a *10 hand.* Then slightly twist the right *10 hand* with a repeated movement, palm facing in and thumb pointing up.

diminish *v.* See signs for DECLINE¹, DECREASE².

dimple *n.* A small indentation usually in the cheek or chin: *He has dimples when he smiles.*

- [Location of dimples in the cheeks] Beginning with both extended index fingers touching the cheeks on each side of the mouth, twist the hands forward with a double movement.

dim sum *n.* Small items of savory Chinese food, as steamed dumplings: *eating dim sum for lunch.*

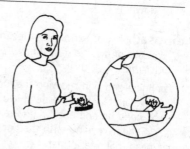

- [Indicates the shape of small dumplings] With the palms of both *modified C hands* facing in opposite directions, place the bent index finger of the right hand against the left thumb. Then move the right hand in an arc in front of the left hand, placing the thumb on the bent left index finger.

dine *v.* See sign for EAT.

dining room *n.* A room in which meals are eaten: *Dinner is served in the dining room.*

■ [**eat** + **room**[1,2]] Tap the fingertips of the right *flattened O hand* to the lips with a double movement. Then, beginning with both *open hands* in front of each side of the body, palms facing each other, turn the hands sharply in opposite directions by bending the wrists, ending with both palms facing in.

dinner[1] *n.* The main meal of the day: *We're having roast chicken for dinner.*

■ [Initialized sign similar to sign for **eat**] Tap the fingertips of the right *D hand*, palm facing in, against the lips with a double movement.

dinner[2] *n.* (alternate sign)

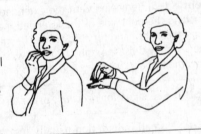

■ [**eat** + **night**] Tap the fingertips of the right *flattened O hand* to the lips with a double movement. Then put the heel of the right *bent hand*, palm facing forward, against the thumb side of the left *open hand* held across the chest, palm facing down.

dinner[3] *n.* (alternate sign) Same sign used for: **supper.**

■ [**eat** + **evening**] Tap the fingertips of the right *flattened O hand*, palm facing down, against the mouth with a repeated movement. Then tap the heel of the right *bent hand*, palm facing down, with a double movement against the index-finger side of the left *B hand* held in front of the chest, palm facing down.

dinosaur *n.* An extinct reptile: *to see the skeleton of a large dinosaur in the museum.*

■ [Initialized sign showing the long neck typical of some dinosaurs] Move the right *D hand* up and back in an arc from the forehead, ending with the hand above the head, palm facing left.

dip *v.* See sign for DYE.

diploma[1] *n.* A document given by a school certifying that a student has successfully completed a designated course of study: *received a high-school diploma.* Same sign used for: **degree.**

- [Shape of rolled diploma] Beginning with the index-finger sides of both *F hands* in front of the chest, palms facing forward, move the hands apart to in front of each side of the chest.

diploma[2] *n.* (alternate sign) Same sign used for: **degree.**

- [Shape of rolled diploma] Beginning with the index-finger sides of both *O hands* in front of the chest, palms facing down, move the hands apart to in front of each side of the chest.

diploma[3] *n.* (alternate sign) Same sign used for: **degree.**

- [Initialized sign similar to sign for **accredit**] Beginning with the right *D hand* in front of the right side of the chest, palm facing left, twist the right wrist until the palm faces back, and then bring it straight down, ending with the back of the right hand on the upturned left *open hand.*

dip switch See sign for TOGGLE.

direct[1] *adj.* Proceeding without interruption in a straight course or line; not deviating or swerving: *The child followed a direct path home.* Related form: **directly** *adv.*

- [Shows direct direction] Beginning with the right *B hand* in front of the right side of the chest, palm facing in and fingers pointing left, and with the left index finger pointing up slightly in front of the left side of the chest, move the right hand to touch the fingers against the left index finger.

direct[2] *v., adj.* See signs for DESCRIBE[1,2], MANAGE, ORDER[1,2], SPECIALIZE[2], STRAIGHT[1]. Related form: **direction** *n.*

Direct Broadcast Satellite (DBS) See signs for SATELLITE TELEVISION[1,2].

director[1] *n.* A person who manages: *The director told the actors what to do.*

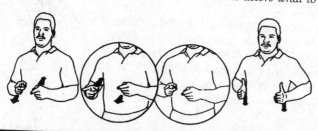

- ■ [**describe**[2] + **person marker**] Beginning with both *D hands* in front of the chest, palms facing each other and index fingers pointing forward, move the hands forward and back with an alternating movement. Then move both *open hands*, palms facing each other, downward along each side of the body.

director[2] *n.* See sign for ADMINISTRATOR[1].

directory *n.* See sign for DICTIONARY[1].

DirecTV (*trademark*) See signs for SATELLITE TELEVISION[1,2].

dirt *n.* **1.** A filthy substance: *to scrub the dirt off the kitchen floor.* **2.** Loose earth or soil: *We need some dirt to repot the plants.* Same sign used for: **ground, land, soil.**

- ■ [Feeling the texture of dirt] Beginning with both *flattened O hands* in front of each side of the body, palms facing up, with a double movement move the thumb of each hand smoothly across each fingertip, starting with the little fingers and ending as *A hands.*

dirty *adj.* Not clean: *Please wash the dirty dishes.* Same sign used for: **filthy, nasty, pollution, soiled.**

- ■ [Represents a pig's snout groveling in a trough] With the back of the right *curved 5 hand* under the chin, palm facing down, wiggle the fingers.

disability *n.* **1.** A disease or injury that renders a person unable to perform his or her usual job. **2.** A physical or mental condition that renders it impossible for a person to hold gainful employment: *the disability of spinal injury.* Same sign used for: **handicap.**

- ■ [Initialized sign] Tap the fingertips of the right *D hand*, palm down, on the base of the thumb of the left *B hand*, palm down.

disagree *v.* To differ in opinion: *I disagree with you about that movie.* Same sign used for: **contrast, dissent, object.**

- ■ [**think**[1] + **opposite**] Move the extended right index finger from touching the right side of the forehead downward to meet the extended left index finger held in front of the chest. Then, beginning with both index fingers pointing toward each other, palms facing in, bring the hands apart to each side of the chest.

disappear[1] *v.* **1.** To cease to be visible: *The sun disappeared behind a cloud.* **2.** To go or be removed to another place: *When I turned my back, my purse disappeared.* Related form: **disappearance** *n.* Same sign used for: **abscond, vanish.**

- [Moving out of sight] Beginning with the extended right index finger, palm facing left, pointing up between the index and middle fingers of the left *5 hand,* palm facing down, pull the right hand straight down a short distance.

disappear[2] *v.* See sign for DISSOLVE.

disappointed *adj.* Feeling that expectations were not satisfied: *to feel disappointed about not getting a promotion.* Related form: **disappointment** *n.* Same sign used for: **miss.**

- Touch the extended right index finger to the chin, palm facing down.

disastrous *adj.* See sign for AWFUL.

discard *v.* See signs for ABANDON[1,2].

discharge *v., n.* See signs for DISMISS, EXCUSE.

disciple[1] *n.* A follower or adherent of someone's teachings: *the master's disciples.*

- [Initialized sign representing marching after another] Beginning with both *D hands* in front of the chest, palms facing forward and the right hand somewhat nearer the chest than the left hand, move both hands forward in a double arc.

disciple[2] *n.* (alternate sign) Same sign used for: **follower.**

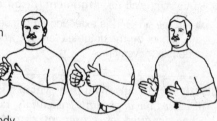

- [follow + person marker] Beginning with the right *A hand* in front of the chest, palm facing left, and the left *A hand* touching the right wrist, palm facing right, move both hands forward. Then move both *open hands,* palms facing each other, down along the sides of the body.

discipline *n.* See sign for DRILL[1].

disco *n.* See sign for DANCE.

disconnect *v.* To break or interrupt the connection of or between: *to disconnect the phone.* Same sign used for: **detach, let go, loose, part from, release, withdraw.**

- [Demonstrates releasing of a connection] Beginning with the thumb and index fingertips of each hand intersecting with each other, palms facing each other and right hand nearer the chest than the left hand, release the fingers and pull the left hand forward and the right hand back toward the right shoulder.

discount[1] *n.* An amount taken off a price: *The coupon entitles you to a 15% discount.*

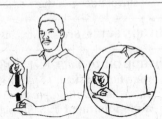

- [Initialized sign similar to sign for **decrease**[3]] Beginning with both *D hands* in front of the chest, right hand above the left hand, palms facing each other, and index fingers pointing forward, bring the hands toward each other.

discount[2] *v.* See sign for SUBTRACT.

discouraged *adj.* See sign for DEPRESSED[1,2,3].

discover *v.* See signs for FIND[1,2].

discriminate *v.* To show a difference in treatment, esp. based on membership in a group or class: *to discriminate against women.* Related form: **discrimination** *n.*

- [Initialized sign similar to sign for **cancel**] With the fingertips of the right *D hand,* palm facing left and index finger pointing up, draw a large X across the palm of the left *open hand.*

discuss[1] *v.* To talk about at length: *It is time to discuss the topic thoroughly.* Related form: **discussion** *n.* Same sign used for: **argument, dispute.**

- Tap the side of the extended right index finger, palm facing in, on the upturned left *open hand* with a double movement.

discuss[2] *v.* To talk about fully within a group: *The committee discussed the applicant's credentials.* Related form: **discussion** *n.* Same sign used for: **argument, dispute.**

- [Indicates a group discussing a topic] Tap the side of the extended right index finger, palm facing in, on the upturned left *open hand* while moving both hands in an arc in front of the body.

disease *n.* An abnormal condition of the body or part of the body: *The dog has a skin disease.*

- ■ [Initialized sign similar to sign for **sick**[2]] Tap the fingertips of the right *D hand* on the forehead and the left *D hand* on the chest simultaneously with a double movement.

disgusted[1] *adj.* Having a strong dislike or repugnance; sickened: *I am disgusted by your rude behavior.* Related form: **disgust** *n., v.* Same sign used for: **aggravated, nausea, revulsion, stomachache, upset.**

- ■ [Represents one's stomach churning in disgust] Move the fingertips of the right *curved 5 hand* in a repeated circle on the stomach.

disgusted[2] *adj.* (alternate sign, used especially when referring to one's own actions or mistakes) Same sign used for: **Now I remember** and **I should have thought of it before.**

- ■ [Represents internal grumbling because of an oversight] Move the fingertips of the right *curved 5 hand*, palm facing in, in a double circle on the chest.

dish[1] *n.* A shallow container for serving food: *a dish of spaghetti.* Same sign used for: **plate, saucer.**

- ■ [Shape of a dish] Beginning with the fingertips of both *curved hands* touching in front of the chest, palms facing in, move the hands away from each other in a circle, ending with the heels together close to the chest.

dish[2] *n.* (alternate sign) Same sign used for: **plate, saucer.**

- ■ [The shape of a dish] Move both *modified hands* downward with a short repeated movement in front of each side of the body, palms facing each other.

dish[3] *n.* A dish-shaped receiver, approximately two or three feet in diameter, used to accept satellite-emitted television signals: *The Smiths have a TV dish on their roof.* Same sign used for: **satellite dish, dish antenna.**

- ■ [T-V + shape of a receiver dish] Form a *T* and a *V* in front of the chest. Then hold the right

curved hand up near the right shoulder, palm facing left and fingers pointing up.

dish antenna *n.* See sign for DISH[3].

disk *n.* A round, flat, plate-like object used for storing electronic computer programs or data: *Oddly enough, you can store more data on the smaller disk.* Same sign used for: **diskette, floppy disk, volume.**

- [Initialized sign similar to sign for **record**[1]] Move the fingertips of the right *D hand,* palm facing down and index finger pointing forward, in a double circle on the upturned left *open hand.*

diskette *n.* See sign for DISK.

dislike *v.* See sign for DON'T LIKE.

dismiss[1] *v.* To send away: *to dismiss the class from school early.* Related form: **dismissal** *n.* Same sign used for: **acquit, discharge, exempt, lay off, pardon, parole, release, waive.**

- [Movement seems to wipe person away] Wipe the right *open hand,* palm down, deliberately across the upturned left *open hand* from the heel off the fingertips.

dismiss[2] *v.* See sign for FIRE[3].

disobey[1] *v.* To fail or refuse to obey: *a defiant child who always disobeys the rules.* Related form: **disobedience** *n.*

- [Hands move as in protest] Beginning with the thumbs of both *A hands* touching each side of the forehead, palms facing down, swing the hands outward to each side of the head by twisting the wrists, ending with both palms facing forward.

disobey[2] *v.* (alternate sign) Same sign used for: **rebel.**

- [**think** + hand moves as in protest] Beginning with the extended right index finger touching the right side of the forehead, palm facing back, swing the hand forward by twisting the wrist while changing into an *S hand.*

disorder *n.* See signs for MESS[1], MESSY, MIX[1].

displacement *n.* The distance between the base address, or the starting location of a section of computer code or data, and another location, or relative address: *the program displacement.* Same sign used for: **offset.**

- [Initialized sign showing removal to another place] Beginning with the index finger sides of both *D hands* together in front of the chest, both palms facing forward, move the right hand to the right.

display[1] *v.* To show or exhibit: *to display your work at the gallery.* Same sign used for: **demonstrate, demonstration.**

- [Initialized sign similar to sign for **show**] With the fingertips of the right *D hand,* palm facing left, touching the palm of the left *open hand,* move both hands forward from the chest.

display[2] *v.* (alternate sign) Same sign used for: **demonstrate, demonstration.**

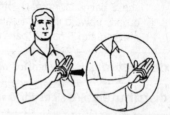

- [Initialized sign similar to sign for **show**[1]] Beginning with the thumb side of the right *D hand,* palm facing forward, against the palm of the left *open hand,* palm facing right, move both hands forward from the chest.

disprove *v.* To prove false: *The evidence will disprove your statement.*

- [**not**[1] + **proof**] Bring the knuckles of the right *Y hand* back against the chin. Then move the right *open hand,* palm facing in, downward from in front of the chest, ending with the back of the right hand in the palm of the upturned left *open hand.*

dispute *v.* See signs for ARGUE[1,2], DISCUSS[1,2].

disseminate *v.* See sign for SPREAD[1].

dissent *v.* See sign for DISAGREE.

dissertation *n.* A research paper written as partial fulfillment of an advanced degree: *to write a dissertation on endangered species.*

- [Initialized sign similar to sign for **write**[1]] Move the fingers of the right *D hand,* palm facing down, from the heel to off the fingers of the left *open hand,* palm facing up.

dissolve *v.* To make or become liquid: *The sugar dissolved in the hot coffee.* Same sign used for: **cure, disappear, evaporate, fade away, melt, perish, resolve, solution, solve.**

- ■ [Something in the hands seems to melt away to nothing] Beginning with both *flattened O hands* in front of the body, palms facing up, move the thumb of each hand smoothly across each fingertip, starting with the little fingers and ending as *10 hands* while moving the hands outward to each side.

distance *n.* See sign for FAR[1]. Related form: **distant** *adj.*

distort *v.* To change or twist the true meaning of: *to distort the facts in a newspaper article.*

- ■ [**not**[1] + **bright**] Move the extended thumb of the right *10 hand,* palm facing left, forward from under the chin. Then, beginning with the fingertips of both *flattened O hands* touching in front of the chest, palms facing each other, move the hands quickly upward in arcs to above each shoulder while opening into *5 hands,* palms facing forward.

distracted *adj.* See sign for DIGRESS.

distribute *v.* See signs for GIVE[4], PASS OUT[1], SELL, SPREAD[1].

distributee *n.* See sign for BENEFICIARY.

district[1] *n.* A designated region established for administrative purposes: *the fifth election district.* Same sign used for: **area.**

- ■ [Indicates an area] Beginning with the left *open hand* held in front of the body, palm facing down, bring the right *open hand* in an arc from the right side of the body forward and back over the left hand.

district[2] *n.* (alternate sign)

- ■ [Initialized sign indicating an area] Bring the right *D hand,* palm facing down, over the back of the left *S hand,* palm facing down, in a large forward circle.

district[3] *n.* (alternate sign)

- ■ [Initialized sign similar to sign for **area**[2]] Beginning with the fingers of both *D hands* touching in front of the chest, palms facing each other, move the hands apart and back in a circular movement back until they touch again near the chest.

distrust *v., n.* See sign for MISTRUST.

disturb *v.* See signs for ANNOY[1,2].

dive[1] *v.* **1.** To plunge into water, esp. headfirst with arms extended above the head: *to dive into the pool.* —*n.* **2.** An act or instance of diving: *a beautiful dive that won her a gold medal.*

- ∎ [Represents legs diving off a diving board] Beginning with the fingertips of the right *U hand*, palm facing right and fingers pointing down, touching the top of the fingers of the left *U hand*, palm facing down and fingers pointing right, bring the right hand over the end of the left fingers and downward in front of the right side of the body, ending with the palm facing left and the fingers pointing up.

dive[2] *v.* (alternate sign)

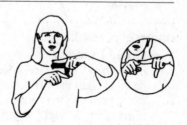

- ∎ [Mime hand position when diving] Beginning with the palms of both *open hands* together in front of the chest, fingers pointing up, move the hands forward and downward in a large arc.

dive into *v. phrase.* See sign for PLUNGE INTO.

diverse *adj.* See sign for VARY.

divide[1] *v.* To separate mathematically into equal parts: *divide by two.* Related forms: **dividend** *n.*, **division** *n.* Same sign used for: **angle.**

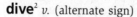

- ∎ [Forms shape of dividend sign] Hold the left *L hand* in front of the chest, palm facing down and index finger pointing right. Then trace along the thumb and extended left index finger with the extended right index finger, palm facing down.

divide[2] *v.* To separate into two or more parts: *to divide the money among the survivors.* Same sign used for: **split, split up.**

- ∎ [Split something as if to divide it] Beginning with the little-finger side of the right *B hand* at an angle across the index-finger side of the left *B hand*, palms angled in opposite directions, move the hands downward and apart, ending with the hands in front of each side of the body, palms facing down.

divine *adj.* Of, like, or from God: *a divine act of charity.*

- ■ [Initialized sign similar to sign for **clean**] Move the fingertips of the right *D hand,* palm facing down, forward across the length of the left upturned *open hand* from the heel off the fingertips.

division *n.* See sign for DEPARTMENT.

divorce[1] *v.* **1.** To terminate a marriage legally: *She had to divorce her husband.* **2.** To break one's marriage contract legally: *a couple planning to divorce.* —*n.* **3.** A legal dissolution of a marriage: *In spite of problems, they want to avoid a divorce.*

- ■ [Initialized sign representing two people moving apart] Beginning with the fingertips of the both *D hands* touching in front of chest, palms facing each other and index fingers pointing up, swing the hands away from each other by twisting the wrists, ending with the hands in front of each side of the body, palms facing forward.

divorce[2] *v., n.* (alternate sign)

- ■ [**marry** + a movement indicating two people moving apart] Beginning with the right *curved hand* clasped over the left *curved hand,* palms facing each other, bring the hands apart, forming *A hands* in front of each shoulder.

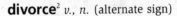

divorce[3] *v., n.* (alternate sign)

- ■ [**marry** + **finish**] Beginning with the right *curved hand,* palm facing down, moving down to clasp the left *curved hand,* palm facing up, bring the hands apart while opening into *5 hands,* fingers pointing up and palms forward.

divorce[4] *v., n.* (alternate sign)

- ■ [Represents removal of a wedding ring] With the fingertips of the right *flattened O hand,* pull upward to the right with a sudden movement from the base of the ring finger of the left *5 hand,* while opening to a *5 hand* with the palm facing down.

dizzy[1] *adj.* Feeling unsteady or giddy: *The merry-go-round made me feel dizzy.*

- [Indicates confusion or a spinning sensation in the head] Beginning with the right *curved 5 hand* near the right side of the head, palm facing left, move the hand in a double circular movement.

dizzy[2] *adj.* (alternate sign)

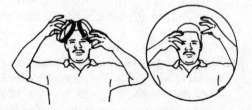

- [Indicates confusion or a spinning sensation in the head] Beginning with both *curved 5 hands* near either side of the head, right hand higher than the left hand, move the hands in alternating circular movements.

do *v.* To engage in or carry out: *Do your homework now, please.* Related forms: **doing**, *n.,* **done** *adj.* Same sign used for: **commit, conduct, deed, perform, performance.**

- [Hands seem to be actively doing something] Move both *C hands,* palms facing down, from side to side in front of the body with a repeated movement.

docile *adj.* Submissive; receptive to training: *The puppy became docile after going to obedience school.*

- [The hands seem to push down disorder or noise] Beginning with both *B hands* crossed in front of the chest, palms angled outward in opposite directions, bring the hands downward and outward with a double movement, ending with both *B hands* in front of each side of the waist, palms facing down.

dock[1] *n.* **1.** A structure extending from land out over water, used as a landing place for ships; wharf; pier: *to anchor the boat at the dock.* —*v.* **2.** To bring a boat to a dock: *to dock the boat to unload the cargo; to dock at 4 p.m.*

- [**water** + a gesture that represents moving a boat close to the dock] Tap the index-finger side of the right *W hand,* palm facing left, against the chin with a double movement. Then move the right *3 hand,* palm facing in, toward the chest against the back of the left *open hand,* palm also facing in.

dock[2] *v.* **1.** To deduct part of (one's wages): *The bosses will dock your pay whenever you're late.* **2.** To deduct something from the wages of: *He was docked for staying home last Monday.*

doctor

■ [**subtract** + **pay**[1,2]] Beginning with the right *curved 5 hand* in front of the chest, palm facing forward, bring the hand downward past the palm of the left *open hand,* palm facing in and fingers pointing right, changing the right hand into an *S hand* as it moves. Then brush the fingers of the right *P hand,* palm facing down, from the heel to off the fingertips of the left *open hand,* palm facing up in front of the chest.

doctor[1] *n.* A person trained and licensed to treat diseases and injuries: *You'd better see the doctor about your cough.* Same sign used for: **physician.**

■ [Initialized sign formed at the location where one's pulse is taken] Tap the fingertips of the right *D hand,* palm facing left and index finger pointing up, on the wrist of the upturned left *open hand* with a double movement.

doctor[2] *n.* (alternate sign) Same sign used for: **medical, physician.**

■ [Formed at the location where one's pulse is taken] Tap the fingertips of the right *M hand,* palm facing left, on the wrist of the upturned left *open hand* with a double movement.

doctrine *n.* A body of principles taught or advocated in a system of belief: *a Christian doctrine.*

■ [Initialized sign similar to sign for **teach**] Beginning with both *D hands* in front of each shoulder, palms facing each other, bring the hands forward with a double movement.

document[1] *n.* Something written, printed, or stored in electronic form that contains information or evidence: *legal documents.* Same sign used for: **documentation.**

■ [Initialized sign similar to sign for **write**[1]] Move the fingers of the right *D hand,* palm facing left, from the heel to off the fingers of the palm of the left *open hand,* palm facing right, with a double movement.

document[2] *v.* See sign for PUT DOWN[1].

document feeder or **automatic document feeder (ADF)** *n.* A feature that enables a set of pages to be fed, one at a time, into multifunction printers, fax machines, photocopiers, and scanners, thus allowing multipage documents to be processed without the user having to manually feed each page: *The document feeder had a paper jam.*

■ [**printer** + the movement of paper through a feeder] Bring the thumb side of the right *G hand,* palm facing down, against the left *open hand,* palm facing up, while pinching the right index finger and thumb together as the hand moves toward the heel of the left hand. Then swing the right *4 hand,* palm facing up, to the left with a repeated movement by bending the wrist.

---

doesn't or **does not** See sign for DON'T[1].

---

doesn't matter See sign for ANYWAY.

---

dog[1] *n.* A domestic, four-legged, flesh-eating mammal, bred in many varieties: *my pet dog.*

■ [Natural gesture for signaling or calling a dog] Pat the right thigh with the right *open hand.* Then snap the right thumb off the right middle finger with a double movement near the right thigh.

---

dog[2] *n.* (alternate sign)

■ [Natural gesture for signaling or calling a dog] With a double movement, snap the right thumb gently off the right middle finger, palm facing up, in front of the right side of the chest.

---

dog[3] *n.* (alternate sign)

■ [Natural gesture for signaling or calling a dog] With a double movement, pat the right thigh with the right *open hand,* fingers pointing down.

---

doing better *slang.* See sign for IMPROVE[1].

---

do it myself See sign for ALONE[2].

doll *n.* A child's toy formed like a human figure: *children playing with their dolls.*
- Bring the index finger of the right *X hand,* palm facing left, downward on the nose with a repeated movement.

dollar *n.* The basic unit of money in the U.S. and Canada: *One dollar doesn't buy much these days.* Same sign used for: **bill.**
- Beginning with the fingertips of the right *flattened O hand* holding the fingertips of the left *open hand,* both palms facing in, pull the right hand to the right with a double movement.

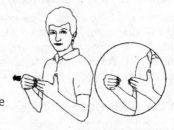

dolphin[1] *n.* A sea mammal: *The dolphin frolicked around in the water.*
- [Initialized sign similar to sign for **whale**] Move the right *D hand,* palm facing down and finger pointing left, along the side of the bent left arm held across the chest, from the wrist to the elbow with a wavy movement.

dolphin[2] *n.* See sign for PORPOISE.

domestic *adj.* See sign for DAILY.

dominoes *n.* A game played with oblong playing pieces marked with dots: *to play a game of dominoes.*
- [Represents moving two dominoes end to end with each other] Bring the fingertips of both *H hands,* palms facing in, together in front of the body with a double movement.

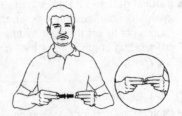

donate *v.* See sign for CHARITY, GIVE[1]. Related form: **donation** *n.*

donation *n.* See signs for ALLOCATE[2], GIFT[1,2].

done *adj.* See signs for FINISH[1,2].

donkey[1] *n.* A long-eared mammal that looks something like a small horse: *ride a donkey.* Same sign used for: **mule.**
- [Represents a donkey's ears] With the thumb side of the right *B hand* against the right side of the forehead, palm facing forward, bend the fingers up and down with a repeated movement.

donkey[2] *n.* (alternate sign) Same sign used for: **mule.**

- [Represents a donkey's ears] With the index-finger side of both *open hands* against each side of the head, palms facing forward, bend the fingers up and down with a repeated movement.

don't[1] Contraction of *do not: Don't do it.* Same sign used for: **do not, doesn't, does not.**

- [Natural gesture of denial] Beginning with both *open hands* crossed in front of the chest, palms angled in opposite directions, swing the hands downward away from each other, ending at each side of the body, palms facing down.

don't[2] Contraction of *do not.* See signs for NOT[1,2].

don't believe See sign for DOUBT[1].

don't care[1] Not to have concern or any other feeling for: *I don't care what they think.* Same sign used for: **don't mind, indifferent, nonchalant.**

- [Outward movement indicates the negative] Beginning with the extended right index finger touching the nose, palm facing down, swing the hand forward by twisting the wrist, ending with the index finger pointing forward in front of the right shoulder.

don't care[2] (alternate sign) Same sign used for: **don't mind, indifferent, nonchalant.**

- [Outward movement indicates the negative] Beginning with the fingertips of the right *flattened O hand* touching the nose, palm facing down, swing the hand forward by twisting the wrist while opening the fingers, ending with the fingers pointing forward in front of the right shoulder.

don't know Not to have knowledge or information (of): *I can't give you the answer because I just don't know it.* Same sign used for: **unaware, unconscious, unknown.**

- [**know** + an outward gesture indicating the negative] Beginning with the fingers of the right *open hand* touching the right side of the forehead, palm facing in, swing the hand forward by twisting the wrist, ending with the fingers pointing forward in front of the right shoulder.

don't like To regard with distaste: *I don't like horror movies.* Same sign used for: **dislike.**

■ [**like**[1] formed with an outward gesture indicating the negative] Beginning with the fingertips of the right *8 hand* touching the chest, palm facing in, swing the hand forward by twisting the wrist, then release the fingers into a *5 hand,* palm facing down.

don't mind See signs for DON'T CARE[1,2].

don't want Not to have a desire for: *We don't want any dessert.* Same sign used for: **unwanted.**

■ [**want** formed with an outward gesture indicating the negative] Beginning with both *curved 5 hands* in front of the body, palms facing up, swing the hands downward by twisting the wrists, ending with the palms facing down.

donut *n.* See sign for DOUGHNUT.

door *n.* A solid barrier that moves to open and close an entrance: *Please close the door when you leave the room.*

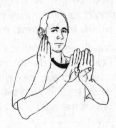

■ [Shows movement of a door being opened] Beginning with the index-finger sides of both *B hands* touching in front of the chest, palms facing forward, swing the right hand back toward the right shoulder with a double movement by twisting the wrist.

dormant *adj.* **1.** Inactive, esp. temporarily: *a dormant volcano.* **2.** Being in a state or condition of rest, with a temporary cessation of growth: *The bulbs lay dormant all summer.* related form: **dormancy** *n.*

■ [Represents a seed breaking through the ground, growing, then going back to its original state] Beginning with the right *flattened O hand,* palm facing back and fingers pointing up, cupped in the left *O hand,* palm facing right, bring the right hand upward and forward around the left hand, ending back in the original position. Repeat.

dormitory *n.* **1.** A residence with many rooms for sleeping: *to live in a double room in the college dormitory.* **2.** A room with beds that serves as communal sleeping quarters: *There's no privacy when you live in a dormitory, surrounded by other people.*

■ [Initialized sign similar to sign for **home**] Touch the fingertips of the right *D hand,* palm facing left, first near the right side of the mouth and then near the right temple.

dorsal *adj.* See sign for BACK[1].

dot *n.* See sign for PERIOD[1].

dots *pl. n.* See sign for SPOTS.

double *n.* See sign for TWICE.

double date *n.* An instance of two unmarried couples socializing together: *It would be fun to go on a double date.* Same sign used for: **couple.**

- [Represents two couples getting together] Tap the fingertips of both *V hands,* palms facing each other, together in front of the chest with a double movement.

doubt[1] *v.* **1.** To be uncertain about; fail to believe or trust: *You may say so, but I doubt it.* —*n.* **2.** An uncertain state of mind: *I should trust her, but I am filled with doubt.* Same sign used for: **don't believe, skeptic, skeptical.**

- [As if one is blind to what is doubted] Beginning with the right bent *V* fingers in front of the eyes, palm facing in, pull the hand downward a short distance while constricting the fingers with a single movement.

doubt[2] *v., n.* (alternate sign) Related form: **doubtful** *adj.* See also sign for RESIST.

- Move the right *S hand,* palm facing in, forward and downward near the right side of the body with a deliberate short double movement.

doubt[3] *v., n.* (alternate sign) Related form: **doubtful** *adj.* Same sign used for: **probability, probable, skeptical.**

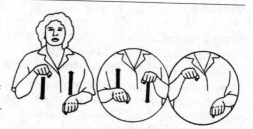

- [Alternating movement indicates indecision] Move both *S hands,* palms facing down, up and down in front of the body with alternating movements.

doubtful[1] *adj.* Same sign as for DOUBT[1] but made with a double movement.

doubtful[2] *adj.* See sign for INDECISION.

doughnut or **donut** *n.* A small, ring-shaped
cake cooked in deep fat: *coffee and doughnuts.*

- [Shape of a doughnut] Beginning with the
fingertips of both *R hands* touching in front of
the body, palms facing in, move the hands
apart and back in a circular movement, ending
with the heels touching near the chest.

down *adv.* **1.** From a higher place or level to a
lower one: *The temperature went down overnight.*
—*prep.* **2.** To a lower place on or along: *rolling
down the hill.*

- [Shows direction] Move the extended right index
finger downward in front of the right side of the
body.

download *v.* To copy a file from a main source
to a peripheral device: *download the file to a
flash drive.* Same sign used for: **import.**

- [Action of information flowing down] Beginning
with both *V hands* near the right shoulder,
palms facing each other and fingers pointing up,
bring the hands down to the left while bending
the extended fingers.

downstairs *adv.* Same sign as for DOWN but made with a double movement. Same
sign used for: **downward.**

doze *v.* See signs for FALL ASLEEP[1,2], SLEEP[1,2].

draft[1] *v.* See signs for DESIGN, DRAW[1].

draft[2] *n.* See signs for DESIGN, ROUGH, SKETCH[1].

drafting *n.* See sign for ENGINEER.

drag *v.* To pull along with effort: *to drag the
heavy suitcase into the airline terminal.*
Same sign used for: **draw, haul, pull, tow.**

- [Mime pulling something] Beginning with
the right *curved hand* in front of the body
and the left *curved hand* somewhat
forward, both palms facing up, bring the
hands back toward the right side of the
body while closing them into *A hands.*

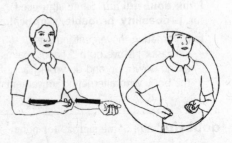

drain *v.* See signs for ABSENT, LEAK[1].

drama *n.* See sign for ACT[2].

drapes *pl. n.* Long curtains, usually of a heavy decorative fabric, hung at a window: *closing the drapes to keep the chill out.*

- [Shape of drapes] Beginning with both *4 hands* in front of each shoulder, palms facing forward, drop the hands downward while turning the palms down.

drat *interj.* See signs for ALAS, DARN.

draw[1] *v.* To make (a picture or a picture of) using a pen, pencil, or the like: *to draw a picture; to draw a house.* Same sign used for: **draft, illustrate, sketch.**

- [The finger moves as if drawing] Move the extended right little finger, palm facing left, down the palm of the left *open hand* with a repeated movement.

draw[2] *v.* See signs for ATTRACT[1], CHOOSE[1,2], DESIGN, DRAG, FIND[1], PULL[1].

draw back *v. phrase.* See sign for RESIGN.

drawing *n.* See signs for ART, DESIGN, SKETCH[1].

draw blood To take blood for medical purposes: *The nurse drew blood from my arm to send to the lab.* Same sign used for: **give blood.**

- [Hand seems to extract blood from the arm] Beginning with the fingers of the right *curved 5 hand,* palm facing up, near the crook of the left arm held extended in front of the left side of the body, pull the right hand to the right while closing the fingers to the thumb, forming a *flattened O hand.*

drawer *n.* A sliding open boxlike compartment in a piece of furniture: *I keep my socks in the top drawer of my bureau.* Same sign used for: **dresser.**

- [Mime opening a drawer] With the fingers of both *A hands* tightly curled in front of each side of the body, palms facing up, pull the hands back toward the body with a repeated movement.

drawl[1] *v.* **1.** To talk or say in a slow way, prolonging the vowels: *drawls his sentences.* —*n.* **2.** An act or utterance or the habitual way of speaking of a person who drawls: *Her Southern drawl is charming.*

- [talk[3] + slow] Beginning with the index finger of the right *4 hand* in front of the chin, palm facing left and fingers pointing up, move the hand forward. Then, beginning

drawl

with the palm of the right *open hand* on the back of the left *open hand*, both palms facing down, pull the right hand up the left hand and wrist with a slow movement.

drawl[2] *v.* (alternate sign)

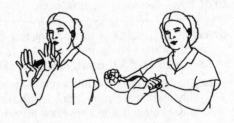

- [**talk**[3] + **exaggerate**] Beginning with the index-finger side of the right *4 hand* against the chin, palm facing left, move the right hand forward. Then, beginning with the thumb side of the right *S hand* against the little-finger side of the left *S hand*, move the right hand forward with a wiggly movement.

dreadful *adj.* See sign for AWFUL.

dream *v.* **1.** To have a series of images pass through the mind during sleep: *I dreamed about you last night.* —*n.* **2.** A series of such images that pass through the mind: *I had a bad dream last week.* Same sign used for: **daydream, fantasize.**

- [Represents an image coming from the mind] Move the extended right index finger from touching the right side of the forehead, palm facing down, outward to the right while bending the finger up and down.

dress[1] *v.* To put clothes on: *to dress yourself.*

- [Location of clothes] Brush the thumbs of both *5 hands* downward on each side of the chest.

dress[2] *n.* See sign for CLOTHES.

dresser *n.* See sign for DRAWER.

dribble *v.* See signs for BOUNCE[2], DRIP.

drill[1] *v.* **1.** To teach by repetition: *Drill the students in French verbs.* —*n.* **2.** Teaching done through repetition: *The class will have a drill in spelling.* Same sign used for: **discipline.**

- [Initialized sign similar to sign for **practice**] Move the fingers of the right *D hand*, palm facing forward and index finger pointing up, from side to side with a double movement across the extended index finger of the left hand, palm facing down and fingers pointing right.

---

drill² *v., n.* See signs for ALARM, PRACTICE.

---

drink¹ *n.* **1.** A liquid suitable for drinking: *Orange juice is a refreshing drink.* **2.** A portion of such a liquid: *a drink of milk.* —*v.* **3.** To swallow something liquid: *Drink some milk.* Same sign used for: **beverage.**

■ [Mime drinking from a glass] Beginning with the thumb of the right *C hand* near the chin, palm facing left, tip the hand up toward the face, with a single movement for the noun and a double movement for the verb.

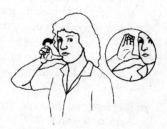

---

drink² *n.* Alcoholic liquor or a portion of this: *to have a mixed drink before dinner.* Same sign used for: **bar, drinking.**

■ [Initialized sign made with **a** to represent an alcoholic drink] Move the thumb of the right *A hand*, palm facing left, back toward the mouth with a double circular movement.

---

drink³ *n.* See sign for COCKTAIL.

---

drip *n.* **1.** The act or sound of liquid falling in drops: *I can hear the drip of rain on the roof.* **2.** The liquid so falling: *Catch the drip in this pan.* —*v.* **3.** To fall or allow liquid to fall in drops: *The faucet drips.* Same sign used for: **dribble, drop, leak.**

■ [Represents action of water dripping] Beginning with the right *S hand*, palm facing down, near the fingertips of the left *open hand*, palm facing down, flick the right index finger downward with a repeated movement.

---

drive¹ *v.* To guide the movement of a vehicle: *to drive carefully through the traffic.*

■ [Similar to sign for **car**¹ except made with a larger movement] Beginning with both *S hands* in front of the chest, palms facing in and one hand higher than the other hand, move the hands in an up-and-down repeated alternating movement.

drive

drive² *v.* See sign for CAR¹.

driver *n.* A person who drives: *The driver shouldn't drink.* Same sign used for: **chauffeur.**

- [**car**¹ + **person marker**] Beginning with both *S hands* in front of the chest, palms facing in and the left hand higher than the right hand, move the hands up and down with a repeated alternating movement. Then move both *open hands,* palms facing each other, downward along the sides of the body.

drive to *v. phrase.* To go in a vehicle to (a particular destination): *to drive to church.*

- [Represents continuous driving] Beginning with both *S hands* in front of the chest, palms facing in, move the hands forward with a deliberate movement.

driveway *n.* A small road leading from a public road to a house or garage: *Please don't park in front of the driveway.*

- [**park** + **road**¹] Bring the little-finger side of the right *3 hand,* palm facing left and fingers pointing forward, down on the palm of the left *open hand,* palm facing up. Then, beginning with both *open hands* in front of each side of the body, palms facing each other and fingers pointing forward, move the hands straight forward.

drool *v.* To let saliva run from the mouth: *to drool just looking at the delicious food.* Same sign used for: **crave.**

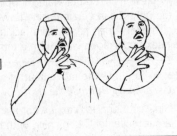

- [Indicates saliva running from corner of mouth] Beginning with the index finger of the right *4 hand* near the right side of the mouth, palm facing in and fingers pointing left, bring the hand downward in front of the chest.

droop *v.* See sign for WILT².

drop[1] *v.* To let fall: *Try not to drop the dish.*

■ [Represents dropping something held in the hands] Beginning with both *flattened O hands* in front of the body, palms facing in and fingers pointing toward each other, drop the fingers of both hands downward while opening into *5 hands,* ending with both palms facing in and fingers pointing down.

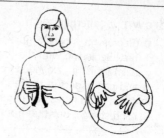

drop[2] *v.* (alternate sign)

■ [Mime dropping something held in the hand] Beginning with the right *flattened O hand* in front of the right side of the body, fingers facing down, drop the fingers downward while opening into a *5 hand.*

drop[3] *v.* See signs for ABANDON[1], DECLINE[4].

drop[4] *n., v.* See sign for DRIP.

drop out *v. phrase.* See sign for RESIGN.

drought *n.* A long period of dry weather: *a long summer drought.*

■ [**water** + **none**[2] + **dry**] Bring the index-finger side of the right *W hand,* palm facing left, back against the chin with a double movement. Then move both *flattened O hands,* palms facing forward, from in front of each side of the chest outward to each side of the body. Then drag the index-finger side of the right *X hand,* palm facing left, from left to right across the chin.

drown[1] *v.* To die or cause to die of suffocation under water: *drown in the pool.*

■ [Symbolizes a person's head going under the water] Beginning with the thumb of the right *10 hand,* palm facing in, extended up between the index finger and middle finger of the left *open hand,* palm facing down and fingers pointing right, pull the right hand straight down.

drown[2] *v.* (alternate sign)

- [Represents a person going under the water head-first] Beginning with the fingers of the right *V hand*, palm facing in, extended up between the middle and ring fingers of the left *open hand*, palm facing down and fingers pointing right, bring the right hand straight down in front of the chest.

drowsy *adj.* See sign for SLEEPY.

drug[1] *n.* A medicinal substance taken by injection: *a new drug administered intravenously.*

- [Initialized sign at the location that drug may be injected] Tap the fingertips of the right *D hand*, palm facing left, in the crook of the extended left arm with a double movement.

drug[2] *n.* (alternate sign used for illicit substances) Same sign used for: **heroin, controlled substance.**

- [Represents injecting a drug] Pound the little-finger side of the right *S hand*, palm facing up, with a double movement near the crook of the extended left arm.

drug[3] *n.* A medicinal substance: *to take drugs twice a day for the illness.*

- [Initialized sign similar to sign for **medicine**] Move the fingertips of the right *D hand*, palm facing down, back and forth on the upturned left *open hand*.

drug[4] *n.* See sign for MEDICINE.

drum[1] *n.* A musical percussion instrument struck with the hands or a pair of sticks: *beat the drum.*

- [Mime playing a snare drum] Move both *modified X hands*, palms facing in and knuckles pointing toward each other, up and down in front of the chest with a repeated alternating movement.

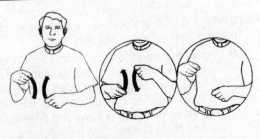

drum[2] *n.* See sign for CYLINDER.

drunk *adj.* Being in a state in which one's faculties are impaired by alcoholic liquor: *He is so drunk that he can't talk coherently.* Same sign used for: **intoxicated.**

- ■ Move the thumb of the right *10 hand*, palm facing left, in an arc from right to left past the chin.

dry[1] *adj.* **1.** Not wet or moist: *suffering from dry, flaky skin.* **2.** Having or characterized by insufficient rain: *a spell of dry weather.* **3.** Dull and uninteresting: *a dry lecture that we could hardly sit through.* Related form: **dried** *adj.* Same sign used for: **boring.**

- ■ [Wiping the chin dry] Drag the index-finger side of the right *X hand*, palm facing down, from left to right across the chin.

dry[2] *adj.* See sign for THIRSTY.

dry cleaners *n.* See sign for CLEANERS.

dryer *n.* See signs for CLOTHES DRYER, HAIRDRYER.

duck *n.* A swimming bird with a short neck, flat bill, and webbed feet: *a wild duck.*

- ■ [A duck's bill] Close the extended index and middle fingers of the right hand, palm facing forward, to the right thumb with a repeated movement in front of the mouth.

due *adj.* See signs for AFFORD, OWE[1].

duel *n.* **1.** A formal fight with deadly weapons to settle a quarrel: *to arrange to fight a duel behind the castle at dawn.* —*v.* **2.** To fight a duel: *to duel with swords.*

- ■ [**meet** + guns pointing at each other] Beginning with both extended index fingers pointing upward in front of each side of the chest, palms facing each other, move the hands slowly, with hesitation, toward each other. Then, with both *L hands* pointing toward each other in front of the chest, palms facing in, bend both thumbs up and down with a double movement.

dull *adj.* See signs for BORING[1,2].

dumb *adj.* **1.** Slow in understanding: *He's good with words but dumb in math.* **2.** revealing lack of intelligence: *That's a dumb idea.* Same sign used for: **stupid.**

- [Natural gesture] Hit the palm side of the right *A hand* against the forehead.

dumbfounded *adj.* See signs for SHOCK[1,2].

dump[1] *v.* To duplicate an image of (the contents of computer memory) into a printer or storage device: *dump the ASCII file to the printer.*

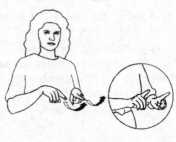

- [Initialized sign] Beginning with the fingers of the right *D hand,* palm facing down and index finger pointing forward, on the palm of the left *open hand,* palm facing up, bring the right hand downward to the right in an arc, ending with the palm facing up in front of the right side of the body.

dump[2] *v.* See signs for THROW[1,2].

duplicate *v., n.* See signs for COPY[1,2,3,4,5].

during *prep.* **1.** Throughout the entire length or existence of: *They're both at the office during the day.* **2.** At some time during the course of: *She sings once during the first act of the opera.* Same sign used for: **meantime, meanwhile, while.**

- [Shows two events occurring simultaneously] Beginning with both extended index fingers in front of each side of the body, palms facing down, move them forward and upward in parallel arcs.

dusk *n., adj.* See sign for DARK.

dust *v.* To wipe the dust, or fine powdery substance, from: *to dust the furniture.* Same sign used for: **wipe.**

- [Mime dusting] Move the right *A hand,* palm facing down, from in front of the left side of the body in a wavy movement to the right side of the body.

Dutch *n., adj.* See signs for HOLLAND[1,2].

duty[1] *n.* Something one is morally or legally required to do; an obligation: *It's my duty to tell the truth.*

- [Initialized sign similar to sign for **work**[1]] Tap the fingertips of the right *D hand,* palm facing down, on the back of the left *curved hand,* palm facing down, with a repeated movement.

duty[2] *n.* See sign for COST[1].

DVD recorder or **burner** *n.* An optical disk recorder, either as a standalone component or installed drive in a computer, that records video onto blank writable DVD media: *Use the DVD recorder to copy the TV show onto a DVD.*

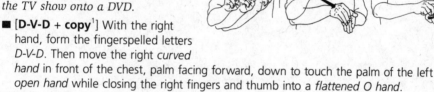

- [D-V-D + **copy**[1]] With the right hand, form the fingerspelled letters *D-V-D.* Then move the right *curved hand* in front of the chest, palm facing forward, down to touch the palm of the left *open hand* while closing the right fingers and thumb into a *flattened O hand.*

dwarf *n.* A person or animal much smaller than the usual size for its kind: *the story of Snow White and the seven dwarfs.* Same sign used for: **midget.**

- [**little**[1] + **people**] Move the right *5 hand,* palm facing down, downward with a double movement in front of the right side of the chest. Then move both *P hands,* palms facing each other, in alternating forward circles in front of each side of the body.

dwell *v.* See sign for LIVE[2].

dwell on *v. phrase.* See signs for OBSESSION[1,2].

dye *n.* **1.** A coloring matter: *Dip the tee shirt in the dye.* —*v.* **2.** To color or stain with a dye, esp. by dipping: *We can dye the cloth blue.* Same sign used for: **dip, rinse.**

- [Dipping cloth in dye] Move both *F hands,* palms facing down, with a slight up and down repeated movement in front of each side of the body.

dynamic *adj.* Pertaining to computer circuitry that performs tasks as needed rather than in advance or to computer memory that must constantly be refreshed: *Dynamic RAM rather than static RAM is used in most personal computers.*

■ [Initialized sign similar to sign for **road**[1]] Beginning with both *D hands* in front of each side of the body, palms facing down and fingers pointing forward, move the hands straight forward simultaneously.

each *adj.* **1.** Being every one out of two or more considered individually: *Each person gets a door prize.* —*pron.* **2.** Each one: *each of us.* —*adv.* **3.** Apiece: *The candies cost 10 cents each.* Same sign used for: **apiece, every, per.**

- Bring the knuckle side of the right *10 hand* down the knuckles of the left *10 hand,* palms facing each other and thumbs pointing up.

each other See sign for ASSOCIATE.

eager[1] *adj.* Filled with enthusiastic desire or interest: *an eager student.* Same sign used for: **enthusiastic.**

- [**excite** + **zeal**] Move the bent middle fingers of both *5 hands,* palms facing in, upward in large alternating circular movements on each side of the chest. Then rub the palms of both *open hands* together with an alternating repeated movement.

eager[2] *adj.* See sign for ZEAL.

eagle *n.* A large predatory bird with a hooked beak, noted for its acute vision: *the keen eyesight of a young eagle.*

- [Represents an eagle's beak] Tap the back of the index finger of the right *X hand,* palm facing forward, against the nose with a double movement.

ear[1] *n.* **1.** The organ of hearing and balance in a mammal: *The noise hurt my ears.* **2.** The external, or outer, ear: *Cover your ears with earmuffs if they're cold.*

- [Location of an ear] Wiggle the right earlobe with the thumb and index finger of the closed right hand.

ear[2] *n.* See sign for HEAR.

earache *n.* A pain in the ear: *I have an earache.*

- [**hurt**[2] formed near the ear] Jab both extended index fingers toward each other with a short repeated movement near the right ear or near the ear with an earache.

earbuds *pl. n.* A tiny pair of loudspeakers, connected to a signal source, that fits within the ear canal: *wear earbuds to listen to music while jogging.*

- [Placing earbuds in ears] Beginning with both *G hands* in front of the body, fingers pointing toward each other, bring the hands upward to each ear.

early *adv.* **1.** Before the usual time: *to arrive early.* **2.** Near the beginning of a period of time, series of events, or the like: *to wake up early in the morning.* —*adj.* **3.** Occurring before the usual time: *an early winter.* **4.** Of or occurring near the beginning, as of a period of time: *born sometime in the early 1950s.*

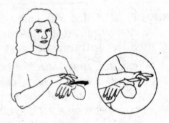

- Push the bent middle finger of the right *5 hand* across the back of the left *open hand*, both palms facing down.

earmold *n.* A device fitting into the outer ear and attached by a cord to a hearing aid receiver: *Wait while I put in my earmold.*

- [Putting in an earmold] Twist the fingertips of the right *F hand,* palm facing in, near the right ear with a repeated movement.

earmuffs *pl. n.* See sign for EARPHONES.

earnings *n.* Money acquired in return for one's work: *the teenager's earnings from his first job.* Same sign used for: **income, salary, wages.**

- [Bringing earned money toward oneself] Bring the little-finger side of the right *curved hand,* palm facing left, across the upturned left *open hand* from fingertips to heel while changing into an *S hand* with a double movement.

earnest *adj.* See sign for ZEAL.

earphones *pl. n.* A set of receivers worn over or in the ears to transmit sound from a sound source: *to wear earphones to listen to the portable tape player.* Same sign used for: **earmuffs.**

■ [Putting on earphones] Tap the fingertips of both *curved 5 hands,* palms facing in, on each side of the head around each ear with a repeated movement.

earring *n.* An ornament for the lobe of the ear: *He now wears an earring in one ear.*

■ [Location of earring] Shake the right earlobe with the index finger and thumb of the right *F hand* with a repeated movement. For the plural, use the same sign but made with both hands, one at each ear.

earth[1] *n.* The planet on which we live; the third planet from the sun: *Dinosaurs once lived on earth.* Same sign used for: **geography.**

■ [Represents the earth rotating on its axis] Grasp each side of the left *S hand,* palm facing down, with the bent thumb and middle finger of the right *5 hand,* palm facing down. Then rock the right hand from side to side with a double movement.

earth[2] *n.* (alternate sign) Same sign used for: **geography.**

■ [Represents the earth rotating on its axis] Grasp each side of the left *open hand* with the bent thumb and middle finger of the right *5 hand,* both palms facing down. Then rock the right hand from side to side with a double movement.

earthquake *n.* A series of vibrations of the earth's crust: *The city was nearly destroyed by the earthquake.* Same sign used for: **tremble.**

■ [**earth**[1,2] + **thunder**[2]] Grasp each side of the left *open hand,* palm facing down, with the bent thumb and middle finger of the right *5 hand,* palm facing down. Then rock the right hand from side to side with a repeated movement. Then, beginning with both *S hands* in front of each side of the body, palms facing down, move the hands forward and back with an alternating repeated movement.

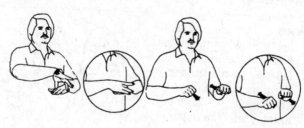

east *n.* **1.** The general direction 90 degrees to the right of north: *The sun rises in the east.* —*adj.* **2.** Lying toward or located in the east: *a house on the east side of the street.* —*adv.* **3.** To, toward, or in the east: *going east to go to college.*

- [Initialized sign showing an easterly direction on a map] Move the right *E hand,* palm facing forward, a short distance to the right in front of the right shoulder.

Easter *n.* The Christian festival celebrating Jesus' rising from the dead: *to go to church on Easter.*

- [Initialized sign] Beginning with the right *E hand* in front of the right shoulder, palm facing back, twist the hand forward and back with a repeated movement.

easy *adj.* Not difficult: *an easy lesson.* Same sign used for: **convenient, simple.**

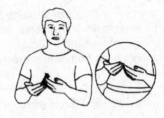

- Brush the fingertips of the right *curved hand* upward on the back of the fingertips of the left *curved hand* with a double movement, both palms facing up.

eat *v.* To take food into the mouth and swallow it for nourishment: *to eat only when you're hungry; to eat dinner.* Same sign used for: **dine.**

- [Putting food in the mouth] Bring the fingertips of the right *flattened O hand,* palm facing down, to the lips.

eat up *v. phrase.* See signs for ACID, CANCER, CONSUME.

eavesdrop *v.* See sign for: LISTEN[3].

echo *n.* **1.** A repeated sound produced when the sound waves of the original are reflected from a surface: *I hear an echo in the auditorium.* —*v.* **2.** To be heard again: *The sound echoed through the valley.*

■ [**hear** + **hit**[1] + a gesture showing sound reflecting off something] Point the extended right index finger to the right ear, palm facing left. Then hit the palm side of the right *A hand*, palm facing left, against the palm of the left *open hand*, palm facing right and fingers pointing forward, causing the left hand to move back slightly. Then draw the right *5 hand*, palm facing left, back from the left *open hand* while wiggling the right fingers as it moves.

eclipse *n.* A darkening of the light of the sun by the intervention of the moon or of the moon by the shadow of the earth obscuring it: *It is exciting to see an eclipse of the moon.*

■ [Represents the changing phases of the moon] Beginning with both *C hands* in front of each shoulder, palms facing each other, bring the hands upward and toward each other, ending in front of the face with the right little finger against the index-finger side of the left hand, palms facing in opposite directions.

economics *n.* See sign for ECONOMY.

economy *n.* **1.** The thrifty use of one's resources: *We practice economy at home by using our leftovers.* **2.** The state or condition of the resources of a place and their management and distribution: *a nation with a rich economy.* Related forms: **economic** *adj.*, **economical** *adj.* Same sign used for: **economics.**

■ [Initialized sign similar to sign for **money**] Tap the back of the right *E hand*, palm facing up, in the upturned left *open hand* with a double movement.

edge *n.* A line or border where an object or surface begins or ends: *trace the edge of the circle.*

■ [Shows edge of fingers] Slide the palm of the right *open hand*, palm facing left and fingers pointing forward, back and forth with a double movement on the fingertips of the left *B hand*, palm facing down and fingers pointing right.

edit[1] *v.* To correct and prepare for publication: *to edit the document.* Same sign used for: **correct.**

■ [Crossing out text in order to correct it] With the extended right index finger, palm facing forward, make small repeated crosses on the palm of the left *open hand*, palm facing in, in front of the chest.

edit[2] *v.* See signs for WRITE[1,2,3].

editor *n.* A person who edits material for publication: *hire an editor to work on the magazine.*

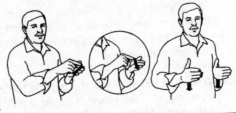

- [**edit**[1] + **person marker**] With the extended right index finger, palm facing forward, make small repeated crosses on the palm of the left *open hand,* palm facing in. Then move both *open hands,* palms facing each other, downward along each side of the body.

educate *v.* See signs for LEARN, TEACH. Related form: **education** *n.*

education *n.* The process of conveying or acquiring knowledge and judgment, as through teaching or reading: *Children are entitled to a good education.* Related form: **educate** *v.*

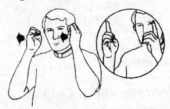

- [Initialized sign **e-d** similar to sign for **teach**] Beginning with both *E hands* near each side of the head, palms facing each other, move the hands forward a short distance while changing into *D hands.* [This sign may also be made with one hand.]

educator *n.* See sign for TEACHER.

eel *n.* A long, snakelike fish with smooth, slippery skin: *difficult to catch an eel.*

- [**fish**[1,2] + **stick**[2]] With the left index finger touching the right wrist, swing the right *B hand,* palm facing forward, back and forth with a double movement, touching the back of the left hand each time. Then, beginning with the index-finger side of both *F hands* touching in front of the chest, palms facing forward, bring the hands apart to in front of each shoulder.

effect *n.* See signs for ADVICE, INFLUENCE.

efficient *adj.* See sign for SKILL.

effort *n.* The use of physical or mental energy or strength to do something: *The students made a real effort to pass the test with high scores.*

- [Initialized sign similar to sign for **try**] Move both *E hands* from in front of each side of the body, palms facing each other, downward and forward simultaneously in an arc.

egg *n.* **1.** A roundish or oval reproductive body produced by the female of some animals: *a bird's nest with three eggs ready to hatch.* **2.** Such a body, oval and with a brittle shell, produced by a domestic bird, especially the hen; used as food for human beings: *eat scrambled eggs.*

■ [Represents cracking eggs] Beginning with the middle-finger side of the right *H hand* across the index-finger side of the left *H hand,* palms angled toward each other, bring the hands downward and away from each other with a double movement by twisting the wrists each time.

egotistic or **egotistical** *adj.* Having or displaying an exaggerated sense of self-importance; vain and selfish: *an egotistic disregard for the feelings of others.* Related forms: **ego** *n.,* **egotism** *n.*

■ [The repeated **1** sign represents concentrating on oneself] Beginning with the right *I hand* in front of the right side of the chest, and the left *I hand* somewhat forward of the left side of the chest, palms facing in opposite directions, bring the right hand forward and the left hand back to the chest with an alternating movement.

Egypt[1] *n.* A country in northeast Africa: *a vacation in Egypt to see the Sphinx and the pyramids.* Related form: **Egyptian** *adj., n.*

■ [Represents the insignia on headdresses worn by Pharaohs] Tap the back of the right *X hand,* palm facing forward, against the center of the forehead with a double movement.

Egypt[2] *n.* (alternate sign) Related form: **Egyptian** *adj., n.*

■ [Reminiscent of Cleopatra's hairstyle] Beginning with the fingers of both *B hands* touching each side of the top of the head, bring the hands downward and outward to in front of each shoulder.

eighth *adj.* **1.** Next after the seventh: *the eighth person who has applied for the job so far.* —*n.* **2.** The one after the seventh in a series of eight or more: *We're having a party on the eighth.* —*adv.* **3.** In the eighth place: *finished eighth in the race.* Same sign used for: **eight dollars.**

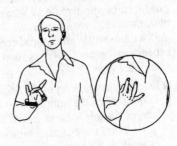

- [**eight** with a twisting movement used for ordinal numbers] Beginning with the right *8 hand* in front of the right side of the body, palm facing forward, twist the hand back, ending with the palm facing back.

either[1] *adj.* **1.** One or the other of two: *We can go either way to get there.* —*pron.* **2.** One or the other: *I'll take either.* —*conj.* **3.** (Used before the first of two words or groups of words that represent alternatives and are separated by **or**): *It will either rain or snow; Either it will rain or it won't.* See also sign for OR[1]. Same sign used for: **alternative, choice.**

- [Shows alternative choices] Tap the fingertips of the right *V hand* with a repeated alternating movement on the fingertips of the left *V hand*, palms facing each other.

either[2] *adj., pron., conj.* (alternate sign) See also sign for OR[1]. Same sign used for: **alternative, choice.**

- [Initialized sign showing alternative choices] Tap the heel of the right *E hand*, palm facing left, first on the thumb and then on the index finger of the left *L hand*, palm facing right.

either[3] *adj., pron., conj.* See signs for CHOOSE[2], NEITHER, WHICH.

either-or *adj.* See sign for WHICH.

ejaculate *v.* to eject or discharge, especially semen from the penis. Related form: **ejaculation** *n.* Same sign used for: **emission.**

- [Shows movement of semen] While touching the wrist of the right *S hand* with the left extended index finger, palms facing in opposite directions, move the right hand forward while opening into a *4 hand*, ending with the right palm facing left and fingers pointing forward.

eject *v.* To propel oneself from a disabled airplane: *Luckily, he ejected before the plane crashed.*

- [Represents a person being ejected from a plane.] Beginning with the little finger, index finger, and thumb of the left hand extended, palm facing down somewhat forward of the chest, and the right *curved 3 hand* across the back of the left hand, tip right hand upward, ending with the palm facing forward.

elaborate[1] *adj.* marked by ornate or excessive details, complicated: *an elaborate design.* Same sign used for: **fancy.**

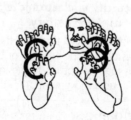

- [Placing decorative items around the room] Beginning with both *curved 5 hands* in front of each side of the head, move both hands in repeated circles outward and downward.

elaborate[2] *v.* To give additional details: *Would you please elaborate on the story?* Same sign used for: **extend.**

- [Stretching out the facts] Beginning with the thumb side of the right *S hand* against the little-finger side of the left *S hand,* move the right hand forward with a wavy movement.

elaborate[3] *v.* See signs for DECORATE, EXAGGERATE.

elapse *v.* (of time) To slip away: *Five hours elapsed while he slept.*

- [**time**[2] + **pass**[1]] Tap the index finger of the right hand, palm facing down, on the back of the left hand, palm facing down. Then, beginning with both *A hands* in front of the body, palms facing each other and left hand somewhat forward of the right hand, move the right hand forward, striking the knuckles of the left hand as it passes.

elastic *adj.* See signs for STRETCH[1,2].

elbow *n.* The joint of the human arm, between the upper arm and the forearm: *I hurt my elbow lifting that chair.*

- [Location of elbow] Touch the bent left elbow with the extended right index finger, palm facing in.

elders *pl. n.* See sign for ADULTS.

eldest *adj.* See sign for OLDEST.

elect *v.* See signs for APPOINT[1], VOTE. Related form: **election** *n.*

electric or **electrical** *adj.* Of or run
  by electricity: *an electric fan.* Related
  form: **electricity** *n.* **electronic** *adj.*
  Same sign used for: **battery.**

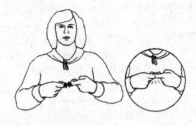

  ■ [An electrical connection] Tap the
  knuckles of the index fingers of both
  X hands together, palms facing in,
  with a double movement.

electronic game See sign for GAME CONTROLLER.

electronic mail See signs for EMAIL[1,2,3].

elegant *adj.* See signs for FANCY[1,2].

elementary *adj.* Dealing with simple, basic, or
  introductory information: *elementary school.*

  ■ [Initialized sign similar to sign for **base**[1]]
  Move the right *E hand,* palm facing forward,
  from side to side with a repeated movement
  below the left *open hand,* palm facing
  down and fingers pointing right, in front of
  the chest.

elephant[1] *n.* A huge mammal with large
  ivory tusks and a long, flexible prehensile
  trunk: *ride an elephant in the circus parade.*

  ■ [Shape of elephant's trunk] Beginning with
  the back of the right *bent B hand* against
  the nose, palm facing down, move the
  hand downward and forward with a large
  wavy movement.

elephant[2] *n.* (alternate sign)

  ■ [Shape of elephant's trunk]
  Beginning with the index-
  finger side of the right *C hand*
  against the nose, palm facing
  left, move the hand
  downward and forward with
  a large wavy movement.

elevate *v.* See sign for ADVANCED. Related forms: **elevated** *adj.* **elevation** *n.*

elevator[1] *n.* A moving platform or compartment used to carry people or things to different levels in a building or other structure: *Take the elevator to the top floor.*

- [Initialized sign showing movement of elevator] Move the right *E hand*, palm facing left, up and down with a repeated movement in front of the right shoulder.

elevator[2] *n.* (alternate sign)

- [Initialized sign showing movement of elevator] Move the index-finger side of the right *E hand*, palm facing forward, up and down with a repeated movement against the left *open hand*, palm facing right and fingers pointing up.

elevator[3] *n.* (alternate sign)

- [Initialized sign showing movement of elevator] Move the knuckles of the right *E hand*, palms facing in, up and down with a repeated movement against the extended left index finger, palm facing forward.

elf[1] *n.* A small, mischievous fairy; common in folklore: *the little pointed ears of an elf.*

- [Initialized sign similar to sign for **fairy**] Beginning with both *E hands* on each shoulder, palms facing down, twist the wrists forward and outward, ending with both palms facing outward near each shoulder.

elf[2] *n.* (alternate sign)

- [Shape of elf's ears] Beginning with the fingertips of the right *G hand* pointing toward the right side of the head, palm facing down, bring the hand upward a short distance while pinching the index finger to the thumb.

eligible *adj.* See sign for APPLY[2].

eliminate[1] *v.* To get rid of: *Try to eliminate sugar and fats from your diet.* Same sign used for: **abolish, abort, delete, omit, remove, repel, rid, terminate.**

- [Natural gesture] Beginning with the back of the right *modified X hand* touching the palm of the left *open hand*, both palms facing in, bring the right hand upward and outward to the right while flicking the thumb upward.

eliminate[2] *v.* (alternate sign) Same sign used for: **abolish, abort, delete, omit, remove, repel, rid, terminate.**

■ [Natural gesture] Beginning with the index finger of the right *modified X hand,* touching the index finger of the left *modified X hand,* both palms facing in, bring the right hand upward and outward to the right while flicking the thumb upward.

eliminate[3] *v.* See sign for SUBTRACT.

elope *v.* To run away to get married secretly: *She eloped with her boyfriend.*

■ [**escape** + **marry**] Beginning with the extended right index finger pointing up between the index and middle fingers of the left *open hand,* palm facing down, bring the right hand quickly outward to the right. Then, bring the right *curved hand* downward to land across the left *curved hand* in front of the chest, palms facing each other.

else *adj., adv.* See sign for OTHER.

elsewhere *adv.* Somewhere else; in or to some other place: *I'll have to look elsewhere for a good winter coat.*

■ [**other** + **where**] Beginning with the right *10 hand* in front of the body, palm facing down and thumb pointing left, flip the hand over to the right, ending with the palm facing up. Then, beginning with the extended right index finger pointing up in front of the right side of the body, move the hand back and forth with a double movement.

elude *v.* See sign for AVOID[1].

email[1] or **e-mail** *n., v. Short for electronic mail.* Correspondence or data transmitted over computer telephone lines: *read your email.* Same sign used for: **mail.**

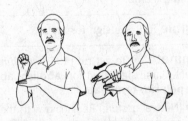

■ [Initialized sign similar to **mail**[1] + **mail**[2]] Hold the index-finger side of the left *B hand,* palm down and fingers pointing right, against the wrist of the right *E hand* held in front of the right shoulder, palm forward.

email[2] or **e-mail** *n., v.* (alternate sign) Same sign used for: **mail.**

- [Email being sent] Starting with the extended right index finger pointing left in front of the chest, move the extended right index finger past the palm side of the left *C hand,* palm right, ending with the right index finger pointing forward.

embarrass *v.* To cause to feel uneasy and self-conscious: *You embarrassed me by mentioning my grades.* Related form: **embarrassed** *adj.* Same sign used for: **ashamed, humiliate.**

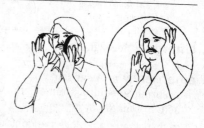

- [Indicates blood rising in the face when embarrassed] Move both *5 hands,* palms facing each other, in repeated alternating circles near each cheek.

embarrassed *adj.* See signs for ASHAMED[1], BASHFUL[1,2]. Related form: **embarrassment** *n.*

embezzle[1] *v.* To steal money left in one's care: *an attorney who embezzled thousands from the children's trust fund.*

- [**money + capture**[1]] Tap the back of the right *flattened O hand,* palm facing up, with a double movement against the palm of the left *open hand,* palm facing up. Then, beginning with both *5 hands* in front of each side of the body, palms facing down, bring the hands back toward the body while forming *S hands.*

embezzle[2] *v.* To convert to one's own use property that is lawfully within another's possession: *embezzle money from the company.* Related form: **embezzlement** *n.*

- [**steal**[1] formed with a double movement] Beginning with the palm side of the right *V hand* on the elbow of the bent left arm, held at an upward angle across the chest, pull the right hand upward toward the left wrist with a double movement while bending the fingers in tightly each time.

emblem *n.* See sign for BADGE[1].

embrace[1] *v.* To take and hold in one's arms: *embraced the child lovingly.* Same sign used for: **dear.**

- [Holding someone near] Hold the arms of both *S hands* crossed at the wrists, palms facing in, against the chest.

embrace

embrace[2] *v.* See signs for HUG[1,2].

embroider *v.* To add ornamental designs with a needle and thread on fabric: *embroidered a flower on her blouse.*

- Move the fingertips of the right *F hand,* palm facing down, in a repeated circular movement on the palm of the left *open hand,* palm facing up.

emerge *v.* See sign for MAINSTREAM[2].

emergency *n.* A sudden occurrence requiring immediate action: *Dial 911 in an emergency.*

- [Initialized sign] Move the right *E hand,* palm facing forward, back and forth with a double movement in front of the right shoulder.

emery board *n.* See signs for FILE[4], PUMICE.

emigrant *n.* A person who leaves his or her own country to settle in another: *A wave of emigrants left Europe to move to America.* Related form: **emigration** *n.* Same sign used for: **immigrant, immigration.**

- [**move**[1] + **outside**[1] + **country**[1,2]] Beginning with both *flattened O hands* in front of the body, palms facing down, move them in large arcs to the right. Then, beginning with the right *flattened O hand,* palm facing in, inserted in the opening formed by the left *C hand,* palm facing right, bring the right hand outward in a large arc to the right. Then rub the palm of the right *Y hand* on the elbow of the bent left arm.

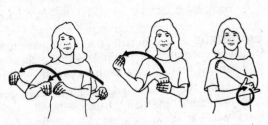

emission *n.* See sign for EJACULATE.

emit[1] *v.* To give off: *emitted a strange light.*

- [Represents a beam of light] Beginning with the left *S hand* on the back of the right *S hand,* both palms facing down, move the right hand forward with a double movement, opening into a *5 hand* each time.

emit[2] *v.* (alternate sign)

- [Represents a radiating light] Beginning with the fingertips of the right *flattened O hand* on the back of the left *S hand,* both palms facing down, bring the right hand upward and forward in several directions, opening into a *5 hand* each time.

emotional *adj.* Involving, experiencing, or likely to have a strong feeling, as joy, love, hate, or sorrow: *an emotional homecoming; a person who is rarely emotional.* Related form: **emotion** *n.*

- [Initialized sign showing feeling welling up in the body] Move both *E hands,* palms facing in and knuckles pointing toward each other, in repeated alternating circles on each side of the chest.

emotionally disturbed *adj.* Having severe psychological problems; agitated and distressed: *an emotionally disturbed person.*

- [**emotional** + **annoy**[1]] Move both *E hands,* palms facing in and knuckles pointing toward each other, in repeated alternating circles on each side of the chest. Then sharply tap the little-finger side of the right *open hand,* palm facing in at an angle, at the base of the thumb and index finger of the left *open hand* with a double movement.

empathy *n.* See signs for MERCY[1,2,3,4].

emperor *n.* The supreme ruler of an empire: *Charlemagne was the first emperor of the Holy Roman Empire.*

- [Initialized sign similar to sign for **king**] Move the right *E hand,* palm facing left, from the left shoulder diagonally down to the right side of the waist.

emphasis *n.* Intensity that attaches importance to something: *The speaker put emphasis on his closing remarks.* Related form: **emphasize** *v.* Same sign used for: **impression, stress.**

- [Movement seems to press something in order to make an impression] With the extended thumb of the right *10 hand,* palm facing down, pressed into the palm of the left *open hand,* palm facing right, twist the right hand downward while keeping the thumb in place.

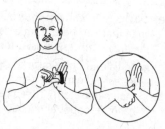

emphasize *v.* See sign for IMPRESS.

employ[1] *v.* To give work with pay to: *tax exemptions for companies that employ many workers.* Related form: **employment** *n.*

- [Initialized sign similar to sign for **work**[1]] Tap the heel of the right *E hand* on the back of the left hand, both palms facing down, with a repeated movement.

employ[2] *v.* See signs for INVITE[1], WORK[2].

employer *n.* A person who employs others for the purpose of conducting business: *The employer held a staff meeting to announce the raises.* Same sign used for: **employee.**

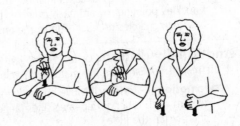

- [**employ**[1] + **person marker**] Tap the heel of the right *E hand* with a double movement on the back of the left *S hand*, both palms facing down. Then move both *open hands*, palms facing each other, downward along each side of the body.

employ me See sign for INVITE[2].

employment *n.* See signs for JOB, WORK[1,2].

empty *adj.* Containing nothing; lacking contents: *an empty can.* Same sign used for: **available, bare, blank, naked, space, vacancy, vacant, void.**

- [Indicates a vacant space] Move the bent middle fingertip of the right *5 hand* across the back of the left *open hand* from the wrist to off the fingertips, both palms facing down.

enable *v.* See sign for SKILL.

encode *v.* To convert information into program code that can be run on a computer: *encode the data.* Same sign used for: **evolution.**

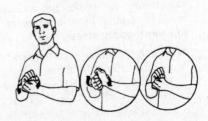

- [Initialized sign similar to sign for **change**[1]] Beginning with the palms of both *E hands* together in front of the chest, twist the hands in opposite directions.

encore[1] *n.* **1.** A demand by an audience for a repeated or additional performance: *The audience shouted, "Encore, encore"!* **2.** The performance itself: *The encore was wildly applauded.*

■ [**more** with a repeated action] Beginning with both *flattened O hands* in front of each shoulder, palms facing each other, bring the fingertips together with a double movement in front of the chest.

encore[2] *n.* See sign for AGAIN.

encounter *v., n.* See sign for FACE[2].

encourage *v.* To give support and confidence to: *encouraged her to go to college.* Related form: **encouragement** *n.* Same sign used for: **bear up, coax, persuade.**

■ [Hands seem to give someone a push of encouragement] Beginning with both *open hands* outside each side of the body, palms and fingers angled forward, move the hands toward each other and forward with a double pushing movement.

encyclopedia *n.* A book or set of books giving detailed information on specific topics or a variety of topics; usually arranged alphabetically: *Let's look up Gothic architecture in the encyclopedia.*

■ [Initialized sign similar to sign for **page**[2]] Move the back of the right *E hand*, palm facing up, upward with a double movement on the heel of the upturned left *open hand.*

end[1] *n.* **1.** The last part or portion: *the end of the year.* **2.** The point where something stops: *This bus goes to the end of the line.* See also sign for LAST[1].

■ [Shows last finger representing the end] Strike the tip of the extended little finger of the left hand, palm facing right, with the tip of the extended little finger of the right hand, palm facing left, as the right hand moves quickly forward in front of the chest.

end[2] *v.* To come to or bring to a conclusion: *The story ended suddenly.* Same sign used for: **complete, conclude, finish, over, wind up.**

■ [Demonstrates going off the end] Beginning with the little-finger side of the right *open hand*, palm facing left, across the index-finger side of the left *open hand*, palms facing in, bring the right hand deliberately down off the left fingertips.

endanger *v.* See sign for DANGER.

endorse *v.* See signs for SIGN[3], SUPPORT[1,2].

endorsement *n.* See sign for CONTRACT.

endure *v.* See signs for CONTINUE[1], PATIENT[1].

enema *n.* The injection of a liquid into the rectum to clear the bowels: *ordered by the doctor to take an enema.*

- ■ [Inserting an enema] Insert the thumb of the right *10 hand,* palm facing left, upward into the little-finger opening of the left *A hand* held in front of the chest, palm facing right.

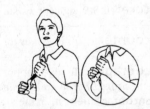

enemy *n.* Someone who hates, opposes, or wishes to harm another: *difficult to face the enemy.* Same sign used for: **foe, opponent, rival.**

- ■ [**opposite + person marker**] Beginning with both extended index fingers touching in front of the chest, palms facing down, pull the hands apart to in front of each side of the chest. Then move both *open hands,* palms facing each other, downward along each side of the body.

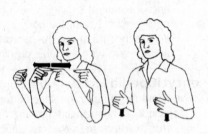

energy *n.* Capacity for or manifestation of vigorous activity: *a young child with a lot of energy.*

- ■ [Initialized sign similar to sign for **authority**] Touch the index-finger side of the right *E hand,* palm facing left, near the left shoulder and then, by twisting the wrist, swing the hand down and touch the little-finger side near the crook of the left arm.

engaged *adj.* Being pledged to marry: *She's engaged to him. They are engaged.* Related form: **engagement** *n.*

- ■ [Initialized sign showing the location of an engagement ring] Beginning with the right *E hand* over the left *open hand,* both palms facing down, move the right hand in a small circle and then straight down to land on the ring finger of the left hand.

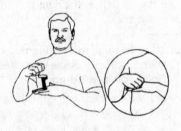

engagement *n.* See sign for APPOINTMENT.

engine[1] *n.* A mechanical device that converts energy into power to produce force and motion: *Start the car's engine by turning the key.* Same sign used for: **cylinders, motor.**

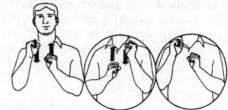

- [Shows the action of a car's cylinders] Beginning with both *S hands* in front of the chest, palms facing in opposite directions and right hand higher than the left hand, move the right hand down and the left hand up with an alternating double movement.

engine[2] *n.* See signs for LOCOMOTIVE, MACHINE.

engineer *n.* A person trained in the design and construction of machines, roads, bridges, electrical systems, computer hardware, software systems, etc.

- [**engineering + person marker**] With the thumbs of both *Y hands* touching in front of the chest, right palm facing forward and left palm facing in, twist the hands in opposite directions. Then move both *open hands*, palms facing each other, downward along each side of the body.

engineering *n.* The design and construction of machines, roads, bridges, electrical systems, computer hardware and software systems, etc.: *The bridge was a remarkable feat of engineering.* Same sign used for: **drafting, measuring.**

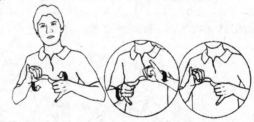

- [Similar to sign for **measure**] With the thumbs of both *Y hands* touching in front of the chest, right palm facing forward and left palm facing in, twist the hands in opposite directions with a double movement.

England *n.* The southern part of Great Britain: *reading about the royal family in England.* Related form: **English** *n., adj.* Same sign used for: **Britain, British.**

- [Suggests an English gentleman with his hands on his cane] With the right *curved hand* grasping the back of the left *curved hand,* both palms facing down, move the hands forward slightly with a shaking movement.

English *adj.* Of or pertaining to England or the people of England: *She is half English and half Scottish.* Same sign used for: **British.**

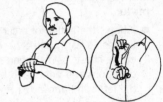

- [**England** + a gesture symbolizing **ish**] With the right *curved hand* grasping the back of the left *curved hand* grasping the back of the left *curved hand,* both palms facing down, move the hands forward slightly. Then bring the extended right index finger, palm facing forward, downward with a wavy movement in front of the right shoulder.

engrave *v.* See sign for CARVE.

enjoin *v.* See sign for FORBID.

enjoy *v.* To be happy with; take pleasure in: *We always enjoy the performance at the opera.* Related form: **enjoyment** *n.* Same sign used for: **appreciate, appreciation, leisure, like, please, pleasure.**

- [Hands rub the body with pleasure] Rub the palms of both *open hands* on the chest, right hand above the left hand and fingers pointing in opposite directions, in repeated circles moving in opposite directions. [This sign can be formed using one hand.]

enlarge *v.* See signs for BIG², EXPAND¹.

enlighten *v.* To furnish knowledge and bring understanding to: *Please enlighten me about the facts of the case before we go to court.*

- Beginning with the index-finger side of both *E hands* touching in front of the chest, palms facing forward, move the hands quickly upward in arcs to in front of each shoulder while opening into *5 hands.*

enlist *v.* To join a branch of the armed services: *to enlist in the Navy.*

- [**accept** + **enter** + **people**] Beginning with both *5 hands* in front of the body, palms facing down and fingers pointing forward, bring both hands back toward the chest while closing into *flattened O hands.* Then move the back of the right *open hand* in a downward arc under the palm of the left *open hand,* both palms facing down. Then move both *P hands,* palms angled toward each other, in alternating forward circles in front of each side of the chest.

enormous *adj.* See sign for LARGE.

enough *adj.* **1.** Adequate to answer a purpose or satisfy a need; sufficient: *enough water for the crops.* —*pron.* **2.** An adequate amount: *Be sure you eat enough for breakfast.* —*adv.* **3.** In or to an adequate quantity or degree: *The room is warm enough.* Same sign used for: **adequate, ample, plenty, sufficient.**

■ [Represents leveling off a container filled to the top] Push the palm side of the right *open hand,* palm facing down, forward across the thumb side of the left *S hand,* palm facing in.

enrage *v.* See sign for ANGER.

enroll *v.* To make into or become an official member: *to enroll the child in school; to enroll in a photography class.*

■ [**enter** + **people**] Move the back of the right *open hand* in a downward arc under the palm of the left *open hand,* both palms facing down. Then move both *P hands,* palms angled toward each other, in alternating forward circles in front of each side of the chest.

enter *v.* To go into: *enter the house.* Related forms: **entrance** *n.,* **entry** *n.* Same sign used for: **access, admit, enroll, go into, immigrate, into.**

■ [Represents movement of entering] Move the back of the right *open hand* forward in a downward arc under the palm of the left *open hand,* both palms facing down.

Enter key or **Return key** *n.* The keyboard key that is pressed to execute a command or to move the cursor down to the next line.

■ [Initialized sign showing a change in direction] Beginning with the right *R hand* in front of the right side of the chest, palm facing down and fingers pointing forward, twist the hand over, ending with the palm facing up.

entertain *v.* To have as a guest: *entertained ten people for dinner.*

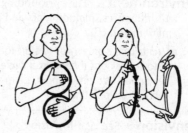

■ [**enjoy** + **people**] Rub the palms of both *open hands* on the chest, right hand above the left hand and fingers pointing in opposite directions, in repeated circles moving in opposite directions. Then move both *P hands,* palms angled toward each other, in alternating forward circles in front of each side of the chest.

enthusiastic *adj.* See signs for EAGER[1], ZEAL.

entice *v.* See sign for TEMPT.

entire *adj.* See sign for ALL[1].

entitle *v.* See signs for BELONG[2], TITLE.

entrance *n.* See sign for ADMISSION. Related form **entry** *n.*

entreat *v.* To ask in an earnest and persistent manner; beg: *She entreated her mother to allow her to go out.* Same sign used for: **plead.**

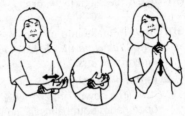

- [beg[1,2] + worship[1]] With the wrist of the right *curved 5 hand,* palm facing up, resting on the back of the left *curved hand,* palm facing up, constrict the right fingers with a double movement. Then, beginning with the right *curved hand* clasped over the back of the left *S hand,* both palms facing down, move the hands up and down with a double movement in front of the chest.

envelope[1] *n.* A flat paper container in which something can be mailed: *Put the letter in an envelope.*

- [letter[2,3] + card[1]] Touch the extended right thumb to the lips, palm facing in, and then move the thumb downward to touch the palm of the left *open hand* held in front of the chest, palm facing up. Then, beginning both *modified C hands* touching in front of the chest, palms facing forward, bring the hands apart to in front of each shoulder and pinch each thumb and index finger together.

envelope[2] *n.* See sign for CARD[1].

envious *adj.* See sign for JEALOUS.

environment *n.* The surrounding conditions and influences, including air and water: *a clean environment.*

- [Initialized sign similar to sign for **atmosphere**] Move the right *E hand* in a circle around the extended left index finger, palm facing right and finger pointing up.

envision *v.* See sign for VISION[1].

envy *n.* **1.** A feeling of discontent, resentment, and unreasoning desire for another's attributes, possessions, accomplishments, or status: *filled with envy over her promotion.* —*v.* **2.** To regard with envy; be envious of: *How I envy her slim figure.* Related form: **envious** *adj.*

■ [Natural gesture used when a person envies another's possessions] Touch the teeth on the right side of the mouth with the right bent index fingertip.

epidemic *n.* The rapid spreading of a disease: *a measles epidemic.* Same sign used for: **plague.**

■ [**sick**[1,2] + **spread**[1]] Touch the bent middle finger of the right *5 hand* to the forehead and the bent middle finger of the left *5 hand* to the chest. Then, beginning with the fingers of both *flattened O hands* together in front of the chest, palms facing down, bring the hands apart to in front of each shoulder while opening into *5 hands.*

epilepsy *n.* See sign for SEIZURE. Related form: **epileptic** *adj.* A disorder or variety of disorders of which seizures are a possible symptom.

Episcopal[1] *adj.* Of or pertaining to the Protestant Episcopal Church: *belong to the Episcopal Church.* Related form: **Episcopalian** *n., adj.*

■ [Indicates the sleeves of bishop's surplice] Touch the side of the right extended index finger, finger pointing left, first to the forearm and then near the elbow of the bent left arm.

Episcopal[2] *adj.* (alternate sign) Related form: **Episcopalian** *n., adj.*

■ [Initialized sign indicating the sleeves of a bishop's surplice] Touch the back of the right *E hand,* palm facing left, first to the forearm and then near the elbow of the bent left arm.

equal *adj.* **1.** Having the same amount, size, value, etc: *equal portions.* —*v.* **2.** To be the same as: *Two nickels equal 10 cents.* Same sign used for: **fair, get even, just, tie.** equal level] Tap the fingertips of both *bent hands,* palms facing down, together in front of the chest with a double movement.

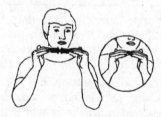

equator *n.* An imaginary circle around the middle of the earth, equally distant from the North Pole and the South Pole: *It is hot and humid near the equator.*

■ [**earth**[1,2] + **ball**[1,2] + location of equator] Grasp each side of the left *open hand,* palm facing down, with the bent thumb and middle finger of the right *5 hand,* palm facing down. Then rock the right hand from side to side with a double movement. Next bring the fingers of both *curved 5 hands,* palms facing each other, together in front of the chest. Finally, move the extended right index finger, palm and finger pointing down, in a circle near the palm of the left *C hand,* palm facing right.

equipment[1] *n.* Articles used or needed for a specific purpose: *camping equipment.* Same sign used for: **device, hardware.**

■ [Initialized sign similar to sign for **thing**[2]] Move the right *E hand,* palm facing up, from in front of the middle of the body to the right in a double arc.

equipment[2] *n.* (alternate sign) Same sign used for: **device, hardware.**

■ [Initialized sign similar to sign for **thing**] Move the right *E hand,* palm facing up, from lying on the upturned palm of the left *open hand* to the right in a double arc.

erase[1] *v.* To remove (something written or typed on a piece of paper) by rubbing: *Try to erase the mistake without making a hole in the paper.*

■ [Mime erasing something] Rub the knuckle of the index finger of the right *X hand,* palms facing in, back and forth with a repeated movement on the upturned palm of the left *open hand.*

erase[2] *v.* **1.** To remove (something written on a chalkboard) by rubbing out: *Erase the answers from the left side of the blackboard.* **2.** To clean off the surface of (a chalkboard) in this way: *It's your turn to erase the blackboard.*

■ [Mime erasing something on a chalkboard] Move the right *A hand,* palm facing forward, from side to side with a repeated movement in front of the right shoulder.

erect[1] *adj.* **1.** Being straight and upright in position: *an erect pole.* —*v.* **2.** To put in an up-right position: *erect the flagpole.*

■ [**make**[1] + **hard**[1] + **freeze**] Beginning with the little-finger side of the right *S hand* on the index-finger side of the left *S hand,* both palms facing in, separate the hands slightly and twist the wrists in opposite directions with a double movement. Then tap the middle finger side of the right *bent U hand,* palm facing left, against the back of the left *S hand,* palm facing down. Then, beginning with both *curved 5 hands* in front of the chest, palms facing down, bring the hands back toward the chest while constricting the fingers.

erect[2] *v.* See sign for SET UP[1].

erosion *n.* The process by which something is eaten away little by little: *erosion of the mountain by centuries of melting snow.*

■ [**wet**[2] + similar to sign **acid** showing dirt being eaten away] Beginning with both *5 hands* near the face, palm facing down, bring the hand forward and downward, closing into *flattened O hands.* Then rub the thumb of both *flattened O hands* against the fingers in front of each shoulder. Then, beginning with the fingers of the right *curved 5 hand* on the back of the bent left forearm, both palms facing down, bring the right hand downward with a double movement, closing into an *S hand* each time.

error *n.* See sign for MISTAKE[2].

erupt[1] *v.* **1.** To burst forth: *Lava erupted from the volcano.* **2.** To explode violently and eject matter: *The volcano erupted.*

■ [Represents an explosion upward] Beginning with the right *S hand* below the left *C hand,* both palms facing in, bring the right hand suddenly upward through the left hand while opening into a *5 hand* in front of the face, palm facing in and fingers pointing up.

erupt[2] *v.* See sign for BLOWUP.

eruption *n.* Same sign as for ERUPT[1] but formed with a double movement.

escape *v.* To get safely away (from): *to escape from prison; to escape the mugger.* See also sign for RUN AWAY. Same sign used for: **abscond, estranged, get away.**

- ■ [Represents one person going off alone] Beginning with the extended right index finger, palm facing down and finger pointing forward, under the palm of the left *open hand*, palm facing down and fingers pointing forward, move the right hand straight forward.

escrow *n.* Money deposited with a third party for delivery upon the fulfillment of some condition: *pay the homeowner's insurance using money from the escrow account.*

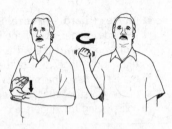

- ■ [**money + hold**[2]] With a double movement, tap the back of the right *flattened O hand* against the palm of the left *open hand*, both palms facing up. Then move the right *S hand*, palm facing up, in a circular movement in front of the right side of the body.

Eskimo[1] *n.* **1.** A member of a people living in arctic regions of North America, Greenland, and eastern Siberia: *the Eskimos of Alaska.* —*adj.* **2.** Of or pertaining to Eskimos: *the Eskimo language.*

- ■ [Initialized sign] Move the right *E hand*, palm facing in, from right to left in front of the nose.

Eskimo[2] *n., adj.* (alternate sign)

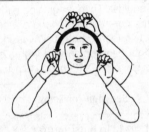

- ■ [Initialized sign showing location of the fur hood on an Eskimo's parka] Beginning with both *E hands* at the top of the head, palms facing forward, move the hands downward on each side of the head to in front of each shoulder.

especially *adv.* See signs for EXCEPT, SPECIAL[1,2].

essential *adj.* See signs for IMPORTANT[1,2].

establish *v.* To set up or bring into being on a firm basis: *establish a schedule to which we can all adhere.* Same sign used for: **based on, founded, set up.**

- ■ [Represents setting something up firmly] Beginning with the right *10 hand* in front of the right shoulder, palm facing down, twist the wrist upward with a circular movement and then move the right hand straight down to land the little-finger side on the back of the left *open hand,* palm facing down.

estimate *n., v.* See signs for ARITHMETIC, GUESS, MULTIPLY, ROUGH.

estranged *adj.* See signs for ASTRAY, ESCAPE.

et cetera *adv.* See sign for VARIETY[1].

eternal[1] *adj.* Without beginning or end; lasting forever: *eternal life.*

■ [**forever**[2] + **continue**[1]] Touch the extended right index finger to the right side of the forehead, palm facing down. Then move the extended right index finger, palm facing in, in a large repeated circle in front of the right side of the chest. Then, beginning with the thumb of the right *10 hand* on the thumb of the left *10 hand,* both palms angled down, move the hands straight forward in front of the chest.

eternal[2] *adj.* See signs for FOREVER[1,2].

etiquette *n.* Conventional rules for appropriate social behavior: *a magazine article discussing proper etiquette at a formal dinner.*

■ [**polite** + **behavior**] Tap the thumb of the right *5 hand,* palm facing left, against the center of the chest. Then move both *B hands,* palms angled forward, simultaneously from side to side in front of each side of the body with a swinging movement.

Europe *n.* A continent west of Asia: *planning to travel in Europe for three weeks.*

■ [Initialized sign] Move the right *E hand,* palm facing back, in a repeated circular movement near the right side of the forehead.

evade *v.* See sign for AVOID[1].

evaluate[1] *v.* To appraise the value or quality of: *a committee to evaluate the effectiveness of the program.* Related form: **evaluation** *n.*

■ [Initialized sign with a movement that signifies weighing choices] Move both *E hands,* palms facing forward, up and down with a repeated alternating movement in front of each side of the chest.

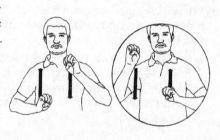

evaluate[2] *v.* See sign for ANALYZE. Related form: **evaluation** *n.*

evangelism[1] *n.* The spreading and promoting of the Christian Gospel: *a preacher known for his effective evangelism.*

- [Initialized sign similar to sign for **preach**[1]] Move the right *E hand*, palm facing left, forward with a short repeated movement in front of the right shoulder.

evangelism[2] *n.* (alternate sign)

- [Initialized sign **e-v** similar to sign for **preach**[1]] Beginning with the right *E hand* in front of the right shoulder, palm facing forward, move the hand to the right a short distance while changing into a *V hand*, palm facing forward.

evangelist *n.* A preacher of Christian gospel: *The evangelist held a revival in a tent.*

- [**evangelism**[1,2] + **person marker**] Move the right *E hand*, palm facing left, forward with a short repeated movement in front of the right shoulder. Then move both *open hands*, palms facing each other, downward along each side of the body.

evaporate[1] *v.* To turn from liquid into vapor: *The water evaporated in the hot sun.*

- [**water** + **dissolve**] Tap the index-finger side of the right *W hand*, palm facing left, against the chin. Then, beginning with both *flattened O hands* in front of each side of the chest, palms facing up, move the hands outward in an arc while rubbing the thumbs against the fingertips and changing into *10 hands*.

evaporate[2] *v.* See signs for DISSOLVE, RAPTURE.

even[1] *adj.* Being at the same level: *The piles of books on the floor were even.* Same sign used for: **fair, level.**

- [Shows things of equal level] Beginning with the fingertips of both *bent hands* touching in front of the chest, both palms facing down, bring the hands straight apart from each other to in front of each shoulder.

even[2] *adj., v.* See sign for CONSTANT[2].

evening *n.* The latter part of the day and early part of the night: *this evening, just before supper.*

- ■ [Represents the sun low on the horizon] Tap the heel of the right *bent hand,* palm facing forward, with a double movement against the thumb side of the left *open hand* held across the chest, palm facing down.

event *n.* See sign for HAPPEN.

even though *conj.* See sign for ANYWAY.

ever[1] *adv.* At any time: *Did you ever go ice-skating?*

- ■ [Initialized sign similar to sign for **always**] Move the right *E hand,* palm facing forward, in a large circle in front of the right shoulder

ever[2] *adv.* See sign for ALWAYS.

everlasting *adj.* See signs for FOREVER[1,2].

ever since See signs for ALL THE TIME[1,2], SINCE[1].

every *adj.* Being each one in a group of three or more: *Every eligible person in our county voted.*

- ■ Bring the knuckle side of the right *10 hand* down the thumb of the left *10 hand* with a double movement, palms facing each other and thumbs pointing up.

every afternoon Each afternoon: *come home from school at the same time every afternoon.*

- ■ [**afternoon** formed with a continuous movement] With the bottom of the right forearm resting on the index-finger side of the left *B hand,* palm facing in and fingers pointing right, move the right *bent hand* from left to right in front of the chest.

everybody[1] *pron.* Each person: *Everybody should vote.*

■ [**every** + **them**[2]] Bring the knuckle side of the right *10 hand* down the thumb of the left *10 hand* with a double movement, palms facing each other and thumbs pointing up. Then move the right *open hand*, palm facing up and fingers pointing forward, from in front of the body outward to the right.

everybody[2] *pron.* (alternate sign)

■ [**every** + **you**[2]] Bring the knuckle side of the right *10 hand* down the thumb of the left *10 hand* with a double movement, palms facing each other and thumbs pointing up. Then move the extended right index finger, palm facing left, from in front of the body to the right with a sweeping movement.

everyday *adj.* See sign for DAILY.

every day See sign for DAILY.

every morning Each morning: *eating breakfast together every morning.*

■ [**morning** formed with a continuous movement] With the left *open hand* in the crook of the right arm bent across the body, right palm facing in, bring the right *open hand* smoothly from left to right in front of the chest, ending with the right palm facing up.

every night Each night: *wine with dinner every night.*

■ [**night** formed with a continuous movement] With the heel of the right *bent hand*, palm facing down, on the index-finger side of the left *B hand*, palm facing in and fingers pointing right, move the arms smoothly across the chest from left to right.

every noon or **at noon every day** Each noon: *eat lunch at noon every day.*

■ [**noon** formed with a continuous movement] With the right elbow, arm extended up and right *open hand* facing left, on the index-finger side of the left *B hand*, palm facing in and fingers pointing right, move the right arm smoothly in front of the chest from left to right, ending with the right palm facing forward in front of the right shoulder.

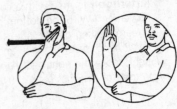

everyone *pron.* Each person: *Everyone must pay to get in.*

■ [**every** + **one**] Bring the knuckle side of the right *10 hand* down the thumb of the left *10 hand* with a double movement, palms facing each other and thumbs pointing up. Then hold up the extended right index finger in front of the right side of the body, palm facing in.

every so often See sign for SOMETIMES.

everything[1] *pron.* Every single thing in a group or total: *I think you should keep everything you bought today.*

■ [**every** + **thing**[1,2]] Bring the knuckle side of the right *10 hand* down the thumb of the left *10 hand* with a double movement, palms facing each other and thumbs pointing up. Then move the right *open hand*, palm facing up and fingers pointing forward, from in front of the body to the right in a double arc.

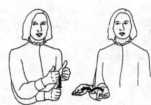

everything[2] *pron.* (alternate sign)

■ Beginning with both *A hands* held in front of each side of the body, palms facing up, bring the knuckles of the right hand to the left, brushing across the top of the left hand and back again to the right while opening into a *5 hand*.

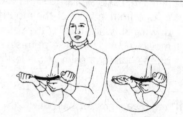

everything[3] *pron.* (alternate sign)

■ [**every** + **thing**[1,2]] Bring the knuckle side of the right *10 hand* down the thumb side of the left *10 hand*. Then, beginning with both *5 hands* together, throw the hands out to each side, palms up.

everything[4] *pron.* See sign for INCLUDE.

every three months See sign for QUARTERLY.

every two months See sign for BIMONTHLY.

every two weeks See sign for BIWEEKLY.

everywhere *adv.* In all places: *looked everywhere.*

■ [**every** + **where**] Bring the knuckle side of the right *10 hand* down the thumb of the left *10 hand* with a double movement, palms facing each other and thumbs pointing up. Then move the extended right index finger, palm facing forward, from side to side with a small repeated movement in front of the right shoulder.

every year See sign for ANNUAL.

evict *v.* See sign for ABANDON[2].

evidence[1] *n.* Anything that tends to prove or disprove something: *required to show the evidence of the accused swindler's guilt in court.*

- ■ [Initialized sign similar to sign for **proof**] Move the right *E hand* from near the right eye, palm facing left, downward to land the back of the right *E hand* in the left *open hand,* both palms facing up.

evidence[2] *n.* See sign for PROOF.

evil[1] *adj.* Morally wrong or bad; wicked: *an evil person, who is entirely unrepentant.*

- ■ [Initialized sign similar to sign for **bad**] Move the right *E hand* from in front of the mouth, palm facing in, downward while turning the palm down as the hand moves, ending with the palm side of the right *E hand* on the upturned palm of the left *open hand* in front of the chest.

evil[2] *adj.* See signs for BAD, DEVIL.

evolution *n.* See sign for ENCODE.

exact *adj.* See sign for PRECISE.

exaggerate *v.* To make claims beyond the limits of truth: *tends to exaggerate the extent of the difficulties.* Related form: **exaggeration** *n.* Same sign used for: **elaborate, prolong, stretch.**

- ■ [Hands seem to stretch the truth] Beginning with the thumb side of the right *S hand,* palm facing left, against the little-finger side of the left *S hand,* palm facing right, move the right hand forward with a large wavy movement.

exalt *v.* See signs for ADVANCE, ADVANCED. Related forms: **exalted** *adj.,* **exaltation** *n.*

examination or **exam** *n.* See signs for TEST[1,2,3].

examine *v.* See signs for ANALYZE, CHECK[1], INVESTIGATE, LOOK FOR[1,2,3]. Related form: **examination** *n.*

example[1] *n.* One thing used to show what others are like or should be like: *This essay is a fine example of what a good student can do.* Same sign used for: **exhibit.**

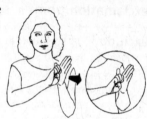

- [Initialized sign similar to sign for **show**[1]] With the index-finger side of the right *E hand*, palm facing forward, against the left *open hand*, palm facing right and fingers pointing up, move the hands forward together a short distance.

example[2] *n.* See sign for SHOW[1].

exceed *v.* See signs for EXCESS, OVER[1].

excellent *adj.* See signs for FINEST, SUPERB, WONDERFUL[1,2].

except *prep.* See signs for SPECIAL[1,2]. Related form: **exceptional** *adj.*

excerpt *n.* **1.** A passage taken from a book, document, or the like: *permission to quote an excerpt from the book in a forthcoming article.* —*v.* **2.** To take (a passage) from a book, document, or the like: *Scenes from the movie were excerpted for use on television.* Same sign used for: **copy, quote, quotation.**

- [Similar to sign for **quote**] Beginning with both *bent V hands* in front each side of the body, palms facing each other, bring the hands back toward the chest while constricting the fingers.

excess *n.* **1.** An amount or degree beyond what is necessary or usual: *If your shopping cart is full, I'll carry the excess.* —*adj.* **2.** Being more than what is necessary or usual: *The airline charges for excess baggage.* Related form: **excessive** *adj.* Same sign used for: **exceed, massive, more than, too much.**

- [Demonstrates an amount that is more than the base] Beginning with the fingers of the right *bent hand* on the back of the left *bent hand*, both palms facing down, bring the right hand upward in an arc to the right.

exchange *n., v.* See signs for BUDGET[1], TRADE[1,2,3].

excite *v.* To stir up feelings in: *The trip excited me.* Related form: **excited** *adj.*, **exciting** *adj.* Same sign used for: **anxious, thrill.**

- Move the bent middle fingers of both *5 hands*, palms facing in and fingers pointing toward each other, in repeated alternating circles on each side of the chest.

exclamation point *n.* See sign for PUNCTUATION.

exclude *v.* To keep out: *excluded from the meeting*. See also signs for REJECT[2,3].

- [Shoving something away to exclude it] Beginning with the heel of the right *curved hand*, palm facing forward, against the heel of the left *open hand*, palm facing up, move the right hand across the left hand and off the fingertips.

excrement *n.* See sign for FECES.

excuse *n.* An explanation offered as justification for an action, apology for a fault, or plea for release from an obligation: *He didn't have a very good excuse for staying home from work*. Same sign used for: **forgiveness, pardon, parole.**

- [The hand seems to wipe away a mistake] Wipe the fingertips of the right *open hand* across the upturned left *open hand* from the heel off the fingertips.

excuse me (A polite expression used to offer an apology): *Excuse me for being late. Excuse me—may I get by?* Same sign used for: **pardon me.**

- [The hand seems to wipe away a mistake] Wipe the fingertips of the right *open hand* across the upturned left *open hand* from the heel off the fingertips with a short double movement.

execute[1] *v.* To process and put into effect (a computer program or command): *Clicking the mouse on this icon will execute the spreadsheet program*. Same sign used for: **run.**

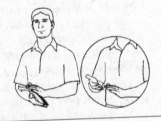

- Slide the palm of the right *open hand*, palm facing up, at an angle across the palm of the left *open hand*, palm facing down, with a double movement.

execute[2] *v.* See sign for CAPITAL PUNISHMENT. Related form: **execution** *n.*

exempt *v., adj.* See signs for DISMISS, SUBTRACT.

exercise[1] *n.* **1.** Activity or an activity designed to make the body healthier, stronger, and more flexible: *lifting weights for exercise; do my exercises every morning.* —*v.* **2.** To perform such activity, as to promote physical fitness: *I exercise by jogging.*

- [Initialized sign miming doing exercises] Beginning with both *E hands* near each shoulder, palms facing down, bring both arms up and down with a double movement.

exercise[2] *v., n.* (alternate sign) Same sign used for: **work out.**

- [Mime exercising] Beginning with both *S hands* near each shoulder, palms facing down, bring both arms up and down with a double movement.

exercise[3] *n., v.* See sign for PRACTICE.

exhausted *adj.* See sign for TIRED.

exhibit[1] *v.* To show publicly: *to exhibit his paintings at the new gallery.* Related form: **exhibition** *n.*

- [Initialized sign similar to sign for **show**[3]] Beginning with the index-finger side of the right *E hand,* palm facing forward, against the palm of the left *open hand,* palm facing right and fingers pointing up, move both hands in a flat circle in front of the chest.

exhibit[2] *v.* (alternate sign) Related form: **exhibition** *n.*

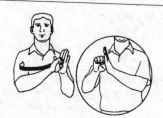

- [Initialized sign] Beginning with the index-finger side of the right *E hand,* palm facing forward, against the palm of the left *open hand,* palm facing right, move both hands from in front of the left shoulder in an arc to in front of the right shoulder.

exhibit[3] *n., v.* See signs for EXAMPLE[1], SHOW[2]. Related form: **exhibition** *n.*

exotic *adj.* Strikingly unusual, strange, or foreign, as in appearance: *exotic butterflies never before seen in this country.*

- [**interest**[1,2] + **strange**] Beginning with the bent thumb and middle fingers of both *5 hands* in front of the chest, palms facing in and right hand above the left hand, pull the hands forward simultaneously while pinching the thumbs and middle fingers together into *8 hands.* Then, beginning with the right *C hand* near the right side of the head, palm facing left, move the hand to the left in a large arc in front of the face.

expand[1] *v.* To make or become larger: *expanding the business by opening another store.* Related form: **expanse** *n.* Same sign used for: **enlarge, explosion, swell.**

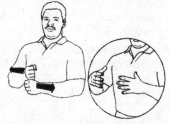

- [Demonstrates something expanding] Beginning with the little-finger side of the right *S hand* on top of the index-finger side of the left *S hand,* palms facing in opposite directions, bring the hands apart while opening into *curved 5 hands* in front of each side of the chest, palms facing each other.

expand[2] *v.* See signs for BALLOON[1,2].

expansion board See sign for BOARD[3].

expansion card See sign for BOARD[3].

expect *v.* See signs for HOPE[1,2]. Related form: **expectation** *n.*

expel *v.* To cut off from membership; to drive out: *to expel from class.*

- [Initialized sign similar to sign for **fire**[3]] Swing the knuckles of the right *E hand*, palm facing up, across the index-finger side of the left *B hand*, palm facing in and fingers pointing to the right.

expense *n.* A charge or the cost incurred from some activity: *My house mortgage is my major expense for the year.*

- [Similar to sign for **cost**[1]] Strike the knuckle of the right *X hand*, palm facing in, downward on the palm of the left *open hand*, palm facing right, with a double movement.

expensive *adj.* High-priced: *an expensive coat.* Same sign used for: **costly.**

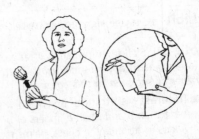

- [**money** + a gesture of throwing it away] Beginning with the back of the right *flattened O hand* in the upturned left *open hand*, bring the right hand upward to the right while opening into a *5 hand* in front of the right shoulder, palm facing down.

experience *n.* **1.** Something lived through or encountered: *a terrifying experience.* **2.** The undergoing of events in the course of time: *My life experiences would make a good novel.* **3.** Knowledge and wisdom gained from these events: *His experience qualifies him for the job.* —*v.* **4.** To have happen to one: *Experience it for yourself.* Same sign used for: **ordeal.**

- Beginning with the fingertips of the right *5 hand* on the right cheek, palm facing in, bring the hand outward to the right while closing the fingers into a *flattened O hand*.

experiment *n.* **1.** A test or trial to discover something: *a scientific experiment.* —*v.* **2.** To conduct such a test or trial: *experiment with combining the chemicals.*

- [Initialized sign similar to sign for **science**] Beginning with both *E hands* in front of the chest, palms facing forward and right hand higher than the left hand, move the hands in repeated alternating circles.

expert *adj.* See signs for ADROIT, GOOD AT, SKILL.

expire *v.* See signs for RUN OUT OF[1,2].

explain *v.* See sign for DESCRIBE[1]. Related form: **explanation** *n.*

explode[1] *v.* To burst or erupt violently; blow up: *The bomb exploded.* Related form: **explosion** *n.* Same sign used for: **blast, bomb, boom.**

- [Demonstrates something blowing up] Beginning with the little-finger side of the right *S hand* on top of the index-finger side of the left *S hand*, palms facing in opposite directions, move the hands suddenly away from each other while twisting the palms forward in front of each side of the chest.

explode[2] *v.* (alternate sign) Related form: **explosion** *n.* Same sign used for: **bomb, boom.**

- [Demonstrates something blowing up] Beginning with the fingers of both *flattened O hands* together in front of the chest, palms facing each other, move the hands suddenly upward and outward while opening into *5 hands*, ending with the palms angled upward near each side of the head.

explode[3] *v.* See sign for BURST[1].

explore *v.* See signs for LOOK FOR[1,2].

explosion *n.* See sign for EXPAND[1].

export *v.* See signs for SELL, UPLOAD.

expose *v.* See signs for SHOW[1], STICK[1].

exposure *n.* **1.** The act of presenting a photosensitive surface, as film, to light: *The exposure didn't work in the afternoon light.* **2.** The amount of time taken or the amount of light received during such an exposure: *The new camera automatically sets the exposure.* **3.** The photographic image thus produced: *This looks like a double exposure.*

■ [Represents the shutter of a camera opening and closing while taking a picture] Beginning with the fingertips of the right *flattened O hand*, palm facing left, against the extended left index finger, palm facing right, bring the right hand back and then forward again to the index finger while changing into a *5 hand*.

express[1] *v.* **1.** To show, reveal, or put into words (one's thoughts or feelings): *to express your anger.* **2.** To reveal the thoughts or feelings of (oneself): *to express yourself.*

■ [Initialized sign similar to sign for **admit**[2]] Beginning with both *E hands* in front of the chest, palms facing each other, move both hands forward in a double arc.

express[2] *n.* **1.** A quick or direct means of sending something or traveling somewhere: *Send the package by express.* —*adj.* **2.** Quick or direct: *an express train.*

■ [Initialized sign similar to sign for **subway**] Move the right *E hand*, palm facing forward, to the right under the palm of the left *open hand*, palm facing down and fingers pointing right.

express[3] *n.* See sign for EMAIL[3].

expression *n.* An outward indication on the face that reveals one's feelings: *a sad expression in her eyes.*

■ [Indicates the face's movement when changing expression] Move both *modified X hands*, palms facing forward, up and down with a repeated alternating movement in front of each side of the face.

expressway *n.* See sign for SUPERHIGHWAY.

extend *v.* See sign for ELABORATE[2].

exterior *adj.* **1.** Located on the outside: *building an exterior wall.* —*n.* **2.** The outside: *the exterior of the house.*

■ [**outside**[1] + a gesture that indicates an exterior surface] Beginning with the right *flattened O hand* cupped inside the opening made by the left *C hand,* palm facing right, bring the right hand upward and back in an arc. Then move the fingertips of the right *open hand* up the back of the left *open hand* and then down again, both palms facing in and fingers pointing in opposite directions.

external *n., adj.* See signs for OUTSIDE[1,2].

extinct *adj.* See sign for ABSENT.

extra *n.* See sign for ADD[2].

eye[1] *n.* One of a pair of organs of the body through which one sees: *I have something in my eye.*

■ [Location of the eye] Point the extended right index finger, palm facing in, toward the right eye with a double movement. For the plural, point to each eye.

eye[2] *v.* See sign for LOOK OVER[1].

eyebrows *pl. n.* The fringes of hair that grow on the bony ridge above the eyes: *She has thin eyebrows.*

■ [Location and shape of eyebrows] Beginning with the fingers of both *G hands* on each eyebrow, palms facing each other, bring the hands outward to the sides while closing the index fingers to the thumbs. [Use one hand for the singular form of this sign.]

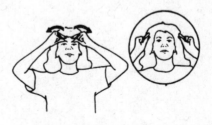

eyeglasses *pl. n.* See sign for GLASSES.

eyelashes *pl. n.* The fringes of hair along the edges of the eyelids: *putting mascara on her eyelashes.*

■ [Mime movement of eyelashes] Beginning with both *4 hands* near each side of the face, palms facing down and fingers pointing forward, bend the hands back, ending with the fingers pointing upward at an angle.

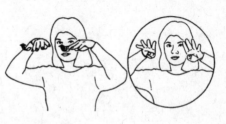

eyepatch *n.* A pad worn to protect an injured eye: *The general never appears without an eyepatch on his left eye.* Same sign used for: **patch, pirate.**

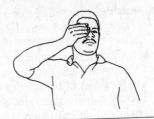

- ■ [Shows location of an eye patch] Place the fingers of the right *open hand* on the right eye, palm facing in and fingers pointing left.

eyesight *n.* See sign for SEE[1].

eyewitness *n.* See sign for WITNESS[3].

fable[1] *n.* A story made up to teach a moral or a practical lesson: *According to the fable about the tortoise and the hare, slow and steady wins the race.*

■ [**tell**[1] + **story**[1,2]] Beginning with the extended right index finger pointing toward the mouth, palm facing in, move the hand forward, ending with the finger pointing up in front of the face. Then, with the thumbs and index fingers of both hands near each other in front of the chest, palms facing each other, pull the hands apart with a repeated movement to each side of the chest while pinching the thumbs and index fingers of each hand together.

fable[2] *n.* See sign for STORY[1,2].

fabric *n.* A woven material: *made of silk fabric.* See also sign for MATERIAL. Same sign used for: **cloth.**

■ [**clothes** + **material**] Brush the thumbs of both *5 hands* downward on each side of the chest with a double movement. Then rub the thumb and fingertips of both *flattened O hands* together in front of each side of the chest, palms facing up.

face[1] *n.* The front part of the head, from the forehead to the chin: *You shouldn't let your hair hide your face.*

■ [Location and shape of face] Draw a large circle around the face with the extended right index finger, palm facing in.

face[2] *n.* (alternate sign)

■ [Location of face] Bring the thumb side of both *L hands,* palms facing forward, against each side of the face.

face

face[3] *v.* To confront directly: *to face the dilemma rationally.* Same sign used for: **approach, confront, encounter, face to face, facing, interface, presence.**

- [Represents two things facing each other] Move both *open hands,* right palm facing down and left palm facing up, upward in front of the body while keeping the palms facing each other, ending with the left hand somewhat forward of the right hand.

face to face See sign for IN FRONT OF.

facing *adj., v.* (*pres. participle of* FACE) See signs for FACE, IN FRONT OF.

fact *n.* See signs for TRUTH[1,2].

factory *n.* See sign for MACHINE.

faculty *n.* The teaching staff at a school or college: *The faculty will have a meeting tomorrow.*

- [Initialized sign similar to sign for **member**[2]] Touch the fingertips of the right *F hand,* palm facing left, first to the left side of the chest and then to the right side of the chest.

fade *v.* See sign for VAGUE.

fade away *v. phrase.* See sign for DISSOLVE.

fail[1] *v.* To not succeed: *failed his final exam.* Related form: **failure** *n.*

- Beginning with the back of the right *V hand* on the heel of the left *open hand,* palm facing up, move the right hand across the left palm and off the fingers.

fail[2] *v.* See sign for FLUNK.

faint *v.* To lose consciousness temporarily: *He fainted from hunger.* Same sign used for: **coma, unconscious.**

- Touch both extended index fingers, palms facing down, to each side of the forehead. Then drop the hands down while opening into *5 hands,* ending with both palms facing in and fingers pointing down in front of each side of the chest.

fair[1] *adj.* Not favoring one over others: *a fair test.*
Related form: **fairly** *adv.*

- [Initialized sign] Tap the middle finger of the right
F hand, palm facing left, against the chin with a
repeated movement.

---

fair[2] *n.* A gathering to show or sell goods, often
combined with entertainment: *We go to the state
fair every year.* Same sign used for: **carnival, ferris
wheel.**

- [Represents seats of a ferris wheel going around]
Beginning with the right *bent V hand* in front of the
right shoulder and the left *bent V hand* in front of
the left side of the chest, palms facing forward,
move the hands forward in large alternating circles.

---

fair[3] *adj.* Neither good nor bad: *I feel
just fair, but I'm getting better.* Same
sign used for: **sort of, so-so.**

- [Natural gesture showing
ambivalence] Rock the right *5 hand*,
palm facing down, from side to side
with a repeated movement in front
of the right side of the body.

---

fair[4] *adj.* See signs for EQUAL, EVEN[1].

---

fairy *n.* A tiny being with magical powers: *In the
story, the fairy gives the princess three wishes.*

- [Initialized sign similar to sign for **angel**[1]] Beginning
with the fingertips of both *F hands* on each
shoulder, palms facing down, twist the wrists
forward and outward, ending with both palms
facing outward and the *F hands* tapping downward
with a double movement near each shoulder.

---

fairy tale[1] *n.* **1.** A story, usually for children, about magical creatures and events: *to
read a fairy tale to the little children.* **2.** A misleading statement or story: *I can't
believe you'd tell me such a
fairy tale as an excuse.*

- [**fairy + story**[1,2]]
Beginning with the
fingertips of both *F hands*
on each shoulder, palms
facing down, twist the
wrists forward and
outward, ending with both palms facing outward and the *F hands* tapping downward
with a double movement near each shoulder.

fairy tale[2] *n.* (alternate sign)

■ [**invent** + **story**[1,2]] Beginning with the index-finger side of the right *B hand* touching the forehead, palm facing left, move the hand forward in an arc. Then, with the thumbs and index fingers of both hands near each other in front of the chest, palms facing each other, pull the hands apart with a repeated movement to each side of the chest while pinching the thumbs and index fingers of each hand together.

faith[1] *n.* Belief without proof: *faith in God.*

■ [**think**[1] + initialized sign similar to sign for **trust**] Move the extended right index finger from touching the right side of the forehead downward while changing into an *F hand*, ending with the bottom of the index finger of the right *F hand* on top of the index finger of the left *F hand* in front of the body, palms facing each other.

faith[2] *n.* (alternate sign)

■ [**think**[1] + **confident**] Move the extended right index finger from touching the right side of the forehead downward while changing into an *S hand*, ending with the little-finger side of the right *S hand* on the thumb side of the left *S hand* in front of the body, palms facing in opposite directions.

faith[3] *n.* (alternate sign)

■ [Initialized sign] Move the right *F hand*, palm facing left, in a circular movement over the left *F hand*, palm facing right, ending with the little-finger side of the right *F hand* landing across the index-finger side of the left *F hand*.

faithful *adj.* Loyal, steady, and reliable: *a faithful friend.*

■ [Initialized sign similar to sign for **regular**] Tap the little-finger side of the right *F hand*, palm facing left, on the thumb side of the left *F hand*, palm facing right, with a double movement.

fake[1] *n.* **1.** A product of the imagination: *The story is a well-constructed fake.* —*adj.* **2.** Of, pertaining to, or created by the imagination: *a fake tale of woe.* Same sign used for: **fiction, hypothetical, virtual.**

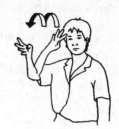

- [Indicates a source in the imagination rather than reality] Beginning with the index finger of the right *4 hand* touching the right side of the forehead, move the hand forward while forming several circles, palm facing left.

fake[2] *adj.* Designed to deceive or trick: *a fake mustache; fake money.* Same sign used for: **artificial, counterfeit, impostor, pseudo, sham, synthetic.**

- [Formed similar to sign for **false** indicating pushing the truth aside.] Brush the extended right index finger, palm facing left, with a double movement across the tip of the nose from right to left by bending the wrist.

fake[3] *adj.* (alternate sign) Same sign used for: **artificial, counterfeit, pseudo, sham, synthetic.**

- Brush index-finger side of the right *bent hand*, palm facing down, across the chin from right to left.

fake[4] *adj.* See sign for HYPOCRITE.

fall[1] *v.* **1.** To come down or drop down quickly from a standing position: *to fall on the ice.* —*n.* **2.** An act or instance of falling down: *I had a bad fall.*

- [Represents legs slipping out from under a person] Beginning with the fingertips of the right *V hand* pointing down, palm facing in, touching the upturned palm of the left *open hand*, flip the right hand over, ending with the back of the right *V hand* lying across the left palm.

fall[2] *v.* **1.** To come down quickly from a higher to a lower position: *to fall from a horse.* —*n.* **2.** An act or instance of falling from a higher to a lower position: *hasn't yet recovered from his fall from the balcony.*

- [Represents legs falling from a higher place] Beginning with the right *V hand* in front of the body, palm facing in and fingers pointing left, flip the right hand over and down, ending with the palm facing up and the fingers pointing forward.

fall³ *n.* The season between summer and winter: *expecting cool weather in the fall.* Same sign used for: **autumn.**

- Brush the index-finger side of the right *B hand,* palm facing down, downward toward the elbow of the left forearm, held bent across the chest.

fall⁴ *v.* To drop or come down slowly from a higher place: *I love to see the leaves fall from the trees.* Related form: **falling** *n., adj.*

- [Movement of falling leaves] Beginning with the right *V hand* near the right side of the head, palm facing forward and fingers pointing up, and the left *V hand* in front of the chest, palm facing up, bring the right hand down slowly with a wiggly movement while turning the palm over, ending with the palm facing up. Repeat with the left hand near the head.

fall asleep¹ To go to sleep: *The baby fell asleep at last.* Same sign used for: **asleep, doze.**

- [**sleep**² + a gesture that represents the head falling forward when dozing off] Beginning with the right *5 hand* in front of the face, palm facing in and fingers pointing up, bring the hand down while changing into an *A hand,* ending with the right hand, palm down, on top of the left *A hand,* palm up, in front of the body.

fall asleep² (alternate sign) Same sign used for: **asleep, doze.**

- [Gesture represents the eyes closing when dozing off] Beginning with the right *B hand* near the right eye, palm facing down and fingers pointing left, bring the hand down, ending with the little-finger side of right *B hand* on the index-finger side of the left *B hand,* held in front of the chest, both palms facing in and fingers pointing in opposite directions.

fall behind *v. phrase.* See sign for AVOID¹.

fall for *v. phrase. Slang.* Same sign used for: **flip over** (slang). To fall in love with: *He fell for her the minute he saw her.* Same sign used for: **adore, fall in love.**

- [One falls into a swoon over another] Beginning with the extended right index finger near the face, palm facing forward, bring the hand down to land on the palm of the left *open hand,* palm facing up, and slide the right hand forward off the left fingertips.

fall in love[1] To become filled with intense passionate affection and tenderness for another: *They fell in love and became engaged.*

- [The heart is touched, causing the person to fall into a swoon] Beginning with the bent middle finger of the right *5 hand* touching the chest, palm facing in, bring the right hand downward while changing into a *V hand* and landing on the palm of the left *open hand,* palm facing up. Then slide the right hand forward off the left fingertips.

fall in love[2] See sign for FALL FOR.

fall into *v. phrase.* See sign for PLUNGE INTO.

fall through *v. phrase.* See sign for BREAK DOWN.

false *adj.* Not true or correct: *a false statement.*

- [Similar to sign for **fake**[3] indicating pushing the truth aside.] Brush the extended right index finger, palm facing left, across the tip of the nose from right to left by bending the wrist.

falsehood *n.* See signs for LIE[1,2].

false teeth[1] *pl. n.* Artificial teeth: *to wear false teeth.* Same sign used for: **dentures.**

- [Mime putting in false teeth] Push upward on the front top teeth with the fingers of the right *flattened O hand,* palm facing in.

false teeth[2] *pl. n.* (alternate sign) Same sign used for: **dentures, partial plate.**

- [**false** + **teeth**] Brush the extended right index finger across the tip of the nose from right to left by bending the wrist. Then move the curved index finger of the right *X hand* from right to left across the top front teeth.

familiar *adj.* See sign for AWARE[1].

family *n.* **1.** A group of closely related people, especially parents and their children: *I live with my family.* **2.** An extended group of related people, including grandparents, uncles, aunts, and cousins: *We're having the family over for Thanksgiving dinner.*

- [Initialized sign similar to sign for **class**] Beginning with the fingertips of both *F hands* touching in front of the chest, palms facing each other, bring the hands away from each other in outward arcs while turning the palms in, ending with the little fingers touching.

famished *adj.* See sign for HUNGRY.

famous *adj.* Very well known: *a famous American.* Related form: **fame** *n.* Same sign used for: **notorious.**

- [Similar to sign for **tell**[1], except spreading the words far and wide] Beginning with both extended index fingers pointing to each side of the mouth, palms facing in, move the hands forward and outward in double arcs, ending with the index fingers pointing upward in front of each shoulder.

fan[1] *n.* A device used to stir the air, as a flat half circle for waving in the hand: *Here—you can cool yourself with this fan.*

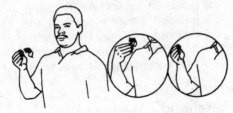

- [Mime fanning oneself] Move the fingers of the right *flattened O hand*, palm facing back, forward and back with a repeated movement near the right side of the face.

fan[2] *n.* An electric device, especially one with blades radiating from a central hub, used to stir the air: *Please turn on the fan.*

- [Represents the movement of an electric fan and the resulting blowing air] Move the extended right index finger, palm facing down and finger pointing forward, in a large circle in front of the right shoulder. Then wave the fingers of the right *5 hand*, palm facing back and fingers pointing up, forward and back near the right side of the face.

fan[3] *n.* (alternate sign)

- [Represents the blades of an electric fan] Beginning with the extended left index finger, palm facing in and finger pointing right, touching the palm of the right *5 hand*, palm facing left, twist the right hand downward with a double movement.

fancy[1] *adj.* Not plain; ornamental; decorative: *a fancy blouse to wear for a special occasion.* Same sign used for: **classical, classy, deluxe, elegant, formal, fussy, grand, luxury, prim, proper.**

■ Move the thumb of the right *5 hand,* palm facing left, upward and forward in a double circular movement in the center of the chest.

fancy[2] *adj.* (alternate sign) Same sign used for: **classical, classy, deluxe, elegant, formal, fussy, grand, luxury, prim, proper.**

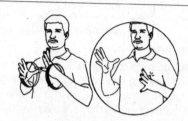

■ Move the thumbs of both *5 hands,* palms facing each other, upward and forward in double alternating circular movements on each side of the chest.

fancy[3] *v., adj.* See signs for DECORATE[2], ELABORATE[1].

fangs *pl. n.* Long, sharp, projecting teeth: *bitten by the snake's fangs.*

■ [Shape and location of fangs] Beginning with both *G hands* in front of the mouth, palms facing each other and forefingers touching, bring the hands downward while pinching the thumb to the index finger of each hand.

fantasize *v.* See sign for DREAM.

fantastic *adj.* See signs for SUPERB, WONDERFUL[1,2].

fantasy[1] *n.* A product of the imagination: *a lovely fantasy about living on a tropical island.* Related form: **fantasize** *v.* Same sign used for: **fiction.**

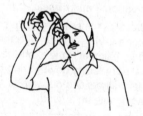

■ [Initialized sign similar to sign for **fake**[1]] Move the right *F hand,* palm facing left, from touching the right side of the forehead forward and upward in a double arc.

fantasy[2] *n.* (alternate sign) Related form: **fantasize** *v.* Same sign used for: **bizarre, fiction.**

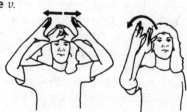

■ [**vision**[2] + **fake**[1,2]] Beginning with the left hand cupped over the right *S hand* in front of the forehead, palms facing each other, move the hands apart while opening into *C hands,* palms facing each other. Then, beginning with the index-finger side of the right *4 hand* touching the right side of the forehead, palm facing left, move the hand forward in an arc.

far[1] *adv.* **1.** At or to a great distance; a long way off: *They live far from here.* —*adj.* **2.** Being at or extending to a great distance: *explored the far frontiers.* Related form: **farther** *adv., adj.* Same sign used for: **distance, distant, remote.**

- [Moves to a location at a far distance] Beginning with the palm sides of both *A hands* together in front of the chest, move the right hand upward and forward in a large arc.

far[2] *adv.* (alternate sign) Same sign used for: **remote.**

- [Indicates a location at a far distance] Move the extended right index finger, palm facing left, upward and forward from in front of the right shoulder with a deliberate movement.

fare *n.* See sign for COST[1].

farewell *interj., n.* See sign for GOOD-BYE.

farm *n.* A tract of land, plus a house, barn, etc., used for raising crops or animals for a livelihood: *lived on a small dairy farm in Vermont.* Same sign used for: **agriculture, bum, casual, ranch, sloppy.**

- Drag the thumb of the right *5 hand,* fingers pointing left, from left to right across the chin.

far-out *adj. Slang.* Exceedingly strange; unconventional and offbeat: *a far-out idea.*

- [Represents something getting smaller as it moves farther away] Beginning with the thumb of the right *C hand,* palm facing left, on the back of the left *open hand,* palm facing down, bring the right hand across the left fingers and outward to the right while changing into an *S hand.*

fascinating *adj.* See signs for INTEREST[1,2].

fashion[1] *n.* The prevailing style of clothes: *dress in the latest fashion.*

- [Initialized sign] Beginning with the right *F hand* in front of the right side of the body, palm facing down, move the hand in an arc to the right.

fashion[2] *n.* (alternate sign) Same sign used for: **style**.

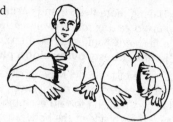

- [Location of clothes on body] Brush the thumbs of both *5 hands* downward on each side of the chest with a repeated alternating movement.

fashion[3] *n.* See sign for CLOTHES.

fast[1] *adj.* **1.** Moving or able to move quickly: *a fast runner.* —*adv.* **2.** Quickly: *ran fast.* Same sign used for: **automatic, immediately, instant, quick, rapid, speedy, spontaneous, sudden, swift**.

- [Natural gesture indicating speed] Beginning with the thumbs of both *A hands* tucked under the index fingers, palms facing each other in front of the body, flick the thumbs out while twisting the wrists quickly forward.

fast[2] *adj., adv.* (alternate sign) Same sign used for: **automatic, immediately, instant, quick, rapid, speedy, spontaneous, sudden, swift**.

- [Demonstrates quickness] Slide the palm of the right *open hand*, palm facing left and fingers pointing forward, with a quick movement from the heel to off the fingers of the left *open hand*, palm facing right and fingers pointing forward.

fast[3] *adj., adv.* (alternate sign) Same sign used for: **automatic, immediately, instant, quick, rapid, speedy, spontaneous, sudden, swift**.

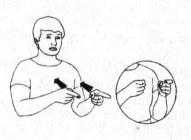

- [Demonstrates quickness] Beginning with both extended index fingers pointing forward in front of the body, palms facing each other, pull the hands quickly back toward the chest while constricting the index fingers into *X hands*.

fast[4] *v.* See sign for ABSTAIN.

fasten *v.* See signs for BELONG[1], STICK[1].

fat

fat[1] *adj.* **1.** Having more flesh than is usual; obese: *dieting to avoid getting fat.* **2.** Well-fed; plump; chubby: *a fat baby.* Same sign used for: **chubby, gain weight, jumbo, obese, overweight, plump.**

■ [Shows shape of fat body] Move both *curved 5 hands* from in front of each side of the chest, palms facing in and fingers pointing toward each other, outward in large arcs to each side of the body.

fat[2] *adj.* (alternate sign) Same sign used for: **chubby, gain weight, obese, overweight, plump.**

■ [Shows shape of fat cheeks] Move both *curved 5 hands* from near each cheek, palms facing each other, outward a short distance while puffing out the cheeks.

fat[3] *adj.* (alternate sign) Same sign used for: **become fat, gain weight.**

■ [Shows shape of fat body] Move both *curved 5 hands* from near each side of the body, palms facing in, outward a short distance.

fat[4] *adj.* (alternate sign) Same sign used for: **fatso** (*disparaging and offensive*), **jumbo, obese, overweight.**

■ Place the knuckles of the right *Y hand,* palm facing in, down on the upturned left *open hand* held in front of the chest.

fate *n.* **1.** What unavoidably happens to one; one's lot or destiny: *Unfortunately, his fate was to be assassinated early in his presidency.* **2.** A higher power that controls the course of events: *Do you believe in fate or free will?* Same sign used for: **prophecy.**

■ [**predict**[1,2] + **future**[2]] Beginning with the fingers of the right *V hand,* palm facing in, pointing toward each eye, move the right hand forward under the left *open hand,* palm facing down in front of the chest. Then move the right *open hand,* palm facing left and fingers pointing up, from near the right cheek forward in a large arc.

father[1] *n.* A male parent: *a picture of my father and mother on their wedding day.* Same sign used for: **dad, daddy, papa.**

- [Formed near male area of the head] Tap the thumb of the right *5 hand,* palm facing left and fingers pointing up, against the middle of the forehead with a repeated movement.

father[2] *n.* (alternate sign) Same sign used for: **dad, daddy, papa.**

- [Formed near male area of the head] With the thumb of the right *5 hand* touching the forehead, palm facing left and fingers pointing up, wiggle the fingers with a repeated movement.

Father *n.* God: *our heavenly Father.*

- [Indicates direction toward heaven] Beginning with the thumb of the right *A hand* touching the right side of the forehead, palm facing left, and the left *A hand* in front of the left side of the head, palm facing right, move both hands upward and forward while changing into *open hands.*

father-in-law *n.* The father of one's husband or wife: *My father-in-law is coming to visit us.*

- [**father**[1,2] + **law**] With the thumb of the right *5 hand* touching the forehead, palm facing left, wiggle the fingers with a repeated movement. Then place the palm side of the right *L hand* first on the fingers and then on the wrist of the left *open hand* held in front of the body, palm facing up.

fatigue *n.* See signs for TIRED, WEAK.

fatso *n.* *Disparaging and offensive.* See sign for FAT[4].

fatten *v.* **1.** To make or become fat: *The actress has to fatten herself for the part.* **2.** To feed (animals) abundantly before slaughter: *to fatten the pigs for market.* Same sign used for: **gain weight.**

- [Shows gaining weight in both face and body] Beginning with both *curved 5 hands* near each side of the face, palms facing each other, bring the hands outward to in front of each shoulder. Then move the hands downward and repeat the movement from in front of each side of the waist.

faucet *n.* A device for turning the flow of water on and off: *Turn on the cold water faucet.*

- [Mime turning on faucets] Beginning with both *curved 3 hands* in front of each side of the body, palms facing down, turn the fingers outward and away from each other with a double movement.

fault[1] *n.* Personal responsibility for doing something wrong, failing to act, or the like: *It was my fault that we were late.*

- [Weight of faults on one's shoulders] Beginning with the fingers of the right *bent hand* on the right shoulder, palm facing down, pivot the hand downward while keeping the fingers in place.

fault[2] *n.* Another's responsibility for doing something wrong, failing to act, or the like: *This argument is all your fault.* Same sign used for: **accusation, blame.**

- [Pushes blame toward another] Push the little-finger side of the right *10 hand,* palm facing left, forward and upward in an arc across the back of the left *S hand,* palm facing down.

fault[3] *n.* See sign for BURDEN.

fault, not my See signs for NOT RESPONSIBLE[1,2].

favor *v.* See sign for PET[1].

favorite[1] *adj.* **1.** Being liked or preferred above others: *Eggdrop soup is my favorite soup.* —*n.* **2.** A contestant with the best chance to win: *Joe is the favorite in the broad-jump.* **3.** A person or thing that is preferred: *I was always daddy's favorite.* Related form: **favor** *v.* Same sign used for: **flavor, prefer, preference, rather, type, typical.**

- [Taste something on the finger] Touch the bent middle finger of the right *5 hand,* palm facing in, to the chin with a double movement.

favorite[2] *adj.* See sign for PARTIAL TO.

fawn *n.* A deer less than a year old: *It's an incredible experience to see a fawn in the woods.*

- [**baby**[1] + **deer**] With the bent right arm cradled on the bent left arm, both palms facing up, swing the arms from left to right in front of the body with a double movement. Then place the thumbs of both *5 hands* on each side of the forehead, palms angled forward.

fear[1] *n.* **1.** A distressing feeling of anxiety and worry, as over impending danger: *shaking with fear during the battle.* —*v.* **2.** To regard with fear; be in dread of: *What they fear most is losing their jobs.* Related form: **fearful** *adj.* Same sign used for: **coward, frightened, scared.**

- [Natural gesture of protecting the body from the unknown] Beginning with both *5 hands* in front of each side of the chest, palms facing in and fingers pointing toward each other, move the hands toward each other with a short double movement.

fear[2] *n.* **1.** Reverence and awe: *fear of God.* —*v.* **2.** To have reverential awe of: *to promise to fear God always.* Related form: **fearful** *adj.*

- [Natural gesture of protecting the body from the unknown] Beginning with both *5 hands* in front of the chest, palms facing forward, move the hands down with a wavy movement.

feast *n.* See sign for BANQUET.

feather[1] *n.* One of the horny shafts, each bearing a series of interlocking barbs, that form the covering of a bird: *fluffy pillows stuffed with feathers.*

- [Shape of feather in a hat] Beginning with the fingers of the right *G hand*, palm facing left, on the right side of the head, bring the hand upward to the right while pinching the index finger and thumb together.

feather[2] *n.* (alternate sign)

- [Shape of a feather] Beginning with both *G hands* in front of the body, fingers touching and palms facing each other, right hand above left hand, pull the right hand upward toward the right shoulder while pinching the index fingers and thumbs of each hand together.

feces *n.* Waste matter discharged from the bowels; excrement: *to flush the feces down the toilet.* Same sign used for: **bowel movement, bullshit** (*vulgar, slang*), **defecation, excrement, manure, shit** (*vulgar*).

- [Secretion of feces] Beginning with the thumb of the right *10 hand*, palm facing left, inserted in the little-finger side of the left *A hand*, palm facing right, bring the right hand deliberately downward.

federal

federal *adj.* Of the central government of a country: *exempt from federal taxes.*

■ [Initialized sign similar to sign for **government**[1]] Beginning with the right *F hand* near the right side of the head, palm facing forward, twist the wrist forward and bring the fingertips against the right temple.

fed up Having reached the limit of tolerance: *We're all fed up with your behavior.*

■ [Indicates filling something to the top] Move the right *B hand,* palm facing down, from the center of the chest upward with a quick deliberate movement, ending with back of the right fingers under the chin.

fee *n.* See sign for COST[1].

feeble *adj.* See sign for WEAK.

feeble-minded[1] *adj.* Mentally deficient; lacking normal mental powers: *a feeble-minded person.*

■ [Indicates weakness in the brain] Beginning with the fingers of the right *curved hand* touching the right side of the forehead, palm facing down, with a double movement push the hand back toward the forehead, bending the fingers each time.

feeble-minded[2] *adj.* See sign for MORON[2].

feed[1] *v.* To give food to: *It's time to feed the baby.* Same sign used for: **nourish, nurture, supply.**

■ [Offering food to another] Beginning with the right *flattened O hand* in front of the mouth and the left *flattened O hand* somewhat forward, both palms facing in, bring the hands down simultaneously, ending with both palms facing up and the hands moving forward with a small repeated movement.

feed[2] *v.* To supply for use: *feed the paper into the copier.* Same sign used for: **supply.**

■ [Offering something to another] Beginning with both *flattened O hands* in front of each side of the body, palms facing up and right hand somewhat forward of the left hand, push the hands forward a short distance with a double movement.

feedback[1] *n.* Reaction and response directed to an original source of information: *Good feedback from his first class allowed him to improve his teaching.*

- [Abbreviation **f-b** moving back into the past] Beginning with the right *F hand* in front of the right side of the body, palm facing left, move the hand back toward the right shoulder while changing into a *B hand,* palm facing in.

feedback[2] *n.* (alternate sign) Same sign used for: **impeach.**

- [Initialized sign indicating information going both ways] Beginning with both *F hands* in front of each side of the chest, right palm facing forward and left palm facing in, move the hands with a double movement in opposite directions to and from the chest.

feel *v.* To sense by touch or awareness: *The wool blanket feels rough. I feel happy.* Related form: **feeling** *n.* Same sign used for: **motive, sensation, sense.**

- [Bent middle finger indicates feeling in sign language] Move the bent middle finger of the right *5 hand,* palm facing in, upward on the chest. Sometimes formed with a repeated movement.

fellowship *n.* See sign for ASSOCIATE.

felony *n.* See signs for CRIME[1,2].

female *n.* See signs for LADY, WOMAN.

fence *n.* A barrier, as of wooden posts or wire, used to enclose a field, yard, etc.: *A fence around the yard will keep the stray dogs out.*

- [Shape of interlocking fence rails] Beginning with both *4 hands* in front of the chest, fingers pointing in opposite directions and overlapping, both palms facing in, move the hands outward to in front of each shoulder.

fencing *n.* The art of fighting with swords or foils: *I enjoy fencing.*

- [Mime fencing] Beginning with the left *curved hand* held near the left side of the head, palm facing right, and the right *A hand* in front of the right side of the body, palm facing left, move the right arm forward a short distance.

ferris wheel *n.* See sign for FAIR[2].

ferry *n.* A boat used to carry people and goods across a narrow stretch of water: *take the ferry.* Alternate form: **ferryboat.**

■ [**boat** + indication of the paddle wheel on a ferry] With the little-finger sides of both *curved hands* together, palms facing up, move the hands forward a short distance. Then move the extended right index finger in a repeated circle near the wrist of the left *open hand,* palm facing right.

fertilize *v.* See sign for CONFLICT[1].

festival *n.* See sign for CELEBRATE.

feud *n.* **1.** A long quarrel, usually between families: *a long, bitter feud over property lines.* —*v.* **2.** To engage in a feud: *The two families feuded for many years.*

■ [**family** + **argue**[1,2]] Beginning with the fingertips of both *F hands* touching in front of the chest, palms facing each other, bring the hands away from each other in outward arcs while turning the palms in, ending with the little fingers touching. Then, beginning with both extended index fingers pointing toward each other in front of the chest, one hand higher than the other and palms facing in, move the hands up and down in opposite directions with a repeated movement by bending the wrists.

fever[1] *n.* A condition in which the body temperature is above normal: *The baby has a slight fever.*

■ [**thermometer**[2] + **temperature**] Beginning with the extended right index finger in the corner of the mouth, palm facing down, move the finger down and rub the back of it, palm facing in, up and down with a repeated movement on the extended left index finger held up in front of the chest.

fever[2] *n.* (alternate sign)

■ [Initialized sign similar to sign for **temperature**] Move the fingertips of the right *F hand,* palm facing left, up and down with a repeated movement on the extended left index finger held up in front of the chest.

fever[3] *n.* See sign for TEMPERATURE.

few *adj.* Not many but more than one: *costs a few dollars more than I would like.* Same sign used for: **several.**

- Beginning with the right *A hand* held in front of the right side of the chest, palm facing up, slowly spread out each finger from the index finger to the little finger, ending with an upturned *4 hand.*

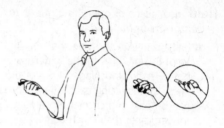

few days ago, a At a recent time in the past, less than a week previous but more than one or two days: *She arrived from Canada a few days ago.*

- [The fingers move into the past] Beginning with the thumb of the right *A hand* on the right cheek, palm facing down, twist the hand up while changing into a *3 hand* and keeping the thumb in place on the cheek.

few seconds ago, a See sign for WHILE AGO, A.

fiancé (or **fiancée**) *n.* A man (or a woman) engaged to be married: *Her parents haven't met her fiancé. My brother's fiancée has a beautiful engagement ring.*

- [Initialized sign similar to sign for **engaged**] Beginning with the right *F hand* over the left *open hand,* both palms facing down, move the right hand in a small circle and then straight down to land on the ring finger of the left hand.

fib *v.* See signs for BETRAY[1], FOOL[1], LIE[1,2].

fiction *n.* See signs for FAKE[1], FANTASY[1,2].

fiddle *n.* See sign for VIOLIN.

field[1] *n.* A range or sphere of interest or of professional activity: *studying the field of biology.*

- [Initialized sign similar to sign for **specialize**[1]] Move the fingertips of the right *F hand,* palm facing down, forward along the length of the index finger of the right *B hand* palm facing right, from the base to the tip.

field[2] *n.* A piece of open land: *plans to plant corn in the field.*

- [Initialized sign showing the area of a field] Beginning with the fingertips of both *F hands* touching in front of the chest, palms facing each other, move the hands apart in a circular movement forward until they touch again.

field[3] *n.* See signs for COLUMN[2], LAND[1], SPECIALIZE[1].

field trip *n.* See sign for TOUR.

fierce[1] *adj.* Violent in force and intensity: *a fierce argument.* Same sign used for: **angry, savage.**

- Beginning with both *curved 5 hands* near each other in front of the chest, palms facing in, bring the hands abruptly upward to near each side of the head.

fierce[2] *adj.* See sign for AWFUL.

fifth *adj.* **1.** Next after the fourth: *the fifth person to telephone.* —*n.* **2.** The one after the fourth in a series of five or more: *He is the fifth in line.* —*adv.* **3.** In the fifth place: *She placed fifth in the competition.* Same sign used for: **five dollars.**

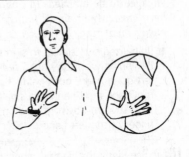

- [**five** formed with a twisting movement used for ordinal numbers] Beginning with the right *5 hand* in front of the right side of the chest, palm angled forward, twist the hand to the left, ending with the palm facing in.

fight[1] *n.* **1.** An angry dispute or a violent struggle: *having a fight over money.* —*v.* **2.** To engage in such a dispute or struggle: *to fight with their fists.* Related form: **fighting.**

- [Mime two people striking at each other] Beginning with both *S hands* in front of each shoulder, palms facing each other, move the hands deliberately toward each other, ending with the wrists crossed in front of the chest.

fight[2] *v.* See signs for ARGUE[1,2], BOXING.

fight[3] *n.* See sign for COMBAT.

figure *n., v.* See signs for ARITHMETIC, COUNT, MULTIPLY, SHAPE[1,2].

figure out *v. phrase.* See signs for ARITHMETIC, MULTIPLY.

file[1] *v.* To put away in convenient order for storage and reference: *File the forms in the drawer.* Same sign used for: **sort.**

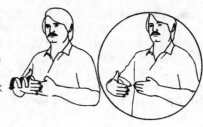

- [Seems to put things in order] Beginning with the palm of the right *open hand*, palm facing in and fingers pointing left, touching the back of the left *open hand*, palm facing in and fingers pointing right, move the right hand forward in a double series of small arcs.

file[2] *v.* (alternate sign) Same sign used for: **sort.**

- [Insert something in order to file it] Slide the little-finger side of the right *B hand*, palm angled up, between the middle finger and ring finger of the left *B hand* held in front of the chest, palm facing in.

file[3] *v.* (alternate sign) Same sign used for: **sort.**

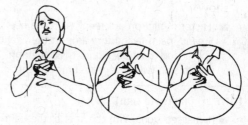

- [Insert things in order to file them] Slide the little-finger side of the right *B hand*, palm angled up, between the fingers of the left *B hand*, palm facing in, beginning with between the index and middle fingers and moving in turn to between the ring and little fingers.

file[4] *n.* **1.** A tool with a rough surface for smoothing or grinding down metal, wood, etc.: *Use a file on the key to make it fit the lock.* —*v.* **2.** To smooth edges or surfaces with or as if with a file: *filing the broken fingernail.* Same sign used for: **emery board, nail file.**

- [Mime filing one's fingernails] Rub the extended fingers of the right *H hand*, palm facing left, forward and back with a short repeated movement on the fingertips of the left *B hand*, palm facing down.

file[5] *n.* Same as sign for FILE[2], but made with a double movement.

file[6] *v.* See signs for APPLY[1], RASP.

fill *v.* See signs for POUR[1,2].

filled *adj.* See sign for FULL[2].

fill in or **fill out** *v. phrase.* To complete, as by supplying information: *fill in the blanks.*

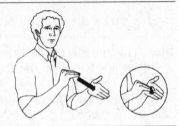

- ■ [Represents documenting something on paper] Touch the fingertips of the right *flattened O hand*, palm facing down, on the upturned left *open hand* in several places.

fill up[1] *v. phrase.* To fill completely: *fill up the tank with gas.*

- ■ [Shows rising level of something in a container] Bring the right *B hand*, palm facing down and fingers angled left, upward until level with the index-finger side of the left *C hand*, palm facing right.

fill up[2] *v. phrase.* See sign for REFILL[2].

film[1] *n.* A series of consecutive pictures projected onto a screen so rapidly that they appear to move, often telling a story; motion picture: *watching a rented film on the VCR.* Same sign used for: **cinema, movie, show.**

- ■ [Flicker of film on a screen] With the heel of the right *5 hand*, palm facing forward, on the heel of the left *open hand*, palm facing in, twist the right hand from side to side with a repeated movement.

film[2] *n.* (alternate sign)

- ■ [Initialized sign] With the heel of the right *F hand*, palm facing forward, on the heel of the left *open hand*, palm facing in, twist the right hand from side to side with a repeated movement.

film[3] *n.* See sign for MOVIE CAMERA.

filmstrip *n.* A series of pictures printed on a reel of film and projected one at a time on a screen: *watched a filmstrip on national parks.*

- ■ [**film**[1,2] + gesture miming unrolling a filmstrip] With the heel of the right *5 hand* on the heel of the left *open hand*, palm facing in, twist the right hand from side to side with a repeated movement. Then, beginning with the thumbs and index fingers of both *G hands* touching, right hand over the left hand and palms facing each other, move the right hand up and the left hand down away from each other.

filthy[1] *adj.* Very dirty: *a filthy room.*

- [Similar to sign for **dirty** except exaggerated] Beginning with the back of the right *S hand* under the chin, palm facing down, flick the fingers open with a deliberate movement, forming a *5 hand.*

filthy[2] *adj.* See sign for DIRTY.

fin *n.* A moveable fan-like organ extending from the body of a fish and used especially for propulsion and steering: *The fish moved its fins slowly as it glided through the water.*

- [**fish**[2] + shows location and action of a fish's fin] With the extended left index finger touching the wrist of the right *B hand,* move the right fingers back and forth with a double movement. Then place the heel of the right *B hand* on the left side of the neck and wiggle the fingers forward and back with a small repeated movement.

final *adj.* See sign for LAST[1]. Related form: **finally** *adv.*

finally[1] *adv.* At last; at the final moment: *They finally decided to move out of town.* Same sign used for: **at last, Pah!, succeed.**

- Beginning with both extended index fingers pointing up near each cheek, palms facing in, twist the wrists forward, ending with the index fingers pointing up in front of each shoulder, palms facing forward.

finally[2] *adv.* (alternate sign) Related form: **final** *adj.*

- [Similar to sign for **end**[2]] Swing the extended right little finger back toward the chest and then straight down, striking the extended little finger of the left hand, palm facing right, as it moves.

finances *pl. n.* Monetary resources and their management: *hiring an accountant to handle your finances.* Related form: **financial** *adj.* Same sign used for: **fund.**

- [Initialized sign similar to sign for **money**] Tap the back of the right *F hand,* palm facing up, with a double movement on the upturned left palm.

find[1] *v.* To locate or come upon, on purpose or by chance: *found a quarter in my pocket.* Same sign used for: **discover, draw.**

- [Picking up a found object] Beginning with the right *curved 5 hand* inserted in palm side of the left *curved 5 hand,* palm facing right in front of the body, bring the right hand upward while closing the thumb and index finger, forming an *F hand.*

find[2] *v.* (alternate sign) Same sign used for: **discover, locate, pick up.**

- [Represents finding something and picking it up] Beginning with right *5 hand* in front of the right side of the body, palm facing down, bring the hand upward while closing the thumb and index finger, forming an *F hand.*

fine[1] *adj.* **1.** Of superior quality; very good: *served a fine wine.* **2.** In good health: *I feel fine, thank you.* Same sign used for: **okay, well.**

- Beginning with the thumb of the right *5 hand* touching the chest, palm facing left, move the hand forward a short distance.

fine[2] *adj.* Consisting of minute particles: *Grind the coffee beans to a fine powder.*

- [The fingers feel a fine texture] Beginning with the right *F hand* in front of the right shoulder, palm facing forward, rub the tip of the index finger and thumb together with a quick small movement.

fine[3] See sign for COST[1].

finest *adj.* Of the best or most desirable quality: *the finest day we've had this week.* Same sign used for: **excellent, terrific, whew.**

- With the thumb of the right *5 hand* touching the chest, palm facing left and fingers pointing up, wiggle the fingers with a repeated movement.

finger *n.* Any of the jointed appendages of the hand (sometimes excluding the thumb): *broke my finger.*

- ■ [Location of finger] Rub the fingertip of the extended right index finger back and forth along the length of the index finger of the left *5 hand* with a repeated movement.

fingernail *n.* The hard covering on the end of each finger: *paint my fingernails with frosted polish.*

- ■ [Location] Tap the right extended index fingertip on the fingernail of the left extended index finger with a repeated movement.

fingernail polish *n.* See sign for POLISH[2].

fingerprint *n.* The pattern of marks made by pressing the tip of the finger on a surface: *The burglar left fingerprints all over the windowsill.*

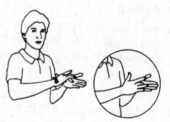

- ■ [Mime having one's fingerprints taken] Beginning with the bent middle finger of the right *5 hand* touching the palm of the left *open hand*, palms facing each other, twist the right hand forward with a double movement.

fingerspell *v.* To spell out words with the hands using the Manual Alphabet: *to fingerspell your name.* Same sign used for: **spell.**

- ■ [Represents action of fingers when fingerspelling] Move the right *5 hand*, palm facing down, from in front of the chest to the right while wiggling the fingers.

fingerspelling *n.* Same as sign for FINGERSPELL, but made with a double movement.

finish[1] *v.* To bring or come to an end; complete: *to finish the project on time; waiting for the movie to finish.* Same sign used for: **already, complete, done, over, then, through.**

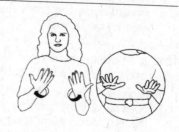

- ■ Beginning with both *5 hands* in front of the chest, palms facing in and fingers pointing up, flip the hands over with a sudden movement, ending with both palms facing down and fingers pointing forward.

finish[2] *v.* (alternate sign) Same sign used for: **already, complete, done, over, then.**

- Beginning with the right *5 hand* in front of the right side of the chest, palm facing in and fingers pointing up, flip the hand over with a sudden movement, ending with the palm facing down and the fingers pointing forward.

finish[3] *v.* See sign for END[2].

finish[4] *v.* See signs for BEEN (THERE), END[2].

Finland[1] *n.* A republic in northern Europe: *The capital of Finland is Helsinki.* Related form: **Finnish** *adj., n.*

- Tap the fingertip of the right *X hand*, palm facing in, against the chin with a double movement.

Finland[2] *n.* (alternate sign) Related form: **Finnish** *adj., n.*

- [Initialized sign] Tap the thumb side of the right *F hand* against the center of the forehead with a double movement.

fire[1] *n.* Flames, heat, and light produced by something burning: *start a fire with a match.* Same sign used for: **blaze, flame.**

- [Represents flames] Move both *5 hands*, palms facing up, from in front of the waist upward in front of the chest while wiggling the fingers.

fire[2] *n.* (alternate sign) Same sign used for: **blaze, flame.**

- Beginning with both *5 hands* in front of the chest, left hand higher than the right hand, palms facing in and fingers pointing upward, move the hands in large forward alternating circles in front of the chest while wiggling the fingers.

fire[3] *v.* To dismiss from a job: *They fired the three employees for theft.* Same sign used for: **dismiss, let go, terminate.**

- [Indicates cutting a job short] Swing the back of the right *open hand*, palm facing up, across the index-finger side of the left *B hand*, palm facing in.

fire[4] *v.* See signs for SHOOT[1,2].

firefighter[1] *n.* A person trained to put out destructive fires: *The firefighters arrived too late to save the house.*

- [**fire**[1,2] + **person marker**] Move both *5 hands,* palms facing in, from in front of the waist upward in front of the chest while wiggling the fingers. Then move both *open hands,* palms facing each other, downward along each side of the body.

firefighter[2] *n.* (alternate sign)

- [Represents the raised front of a firefighter's helmet] Bring the back of the right *B hand,* fingers pointing up and palm facing forward, against the center of the forehead with a double movement.

fireman *n.* A person whose job is to put out fires: *The fireman rescued the children from the burning house.* Same sign used for: **firefighter.**

- [**fire**[1,2] + **man**[1,2,3]] Move both *5 hands,* palms facing up, from in front of the waist upward in front of the chest while wiggling the fingers. Then, beginning with the right *flattened C hand* near the forehead, palm facing down, move the hand forward while closing the fingers to the thumb.

fire truck *n.* A vehicle equipped to extinguish a fire; a fire engine: *rushed out of the fire truck into the burning building.*

- [**fire**[1,2] + **truck**] Move both *5 hands,* palms facing up, from in front of the waist upward in front of the chest while wiggling the fingers. Then, beginning with the little-finger side of the right *T hand,* palm facing left, touching the index-finger side of the left *T hand,* palm facing right, move the right hand back toward the chin and the left hand forward.

firewall *n.* A computer system that prevents unauthorized access to or from a private network by examining each message and blocking those that do not meet specified security criteria: *The firewall prevented spam from infecting the computer.*

■ **[Internet + protect]** Beginning with the bent middle fingers of both *5 hands* pointing toward each other in front of the chest, twist both wrists to change positions. Then, with the wrists of both *open hands* crossed in front of the chest, palms facing in opposite directions, move the hands forward a short distance.

firewood *n.* Wood suitable for burning as fuel: *stock up on firewood for the winter.*

■ **[fire**[1,2] **+ wood**[1,2] **+ loaf**[2] indicating the shape of logs] Beginning with both *5 hands* in front of the chest, left hand higher than the right hand, palms facing in and fingers pointing upward, move the hands in large forward alternating circles in front of the chest while wiggling the fingers. Then move the little-finger side of the right *B hand,* palm facing left, forward and back on the index-finger side of the left *B hand,* palm facing in. Then, beginning with both *C hands* near each other in front of the chest, palms facing down, move the hands straight apart.

fireworks *n.* A display of patterns of color and light produced by explosive devices (firecrackers) that burst loudly into the air: *watching the fireworks on the Fourth of July.*

■ [Represents the bursting of fireworks] Beginning with both *S hands* in front of each side of the body, palms facing forward, bring the hands upward and together in front of the chest and then upward and outward to each side near the head while opening into *5 hands.*

firm[1] *adj.* Not easily changed: *a firm decision.*

■ **[strict + gesture showing firmness]** Bring the index-finger side of the bent fingers of the right *U hand* back against the nose, palm facing left. Then, beginning with both *S hands* in front of the chest, palms facing in, move the hands firmly downward.

firm[2] *adj.* Having a solid consistency: *Bake the pudding until it is firm.*

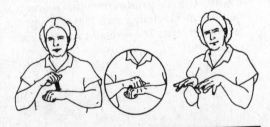

■ **[rock**[1,2] **+ showing the shape of something firm]** Hit the palm side of the right *A hand* with a double movement on the back of the left *A hand,* both palms facing down. Then place both *curved 5 hands*

tensely in front of each side of the body, palms facing down and fingers pointing forward.

firm³ *adj.* See sign for STRICT.

first¹ *adj.* **1.** Coming before others, as in time or order: *the first book I ever read.* —*n.* **2.** The one before all others, as in rank or order, in any series: *the first to finish.* —*adv.* **3.** In the first place; before others: *You can eat first.* Same sign used for: **one dollar.**

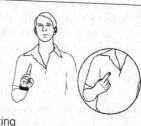

■ [**one** formed with a twisting movement used for ordinal numbers] Beginning with the extended right index finger pointing up in front of the right side of the chest, palm facing forward, twist the hand, ending with the palm facing in.

first² *adj.* (alternate sign) Same sign used for: **original.**

■ [Touches first finger] Touch the extended right index finger, palm facing in, against the extended thumb of the left *10 hand*, palm facing right.

first³ *adj.* (alternate sign) Same sign used for: **first place.**

■ Bring the extended right index finger, palm facing in and finger pointing left, from left to right in front of the chest.

fish¹ *n.* Any of various cold-blooded animals with gills and fins that live in water: *a beautiful fish swimming in the stream.*

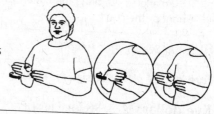

■ [Movement of fish swimming] Beginning with the fingertips of the left *B hand* touching the heel of the right *B hand*, palms facing in opposite directions and fingers pointing forward, wave the right hand back and forth with a repeated movement.

fish² *n.* (alternate sign)

■ [The movement of a fish in water] While touching the wrist of the right *open hand*, palm facing left, with the extended left index finger, swing the right hand back and forth with a double movement.

fish[3] *v.* To use a hook, line, and fishing pole to try to catch fish: *fish all day for trout.* Related form: **fishing** *n.*

- ■ [Mime fishing with a fishing pole] Beginning with both *modified X hands* in front of the body, right hand forward of the left hand and palms facing in opposite directions, move the hands upward by bending the wrists with a double movement.

fist[1] *n.* A hand with the fingers closed tightly into the palm: *He hit me with his fist.*

- ■ [Shows fist] Beginning with the right *S hand* near the face, palm facing in, move the hand forward with a short deliberate double movement.

fist[2] *n.* (alternate sign)

- ■ [Shows fist] While tightly grasping the wrist of the right *S hand* with the left hand, both palms facing back, move the right hand forward a short distance with a deliberate movement.

fit[1] *v.* **1.** To be of the right size (for): *Does the dress fit? Will it fit me if I shorten it?* **2.** Same sign used for: **suit.** To be adapted to or suitable for: *a speech that fits the occasion.* —*n.* **3.** The way in which something fits: *The fit of the jacket is perfect.*

- ■ [Initialized sign showing that two things fit together] Beginning with the right *F hand* in front of the right shoulder, palm angled down, and the left *F hand* in front of the left side of the body, palm angled up, bring the fingertips together in front of the chest.

fit[2] *v., n.* See sign for MATCH[1].

five cents *pl. n.* See sign for NICKEL.

five dollars *pl. n.* See sign for FIFTH.

fix[1] *v.* To mend or repair: *fix the flat tire.* Same sign used for: **maintain, mend, repair.**

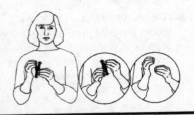

- ■ [The fingers seem to put things together] Brush the fingertips of both *flattened O hands* across each other repeatedly as the hands move up and down in opposite directions in a double movement.

fix[2] *v.* (alternate sign) Same sign used for: **maintain, mend, repair.**

■ [Initialized sign similar to sign for **make**[2]] Beginning with the little-finger side of the right *F hand* on the index finger of the left *F hand*, palms facing in opposite directions, twist the right hand inward with a double movement.

flabbergast[1] *v.* To overcome with shock and surprise; astound: *The news flabbergasted her.* Same sign used for: **astound, awesome, startle.**

■ [Represents a person's mouth opening in amazement] Beginning with the palms of both *bent V hands* together in front of the chest, move the hands apart by bringing the right hand up and the left hand down, and open the mouth at the same time.

flabbergast[2] *v.* (alternate sign) Same sign used for: **astound, awesome, startle.**

■ [Represents a person's mouth opening in amazement] Beginning with the right *S hand* near the right side of the chin, palm facing forward, open the fingers into a *bent 3 hand* while opening the mouth.

flabby *adj.* See sign for LOOSE[1].

flag[1] *n.* A piece of cloth, typically rectangular, marked with distinctive colors or designs and used often as a symbol, as of a country: *watching the parade and waving the American flag.*

■ [Represents a waving flag] While holding the elbow of the raised right arm in the left palm, wave the right *open hand* back and forth with a repeated movement in front of the right shoulder.

flag[2] *n.* (alternate sign)

■ [Represents a waving flag] With the extended left index finger touching the right wrist, wave the right *open hand* back and forth with a repeated movement in front of the right shoulder.

flame *n.* See signs for CANDLE, FIRE[1,2].

flap *v.* **1.** To move about loosely and with some noise: *The flag flapped in the wind.* **2.** To move up and down, as arms: *The bird flew away with wings flapping wildly.*

- [Mime flapping wings] Beginning with both *open hands* in front of the shoulders, fingers pointing up and palms facing forward, bend the wrists of each hand while swinging the arms upward and downward with alternating movements.

flare up *v. phrase.* See sign for BOILING MAD.

flash[1] *n.* **1.** A sudden, brief, bright light from a camera attachment: *The flash hurt my eyes.* **2.** The attachment producing this light: *Use a flash to take a picture in dim indoor light.*

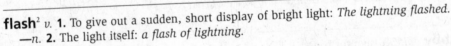

- [Shows a flash of light] Beginning with the heel of the right *flattened O hand*, palm facing down, on the index-finger side of the left *B hand*, palm facing in, flick the right fingers quickly to form a *curved 5 hand* and back again to form a *flattened O hand*.

flash[2] *v.* **1.** To give out a sudden, short display of bright light: *The lightning flashed.* —*n.* **2.** The light itself: *a flash of lightning.*

- [Shows a flash of light] Beginning with the right *flattened O hand*, fingers pointing down, held near the right side of the head, flick the fingers open with a quick repeated movement. [This sign can be formed with two hands.]

flash[3] *n.* See sign for TAKE PICTURES[2].

flashlight[1] *n.* A small portable electric light, often shaped like a cylinder and usually powered by batteries: *Keep a flashlight handy in case the electricity goes out.*

- [Light from a flashlight] While holding the wrist of the right *flattened O hand* with the left hand, flick the right fingers open into a *5 hand*, palm facing down.

flashlight[2] *n.* (alternate sign)

- [Mime holding a flashlight] Move the right *modified C hand,* palm facing left, back and forth in front of the waist with a repeated movement.

flat *adj.* Smooth and level: *a flat surface to write on.*

- [Shows flat surface] Beginning with the index-finger side of the right *bent hand* against the little-finger side of the left *bent hand,* both palms facing down, move the right hand forward a short distance.

flat panel display See sign for FLAT SCREEN DISPLAY.

flat screen display Large-screen televisions or monitors that use alternative technologies to replace the bulky cathode ray tube (CRT), allowing for thinner and larger screens. Same sign used for **flat panel display, liquid crystal display (LED), plasma.**

- [**box + wall**[1]] Beginning with both *open hands* in front of each side of the chest, palms facing each other and fingers pointing forward, move the hands deliberately in opposite directions, ending with the left hand near the chest and the

right hand several inches forward of the left hand, both palms facing in. Then, beginning with both *open hands* together in front of the chest, palms facing forward and fingers pointing up, bring the hands apart, one in front of each shoulder.

flatter *v.* To praise or compliment excessively and insincerely: *Don't try to flatter me just because you want a job.* Related form: **flattery** *n.* Same sign used for: **bluff, floppy.**

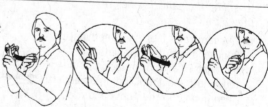

- Swing the right *B hand* back and forth with a repeated movement, brushing the fingers against the extended left index finger held in front of the chest, palm facing right, each time it passes.

flat tire *n.* A tire with too little air for proper support: *My car has a flat tire.*

- [Represents air going out of a tire] Beginning with the thumb of the right *open hand,* palm facing down, on the palm of the upturned left *open hand,* close the right fingers to the thumb, forming a *flattened O hand.*

flatulence *n.* A chronic accumulation of gas in the intestinal tract: *Her flatulence caused her to pass gas.* Related form: **flatus** *n.* Same sign used for: **gas, pass gas.**

- [Action of released gas] Beginning with the wrists of both *S Hands* crossed in front of the body, palms facing down, right hand under the left hand, push the right hand forward while opening into a *5 hand.*

flavor *n.* See sign for FAVORITE.

flee *v.* See sign for RUN AWAY.

flesh *n.* See signs for MEAT, SKIN[1,2].

flexible[1] *adj.* Being easily bent: *a flexible plastic straw.* Same sign used for: **floppy.**

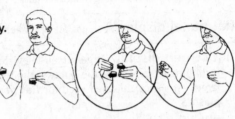

- [Shows something easily bent] With both *flattened O hands* in front of each side of the chest, palms facing in, bend the wrists to move the hands forward and back with an alternating repeated movement.

flexible[2] *adj.* See signs for PLIABLE[1,2].

flier *n.* See sign for PILOT.

flight *n.* See sign for FLY[2].

flip[1] *v.* To turn over with a quick toss: *Flip the pancakes before they burn.*

- [Demonstrates flipping something] Beginning with the middle finger of the right *P hand,* palm facing down, touching the palm of the upturned left *open hand,* flip the right hand over, ending with the back of the right hand in the left palm.

flip[2] *v.* See sign for COOK[1].

flip-flop *v., n.* See signs for SANDAL, TOGGLE.

flip over *v. phrase. Slang.* See sign for FALL FOR.

flirt *v.* To behave amorously without having serious intentions: *He flirted with every girl at the party.* Same sign used for: **philander.**

■ [Represents batting one's eyelashes] Beginning with the thumbs of both *5 hands* touching in front of the chest, palms facing down and fingers pointing forward, wiggle the fingers up and down with an alternating movement.

float *n.* The amount of time following the completion of one computer activity and the start of the next activity: *Start the printer during the float.* Related form: **floating** *adj.*

■ [Initialized sign] Beginning with the right *F hand* in front of the right side of the chest, palm facing forward, move the hand with a wavy movement to the right.

flock[1] *n.* **1.** A large group, as of sheep or birds, that live and travel together: *a flock of geese.* **2.** A large group of people or things gathered together: *a flock of teenagers around the rock star.* —*v.* **3.** To go or gather in a large group: *The people flocked to the carnival.* Same sign used for: **flow.**

■ [Shows movement of a flock of geese] Beginning with the right *S hand* near the right side of the face and the left *S hand* in front of the left shoulder, move both hands forward while opening into *5 hands,* palms facing down and fingers pointing forward.

flock[2] *v.* See signs for GATHER[2,3].

flood *n.* **1.** A great flow or overflow of water, especially covering land not usually submerged: *The basement was damaged in the flood.* —*v.* **2.** To cover with a flood: *Water flooded the kitchen floor.* **3.** To overflow: *The river flooded during the heavy rain.*

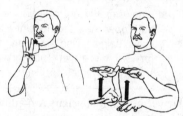

■ [**water** + showing level of water rising] Tap the index finger of the right *W hand,* palm facing left, against the chin. Then, beginning with both *5 hands* in front of the waist, palms facing down and fingers pointing forward, raise the hands to in front of the chest.

floor *n.* The horizontal surface that is walked upon at the bottom of a room: *mop the floor.*

■ [Shows flatness of a floor's surface] Beginning with the index-finger side of both *B hands* touching in front of the waist, palms facing down and fingers pointing forward, move the hands apart to each side.

floppy

floppy[1] *adj.* See sign for FLATTER. Shared idea of lack of steadiness.

floppy[2] *adj.* See sign for FLEXIBLE[1].

floppy disk *n.* See sign for DISK.

florist *n.* A person who sells flowers and plants in a retail store: *We'll have the florist send a bouquet of roses to the hostess.*

- ■ [**flower + person marker**] Touch the fingertips of the right *flattened O hand*, palm facing down, first to the right side of the nose and then to the left side. Then move both *open hands*, palms facing each other, downward along each side of the body.

floss *n.* **1.** A strong, thin thread, sometimes waxed, for dislodging food particles from between the teeth: *cleaned his teeth with dental floss.* —*v.* **2.** To use dental floss to clean the teeth: *She flosses her teeth daily.*

- ■ [Mime flossing] Beginning with the right *F hand* in front of the right side of the face, palm facing left, and the left *modified X hand* pinched together near the left side of the mouth, palm facing right, move the hands forward and back with an alternating double movement.

flow[1] *n.* The sequence of events in a computer program: *to print a chart of the program's flow from beginning to end.*

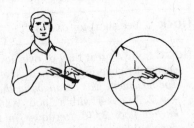

- ■ [Shows movement of a flow] Beginning with both *open hands* in front of each side of the chest, palms facing down and fingers pointing forward, move the hands forward with a smooth movement.

flow[2] *n.* (alternate sign) A nonlinear movement or transmission of signals from one location to another.

- ■ [Shows movement of a flow] Beginning with both *open hands* in front of the right side of the body, right palm facing up and left palm facing down, swing the hands to the left with a double movement.

flow[3] *n., v.* See signs for FLOCK[1], STREAM. Shared idea of smooth movement, as of birds flying.

flower *n.* The blossom part of a plant, often having a pleasing color and fragrance: *Smell the flowers.*

- ■ [Holding a flower to the nose to smell it] Touch the fingertips of the right *flattened O hand*, palm facing down, first to the right side of the nose and then to the left side.

---

fluent *adj.* See signs for SMOOTH², SMOOTHLY. Related form: **fluently** *adv.*

---

fluid *n.* Something, especially a liquid, that is capable of flowing: *I must have spilled some kind of fluid on the floor.*

- ■ [**water** + action showing movement of a fluid] Tap the index-finger side of the right *W hand*, palm facing left, against the chin. Then swing the right *5 hand*, palm facing down and fingers pointing forward, from side to side near the palm of the left *5 hand*, palm facing right and fingers pointing forward.

---

flunk *v. Informal.* **1.** To fail in a course or exam: *The teacher says I just flunked.* **2.** To get a failing grade in: *to flunk math.* **3.** To give a failing grade to: *I was shocked when the teacher flunked me.* Same sign used for: **fail.**

- ■ [Initialized sign] Strike the index-finger side of the right *F hand*, palm facing forward, against the palm of the left *open hand*, palm facing right and fingers pointing up.

---

flush *v.* See sign for BLUSH.

---

flush a toilet To send a sudden flow of water through a toilet: *Don't forget to flush the toilet.*

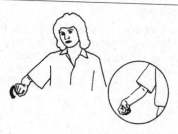

- ■ [Mime flushing a toilet] Beginning with the right *S hand* held in front of the right side of the body, palm facing down, twist the wrist downward with a deliberate movement.

---

flute *n.* A slender pipelike musical instrument with a high range played by holding it to the side and blowing: *plays a flute in the school orchestra.*

- ■ [Mime playing a flute] Move both *curved 5 hands*, palms facing in, with a repeated movement from side to side in front of the mouth while wiggling the fingers.

fly

fly[1] *v.* To move through the air with wings: *watching the birds fly south.* Same sign used for: **wings.**

- [Mime flapping wings to fly] Beginning with both *open hands* near each shoulder, palms facing down and fingers pointing outward in opposite directions, bend the wrists repeatedly, causing the hands to wave.

fly[2] *v.* To travel in an aircraft: *fly home by plane.* Same sign used for: **flight.**

- [Represents an airplane flying] With the thumb, index finger, and little finger of the right hand extended, palm angled down, move the hand forward and upward in front of the right shoulder.

focus[1] *v.* To adjust the lens of so as to make an image clear: *focusing the camera on a cloudy day.*

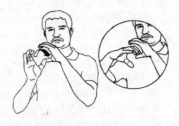

- [Mime adjusting the focus on a lens] Beginning with both *C hands* near each other in front of the chest, palms facing each other and left hand nearer the chest than the right hand, twist the right hand downward to the left.

focus[2] *v.* **1.** To concentrate on a single thing: *Focus on your work.* —*n.* **2.** The central point of attention: *the focus of the conversation.*

- [Directing one's attention] Beginning with both *B hands* near each side of the face, palms facing each other and fingers pointing up, bring the hands down while tipping the fingers downward and toward each other.

focus[3] *v., n.* (alternate sign)

- [The hands seem to turn to focus a spyglass] Beginning with both *C hands* in front of the face, right hand closer to the face than the left hand and the little-finger side of the right hand touching the index-finger side of the left hand, palms facing in opposite directions, twist the hands downward in opposite directions.

focus[4] *v., n.* (alternate sign) Same sign used for: **zoom**.

- [Moving something toward the eye to bring it into focus] Move the right *curved hand* forward and back toward the face with a double movement.

focus on *v. phrase.* See signs for ATTENTION, NARROW DOWN.

foe *n.* See sign for ENEMY.

fold *v.* To bend over on itself: *Fold the letter before putting it in the envelope.*

- [Mime folding paper in half] Beginning with both *open hands* near each other in front of the chest, palms facing up, flip the right hand over in an arc, ending with the right palm on the left palm.

folder[1] *n.* A folded piece of cardboard used for holding papers: *Put the new information in the sales folder.*

- [Represents inserting papers into a folder] Slide the little-finger side of the right *open hand*, palm facing up, with a double movement into the opening formed by the left *flattened C hand*, palm facing up.

folder[2] *n.* See sign for DICTIONARY.

folk *n.* See sign for PEOPLE.

follow *v.* To come after, as in sequence or time: *Look at the children following the parade. The late night movie follows the news.* Same sign used for: **go after, track down, trail**.

- [One hand follows the other hand] With the knuckles of the right *10 hand*, palm facing left, near the wrist of the left *10 hand*, palm facing right, move both hands forward a short distance.

follower *n.* See sign for DISCIPLE[2].

fond of See signs for LIKE[1,2].

food *n.* Anything eaten that sustains life: *to shop for food for dinner.* Same sign used for: **groceries, meal.**

■ [Putting food in one's mouth] Bring the fingertips of the right *flattened O hand,* palm facing in, to the lips with a double movement.

fool[1] *n.* **1.** A person who lacks good sense; a silly or stupid person: *acts like a fool at parties.* **2.** A person who has been tricked or deceived: *You were a fool to believe them.* —*v.* **3.** To trick or deceive: *You can't fool all of the people all of the time.* **4.** To pretend; make believe: *I was only fooling when I said I was leaving.* Related form: **foolish** *adj.* Same sign used for: **fib, pretend.**

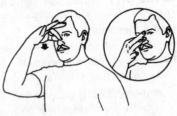

■ With the fingertips of the right *F hand* pinching the bridge of the nose, drop the hand slightly while keeping the fingers in place.

fool[2] *v.* See signs for BETRAY[1], BLOW[1], TRICK.

fool around *v. phrase.* See sign for RUN AROUND.

foolish *adj.* See signs for SILLY[1,2].

foot *n.* The end part of the leg, below the ankle joint, that is stood upon or is moved for walking: *These shoes hurt my feet.*

■ Move the bent middle finger of the right *5 hand,* palm facing down, up and down the length of the left *open hand,* palm facing down, with a repeated movement.

football *n.* A game, played by two teams defending goals at opposite ends of a large field, in which an oval leather ball is kicked, carried, or thrown so as to get it across the opposing team's goal line: *played football in high school.*

■ [Represents scrimmage between two teams] Beginning with both *5 hands* in front of each side of the chest, palms facing in and fingers pointing toward each other, bring the hands together with a short double movement, interlocking the fingers of both hands each time.

for *prep.* **1.** With the purpose of: *reads for pleasure.* **2.** Intended to be used by: *art supplies for the students.* **3.** So as to obtain: *sells them for profit.* **4.** With regard to: *bad for your health.* **5.** During or to the extent of: *worked there for several years.* **6.** Instead of: *a replacement for the retiring secretary.* **7.** Because of: *shouting for joy.*

■ Beginning with the extended right index finger touching the right side of the forehead, palm facing down, twist the hand forward, ending with the index finger pointing forward.

forbid *v.* To not allow: *to forbid visitors.* Same sign used for: **ban, enjoin, illegal, prohibit.**

■ Bring the palm side of the right *L hand*, palm facing left, sharply against the palm of the left *open hand*, palm facing right and fingers pointing up.

fore *adj.* See sign for FRONT.

forecast *v.* See signs for PREDICT[1,2].

foreign *adj.* Of or having to do with another country: *a foreign language.*

■ [Initialized sign similar to sign for **country**[2]] Move the thumb side of the right *F hand*, palm facing left, in a double circular movement near the bent left elbow.

foresee *v.* See signs for PREDICT[1,2], VISION[1].

forest[1] *n.* A tract of land covered with trees: *to walk through the forest.* Same sign used for: **jungle, orchard, woods.**

■ [**tree** is repeated] Beginning with the bent right elbow resting on the back of the left hand held across the body, palm facing down, twist the right *5 hand* forward with a double movement, moving the arms to the right each time.

forest[2] *n.* (alternate sign) Same sign used for: **jungle, orchard, woods.**

■ [**many + tree + horde**] Beginning with both *S hands* in front of each side of the chest, palms facing in, move the hands forward with a deliberate double movement while opening the fingers into *5 hands* each time. Then, beginning with the

bent elbow of the right *5 hand* resting on the back of the left *open hand* held across the body, wiggle the right hand with a repeated movement, palm facing in. Next move both *curved 5 hands,* palms facing down, from in front of each side of the chest forward with a simultaneous movement.

foretell *v.* See signs for PREDICT[1,2].

forever[1] *adv.* Without coming to an end: *music whose beauty will last forever.* Same sign used for: **eternal, everlasting.**

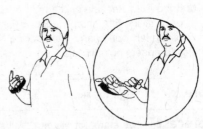

- ■ [**always** + **still**[1]] Move the right *1 hand,* palm facing up, in a circle in front of the right side of the body. Then move the right *Y hand* from in front of the right side of the body, palm facing down, forward and upward in an arc.

forever[2] *adv.* (alternate sign) Same sign used for: **eternal, everlasting.**

- ■ [**for** + **always**] Beginning with the extended right index finger touching the right side of the forehead, palm facing down, move the hand downward and form a large circle in front of the right side of the body, palm facing in and finger pointing up.

forgery *n.* The crime of falsely making a writing, recording, coin, document, etc., and passing it off as genuine: *The signature was a forgery.* Alternate form: **forge** *v.*

- ■ [**contract** + **lie**[2]] With a double movement, place the extended fingers of the right *H hand,* palm down, on the upturned palm of the left *open hand* held in front of the chest. Then move the index-finger side of the right *bent hand,* palm down and fingers pointing left, across the chin from right to left.

forget *v.* To cease to remember: *I'm sorry, but I forgot your name.*

- ■ [Wipes thoughts from one's memory] Wipe the fingers of the right *open hand,* fingers pointing left, across the forehead from left to right while closing into a *10 hand* near the right side of the forehead.

forgiveness *n.* See sign for EXCUSE.

fork *n.* An instrument with a handle and two or more projecting prongs used for piercing food: *a toddler learning to eat with a fork.*

■ [Tines of a fork] Touch the fingertips of the right *V hand*, palm facing down, on the palm of upturned left *open hand*. Then quickly turn the right hand so the palm faces the body and touch the left palm again.

form[1] *n.* A printed document with blank spaces, usually labeled, to be filled in with information: *Fill out the application form and hand it to the clerk.* See also sign for FRAME[2]. Same sign used for: **format.**

■ [Initialized sign showing the shape of a form] Beginning with the fingertips of both *F hands* touching in front of the chest, palms facing each other, bring the hands away from each other to about shoulder width and then straight down a short distance, ending with the palms facing forward.

form[2] *v.* To make or shape: *Form a ball with the clay.*

■ [Initialized sign similar to sign for **make**] Beginning with the little-finger side of the right *F hand* on the index-finger side of the left *F hand*, twist the hands with a double movement in opposite directions.

form[3] *n., v.* See signs for FIGURE, MAKE[1,2], SHAPE[1,2].

formal *adj.* See signs for FANCY[1,2].

format[1] *n.* **1.** The specific arrangement of computer data: *a logical format for the database structure.* —*v.* **2.** To prepare (a computer disk) for storing programs or data: *You'll have to format these disks before you can use them.* Related form: **formatted** *adj.*

■ [Initialized sign similar to sign for **disk**] Beginning with the right *F hand* in front of the right side of the chest, palm facing forward, and the left *open hand* in front of the left side of the chest, palm facing right, move the right hand forward in a circular movement and then against the palm of the left *open hand.*

format[2] *n.* (alternate sign) Related form: **formatted** *adj.*

■ [Initialized sign] Beginning with the fingers of both *F hands* touching in front of the chest, palms facing each other, bring the right hand outward to the right.

format[3] *n.* See signs for FORM[1], FRAME[2].

former *adj.* Of, pertaining to, or having existed in the past: *a former roommate.* Same sign used for: **previous.**

■ [Hand moves back into the past] Move the right *5 hand*, palm facing left and fingers pointing up, back toward the right shoulder in a double circular movement.

formerly *adv.* See signs for LONG AGO[1,2].

formula *n.* A mathematical rule expressed in algebraic symbols: *Use the right formula to solve the equation.*

■ [Initialized sign similar to sign for **law**] Beginning with the index-finger side of the right *F hand*, palm facing forward, against the fingers of the left *open hand*, palm facing right, move the right hand downward to touch the left hand near the heel.

formulate *v.* See signs for MAKE[1,2].

forsake[1] *v.* To leave completely; desert: *to forsake your home and friends.* Same sign used for: **depart, withdraw.**

■ [Represents picking things up to leave] Beginning with both *open hands* in front of the body, palms facing down and fingers pointing forward, bring the hands back toward each side of the chest with a quick movement while closing into *A hands.*

forsake[2] *v.* See signs for ABANDON[1], IGNORE[1,2], LEAVE[3].

fortress *n.* See sign for RAMPART.

fortunate *adj.* See sign for LUCK.

fortune *n.* A great deal of wealth: *to make a fortune in the stock market.* Same sign used for: **cash.**

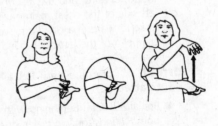

■ [**money** + **rich**] Tap the back of the right *flattened O hand*, palm facing up, with a double movement against the palm of the left *open hand*, palm facing up. Then raise the right *curved 5 hand* over the left *curved hand* in front of the chest, palms facing each other.

forward *adv.* See signs for AHEAD[1,2], GO ON[1].

forward slash See sign for SLASH[2].

founded *adj.* See signs for ESTABLISH, RECOVER[1].

fountain *n.* A structure producing a spray of water rising in the air: *There are colored lights in the fountain.*

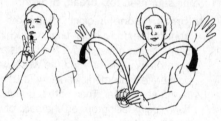

- ■ [**water** + spray of water coming up in a fountain] Tap the index-finger side of the right *W hand*, palm facing left, against the chin. Then, beginning with the fingers of both *flattened O hands* touching in front of the body, palms facing down, bring the hands upward and forward in large arcs while opening into *5 hands* in front of each shoulder, palms facing forward.

four dollars *pl. n.* See sign for FOURTH.

fourth *adj.* **1.** Next after the third: *the fourth quarter of the year.* —*n.* **2.** The one after the third in a series of four or more: *the fourth in line.* —*adv.* **3.** In the fourth place: *came in fourth in the marathon.* Same sign used for: **four dollars.**

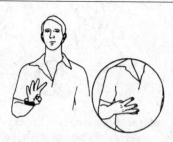

- ■ [**four** formed with a twisting movement used for ordinal numbers] Beginning with the right *4 hand* in front of the right side of the chest, palm facing forward, twist the hand to the left, ending with the palm facing up.

fowl *n.* See sign for BIRD.

fox *n.* A wild animal of the dog family having a bushy tail and pointed face: *hunting for foxes in England.*

- ■ [Initialized sign showing the shape of a fox's nose] With the index finger and thumb of the right *F hand* encircling the nose, palm facing left, twist the hand with a repeated movement, ending with the palm facing down.

fraction[1] *n.* A number showing one or more equal parts of a whole: *to write one-third as the fraction 1/3.*

- ■ [Initialized sign showing that a fraction is expressed above and below a dividing line] Move the right *F hand*, palm facing forward, downward in front of the chest, past the index-finger side of the left *open hand* held in front of the chest, palm facing down.

fraction[2] *n.* See sign for PART[1].

fracture[1] *n.* **1.** A broken bone.—*v.* **2.** To break a bone: *She fractured her shoulder in the fall.* Same sign used for: **break, broken.**

■ **[break + bone]** Beginning with both *S hands* in front of the body, index fingers touching and palms facing down, move the hands away from each other while twisting the wrists with a deliberate movement, ending with the palms facing each other. Then with a double movement, tap the back of the right bent *V hand*, palm facing up, on the back of the left *S hand*, palm facing down.

fracture[2] *v., n.* See sign for BREAK[1].

fragile *adj.* Easily broken: *a fragile vase.*

■ **[carefully + easy + break]** With the little-finger side of the right *K hand* across the index-finger side of the left *K hand*, palms facing in opposite directions, move the hands upward and forward in a large circular movement. Then brush the fingertips of the right *curved hand* upward on the back of the fingertips of the left *curved hand* with a double movement, both palms facing up. Then, beginning with both *S hands* in front of the chest, index fingers touching and palms facing down, move the hands away from each other while twisting the wrists with a deliberate movement, ending with the palms facing each other.

fragrance *n.* See sign for SMELL[1].

frail[1] *adj.* Not very strong; having delicate health: *a frail child, unable to run and play with his friends.*

■ **[sick**[1,2] **+ weak]** Touch the bent middle finger of the right *5 hand*, to the forehead and the bent middle finger of the left *5 hand* to the lower torso. Then, beginning with the fingertips of the right *curved 5 hand* on the palm of the left *open hand*, palm facing up, bend the right fingers up and down with a double movement, palm facing in.

frail[2] *adj.* See sign for WEAK.

frame[1] *n.* **1.** A decorative border or supporting structure in which a picture, mirror, or the like can be set or enclosed: *an ornately carved picture frame.* —*v.* **2.** To provide with or place into a frame: *three photographs that I want to frame.*

- [Shape of a frame] Beginning with the extended fingers of both *G hands* touching in front of the chest, palms facing each other, move the hands apart to in front of each shoulder, then straight down, and finally back together in front of the lower chest.

frame[2] *n.* (alternate sign) See also sign for FORM[1]. Same sign used for: **format.**

- [Initialized sign showing shape of a frame] Beginning with the index-finger side of both *F hands* touching in front of the chest, palms facing forward, bring the hands apart to in front of each shoulder, then straight down, and finally back together in front of the lower chest.

France[1] *n.* A country in western Europe: *France is famous for its food and wine.* Related form: **French** *n., adj.*

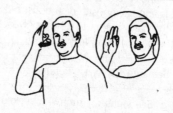

- [Initialized sign] Beginning with the right *F hand* near the right side of the head, palm facing back, twist the hand quickly forward.

France[2] *n.* (alternate sign) Related form: **French** *n., adj.*

- [Initialized sign] Beginning with the index-finger side of the right *F hand*, palm facing down, touching the left side of the chest, twist the hand forward, ending with the palm facing in.

frank *adj.* See sign for HONEST. Related form: **frankly** *adv.*

fraternity *n.* See sign for ASSOCIATE.

fraud[1] *n.* The obtaining of money or property by means of a false portrayal of facts: *The bookkeeper committed fraud to move money into his own account.* Related form: **fraudulent** *adj.* Same sign used for: **deceit, defraud.**

- [The hands seem to smear things] With the heel of the right *5 hand* on the palm of the left *5 hand*, twist the wrist down to the left.

fraud[2] *n.* See signs for CHEAT[1,2], COVER-UP, DECEIVE[1].

freak *n., adj.* See sign for STRANGE.

freckles *pl. n.* Small, light brown spots on the skin: *nose and cheeks covered with freckles.*

- [Location of freckles on the face] Beginning with the fingertips of both *curved 5 hands* touching the face near each side of the nose, palms facing in, tap the fingertips on the face in several locations as the hands move down the cheeks. [This sign can be formed with one hand.]

free[1] *adj.* **1.** Not under another's control; having personal, political, or civil liberties: *a free nation.* **2.** Provided without charge: *The neighborhood newspaper is free.* Related form: **freedom** *n.* Same sign used for: **liberty.**

- [Initialized sign similar to sign for **save**[1]] Beginning with both *F hands* crossed at the wrists in front of the chest, palms facing in opposite directions, twist the wrists to move the hands apart to in front of each shoulder, ending with the palms facing forward.

free[2] *adj.* See sign for SAVE[1]. Related form: **freedom** *n.*

freeway *n.* See signs for HIGHWAY, SUPERHIGHWAY.

freeze *v.* To become hard because of loss of heat, especially to turn into ice: *so cold out that the lake froze over.* Same sign used for: **frost, frozen, ice, rigid, solidify.**

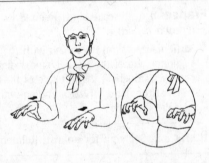

- [Shows things hardening when frozen] Beginning with both *5 hands* in front of each side of the body, palms facing down and fingers pointing forward, pull the hands back toward the body while constricting the fingers.

freezer[1] *n.* A refrigerated cabinet or compartment for freezing and storing food: *Keep the extra steaks in the freezer.*

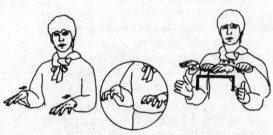

- [freeze + shape of freezer] Beginning with both *5 hands* in front of each side of the body, palms facing down and fingers pointing forward, pull the hands back toward the body while constricting the fingers. Then, beginning with the index fingers of both *B hands* touching in front of the chest, palms facing down and fingers pointing forward, move the hands away from each other to about shoulder width and then turn the palms toward each other and move the hands straight down a short distance.

freezer[2] *n.* Same sign as for FREEZE but formed with a double movement.

French *n., adj.* See signs for FRANCE[1,2].

french fries *pl. n.* Strips of potato cooked by deep-frying in hot oil: *I always put catsup on french fries.*

■ [Abbreviation **f-f**] Form an *F* with the right hand, palm facing forward, in front of the right side of the body and then again slightly to the right.

frequently *adv.* See sign for OFTEN.

fresh[1] *adj.* **1.** Not preserved, as by freezing or canning: *serving fresh vegetables.* **2.** Not stale or worn: *to change into fresh clothing.* **3.** Pure, clean, and refreshing: *fresh air.* **4.** Newly made: *a pot of fresh coffee.*

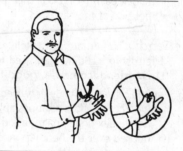

■ [Initialized sign similar to sign for **clean**] Brush the little-finger side of the right *F hand,* palm facing in, from the fingers to the heel of the palm of the left *open hand,* palm facing in.

fresh[2] *adj.* See sign for NEW.

freshman *n.* A student in the first year of high school or college: *a college freshman.*

■ [Indicates second year in school after preparatory year] Touch the ring finger of the left *5 hand* with the extended right index finger, both palms facing in.

friction *n.* Surface resistance to the rubbing of one thing against another: *Oil reduces friction.*

■ [Demonstrates friction caused by rubbing] Rub the palm of the right *open hand* back and forth with a repeated movement on the extended left index finger, palm facing in.

Friday *n.* The sixth day of the week, following Thursday: *to get out of work early on Friday.*

- [Initialized sign] Move the right *F hand*, palm facing in, in a repeated circle in front of the right shoulder.

---

fried *v.* See sign for FRY[1].

---

friend[1] *n.* A person whom one knows and likes well: *She's been my best friend for many years.* Related form: **friendship** *n.* Same sign used for: **comrade, pal.**

- [Indicates the entwined lives of friends who have a close relationship] Hook the bent right index finger, palm facing down, over the bent left index finger, palm facing up. Then repeat, reversing the position of the hands.

---

friend[2] *n.* (alternate sign) Related form: **friendship** *n.* Same sign used for: **best friend, close friend, comrade, good friend, pal.**

- [Indicates the tightly entwined lives of friends who have a close relationship] With the bent right index finger, palm facing down, tightly hooked over the bent left index finger, palm facing up, move the hands forward and back toward the chest with a shaking movement.

---

friendly *adj.* Characteristic of or like a friend, as in attitude and behavior: *a friendly smile.* Same sign used for: **cheerful, pleasant.**

- With both *5 hands* near the cheeks, palms facing back, wiggle the fingers.

---

fright *n.* See sign for AFRAID. Related form: **frightened** *adj.*

---

frightened *adj.* See sign for FEAR[1].

---

frigid *adj.* See signs for ARCTIC, COLD[2].

---

frivolous *adj.* See sign for WORTHLESS.

frog *n.* A small, leaping animal with hairless skin and webbed feet, living in water or on land: *a green frog near the pond.*

- Beginning with the index-finger side of the right *S hand* against the chin, palm facing left, flick the index and middle fingers outward to the left with a double movement.

frolic *v.* To play together joyously: *The children frolicked in the playground.*

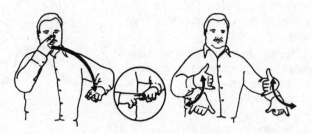

- [**fun** + **play**[1]] Bring the fingers of the right *H hand* from near the nose downward, ending with these fingers across the fingers of the left *H hand* in front of the chest, both palms facing down. Then swing both *Y hands* up and down by twisting the wrists in front of each side of the body with a repeated movement.

from *prep.* Out of or starting at: *took a bus from New York to Boston.*

- [Moving from another location] Beginning with the knuckle of the right *X hand,* palm facing in, touching the extended left index finger, palm facing right and finger pointing up, pull the right hand back toward the chest.

from now on See sign for AFTER[1].

front *n.* **1.** The first part: *The preface is in the front of the book.* **2.** The part that faces forward: *a large door on the front of the house.* —*adj.* **3.** Situated in or at the front: *the front door.* Same sign used for: **fore.**

- [Location in front of the person] Move the right *open hand,* palm facing in and fingers pointing left, straight down from in front of the face to in front of the chest.

frost *v.* See sign for FREEZE.

frosted *adj.* Of or referring to hair that is highlighted by bleaching certain strands: *She has frosted hair.*

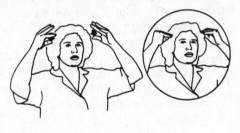

- [Indicates putting frosting on the hair] Beginning with both *flattened C hands* near each side of the head, palms facing each other, close the fingers into *flattened O hands* with a double movement.

frosting *n.* A mixture of sugar and liquid forming a creamy or brittle mixture used to cover a cake: *I like to lick frosting from the bowl.* Same sign used for: **icing.**

- [Spreading frosting on a cake] Drag the fingers of the right *H hand,* palm facing down, down the length of the upturned left *open hand* from the fingers to the heel.

frown *v.* **1.** To wrinkle the forehead by contracting the brow, as to show disapproval: *He frowned at the naughty boy.* —*n.* **2.** A frowning look: *The teacher's face always had a frown.*

- [Eyebrows turning down when frowning] Beginning with both extended index fingers near each side of the forehead, palms facing each other and fingers pointing up, bend the fingers downward to form *X hands* near the side of each eye.

frozen *adj.* See sign for FREEZE.

fruit *n.* A juicy or fleshy, often sweet product of a plant: *to eat a piece of fruit.*

- [Initialized sign] Beginning with the fingertips of the right *F hand* on the right side of the chin, palm facing left, twist the hand forward with a double movement, ending with the palm facing in.

frustrate[1] *v.* To thwart, get in the way of, or disappoint: *frustrated in trying to get a perfect score.* Related form: **frustration** *n.*

- Bring the back of the right *B hand,* palm facing forward, back against the mouth with a double movement or, sometimes, a single movement.

frustrate[2] *v.* (alternate sign) Related form: **frustration** *n.*

- [Initialized sign] Bring the back of right *F hand* and then the back of the left *F hand,* palms facing forward, back against the mouth with an alternating movement.

frustrate[3] *v.* (alternate sign) Related form: **frustration** *n.*

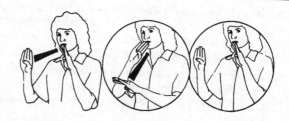

- Bring the back of the right *B hand* and then the back of the left *B hand,* palms facing forward, back against the mouth with an alternating movement.

fry[1] *v.* To cook in hot grease, especially over direct heat: *fry the chicken.* Same sign used for: **fried.**

- [Initialized sign showing turning food over in a frying pan] Beginning with the fingers of the right *F hand,* palm facing down, touching the palm of the left *open hand,* flip the right hand over, ending with the back of the right hand on the left palm.

fry[2] *v.* See sign for COOK[1].

fuel *n.* See sign for GAS.

fugitive *n.* A person who runs away, especially to escape from danger or the law: *a fugitive from jail.*

- [jail[1,2] + runaway] Bring the back of the right *5 hand* from the chest forward against the palm of the left *5 hand,* ending with the fingers crossed at angles, both palms facing in. Then, beginning with the extended right index finger, palm facing left, pointing upward between the index finger and middle finger of the left *5 hand,* palm facing down, bring the right hand quickly outward to the right.

full[1] *adj.* Filled to capacity; unable to eat more without becoming uncomfortable: *too full for dessert.* Same sign used for: **sated, satisfied, stuffed.**

- [Represents feeling full] Move the right *B hand,* palm facing down, from the center of the chest upward with a deliberate movement, ending with back of the right fingers under the chin.

full[2] *adj.* Unable to hold more: *a full cup.* Same sign used for: **complete, filled.**

- [Leveling off something that is full] Slide the palm of the right *open hand*, palm facing down, from right to left across the index-finger side of the left *S hand*, palm facing right.

fumble *v.* **1.** To handle awkwardly and ineptly: *He fumbled his first meeting with his new boss.* **2.** To drop (something, as a ball) after having touched or carried it: *The home team fumbled the ball again in the middle of the game.*

- [Something slipping out of one's hands] Beginning with the left *open hand* in front of the right *S hand*, both palms facing in, bring the right hand downward with a deliberate movement.

fume *n., v.* See signs for BOILING MAD, SMELL[1].

fun *n.* **1.** Something that provides enjoyment, pleasure, or amusement: *Playing tennis is fun.* **2.** The pleasurable feelings so provided: *We had fun at the party.* Same sign used for: **leisure, recreation.**

- Bring the fingers of the right *H hand* from near the nose downward, ending with the fingers of the right *H hand* across the fingers of the left *H hand* in front the chest, both palms facing down.

function *n.* **1.** The normal action, activity, or work of a person or thing: *The chief function of the manager is to see that the work gets done.* —*v.* **2.** To perform a particular action or activity: *I don't understand the way the old pendulum clock functions.*

- [Initialized sign similar to sign for **practice**] Move the fingertips of the right *F hand*, palm facing forward, back and forth across the length of the left *open hand*, palm facing down, with a double movement.

fund *n.* See signs for FINANCES, MONEY, SUPPORT[1,2].

fundamental *adj.* Essential or basic: *fundamental principles.*

- [Initialized sign similar to sign for **base**[1]] Move the right *F hand*, palm facing forward, in a circular movement under the left *open hand* held across the chest, palm facing down.

funeral *n.* A ceremony performed before the burial or cremation of someone who has died: *left town to attend his grandfather's funeral.*

■ [Represents a procession following a casket] Beginning with both *V hands* in front of the chest, right hand closer to the chest than the left hand and both palms facing forward, move the hands forward simultaneously in a double arc.

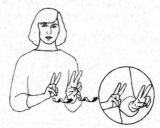

funnel *n.* A cone-shaped tube: *pour the gas through a funnel.*

■ [Represents something becoming concentrated at the narrow opening of a funnel] Beginning with both *open hands* in front of each shoulder, palms angled upward, bring the hands toward each other in front of the chest. Then, with the little-finger side of the left *O hand* on the index-finger side of the right *O hand,* palms facing in, bring the right hand straight downward in front of the chest.

funny *adj.* **1.** Causing laughter; providing fun: *a funny joke.* **2.** Able to amuse: *a genuinely funny comedian.* Same sign used for: **amusing, humorous.**

■ With a double movement, brush the nose with the fingertips of the right *U hand,* palm facing in and thumb extended, bending the fingers of the *U hand* back into the palm each time.

fur[1] *n.* The fine, soft hair covering the skin of some mammals: *a rabbit's white fur.*

■ [Initialized sign feeling the nap of a fur sleeve] Move the thumb side of the right *F hand,* palm facing left, up and down the length of the extended left arm with a double movement.

fur[2] *adj.* (alternate sign) Made of animal fur: *a fur coat.*

■ [Shape of a fur collar] Beginning with the fingers of both *C hands* touching each shoulder, bring the hands down toward each other until they meet in the center of the chest.

furious[1] *adj.* Full of fierce anger: *I was furious with the store for overcharging me.*

■ [Feeling rising in the body] Beginning with the index-finger sides of both *B hands* on each side of the body, palms facing down and fingers pointing toward each other, raise the hands upward on the chest with a double movement.

furious[2] *adj.* See signs for ANGER[2], BOILING MAD.

furniture *n.* Movable articles, as tables, chairs, and storage units, used in a house or office: *to polish the furniture.*

■ [Initialized sign] Move the right *F hand*, palm facing forward, from side to side in front of the right side of the chest with a repeated movement.

further *adv.* See signs for AHEAD[1,2].

fury *adj.* See sign for ANGER.

fuse[1] *n.* A protective device in an electric circuit, with a conductor that melts when current is too strong, shutting electricity off: *replace the fuse.*

■ [electric + screwing a small fuse into a fuse box] Tap the knuckles of both *modified X hands* together with a double movement in front of the chest, palms facing in. Then twist the right *modified X hand* on the palm of the left *open hand*, palm facing right, with a double movement.

fuse[2] *n.* (alternate sign)

■ [electric + turn on] Tap the knuckles of both *modified X hands* together with a double movement, palms facing in. Then twist the bent thumb and index finger of the right hand, palm facing down, with a double movement in front of the chest.

fuss *n.* Bother about small matters: *too much fuss about the party.* Related form: **fussy** *adj.*

■ Beginning with the thumb of the right *5 hand* touching the body, palm facing left, bring the hand upward and forward in front of the chest, ending with the fingers pointing forward.

fussy *adj.* See signs for FANCY[1,2].

future[1] *n.* Time that is to come: *I don't know what the future will bring.*

■ [Initialized sign moving forward into the future] Move the right *F hand* from near the right cheek, palm facing left, forward in a double arc.

future[2] *n.* (alternate sign) Same sign used for: **someday.**

■ [Hand moves forward into the future] Move the right *open hand,* palm facing left and fingers pointing up, from near the right cheek forward in a double arc.

gab *v., n. Informal.* See sign for BLAB.

gag *v.* **1.** To stop up the mouth with a covering to prevent speech, screaming, etc.: *The bandits gagged the watchman.* —*n.* **2.** A covering put over a person's mouth: *They bound his mouth with a gag.*
- ■ [**muffle** + **choke**[1]] Move the right *C hand,* palm facing in, firmly over the mouth and then around the neck.

gain *v., n.* See signs for INCREASE[1,2], PROFIT.

gain weight See signs for FAT[1,2,3].

gait *n.* See sign for LIMP[1].

gala *adj., n.* See signs for CELEBRATE, DANCE.

gale *n.* A very strong wind: *The gales were so powerful that they blew the tree down.*
- ■ [**strong**[1] + **wind**[1]] Beginning with both *S hands* in front of each side of the chest, palms facing in, move the hands firmly forward. Then, beginning with both *5 hands* above the right shoulder, palm facing forward and fingers pointing up, move the hands down in arcs to the left, turning the palms inward as the hands move with a double movement.

gallop *n.* **1.** A horse's fastest gait: *The horse ran off at a gallop.* **2.** A ride on a horse at this gait: *an early morning gallop on my favorite horse.* —*v.* **3.** To run at a gallop: *The horse galloped toward the stables.* **4.** To ride a horse at a gallop: *The ranger galloped speedily on his powerful horse.*
- ■ [**horse** + a movement that represents a horse's front legs] With the extended thumb of the right *U hand* against the right side of the forehead, palm facing

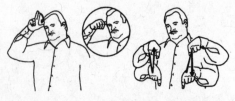

forward, bend the fingers up and down with a double movement. Then, with the index fingers of both hands pointing down in front of each side of the chest, move the hands up and down in an alternating movement.

galoshes *pl. n.* See signs for BOOTS[1,2].

gamble[1] *v.* **1.** To play a game of chance, especially for money: *They go to Las Vegas to gamble.* **2.** To bet or take a risk on an uncertain outcome: *to gamble on the results of the election.* —*n.* **3.** A risky undertaking: *to leave the organization and take a gamble on getting a better job.* Same sign used for: **dice.**

■ [Mime tossing dice] Beginning with the right *A hand* in front of the right side of the body, palm facing up, thrust the hand forward to the left while opening into a *5 hand.*

gamble[2] *n., v.* See sign for BET.

game *n.* A contest played according to a set of rules, often between two opposing teams of players: *Now that everyone is here, we can play the game.*

■ [Represents opposing teams sparring] Bring the knuckles of both *10 hands,* palms facing in, against each other with a double movement in front of the chest.

game controller An input device that governs movement and action in the playing of electronic games. A game controller can be a joystick, mouse, keyboard, paddle, game pad, steering wheel or any other input device designed for gaming: *The boy used his game controller to play games after school.* Same sign used for: **electronic game.**

■ [**game** + **joystick**] Bring the knuckles of both *10 hands,* palms facing in, against each other in front of the chest. Then move the little-finger side of the right *A hand,* palm facing in, in a circular movement on the palm of the left *open hand.*

gang[1] *n.* A group of persons associated for criminal or antisocial purposes: *Since he joined a gang, he just hangs out on the street.* Related form: **gangster** *n.* Same sign used for: **dare, tough.**

■ Move the right *S hand,* palm facing in, downward on the right side of the chest with a double movement.

gang[2] *n.* (alternate sign)

■ [**gang**[1] + **group**[1]] Move the right *S hand,* palm facing in, downward on the right side of the chest with a double movement. Then, beginning with both *G hands* in front of the chest, palms facing each other, bring the hands away from each other in outward arcs while turning the palms in, ending with the little fingers near each other.

gangster *n.* A member of a gang of criminals: *The gangsters were arrested and sent to jail.*

■ [**gang**[1] + **person marker**] Move the right *S hand*, palm facing in, downward on the right side of the chest with a double movement. Then move both *open hands*, palms facing each other, downward along each side of the body.

gap *n.* See sign for BETWEEN.

garage *n.* A building or other shelter for vehicles: *Park in the garage.*

■ [Represents a car moving into a garage] Move the right *3 hand*, palm facing left, forward with a short repeated movement under the palm of the left *open hand*, palm facing down and fingers pointing right.

garbage *n.* Scraps of waste, as animal and vegetable matter from a kitchen, to be thrown away: *to take out the garbage.* Same sign used for: **gross, junk, trash.**

■ [Natural gesture of holding one's nose when something smells bad] Beginning with the fingertips of the right *F hand* touching the nose, palm facing in, bring the right hand forward a short distance while opening the index finger and thumb in front of the face.

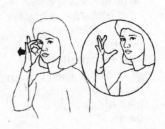

garbled *adj.* See signs for MESSY, MIX[1].

garden *n.* A plot of ground, usually near a house, for growing flowers, shrubs, vegetables, and other plants: *gathered a bouquet from my own garden.*

■ [Initialized sign encircling an area of land] Move the right *G hand*, palm facing left, in a large circular movement over the bent left arm, beginning near the left fingers and ending near the elbow.

gardener *n.* **1.** A person who cares for a garden: *She considers herself an expert gardener because of her large tomatoes.* **2.** A person employed to care for a garden: *The gardener pruned back the roses before the first frost.*

■ [**plant**[2] + **person marker**] Beginning with the right *flattened O hand* in front of the right side of the body, palm facing down, quickly close the fingers, forming an *A hand*, while bending the wrist up. Then move both *open hands*, palms facing each other, downward along each side of the body.

gargle *v.* **1.** To rinse the mouth and throat with a liquid kept in motion by air from the lungs: *I gargle after I brush my teeth.* —*n.* **2.** The liquid used for gargling: *a new brand of mint-flavored gargle.*

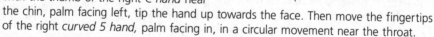

- ■ [**drink**[1] + showing the movement of mouthwash in the mouth] Beginning with the thumb of the right *C hand* near the chin, palm facing left, tip the hand up towards the face. Then move the fingertips of the right *curved 5 hand*, palm facing in, in a circular movement near the throat.

garment *n.* See sign for CLOTHES.

gas[1] *n.* A liquid used as fuel to propel a vehicle: *We have to fill the tank with gas before the trip.* Alternate form: **gasoline.** Same sign used for: **fuel.**

- ■ [Mime pouring gas into the gas tank of a vehicle] Tap the extended thumb of the right *10 hand*, palm facing forward, downward with a repeated small movement into the thumb-side opening of the left *S hand*.

gas[2] *n.* See sign for FLATULENCE.

gasp *v.* See sign for GULP[1].

gate *n.* A movable section of a fence, usually on hinges, that can be swung back and forth for opening or closing: *Unlock the gate for the letter carrier.*

- ■ [Shows a gate swinging open] Beginning with both *open hands* in front of the body, palms facing in and the fingers touching, swing the fingers of the right hand forward and back with a double movement.

gather[1] *v.* To bring or come together into one group: *to gather the eggs; We will all gather in front of the restaurant.* Same sign used for: **assemble, get together.**

- ■ [Represents people coming together] Beginning with both *curved 5 hands* in front of each side of the body, palms facing each other, bring the fingers together in front of the body.

gather[2] *v.* (alternate sign) Same sign used for: **assemble, attend, congregate, flock, get together, go to.**

- ■ [Represents people coming together] Beginning with both *5 hands* in front of each shoulder, palms angled forward, bring the hands forward toward each other, ending with the palms facing down.

gather³ *v.* (alternate sign) Same sign used for: **assemble, attend, congregate, flock, get together, go to.**

- [**gather²** + **together**] Beginning with both *5 hands* in front of each shoulder, palms angled forward, bring the hands forward toward each other, ending with the palms facing down. Then with the palm sides of both *A hands* together, move the hands in a flat circle in front of the body.

gather⁴ *v.* (alternate sign) Same sign used for: **assemble, get together.**

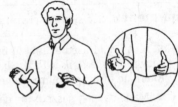

- [The hands seem to pull a group together] Beginning with both *C hands* in front of each side of the chest, palms angled toward each other, bring the hands toward each other with a short movement, ending with palms facing each other.

gather⁵ *v.* See signs for COLLECT[1,2].

gauge *v.* See sign for ANALYZE.

gaunt *adj.* See sign for THIN³.

gay¹ *adj.* **1.** Pertaining to or being a homosexual person: *a gay employee.* **2.** Pertaining to homosexuality: *gay rights.* —*n.* **3.** A homosexual person: *gays demonstrating on behalf of AIDS research.* Same sign used for: **homosexual, queer** (*disparaging and offensive*).

- [Initialized sign] Bring the fingertips of the right *G hand*, palm facing in, back to touch the chin with a double movement.

gay² *adj.* See sign for HAPPY.

gelatin *n.* A food product made of a nearly transparent, glutinous, jellylike substance: *A strawberry gelatin was served for dessert.* Same sign used for: **Jell-O** (*trademark*).

- [Shows the shaking movement of gelatin] Shake the right *curved 5 hand*, palm facing down, with a repeated back and forth movement over the left *open hand*, palm facing up.

gem *n.* A mineral or other natural substance valued for its beauty and rarity; precious stone: *A diamond is a highly valued gem in jewelry making.*

■ [**rock**[1,2] + pointing to something glittering on the back of the hand] Knock the palm side of the right *A hand*, palm facing down, against the back of the left *open hand* with a double movement. Then point to the ring finger of the left *open hand*, palm facing down. Then, with the back of the right *flattened O hand* on the back of the left *open hand*, open the right hand and wiggle the fingers.

gender *n.* See sign for SEX.

general[1] *adj.* **1.** Not specific or definite; approximate: *traveling in the general direction of New York.* **2.** Concerned or dealing with extensive or important aspects rather than details: *The college catalogue provides a general description of the biology course.* Same sign used for: **broad.**

■ [Hands open up broadly] Beginning with both *open hands* in front of the chest, fingers angled toward each other, swing the fingers away from each other, ending with the fingers angled outward in front of each side of the body.

general[2] *adj.* See sign for WIDE.

general[3] *n.* See sign for CAPTAIN.

generate *v.* To bring into existence; produce: *to generate the printout; to generate electricity.* Related form: **generator** *n.*

■ [Initialized sign similar to sign for **make**[1]] Beginning with the little-finger side of the right *G hand* on the index-finger side of the left *G hand*, palms facing in opposite directions, twist the hands in opposite directions by bending the wrists.

generation *n.* **1.** The body of individuals born and living in the same period of time: *books aimed at an audience of the younger generation.* **2.** The average period of time between the birth of parents and the birth of their children, usually 30 years: *to wear clothing fashionable during the previous generation.* **3.** A new development in a particular technology: *Will there be voice-activated commands in the next generation of personal computers?*

■ [Initialized sign similar to sign for **ancestor**[2] but moving in an opposite direction] Beginning with both *G hands* in front of the right shoulder, palms facing in opposite directions and right hand above the left hand, roll the hands over each other with an alternating movement while moving the hands forward.

generous *adj.* See signs for KIND[1,2].

genius *n.* See signs for INTELLIGENT[1], SCHOLARLY, SMART[3].

gentle[1] *adj.* Kindly and agreeable: *a gentle manner.*
■ Wipe the fingertips of the right *open hand,* palm facing in and fingers pointing up, downward with a double movement off the chin while bending the fingers each time.

gentle[2] *adj.* See signs for KIND[1,2], POLITE[1,2], SOFT, SWEET.

gentleman *n.* See signs for MAN[1,2].

genuine *adj.* See sign for REAL.

geography[1] *n.* The study of the earth's climate, surface, political divisions, etc.: *to study the capitals of Europe in the geography class.*
■ [Initialized sign similar to sign for **earth**[2]] With the extended finger tips of the right *G hand* touching the back of the left *open hand,* both palms facing down, rock the right hand from side to side with a double movement.

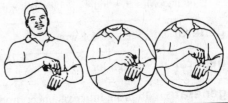

geography[2] *n.* See signs for EARTH[1,2].

geometry *n.* The branch of mathematics that deals with the relationships of points, lines, angles, and figures in space: *learning how to derive the area of a circle from the radius in the geometry class.*
■ [Initialized sign similar to sign for **arithmetic**] With a double movement, move both *G hands* in opposite directions, brushing the back of the right hand, palm facing left, across the thumb side of the left hand, palm facing right.

gerbil *n.* A small rodent with long hind legs, popular as a pet: *a cage for my pet gerbil.*
■ [Initialized sign similar to sign for **mouse**] Brush the thumb side of the right *G hand,* palm facing left, downward across the nose with a repeated movement.

germ *n.* A microscopic organism, especially one that produces disease: *Stop, there are germs on that glass!*

■ [**dirty** + **give**³] With the back of the right *5 hand* under the chin, palm facing down, wiggle the fingers. Then, beginning with both *flattened O hands* in front of each side of the body, palms facing up, move the hands forward simultaneously in double arcs.

Germany¹ *n.* A republic in central Europe: *East and West Germany were reunited in 1990.* Related form: **German** *n., adj.*

■ [Represents the raised insignia on a German helmet] Bring the back of the right *1 hand,* palm facing forward, against the center of the forehead.

Germany² *n.* (alternate sign) Related form: **German** *n., adj.*

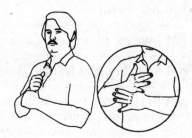

■ [Represents the eagle on the German insignia] Beginning with right *A hand* holding the thumb of the left *A hand* in front of the chest, both palms facing in, quickly flick the fingers of both hands outward, ending with *5 hands.*

Germany³ *n.* (alternate sign) Related form: **German** *n., adj.*

■ [Represents the eagle on the German insignia] With the little-finger side of the right *5 hand* at the base of the thumb and index finger of the left *5 hand,* both palms angled in, wiggle the fingers of both hands with a repeated movement.

gesture *n.* A movement of the hands, arms, and body used in sign language: *The gestures used in signing are very expressive.*

■ [Mime gesturing with the hands; similar to sign for **sign**¹] Beginning with both *curved 5 hands* in front of the chest, left hand higher than the right hand and palms facing in opposite directions, move both hands in alternating forward circles.

get *v.* To gain possession of: *They want to get a new car.* Same sign used for: **acquire, attain, obtain, receive, retrieve.**

■ [Reaching for something and bringing it to oneself] Beginning with both *curved 5 hands* in front of the chest, right hand above the left and palms facing in opposite directions, bring the hands back toward the chest while closing into *S hands,* ending with the little-finger side of the right hand on the index-finger side of the left hand.

---

get along *v. phrase.* See sign for GO ON[1].

---

get a ticket *v. phrase.* To receive an official summons to appear before a court. Same sign used for: **cited.**

■ [Represents punching a ticket to show it has been used] Insert the bent fingers of the right *V hand,* palm facing down, around the little-finger side of the left *open hand* held in front of the chest, palm facing in and fingers pointing up.

---

get away *v. phrase.* See signs for AVOID[1], AWAY, ESCAPE, RUN AWAY.

---

get even See signs for EQUAL, REVENGE.

---

get in or **into a vehicle** To enter a vehicle as a passenger or driver: *Get in the car quickly, so we can drive to the party.*

■ [The fingers represent legs getting into a vehicle and sitting] Beginning with the right *bent U hand* in front of the right side of the body, palm facing up, flip the hand over to the left to hook the bent fingers over the thumb of the left *C hand,* palm facing right.

---

get on *v. phrase.* To get astride; climb aboard: *Can you get on the horse without help?*

■ [The fingers represent legs astride something] Beginning with the right *V hand* in front of the right side of the body, palm facing in and fingers pointing left, flip the hand over to the left to straddle the index-finger side of the left *B hand,* palm facing right.

get out *v. phrase.* To leave (often followed by *off*): *Get out of here.* See also sign for OUT. Same sign used for: **take a hike** (*slang*).

- [Natural gesture for ejecting a player from a game] Beginning with the right *10 hand* in front of the right shoulder, palm facing in, jerk the hand abruptly backward over the shoulder.

get pinned See sign for BADGE[1].

get rid of See sign for ABANDON[2].

get together See signs for GATHER[1,2,3,4].

get up[1] *v. phrase.* **1.** To rise to one's feet: *to get up from the chair.* **2.** To rise from bed: *I get up at 7 o'clock every morning.* Same sign used for: **arise, stand up.**

- [The fingers represent legs moving to a standing position] Beginning with the right *bent V hand* in front of the right side of the body, palm facing up, flip the hand over to the left to touch the fingers on the upturned left *open hand.*

get up[2] *v. phrase.* See signs for RAISE[2], RESURRECTION[1].

ghastly *adj.* See sign for HORROR.

ghost *n.* See signs for SPIRIT[1,2].

giant *n.* Someone of great size: *He is a giant, who can't find clothes large enough to fit.*

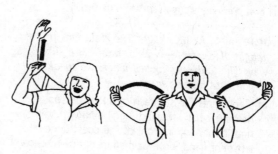

- [Shows tall height + **huge**] Raise the right *open hand,* palm facing down, upward from in front of the right shoulder. Then, beginning with both *modified C hands* in front of each shoulder, palms facing each other, move the hands outward to each side in large arcs.

gift

gift[1] *n.* **1.** A present, as for a special occasion: *Bring a gift to the birthday party.* **2.** Something given to provide aid to another: *a gift to your favorite charity.* **3.** A presentation to honor a person or an occasion: *presented with a $1,000 gift at the awards banquet.* Same sign used for: **award, contribution, donation, grant, present, reward, tribute.**

■ [Presenting something to another] Move both *X hands* from in front of the body, palms facing each other, forward in simultaneous arcs.

gift[2] (alternate sign) Same sign used for: **present.**

■ [**gift**[1] + **box**] Move both *X hands* forward from in front of the body, palms facing each other, in simultaneous arcs. Then, beginning with both *open hands* in front of each side of the chest, palms facing each other and fingers pointing forward, move the hands deliberately in opposite directions, ending with the left hand near the chest and the right hand several inches forward of the left hand, both palms facing in.

gift[3] *n.* (alternate sign) Same sign used for: **award, bequeath, contribution, donation, grant, reward, tribute.**

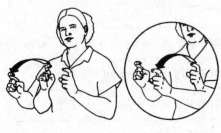

■ [Presenting things to a number of others] Beginning with the right *X hand* in front of the right shoulder and the left *X hand* in front of the left side of the body, palms facing in opposite directions, move the right hand downward in an arc and the left hand upward with a double alternating movement.

gift[4] *n.* See signs for ALLOCATE[2], CHARITY.

giggle[1] *n.* **1.** A silly laugh: *The child was full of delightful giggles.* —*v.* **2.** To laugh in a silly way: *The audience giggled when the speaker forgot what he was saying.*

■ [Represents the stomach of a jolly person heaving when laughing] Beginning with the right *bent hand* in front of the chest under the left *bent hand*, both palms facing down, curve the right hand toward the chest with a double movement by bending the wrist.

giggle[2] *n., v.* (alternate sign)

- [Shows smile when giggling] Beginning with both extended index fingers pointing to each side of the mouth, brush the fingers back toward the sides of the face with a double movement.

gingerbread *n.* A cake flavored with ginger and molasses: *I like whipped cream on my gingerbread.*

- [Initialized sign like slicing bread + **bread**] Move the fingertips of the right *G hand* over the back of the left *open hand,* palm facing in. Then move the little fingertip sides of the right *bent hand* downward on the back of the left hand with a double movement.

gingivitis *n.* See sign for GUMS. Related form: **gingiva** *n.*

giraffe[1] *n.* A tall spotted African mammal with long, slender legs and a long neck: *We saw a giraffe at the zoo nibbling leaves from a tree.*

- [Shows shape of giraffe's neck] Beginning with the little-finger side of the right *C hand* on the index-finger side of the left *C hand,* both palms facing in at the neck, move the right hand upward in front of the face.

giraffe[2] *n.* (alternate sign)

- [Shows shape of giraffe's neck] Move the right *C hand,* palm facing in, from in front of the chin upward in front of the face.

girdle *n.* An elasticized or boned undergarment for supporting the abdomen, lower back, hips, and buttocks; corset: *wears a girdle to look slimmer.*

- [Shows wrapping an elastic around one's waist] Move both *10 hands* from near each side of the body in large arcs toward each other, striking both sides of the waist, and then in an arc away from each other in front of the body.

girl[1] *n.* A female child: *boys and girls in the school playground.* Same sign used for: **female.**

- [Formed in the female area of the head] Move the thumb of the right *A hand,* palm facing left, downward on the right cheek to the right side of the chin.

girl[2] *n.* (alternate sign)

- [**girl**[1] + **little**[2]] Move the thumb of the right *A hand,* palm facing left, downward on the right cheek to the right side of the chin. Then place the right *open hand,* palm facing down and fingers pointing forward, near the right side of the body.

Girl Scout *n.* A member of the Girl Scouts, an organization fostering character, health, and skills in young women: *My daughter is now old enough to be a Girl Scout.*

- [**girl**[1] + **Scout**[1]] Move the thumb of the right *A hand,* palm facing left, downward on the right cheek to the right side of the chin. Then bring the index-finger side of the extended three middle fingers of the right hand against the right side of the forehead, palm facing forward.

give[1] *v.* To present or donate: *to give a donation to the fund.* Same sign used for: **award, contribute, donate, grant, present, provide, reward.**

- [Presenting something to another] Move the right *X hand* from in front of the right side of the chest, palm facing left, forward in a large arc.

give[2] *v.* (alternate sign) Same sign used for: **grant, present, provide.**

- [Presenting something to another] Beginning with both *flattened O hands* in front of each side of the chest, palms facing down, move both hands forward while flipping the hands over and opening into *5 hands.*

give³ *v.* (alternate sign) Same sign used for: **present, provide.**

■ [Presenting something to another] Beginning with both *flattened O hands* in front of the body, palms facing up, move the hands forward in simultaneous arcs.

give⁴ *v.* To give out; issue; distribute: *Give these papers to everyone in the class.* Same sign used for: **distribute, hand out, pass out.**

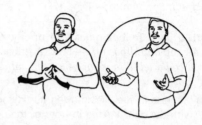

■ [Hands seem to distribute broadly] Beginning with the back of both *flattened O hands* touching in front of the chest, palms facing up, move the hands forward and apart while opening into *curved 5 hands,* ending in front of each side of the body, palms facing up.

give blood See sign for DRAW BLOOD.

give me¹ To give to (the speaker): *Please give me your sister's address.*

■ [**give**³ formed toward oneself] Beginning with both *flattened O hands* in front of the body, palms facing up, bring the hands in to touch the fingertips on each side of the chest, palms facing in.

give me² (alternate sign) Same sign used for: **bonus.**

■ [**give**¹ formed toward oneself] Beginning with the right *X hand* in front of the body, palm facing left, bring the hand back toward the chest in an arc, ending with the index-finger side of the right *X hand* against the chest, palm facing left.

give me³ To give to (the listener): *Give me the notes for the class I missed.* Same sign used for: **present.**

■ [Natural gesture for handing something to another] Beginning with the right *flattened O hand* in front of the right side of the chest, palm facing up and fingers pointing left, move the hand in toward the chest.

give up *v. phrase.* To surrender: *I give up—you've convinced me.* Same sign used for: **relinquish, renounce, surrender, waive, yield.**

- [Natural gesture used when surrendering] Beginning with both *open hands* in front of the body, palms facing down, flip the hands upward in large arcs while opening into *5 hands,* ending in front of each shoulder, palms facing forward.

glad *adj.* See sign for HAPPY.

glance[1] *v.* **1.** To look quickly or briefly: *She glanced at the map and drove off.* —*n.* **2.** A quick or brief look: *You could tell at a glance that the paintings were wonderful.*

- [Represents the eyes moving quickly around] Beginning with the right *V hand* in front of the right side of the face, palm facing down and fingers pointing to the right eye, move the hand forward and outward to the right by twisting the wrist outward with a quick movement, following the fingers with the eyes.

glance[2] *v., n.* (alternate sign)

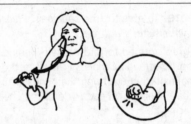

- [**eye**[1] + **grab**[1]] Beginning with the extended right index finger pointing to the right eye, twist the hand forward while opening to a *curved 5 hand* and then closing it quickly to an *S hand* in front of the right side of the chest.

glare *n.* **1.** A strong, harsh, dazzling light: *She turned her head away from the glare.* —*v.* **2.** To shine with a harsh, dazzling light: *The sun glared off the windshield.*

- [Represents light shining down and reflecting off the face] Move the right *flattened O hand,* palm facing left, downward from near the right side of the head toward the face with a double movement, opening into a *curved 5 hand* each time.

glass[1] *n.* A hard, brittle, transparent substance: *large windows made of glass.*

- [Shows porcelain on teeth] Tap the fingertip of the right bent index finger against the front teeth with a repeated movement.

glass[2] *n.* See signs for BOTTLE[1], CUP.

glasses *pl. n.* Corrective eyewear consisting of two glass or plastic lenses set in a frame, usually with earpieces: *had to wear glasses for nearsightedness.* Same sign used for: **eyeglasses, spectacles.**

- ■ [Shape and location of eyeglasses] Tap the thumbs of both *modified C hands,* palms facing each other, near the outside corner of each eye with a repeated movement.

glimpse[1] *n.* **1.** A brief view: *trying to catch a glimpse of a movie star.* —*v.* **2.** To look briefly (at): *glimpse at the photos; to glimpse a deer running past.*

- ■ [Represents the eyes seeing something only briefly] Beginning with the right *V hand* near the right eye, palm facing left, move the hand forward and downward. Then swing the fingertips to the left while turning the head to follow the hands' movement.

glimpse[2] *n.* (alternate sign)

- ■ Beginning with the right *F hand* near the right shoulder and the left *F hand* near the center of the chest, swing both *F hands,* palms facing each other, in an arc to the left in front of the chest while following the hands' movement with the eyes.

glitter *v., n.* See sign for SHINY[1].

globe[1] *n.* **1.** The planet Earth: *a political leader known over the globe.* **2.** A sphere with a map of the earth covering its surface: *See if you can find Europe on the globe.* Related form: **global** *adj.*

- ■ [Initialized sign showing the movement of the sun around the earth] Beginning with both *G hands* in front of the body, right hand above the left, palms facing in opposite directions, roll the hands over each other in a forward circle, ending with the little-finger side of the right *G hand* on the index-finger side of the left *G hand.*

globe[2] *n.* See sign for BALL[2].

gloomy *adj.* See sign for SAD.

glory *n.* Worshipful praise: *Glory to God.*

■ [Shows light and splendor rising from something glorified] Beginning with the palm of the right *open hand* on the upturned left *open hand*, bring the right hand upward in front of the chest while opening the fingers and wiggling them.

gloss[1] *n.* A smooth, extremely shiny surface: *The kitchen floor is shined to a high gloss.*

■ [**smooth**[1] + **shiny**[1]] Move the palm of the right *open hand* across the top of the left *open hand* held in front of the chest, palm facing down. Then, beginning with the bent middle finger of the right *5 hand*, palm facing down, touching the back of the left *open hand*, palm facing down, bring the right hand upward in front of the chest with a wiggly movement.

gloss[2] *v.* See sign for INTERPRET.

glossy *adj.* See sign for SHINY[1].

glove *n.* A covering for the hand with a close-fitting cover for each finger and the thumb: *He lost a glove on the bus.*

■ [Represents pulling on a glove] Pull the right *5 hand*, palm facing down, from the fingers up the length of the back of the left *5 hand*, palm facing down. To indicate the plural, repeat with the other hand.

glow *v., n.* See signs for BEAM, CANDLE, SHINY[1].

glue[1] *n.* **1.** An adhesive substance that causes two surfaces to stick together: *Use glue to mount the pictures.* —*v.* **2.** To cause to adhere with or as if with glue: *Glue the address label to the envelope.*

■ [Initialized sign seeming to squeeze glue on paper] Move the fingertips of the right *G hand*, palm and fingers facing down, in a circular movement over the upturned left *open hand.* [Repeat the movement for the noun form.]

glue² *n., v.* (alternate sign)

- [Initialized sign seeming to seal something closed] Drag the index-finger side of the right *G hand*, palm facing left and fingers pointing left, with a double movement from left to right in front of the mouth.

gnat *n.* A small flying insect that bites: *trying to brush the gnat away from my face.*

- [**bug¹** + natural gesture for shooing away a gnat] With the thumb of the right *3 hand* on the nose, palm facing left, bend the extended index and middle fingers with a repeated movement. Then, beginning with the left *open hand* above the left shoulder and the right *open hand* above the right shoulder, palms angled up, bring the hands downward at an angle in front of the chest with an alternating movement as if swatting away an insect.

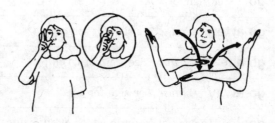

gnaw *v.* To bite or chew on with tiny, repeated nibbles: *The dog gnawed the bone.*

- [Similar to sign for **acid** showing something being eaten up slowly] Beginning with the fingertips of the right *curved 5 hand* on the fingers of the left *open hand*, palms facing each other, move the right hand downward, opening and closing the fingers as the hand moves.

go¹ *v.* To move along, especially to or from somewhere: *She didn't want to go home from the park.* Same sign used for: **go out, gone.**

- [Shows movement going forward] Beginning with both extended index fingers pointing toward each other in front of the chest, palms facing in, move the hands forward in arcs with a double movement.

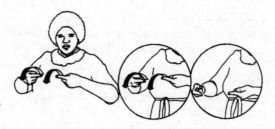

go[2] *v.* To leave or depart, especially to a place distant from the starting location: *to go on vacation.* Same sign used for: **depart, go away, go out, leave.**

■ [Represents something getting smaller as it disappears into the distance] Beginning with the *flattened C hand* in front of the right shoulder, fingers pointing left, move the hand quickly to the right while closing the fingers into a *flattened O hand.*

go[3] *v.* See sign for AWAY.

go after *v. phrase.* See sign for FOLLOW.

go ahead *v. phrase.* See sign for GO ON[1].

go away *v. phrase.* See sign for GO[2].

goal[1] *n.* The end or result to which effort is directed: *The store manager will exceed her goal this week by $10,000.* Same sign used for: **aim, ambitious, objective, target.**

■ [Indicates directing something toward something else] Move the extended right index finger from touching the right side of the forehead, palm facing down, forward to point toward the extended left index finger held in front of the face, palm facing forward and finger angled up.

goal[2] *n.* (alternate sign)

■ [Initialized sign similar to sign for **goal**[1]] Move the extended right index finger from touching the right side of the forehead, palm facing down, forward to point toward the left *G hand* held in front of the face, palm facing forward and fingers angled toward the right.

goal[3] *n.* An area or object toward which players try to go or to carry or propel an object in certain games, as football or hockey: *scored only one goal in the first half of the game.*

■ [Represents a football going through the goalposts] Beginning with the extended right index finger in front of the right shoulder, palm facing left, move the finger to the left, ending with it between the extended fingers of the left *V hand*, palm facing right and fingers pointing up.

goat[1] *n.* A cud-chewing, horned mammal closely related to sheep and found in mountainous regions: *a goat with a small, pointed beard.*

■ [Represents a goat's beard and horns] Beginning with the right *S hand* on the chin, palm facing in and the heel of the hand pointing down, move the hand upward to the forehead while flicking up the index and middle fingers.

goat[2] *n.* (alternate sign)

■ [Represents a goat's beard and horns] Move the right *S hand* from the chin, palm facing in and the heel of the hand pointing down, forward a short distance while flicking up the index and middle fingers. Then repeat the same movement from the forehead.

go by train See sign for TRAIN[1].

God *n.* The Supreme Being; the Creator: *to believe in God.*

■ [Indicates the spirit of God moving down from above] Move the right *B hand*, palm facing left and fingers angled upward, from above the head downward in front of the face in an inward arc.

goggles *pl. n.* Large spectacles with close-fitting rims worn to protect the eyes, as from flying objects: *Wear your goggles when you ride your motorcycle.* Same sign used for: **safety glasses.**

■ [Shape and location of goggles] Tap the index-finger side of the both *C hands*, palms facing each other, against each side of the face near the eyes.

go into *v. phrase.* See sign for ENTER.

gold[1] *n.* **1.** A valuable yellow metallic element, used in jewelry: *a bracelet made of gold.* —*adj.* **2.** Made of gold: *gold coins.* See also sign for CALIFORNIA. Same sign used for: **golden.**

■ [Shows a gold earring + **yellow**] With the thumb, index finger, and little finger of the right hand extended, palm facing in, touch the index finger near the right ear. Then bring the right hand downward and forward with a shaking movement while turning the wrist forward and changing into a *Y hand.*

gold[2] *n.* (alternate sign) Same sign used for: **golden.**

- [Shows a gold earring + **yellow**] Touch the extended right index finger, palm facing in, near the right ear. Then bring the right hand downward and forward with a shaking movement while turning the wrist forward and changing into a *Y hand.*

golden *adj.* See signs for GOLD[1,2]. Shared idea of yellow color.

golf *n.* An outdoor game played by hitting a small ball into a series of holes with as few strokes as possible, using a set of long-handled clubs: *plays nine holes of golf every Saturday.*

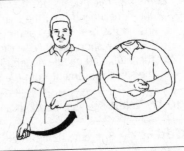

- [Mime swinging a golf club] Beginning with the right *modified X hand* near the right hip, palm facing left, and the left *modified X hand* in front of the right side of the body, palm facing in, swing the right hand upward and to the left.

gone *v., adj.* See signs for ABSENT, GO[1], NOTHING[5].

good *adj.* **1.** Of a favorable character; virtuous: *good people, who care about others.* **2.** Satisfactory in quality or degree: *a good doctor; in good health.* **3.** Palatable or tasty: *This is a good hamburger.* Same sign used for: **benevolent, well.**

- [Presents something good for inspection] Beginning with the fingertips of the right *open hand* near the mouth, palm facing in and fingers pointing up, bring the hand downward, ending with the back of the right hand across the palm of the left *open hand,* both palms facing up.

good at[1] Skilled in doing, performing, or playing: *good at volleyball.* Same sign used for: **expert, proficient.**

- Bring the fingertips of the right *F hand,* palm facing in, back against the chin.

good at[2] See signs for ADROIT, SKILL.

good-bye *interj.* **1.** (A conventional expression used as a parting remark): *Good-bye, everyone, we're leaving.* —*n.* **2.** An act of saying good-bye: *Say your good-byes and go.* Same sign used for: **bye, farewell.**

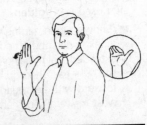

- [Natural gesture for waving good-bye] Beginning with the right *open hand* in front of the right shoulder, palm facing forward and fingers pointing up, bend the fingers up and down with a repeated movement.

good enough See sign for MAKESHIFT.

good friend See sign for FRIEND².

good-looking *adj.* See sign for APPEARANCE².

good luck¹ *interj.* (A conventional expression used to wish someone favorable circumstances and good fortune): *Good luck to you in the competition.*

- **[good** + a natural "thumbs up" gesture for wishing luck] Beginning with the fingertips of the right *open hand* near the mouth, palm facing in and fingers pointing up, bring the hand downward and forward while changing into a *10 hand,* ending with the thumb pointing up, palm facing left, in front of the right shoulder.

good luck² *interj.* (alternate sign)

- [Natural gesture for "thumbs up"] Push the thumb of the right *10 hand,* palm facing left, forward with a short double movement in front of the right shoulder.

good luck³ *interj.* (alternate sign)

- **[good + luck]** Bring the fingertips of the right *open hand,* palm facing in and fingers pointing up, downward from near the mouth. Then, beginning with the bent middle finger of the right *5 hand* touching the chin, palm facing in, twist the wrist to swing the hand forward with a quick movement, ending with the palm facing forward.

good time See sign for PARTYING.

Google *Trademark.* or **google** *v.*
1. A computer search engine used to obtain information on the World Wide Web: *Use Google to find tomorrow's weather forecast for Greece.—v.* 2. To search for information on the World Wide Web using any search engine: *He googled the name of the author to find out the title of the book.*

- **[Internet + look for**¹**]** Beginning with the bent middle fingers of both *5 hands* pointing toward each other in front of the chest, twist both wrists to change positions. Then move the right *C hand,* palm facing left, with a double *circular* movement in front of the face.

go on[1] *v. phrase.* **1.** To move forward: *too tired from walking to go on.* **2.** To continue: *Let's go on with the meeting.* Same sign used for: **all along, continue, forward, get along, go ahead, move on, onward, proceed.**

- [Shows shoving something along ahead of oneself] Beginning with both *open hands* in front of the body, palms facing in and fingers pointing toward each other, move the hands forward a short distance simultaneously.

go on[2] *v. phrase.* (alternate sign)

- [Natural gesture telling someone to leave] Beginning with the extended right index finger pointing down in front of the right side of the body, palm facing in, twist the hand forward and upward, ending with the palm facing down and the finger pointing forward.

goose *n.* **1.** A long-necked, web-footed, swimming bird, resembling but larger than a duck: *watching ducks and geese swimming in the pond.* **2.** The flesh of this fowl used as food: *serving a Christmas goose.*

- [Shows long neck of a goose and the movement of a goose's bill] With the left *open hand* held across the chest, palm facing down, rest the right forearm on the back of the left wrist while closing the extended right index and middle fingers to the right thumb, palm facing forward, with a repeated movement.

go out *v. phrase.* See signs for GO[1,2], OUT.

gorilla[1] *n.* A large and powerful ape: *Gorillas live in the jungles of Africa.* Same sign used for: **ape.**

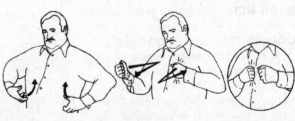

- [**monkey** + miming a gorilla beating its chest] Beginning with the fingertips of both *curved 5 hands* against each side of the body near the waist, palms facing in, brush the fingertips upward with a double movement. Then pound the palm side of both *S hands* against the chest with an alternating double movement.

gorilla[2] *n.* See sign for MONKEY.

Gospel[1] *n.* The teachings of Jesus and the apostles, as contained in the first four books of the New Testament of the Bible: *to proclaim the Gospel.*

- ■ [Initialized sign similar to sign for **new**] Brush the little-finger side of the right *G hand,* palm facing left, across the left upturned palm from the fingers to the heel with a repeated movement.

Gospel[2] *n.* (alternate sign)

- ■ [**good** + **new**] Beginning with the fingertips of the right *open hand* near the mouth, palm facing in and fingers pointing up, bring the hand downward and forward in an arc, brushing the back of the right upturned hand across the left upturned palm.

Gospel[3] *n.* (alternate sign)

- ■ [**true** + **new**] Beginning with the extended right index finger in front of the mouth, palm facing left and fingers pointing up, bring the hand downward while changing into an *open hand.* Then brush the back of the right upturned hand across the left upturned palm.

gossip[1] *n.* **1.** Idle talk filled with rumors about the private lives of others: *There has been malicious gossip about her since she started working here.* **2.** Chatty, light, convivial talk: *to enjoy a bit of harmless gossip over coffee.* —*v.* **3.** To engage in gossip: *They never gossip about their friends.* Same sign used for: **rumor.**

- ■ [Represents mouths opening and closing repeatedly] Move both *G hands,* palms facing each other, in a flat circular movement in front of the chest while pinching the index finger and thumb of each hand together with a repeated movement.

gossip[2] *n., v.* See signs for BLAB, HEARSAY, PRATTLE.

go smoothly See signs for SMOOTH[2], SMOOTHLY.

go steady See sign for STEADY[1].

go to[1] *v. phrase.* (Used as a command directing someone to a specified place): *Go to your seat.*

- ■ [Natural gesture directing someone away from oneself] Move the extended right index finger from pointing forward in front of the right side of the body, palm facing down, deliberately to the right.

go to[2] *v. phrase.* See signs for ATTEND[1], GATHER[2,3].

go to bed

■ [Indicates a person's legs getting under a blanket] Insert the fingers of the right *U hand*, palm facing down, into the hole formed by the left *O hand*, palm facing down.

go to bed together Same sign used for: **sleep together.**

■ [Represents the legs of two people lying down side by side] Beginning with both *H hands* in front of each side of the chest, palm facing down and fingers angled forward, bring the hands forward toward each other, ending with the index-finger side of both hands touching in front of the chest, palms facing down.

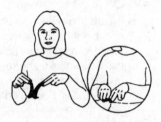

go to regularly See sign for ATTENDANCE.

got you! or **gotcha!** See sign for ZAP.

govern *v.* See sign for MANAGE.

government[1] *n.* A political unit that directs and restrains the actions of its citizens: *the federal government; the state government.*

■ Beginning with the extended right index finger pointing upward near the right side of the head, palm facing forward, twist the wrist to touch the finger to the right temple.

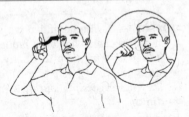

government[2] *n.* (alternate sign)

■ [Initialized sign] Beginning with the right *G hand* near the right side of the head, palm facing forward, twist the wrist to touch the fingers to the right temple.

go with[1] *v. phrase.* To accompany: *He may go with his sister to the movies.* Same sign used for: **accompany.**

■ [Similar to sign for **with** but moving toward a destination] With the palm sides of both *A hands* together in front of the chest, move the hands forward and downward with a deliberate movement.

go with[2] *v. phrase*. See sign for ACCOMPANY[2].

---

grab[1] *v.* To snatch suddenly: *Grab your hat and let's get out of here.*

- [Natural gesture of snatching something] Bring the right *curved 5 hand* from in front of the right side of the body, palm facing left and fingers pointing forward, in toward the body with a quick movement while changing into an *S hand*.

---

grab[2] *v.* (alternate sign, used especially when referring to seizing an opportunity) Same sign used for: **take a chance.**

- [Hand seems to snatch something from the other hand] Bring the right *curved 5 hand* from in front of the right side of the body, palm facing left and fingers pointing forward, in toward the body in a downward arc while changing into an *S hand*, brushing the little-finger side of the right *S hand* across the palm of the left *open hand*, palm facing up in front of the chest.

---

grace[1] *n.* The influence, spirit, or mercy of God: *the grace of God.*

- [Initialized sign moving from pointing to the location of God to pointing to one's heart] Bring the right *G hand* from near the right side of the head, palm facing left and fingers pointing up, downward and to the left in an arc, ending with the little-finger side of the right hand against the left side of the chest, palm and fingers pointing up.

---

grace[2] *n.* See sign for SUN[2].

---

gracious *adj.* See signs for KIND[1,2].

---

grade *n.* A slope in the terrain: *The road has a steep grade.* Same sign used for: **incline, slope.**

- [Demonstrates the shape of an incline] Beginning with the right *B hand* on top of the left *B hand* in front of the chest, both palms facing down, move the right hand upward and forward at an angle.

---

graduate *v.* To receive an academic degree upon completion of a course of study: *graduate from high school.* Related form: **graduation** *n.*

- [Initialized sign similar to sign for **accredit**] Beginning with the right *G hand* in front of the right side of the chest, palm facing left and fingers angled forward, move the hand in a small circular movement and then straight down, ending with the little-finger side of the right hand on the left upturned open palm.

graduate school (first year) A division of a
university devoted to studies beyond the
bachelor's degree, as attended during the first year
of such studies: *in her first year of graduate
school.*

- Place the back of the right *1 hand* across the wrist
  of the left *5 hand,* both palms facing in.

graduate school (second year) A division of
a university devoted to studies beyond the
bachelor's degree, as attended during the second
year of such studies: *in his second year of graduate
school.*

- Place the back of the right *2 hand* across the wrist
  of the left *5 hand,* both palms facing in.

grammar *n.* **1.** The ways in which the words and
sentences of a language are structured: *spent several
years studying the grammar of French.* **2.** A set of rules
derived from such structure: *to produce a grammar of
English.* **3.** Language constructed according to these
rules: *They always use good grammar.* Same sign used
for: **syntax.**

- [Initialized sign similar to sign for **sentence**] Beginning
  with both *G hands* in front of the chest, fingers pointing
  toward each other, bring the hands apart with a wavy
  movement to in front of each side of the body.

grand *adj.* See signs for BIG[1], FANCY[1,2].

grandfather[1] *n.* The father of one's father or
mother: *One of my grandfathers was born in
Vermont.* Alternate form: **grandpa** *(informal).*

- [**father**[1] + moving forward to future
  generations] Beginning with the thumb of the
  right *5 hand* touching the forehead, palm
  facing left, move the hand forward in a double
  arc.

grandfather[2] *n.* (alternate sign) Alternate form:
grandpa *(informal).*

- [**man**[2] + moving forward one generation] Beginning
  with the thumb of the right *A hand* touching the right
  side of the forehead, palm facing left, bring the hand
  downward while opening into a *curved 5 hand* in front
  of the face, palm angled up.

grandma *n. Informal.* See signs for GRANDMOTHER[1,2].

grandmother[1] *n.* The mother of one's father or mother: *My grandmother owns a store.* Alternate form: **grandma** (*informal*).

■ [**mother**[1] + moving forward to future generations] Beginning with the thumb of the right *5 hand* touching the chin, palm facing left, move the hand forward in a double arc.

grandmother[2] *n.* (alternate sign) Alternate form: **grandma** (*informal*).

■ [**girl**[1] + moving forward one generation] Beginning with the thumb of the right *A hand* touching the chin, palm facing left, bring the hand downward while opening into a *curved 5 hand* in front of the chest, palm facing up.

grandpa *n. Informal.* See signs for GRANDFATHER[1,2].

grant[1] *n.* See signs for GIFT[1,2].

grant[2] *v.* See signs for GIVE[1,2], LET[2].

grapes *pl. n.* Smooth-skinned, edible berries that grow in clusters on vines: *to buy a bunch of grapes.*

■ [Shows bumpy shape of a bunch of grapes] Tap the fingertips of the right *curved 5 hand*, palm facing down, down the back of the left *open hand*, palm facing down, from the wrist to the fingers with a bouncing movement.

graph *n.* See sign for SCHEDULE[1].

graphic *adj.* **1.** Being visual, especially in containing diagrams, graphs, etc.: *a graphic presentation to the board of directors.* —*n.* **2.** A diagram, chart, graph, etc.: *The paper contained numerous graphics.*

■ [Initialized sign similar to sign for **picture**] Move the right *G hand*, palm facing forward, from the right cheek downward to touch the left *open hand* held in front of the chest, palm facing right and fingers pointing up.

grass[1] *n.* A plant with bladelike leaves used as ground cover: *time to cut the grass.*

■ [Represents grass growing] Insert the fingers of the right *5 hand* between the fingers of the left *5 hand*, both palms angled up, with a short double movement while wiggling the fingers.

grass[2] *n.* (alternate sign) Same sign used for: **hay.**

■ Push the heel of the right *curved 5 hand,* palm facing up, upward a short distance on the chin.

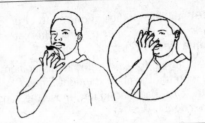

grass[3] *n.* (alternate sign)

■ [**green** + **grow**] Twist the right *G hand,* palm facing left, back and forward with a small repeated movement in front of the right shoulder. Then bring the right *flattened O hand,* palm facing in, up through the left *C hand,* palm facing in and fingers pointing right, while spreading the right fingers into a *5 hand.*

grateful *adj.* Warmly appreciative of kindness or a favor received: *I am grateful for your help.* Same sign used for: **appreciative, thankful.**

■ [**thank you** moving forward toward another] Beginning with the right *bent hand* near the mouth and the left *bent hand* somewhat forward, palms facing in and fingers pointing up, move both hands forward.

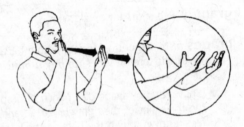

grave *n., adj.* See signs for BURY[1,2], SAD.

graveyard *n.* See sign for CEMETERY.

gravity *n.* **1.** The natural force that pulls objects toward earth: *using the pull of gravity to roll the boulder downhill.* **2.** The attraction between any two masses: *less gravity on the moon than on the earth.*

■ [**earth**[1,2] + a movement showing being pulled downward] Grasping the top of the left hand, palm facing down, with the bent thumb and middle finger of the right *5 hand,* palm facing down, rock the right hand from side to side with a double movement. Then bring the back of the right *S hand,* palm facing in, downward past the thumb side of the left *open hand,* palm facing down.

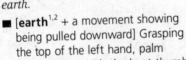

gravy *n.* Sauce for meat, potatoes, and other food made from the juices of cooked meat: *Put beef gravy on the potatoes.* Same sign used for: **grease, oil, syrup.**

- [Represents dripping gravy] Beginning with the extended thumb and index finger of the right *G hand* grasping the little-finger side of the left *open hand*, both palms facing in, bring the right hand downward with a double movement while closing the index finger to the thumb each time.

gray¹ *adj.* Having a neutral color between black and white: *a gray, cloudy sky.*

- [Initialized sign similar to sign for **tan**] Move the index-finger side of the right *G hand*, fingers pointing up, downward on the right cheek with a repeated movement.

gray² *adj.* (alternate sign)

- Beginning with both *5 hands* in front of the chest, fingers pointing toward each other and palms facing in, move the hands forward and back in opposite directions, lightly brushing fingertips as the hands pass each other.

gray³ *adj.* (alternate sign)

- [Initialized sign] Tap the thumb of the right *G hand*, palm facing in and fingers pointing up, against the chin with a double movement.

gray⁴ *adj.* (alternate sign)

- [Initialized sign similar to sign for **black**] Slide the thumb side of the right *G hand*, palm facing left, with a double movement from left to right across the forehead.

grease *n.* See signs for GRAVY, OIL. Related form: **greasy** *adj.*

greasy *adj.* See sign for OILY.

great[1] *adj.* **1.** Unusually large in size: *a great mountain towering over the village.* **2.** Unusually large in number: *The president's visit attracted a great crowd.*

- [Initialized sign similar to sign for **big**[1]] Beginning with both *G hands* in front of the chest, fingers pointing toward each other, bring the hands outward in large arcs, ending near each shoulder.

great[2] *adj.* See signs for BIG[1], WONDERFUL[1,2].

Great Britain *n.* See sign for UNITED KINGDOM.

Greece[1] *n.* A European country in the Balkan Peninsula: *Many tourists travel to see the ruins in ancient Greece.* Related forms: **Greek** *adj.*, **Grecian** *n.*

- Cross the extended index fingers of both hands, fingers angled downward and palms facing in, in the front of the lower chest.

Greece[2] *n.* (alternate sign) Related forms: **Greek** *adj.*, **Grecian** *n.*

- [Initialized sign indicating a Grecian nose] Move the index-finger side of the right *G hand*, palm facing left and fingers pointing up, downward in front of the forehead and nose with a double movement.

greedy[1] *adj.* Having an excessive, selfish desire: *greedy for wealth.* Same sign used for: **covetous, miserly, possessive.**

- Beginning with the right *curved 5 hand* in front of the chin, palm facing in, bring the hand downward with either a single or double movement while closing the hand into an *S hand.*

greedy[2] *adj.* See sign for SELFISH.

green *adj.* Of a color between blue and yellow: *the rich green shades of summer foliage.*

- [Initialized sign] Twist the right *G hand*, palm facing left, back and forward with a small repeated movement in front of the right shoulder.

greet *v.* See signs for INVITE[1], MEET.

greet me See sign for INVITE[2].

grenade *n.* A small explosive shell, usually thrown by hand: *The soldier threw a grenade into the enemy camp.*

- [Mime pulling the pin out of a grenade with one's teeth and then throwing the grenade] Beginning with the right *S hand* near the right side of the face, palm facing left, move the hand outward a short distance and then downward with a deliberate movement while opening into a *5 hand,* ending with the right *5 hand* in front of the right side of the body, palm facing left.

grievance *n.* See sign for PROTEST[1].

grimace *n.* **1.** A twisted or contorted facial expression: *With a grimace of pain, he lifted the heavy box.* —*v.* **2.** To contort the face in a grimace: *grimaced at the site of the mess all over the floor.*

- [Shows shape of face when grimacing] Place the right *5 hand,* palm facing in, near the right side of the face. Then constrict the fingers into a *curved 5 hand.*

grin *v., n.* See signs for SMILE[1,2].

grind[1] *v.* **1.** To reduce to fine particles by crushing or pounding: *to grind the kernels of corn into cornmeal.* **2.** To rub harshly; grate together: *to grind one's teeth.*

- [Represents teeth grinding together] Beginning with the palm sides of both *A hands* together in front of the chest, right hand over the left hand, move the hands in opposite directions in double circles while rubbing on each other.

grind[2] *v.* (alternate sign)

- [Demonstrates movement of grinding something with a rock] Move the right *S hand,* palm facing left, in a circular movement on the palm of the left *open hand,* palm facing up.

grind[3] *v.* See sign for CHEW.

grind out *v. phrase.* To produce in a mechanical way: *The students ground out their homework assignments day after day.* Same sign used for: **monotonous.**

- Beginning with the extended right index finger touching the nose, palm facing in, move the hand forward while changing into an *S hand.* Then rub the index-finger side of the right *S hand,* palm facing forward, on the palm of the left *open hand,* palm facing right and fingers pointing up, with a double movement.

grip *n., v.* See sign for HOLD[1].

gripe *v.* See sign for COMPLAIN.

groceries *pl. n.* See sign for FOOD.

grocery store *n.* A store displaying and selling food: *Our local grocery store has the brand of frozen food you want.* Same sign used for: **market.**

- [**food** + **store**[1,2]] Bring the fingertips of the right *flattened O hand,* palm facing in, to the lips with a repeated movement. Then, beginning with both *flattened O hands* in front of the body, fingers pointing down, swing the fingertips upward and downward from the wrists with a repeated movement.

gross *adj.* See signs for GARBAGE, PROFIT.

grouchy *adj.* See sign for ANGER[2].

ground *n.* See sign for DIRT.

group[1] *n.* A number of people or things considered as a unit: *a group of children.*

- [Initialized sign similar to sign for **class**] Beginning with both *G hands* in front of the chest, palms facing each other, bring the hands away from each other in outward arcs while turning the palms in, ending with the little fingers near each other.

group[2] *n.* See sign for CLASS.

groups *pl. n.* See sign for PACKET.

grovel *v.* **1.** To crawl or lie at someone's feet, as in humility or fear: *He groveled in front of his master.* **2.** To humble oneself: *She refuses to grovel in front of her boss.*

■ [Bent fingers represents crawling on one's knees to grovel] With the knuckles of the right *bent V hand,* palm facing in, on the palm of the left *open hand,* move the knuckles of the right hand in an alternating movement across the left palm.

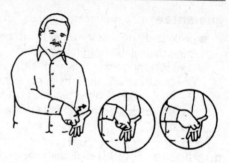

grow *v.* **1.** To develop to maturity, as a plant: *The rose bush has grown another six inches.* **2.** To cause to grow: *They grow tulips in the Netherlands.* Same sign used for: **sprout.**

■ [Represents a plant coming up through the soil] Bring the right *flattened O hand,* palm facing in, up through the left *C hand,* palm facing in and fingers pointing right, while spreading the right fingers into a *5 hand.*

grow up *v. phrase.* To develop to maturity: *grow up on a farm.* Same sign used for: **raise, rear.**

■ [Shows height as one grows] Bring the right *open hand,* palm facing down and fingers pointing left, from in front of the chest upward.

grow big *v. phrase.* See signs for BIG[1,2].

grown-up *n.* See signs for ADULT, ADULTS.

grumble *v.* See sign for COMPLAIN.

grumpy *adj.* See sign for ANGER[2].

guarantee[1] *n.* **1.** A promise to do something; a pledge: *Give us a guarantee that you will stop smoking.* **2.** An assurance, especially in writing, that something will remain of satisfactory quality for a specified amount of time: *The computer comes with a 90-day money-back guarantee.* —*v.* **3.** To make oneself responsible for the quality, performance, or lasting reliability of something: *She guarantees the value of her company's software.*

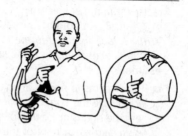

■ [Initialized sign similar to sign for **accredit**] Move the right *G hand,* fingers pointing left, from in front of the right shoulder in an arc downward and then upward to land the little-finger side of the right *G hand* on the upturned palm of the left *open hand* held in front of the chest.

guarantee[2] *n., v.* (alternate sign)

- [Initialized sign similar to sign for **accredit**] Bring the right *G hand* from in front of the right shoulder, fingers pointing left, downward to land the little-finger side of the right *G hand* on the upturned palm of the left *open hand* held in front of the chest.

guarantee[3] *n., v.* See signs for PROMISE[1], STAMP[2].

guard *v.* To protect from danger or invasion: *We bought a dog to guard the house.* See also signs for DEFEND[1,2]. Same sign used for: **protect.**

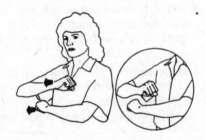

- [Arms place a barrier in front of body] With the arms of both *S hands* bent across the front of the chest, right arm above the left, move both arms forward with a short double movement.

guardian *n.* A person with responsibility for the care of, and control over the affairs of, a child or incompetent adult: *The girl lived with a guardian when her mother went to jail.*

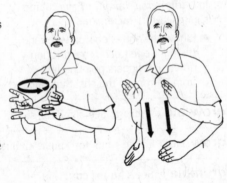

- [**care**[1] + **person**] With the little-finger side of the right *K hand* on the thumb side of the left *K hand*, palms facing in opposite directions, move the hands in a flat circle in front of the body. Then move both *open hands*, palms facing each other, downward along the sides of the body.

guess *v.* **1.** To make assumptions based on limited facts; estimate; conjecture: *I can't begin to guess your age.* —*n.* **2.** An opinion based on limited facts: *Without looking the information up, I can only give you an educated guess.* Same sign used for: **assume, estimate.**

- [Hand seems to snatch at an idea as it passes the face] Move the right *C hand*, palm facing left, from near the right side of the forehead in a quick downward arc in front of the face while closing into an *S hand*, ending with the palm facing down in front of the left shoulder.

guest *n.* See signs for COMPANY, VISITOR.

guide[1] *n.* A person who guides, particularly tourists, visitors, etc.: *The visitors followed the guide on the plant tour.* Same sign used for: **host, leader, ringleader.**

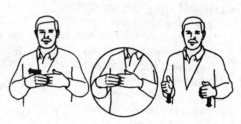

■ [**lead**[1] + **person marker**] With the fingers of the left *open hand* being held by the fingers and thumb of the right hand, both palms facing in, pull the left hand a short distance to the right. Then move both *open hands,* palms facing each other, downward along each side of the body.

guide[2] *v.* See signs for LEAD[1,2].

guideline *n.* An outline of policy, including recommendations for a specific course of action: *It's wise to follow the guidelines in writing your proposal for a grant.*

■ [**lead**[1] + **line**] With the fingers of the left *open hand,* palm facing right, being held by the fingers and thumb of the right hand, palm facing in, pull the left hand a short distance to the right. Then, beginning with both extended little fingers touching in front of the chest, palms facing in, move the hands apart in front of the chest.

guilt[1] *n.* **1.** A feeling of remorse for committing an offense: *A feeling of guilt for lying stayed with her all day.* **2.** The fact that one has committed an offense: *The accomplice denied his guilt.* Related form: **guilty** *adj.*

■ [Initialized sign formed near the heart] Bring the thumb side of the right *G hand,* palm facing left, back against the left side of the chest.

guilt[2] *n.* (alternate sign) Related form: **guilty** *adj.*

■ [Initialized sign formed near the heart] Bring the extended right index finger, palm facing left, back against the left side of the chest.

guinea pig *n.* A tailless rodent similar to a rat, kept as a pet and used for experiments: *a pet guinea pig.*

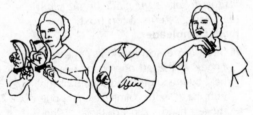

■ [**test**[1,2] + **pig**] Beginning with both extended index fingers pointing up in front of each side of the chest, palms facing forward, bend the fingers down while moving the hands forward and extending the fingers again, ending with the palms facing down and the fingers pointing forward. Then, beginning with the back of the right *bent hand* under the chin, palm facing down and fingers pointing down, wiggle the fingers up and down.

guitar *n.* A stringed instrument with a flat, violinlike body, played with the fingers or a pick: *He learned to play the guitar when he was 12 and joined a rock band at 16.*

■ [Mime playing a guitar with a pick] With the left *curved 5 hand* in front of the left shoulder, palm facing right, and the right *F hand* in front of the right side of the body, palm facing in, twist the right hand downward with a double movement.

gullible *adj.* See sign for CONSUME.

gulp[1] *v.* To swallow greedily: *The baby gulped her milk.* Same sign used for: **gasp.**

■ [Represents the throat constricting as one swallows] Beginning with the right *C hand* near the throat, palm facing in, close the fingers to change into an *S hand.*

gulp[2] *v.* See signs for SWALLOW[1,2].

gum *n.* See sign for CHEWING GUM.

gums *pl. n.* The firm, fleshy tissue along the jaws that surrounds the necks of the teeth: *The gums were inflamed from an infection.* Same sign used for: **gingivitis.**

■ [Point to location] Touch the upper gums with the extended right index finger.

gun *n.* A portable firearm: *According to the movies, you had to carry a gun in the old west.* Same sign used for: **pistol.**

■ [Demonstrates pulling back the hammer on a pointed gun] With the index finger of the right *L hand* pointing forward in front of the right side of the body, palm facing left, wiggle the thumb up and down with a repeated movement.

gust *n.* A sudden rush of wind: *The sails caught a gust of wind.*

■ [Shows movement of a gust of wind] Move the right *5 hand* from in front of the right shoulder, palm facing left and fingers pointing forward, with a swooping movement in front of the chest.

gut *slang.* See signs for ABDOMEN[1,2].

guy *n.* See signs for MAN[1,2].

gym *n.* A class for training in sports and exercises: *time to go to gym.*

■ Beginning with the *modified X hands* in front of each shoulder, palms facing each other, move the hands forward in small double circles by moving the arms and the wrists.

gymnasium *n.* A room or building equipped for exercises or sports: *The basketball team practices in the gymnasium.* Alternate form: **gym.**

■ [**gym** + **house**] Beginning with the *modified X hands* in front of each shoulder, palms facing each other, move the hands forward in small double circles by moving the arms and the wrists. Then, beginning with the fingertips of both *open hands* touching in front of the chest, palms angled toward each other, bring the hands at a downward angle outward to in front of each shoulder and then straight down, ending with the fingers pointing up and the palms facing each other.

gymnastics *n.* Physical exercises and acrobatic feats for developing strength, balance, and flexibility, often performed as a competitive sport: *If you practice your gymnastics, you may be in the Olympics some day.*

■ [Represents a person's legs flipping around when tumbling] Beginning with the right *H hand* in front of the right shoulder, palm facing forward and fingers pointing up, and the left extended index finger pointing right in front of the chest, palm facing down, move the right fingers around the left finger in a forward circle by twisting the right wrist.

gynecologist *n.* A doctor specializing in health maintenance and the diseases of women, especially concerning the reproductive organs: *It's time for her yearly appointment with the gynecologist.*

■ [**doctor**[1,2] + **woman** + **specialize**[1]] Tap the fingertips of the right *M hand,* palm facing left, on the heel of the left *open hand* with a double movement. Then bring the thumb of the right *A hand,* palm facing left, downward from the chin while opening into a *5 hand,* ending by tapping the thumb of the right *5 hand* in the center of the chest. Then move the little-finger side of the right *B hand,* palm facing left, from the thumb forward across the index finger of the left *B hand,* palm facing right.

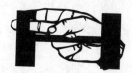

ha ha

ha ha *interj.* (A conventionalized exclamation of joy representing the sound of laughter or, sometimes, sarcastic laughter): *"Ha, ha," the man laughed at the joke.*

- [Spell **h-a, h-a**] Beginning with the right *H hand* in front of the right shoulder, palm facing in and the thumb extended up, close the fingers with a double movement, forming an *A hand* each time.

habit *n.* A pattern of behavior acquired through repeated experience or exposure: *an irritating habit of turning her head away and mumbling.* Same sign used for: **accustomed to, custom.**

- [Symbolizes being bound by tradition] With the heel of the right *S hand* across the wrist of the left *S hand,* both palms facing down, move the hands down simultaneously in front of the chest.

hack *v.* To cut, chop, or sever with repeated blows (often followed by *off, up,* or *down*): *to hack off the tree branch.* Same sign used for: **karate.**

- [Mime hacking something down] Beginning with the right *B hand* in front of the left shoulder, palm facing down, bring the hand deliberately down across the body to in front of the right side of the body. Then, beginning with the right *B hand* near the right shoulder, palm facing left, bring the hand down across the body, ending in front of the left side of the body.

had[1] *v.* Past tense of *have: had a good time.*

- [Initialized sign similar to sign for **have**[1]] Bring the fingertips of both *D hands,* palms facing in, back to touch each side of the chest.

had[2] *v.* See sign for HAVE[1].

hail[1] *n.* **1.** Precipitation in the form of small lumps of ice that form in and fall from cumulonimbus clouds: *Hail hit the roof.* **2.** A shower of hail: *The hail started at noon.* —*v.t.* **3.** To pour down hail: *It hailed all morning.*

- [Shapes and movement of hail] Beginning with the right *F hand* above the right shoulder and the left *F hand* in front of the left side of the body, both palms facing forward, lower the right hand and raise the left hand in a repeated alternating movement.

hail[2] *v.* To greet with respect, as by bowing: *The crowd hailed the king.* Same sign used for: **bow, worship.**

- [Mime bowing before someone] Beginning with both *open hands* in front of the face, left hand somewhat higher than the right hand, both palms facing forward and fingers pointing up, move the hands downward with a double movement.

hair *n.* **1.** A thread-like filament growing from the skin: *I found another gray hair this morning.* **2.** A collection of such filaments on the human head: *He has brown hair.*

- [Location of hair] Hold a strand of hair with the thumb and forefinger of the right *F hand,* palm facing left, and shake it with a repeated movement.

hairbrush *n.* See sign for BRUSH.

haircut[1] *n.* **1.** An act of shaping the hair by cutting it: *to get a haircut every six weeks.* **2.** The style in which the hair is cut: *an attractive haircut.*

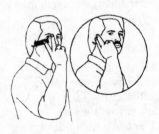

- [Mime cutting one's hair] Move the right *V hand,* palm facing left and fingers pointing up, from near the right cheek back to near the right ear while opening and closing the index and middle fingers with a double movement.

haircut[2] *n.* See sign for CUT[2].

hair dryer *n.* An electrical device used to dry hair: *She used a hair dryer before curling her hair.* Same sign used for: **dryer.**

■ [**dry** + the movement used to dry one's hair with a hair dryer] Drag the index-finger side of the right *X hand,* palm facing down, from left to right across the chin. Then move the extended index finger of the right *L hand,* palm facing down, in a repeated circular movement near the right side of the head.

hair roller[1] *n.* A cylindrical object around which hair is rolled for setting, as in curls or waves: *Every night she puts up her hair in hair rollers.* Same sign used for: **curler, roller.**

■ [Initialized sign showing rolling one's hair] Beginning with both *R hands* on top of each side of the head, palms facing forward, flip the hands backward with a double movement by twisting the wrists.

hair roller[2] *n.* See sign for ROLL ONE'S HAIR.

hair spray *n.* A fixative used on hair after styling: *The beautician sprayed hair spray on the woman's hair.*

■ [**spray** formed near one's hair] Repeatedly bend the extended right index finger while moving the hand back and forth near the right side of the head.

half *n.* See signs for ONE HALF[1,2,3].

half hour *n.* Thirty minutes: *I waited a half hour.*

■ [Shows thirty-minute movement of minute hand on a clock] With the right index finger extended, palm facing forward, move the thumb side of the right hand in a half circle on the palm of the left *open hand,* palm facing right and fingers pointing upward, ending with the right index finger pointing straight down and palm facing in.

halftime *n.* A break in the middle of a
football, basketball, or other game: *There
was entertainment during halftime.* See also
sign for INTERMISSION. Same sign used for:
break.

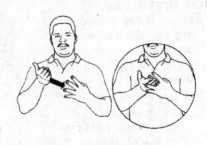

- [Indicates a time in the middle] Insert the
  little-finger side of the right *open hand,*
  palm angled up and fingers pointing
  forward, between the middle finger and ring
  finger of the left *4 hand,* palm facing in.

hall *n.* A corridor in a building: *Her
office is down the hall.* Alternate
form: **hallway.** Same sign used for:
corridor.

- [Shape of a hallway] Move both
  open hands, palms facing each other
  and fingers pointing up, from in front
  of each shoulder straight forward.

hallelujah[1] *interj.* (Used to
express praise to the Lord):
Hallelujah to God!

- [Initialized sign similar to sign
  for **celebrate**] Move both *H
  hands,* palms angled forward,
  in small repeated circles in
  front of each shoulder.

hallelujah[2] *interj.* (alternate sign)

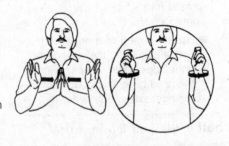

- [**applaud** + **celebrate**] Beginning with
  both *open hands* in front of each
  shoulder, palms facing each other and
  fingers pointing upward, bring the palms
  together in front of the chest. Then move
  both modified *X hands,* palms facing each
  other, in small repeated circles in front of
  each shoulder.

hallowed *adj.* See sign for HOLY.

Halloween[1] *n.* A holiday celebrated, especially by
children, on the evening of October 31, the eve of
All Saints' Day: *It's customary for children to wear
costumes and play trick or treat on Halloween.*

- [Initialized sign similar to sign for **mask**] Move both
  H hands from in front of each eye, palms facing in
  and fingers pointing up, around to each side of the
  head, ending with the palms facing forward.

Halloween[2] *n.* (alternate sign) Same sign used for: **mask, masquerade.**

- [Represents a Halloween mask] Move both *curved hands* from in front of each eye, palms facing in and fingers pointing up, around to each side of the head, ending with the palms angled forward.

hallucination *n.* See sign for HIGH[2].

halo *n.* See sign for BALD.

halt *v.* See signs for HOLD[2,3], STOP[1], SUSPEND.

halve *v.* **1.** To divide into two equal parts: *to halve the pie so you can take some home.* **2.** To share equally between two: *Halve the dinner check between us.*

- [Demonstrates cutting something in half] Move the right *B hand,* palm facing left, from in front of the right side of the face, downward behind the palm of the left *open hand* held across the chest, palm facing in and fingers pointing right.

ham *n.* See sign for PIG.

hamburger *n.* **1.** A patty of ground beef: *to broil a hamburger.* **2.** A sandwich made with such a patty, usually served on a round bun: *to eat a hamburger with tomato and raw onion.*

- [Mime making a hamburger patty] Clasp the right *curved hand,* palm facing down, across the upturned left *curved hand.* Then flip the hands over and repeat with the left hand on top.

hammer *n.* **1.** A hand tool with a solid head at one end of a handle, used especially for driving nails: *Hit the nail with a hammer.* —*v.* **2.** To drive (nails) with a hammer: *hammering nails into the roof.* **3.** To fasten or assemble using a hammer and nails: *hammered the roof into place.*

- [Mime hitting something with a hammer] Move the right *A hand,* palm facing left, up and down with a repeated movement in front of the right side of the body.

hammock *n.* A bed or couch as of netted cord, that hangs between two supports so that it can swing from side to side: *It's relaxing to sleep in a hammock.*

■ [**sleepy** + showing the swinging action of a hammock] Beginning with the fingers of the right *open hand* pointing toward the face, move the hand downward while closing the fingers and thumb together, forming a *flattened O hand.* Then move the right *H hand,* palm facing down and fingers pointing forward, in a swinging, back-and-forth, double movement over of the palm of the left *open hand.*

hamper *n.* A large container for storing dirty clothes before washing: *Throw your laundry in the hamper in the closet.*

■ [**dirty** + **clothes** + **throw**[1]] With the back of the right *5 hand* under the chin, palm facing down, wiggle the fingers. Then brush the thumbs of both *5 hands* downward on each side of the chest with a double movement. Then, beginning with the right *O hand* near the right side of the head, palm angled to the left, move the hand deliberately downward while opening into a *5 hand* near the left *curved hand* held in front of the left side of the body, palm facing right.

hamster *n.* A short-tailed rodent with large cheek pouches: *bought the first-grade class a pet hamster.*

■ [**mouse** + showing a hamster's fat cheeks] Brush the extended right index finger, palm facing left, across the tip of the nose with a double movement. Then touch the fingertips of both *curved 5 hands* to each cheek, palms facing in.

hand *n.* The free prehensile part of the end of the arm, consisting of the wrist, the thumb and fingers, and the area between, used for touching, grasping, seizing, manipulating, etc.: *She broke her left hand.*

■ [Location of hand] Pat the fingers of the left *curved hand,* palm facing down, with a double movement on the back of the left *open hand,* palm facing down.

handball *n.* A game played by two to four persons by hitting a small ball against a wall with the hand: *a game of handball.*

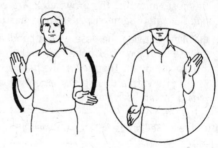

■ [Indicates two people hitting a handball] Beginning with the right *open hand* in front of the right shoulder, palm facing forward and fingers pointing up, and the left *open hand* near the left side of the body, palm facing forward and fingers angled to the left, move the right hand down and the left hand up by twisting the wrists and keeping the elbows close to the body with an alternating double movement.

handcuffs *pl. n.* **1.** A pair of steel bracelets joined by a short chain and used to fasten the wrists of a prisoner: *The detectives put handcuffs on the burglar and led him away.* —*v.* **2. handcuff** To put handcuffs on: *Handcuff him quickly and get him into the police car.*

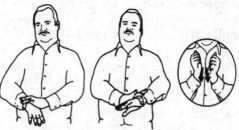

■ [Location of handcuffs on each wrist and then showing them locked in place] With the curved thumb and index finger of the left hand, palm facing down, grasp the wrist of the right *open hand*. Then repeat with the right hand on the wrist of the left hand. Then, beginning with the wrists of both *A hands* near each other in front of the chest, move the hands forward with a short deliberate movement.

hand down *v. phrase.* See sign for PASS DOWN.

handicap *n.* See sign for DISABILITY. Related form: **handicapped** *adj.*

handicraft *n.* **1.** An art or craft requiring skilled work with the hands: *The students will work on jewelry making and other handicrafts.* **2.** Articles fashioned by handicraft: *buying handicraft at the craft fair.* Same sign used for: **handmade.**

■ [**hands** + **make**[1]] Beginning with the little-finger side of the right *B hand* at an angle on the thumb side of the left *B hand,* palms facing in opposite directions, bring the right hand down and under the left hand in order to exchange positions. Repeat the movement with the left hand. Then, beginning with the little-finger side of the right *S hand,* palm facing left, on the index-finger side of the left *S hand,* palm facing right, separate the hands slightly in order to twist the hands in opposite directions and then touch each other again.

handkerchief *n.* A cloth square used for wiping or blowing the nose, mopping the brow, etc.: *Are you carrying a handkerchief?* Same sign used for: **tissue.**

- [Mime blowing the nose with a handkerchief] Grasp the nose with the index finger and thumb of the right *G hand*, palm facing in. Then move the hand forward a short distance with a double movement, closing the index finger and thumb each time.

handle *v.* See signs for MANAGE, PIPE[3].

handmade *adj.* See sign for HANDICRAFT.

hand-me-down *n., adj.* See sign for PASS DOWN.

hand out *v. phrase.* See sign for GIVE[4].

hands *pl. n.* The two end parts of the arms of humans and other primates: *to put gloves on my hands.*

- [Location of one's hands] Beginning with the little-finger side of the right *B hand* at an angle on the thumb side of the left *B hand*, palms facing in opposite directions, bring the right hand down and under the left hand in order to exchange positions. Repeat the movement with the left hand.

handshake *n.* The act of grasping hands with another in friendship or greeting: *She has a firm handshake.* Same sign used for: **shake hands.**

- [Mime shaking one's own hand] Grasp the left *open hand* with the right *curved hand*, both palms facing in, and shake the hands up and down with a double movement.

hands off See signs for NOT RESPONSIBLE[1,2].

handsome[1] *adj.* Having an attractive and imposing appearance; good looking: *He is a handsome man.*

- [**face**[1,2] + **clean**] Move the right extended index finger in a circle in front of the face, palm facing in. Then slide the palm of the right *open hand* from the heel to the fingers of the upturned left *open hand*.

handsome[2] *adj.* See signs for HAWAII[1], APPEARANCE[2].

handwriting *n.* **1.** Writing, especially in flowing strokes with the letters joined together, done with a pen or pencil: *The new scanner can read handwriting into the computer.* **2.** A style or manner of writing by hand; a person's penmanship: *poor handwriting that is difficult to read.*

■ [**hands** + **write**[1,2]] Beginning with the little-finger side of the right *B hand* at an angle on the thumb side of the left *B hand*, palms facing in opposite directions, bring the right hand down and under the left hand in order to exchange positions. Repeat the movement with the left hand. Then move the fingertips of the right *modified X hand*, palm facing down, across the upturned left *open hand* from the heel to the fingertips.

handy *adj.* See sign for SKILL.

hang[1] *v.* To suspend without support from below: *Hang your coat in the closet.*

■ [Represents placing hangers on a rod] With the index finger of the right *X hand*, palm facing left, over the left extended index finger, palm facing down, move both hands downward a short distance.

hang[2] *v.* (alternate sign)

■ [Indicates something hanging down from a hook] With the index fingers of both *X hands* hooked together, right palm facing forward and left palm facing down, move both hands upward a short distance.

hang[3] *v.* To kill by suspension from a rope knotted around the neck: *They set up the gallows, where they hanged the convicted murderer.* Same sign used for: **lynch.**

■ [Location of a noose around the neck] Beginning with the right *S hand* near the right side of the neck, palm facing forward, bring the hand upward and outward to the right.

hang up *v. phrase.* To break the connection and end a telephone call, especially by placing the receiver back on its cradle: *I have to hang up the phone now.*

■ [Mime moving the telephone receiver from the ear to its cradle to hang it up] Beginning with the palm side of the right *Y hand* on the right side of the face, palm facing left, move the hand downward, ending with the right *Y hand* in front of the right side of the body, palm facing back.

hanger *n.* A device, often made of metal or wood, used to suspend clothes, equipment, etc.: *The dry cleaner needs the hangers back.* Same sign used for: **clothes hanger.**

■ [Represents a hanger on a rod] Tap the index finger of the right *X hand,* palm facing left, repeatedly on the left extended index finger, palm facing down.

Hanukkah[1] or **Chanukah** *n.* An eight-day Jewish festival, usually in December, commemorating the rededication of the Temple in Jerusalem in 165 B.C.: *to celebrate Hanukkah by lighting the candles in the menorah.*

■ [Represents the shape of a Hanukkah menorah] Beginning with both *B hands* in front of the chest, palms facing forward, bring the hands outward to each side while opening the fingers into *4 hands.*

Hanukkah[2] or **Chanukah** *n.*
(alternate sign)

■ [Represents the shape of a Hanukkah menorah] Beginning with the little fingers of both *4 hands* touching in front of the chest, palms facing in and fingers pointing up, move the hands apart in an arc, ending with the hands in front of each shoulder.

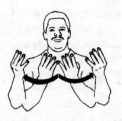

happen *v.* To take place: *Let's find out what happened at the meeting.* Same sign used for: **accident, coincidence, event, incident, occur, occurrence.**

■ Beginning with both extended index fingers in front of the body, palms facing up and fingers pointing forward, flip the hands over toward each other, ending with the palms facing down.

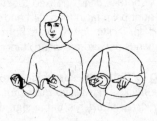

happy *adj.* **1.** Enjoying a sense of well-being; delighted; pleased: *He always seems to be a happy person.* **2.** Characterized by pleasure or joy: *led a happy life.* Same sign used for: **cheer, cheerful, delighted, gay, glad, jolly, joy, merry.**

■ [Represents joy rising in the body] Brush the fingers of the right *open hand,* palm facing in and fingers pointing left, upward in a repeated circular movement on the chest.

harassment *n.* See sign for DANGER.

hard¹ *adj.* Not easily penetrated: *a hard rock.*
Same sign used for: **solid.**

- [Indicates a hard surface] Strike the little-finger side of the right *bent V hand* sharply against the index-finger side of the left *bent V hand,* palms facing in opposite directions.

hard² *adj.* (alternate sign) Same sign used for: **solid.**

- [Indicates a hard surface] Strike the middle finger side of the right *bent V hand,* palm facing in, against the back of the left *S hand,* palm facing down.

hard³ *adj.* See sign for DIFFICULT.

hardly¹ *adv.* Barely; almost not: *We hardly had time to finish dinner.* Same sign used for: **infrequent.**

- [**not**¹ + **often**] Bring the extended thumb of the right *10 hand* from under the chin, palm facing left, forward with a deliberate movement. Then tap the fingertips of the right *bent hand,* palm facing down, from the heel to the fingertips of the left *open hand* in a repeated movement.

hardly² *adv.* See sign for ANYWAY.

hard-of-hearing¹ *adj.* Having a reduced ability to hear: *hired a hard-of-hearing person.*

- [Abbreviation **h-h**] Move the right *H hand,* palm facing left, downward first in front of the right side of the body and then again to the right.

hard-of-hearing² *adj.* (alternate sign)

- [**hear** + abbreviation **h-h**] Touch the extended right index finger to near the right ear, palm facing left. Then move the right *H hand,* palm facing left, downward first in front of the right side of the body and then again to the right.

hardware *n.* See sign for EQUIPMENT[1,2].

hare *n.* See signs for RABBIT[1,2].

harm *v.* See signs for DANGER, HURT[1].

harmful *adj.* Causing or able to cause harm: *harmful gossip.*

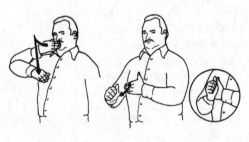

- [**bad** + **danger**] Move the fingers of the right *open hand* from the mouth, palm facing in, downward while flipping the palm quickly down as the hand moves. Then move the thumb side of the right *10 hand,* palm facing left, upward on the back of the left *open hand,* palm facing in, with a double movement.

harmless *adj.* Unable or unwilling to cause harm; innocuous: *harmless gossip.*

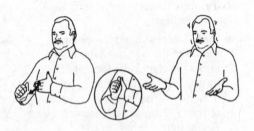

- [**danger** + **none**[4]] Move the thumb side of the right *10 hand,* palm facing left, upward on the back of the left *open hand,* palm facing in, with a double movement. Then place both *open hands* in front of each side of the body, palms facing up, while shaking the head from side to side with a slight movement.

harmonica *n.* A small rectangular musical instrument played by blowing: *to play a harmonica while strolling down the street.*

- [Mime playing a harmonica] Beginning with both *flattened C hands* in front of left side of the face, palms facing each other and fingers pointing toward each other, move the hands back and forth in front of the mouth with a double movement.

harness race *n.* A contest involving horses running at a trot while pulling a buggy by harnesses: *going to a harness race at the local track.* Same sign used for: **reign, wagon.**

- [Mime holding the reins in a harness race] Shake both *A hands,* palms angled up, up and down with a double movement in front of each side of the body.

harp *n.* A large musical instrument with vertical strings in a triangular frame, played by plucking: *Harpo Marx played a harp in the Marx brothers movies.*

- [Mime plucking the strings of a harp] Beginning with the right *5 hand* nearer the chest than the left *5 hand*, palms facing each other and fingers pointing forward, bring the hands back toward the chest with a double movement while constricting the fingers each time into *curved 5 hands.*

---

harsh *adj.* See sign for MEAN[1].

---

harvest[1] *n.* **1.** The reaping of grain or other food crops: *a fall harvest.* —*v.* **2.** To gather grain or other food crops: *to harvest the wheat.* Same sign used for: **chop, cut down.**

- [Represents cutting down a plant close to the ground] Move the fingers of the right *open hand,* palm facing up and fingers pointing forward, with a double movement under the elbow of the bent left arm, hand pointing up.

---

harvest[2] *v.* See sign for REAP.

---

has *v.* Third person present tense of *have*: *She has a dog.* See also sign for HAVE[1].

- [Initialized sign similar to sign for **have**] Bring both *S hands,* palms facing in, back to touch each side of the chest.

---

hassle *v.* See signs for HURRY[1,2].

---

haste *n.* See signs for HURRY[1,2].

---

hat *n.* A shaped head covering, as one with a crown and brim: *to wear a hat in the winter.*

- [Location of a hat on one's head] Pat the top of the head with the fingers of the right *open hand,* palm facing down, with a double movement.

hatch *v.* **1.** To cause young to emerge from (the egg): *After weeks of incubation, the eggs were hatched.* **2.** To be hatched: *Three little robins hatched in the nest.*

■ [Represents an egg breaking open at the top] Beginning with the fingertips of both *C hands* touching in front of the chest, palms facing each other, move the fingers apart from each other while keeping the thumbs together.

hate *v.* To feel extreme dislike or aversion for: *I've always hated peas.* Same sign used for: **despise, detest.**

■ [The fingers flick away something distasteful] Beginning with both *8 hands* in front of the chest, palms facing each other, flick the middle fingers forward, changing into *5 hands.*

haughty *adj.* Disdainfully proud: *She had a haughty attitude about living uptown in a condominium.* Same sign used for: **arrogant, egotistic.**

■ [own¹,² + **proud**] Bring the thumb side of the right *A hand*, palm facing left, back against the center of the chest. Then move the thumb of the right *10 hand*, palm facing down, from the center of the lower chest upward with a smooth movement.

haul¹ *v.* **1.** To pull or drag (something heavy): *Haul that firewood over here.* **2.** To transport; carry: *The trucks haul coal across several states.* Same sign used for: **pull, tow.**

■ [Shows action of pulling another with a hitch] With the index fingers of both *X hands* hooked around each other, right palm facing in and left palm facing down, move both hands from left to right in front of the chest.

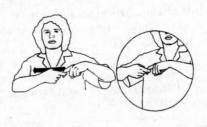

haul² *v.* See sign for DRAG.

haunt *v.* See sign for MONSTER. Related form: **haunted** *adj.*

have¹ *v.* To possess; own: *always wanted to have a dog.* See also sign for HAS. Same sign used for: **had, possess.**

■ [Brings something toward oneself] Bring the fingertips of both *bent hands*, palms facing in, back to touch each side of the chest.

have[2] *v.* (alternate sign)

- [Initialized sign similar to sign for **have**[1]] Bring the fingertips of both *V hands,* palms facing in, back to touch each side of the chest.

have to See sign for MUST.

havoc *n.* See sign for MOB.

Hawaii[1] *n.* A state of the United States located in the North Pacific: *Do they really dance the hula in Hawaii?* Related form: **Hawaiian** *n., adj.* Same sign used for: **handsome.**

- [Initialized sign] Move the fingers of the right *H hand,* palm facing in, around the face with a circular movement.

Hawaii[2] *n.* (alternate sign) Related form: **Hawaiian** *n., adj.*

- [Mime doing a hula dance] Beginning with the left *open hand* somewhat to the left side of the body and the right *open hand* in front of the left side of the body, both palms facing down and fingers pointing left, move the hands upward while bending the fingers down with a swaying movement. Repeat the same movement from the right side of the body.

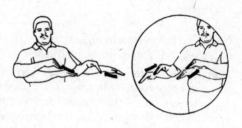

hawk *n.* A small- to medium-sized bird of prey with a short, hooked beak and curved talons: *a hawk hovering over the frightened squirrel.*

- [Shows a hawk's claws] Beginning with the back of the right *bent V hand* in front of the mouth, palm facing forward and fingers bent, bring the hand back against the mouth with a double movement while constricting the fingers each time.

hay *n.* See signs for GRASS[2,3].

hazard *n.* See sign for DANGER.

haze *v.* See sign for TORTURE.

hazy *adj.* See sign for VAGUE.

he[1] *pron.* The male person or animal specified, under discussion, or last mentioned: *He is the man who approached me.* Same sign used for: **her, him, it, she.**

- [Directional sign toward another] Point the extended right index finger, palm facing down, outward to the right or in the direction of the referent.

he[2] *pron.* (alternate sign)

- [Initialized sign formed near the male area of the head] Beginning with the index-finger side of the right *E hand* touching the right side of the forehead, palm facing left, move the hand slightly forward.

head[1] *n.* The upper part of the body, containing the skull, the brain, and the face: *I hit my head on a low branch of the tree.* Same sign used for: **cerebral.**

- [Location of the head] Touch the fingertips of the right *bent hand,* palm facing down, first to the right side of the forehead and then to the right side of the chin.

head[2] *n.* The person in highest authority; leader; chief: *the head of the company.*

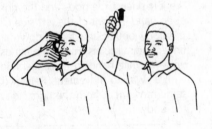

- [head[1] + **chief**] Touch the fingertips of the right *bent hand,* palm facing down, first to the right side of the forehead and then to the right side of the chin. Then move the right *10 hand* upward near the right side of the head, palm facing left and thumb pointing up.

head[3] *v.* See signs for LEAD[1,2].

headache[1] *n.* A pain located in the head, as at the temples: *I have a headache from all that noise.* Same sign used for: **migraine.**

- [hurt[1] formed near the forehead] With both extended index fingers pointing toward each other in front of the forehead, palms facing down, jab them toward each other with a short double movement.

headache[2] *n.* (alternate sign) Same sign used for: **migraine.**

- [Location of a headache] Beginning with the thumb side of the right *modified C hand* against the forehead, bring the hand forward a short distance.

headlight *n.* A light on the front of a vehicle: *The approaching car's headlights were far too bright.*

■ [Shows headlight beams] Beginning with both *flattened O hands* in front of the chest, palms facing down and fingers pointing forward, open the hands into *5 hands.*

headline *n.* A heading, as in a newspaper, printed in heavy type to indicate the subject of an article: *I have no time to read anything but the headlines.*

■ [**head** + **line**] Touch the fingertips of the right *bent hand,* palm facing down, first to the right side of the forehead and then to the right side of the chin. Then, beginning with both extended little fingers touching in front of the chest, palms facing in, move the hands apart to in front of each side of the chest.

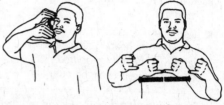

heal *v.* See sign for WELL[1].

health *n.* The general condition of one's body with regard to soundness, vigor, etc.: *in good health.* Same sign used for: **human, hygiene.**

■ [Initialized sign similar to sign for **body**] Touch the fingertips of both *H hands,* palms facing in, first to each side of the chest and then to each side of the waist.

healthy *adj.* See sign for WELL[1].

heap *n.* See signs for AMOUNT[1,2].

hear *v.* To perceive through the ear: *hear a sound.* Related form: **hearing** *n.* Same sign used for: **ear, sound.**

■ [Location of the organ of hearing] Bring the extended right index finger to the right ear.

hearing *adj.* Having the ability to hear: *She is a hearing person who knows sign language.* Same sign used for: **public.**

■ [Indicates a person who talks] Move the side of the extended right index finger, pointing left, in a small double circular movement upward and forward in front of the lips.

hearing aid[1] *n.* An electronic device worn behind the ear to amplify sound: *Wearing a hearing aid is helpful with some kinds of hearing loss.*

- [Shape of a hearing aid showing the location behind the ear where it is worn] Tap the index-finger side of the *modified C hand,* palm facing forward, against the head near the right ear.

hearing aid[2] *n.* (alternate sign, used to refer to an in-the-ear hearing aid)

- [Demonstrates putting the earmold of a hearing aid in one's ear] Twist the right *modified X hand* forward near the right ear.

hearing-impaired[1] *adj.* Having reduced hearing ability: *an interpreter for a hearing-impaired person.*

- [Abbreviation **h-i**] Beginning with the fingers of the right *H hand* pointing to the right ear, palm facing down, move the hand forward while changing into an *I hand,* palm facing forward.

hearing-impaired[2] *adj.* (alternate sign)

- [Abbreviation **h-i** ending with **impair**[1]] Beginning with the fingers of the right *H hand* pointing to the right ear, palm facing down, move the hand forward while changing into an *I hand,* ending with the little-finger side of the right *I hand,* palm facing left, against the index-finger side of the left *B hand,* palm facing down and fingers pointing up.

hearsay *n.* Unverified information received from another: *Pay no attention to hearsay.* Same sign used for: **gossip, rumor.**

- [**hear** + a movement representing talking going around] Move the extended right index finger from touching the right ear forward to in front of the right shoulder. Then move both extended index fingers, palms facing forward and fingers pointing up, from in front of the chest forward and to the left in arcs while shaking the index fingers.

heart[1] *n.* The muscular organ of the body that acts as a pump to circulate the blood: *Luckily, the premature baby was born with a strong heart.* Same sign used for: **cardiac.**

- [Location and action of a heartbeat] Tap the bent middle finger of the right *5 hand,* palm facing in, with a repeated movement on the left side of the chest.

heart[2] *n.* Something having the conventional shape of a heart, with rounded sides curving in at the top and narrowing to a point at the bottom: *three hearts on the charm bracelet.* Same sign used for: **valentine.**

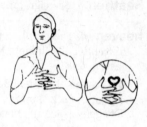

- [Conventionalized shape of a heart formed on the chest at the location of the heart] Beginning with the bent middle fingers of both *5 hands* touching on the left side of the chest, palms facing in, move the hands downward, tracing the shape of a heart on the chest.

heart[3] *n.* (alternate sign) Same sign used for: **valentine.**

- [Conventional shape of a heart formed on the chest at the location of the heart] Beginning with the extended index fingers of both hands touching on the left side of the chest, palms facing in, move the hands downward, tracing the shape of a heart on the chest.

heart attack *n.* A acute episode of heart disease, in which heart function is severely disrupted: *We called an ambulance for the man who was having a heart attack.* Same sign used for: **coronary.**

- [**heart**[1] + **beat**[2]] Beginning with the bent middle finger of the right *5 hand* on the left side of the chest, palm facing in, bring the back of the right hand forward to touch the palm of the left *open hand,* palm facing in and fingers pointing right.

heartbeat *n.* The pulsing rhythm of the heart: *checking on my heartbeat after jogging.*

- [**heart**[1] + the action of a heartbeat] Touch the bent middle finger of the right *5 hand* on the left side of the chest, palm facing in. Then tap the palm side of the right *A hand* against the chest with a double movement.

heat[1] *n.* **1.** The condition or quality of being hot: *There is too much heat in the house.* —*v.* **2.** To make or become warm or hot (sometimes followed by *up*): *Heat some water until it boils. The oven won't heat up.*

- [Movement of a flame heating something on the stove] Move the right *curved 5 hand,* palm facing up, in a double circular movement under the upturned left *open hand.*

heat[2] *v.* See sign for BOIL.

heat[3] *n.* See sign for HOT.

heathen *n.* See sign for PAGAN.

heaven[1] *n.* The dwelling place of God and the angels, conventionally thought to be in the sky: *Grandpa is in heaven now.*

■ [Location of heaven] Beginning with both *open hands* in front of each shoulder, palms facing each other and fingers angled up, bring the hands upward toward each other, passing the right hand forward under the left *open hand,* both palms facing down, as the hands meet above the head.

heaven[2] *n.* (alternate sign)

■ [Location of heaven] Beginning with both *open hands* above each shoulder, palms facing down and fingers pointing toward each other, move the hands upward, rolling the right hand over the left hand, then bringing the hands apart to above each shoulder, ending with the palms facing down and the fingers pointing toward each other.

heavy *adj.* Having great weight: *a box of books too heavy for me to lift.*

■ [The hands seem to be weighted down with something heavy] Beginning with both *curved 5 hands* in front of each side of the chest, palms facing up, move the hands downward a short distance.

hectic *adj.* Characterized by excitement, confusion, and frantic activity: *another hectic day at work.*

■ [Natural gesture used when someone describes rushing around] Beginning with both *5 hands* in front of each side of the chest, palms facing in and fingers pointing toward each other, twist the wrists forward in opposite directions with a repeated movement.

heel *n.* **1.** The back part of a shoe that supports the human heel: *The heel of my left shoe is too tight.* **2.** A solid base raised from the under part of the back of the shoe: *She wears high heels to the office.*

■ [Represents the location of a heel under a shoe] Place the thumb of the right *modified C hand,* palm facing up, on the heel of the left *open hand,* palm facing down.

height[1] *n.* The distance between the lowest and highest points of an upright person: *The child has grown to a height of four feet.*

- [Indicates the top of oneself] Tap the extended right index finger, palm facing up, on the top of the head with a double movement.

height[2] *n.* See sign for TALL[2].

heir *n.* A person designated to receive property from a deceased person's estate: *She is heir to her uncle's entire estate.*

- [**family** + **pass down**] Beginning with the fingers of both *F hands* touching in front of the chest, palms facing each other, bring the hands away from each other in outward arcs while turning the palms in, ending with the little fingers touching. Then, beginning with both *flattened O hands* in front of the left shoulder, palms facing back, move the hands downward to the right in front of the chest in small arcs.

helicopter[1] *n.* An aircraft supported in the air by propellers revolving on a vertical axis: *to hover in the air in a helicopter.*

- [Represents a helicopter's propeller] With the extended thumb of the left *10 hand,* palm facing right, pointing up into the palm of the right *5 hand,* palm facing down, wiggle the right fingers while moving both hands forward a short distance.

helicopter[2] *n.* (alternate sign)

- [Represents a helicopter's propeller] With the extended thumb of the left *3 hand,* palm facing right, pointing up into the palm of the right *5 hand,* palm facing down, wiggle the right fingers while moving both hands forward a short distance.

helicopter[3] *n.* (alternate sign)

- [Represents a helicopter's propeller] With the extended left index finger, palm facing right, pointing up into the palm of the right *5 hand,* palm facing down, wiggle the right fingers while moving both hands forward a short distance.

hell *n.* The abode of evil and condemned souls after death: *The wicked are doomed to go to hell.*

■ [Initialized sign moving downward to the traditional location of hell] Move the right *H hand* from in front of the left shoulder, palm facing in and fingers angled up, downward with a deliberate movement to the right, ending with the hand in front of the right side of the body, fingers pointing forward and palm facing left.

hello *interj.* **1.** (Used to express a greeting): *Hello, there. How are you?* —*n.* **2.** An act or instance of saying "hello": *Say your "hellos" to your friends and then let's go.* Same sign used for: **greet, hi, salute.**

■ [Natural gesture for a salute to greet someone] Beginning with the fingertips of the right *B hand* near the right side of the forehead, palm angled forward, bring the hand forward with a deliberate movement.

helmet *n.* A rigid covering to protect the head: *Football players now wear helmets made of a hard plastic.*

■ [Shape and location of a helmet on the head] Beginning with both *curved 5 hands* near each other at the top of the head, palms facing each other and fingers angled up, move the hands downward along the shape of the head, stopping abruptly near each side of the head.

help[1] *v.* **1.** To provide needed effort, materials, etc.; give assistance: *Will you help us wash the dishes?* —*n.* **2.** The act of giving assistance: *We appreciate your help in organizing the class trip.* Same sign used for: **aid, assist.**

■ [The lower hand seems to give assistance to the other hand] With the little-finger side of the left *A hand* in the upturned right *open hand,* move both hands upward in front of the chest.

help[2] *v., n.* (alternate sign) See sign used for: **aid, assist.**

■ [One hand gives a boost or aid to the other] Bring the palm of the left *open hand,* palm facing up, against the little-finger side of the right *A hand,* palm facing left, with a double movement.

helpless *adj.* See sign for APATHY.

hen *n.* See sign for CHICKEN[1].

henpeck *v.* See sign for PICK ON.

her *pron.* See signs for HE[1], HIS[1].

here[1] *adv.* **1.** In or at this place: *The meeting will take place here.* **2.** To or toward this place: *Come here.* —*n.* **3.** This place: *From here, you go left one mile.* Same sign used for: **present.**

■ [Indicates a location near oneself] Beginning with both *curved hands* in front of each side of the body, palms facing up, move the hands toward each other in repeated flat circles.

here[2] *adv., n.* (alternate sign) Same sign used for: **present.**

■ [Points at an exact location near oneself] Point the extended right index finger, palm facing down, downward in front of the right side of the body. [This sign can be formed using both hands.]

heritage *n.* **1.** Something, as a principle or a set of values, that belongs to one by reason of birth, membership in a cultural group, etc.: *proud of our heritage of freedom of speech.* **2.** Something handed down as part of an inheritance: *Grandmother's jewelry is part of the family heritage.* Same sign used for: **heredity.**

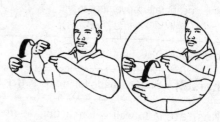

■ [Initialized sign similar to sign for **generation**] Beginning with the left *H hand* near the right shoulder and the right *H hand* somewhat forward, both palms facing in and fingers pointing in opposite directions, roll the hands over each other with an alternating movement while moving the hands forward.

hermit[1] *n.* A person who lives alone in seclusion, especially in a solitary, isolated place: *She lives like a hermit, never seeing anyone or going out.* Same sign used for: **isolated.**

■ Beginning with both *I hands* in front of the face, palms facing in, bring the little fingers together with a double movement.

hermit[2] *n.* See sign for RECLUSE.

hero *n.* **1.** A courageous man, admired for his bravery: *He was considered a hero for stopping the runaway bus.* **2.** The most important male character in a story, film, etc.: *The hero married the princess at the end of the story.*

■ [**boy**[1] + **brave**] Beginning with the index-finger side of the *flattened C hand* near the right side of the forehead, palm facing left, close the fingers to the thumb with a double movement. Then, beginning with the fingers of both *curved 5 hands* near the shoulder, palms facing in, bring the hands forward with a deliberate movement while closing the *S hands*.

---

heroin *n.* See sign for DRUG[2].

---

heroine *n.* **1.** A courageous woman, admired for her bravery: *a true heroine, who saved many lives while risking her own.* **2.** The most important female character in a story, film, etc.: *The heroine of the story is Cinderella.*

■ [**girl**[1] + **brave**] Move the thumb of the right *A hand,* palm facing left, downward on the right cheek to the right side of the chin. Then, beginning with the fingers of both *curved 5 hands* near each shoulder, palms facing in, bring the hands forward with a deliberate movement while closing into *S hands*.

---

hers *pron.* See sign for HIS[1].

---

herself *pron.* See signs for HIMSELF, ITSELF.

---

hesitate *v.* To wait before acting, as from fear or indecision: *He hesitated to answer the question.*

■ [Natural gesture used to balk at something] With both *open hands* in front of each side of the chest, palms facing forward and fingers pointing up, pull the head and body backward with a short repeated movement.

---

hexadecimal *adj.* Of or pertaining to a numbering system using a base of sixteen and representing digits greater than 9 with the letters A through F: *translating the ASCII codes into hexadecimal digits that my software program can use.*

■ [Abbreviation **b-16** indicating base-sixteen] Beginning with the right *B hand,* palm facing forward and fingers pointing up, under the palm of the left *open hand,* palm facing down and fingers pointing right, move the right hand to the right while forming the number "16."

hi *interj.* (Used as an informal greeting): *Hi, everyone!*

- [Natural gesture for waving in greeting] Move the right *open hand,* palm facing forward and fingers pointing up, from in front of the chest to the right in a smooth arc.

hiccup[1] *n.* **1.** An involuntary, spasmodic inhalation, producing a short, sharp sound: *Gulping a drink gives me the hiccups.* —*v.* **2.** To have the hiccups: *Don't make me laugh or I'll hiccup.*

- [Shows action of hiccuping] Beginning with the bent index finger of the right hand tucked under the right thumb, palm facing in, flick the index finger upward with a double movement in front of the chest.

hiccup[2] *n., v.* (alternate sign)

- [Shows action of hiccuping] Beginning with the fingers of the right *curved hand* on the chest, palm facing in, move the hand abruptly upward and then downward, keeping the fingers on the chest while closing into an *S hand.*

hickey *n. Slang.* A reddish mark left on the skin after a passionate kiss: *She had a hickey on her neck.*

- [Represents sucking someone's neck] Beginning with the fingertips of the right *curved 5 hand* on the right side of the neck, palm facing left, pull the hand outward to the right with a double movement, closing the fingers to form a *flattened O hand* each time.

hide[1] *v.* To put or get out of view: *Hide the money in the desk. You'd better hide from them.* Same sign used for: **conceal, mystery, secluded.**

- [**secret** + a gesture putting something under the other hand as if to hide it] Move the thumb of the right *A hand,* palm facing left, from near the mouth downward in an arc to under the left *curved hand* held in front of the chest, palm facing down.

hide[2] *v.* See sign for COVER-UP.

hierarchic or **hierarchical** *adj.* Of or pertaining to an order or sequence resembling an inverted tree, in which the topmost item has branches that in turn branch to other items, with further branching as necessary: *A hierarchic structure is typical in computer file systems.* Related form: **hierarchy** *n.*

■ [Initialized sign showing things moving down in a hierarchy] Beginning with the fingertips of both *H hands* touching in front of the chest, palms facing in, bring the hands apart to in front of each shoulder. Then move the *H hands* downward, palms facing each other and fingers pointing forward, outward to in front of each side of the chest, and downward again.

high¹ *adj.* **1.** Having a great height; tall: *a high hill.* **2.** Having a specified height: *The table is three feet high.* **3.** Raised to an elevated position: *The shelf is too high for me to reach.* —*adv.* **4.** To or at an elevated place: *Hang the hook high enough to be out of the way.* Same sign used for: **altitude.**

■ [Initialized sign showing a location at a higher elevation] Move the right *H hand*, palm facing left and fingers pointing forward, from in front of the right side of the chest upward to near the right side of the head.

high² *n.* A state of elation induced by drugs: *on a high for the past few hours.* Same sign used for: **hallucination.**

■ [Initialized sign indicating that the brain is high] Move the fingers of the right *H hand*, palm facing down, from the right side of the forehead upward a short distance.

high-definition or **HDTV** *adj.* Referring to a television system that has twice the standard number of scanning lines per frame as a standard television, and therefore produces pictures with greater detail.

■ [**picture + bright**] Move the right *C hand* downward, palm facing forward, from near the right side of the face, ending with the index-finger side of the right *C hand* against the palm of the left *open hand*, palm facing right. Then, beginning with the fingertips of both *flattened O hands* touching in front of the chest, palms facing each other, move the hands quickly upward in arcs to above each shoulder while opening to *5 hands.*

higher *adj.* See sign for ADVANCED.

high-resolution *adj.* The fineness of detail in an image, resulting from the close proximity of the lines or pixels comprising the image, as seen on a television or video display terminal, or in digital pictures.

- [**high**¹ + **pixels**] Move the right *H hand* upward, palm facing in and fingers pointing left, from in front of the right side of the chest. Then tap the fingertips of the right *curved 5 hand* with a small repeated movement from the fingers to the heel of the left *open hand* held in front of the chest, palm facing right and fingers pointing up.

high school *n.* A secondary school, usually consisting of grades 9 or 10 through 12: *attends high school in another neighborhood.*

- [Abbreviation **h-s**] Form the fingerspelled letters H and S in front of the right side of the chest, palm facing in.

highway *n.* A main public road, especially one between towns or cities: *Follow the highway to the next turnoff.* Same sign used for: **freeway.**

- [Initialized sign representing two streams of traffic going in opposite directions] Beginning with both *H hands* held in front of each side of the chest, palms facing down and fingers pointing toward each other, move the hands past each other toward the opposite sides of the chest with a repeated movement.

hill¹ *n.* A rounded elevation of earth, smaller than a mountain: *to climb the hill on foot.*

- [Shows shape of a hill] Move the right *open hand,* palm facing down, from in front of the left side of the chest in an arc upward to the right and then down again.

hill² *n.* (alternate sign)

- [Shows shape of a hillside] Beginning with both *open hands* in front of each side of the waist, palms angled forward and fingers angled up, move the hands forward and upward with a large wavy movement.

him *pron.* See sign for HE¹.

himself *pron.* A reflexive form of *him*, used to refer back to the male last mentioned: *He will be able to do it himself.* See also sign for ITSELF. Same sign used for: **herself, itself.**

■ [Directional sign toward the person you are referring to] Push the extended thumb of the right *10 hand*, palm facing left, forward with a short double movement in front of the right side of the body.

hinder *v.* See sign for PREVENT.

hindsight *n.* The perception of the significance of an event only after it has occurred: *Their insincerity became clear in hindsight.* Same sign used for: **look back, recollect, recollection, retrospect.**

■ [Represents the eyes looking back into the past] Beginning with the fingertips of the right *V hand* pointing toward the right eye, palm facing down, move the hand around to the right side of the head, ending with the fingers pointing back.

hinge *n.* The joint on which a door or gate moves back and forth: *The gate swung open on its hinges.*

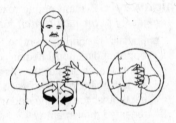

■ [Shows action of a door opening on hinges] Beginning with the fingers of both *curved 5 hands* meshed together in front of the chest, palms facing in, bend the fingers forward and back with a double movement by twisting the wrists.

hip *n.* The projecting portion on each side of the body below a person's waist, below which the leg joins the body: *She tends to carry the child on her hip.*

■ [Location of the hip] Tap the fingertips of the right *bent hand,* palm facing up, against the right hip with a double movement.

hire[1] *v.* To engage the services of; employ: *to hire a new assistant.*

■ [Initialized sign similar to sign for **invite**[1]] Swing the right *H hand* from in front of the right side of the body, palm facing up, downward and to the left in front of the body.

hire[2] *v.* See sign for INVITE[1].

hire me See sign for INVITE[2].

his[1] *pron.* The possessive adjective form of *he: His name is Bob.* Same sign used for: **her, hers, its.**

- [Directional sign toward the person referred to] Push the right *open hand,* palm facing forward, at an angle forward in front of the right side of the body.

Hispanic *n., adj.* See signs for Mexico[2], Spain[1,2].

historic *adj.* See signs for LONG AGO[1,2]

history *n.* **1.** The branch of knowledge dealing with significant past events: *to study history in college.* **2.** An account or record of these events regarding a particular people, period, etc.: *I am reading a history of England.* Related form: **historical** *adj.*

- [Initialized sign] Move the right *H hand,* palm facing left, downward with a double movement in front of the right side of the body.

hit[1] *v.* To strike with force: *He hit the wall with his fist.* Same sign used for: **attack, impact, strike.**

- [Demonstrates action of hitting] Strike the knuckles of the right *A hand,* palm facing in, against the extended left index finger held up in front of the chest, palm facing right.

hit[2] *v.* See signs for BEAT[4], BEAT UP, PUNCH.

hit me To strike the speaker: *The ball hit me.* Same sign used for: **inflict.**

- [Directional sign toward oneself] Bring the knuckles of the right *S hand,* palm facing right, in toward the chest to hit the extended right index finger held up in front of the chest, palm facing right.

hitchhike *v.* To travel by getting rides from passing vehicles, especially by standing at the side of road and gesturing with the thumb: *He hitchhiked across the nation.* Related form: **hitch** *v.*

- [Natural gesture for hitchhiking] Move the thumb of the right *10 hand,* palm facing in, from the front of the right shoulder to the right with a double movement.

hockey *n.* A game played on a field or on ice by two teams attempting to score goals at opposite ends of the playing area: *plays ice hockey on the school team.*

- Brush the index finger of right *X hand* against the upturned palm of the left *open hand* as the right hand moves in a double circular movement.

hoe *n.* See sign for RAKE.

hog *n.* See sign for PIG.

hold[1] *v.* **1.** To have or keep in one's hand: *Please hold the package while I tie my shoe.* **2.** To have possession or use of: *to hold a job.* Same sign used for: **grip.**

- [The hands seem to hold something securely] Beginning with the little-finger side of the right *C hand* on the index-finger side of the left *C hand*, both palms facing in, move the hands in toward the chest while closing the fingers of both hands into *S hands.*

hold[2] *v.* **1.** To keep or remain in a specified state: *Hold still.* **2. hold on** To stop or halt: *Hold on, the traffic light is changing.* Same sign used for: **halt, pause.**

- [The hand seems to hold something] Move the right *S hand,* palm facing up, in a circular movement in front of the right side of the chest.

hold[3] or **hold on** *v.* or *v. phrase.* To restrain or delay (oneself): *Hold on until later.* See also sign for SUSPEND. Same sign used for: **halt, pause.**

- [One hand seems to suspend the other] With the index fingers of both *X hands* hooked together, palms facing down, pull both hands upward.

hold up *v. phrase.* See signs for ROB[1,2].

hole[1] *n.* An opening in or through something: *There is a hole in the road. I have a hole in my sock.*

- [Shape of a hole] Move the extended right index finger, palm facing back and fingers pointing down, in a large circle around the index-finger side of the left *C hand,* palm facing down.

hole[2] *n.* (alternate sign)

- [Shape of a hole] Bring the thumb side of the right *F hand,* palm facing forward, with a double movement against the palm of the left *open hand,* palm facing right and fingers pointing up.

holiday *n.* **1.** A day officially honoring a well-known person or commemorating an important event: *to celebrate the holiday with fireworks.* **2.** A day or sequence of days of exemption from work: *I spent the holiday shopping.*

- [Gesture often used when one is carefree] Tap the thumbs of both *5 hands* near each armpit, palms facing each other and fingers pointing forward, with a double movement.

Holland[1] *n.* A country in western Europe, on the North Sea: *Holland is famous for its tulips.* Same sign used for: **Dutch, the Netherlands.**

- [Shape of a traditional Dutch hat] Beginning with the thumb of the right *Y hand* on the forehead, palm facing left, move the right hand forward in an arc.

Holland[2] *n.* (alternate sign) Same sign used for: **Dutch, the Netherlands.**

- [Shape of a traditional Dutch hat] Beginning with the fingertips of both *C hands* touching each side of the head, palms facing each other, bring the hands outward to each side while closing the fingers, forming *flattened O hands.*

holler *v.* See sign for CALL[4].

Hollywood *n.* The northwest part of Los Angeles, California, known as the center of the movie industry: *Many movie stars work in Hollywood but live somewhere else.*

- Bring the thumbs of both *5 hands,* palms angled toward each other, back toward each side of the chest with an alternating double movement.

holy *adj.* **1.** Declared by religious authority to be sacred: *a holy place.* **2.** Spiritually pure: *a holy love of God.* Related form: **holiness** *n.* Same sign used for: **hallowed.**

- [Initialized sign similar to sign for **clean**] Move the right *H hand* in a circular movement over the upturned left *open hand.* Then slide the little-finger side of the right *H hand* from the base to the fingertips of the left hand.

home *n.* **1.** The house, apartment, or other shelter that is the principal residence of a person, family, or household: *Their home is in Montana.* —*adv.* **2.** To, toward, or at home: *It's past time for you to go home.*

- [A modification of the signs **eat** and **sleep**[2] indicating that a home is a place where you eat and sleep] Touch the fingertips of the right *flattened O hand* first to the right side of the chin, palm facing down, and then to the right cheek.

homework *n.* Work, especially school lessons, to be done at home: *I have a lot of math homework due tomorrow.*

- [**home** + **work**[1,2]] Touch the fingertips of the right *flattened O hand* to the right cheek, palm facing down. Then move the right hand down while changing into an *S hand* and tap the base of the right *S hand* on the back of the left *S hand* held in front of the chest, palm facing down.

homosexual[1] *n.* **1.** A person who is sexually attracted to persons of the same sex: *He told the people where he works that he is a homosexual.* —*adj.* **2.** Of or pertaining to homosexuals or homosexuality: *a homosexual group.* Related form: **homosexuality** *n.* Same sign used for: **queer** (*disparaging and offensive*).

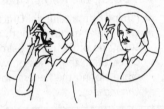

- Touch the bent middle finger of the right *5 hand,* palm facing in, first to the lips and then upward off the right eyebrow. The sign is used disparagingly.

homosexual[2] *adj., n.* See sign for GAY[1].

honest *adj.* Tending not to lie or cheat; truthful: *an honest appraisal of their work.* Related forms: **honestly** *adv.,* **honesty** *n.* Same sign used for: **frank, frankly, sure, truth.**

- [Initialized sign similar to sign for **clean**] Slide the extended fingers of the right *H hand,* palm facing left, forward from the heel to the fingers of the upturned left *open hand.*

honey[1] *n.* A thick, sweet liquid prepared by bees from floral nectar: *I like to put honey in my tea.*

- [Initialized sign similar to sign for **sweet**] Beginning with the fingers of the right *H hand* near the right side of the mouth, palm facing back and fingers pointing left, move the fingers to the right with a double movement, bending the fingers back into the palm to change into an *A hand* each time.

honey[2] *n.* See sign for SWEETHEART.

honeymoon *n.* A holiday spent by a newly married couple: *They plan to go to Bermuda on their honeymoon.*

- Touch the bent middle finger of the right *5 hand,* palm facing in, first to the left side of the chin and then to the right side of the chin.

honor *n.* **1.** A source of credit or distinction: *It is an honor to know you.* **2.** Credit, respect, or recognition given, as for special worth or merit: *gave him the honor of speaking at the dinner.* —*v.* **3.** To show respect: *Honor your parents.* Related form: **honorary** *adj.*

- [Initialized sign similar to sign for **respect**] Beginning with both *H hands* in front of the face, right hand higher than the left hand and palms facing in opposite directions, bring both hands downward and forward in a slight arc.

hood[1] *n.* A soft covering for the head and the neck, often attached to the back of a jacket or sweater: *It's cold enough for you to pull your hood up over your head.*

- [Shape and location of a hood] Beginning with the fingertips of both *bent hands* near the back of the head, palms facing forward, pull the hands upward and over the head to near each side of the forehead, ending with the palms facing back and fingers pointing toward each other.

hood[2] *n.* See sign for PONCHO.

hook *n.* **1.** A curved or angled piece of metal, plastic, or the like for holding and suspending something: *Put your jacket on the coat hook.* —*v.* **2.** To hang on or suspend from a hook: *hooked my sweater on a nail.*

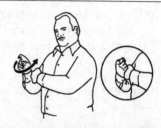

- [Demonstrates hooking something] Beginning with the right *X hand* in front of the right side of the body, palm facing left, and the left arm bent across the chest, swing the right index finger in an arc to the left, ending with the palm facing in.

hooked *adj.* See sign for ADDICTED.

hook up *v. phrase.* See sign for BELONG[1].

hop[1] *v.* To spring on one foot: *hop around the room.*

- [Shows action of hopping] Touch the middle finger of the right *P hand,* palm facing down, first to heel and then to the fingers of the upturned open left palm.

hop[2] *v.* (alternate sign)

- [Shows action of hopping] Beginning with the knuckles of the right *bent V hand,* palm facing back, on the heel of the left *open hand* held in front of the chest, palm facing up, raise the right hand while straightening the fingers into a *V hand,* and then bend the fingers again to touch down on the left palm. Repeat, touching farther toward the left fingers each time.

hope[1] *v.* **1.** To wish or wish for and expect: *We hope for rain after the dry summer.* —*n.* **2.** A feeling that what one desires might happen: *My hope is to go to college.* Same sign used for: **anticipate, anticipation, expect, expectation.**

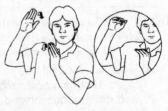

- [The hands seem to compare a thought with the anticipated future] Beginning with the right *open hand* near the right side of the head, palm angled left and fingers pointed up, and the left *open hand* in front of the chest, palm facing right and fingers pointing up, bend the fingers toward each other with a double movement.

hope[2] *v., n.* (alternate sign) Same sign used for: **anticipate, anticipation, expect, expectation.**

- [**think**[1] + **hope**[1]] Beginning with the extended right index finger touching the right side of the forehead, palm facing down, and the left *bent hand* in front of the chest, palm facing right, bring the right hand downward to in front of the right shoulder while changing into a *bent hand* and bend the fingers of both hands toward each other.

hopeless *adj.* See sign for WORTHLESS.

horde *n.* A multitude; crowd: *A horde of people attended the concert.* See also signs for AUDIENCE[1,2]. Same sign used for: **crowd, mass.**

- [Indicates large crowds of people] Move both *curved 5 hands,* palms facing down, from in front of each side of the body forward with a simultaneous movement.

horn[1] *n.* A musical instrument sounded by blowing into the smaller end; wind instrument: *Sound the horn before the hunt.*

- [Mime holding a horn and blowing into it] Hold the left *S hand* in front of the mouth, palm facing right, and the right *C hand* in front of the face, palm facing left.

horn[2] *n.* See sign for MEGAPHONE.

horns[1] *pl. n.* A pair of hard bony growths on the head of many hoofed animals: *The steer's horns got caught in the bushes.*

- [Shape and location of horns on the head] Beginning with the thumb side of both *O hands* on each side of the head, palms facing forward, bring the hands upward and outward in small arcs while closing into *S hands.*

horns[2] *pl. n.* See sign for PRESIDENT. Shared idea of corrupt politician.

horny *adj. Slang (often considered vulgar).* Having a strong desire for sex; feeling lust: *always horny after a couple of drinks.*

- [Represents sexual thoughts] Bring the back of the right *1 hand,* palm facing forward and finger pointing up, back against the forehead with a double movement.

horror *n.* A terrifying and overwhelming feeling of revulsion and fear: *feels a sense of horror about the victims of the famine.* Related forms: **horrible** *adj.,* **horrific** *adj.* Same sign used for: **ghastly, terrible, terror.**

- [**awful** formed near the head] Beginning with both *8 hands* near each side of the forehead, palms facing each other, flick the fingers open quickly into *5 hands,* palms facing forward.

horrible *adj.* See sign for AWFUL.

horrified *adj.* See sign for AGHAST.

horse *n.* A large, four-legged mammal with solid hoofs, bred for riding, pulling loads, etc.: *learned to ride a horse as a child.*

■ [Represents a horse's ears] With the extended thumb of the right *U hand* against the right side of the forehead, palm facing forward, bend the fingers of the *U hand* up and down with a double movement.

horseback riding[1] *n.* The act or skill of traveling while mounted on the back of a horse: *She's always been excellent at horseback riding.*

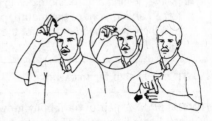

■ [horse + ride a horse] With the extended thumb of the right *U hand* against the right side of the forehead, palm facing forward, bend the fingers of the *U hand* up and down with a double movement. Then, with the index finger and middle finger of the right *3 hand,* palm facing in and fingers pointing down, straddling the index-finger side of the left *open hand,* palm facing right and fingers pointing forward, move the hands forward.

horseback riding[2] *n.* See sign for RIDE A HORSE.

hose[1] *n.* A narrow tube for conveying water from a faucet to some desired point: *watering the lawn with the large garden hose.*

■ [water + mime holding a hose to water something] Tap the index-finger side of the right *W hand,* palm facing left, against the chin with a double movement. Then, with the little-finger side of the right *modified X hand* touching the index-finger side of the left *S hand,* palms facing in opposite directions, swing the hands from side to side with a double movement in front of the body.

hose[2] *n.* See signs for PANTYHOSE, STOCKING.

hospital[1] *n.* An institution, staffed with doctors and nurses, in which sick and injured people are treated and cared for: *had to go to the hospital for major surgery.* Same sign used for: **infirmary.**

■ [Initialized sign following the shape of a cross, symbolic of the American Red Cross, a healthcare organization] Bring the fingertips of the right *H hand,* palm facing right, first downward a short distance on the upper left arm and then across from back to front.

hospital[2] *n.* (alternate sign) Same sign
used for: **infirmary.**

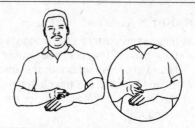

- ■ [Initialized sign] Move the middle finger
  side of the right *H hand,* palm facing left,
  in a small arc down the back of the left
  open hand, palm facing down and fingers
  pointing right.

host *n., v.* See signs for GUIDE[1], LEAD[1,2], SERVE.

hostage *n.* A person held captive, as by an enemy,
until certain conditions are met: *held as a hostage by
terrorists demanding ransom.*

- ■ [Initialized sign similar to sign for **jail**[1,2]] Beginning
  with both *H hands* in front of the chest, palms facing
  in and fingers pointing upward at angles in opposite
  directions, bring the fingers of the right *H hand* in
  against the left fingers.

hostile *adj., v.* See sign for OBSESSION[1].

hot *adj.* Having or giving off heat; having a high temperature:
a hot fire. Same sign used for: **heat.**

- ■ [Hands seems to take something hot from the mouth and
  throw it away] Beginning with the right *curved 5 hand* in
  front of the mouth, palm facing in, twist the wrist forward
  with a deliberate movement while moving the hand
  downward a short distance.

hot dog[1] *n.* **1.** A cooked and smoked
sausage; frankfurter; wiener: *to grill
hot dogs.* **2.** A sandwich made with a
hot dog, usually on a long bun: *to eat
a hot dog with mustard and relish.*

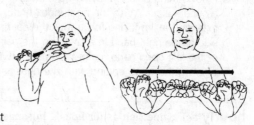

- ■ [**hot** + **sausage**] Beginning with the
  right *curved 5 hand* in front of the
  mouth, palm facing in, twist the wrist
  forward with a deliberate movement while moving the hand downward a short
  distance. Then, beginning with the index-finger sides of both *C hands* touching in
  front of the body, palms facing forward, bring the hands outward to each side while
  squeezing them open and closed from *C* to *S hands* repeatedly as the hands move.

hot dog[2] *n.* (alternate sign)

- ■ [Shows links of frankfurters] Beginning with the
  thumbs and index fingers of both *G hands* touching
  in front of the chest, palms facing each other, bring
  the hands outward to each side while pinching the
  thumbs and index fingers together repeatedly as
  the hands move.

hot dog[3] *n.* (alternate sign)

- [Represents putting a hot dog in a bun] Bring the extended fingers of the right *H hand,* palm facing left, from in front of the lips downward to land between the thumb and index finger of the left *C hand* held in front of the body, palm facing up.

hotel *n.* A large commercial building with rooms or suites for travelers, frequently with restaurants, stores, and other service facilities: *We plan to stay for a week in a hotel in the city.*

- [Initialized sign] Place the fingers of the right *H hand,* palm facing in and fingers pointing left, on the back of the extended left index finger, palm facing in and index finger pointing up in front of the chest.

hour[1] *n.* A period of time consisting of 60 minutes: *It will take me one hour to finish.* Same sign used for: **one hour.**

- [Shows minute hand moving 60 minutes around a clock] With the right index finger extended, palm facing left, move the palm side of the right hand in a circle on the palm of the left *open hand,* palm facing right and fingers pointing up.

hour[2] *n.* (alternate sign) Same sign used for: **one hour.**

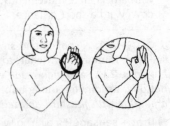

- [Shows minute hand moving 60 minutes around a clock] With the right index finger extended, palm facing left, move the palm side of the right hand in a circle on the palm of the left *open hand,* palm facing right, while twisting the wrist, ending with the right palm facing in.

hourly *adj.* Same sign as for HOUR[1,2] but made with a double movement.

house *n.* A building in which people live, typically for one or two families: *They want to own a house in the suburbs.*

- [Shape of house's roof and walls] Beginning with the fingertips of both *open hands* touching in front of the neck, palms angled toward each other, bring the hands at a downward angle outward to in front of each shoulder and then straight down, ending with the fingers pointing up and the palms facing each other.

how *adv.* **1.** By what means: *How did this happen?* **2.** To what degree or extent: *How tired are you?* **3.** In what condition: *How are you?* **4.** For what reason: *How can you say that?* —*conj.* **5.** The way in which: *I can't figure out how to do it.* **6.** About the way or condition in which: *Think how the project started!*

- [Similar to gesture used with a shrug to indicate not knowing something] Beginning with the knuckles of both *curved hands* touching in front of the chest, palms facing down, twist the hands upward and forward, ending with the fingers together pointing up and the palms facing up.

however *adv.* See signs for ANYWAY, BUT.

how many[1] (Used to request information about the number of things, persons, etc., in question): *How many people work for you?*

- [**how** + **many**] Beginning with the knuckles of both *curved hands* touching in front of the chest, palms facing down, twist the hands upward and forward, ending with the fingers together pointing up and the palms facing up. Then, beginning with both *S hands* in front of each side of the chest, palms facing up, flick the fingers open quickly into *5 hands*.

how many[2] See sign for HOW MUCH[2].

how much[1] (Used to request information about the extent of something): *How much time will it take to finish?*

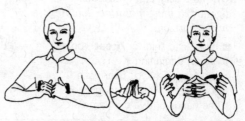

- [**how** + **much**] Beginning with the knuckles of both *curved hands* touching in front of the chest, palms facing down, twist the hands upward and forward, ending with the fingers together pointing up and the palms facing up. Then, beginning with the fingertips of both *curved 5 hands* touching in front of the chest, palms facing each other, bring the hands outward to in front of each side of the chest.

how much[2] (alternate sign) Same sign used for: **how many.**

- [An abbreviated form] Beginning with the right *S hand* in front of the right side of the chest, palm facing up, flick the fingers open quickly into a *5 hand*.

huddle *n.* **1.** A gathering of the football players on a team during a game to receive signals about the next play from the quarterback: *a huddle behind the scrimmage line at the start of the second quarter.* —*v.* **2.** To gather together closely: *huddled around the fireplace.*

■ [Initialized sign similar to sign for **class**] Beginning with the index-finger sides of both *H hands* touching in front of the chest, palms facing forward, bring the hands away from each other in outward arcs while turning the palms in, ending with the little fingers together in front of the chest, palms facing in.

hug[1] *v.* To put the arms around and hold close, especially as an expression of affection: *hugging the baby.* Same sign used for: **affection, affectionate, embrace.**

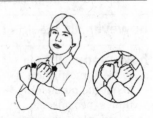

■ [Mime hugging someone] With the arms of both *S hands* crossed at the wrists, palms facing in, pull the arms back against the chest with a double movement.

hug[2] *v.* (alternate sign) Same sign used for: **embrace.**

■ [Mime hugging someone] Beginning with both *S hands* in front of each side of the body, palms facing each other, bring the hands back against the opposite shoulder by crossing the wrists, ending with the palms facing in.

huge[1] *adj.* Very big; enormous; gigantic: *a huge mountain looming on the horizon.*

■ [Similar to sign for **great**[1], only larger] Beginning with both *modified C hands* near each shoulder, palms facing in, move the hands outward in large arcs.

huge[2] *adj.* See sign for LARGE.

hulk *n.* A large, muscular person: *The boxer is a real hulk.* Same sign used for: **husky.**

■ [Shows shape of a hulk's shoulders] Beginning with both *modified C hands* near each side of the neck, move the hands forward from each shoulder, ending with the palms facing in.

hum *v.* **1.** To make a continuous droning sound: *The fan in my computer keeps humming.* **2.** To sing without words through closed lips: *The boy hummed a song.* —*n.* **3.** The sound of humming: *I heard the hum of the bees.*

- [Initialized sign using **m** indicating the sound that is made when humming] Beginning with the index-finger side of the right *M hand* near the right side of the face, palm facing left, bring the hand forward with a wavy movement.

human *adj., n.* See sign for HEALTH. Shared idea of ideal state of human being.

humble[1] *adj.* Not proud; modest: *a humble man without any pretensions.* Related form: **humility** *n.* Same sign used for: **meek, modest, modesty.**

- [Shows moving oneself under another when humbled] Bring the extended right index finger from in front of the mouth, palm facing left, downward and forward while opening into a *B hand* and moving under the left *open hand* held in front of the chest, palm facing down.

humble[2] *adj.* (alternate sign) Related form: **humility** *n.* Same sign used for: **meek, modest, modesty.**

- [Shows moving oneself under another when humbled] Bring the right *B hand*, palm facing left and fingers pointing up, from in front of the mouth downward and forward under the left *open hand* held in front of the chest, palm facing down.

humid[1] *adj.* Filled with moisture; containing damp air: *a humid climate.*

- [**hot** + as if feeling sweat dripping off one's face] Beginning with the right *curved 5 hand* in front of the mouth, palm facing in, twist the wrist forward with a deliberate movement. Then, beginning with the fingers of both *5 hands* near the chin, palms facing in, move the hands downward and forward slightly, changing into *flattened O hands* in front of each shoulder and rubbing the thumbs and fingers together.

humid[2] *adj.* See signs for SWEAT[2], WET[1,2].

humiliate *v.* See signs for EMBARRASS, SWALLOW[2]. Related form: **humiliation** *n.*

humorous[1] *adj.* Characterized by humor; funny: *a humorous story.* Same sign used for: **comical.**

- [Similar to sign for **silly**[1], except more exaggerated and formed with both hands] With the thumb of the right *Y hand* near the nose, and with the left *Y hand* somewhat lower and forward, palms facing each other, move both hands downward with repeated circular movements.

humorous[2] *n.* See sign for FUNNY.

hundred *n.* A cardinal number equal to ten times ten: *I have a hundred pages of the manuscript finished.*

- [Abbreviation **c** representing the Roman numeral for **hundred**] Move the right *C hand*, palm facing left, from in front of the chest a short distance to the right.

Hungary *n.* A republic in central Europe: *The capital of Hungary is Budapest.* Related form: **Hungarian** *adj., n.*

- Move the thumb side of the right *X hand*, palm angled left, from under the nose to the right and downward to the right side of the mouth.

hungry *adj.* Having a strong desire for food: *hungry for a steak.* Related form: **hunger** *n.* Same sign used for: **appetite, crave, famished, ravenous, starved, yearn.**

- [Shows passage to an empty stomach] Beginning with the fingertips of the right *C hand* touching the center of the chest, palm facing in, move the hand downward a short distance.

hunt *v.* To go after or search for (wild animals) to catch or kill: *to hunt for deer.* Related form: **hunting** *n., adj.*

- [Mime aiming a rifle or shotgun] With both *L hands* in front of the chest, right hand closer to the chest than the left, palms facing in opposite directions and index fingers angled up, move the hands downward with a double movement.

hunt for *v. phrase.* See signs for LOOK FOR[1,2,3].

hurdle *n.* An obstacle or barrier: *to jump the hurdle.*

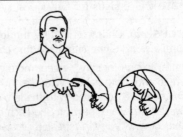

- [Demonstrates legs moving over a hurdle] Move the right *P hand* from near the chest, palm facing down, forward in a small arc over the extended left index finger, palm facing in and finger pointing right.

hurrah *n.* See sign for RALLY.

hurry[1] *v.* **1.** To move or cause to move quickly: *Hurry home. Don't hurry me.* —*n.* **2.** An eagerness to act quickly: *always in a hurry.* Same sign used for: **hassle, haste, hustle, rush, urgent.**

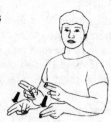

■ [Initialized sign showing hurried movement] Beginning with both *H hands* in front of each side of the body, palms facing each other, move the hands up and down with a quick short repeated movement.

hurry[2] *v., n.* (alternate sign) Same sign used for: **hassle, haste, hustle, rush, urgent.**

■ [Initialized sign showing hurried movement] Beginning with both *H hands* in front of each side of the body, palms facing each other, move the hands up and down with a quick repeated alternating movement.

hurt[1] *v.* **1.** To cause pain or injury: *I hurt my wrist when I twisted it.* **2.** To feel pain: *Does your head hurt?* —*n.* **3.** An injury, wound, pain, etc.: *How is the hurt on your finger?* See also signs for PAIN[1,2]. Same sign used for: **ache, harm, injury, sore, wound.**

■ [Fingers indicate a stabbing pain] Beginning with both extended index fingers pointing toward each other in front of the chest, palms facing in, jab the fingers toward each other with a short repeated movement.

hurt[2] *adj.* (alternate sign) See also signs for PAIN[1,2]. Same sign used for: **bear, sore, wound.**

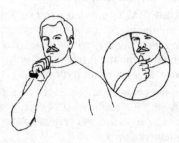

■ [Symbolizes patience when having pain] Beginning with the thumb of the right *A hand* touching the chin, palm facing left, twist the wrist back, ending with the palm facing in.

husband *n.* A married man, especially in relation to his wife: *My husband will be home in an hour.*

- [Hand moves from the male area of the head + **marry**] Move the right *C hand* from the right side of the forehead, palm facing left, down to clasp the left *curved hand* held in front of the chest, palm facing up.

husk *n.* The dry outer covering of an ear of corn: *Peel back the husk so we can see if the corn is still good.*

- [**corn** + a gesture showing pulling down husks on an ear of corn] With both *S hands* held near each side of the mouth, palms facing forward, twist the hands forward from the wrists. Then pull the fingertips of the right *curved 5 hand* forward and downward across the back of the left *open hand* with a double movement.

husky *adj.* See sign for HULK.

hustle *v.* See signs for HURRY[1,2].

hyena *n.* A wild carnivorous animal of Africa and Asia, much like a large dog, one kind of which is noted for its noisy, laughlike call: *a laughing hyena.*

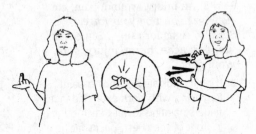

- [**dog**[1,2,3] + **hysterical**[1,3]] Snap the right thumb gently off the right middle finger, palm facing up, in front of the right side of the chest. Then, with the right *curved 5 hand* over the left *curved 5 hand* in front of the chest, move the hands forward and back with a repeated alternating movement.

hygiene *n.* See sign for HEALTH.

hymn *n.* See sign for MUSIC.

hypnotize *v.* **1.** To put into a trance or trancelike state; make vulnerable to control: *When hypnotized, she was able to remember the terrible experience she had blocked.* **2.** To hold spellbound; transfix; fascinate: *to hypnotize the audience.* Related form: **hypnosis** *n.*

- [The fingers seem to put a spell on someone] Beginning with both *5 hands* in front of each side of the chest, palms facing down and fingers pointing forward, wiggle the fingers slowly.

hypocrite *n.* A person who espouses or pretends to exhibit virtues but is not sincere: *He is a hypocrite, who spoke against crime but embezzled funds.* Same sign used for: **fake, impostor.**

■ [Hands indicate someone covering the truth] With the palm of the right *open hand* on the back of the left *open hand,* the fingers of both hands pointing forward and palms facing down, push the fingers of the left hand down with the right fingers.

hypodermic[1] *adj.* **1.** Of or characterized by the injection of drugs under the skin: *a hypodermic needle.* —*n.* **2.** A hypodermic syringe: *Hand the doctor the hypodermic.* **3.** A dose of medicine administered by syringe: *prescribed a hypodermic of morphine every four hours for the pain.*

■ [Mime giving a shot in the arm with a hypodermic] Move the index finger of the right *3 hand* from in front of the right shoulder, palm facing right, back against the right upper arm while closing the middle finger to the thumb.

hypodermic[2] *n.* See sign for SHOT.

hypothesis *n.* A provisional theory based on certain assumptions: *He did research to prove the hypothesis.*

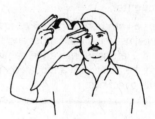

■ [Initialized sign similar to sign for **invent**] Move the fingers of the right *H hand,* palm facing down, from the right side of the forehead forward in a double arc.

hypothetical *adj.* See sign for FAKE[1].

hysterectomy *n.* An operation in which the uterus is removed: *She had a hysterectomy after developing benign tumors.*

■ [**woman** + **operate**[2] + **remove**[1]] Bring the thumb of the right *A hand,* palm facing left, downward from the chin while opening into a *5 hand,* ending by tapping the thumb of the right *5 hand* in the center of the chest. Then pull the thumb of the right *A hand,* palm facing down, from left to right across the abdomen. Next, bring the fingertips of the right *curved hand* against the left *open hand,* palms facing each other, while changing the right hand into an *A hand.* Finally, bring the right *A hand* downward off the left fingertips while opening into a *curved 5 hand,* palm facing down.

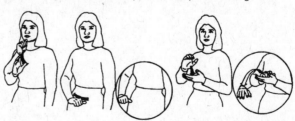

hysterical[1] *adj.* Showing or characterized by uncontrollable outbursts: *hysterical laughter.* Same sign used for: **laugh, laughter.**

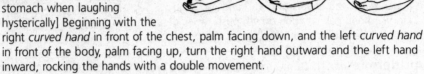

■ [Shows the movement of the stomach when laughing hysterically] Beginning with the right *curved hand* in front of the chest, palm facing down, and the left *curved hand* in front of the body, palm facing up, turn the right hand outward and the left hand inward, rocking the hands with a double movement.

hysterical[2] *adj.* (alternate sign) Same sign used for: **laugh, laughter.**

■ [Represents one rolling around on the floor with laughter] Beginning with the back of the right *V hand,* palm facing up, on the palm of the left *open hand,* palm facing up, move the right hand in a circle while bending and extending the *V* fingers with a double movement.

hysterical[3] *adj.* (alternate sign) Same sign used for: **laugh, laughter.**

■ Beginning with both *curved 5 hands* in front of the chest, palms facing each other and the right hand above the left hand, move the hands forward and back to the chest with a repeated movement and in opposite directions.

I[1] *pron.* The first person singular pronoun; the person speaking: *I am happy to see you.*

■ [Initialized sign formed toward oneself] Bring the thumb side of the right *I hand,* palm facing left, back against the chest.

I[2] *pron.* See sign for ME.

ice *n., v.* See sign for FREEZE.

ice box *n.* See sign for REFRIGERATOR[2].

ice cream *n.* A smooth, frozen dessert made with cream or milk, sugar, and flavorings: *vanilla ice cream.*

■ [Mime eating from an ice cream cone] Bring the index-finger side of the right *S hand,* palm facing left, back in an arc toward the mouth with a double movement.

ice skate *n., v.* See sign for SKATE[2].

icing *n.* See sign for FROSTING.

idea *n.* A thought, conception, or notion occurring in the mind: *Having this party was a good idea.*

■ [Initialized sign similar to sign for **invent**] Move the extended right little finger from near the right temple, palm facing down, upward in a double arc.

ideal *n., adj.* See sign for PERFECT.

identical *adj.* See signs for ALIKE[1,2].

identify

identify *v.* To recognize as being a particular person or thing: *to identify the picture.*

- [Initialized sign similar to sign for **show**[1]] Tap the thumb side of the right *I hand*, palm facing left, with a double movement against the left open palm held in front of the chest, palm facing forward and fingers pointing up.

identification *n.* Same as sign for: IDENTIFY, but made with a double movement. Related form: **identity** *n.*

idiom[1] *n.* A phrase or expression with a meaning different from the sum of the individual words within it: *Since "bite the bullet" is an English idiom, you should not take it literally.*

- [Initialized sign similar to sign for **quotes**] While holding both *I hands* near each side of the head, palms angled forward, bend the little fingers.

idiom[2] *n.* (alternate sign)

- [Initialized sign similar to sign for **quote**] Beginning with both *I hands* near each side of the chin, palms facing each other and extended little fingers pointing up, move the hands outward while changing into *bent V hands.*

idiom[3] *n.* See sign for QUOTATION[1].

idiot *n.* A very stupid or foolish person: *always acts like an idiot in public.* Same sign used for: **ignorant.**

- [Initialized sign similar to sign for **ignorant**[1]] Bring the thumb side of the right *I hand*, palm facing left, against the forehead.

idle *adj.* See signs for APATHY, REST[1].

idol[1] *n.* **1.** An object, as a statue, worshipped as a god: *to pray to an idol.* **2.** Someone or something excessively admired or adored: *made the rock star into an idol.* Same sign used for: **worship.**

- [Indicates legs kneeling in worship] Bring the right *V hand,* palm facing out, from touching the right side of the forehead downward in an arc and then straight down, ending with the knuckles of the *bent V hand* resting on the upturned left *open hand.*

idol[2] *n.* See sign for IMAGE[1].

if[1] *conj.* **1.** On condition that: *If you can, please hand that large book to me.* **2.** Whether: *I wonder if he will go.*

- [Initialized sign using **f** formed with a movement indicating indecision] Move both *F hands,* palms facing each other, up and down with an alternating movement in front of the chest.

if[2] *conj.* See sign for SUPPOSE.

ignite[1] *v.* To set on fire: *used several matches to ignite the campfire.* Same sign used for: **light a match, strike a match.**

- [strike a match[1] + candle] With the right *modified X hand,* palm facing down, touching the left *open hand,* palm facing right, in front of the chest, move the right hand upward to the right with a quick movement. Then wiggle the fingers of the right *5 hand* in front of the chest, palm facing back and fingers pointing forward, while touching the right wrist with the left index finger.

ignite[2] *v.* See sign for START[2].

ignition *n.* See sign for STARTER.

ignorant[1] *adj.* **1.** Knowing little or nothing: *an ignorant person whose insults you should ignore.* **2.** Revealing lack of knowledge, poor training, or insensitivity: *an ignorant remark.* Related form: **ignorance** *n.* Same sign used for: **stupid.**

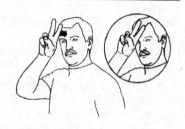

- Bring the back of the right *V hand,* palm facing forward, against the forehead with a deliberate movement.

ignorant[2] *adj.* See sign for IDIOT.

ignore

ignore[1] *v.* To refrain from paying attention to; disregard: *Don't let the townspeople ignore the storm warning.* Same sign used for: **forsake, neglect.**

- [Indicates attention moving away from object or person in view] While looking forward, place the index finger of the right *4 hand,* palm facing forward and fingers pointing up, near the right side of the face. Then move the hand outward to the right with a quick deliberate movement.

ignore[2] *v.* (alternate sign) Same sign used for: **forsake, neglect.**

- [Shows not paying attention to someone or something] Beginning with the index-finger side of the right *S hand* near the right ear, move the hand outward with a quick deliberate movement while extending the index finger and pointing outward.

ignore[3] *v.* (alternate sign, used to indicate disregarding the presence or wishes of the speaker) Same sign used for: **neglect me.**

- [Directional sign toward oneself] Beginning with the index-finger side of the right *4 hand* touching the nose, palm facing down and fingers pointing left, bring the hand downward in an arc, ending with the little-finger side of the hand touching the chest, palm facing up.

ill *adj.* See signs for SICK[1,2]. Related form: **illness** *n.*

illegal *adj.* See signs for CRIME[1,2], FORBID.

illegible *adj.* See sign for VAGUE.

illustrate *v.* See sign for DRAW[1].

illustration *n.* See signs for ART, SKETCH[1].

illustrator *n.* See sign for ARTIST.

I love you (A special handshape in American Sign Language).

- [Abbreviation **i-l-y** formed simultaneously in a single handshape] Hold up the right hand with the thumb, index finger, and little finger extended, palm facing forward, in front of the right shoulder.

image[1] *n.* **1.** A physical likeness, as a photograph, painting, or statue, representing a particular person, animal, or thing: *an image of George Washington.* **2.** Something or someone strongly resembling another; counterpart; copy: *She is the image of her mother.* Same sign used for: **idol.**

- [Initialized sign similar to sign for **statue**] Beginning with both *I hands* near each side of the head, palms facing each other, move the hands downward with a wavy movement, first toward each other in front of the chest and then away from each other again as the hands move down.

image[2] *n.* (alternate sign)

- [Initialized sign similar to sign for **picture**] Beginning with the index-finger side of the right *I hand* near the right side of the chin, palm facing forward, move the right hand downward, ending with the index-finger side of the right *I hand* against the palm of the left *open hand,* palm facing right and fingers pointing up.

image[3] *n.* (alternate sign) Same sign used for: **indicate, indicator.**

- [Initialized sign similar to sign for **show**[1]] Beginning with the index-finger side of the right *I hand* against the palm of the left *open hand,* palm facing right and fingers pointing up, move both hands forward simultaneously.

image[4] *n.* See signs for PICTURE, SHAPE[1,2].

imagination *n.* The ability to form mental images of things not actually present: *a vivid imagination.* Same sign used for: **superstition, superstitious.**

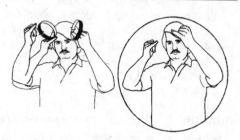

- [Initialized sign showing ideas coming from the head] Move the extended little fingers of both *I hands,* palms facing back, in double alternating circles near each side of the head.

imagine *v.* To form a picture or concept in one's mind: *Imagine what it must be like to fly a plane.* Same sign used for: **make believe.**

- [Initialized sign similar to sign for **dream**] Move the extended right little finger from near the right temple, palm facing down, upward in a double circular movement.

imitate *v.* See sign for COPY[1].

immaterial *adj.* Not important: *The story was immaterial to the conversation.*

- **[not + connect]** Bring the thumb of the right *10 hand* forward from under the chin with a deliberate movement. Then, beginning with both *curved 5 hands* in front of each side of the body, palms facing each other, bring the hands together with a double movement while touching the thumb and index fingertips of each hand to form two interlocking circles with the fingers.

immature *adj.* **1.** Not yet mature: *just an immature child from whom you expect too much.* **2.** Emotionally undeveloped: *too immature to take on those responsibilities.*

- **[not[1] + advanced]** Bring the extended thumb of the right *10 hand* from under the chin, palm facing left, forward with a deliberate movement. Then move both *bent hands,* palms facing each other, from in front of each shoulder upward a short distance in deliberate arcs.

immediately *adv.* See signs for FAST[1,2,3].

immigrant *n.* See sign for EMIGRANT. Related form: **immigration** *n.*

immigrate *v.* See sign for ENTER.

immovable *adj.* Unable to be moved; firmly fixed: *an immovable object.*

- **[can't + move]** Bring the extended right index finger downward, striking the extended left index finger held in front of the chest, palm facing down and finger pointing right. Then, beginning with both *flattened O hands* in front of the body, palms facing down, move them in large arcs to the right.

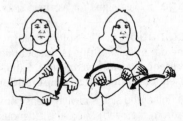

immune[1] *adj.* Protected from a disease: *She is immune to poison ivy.*

- **[protect + from + sick[1,2]]** With the wrists of both *S hands* crossed in front of the chest, palms facing in opposite directions, move the hands forward with a short double movement. Then, beginning with the index fingers of both *X hands* touching, left hand forward of right hand, pull the right hand back toward the chest. Then touch the bent middle finger of the right *5 hand* to the forehead and the bent middle finger of the left *5 hand* to the chest, both palms facing in.

immune[2] *adj.* See sign for RESIST.

impact *n.* See sign for HIT[1].

impair[1] *v.* To make worse; damage: *The smog impaired his vision.* Related form: **impaired** *adj.*

■ [Initialized sign similar to sign for **annoy**[1]] Strike the little-finger side of the right *I hand,* palm facing left, with a double movement against the index-finger side of the left *B hand,* palm facing down and fingers pointing right.

impair[2] *v.* See sign for PREVENT.

impassive *adj.* See sign for APATHY.

impeach *v.* See signs for FEEDBACK[2], REJECT[2].

imperfect *adj.* Characterized by defects; not perfect: *an imperfect character.*

■ [**not** + **perfect**] Bring the extended thumb of the right *10 hand* from under the chin, palm facing left, forward with a deliberate movement. Then move the right *P hand,* palm facing down, in a small circle above the left *P hand,* palm facing up, before moving the right hand downward to touch both middle fingers together.

implement *v.* See sign for APPLY[1].

implore *v.* See signs for BEG[1,2].

imply *v.* See sign for SEEM.

import[1] *v.* To bring in from a foreign country for sale or use: *to import televisions from Japan.* Same sign used for: **sell to me, sell to us.**

■ [Directional sign **sell** formed toward oneself] Beginning with both *flattened O hands* somewhat forward of each side of the chest, palms facing down and fingers pointing forward, swing the hands back toward the chest, ending with the fingers pointing toward each side of the chest and palms facing back.

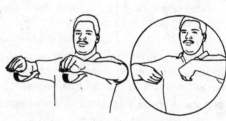

import[2] *v.* See sign for DOWNLOAD.

important[1] *adj.* Having value or significance: *an important document.* Same sign used for: **crucial, essential, key, main, significance, significant, value, worth.**

- Beginning with the fingertips of both *F hands* touching, palms facing down, bring the hands upward in a circular movement, ending with the index-finger sides of the *F hands* touching in front of the chest.

important[2] *adj.* (alternate sign) Same sign used for: **crucial, essential, key, main, significance, significant, value, worth.**

- Beginning with the little-finger sides of both *F hands* touching, palms facing up, bring the hands upward in a circular movement while turning the hands over, ending with the index-finger sides of the *F hands* touching in front of the chest.

impossible[1] *adj.* Not possible: *impossible to lift the desk.*

- Strike the palm side of the right *Y hand* against the upturned open left palm with a double movement.

impossible[2] *adj.* (alternate sign)

- [**not**[1] + **possible**] Bring the extended thumb of the right *10 hand,* palm facing left, from under the chin forward with a deliberate movement. Then move both *S hands,* palms angled forward, downward simultaneously in front of each side of the body with a double movement by bending the wrists.

impossible[3] *adj.* (alternate sign)

- [**can't** formed with a double movement] Bring the extended right index finger downward in front of the chest with a double movement, striking the extended left index finger, palm facing down and finger pointing right, each time.

impostor[1] *n.* A person who assumes a false identity or name: *We were horrified when the surgeon turned out to be an impostor.*

- [**false** + **name**[1]] Brush the extended right index finger, palm facing left, with a double movement across the tip of the nose from right to left by bending the wrist. Then tap the middle finger side of the right *H hand* across the index-finger side of the left *H hand*, palms angled in, with a double movement.

impostor[2] *n.* See sign for HYPOCRITE.

impoverished *adj.* See sign for POOR[1].

impress *v.* To have a strong effect on oneself: *The report impressed me with the facts.* Related form: **impression** *n.* Same sign used for: **emphasize, stress.**

■ [Directional sign toward oneself] With the thumb of the right *A hand* against the palm of the left *open hand*, palm facing right, bring both hands back toward the chest.

imprisoned *adj.* See signs for JAIL[1,2].

improve[1] *v.* To make or become better: *Try to improve your handwriting. The students' reading has improved.* Related form: **improvement** *n.* Same sign used for: **doing better.**

■ [Hands seems to measure out an amount of improvement] Touch the little-finger side of the right *open hand*, palm facing back, first to the wrist and then near the crook of the extended left arm.

improve[2] *v.* To increase the value of: *We improved our house by adding an extra room.* Related form: **improvement** *n.* Same sign used for: **remodel, renovate, upgrade.**

■ [**improve**[1] formed with a movement that indicates continued improvements] Brush the little-finger side of the right *open hand*, palm facing in and fingers pointing left, upward with a circular movement on the forearm of the bent left arm.

impulse *n.* A sudden, involuntary driving force or inclination: *bought a new hat on impulse.*

■ [Shows spontaneity] Beginning with both *S hands* near the chest, palms facing in, move the hands suddenly forward while extending the index fingers, palms facing down and index fingers pointing forward.

impure *adj.* Not pure; mixed with material of inferior quality: *impure air.* Related form: **impurity** *n.*

■ [**not**[1] + **pure**[1,2]] Bring the extended thumb of the right *10 hand* from under the chin, palm facing left, forward with a deliberate movement. Then move the middle finger of the right *P hand,* palm facing down, along the length of the upturned left *open hand.*

in *prep.* (Used to indicate inclusion within something, as a place or time): *keeps the jewelry in a box.* Related form: **inner** *adj.* Same sign used for: **internal.**

■ [Shows location in something] Insert the fingertips of the right *flattened O hand,* palm facing down, into the center of the thumb side of the left *O hand,* palm facing right in front of the chest.

inability *n.* Lack of ability: *inability to read music.*

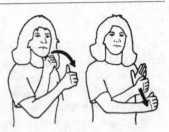

■ [**not**[1] + **skill**] Bring the extended thumb of the right *10 hand* from under the chin, palm facing left, forward with a deliberate movement. Then, while grasping the little-finger side of the left *open hand* with the curved right fingers, pull the right hand downward and forward while closing the fingers into as *A hand.*

in accord See sign for AGREE[1].

inaccurate *adj.* Not accurate; incorrect or untrue: *an inaccurate calculation.* Related form: **inaccuracy** *n.*

■ [**not**[1] + **precise**] Bring the extended thumb of the right *10 hand* from under the chin, palm facing left, forward with a deliberate movement. Then, with the palms of both *modified X hands* facing each other, right hand higher than the left hand, bring the hands together in front of the chest.

inadequate *adj.* See sign for DEFICIENCY.

in agreement See sign for AGREE[1].

inauguration *n.* See sign for OATH. Related form: **inaugural** *n.*

in behalf of See signs for SUPPORT[1,2].

incapable *adj.* Not capable; not having the necessary qualifications, strength, etc.: *incapable of doing the work.* Same sign used for: **unable.**

■ [**not**[1] + **able**[1]] Bring the extended thumb of the right *10 hand* from under the chin, palm facing left, forward with a deliberate movement. Then move both *S hands,* palms facing down, downward simultaneously in front of each side of the body with a double movement.

in case of See sign for SUPPOSE.

incense *n.* A substance giving off a sweet smell when burned: *to burn incense at the ceremony.*

■ [Mime swinging an incense burner] With the left *S hand,* palm facing back, held extended across the chest, swing the right *S hand* back and forth under the left arm with a repeated movement while twisting the right palm up and down each time.

inch *n.* A unit of measure equivalent to one-twelfth of a foot: *He let his hair grow about six inches long.*

■ Place the fingertips of the right *modified C hand,* palm facing left, against the extended thumb of the left *10 hand* held up in front of the chest, palm facing right.

in charge of See sign for MANAGE.

incident *n.* See signs for HAPPEN, SHOW UP.

incision *n.* A surgical cut into a tissue or an organ: *The surgeon made an incision across the stomach.* Same sign used for: **cut.**

■ [**cut** + **knife**] Slide the side of the extended right index finger, palm in, across the palm of the left *open hand.* Then with a double movement, slide the side of the extended right index finger, palm facing in, at an angle down the length of the extended left index finger, palm facing right, turning the right palm down each time as it moves off the end of the left index finger.

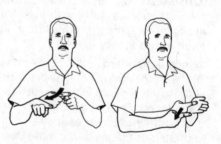

incline *v., n.* See sign for GRADE.

inclined to *v. phrase.* See sign for TEND.

include *v.* To contain as part of a whole: *The price of the hotel room includes tax.* Same sign used for: **contained in, everything, involve, vested, within.**

- ■ [The hand seems to encompass everything to gather it into one space] Swing the right *5 hand,* palm facing down, in a circular movement over the left *S hand,* palm facing in, while changing into a *flattened O hand,* ending with the fingertips of the right hand inserted in the center of the thumb side of the left hand.

income[1] *n.* Earnings that come from work, the sale of goods, investments, or other sources: *to have an annual income of $30,000.* Same sign used for: **revenue, salary, wages.**

- ■ [**money** + **earn**] Tap the back of the right *flattened O hand,* palm facing up, with a double movement against the left *open hand,* palm facing up. Then bring the little-finger side of the right *C hand,* palm facing left, with a double movement across the palm of the left *open hand,* closing the right hand into an *S hand* each time.

income[2] *n.* See sign for EARN.

incomplete *adj.* Not complete; lacking some portion of the whole: *The homework was incomplete.*

- ■ [**not**[1] + **finish**[1]] Bring the extended thumb of the right *10 hand* from under the chin, palm facing left, forward with a deliberate movement. Then, beginning with both *5 hands* in front of the chest, palms facing in and fingers pointing up, flip the hands over with a sudden movement, ending with both palms facing down and fingers pointing forward.

inconsistent *adj.* Not consistent; including elements not compatible with one another: *The quality of the work was inconsistent.* Related form: **inconsistency** *n.*

- ■ [**not**[1] + **standard**[1,2]] Bring the extended thumb of the right *10 hand* from under the chin, palm facing left, forward with a deliberate movement. Then, beginning with the thumbs of both *Y hands* near each other in front of the chest, palms facing down, move the hands in a flat circle in front of the body.

incorrect *adj.* See sign for WRONG.

increase[1] *v.* To make or become greater, as in size, number, or quality: *to increase your speed in running; sales that increase every year.* Same sign used for: **gain.**

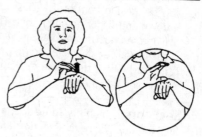

■ [Shows something increasing in volume] Beginning with the thumb of the right *flattened O hand* on the back of the left *curved hand,* palm facing down, open the right fingers to form a *flattened C hand.*

increase[2] *n.* **1.** An act or instance of growing greater: *an increase in spending.* —*v.* **2.** To make or become greater: *increase the amount of salt.* Same sign used for: **gain, increment, raise.**

■ [Shows more and more things adding to a pile to increase it] Beginning with the right *U hand,* palm facing up, slightly lower than the left *U hand,* palm facing down, flip the right hand over, ending with the right fingers across the left fingers.

increase[3] *v.* See sign for BUILD[2].

incredible[1] *adj.* Extraordinary; unbelievable: *This is an incredible performance.* Same sign used for: **amazed, stunned.**

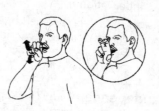

■ [Represents one's mouth dropping open when amazed] Beginning with the back of the right *S hand* against the open mouth, palm facing forward, deliberately open the hand into a *bent 3 hand.*

incredible[2] *adj.* (alternate sign)

■ [**hard**[1] + **believe**] Bring the right *bent V hand,* palm facing left, downward in front of the chest to rest on top of the left *bent V hand,* palm facing right. Then, with the right index finger near the right eye, bring the right hand downward, changing into a *curved hand* and clasping the left *curved hand* held in front of the body, ending with the palms facing each other.

incredible[3] *adj.* See signs for WONDERFUL[1,2].

increment *n.* See sign for INCREASE[2].

incurable *adj.* Of or designating an illness that cannot be cured: *an incurable disease.*

■ [**can't** + **well**[1]] Bring the extended right index finger downward striking the extended left index finger held in front of the chest, palm facing down and finger pointing right. Then, beginning with the fingertips of both *curved 5 hands* on each shoulder, palms facing in, bring the hands forward with a deliberate movement while changing into *S hands*.

indecision *n.* Inability to decide; an act or instance of being unable to make up one's mind: *The coach has no time for indecision on the playing field.* Same sign used for: **doubt, doubtful, juggle, uncertain, undecided.**

■ [Represents "sitting on the fence" when one is undecided] Beginning with the fingers of the right *V hand,* palm facing back and fingers pointing down, straddling the index-finger side of the left *B hand,* palm facing right and fingers pointing forward, rock the right hand back and forth with a double movement.

indent *v.* To position text a specific distance from the left or right edge of a page: *indent one inch from the edge of the paper.* Related form: **indentation** *n.*

■ [Shows the space left by an indentation] With a deliberate movement, move the right *B hand,* palm facing left, from in front of the left side of the chest to the right.

independent *adj.* Thinking or acting for oneself: *an independent person who doesn't rely on others.* Related form: **independence** *n.*

■ [Initialized sign similar to sign for **free**[1]] Beginning with the wrists of both *I hands* crossed in front of the chest, palms facing in, swing the arms apart, ending with the *I hands* in front of each shoulder, palms facing forward.

in-depth See sign for DEEP.

India[1] *n.* A country in south Asia: *looking at the traditional costumes of India.* Related form: **Indian** *n., adj.*

■ [Shows location of spot on Hindu woman's forehead] With the extended right 10 thumb pressed against the center of the forehead, palm facing left, twist the hand downward.

India[2] *n.* (alternate sign) Related form: **Indian** *n., adj.*

- [Shows location of spot on Hindu woman's forehead] Flick the extended right 10 thumb upward and forward on the middle of the forehead with a double movement.

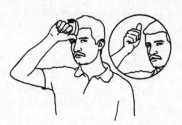

Indian *n.* **1.** An American Indian; native American: *Many Indians still live in the Southwest.* —*adj.* **2.** Belonging to or characteristic of American Indians: *Indian languages.* Same sign used for: **American Indian, Native American.**

- Move the fingertips of the right *F hand,* palm facing in, from touching the right side of the mouth upward to touch near the right temple.

Indiana *n.* One of the central states in the United States: *to live in Indiana.*

- [Initialized sign] Move the right *I hand,* palm facing forward, from in front of the right shoulder outward to the right and then downward to in front of the waist.

indicate *v.* See signs for IMAGE[3], SHOW[1]. Related forms: **indicator** *n.,* **indication** *n.*

indifferent *adj.* See signs for DON'T CARE[1,2].

individual *n.* **1.** A single person, as distinguished from a group: *Each individual in the class is responsible for doing all the assignments.* —*adj.* **2.** Intended for a single person: *individual attention.*

- [Initialized sign similar to sign for **person**] Bring both *I hands,* palms facing each other, from the chest down along the sides of the body.

individuals *pl. n.* Several persons, each considered separately: *All individuals must sign up one at a time.*

- [Initialized sign repeated to indicate more than one person] Bring both *I hands,* palms facing each other, downward first in front of the right side of the body and then again in front of the left side of the body.

indoctrinate *v.* See sign for TEACH. Related form: **indoctrination** *n.*

indolence *n.* A tendency to avoid work; laziness: *the indolence of the staff has led to reduced productivity.*

■ [**lazy** + **apathy**] Tap the palm side of the right *L hand* against the left side of the chest. Then limply hang both *open hands* in front of each side of the body, palms facing down and fingers dangling down.

Indonesia *n.* A country in the Far East, in the Malay Archipelago: *vacationed in the islands of Indonesia.*

■ Beginning with the right *H hand* in front of the body, palm facing in and fingers pointing left, bring the hand with a wavy in-and-out movement to the right.

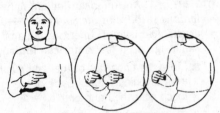

indoor[1] *adj.* Located, used, or done inside a building: *to have an indoor picnic.* Related form: **indoors** *adv.*

■ [**inside** + **house**] Insert the fingertips of the right *flattened O hand,* palm facing down, with a double movement into the opening formed by the left *O hand,* palm facing right in front of the chest. Then, beginning with the fingertips of both *open hands* touching near the face, palms angled toward each other, bring the hands at a downward angle outward to in front of each shoulder and then straight down, ending with the fingers pointing up and the palms facing each other.

indoor[2] *adj.* See sign for INSIDE. Related form: **indoors** *adv.*

induce *v.* To influence; move to action by persuasion: *induced me to come along to the party.*

■ [Similar to sign for **hypnotize** moving toward oneself] Beginning with both *curved 5 hands* in front of the face, palms facing each other, wiggle the fingers while moving the hands in toward the eyes, closing into *S hands.*

industrial *adj.* **1.** Of or pertaining to manufacturing, business, or trade: *a country's industrial progress.* **2.** Engaged in industry: *industrial workers.* Related form: **industry** *n.*

■ [Initialized sign similar to sign for **busy** + **machine**] Slide the little-finger side of the right *I hand,* palm facing left, back and forth on the extended left index finger, palm facing down and finger pointing right. Then, with the fingers of both *curved 5 hands* loosely meshed together, palms facing in, move the hands up and down in front of the chest with a repeated movement.

industry *n.* See sign for MACHINE.

inexpensive *adj.* See sign for CHEAP.

inexperienced *adj.* See signs for CLUMSY[1], UNSKILLED.

inexpensive *adj.* Not expensive; costing relatively little: *an inexpensive wristwatch.*

■ [**not**[1] + **expensive**] Bring the extended thumb of the right *10 hand* from under the chin, palm facing left, forward with a deliberate movement. Then, beginning with the back of the right *flattened O hand* in the palm of the left *open hand*, both palms facing up, bring the right hand upward and then downward with a quick movement while opening into a *curved 5 hand,* ending with the palm facing down.

infant *n.* See sign for BABY[1].

in favor of See signs for AGREE[1], SUPPORT[1,2].

infection *n.* See sign for INSURANCE.

inferior *adj.* Below average, as in quality or grade: *a cheap car of inferior quality.*

■ [Initialized sign similar to sign for **base**[1]] Move the extended finger of the right *I hand,* palm angled forward, in a double circular movement under the left *open hand,* palm facing down.

infest *v.* To invade and overrun in large numbers: *The house was infested with roaches.*

■ [Similar to sign for **enter** except spreading when hand emerges] Move the back of the right *flattened O hand,* palm facing down, into the opening formed by the left *flattened C hand,* palm facing right. Then open both hands into *5 hands* as they move forward and outward to in front of each side of the chest.

infirmary[1] *n.* A hospital in a school or other institution: *sent by the Dean to rest in the infirmary.*

- ■ [Initialized sign similar to sign for **hospital**[1]] Move the extended fingertip of the right *I hand,* palm facing in, first down and then across on the upper left arm from back to front.

infirmary[2] *n.* See signs for HOSPITAL[1,2].

inflict *v.* See sign for HIT ME.

influence *v.* **1.** To have an effect on: *Nothing you say will influence my thinking.* —*n.* **2.** The power to affect others without force: *Their teacher has a lot of influence on the rest of the faculty.* **3.** Someone or something that exerts influence: *Her new friend is a good influence.* Same sign used for: **affect, effect.**

- ■ [Similar to sign for **advice** except spread outward to others] Beginning with the fingertips of the right *flattened O hand* on the back of the left *open hand,* palm facing down, move the right hand forward while opening into a *5 hand* and bringing the hand in a sweeping arc to in front of the right side of the body.

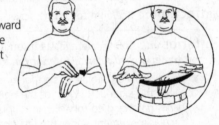

inform[1] *v.* To give knowledge or information to: *I had to inform you of the news myself.* Same sign used for: **issue, let know, notice, notify.**

- ■ [Indicates taking information from one's head and giving it to others] Beginning with the fingertips of the right *flattened O hand* near the forehead and the left *flattened O hand* in front of the chest, move both hands forward while opening into *5 hands,* palms facing up.

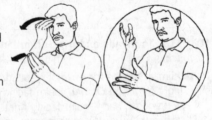

inform[2] *v.* (alternate sign, used when information is to be given to the speaker) Same sign used for: **let me know, notify me.**

- ■ [Directional sign **inform**[1] formed toward oneself] Beginning with the fingertips of the right *flattened O hand* near the forehead and the left *flattened O hand* in front of the chest, move both hands down and back to the chest while opening into *5 hands,* palms facing up.

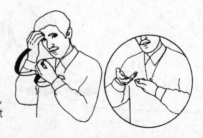

inform[3] *v.* (alternate sign, used to direct information toward a large group) Same sign used for: **make public.**

- [A broader form of **inform**[1]] Beginning with the fingertips of both *flattened O hands* touching the center of the forehead, palms facing in, bring the hands forward and outward in arcs while opening the fingers into *curved 5 hands,* ending with both *curved 5 hands* beside the head, palms facing each other.

information *n.* Same sign as for **inform**[1] but made with a double movement. Same sign used for: **data.**

information superhighway See sign for INTERNET.

infraction *n.* See signs for CRIME[1,2].

infrequent *adj.* See sign for HARDLY[1].

in front of Outside or facing the front part of; before: *in front of the house.* Same sign used for: **before, face to face, facing.**

- [Shows two things facing each other] Beginning with both *open hands* in front of the chest, palms facing each other and fingers pointing up, move both hands forward simultaneously.

infuse *v.* See signs for INTERFACE[1], MESH.

inhale[1] *v.* To breathe in: *to inhale fresh air.*

- [Represents air being brought in through the nose] Move the back of the right *5 hand,* palm facing down and fingers pointing forward, back toward the nose while closing into a *flattened O hand.*

inhale[2] *v.* See sign for BREATH.

inherit *v.* See sign for PASS DOWN.

initiate *v.* See sign for START[2].

inject *v.* To cause (liquid) to enter the body through a needle piercing the skin: *to inject insulin daily.* Same sign used for: **innoculate, shoot, vaccinate.**

- [Represents getting an injection in one's arm] Move the extended index finger of the right *L hand,* palm facing right, against the left upper arm.

injection

injection *n.* See sign for SHOT.

---

injure *v.* To cause harm to: *The car injured the dog.*

- [**pain**[2] + **suffer**[1]] Beginning with both extended index fingers pointing in opposite directions in front of the chest, palms facing in and the right hand slightly higher than the left, jab the fingers across the body. Then bring the right *A hand,* palm facing left, with a twisting movement down from the chin.

---

injury *n.* See signs for PAIN[1,2].

---

innocent *adj.* Being free from moral or legal wrong: *an innocent baby; proved innocent in a court of law.* Same sign used for: **naive.**

- Beginning with the fingers of both *U hands* touching the mouth, palms facing in, move the hands forward and outward to in front of each shoulder.

---

innoculate *v.* See sign for INJECT.

---

inoperable *adj.* Not treatable with surgery: *an inoperable tumor.*

- [**can't** + **operate**] Bring the extended index finger of the right *1 hand* downward, hitting the extended index finger of the left *1 hand* as it moves. Then move the thumb of the right *A hand,* palm facing down, across the upturned palm of the left *open hand* held in front of the chest.

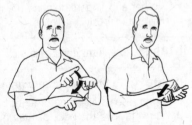

---

in order See signs for PLAN[2], PREPARE.

---

inquire *v.* See signs for TEST[1,2].

---

insane[1] *adj.* **1.** Mentally deranged; demented; crazy: *a hospital for insane people.* **2.** Of or characteristic of insane persons: *insane behavior.*

- [**think**[1] + a gesture indicating the brain not working straight] Touch the extended right index finger to the right side of the forehead, palm facing down. Then wave the fingers of the right *bent hand,* palm facing down, with a double movement in front of the forehead.

insane[2] *adj.* (alternate sign)

- [**think**[1] + **bend**[3]] Touch the extended right index finger to the right side of the forehead, palm facing down. Then, with the little-finger side of the right *open hand*, palm facing left, across the fingers of the left *open hand*, palm facing up, bend the right hand back toward the chest, ending with the palm facing in.

insect *n.* See sign for BUG[1].

insecure *adj.* Subject to self-doubt; not confident: *seems to be a nervous and insecure person.*

- [**not**[1] + **sure**[1] + **myself**[1,2]] Bring the thumb of the right *10 hand* from under the chin, palm facing left, forward with a deliberate movement. Then move the extended right index finger, palm facing left, straight forward from the mouth. Then move the thumb of the right *A hand* back against the chest with a double movement.

insert *v.* **1.** To put in: *insert the memory card in the camera.* —*n.* Something that is put in: *The bulletin insert gave details about the meeting.*

- [Action of inserting] Slide the little-finger side of the right *open hand*, palm facing up, between the right and middle fingers of the left *4 hand*, palm facing right.

inside *prep.* **1.** On the inner side of; in or within: *inside the box.* —*adv.* **2.** In or into the inner part: *Come inside.* —*n.* **3.** The inner surface; the interior: *the inside of the room.* —*adj.* **4.** Being on the inside: *an inside seat.* Same sign used for: **indoors, internal, stuffing.**

- [Shows location inside] Insert the fingertips of the right *flattened O hand*, palm facing down, into the center of the thumb side of the left *O hand*, palm facing right in front of the chest, with a repeated movement.

insignificant *adj.* See sign for NOTHING[4].

insist *v.* See sign for DEMAND[2].

insomnia[1] *n.* Inability to fall or stay asleep: *Too much coffee gives me insomnia.* Same sign used for: **alert, awake.**

- [Represents the eyes being wide open when one can't sleep] Place both *C hands* around the wide-open eyes with the thumbs near each side of the nose, palms facing forward.

insomnia[2] *n.* (alternate sign)

- **[can't + sleep**[1,2]**]** Bring the extended index finger of the right *1 hand* downward, hitting the extended index finger of the left *1 hand* as it moves. Then, beginning with the fingers of the right *curved 5 hand* pointing toward the face, move the hand forward and down while changing to a *flattened O hand*.

inspect *v.* See signs for CHECK[1], INVESTIGATE. Related form: **inspection** *n.*

inspire *v.* To fill with feeling: *inspired with hope.* Related form: **inspiration** *n.* Same sign used for: **pep, revive.**

- [Represents inspiration moving up in one's body] Beginning with both *flattened O hands* in front of each side of the chest, palms facing in and fingers pointing up, move the hands upward while opening into *5 hands* in front of each shoulder.

install *v.* See signs for APPLY[1], PUT.

installment *n.* One of a series of payments required by a contract: *pay an installment on a loan.* Same sign used for: **payment.**

- [Shows small increments] With repeated short movements, move the little-finger side of the right *open hand*, palm facing left, across the palm of the upturned left *open hand*.

instant[1] *n.* A short moment of time: *He stopped for an instant, then went on.*

- **[abrupt**[2] **+ minute]** Beginning with the thumb of the right *A hand* tucked under the index finger, palm facing left, flick the thumb out while lowering the hand beside the palm of the left *open hand* held in front of the chest, palm facing right and fingers pointing forward. Then move the extended right index finger, palm facing left, forward a short distance by pivoting the closed fingers of the right hand on the palm of the left *open hand*, palm facing right and fingers pointing forward.

instant[2] *adj.* See signs for FAST[1,2,3].

instead *adv.* As a substitute: *tea instead of coffee.* Same sign used for: **instead.**

- [Represents substituting one thing for another] Move the fingertips of the right *F hand* forward in a circle around the fingertips of the left *F hand*, ending with the fingertips touching, palms facing each other.

institute[1] *n.* An organization established for a specific purpose: *decided to go to an art institute after college.*

- [Initialized sign similar to sign for **establish**] Beginning with the right *I hand* in front of the right side of the body, palm facing in, and the left *open hand* held across the chest, palm facing down and fingers pointing right, bring the right hand back toward the chest in a large upward arc and then down, ending with the little-finger side of the right *I hand* on the back of the left hand.

institute[2] *n.* (alternate sign) Alternate form: **institution.** Same sign used for: **residential school.**

- [Initialized sign] Tap the little-finger side of the right *I hand,* palm facing left, on the index finger side of the left *I hand,* palm facing right, with a double movement.

instruct[1] *v.* To give knowledge to, especially in a systematic way; teach; train: *to instruct the class in grammar.* Related form: **instruction** *n.*

- [Initialized sign similar to sign for **teach**] Move both *I hands* forward a short distance with a double movement from in front of each side of the chest, palms facing each other.

instruct[2] *v.* See signs for DESCRIBE[1], TEACH. Related form: **instruction** *n.*

instructor[1] *n.* A person who teaches: *Listen to the instructor.*

- [**instruct**[1] + **person marker**] Move both *I hands* forward a short distance with a double movement from in front of each side of the chest, palms facing each other. Then move both *open hands,* palms facing each other, down along the sides of the body.

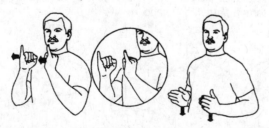

instructor[2] *n.* See sign for TEACHER.

insufficient *adj.* See sign for DEFICIENCY.

insult[1] *v.* **1.** To say something harsh, rude, or insolent to: *She insulted me.* —*n.* **2.** A harsh, rude, or insolent statement or deed: *Not inviting me is an insult.* Related form: **insulting** *adj.* Same sign used for: **affront, put down.**

- [Finger seems to direct an insult at another] Move the extended right index finger from in front of the right side of the body, palm facing left and finger pointing forward, forward and upward sharply in an arc.

insult[2] *v., n.* (alternate sign) Related form: **insulting** *adj.* Same sign used for: **affront.**

- [Finger seems to direct an insult at another] With a deliberate movement, insert the extended right index finger, palm facing left and finger pointing forward, between the index finger and middle finger of the left *5 hand* held in front of the chest, palm facing in and fingers pointing up.

insurance *n.* **1.** Coverage by contract with a business offering monetary reimbursement as protection from loss in return for payment of a premium: *It is considered important to have life insurance.* **2.** The premium paid for this coverage: *The insurance is $20 a month.* Related form: **insure** *v.* Same sign used for: **infection.**

- [Initialized sign] Move the right *I hand,* palm facing forward, from side to side with a repeated movement near the right shoulder.

intake *n.* An act, instance, or process of taking in: *to complete the intake of patients at the hospital admittance office.*

- [inside + write[1,2] + copy[1]] Insert the fingertips of the right *flattened O hand,* palm facing down, into the center of the thumb side of the left *O hand,* palm facing right, in front of the chest, with a double movement. Then slide the palm side of the right *modified X hand* across the palm of the left *open hand* with a double movement. Then move the right *5 hand* from in front of the right side of the chest, palm facing forward, down to touch the palm of the left *open hand* while closing the right fingers and thumb to form a *flattened O hand.*

integrate *v.* See signs for MAINSTREAM[2], MESH.

intelligent[1] *adj.* Having an ability to learn quickly and understand comprehensively: *an intelligent child with a lot of promise.* Same sign used for: **brilliant, genius.**

- Beginning with the index-finger side of the right *G hand* near the right side of the forehead, palm facing left, bring the hand forward while closing the thumb and index finger together.

intelligent[2] *adj.* See signs for SMART[1,2,3]. Related form: **intelligence** *n.*

intend[1] *v.* To have in mind to do or bring about: *We intend to have a party if it doesn't rain.* Related form: **intention** *n.* Same sign used for: **purpose.**

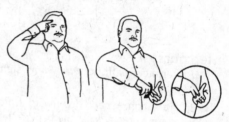

- [**think**[1] + **mean**[2]] Touch the extended right index finger to the right side of the forehead, palm facing down. Then touch the fingertips of the right *V hand,* palm facing down, to the palm of the left *open hand,* palm facing right and fingers pointing up, and then twist the right wrist to touch the fingertips down again.

intend[2] *v.* (alternate sign) Same sign used for: **mean, meaning, purpose, stand for.** Related form: **intention** *n.*

- [The fingers change positions to signify a change in intent] Touch the fingertips of the right *V hand,* palm facing down, in the palm of the left *open hand,* palm facing up and fingers pointing forward. Then twist the right wrist and touch the fingertips down again.

intensity *n.* **1.** The condition of being strong, as in force or strength: *The intensity of his voice frightened me.* **2.** The degree to which something has such force or strength: *the intensity of light.*

- [Initialized sign similar to sign for **power**[2]] Beginning with the thumb side of the right *I hand* near the left shoulder, palm facing down, turn the hand over in an arc, ending with the little-finger side of the right *I hand* in the crook of the extended left arm.

interact *v.* See sign for ASSOCIATE. Related form: **interactive** *adj.*

intercept[1] *v.* To seize en route: *tried to intercept the package before it got mailed.* Same sign used for: **cut off.**

- [The hand moves forward to stop or intercept the other hand] Move the right *V hand,* palm facing left, forward while closing the index and middle fingers together near the end of the extended left index finger held in front of the chest, palm facing down and finger pointing right.

intercept² *v.* See sign for SOLICIT.

intercom *n.* A device, with speakers and receivers at two or more points, for communication within a building: *Call me on the intercom.*

■ [**inside + communication**] Insert the fingertips of the right *flattened O hand*, palm facing down, into the center of the thumb side of the left *O hand*, palm facing right in front of the chest, with a double movement. Then move both *C hands*, palms facing each other, forward and back from the chin with an alternating movement.

intercourse *n.* Sexual relations: *The man had intercourse with his wife.* Same sign used for: **sex.**

■ Bring the right *V hand* downward in front of the chest to tap against the heel of the left *V hand* with a double movement, palms facing each other.

interest¹ *n.* A feeling of concern, involvement, and curiosity: *to have an interest in stamp collecting.* Related form: **interested** *adj.* Same sign used for: **fascinating.**

■ Beginning with the right *modified C hand* in front of the face and the left *modified C hand* in front of the chest, both palms facing in, move the hands forward simultaneously while closing into *A hands*.

interest² *n.* (alternate sign) Related forms: **interested** *adj.*, **interesting** *adj.* Same sign used for: **fascinating.**

■ Beginning with the bent thumb and middle fingers of both *5 hands* in front of the chest, palms facing in and right hand above the left hand, move the hands forward simultaneously while pinching the thumbs and middle fingers together into *8 hands*.

interest³ *n.* Money paid or charged for the use of money or for borrowing money: *The bank will earn interest on the loan.*

■ [Initialized sign] Rub the little-finger side of the right *I hand*, palm facing the chest, in a repeated circle on the back of the left *open hand*, palm facing down.

interface[1] *n.* **1.** The connection between a computer and another entity: *an interface between the printer and the computer.* **2.** Software and hardware designed to allow communication between a computer and a user: *an easy, intuitive user interface.* Same sign used for: **infuse, merge.**

- [The hands represent things interfacing with each other] Beginning with both *5 hands* in front of each side of the chest, palms facing in and fingers pointing toward each other, push the hands toward each other, causing the fingers to mesh together.

interface[2] *v.* See sign for FACE[3].

interfere *v.* See signs for ANNOY[1,2], MEDDLE.

intermediate *adj.* Occurring or situated between two points, things, persons, etc.: *the intermediate level in school.*

- [Shows a location in the middle] Slide the little-finger side of the right *open hand,* palm facing up, with a double movement between the middle and ring fingers of the left *5 hand,* palm facing right.

intermission *n.* **1.** A short interval between acts of a play or other performance: *saw friends in the lobby during the intermission.* **2.** A pause between periods of activity: *took a short intermission between tasks around the house.* See also sign for HALFTIME. Same sign used for: **break.**

- [Shows something being inserted halfway through something] Slide the index-finger side of the right *open hand,* palm facing down, between the index and middle fingers of the left *5 hand,* palm facing in.

internal[1] *adj.* Within the body: *internal organs.*

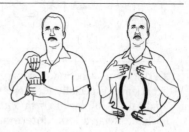

- [**inside** + **body**] With a short double movement, move the fingers of the right *flattened O hand* downward into the thumb side of the left *O hand* held in front of the chest. Then pat the palm side of both *open hands,* first on each side of the chest and then on each side of the abdomen.

internal[2] *adj.* See signs for IN, INSIDE.

international *adj.* Among nations; involving two or more nations: *Trade talks are an international affair.*

■ [Initialized sign similar to sign for **world**] Move both *I hands* in circles around each other, palms facing each other, ending with the little-finger side of the right hand on the index-finger side of the left hand in front of the chest.

Internet *n.* An electronic network that connects computers all over the world, allowing them to communicate with each other and to send, receive, and store information. Same sign used for: **information superhighway, the Net.**

■ [**connect** repeated to show network connections] Beginning with the bent middle fingers of both *5 hands* pointing toward each other in front of the chest, twist both wrists to change positions.

Internet security Techniques or programs utilized to ensure that data stored in a computer cannot be read or compromised: *The system of Internet security prevented spam from infecting the computer.*

■ [**Internet** + **defend**[1]] Beginning with the bent middle fingers of both *5 hands* pointing toward each other in front of the chest, twist both wrists to change positions. Then, with the wrists of both *S hands* crossed in front of the chest, palms facing in opposite directions, move the hands forward a short distance.

internship *n.* A period of supervised experience, especially for a recent graduate of medical school: *an internship at the local hospital.* Related form: **intern** *n.*

■ [Initialized sign similar to sign for **practice**] Slide the little-finger side of the right *I hand*, palm facing left, back and forth with a double movement on the back of the left *open hand*, palm facing down and fingers pointing right.

interpret *v.* **1.** To explain or provide the meaning of: *to interpret the story for the class.* **2.** To translate, as from one language into another: *She interprets from Russian to French and English at the United Nations.* Same sign used for: **gloss.**

- [Uses the same movement as **change**[1]] With the fingertips of both *F hands* touching in front of the chest, palms facing each other, twist the hands in opposite directions to reverse positions.

interpreter *n.* A person whose business is translation, as between English and American Sign Language: *easy to follow what the interpreter is doing.*

- [**interpret** + **person marker**] With the fingertips of both *F hands* touching in front of the chest, palms facing each other, twist the hands in opposite directions to reverse positions. Then move both *open hands,* palms facing each other, down along the sides of the body.

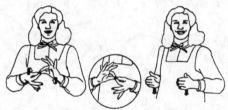

interrupt *v.* See signs for ANNOY[1,2], MEDDLE[1].

intersection[1] *n.* A place where one thing, especially a road, crosses another: *the famous intersection of Broadway and Forty-second Street.* Same sign used for: **crossing.**

- [Represents two roads crossing each other] Bring the side of the extended right index finger, palm facing left, with a double movement across the extended left index finger, palm facing down.

intersection[2] *n.* (alternate sign) Same sign used for: **crossing.**

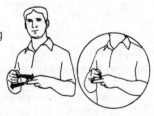

- [Seems to be the point where traffic crosses] Beginning with both *H hands* in front of each side of the chest, palms angled toward each other, move the hands at an angle forward, ending with the middle-finger side of the right hand crossed over the index-finger side of the left hand.

intervene *v.* See sign for ANNOY.

interview *v.* **1.** To meet and talk with, as to obtain information: *to interview a movie star for a magazine article.* —*n.* **2.** A formal meeting to evaluate someone's qualifications: *to have a job interview.*

■ [Initialized sign similar to sign for **communication**] Move both *I hands*, palms facing each other, forward and back toward the mouth with an alternating movement.

---

in the near future See signs for SOON[1,2].

---

intimidate *v.* To influence by fear: *The video camera intimidated the speaker.* Related form: **intimidation** *n.*

■ [**feel** + a gesture that shows someone being pushed over] Brush the bent middle finger of the right *5 hand* upward on the chest with a double movement. Then bring the right *open hand* in toward the chest, pushing the extended left index finger held up in front of the chest, palm facing right.

---

into *prep.* See sign for ENTER.

---

in touch with See signs for CONTACT[1,2].

---

intoxicated *adj.* See sign for DRUNK.

---

introduce *v.* To present (one or more persons) to another or to each other so as to make acquainted: *Introduce yourself to the committee.* Related form: **introduction** *n.* Same sign used for: **present.**

■ [The hands seem to bring two people together] Bring both *bent hands* from in front of each side of the body, palms facing up and fingers pointing toward each other, toward each other in front of the waist.

---

intrude *v.* To enter without permission: *to intrude on the private meeting.*

■ [**enter** + **conceited**] Move the back of the right *open hand*, palm facing down, in a downward movement under the palm of the left *open hand*, palm facing down. Then, beginning with both *modified C hands* in front of each side of the forehead, index fingers pointing toward each other and palms facing in, bring the hands outward, away from each other a short distance.

invade *v.* To enter with force: *The soldiers invaded the small country.*

■ [**enter** + **capture**[1]] Move the back of the right *open hand*, palm facing down, in a downward movement under the palm of the left *open hand*, palm facing down. Then, beginning with both *5 hands* in front of each side of the chest, palms facing down and fingers pointing forward, move the hands quickly downward while closing into *S hands*.

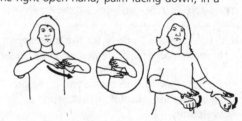

invent *v.* **1.** To create (something new) as a result of one's own planning and ingenuity: *to invent a gadget that will peel apples.* **2.** To make up out of one's imagination: *to invent a song.* **3.** To devise for one's own purposes: *to invent an excuse.* Same sign used for: **create, make up, originate.**

■ [The hand seems to take ideas from the head] Move the index-finger side of the right *4 hand*, palm facing left, upward from the forehead in a forward arc.

invest[1] *v.* To use money to buy something that is expected to return a profit: *invest in stocks.* Related form: **investment** *n.* Same sign used for: **deposit, stocks.**

■ [Represents depositing money in a bank] Insert the fingertips of the right *flattened O hand*, palm facing left, into the center of the thumb side of the left *O hand*, palm angled forward.

invest[2] *v.* (alternate sign) Same sign used for: **save, savings, stocks.**

■ [Represents placing stacks of money forward] Move the curved middle index fingers and thumbs of both hands from in front of each side of the chest, palms facing forward, upward and forward in deliberate arcs.

investigate[1] *v.* To examine the details (of), especially to find a cause or motive: *We'll investigate to find out what went wrong with your travel plans. The police investigated the murder.* Related form: **investigation** *n.* Same sign used for: **examination, examine, inspect, inspection.**

■ [The finger seems to be paging through pages of documents] Brush the extended right index finger with a repeated movement from the heel to the fingertips of the upturned palm of the left *open hand*.

investigate[2] *v.* See sign for ANALYZE.

invisible *adj.* See sign for WORTHLESS.

invite[1] *v.* To ask politely for the presence or participation of, as at a gathering of friends or a meeting: *I am inviting you to my party.* Related form: **invitation** *n.* Same sign used for: **employ, greet, hire, welcome.**

- ■ [The hand brings another to oneself] Bring the upturned right *curved hand* from in front of the right side of the body in toward the center of the waist.

invite[2] *v.* (alternate sign, used when an invitation, welcome, etc., is issued to the speaker) Same sign used for: **employ me, greet me, hire me, welcome me.**

- ■ [Directional sign toward another] Bring the upturned right *curved hand* from in front of the center of the waist outward in an arc.

involuntary *adj.* Not voluntary; occurring without one's consent or intention: *He has an involuntary twitch in his eye.*

- ■ [**not**[1] + **apply**[2]] Bring the extended thumb of the right *10 hand* from under the chin, palm facing left, forward with a deliberate movement. Then pinch a small amount of clothing on the right side of the chest with the fingers of the right *F hand* and pull forward with a short double movement.

involve *v.* See sign for INCLUDE.

iPod *Trademark.* See sign for DIGITAL AUDIO PLAYER (DAP).

Iran *n.* An Islamic republic in southwest Asia: *The capital of Iran is Teheran.* Related form: **Iranian** *adj., n.*

- ■ [Similar to sign for **gas** indicating Iran's primary natural resource] Touch the extended thumb of the right *10 hand,* palm facing forward, to the upturned palm of the left *open hand.*

Ireland *n.* One of the British Isles, comprising Northern Ireland and the Republic of Ireland: *the green fields of Ireland.* Related form: **Irish** *adj., n.*

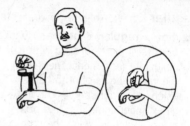

■ [Similar to sign for **potato** because Ireland is known for its potatoes] Move the right *bent V hand,* palm facing down, in a circle and then straight down, ending with the fingertips of the *bent V hand* on the back of the left *curved hand* held in front of the body, palm facing down.

iron[1] *n.* **1.** A silver-colored metal valued for its strength and commonly used for making tools, machinery, etc.: *The hammer was made of iron.* —*adj.* **2.** Made of iron: *an iron fence.*

■ [Initialized sign] Slide the base of the extended little finger of the right *I hand,* palm facing left, with a double movement across the extended left index finger, palm facing down and finger pointing right in front of the chest.

iron[2] *n.* **1.** An appliance with a flat, smooth surface that can be heated for pressing and smoothing cloth: *The steam iron will get the wrinkles out of this jacket.* —*v.* **2.** To smooth or press cloth with an iron: *to iron the cotton shirts.*

■ [Mime using an iron] Rub the knuckle side of the right *S hand,* palm facing in, back and forth along the length of the upturned left *open hand* with a repeated movement.

irony[1] *n.* **1.** The sarcastic use of words to communicate a meaning that is the opposite of what is actually said: *The irony of his words is apparent from his sarcastic tone.* **2.** A situation in which an otherwise favorable outcome cannot be enjoyed or appreciated: *The irony is that she won an award after her show was canceled.* Related form: **ironic** *adj.* Same sign used for: **sarcastic.**

■ With the little finger and index finger of the right hand extended, palm facing left near the nose, and the little finger and index finger of the left hand extended in front of the chest, palm facing down, move the right hand forward and the left hand back until the hands are facing each other in front of the chest. Then push the hands past each other, ending with the wrists crossed in front of the chest.

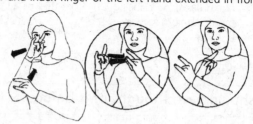

irony[2] *n.* (alternate sign)

■ With the index fingers and middle fingers of both hands extended, bring the right hand downward from the nose, passing the left hand in front of the chest, ending with the right hand in front of the body, palm facing down.

irregular *adj.* Not regular; erratic: *He has irregular attendance.*

■ [**not**[1] + **regular**] Bring the extended thumb of the right *10 hand* from under the chin, palm facing left, forward with a deliberate movement. Then, with the index fingers of both hands extended at right angles, right index finger angled up and both palms angled in, bring the little-finger side of the right hand sharply down across the thumb side of the left hand with a double movement.

irresponsible *adj.* See signs for NOT RESPONSIBLE[1,2].

irrigation *n.* The act or process of supplying water artificially to otherwise dry land: *The crops will grow with proper irrigation.* Related form: **irrigate** *v.*

■ [**water** + **spread**[1]] Tap the index-finger side of the right *W hand,* palm facing left, against the chin with a double movement. Then, beginning with the thumbs of both *flattened O hands* together in front of the chest, palms facing down and fingers pointing forward, move the hands forward and apart from each other while opening into *5 hands.*

irritate *v.* See signs for ANNOY[1,2], ITCH.

is[1] *v.* The third-person singular form of the verb *to be: He is here.*

■ [Initialized sign similar to sign for **be**[2]] Move the extended little finger of the right *I hand,* palm facing left, from the mouth straight forward a short distance.

is[2] *v.* See sign for BE[2].

I should have thought of it before See sign for DISGUSTED[2].

island[1] *n.* A relatively small body of land surrounded by water: *We plan to take a trip to an island in the Bahamas.*

■ [Initialized sign] Rub the side of the extended little finger of the right *I hand,* palm facing left, with a double movement in a circle on the back of the left *S hand,* palm facing down.

island[2] *n.* (alternate sign)

- [Initialized sign similar to sign for **area**[2]] Beginning with the extended little fingers of both *I hands* touching in front of the body, palms facing in, bring the hands away from each other in arcs until they touch again in front of the chest.

isolated *adj.* See signs for ALONE[1,2], HERMIT[1].

Israel *n.* A country in southwest Asia: *The modern state of Israel was formed in 1948.* Related form: **Israeli** *n., adj.*

- [Initialized sign showing the location of a traditional Jewish beard] Bring the extended little finger of the right *I hand,* palm facing in, downward first on the left side of the chin and then on the right side of the chin.

Israelite *n.* See sign for JEW.

issue *v.* See signs for INFORM[1], NEWSPAPER.

it[1] *pron.* (Used to represent an inanimate thing spoken about or present): *If you don't have the report, you'll have to find it.*

- [Initialized sign] Touch the extended little finger of the right *I hand,* palm facing in, into the center of the open left palm.

it[2] *pron.* See sign for HE[1].

Italy[1] *n.* A country in southern Europe: *We ate wonderful pasta dishes in Italy.* Related form: **Italian** *n., adj.* Same sign used for: **Pepsi.**

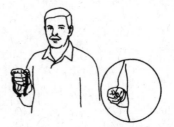

- [Shows the shape of the Italian peninsula] Beginning with the right *modified C hand,* palm facing forward, in front of the right side of the body, move the hand downward while pinching the thumb and index finger together.

Italy[2] *n.* (alternate sign) Related form: **Italian** *adj., n.*

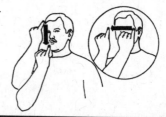

- [Initialized sign similar to sign for **Catholic**] Bring the extended little finger of the right *I hand,* palm facing in, first from the forehead downward in front of the face and then from left to right across the forehead.

itch *n.* **1.** A prickly, irritated feeling making one want to scratch the affected part: *If you have an itch, you can use this ointment.* —*v.* **2.** To manifest such a feeling: *My mosquito bites itch terribly.* Related form: **itchy** *adj.* Same sign used for: **irritate.**

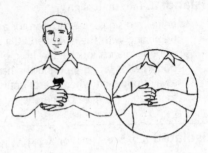

■ [Mime scratching an itchy place] Move the fingertips of the right *curved 5 hand,* palm facing in, back and forth with a double movement on the back of the left *open hand,* palm facing in and fingers pointing right.

its *pron.* See sign for HIS[1].

itself *pron.* A reflexive form of *it,* used to refer back to the object last mentioned: *The door closed by itself.* See also sign for HIMSELF. Same sign used for: **herself.**

■ Bring the knuckles of the right *10 hand,* palm facing left, firmly against the side of the extended left index finger, palm facing right and finger pointing up in front of the chest.

jab *v.* **1.** To poke: *jabbed him with her elbow.* —*n.* **2.** A thrust with something pointed: *feel a jab in my side.*

- [Mime jabbing someone in the ribs] Poke the extended right index finger, palm facing back, against the right side with a double movement.

jabber *v.* To talk very fast in a senseless way: *They jabbered away about nothing for hours.* Same sign used for: **chatter.**

- [**talk**² formed with a fast repeated movement] Beginning with the right *5 hand* in front of the mouth, palm facing left and fingers pointing up, and the left *5 hand* near the little finger of the right hand, palm facing right and fingers pointing up, wiggle the fingers repeatedly.

jacket¹ *n.* A short coat: *bought a new winter jacket.*

- [Initialized sign similar to sign for **coat**] Move the extended little fingers of both *J hands,* palms facing in, from near each shoulder in an arc downward toward each other, ending near each other at the waist.

jacket² *n.* See sign for COAT.

jack-o'-lantern¹ *n.* A hollow pumpkin with openings in the shell carved to look like a face: *to put a candle in a jack-o'-lantern on Halloween.*

- [Abbreviation **j-o-l**] On the back of the left *S hand,* palm facing down, first brush the little-finger side of the right *J hand* as it moves in an upward arc, then form an *O* followed by an *L* with the right hand.

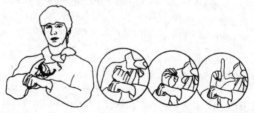

jack-o'-lantern² *n.* (alternate sign)

- [Represents showing a jack-o-lantern's face] With the index-finger side of both *open hands* near each side of the face, the thumbs of both *open hands* near each side of the chin, palms facing forward, bend the head sideways toward each shoulder.

jagged *adj.* See sign for RAGGED.

jail[1] *n.* A place for holding accused persons awaiting trial or sentenced prisoners; prison: *sentenced to jail for a minor crime.* Same sign used for: **imprisoned, penitentiary, prison.**

■ [Represents jail bars] Bring the back of the fingers of the right *V hand* from near the chest forward to meet at an angle across the fingers of the left *V hand,* both palms facing in.

jail[2] *n.* (alternate sign) Same sign used for: **imprisoned, penitentiary, prison.**

■ [Represents jail bars] Bring the back of the right *4 hand* from near the chest forward with a double movement while bringing the left *4 hand* in to meet the right hand, ending with the fingers crossed at an angle, both palms facing in.

jam[1] *v.* **1.** To squeeze into a small space: *jammed many people into the bus.* —*n.* **2.** A mass of objects, especially vehicles, crowded together in a way that hinders movement: *caught in a traffic jam.* Same sign used for: **crowded.**

■ [**crowded**[2] + **stuck**] Beginning with both *curved 5 hands* in front of each shoulder, palms facing each other, bring the hands together while bending the fingers and meshing them with each other in front of the chest. Then push the fingers of the right *V hand* against the neck, palm facing down.

jam[2] *v., n.* (alternate sign) Same sign used for: **crowded.**

■ [Represents things merging into a narrow area] Move both *5 hands,* palms facing down, from in front of each shoulder forward toward each other, ending with the right hand slightly above the left hand in front of the body.

jam[3] *n.* See sign for JELLY.

janitor[1] *n.* A person hired to clean and maintain public areas in a building, as a school or apartment house: *The janitor will turn the furnace on.* Same sign used for: **custodian.**

■ [**sweep**[1] + **person marker**] Brush the little-finger side of the right *open hand,* palm facing in, with a small, repeated upward movement on the open left palm. Then bring both *open hands,* palms facing each other, downward along the sides of the body.

janitor[2] *n.* (alternate sign) Same sign used for: **custodian.**

■ **[clean + mop + person marker]**
Slide the palm of the right *open hand* from the heel to the fingers of the palm of the left *open hand,* with a double movement. Then, with the right *modified X hand* forward of the left *modified X hand* in front of the body, push the

hands forward and back with a double movement. Then bring both *open hands,* palms facing each other, downward along the sides of the body.

Japan[1] *n.* A country in the west Pacific, off the East coast of Asia: *The monitor for your computer was made in Japan.* Related form: **Japanese** *n., adj.*

■ Beginning with the extended fingers of both *G hands* pointing toward each other in front of the body, palms facing in, pull the hands apart to in front of each side of the body while pinching the fingers of the *G hands* closed.

Japan[2] *n.* (alternate sign, sometimes considered offensive) Related form: **Japanese** *n., adj.*

■ [Initialized sign showing the shape of a Japanese person's eyes] Beginning with the extended little finger of the right *J hand* touching the outside corner of the right eye, twist the hand upward with a double movement.

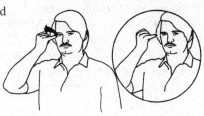

Japan[3] *n.* (alternate sign) Related form: **Japanese** *n., adj.*

■ Beginning with both *D hands* near each other in front of the chest, palms angled down, bring the extended index fingers toward each other.

jar[1] *n.* A deep cylindrical container made of glass and having a broad mouth: *to open a jar of jelly.*

■ **[bottle**[1] **+ can**[1]**]** Beginning with the little-finger side of the right *C hand,* palm facing left, on the upturned left *open hand,* raise the right hand. Then, with the right *curved 5 hand,* palm facing down, over the thumb side of the left *S hand,* twist the right hand with a double movement.

jar[2] *n.* See sign for CUP.

jaunty *adj.* Easy, buoyant, and carefree: *walked with jaunty steps.*
- [**walk** with a light, bouncy movement] Beginning with the right *open hand* in front of the right shoulder and the left *open hand* near the center of the chest, both palms facing down and fingers pointing forward, move the hands to the left in repeated arcs.

jaw[1] *n.* The bony structure of the lower part of the face, supporting the mouth and teeth: *He has a square jaw.*
- [Location of jaws] Beginning with the fingertips of both *curved hands* on each side of the face, palms facing in, bring the hands downward toward the chin.

jaw[2] *n.* (alternate sign)
- [Location of jaws] Move the extended index fingers of both *1 hands* from the outside of each cheek downward toward the chin.

jaws *pl. n.* See sign for ALLIGATOR.

jaywalk *v.* To walk into the street without obeying traffic rules, especially by crossing against the traffic light or at a place other than a designated crosswalk: *You will have to pay a fine if you're caught jaywalking.* Related form: **jaywalking** *n.*
- [**wrong** + **across** + **walk**[1,2]] Bring the knuckles of the right *Y hand* back against the chin. Then push the little-finger side of the right *open hand,* palm facing left, across the back of the left *open hand,* palm facing down. Then, beginning with both *open hands* in front of each side of the body, swing the fingertips forward and back with an alternating double movement.

jealous *adj.* **1.** Being suspicious that a rival can attract the love and attention of someone you care for: *a jealous lover.* **2.** Envious and covetous of another's accomplishments, possessions, etc.: *I'm jealous of his good luck.* Same sign used for: **envious.**

- [Initialized sign] Beginning with the extended little finger of the right *J hand* touching the right corner of the mouth, palm facing forward, twist the hand down and forward, ending with the palm facing back.

jeans *pl. n.* See sign for PANTS.

Jell-O *Trademark.* See sign for GELATIN.

jelly *n.* A sweet, sticky spread, often translucent, made from fruit or fruit juice: *The coffee shop serves jelly with the toast.* Same sign used for: **jam.**

- [Initialized sign miming spreading jelly on bread] Strike the extended little finger of the right *J hand* on the upturned left *open hand* as it moves upward in an arc with a double movement.

jest *v.* See sign for TEASE.

Jesus *n.* The source of the Christian religion; Jesus Christ: *Jesus, Son of God.*

- [Shows location of wounds in Jesus' hands made when he was nailed to the cross] Touch the bent middle finger of the left *5 hand* into the palm of the right *open hand,* palms facing each other in front of the right side of the chest. Then touch the bent middle finger of the right *5 hand* into the palm of the left *open hand,* palms facing each other in front of the left side of the chest.

jet *n.* See sign for AIRPLANE.

Jew *n.* **1.** A person descended from the Biblical followers of Moses: *Many Jews emigrated to Israel after World War II.* **2.** An adherent of the Jewish religion: *a practicing Jew who attends religious services on Friday nights.* Related form: **Jewish** *adj.* Same sign used for: **Israelite.**

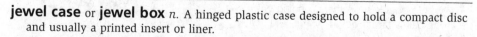

- [Shape of traditional Jewish beard] Slide the fingertips of the right *flattened C hand* from touching the chin, palm facing in and fingers pointing up, downward with a double movement while closing into a *flattened O hand* each time.

jewel case or **jewel box** *n.* A hinged plastic case designed to hold a compact disc and usually a printed insert or liner.

■ [**disk** + mime sliding a disk in and closing a jewel case] Move the fingertips of the right *D hand*, palm facing down and index finger pointing forward, in a double circle on the upturned left *open hand*. Then slide the back of the right *bent hand*, palm facing up, from the fingers to the heel of the upturned left *open hand*. Then, beginning with the little-finger sides of both *open hands*, palms angled up, touching in front of the chest, bring the palms together.

jewelry *n*. Necklaces, bracelets, rings, etc., made of precious metals and gemstones or imitations of these: *We bought some handcrafted jewelry on our trip.*

■ [Location of necklace and bracelet] Beginning with the fingers of both *5 hands* in front of the chest, palms facing in, bring the hands upward to on top of each shoulder. Then grasp the left wrist with the bent middle finger and thumb of the right hand.

jigsaw puzzle *n*. See sign for PUZZLE.

jingle *n*. **1.** A tinkling sound like that made by little bells: *I heard the jingle of the coins in his pocket.* —*v.* **2.** To make such a sound: *tiny bells on her charm bracelet that jingle as she walks.*

■ [Shows ringing of a small bell] Strike the index-finger side of the right *flattened O hand*, palm facing down, against the palm of the left *open hand*, palm facing right and fingers pointing up, with a small double movement.

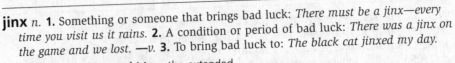

jinx *n*. **1.** Something or someone that brings bad luck: *There must be a jinx—every time you visit us it rains.* **2.** A condition or period of bad luck: *There was a jinx on the game and we lost.* —*v.* **3.** To bring bad luck to: *The black cat jinxed my day.*

■ [**always** + **happen**] Move the extended right index finger, palm facing in, in a large repeated circle in front of the right side of the chest. Then, beginning with both extended index fingers in front of the body, palms facing in, flip the hands over toward each other and downward with a double movement, ending with the palms facing down.

job[1] *n.* **1.** A position of employment: *trying to find a good job.* **2.** A specific task done for an agreed-upon price: *The job will take three weeks.*

- [Initialized sign similar to sign for **work**[1]] With the palm side of the right *J hand* on the back of the left *S hand*, both palms facing down, twist the wrist of the right hand upward.

job[2] *n.* See signs for WORK[1,2].

jog[1] *v.* To run slowly and steadily, especially as part of an exercise program: *jog every day.* Related form: **jogging** *n.*

- [Mime how the hands are thought to move when jogging] Move both *S hands,* palms facing each other, in repeated alternating outward circles in front of each side of the chest.

jog[2] *v.* See signs for RUN[1,2]. Related form: **jogging** *n.*

join[1] *v.* To become a member of: *to join the club.* Same sign used for: **participate.**

- [Represents a person's legs entering a place where there are other people with whom one can have social exchanges] Beginning with the right *H hand* in front of the chest, palm facing left and fingers pointing forward, and the left *C hand* in front of the lower left side of the chest, palm facing right, bring the right hand down in an arc into the palm side of the left hand while closing the left fingers around the fingers of the right *H hand.*

join[2] *v.* See sign for BELONG[1].

joint[1] *n.* Structure made up of ligaments and cartilage that holds bones together and enables them to move easily in relation to each other: *My knee joint hurts.* Same sign used for: **socket.**

- [A bone in its socket] Cover the left *S hand,* palm facing in, with the palm side of the right *curved hand.*

joint[2] *n.* See sign for BELONG[1].

joke *v.* See sign for TEASE. Related form: **joking** *n.*

jolly *adj.* See sign for HAPPY.

jolt *v.* See sign for SHOCK[2].

jostle *v.* **1.** To bump against or elbow roughly: *We were jostled by the people on the bus.* —*n.* **2.** The act of being jostled; a rough bump or push: *upset by the jostle of the crowd.*

- [Mime how one is jostled on a bumpy bus] With both elbows extended and the *A hands* in front of the chest, wiggle the arms around with an irregular repeated movement.

journal[1] *n.* A written account of the events of one's life: *I keep a journal of my activities.* See also sign for MAGAZINE. Same sign used for: **monograph.**

- [**write**[1,2] + **article**] Slide the palm side of the right *modified X hand* across the length of the upturned left *open hand* with a double movement. Then move the right *modified C hand* down across the palm of the left *open hand.*

journal[2] *n.* See signs for ARTICLE, DIARY.

journalist *n.* See sign for AUTHOR.

journey *n.* See sign for TRIP[2].

jovial *adj.* Good-humored and full of fun: *a jovial Santa Claus in the department store.*

- [**friendly** + **person**] Move both *5 hands* back and upward near each cheek, palms facing back, while wiggling the fingers. Then move both *P hands*, palms facing each other, downward along each side of the body.

joy[1] *n.* A feeling of happiness and delight: *I nearly jumped for joy when I heard you were here.*

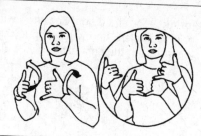

■ [Initialized sign with **y** similar to sign for **happy**] Beginning with both *Y hands* in front of each side of the chest, swing the little fingers back toward the chest with a double movement.

joy² *n.* See sign for HAPPY.

joystick *n.* A device that can be attached to a computer to control the action of a game on its display screen.

■ [Action of using a joystick] With the little-finger side of the right *S hand*, palm facing left, in the palm of the left *open hand*, palm facing up, rock the right hand in different directions with a repeated movement.

judge¹ *v.* To form an opinion or make a decision: *to judge the case on its merits.* Same sign used for: **court, justice, trial.**

■ [The hands move up and down indicating weighing a decision] Move both *F hands*, palms facing each other, up and down in front of each side of the chest with a repeated alternating movement.

judge² *n.* A public official who is authorized to hear and decide cases in a court of law: *The judge assigned to the case gives harsh sentences to offenders.*

■ [**judge**¹ + **person marker**] Move both *F hands*, palms facing each other, up and down in front of each side of the chest with a repeated alternating movement. Then bring both *open hands*, palms facing each other, downward along the sides of the body.

juggle *v.* See sign for INDECISION.

juice *n.* Liquid extracted from fruits: *to drink orange juice for breakfast.*

■ [**drink**[1] + initialized sign] Beginning with the thumb of the right *C hand* near the chin, palm facing left, tip the hand up toward the face. Then form a *J* near the right side of the face with the right hand.

jumbo[1] *adj.* Very large: *a jumbo ice cream cone.*

■ [**large** + **fat**[2]] Beginning with both *L hands* in front of each side of the body, palms facing each other, move the hands outward to each side in large arcs. Then, beginning with both *curved 5 hands* in front of each side of the face, palms facing each other, move the hands outward away from each other.

jumbo[2] *adj.* See sign for FAT[1,4].

jump *v.* **1.** To spring up from the ground: *Jump over the puddle.* —*n.* **2.** An act or instance of jumping: *It's a long jump from here to there.*

■ [Demonstrates the action of jumping] Beginning with the extended fingers of the right *V hand*, palm facing in, pointing down and touching the open left palm, move the right hand up and down in front of the chest with a double movement.

jump over *v. phrase.* To spring up and leap over (an object, hole, etc.): *to jump over the hole.*

■ [Demonstrates legs jumping over something] Move the right *V hand*, palm facing down, from near the chest forward in an arc over the thumb side of the left *open hand*, palm facing in and fingers pointing right.

jump rope *n.* **1.** A children's game in which a rope is swung over the head and around under the feet of the player, who leaps over it every time it comes around again: *learned to play jump rope as a child.* **2.** The rope used in this game: *Hand me the jump rope so I can see how many times I can jump.*

■ [Mime using a jump rope oneself, with one end of the rope in each hand] Move both *A hands,* palms facing up, in simultaneous outward circles in front of each side of the body.

junction *n.* The place where two things join or meet: *The stop sign is at the junction of Smith Street and Anderson Avenue.*

- [**intersection**[1] + pointing to the place where two things are crossing] Place the extended right index finger, palm facing left and finger angled forward, across the extended left index finger, palm facing in and finger pointing right. Then touch the extended right index fingertip, palm facing down and finger pointing down, on the top of the extended left index finger.

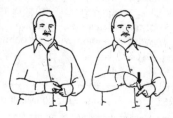

jungle *n.* See signs for FOREST[1,2].

junior *adj.* **1.** Of or pertaining to students in the third year of high school or college: *the junior class.* —*n.* **2.** A person in the third year of high school or college: *She is a junior, who has started applying to colleges.*

- Touch the extended right index finger to the index finger of the left *5 hand,* both palms facing in.

junk[1] *n.* Old rubbish: *A lot of junk is in the attic.*

- [**old** + **things**[2] + **pack**[1]] Beginning with the index-finger side of the right *C hand* against the chin, palm facing left, bring the hand forward while closing into an *S hand.* Then, beginning with the right *open hand* in front of the left side of the body, palm facing up, resting on the upturned left *open hand,* move the hand in a sequence of arcs to the right. Then, beginning with both *flattened O hands* in front of the chest, palms facing down, move the hands downward with an alternating double movement.

junk[2] *n.* See sign for GARBAGE.

jury *n.* A group of citizens called upon to hear the evidence at a trial, decide the facts, and render a verdict: *The jury listened to the defendant's case.* Same sign used for: **petit jury.**

- [Represents people in a jury box] Beginning with the little-finger sides of both *bent 4 hands,* palms facing in, together in front of the chest, move the hands apart to each side.

just

just¹ *adv.* No more than: *just one more.*

■ Beginning with the extended right index finger pointing up in front of the right shoulder, palm facing forward, twist the wrist in, ending with the palm facing back.

just² *adv.* See signs for EQUAL, PRECISE, RECENTLY².

justice *n.* See sign for JUDGE¹.

justify *v.* See sign for CHANGE¹.

juvenile *n.* **1.** A young person: *Juveniles pay half-price.* —*adj.* **2.** Young: *a juvenile crowd at the movie.* **3.** Of, characteristic of, or suitable for young people: *a shelf of juvenile books.*

■ [**young** + **little²**] Beginning with the fingertips of both *bent hands* on each side of the chest, palms facing in and fingers pointing toward each other, brush the fingers upward in a double arc. Then move the right *bent hand* downward with a double movement in front of the right side of the body, palm facing down.

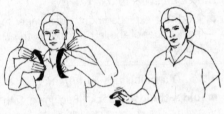

kaleidoscope

kaleidoscope *n.* A tube containing loose bits of colored glass at one end that are reflected in mirrors to make symmetrical patterns as the tube is turned: *looking through the kaleidoscope at the changing patterns.*

■ [**focus**[1,3] + **vague**] Beginning with both *C hands* in front of the face, right hand closer to the face than the left hand and the little-finger side of the right hand touching the index-finger side of the left hand, palms facing in opposite directions, twist the hands in opposite directions. Then open the hands into *5 hands* in front of the chest, twisting the palms against each other in opposite directions.

kangaroo[1] *n.* A mammal having short forelegs and strong hind legs for leaping, with young that continue their development after birth in a pouch on the mother's abdomen: *We saw kangaroos on our trip to Australia.*

■ [Shows posture of a kangaroo] Move both *bent hands* from in front of each side of the body, palms facing in, forward in small upward arcs.

kangaroo[2] *n.* (alternate sign)

■ [Initialized sign showing a kangaroo jumping] Tap the little-finger side of the right *K hand*, palm facing left, in a series of arcs from the heel to the fingers of the open left palm as the left hand moves forward in a series of arcs at the same time.

karate[1] *n.* A Japanese system of self-defense that uses quick, hard blows of the hands and feet: *learning karate from an expert.*

■ [Mime a karate chop] Beginning with the right *B hand* in front of the left side of the face, palm facing left and fingers angled up, and the left *B hand* in front of the left side of the chest, palm facing right and fingers angled up, move the right hand forward with a deliberate movement while turning the palm down as the left hand moves back toward the left side of the chest. Then reverse the action, moving the right hand back toward the chest and the left hand forward and downward to the left.

karate[2] *n.* See sign for HACK.

kayak *v., n.* See sign for CANOE. Related form: **kayaking** *n.*

keel *n.* The main supporting structural piece of a ship that extends along the whole length of the bottom: *The keel of the boat is scratched from scraping bottom in shallow water.*

■ [**ship** + the shape of the bow of a boat] Move the right *3 hand*, palm facing left and fingers pointing forward, in a double arc in front of the chest. Then, beginning with the fingertips of both *open hands* touching in front of the chest, bring the hands at an angle back a short distance and then straight back toward the chest, ending with the palms facing each other and fingers pointing forward.

keen *adj.* See sign for SHARP.

keep[1] *v.* **1.** To hold in one's possession: *to keep the idea in mind.* **2.** To put or store: *to keep the flour in a canister.* Same sign used for: **maintain.**

■ Tap the little-finger side of the right *K hand* across the index-finger side of the left *K hand*, palms facing in opposite directions.

keep[2] *v.* See signs for SAVE[2,3,4].

keep one's hands off See signs for NOT RESPONSIBLE[1,2].

keep quiet See signs for SEAL ONE'S LIPS[1], SHUT UP (*informal*).

keep secret See sign for SEAL ONE'S LIPS[1].

kennel *n.* **1.** A small structure where a dog may be kept: *We built a kennel in the back yard.* **2.** An establishment where dogs or cats are sheltered or boarded: *We'll put the dog in a kennel while we're away.*

■ [**dog**[1,2,3] + **home**] Snap the right thumb gently off the right middle finger, palm facing up in front of the right side of the chest. Then touch the fingertips of the right *flattened O hand* first to the right side of the chin, palm facing down, and then to the right cheek.

ketchup *n.* A sauce made of tomatoes, vinegar, sugar, spices, and other flavorings: *Please put ketchup on my hotdog.* See also sign for CATSUP.

■ [Initialized sign] Shake the right *K hand,* palm facing left, up and down with a short repeated movement in front of the right side of the body.

---

key[1] *n.* A small instrument used to move the bolt in a lock, especially for opening and closing: *a brass key for the antique door.*

■ [Mime turning a key in a lock] Twist the knuckle of the right *X hand,* palm facing down, in the palm of the left *open hand,* palm facing right and fingers pointing forward, with a repeated movement.

---

key[2] *n.* A button on a keyboard: *press on a key.* Same sign used for: **keystroke.**

■ [Action of pressing on a key] Push the extended thumb of the right *10 hand* downward a short distance in front of the right side of the body.

---

key[3] *adj.* See signs for IMPORTANT[1,2].

---

keyboard *n.* **1.** The row of keys on a piano, organ, or similar musical instrument: *trying to pick out a tune on the keyboard.* **2.** The set of alphanumeric and other functional keys, usually in tiers, for operating a typewriter, computer, etc.: *learned to type on a computer keyboard.*

■ [**type** + the shape of a keyboard] Beginning with both *5 hands* in front of the body, palms facing down and fingers pointing forward, wiggle the fingers with alternating movements. Then, beginning with the fingers of both *G hands* touching in front of the chest, palms facing down, move the hands away from each other to in front of each side of the chest and pinch the index fingers to the thumb of each hand.

---

keystroke *n.* See sign for KEY[2].

---

kick[1] *v.* To strike with the foot: *to kick the football through the goalposts.* Same sign used for: **kick off.**

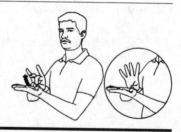

■ [Represents the action of kicking something] Beginning with the thumb of the right *8 hand,* palm facing forward, on the upturned open left palm, flick the right fingers open into a *4 hand.*

kick² *v.* (alternate sign)

- [Demonstrates the action of kicking something] Bring the right *B hand* in front of the right side of the body, palm facing left and fingers angled down, upward to strike the index-finger side of the right hand against the little-finger side of the left *B hand* held in front of the body, palm facing in and fingers pointing right.

kick off *v. phrase.* See sign for KICK¹.

kick the bucket *Slang.* See sign for DIE².

kid¹ *n. Informal.* A child: *a family with two kids and a dog.*

- With the right index finger and little finger extended, palm facing down, put the extended index finger under the nose and twist the hand up and down with a small repeated movement.

kid² *n. Informal.* (alternate sign)

- [Initialized sign] Tap the palm side of the right *K hand* against the nose with a short double movement.

kid³ *v.* See sign for TEASE. Related form: **kidding** *n.*

kidnap *v.* See sign for ABDUCT¹,².

kidney¹ *n.* One of a pair of organs in the abdominal cavity that filter waste matter from the blood: *donated a healthy kidney to her desperately ill sister.*

- [Location of one's kidneys] Tap the fingertips of the right *open hand,* palm facing up, against the right side of the lower back with a double movement.

kidney² *n.* (alternate sign)

- [Location of one's kidneys] Place the palm side of the right *F hand* against the right side of the body.

kill[1] *v.* To cause to die: *A stroke of lightning killed the old tree.* Same sign used for: **murder, slaughter, slay.**

- [Represents a knife being inserted] Push the side of the extended right index finger, palm facing down, across the palm of the left *open hand,* palm facing right, with a deliberate movement.

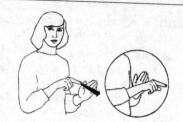

kill[2] *v.* (alternate sign)

- [Initialized sign representing a knife being inserted] Push the thumb side of the right *K hand,* palm facing down, across the palm of the left *open hand,* palm facing right, with a deliberate movement.

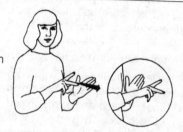

killer *n.* See sign for ASSASSIN.

kilt *n.* A pleated skirt worn by men in some parts of Scotland, especially the Scottish Highlands: *to wear a kilt with the plaid pattern of his ancestral clan.*

- [**Scotland**[1] + **skirt**] First bring the fingertips of the right *4 hand* from back to front and then bring the back of the fingers downward on the upper left arm. Then move both *5 hands* downward in front of each side of the waist, palms facing in and fingers pointing down.

kind[1] *adj.* Having a nature that prompts one to be helpful, generous, charitable, etc.: *a kind person, always generous with his time.* Same sign used for: **generous, gentle, gracious.**

- [**good** + **kind**[2]] Bring the right *open hand* from the mouth, palm facing in, downward and over the left *open hand,* palm facing in, while moving the left hand in a circle over the right hand, ending with the back of the right hand in the left palm.

kind[2] *adj.* (alternate sign) Same sign used for: **generous, gentle, gracious.**

- [A comforting movement] Bring the right *open hand,* palm facing in near the middle of the chest, in a forward circle around the back of the left *open hand,* palm facing in, as it moves in a circle around the right hand.

kind[3] *n.* A group having characteristics in common: *can use computers of the same kind we have in the office.* Same sign used for: **sort, type.**

- [Initialized sign showing a comforting movement] Move the right *K hand,* palm facing left, in a forward circle around the left *K hand,* palm facing right, as it moves in a circle around the right hand, ending with the little-finger side of the right hand landing on the index-finger side of the left hand.

kind[4] *n.* (alternate sign) Same sign used for: **sort, type.**

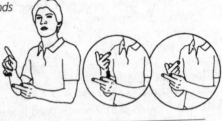

- [Initialized sign] Beginning with both *K hands* in front of the chest, right hand higher than the left hand and palms angled toward each other, twist the right wrist forward and bring the little-finger side of the right *K hand* down on the thumb side of the left *K hand,* ending with the palms facing in opposite directions.

kind[5] *adj.* See sign for SOFT-HEARTED.

kindergarten[1] *n.* A school class for five-year-old children prior to first grade: *Attending kindergarten was a real help to the child's social development.*

- [Initialized sign similar to sign for **school**] Brush the thumb side of the right *K hand,* palm facing down, with a repeated movement downward on the palm of the left *open hand,* palm facing right.

kindergarten[2] *n.* (alternate sign)

- [Initialized sign similar to sign for **base**] Move the right *K hand,* palm facing left, with a repeated back and forth movement under the left *open hand,* palm facing down.

king *n.* The male ruler of a country: *the king of Spain.*

- [Initialized sign following the location of a royal sash] Move the right *K hand,* palm facing in, from touching the left side of the chest near the shoulder downward to touch again near the right side of the waist.

kingdom *n.* The land ruled by a king or queen: *local laws that spread throughout the kingdom.*

■ [**king** + **area**³] Move the right *K hand*, palm facing in, from touching the left side of the chest near the shoulder downward to touch again near the right side of the waist. Then, with the right elbow on the back of the left *open hand* held across the chest, move the right *open hand* forward in a large arc from in front of the right side of the body to in front of the left side of the body.

kink *n., v.* See sign for KNOT¹.

kiss¹ *v.* **1.** To touch with the lips, as to show affection or veneration: *kissed her hand.* —*n.* **2.** An act or instance of kissing: *Give me a big kiss on the cheek.*

■ [The hand takes a kiss from the mouth and puts it on the cheek] Touch the fingertips of the right *bent hand*, palm facing down, first to the right side of the mouth and then to the right cheek.

kiss² *v., n.* (alternate sign)

■ [Represents two mouths coming together to kiss] Beginning with both *flattened O hands* in front of the chest, right hand somewhat forward of the left hand, palms facing each other, bring the fingertips together.

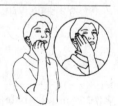

kiss³ *v., n.* (alternate sign)

■ [The hand takes a kiss from the mouth and puts it on the cheek] Touch the fingertips of the right *flattened O hand*, palm facing down, to the right side of the mouth, and then open the right hand and lay the palm of the right *open hand* against the right side of the face.

kitchen *n.* A room equipped for preparing and cooking food: *Everyone came into the kitchen while I made dinner.*

■ [Initialized sign similar to sign for **cook**] Beginning with the palm side of the right *K hand* on the upturned left *open hand*, flip the right hand over, ending with the back of the right hand in the left palm.

kite *n.* A lightweight device, made of thin material stretched on a frame, that is flown in the wind on the end of a long string: *fly a kite.*

■ [Represents a kite on a string] With the extended right index finger, palm facing left, in the palm of the left *open hand*, palm facing right and fingers pointing up, move both hands upward and outward to the left with a double movement.

kitten *n.* A young cat: *to pet the kitten.*

■ [**baby** + **cat**[1,2]] With the bent right arm cradled on the bent left arm, both palms facing up, swing the arms from left to right in front of the body with a double movement. Then, beginning with the index finger and thumb of both *5 hands* touching each cheek, palms facing each other, bring the hands outward with a double movement while pinching the index fingers and thumbs together each time.

Kleenex *Trademark.* See sign for TISSUE[1].

---

knead *v.* To work and shape (clay, dough, etc.) by molding in the hands: *to knead the dough for baking bread.*

■ [Mime kneading dough] Beginning with both *curved 5 hands* in front of the chest, palms facing down, repeatedly close the fingers into *S hands*. Then, beginning with the right *5 hand* over the left *5 hand*, with a double movement move the hands to touch each other while changing to *A hands* and twist them in opposite directions.

---

knee[1] *n.* The joint between the thigh and the lower leg: *bumped my knee.*

■ [Location of the knee] Tap the fingertips of the right *open hand,* palm facing in, on the bent right knee with a double movement.

---

knee[2] *n.* (alternate sign)

■ [Location of the knee] Tap the extended right index finger, palm facing in, on the bent right knee with a double movement.

---

kneel *v.* To go down on one's knees: *kneel at the altar.*

■ [Represents a person's bent knees] Bring the knuckles of the bent fingers of the right *V hand,* palm facing in, down on the upturned left *open hand.*

knife *n.* A thin, flat metal blade fastened in a handle and used for cutting and spreading: *to cut meat with a knife.*

- [Represents the slicing movement done with a knife] Slide the side of the extended right index finger, palm facing in, with a double movement at an angle down the length of the extended left index finger, palm facing right, turning the right palm down each time as it moves off the end of the left index finger.

knit *v.* See sign for CROCHET.

knob *n.* A rounded projection forming a handle on a door or drawer, or a controlling device on an appliance: *Turn the volume down on the television with the knob on the left.*

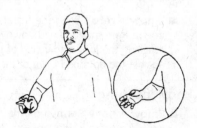

- [Mime turning a knob] Beginning with the right *curved 5 hand* in front of the right side of the body, palm facing forward, twist the hand, ending with the palm facing left.

knock *v.* To strike a blow with the knuckles: *knock on the door.* Same sign used for: **rap.**

- [Mime knocking on something] Hit the palm side of the right *A hand*, palm facing left, with a double movement on the palm of the left *open hand*, palm facing right and fingers pointing up.

knot[1] *n.* **1.** A fastening made by tying pieces or ends of rope, string, etc., together by looping or interlacing them: *Tie a tight knot in the shoelace.* **2.** A tangled mass: *terrible knots in my hair.* —*v.* **3.** To tie in a knot: *Knot the rope on each end.* Same sign used for: **kink.**

- [Represents a knotted rope] Beginning with the index finger of the right *X hand*, palm facing down, hooked over the bent left index finger, palm facing up, twist the hands in opposite directions, reversing positions.

knot[2] *n.* A hard mass where a tree branch grows out of a trunk: *a knot on the tree.* Same sign used for: **knothole.**

- [**wood** + the shape of a knothole] Slide the little-finger side of the right *B hand*, palm facing left and fingers pointing forward, with a double movement forward and back on the index-finger side of the left *B hand*, palm facing in and fingers pointing right. Then bring the thumb side of the right *F hand*, palm facing forward, with a repeated movement against the palm of the left *open hand*.

knot[3] *v.* See signs for TIE[1,2].

knothole *n.* See sign for KNOT[2].

know

know *v.* To have the facts; perceive; understand: *to know about the accident.*

- [Location of knowledge in the brain] Tap the fingertips of the right *bent hand*, palm facing down, on the right side of the forehead.

knowledge *n.* See sign for AWARE[1].

know nothing[1] Not to have the facts; be unaware: *know nothing about it.*

- [**know** + **zero**[1]] Bring the fingers of the right *bent hand*, palm facing down, from the forehead downward while changing into an *O hand*, touching the little-finger side of the right *O hand*, palm facing left, against the upturned palm of the left *open hand*.

know nothing[2] (alternate sign)

- [**know** + **none**[4] formed on the brain + a shrug indicating ignorance] Tap the fingers of the right *bent hand*, palm facing down, against the right side of the forehead. Then bring the index-finger side of the right *O hand* against the right side of the forehead. Then, with both *open hands* held up in front of each shoulder, palms facing up and elbows close to the body, shrug the shoulders with a double movement.

Korea[1] *n.* A former country in East Asia now divided into North Korea and South Korea: *diplomatic discussions about unifying Korea.* Related form: **Korean** *n., adj.*

- [Initialized sign] With the middle finger of the right *K hand* touching near the outer corner of the right eye, palm facing in, twist the hand forward with a double movement.

Korea[2] *n.* (alternate sign) Related form: **Korean** *n., adj.*

- [Shows shape of Korean hat] Beginning with the fingertips of both *open hands* touching each side of the head, palms angled down, bring the hands downward and outward in an arc while bending the fingers.

kosher *adj.* Clean, fit, and appropriate for eating or using according to Jewish law: *a grocery store that sells kosher food.*

- [**Jew** + **food**] Slide the fingertips of the right *flattened C hand* from touching the chin, palm facing in and fingers pointing up, downward with a double movement while closing into a *flattened O hand* each time. Then bring the fingertips of the right *flattened O hand*, palm facing down, to the lips.

label[1] *n.* **1.** A strip of paper attached to an object to specify its contents, purpose, destination, or other information: *Put a label on each file folder.* —*v.* **2.** To mark with a label; attach a label to: *to label the jelly jars.* Same sign used for: **apply, brand, decal, tag.**

- [Demonstrates applying a label] Wipe the extended fingers of the right *H hand,* palm facing left, from the fingers to the heel of the left *open hand,* palm facing right and fingers pointing forward.

label[2] *n.* See sign for NAME[1].

labor[1] *v.* See signs for WORK[1,2].

labor[2] *n.* See signs for ACTIVE[1], JOB, WORK[1,2].

laboratory *n.* See sign for SCIENCE.

lack *n.* See sign for SKIP[1].

lacrosse *n.* A game played by two teams attempting to score goals at opposite ends of the playing field by throwing and catching a ball using sticks with webbed baskets at the ends: *learned to play lacrosse at camp.*

- With the elbow of the bent right arm, *bent hand* facing forward, on the back of the left *open hand* held across the body, palm facing down and fingers pointing right, move the right hand forward with a double movement.

ladder *n.* See signs for CLIMB[1,2,3].

laden *adj.* Heavily burdened: *a ship laden with cargo.*

- [**weigh + heavy + push down**[2]] Beginning with the middle finger side of the right *H hand,* palm angled left, across the index-finger side of the left *H hand,* palm angled right, shake the hands up and down with a double movement. Then, beginning with both *curved 5 hands* in front of each side of the body, palms facing up, move the hands downward a short distance with a double movement. Then, with the palm of the right *curved 5 hand* resting across the palm of the left *open hand* in front of the chest, push the hands downward a short distance.

ladle *n.* A large, cup-shaped spoon with a long handle: *to serve the gravy with a ladle.*

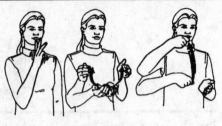

- [**water** + **bowl** + mime eating from a bowl] Tap the index finger of the right *W hand,* palm facing left, against the chin with a double movement. Then, beginning with the little fingers of both *C hands* touching, palms facing up, bring the hands apart from each other and upward, ending with the palms facing each other in front of each side of the chest. Then, with the right *modified X hand* in front of the chest, palm facing in, and the left *curved hand* in front of the left side of the chest, palm facing right, scoop the right hand upward toward the mouth with a double movement.

lady *n.* A well-bred woman: *She is quiet and refined and always acts like a lady.* Same sign used for: **female.**

- [**girl**[1] + **polite**[2]] Bring the thumb of the right *A hand,* palm facing left, downward from the right side of the chin while opening into a *5 hand,* ending by tapping side of the thumb of the right *open hand* in the center of the chest.

ladybug *n.* A small, round beetle with black spots: *Ladybugs protect the plants from aphids.*

- [**woman** + **bug**[1]] Move the thumb of the right *5 hand,* palm facing left and fingers pointing forward, from the center of the chin to touch the center of the chest. Then, beginning with the extended thumb of the right *3 hand* on the nose, palm facing left, bend the extended index and middle fingers with a repeated movement.

laid up *adj. phrase.* Temporarily incapacitated or disabled, especially when confined to bed: *He was laid up with the flu.*

- Bring both *bent V hands,* palms facing each other, from in front of each side of the body back toward each side of the chest.

lake[1] *n.* A body of water surrounded by land: *to fish for trout in the lake.*

- [**water** + shape of a lake] Tap the index finger of the right *W hand,* palm facing left, against the chin with a double movement. Then, with the *modified C hands,* palms facing each other, in front of each side of the body, move the hands downward a short distance.

lake[2] *n.* (alternate sign)

- [**water** + **location**] Tap the index finger of the right *W hand,* palm facing left, against the chin with a double movement. Then, beginning with the thumbs of both *L hands* touching in front of the body, palms facing down, move the hands apart in a circular movement back until they touch again near the chest.

lamb[1] *n.* **1.** A young sheep: *a little white lamb bleating for its mother.* **2.** The meat of a young sheep: *serving braised lamb for dinner.*

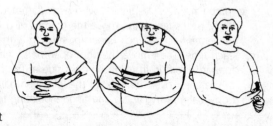

- [**baby**[1] + **sheep**] With the bent right arm cradled on the bent left arm, both palms facing up, swing the arms from left to right in front of the body with a double movement. Then slide the back of the right *K hand,* palm facing up, with a double movement from the wrist up the inside forearm of the bent left arm.

lamb[2] *n.* (alternate sign)

- [**sheep** + a gesture indicating small size] Slide the back of the right *K hand,* palm facing up, with a double movement from the wrist up the inside forearm of the bent left arm. Then, with the right *open hand* a few inches above the left *open hand,* palms facing each other and fingers pointing in opposite directions, move the hands toward each other with a short double movement.

lamp[1] *n.* Any of several devices that give out artificial light: *Turn on the lamp in the hallway.* Same sign used for: **light.**

- [Represents light coming out of a table lamp] With the elbow of the raised right arm resting on the palm of the left *open hand* in front of the right side of the chest, open the right *flattened O hand,* forming a *curved hand,* palm facing down and fingers pointing forward.

lamp[2] *n.* (alternate sign) Same sign used for: **light.**

- [**light**[1] + represents a lamp on a table] Beginning with the fingertips of the right *8 hand* near the chin, palm facing in, flick the middle finger upward and forward with a double movement, while opening into a *5 hand* each time. Then, with the right *5 hand* bent at the wrist, palm facing down

land

and fingers pointing left, place the elbow of the right bent arm on the back of the left *open hand* held across the body, palm facing down and fingers pointing right.

---

land[1] *n.* **1.** Any part of the earth not covered by water: *The lost ship finally approached land.* **2.** Soil on an area of ground with reference to its composition and potential use: *good land for planting.* Same sign used for: **acreage, field, property.**

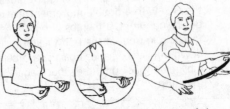

- [**dirt** + **area**[1,2,3]] Beginning with both *flattened O hands* in front of each side of the body, palms facing up, move the thumbs of both hands smoothly with a double movement across each fingertip, starting with the little fingers and ending as *A hands* each time. Then move the right *open hand,* palm facing down and fingers pointing forward, from in front of the right side of the body in a large arc forward and in front of the chest over the back of the left *open hand,* held in front of the left side of the body, palm facing down and fingers pointing forward.

---

land[2] *n.* See signs for COUNTRY[1,2], DIRT.

---

lane *n.* See sign for ROAD[1].

---

language *n.* Structured communication using a system of arbitrary symbols, sounds, gestures, etc., to express thought: *knows the French language well.* Same sign used for: **dialect, tongue.**

- [Initialized sign] Beginning with the thumbs of both *L hands* near each other in front of the chest, palms angled down, bring the hands outward with a wavy movement to in front of each side of the chest.

---

lantern[1] *n.* A portable light contained in a protective case: *to carry a lantern into the woods.*

- [Represents the movement of a swinging lantern] Beginning with the right *S hand,* palm facing down, over the back of the left *5 hand,* palm facing down, swing both hands across the chest in an arc, ending in front of the left side of the chest.

---

lantern[2] *n.* (alternate sign)

- [**light**[1] + a gesture showing the movement of a swinging lantern] Beginning with the fingertips of the right *8 hand* near the chin, palm facing in, flick the middle finger upward and forward with a double movement, opening into a *5 hand* each time. Then, with the right elbow extended, place the extended right index finger, palm facing right and finger pointing down, on the wrist of the left *5 hand,* palm facing left and fingers dangling down, and swing both arms from side to side in front of the body with a double movement.

lap[1] *n.* The front part of the body from the waist to the knees formed when a person sits: *the kitten asleep on my lap.*

■ [The location of one's lap] Pat the palm of the right *open hand* on top the right thigh with a double movement. [This sign can be formed with two hands.]

lap[2] *n.* One complete circuit of a race course: *run a lap; swam two laps before breakfast.* Same sign used for: **run around.**

■ [Represents movement of going around a lap] Move the extended right index finger, pointing up and palm facing in, in a large circle in front of the right shoulder.

lap[3] *n.* (alternate sign) Same sign used for: **run around.**

■ [Represents movement of going around a lap] Move the right *10 hand,* thumb pointing up and palm facing in, in a large double circle in front of the right shoulder.

lapse *n.* See sign for BETWEEN.

laptop computer *n. phrase.* A portable computer with an integrated screen and keyboard, usually weighing less than 10 pounds: *take the laptop computer on the trip.* Same sign used for: **notebook computer.**

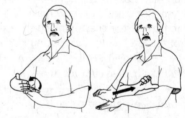

■ [Opening of a laptop + **computer**[1]] Beginning with the palms of both *open hands* together, right hand on top of left hand and fingers pointing in opposite directions, flip the thumb side of the right hand up while keeping the little finger on the left palm. Then move the thumb side of the right *C hand* upward, palm facing left, from touching the lower part of the extended left arm to touching the upper arm.

large *adj.* Of more than the usual size, quantity, degree, etc.: *a large amount of money.*

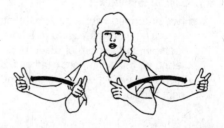

■ [Initialized sign showing a large size] Move both *L hands* from in front of each side of the chest, palms facing each other, in large arcs beyond each side of the body.

larva *n.* The immature, feeding stage of an insect, before metamorphosis: *The caterpillar is the larva of the butterfly.*

- [**bug**[1] + demonstrates the movement of a worm crawling] With the extended thumb of the right *3 hand* on the nose, palm facing left, bend the extended index and middle fingers with a repeated movement. Then, with the palm side of the extended right index finger resting on the upturned palm of the left *open hand,* move the right hand forward a short distance while wiggling the index finger up and down with a double movement.

larynx *n.* See sign for THROAT.

laser *n.* A device that emits intense light of a precise wavelength: *burn a design in the wood with a laser.* Same sign used for: **burn.**

- [Action of a laser beam] With the index finger of the right *L hand* pointing at the palm of the left *open hand,* move the right hand back and forth with a double movement.

last[1] *adj.* **1.** Coming after all others: *the last cookie in the box.* —*adv.* **2.** After all others: *He finished last.* —*n.* **3.** Something or someone that is last: *the last to arrive.* See also sign for END[1]. Same sign used for: **final, finally.**

- [Indicates the last thing] Move the extended little finger of the right *I hand,* palm facing left, downward in front of the chest, striking the extended little finger of the left *I hand,* palm facing in, as it passes.

last[2] *adj., adv.* See sign for AGO[1].

last[3] *adv.* See sign for BEFORE[1].

last[4] *v.* See sign for CONTINUE[1].

lasting *adj.* See sign for CONTINUE[1].

last week During the week before this one: *went to the opera last week.*

- [**week** formed with a movement into the past] Beginning with the back of the right *1 hand,* palm facing in, in the palm of the left *open hand,* palm facing in, bring the right hand across the palm and then back with a sweeping movement over the right shoulder.

last year[1] During the year before this one: *attended college last year.*

- [An abbreviated form of **year** formed with a movement into the past] Beginning with the little-finger side of the right *S hand,* palm facing left, on the index-finger side of the left *S hand,* palm facing right, bring the right hand back with a sweeping movement over the right shoulder.

last year[2] (alternate sign)

- [An abbreviated form of **year** moving into the past] With the back of the right *1 hand,* palm facing up, on the index-finger side of the left *S hand,* palm facing down, bend the right extended index finger down toward the chest with a double movement.

late *adj.* **1.** Occurring after the usual time: *a very late summer.* **2.** Continued past the usual time: *I just rushed over from a late meeting.* —*adv.* **3.** After the usual time: *you got here late.* **4.** Until past the usual time: *had to work late again.* Same sign used for: **delay, tardy.**

- [Hand moves into the past] Bend the wrist of the right *open hand,* palm facing back and fingers pointing down, back near the right side of the waist with a double movement.

lately *adv.* See sign for SINCE[1].

later[1] *adv.* After the present time: *talk about it later.* Alternate form: **later on.** Same sign used for: **after a while, afterward.**

- [Initialized sign representing the minute hand on a clock moving to indicate the passing of time] With the thumb of the right *L hand,* palm facing forward, on the palm of the left *open hand,* palm facing right and fingers pointing forward, twist the right hand forward, keeping the thumb in place and ending with the right palm facing down.

later[2] *adv.* (alternate sign) Alternate form: **later on.** Same sign used for: **after a while, afterward.**

- [Initialized sign moving forward into the future] Beginning with the thumb of the right *L hand* near the right side of the chin, palm facing left and index finger pointing up, move the right hand forward, ending with the index finger pointing forward.

Latin

Latin[1] *n.* **1.** The language of ancient Rome: *learned to read Latin in high school.* —*adj.* **2.** Of or pertaining to Latin: *Latin grammar.*

- [Shows the shape of a Roman nose] Touch the fingertips of the right *H hand* first to the bridge of the nose, palm facing in, and then to the tip of the nose.

Latin[2] *n.* See sign for ROME.

latter *adj.* Occurring toward the end: *the latter part of the week.*

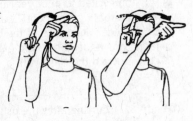

- [Initialized sign moving forward, indicating the future] Beginning with the right *L hand* near the right side of the forehead, palm facing forward and index finger pointing up, tip the right index finger forward with a double movement as the hand moves forward in a double arc.

laugh[1] *v.* To make sounds, as chuckles, giggles, or loud guffaws, expressing amusement or happiness: *The children are laughing hysterically at the clown.*

- [Initialized sign showing the shape of the mouth when one laughs] Beginning with the extended index fingers of both *L hands* at each corner of the mouth, palms facing back, pull the hands outward to each side of the head with a double movement while closing the hands into *10 hands* each time.

laugh[2] *v.* See signs for HYSTERICAL[1,2,3]. Related form: **laughter** *n.*

laugh at *v. phrase.* See sign for MOCK.

launch[1] *v.* To set (a boat, especially a newly constructed ship) afloat in the water: *launched the new ocean liner with great ceremony.*

- [Hand shape represents a boat moving into the water] Beginning with the little-finger side of the right *3 hand*, palm facing right and fingers pointing in, on the palm of the left *open hand*, palm facing up and fingers pointing forward, slide the right hand forward.

launch[2] *v.* To set forth into the air: *to launch a rocket.*

- [Represents a rocket being launched upward] Beginning with the wrist of the right *R hand*, palm facing forward and fingers pointing up, on the back of the left *S hand*, palm facing down, raise the hands in front of the chest while dangling the left fingers downward and wiggling them as the hands move up.

546

lava *n.* Hot, molten rock flowing from a volcano: *The lava flowed down the mountain.*

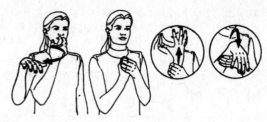

■ [**hot** + **erupt**[1] + a movement indicating the lava running down the mountain side] Beginning with the right *curved 5 hand* in front of the mouth, palm facing in, twist the wrist forward with a deliberate movement. Then, beginning with the right *S hand* cupped in the fingers of the left *C hand,* both palms facing in, raise the right hand in front of the chest while opening into a *5 hand.* Then twist the right wrist and drop the fingers down over the back of the left *C hand.*

lavatory *n.* See sign for TOILET.

law *n.* **1.** The combination of regulations made by a government: *sworn to obey the law of the land.* **2.** An individual rule, prescribed by a city, state, or national authority, governing the behavior of its citizens: *broke the law against jaywalking.* Same sign used for: **legal.**

■ [Initialized sign representing recording laws on the books] Place the palm side of the right *L hand,* palm facing left, first on the fingers and then the heel of the left *open hand,* palm facing right and fingers pointing up.

lawyer *n.* See sign for ATTORNEY.

layer[1] *n.* One thickness spread on a surface or forming a level below or beneath other thicknesses: *a layer of dust.* Same sign used for: **plush.**

■ [Shows the shape of a layer on top of something] Slide the thumb of the right *modified C hand,* palm facing left, from the heel to off the fingers of the upturned palm of the left *open hand* held in front of the chest.

layer[2] *n.* (alternate sign) Same sign used for: **plush.**

■ [Shows the shape of a layer on top of something] Slide the thumb of the right *G hand,* palm facing left, from the wrist to off the fingers of the back of the left *open hand* held in front of the chest, palm facing down and fingers pointing right.

lay off *v. phrase. Informal.* See sign for DISMISS.

lazy *adj.* Not inclined to work or be active: *a lazy person, who hangs around the house all day doing nothing.* Same sign used for: **slothful.**

- [Initialized sign] Tap the palm side of the right *L hand* against the left side of the chest with a double movement.

LCD (liquid crystal display) See sign for FLAT SCREEN DISPLAY.

lead[1] *v.* To show the way (to): *to lead the way; to lead the group on a hike.* Same sign used for: **conduct, guide, head, host, steer.**

- [One hand leads the other by pulling it] With the fingers of the left *open hand,* palm facing right, being held by the fingers and thumb of the right hand, palm facing in, pull the left hand forward a short distance.

lead[2] *v.* (alternate sign) Same sign used for: **conduct, guide, head, host, steer.**

- [One hand seems to lead the other hand] Grasp the middle finger of the left *open hand,* palm facing in and fingers pointing right, with the index finger and thumb of the right hand, palm facing in, and pull the left hand a short distance to the right.

leader *n.* See sign for GUIDE[1].

leaf *n.* A thin, flat green part that grows on the stem of a plant and absorbs energy from the sun: *Rake the dried leaves that have fallen from the tree.*

- [Represents a leaf blowing in the wind on a branch] With the extended left index finger on the wrist of the right *5 hand,* angled in down and bent at the wrist, swing the right hand forward and back with a double movement.

leak[1] *v.* **1.** (of liquid) To escape from a hole or crack: *The water leaked onto the floor through a small hole in the pipe.* —*n.* **2.** A hole or crack that lets liquid out: *a leak in the bucket.* **3.** An act or instance of leaking: *furniture damaged by the leak in the ceiling.* Same sign used for: **drain.**

- [Represents the flow of a leaking liquid] Beginning with the index-finger side of the right *4 hand,* palm facing in and fingers pointing left, touching the palm of the left *open hand,* palm facing down and fingers pointing right, move the right hand down with a double movement.

leak[2] *n., v.* See sign for DRIP.

lean *adj.* See signs for DIET, THIN[2,3].

learn *v.* To gain knowledge of or skill in: *learn a trade.* Same sign used for: **acquire, educate, education.**

■ [Represents taking information from paper and putting it in one's head] Beginning with the fingertips of the right *curved hand,* palm facing down, on the palm of the upturned left *open hand,* bring the right hand up while closing the fingers and thumb into a *flattened O hand* near the forehead.

least[1] *adj.* Smallest in size, amount, degree, etc.: *the least amount.*

■ [**less**[1] + **most**] Move the right *bent hand,* palm facing down and fingers pointing left, from in front of the chest downward a few inches above the left *open hand,* palm facing up and fingers pointing right. Then, beginning with the palm sides of both *10 hands* together in front of the chest, bring the right hand upward, ending with the right hand in front of the right shoulder, palm facing left.

least[2] *adj.* See sign for MINIMUM[1].

leather *n.* **1.** Material made from the processed skin of an animal: *The jacket is made of leather.* —*adj.* **2.** Made of leather: *leather shoes.*

■ [Initialized sign] Beginning with both *L hands* on each side of the chest, palms facing in and index fingers pointing toward each other, brush the hands downward with a double movement while turning the index finger down. [This sign can be formed with one hand.]

leave[1] *v.* To go away (from): *to leave without saying good-bye; to leave home.* Same sign used for: **depart, desert, withdraw.**

■ Beginning with both *curved 5 hands* in front of each side of the chest, palms facing down, pull the hands back toward the right shoulder while closing the fingers and thumbs into *flattened O hands.*

leave[2] *v.* To let stay or be: *Leave your shoes outside.* Same sign used for: **leftover, rest.**

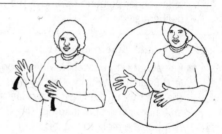

■ [The hands seem to leave something by thrusting it down] Beginning with both *5 hands* in front of each side of the body, palms facing each other and fingers angled up, thrust the fingers downward with a deliberate movement.

leave

leave[3] *v.* To let stay permanently or for a long time: *The pioneers had to leave many of their possessions behind.* Same sign used for: **abandon, forsake, neglect.**

- [The circular movement indicates a continuing abandonment of something] Beginning with both *5 hands* in front of each side of the body, palms facing each other and fingers pointing forward, move the hands in forward circles with a double movement.

leave[4] *v.* See sign for GO[2].

leave alone (used with reference to the speaker) To let stay in isolated or undisturbed circumstances: *I was left alone to read.*

- [Directional sign toward oneself] Beginning with both *curved 5 hands* in front of each side of the chest, palms facing up, bring the fingertips back to touch the right side of the chest.

lecture *v.* See sign for SPEAK[2].

leech *n.* A person who habitually tries to get something from others without giving anything in return: *He is a leech when it comes to cigarettes—borrowing them from everyone.* Same sign used for: **mooch** (*slang*), **take advantage of.**

- [One hand seems to "put the bite on" the other hand] Tap the fingers of the right *U hand* and extended thumb of the right hand, palm facing left, with a double movement on the fingertips of the left *U hand*, palm facing down and fingers pointing right.

left[1] *adj.* **1.** Belonging to the left side: *his left arm.* —*adv.* **2.** On or toward the left side: *Turn left at the next light.* —*n.* **3.** The left side: *leaning toward the left.*

- [Initialized sign indicating a direction to the left] Beginning with the right *L hand* in front of the right side of the chest, palm facing forward and index finger pointing up, move the hand deliberately to the left.

left[2] *adj., adv.* (alternate sign)

- [Initialized sign indicating a direction to the left] Beginning with the left *L hand* in front of the left side of the chest, palm facing forward and index finger pointing up, move the left hand deliberately to the left.

left-handed[1] *adj.* **1.** Having the left hand more easily used and controlled than the right: *a left-handed person.* **2.** Made or modified for use by a left-handed person: *a left-handed pair of scissors.* **3.** Done by someone using the left hand: *made a left-handed catch in center field.*

■ [**left**[1] + **hand**] Move the right *L hand,* palm facing forward and index finger pointing up, to the left with a deliberate movement. Then pat the palm of the right *curved hand* with a double movement on the back of the left *curved hand,* both palms facing down.

left-handed[2] *adj.* (alternate sign)

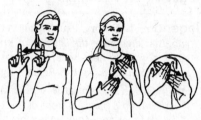

■ [**left**[1] + **hands**] Move the right *L hand,* palm facing forward and index finger pointing right, to the right with a deliberate movement. Then bring the back of the right *open hand* downward across the palm of the left *open hand,* both palms facing in, and repeat the movement with the left hand.

left justify To align text along the left margin: *We're designing the cookbook so that we left justify the copy, leaving a ragged right margin.* Same sign used for: **left side.**

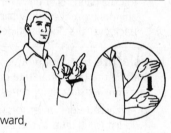

■ [**left**[2] + a gesture showing the left margin] Move the left *L hand,* palm facing forward, from in front of the left side of the chest to the left. Then move the left *open hand,* palm facing right and fingers pointing forward, downward in front of the left side of the chest.

leftover *n., adj.* See sign for LEAVE[2].

left side See sign for LEFT JUSTIFY.

left turn[1] A turn to the left to proceed along a street, hallway, etc.: *made a left turn on Main Street.*

■ [Initialized sign demonstrating a left direction] Move the left *L hand,* palm facing in and index finger pointing right, to the left while twisting the wrist, ending with the palm facing forward and the index finger pointing left.

left turn[2] (alternate sign)

■ [Demonstrates a left turn] Beginning with the right *open hand* in front of the right side of the chest, palm facing left and fingers pointing up, move the hand to the left while twisting the wrist, ending with the palm facing in.

leg *n.* Either of the two lower limbs used for standing, walking, etc.: *I hurt my leg on the corner of the coffee table.*

■ [Location of the leg] Pat the palm of the right *open hand,* palm facing left, against the side of the right thigh with a double movement.

legal *adj.* See sign for LAW.

legend *n.* **1.** A story, usually not verified, handed down by tradition and given popular credence: *the legends of King Arthur and his Knights of the Round Table.* **2.** A popularly held belief about a well-known person: *His reputation is legend.* Related form: **legendary** *adj.*

■ [Initialized sign similar to sign for **ancestor**[2]] Beginning with both *L hands* in front of the body, palms facing each other and index fingers pointing forward, roll the hands over each other with an alternating movement while moving the hands back over the right shoulder.

legislature *n.* A group of people responsible for making the laws of a state or country: *a vote of the state legislature for a new bond issue.*

■ [Initialized sign similar to sign for **Congress**] Touch the thumb of the right *L hand,* palm facing left, first to the left side of the chest and then to the right side.

leisure[1] *n.* **1.** Free time to relax: *Many people dream of a life of leisure.* —*adj.* **2.** Not occupied with work; free: *I use my leisure time to sew.*

■ [Formed similarly to sign for **vacation**] Tap the thumbs of both *5 hands* with a double movement near each armpit, palms facing in and fingers pointing toward each other.

leisure[2] *n.* See signs for ENJOY, FUN.

lemon[1] *n.* A sour, juicy, citrus fruit, yellow in color: *to put lemon in the tea.*

■ [Initialized sign similar to sign for **sour**] Tap the thumb of the right *L hand,* palm facing left, against the chin with a double movement.

lemon[2] *n.* (alternate sign)

- [Similar to sign for **sour** but formed with a double movement] With the extended right index finger on the right side of the chin, palm facing left, twist the hand downward with a double movement, turning the palm toward the back.

lemonade *n.* A drink made of lemon juice, sugar, and water: *Have some cold lemonade.*

- [**lemon**[1] + **drink**[1]] Tap the thumb of the right *L hand,* palm facing left and index finger pointing up, against the chin. Then, beginning with the thumb of the right *C hand* near the chin, palm facing left, tip the hand up toward the face.

lend *v.* To let someone have temporary use of: *I will lend you my umbrella.* Same sign used for: **loan.**

- [Directional sign toward the person to whom something is lent] With the little-finger side of the right *V hand* across the index-finger side of the left *V hand,* move the hands from near the chest forward and down a short distance.

lend me See sign for BORROW.

length *n.* The extent of something as measured from end to end: *What is the length of that table?* See also sign for LONG.

- [The finger measures off a designated distance] Beginning with the extended right index finger, palm facing in and finger pointing down, touching the extended left index finger, palm facing in and finger pointing right, move the right finger outward to the right.

lens[1] *n.* A thin, curved piece of transparent glass, plastic, etc., used in an optical device: *the lens of a telescope.*

- [**picture** + **focus**[1,3]] Move the right *C hand* from near the right side of the face, palm facing forward, downward, ending with the index-finger side of the right *C hand* against the palm of the left *open hand,* palm facing right. Then, beginning with the left *C hand* near the right eye, palm facing right, and the right *C hand* touching the little-finger side of the left *C hand,* palm facing left, twist the hands in opposite directions.

lens[2] *n.* (alternate sign)

-  [A gesture representing a lens closing + **glass**[1] + the shape of a lens held up in front of the eye] Beginning with both *G hands* near the outside of each eye, palms facing each other, bring the hands forward a short distance and pinch the index fingers to each thumb. Then tap the fingertip of the right bent index finger against the teeth with a repeated movement. Then, with the left *modified C hand* around the outside edge of the left eye, move the bent right index finger in a circle inside the form shaped by the left hand.

Lent *n.* See sign for ANOINT[2].

lesbian *n.* **1.** A woman who is sexually attracted to other women; female homosexual: *She realized in her twenties that she was a lesbian.* —*adj.* **2.** Of or pertaining to lesbians or lesbianism. Related form: **lesbianism** *n.*

-  [Initialized sign] Bring the palm side of the right *L hand*, palm facing in and index finger pointing left, back against the chin with a double movement, ending with the chin within the crook between the right index finger and thumb.

less[1] *adj.* **1.** Being smaller in amount, quantity, or size: *less rain this year.* —*adv.* **2.** To a smaller extent or degree: *charity for those less fortunate.* Related form: **lessen** *v.* Same sign used for: **below, cut back, low, reduce.**

-  [The hands demonstrate a decreasing amount] Move the right *open hand*, palm facing down and fingers pointing left, from in front of the chest downward a few inches above the left *open hand*, palm facing up and fingers pointing right.

less[2] *adj.* See sign for MINIMUM[1].

lessen *v.* See signs for DECREASE[1,3].

lesson[1] *n.* **1.** A section of a course of study: *Did you study your French lesson for tomorrow?* **2.** Something to be learned or taught, especially of a moral nature: *learning from the lessons of history.*

-  [The movement represents breaking up information on a page into lessons] Move the little-finger side of the right *bent hand*, palm facing in, from the fingers to the heel of the left *open hand*, palm facing up.

lesson[2] *n.* See sign for COURSE.

let[1] *v.* To allow to: *Let me do it.* Same sign used for: **allow, grant, permit.**

- [The hands outline a path for a person to pass] Beginning with both *open hands* in front of the waist, palms facing each other and fingers pointing down, bring the fingers forward and upward by bending the wrists.

let[2] *v.* (alternate sign) Same sign used for: **allow.**

- [Initialized sign outlining a path for a person to pass through] Beginning with both *L hands* in front of the waist, palms facing each other and index fingers pointing forward, bring the index fingers forward and upward by bending the wrists.

let go *v. phrase.* See signs for DISCONNECT, FIRE[3].

let know See sign for INFORM[1].

let me know See sign for INFORM[2].

let's see **1.** (Used to recommend the postponement of action or judgment until something specified occurs): *Let's see what happens before you make up your mind.* **2.** (Used to indicate an impending investigation): *Let's see how our patient is doing.* Same sign used for: **speculate, speculation.**

- [The fingers represent one's eyes] Tap the fingertips of the right *V hand,* palm facing left and fingers pointing up, with a double movement near the right eye.

letter[1] *n.* One of the 26 symbols forming the English alphabet, used in printing and writing to represent the sounds of the spoken language: *the letters A to Z.* Same sign used for: **literal.**

- [Initialized sign similar to sign for **word**] Tap the thumb of the right *L hand,* palm facing forward, with a double movement against the extended left index finger, palm facing right.

letter[2] *n.* A written communication sent through the postal service: *to write a letter of complaint to the utility company.* Same sign used for: **mail.**

- [Shows licking a stamp and placing it on an envelope] Touch the extended thumb of the right *10 hand* to the lips, palm facing in, and then move the thumb downward to touch the fingertips of the left *open hand* held in front of the body, palm facing up.

letter³ *n.* (alternate sign) Same sign used for: **mail.**

- [Shows licking a stamp and placing it on an envelope] Touch the extended thumb of the right *10 hand* to the lips, palm facing in, and then move the thumb downward to touch the thumb of the left *10 hand* held in front of the chest, palm facing right.

lettuce¹ *n.* A plant with crisp, green leaves used in salad: *to put lettuce on my sandwich.*

- [Initialized sign similar to sign for **cabbage**] Touch the thumb of the right *L hand,* palm facing forward and index finger pointing up, to the right side of the forehead.

lettuce² *n.* (alternate sign)

- [Initialized sign similar to sign for **cabbage**] Tap the palm side of the right *L hand* against the right side of the forehead with a double movement.

lettuce³ *n.* See sign for CABBAGE.

level *adj.* See sign for EVEN¹.

lever¹ *n.* A bar, which rests on a raised central fulcrum, used for moving a weight supported on one end by pushing down on the other end: *Lift the rock with a lever.*

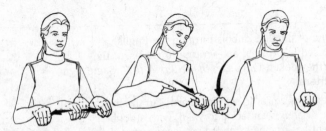

- [**pipe**³ + a gesture indicating where a lever is inserted + mime moving a lever] Beginning with the index-finger sides of both *O hands* in front of the body, palms facing down, move the hands away from each other to in front of each side of the body. Then insert the extended right index finger, palm facing down and finger pointing left, into the opening formed by the left *S hand,* held in front of the left side of the body, palm facing down. Then keeping the left *S hand* in front of the left side of the body, move the right *S hand* downward in front of the right shoulder.

lever² *n.* See sign for PIPE³.

liability *n.* See signs for AFFORD[1], BURDEN.

liberal *adj., n.* See signs for BROAD-MINDED, LIBERTY[1].

liberate *v.* See sign for SAVE[1].

liberty[1] *n.* Freedom from governmental or other external control: *We are proud of the liberty of our citizens.* Same sign used for: **liberal.**

- ■ [Initialized sign similar to sign for **save**[1]] Beginning with the wrists of both *L hands* crossed in front of the chest, palms facing in, twist the wrists to move the hands outward, ending with the hands in front of each shoulder, palms facing forward.

liberty[2] *n.* See signs for FREE[1], SAVE[1].

library *n.* **1.** A collection of books or other materials useful for reference, especially one that is organized and catalogued: *The university has a fine library.* **2.** The building in which such a collection is housed: *We can go to the library to study.*

- ■ [Initialized sign] Move the right *L hand,* palm facing forward, in a circle in front of the right shoulder.

license *n.* A permit to do something: *a driver's license.* Same sign used for: **permit.**

- ■ [Initialized sign similar to sign for **certificate**[2]] Tap the thumbs of both *L hands* with a double movement in front of the chest, palms facing forward.

lick *v.* To stroke with the tongue: *The dog licked my hand.*

- ■ [The fingers represent the tongue licking something] Brush the fingertips of the right *U hand,* palm facing back and fingers pointing down, forward with a double movement along the length of the palm of the upturned left *open hand,* held in front of the chest.

lid[1] *n.* A removable cover, as for a jar: *Put the lid back on the peanut butter, please.* Same sign used for: **cover, top.**

- ■ [Mime putting a lid on a jar] Bring the fingers of the right *open hand* from in front of the right shoulder, palm facing left and fingers pointing forward, in an arc down on top of the index-finger side of the left *C hand,* palm facing right in front of the left side of the chest.

lid[2] *n.* (alternate sign) Same sign used for: **cover, top.**

- [**bowl** + a gesture representing putting a cover over something] Beginning with the little fingers of both *curved hands* touching, palms facing up, bring the hands apart from each other and upward, ending with the palms facing each other. Then, beginning with the palm side of the right *curved hand* on the back of the left *curved hand,* both palms facing right, move the right hand in an arc to the right ending with the palms facing each other.

lie[1] *v.* **1.** To speak or write falsely with the intention of deceiving: *lied to his lawyer about the accident.* —*n.* **2.** Something said or written that is intended to deceive: *Don't tell your mother a lie.* Same sign used for: **falsehood, fib, perjury.**

- [The finger indicates that a person is speaking out of the side of the mouth when telling a lie] Move the side of the extended right index finger, palm facing down and finger pointing left, across the chin from right to left.

lie[2] *v., n.* (alternate sign) Same sign used for: **falsehood, fib, perjury.**

- [The hand movement indicates that a person is speaking out of the side of the mouth when telling a lie] Slide the index-finger side of the right *bent hand,* palm facing down, with a double movement across the chin from right to left.

lie[3] or **lie down** *v.* or *v. phrase.* To recline the body in a horizontal position: *to lie down on the couch.* Same sign used for: **recline.**

- [The fingers represent a person's legs in a reclining position] Beginning with the back of the right *V hand,* palm facing up, on the palm of the left *open hand,* palm facing up, pull the right hand in toward the body.

life *n.* See sign for LIVE[1].

lifeguard *n.* A person expert in swimming employed at a beach or swimming pool to assist bathers in danger: *The lifeguard watched the swimmers from the platform.*

- [**live**[1] + **guard**[1]] Beginning with both *L hands* in front of each side of the body, palms facing in and index fingers pointing toward each other, move the hands upward on each side of the chest. Then, with the wrists of both *S hands* crossed in front of the chest, palms facing in opposite directions, move the hands forward with a short double movement.

life jacket *n.* A sleeveless canvas jacket used as a life preserver to buoy one's body in water: *You'll have to wear a life jacket if you go sailing with us.*

- **[live¹ + stole]** Beginning with both *L hands* in front of each side of the body, palms facing in and index fingers pointing toward each other, move the hands upward on each side of the chest. Then move the fingertips of both *C hands* downward on each side of the chest.

lift *v.* See signs for RAISE¹˒².

light¹ *adj.* Bright; well-lighted; not dark: *Turn on the lamp to make the room lighter.* Same sign used for: **light bulb.**

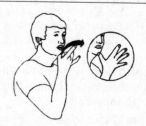

- Beginning with the fingertips of the right *8 hand* near the chin, palm facing in, flick the middle finger upward and forward with a double movement while opening into a *5 hand* each time.

light² *n.* Something that gives off light, as a lamp: *Turn on the light in the hallway.* Same sign used for: **shine.**

- [The hand shows the rays of light beaming from a lamp] Beginning with the right *flattened O hand* held above the right shoulder, palm facing down, open the fingers into a *5 hand.*

light³ *adj.* Not heavy: *a light load.*

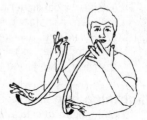

- [The gesture represents something light floating upward] Beginning with both *5 hands* with bent middle fingers in front of the waist, palms facing down, twist the wrists to raise the hands quickly toward each other and upward, ending with the hands in front of each side of the chest, bent middle fingers pointing in.

light⁴ *adj.* See sign for BRIGHT.

light a match See signs for IGNITE¹, STRIKE A MATCH.

light bulb *n.* See sign for LIGHT¹.

lighter *n.* A device with a spark used to ignite a cigarette: *He'd rather use a lighter than a match.*

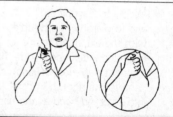

- [Mime starting a lighter] Bend the extended thumb of the right *10 hand*, palm facing in, up and down with a double movement in front of the right side of the chest.

lighthouse *n.* A tower with a bright light to guide ships through dangerous water: *The lighthouse beamed a light over the water.*

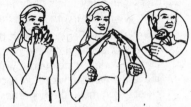

■ [**light**[1] + **house** + showing the moving light of a lighthouse] Beginning with the fingertips of the right *8 hand* near the chin, palm facing in, flick the middle finger upward and forward with a double movement while opening into a *5 hand* each time. Next, beginning with the fingertips of both *open hands* touching in front of the face, palms angled toward each other, bring the hands at a downward angle outward to in front of each shoulder and then straight down, ending with the fingers pointing forward and the palms facing each other. Then, with the left hand grasping the wrist of the right hand in front of the right shoulder, move the right *flattened O hand* in a circular movement by repeatedly twisting the wrist and opening the fingers into a *5 hand* each time.

---

lightning[1] *n.* A flash of electric sparks discharged in the atmosphere: *The lightning hit the tree.* Same sign used for: **bolt, thunderbolt.**

■ [Shows shape of lightning bolt] Beginning with the extended index fingers of both hands touching above the left shoulder, move the right hand downward with a jagged movement in front of the chest, ending in front of the waist, finger pointing forward and palm facing down.

---

lightning[2] *n.* (alternate sign) Same sign used for: **bolt, thunderbolt.**

■ [Shows shape of a lightning bolt] Beginning with the right extended index finger pointing up near the right side of the head, palm facing forward, move the right hand downward with a jagged movement to touch the index finger to the left extended index finger held up in front of the chest, palm facing forward.

---

lightning bug *n.* A beetle, active at night, with an organ near its tail that produces flashing light: *to watch lightning bugs at dusk.*

■ [**light**[1] + **bug**[1] + a gesture showing a lightning bug flashing its light] Beginning with the fingertips of the right *8 hand* near the chin, palm facing in, flick the middle finger upward and forward with a double movement while opening into a *5 hand* each time. Then, with the extended thumb of the right *3 hand* on the nose, palm facing left, bend the extended index and middle fingers with a repeated movement. Then, beginning with the right *flattened O hand* in front of the left shoulder, palm facing left, move the hand to the right in front of the chest with a wavy movement, opening and closing into a *curved hand* as the hand moves.

lightning rod *n.* A metal rod fixed to a building to conduct lightning safely away from the building and into the ground: *Luckily, the lightning struck the lightning rod and didn't hurt anyone.*

■ [**house** + a gesture indicating the location of a lightning rod on top of the roof + **lightning**²] Beginning with the fingertips of both *open hands* touching in front of the face, palms angled toward each other, bring the hands at a downward angle outward to in front of each shoulder and then straight down, ending with the fingers pointing forward and palms facing each other. Then place the fingertips of the left *B hand,* palm angled downward, at the wrist of the right hand, with extended right index finger pointing up in front of the face, palm facing forward. Then, beginning with the extended right index finger pointing up near the right side of the head, palm facing forward, and the left extended index finger pointing up in front of the left shoulder, palm facing forward, bring the right hand downward with a repeated jagged movement to touch the right index finger to the left index finger.

like¹ *v.* To be pleased with; find agreeable; enjoy: *like to watch TV.* Same sign used for: **fond of.**

■ Beginning with the bent thumb and middle finger of the right *5 hand* touching the chest, palm facing in, bring the hand forward while closing the fingers to form an *8 hand.*

like² *v.* (alternate sign) Same sign used for: **fond of.**

■ [Mime kissing the back of one's hand to show fondness] Bring the back of the right *S hand,* palm facing forward, back to the lips and then forward again.

like³ *prep.* **1.** Resembling; similar to: *sounds like a train.* **2.** As if there are indications of: *It feels like a storm brewing.* **3.** With characteristics of: *hungry like a bear.* See also sign for SAME¹.

■ [A directional sign in which the hand moves back and forth between the two objects being compared] Move the right *Y hand,* palm facing forward, from side to side with a double movement in front of the right side of the body.

like⁴ *v.* See sign for ENJOY.

likely *adj.* **1.** Probably destined to happen: *It is likely that it will rain.* **2.** Believable: *a likely excuse.* —*adv.* **3.** Probably: *They will very likely not pass the exam.* Same sign used for: **look like.**

limb

■ [A gesture moving from the eye + **like**[3]] With the thumb, index finger, and little finger of the right hand extended, bring the right hand from near the right side of the face, palm facing left, downward while changing into a *Y hand,* and move the right *Y hand* back and forth with a double movement in front of the right side of the chest, palm facing down.

limb *n.* A branch of a tree: *cut off a limb.* Same sign used for: **branch.**

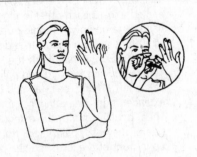

■ [**tree** + the fingers representing limbs growing from the tree] With the bent elbow of the left *5 hand* resting on the thumb side of the right *S hand,* wiggle the left fingers, palm facing back. Then slide the extended index finger and thumb of the right *G hand,* palm facing forward, along the length of the little finger of the left *5 hand,* palm facing in.

lime *n.* A sour, juicy, citrus fruit, green in color: *I like to put lime in my soda.*

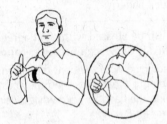

■ [Initialized sign showing slicing a lime] Slide the thumb of the right *L hand,* palm facing left and index finger pointing up, down the back of the left *S hand,* palm facing in, in front of the chest.

limit *v.* See sign for RESTRICT[1].

limp[1] *n.* **1.** A faltering walk as if lame: *to walk with a limp.* —*v.* **2.** To walk with a faltering gait: *to limp because of a sprained ankle.* Same sign used for: **gait.**

■ [**walk**[1,2] formed with an uneven movement] Beginning with both *open hands* in front of each side of the body, the right hand somewhat higher than the left hand and both palms facing down, move the hands forward in unequal arcs.

limp[2] *n.* See sign for CRIPPLED.

Lincoln, Abraham *n.* The sixteenth president of the United States: *Abraham Lincoln was president during the Civil War.*

■ [Abbreviation a-l] Touch the thumb of the right *A hand* to the forehead, palm facing left. Then touch the thumb of the right *L hand* to the forehead, palm facing left.

line *n.* **1.** A long, thin fiber, as a cord, wire, or rope: *Unwind the line and tie the boat to the dock.* **2.** A particular set of points when connected form a straight line: *Draw a line around the right answer.* **3.** A row of text in a document: *the last line of the paragraph.* Same sign used for: **string, thread.**

- [Shows shape of a line] Beginning with the extended little fingers of both *I hands* touching in front of the chest, palms facing in, move both hands outward.

line up *v. phrase.* To stand or cause to stand one behind the other in a row; form or cause to form a line: *Let's have the first graders line up on the playground.* Same sign used for: **align, queue, row.**

- [Represents people lined up in a row] Beginning with the little finger of the right *4 hand,* palm facing left, touching the index finger of the right *4 hand,* palm facing right, move the right hand back toward the chest and the left hand forward.

linguistics *n.* The study of language, including the examination of the patterns of words and sentences in one or more languages: *majored in linguistics in graduate school.*

- [Abbreviation **l-s** formed with a movement similar to sign for **language**] Beginning with the thumbs of both *L hands* touching in front of the body, palms facing down and index fingers pointing forward, bring the hands away from each other while changing into *S hands,* ending with both *S hands* in front of each side of the body, palms facing down.

link[1] *v.* See sign for BELONG[1].

link[2] *n.* See sign for RELATIONSHIP.

lint *n.* Miscellaneous pieces of fiber, as shed from fabric: *I have to pick the lint off my sweater.*

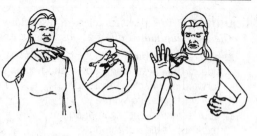

- [**dirty** + **white** + mime picking lint off oneself and tossing it away] With the back of the right *curved 5 hand* under the chin, palm facing down and fingers pointing left, wiggle the fingers. Then, beginning with the fingers of the right *5 hand* on the chest, pull the hand forward while closing the fingers to the thumb, forming a *flattened O hand.* Then touch the fingertips of the right *9 hand* near the right shoulder and the left hand near the left side of the body, palms facing in, and flick the right hand forward while opening into a *5 hand.*

lion *n.* A large, tawny-colored, flesh-eating member of the cat family, the male of which has a large mane on the back of the neck: *Lions are found in Africa and Asia.*

- [Shows shape and location of lion's mane] Beginning with the fingers of the right *curved 5 hand* pointing down over the forehead, palm facing down, move the hand back over the top of the head.

lip *n.* Either of the two moveable fleshy folds forming the edges of the mouth: *Watch my lips move when I speak.*

- [Location of one's lips] Draw a rectangle around the edge of the mouth with the extended right index finger, palm facing in.

lipread *v.* To understand speech by watching and interpreting the movements of a person's lip's while that person is speaking: *does not find it easy to lipread.* Same sign used for: **speechread.**

- [Sign **read**[1] over the lips] Move the fingertips of the right *V hand,* palm facing down, back and forth in front of the mouth with a double movement.

lipstick *n.* A cosmetic used for coloring the lips: *to put on lipstick before going out.*

- [Mime putting on lipstick] Move the fingers of the right *modified X hand* back and forth in front of the mouth with a double movement.

liquid crystal display (LCD) See sign for FLAT SCREEN DISPLAY.

liquidate *v.* To sell assets for cash, especially outside the ordinary course of business: *The office liquidated all of its equipment.* Related form: **liquidation** *n.*

- [**sell** + **everything**[1,2,3]] Beginning with both *flattened O hands* held in front of each side of the chest, palms down and fingers pointing down, swing the fingertips forward and back by twisting the wrists upward with a double movement. Then bring the knuckle side of the right *10 hand* down the thumb side of the left *10 hand.* Then, beginning with both *5 hands* together, throw the hands out to each side, palms up.

liquor *n.* See signs for COCKTAIL, WHISKEY.

lisp *v.* To talk imperfectly, especially with defective pronunciation of the sounds symbolized by *s* and *z*: *Some young children lisp.*

■ Move the fingers of the right *bent V hand* in a circle around the mouth, palm facing in.

list¹ *n.* **1.** A series of items written or printed in a sequence: *A shopping list for Christmas.* —*v.* **2.** To record in such a sequence: *She listed all her reasons for changing schools.* Same sign used for: **record, score.**

■ [The hand moves down a list of items on a page] Touch the little-finger side of the right *bent hand,* palm facing in, several times on the palm of the left *open hand,* palm facing right and fingers pointing up, as it moves from the fingers downward to the heel.

list² *n., v.* (alternate sign) Same sign used for: **record, score.**

■ [The finger points out items on a list] Touch the bent middle finger of the right *5 hand,* palm facing left, several times on the palm of the left *open hand,* palm facing right and fingers pointing up, as it moves from the fingers downward to the heel.

list³ *n., v.* (alternate sign) Same sign used for: **record, score.**

■ [The hand moves down a list of items on a page] Touch the index-finger side of the right *B hand,* palm facing down, several times on the palm of the left *open hand,* palm facing right and fingers pointing up, as it moves from the fingers downward to the heel.

list⁴ *n., v.* (alternate sign) Same sign used for: **record, score.**

■ [The hand moves down a list of items on a page] Touch the fingers of the right *flattened O hand,* palm facing down, several times on the palm of the left *open hand,* palm facing right and fingers pointing up, as it moves from the fingers downward to the heel.

list[5] *n.* (Used to designate a long series of items recorded in a sequence): *a long Christmas list.* Same sign used for: **long list, menu.**

- [The hand moves down a long list of items on a page] Touch the little-finger side of the right *bent hand*, palm facing in, from the fingertips of the left *open hand* down the left forearm to near the crook of the bent left arm.

listen[1] *v.* To attend with the ears: *listen to the music.*

- [The hand cups the ear in order to listen] Touch the thumb of the right *C hand*, palm facing left, near the right ear.

listen[2] *v.* (alternate sign)

- [Initialized sign] Touch the thumb of the right *L hand*, palm facing left, near the right ear.

listen[3] *v.* (alternate sign) Same sign used for: **eavesdrop.**

- [The fingers bring sound to the ear] With the thumb of the right *curved 3 hand*, palm facing left, touching the right ear, bend the extended index and middle fingers down with a short double movement.

listen[4] *v.* (alternate sign)

- [The fingers bring sound to the ear] Bring the thumb of the right *curved 3 hand*, palm facing left, back to touch near the right ear with a double movement, bending the index and middle fingers downward each time.

literal[1] *n.* A number that stays constant during programming: *In this program, the number "2" is a literal.*

- [**itself + number**] Move the knuckles of the right *10 hand*, palm facing left, against the extended left index finger, palm facing right and index finger pointing up. Then, with the fingertips of both *flattened O hands* touching, left palm facing up and right palm facing down, twist the wrists in opposite directions and touch the fingers again, ending with the left palm facing down and the right palm facing up.

literal[2] *adj.* See sign for LETTER[1].

litigate *v.* To make something the subject of a lawsuit; to perform the tasks entailed in the pursuit of a court case. Related form: **litigation** *n.*

- [An attacking gesture] Throw both *bent V hands* forward while opening into *V hands*, palms facing each other, and then pull the hands back while closing into *bent V hands* again near the chest.

litter *n.* See sign for TRASH[1].

little[1] *adj.* Not large: *a little box that fits in a purse or pocket.* See also signs for SMALL[1,2].

- [Shows a small size] Move both *open hands*, palms facing each other, toward each other with a short double movement in front of body.

little[2] *adj.* Not tall: *a little girl.* See also signs for SMALL[1,2]. Same sign used for: **short.**

- [Shows someone or something short in size] Move the right *bent hand*, palm facing down, with a short double movement in front of the right side of the body.

little bit See signs for TINY[1,2].

live[1] *v.* To exist or dwell: *to live in Ohio.* Same sign used for: **alive, life, revive, survival, survive.**

- [Initialized sign] Beginning with both *L hands* in front of each side of the body, palms facing in and index fingers pointing toward each other, move the hands upward on each side of the chest.

live[2] *v.* (alternate sign) Same sign used for: **alive, dwell, reside, residence, survival, survive.**

- Move both *A hands*, palms facing in, upward on each side of the chest.

living room *n*. A room for use by the family for leisure activities and for entertaining guests: *to sit in the living room reading*.

- [**fancy**[1] + **room**[1,2]] Brush the thumb of the right *5 hand*, palm facing left, upward on the chest with a double movement. Then, beginning with both *open hands* in front of each side of the body, palms facing each other, turn the hands sharply in opposite directions, ending with both palms facing in.

---

load *n*. See sign for PILE[1].

---

loaf[1] *v*. To be idle: *to loaf all afternoon*.

- [Initialized sign similar to sign for **vacation**] Touch the extended thumbs of both *L hands*, palms facing each other, near each armpit.

---

loaf[2] *n*. Anything, especially baked food, shaped in an oblong mass with a slightly rounded top: *a loaf of bread*.

- [Shows shape of a loaf] Beginning with the index fingers of both *C hands* touching in front of the body, palms facing down, bring the hands outward to in front of each side of the body.

---

loan *v*. See sign for LEND.

---

loath *adj*. Unwilling; reluctant: *loath to leave for college*. Same sign used for: **unwilling.**

- [**not**[1] + **admit**[1]] Bring the extended thumb of the right *10 hand* from under the chin, palm facing left, forward with a deliberate movement. Then move the right *open hand*, palm facing in and fingers pointing left, from the chest forward in an arc.

---

loathe *v*. See signs for ABHOR, DETEST[1,2].

---

lobster *n*. **1.** A large shellfish with prominent asymmetrical pincers: *setting traps for lobsters in the bay*. **2.** The edible meat of this shellfish: *a fancy seafood restaurant where we ate lobster*.

- [Represents a lobster's claws] Beginning with both *V hands* in front of each shoulder, palms facing forward, close the index and middle fingers with a double movement.

---

location[1] *n.* **1.** A position occupied by something: *looking for the location of the document.* **2.** An area where people have settled or reside or where a particular activity can take place: *a good location to camp.* Same sign used for: **local.**

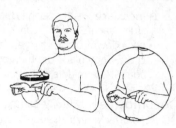

- [Initialized sign similar to sign for **area**[2]] Beginning with the thumbs of both *L hands* touching in front of the body, palms facing down, move the hands apart and back in a circular movement until they touch again near the chest.

location[2] *n.* See sign for PLACE[1].

lock[1] *n.* **1.** A device for securing something when it is closed, as a door, drawer, etc.: *a house protected with a new electronic lock.* —*v.* **2.** To secure an object, as a door or drawer, with a lock: *Lock the front door.*

- [Represents the wrists locked together] Beginning with both *S hands* in front of the body, right hand above left and both palms facing down, turn the right hand over by twisting the wrist, ending with the back of the right *S hand,* palm facing up, on the back of the left *S hand,* palm facing down.

lock[2] *v.* (alternate sign)

- [Shows twisting a key in a lock] Twist the knuckle of the right *X hand,* palm facing down, in the palm of the left *open hand,* palm facing right and fingers pointing forward.

locked into See sign for BIND.

locker *n.* See sign for CLOSET[2].

locket[1] *n.* A case, as of gold or silver, usually worn on a chain as a necklace and holding a picture or other trinket or memento: *wears an antique locket around her neck with a picture of her grandparents.*

- [**necklace**[2,3] + location of a locket hanging from a chain] Beginning with both *curved 5 hands* in front of each shoulder, palms facing each other, bring the hands downward and together, interlocking the index fingers and thumbs in front of the chest. Then bring the fingers of both *modified C hands* together in front of the chest, palms facing in.

locket[2] *n.* (alternate sign) Same sign used for: **pendant**.

■ [**necklace**[2,3] + the shape of a locket] Bring the extended index fingers of both hands from near each side of the neck downward toward each other to the middle of the chest. Then place the thumb side of the right *F hand* against the middle of the chest, palm facing left.

locomotive *n.* An engine that pulls a train or individual cars on a railroad: *The locomotive pulled twenty cars along the tracks.* Same sign used for: **engine.**

■ [**front** + **train**[1] + a gesture showing smoke coming from the smokestack] Move the right *open hand*, palm facing in, downward from in front of the forehead to in front of the chest. Then rub the fingers of the right *H hand* with a double movement across the fingers of the left *H hand*, both palms facing down. Then, with the left hand grasping the wrist of the right *E hand*, palm facing in, open the right hand into a *5 hand* with a double movement.

loft *n.* **1.** A space, as a storage area or room, just under the roof: *a teenager who prefers to sleep in the loft.* **2.** An upper story of a business building, warehouse, etc., used for work, storage, or sometimes converted to provide living quarters: *made an enormous apartment out of a loft downtown.*

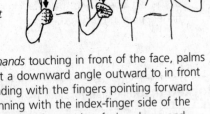

■ [**house** + **floor** formed at an elevated level] Beginning with the fingertips of both *open hands* touching in front of the face, palms angled toward each other, bring the hands at a downward angle outward to in front of each shoulder and then straight down, ending with the fingers pointing forward and the palms facing each other. Then, beginning with the index-finger side of the both *bent hands* touching each other in front of the face, palms facing down and fingers pointing forward, bring the hands apart a short distance.

logic *n.* **1.** The science investigating the basic principles of reliable reasoning and thought: *a fine mind equipped to study logic.* **2.** Sound judgment based on reason: *She always uses logic in her arguments.* Related form: **logical** *adj.*

■ [Initialized sign similar to sign for **theory**] Move the right *L hand*, palm facing left, in a double circle in front of the right side of the forehead.

log off *v. phrase.* (of a computer user) To terminate a communication session with a networked or multiuser computer: *log off the computer for the evening.* Same sign used for: **sign off.**

■ [**sign**[3] + **disconnect**] Place the fingers of the right *H hand* firmly down on the palm of the left *open hand* held in front of the chest, palm angled right. Then, beginning with the thumb and index fingertips of each hand intersecting, palms facing each other and right hand nearer the chest than the left hand, release the fingers and pull the left hand forward and the right hand back toward the right shoulder.

loiter *v.* To spend time idly lingering in or around a place: *not allowed to loiter at the bus station.*

■ [**lazy** + **apathy**] Tap the palm side of the right *L hand* against the left side of the chest. Then drop both *5 hands*, palms facing down, downward in front of each side of the chest.

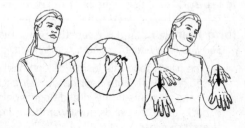

lollipop *n.* A piece of hard candy on a stick: *Some people suck on a lollipop instead of smoking.* Same sign used for: **Popsicle** (*trademark*), **sucker.**

■ [Mime holding and licking a lollipop] Bring the thumb side of the right *X hand*, palm facing left, in a double circular movement back toward the mouth.

lone *adj.* See signs for ALONE[1,2].

lonely[1] *adj.* Affected with a depressed sensation resulting from feeling alone: *a lonely person who finds it difficult to make friends.* Alternate form: **lonesome.**

■ Bring the side of the extended right index finger, palm facing left, from near the nose slowly downward in front of the mouth.

lonely[2] *adj.* See signs for ALONE[1,2].

long *adj.* Having a greater than usual extent in space or time: *to walk a long way; to wait a long time.* See also sign for LENGTH.

■ [The finger measures out a long length] Move the extended right index finger from the wrist up the length of the extended left arm to near the shoulder.

long ago[1] In the distant past: *fossils of creatures that existed long ago.* Same sign used for: **ancient, formerly, historic, primitive, used to.**

- [Indicates a time far in the past] Beginning with both *5 hands* in front of the right side of the body, left hand forward of the right hand and palms facing in opposite directions, move the hands upward in large alternating arcs back over the right shoulder.

long ago[2] *adv.* See signs for AGO[2], PRIMITIVE.

long hair Hair that has a length greater than usual: *She has long hair that she has never cut.*

- [The hands show the length of long hair] Beginning with both *bent hands* near each side of the head, palms facing in and fingers pointing back, bring the hands downward to in front of each shoulder.

long list See sign for LIST[5].

long sleeve A sleeve that extends to the wrist: *a shirt with long sleeves.*

- [Shows length of long sleeve] Touch the little-finger side of the right *open hand,* palm facing back, near the shoulder and then the back of the wrist of the bent left arm.

look at *v. phrase.* To direct the eyes toward in order to see (a specific thing): *look at the picture.*

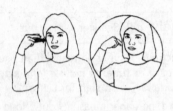

- [**look** directed toward something] Move the right *V hand,* palm facing down and extended fingers pointing forward, forward a short distance in the direction of the referent.

look back[1] *v. phrase.* To recall the past: *to look back on the major events in American history.* Same sign used for: **memorial, memory.**

- [**look at** directed toward the past] Move the fingers of the right *V hand,* palm facing down and fingers pointing back, back beside the right side of head.

look back[2] *v. phrase.* See sign for HINDSIGHT.

look down at or **on** *v. phrase.* See sign for CONTEMPT.

look for[1] *v. phrase.* To search for: *Wait while I look for my keys.* Same sign used for: **check for, examine, explore, hunt for, scour, search for, seek.**

- [Shows repeated searching for something] Move the right C *hand,* palm facing left, with a double movement in a circle in front of the face.

look for[2] *v. phrase.* (alternate sign) Same sign used for: **check for, examine, explore, hunt for, scour, search for, seek.**

- [Shows repeated searching for something] Move both C *hands,* palms facing in opposite directions, with an alternating movement in front of the face.

look for[3] *v. phrase.* (alternate sign) Same sign used for: **check for, physical examination, examine, hunt for, scour, search for, seek.**

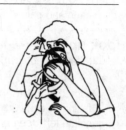

- [Shows repeated searching for something] Move both C *hands,* palms facing in opposite directions, with a repeated alternating movement beginning in front of the face and moving down to in front of the chest with each movement.

look out *v. phrase.* To watch carefully for danger: *Look out for cars crossing the street.* Same sign used for: **watch out, yield.**

- [Represents the eyes moving quickly to observe something] Beginning with the right V *hand* near the right side of the nose, palm facing left and fingers pointing up, bring the hand forward and outward to the right and then downward in front of the chest, ending with the palm facing down and the fingers angled to the left.

look over[1] *v. phrase.* To inspect or examine (a person): *Look him over to see the way he's dressed.* Same sign used for: **browse, eye.**

- [Represents the eyes moving up and down someone to inspect him or her] Move the fingers of the right V *hand,* palm facing down and fingers pointing forward, up and down with a double movement in front of the right side of the chest, following the fingers with the eyes as the hand moves.

look over[2] *v. phrase.* To inspect or examine (something): *to look over the work he did.* Same sign used for: **browse, observe, view.**

look over

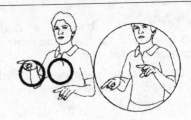

- [Represents the eyes surveying something] Beginning with both *V hands* in front of each side of the chest, right hand higher than the left hand, both palms facing down and fingers pointing forward, move the hands in double alternating circles. [This sign can be formed with one hand.]

look over[3] *v. phrase.* See signs for SCAN[1,2,3].

look up[1] *v. phrase.* **1.** To raise one's eyes: *I looked up when he passed.* **2. look up to** *v. phrase.* To have respect for: *He looks up to his teacher.* Same sign used for: **admire.**

- [Represents the eyes looking up at something] Beginning with both *V hands* in front of the chest, palms facing down and fingers pointing forward, move the hands upward while tipping the palms forward, ending with the hands in front of the face, right hand higher than the left hand and palms facing forward.

look up[2] *v. phrase.* To search for, as in a reference book or online database: *to look up a phone number.*

- [The fingers seem to paging through a book to look up something] Brush the extended thumb of the right *10 hand*, palm facing down, with a double movement in an arc across the palm of the left *open hand*, palm facing up.

look alike To have a similar appearance: *The three sisters really look alike.* See also sign for ALIKE[1]. Same sign used for: **resemblance.**

- [**looks** + **like**[3]] Move the extended right index finger in a circle around the face, finger pointing in. Then move the right *Y hand*, palm facing forward, from side to side with a double movement in front of the right side of the chest.

look like See signs for LIKELY, SEEM.

looks *n.* See sign for APPEARANCE[2].

loop *n.* A sequence of computer instructions that is repeatedly executed until some specified condition is met: *caught in an endless loop because of bad programming.*

- [Shape of a loop] Move the extended right index finger, palm facing down and finger pointing left, in a large circle with a double movement around the extended left index finger, palm facing in and finger pointing right.

loose[1] *adj.* Not firmly fastened: *a loose button.* Same sign used for: **flabby.**

■ [Demonstrates something that is loose and moves easily] With the extended left index finger, palm facing down and finger pointing right, grasped between the thumb and bent middle finger of the right *5 hand,* palm facing left, move the right hand up and down with a double movement.

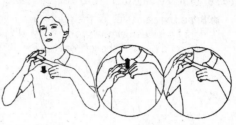

loose[2] *adj.* See sign for DISCONNECT.

loose tooth A tooth that is not firmly fastened: *The child has a loose tooth.*

■ [Shows location of a loose tooth] Wiggle a front tooth with the right thumb and index finger.

lopsided *adj.* **1.** Not level; leaning to one side: *a lopsided shelf.* **2.** Larger or heavier on one side; not balanced: *trying to carry a bulky, lopsided package.*

■ Beginning with both *open hands* in front of each side of the chest, palms facing down and fingers pointing forward, and hands angled downward to the right, drop the right hand while tipping the right side of the body downward at the same time.

Lord *n.* **1.** The Supreme Being; God: *religions that share a belief in the Lord.* **2.** Jesus Christ: *Christians who believe in the Lord.*

■ [Initialized sign similar to sign for **king**] Move the right *L hand,* palm facing left, from the left shoulder diagonally down to the right side of the waist, ending with the palm facing down and the index finger pointing forward.

lose[1] *v.* To come to be without: *I lost my wallet at the supermarket.*

■ [The hands seem to drop something as if to lose it] Beginning with the fingertips of both *flattened O hands* touching in front of the body, palms facing up, drop the fingers quickly downward and away from each other while opening into *5 hands,* ending with both palms angled down and fingers angled downward.

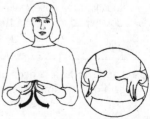

lose

lose[2] *v.* To be defeated in: *to lose the game.*
- Bring the palm side of the right *V hand* from in front of the right shoulder, palm facing forward, downward to land in the upturned palm of the left *open hand* in front of the body.

lose[3] *v.* See sign for DECREASE[1].

loss *n.* See sign for DECREASE[1].

lots *adj.* See signs for A LOT, MANY, MUCH.

lotion *n.* A liquid preparation for cleansing, soothing, disinfecting, or smoothing the skin: *She put lotion on her rough hands.*
- [Shows pouring lotion from a bottle into one's hand] Bring the thumb of the right *Y hand* from in front of the right shoulder, palm facing right, downward to touch the left *open hand* held in front of the chest, palm facing up and fingers pointing right.

lots to do See sign for BUSY[2].

loud[1] *adj.* (Of sound) Having marked intensity or great volume: *The horn made a loud blast.*
- [**hear** formed with both hands + **noise**] Move both extended index fingers from pointing to each ear forward while changing into *S hands* and shake them with a repeated movement.

loud[2] *adj.* See sign for NOISE.

lousy *adj.* Slang. Of low quality; extremely poor: *did a lousy job painting the living room.* Related form: **louse** *n.* Same sign used for: **worse.**
- Beginning with the thumb of the right *3 hand* touching the nose, palm facing left, bring the hand downward in front of the chest.

love[1] *v.* **1.** To have a deep affectionate feeling for: *I really love my dog.* —*n.* **2.** A warm regard or affectionate feeling: *to have a great love of books.*

■ [The hands bring something that is loved close to oneself] With the wrists of both *S hands* crossed in front of the chest, palms facing in, bring the arms back against the chest.

love[2] *v.* See sign for I LOVE YOU.

lovely *adj.* See signs for BEAUTIFUL[1,2].

lover *n.* See sign for SWEETHEART.

low[1] *adj.* Existing close to the floor or ground; not high: *a low shelf.* Related form: **lower** *adj.*
■ [Initialized sign moving to a lower location] Move the right *L hand* downward in front of the right side of the chest, palm facing forward.

low[2] *adj.* (alternate sign) Related form: **lower** *adj.* Same sign used for: **demote.**
■ [Indicates a location lower than another location] Beginning with both *bent hands* in front of each shoulder, palms facing each other, move them downward in front of each side of the chest.

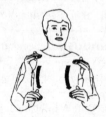

low[3] *adv.* See sign for LESS[1].

loyal *adj.* Faithful and devoted, as to one's country or friends: *to be a loyal follower of the cause.*
■ [Initialized sign formed similar to the sign for **respect**] Beginning with the thumb of the right *L hand,* palm facing left, touching the forehead, move the right hand forward in an arc.

LP *n.* Short for *long-playing.* See signs for RECORD[1,2].

lubrication *n.* See sign for OIL.

luck *n.* **1.** Something that seems to cause things, whether good or bad, to happen by chance: *We wish you good luck.* **2.** Success; good fortune: *She's had a lot of luck in her job.* Related form: **lucky** *adj.* Same sign used for: **fortunate.**

luggage

■ Beginning with the bent middle finger of the right *5 hand*, palm facing in, touching the chin, twist the wrist to swing the hand forward with a quick movement, ending with the palm angled forward.

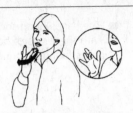

luggage *n.* See signs for BAGGAGE, PURSE[1].

lullaby *n.* A quiet song used to lull a child to sleep: *singing a lullaby to the baby.*

■ [**music** + **sleep**[1]] Swing the little-finger side of the right *open hand* with a double movement along the length of the curved left arm held in front of the body. Then, beginning with the right *curved 5 hand* in front of the face, bring the hand downward while closing the fingers into a *flattened O hand* in front of the chest.

lumbago *n.* See sign for BACKACHE.

lumbar *adj.* See sign for BACK[1].

lumber *n.* See signs for WOOD[1,2].

luminous *adj.* See sign for SHINY[1].

lump *n.* See signs for AMOUNT[1,2], BUMP[1,2,3].

lunch[1] *n.* A light meal eaten at midday: *time for lunch.*

■ [Initialized sign similar to sign for **eat**] Tap the thumb of the right *L hand*, palm facing left, against the chin with a double movement.

lunch[2] *n.* (alternate sign)

■ [**eat** + **noon**[1,2]] Bring the fingers of the right *flattened O hand* to the lips, palm facing down. Then place the elbow of the bent right arm, arm extended up and open right palm facing forward, on the back of the left *open hand* held in front of the body, palm facing down.

lung *n.* Either of the two respiratory organs in humans and other vertebrates used for the exchange of air so as to bring oxygen to the blood: *to take fresh air into the lungs by breathing deeply.*

■ [Shows location of one's lungs] Rub the fingertips of both *bent hands*, palms facing in opposite directions, up and down near the center of the chest with a repeated movement.

lurch *v.* To jerk suddenly: *The train lurched forward.*

■ [Demonstrates movement when one lurches] With the body held at an angle, left shoulder higher than the right shoulder, hold both *open hands* in front of the body, left hand higher than the right and the palms angled left. Then change into *1 hands* in the same positions and alternately move each hand forward in lurching arcs.

lush *adj.* See sign for LUXURIANT.

lust[1] *n.* **1.** A strong desire, as a sexual desire, or intense craving: *to feel overwhelming lust for someone.* —*v.* **2.** To have a strong desire: *to lust after money.*

■ [Initialized sign similar to sign for **passionate**] Move the palm side of the right *L hand* downward on the chest with a double movement.

lust[2] *n., v.* (alternate sign)

■ [Similar to sign for **thirsty**, representing an insatiable thirst] Move the extended right index finger, palm facing in and finger pointing up, downward with a double movement on the length of the neck, bending the finger down each time as it moves.

Lutheran *n.* A member of the church founded by Martin Luther: *Lutherans form the majority in the Scandinavian countries.*

■ [Initialized sign] Tap the extended thumb of the right *L hand*, palm facing forward, with a double movement against the palm of the left *open hand*, palm facing right.

luxuriant *adj.* Being lush and green; abundant in growth: *a luxuriant forest.* Same sign used for: **lush.**

■ [**tree** + **thick**[4] + **horde**] With the elbow of the bent right arm on the back of the left hand held across the body, shake the right *5 hand*, palm facing in, with a repeated movement near the right side of the head. Then bring the right *modified C hand*, palm facing in, from in front of the mouth forward in an arc. Then move both *curved 5 hands*, palms facing down, forward from in front of the face.

luxury *n.* See signs for FANCY[1,2].

lynch *v.* See sign for HANG[3].

lyrics *pl. n.* The words of a song: *George Gershwin wrote the music and Ira Gershwin the lyrics.*

■ [**short**[1] + a gesture showing the rhythm of lyrics] Rub the middle-finger side of the right *H hand* with a short repeated movement on the index-finger side of the left *H hand*. Then swing the extended right index finger with a double movement along the length of the left *curved hand* held in front of the body.

M

macaroni *n.* A pasta in the form of small hollow tubes: *We'll have macaroni and cheese for dinner.*

- [Initialized sign similar to sign for **spaghetti**[1]] Move both *M hands* downward from in front of each side of the body toward each other with a circular double movement.

machine *n.* An apparatus consisting of fixed and moving parts functioning together to do specific work: *a washing machine.* Same sign used for: **engine, factory, industry, manufacture, mechanism, motor, plant, run.**

- [Represents movement of gears meshing together] With the fingers of both *curved 5 hands* loosely meshed together, palms facing in, move the hands up and down in front of the chest with a repeated movement.

machine gun *n.* An automatic gun capable of continuous fire: *to fight the enemy with machine guns.*

- [Mime holding a machine gun] Beginning with both *S hands* in front of the right side of the body, right hand forward of the left hand and palms facing in opposite directions, shake the hands with a repeated movement as the hands move slightly forward.

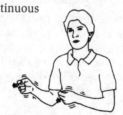

macro *n.* A set of abbreviated keystrokes that activate a sequence of computer instructions: *to write and execute macros in a word processing program.* Alternate form: **macroinstruction.**

- [Initialized sign] Beginning with the fingertips of both *M hands* touching in front of the chest, palms facing each other, bring the hands straight apart to in front of each side of the chest.

mad *adj.* See signs for ANGER[2], CROSS[2].

magazine *n.* A periodical publication containing stories, articles, photographs, etc.: *to read a magazine during the plane trip.* See also sign for JOURNAL[1]. Same sign used for: **brochure, catalog, pamphlet.**

■ [Shows the spine of a magazine] Grasp the little-finger side of the left *open hand*, palm angled up, with the index finger and thumb of the right *A hand*, and slide the right hand from heel to fingertips of the left hand with a double movement.

maggot *n.* A soft, legless, immature larva, representing the early feeding stage of a fly's development: *The decayed body was covered with maggots.*

■ [**bug**[1] + showing the movement of a worm] With the extended thumb of the right *3 hand* on the nose, palm facing left, bend the extended index and middle fingers with a repeated movement. Then move the palm side of the right *X hand* across the palm of the left *open hand* from the heel to the fingers while bending the right index finger up and down as the hand moves.

magic *n.* **1.** The art of commanding supernatural powers to influence events or produce effects normally considered impossible: *a fictional world in which people appear and disappear by magic.* **2.** The art of creating the illusion of magical acts: *By magic, he pulled a dove out of the hat.*
—*adj.* **3.** Accomplished as if by magic: *learning to do magic tricks.*

■ [The hands seem to cast a spell] Beginning with both *S hands* in front of each side of the body, palms facing forward, drop the hands downward and forward with a quick double movement while opening into *5 hands* each time.

magician *n.* **1.** A person who attempts or purports to exercise supernatural powers: *The ancient magician cast a spell on the entire kingdom.* **2.** A person who entertains by performing magic tricks, as sleight-of-hand: *The magician seemed to find coins in the children's ears!*

■ [**magic** + **person marker**] Beginning with both *A hands* in front of each side of the chest, palms facing forward, drop the hands downward and forward with a quick movement while opening into *5 hands*, palms facing down and fingers pointing forward. Then move both *open hands*, palms facing each other, downward along each side of the body.

magnet[1] *n.* A piece of metal that has the property of attracting smaller pieces of metal: *cars drawn upward by the giant magnet in the junkyard.* Related form: **magnetic** *adj.*

■ [Demonstrates action of a magnet pulling something to itself] Beginning with the right *flattened C hand,* palm angled forward, near the palm of the left *open hand,* palm facing right and fingers pointing up, bring the index-finger side of the right hand against the left palm while closing the right fingers into a *flattened O hand.*

magnet[2] *n.* (alternate sign) Related form: **magnetic** *adj.*

■ [Initialized sign showing the action of a magnet pulling something to itself] Beginning with both *M hands* near each other in front of the chest, palms and fingers pointing down, swing the fingers toward each other to overlap in front of the chest with a double movement.

magnetic *adj.* See sign for ABSORB[1].

magnifying glass *n.* A lens that causes things to look larger than they are: *to look at the small print through a magnifying glass.*

■ [**expand**[1] + mime holding a magnifying glass to look at something] Beginning with the little-finger side of the right *S hand* on top of the index-finger side of the left *S hand,* palms facing in opposite directions, move the hands away from each other while opening the fingers into *curved hands* in front of each side of the chest. Then, with the right *modified X hand* in front of the right shoulder, palm facing left, bring the right hand downward with a short double movement toward the palm of the left *open hand* held in front of the body, palm facing up and fingers pointing right.

magnitude *n.* Greatness of size, amount, or importance: *I have a problem of great magnitude.*

■ [**huge** formed with an exaggerated movement] Beginning with the palm sides of both *modified C hands* touching each other in front of the chest, move the right hand upward with a large circular movement to near the right side of the head and the left hand downward with a large circular movement to in front of the left side of the body.

mail[1] *n.* **1.** Letters, packages, etc., sent by means of the postal service or an alternate agency: *The mail doesn't get delivered on holidays.* —*v.* **2.** Alternate form: **mail out.** To send by mail: *to mail a letter; to mail out form letters to prospective clients.* Same sign used for: **send, send out.**

mail

■ [Natural gesture for tossing something forward] Beginning with the right *O hand* in front of the right shoulder, palm facing forward, move the hand quickly forward while opening into a *curved 5 hand.*

---

mail[2] *v.* (alternate sign) Alternate form: **mail out.** Same sign used for: **send, send out.**

■ [Shows sending something forward] Flick the fingertips of the right *bent hand* forward across the back of the left *open hand,* both palms facing down, with a quick movement, straightening the right fingers as the right hand moves forward.

---

mail[3] *n.* See signs for EMAIL[1,2], LETTER[2,3].

---

mailbox *n.* **1.** A public box from which mail is collected and distributed: *Put the letter in the mailbox on the corner.* **2.** A private box into which one's mail is delivered: *new magazines in my mailbox.*

■ [**letter**[2,3] + **room**[2]] Touch the extended thumb of the right *10 hand* to the lips, palm facing in, and then move the thumb downward to touch the thumb of the right *A hand* held in front of the body, palm facing in. Then, beginning with both *B hands* in front of each side of the chest, palms facing each other and fingers pointing forward, move the hands deliberately in opposite directions, ending with the left hand near the chest and the right hand several inches forward of the left hand, both palms facing in.

---

maim *v.* To disable by depriving of some part of the body or its use: *He was maimed in the war, when he lost a leg.*

■ [Represents cutting off a limb to maim] Bring the fingers of the right *B hand,* palm facing left, downward with a double movement near the bent left forearm held in front of the body.

---

main *adj.* See signs for IMPORTANT[1,2], SPECIALIZE[1].

---

mainboard *n.* See sign for MOTHERBOARD.

Maine *n.* See sign for PITTSBURGH.

---

mainstream[1] *n.* **1.** The principal course, trend, or direction: *This artist's work has always been in the mainstream.* —*adj.* **2.** Belonging to the most widely accepted group: *a radio station that plays mainstream music.* **3.** Being integrated into regular, especially public school programs: *to attend mainstream classes rather than special ones.* —*v.* **4.** To place in mainstream classes: *These children are ready to be mainstreamed.* Same sign used for: **merge.**

■ [Initialized sign indicating things coming together] Beginning with both *M hands* in front of each side of the chest, palms facing down and fingers angled toward each other, move the hands forward and toward each other, ending with the index fingers of both hands together in front of the chest.

mainstream[2] *n., adj.* (alternate sign) Same sign used for: **blend, emerge, integrate, integration, merge.**

■ [Represents things coming together to merge] Beginning with both *5 hands* in front of each side of the chest, palms facing down and fingers pointing toward each other, move the hands downward and forward toward each other, ending with the right hand on the back of the left hand in front of the chest.

maintain *v.* See signs for FIX[1,2], KEEP.

maintenance *n.* See signs for ALIMONY, WRENCH.

major *v.* See sign for SPECIALIZE[1].

majority *n.* The larger number, especially a number larger than half the total: *The majority of the first-grade class has learned to read.*

■ [**specialize**[1] + **class**] Slide the little-finger side of the right *B hand*, palm facing left and fingers pointing forward, along the length of the index finger of the left *B hand*, palm facing right and fingers pointing forward. Then, beginning with both *C hands* in front of each side of the chest, palms facing each other, bring the hands away from each other in outward arcs while turning the palms in.

make[1] *v.* To put together or bring into being: *to make a cake.* Same sign used for: **create, form, formulate, manufacture, produce.**

■ [The hands seem to be molding something] Beginning with the little-finger side of the right *S hand* on the index-finger side of the left *S hand*, separate the hands slightly, twist the wrists in opposite directions, and touch the hands together again.

make[2] *v.* (alternate sign) Same sign used for: **create, form, formulate, manufacture, produce.**

■ [The hands seem to be molding something] Beginning with the little-finger side of the right *S hand* on the index-finger side of the left *S hand*, twist the wrists in opposite directions with a small, quick, grinding movement.

make an effort See sign for ATTEMPT.

make believe[1] To pretend or imagine: *Let's make believe we're king and queen.*

- ■ [**make**[1] + **believe**] Beginning with the little-finger side of the right *S hand* on the index-finger side of the left *S hand*, palms facing in opposite directions, separate the hand slightly, twist the wrists in opposite directions, and touch the hands together again. Then move the extended right index finger from in front of the face downward while opening the hand, ending with the right hand clasping the left hand in front of the body, palms facing each other.

make believe[2] (alternate sign)

- ■ Move the extended right index finger from in front of the face, palm facing forward and finger pointing up, downward while forming a *flattened O hand* near the heel of the left hand held in front of the chest, palm facing up and fingers pointing forward. Then move the right hand forward on the left palm while opening and closing the fingers with a repeated movement.

make believe[3] See sign for IMAGINE.

make love See sign for PET[2].

make public See sign for INFORM[3].

makeshift *adj.* Serving as a temporary replacement or substitute: *a makeshift handle for the pot.* Same sign used for: **good enough.**

- ■ Beginning with the bent middle finger of the right *5 hand* touching the chin, palm facing in, move the hand forward while twisting the wrist, ending with the palm facing down.

make up *v. phrase.* See sign for INVENT.

make-up[1] or **makeup** *n.* Cosmetics for the face: *to put on your make-up before the party.* Same sign used for: **cosmetics.**

- ■ [Mime dabbing make-up on one's face] Move the fingertips of both *flattened O hands*, palms facing each other, in double alternating circles near each cheek.

make-up[2] or **makeup** *n.* (alternate sign) Same sign used for: **cosmetics**.

■ [Mime taking make-up from a container and applying it to the face] Beginning with the fingers of the right *flattened O hand*, palm facing down, on the index-finger side of the left *S hand*, palm facing right, move the right hand upward and rub the fingertips with a circular movement on the right cheek.

make up your mind See sign for DECIDE[1].

malady *n.* See signs for SICK[1,2].

Malaysia *n.* A country in southeast Asia: *The capital of Malaysia is Kuala Lumpur.*

■ Beginning with both *open hands* on each side of the head, palms facing each other and fingers pointing up, move the hands up and down with an alternating movement.

male *n.* See signs for MAN[1,2,3], BOY[1].

malignant *adj.* See sign for CANCER. Related form: **malignancy** *n.*

malleable *adj.* Capable of being hammered or pressed into various shapes: *Gold is a malleable metal.*

■ [hammer + a gesture seeming to mold something in one's hand] With the right *modified X hand* in front of the right shoulder, palm facing left, bring the right hand downward in a large arc to the palm of the left *open hand* held in front of the body, palm facing up and fingers pointing right. Then, beginning with the right *curved 5 hand* in front of the right shoulder and the left *curved 5 hand* in front of the left side of the chest, palms facing each other, bring the hands toward each other while bending the fingers up and down, ending with the fingertips of both hands touching in front of the body.

maltreatment *n.* See sign for TORTURE.

mama *n.* See signs for MOTHER[1,2].

mammillary *adj.* See signs for NIPPLE[1,2].

mammoth *n.* A huge hairy elephant with long, curved tusks, now extinct: *The woolly mammoth was nine feet high at the shoulder.*

man

■ [**huge** + **elephant**[1] + showing the shape of a mammoth's tusks] Beginning with both *modified C hands* together in front of the chest, palms facing each other, move the hands straight outward to in front of each shoulder. Then, beginning with the back of the right *B hand* against the nose, palm angled forward, move the hand downward and forward in a large wavy movement. Finally, beginning with the thumb side of both *F hands* near each side of the chin, palms facing each other, move the hands downward in forward arcs to in front of the chest.

man[1] *n.* An adult male person: *a man who owns his own business.* Same sign used for: **gentleman, guy, male.**

■ [A combination of **boy**[1] + indicating the height of a man] Beginning with the thumb side of the right *flattened C hand* in front of the right side of the forehead, palm facing left, bring the hand straight forward while closing the fingers to the thumb.

man[2] *n.* (alternate sign) Same sign used for: **gentleman, guy, male.**

■ [A gesture beginning near the male area of the head + **polite**] Beginning with the thumb of the right *10 hand* touching the right side of the forehead, palm facing left, bring the hand downward while opening into a *5 hand,* ending with the thumb touching the chest, palm facing left.

man[3] *n.* (alternate sign) Same sign used for: **male.**

■ [A gesture beginning near the male area of the head + **polite**] Beginning with the thumb of the right *5 hand* touching the right side of the forehead, palm facing left, bring the hand downward to touch the thumb to the chest.

manage *v.* To take charge of: *to manage a business.* Same sign used for: **administer, control, direct, govern, handle, in charge of, manipulate, operate, preside over, regulate, reign, rule, run (a meeting).**

■ [Mime holding a horse's reins indicating being in a position of management] Beginning with both *modified X hands* in front of each side of the body, right hand forward of the left hand

and palms facing each other, move the hands forward and back with a repeated alternating movement.

---

management *n.* The control or handling of something, as a corporation or department: *The company has good management.*

■ **[manage + -ment]** Beginning with both *X hands* in front of each side of the chest, right hand slightly forward of the left hand and palms facing each other, move the hands forward and back with a repeated alternating movement. Then, beginning with the ring-finger side of the right *M hand,* palm facing forward, on the back of the left *open hand,* palm facing right and fingers pointing up, bring the right hand up over the left fingertips and then down the left palm to the heel.

---

manager *n.* See sign for ADMINISTRATOR[1].

---

mandate *n.* See sign for MUST.

---

mandatory *adj.* See sign for DEMAND[2].

---

mane *n.* The long hair around the neck of a horse or lion: *The male lion is distinguished by a long, thick mane.*

■ **[long** + a gesture showing long hair] Move the extended right index finger from the wrist up the length of the extended left arm to near the shoulder. Then, beginning with the fingers of both *curved hands* touching at the top of the head, palms facing down, bring the hands downward near each side of the head with a wavy movement while opening the fingers, ending with both *open hands* near each shoulder, palms facing down and fingers pointing toward each other.

---

maneuver *n.* **1.** A skillful, complex movement involving changes in direction and the avoidance of obstacles: *His maneuvers through the traffic amazed us.* —*v.* **2.** To move skillfully in this way: *She quickly maneuvered her way through the crowd.*

■ [Initialized sign showing the action of maneuvering] Beginning with both *M hands* in front of the chest, fingers pointing forward, move the hands forward with a wavy movement.

---

mangle *v.* To ruin, injure, or disfigure, as by slashing or crushing: *He mangled his car in the accident.*

■ **[damage[1] + mix[1] + explode[2]]** Beginning with both *5 hands* in front of the chest, right hand crossed over the left hand, right palm facing down and left palm facing up, move the hands in opposite directions past each other while changing into *A hands* and then opening again into *curved 5 hands.* Then, with the right *curved 5 hand* over

---

the left *curved 5 hand*, palms facing each other, move the hands in repeated circles in front of the chest in opposite directions. Then, beginning with the fingers of both *curved 5 hands* touching in front of the chest, bring the hands suddenly upward and outward to near each side of the head while opening into *curved 5 hands*.

Manhattan *n.* See sign for NEW YORK.

---

manicure *n.* **1.** A cosmetic treatment of the fingernails, including cleaning and often the application of nail polish: *I will get a manicure at the beauty shop.* —*v.* **2.** To give a manicure to (the fingernails): *She manicures her nails every week.*

■ [Mime trimming fingernails and applying nail polish] Beginning with the right *3 hand,* palm facing left, near the fingertips of the left *open hand,* palm facing down and fingers pointing forward, move the right hand around the left fingertips while opening and closing the index and middle fingers. Then move the extended right index finger back and forth with a repeated movement on the fingernails of the left *open hand.*

---

manipulate[1] *v.* To handle or influence skillfully, often for one's own purposes: *He manipulated the numbers in the account to disguise his thievery.*

■ [**smooth**[2] + **manage**] Beginning with both *flattened O hands* in front of the chest, both palms facing in and fingers pointing up, move the hands forward while sliding the thumbs of each hand across the fingers, forming *A hands.* Then, beginning with both *modified X hands* in front of each side of the chest, right hand forward of the left hand and palms facing each other, move the hands forward and back with a repeated alternating movement.

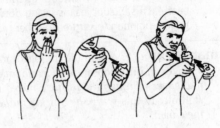

---

manipulate[2] *v.* See sign for MANAGE.

---

man-made *adj.* Not arising from natural processes; produced by human beings: *a man-made lake.*

■ [**man**[1,2] + **make**[1]] Beginning with the thumb side of the right *flattened C hand* in front of the right side of the forehead, palm facing left, bring the hand straight forward while closing

the fingers to the thumb. Then, beginning with the little-finger side of the right *S hand* on the index-finger side of the left *S hand,* separate the hands slightly, twist the wrists in opposite directions, and touch the hands together again.

manners *pl. n.* See signs for POLITE[1,2].

mantel[1] *n.* The shelf above a fireplace: *Put the candlestick on the mantel.*

■ **[flame**[1] + the shape of a mantel] Move both *5 hands* upward with an alternating movement while wiggling the fingers in front of each side of the chest, palms facing up. Then, beginning with the index-finger sides of both *B hands* touching in front of the chest, palms facing down and fingers pointing forward, move the hands apart to in front of each shoulder and then straight downward, ending with the palms facing each other and the fingers pointing forward.

mantel[2] *n.* See sign for SHELF.

manual *n.* See sign for BOOK.

manufacture *v.* See signs for MACHINE, MAKE[1,2].

manure *n.* See sign for FECES.

many *adj.* **1.** Consisting of a great number: *They own many cats.* —*pron.* **2.** A large number of persons or things: *Many couldn't come to the annual dinner this year.* Same sign used for: **a lot, lots, numerous.**

■ [Natural gesture for indicating many things] Beginning with both *S hands* in front of each side of the chest, palms facing up, flick the fingers open quickly with a double movement into *5 hands.*

marbles *n.* A children's game played with small glass balls: *played marbles in the front yard.*

■ [Mime shooting a marble] Beginning with the right *modified X hand* in front of the right shoulder, palm facing left, flick the thumb upward with a double movement.

march *v.* **1.** To advance steadily: *Time marches on.* **2.** To move forward in time to music or in step with others: *marched in the parade.* Same sign used for: **parade, procession.**

■ [The hands represent people moving forward in a procession] Beginning with both *4 hands* in front of the body, the right hand somewhat forward of the left hand, both palms facing in and fingers

mare

pointing down, flip the fingers forward and back with a double movement by bending the wrist.

mare *n.* A mature female horse: *The mare won the race.*
- ■ [**girl**[1] + **horse**] Move the extended thumb of the right *10 hand,* palm facing in, downward on the right cheek to off the right side of the chin. Then, with the thumb of the right extended *U hand* against the right side of the forehead, palm facing forward, move the fingers up and down with a double movement.

margarine[1] *n.* A spread made of vegetable oils, used as a substitute for butter: *to put margarine on the toast.* Same sign used for: **oleomargarine.**
- ■ [**not**[1] + **real** + **butter**] Bring the extended thumb of the right *10 hand* from under the chin, palm facing left, forward with a deliberate movement. Next move the extended right index finger from in front of the mouth, palm facing left and finger pointing up, upward and forward in an arc. Then wipe the extended fingers of the right *U hand,* palm facing down, across the upturned palm of the left *open hand* with a double movement, bending the right fingers back into the palm each time.

margarine[2] *n.* (alternate sign) Same sign used for: **oleomargarine.**
- ■ [**false** + **butter**] Brush the extended right index finger, palm facing left and finger pointing up, across the nose from right to left by bending the wrist. Then wipe the extended fingers of the right *U hand,* palm facing down, across the upturned palm of the left *open hand* with a double movement, bending the right fingers back into the palm each time.

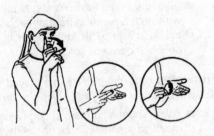

margarine[3] *n.* See sign for BUTTER.

margin *n.* The blank border around a printed page: *Leave a wide margin on your report.*
- ■ [Shows a column of text along an edge or margin] Move the thumb side of the right *modified C hand,* palm facing left, downward along the little-finger side of the left *open hand,* palm facing right and fingers pointing up.

marijuana *n.* The dried leaves and flowers of the hemp plant, used especially as an intoxicant: *to smoke a marijuana cigarette*. Same sign used for: **pot** (*slang*).

- [Mime holding and smoking a marijuana cigarette] Move the right *F hand,* palm facing left, from near the pursed mouth forward with a short double movement.

marionette *n.* See signs for PUPPET[1,2].

mark *v.* See sign for CHECK[2].

market[1] *n.* **1.** An open place or large building for buying and selling various goods: *a weekly market set up on the village green.* **2.** A store where food is sold: *to buy groceries at the market.* Same sign used for: **mart.**

- [Initialized sign similar to sign for **sell**] Beginning with both *M hands* held in front of each side of the chest, palms facing down and fingers pointing down, swing the fingertips forward and back by twisting the wrists upward with a double movement.

market[2] *n.* See signs for GROCERY STORE, STORE[1,2].

marksman *n.* A person who shoots well: *He is a good marksman who always hits the target.*

- [**precise** + **shoot**[1,2]] Bring both *modified X hands* together in front of the chest, palms facing each other. Then, with the right *L hand* in front of the right shoulder and the left *L hand* somewhat forward of the left shoulder, palms facing each other and index fingers pointing forward, wiggle the thumbs of both hands up and down with a repeated movement.

marrow *n.* The soft tissue in the hollow center of most bones: *He had a bone marrow transplant.*

- [**skeleton**[1] + showing the center opening of a bone] With the arms crossed at the wrists and each *bent V hand* near the opposite shoulder, bring the hands forward and back with a double movement. Then move the extended right index finger, palm facing in and finger pointing left, in a circular movement around the opening of the thumb side of the left *O hand.*

marry *v.* **1.** To join one another officially as husband and wife: *They will marry in the spring.* **2.** To take in marriage as husband or wife: *Will you marry me?* **3.** To officiate at the marriage ceremony of: *They were married by a justice of the peace.*

- [Symbolizes joining hands in marriage] Bring the right *curved hand*, palm facing down, downward in front of the chest to clasp the left *curved hand*, palm facing up.

marshal *n.* See signs for POLICE[1,2].

mart *n.* See signs for MARKET[1], STORE[1,2].

martial law *n. phrase.* Government by the military, making use of military law and institutions as opposed to civilian: *The military imposed a curfew when the president declared martial law.* Same sign used for: **military law.**

- [army + law] Tap the palm side of both *A hands* against the right side of the chest, right hand above the left hand, with a repeated movement. Then place the palm side of the right *L hand*, palm facing left, first on the fingers and then on the heel of the left *open hand*, palm facing right and fingers pointing up.

marvel *n.* See signs for WONDERFUL[1,2]. Related form: **marvelous** *adj.*

mash[1] *v.* To crush or beat into a soft, uniform, pulpy mass: *to mash the potatoes.* Same sign used for: **smash.**

- [Demonstrate action of mashing something] Bring the right *S hand*, palm facing left, downward in a double arc across the palm of the left *open hand*, palm facing up in front of the body.

mash[2] *v.* (alternate sign) Same sign used for: **smash.**

- [Mime mashing something with the heel of the hand] Bring the heel of the right *open hand* downward on the heel of the left *open hand*, palms facing each other, while twisting the right wrist and grinding the heel on the left palm.

mask[1] *n.* A covering to hide all or part of the face: *The burglar wore a mask.*

- [Initialized sign showing the location of a mask] Beginning with both *M hands* in front of the face, palms facing in and fingers pointing up, move the hands to each side of the face while turning the palms toward each other.

mask[2] *n.* (alternate sign)

- [Shows location of the type of face mask used in football or to give oxygen] Bring the right *curved 5 hand*, palm facing in and fingers pointing up, toward the face with a deliberate movement.

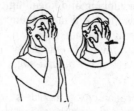

mask[3] *n.* See sign for HALLOWEEN[2].

masquerade *n.* See sign for HALLOWEEN[2].

masquerade ball *n.* A dance at which costumes are worn: *to go to a masquerade ball at Halloween.*

- [**Halloween**[1,2] + **dance**] Beginning with both *open hands* in front of the face, palms facing in and fingers pointing up, bring the hands apart to each side of the face, turning the palms toward each other. Then swing the fingers of the right *V hand*, palm facing in and fingers pointing down, back and forth over the palm of the left *open hand*, palm facing up.

Mass *n.* The central service of worship in some churches, especially the Roman Catholic church: *to attend a midnight Mass.*

- [Represents consecrating the host during Mass] With the fingertips of both *F hands* touching, palms facing down, bring the hands upward from in front of the chest to above the head.

mass *n.* See signs for CLASS, HORDE.

massacre *n.* **1.** A cruel and reckless slaughter of a large number of people or animals: *There was a massacre in which the people of the town were killed by terrorists.* —*v.* **2.** To kill many people or animals in a massacre: *They massacred all of the wild ponies.*

- [**kill**[1,2] + **audience**[2]] Push the thumb side of the right *G hand*, palm facing down, across the palm of the left *open hand*, palm facing right, with a deliberate movement. Then move both *curved 5 hands*, palms facing down, from in front of each side of the chest forward with a simultaneous movement.

massage *n.* **1.** The rubbing and kneading of muscles to relax them and make them work more efficiently: *The massage eased the tension in my back.* —*v.* **2.** To rub and knead muscles: *Let me massage your back.*

■ [Indicates the location of the shoulders + mimes the action of massaging] Touch the bent middle fingers of both *5 hands* to each shoulder. Then, with both *5 hands* in front of each side of the chest, palms facing down and fingers pointing forward, open and close the fingers of both hands with a repeated simultaneous movement.

massive *adj.* See signs for BIG, EXCESS.

mass-produce *v.* See sign for ASSEMBLY LINE.

mast *n.* The long pole that supports a ship's sails and other rigging: *to hoist the sails up the mast.*

■ [A handshape representing a boat + showing the shape of a ship's mast] Place the right *3 hand* in front of the body, palm facing left and fingers pointing forward. Then, beginning with the little-finger side of the right *C hand,* palm facing left, on the index-finger side of the left *C hand,* palm facing right, raise the right hand in front of the body.

master *n.* **1.** A person who has autonomy and can exercise authority over others: *On a ship, the captain is master.* **2.** The head of a household: *master of the house.*

■ [Initialized sign similar to sign for **area**[3]] Beginning with the right *M hand,* palm facing down, over the back of the left *open hand,* palm facing down and fingers pointing right, move the right hand in a large forward circle over the left arm.

masterpiece *n.* An excellent piece of workmanship, representing the finest of its kind: *That painting is a masterpiece.*

■ [**wonderful**[1,2] + **work**[1,2]] Beginning with both *5 hands* in front of each shoulder, move the hands in outward circles while raising them beside the head. Then tap the heel of the right *S hand,* palm facing down, with a double movement on the back of the left *S hand,* palm facing down.

masturbation[1] *n.* Manipulation of one's genitals in order to stimulate an orgasm. Related form: **masturbate** *v.*

- [Male sign] With a repeated movement in front of the chest, move the right *5 hand,* palm facing up, forward and back at an angle.

masturbation[2] *n.* (alternate sign) Related form: **masturbate** *v.*

- [Female sign] With a double movement, insert the bent middle finger of the right *5 hand,* palm facing down, up and down in the thumb-side opening of the left *S hand* held in front of the chest, palm facing in.

mat *n.* See sign for PAD[2].

match[1] *v.* **1.** To correspond in essential aspects, as material, style, or color: *The chair matches the sofa.* **2.** To go well together: *These colors match quite well.* —*n.* **3.** A person or thing that matches: *This jacket is a match to that skirt.* Same sign used for: **combine, fit, mate, merge, suit.**

- [The fingers move together to match with each other] Beginning with both *5 hands* in front of each side of the chest, palms facing in, bring the hands together, ending with the bent fingers of both hands meshed together in front of the chest.

match[2] *n.* A short, slender stick or piece of cardboard with a tip that ignites when struck: *to light the candles with a match.*

- [Mime striking a match] Flick index-finger knuckle of the right *modified X hand,* palm facing left, upward with a double movement on the palm of the left *open hand,* palm facing right and fingers pointing forward.

match[3] *n.* See signs for TOURNAMENT, VERSUS[1]. Shared idea of competition.

mate *n.* See sign for MATCH[1].

material *n.* **1.** What a thing is made of: *The material of this appliance is plastic.* **2.** Fabric; cloth: *a loosely woven material.* See also sign for FABRIC. Same sign used for: **cloth, texture.**

- [The hands seem to feel material with the fingers] Rub the thumbs of both *flattened O hands* against the fingers of each hand in front of each side of the chest, palms facing up.

materialize *v.* See sign for SHOW UP.

materials *pl. n.* Supplies for doing or making something: *You'll have to use your own materials to make the collage.* Same sign used for: **media.**

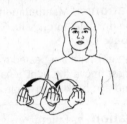

- [Initialized sign similar to sign for **thing**] Beginning with the right *M hand* in front of the body, palm facing up, move the hand in a double arc to the right.

mathematics *n.* The science dealing with measurements, quantities, and other quantitative properties as expressed with numbers: *solved an equation using higher mathematics; to study math for an engineering degree.* Alternate form: **math.** Same sign used for: **multiplication.**

- [Initialized sign similar to sign for **arithmetic**] Brush the back of the right *M hand* across the index-finger side of the left *M hand,* both palms facing in, as the hands cross with a double movement in front of the chest.

matinee *n.* See sign for AFTERNOON.

mattress *n.* A large cushion or pad used on the length of a bed to support the body when lying down: *to sleep on a firm mattress.*

- [**bed**[1,2] + **soft**] Rest the right cheek at an angle on the open right palm. Then, beginning with both *curved 5 hands* in front of each side of the chest, palms facing up, bring the hands downward while closing the fingers to the thumbs of each hand with a double movement.

mature *adj.* **1.** Completely developed; fully grown: *a mature plant; evening classes for mature students.* **2.** Sensible and reliable, as befitting an adult: *a mature person whose judgment you can trust.* —*v.* **3.** To become mature: *She has matured a great deal since graduating.* Related form: **maturity** *n.*

- [Initialized sign similar to sign for **tall**[1]] Move the index-finger side of the right *M hand,* palm facing down, upward from the heel to the fingers of the left *open hand* held in front of the chest, palm facing right and fingers pointing up.

matzo *n.* See sign for CRACKER.

maximum *n.* **1.** The greatest possible amount: *The class score was the maximum.* —*adj.* **2.** Being the maximum: *achieved maximum production levels.* Same sign used for: **up to.**

- [Shows reaching the top] Beginning with the right *B hand* a few inches under the left *open hand,* both palms facing down, bring the back of the right hand up against the left palm.

may *auxiliary v.* See signs for CAN², MAYBE.

maybe *adv.* Possibly: *Maybe it will snow.* Same sign used for: **may, might, perhaps, probability, probable, probably.**

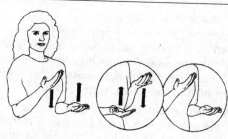

- [Indicates weighing possibilities] Beginning with both *open hands* in front of each side of the chest, palms facing up and fingers pointing forward, alternately move the hands up and down with a double movement.

mayonnaise *n.* A dressing made chiefly of egg yolk, vegetable oil, and lemon juice: *I always put mayonnaise on my hamburger.*

- [Initialized sign miming spreading mayonnaise on bread] Move the fingers of the right *M hand,* palm facing down, in a double circular movement on the palm of the left *open hand,* palm facing up.

me *pron.* The objective case of *I,* used as a direct or indirect object: *He gave it to me.* Same sign used for: **I.**

- Point the extended right index finger to the center of the chest.

meadow *n.* An area of grassy land, typically used for grazing: *The sheep were in the meadow.*

- [**eat** formed with both hands to indicate an animal eating + a gesture showing the expanse of a meadow] Bring the fingertips of both *flattened O hands* together in front of the mouth and wiggle the hands. Then bring both *5 hands* from in front of the mouth downward and forward in outward arcs, ending with the hands in front of each side of the chest, palms facing down and fingers pointing forward.

---

meager *adj.* See sign for SMALL[2].

---

meal *n.* See sign for FOOD.

---

mealtime *n.* The usual time for eating a meal: *We don't want to be interrupted at mealtime.*

■ [**eat** + **time**[2]] Bring the fingertips of the right *flattened O hand,* palm facing in, to the lips with a short repeated movement. Then tap the index finger of the right *X hand,* palm facing down, against the left wrist with a double movement.

---

mean[1] *adj.* Unkind; nasty; bad-tempered: *a mean person who never loses an opportunity to insult others.* Related form: **meanness** *n.* Same sign used for: **bust, cruel, harsh, rude, unkind.**

■ Beginning with both *5 hands* in front of the body, palms facing in opposite directions and the right hand above the left hand, close the hands into *A hands* while quickly moving the right hand down, brushing the knuckles against the left knuckles as it passes.

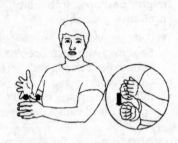

---

mean[2] *v.* See signs for INTEND[1,2]. Related form: **meaning** *n.*

---

mean[3] *n., adj.* See signs for AVERAGE[1,2].

---

meanness[1] *n.* **1.** One or more instances of being mean and cruel: *We were shocked by their meanness to the child.* **2.** The state or quality of being mean or cruel: *notorious for their meanness.* Same sign used for: **cruel, rude.**

■ Beginning with the index finger of the right *5 hand,* palm facing left, touching the nose, close the right hand into an *A hand* while quickly moving it down, brushing the knuckles against the knuckles of the left *A hand,* palm facing right, as it passes.

---

meanness[2] *n.* (alternate sign) Same sign used for: **cruel, tough.**

■ Bring the knuckles of the right *bent V hand,* palm facing in, downward, brushing the knuckles of the left *bent V hand,* palm facing in, as the right hand passes.

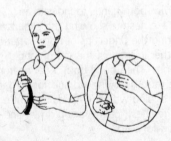

meantime *n., adv.* See sign for DURING.

meanwhile *n., adv.* See sign for DURING.

measles *n.* Any of several contagious diseases caused by viruses and characterized by symptoms resembling those of a cold and by red spots or a red rash on the skin: *vaccinated against the measles.*

■ [Shows location of measles spots] Beginning with the fingers of both *curved 5 hands,* palms facing each other, on each side of the chin, move the hands upward, touching the fingertips to several places on the cheeks and then to each side of the forehead.

measure *v.* To find out the size or amount of: *to measure the room.* Related form: **measurement** *n.* Same sign used for: **size.**

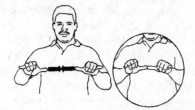

■ [The fingers seem to measure something] Tap the thumbs of both *Y hands,* palms facing down, together in front of the chest with a double movement.

measure up *v. phrase.* See sign for MEET.

measuring *n., adj.* See sign for ENGINEER.

meat *n.* Animal flesh used for food: *prefers to eat meat for dinner.* Same sign used for: **beef, content, flesh, steak, substance.**

■ [Indicates the meaty part of the hand] With the bent index finger and thumb of the right *5 hand,* palm facing down, grasp the fleshy part of the left *open hand* near the thumb, palm facing right and fingers pointing forward, and shake the hands forward and back with a double movement.

mechanic *n.* See sign for PLUMBER.

mechanism *n.* See sign for MACHINE.

medal *n.* An award, typically in the form of a metal disk, usually bearing an inscription: *won the gold medal in figure skating at the Olympics.* Same sign used for: **prize, ribbon.**

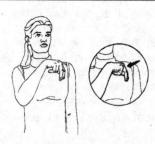

■ [Symbolizes pinning on a medal] Bring the index-finger side of the right *H hand,* palm facing down and fingers pointing down, back against the left side of the chest with a deliberate movement.

medallion *n.* A large medal or an ornament resembling one: *to wear a medallion on a chain.*

- [Shows shape of medallion] Touch the thumbs and index fingers of both *modified C hands* together in front of the chest.

meddle[1] *v.* To interfere in others' affairs without their consent: *not wise to meddle in their business.* Same sign used for: **interfere, interrupt.**

- [Hand seems to interrupt in the middle of something] Bring the little-finger side of the right *open hand,* palm facing left, downward sharply between the middle finger and ring finger of the left *5 hand* held in front of the chest, palm facing in and fingers pointing up.

meddle[2] *v.* See sign for NOSY[2].

media *pl. n.* See sign for MATERIALS.

media card[1] *n.* A small card having a built-in computer chip on which digital photographic images are stored: *use a 2GB media card in the digital camera.* Same sign used for: **memory card, smart media card.**

- [**picture** + **card**] Move the right *C hand,* palm facing forward, from near the right side of the face downward, ending with the index-finger side of the right *C hand* against the palm of the left *open hand,* palm facing right. With the fingertips of both *L hands* touching in front of the chest, palms facing forward, bring the hands apart to in front of each shoulder, and then pinch each thumb and index finger together.

media card[2] (alternate sign) Same sign used for **memory card, smart media card.**

- [**memorize**[2] + **insert**] Beginning with the fingertips of the right *curved hand* touching the right side of the forehead, palm facing down, bring the hand forward and down while closing the fingers into an *S hand,* palm facing in. Then slide the little-finger side of the right *open hand,* palm facing up, between the right and middle fingers of the left *4 hand,* palm facing right.

medical *adj.* See sign for DOCTOR[2].

medicine *n.* A drug or other substance used to treat or prevent disease: *It's time to take your medicine.* Related forms: **medical** *adj.*, **medication** *n.* Same sign used for: **drug, poison.**

- [Represents mixing a prescription with a mortar and pestle] With the bent middle finger of the right *5 hand*, palm facing down, in the palm of the left *open hand*, rock the right hand from side to side with a double movement while keeping the middle finger in place.

meditate[1] *v.* **1.** To think quietly and consider: *meditated about the problem.* **2.** To engage in devout religious contemplation: *The monks meditated for many hours.* Related form: **meditation** *n.*

- [Initialized sign similar to sign for **wonder**] Move the fingers of the right *M hand*, palm facing in, in a circular movement near the right side of the forehead.

meditate[2] *v.* See signs for TALK[1], WONDER. Related form: **meditation** *n.*

medium *adj.* See signs for AVERAGE[1,2].

meek *adj.* See signs for HUMBLE[1,2].

meet *v.* **1.** To come face to face with; encounter: *to meet a friend for lunch.* **2.** To become acquainted with; be introduced to: *It's good to meet you at last.* **3.** To be in accordance with; deal with appropriately: *Your report meets our expectations.* Same sign used for: **greet, measure up.**

- [Represents two people approaching each other when meeting] Beginning with the extended index fingers of both hands pointing up in front of each shoulder, palms facing each other, bring the hands together in front of the chest.

meeting *n.* **1.** The act of coming together: *Our meeting was a lucky event.* **2.** A gathering or assembly of people for some purpose: *to attend the meeting.* Related form: **meet** *v.* Same sign used for: **assembly, conference, convention, convocation, council, session.**

- [Represents many people coming together for a meeting] Beginning with both *open hands* in front of the chest, palms facing forward and fingers pointing up, close the fingers with a double movement into *flattened O hands* while moving the hands together.

megaphone *n.* A large horn that magnifies the voice: *The cheerleader used a megaphone.* Same sign used for: **horn.**

■ [Shows the shape of a megaphone held to the mouth] Beginning with the index-finger side of the right *S hand* against the little-finger side of the left *S hand* held in front of the mouth, palms facing in opposite directions, move the right hand forward while opening into a *curved 5 hand.*

mellow *adj.* See sign for SOFT.

melody *n.* See sign for MUSIC.

melon *n.* See sign for PUMPKIN.

melt *v.* See sign for DISSOLVE.

melted *adj.* See sign for MOLTEN.

member[1] *n.* A person or thing belonging to a group: *a member of the committee.*

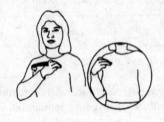

■ [Initialized sign similar to sign for **committee**] Move the fingertips of the right *M hand* from the left side of the chest in an arc around to touch again at the right side of the chest.

member[2] *n.* (alternate sign)

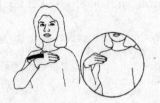

■ [Similar to sign for **committee**] Touch the fingertips of the right *bent hand,* first to the left side of the chest and then to the right side of the chest.

membrane *n.* See sign for SMOOTH[1].

memorable *adj.* Worth remembering: *The anniversary party was a memorable occasion.*

■ [Bringing a thought from the mind to the forefront for inspection] Move the thumb of the right *10 hand,* palm facing left, from the right side of the forehead smoothly down with a double movement to touch the thumb of the left *10 hand* held in front of the body, palm facing down.

memorial *n.* See signs for LOOK BACK[1], MEMORY[1]. Shared idea of preserving the memory of a person or event.

memorize[1] *v.* To commit to memory: *to memorize the telephone number.*

■ [**think**[1] + a gesture symbolizing holding a thought in one's memory] Beginning with the extended right index finger touching the right side of the forehead, palm facing down, bring the hand forward and down while closing the fingers into an *S hand,* palm facing in.

memorize[2] *v.* (alternate sign) Related form: **memory** *n.*

■ [The hand seems to take information from the brain and then hold on to it tightly, as if to keep it in the memory] Beginning with the fingertips of the right *curved hand* touching the right side of the forehead, palm facing down, bring the hand forward and down while closing the fingers into an *S hand,* palm facing in.

memory[1] *n.* **1.** The ability to retain and recall facts, experiences, etc.; capacity to hold in the mind: *She has an excellent memory.* **2.** A person, thing, or event remembered; recollection: *I have fond memories of my childhood.* Same sign used for: **memorial.**

■ [Initialized sign similar to sign for **look back**[1]] Move the right *M hand,* palm facing back, from in front of the right side of the head back along the side of the head.

memory[2] *n.* (alternate sign)

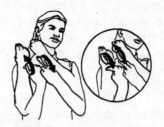

■ [Initialized sign similar to sign for **ancestor**[2]] Beginning with both *M hands* over the right shoulder, palms facing back and fingers pointing back, move the hands back with a rolling alternating movement over each other.

memory[3] *n.* See sign for LOOK BACK[1].

memory card *n.* See signs for MEDIA CARD[1,2].

mend *v.* See signs for FIX[1,2].

Mennonite

Mennonite *n.* See sign for SCARF[1]. Shared idea relating to Mennonite costume.

menopause *n.* The period in midlife during which menstruation naturally ceases: *She is 48 and is going through menopause.*

- ■ [**old** + **menstruation** + **stop**] Move the right *C hand*, palm facing left, downward a short distance from the chin while changing into an *S hand*. Next tap the palm side of the right *A hand* against the right side of the chin with a double movement. Then bring the little-finger side of the right *open hand*, palm facing left and fingers pointing forward, downward with a deliberate movement on the upturned palm of the left *open hand*.

menstrual cramps *pl. n.* The involuntary, painful spasms of the abdomen that can occur during menstruation: *She has menstrual cramps every other month.*

- ■ [**menstruation** + a gesture indicating a cramp] Tap the palm side of the right *A hand* against the right side of the chin with a double movement. Then, beginning with both *A hands* in front of each side of the body, right palm facing down and left palm facing up, twist the hands in opposite directions.

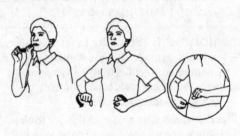

menstruation *n.* A discharging of blood and tissue from the uterus at monthly intervals, between puberty and menopause, by a nonpregnant female: *If she's almost 13, it is time to talk to her about menstruation.* Same sign used for: **period.**

- ■ Tap the palm side of the right *A hand* against the right side of the chin with a double movement.

-ment *suffix.* (Used to form nouns, especially from verbs, that indicate an act, state, or condition): *The word* amazement *means "the act, state, or condition of being amazed."*

- ■ [Initialized sign] Bring the index-finger side of the right *M hand*, palm facing forward, downward on the palm of the left *open hand*, palm facing right and fingers pointing up.

mental *adj.* Of or pertaining to the mind: *mental alertness.*

■ [Initialized sign similar to sign for **know**] Tap the fingertips of the right *M hand,* palm facing in, against the right side of the forehead with a double movement.

mentally retarded[1] Having a developmental disorder characterized by a limited ability to learn: *assessing the abilities of a mentally retarded person.*

■ [Abbreviation **m-r** similar to sign formed for **know**] Touch the fingertips of first the right *M hand* and then the right *R hand,* palm facing down, to the right side of the forehead.

mentally retarded[2] See sign for RETARDED[1].

mention *v.* To speak about briefly or in passing: *Did you mention something about a rehearsal?*

■ [**say**[1] + **call**[5]] Beginning with the extended right index finger near the mouth, palm facing in and finger pointing up, bring the right hand downward while changing into an *H hand,* ending with the middle-finger side of the right *H hand* across the index-finger side of the left *H hand* in front of the chest.

menu[1] *n.* A list of foods or prepared dishes available to be served at a restaurant: *I need to look at a menu before I order.*

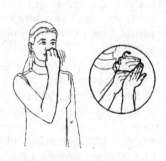

■ [**food** + **list**[1,2,3,4]] Bring the fingertips of the right *flattened O hand,* palm facing down, to the lips with a repeated movement. Then touch the little-finger side of the right *bent hand,* palm facing left, several times on the palm of the left *open hand,* palm facing in and fingers angled upward as it moves from the fingertips downward to the heel of the left palm.

menu[2] *n.* See sign for LIST[5].

meow *n.* **1.** The characteristic sound made by a cat: *the loud, low-pitched meow of the Siamese cat.* —*v.* **2.** To make this sound or a sound resembling it: *The cat meowed for its dinner.* Same sign used for: **mew.**

merchandise

■ [cat[1,2] + scream[1,2]] Beginning with the index finger and thumb of the right *5 hand* touching the right cheek, palm facing left, bring the hand outward to the right with a double movement while pinching the index finger and thumb together each time. Then, beginning with the right *curved 5 hand* in front of the mouth, palm facing in, bring the hand forward in a small arc.

merchandise *n.* See sign for SELL.

merciless *adj.* Having no pity; cruel: *The merciless boss made everyone work on Christmas Eve.*

■ [mercy[1,2,3,4] + zero[1,2]] With the bent middle fingers of both *5 hands* pointing forward in front of each shoulder, move the hands forward in repeated circular movements. Then, beginning with the index-finger side of the right *O hand* near the chin, palm facing left, bring the hand forward.

mercy[1] *n.* Kindness or compassion, especially as shown to an offender or enemy: *The judge showed mercy to the young offender.* Related form: **merciful** *adj.* Same sign used for: **compassion, empathy, pathetic, pity, poor, Poor baby! (sarcasm), poor thing, sympathy.**

■ [The finger used to show feeling is directed toward another] Beginning with the bent middle finger of the right *5 hand* pointing forward in front of the right shoulder, move the hand forward in a repeated circular movement.

mercy[2] *n.* (alternate sign) Related form: **merciful** *adj.* Same sign used for: **compassion, empathy, pathetic, pitiful, pity, poor, Poor baby! (sarcasm), poor thing, sympathy.**

■ [The finger used to show feeling is directed toward another] Beginning with the bent middle fingers of both *5 hands* pointing forward in front of each shoulder, move the hands forward in repeated circular movements.

mercy[3] *n.* (alternate sign) Related form: **merciful** *adj.* Same sign used for: **compassion, empathy, pathetic, pitiful, poor, Poor baby! (sarcasm), poor thing, sympathy.**

■ [Feeling is moved from oneself toward another] Beginning with the bent middle finger of the right *5 hand* touching the chest and the bent middle finger of the left *5 hand* pointing forward, twist the right hand forward and move both hands forward in repeated circular movements.

mercy[4] *n.* (alternate sign) Related form: **merciful** *adj.* Same sign used for: **compassion, empathy, pathetic, pitiful, pity, poor, Poor baby! (sarcasm), poor thing, sympathy.**

■ [**feel** + **mercy**[1]] Beginning with the bent middle finger of the right *5 hand* touching the chest, twist the hand forward and then move the bent finger downward in the air with a double movement.

merge *v.* See signs for CIRCULATE[1], INTERFACE[1], MAINSTREAM[1,2], MATCH[1], MESH.

mermaid *n.* A mythical sea maiden whose head, torso, and arms are human and who is shaped like a fish from the waist down: *They made a movie from the fairy tale about a little mermaid.*

■ [**girl**[1] + **fish**[1,2]] Move the extended thumb of the right *10 hand,* palm facing left, downward on the right cheek to the right side of the chin. Then, beginning with the fingertips of the left *open hand* touching the heel of the right *open hand,* palms facing in opposite directions and fingers pointing forward, wave the right hand back and forth with a repeated movement as the hand moves forward a short distance.

merry *adj.* See sign for HAPPY.

merry-go-round *n.* A round, revolving platform containing a set of horses, chairs, or other figures on which people ride: *to ride the merry-go-round at the fair.*

■ [Represents sitting on a merry-go-round with an up-and-down movement + **round**[1]] Beginning with both *bent V hands* in front of the body, one hand higher than the other and palms facing forward, move the hands forward in large alternating circles. Then move the extended right index finger, palm facing right and finger pointing down, in a large flat circle in front of the body.

mesh *v.* To fit together and engage, as gear teeth: *The gears are grinding because they don't mesh.* Same sign used for: **blend, combine, infuse, integrate, merge.**

■ [Shows the fingers coming together to merge] Beginning with both *curved 5 hands* in front of each side of the chest, palms facing up, drop the hands down while meshing the fingers together, and then drop them apart in front of each side of the body.

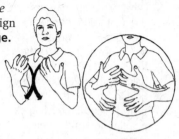

mess[1] *n.* **1.** An untidy condition: *Your room is in a mess.* **2.** A person or thing that is untidy or disordered: *My hair is a mess.* Related form: **messy** *adj.* Same sign used for: **chaos, disorder.**

■ [**mix**[1] + **dirty**] With the right *curved 5 hand* over the left *curved 5 hand*, palms facing each other, move the hands in repeated circles in opposite directions. Then, beginning with the right *S hand* under the chin, palm facing left, quickly open the fingers, forming a *5 hand* under the chin, palm facing down and fingers pointing left, and wiggle the fingers with a repeated movement.

mess[2] *n.* See sign for MOB. Shared idea of unmanageableness.

message[1] *n.* A communication sent by written, spoken, or other means: *Please give your mother a message for me.* Same sign used for: **phrase.**

■ [Similar to sign for **caption** but formed with a single movement] Beginning with the fingertips of both *F hands* touching in front of the chest, bring the hands apart.

message[2] *n.* (alternate sign) Same sign used for: **phrase.**

■ [Similar to sign for **sentence** but formed with a single movement] With the bent thumbs and index fingers of both *5 hands* near each other in front of the chest, pull the hands apart while pinching the thumbs and index fingers of each hand together.

messenger *n.* A person who carries messages or mail to another: *The messenger brought a telegram to my door.* Same sign used for: **courier.**

■ [**message**[1,2] + a gesture indicating sending something + **person marker**] With the bent thumbs and index fingers of both *5 hands* near each other, palms facing each other, pull the hands apart with a repeated movement to in front of each side of the chest while pinching the thumbs and index fingers of each hand together. Then brush the bent middle finger of the right *5 hand*, palm facing down, from the heel to off the fingers of the palm of the left *open hand* held in front of the chest, palm facing up and fingers pointing forward. Then move both *open hands*, palms facing each other, downward along each side of the body.

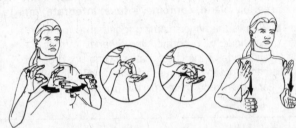

messy *adj.* Untidy: *a messy desk.* Same sign used for: **chaos, disorder, garbled, riot, stir, storm.**

- ■ [Represents something turned upside down, causing a mess] Beginning with both *curved 5 hands* in front of the body, right hand over the left hand, twist the hands with a deliberate movement, reversing the positions.

metal *n.* **1.** Any of a group of elementary substances, as gold, silver, or iron, particularly the stronger metals and alloys used for construction: *The file cabinet is made of metal.* —*adj.* **2.** Made of metal: *a metal container.* Same sign used for: **rock, steel.**

- ■ Bring the top of the bent index finger of the right *X hand*, palm facing left, forward from under the chin with a double movement.

meter *n.* A length in metric measure roughly equivalent to 40 U.S. inches: *The room was ten meters long.*

- ■ [Initialized sign similar to sign for **temperature**] Slide the middle-finger side of the right *M hand*, palm facing left, up and down on the extended left index finger, palm facing right and finger pointing up.

method *n.* A procedure or technique for doing something: *developed a method for manufacturing the parts more cheaply.*

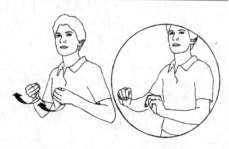

- ■ [Initialized sign similar to sign for **road**[1]] Move both *M hands* from in front of each side of the body, palms facing in and fingers angled up, downward and forward simultaneously while twisting the palms down.

me too *Slang.* See sign for AGREE[2].

metronome *n.* An adjustable mechanical device used to set time for music by marking the rhythm with a series of clicks: *Set the metronome at a slower speed.*

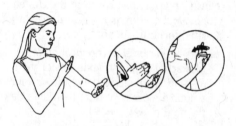

- ■ [**music** + showing the movement of a metronome] Swing the little-finger side of the right *open hand*, palm facing in, back and forth across the length of the bent left forearm held in front of the chest. Then move the extended right index finger, palm facing forward and finger pointing up, back and forth with a repeated movement in front of the chest.

metropolis *n.* **1.** The most important city in an area: *businesses moving out of the metropolis.* **2.** Any large, busy city: *The town is becoming a busy, thriving metropolis.*

■ [**important**[1,2] + **large** + **town**] Beginning with the fingertips of both *F hands* touching, palms facing each other, bring the hands upward in a circular movement, ending with the index-finger sides of the *F hands* near each other in front of the chest, palms facing forward. Then, beginning with both *modified C hands* near each other in front of the chest, palms facing each other, move the hands outward to in front of each shoulder. Then tap the fingertips of both *open hands,* palms angled toward each other, in front of the chest with a double movement.

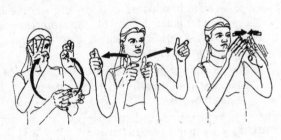

metropolitan *adj.* **1.** Of, pertaining to, or characteristic of a large city: *The decor shows sophisticated metropolitan taste.* **2.** Of or pertaining to a large city and the area surrounding it: *This service is now available in the New York metropolitan area.*

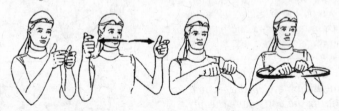

■ [**large** + **area**[1,2,3,4]] Beginning with both *modified C hands* near each other in front of the chest, palms facing each other, move the hands outward to in front of each shoulder. Then, beginning with the thumbs of both *A hands* touching in front of the chest, palms facing down, move the hands apart and back in a circular movement until they touch again near the chest.

mew *n., v.* See sign for MEOW.

Mexico[1] *n.* A country in the southern part of North America, just south of the United States: *Mexico City is the capital of Mexico.* Related form: **Mexican** *n., adj.*

■ [Initialized sign showing location of mustache] Wipe the fingertips of the right *M hand,* palm facing down, downward with a double movement from the right side of the mouth.

Mexico² *n.* (alternate sign) Related
form: **Mexican** *n., adj.* Same sign used
for: **Hispanic.**

- ■ [Shows the brim of a Mexican
  sombrero] Move the right *V hand,*
  fingers pointing down, from in front
  of the forehead in an arc to near the
  right side of the head.

Mexico³ *n.* See sign for SPAIN³. Related form: **Mexican** *n., adj.*

microphone *n.* An electric device used for
magnifying small sounds for broad
transmission: *The speaker's voice was so
strong that he didn't have to use a
microphone.*

- ■ [Mime holding a microphone] Hold the right
  S hand in front of the chin, palm facing in.

microscope¹ *n.* An optical instrument with a lens for magnifying objects too small to
be seen with the naked eye, as tiny organisms: *examining a human hair through a
microscope.*

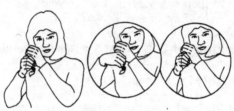

- ■ [Mime looking through a microscope
  and adjusting the lens] Beginning
  with the little-finger side of the left
  O hand on the index-finger side of
  the right *O hand,* palms facing in
  opposite directions, twist the right
  hand forward and back.

microscope² *n.* (alternate sign)

- ■ [Mime looking through a microscope]
  Beginning with the little-finger side of the
  left *O hand* against the index-finger side of
  the right *O hand* in front of the left eye,
  palms facing in opposite directions, bring the
  right hand straight down while changing into
  a *C hand.*

microwave *n.* **1.** Alternate form: **microwave oven.** An oven in which food is cooked
by the penetration of microwaves: *It saves time to
cook dinner in the microwave.* —*v.* **2.** To cook food
in a microwave oven: *I microwave my vegetables
because they stay crunchy.*

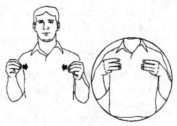

- ■ [Abbreviation **m-w**] Beginning with both *M hands*
  in front of each side of the chest, palms facing in,
  move the hands toward each other while extending
  the fingers toward each other with a double
  movement, changing into *W hands* each time.

midday *n.* See sign for NOON[1].

middle *adj.* **1.** Located in the center: *the middle chair.* —*n.* **2.** The point that is the same distance from each end or side: *to sit in the middle of the aisle.* See also sign for CENTER. Same sign used for: **central.**

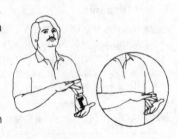

- ■ [Indicates the middle of something] Move the bent middle finger of the right *5 hand,* palm facing down, in a circular movement and then down into the palm of the left *open hand* held in front of the chest, palm facing up.

middle age *n.* The period of human life ranging approximately from the ages of forty to sixty-five: *Middle age is the prime of life.* Related form: **middle-aged** *adj.*

- ■ [**center** + **age**] Move the right *bent hand,* palm facing down, in a circular movement near the palm of the left *open hand,* ending with the fingertips of the right *bent hand* touching the middle of the left palm. Then move the right *O hand,* palm facing left, downward a short distance from the chin while changing into an *S hand.*

middle of the night See sign for MIDNIGHT.

midget *n.* See sign for DWARF.

midnight *n.* Twelve o'clock at night: *They were told to be home by midnight.* Same sign used for: **middle of the night.**

- ■ [Represents the sun being on the other side of the world at midnight] With the fingertips of the left *open hand,* palm facing in, touching the crook of the extended right arm, fingers pointing down and palm facing left, move the right *B hand* to the left with a short double movement.

midst *prep.* See sign for AMONG.

midwest *n.* A region in the north central part of the United States: *to travel to several states in the midwest, including Illinois and Michigan.* Alternate form: **middle west.**

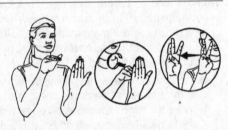

- ■ [**center** + **west**[1,2]] Move the right *bent hand,* palm facing down, in a circular movement near the palm of the left *open hand,* ending with the fingertips of the right *bent hand* touching the middle of the left palm. Then move the right *W hand,* palm facing forward, to the right in front of the right shoulder.

might *auxiliary v.* See sign for MAYBE.

mighty *adj.* See sign for POWER[1], STRONG[1].

migraine *n.* See signs for HEADACHE[1,2].

migrate *v.* To move from one region to another, as with the change of seasons: *The birds migrated south for the winter.* Related form: **migration** *n.*

- [**bird** + a movement representing a flock of birds flying] Close the index finger and thumb of the right *G hand,* palm facing forward, with a repeated movement in front of the mouth. Then, beginning with both *open hands* over the head, palms facing down and fingers pointing forward, move the hands forward simultaneously.

mildew *n.* A fungus that grows on objects exposed to prolonged moisture: *The wet clothes we forgot about developed mildew.*

- [**wet**[2] + **layer**[2]] Beginning with both *curved 5 hands* in front of the face, palms facing in and fingers pointing up, close the fingers to the thumbs of each hand, forming *flattened O hands* in front of the chest. Then move the thumb side of the right *G hand,* palm facing forward, from the wrist to off the fingers of the left *open hand* held in front of the chest, palm facing down and fingers pointing right.

military *n.* See signs for ARMY, SOLDIER.

military law *n. phrase.* See sign for MARTIAL LAW.

milk[1] *n.* **1.** The white liquid secreted by female mammals to feed their young: *The mother cat had enough milk for her six kittens.* **2.** This liquid, secreted by certain animals, especially cows and goats, used by humans as food: *Drink your milk.*

- [Mime squeezing a cow's udder to get milk] Beginning with the right *C hand,* palm facing left, in front of the right side of the body, squeeze the fingers together with a double movement, forming an *S hand* each time.

milk² *v.* To draw milk from the udders of a cow, goat, or the like: *The cows must be milked every day.*

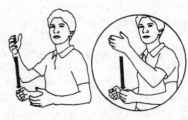

■ [Mime milking a cow] Beginning with the right *C hand* in front of the right shoulder and the left *C hand* in front of the left side of the body, palms facing in opposite directions, bring the right hand down while closing in an *S hand,* and repeat the movement with the left hand in front of the left side of the body.

milkman *n.* A man who delivers milk to customers: *Remember when we had milkmen bringing bottles of milk to the door?*

■ [**milk¹** + **man**[1,2,3]] Beginning with the right *C hand,* palm facing left, in front of the right side of the body, squeeze the fingers together with a double movement, forming an *S hand.* Then, beginning with the thumb side of the right *flattened C hand* in front of the right side of the forehead, palm facing left, bring the hand straight forward while closing the fingers to the thumb.

milky *adj.* Like milk, as in appearance or texture: *The material has a milky color.*

■ [**white** + **milk¹** + **overflow**] Beginning with the fingertips of the right *curved 5 hand* against the chest, bring the hand forward while closing into a *flattened O hand.* Then, beginning with the right *C hand,* palm facing left, in front of the right side of the body, squeeze the fingers together with a double movement, forming an *S hand.* Then, beginning with the palm side of the right *A hand,* palm facing down, on the thumb side of the left *S hand,* palm facing right, move the right hand forward and down on the back of the left hand while opening into a *5 hand.*

million¹ *adj.* One thousand times one thousand: *a million stars.*

■ [Initialized sign similar to sign for **thousand** except repeated] Touch the fingertips of the right *M hand,* palm facing down, first on the heel, then in the middle, and then on the fingers of the upturned left *open hand.*

million² *adj.* (alternate sign)

■ [Similar to sign for **thousand** except made with a double movement] Touch the fingertips of the right *bent hand,* palm facing left, first on the palm and then on the fingers of the left hand, palm facing right.

millionaire *n.* A very wealthy person, especially one whose assets amount to more than one million in some currency: *The young millionaire made money by investing in stocks.*

■ [**million**¹·² + **person marker**] Touch the fingertips of the right *bent hand,* palm facing down, first on the heel, then in the middle, and then on the fingers of the upturned left *open hand.* Then move both *open hands,* palms facing each other, downward along each side of the body.

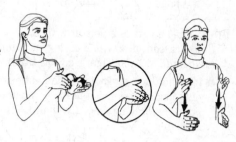

Milwaukee¹ *n.* A city in southeast Wisconsin: *Milwaukee is a port on Lake Michigan.*

■ [Initialized sign representing wiping Milwaukee beer from the chin] Slide the index-finger side of the right *M hand,* palm facing left, from right to left with a double movement across the chin.

Milwaukee² *n.* (alternate sign)

■ [Represents wiping Milwaukee beer from the chin] Slide the index finger of the right *G hand,* palm facing left, from left to right across the chin with a double movement.

mimic *v.* To imitate or copy: *The comedian mimicked the President.*

■ [Represents copying another repeatedly] Move the right *5 hand* from in front of the chest, palm angled forward, down with a repeated movement to touch the upturned palm of the left *open hand* while closing the right fingers and thumb into a *flattened O hand* each time.

mince *v.* To chop into tiny pieces: *Mince the onion before adding it to the sauce.*

- [**chop**[1] + a gesture showing small tidbits + **little**[1]] Hit the middle-finger side of the right *open hand,* palm facing left, with a double movement on the upturned left *open hand.* Next move the thumb side of the right *G hand,* palm facing forward, from the heel to the fingers in a small repeated movement on the upturned left *open hand.* Then move both *open hands* toward each other with a short double movement in front of the chest, palms facing each other and fingers pointing forward.

mind *n.* The part of a person with the capacity to think, reason, perceive, etc.: *a good mind for mathematics.* Same sign used for: **brain, sense.**

- [Location of the mind] Tap the bent extended right index finger, palm facing in, against the right side of the forehead with a double movement.

mine[1] *n.* **1.** An excavation in the earth set up for the retrieval of valuable minerals, as metal ore or precious stones: *The miners were trapped in the coal mine.* —*v.* **2.** To dig a mine: *to mine for silver.*

- [The finger seems to dig as if mining] Bring the tip of the index finger of the right *X hand,* palm facing down, in a double movement across the palm of the left *open hand,* palm facing up.

mine[2] *pron.* See sign for MY.

mingle *v.* See sign for ASSOCIATE.

mini *adj.* See signs for SMALL[1,2].

miniature *adj.* **1.** Done or represented on a small scale: *the miniature furniture in the doll house.* —*n.* **2.** An object, as an image or representation, done on a small scale: *wearing a miniature made into a brooch.*

- [**small**[2] + a gesture showing several little things] Beginning with both *open hands* in front of each side of the chest, palms facing each other and fingers pointing forward, bring the hands toward each other in front of the chest. Then move the right *G hand,* palm facing down, from left to right in front of the body in small arcs.

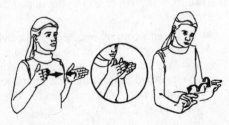

minimum[1] *n.* **1.** The least possible or allowable amount: *had to take the minimum for their house.* —*adj.* **2.** Least possible: *Use the minimum amount of salt.* Same sign used for: **below, least, less.**

- ■ [Indicates that something exceeds the base or minimum] Beginning with the back of the right *B hand,* palm facing down and fingers pointing left, touching the palm of the left *open hand,* palm facing down and fingers pointing right, bring the right hand downward a few inches.

minimum[2] *n., adj.* (alternate sign)

- ■ [Indicates that something falls short of the base or minimum] Beginning with the palm side of the right *open hand* on the back of the left *open hand,* both palms facing down and fingers pointing in opposite directions, raise the right hand upward in front of the chest.

minister[1] *v.* To serve others by giving comfort, aid, etc.: *to minister to the sick.*

- ■ [Initialized sign similar to sign for **preach**[1]] Move the right *M hand* forward with a short double movement in front of the right shoulder, palm facing forward.

minister[2] *v.* (alternate sign)

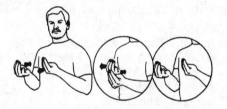

- ■ [Initialized sign similar to sign for **serve**] Beginning with both *M hands* in front of each side of the body, palms facing up, move them forward and back with an alternating movement

minister[3] *n.* A person who serves a religious group, as by conducting religious services, counseling the congregation, etc.: *The new minister preached the sermon.*

- ■ [**minister**[1,2] + **person marker**] Beginning with both *M hands* in front of each side of the body, palms facing up, move them forward and back with an alternating movement. Then move both *open hands,* palms facing each other, downward along each side of the body.

minister[4] *v.* See signs for PREACH, SERVE.

minister[5] *n.* See sign for PREACHER.

ministry *n.* The duties and service of a clergy: *a ministry to deaf people.* Same sign used for: **mission.**

- [Initialized sign similar to sign for **church**] Tap the heel of the right *M hand*, palm facing forward, on the back of the left *S hand* held in front of the chest, palm facing down.

Minneapolis *n.* A large city in southeast Minnesota: *Minneapolis is on the Mississippi River.*

- Tap the fingertips of the right *D hand*, palm facing in, against the left side of the chest with a double movement.

minor[1] *adj.* Less, as in size, amount, or importance: *a few minor problems.*

- [Shows something taking a lesser position under another] Slide the index-finger side of the right *B hand*, palm facing left and fingers pointing forward, forward under the little-finger side of the left *B hand*, palm facing right and fingers pointing forward.

minor[2] *adj.* See sign for NOTHING[4].

minority *n.* The smaller part, forming less than half of the whole: *The minority of the group voted to stay home.*

- [**minor** + **class**] Slide the index-finger side of the right *B hand*, palm facing left and fingers pointing forward, forward under the little-finger side of the left *B hand*, palm facing right and fingers pointing forward. Then, beginning with both *C hands* in front of the chest, palms facing each other, bring the hands away from each other in outward arcs while turning the palms in, ending with the little fingers near each other.

minus[1] *prep.* Less by the subtraction of: *Ten minus five equals five.*

- [Shape of a minus sign] Touch the thumb side of the extended right index finger, palm facing down and finger pointing forward, against the palm of the left *open hand*, palm facing right.

minus[2] *prep.* See sign for SUBTRACT.

minute *n.* **1.** One of the 60 equal periods of time that make up an hour: *The dinner will come out of the microwave in two minutes.* **2.** A very short period of time; moment: *Wait a minute.* Same sign used for: **moment, momentarily, one minute.**

- [The finger represents the movement of the minute hand on a clock] Move the extended right index finger, palm facing left, forward a short distance, pivoting the closed fingers of the right hand on the palm of the left *open hand,* palm facing right and fingers pointing up.

miracle *n.* A marvelous happening that defies nature: *It was a miracle that he survived the accident.*

- [**wonderful**[1,2] + **neat**[2]] Beginning with both *5 hands* in front of each shoulder, palms facing forward and fingers pointing up, bring the hands forward and upward in large arcs to near each side of the head. Then bring the thumb and index finger of the right *F hand,* palm facing in, back against the chin with a double movement.

mirror *n.* A smooth, shiny surface, usually a piece of glass with a silver or amalgam backing, that reflects images: *to look in a mirror to check your hair.*

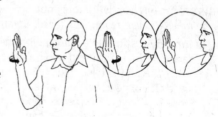

- [The hand represents a mirror] Beginning with the right *open hand* held up near the right shoulder, palm facing left, twist the wrist to turn the palm forward and back with a double movement.

misbehavior *n.* Bad or inappropriate conduct: *The teacher won't tolerate misbehavior.*

- [**bad** + **behavior**] Move the fingers of the right *open hand* from the mouth, palm facing in, downward while flipping the palm quickly down as the hand moves. Then move both *B hands,* palms facing down and fingers pointing forward, simultaneously from side to side in front of the body with a swinging movement.

mischief *n.* See sign for DEVIL. Related form: **mischievous** *adj.*

misconception *n.* See sign for MISUNDERSTAND.

misconduct *n.* Improper or unlawful behavior: *The treasurer of the corporation was fired for gross misconduct.* Same sign used for: **misdeed.**

misdeal

■ **[bad + act¹]** Move the fingers of the right *open hand* from the mouth, palm facing in, downward while flipping the palm quickly down as the hand moves. Then move both *C hands,* palms facing down, simultaneously back and forth in front of the body with a swinging movement.

misdeal *v.* **1.** To deal cards incorrectly: *You misdealt the hand.* —*n.* **2.** An incorrect deal at cards: *We started over because of the misdeal.*

■ **[wrong + play¹ + deal²]** Bring the middle fingers of the right *Y hand,* palm facing in, against the chin. Then swing both *Y hands* up and down by twisting the wrists in front of each side of the chest. Then, beginning with the back of the right *flattened O hand* in the palm of the left *open hand* held in front of the body, both palms facing up, move the right hand forward with a repeated movement in several directions.

misdeed *n.* See sign for MISCONDUCT.

misdemeanor *n.* See signs for CRIME[1,2].

miser¹ *n.* A person who holds onto money for its own sake; a stingy person: *a miser who won't even repair the house.* Related form: **miserly** *adv.*

■ **[greedy + stingy]** Beginning with the right *curved 5 hand* in front of the chin, palm facing in, bring the hand downward while closing the hand into an *S hand.* Then, beginning with the fingers of the right *curved 5 hand* on the palm of the left *open hand,* palms facing each other, bring the right hand back toward the heel of the left hand while closing into an *A hand.*

miser² *n.* See sign for STINGY. Related form: **miserly** *adv.*

miserable *adj.* Very uncomfortable or unhappy; wretched: *I was miserable waiting for two hours in the hot sun.*

■ With a repeated alternating movement, touch the chin with the extended right index finger and then the left.

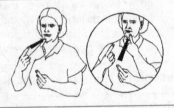

misfit *n.* **1.** A person who is not well suited to the prevailing situation, social environment, etc.: *That boy is a misfit at his school.* **2.** Something, as a garment, that does not fit properly: *The plaid jacket is a misfit.*

■ [**wrong** + **match**[1]] Tap the middle fingers of the right *Y hand,* palm facing in, against the chin with a double movement. Then, beginning with both *curved 5 hands* in front of the chest, palms facing in, bring the hands together, ending with the bent fingers of both hands meshed together in front of the chest.

misfortune *n.* Bad luck: *Her life has been full of misfortune since childhood.*

■ [**bad** + **trouble**[1,2]] Move the fingers of the right *open hand* from the mouth, palm facing in, downward while flipping the palm quickly down as the hand moves. Then, beginning with both *B hands* near each side of the head, palms angled toward each other, move the right hand to the left and the left hand to the right with an alternating double movement.

misguided *adj.* Led into wrongdoing: *The boy is not evil—simply misguided.* Same sign used for: **mislead.**

■ [**wrong** + **lead**[1,2]] Tap the middle fingers of the right *Y hand,* palm facing in, against the chin with a double movement. Then, with the right fingers grasping the fingers of the left *open hand,* both palms facing in, in front of the left side of the body, pull the left hand to the right.

misjudge *v.* To judge wrongly or unjustly: *The teacher misjudged the student's honesty.*

■ [**wrong** + **judge**[1]] Tap the middle fingers of the right *Y hand,* palm facing in, against the chin with a double movement. Then move both *F hands,* palms facing each other, up and down in front of each side of the chest with a repeated alternating movement.

mislay *v.* See signs for MISPLACE[1,2].

mislead *v.* See sign for MISGUIDED.

mismanage *v.* To manage badly, inefficiently, or dishonestly: *to mismanage the business and drive it into bankruptcy.* Related form: **mismanagement** *n.*

■ [**not**[1] + **right**[3] + **manage**] Bring the extended thumb of the right *10 hand* from under the chin, palm facing left, forward with a deliberate movement. Then, with the index fingers of both hands extended forward at right angles, palms angled in, bring the little-finger side of the right hand sharply down

across the thumb side of the left hand. Then, beginning with both *X hands* in front of each side of the body, right hand forward of the left hand and palms facing each other, move the hands forward and back with a repeated alternating movement.

misplace[1] *v.* To put somewhere and not remember where: *to misplace your keys.* Same sign used for: **mislay.**

■ [**lose**[1] + **place**[1]] Beginning with the fingertips of both *flattened O hands* touching in front of the chest, palms facing in, drop the hands quickly downward and away from each other while opening into *5 hands,* ending with both palms facing down and

fingers pointing forward. Then, beginning with the middle finger of both *P hands* touching in front of the body, palms facing each other, move the hands apart and back in a circular movement until they touch again near the chest.

misplace[2] *v.* (alternate sign) Same sign used for: **mislay.**

■ [**careless**[1,2] + **put**] Beginning with both *V hands* in front of the face, palms facing in opposite directions, move the right hand to the left in front of the eyes and the left hand to the right in front of the eyes with an alternating movement. Then, beginning with both *flattened O hands* in front of the body, palms facing down, move the hands upward and forward in a small arc.

misprint *n.* **1.** A mistake in printing: *I found a misprint in this book.* —*v.* **2.** To print incorrectly, as by misspelling: *The bank misprinted my name on my checks.*

■ [**careless**[1,2] + **print** + **this**[1]] Beginning with both *V hands* in front of the face, palms facing in opposite directions, move the right hand to the left in front of the eyes and the left hand to the right in front of the eyes with an alternating movement. Then, beginning with the thumb of the right *G hand,* palm facing down, resting on the heel of the left *open hand,* palm facing up, close the right index finger to the thumb with a double movement.

mispronounce *v.* To pronounce incorrectly: *The speaker mispronounced the name of this city.*

■ [**careless**[1,2] + **talk**[2,3]] Beginning with both *V hands* in front of the face, palms facing in opposite directions, move the right hand to the left in front of the eyes and the left hand to the right in front of the eyes with an alternating movement. Then, beginning with the index-finger side of the right *4 hand* in front of the chin, palm facing left and fingers pointing up, move the hand forward with a double movement.

misread *v.* To read and interpret incorrectly: *I misread your article and thought you meant something else.*

■ [**wrong** + **read**[1]] Tap the middle fingers of the right *Y hand*, palm facing in, against the chin with a double movement. Then move the fingertips of the right *V hand*, palm facing down, from the fingers to the heel of the left *open hand*, palm facing up.

miss[1] *v.* **1.** To fail to hit or strike: *The batter swung at the ball and missed.* **2.** To fail to catch or come into the presence of: *to miss the bus.* **3.** To overlook or let go by, as an opportunity: *to miss a chance.*

■ [The hand seems to snatch at something as it passes] Move the right *C hand*, palm facing left, from near the right side of the forehead in a quick downward arc in front of the face while closing into an *S hand*, ending with the palm facing down in front of the left shoulder.

miss[2] *v.* To fail to notice or pay attention to (something said); used especially as an informal sign indicating that the speaker is unwilling to repeat: *The coach told the late player that he would have to sit the game out because had missed the game plan.* Same sign used for: **You're too late.**

■ [**train**[1] + **zoom**[1]] Rub the extended fingers of the right *H hand* across the back of the extended fingers of the left *H hand*, both palms facing down. Then, beginning with the thumb of the right *L hand*, palm angled forward, on the base of the extended left index finger, palm facing down, move the right hand quickly to the right while closing the index finger to the thumb.

miss[3] *v.* See signs for ABSENT, DISAPPOINTED, SKIP[1]. Related form: **missing** *adj.*

missile[1] *n.* A weapon propelled by a rocket: *launched the missile at the enemy target.*

■ [Shows movement of a missile ejecting] Beginning with the heel of the right *1 hand*, palm facing forward, on the back of the left *open hand*, palm facing down, raise the right hand upward in front of the face.

missile[2] *n.* See signs for ROCKET[1,2].

mission *n.* See sign for MINISTRY.

missionary *n.* A person sent by a church to a foreign country to do religious work and perform humanitarian services: *The missionary set up a hospital, a school, and a church.*

- ■ [Initialized sign] Move the index-finger side of the right *M hand,* palm facing left, in a double circle on the left side of the chest.

mistake[1] *n.* A blunder or error, as in action or judgment: *It was a mistake to leave without resolving the argument.* Related form: **mistaken** *adj.* Same sign used for: **accident.**

- ■ [Similar to sign for **wrong** but made with a double movement] Tap the middle fingers of the right *Y hand,* palm facing in, against the chin with a double movement.

mistake[2] *n.* (alternate sign) Related form: **mistaken** *adj.* Same sign used for: **error.**

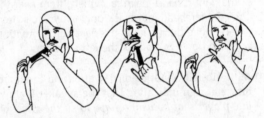

- ■ [Similar to sign for **wrong** except with a repeated movement] Alternatingly bring the middle fingers of first the left *Y hand,* and then the right *Y hand,* and then the left hand again against the chin with an alternating movement, palms facing in.

mistrust *v.* **1.** To lack confidence in; doubt; suspect: *I wish I didn't mistrust my ability to handle the job.* —*n.* **2.** Lack of confidence or trust: *filled with mistrust of their motives.* Related form: **mistrustful** *adj.* Same sign used for: **distrust.**

- ■ [**not**[1] + **confident**] Bring the extended thumb of the right *10 hand* from under the chin, palm facing left, forward with a deliberate movement. Then, beginning with the little-finger side of the left *curved 5 hand* against the index-finger side of the right *curved 5 hand,* both palms facing up, close the hands quickly into *S hands* while moving the hands downward a short distance in front of the chest.

misty *adj.* See signs for WET[1,2].

misunderstand *v.* To understand incorrectly: *I misunderstood the directions.* Related form: **misunderstanding** *n.* Same sign used for: **misconception.**

- ■ [The fingers indicate something turned around in the mind] Touch the index finger of the right *V hand* to the right side of the forehead, palm facing forward, and then twist the wrist and touch the middle finger to the forehead, ending with the palm facing back.

misuse *v.* **1.** To use for the wrong purpose: *He misused the chain saw to trim the bushes.* **2.** To use inappropriately: *If you misuse polysyllabic words, you'll sound both pompous and foolish.*

■ [**not**[1] + **right**[3] + **use**[1,2]] Bring the extended thumb of the right *10 hand* from under the chin, palm facing left, forward with a deliberate movement. Then, with the index fingers of both hands extended forward at right angles, palms angled in, bring the little-finger side of the right hand sharply down across the thumb side of the left hand. Then move the right *U hand*, palm facing forward and fingers pointing up, in a small circle in front of the right shoulder.

mitten *n.* A long, sometimes padded glove with a single enclosure for the four fingers and a separate one for the thumb: *wearing mittens in cold weather; an oven mitt.* Alternate form: **mitt.**

■ [Shape of a mitten] With the extended right index finger, palm facing down and finger pointing forward, trace the shape of the left *open hand*, palm facing in and fingers pointing up, beginning at the base of the thumb and ending at the base of the little finger.

mix[1] *v.* To put together; combine: *to mix the ingredients for the cake.* Same sign used for: **blend, complex, complicate, confuse, disorder, garbled, scramble, stir.**

■ [Mime mixing things up] Beginning with the right *curved 5 hand* over the left *curved 5 hand*, palms facing each other, move the hands in repeated circles in front of the chest in opposite directions.

mix[2] *v.* See signs for BEAT[1,2], CIRCULATE[1].

mixed up See sign for CONFUSE[1].

moat *n.* A deep, wide ditch dug around a fortified place, as a castle or town, and usually filled with water: *The knight's enemies crossed the moat and stormed the castle.*

■ [**water** + location and shape of a moat] Tap the index-finger side of the right *W hand*, palm facing left and fingers pointing up, against the chin with a double movement. Then, beginning with the right *C hand*, palm facing down, crossed over the left *C hand*, palm facing right, move the right hand in a forward arc to the right, ending near the left fingertips.

mob *n.* A large number of people, usually unruly: *The mob pushed at the gate.* Same sign used for: **havoc, mess, riot.**

mobile

■ [Indicates that a mob is out of control] Beginning with the right *curved 5 hand* over the left *curved 5 hand,* palms facing each other, twist the hands with a sharp deliberate movement, pulling the right hand upward and the left hand downward, ending with the right hand in front of the right shoulder and the left hand in front of the left side of the body.

mobile *adj.* Easy to move: *a mobile hospital.*
Same sign used for: **moveable.**

■ [Sign similar to sign for **move**[1] except indicates moving in different directions] Beginning with both *flattened O hands* in front of the right side of the body, palms facing down, move the hands forward with a wavy movement.

mobilize *v.* See sign for TRIP[2].

moccasin *n.* A heelless shoe made of soft leather and having a characteristic U-shaped seam on the top: *These deerskin shoes look like authentic Indian moccasins.*

■ [**Indian** + **shoe**] Move the fingertips of the right *F hand* from near the right side of the mouth to the right temple, palm facing left. Then tap the index-finger side of both *S hands,* palms facing down, together in front of the chest with a double movement.

mock *v.* To ridicule; make fun of: *It is insensitive of them to mock her foreign accent.* Same sign used for: **jeer, laugh at.**

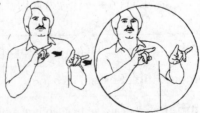

■ [The fingers seem to jeer at another] Move both *Y hands,* palms facing down, forward a short distance with a double movement from in front of each side of the chest

model *n.* **1.** Something or someone worth imitating; exemplar: *The teacher was a good model for the children.* **2.** A person whose profession is posing, displaying products for advertising, or wearing and displaying clothing, as for photographers: *a young model whose work has taken her all over the world.* —*v.* **3.** To serve as a model for: *to model dresses.* Related form: **modeling** *n.*

■ [Initialized sign similar to sign for **show**[1]] With the index-finger side of the right *M hand,* palm angled left, against the palm of the left *open hand,* palm angled forward, move both hands forward a short distance.

modem *n.* Acronym for *modulator-demodulator.* A device used by a computer to communicate with remote computers through telephone lines.

- **[telephone + insert]** Bring in the knuckles of the right *Y hand* to touch the lower right cheek, holding the right thumb near the right cheek and the little finger in front of the mouth. Then slide the little-finger side of the right *open hand*, palm facing up, between the right and middle fingers of the left *4 hand*, palm facing right.

modest *adj.* See signs for HUMBLE[1,2]. Related form: **modesty** *n.*

modify[1] *v.* To change somewhat; alter partially: *You'd better modify the tone of your letter.* Related form: **modification** *n.*

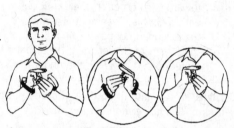

- [Initialized sign similar to sign for **change**[1]] Beginning with the palm sides of both *M hands* facing each other in front of the chest, twist the hands in opposite directions with a double movement.

modify[2] *v.* See signs for CHANGE[1], CONVERT[2].

modular *adj.* **1.** Made of standardized units or sections that can be rearranged: *a modular home.* **2.** (of a computer program) Having a series of routines that can be programmed independently and reused: *a modular program.* Related form: **module** *n.* Same sign used for: **classification, classify.**

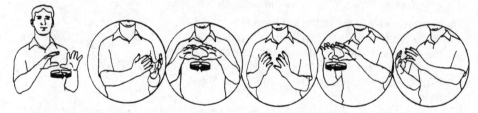

- **[class-class-class]** Beginning with both *C hands* in front of the left side of the chest, palms facing each other, bring the hands away from each other in outward arcs while turning the palms in. Repeat again in front of the chest and a third time in front of the right shoulder.

modules *pl. n.* See sign for ROUTINE[1].

moist *adj.* See signs for WET[1,2]. Related forms: **moisten** *v.*, **moisture** *n.*

mole[1] *n.* A small furry mammal with rudimentary eyes that lives primarily underground: *The mole burrowed under the lawn.*

mole

■ [Represents the action of mole burrowing through dirt] Beginning with the back of both *open hands* together in front of the chest, palms facing in opposite directions, bend the fingers of each hand downward toward each palm with a double movement.

mole² *n.* (alternate sign)

■ [**animal** + a gesture indicating something crawling underground] Beginning with the fingertips of both *bent hands* on the chest near each shoulder, keep the fingers in place and roll the fingers toward each other on their knuckles with a double movement. Then move the extended right index finger, palm facing down and finger pointing forward, under the fingers of the left *bent hand,* palm facing right, while wiggling the right index finger up and down as the finger moves forward.

mole³ *n.* A small, often dark, raised spot on the skin: *She has a mole on her cheek.*

■ [**brown** + shape and location of a mole on the face] Slide the index-finger side of the right *B hand,* palm facing left, down the right cheek with a repeated movement. Then bring the thumb side of the right *F hand,* palm facing forward, against the right side of the chin.

molest *v.* To disturb or annoy, especially in a way that may cause harm: *Don't molest the animals in the cages.*

■ With the index finger of the left hand extended in front of the chest, palm facing right, and the index finger of the right hand extended, palm facing forward, rub the knuckles of the right hand back and forth with a double movement against the thumb side of the left hand.

molten *adj.* **1.** Liquified by heat: *molten lava pouring down the hillside.* **2.** Made from material that has been melted: *a molten statue.* Same sign used for: **melted.**

■ [**hot** + **dissolve**] Beginning with the right *curved 5 hand* held in front of the mouth, palm facing in, twist the wrist forward with a deliberate movement while moving the hand downward in front of the chest. Then, beginning with both *curved 5 hands* together in front of the chest, palms facing up, move the hands downward while sliding the thumb of each hand smoothly across each fingertip, starting with the little finger and ending as *A hands* in front of each side of the body, palms facing up.

mom *n.* See signs for MOTHER[1,2]. Diminutive form: **mommy**.

moment *n.* See sign for MINUTE. Related form: **momentarily** *adv.*

momentum *n.* See sign for CONSTANT[1].

monarch *n.* The hereditary ruler of a land: *the monarch of Russia.*

- **[king + chief[1]]** Move the right *K hand*, palm facing in, from touching the left side of the chest near the shoulder downward to touch again near the right side of the waist. Then move the right *10 hand*, palm facing in and thumb pointing up, upward from in front of the right side of the chest.

monastery *n.* A residence for the members of a religious order, especially monks living in relative seclusion: *a monastery supported in part by sale of its homemade bread.* Same sign used for: **convent, parsonage, rectory.**

- **[church + house]** Tap the thumb of the right *C hand*, palm angled left, on the back of the left hand, palm facing down, with a double movement. Then, beginning with the fingertips of both *B hands* touching in front of the face, palms angled toward each other, bring the hands at a downward angle outward to in front of each shoulder and then straight down, ending with the fingers pointing forward and the palms facing each other.

Monday *n.* The second day of the week, after Sunday: *The work week begins on Monday.*

- [Initialized sign] Move the right *M hand*, palm facing up, in a double circle in front of the right shoulder.

money *n.* Coins and paper notes issued by a government for use in buying and selling: *Don't spend all your money at once.* Same sign used for: **fund.**

- [Represents putting money in one's hand] Tap the back of the right *flattened O hand*, palm facing up, with a double movement against the palm of the left *open hand*, palm facing up.

mongrel *n.* **1.** An animal, especially a dog, of mixed or undetermined breed: *Our new dog is a mongrel with a great personality.* —*adj.* **2.** Of mixed breed: *a mongrel dog.*

monitor

■ [**conflict**[1] + **dog**[1,2]] Beginning with both extended index fingers in front of each side of the body, palms facing in and fingers angled toward each other, move the hands toward each other, ending with the fingers crossed. Then, with a double movement, snap the right thumb gently off the right middle finger, palm facing up, in front of the right side of the chest.

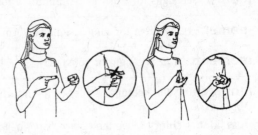

monitor[1] *v.* To observe for a special purpose: *a camera that will monitor the kids in the playground.*

■ [The fingers represent the eyes watching something to monitor it] Beginning with both *V hands* in front of the body, palms facing down and fingers pointing forward, move the hands from side to side in front of the body with a simultaneous double movement.

monitor[2] *v.* See sign for CARE[1].

monitor[3] *n.* See sign for TERMINAL[1].

monkey *n.* A small primate, usually having a long tail: *Watch the monkey swing from the bars by its tail.* Same sign used for: **ape, chimpanzee.**

■ [Mime the scratching motion done by monkeys] Beginning at the waist, scratch the fingertips of both *curved 5 hands*, palms facing in, upward on each side of the body with a double movement.

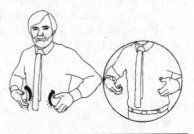

monkey wrench *n.* A wrench with an adjustable moveable jaw for grasping: *tighten the bolt with a monkey wrench.*

■ [**monkey** + **wrench**] Beginning at the waist, scratch the fingertips of both *curved 5 hands*, palms facing in, upward on each side of the body with a double movement. Then, with the extended left index finger inserted between the index finger and middle finger of the right *3 hand*, palm facing left, twist the right hand up and down with a double movement.

monogram *n.* A design formed from one or more letters, usually a person's initials, used to mark or identify objects, as towels or note paper: *a tasteful monogram on the hotel towels.*

■ [**name** + the location of a monogram on a sweater] Tap the middle-finger side of the right *H hand* across the index-finger side of the left *H hand* with a double movement. Then place the fingertips of the right *curved 5 hand* on the left side of the chest.

monograph *n.* See sign for JOURNAL[1].

monologue *n.* **1.** A piece spoken by a single performer: *The comic starts his show with a monologue.* **2.** A long speech by one person: *a boring monologue delivered on the Senate floor.*

■ [**alone**[1,2] + **talk**[3]] With the right index finger extended up, move the right hand, palm facing back, in a small circle in front of the right shoulder. Then, beginning with the right *4 hand* in front of the chin, palm facing left and fingers pointing up, move the hand forward with a double movement.

monotonous[1] *adj.* Lacking variety: *Working on an assembly line can be monotonous work.* Related form: **monotony** *n.* Same sign used for: **monotone.**

■ [Shows repetitive activity] Rub the index-finger side of the right *S hand*, palm facing down, in a repeated circular movement on the palm of the left *open hand* held in front of the chest, palm facing right.

monotonous[2] *adj.* See signs for BORING[1], GRIND OUT.

monsignor *n.* See sign for SASH[1]. Shared idea of the sash that is part of a monsignor's ceremonial costume.

monster *n.* A creature, imaginary or not, with exaggerated features unlike those usually found in nature: *They claim they saw a monster rising up from the ocean.* Same sign used for: **haunt, haunted, spooky.**

■ [Mime the action and facial expression of a monster] Beginning with both *curved 5 hands* held near each side of the head, palms facing down, move the hands up and down with a double movement accompanied by a menacing facial expression.

Monster Cable *Trademark.* A brand of consumer cable whose name has become synonymous with any boutique cable claiming to provide higher quality sound or video when used to connect audio and video components.

month

■ [Size and shape of large cable] Beginning with the index-finger side of both *C hands* touching in front of the body, palms facing down, bring the hands to each side apart from each other.

month *n.* **1.** One of the 12 parts into which a year is divided: *April is my favorite month.* **2.** A period of time of approximately 30 days: *I'll see you in one month.* Same sign used for: **one month.**

■ [The finger moves down the weeks on a calendar] Move the extended right index finger, palm facing in and finger pointing left, from the tip to the base of the extended left index finger, palm facing right and finger pointing up in front of the chest.

monthly *adv.* Same sign as for MONTH but formed with a double movement.

monument *n.* A structure constructed in memory of a person or event: *the Washington Monument.*

■ [Shows the shape of the top of a monument] Beginning with both *B hands* in front of each shoulder, palms angled down, bring the hands upward toward each other, ending with the fingertips touching in front of the head.

moo *n.* **1.** The sound made by a cow: *I heard the cow's moo.* —*v.* **2.** To make the sound of a cow: *the cow mooed.*

■ [**cow**[1,2] + **scream**[1,2]] With the thumb of the right *Y hand* on the right side of the forehead, palm facing down, twist the hand forward with a repeated movement. Then, beginning with the right *curved 5 hand* in front of the mouth, palm facing in, bring the hand forward.

mooch *v. Slang.* See sign for LEECH.

moody *adj.* See sign for MOPE.

moon *n.* **1.** The natural heavenly body that revolves around the earth: *Look at the full moon shining through those trees.* **2.** Any similar body orbiting another planet: *Io is one of the moons of Jupiter.*

■ [The shape of the crescent moon] Tap the thumb of the right *modified C hand*, palm facing left, against the right side of the forehead with a double movement.

moonlight *n.* The light reflected from the surface of the moon: *He could see an outline of the bear in the moonlight.* Same sign used for: **moonbeam, moonshine.**

■ [**moon** + **light**[2]] Hold the thumb side of the right *modified C hand,* palm facing left, against the right side of the forehead. Then, beginning with the right *flattened O hand* near the right side of the head, palm facing down, move the hand downward and forward while opening into a *5 hand.*

mop *n.* **1.** A cleaning tool with an absorbent head and long handle: *Let's use a mop to clean the kitchen floor.* —*v.* **2.** To clean with a mop: *to mop the floor.*

■ [Mime using a mop] Beginning with both *modified X hands* in front of the body, the left hand lower than the right hand, palms angled up, move the hands forward and downward with a double movement.

mope *v.* To be sad and sullen; brood: *He moped around the house for days.* Same sign used for: **moody.**

■ [**always** + **sad**] With the right index finger extended up, move the right hand, palm facing back, in a repeated circle in front of the right shoulder. Then move both *5 hands* from in front of each side of the face, palms facing in and fingers pointing up, downward a short distance.

moped *n.* See sign for MOTORCYCLE.

moral *adj.* Being of good character; concerned with right conduct; ethical: *She's a highly moral person, so don't ask her to lie for you.* Related form: **morals** *pl. n.*

■ [**good** + **character**[1,2]] Beginning with the fingertips of the right *open hand* near the mouth, palm facing in and fingers pointing up, bring the hand downward, ending with the back of the right hand across the palm of the left *open hand,* both palms facing up. Then move the right *C hand,* palm facing left, in a small circle and then back against the left side of the chest.

more *adj.* **1.** Greater in amount, quantity, degree, etc.: *more food.* —*adv.* **2.** In or to a greater degree: *It's a more interesting excuse than most.* **3.** In addition or additionally; again: *We need to exercise more.*

■ [The hands seem to add more and more things together] Tap the fingertips of both *flattened O hands,* palms facing down, together in front of the chest with a double movement.

more than See sign for EXCESS.

Mormon *n.* A member of the Church of Jesus Christ of Latter-Day Saints founded by Joseph Smith in 1830: *Although their religion has spread, many Mormons still live in Utah.*

■ [Initialized sign] Wipe the fingertips of the right *M hand,* palm facing down, with a double movement forward from the right side of the forehead, bending the fingers down each time.

morning *n.* The early part of the day, before noon: *to eat breakfast in the morning.*

■ [Represents the sun coming up over the horizon] With the left *open hand* in the crook of the bent right arm, bring the right *open hand* upward

moron¹ *n.* **1.** A stupid person: *He is a moron for forgetting to notify us.* **2.** (in a classification of mental retardation no longer in use) A person with an IQ above 50 and below 70: *tested as a moron on the intelligence test.* Same sign used for: **blockhead, square.**

■ [Indicates the small size of a moron's brain] Touch the fingertips of the right *G hand,* palm facing left, to the right side of the forehead, then twist the wrist and touch the fingers to the forehead again.

moron² *n.* (alternate sign) Same sign used for: **blockhead, feeble-minded, weak-minded.**

■ [Form the sign **weak** on the head to indicate weakness of intellect] Touch the fingertips of the right *curved hand* to the right side of the forehead, palm facing down, and then collapse the fingers with a double movement, bringing the palm close to the forehead each time.

morsel *n.* A small portion of food: *scattered morsels of bread for the birds.*

- [**food** + a gesture that seems to take a small amount of something from the hand + **amount**[1]] Bring the fingertips of the right *flattened O hand,* palm facing down, to the lips with a repeated movement. Then, with the index finger and thumb of the right hand pinched together, palm facing left, place the right fingertips on the palm of the left *open hand,* palm facing up. Then move the side of the extended right index finger, palm facing in, in a small arc from the heel to the center of the palm of the left *open hand,* palm facing up.

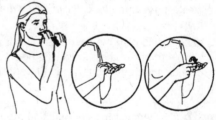

mortgage *n.* An agreement conveying interest in property in return for financial obligations to pay for it: *The mortgage payment is due on the first of each month.*

- [Initialized sign similar to sign for **lend**] With the little finger of the right *M hand* on the index finger of the left *M hand,* fingers pointing in opposite directions and palms facing in, tip the hands forward.

mosaic *n.* A design or picture made of small pieces of stone or glass applied to a surface: *The floor was a mosaic of colored tiles.*

- [**glass**[1] + showing how the pieces of a mosaic fit together] Tap the fingertip of the bent right index finger against the front teeth with a repeated movement. Then, with the fingers of the right *H hand* across the fingers of the left *H hand,* both palms facing down, twist the hands in opposite repeated movements, shifting the angle of the fingers.

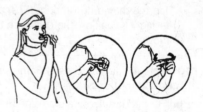

mosquito[1] *n.* A small slender insect, the female of which sucks the blood of humans and animals: *bitten by a mosquito.*

- [Represents a mosquito biting one's cheek, causing one to hit it in order to kill it] Touch the fingertips of the right *F hand,* palm facing left, on the right cheek. Then place the palm of the right *open hand* against the same place on the right cheek.

mosquito[2] *n.* (alternate sign)

- [Represents a mosquito biting one's hand, causing one to hit it in order to kill it] Touch the fingertips of the right *F hand,* palm facing down, on the back of the left hand held in front of the chest. Then place the palm of the right *open hand* against the same place on the back of the left hand.

mosquito[3] *n.* See signs for BEE[1,2,3].

most *adj., adv.* **1.** To or in the highest degree, amount, etc.: *the most money; the most cooperative.* —*n.* **2.** The greatest amount: *Of all those at the dinner, he ate the most.*

■ Beginning with the palm sides of both *10 hands* together in front of the chest, bring the right hand upward, ending with the right hand in front of the right shoulder, palm facing left.

moth *n.* A winged insect similar to a butterfly: *Moths fly at night.*

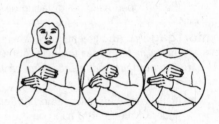

■ [Initialized sign similar to sign for **butterfly**] Beginning with the little-finger side of the right *M hand* across the index-finger side of the left *M hand,* both palms facing in, bend the fingers of both hands back toward each palm with a double movement.

mother[1] *n.* A female parent: *Her hair is the same color as her mother's.* Same sign used for: **mama, mom, mommy.**

■ [Formed in the female area of the head] Tap the thumb of the right *5 hand,* palm facing left, against the chin with a double movement.

mother[2] *n.* (alternate sign) Same sign used for: **mama, mom, mommy.**

■ [Formed in the female area of the head] With the thumb of the right *5 hand* on the chin, palm facing left, wiggle the fingers with a repeated movement.

motherboard *n.* In a computer, the primary circuit board into which circuit cards, boards, or modules are plugged: *The computer's motherboard needs repair.* Same sign used for: **controller, mainboard.**

■ [**specialize**[2] + **board**[3]] Slide the extended right index finger from the base to the fingertip of the index finger of the left *B hand.* Then bring the little-finger side of the right *B hand,* palm left, sharply against the palm of the left *C hand* held in front of the chest, palm facing up.

mother-in-law *n.* The mother of one's husband or wife: *cleaning house before a visit from my mother-in-law.*

- ■ [**mother**^{1,2} + **law**] With the thumb of the right *5 hand* touching the chin, palm facing left, wiggle the fingers with a repeated movement. Then place the palm side of the right *L hand* first on the fingers and then on the heel of the upturned left *open hand* held in front of the body.

motion¹ *n.* The action or process of changing position or place: *I feel the motion of the train.* Same sign used for: **movement.**

- ■ [Initialized sign similar to sign for **do**] Move both *flattened O hands,* palms facing down, simultaneously back and forth in front of the body with a swinging movement.

motion² *n.* See sign for SUGGEST. Related form: **move** *v.*

motive *n.* See signs for FEEL, ZEAL. Related form: **motivation** *n.*

motor *n.* See signs for MACHINE, ENGINE¹.

motorcycle *n.* A two-wheeled motorized vehicle: *ride a motorcycle.* Same sign used for: **moped, snowmobile.**

- ■ [Mime the action of one's hands on a motorcycle's handlebars] Beginning with both *S hands* held near each side of the waist, palms facing back, twist the wrists to move the hands up and down with a repeated movement.

motto *n.* **1.** A brief phrase adopted as a rule of conduct: *"Try, try again,"* is my motto. **2.** A saying expressing the spirit or aims of an organization: *After a series of defeats, the team decided they needed a new motto.*

- ■ [**say**^{1,2} + **sentence** + **quotation**¹] Move the extended right index finger in a repeated circular upward movement in front of the chin, palm facing in and finger pointing left. Next, beginning with the fingertips of both *F hands* together in front of the chest, palms facing each other, bring the hands apart to in front of each shoulder with a wavy movement. Then, beginning with both *V hands* held near each side of the head, palms facing forward, bend the fingers downward with a double movement.

mount

mount[1] *v.* To put in proper position, as on a support or backing: *to mount the pictures on the page.* Same sign used for: **overlap.**

- [Demonstrates the position of two things that are overlapped] Beginning with the left *open hand* in front of the left side of the chest, palm facing down and fingers pointing right, bring the right *curved hand*, palm facing up, over to land on the back of the left hand, ending with both palms facing down.

mount[2] *v.* See sign for PUT.

mountain *n.* A very high elevation of land, higher than a hill: *the beautiful craggy mountains of Montana.*

- [**rock**[1,2] + **hill**[2]] Tap the palm side of the right *S hand* on the back of the left *S hand,* both palms facing down in front of the body. Then, beginning with both *open hands* in front of each side of the waist, palms facing down and fingers angled up, move the hands upward and forward at an angle with a large wavy movement.

mournful *adj.* See sign for SAD.

mouse[1] *n.* **1.** A small gnawing rodent with pointed ears and a long, thin tail: *Don't be surprised if you see a mouse in the pantry.* **2.** A small device for controlling the pointer on a computer's display screen: *To open the file, click twice on the file name with the left button on your mouse.*

- [Represents the twitching of a mouse's nose] Flick the extended right index finger, palm facing left, across the tip of the nose with a double movement.

mouse[2] *n.* (alternate sign)

- [Action of moving a computer mouse] Move the right *modified C hand*, palm forward, around in front of the right side of the body

mouth *n.* The opening through which one takes in food: *You'll have to open your mouth wide for that sandwich.*

- [Location of the mouth] Draw a circle around the mouth with the extended right index finger, palm facing in.

mouthful *n.* The amount a mouth can easily hold: *a mouthful of food.*

- [**mouth + full**[2]] Draw a circle around the mouth with the extended right index finger, palm facing in. Then slide the palm of the right *open hand* from right to left across the index-finger side of the left *S hand*, palm facing right.

---

movable *adj.* See sign for MOBILE.

---

move[1] *v.* **1.** To change the position of: *Move the chair to the other side of the room.* **2.** To change the location of one's business or residence: *We're moving to the third floor.* Related form: **movement** *n.* Same sign used for: **relocate.**

- [The hands seem to move something from one place to another] Beginning with both *flattened O hands* in front of the body, palms facing down, move the hands in large arcs to the right.

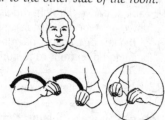

---

move[2] *v.* (alternate sign) Related form: **movement** *n.* Same sign used for: **relocate.**

- [The hands seem to move something from one place to another] Beginning with both *flattened O hands* in front of the body, palms facing down and right hand somewhat forward of the left hand, move the hands forward in simultaneous arcs.

---

move around *v. phrase.* **1.** To change the positions of (several things): *to move the furniture around.* **2.** To change (something) from one position or place to another several times: *We moved the picture around until the effect was right.*

- [The hands seem to move things around] Beginning with both *flattened O hands* in front of each side of the body, palms facing down, move the hands in a simultaneous flat circle in front of the body.

---

movement *n.* See sign for MOTION[1].

---

move on *v. phrase.* See sign for GO ON[1].

---

move out *v. phrase.* To change one's residence or place of business by moving one's belongings to another place: *She moved out of her parents' house when she was eighteen.* Same sign used for: **move away.**

movie

■ [The hands seem to toss one out] Beginning with both *flattened O hands* in front of the chest, palms facing down and elbows extended, move the hands in a large upward arc to the right while opening both hands into *5 hands*.

movie *n*. See sign for FILM[1].

movie camera *n*. A camera used for making motion pictures: *Film the birthday party with a movie camera.* Same sign used for: **camera, film, shoot, video camera, videotape.**

■ [Shows the action of movie film going through the camera] Move the right *modified X hand*, palm facing down, in a forward circular movement near the palm of the left *open hand*, palm facing right and fingers pointing up, in front of the upper chest.

MP3 player See sign for DIGITAL AUDIO PLAYER (DAP).

much *n*. **1.** A great amount: *carried too much.* —*adj.* **2.** In a great amount: *not much time.* —*adv.* **3.** Greatly: *much pleased.* Same sign used for: **a lot, lots.**

■ [The hands expand to encompass something large] Beginning with the fingertips of both *curved 5 hands* touching each other in front of the body, palms facing each other, bring the hands outward to in front of each side of the chest.

muck *n*. **1.** Moist, dark dirt; mud: *to walk through the muck.* **2.** Filth or slime: *What's this muck on the stove?*

■ [**dirty** + **scratch**[2]] With the back of the right *curved 5 hand* under the chin, palm facing down, wiggle the fingers. Then move the fingertips of the right *curved 5 hand*, palm facing down, from the fingers to the heel of the upturned palm of the left *open hand* with a double movement, bending the fingers back toward the palm each time.

mud *n*. Wet and sticky dirt: *They tracked mud in from the backyard.*

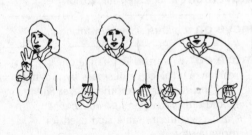

■ [**water** + **dirt**] Tap the index finger of the right *W hand*, palm facing left, against the chin with a double movement. Then, beginning with both *flattened O hands* in front of each side of the body, palms facing up, move the thumb of each hand smoothly across each fingertip, starting with the little fingers and ending as *A hands*.

muffle *v.* To stop (sound) from being emitted from the mouth by covering the mouth with the hand: *The girls muffled their giggling by hiding under the covers.* Same sign used for: **cover one's mouth.**

- [Natural gesture] Place the palm side of the right *C hand* over the mouth.

muggy *adj.* (of the weather) Oppressively warm and damp: *a muggy day.*

- [**hot** + **day**] Beginning with the right *curved 5 hand* in front of the mouth, palm facing in, twist the wrist forward with a deliberate movement while moving the hand downward a short distance. Then, beginning with the bent right elbow resting on the back of the left hand held across the body, palm facing down, bring the extended right index finger from pointing up in front of the right shoulder, palm facing left, downward toward the left elbow.

mule *n.* See signs for DONKEY[1,2].

mull or **mull over** *v.* To think about carefully: *to mull over a decision.* Same sign used for: **cogitate, deliberate, ponder.**

- [Represents the brain as it cogitates] Wiggle the fingers of the right *4 hand* in a small repeated circle near the forehead, palm facing in.

multiple *adj.* Consisting of a great number: *to finish multiple tasks on Saturday.* Same sign used for: **numerous.**

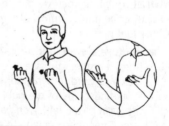

- [Natural gesture for indicating multiple things] Beginning with both *S hands,* palms facing in, in front of each side of the chest, with a repeated movement flick the fingers open quickly into *5 hands* each time, palms angled up.

multiplication *n.* See signs for ARITHMETIC, MATHEMATICS.

multiply *v.* To add a number to itself a given number of times: *If you multiply the number 12 by 7, you get 84.* Same sign used for: **estimate, figure, figure out.**

- Brush the back of the right *V hand* across the palm side of the left *V hand,* both palms facing up, as the hands cross in front of the chest.

mumble *v.* **1.** To speak indistinctly: *He mumbled in his sleep.* —*n.* **2.** Indistinct speech: *I couldn't understand the speaker's mumble.*

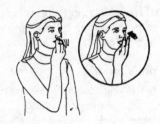

■ [Initialized sign showing that words are garbled in the mouth] Beginning with the *M hand* in front of the mouth, palm facing in and fingers pointing up, open and close the fingers with a small repeated movement.

mumps *n.* A contagious viral disease marked by swollen glands: *vaccinated against the mumps.*

■ [Shows the shape of one's swollen jaws from mumps] Beginning with both *curved 5 hands* in front of each shoulder, palms facing each other, bring the hands in to touch each side of the neck.

munch *v.* To chew steadily: *to munch on popcorn during the movie.*

■ [Represents a person biting to munch on something + **bite**] Beginning with the back of the right *curved 5 hand* against the mouth, palm facing forward, open and close the hand into a *flattened O hand* with a repeated movement. Then, with the thumb of the right *C hand,* palm facing left, in the thumb-side opening of the left *flattened O hand* held in front of the chest, palm facing down and fingers pointing forward, open and close the fingertips of the right hand on the left index finger.

mural *n.* A large picture painted directly on a wall or ceiling: *a mural of the Civil War in the lobby.*

■ [**picture** + **wall**[1]] Move the right *C hand* from near the right side of the face, palm facing forward, downward, ending with the index-finger side of the right *C hand* against the palm of the left *open hand,* palm facing right. Then, beginning with the index-finger sides of both *B hands* together in front of the chest, palms facing forward and fingers pointing up, move the hands apart to in front of each shoulder.

murder[1] *n.* **1.** The unlawful killing of someone: *to get away with murder.* —*v.* **2.** To kill: *The drug dealer was murdered by a gang.*

■ [Initialized sign similar to the sign for **kill**] Slide the index-finger side of the right *M hand,* palm facing down, across the palm of the left *open hand,* palm facing right.

murder[2] *v.* See sign for KILL[1].

murderer[1] *n.* A person who has committed murder: *The murderer wasn't identified until one year after the killings.*

- [**murder + person marker**] Slide the index-finger side of the right *M hand*, palm facing down, across the palm of the left *open hand*, palm facing right. Then move both *open hands*, palms facing each other, downward along each side of the body.

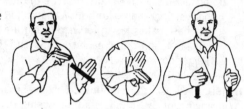

murderer[2] *n.* See sign for ASSASSIN.

murky *adj.* Clouded and dark: *murky water.*

- [Shows the swirling of murky water around an object] Beginning with the bent right arm extended over the left *open hand*, palm facing right and fingers pointing up, move the right *open hand*, palm facing right and fingers pointing down, in an arc around the little-finger side of the left hand while the left hand moves around the right hand.

muscle[1] *n.* A special bundle of tissue in the body composed of long cells that contract to produce movement: *The weight lifter has enormous muscles.*

- [Location of a muscle in the arm] Tap the extended right index finger against the upper part of the bent left arm with a double movement.

muscle[2] *n.* (alternate sign)

- [Initialized sign showing location of a muscle in the arm] Tap the fingertips of the right *M hand* against the upper part of the bent left arm with a double movement.

muscle[3] *n.* (alternate sign)

- [Initialized sign similar to sign for **strong**[2] showing the shape of a muscle in the arm] Beginning with the index-finger side of the right *M hand*, palm facing down and fingers pointing left, against the upper bent left arm, bring the right hand downward while twisting the palm up, ending with the little-finger side of the right hand on the left forearm.

museum *n.* A building intended for the display of objects of public interest: *The city has a wonderful art museum.*

- [Initialized sign showing the shape of museum shelves] Beginning with both *M hands* in front of the chest, palms facing forward, bring the hands outward to in front of each shoulder and then straight down.

music *n.* Pleasant or emotionally expressive arrangements of sounds, as those using rhythm, melody, and harmony: *Play some soft music.* Same sign used for: **chant, hymn, melody, sing, song.**

- [Demonstrates the rhythm of music] Swing the little-finger side of the right *open hand,* palm facing in, back and forth with a double movement across the length of the bent left forearm held in front of the chest.

musician *n.* See sign for SINGER.

must *auxiliary v.* (Used to express obligation, requirement, compulsion, preference, etc.): *We must attend the next concert.* Same sign used for: **have to, mandate, necessary, obligated to, ought to, should.**

- Move the bent index finger of the right *X hand,* palm facing forward, downward with a deliberate movement in front of the right side of the body by bending the wrist down.

mustache[1] *n.* Hair growing on the upper lip: *He wears a mustache.*

- [Location of a mustache] Beginning with the index finger and thumb of each hand pinched together under the nose, palms facing each other, bring the hands straight apart to near each side of the mouth.

mustache[2] *n.* (alternate sign)

- [Location and shape of a mustache] Beginning with both *G hands* near each side of the nose, palms facing each other and fingers pointing toward each other, bring the hands downward to each side of the mouth while pinching the index fingers to the thumbs of each hand.

mute *adj.* See sign for QUIET².

mutilate *v.* See sign for TORTURE.

mutton *n.* Meat from a sheep: *to eat mutton for dinner.*

■ [**sheep** + **meat**] Slide the back of the fingers of the right *K hand,* palm facing up, from the wrist up the inside forearm of the bent left arm with a short repeated movement. Then, with the bent index finger and thumb of the right *5 hand,* palm facing down, grasp the fleshy part of the left *open hand,* palm facing in and fingers pointing right, and shake the hands forward and back with a double movement.

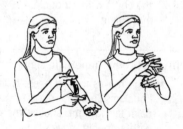

mutual *adj.* See signs for ASSOCIATE, SAME.

muzzle *n.* A cover to put over an animal's mouth to keep it from biting or barking: *They'll have to put a muzzle on the vicious dog.*

■ [**nose** + **mask**²] Touch the nose with the extended right index finger, palm facing in. Then bring the right *curved 5 hand,* palm facing in and fingers pointing up, toward the face with a deliberate movement.

my *pron.* A form of the possessive case of *I,* indicating that something specified or indicated belongs to the speaker: *my book.* Same sign used for: **mine, own.**

■ [Pulling something to oneself] Place the palm of the right *open hand* on the chest, fingers pointing left.

myopic¹ *adj.* Designating a condition of the eye in which objects appear distinct only when close; nearsighted: *myopic vision.*

■ [Shows that one sees only something near] Beginning with the extended fingers of the right *V hand* pointing toward each eye, palm facing in, bring the right hand forward, ending with the back of the right fingers against the back of the left *open hand* held forward of the face, palm facing forward and fingers pointing right.

myopic² *adj.* See sign for NEARSIGHTED.

myself

myself[1] *pron.* A reflexive form of *me: Let me do it myself.*

■ [Sign moves toward oneself] Tap the thumb side of the right *A hand,* palm facing left, against the chest with a double movement.

myself[2] *pron.* (alternate sign)

■ [Sign moves toward oneself] Tap the knuckle side of the right *10 hand,* palm facing right, against the chest with a double movement.

mystery[1] *n.* **1.** Something that is hidden or unknown: *Her whereabouts are a mystery.* **2.** A book, film, or the like, often suspenseful, that focuses on unearthing the explanation of an event, especially a crime: *curled up in an easy chair reading a British mystery.*

■ [**strange** + **story**[1,2]] Beginning with the right *C hand* near the right side of the head, palm angled up, bring the hand downward in front of the face in an arc, ending with the palm facing down near the left side of the face. Then, with the thumb and index finger of each *5 hand* near the other hand in front of the chest, palms facing each other, pull the hands apart with a repeated movement to each side of the chest while pinching the thumbs and index fingers of each hand together into *F hands.*

mystery[2] *n.* See sign for HIDE.

---

nab[1] *v.* To catch or seize: *nabbed the rabbit before it ruined the garden.* Same sign used for: **capture, catch, corner, caught in the act.**

■ [The fingers seem to nab a suspect] Bring the right *bent V* fingers, palm facing down, sharply forward on each side of the extended left index finger held up in front of the chest, palm facing right.

---

nab[2] *v.* See signs for CAPTURE[2,3], SOLICIT.

---

nag *v.* See signs for PICK ON, PREACH[1].

---

nail *n.* **1.** A long, slender piece of metal, pointed at one end, used to fasten one object to another: *to hammer the nail into the wood.* —*v.* **2.** To fasten or hold in place with a nail: *nailed the picture to the wall.*

■ [**hammer** + a gesture showing a nail piercing through something] Move the right *modified X hand*, palm facing left, from the right shoulder downward toward the palm of the left *open hand* held in front of the chest, palm facing up and fingers pointing right. Then move the extended right index finger, palm facing down, forward between the index finger and middle finger of the left *open hand* with a deliberate movement.

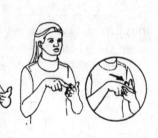

---

nail file *n.* See sign for PUMICE.

---

naive *adj.* See sign for INNOCENT.

---

naked *adj.* See signs for EMPTY, NUDE.

---

name[1] *n.* A word that designates or identifies a person or thing: *The baby's name is John.* Same sign used for: **label.**

■ Tap the middle-finger side of the right *H hand* across the index-finger side of the left *H hand* with a double movement. The verb is the same sign as the noun but made with a single movement.

---

name[2] *v.* See sign for CALL[5].

---

nap[1] *n.* **1.** A short period of sleep during normal waking hours: *to take a nap.* —*v.* **2.** To sleep for a short while: *to nap after lunch.*

- [**sleep**[1,2] + **short**[1]] Beginning with the fingers of the right *curved 5 hand* pointing toward the face, move the hand forward and down while closing the fingers and thumb together, forming a *flattened O hand* in front of the face, palm facing in. Then rub the middle finger side of the right *H hand,* palm angled left, back and forth with a double movement on the index finger of the left *H hand,* palm angled right.

nap[2] *v., n.* See signs for SLEEP[1,2].

napkin[1] *n.* A paper or cloth towel used for wiping the mouth, protecting the clothing, etc., during meals: *Your napkin is on the table.*

- [Mime wiping one's mouth with a napkin] Wipe fingertips of the right *open hand* from side to side over the lips with a double movement, palm facing in.

napkin[2] *n.* (alternate sign)

- [Mime wiping one's mouth with a napkin] Wipe the fingertips of the right *open hand* in a small circle over the lips with a double movement, palm facing in.

narrative *n.* See signs for STORY[1,2].

narrator *n.* A person who delivers spoken commentary, as in a film, or tells stories: *The narrator announced the program.* Same sign used for: **storyteller.**

- [**story**[1,2] + **tell**[1] + **person marker**] Beginning with the thumb and index finger of each *5 hand* near each other in front of the chest, palms facing each other, pull the hands apart with a double movement to in front of each side of the chest while pinching the thumbs and index fingers together. Then, beginning with the extended right index finger under the chin, palm facing in and finger pointing up, move the hand forward, ending with the index finger angled forward. Then move both *open hands,* palms facing each other, downward along each side of the body.

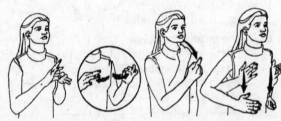

narrow *adj.* Not wide; constricted in width: *walked down a narrow hallway.*

- [The hands demonstrate something getting narrower] Bring both *open hands* from in front of each side of the body, palms facing each other, toward each other in front of the waist.

narrow down *v. phrase.* To restrict, as in amount or number, so as to eliminate what is not essential: *narrow down the number of candidates.* Same sign used for: **convey, focus on.**

- [The hands move downward from wider to narrower] Beginning with both *open hands* in front of each shoulder, palms facing each other and fingers pointing forward, bring the hands downward toward each other in front of the body.

nasal *adj.* See sign for NOSE.

nasty *adj.* See signs for BAD, DIRTY.

nation *n.* A country and its people: *a great nation.* Related form: **national** *adj.* Same sign used for: **native, natural, naturally, nature, normal, of course.**

- [Initialized sign] Beginning with the right *N hand,* palm facing down, over the left *open hand,* palm facing down, move the right hand in a small circle and then straight down to land on the back of the left *open hand.*

nationwide *adj.* Extended throughout a nation: *a nationwide celebration.*

- [**nation** + **area**¹] Beginning with the right *H hand,* palm facing down, over the left *A hand,* palm facing down, move the right hand in a small circle and then straight down to land the extended right fingers on the back of the left hand. Then, beginning with the thumbs of both *5 hands* touching in front of the chest, palms facing down and fingers pointing forward, move the hands outward to each side of the body.

native¹ *n.* **1.** A person born in a specified place: *a native of Ireland.* —*adj.* **2.** Being the place in which a person was born: *my native country.* **3.** Belonging to or typical of a particular place: *native costumes.* **4.** Natural to one; inherent: *native abilities.*

- [**your**¹ + **nation** + **person marker**] Beginning with the right *open hand* in front of the right side of the chest, palm facing forward and fingers pointing up, push the

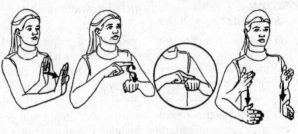

hand straight forward. Then, beginning with the right *H hand,* palm facing down, over the left *A hand,* palm facing down, move the right hand in a small circle and then straight down to land the extended right fingers on the back of the left hand. Then move both *open hands,* palms facing each other, downward along each side of the body.

native[2] *n., adj.* See sign for NATION.

Native American *n.* See sign for INDIAN.

natural *n.* See sign for NATION. Related form: **naturally** *adv.* Shared idea of inherent rights of the citizens of a nation.

natural resources *pl. n.* Raw materials, as minerals, forests, water, etc., that constitute the natural wealth of an area or country: *concerted efforts to preserve the natural resources of the country.*

■ [**nation** + **dirt**] Beginning with the right *H hand,* palm facing down, over the left *A hand,* palm facing down, move the right hand in a small circle and then straight down to land the extended right fingers on the back of the left hand. Then, beginning with both *flattened O hands* in front of each side of the chest, palms facing up, slide the thumbs of each hand across each finger, ending with *A hands.*

nature[1] *n.* A person's disposition: *It's her nature to be cheerful.*

■ [Initialized sign similar to sign for **character**[1]] Move the right *N hand,* palm facing down, in a small circle in front of the left side of the chest with a double movement.

nature[2] *n.* See sign for NATION.

naughty *adj.* See signs for BAD, DEVIL.

nausea *n.* See sign for DISGUSTED[1]. Related form: **nauseous** *adj.*

navel *n.* A depression in the abdomen at the point that the umbilical cord was attached: *Her navel showed above her bikini.* Same sign used for: **belly button, umbilicus.**

- [Location of navel] Place the index-finger side of the left *F hand* on the abdomen.

navigate *v.* To plot the course of and maneuver a vehicle artfully: *to navigate through the heavy storm.*

- [**drive**[1] + **through**] Beginning with both *S hands* in front of the chest, palms facing each other and left hand higher than the right hand, move the hands up and down with a repeated alternating movement. Then move the right *B hand,* palm facing left and fingers pointing forward, with a wavy movement from the right side of the chest forward between the middle finger and ring finger of the left *5 hand,* palm facing in and fingers pointing up.

Navy[1] *n.* A branch of a nation's armed forces comprising warships, their crews, and auxiliary services: *joined the Navy and sailed all over the world.*

- [Shows the location of the flaps on a naval uniform] Beginning with the index-finger side of both *flattened O hands* touching, palms facing in and fingers pointing down, touch the fingertips first to the right side and then the left side of the waist.

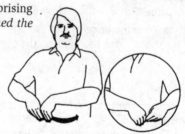

Navy[2] *n.* (alternate sign)

- [Abbreviation **n-y**] Touch the extended fingertips of the right *N hand* and then the knuckles of the right *Y hand* to the right side of the forehead, palm facing in.

navy[3] *adj.* See sign for BLUE.

nay *adv.* Archaic. See sign for NEVER MIND.

near *adv.* See signs for APPROACH[1], BESIDE[2], CLOSE[1,2].

near future, in the See signs for SOON[1,2].

---

nearly *adv.* See sign for ALMOST[1].

---

nearsighted *adj.* Seeing clearly only at a short distance; myopic: *a nearsighted person who wears glasses for distance vision.* Same sign used for: **myopic.**

■ [**beside**[2] + **see**[1]] Beginning with the left *open hand*, palm facing in and fingers pointing right, closer to the chest than the right *open hand*, palm facing in and fingers pointing left, move the right hand in toward the back of the left hand. Then bring the fingers of the right *V hand* from pointing at the eyes, palm facing in, forward a short distance.

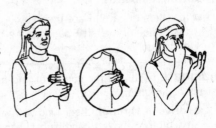

---

neat[1] *adj.* In an orderly condition: *It's easy to find things in a neat closet.*

■ [Initialized sign similar to sign for **clean**] Slide the extended fingers of the right *N hand*, palm facing down, from the heel to the fingers of the upturned left *open hand*, fingers pointing forward.

---

neat[2] *adj.* Clever; adroit: *a neat trick.* Same sign used for: **clever, skillful.**

■ Bring the fingertips of the right *9 hand*, palm facing in, to the center of the chin.

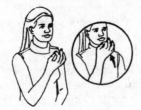

---

neat[3] *adj. Slang.* Fine; wonderful: *That's a neat card trick.* Same sign used for: **cool.**

■ With the knuckle of the right *X hand* near the right side of the mouth, twist the wrist downward with a short movement.

---

neat[4] *adj.* See sign for CLEAN.

---

necessary *adj.* See signs for MUST, NEED.

---

neck[1] *n.* The part of the body that connects the head and the shoulders: *to wrap a scarf around your neck.*

■ [Location of the neck] Tap the fingertips of the right *bent hand*, palm facing down, against the neck with a double movement.

neck[2] *n.* (alternate sign)

■ [Location of the neck] Touch the extended right index finger to the neck.

---

neck[3] *v.* See sign for PET[2].

---

necklace[1] *n.* A piece of jewelry, as a chain or string of beads, worn around the neck as an ornament: *to wear a pearl necklace.*

■ [Location of a necklace] Beginning with the bent middle finger and thumb of the right *5 hand* touching the chest, bring the hand downward while closing the fingers into an *8 hand.*

---

necklace[2] *n.* (alternate sign)

■ [Location of a necklace] Beginning with both extended index fingers touching near each side of the neck, bring the hands downward to touch near the middle of the chest.

---

necklace[3] *n.* (alternate sign)

■ [Location of a necklace] Beginning with the thumb sides of both *curved 5 hands* touching near each shoulder, palms facing forward, bring the hand downward while closing the index fingers and thumbs of each hand together as the hands intersect near the middle of the chest.

---

necklace[4] *n.* (alternate sign)

■ [Location of a necklace] Beginning with the fingers of both *5 hands,* palms facing in and fingers angled down, near each other at the center of the chest, move the hands upward to near each shoulder.

---

necklace[5] *n.* See sign for BEADS.

necktie *n.* A narrow length of cloth worn around the collar and tied so that the two ends hang down the front: *The restaurant won't let a man in unless he's wearing a necktie.* Same sign used for: **tie.**

- ■ [Initialized sign showing the location of a necktie] Touch the fingertips of the right *N hand* first to near the neck and then to the lower chest, palm facing in.

need *v.* **1.** To be in want of; require: *I need a pen so I can sign this.* —*n.* **2.** A requirement, as from lack or want: *to have an acute need for more sleep.* Same sign used for: **necessary, supposed to.**

- ■ Tap the bent index finger of the right *X hand,* palm facing down, with a short, repeated downward movement in front of the right side of the body.

needle *n.* A slender, pointed metal tool used in sewing: *to sew a fine stitch with a small needle.*

- ■ [Represents threading a needle] With the extended thumb of the left hand, palm facing right, touching the extended right index finger, palm facing left and finger pointing up, brush the left extended index finger on the right index fingertip with a double movement.

needless *adj.* Not needed or wanted: *a needless waste of time.* Same sign used for: **unnecessary.**

- ■ [**need** + **none**[1,2,3]] Tap the bent index finger of the right *X hand,* palm facing down, with a short double movement in front of the right side of the chest. Then, beginning with the fingers of both *flattened O hands* in front of the chest, palms facing forward, move the hands apart to in front of each side of the chest.

needlework *n.* The art or process of working with a needle, as in quilting, hand sewing, or embroidery: *Mother does needlework while watching television.* Same sign used for: **sew.**

- ■ [Mime sewing] Beginning with the right *F hand,* palm facing down, above the left *F hand,* palm facing up, move the right hand upward with a short repeated movement.

negative *adj.* **1.** Expressing refusal or denial: *a negative answer.* **2.** Lacking positive qualities: *a negative attitude.*

■ [Shape of a minus sign] Tap the thumb side of the extended right index finger, palm facing down and finger pointing forward, against the palm of the left *open hand*, palm facing right and fingers pointing up, with a double movement.

neglect *v.* See signs for IGNORE[1,2], LEAVE[3]. Related forms: **negligence** *n.*, **negligent** *adj.*

neglect me *v. phrase.* See sign for IGNORE[3].

negligence *n.* See signs for IGNORE[1,2]. Related form: **negligent** *adj.*

negotiate *v.* **1.** To discuss and arrange terms for: *to negotiate a settlement of the strike.* **2.** To deal or bargain with others so as to reach an understanding: *The management and the workers refuse to negotiate.* Related form: **negotiation** *n.*

■ [Initialized sign similar to sign for **communication**] Move both *N* hands, palms facing each other, forward and back from the chin with an alternating movement.

neigh *n.* **1.** The high-pitched whinnying sound made by a horse: *I heard the neigh of horses in the barn.* —*v.* **2.** To utter such a sound: *The horse neighed loudly.*

■ [**horse** + **scream**[1,2]] With the extended thumb of the right *U hand* against the right side of the forehead, palm facing forward, bend the fingers of the right *U hand* up and down with a double movement. Then, beginning with the right *curved 5 hand* in front of the mouth, palm facing in, bring the hand forward and down in a short arc.

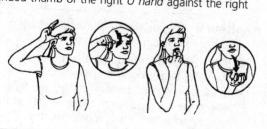

neighbor *n.* A person who lives near another: *to borrow a cup of sugar from my neighbor.*

■ [**next door** + **person marker**] Beginning with the palm of the right *open hand*, palm facing in and fingers pointing left, touching the back of the left *open hand*, palm facing in and fingers pointing right, move the right hand forward in a small arc. Then move both *open hands*, palms facing each other, downward along each side of the body.

neighborhood[1] *n.* A localized area, as in a town or city, considered a definable district by the people who live there: *a friendly neighborhood.*

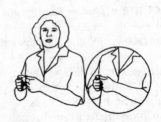

- [**next door** + **area**[1,2,3,4]] Beginning with the palm of the right *bent hand*, palm facing in and fingers pointing left, touching the back of the left *bent hand*, palm facing in and fingers pointing right, move the right hand forward in a small arc. Then, beginning with the left *A hand* held in front of the body, palm facing in, bring the right *open hand*, palm facing down, in a large circle from the right side of the body forward and back over the left hand.

neighborhood[2] *n.* (alternate sign)

- [Similar to sign for **beside**[2] but formed with a double movement to indicate the area nearby] Bring the palm side of the right *bent hand*, palm facing in and fingers pointing left, in against the back of the left *bent hand*, palm facing in and fingers pointing right, with a double movement.

neither *conj.* **1.** Not either (used with *nor*): *Neither you nor I can go.* —*pron.* **2.** Not one person or thing or the other: *Neither of us can go.* —*adj.* **3.** Not the one or the other: *Neither car is working.* Same sign used for: **either, nor, or.**

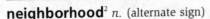

- [Indicates alternatives] Touch the fingertips of the right *9 hand*, palm facing down, alternately on the extended fingertips of the left *V hand*, palm facing in and fingers pointing up.

nephew *n.* The son of one's brother or sister: *taking my nephew to the toy store.*

- [Initialized sign formed near the male area of the head] Beginning with the extended fingers of the right *N hand* pointing toward the right side of the forehead, palm facing left, twist the wrist to point the fingers forward with a double movement.

nerve *n.* One or more bundles of fibers that, as part of a system, convey impulses of sensation, motion, etc., between the brain or spinal cord and other parts of the body: *The needle hit a nerve in my arm.*

- [Initialized sign] Move the fingertips of the right *N hand*, palm facing down, from the wrist to the elbow of the back of the bent left arm.

nervous *adj.* **1.** Extremely uneasy and apprehensive; worried: *nervous about the interview.* **2.** Agitated and jittery: *Your drumming on the table is making me nervous.* Related form: **nervously** *adv.* Same sign used for: **anxiety, anxious, apprehensive.**

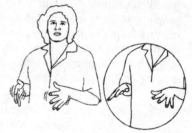

■ [Natural gesture of shaking when nervous] Shake both *5 hands* with a loose, repeated movement in front of each side of the body, palms facing each other and fingers pointing forward.

nervy *adj. Informal.* **1.** Rude; insolent; pushy: *a nervy reporter who won't stop bothering them.* **2.** Requiring courage: *It was nervy of me to ask for a raise so soon.* Related form: **nerve** *n.*

■ Beginning with the bent fingers of the right *U hand* against the right cheek, palm facing forward, twist the wrist, ending with the palm facing back.

nest *v.* (in computer programming) To insert (a command) within another command: *Too many nested loops will slow the program down.*

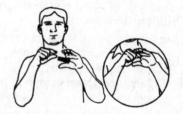

■ [Represents inserting something between other things] Insert the fingers of the right *G hand,* palm facing left, in the thumbside opening of the left *C hand,* palm angled forward.

net[1] *n.* A loosely woven fabric, usually made with knotted string: *to hit the volleyball over the net.* Same sign used for: **screen.**

■ [Shows the mesh of a net] Beginning with the fingers of the right *4 hand* across the back of the fingers of the left *4 hand,* both palms facing forward, move the fingers of both hands slightly upward with a double movement.

net[2] *n.* (alternate sign)

■ [Shape of a net] Beginning with the fingers of both *curved 5 hands* meshed together in front of the body, palms facing up, bring the hands apart and upward in large arcs, ending with the palms facing each other in front of each side of the body.

Net, the *n.* See sign for INTERNET.

Netherlands, the *n.* See signs for HOLLAND[1,2].

network *n.* **1.** A system of interconnected elements, as a group of electronically linked computers: *The data file is accessed through the network.* **2.** A group of people who share information and services, as for career advancement: *Someone in my network will know where to find a good accountant.* —*v.* **3.** To connect to a network: *to network the computer with an information system.* **4.** To get into or stay in touch with a group of people who share information and services: *learning to network early in one's career.*

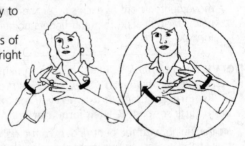

■ [The sign **contact** is formed repeatedly to indicate many contacts in a network] Beginning with the bent middle fingers of both *5 hands* touching in front of the right side of the chest, right palm angled forward and left palm facing in, twist both wrists and touch again in front of the left side of the chest, ending with the right palm facing in and left palm angled forward.

neutral *adj.* Being uncommitted to one side or another in a conflict: *Switzerland was a neutral country during World War II.*

■ [Initialized sign] Move the right *N hand*, palm facing forward, from side to side with a small double movement in front of the right shoulder.

never *adv.* Not ever: *never got married.*

■ Move the right *open hand* from near the right side of the face, palm facing left, downward with a large wavy movement to in front of the right side of the body

never mind (Used as an informal or slang sign to tell listeners that they need not concern themselves with the matter under discussion; often said ironically): *I was going to carry that for you, but never mind.* Same sign used for: **blah** (*slang*)**, nay** (*archaic*).

■ [Natural gesture] Beginning with the right *open hand* in front of the right shoulder, palm facing forward and fingers pointing up, bend the wrist to bring the hand downward to the right side of the body, ending with the fingers pointing down and the palm facing back.

nevertheless *adv.* See sign for ANYWAY.

new *adj.* **1.** Existing or known for the first time: *a new idea.* **2.** Newly produced or purchased: *bought a new coat.* Same sign used for: **fresh.**

■ Slide the back of the right *curved hand,* palm facing up, from the fingertips to the heel of the upturned left *open hand* with a double movement.

New England *n.* An area in the northeastern part of the United States that includes the states of Connecticut, Maine, Massachusetts, New Hampshire, Rhode Island, and Vermont: *to visit New England to see the fall foliage.*

■ [**new** + **England**] Slide the back of the right *curved hand,* palm facing up, from the fingertips to the heel of the upturned left *open hand.* Then, with the right *curved hand* grasping the back of the left *curved hand,* both palms facing down, move the hands forward slightly with a shaky movement.

Newfoundland *n.* See sign for RUSSIA[1].

New Orleans *n.* A city in southeast Louisiana, on the Mississippi River: *to go to New Orleans for the Mardi Gras.*

■ Brush the index-finger side of the right *O hand,* palm facing left, across the palm of the left *open hand,* palm facing right, with a double movement.

newsletter *n.* A printed bulletin, with information, small articles, etc., issued by or for a special interest group: *The company issues a newsletter every three months.*

■ [**inform**[3] + **letter**[3]] Beginning with the finger-tips of both *flattened O hands* near each other on the forehead, palms facing in, move both hands forward and outward while opening into *curved 5 hands,* palms facing each other. Then touch the extended thumb of the right *10 hand* to the lips, palm facing in, and move the thumb downward to touch the thumb of the left *A hand* held in front of the body, palm facing in.

newspaper *n.* A daily or weekly publication containing news, feature articles, advertising, etc.: *a newspaper with an excellent editorial page.* See also sign for PRINT[1]. Same sign used for: **issue, press, publication.**

newsreel

- [Represents putting moveable type into place to set up a newspaper] Beginning with the right *G hand*, palm facing forward, above the left *open hand*, palm facing up, pull the right hand down toward the heel of the left hand with a double movement, closing the right thumb and index finger together each time.

newsreel *n.* A short movie showing current events: *I used to watch the newsreel at the movies.*

- [**film**[1,2] + the shape of a reel] With the heel of the right *5 hand*, palm facing forward, on the heel of the left *open hand*, palm facing in, twist the right hand from side to side with a repeated movement. Then move the extended right index finger, palm facing down, in a circle around the palm of the left *open hand* held in front of the left side of the chest, palm facing right and fingers pointing up.

newsstand *n.* A booth or stand where magazines and newspapers are sold: *to buy a magazine at the newsstand.*

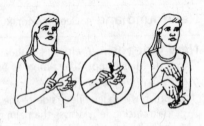

- [**newspaper** + **stand**] Beginning with the right *G hand*, palm facing forward, above the left *open hand*, palm facing up, pull the right hand down toward the heel of the left hand with a double movement, closing the right thumb and index finger together each time. Then bring the fingertips of the right *V hand*, palm facing down and fingers pointing down, downward into the palm of the left *open hand*.

New Testament[1] *n.* The part of the Christian Bible containing the life and teachings of Jesus; the books of this portion of the Bible: *reads a chapter of the New Testament every day.*

- [**new** + an initialized sign similar to the sign for **law**] Slide the back of the right *curved hand*, palm facing up, across the upturned palm of the left *open hand* from the fingertips to the palm. Then touch the index-finger side of the right *T hand*, palm facing left, first to the fingers and then to the heel of the palm of the left *open hand*, held in front of the chest, palm facing forward.

New Testament[2] *n.* (alternate sign)

- [**new** + **Jesus** + **story**[1,2]] Slide the back of the right *curved hand*, palm facing up, from the fingertips to the heel of the upturned left *open hand*. Next touch the bent middle finger of the left *5 hand* to the middle of the palm of the right *open hand,* palms facing each other in front of the right side of the chest. Then touch the bent middle finger of the right *5 hand* into the middle of the palm of the left *open hand.* Finally, with the thumb and index finger of each *5 hand* near the other hand in front of the chest, palms facing each other, pull the hands apart with a repeated movement to each side of the chest while pinching the thumb and index finger of each hand together.

New Year or **New Year's Day** *n.* January 1, the start of the new year in many countries, celebrated as a holiday: *"Happy New Year!"*

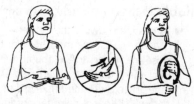

■ [**new + year**] Slide the back of the right *curved hand,* palm facing up, from the fingers to the heel of the upturned left *open hand.* Then, beginning with both *S hands* in front of the chest, palms facing in, move the right hand in a forward circle over the left hand while moving the left hand in a smaller circle over the right hand.

New York *n.* **1.** A state in the northeast United States: *The capital of New York is Albany.* **2.** Same sign used for: **Manhattan.** A city in New York State at the mouth of the Hudson River: *to go to a Broadway play in New York.*

■ Brush the palm side of the right *Y hand,* palm facing down, with a double movement across the palm of the upturned left *open hand.*

next[1] *adj.* **1.** Immediately following: *the next train.* **2.** Nearest; closest in position: *Could you move to the next chair? —adv.* **3.** In the time or position that is nearest: *You are speaking next. She has the next highest score. —prep.* **4. next to** Nearest to: *the chair next to the window.*

■ [Demonstrates one hand overcoming an obstacle to move on to the next thing] Beginning with the right *open hand,* palm facing in and fingers pointing left, closer to the chest than the left *open hand,* palm facing in and fingers pointing right, move the right hand up and over the left hand, ending with the right palm on the back of the left hand.

next[2] *adj.* See sign for TURN[2].

next door or **next-door** *adv.* At, in, or to the next house or apartment: *he lives next door.*

■ [Shows a location next to another thing] Beginning with the palm of the right *curved hand,* palm facing in and fingers pointing left, touching the back of the left *curved hand,* palm facing in and fingers pointing right, move the right hand forward in a small arc.

next to *prep.* See signs for BESIDE[1,2,3].

next year *n.* During the year following this one: *We will vacation in Wyoming next year.*

■ [Similar to the sign for **year** except moving into the future] Beginning with the little-finger side of the right *S hand* on the thumb side of the left *S hand*, palms facing in opposite directions, move the right hand forward in an arc while flicking the right index finger forward.

nibble *v.* To eat delicately, with tiny bites: *The mouse nibbled at the cheese.*

■ [A gesture showing the action of nibbling] Beginning with the back of the right *C hand* against the mouth, palm facing forward, close the fingers to the thumb with a double movement, forming a *flattened O hand* each time. Then, with the fingertips of the right *flattened O hand*, palm facing down, on the index-finger side of the left *B hand*, palm facing in and fingers pointing right, open and close the fingertips of the right hand with a repeated movement on the left index finger.

nice *adj.* See sign for CLEAN.

nickel *n.* A coin of the U.S. valued at five cents: *Remember when candy cost a nickel?* Same sign used for: **five cents.**

■ [Similar to sign for **cent** but formed with a *5 hand*] Beginning with the bent index finger of the right *5 hand*, palm facing left, touching the right side of the forehead, bring the hand forward with a double movement.

nickname[1] *n.* A name, as an affectionate shortened form, used instead of a person's given name: *Elizabeth's nickname at school was Lizard!*

■ [**short**[1] + **name**[1]] Rub the middle-finger side of the right *H hand*, palm angled left, back and forth with a repeated movement on the index-finger side of the left *H hand*, palm angled right. Then place the middle-finger side of the right *H hand* across the index-finger side of the left *H hand*.

nickname[2] *n.* (alternate sign)

■ [**brief**[1] + **name**[1]] Beginning with both *C hands* in front of each side of the chest, palms facing each other, bring the hands toward each other while closing the fingers into *S hands*, ending with the little-finger side of the right *S hand* on the index-finger side of the left *S hand*, palms facing in opposite directions. Then place the middle-finger side of the right *H hand* across the index-finger side of the left *H hand*.

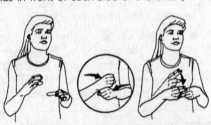

niece *n.* The daughter of one's brother or sister: *babysat for my niece.*

- [Initialized sign formed near the female area of the head] Beginning with the extended fingers of the right *N hand* pointing toward the right cheek, palm facing left, twist the wrist to point the fingers forward with a double movement.

niggardly *adj.* See sign for STINGY.

night *n.* The time between evening and morning: *The job requires him to work at night.* Same sign used for: **tonight.**

- [Represents the sun going down over the horizon] Tap the heel of the right *bent hand,* palm facing down, with a double movement on the back of the left *open hand* held across the chest, palm facing down.

nightgown[1] *n.* A loose garment worn by a woman or child for sleeping: *to wear a nightgown to bed instead of pajamas.*

- [Initialized sign] Beginning with the extended fingers of both *N hands* touching each side of the forehead, palms facing each other, bring the hands downward with a long wavy movement, ending with the *N hands* in front of each side of the body, fingers pointing toward each other and palms facing in.

nightgown[2] *n.* (alternate sign)

- [**night** + **clothes**] Tap the heel of the right *bent hand,* palm facing forward, on the back of the left *open hand* held across the chest, palm facing down. Then brush the thumbs of both *5 hands* downward on each side of the chest with a double movement.

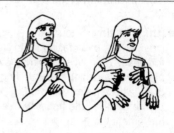

nimble *adj.* Quick and light in movement; agile: *a nimble maneuver while running.*

- [**skill** + **tiptoe**[2]] Grasp the little-finger side of the left *open hand* with the curved right fingers and pull the right hand forward while closing the fingers into the palm. Then, beginning with both extended index fingers pointing down in front of each side of the chest, palms facing down, and the right hand higher than the left, move the hands up and down with an alternating repeated movement.

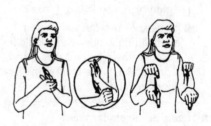

ninth *adj.* **1.** Next after the eighth: *That's your ninth piece of cake!* —*n.* **2.** The one after the eighth in a series of nine or more: *Your seat is the ninth on the left.* —*adv.* **3.** In the ninth place: *came in ninth in the standings.* Same sign used for: **nine dollars.**

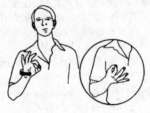

- [The sign **nine** is formed with a twisting movement that is used for ordinal numbers] Beginning with the right *9 hand* in front of the right side of the body, palm facing forward, twist the hand toward the body, ending with the palm facing back.

nipple[1] *n.* The small projection on a breast that, in females, contains the conduit for the milk glands: *The baby grasped the mother's nipple and began to nurse.* Same sign used for: **mammillary.**

- [Indicates position of nipples] Beginning with both *S hands* in front of the chest, palms facing down, flick each index finger forward with a double movement.

nipple[2] *n.* (alternate sign) Same sign used for: **mammillary.**

- [Shows location of nipples] Place the thumb side of the right *F hand,* palm facing left, first on the left side of the chest and then on the right side.

nitwit *n.* A stupid person: *She acts like a nitwit.*

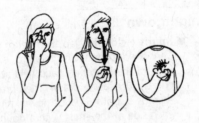

- [**think**[1] + **tiny**[1,2]] Touch the extended right index finger, palm facing in, to the forehead. Then, with the thumb of the right hand touching the little finger in front of the chest, palm facing up, flick the thumb off the little finger with a deliberate movement.

no[1] *adv.* (A negative expressing dissent, denial, or refusal, as in response to a question or request): *No, I won't.*

- [Fingerspell **n-o** quickly] Snap the extended right index and middle fingers closed to the extended right thumb, palm facing down, while moving the hand down slightly.

no[2] *adv.* See signs for NONE[1,2,3,5].

noble *adj.* Of high character: *a noble deed.*
Related form: **nobleness** or **nobility** *n.*

■ [Initialized sign similar to sign for **character**[1]]
Move the right *N hand,* palm facing down, in a
small circle and then back against the left side
of the chest.

nobody[1] *pron.* No person; not anyone: *Nobody
knows where we hid it.* Same sign used for:
no one.

■ [Similar to sign for **none**[1] but formed with
one hand] Move the right *O hand,* palm
facing forward, from side to side with a
double movement in front of the right
shoulder.

nobody[2] *pron.* See sign for NONE[1].

nod *v.* See sign for BOW[1].

node *n.* See signs for BUMP[1,2,3].

no good Not of good quality; valueless:
The term paper is no good.

■ [Abbreviation **n-g**] Beginning with the
right *N hand* in front of the right side of
the chest, palm facing down, quickly
twist the wrist to form a *G hand,* palm
facing left.

noise *n.* **1.** A loud, harsh, or grating sound: *awakened by a
loud noise.* **2.** Loud sound: *I hate noise.* Same sign used for:
aloud, loud, sound.

■ [Indicates the vibration of a loud sound coming from the
ears] Beginning with the bent index fingers of both *5 hands*
touching each ear, palms facing in, move the hands forward
with a deliberate movement while shaking the hands.

nominate[1] *v.* To propose (a person) for office:
nominated Joe for the office of class president.
Related form: **nomination** *n.*

■ [Initialized sign] Beginning with both *N hands* in
front of the chest, palms facing in and fingers
pointing up, move the hands upward with a
double alternating movement.

nominate[2] *v.* (alternate sign) Related form: **nomination** *n.* See also sign for SUGGEST. Same sign used for: **proposal, propose.**

■ [Represents offering names in nomination] Beginning with both *open hands* in front of each side of the chest, move the hands upward with a double alternating movement.

nominate[3] *v.* See sign for APPLY[2].

nonchalant *adj.* See signs for DON'T CARE[1,2].

none[1] *pron.* Not any: *I have none left.* Same sign used for: **no, nobody.**

■ [Indicates zero amount of something in the hand] Move both *flattened O hands,* palms facing forward, from side to side with a repeated movement in front of each side of the chest.

none[2] *pron.* (alternate sign) Same sign used for: **no.**

■ [Indicates zero amount of something in the hand] Beginning with the fingertips of both *flattened O hands,* palms facing forward, together in front of the chest, move the hands apart to in front of each side of the chest.

none[3] *pron.* (alternate sign) Same sign used for: **no.**

■ [Indicates zero amount of something in the hand] Beginning with the little-finger side of the right *O hand* on the index-finger side of the left *O hand* in front of the chest, palms facing in opposite directions, move the hands apart to in front of each side of the chest.

none[4] *pron.* (alternate sign)

■ [Natural gesture showing that there is nothing in the hands] With both *5 hands* in front of each side of the body, palms facing up and elbows tight to the body, shrug the shoulders while shaking the head with a negative movement.

none[5] *pron.* (alternate sign) Same sign used for: **no.**

- [Indicates zero amount of something in both hands] Move both *O hands*, palms facing forward, from in front of the chest forward with a deliberate movement while opening into *5 hands*.

none[6] *pron.* (alternate sign) Same sign used for: **zero.**

- [Indicates zero amount of something] Move the right *O hand*, palm facing left, from in front of the chest forward, ending with the little-finger side of the right hand on the palm of the left *open hand*.

none[7] *pron.* (alternate sign)

- [Shows an empty hole] Move the extended right index finger, palm facing down, in a circular movement around the index-finger-side opening of the left *O hand*.

none[8] *pron.* See signs for NOTHING[5], ZERO[1].

nonstop *adj.* **1.** Being without any stops along the route: *a nonstop flight.* —*adv.* **2.** Without interruption: *worked nonstop all weekend.*

- [**none**[1,2,3] + **stop**] Beginning with the little-finger side of the right *O hand* against the index-finger side of the left *O hand* in front of the chest, palms facing in opposite directions, move the hands outward to in front of each side of the chest. Then bring the little-finger side of the right *open hand* from in front of the right side of the face, palm facing left and fingers pointing up, downward to land on the palm of the left *open hand* held in front of the chest.

noodle *n.* A typically flat, solid strip of pasta made of flour and eggs: *chicken and noodles.*

- [The shape of a thin noodle] Beginning with the fingertips of both *I hands* touching in front of the chest, palms facing in, bring the hands apart with a double movement, bending the little finger back toward the palm each time.

nook *n.* A corner or small recess, as in a room: *a breakfast nook off the kitchen.*

- [Shows shape of a nook] Move the right *curved hand,* palm facing down, in an arc over the left *S hand,* palm facing in. Then move the right *curved hand* in toward the left *S hand* from several directions.

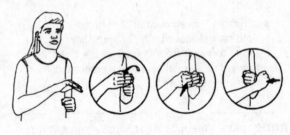

noon[1] *n.* The middle of the day: *eat at 12 noon.* Alternate form: **noontime.** Same sign used for: **midday.**

- [Represents the sun straight overhead at noon] Place the right elbow, arm extended up and right *open hand* facing forward, on the back of the left *open hand* held across the body, palm facing down.

noon[2] *n.* (alternate sign) Alternate form: **noontime.**

- [Represents the sun straight overhead at noon + **twelve**] With the elbow of the bent right arm on the back of the left *open hand* held across the body, palm facing down, flick the index and middle fingers of the right *S hand* upward, forming a *12.*

no one *pron.* See sign for NOBODY[1].

nor *conj.* See sign for NEITHER.

normal *adj.* See sign for NATION. Shared idea of normal life in a well governed nation.

north *n.* **1.** The general direction 90 degrees to the left of east and to the right of west: *moved to a suburb just north of the city.* —*adj.* **2.** Lying toward or located in the north: *the north end of town.* —*adv.* **3.** To, toward, or in the north: *Go north for three miles.*

- [Initialized sign moving in the direction of north on a map] Move the right *N hand,* palm facing forward, upward in front of the right shoulder.

North America *n.* The northern continent in the Western Hemisphere: *The United States and Canada are in North America.*

■ [**north** + **America**] Move the right *N hand*, palm facing down, upward in front of the right shoulder. Then, with the fingers of both *5 hands* loosely entwined, palms facing in, move the hands in a circle in front of the chest.

northeast *n.* **1.** The general direction midway between north and east: *a storm coming from the northeast.* —*adj.* **2.** Lying toward or facing the northeast: *a northeast view from the livingroom window.* **3.** Coming from the northeast: *a northeast wind.* —*adv.* **4.** Toward the northeast: *Drive northeast on Main Street.*

■ [**north** + **east**] Move the right *N hand*, palm facing forward, upward in front of the right shoulder. Then move the right *E hand*, palm facing forward, to the right.

North Star *n.* A bright star over the North Pole: *Another name for the North Star is Polaris.*

■ [**north** + **star**] Move the right *N hand*, palm facing down, upward in front of the right shoulder. Then, beginning with both extended index fingers pointing up in front of the chest, palms facing forward, move the hands up and down with a repeated alternating movement.

northwest *n.* **1.** The general direction midway between north and west: *northwest of the city.* —*adj.* **2.** Lying toward or facing the northwest: *the northwest corner of the room.* **3.** Coming from the northwest: *a cool northwest breeze.* —*adv.* **4.** Toward the northwest: *They're sailing northwest to Hawaii.*

■ [**north** + **west**] Move the right *N hand*, palm facing forward, upward in front of the right shoulder. Then move the right *W hand*, palm facing forward and fingers pointing up from in front of the right shoulder, left in front of the chest.

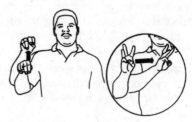

Norway[1] *n.* A kingdom in northern Europe; part of the Scandinavian peninsula: *Oslo is the capital of Norway.* Related form: **Norwegian** *adj., n.*

■ [Initialized sign showing the movement of waves in the sea surrounding Norway] Move the right *N hand*, palm facing down, from in front of the left side of the chest in a large up-and-down movement as the hand moves to the right.

Norway[2] *n.* (alternate sign) Related form: **Norwegian** *adj.*, *n.*

- [Initialized sign] Touch the extended fingers of the right *N hand*, palm facing down, to the right side of the forehead with a double movement.

nose *n.* The part of the face protruding above the lips and having openings for breathing and smelling: *a broken nose*. Same sign used for: **nasal.**

- [Location of the nose] Touch the extended right index finger to the right side of the nose, palm facing down.

nosebleed *n.* See sign for RUN[5].

nosedive *n.* A sudden plunge downward with the forward part pointing down: *the plane took a nosedive.*

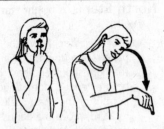

- [**nose** + the direction of diving down] Beginning with the extended right index finger touching the nose, palm facing in, bring the hand forward and downward in a large arc, ending with the finger pointing down and the palm facing down in front of the body.

nose mask *n.* See sign for OXYGEN.

nose ring *n.* See sign for BULL[1].

nostril *n.* Either of the two external openings in the nose: *You breathe through your nostrils.*

- [Location and shape of a nostril] Move the extended right index finger in a small circle near the bottom of the nose.

nosy[1] *adj. Informal.* Prying: *a nosy person.*

- [Shape of a large nose] Beginning with the extended right index finger touching the nose, palm facing down, twist the wrist to bring the finger around the end of the nose, ending with the finger under the nose, palm facing in.

nosy[2] *adj. Informal.* (alternate sign) Same sign used for: **butt in, meddle, peek, pry, snoop.**

- [Represents one's nose extending to insert it into another's business] Beginning with the bent index finger of the right *X hand* beside the nose, palm facing left, bring the right hand downward and insert the bent index finger in the thumb-side opening of the left *O hand,* palm facing right.

not[1] *adv.* (Used to express negation, denial, refusal, etc.): *I'm not tired any more.* Same sign used for: **don't.**

- Bring the extended thumb of the right *10 hand* from under the chin, palm facing left, forward with a deliberate movement.

not[2] *adv.* (alternate sign) Same sign used for: **don't.**

- [Natural gesture forbidding something] Beginning with the right *open hand* crossed over the left *open hand* in front of the body, palms facing down, swing the hands outward to in front of each side of the body.

notable *adj.* See sign for NOTICE[1].

note *v.* See sign for NOTICE[1].

notebook computer *n.* See sign for LAPTOP COMPUTER.

nothing[1] *pron.* **1.** Not anything: *Nothing has arrived in the mail today.* **2.** Something of no importance or value or something requiring little effort: *Don't worry about the trip— it's nothing.*

- [The hand opens to reveal nothing in it] Beginning with the index-finger side of the right *O hand* under the chin, palm facing forward, bring the hand downward and forward while opening into a *5 hand,* palm facing down.

nothing[2] *pron.* (alternate sign)

- [The hands open to reveal nothing in them] Beginning with the index-finger sides of both *O hands* under the chin, palms facing each other, bring the hands downward and forward while opening into *5 hands,* palms angled down.

nothing[3] *pron.* (alternate sign)

- [Showing nothing in the hands] Beginning with both *open hands* in front of the face, left palm on the back of the right hand and fingers pointing in opposite directions, bring the hands upward to each side while blowing on them, ending with the fingers pointing up in front of each shoulder.

nothing[4] *pron.* (alternate sign) Same sign used for: **insignificant, minor, puny, trivial.**

- [Used when something is trivial] Move both *F hands,* palms facing forward, from side to side with a repeated movement in front of each side of the chest.

nothing[5] *n.* (alternate sign) Same sign used for: **all gone, gone, none.**

- [Natural gesture for showing nothing in one's hand] With the right *curved hand* in front of the upper chest, palm facing up, blow across the palm.

notice[1] *v.* To observe; become aware of: *I noticed a big hole in the wall.* Same sign used for: **aware, notable, note, recognize.**

- [Brings the eye down to look at something in the hand] Bring the extended curved right index finger from touching the cheek near the right eye, palm facing left, downward to touch the palm of the left *open hand,* palm facing right in front of the chest.

notice[2] *n.* See sign for INFORM[1].

notify *v.* See sign for INFORM[1].

notify me *v. phrase.* See sign for INFORM[2].

notorious *adj.* See sign for FAMOUS.

not responsible[1] *adj.* Without culpability: *My dog is not responsible for the holes in the yard.* Same sign used for: **carefree, hands off, irresponsible, keep one's hands off, not my fault.**

- [Natural gesture for flicking away responsibility] Beginning with the fingertips of both *8 hands* touching each shoulder, palms facing each other, flick the hands quickly forward while opening into *5 hands.*

not responsible[2] *adj.* (alternate sign) Same sign used for: **carefree, hands off, irresponsible, keep one's hands off, not my fault.**

- [Natural gesture for flicking away responsibility] Beginning with the fingertips of both *8 hands* touching the opposite shoulder, palms facing in opposite directions, quickly flick the hands open into *5 hands.*

not yet See signs for YET[1,2].

nourish *v.* See sign for FEED[1].

nourishment *n.* See sign for NUTRITION.

novel *n.* See signs for STORY[1,2].

now[1] *adv.* At this time or moment: *Come here now!* Same sign used for: **current, present, prevailing, urgent.**

- Bring both *bent hands,* palms facing up, downward in front of each side of the body.

now[2] *adv.* (alternate sign) Same sign used for: **current, prevailing, present, urgent.**

- Bring both *Y hands,* palms facing up, downward in front of each side of the body.

Now I remember See sign for DISGUSTED[2]. Shared idea of disgust with oneself for having forgotten.

nozzle *n.* A tip, as a spout, attached to a hose to control the spray: *Don't water the grass without attaching the nozzle to the hose.*

- [**water** + the shape of a nozzle + mime holding a hose nozzle] Tap the index-finger side of the right *W hand,* palm facing left, against the chin with a double movement. Then, with the fingers of the right *G hand,* palm facing left, on either side of the left index finger, palm facing down, slide the right hand

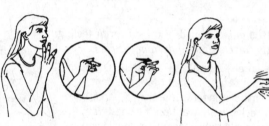

forward. Then, with the right *X hand* held in front of the right side of the body, palm facing up, wiggle the hand back and forth with a repeated movement.

nude *adj.* Wearing no clothes: *a nude model*. Same sign used for: **bare, naked.**

- ■ [The sign **empty** formed downward on the hand representing a person's body] Move the bent middle finger of the right *5 hand*, palm facing in, downward on the back of the left *open hand*, palm facing in and fingers pointing down, from the wrist to off the fingertips.

nudge *v.* To push slightly, as to get attention: *to nudge the next person in line so he'll move along.* Same sign used for: **push.**

- ■ [Natural gesture of nudging someone] Move the palm of the right *open hand*, palm facing forward, with a short double movement in front of the right side of the chest.

nuisance[1] *n.* Something or someone that annoys: *The constant phone calls are a nuisance.*

- ■ [**annoy**[1] + **away**] Sharply tap the little-finger side of the right *open hand*, palm facing in at an angle, at the base of the thumb and index finger of the left *open hand*, palm facing in, with a double movement. Then, beginning with the right *5 hand* in front of the chest, palm facing in and fingers pointing up, flip the hand over with a sudden movement, ending with the palm facing forward and the fingers angled up.

nuisance[2] *n.* (alternate sign)

- ■ Move the bent middle finger of the right *5 hand* forward and back with a short, quick movement in front of the chest, palm facing forward.

numb *adj.* Stripped of the power of feeling: *My fingers are numb from the cold.*

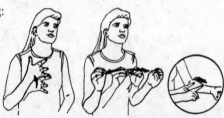

- ■ [**feel** + **none**[1,2,3] + a gesture indicating the skin can't feel] Move the bent middle finger of the right *5 hand*, palm facing in, upward on the chest with a double movement. Then, beginning with the fingers of both *flattened O hands* together in front of the chest, palms facing forward, move the hands apart to in front of each side of the chest. Then move the extended right index finger, palm facing down, back and forth with a repeated movement on the bent left forearm.

number *n.* **1.** Alternate form: **numeral.** A word, letter, or symbol representing a count of things or persons: *Write down the number of people in attendance.* **2.** A mathematical unit expressing an amount or quantity: *The number of people here is twenty-six.* Related form: **numeric** *adj.* Same sign used for: **digit.**

- Beginning with the fingertips of both *flattened O hands* touching, left palm angled forward and right palm facing in, bring the hands apart while twisting the wrists in opposite directions and touch the fingertips again, ending with the left palm facing in and the right palm angled forward.

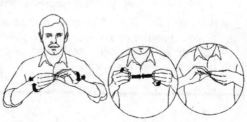

numerous *adj.* See signs for MANY, MULTIPLE.

nun *n.* A woman who is a member of a religious order, especially one bound by vows of poverty, chastity, and obedience: *The nuns who teach in the parish school live in a nearby convent.*

- [Initialized sign showing the shape of a nun's headcloth] Beginning with the extended fingers of both *N hands* near each side of the head, palms facing each other, bring the hands downward to near each shoulder, ending with the palms facing down and the fingers pointing toward each other.

nurse *n.* A person trained to care for ill people: *The family of the sick child hired a private registered nurse.*

- [Initialized sign similar to sign for **doctor²**] Tap the extended fingers of the right *N hand*, palm facing down, with a double movement on the wrist of the left *open hand* held in front of the body, palm facing up.

nursery school *n.* A school for preschool children: *The three-year-old goes to nursery school.*

- [**nurse** + **school**] Tap the extended fingers of the right *N hand*, palm facing down, with a double movement on the wrist of the left *open hand* held in front of the body, palm facing up. Then tap the fingers of the right

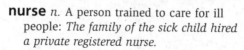

open hand, palm facing down, with a double movement on the palm of the upturned left *open hand.*

nurture *v.* See sign for FEED[1].

nut *n.* See sign for PEANUT[1].

nutrition *n.* The act or process of providing nourishing food: *It is important even in adulthood to have good nutrition.* Same sign used for: **nourishment.**

■ [Initialized sign similar to sign for **restaurant**] Move the extended fingers of the right *N hand,* palm facing in, from the left side of the mouth in an arc around to touch the right side of the mouth.

oar *n.* See sign for CANOE.

oath *n.* A solemn pledge to speak the truth, keep a promise, etc.: *I took an oath in the courtroom to tell the truth.* Same sign used for: **inaugural, inauguration, pledge, testify, testimony.**

■ [Natural gesture for taking an oath with one's hand on the Bible] Hold the left *open hand* in front of the left side of the body, palm facing down and fingers pointing forward, and the right *open hand* in front of the right shoulder, palm facing forward and fingers pointing up.

obese *adj.* See signs for FAT[1,2,4].

obey *v.* To comply with the orders, instructions, or wishes of: *to obey the rules.* Related forms: **obedience** *n.,* **obedient** *adj.*

■ [Represents placing one's own ideas in a position subservient to another's] Beginning with the right *O hand* in front of the forehead and the left *O hand* in front of the left shoulder, both palms facing in, bring the hands downward simultaneously while opening the fingers, ending with both *open hands* in front of the body, palms facing up and fingers pointing forward.

object *v.* See signs for COMPLAIN, DISAGREE.

objection *n.* See sign for PROTEST[1].

objective[1] *n.* A goal or purpose to be achieved: *The objective of the game is to capture all the pieces.*

■ [Initialized sign similar to sign for **goal**[1]] Move the extended right index finger from in front of the right side of the forehead, palm facing left and finger pointing up, forward toward the thumb side opening of the left *O hand* held in front of the left shoulder, palm facing right.

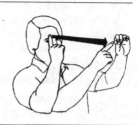

objective[2] *n.* See sign for GOAL[1].

obligate *v.* See signs for PROMISE[1], VOW[1]. Related form: **obligation** *n.*

obligated to See sign for MUST.

obligation *n.* See sign for BURDEN, PROMISE¹.

obscene *adj.* Relating to sex in a manner so offensive as to be outside the protections of the First Amendment: *The movie was R-rated because it featured obscene language.* Related form: **obscenity** *n.*

- Twist the wrist of the right *Y hand* up and down with a repeated movement striking the extended left index finger each time.

observant *adj.* Strict and careful in adhering to religious laws or customs: *an observant Jew.*

- [Pounding one's heart in reverence] Tap the palm side of the right *A hand* with a double movement on the left side of the chest.

observe¹ *v.* **1.** To see and notice: *driving around and observing the scenery.* **2.** To watch carefully so as to learn from: *I observed the procedure in the operating room.* Related form: **observant** *adj.* Same sign used for: **watch.**

- [Represents one's eyes surveying the surroundings] Beginning with both *V hands* in front of the right side of the chest, palms facing down and fingers pointing forward, swing the hands to the left, following the fingers with the eyes.

observe² *v.* See sign for LOOK OVER².

obsession¹ *n.* The domination of one's thoughts by a persistent idea, desire, etc.: *an obsession with neatness.* Related forms: **obsess** *v.*, **obsessive** *adj.* Same sign used for: **dwell on, hostile, persevere, persistent.**

- With the bent middle finger of the right *5 hand* on the back of the left *open hand*, both palms facing down, move the hands forward in a repeated circular movement in front of the body.

obsession² *n.* (alternate sign) Related forms: **obsess** *v.*, **obsessive** *adj.* Same sign used for: **dwell on, persevere, persistent.**

- [Shows thoughts being brought forward to contemplate] Bring the bent middle finger of the right *5 hand*, palm facing in, from the forehead down to touch the back of the left *bent hand* held in front of the chest, palm facing down.

obsolete[1] *adj.* No longer in use: *an obsolete style.*

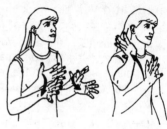

- [**finish**[1,2] + **long time ago, a**[1]] Beginning with both *5 hands* in front of the chest, palms facing in and fingers angled upward, flip the hands over with a sudden movement, ending with both palms angled down and fingers pointing forward. Then, beginning with the right *5 hand* in front of the right shoulder, palm facing left and fingers pointing up, bring the hand back to behind the right shoulder.

obsolete[2] *adj.* (alternate sign)

- [**old** formed with an exaggerated movement to indicate that something is extremely old] Beginning with the index-finger side of the right *C hand* touching the chin, palm facing left, bring the hand straight down with a sudden movement to in front of the body while closing into an *S hand,* palm facing left.

obstinate *adj.* See sign for STUBBORN.

obstruct *v.* See sign for PREVENT.

obtain *v.* See sign for GET.

obvious *adj.* Easily recognized or understood; evident: *the obvious solution to the problem.* Related form: **obviously** *adv.* Same sign used for: **clearly.**

- [Similar to sign for **bright,** indicating that something is clearly known] Beginning with the fingertips of both *flattened O hands* touching in front of the body, palms facing down, move the hands quickly upward in arcs to in front of each side of the chest while opening into *5 hands,* ending with the palms facing forward and the fingers pointing up.

occasional[1] *adj.* Happening irregularly or infrequently: *We have an occasional snowstorm.* Related form: **occasionally** *adv.* Same sign used for: **once in a while, periodically, sometimes.**

- [Shows a series of events moving into the future] Beginning with the right *bent hand* in front of the right side of the chest, palm facing left and fingers pointing left, move the hand forward in a series of arcs.

occasional[2] *adj.* (alternate sign) Related form: **occasionally** *adv.* Same sign used for: **once in a while, periodically, sometimes.**

- [The sign **once** is repeated with a circular movement that indicates a periodic activity] Bring the extended right index finger, palm facing left, upward with a double circular movement off the palm of the left *open hand* held in front of the chest, palm facing up and fingers pointing forward.

occupation

occupation[1] *n.* The work one does to earn a living: *His occupation is teaching.*

- [Initialized sign similar to sign for **work**[1]] Tap the heel of the right *O hand*, palm facing left, with a double movement on the back of the left *S hand*, palm facing down, held across the chest.

occupation[2] *n.* See signs for WORK[1,2].

occupy *v.* See sign for CAPTURE[1].

occur *v.* See signs for HAPPEN, SHOW UP. Related form: **occurrence** *n.*

ocean *n.* **1.** The great body of salt water that covers most of the earth's surface: *Three quarters of the planet is covered by the ocean.* **2.** Any of the divisions of this body: *the Atlantic Ocean.*

- [**water** + the shape of an ocean wave] Tap the index-finger side of the right *W hand*, palm facing left, against the chin with a double movement. Then, beginning with both *5 hands* in front of the body, palms facing down and fingers pointing forward, move the hands upward and forward in a large wavy movement.

octagon *n.* A figure having eight sides and eight angles: *The new building on campus is shaped like an octagon.*

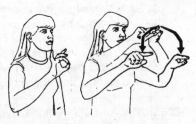

- [**eight** + the shape of an octagon] Form an *8 hand* with the right hand in front of the right shoulder. Then, beginning with both extended index fingers touching in front of the face, palms facing down and fingers pointing forward, move the hands apart from each other at a slight angle downward and then downward at another angle and then straight down, ending with the fingers pointing forward in front of each shoulder, palms facing down.

octal *adj.* Of or pertaining to a numbering system using a base of 8: *The octal numerals are 0 through 8.* Same sign used for: **base eight.**

- [**base** + **eight**] Beginning with the right *B hand*, palm facing forward and fingers pointing up, under the left *open hand*, palm facing down and fingers pointing right, move the right hand to the right while changing into an *8 hand*.

octopus *n.* A sea animal with a soft oval body and eight arms, or tentacles, each with two rows of suckers: *A large octopus can have an armspan of 30 feet.*

- [Represents the tentacles of an octopus] With the fingertips of the right *flattened O hand* touching the back of the left *curved 5 hand*, both palms facing down, wiggle the left fingers with a repeated movement.

odd *adj.* See sign for STRANGE.

odor *n.* See sign for SMELL[1].

odorless *adj.* Without an odor; lacking a smell: *Water is odorless.*

- [smell[1] + none[2]] Brush the fingers of the right *open hand*, palm facing in and fingers pointing left, upward in front of the nose with a double movement. Then, beginning with the fingers of both *O hands* together in front of the chest, palms facing forward, bring the hands apart to in front of each side of the chest.

of course See sign for NATION.

off *prep.* **1.** So as to be away from, no longer resting on, etc.: *Take your feet off the chair.* —*adv.* **2.** So as to be away from the usual position, no longer attached or supported, or the like: *My button fell off.*

- [Shows moving one hand off the other hand] Beginning with the palm of the right *open hand* across the back of the left *open hand* at an angle, both palms facing down in front of the body, raise the right hand upward in front of the chest.

offender *n.* See sign for CRIMINAL.

offense[1] *n.* **1.** The act of attacking, especially in sports: *Our team's offense was terrible in today's game.* **2.** A member or group of members on a team who are responsible for scoring points: *The offense ran with the ball.*

- [Initialized sign similar to sign for **defend**[1]] Beginning with both *O hands* in front of the chest, the left hand somewhat forward of the right hand and palms facing in opposite directions, bring the hands together with a double movement.

offense[2] *n.* (alternate sign)

- [Similar to sign for **defend**[2] but with a different movement] Beginning with both *D hands* in front of the chest, left hand somewhat forward of the right hand and palms facing in opposite directions, bring the hands together with a double movement.

offense[3] *n.* See signs for CRIME[1,2].

offer *v., n.* See sign for SUGGEST.

office *n.* The place in which the work of running a business is done: *Please send copies of the annual report to the office.*

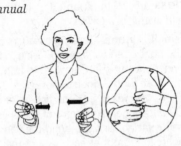

- [Initialized sign similar to sign for **room**[2]] Beginning with both *O hands* in front of each side of the body, palms facing each other, move the hands deliberately in opposite directions, ending with the left hand near the chest and the right hand several inches forward of the left hand, both palms facing in.

officer *n.* See signs for CAPTAIN, CHIEF[1], POLICE[2].

officially *adv.* See sign for DECIDE[1].

offset *n.* See sign for DISPLACEMENT.

offshoot *n.* See sign for ASTRAY.

off the point See signs for ASTRAY, DIGRESS.

off the subject See signs for ASTRAY, DIGRESS.

off track See signs for ASTRAY, DIGRESS.

often *adv.* Many times; frequently: *We often go to the movies.* Same sign used for: **frequently.**

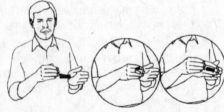

- [The sign **again** formed with a repeated movement to indicate frequency of occurrence] Touch the fingertips of the right *bent hand,* palm facing left, first on the heel and then on the fingers of the left *open hand,* palm angled up.

Oh *interj.* (Used to indicate surprise or understanding): *Oh, I see what you mean.*

- Tap the right *Y hand*, palm angled down, with a double movement in front of the right side of the body.

oil[1] *n.* Any of various kinds of thick, greasy liquids used as fuel, for cooking, etc.: *I now cook in vegetable oil.* Related form: **oily** *adj.* Same sign used for: **grease, greasy, lubrication.**

- [Shows oil dripping off something] Beginning with the bent thumb and middle finger of the right *5 hand*, palm facing up, on each side of the little-finger side of the left *open hand*, palm facing right and fingers pointing forward, bring the right hand downward with a double movement, pinching the thumb and middle finger together each time.

oil[2] *n.* See sign for GRAVY.

oily *adj.* Covered with or full of oil: *oily rags; oily hair.* Same sign used for: **greasy.**

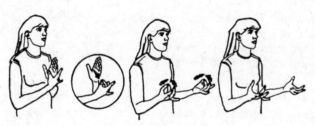

- [**oil** + **sticky**[1]] Beginning with the bent thumb and middle finger of the right *5 hand*, palm facing up, on each side of the little-finger side of the left *open hand*, palm facing right, bring the right hand downward with a double movement, pinching the thumb and middle finger together each time. Then, beginning with both *8 hands* in front of each side of the body, palms facing up, open and close the thumbs and bent middle fingers with a double movement.

ointment *n.* A substance applied to the skin, as to heal or soften: *to put ointment on a cut.*

- [**medicine** + mime rubbing ointment on the hand] With the bent middle finger of the right *5 hand*, palm facing down, in the upturned palm of the left *open hand*, rock the right hand from side to side with a double movement while keeping the middle finger in place. Then rub the fingers of the right *open hand* with a double movement on the back of the left *open hand* held in front of the chest, both palms facing down.

okay or OK or O.K.

okay or **OK** or **O.K.**¹ *interj.* **1.** (Used to express approval or agreement): *"OK," he yelled, "you can go ahead now."* —*adj.* **2.** All right; satisfactory: *The schedule is okay.* **3.** Feeling well: *I was sick, but now I'm O.K.* **4.** Adequate: *His work is OK, but he could do better.*

■ [Fingerspell **o-k**] Form an *O* and a *K* quickly in front of the right side of the chest, palm facing forward.

okay² *adj.* See signs for FINE¹, RIGHT², SUPERB.

old *adj.* Having existed for a long time; not young: *an old house.* Same sign used for: **quaint.**

■ [Shows the shape of a beard on an old man] Move the right *C hand* from near the chin, palm facing left, downward a short distance while closing into an *S hand.*

older *adj.* A comparative form of *old*: *I am older than my sister.*

■ [**old** formed with an upward movement indicating the comparative form] Move the right *C hand* from near the chin, palm facing left, upward in an arc to the right while closing into an *S hand.*

oldest *adj.* A superlative form of *old*: *I am the oldest child in the family.* Same sign used for: **eldest.**

■ [**old** formed with a exaggerated upward movement indicating the superlative form] Move the right *C hand* from near the chin, palm facing left, upward in a large arc to the right while closing into a *10 hand.*

old-fashioned *adj.* Of or characteristic of an earlier era: *old-fashioned ideas.*

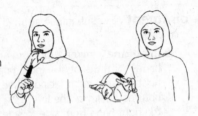

■ [**old** + **fashion**¹] Move the right *C hand* from near the chin, palm facing left, downward a short distance while closing into an *S hand.* Then move the right *F hand*, palm facing down and fingers pointing forward, from in front of the right side of the body to the right a short distance in a small arc.

Old Testament *n.* The complete Bible of the Jews, and the first of two main divisions of the Christian Bible: *The story of the Creation is in the Old Testament.*

■ [**old** + an initialized sign similar to the sign for **law**] Move the right *C hand*, palm facing left, downward a short distance from near the chin while closing into an

S hand. Then touch the index-finger side of the right *T hand,* palm facing left, first to the fingers and then to the heel of the palm of the left *open hand* held in front of the chest, palm facing forward.

oleomargarine *n.* See signs for MARGARINE[1,2].

Olympics or **Olympic Games** *pl. n.* See sign for CHAIN.

omelette *n.* A dish of eggs beaten with milk and often folded over a filling: *to eat a ham and cheese omelette.*

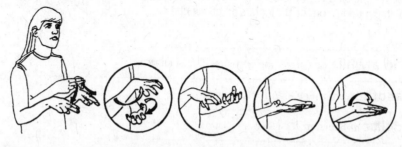

■ [**egg** + **mix**[1] + showing flipping an omelette over] Beginning with the middle finger side of the right *H hand* across the index-finger side of the left *H hand,* palms angled toward each other, bring the hands downward and away from each other with a double movement, twisting the wrists each time. Then, with the right *curved 5 hand* over the left *curved 5 hand,* palms facing each other, move the hands simultaneously in repeated circles going in opposite directions. Then, beginning with both *open hands* near each other in front of the chest, palms facing up and fingers pointing forward, flip the right hand over in an arc, ending with the right palm on the left palm.

omit *v.* See signs for ELIMINATE[1,2].

omnipotent *adj.* Having complete, unlimited power: *the omnipotent Lord.*

■ [**most** + **strong**[2]] Beginning with the palm sides of both *10 hands* together in front of the body, bring the right hand upward in front of the right side of the chest. Then, beginning with the index-finger side of the right *curved hand* near the shoulder of the extended left arm, palm facing down, move the right hand in an arc downward while turning the wrist, ending with the little-finger side near the crook of the left arm, palm facing in.

on *prep.* **1.** Above and supported by: *The purse is on the chair.* **2.** Suspended by: *a pendant on a chain.* **3.** Affixed to: *The label is on the back of the collar.* Same sign used for: **upon.**

■ [Shows moving one hand on the other] Bring the palm of the right *open hand* downward on the back of the left *open hand* held in front of the body, both palms facing down.

once *adv.* One single time: *I'll tell you this just once.*

■ Beginning with the extended right index finger touching the left *open hand* held in front of the body, palm facing right and fingers pointing forward, bring the right finger upward with a quick movement while twisting the right wrist in, ending with the palm facing in and finger pointing up in front of the right side of the chest.

once in a while See signs for OCCASIONAL[1,2], SOMETIMES.

one another *pron.* See sign for ASSOCIATE.

one dollar *n.* See sign for FIRST.

one fourth[1] *n.* One of the four equal parts into which a whole may be divided: *one fourth of a cake.* Related form: **one-fourth** *adj.* Same sign used for: **quarter.**

■ [**one** + **four** formed over each other as in a fraction] Beginning with the extended right index finger pointing up in front of the right side of the chest, palm facing in, drop the hand while opening into a *4 hand.*

one fourth[2] *n.* (alternate sign) Related form: **one-fourth** *adj.* Same sign for: **quarter.**

■ [**one** + **four** formed over each other as in a fraction] Beginning with extended right index finger pointing up in front of the right side of palm facing forward, drop the hand while opening into a *4 hand.*

one half[1] *n.* One of the two equal parts into which a whole may be divided: *one half of the pie.* Related form: **one-half** *adj.* Same sign used for: **half.**

■ [**one** + **two** formed over each other as in a fraction] Beginning with the extended right index finger pointing up in front of the right side of the chest, palm facing in, drop the hand while opening into a *2 hand.*

one half[2] *n.* (alternate sign) Related form: **one-half** *adj.* Same sign used for: **half.**

■ [Shows **one** and **two** formed over each other like a fraction] Beginning with the extended right index finger pointing up in front of the right shoulder, palm facing forward, bring the hand downward while changing into a *2 hand.*

one half[3] *n.* (alternate sign) Related form: **one-half** *adj.* Same sign used for: **half.**

■ [**one** + **two** formed over each other as in a fraction] Beginning with the right *1 hand* in front of the right shoulder, palm facing left and finger angled up, drop the hand quickly while forming a *2 hand,* ending with the palm facing down and fingers pointing left.

one hour *n.* See signs for HOUR[1,2].

one minute *n.* See sign for MINUTE.

one month *n.* See sign for MONTH.

one tenth *n.* See sign for TITHE.

one third *n.* One of the three equal parts into which a whole may be divided: *We gave a grade of B to one-third of the class.* Related form: **one-third** *adj.* Same sign used for: **third.**

■ [**one** + **three** formed over each other as in a fraction] Beginning with the extended right index finger pointing up in front of the right side of the chest, palm facing in, drop the hand while opening into a *3 hand.*

on-line or **online** *adv.* See sign for BELONG[1].

one-way *adj.* Moving or allowing movement in only one direction: *one-way traffic; a one-way street.*

■ [**one** + **way**[1]] Form a *1 hand* in front of the right shoulder, palm facing forward and finger pointing up. Then, beginning with both *W hands* in front of each side of the body, palms facing each other and fingers pointing forward, move the hands straight forward.

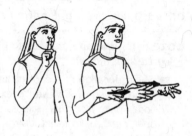

one week *n.* See sign for WEEK.

one year old One year in age: *The baby is one year old.*
Related form: **one-year-old** *adj.*

- Beginning with the extended right index finger pointing up in front of the chin, palm facing left, bring the hand forward and wiggle the right hand with a repeated movement in front of the chest.

onion *n.* An edible round bulb with a strong, pungent smell and taste, having tightly packed layers: *I like to put onions on my hamburger.*

- [As if wiping away a tear from onion fumes] Twist the knuckle of the bent index finger of the right *X hand*, palm facing forward, with a double movement near the outside corner of the right eye.

only[1] *adj.* **1.** Being the single one: *only one ticket left.* —*adv.* **2.** Without others; solely: *This memo is for you only.* **3.** Merely; just: *She is only ten years old.*

- Beginning with the extended right index finger pointing up in front of the right shoulder, palm facing forward, twist the wrist in, ending with the palm facing in near the right side of the chest.

only[2] *adj., adv.* See signs for ALONE[1,2].

onslaught *n.* A vigorous attack: *an onslaught of cold air.*

- [Represents many people or things coming toward one at one time] Beginning with the left extended index finger pointing up in front of the chest, palm facing right, bring the right *curved 5 hand*, palm facing in, toward the body with a deliberate movement, pushing the left finger against the chest.

onward *adv.* See sign for GO ON[1].

ooze *v.* (of moisture, liquid, etc.) To come slowly through a small opening: *Blood oozed from the cut.*

- [Shows location of a cut on the hand and then blood oozing out] Move the extended right index finger, palm facing left, across the back of the left *open hand*, palm facing down. Then bring the right *5 hand* downward with a repeated movement off the back of the left *open hand* while wiggling the right fingers.

open[1] *adj.* **1.** Not closed: *an open box.* —*v.* **2.** To make or become open: *The boy opened the birthday presents eagerly. Does the box open?* Same sign used for: **retrieve.**

- [Represents doors opening] Beginning with the index-finger side of both *B hands* touching in front of the chest, palms facing forward, twist both wrists while bringing the hands apart to in front of each side of the chest, ending with the palms facing each other and the fingers pointing forward.

open[2] *v.* (of a door or doors) To make or become open: *I can't open this door without a key. The door opened when I fell against it.*

- [Represents a door being opened] Beginning with the index-finger sides of both *B hands* touching in front of the chest, palms facing forward, swing the right hand back toward the right shoulder by twisting the wrist.

open[3] *v.* (of a window or windows) To make or become open: *Please open the window. The window opens easily.*

- [Represents a window being opened] Beginning with the little-finger side of the right *B hand* on the index-finger side of the left *B hand,* both palms facing in and fingers pointing in opposite directions, raise the right hand straight up in front of the chest.

open[4] *v.* (of the mouth) To make or become open: *Open your mouth and taste this. Her mouth opened in surprise.*

- [Indicates one's mouth opening] Beginning with the finger and thumb of the right *G hand* pinched together in front of the mouth, palm facing left, separate the thumb and index finger into a *G hand* while opening the mouth.

open-minded *adj.* See sign for BROAD-MINDED.

operate[1] *v.* To treat diseases or injuries by manipulating the body with surgical instruments: *The doctor operated on the man's arm.* Related form: **operation** *n.* Same sign used for: **surgery.**

- [Represents the action of cutting during surgery] Move the thumb of the right *A hand,* palm facing down, from the fingers to the heel of the left *open hand,* palm facing right and fingers pointing forward.

operate[2] *v.* (alternate sign) Related form: **operation** *n.* Same sign used for: **surgery.**

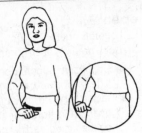

■ [Same as **operate**[1] except formed on the location of abdominal surgery] Move the extended thumb of the right *10 hand*, palm facing down, from the left to right across the abdomen. This sign may be formed near any part of the body where surgery is performed, e.g., for cataract surgery one would form the sign **operate** near the eye.

operate[3] *v.* To work, function, or run: *The machine operates smoothly.* Related forms: **operation** *n.*, **operational** *adj.*

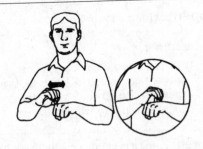

■ [Initialized sign similar to sign for **busy**] Move the thumb side of the right *O hand*, palm facing forward, back and forth with a double movement across the back of the left *S hand* held across the chest, palm facing down.

operate[4] *v.* See signs for MANAGE, RUN[6].

operating system or **OS** *n. phrase.* A set of programs that enables the components of a computer to function together smoothly: *The computer runs on a Windows operating system.*

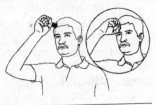

■ [**run**[6] + **system**[2]] With a double movement, brush the palm of the right *open hand* upward on the palm of the left *open hand* held up in front of the chest. Then, beginning with the index-finger sides of both *S hands* touching in front of the chest, palms facing down, move the hands outward to in front of each shoulder and then straight down a short distance.

opinion *n.* A belief or judgment, especially one based on inadequate proof: *It's my opinion that he's innocent.*

■ [Initialized sign] Move the right *O hand*, palm facing left in front of the forehead, toward the head with a double movement.

opossum *n.* A small mammal, with a tail adapted for seizing and grasping, that carries its young in a pouch: *The opossum pretends to be dead whenever it's in danger.*

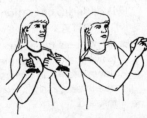

■ [**animal** + showing how an opossum hangs by its tail] Beginning with the fingertips of both *bent hands* on the chest near each shoulder, palms facing in opposite directions, roll the fingers toward each other on their knuckles with a double movement while keeping the fingers in place. Then hang the bent index finger of the right *X hand*, palm facing forward, on the extended left index finger, palm facing down and finger pointing right.

opponent *n.* See sign for ENEMY.

opportunity *n.* A favorable chance or appropriate occasion: *an opportunity to earn some money.*

- ■ [Abbreviation **o-p** formed in a way that is similar to the sign for **permit**] Beginning with both *O hands* in front of the chest, palms facing down, move the hands forward and upward in an arc while changing into *P hands.*

opposed to See sign for AGAINST.

opposite *adj.* Being extremely different, as in character or quality; opposed: *We have opposite opinions on that issue.* Related form: **oppose** *v.* Same sign used for: **contrary, contrast, counter.**

- ■ [Shows two things repelled by each other] Beginning with the fingertips of both extended index fingers touching in front of the chest, palms facing in, bring the hands straight apart to in front of each side of the chest.

opposition *n.* See sign for STRUGGLE.

oppress *v.* To weigh down: *The weather oppressed my spirits.* Related form: **oppression** *n.*

- ■ [Demonstrates pushing an oppressed thing down] Push the palm of the left *5 hand* downward on the extended right index finger, palm facing left and finger pointing up, forcing the right hand downward with a double movement.

optical *adj.* Relating to vision, light, or optics: *an optical illusion.*

- ■ [Turning an optical instrument to adjust its focus] Beginning with the right *C hand*, palm facing down, near the right eye, twist the wrist to turn the palm up.

optical mouse *n.* An advanced computer pointing device that uses a light-emitting diode, optical sensor, and digital signal processing in place of the traditional wired mouse. Movement is

detected by sensing changes in reflected light, rather than by interpreting the motion of a rolling sphere: *Use an optical mouse to move the cursor on the laptop.*

■ [**mouse**[2] + **none**[2] + **wire**[1]] Move the right *modified C hand*, palm facing forward, around in front of the right side of the body. Then, beginning with both *flattened O hands*, palms facing forward, in front of the chest, move the hands apart to each side. Then, beginning with both extended little fingers pointing toward each other in front of the chest, palms facing in, move the hands apart from each other.

optical zoom *n.* The feature on a camera that allows an image to be magnified: *He used the optical zoom to take a close-up picture of the spider.*

■ [**optical + focus**[4]] Beginning with the right *C hand*, palm facing down, near the right eye, twist the wrist to turn the palm up. Then move the right *curved hand* forward and back toward the face with a double movement.

optimistic *adj.* Tending to expect the best: *I am optimistic about tomorrow's weather.*

■ [**feel + plus**] Move the bent middle finger of the right *5 hand*, palm facing in, upward on the chest with a double movement. Then bring the side of the extended right index finger, palm facing left and finger pointing up, with a double movement against the extended left index finger, palm facing down and finger pointing right in front of the chest.

option *n.* See signs for CHOOSE[1,2,3].

or[1] *conj.* (Used to connect alternative words, phrases, etc.): *Do you want apples or oranges?* See also signs for EITHER[1,2]. Same sign used for: **then.**

■ [Touches two choices] Tap the extended right index finger, palm facing in, first to the thumb tip and then to the end of the index finger of the left *L hand*, palm facing right and index finger pointing forward.

or[2] *conj.* See sign for NEITHER.

oral[1] *adj.* **1.** Using speech; spoken: *an oral presentation.* **2.** Pertaining to a method of communication used by some deaf people that involves speechreading and learning to speak: *She went to an oral school for the deaf.*

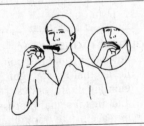

■ [Initialized sign] Move the thumb side of the right *O hand*, palm facing left, in an arc from left to right in front of the mouth with a double movement.

oral[2] *adj.* (alternate sign for the method of communication that involves speechreading and learning to speak)

■ [Used sarcastically to represent the movements of people's jaws when talking] Beginning with the bent arms of both *S hands* across the chest, right arm above the left arm, move the right arm up and down with a short double movement.

---

orange[1] *n.* **1.** A juicy, acidic, often sweet citrus fruit: *to eat an orange at breakfast.* —*adj.* **2.** Reddish-yellow in color: *an orange pumpkin.*

■ [The hand seems to squeeze an orange] Beginning with the right *C hand* in front of the mouth, palm facing left, squeeze the fingers open and closed with a repeated movement, forming an *S hand* each time.

---

orange[2] *adj.* (alternate sign)

■ Move the bent fingers of the right *Y hand,* palm facing down, back and forth on the palm of the left *open hand,* palm facing up, with a double movement by twisting the wrist.

---

orator *n.* A person who speaks well in public; a public speaker: *She is an excellent orator.* Related forms: **oration** *n.,* **oratory** *n.*

■ [**speak**[2] + **smoothly** + **person marker**] Beginning with the right *open hand* in front of the right shoulder, palm angled up and fingers pointing up, bring the hand forward with a double movement by bending the wrist. Then, beginning with both *8 hands* in front of each side of the chest, palms facing up, slide the thumb of each hand across the fingertips from the little to the index fingers with a smooth movement, ending with *flattened O hands.* Then move both *open hands,* palms facing each other, downward along each side of the body.

---

orbit[1] *n.* **1.** The curved path of a heavenly body around another heavenly body: *studying the moon's orbit around the earth.* —*v.* **2.** To travel in a circular movement around another object in space: *The satellite orbits the earth every twenty-four hours.*

■ [Shows movement of one thing around another] Move the extended right index finger, palm facing down, in a circle around the fingers of the left *flattened O hand,* palm facing down in front of the chest.

---

orbit[2] *n.* See signs for AROUND[1,2], YEAR-ROUND.

orchard *n.* See signs for FOREST[1,2].

orchestra[1] *n.* A group of musicians, playing a variety of musical instruments, who perform together: *to conduct the orchestra during the concert.* Same sign used for: **conductor.**

■ [**conduct**[1] + **person marker**] Beginning with both extended index fingers angled forward in front of the chest, palms facing toward each other, swing the hands outward away from each other with a repeated movement. Then move both *open hands,* palms facing each other, downward along each side of the body.

orchestra[2] *n.* See signs for BAND[1,2].

ordain *v.* To consecrate as a member of the clergy: *to ordain a new pastor.*

■ [Represents the laying on of hands to bless one who is being ordained] Move the fingers of the right *open hand* from touching the right side of the forehead, palm angled in, downward to land across the fingers of the left *open hand* held across the chest, both palms facing down.

ordeal *n.* See sign for EXPERIENCE.

order[1] *n.* **1.** An instruction or command issued with authority: *When I give you an order, I expect you to obey it.* —*v.* **2.** To give an order or command to: *I order you to leave the house.* Same sign used for: **command, direct.**

■ [Represents taking words from the mouth and directing them at another] Move the extended right index finger, palm facing left and finger pointing up, from in front of the mouth straight forward while turning the palm down, ending with the finger pointing forward.

order[2] *n., v.* (alternate sign) Same sign used for: **command, direct.**

■ Beginning with the extended right index finger pointing up in front of the mouth, palm facing left, and the extended left index finger pointing up somewhat forward of the chest, palm facing right, move both hands forward simultaneously, ending with the fingers pointing forward and the palms facing down.

order[3] *n.* A body of persons bound by vows to obey shared religious rules and goals: *a religious order dedicated to prayer and contemplation.*

■ [Initialized sign similar to sign for **organization** but representing a smaller group] Beginning with the fingertips of both *O hands* touching in front of the chest, palms angled forward, while keeping the fingers together, turn the hands in small outward arcs, ending with the little fingers touching and palms facing in.

ordinance *n.* A rule or law of a community: *the city ordinance against loitering.*

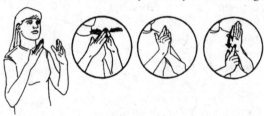

■ [**town** + **law**] Tap the fingertips of both *open hands,* palms angled toward each other, together in front of the chest with a double movement. Next place the palm side of the right *L hand,* palm facing left, first on the fingers and then the heel of the left *open hand,* palm facing right.

ordinary[1] *adj.* Usual; commonplace: *an ordinary day.*

■ [**daily** + **same**] Move the palm side of the right *10 hand* forward on the right side of the chin with a double movement. Then, beginning with both index fingers pointing forward in front of the each side of the body, palms facing down, bring the hands together, ending with the index fingers side by side in front of the body.

ordinary[2] *adj.* See signs for DAILY, REGULAR.

organ *n.* See sign for PIANO.

organist *n.* See sign for PIANIST.

organization *n.* A group of people united for some purpose: *to belong to a political organization.* Related form: **organize** *v.*

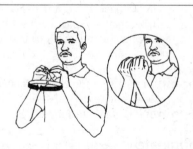

■ [Initialized sign similar to sign for **class**] Beginning with the fingertips of both *O hands* touching in front of the chest, palms angled forward, bring the hands away from each other in outward arcs while turning the palms in, ending with the little fingers touching.

organize

organize *v.* See sign for PREPARE. Related form: **organization** *n.*

orgasm *n.* See sign for CLIMAX.

Oriental *adj.* **1.** Of, pertaining to, or characteristic of the countries of Asia, especially East Asia: *wore an Oriental costume.* —*n.* (sometimes considered an offensive term) **2.** A native of Asia: *According to the history books, signs on factory doors used to read, "No Orientals need apply."*

■ [Initialized sign similar to sign for **China**²] Beginning with the fingertips of the right *flattened O hand* touching the temple near the outer corner of the right eye, palm facing left, twist the hand forward with a double movement, turning the palm back.

Oriental² *adj., n.* See sign for CHINA².

orientation¹ *n.* An introduction or short program of training, as for a new job: *The new employees will attend an orientation.*

■ [Initialized sign similar to sign for **situation**] Move the palm side of the right *O hand* in a circle around the extended left index finger held in front of the chest, palm facing in and finger pointing up.

orientation² *n.* (alternate sign)

■ [Initialized sign similar to sign for **practice**] Swing the palm side of the right *O hand* with a double movement across the length of the extended left index finger held across the chest, palm facing down and finger pointing right.

origin¹ *n.* The starting point of something; beginning; source: *the origins of humankind.* Related form: **original** *n.*

■ [Initialized sign similar to sign for **start**¹] Beginning with the fingertips of the right *O hand,* palm facing left, touching the palm of the left *open hand,* palm facing right and fingers pointing forward, twist the right hand forward with a double movement.

origin² *n.* See sign for START¹. Related form: **origination** *n.*

original *adj.* See sign for FIRST².

originate *v.* See signs for INVENT, START².

ornament[1] *n.* A small decorative item: *to put an ornament on the Christmas tree.*

■ [**pretty** + **fix**[1] + a gesture showing lights flashing on and off on a Christmas tree] Move the right *5 hand* in a circular movement in front of the face while closing the fingers to the thumb, forming a *flattened O hand,* palm facing in. Then brush the fingertips of both *flattened O hands* across each other repeatedly as the hands twist in opposite directions with a double movement. Then, beginning with the right *flattened O hand* in front of the right side of the chest and the left *curved hand* in front of the left shoulder, both palms facing forward, open the right hand into a *curved hand* and close the left hand into a *flattened O hand* with an alternating repeated movement.

ornament[2] *n.* See sign for DECORATE[2].

orphan *n.* A child whose parents are dead: *an orphan available for adoption.*

■ [**none**[1,2,3] + **mother**[1,2] + **father**[1,2]] Beginning with both *O hands* in front of the chest, right hand closer to the chest than the left hand and palms facing in opposite directions, bring the hands outward to in front of each side of the chest while turning the palms forward. Next tap the thumb of the right *5 hand,* palm facing left, against the chin with a double movement. Then tap the thumb of the right *5 hand,* palm facing left, against the forehead with a double movement.

orthodox *adj.* Conforming to generally accepted religious or other doctrinal views: *holds orthodox beliefs about behavior.*

■ [Initialized sign similar to sign for **clean**] Slide the little-finger side of the right *O hand,* palm facing in, from the heel to the fingertips of the left *open hand* held in front of the chest, palm facing up and fingers angled forward.

other[1] *adj.* **1.** Additional; further: *There is no other choice.* **2.** Different from the one under discussion: *If this pen doesn't work, try the other one.* —*n.* **3.** The other one: *I will choose the other.* Same sign used for: **else.**

■ [The thumb points over to another] Beginning with the right *10 hand* in front of the chest, palm facing down, twist the hand upward to the right, ending with the palm facing up and the extended thumb pointing right.

other[2] *adj.* See sign for ANOTHER.

ought to See sign for MUST.

our *adj.* Belonging to us: *This is our car.* Related form: **ours** *pron.*

- ■ [The hand seems to draw a possession to oneself] Beginning with the thumb side of the right *C hand* on the right side of the chest, palm facing left, bring the hand forward in an arc across the chest, ending with the little-finger side of the left hand on the left side of the chest, palm facing right.

ourselves *pl. pron.* A reflexive form of *we* or *us*, used as an object or an intensifier: *We cooked for ourselves. We ourselves would never do that.*

- ■ [Uses the handshape used for reflexive pronouns] Beginning with the thumb of the right *A hand* touching the right side of the chest, palm facing left, bring the hand in an arc across the chest and touch again on the left side of the chest.

out *prep.* Movement or direction from the inside to the outside of something: *She took money out of the jar.* Same sign used for: **go out.**

- ■ [Demonstrates a movement out of something] Beginning with the right *5 hand,* palm facing down, inserted in the thumb-side opening of the left *C hand,* palm facing right, bring the right hand upward, closing the fingers and thumb together into a *flattened O hand.*

outboard motor *n.* A small portable motor attached to a boat: *Start the outboard motor.*

- ■ [**boat** + mime pulling on a motor to start it] With the little-finger sides of both *curved hands* together, palms angled up, move the hands forward with a bouncing double arc. Next move the right *S hand,* palm facing in, from in front of the left side of the body upward to the right. Then, with the right elbow extended, shake the right *S hand* near the right side of the body, palm facing left.

outbreak *n.* See sign for SPREAD[1].

outburst *n.* A sudden and violent bursting forth: *an outburst of laughter.*

- **[mind[1] + explode[1,2]]** Tap the right side of the forehead with the right curved index finger. Then, beginning with the fingers of both *O hands* together in front of the chest, palms facing down, move the hands upward and apart quickly while opening into *5 hands* near each side of the head, palms facing forward.

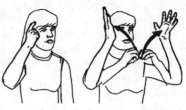

outcome *n.* See signs for RESULT[1,2].

outdated *adj.* Old fashioned; no longer current: *an outdated style.*

- **[old + long time ago]** Move the right *C hand*, palm facing left, downward a short distance from the chin while changing into an *S hand*. Then, beginning with the right *5 hand* in front of the right shoulder, palm facing left, bring the hand back to behind the right shoulder.

outdoors *adv.* See signs for OUTSIDE[1,2].

outfit *n.* A set of clothes appropriate for wearing together: *I have a new outfit to wear to the party.*

- **[The hand indicates what is being worn]** Brush the thumb of the right *5 hand*, palm facing in, downward on the right side of the chest with a double movement.

outgrow *v.* **1.** To grow too large for: *The boy has outgrown all his clothes.* **2.** To discard or lose as one matures: *I've outgrown my allergies.*

- **[outside[1] + grow]** Beginning with the fingertips of the right *flattened O hand*, palm facing down, inserted in the thumb-side opening of the left *C hand*, palm facing right, bring the right hand upward and forward in an arc, ending with the palm facing in. Then bring the right *flattened O hand*, palm facing in, up through the left *C hand*, palm facing in and fingers pointing right, while spreading the right fingers into a *5 hand* in front of the chest.

outline[1] *n.* A brief organized plan showing the main features: *an outline of the book.*

- **[outside[1] + line]** Beginning with the fingers of the right *flattened O hand*, palm facing down, inserted in the thumb-side opening of the left *C hand*, palm facing right, bring the right hand upward and outward in an arc, ending with the palm facing in. Then, beginning with the extended little fingers of both *I hands* touching in front of the chest, palms facing in, bring the hands straight apart to in front of each side of the chest.

outline[2] *n.* (alternate sign)

■ [**brief**[1] + **list**[1,2,3,4]] Beginning with both *curved hands* in front of the chest, right hand above the left hand and fingers pointing in opposite directions, bring the hands toward each other while squeezing the fingers together, ending with the little-finger side of the right *S hand* on top of the thumb side of the left *S hand*. Then touch the little-finger side of the right *bent hand*, palm facing left, several times on the palm of the left *open hand*, palm facing up, beginning at the left fingers and ending at the heel.

outnumber *v.* To exceed in number: *The boys outnumbered the girls.*

■ [**defeat**[1] + **me** + **number**] Move the right *S hand* from in front of the right shoulder, palm facing forward, downward and forward, ending with the right wrist across the wrist of the left *S hand*, both palms facing down. Next touch the extended right index finger to the chest, palm facing in. Then, with the fingertips of both *flattened O hands* touching, left palm facing up and right palm facing down, twist the wrists in opposite directions and touch the fingertips again, ending with the left palm facing down and the right palm facing up.

out of the way See sign for ASTRAY.

output *n.* **1.** Anything, whether meaningful data or garbled nonsense, sent out from a computer, as to a display or printer: *to analyze the printed output.* —*adj.* **2.** Having to do with the transfer of data: *an output buffer.*

■ Beginning with the fingertips of the right *flattened O hand*, palm facing down, inserted in the thumb-side opening of the left *flattened O hand*, palm facing in, bring the right hand upward in an arc to the right while opening into a *flattened C hand*, palm facing left.

outrage *n.* See sign for ANGER[1].

outreach *n.* **1.** An act, instance, or program of extending services and information to the larger community: *an organization engaged in outreach to the elderly.*

—*adj.* **2.** Being part of an information and services network: *an outreach program providing food to the homeless.*

■ [**out** + **touch**[1]] Beginning with the fingertips of the right *flattened O hand,* palm facing down, inserted in the thumb-side opening of the left *C hand,* palm facing right, bring the right hand upward to the right. Then touch the bent middle finger of the right *5 hand,* palm facing down, to the back of the left *open hand* held across the chest, palm facing down.

---

outside[1] *n.* **1.** The external side or surface or the area near it: *the outside of a house.* —*adj.* **2.** Located on the outside: *painting the outside walls.* —*adv.* **3.** On or to the outside: *Go outside and play.* —*prep.* **4.** Beyond the boundaries of: *outside the fence.* Same sign used for: **external, outdoors.**

■ Beginning with the right *5 hand,* palm facing down, inserted in the thumb-side opening of the left *C hand,* palm facing right, bring the right hand upward and forward in an arc while closing the fingers and thumb together into a *flattened O hand* in front of the chest, fingers pointing in.

---

outside[2] *adv.* (alternate sign) Same sign used for: **external, outdoors.**

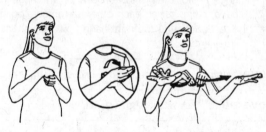

■ [**outside**[1] + **spread**[1]] Beginning with the fingers of the right *flattened O hand,* palm facing down, inserted in the thumb-side opening of the left *C hand,* palm facing right, bring the right hand upward and forward in an arc, ending with the palm facing in. Then, beginning with the fingertips of both *flattened O hands* touching in front of the chest, both palms facing down, move the hands forward and outward while opening into *5 hands,* ending with both *5 hands* in front of each side of the body, palms facing down and fingers pointing forward.

---

outspoken *adj.* Frank; bold; candid: *an outspoken person who won't hesitate to tell you the truth.*

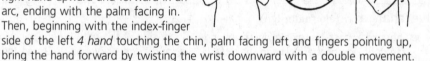

■ [**outside**[1] + **speak**[1]] Beginning with the fingers of the right *flattened O hand,* palm facing down, inserted in the thumb-side opening of the left *C hand,* palm facing right, bring the right hand upward and forward in an arc, ending with the palm facing in. Then, beginning with the index-finger side of the left *4 hand* touching the chin, palm facing left and fingers pointing up, bring the hand forward by twisting the wrist downward with a double movement.

ovary

ovary *n.* The female sexual gland in which eggs mature and ripen for fertilization.

■ [Location of ovaries] Place the palm side of both *F hands*, fingers pointing down, against each side of the abdomen.

ovation *n.* See sign for APPLAUD.

oven *n.* An enclosed place, as in a stove, for baking or roasting food: *Let's bake the pie in the smaller oven.*

■ [The hand seems to put something in the oven] Move the fingers of the right *open hand*, palm facing up and fingers pointing forward, forward with a double movement under the left *open hand* held in front of the chest, palm facing down and fingers pointing right.

over[1] *prep.* In excess of: *He charged over his credit limit.* See also sign for ABOVE[1]. Same sign used for: **exceed, too much.**

■ [Shows a location higher than another] Beginning with the fingertips of the right *bent hand* on the fingertips of the left *bent hand*, palms facing each other and fingers pointing in opposite directions, bring the right hand upward a short distance in a small arc.

over[2] *prep., adv.* See signs for ACROSS, AGAIN, END[2], FINISH[1,2].

overall *adj., adv.* See sign for ALL OVER.

overcharge[1] *v.* To charge too high a price to: *I was overcharged for the groceries.*

■ [**over**[1] + **cost**[1]] Beginning with the right *bent hand* on the back of the left *bent hand*, both palms facing down and fingers pointing in opposite directions, bring the right hand in toward the chest and upward in an arc. Then move the right *X hand* from in front of the right side of the chest, palm facing left, downward, striking the palm of the left *open hand*, palm facing in and fingers pointing right, as it moves.

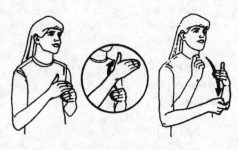

overcharge[2] *v.* (alternate sign)

■ [**absurd** + **cost**[1]] Beginning with the index-finger side of the right *4 hand* touching the right side of the forehead, palm facing left and fingers pointing up, bring the hand

forward in a circular movement. Then move the
right *X hand,* palm facing left, downward, striking
the palm of the left *open hand,* palm facing in and
fingers pointing right, as it moves.

overcoat[1] *n.* A heavy coat worn over
regular clothing: *to wear an overcoat
in cold weather.*

■ [**over**[1] + **coat**] Beginning with the
right *bent hand* on the back of the
left *bent hand,* both palms facing
down and fingers pointing in
opposite directions, bring the right
hand in an arc back toward the
chest and upward. Then bring the thumbs of both *A hands* from near each shoulder,
palms facing each other, downward, ending near the waist, palms facing down.

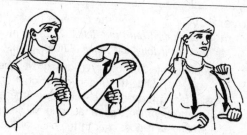

overcoat[2] *n.* See sign for COAT.

overcome *v.* See signs for DEFEAT[1,2,3].

overdose[1] *n.* **1.** Too large a dose of a drug:
*a bad reaction from an overdose of
medicine.* —*v.* **2.** To take an excessive,
harmful, or fatal amount of a drug: *to
overdose on heroin.*

■ [**over**[1] + **medicine**] Beginning with
the right *bent hand* on the back of
the left *bent hand,* both palms facing
down and fingers pointing in
opposite directions, bring the right hand in an arc toward the chest and upward a
short distance. Then, with the bent middle finger of the right *5 hand,* palm facing
down, in the upturned palm of the left *open hand,* rock the right hand from side to
side with a double movement while keeping the middle finger in place.

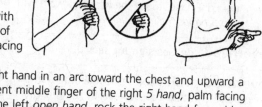

overdose[2] *n., v.* (alternate sign)

■ [**over**[1] + **drug**[2]] Beginning with the
right *bent hand* on the back of the
left *bent hand,* both palms facing
down and fingers pointing in opposite
directions, bring the right hand in an
arc toward the chest and upward.
Then move the little-finger side of the
right *S hand,* palm facing up, against
the upper part of the bent left forearm with a double movement. This sign is used
only when referring to an overdose of illegal drugs.

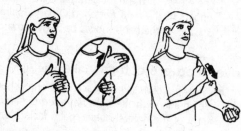

overdose[3] *n., v.* (alternate sign)

- [Abbreviation **o-d**] Form an *O hand* and then a *D hand* in front of the right side of the chest, palm facing forward.

overflow *v.* **1.** To have the contents flow or spill over: *The river overflowed onto the fields.* **2.** To be plentifully supplied: *My heart overflows with love.* Same sign used for: **run over.**

- [Demonstrates a substance flowing over the sides of a container] Slide the fingers of the right *open hand*, palm facing forward, over the index-finger side of the left *open hand*, palm facing in, while opening into a *5 hand* as it goes over to the back of the left hand.

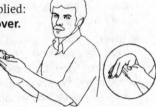

overhaul *v.* To repair so as to restore completely to working condition: *to overhaul the old car.*

- [**break** + **cause**] Beginning with both *S hands* together in front of the body, palms facing down, move the hands away from each other while twisting the wrists with a deliberate movement, ending with the palms facing each other in front of each side of the body. Then, beginning with the little-finger side of the right *S hand* touching the index-finger side of the left *S hand,* palms angled up and left hand closer to the body than the right hand, move the hands forward with a deliberate movement while opening into *5 hands,* palms facing up.

overhead *adv.* See sign for ABOVE[2].

overhead projector[1] *n.* A machine that projects transparencies on a screen that can be seen by an audience: *The speaker will show the information on the overhead projector.*

- [Shows a light shining back over one's shoulder] While holding the elbow of the right *bent hand* in the left palm, open the fingers of the right *flattened O hand*, palm facing in, into a *5 hand* as the hand moves back over the right shoulder.

overhead projector[2] *n.* (alternate sign)

- [Shows a light shining back over one's shoulder] Beginning with the right *flattened O hand* in front of the right shoulder, palm facing forward, twist the hand quickly around while opening into a *5 hand,* palm facing back, and thrust the hand over the right shoulder.

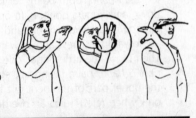

overlap *v.* See sign for MOUNT[1].

overlay *n.* A segment of a program called into computer memory from the disk as needed: *a word processor that uses overlays to make it run more quickly.*

■ [Shows laying something over another thing] Beginning with the right *open hand,* palm facing down and fingers pointing forward, in front of the right side of the chest, move the hand forward in an outward arc to land across the back of the left *open hand* held in front of the chest, palm facing down.

overlook[1] *v.* **1.** To fail to see or notice: *He overlooked too many mistakes to be a good proofreader.* **2.** To disregard or forget: *I'm sorry I overlooked answering your letter.* Same sign used for: **oversight.**

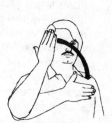

■ [Represents something passing in front of the eyes without notice] Beginning with the right *open hand* near the right side of the head, palm facing left and fingers pointing up, move the hand in an arc in front of the face to the left, ending with the fingers pointing left and the palm facing in, in front of the left side of the chest.

overlook[2] *v.* To have a view of from above: *The house overlooks the ocean.* Same sign used for: **view.**

■ [Represents the eyes pointing down and around as if to keep an eye on something] Beginning with both *V hands* in front of the left side of the body, palms facing down and fingers angled left, swing the hands in a large arc in front of the body, ending with the fingers pointing right in front of the right side of the body, palms facing down.

overnight *adj., adv.* See sign for ALL NIGHT.

overrule[1] *v.* **1.** To rule against or disallow the arguments of. **2.** To rule unfavorably upon an objection raised in court: *The judge overruled the lawyer's objection.*

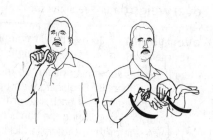

■ [not[1] + accept] Bring the thumb of the right *10 hand* forward from under the chin with a deliberate movement. Then, beginning with both *5 hands* in front of the body, fingers pointing forward and palms facing down, pull both hands back to the chest while changing to *flattened O hands.*

overrule[2] *v.* (alternate sign)

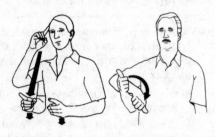

- ■ [**decide**[2] + **reject**[1]] Move the extended right index finger from the right side of the forehead, palm facing left, down in front of the body, palms facing each other. Then, beginning with the right *10 hand* in front of the right shoulder, elbow extended and palm facing down, twist the wrist downward, ending with the thumb pointing down and the palm facing right.

overrule[3] *v.* (alternate sign)

- ■ [**judge**[1] + **manage**] Move both *F hands*, palms facing each other, up and down in front of each side of the chest with a repeated alternating movement. Then, with both *modified X hands* in front of each side of the chest, palms angled up and right hand farther from the chest than the left hand, move the hands forward and back with a repeated alternating movement.

oversight *n.* See sign for OVERLOOK[1].

oversleep *v.* To sleep too long: *I overslept this morning.*

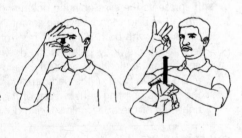

- ■ [**sleepy** + **sunrise**[2]] Beginning with the right *curved 5 hand* in front of the forehead, palm facing in, bring the hand downward while closing the fingers and thumb together, forming a *flattened O hand* in front of the nose. Then, beginning with the right *F hand* in front of the body, palm facing forward, bring the hands straight upward in front of the little-finger side of the left *open hand* held across the chest, palm facing down and fingers pointing right, ending with the right *F hand* in front of the face.

overweight *adj.* See signs for FAT[1,2,4].

overwhelm[1] *v.* To overpower completely; burden; engulf: *overwhelmed with work.*

- ■ [Indicates something being too much for the mind to handle] Beginning with both *modified X hands* in front of each side of the face, palms facing in, bring the hands back along each side of the head while flicking the index fingers open.

overwhelm[2] *v.* (alternate sign)

- [Represents everything coming at one at once, as if to overwhelm] Beginning with both *A hands* in front of each side of the face, palms facing in, bring the hands back along each side of the head while opening into *5 hands*.

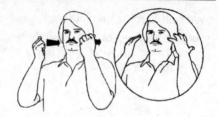

overwhelm[3] *v.* (alternate sign)

- [Indicates being burdened beyond one's ability to cope] Beginning with both *curved hands* in front of each side of the chest, palms facing up, bring the hands in simultaneous arcs upward and back over each shoulder, ending with the palms facing down and the fingers pointing back.

overwork[1] *n.* **1.** Too much work; work beyond one's capacity: *tired from overwork.* —*v.* **2.** To work too long or too hard: *I overworked in the yard today.*

- [**over**[1] + **work**[1,2]] Beginning with the right *bent hand* on the back of the left *bent hand,* both palms facing down and fingers pointing in opposite directions, bring the right hand in toward the chest and upward in an arc. Then tap the heel of the right *S hand,* palm facing forward, on the back of the left *S hand,* palm facing down, with a double movement.

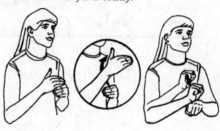

overwork[2] *n.* See sign for WORKAHOLIC.

owe *v.* See sign for AFFORD[1].

owl *n.* A bird of prey active at night, characteristically having a large head and large eyes framed in flat planes: *Owls fly at night.*

- [Shows the shape of an owl's eyes] With the thumb side of each *O hand* in front of each eye, palms angled toward each other, twist the hands downward toward the nose with a repeated movement.

own[1] *adj.* **1.** Belonging to oneself: *I have my own car.* —*pron.* **2.** Something that belongs to oneself: *She has her own.* Same sign used for: **self.**

- [The hand moves back toward oneself] Bring the knuckles of the right *10 hand,* palm facing right, back against the center of the chest.

own[2] *adj., pron.* (alternate sign) Same sign used for: **self.**

■ [The hand moves back toward oneself] Bring the thumb side of the right *A hand,* palm facing left, back against the center of the chest.

own[3] *pron.* See sign for MY.

oxygen *n.* A gas without color or odor that forms part of the breathable atmosphere: *The patient needed more oxygen.* Same sign used for: **nose mask.**

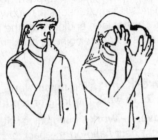

■ [**nose + mask**[2]] Touch the extended right index finger to the nose, palm facing in and finger pointing up. Then bring the right *curved 5 hand* from in front of the face, palm facing in, back toward the face.

pace[1] *n.* See sign for PROCEDURE. Shared idea of taking orderly steps.

pace[2] *n.* See signs for STEP[1,2].

pacify *v.* To make calm: *to pacify the crying baby by rocking him.*

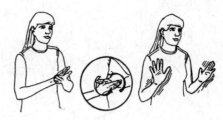

- **[become + settle]** Beginning with the open right palm lying across the open upturned left palm, rotate the hands, exchanging positions while keeping the palms together. Then, beginning with both *5 hands* in front of each side of the body, palms angled forward and fingers angled up, push the hands downward with a short repeated movement.

pack[1] *v.* To place and tightly arrange articles in: *to pack your suitcase.*

- [Mime putting things into a suitcase] Beginning with both *flattened O hands* in front of each side of the chest, palms facing down, move the hands downward with an alternating double movement.

pack[2] *v.* To store several units of data together on disk, especially in a compressed format: *a program that packs the data efficiently.*

- [Indicates things packed together] Beginning with the right *S hand,* palm facing in, above the palm of the left *open hand,* palm facing up, move both hands upward in front of the chest.

pack[3] *v.* (alternate sign)

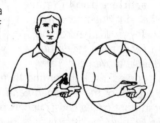

- [Demonstrates condensing something to a smaller size] Beginning with the thumb of the right *C hand,* palm facing left, on the palm of the left *open hand,* palm facing up, bring the right fingers downward to form a *flattened C hand.*

pack

pack[4] *v.* (alternate sign)

■ [Initialized sign similar to sign for **record**[1]] Beginning with the right *P hand,* palm facing down, over the palm of the left *open hand,* palm facing up, move the right hand in a double circular movement.

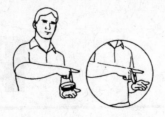

package *n.* See sign for BOX.

packet *n.* A block of data for transmission with other packets over a modem: *The packets of data are sent by your communications software.* Same sign used for: **groups.**

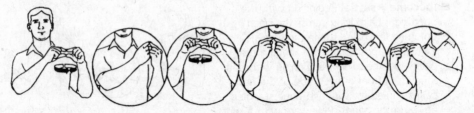

■ [Similar to sign for **group**[1] except repeated three times] Beginning with both *G hands* in front of the left side of the chest, palms facing each other and fingertips touching, bring the hands away from each other in outward arcs while turning the palms in, ending with the little fingers touching. Repeat in front of the chest and again in front of the right side of the chest.

pact *n.* An agreement, compact, or treaty: *Both parties signed the pact.*

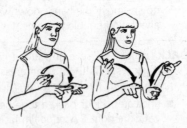

■ [**sign**[3] + gesture similar to **agree**[1]] Place the extended fingers of the right *H hand* firmly down on the upturned palm of the left *open hand,* held in front of the chest. Then, beginning with both extended index fingers in front of each side of the chest, palms facing up and fingers pointing forward, flip the hands over toward each other, ending with the palms facing down.

pad[1] *n.* Sheets of paper fastened by glue on one end: *to write notes for the meeting on a pad.*

■ [**paper** + **article** + **book**[1]] Pat the heel of the right *open hand,* palm facing down, on the heel of the left *open hand,* palm facing up, with a double movement. Then move the curved index finger and thumb of the right *modified C hand* downward across the palm of the left *open hand.* Then, beginning with the palms of both hands together in front of the chest, fingers pointing forward, bring the hands apart at the top while keeping the little fingers together.

pad[2] *n.* A cushion for resting or leaning on: *to take a nap on the quilted pad.* Same sign used for: **mat.**

- [**bed**[1,2] + **floor**] With the left open palm on top of the right open palm, rest the right cheek at an angle on the back of the left hand. Then, beginning with the index fingers of both *open hands* together in front of the body, palms facing down and fingers pointing forward, move the hands away from each other to in front of each side of the body.

paddle *v.* To beat with a short, flat-bladed oar: *The teacher paddled the child for being naughty.* Same sign used for: **spank, whip.**

- [Mime hitting something with a paddle while holding it with the other hand] Beginning with the right *S hand* in front of the right shoulder, palm facing left, and the left *curved hand* in front of the left side of the body, palm facing down, bring the right hand downward with a double movement to near the left hand.

pagan *n.* **1.** A member of a religion that worships more than one god; a person who is not a Christian, Jew, or Muslim: *The ancient Greeks were pagans.* **2.** An irreligious person: *If you won't go to church, people will think you're a pagan.* Same sign used for: **heathen.**

- [**believe** + shaking head in the negative + **God**] Move the extended right index finger from in front of the face, palm facing forward and finger pointing up, downward while opening the hand, ending with the right hand clasping the upturned left palm in front of the body. Then, while shaking the head from side to side in a negative manner, move the right *B hand,* palm facing left and fingers angled forward, from the head downward in front of the face in an inward arc.

page[1] *n.* One side of a leaf of paper in something printed, as a book or manuscript: *to turn the page.*

- [Initialized sign showing turning the pages of a book] Strike the middle finger of the right *P hand,* palm facing left, against the left open palm with a double circular upward movement.

page[2] *n.* (alternate sign) Same sign used for: **dictionary.**

- [The thumb seems to flip through the pages of a book] Strike the extended thumb of the right *10 hand,* palm facing down, against the left open palm with a double circular upward movement.

pagoda

pagoda *n.* A Far Eastern temple in the form of a tower with an upward-curving roof: *a Chinese pagoda.*

- [**China**[2] + **home** + **monument**] With the extended right index finger touching the outer corner of the right eye, palm facing down, twist the finger with a double movement. Next, touch the fingertips of the right *flattened O hand* first to the right side of the chin and then to the right cheek, palm facing down. Then, beginning with the fingertips of both *open hands* touching in front of the face, palms angled toward each other, bring the hands at a downward angle outward to in front of each shoulder and then straight down, ending with the fingers pointing up and the palms facing each other.

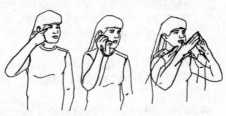

Pah! *interj.* (Deaf community expression meaning Finally! or At last!) See sign for FINALLY[1].

pail *n.* See sign for BUCKET.

pain[1] *n.* Physical suffering associated with disease or injury: *a pain in my chest.* See also signs for HURT[1,2]. Same sign used for: **ache, injury, sore, tender.**

- [Similar to sign for **hurt**[1] except with a twisting movement] Beginning with both extended index fingers pointing toward each other in front of the chest, right palm facing down and left palm facing up, twist the wrists in opposite directions, ending with the right palm facing up and the left palm facing down.

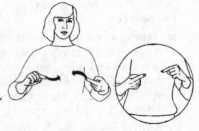

pain[2] *n.* (alternate sign) See also sign for HURT[1,2]. Same sign used for: **ache, injury.**

- [Shows the jabbing feeling of pain] Beginning with both extended index fingers pointing in opposite directions in front of the body, right hand above the left and palms facing in, push the fingers in opposite directions.

painless *adj.* Without pain; causing no pain: *The operation is painless.*

- [**hurt**[1] + **none**[1,2,3]] Beginning with both extended index fingers pointing toward each other in front of the chest, palms facing in, push the fingers toward each other with a double movement. Then move both *O hands*, palms facing forward, from touching in front of the chest outward to in front of each side of the chest.

paint[1] *n.* **1.** Liquid or creamy coloring matter that can be applied to a surface with a brush, as to protect or decorate: *to buy a can of paint.* —*v.* **2.** To apply paint or pigments to: *to paint the bookcase.* **3.** To produce with paint: *to paint a picture.* Same sign used for: **brush, paintbrush.**

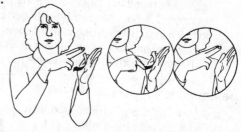

■ [Mime the action of a paintbrush's bristles moving when painting] Brush the extended fingers of the right *U hand* across the left *open hand,* palms facing each other, with a double movement, pulling the back of the fingers of the right *U hand* up the left palm each time.

paint[2] *v.* (alternate sign, used to indicate the application of paint to a large surface) Same sign used for: **brush, paintbrush.**

■ [Mime the action of a paintbrush's bristles moving when painting] Bring the fingertips of the right *open hand* down the length of the left palm from the fingertips to the base with a double movement, pulling the back of the right fingers up the left palm to the fingertips each time.

paint[3] *v.* (alternate sign)

■ [Represents painting with a paintbrush] With the thumb, index finger, and middle finger of the right hand extended, palm facing left, move the right hand with a swinging movement back and forth in front of the chest while holding the right forearm with the left hand.

paintbrush *n.* See signs for PAINT[1,2].

painter *n.* A person who paints: *The painter worked all day.*

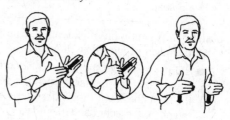

■ [paint[1,2,3] + **person marker**] Bring the fingertips of the right *open hand* down the length of the left open palm from the fingertips to the base. Next pull the back of the right hand up the left palm to the fingertips. Then move both *open hands,* palms facing each other, downward along each side of the body.

pair *n.* See signs for BOTH, COUPLE[1].

pajamas[1] *pl. n.* Loose clothes consisting of a jacket or shirt and trousers, designed to be worn while sleeping: *She'd rather wear pajamas than a nightgown.*

pajamas

■ [sleep[1,2] + clothes] Beginning with the fingers of the right *5 hand* in front of the face, move the hand forward and down while drawing the fingertips and thumb together, forming a *flattened O hand*. Then brush the fingertips of both *5 hands*, palms facing in and fingers pointing toward each other, up and down on each side of the chest with a double movement.

pajamas[2] *pl. n.* (alternate sign)

■ [Abbreviation **p-j**] Form a *P* and then a *J* with the right hand in front of the right side of the chest.

pal[1] *n.* A close friend; chum: *I can always relax with my best pal.*

■ Touch the thumb of the right *L hand*, palm facing left, first to the left side of the chin and then to the right side of the chin.

pal[2] *n.* See signs for FRIEND[1,2].

pale *adj.* Lacking warm or intense skin color: *She looks pale after weeks indoors.* Same sign used for: **Caucasian, wan, white person.**

■ [white + a gesture indicating that a person's face is white] Beginning with the fingertips of the right *5 hand* on the chest, pull the hand forward while closing into a *flattened O hand*. Then move the hand upward toward the face while changing into a *5 hand*.

pallor *n.* A condition of extreme paleness, as from illness: *His deathly pallor and sunken eyes showed how ill he was.*

■ [skin[2] + a gesture showing the blood moving downward from the face] Pinch the skin of the right cheek with the index finger and thumb of the right hand, palm facing down. Then bring the palm side of the right *open hand*, fingers pointing up, downward on the right cheek.

palpitate[1] *v.* To beat rapidly; flutter: *His heart palpitates whenever he looks at her.* Related form: **palpitation** *n.*

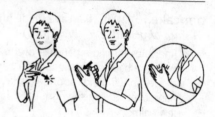

■ [**heart**[1] + **beat**[4]] Tap the bent middle finger of the right *5 hand* against the left side of the chest with a double movement. Then hit the back of the right *S hand*, palm facing in, against the palm of the left *open hand*, palm facing in, with a double movement.

palpitate[2] *v.* See sign for PULSE[1,2]. Related form: **palpitation** *n.*

palsy *n.* Any of several conditions characterized by paralysis or uncontrolled shaking of parts of the body: *We wondered if the man had palsy when we saw his hands shaking.*

■ [Demonstrate how a person with palsy shakes all over] With both *open hands* dangling from the wrist and held in front of each side of the body, shake the head, shoulders and arms loosely while opening the mouth.

pamper *v.* To treat with too much indulgence or care; spoil: *They pamper the dog as if it were a child.*

■ [**mercy**[1,2,3,4] + **pet**[1]] Move the bent middle finger of both *5 hands*, palms facing forward, in alternating forward circles in front of each side of the chest. Then pull the fingertips of the right *open hand*, palm facing down, from the fingers upward on the back of the left *open hand*, palm facing down.

pamphlet *n.* See sign for MAGAZINE.

pan *n.* A shallow, metal dish, often with a long handle, used for cooking: *to fry the meat in a pan.*

■ [**cook**[1] + showing the shape of a frying pan and holding it by the handle] Beginning with the fingers of the right *open hand*, palm facing down, across the upturned palm of the left *open hand*, flip the right hand over, ending with the back of the right hand on the left palm. Next place both *C hands* in front of each side of the body, palms facing each other. Then shake the right *modified X hand*, palm facing left, up and down with a small repeated movement in front of the right side of the body.

pancake *n.* A thin, flat cake made on a griddle: *ordered a stack of pancakes for breakfast.*

■ [Indicates turning a pancake over while cooking] Beginning with the back of the right *open hand* across the palm of the left *open hand,* both palms facing up, flip the right hand over, ending the right palm facing down across the left palm.

pane *n.* A single flat piece of glass set in a frame to form one of several divisions in a window or door: *a broken pane of glass.*

■ [**glass**[1] + **square**[1]] Tap the tip of the bent right index finger against the front teeth with a double movement. Then, beginning with both extended index fingers touching in front of the chest, palms angled down, move the hands apart to in front of each shoulder, then down, and then back together in front of the body.

panel[1] *n.* A board containing instruments, switches, gauges, and other related controls: *a control panel on an airplane.*

■ [Initialized sign showing the shape of a panel] Beginning with the thumb side of both *P hands* together in front of the chest, palms facing down, bring the hands apart to in front of each shoulder, then down, and then back together in front of the body.

panel[2] *n.* A group formed to conduct a public discussion, judge a contest, etc.: *a panel of experts.*

■ [**discuss**[1] + **circle**[3]] Tap the side of the extended right index finger, palm facing in, on the upturned open left palm with a double movement. Then, beginning with the knuckles of both *bent V hands* together in front of the body, palms facing down, bring the hands away from each other in outward arcs while turning the palms out, ending in front of each side of the body.

panic *n., v.* See signs for AFRAID, SHOCK[2].

pant *v.* See sign for BREATH.

panties[1] *pl. n.* Short underpants for a woman or a child: *bought lace panties.*

■ [Mime pulling up panties] Beginning with the fingertips of both *F hands,* palms facing in, touching each hip, move the hands up to touch the fingertips again at the waist.

panties[2] *pl. n.* (alternate sign)

- [Show location of panties] Beginning with the bent middle finger of both *5 hands* touching each hip, palms facing in, move the hands upward to touch the bent middle fingers again at the waist.

pants *pl. n.* A loose-fitting garment for the part of the body from the waist to the ankles; trousers: *tore his pants at the knee.* Same sign used for: **jeans, slacks, trousers.**

- [Shows location of pants on both legs] Beginning with the fingertips of both *open hands* touching each hip, palms facing in, move the hands upward toward the waist with a double movement.

pantyhose *pl. n.* A one-piece garment consisting of hosiery combined with panties: *I tear or snag a pair of pantyhose every day.* Same sign used for: **hose.**

- [Mime pulling up pantyhose] Move the fingertips of both *F hands* upward on the upper part of either leg.

papa *n.* See signs for FATHER[1,2].

papal *adj.* See sign for POPE.

paper *n.* **1.** A substance made from wood pulp and formed into thin sheets, used to write or print on, for wrapping, etc.: *We use plain white paper for the laser printer.* —*adj.* **2.** Made of paper: *a paper container.*

- Brush the heel of the right *open hand,* palm facing down, on the heel of the left *open hand,* palm facing up, in front of the body with a double movement.

paper clip[1] *n.* A link of bent wire used to hold papers together: *to attach the letter to the check with a paper clip.* Same sign used for: **clip.**

- [Represents clipping a paper clip on the edge of paper] With the index finger, middle finger, and thumb of the right hand extended, palm facing down, slide the right hand down over the index-finger side of the left *B hand,* palm facing in and fingers pointing right.

paper clip[2] *n.* (alternate sign) Same sign used for: **clip.**

- [Demonstrates clipping a paper clip on the edge of paper] Beginning with the extended thumb of the right *U hand* against the palm side of the left *B hand,* palm facing down, close the extended right middle and index fingers down against the back of the left hand.

parable *n.* See signs for STORY[1,2].

parachute *n.* **1.** A device, consisting of a silk or nylon expanse attached by strings to a harness, to allow something to be lowered without harm from a great height: *The parachute caught in the tree.* —*v.* **2.** To come down by parachute: *to parachute from the plane.*

- [Represents the shape of a parachute circling around] Beginning with the right *curved 5 hand,* palm facing down, over the extended right index finger, palm facing right and finger pointing up, in front of the right side of the body, move the hands to the left side of the chest and then outward in an arc back to the right side of the chest.

parade *n.* See sign for MARCH.

paradox *n.* See sign for PUZZLED.

paragraph *n.* A portion or subsection of a written document that deals with one aspect of a subject and usually starts on a new line: *a paragraph about whales and another about dolphins.* Same sign used for: **section.**

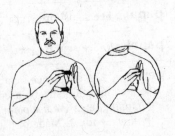

- [Marks off the size of a paragraph] Tap the fingertips of the right *C hand,* palm facing left, against the palm of the left *open hand,* palm facing right and fingers pointing up, with a double movement.

parakeet *n.* A small to medium-sized variety of parrot: *a parakeet in its cage.*

- [Shows the action of a parakeet's beak closing] Pinch the bent index finger and thumb of the right hand together near the right side of the mouth with a double movement, palm facing forward.

parallel[1] *adj.* Extending in the same direction and being always the same distance apart: *parallel lines.*

■ [Shows two things that are parallel to each other] Beginning with the index fingers of both hands in front of each side of the chest, palms facing down and index fingers pointing forward, move the hands forward simultaneously.

parallel² *adj.* (alternate sign) Same sign used for: **path, pathway.**

■ [Initialized sign showing the location of two things that are parallel to each other] With both *P hands* in front of each side of the chest, palms facing down, move both hands forward simultaneously.

paralysis *n.* A condition in which all or part of the body has lost the ability to move or feel sensation: *He had paralysis of the left leg after his stroke.* Related form: **paralyze** *v.*

■ [Mime the rigid body of a person with paralysis] Beginning with both *5 hands* held limply in front of each side of the body, fingers pointing down and palms facing back, jerk the right hand upward in front of the right side of the chest while dropping the left hand downward, bending the hand awkwardly at the wrist near the left hip.

paranoid *adj.* Having exaggerated and unfounded feelings of persecution and distrust of others: *It's difficult to deal with a paranoid person.*

■ [Initialized sign] Beginning with the extended middle finger of the right *P hand* touching the right side of the forehead, palm facing left, move the right hand quickly forward with a double movement while bending the middle finger down.

parasol *n.* A light umbrella used for protection from the sun: *a pink parasol.*

■ [**little¹** + **umbrella**] Move both *curved hands,* palms facing, toward each other with a short double movement in front of the body. Then, beginning with the little-finger side of the right *S hand* on the index-finger side of the left *S hand* in front of the body, palms facing in opposite directions, raise the right hand upward in front of the chest.

parched *adj.* See sign for THIRSTY.

pardon

pardon *v.* See signs for DISMISS[1], EXCUSE.

---

pardon me See sign for EXCUSE ME.

---

pare *v.* See sign for PEEL[1].

---

parentheses *pl. n.* The curved lines used as delimiters to set off something, as a group of numbers or a qualifying word or phrase: *to put parentheses around the explanatory comments.*

- [Draw a pair of parentheses in the air] Beginning with both extended index fingers pointing upward in front of each shoulder, palms facing forward, move both hands in outward and downward arcs while turning the wrists in.

---

parents[1] *pl. n.* One's father and mother: *still lives with his parents.*

- [**mother**[1] + **father**[1]] Touch the thumb of the right *5 hand*, palm facing left, first to the chin, then to the forehead.

---

parents[2] *pl. n.* (alternate sign)

- [Initialized sign formed first near the female area of the head and then near the male area of the head] Touch the middle finger of the right *P hand*, palm facing in, first to the chin, then to the forehead.

---

pariah *n.* An outcast: *He was a pariah, despised by his community.*

- [Similar to sign for **alone**[2] except with an exaggerated movement] Beginning with the extended right index finger pointing up in front of the right side of the body, palm facing in, swing the hand inward toward the chest and back outward with a double movement.

Paris *n.* See sign for TOWER.

---

parish *n.* A section of a diocese served by its own priest or clergy: *A member of the parish greeted visitors to the church.*

- [Initialized sign similar to sign for **church**] Tap the heel of the right *P hand* on the back of the left *S hand*, both palms facing down.

park *v.* To leave a vehicle for a period of time in an appropriate place, as at curbside or in a garage: *to park downtown; to park your car.*

- ■ [The handshape represents a vehicle that is set on the other hand as if to park] Tap the little-finger side of the right *3 hand,* palm facing left and fingers pointing forward, on the palm of the left *open hand,* palm facing up, with a repeated movement.

Parkinson's disease *n.* See sign for TREMOR.

parliamentarian *n.* An expert in parliamentary procedure: *The parliamentarian called for order.*

- ■ [**parliamentary** + **person marker**] Touch the thumb side of the right *P hand* first to the forearm and then near the elbow of the bent left arm held across the chest. Then move both *open hands,* palms facing each other, downward along each side of the body.

parliamentary *adj.* Being in accordance with the rules of a deliberative body: *parliamentary order.* Related form: **Parliament** *n.*

- ■ [Initialized sign] Touch the thumb side of the right *P hand* first to the forearm and then near the elbow of the bent left arm held across the chest.

parliamentary law *n.* The body of rules governing legislative and other deliberative procedure: *to follow strict parliamentary law during the meeting.*

- ■ [**parliamentary** + **law**] Touch the thumb side of the right *P hand* first to the forearm and then near the elbow of the bent left arm held across the chest. Then place the palm side of the right *L hand,* palm facing left, first on the fingers and then on the heel of the left *open hand,* palm facing right and fingers pointing up.

parole *n., v.* See signs for DISMISS[1], EXCUSE.

parrot[1] *n.* A tropical bird of the Southern Hemisphere having a hooked bill and brightly colored feathers: *Some parrots can imitate human speech.*

- ■ [Shows the action of a parrot's beak closing] Pinch the bent index and middle fingers and thumb of the right hand together near the right side of the mouth with a double movement, palm facing forward.

---

parrot[2] *v.* See sign for COPY[1].

---

parsonage *n.* See sign for MONASTERY.

---

part[1] *n.* A separate or distinct portion or fraction of a whole: *This is my part of the pie.* Related form: **partial** *adj.* Same sign used for: **fraction, phase, piece, portion, section, segment.**

- [The hand seems to divide what is in the other hand into parts] Slide the little-finger side of the right *open hand,* palm facing left, across the palm of the left *open hand,* palm facing up, with a curved movement.

---

part[2] *n.* (alternate sign) Related form: **partial** *adj.* Same sign used for: **piece.**

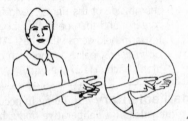

- [Initialized sign] Slide the middle finger of the right *P hand,* palm facing left, across the palm of the left *open hand,* palm facing up, with a curved movement.

---

part[3] *v.* To separate: *We parted the two boys who were fighting. The couple have parted.* Same sign used for: **apart, separate.**

- [The hands separate two things] Beginning with the fingers of both *10 hands* together in front of the chest, palms facing in, bring the hands apart to in front of each side of the chest

---

part[4] *n., adj.* See sign for SOME.

---

part from *v. phrase.* See sign for DISCONNECT.

---

partial to *adj.* Favoring or especially fond of: *I'm partial to mint chocolate-chip ice cream.* Same sign used for: **favorite.**

- [Pointing out a favorite] Tap the fingertips of the right *B hand,* palm facing left, with a double movement against the index finger of the left *B hand* held up in front of the chest, palm facing right.

---

partial plate *n.* See signs for FALSE TEETH[2].

---

participate *v.* To take part: *to participate in the discussion.* Related form: **participation** *n.*

■ [Initialized sign similar to sign for **join**[1]] Insert the middle finger of the right *P hand*, palm facing down, into the thumb-side opening of the left *O hand* held in front of the body, palm facing right.

particular *adj.* See sign for POINT[3].

parting *n.* An act or instance of going away: *It was a sad parting.* Same sign used for: **depart, departure.**

■ [Represents two people moving apart when parting] Beginning with both extended index fingers pointing up in front of the chest, palms facing forward, bring the hands apart to in front of each shoulder.

partner *n.* A person who shares with another in some common activity: *My partner and I run the business.*

■ [**share + person marker**] Move the little-finger side of the right *open hand*, palm facing left, back and forth with a double movement at the base of the index finger of the left *open hand*, palm facing in. Then move both *open hands*, palms facing each other, downward along each side of the body.

partners *pl. n.* See sign for COUPLE[1].

party *n.* A social gathering: *to have a party to celebrate her promotion.*

■ [Initialized sign] Beginning with both *P hands* in front of the right side of the body, palms facing down, swing the hands from side to side in front of the body with a large double arc.

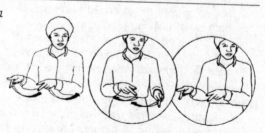

partying *n.* The act of going to parties: *We went partying all night.* Same sign used for: **good time, party.**

■ Beginning with both *5 hands* near each side of the head, palms facing each other and fingers pointing up, flip the hands forward with a double movement, turning the palms forward each time.

pass[1] *v.* To move beyond: *to pass the truck on the highway.* Same sign used for: **by, ratification, ratify.**

- [One hand moves past the other hand] Beginning with both *A hands* in front of the body, palms facing in opposite directions and left hand somewhat forward of the right hand, move the right hand forward, striking the knuckles of the left hand as it passes.

pass[2] *v.* To transfer (a ball) from one player to another: *The coach wants the quarterback to pass the football.*

- [Mime throwing a football] Move the right *C hand,* palm facing left, from above the right shoulder forward with a double movement

pass around *v. phrase.* To distribute: *to pass the bread around.* Same sign used for: **deal, pass out.**

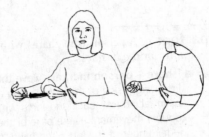

- [Mime passing something around] Beginning with the fingers of both *flattened O hands* together in front of the body, palms facing up, move the right hand forward and then twist it around to the right, ending with the palm facing left.

pass by *v. phrase.* To move past someone who is going in the opposite direction: *passed by an old friend while walking.*

- [Indicates two persons passing each other while moving in opposite directions] Beginning with the extended forefingers of both hands pointing upward in front of each side of the body, right palm facing forward, left palm facing back, and right hand closer to the body than left hand, move the right hand forward while moving the left hand back toward the chest.

pass down *v. phrase.* **1.** To give as a legacy to a descendant or other younger person after use: *This ring was passed down to me by my mother.* **2.** To pass along (a cultural or historical heritage) to subsequent generations: *The unique way we celebrate birthdays has been passed down in my family for generations.* Same sign used for: **hand down, hand-me-down, inherit.**

- [The hands bring something from the past down into the future] Beginning with both *flattened O hands* near the right shoulder, palms facing in, bring them downward and forward to the left in a series of arcs.

pass gas *v. phrase.* See sign for FLATULENCE.

pass out[1] *v. phrase.* To distribute among those present: *to pass out homework assignments to the class.* Same sign used for: **deal, distribute.**

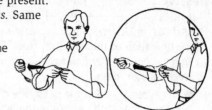

- [Mime passing out papers] Beginning with the thumbs of both *modified X hands* together in front of the chest, palms facing in, move the right hand forward with a repeated movement in different directions.

pass out[2] *v. phrase.* (alternate sign)

- [Shows passing cards to players] Beginning with the back of the right *flattened O hand* in the palm of the left *open hand,* both palms facing up, move the right hand forward and back with a double movement

pass out[3] *v. phrase.* To lose consciousness: *to pass out from the heat.*

- [Abbreviation **p-o**] Place the thumb side of the right *P hand,* and then the right *O hand,* against the forehead, palm facing left.

pass out[4] *v. phrase.* See signs for GIVE[4], PASS AROUND.

passenger *n.* A traveler, who is not the operator, in a vehicle: *room enough to take another passenger in the car.* Same sign used for: **rider.**

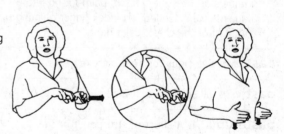

- [**ride in a car** + **person marker**] With the bent fingers of the right *U hand,* palm facing down, hooked over the thumb of the left *C hand,* palm facing right, move the hands forward. Then move both *open hands* down each side of the body, palms facing each other.

passion *n.* See sign for WANT.

passionate *adj.* Having or expressing strong, intense feelings, as fondness or desire: *She had passionate feelings for him.* Related form: **passion** *n.*

- [Shows the location of deep feelings] Move the fingertips of the right *C hand* down the center of the chest with a deliberate double movement.

passive *adj.* See sign for QUIET[1].

Passover[1] *n.* A Jewish holiday commemorating the liberation of the Israelites from slavery in Egypt: *The Passover holiday is celebrated for seven or eight days.*

- ■ [Initialized sign] Tap the palm side of the right *P hand* against the elbow of the left bent arm with a double movement.

Passover[2] *n.* (alternate sign)

- ■ [Initialized sign indicating passing over something] Move the little-finger side of the right *P hand* in an arc over the back of the left *open hand,* palm facing down, held bent across the body.

Passover[3] *n.* See sign for CRACKER.

password *n.* A secret series of characters that enables a user to access a file, computer, or program, and that is intended to prevent access by unauthorized users: *Type in a six-letter password.* Same sign used for: **access code, secretively.**

- ■ [**secret + word**] With a repeated movement, tap the thumb side of the right *A hand,* palm facing left, against the mouth. Then touch the extended fingers of the right *G hand,* palm facing left, against the extended left index finger pointing up in front of the chest, palm right.

past[1] *adv.* See signs for AGO[1], BEFORE[1], PASS[1].

past[2] *adj., n.* See sign for WAS[1].

paste-up *n.* **1.** A sheet of stiff paper on which text and artwork have been pasted to be photographed for making printing plates: *The art department is preparing paste-ups for the book. —v. phrase.* **2. paste up** *v.* To prepare one or more paste-ups for printing: *to paste up the art work.*

- ■ [Represents pasting things on paper] Beginning with the thumbs of both *10 hands* touching in front of the chest, palms facing down, bring the hands downward and apart with a double movement by twisting the wrists.

pasteurize *v.* To heat (milk) for a long enough time to kill germs without altering flavor: *Milk sold commercially is usually pasteurized.* Related form: **pasteurized** *adj.*

■ [**milk**[1] + **boil**] Beginning with the right *C hand,* palm facing left, in front of the right side of the body, squeeze the fingers together with a double movement, forming an *S hand* each time. Then, beginning with both *5 hands* in front of the chest, right hand higher than the left hand, palms facing in, and fingers pointing upward, move the hands upward and forward in alternating repeated circles while wiggling the fingers.

pastor *n.* See signs for PREACHER, PRIEST[1].

pat *v.* **1.** To tap gently with the hand: *to pat the child on the head.* —*n.* **2.** A light tap with the hand: *Give the dog a quick pat.*

■ [Mime patting someone on the shoulder] Tap the palm of the right *open hand* on the left shoulder with a double movement. The hand should pat wherever the patting occurs, as on the head or back.

patch[1] *n.* A piece of material used either to mend a hole or as an ornament: *He wore a patch on his uniform to show his rank.*

■ [Shows the location of a patch on one's sleeve] Move the little-finger side of the right *C hand,* palm facing up, against the left upper arm with a double movement.

patch[2] *n.* See sign for EYEPATCH.

path *n.* See signs for CHANNEL[2], PARALLEL[2], ROAD[1]. Related form: **pathway** *n.*

pathetic[1] *adj.* Causing or evoking pity; pitiful: *a pathetic expression on the hungry child's face.*

■ [**sad** + **mercy**[1,2,3,4]] Move both *5 hands* from in front of each side of the face, palms facing in and fingers pointing up, downward a short distance. Then, beginning with the bent middle finger of the right *5 hand* pointing forward in front of the right side of the chest, move the hand forward in a repeated circle.

pathetic[2] *adj.* See signs for MERCY[1,2,3,4].

patient

patient¹ *adj.* **1.** Bearing annoyance, suffering, etc., calmly or without complaint: *The children were remarkably patient during the long trip.* **2.** Persevering and diligent: *The teacher is patient with the slow learners in class.* Related form: **patience** *n.* Same sign used for: **bear, endure, put up with, tolerate, tolerant.**

- ■ [The thumb seems to seal the lips as a person tolerates something] Move the right *A hand,* palm facing left, downward in front of the chin.

patient² *n.* A person under medical care or treatment: *The little girl is a good patient.*

- ■ [Initialized sign similar to sign for **hospital**¹] Move the extended middle finger of the right *P hand,* palm facing in, first down and then forward on the left upper arm.

patrol *v.* See signs for CARE¹, WATCH⁵.

pattern¹ *n.* A design or guide for something to be made: *a pattern for sewing a skirt.*

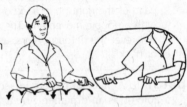

- ■ [**same**¹-**same**¹-**same**¹ indicating a repetition as in a pattern] Beginning with both *Y hands* in front of the left side of the body, palms facing down, move the hands in simultaneous repeated arcs to in front of the right side of the body.

pattern² *n.* (alternate sign)

- ■ [Initialized sign + **establish**] Sweep the middle finger of the right *P hand,* palm facing down, back toward the chest across the back of the left *S hand* held in front of the body, palm facing down. Then change the right hand into a *10 hand* and move the little-finger side downward to land on the back of the left *S hand.*

pauper *n.* See sign for POOR¹.

pause *v.* See signs for HOLD²,³.

pave *v.* To cover (a road or walk), as with concrete, so as to make smooth: *paved the road with asphalt.*

- ■ [Demonstrates the action of moving dirt in order to pave] Slide the little-finger side of the right *bent hand,* palm facing in, from the wrist to off the fingertips of the left *open hand,* palm facing up and fingers pointing forward.

pawn *v.* See sign for SELL.

pay[1] *v.* **1.** To give money in return for goods or services: *to pay $5.00; to pay the cashier.* —*n.* **2.** Money received for goods or services: *The workers received their pay on Fridays.* Same sign used for: **compensate, compensation.**

■ [Represents directing money from the hand to pay another person] Beginning with the extended right index finger touching the palm of the left *open hand,* palms facing each other, move the right finger forward and off the left fingertips.

pay[2] *v., n.* (alternate sign) Same sign used for: **compensate, compensation.**

■ [Initialized sign] Beginning with the middle finger of the right *P hand* touching the palm of the left *open hand,* palms facing each other, move the right finger forward and off the left fingertips.

pay[3] *v., n.* (alternate sign) Same sign used for: **compensate, compensation.**

■ [Represents money slipping through one's fingers] Beginning with the right *flattened O hand* in front of the right side of the body, palm facing up, move the hand forward while quickly sliding the thumb off each finger.

pay[4] *v.* (alternate sign) Same sign used for: **compensate, compensation.**

■ [Represents taking money from the pocket and putting it down to pay for something] Beginning with the right *F hand* near the right side of the body, palm facing down, move the hand upward and forward while opening into a *5 hand.*

payable *adj.* See sign for AFFORD[1].

pay attention *v. phrase.* See sign for ATTENTION.

pay for[1] *v. phrase.* To offer all the money required in exchange for: *Be sure you have enough money to pay for the groceries.* Same sign used for: **pay in full, pay off.**

■ [Represents directing money from the hand to pay another person + **clean**] Touch the bent middle finger of the right *5 hand* to the palm of the left *open hand,* palms facing each other and fingers pointing forward. Then wipe the right *open hand* across the left *open hand* from the heel to off the fingertips with a deliberate movement.

pay for

pay for[2] *v. phrase.* (alternate sign) Same sign used for: **pay in full, pay off.**

- [Initialized sign + **clean**] Beginning with the middle finger of the right *P hand* touching the upturned palm of the left *open hand,* move the right finger forward off the left fingertips. Then wipe the right *open hand* across the left *open hand* from the heel to off the fingertips with a deliberate movement.

pay in full See signs for PAY FOR[1,2].

payment[1] *n.* Same sign as for PAY[1] but formed with a double movement.

payment[2] *n.* Same sign as for PAY[2] but formed with a double movement.

payment[3] *n.* See sign for INSTALLMENT.

pay off *v. phrase.* See signs for PAY FOR[1,2].

PDA (personal digital assistant) *n.* See sign for TEXT MESSAGE.

peace *n.* **1.** Freedom from war: *peace among nations.* **2.** A state of harmony in personal relations or among groups: *hoping for peace among the factions on campus.* **3.** Tranquility; calm: *All I want is a little peace and quiet.* Related form: **peaceful** *adj.*

- [**become** + **settle**] Beginning with the palms of both *open hands* together in front of the chest, right palm facing forward and left palm facing in, twist the wrist to reverse positions. Then move the hands downward, ending with both *open hands* in front of each side of the waist, palms facing down and fingers pointing forward.

peaceful *adj.* See signs for QUIET[1,2].

peach[1] *n.* **1.** A sweet, juicy fruit with yellow flesh and soft, fuzzy skin: *He won't eat a peach without peeling it.* —*adj.* **2.** a yellowish pink color: *Use peach paint on the wall.*

- [The fingers seem to feel peach fuzz] Beginning with the fingertips of the right *curved 5 hand* on the right cheek, palm facing left, bring the fingers down with a double movement, forming a *flattened O hand* near the right side of the chin.

peach[2] *n.* (alternate sign)

- With the fingertips of both *flattened O hands* touching in front of the chest, twist the wrists in opposite directions with a double movement, touching the fingertips each time.

peacock *n.* A bird with beautiful, colorful, iridescent tail feathers that can be spread wide like a fan: *The spots on the peacock's tail look like eyes.*

- [**bird** + a gesture indicating a peacock's tail feathers] Close the index finger and thumb of the right *G hand,* palm facing forward, with a repeated movement in front of the mouth. Then, beginning with the right *O hand,* palm facing in, near the crook of the bent left arm held across the chest, raise the right hand upward in an arc while opening into a *4 hand* as it passes in front of the face.

peak[1] *n.* The pointed top of a mountain or ridge: *The mountain climbers reached the peak.*

- [The shape of a peak] Move both extended index fingers from in front of each shoulder upward toward each other until they meet in front of the head.

peak[2] *adj.* See sign for TOP[1].

peanut[1] *n.* A pod with oily, edible seeds: *Don't leave the shells around when you eat peanuts.* Same sign used for: **nut.**

- [Represents peanut butter sticking to the back of one's teeth] Flick the extended right thumb, palm facing left, forward off the edge of the top front teeth with an upward double movement.

peanut[2] *n.* (alternate sign)

- Twist the palm side of the right *A hand,* palm facing down, with a double movement on the tip of the extended left index finger pointing up in front of the body, palm facing in.

peanut butter *n.* An edible paste, used as a spread, made of browned roasted peanuts: *to eat a peanut butter and jelly sandwich.*

- [**peanut**[1] + **butter**] Flick the extended right thumb, palm facing left, forward off the edge of the top front teeth with an upward double movement. Then wipe the extended middle and index fingers of the right hand, palm facing left, on the palm of the left *open hand,* palm facing right, toward the heel with a double movement, drawing the fingers back into the right palm each time.

pear *n.* A fleshy, juicy fruit, usually with a yellow to green skin: *I ate a pear that wasn't ripe.*

■ [Shows the shape of a pear] Beginning with the fingertips of the right *curved 5 hand* cupped around the fingertips of the left *flattened O hand,* both palms facing in, bring the right hand outward to the right while closing the fingers to the thumb, forming a *flattened O hand.*

pearl *n.* A smooth, spherical, usually white bead found inside an oyster, used as a gem: *to wear pearls with the black dress.*

■ [**white** + **beads**] Beginning with the fingers of the right *5 hand* touching the chest, palm facing in, bring the hand forward while closing into a *flattened O hand.* Then, beginning with the thumb side of the right *F hand* near the left side of the neck, palm facing left, touch the hand in several positions across the chest as the hand moves to the right side of the neck.

peas *pl. n.* The round edible seeds from the pod of a plant of the legume family: *I always put peas in the tuna casserole.*

■ [The finger points to peas in a pod] Touch the fingertips of the right *modified X hand,* palm facing down, on the extended left index finger, palm facing in and finger pointing right, moving from the base to the tip and touching down in several places.

pecan[1] *n.* An edible oval nut with a smooth shell: *The pie was made with pecans and raisins.*

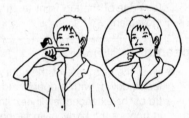

■ Beginning with the extended right index finger in front of the mouth, palm facing down, twist the hand forward with a double movement, turning the palm in.

pecan[2] *n.* (alternate sign)

■ Beginning with the extended thumb of the right *10 hand* behind the front teeth, palm facing left, bring the hand forward in a small arc in front of the mouth. Then move the extended thumb of the right *10 hand* upward into the little finger opening of the left *S hand* held in front of the chest, palms facing in opposite directions.

peck *v.* See sign for PICK ON.

peculiar *adj.* See sign for STRANGE.

pedal[1] *n.* A lever worked by the foot, used to activate or control a mechanism: *to step on the soft pedal of the piano.* Same sign used for: **brake.**

- [Demonstrates the movement of a pedal] Beginning with the right *B hand* in front of the right shoulder, palm facing forward and fingers pointing up, flip the hand downward with a double movement.

pedal[2] *v., n.* See sign for BICYCLE.

peddle *v.* See sign for SELL.

pedometer *n.* An instrument used to measure the distance walked: *I went three miles as measured on the pedometer.*

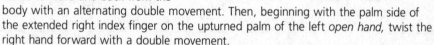

- [**walk**[1,2] + showing the movement of a dial on a meter] Beginning with both *3 hands* in front of each side of the body, palms facing down and left hand somewhat forward of the right hand, move the hands forward and back from the body with an alternating double movement. Then, beginning with the palm side of the extended right index finger on the upturned palm of the left *open hand,* twist the right hand forward with a double movement.

pee *n.* Slang (*sometimes vulgar*). See sign for PENIS[1].

peek[1] *v.* **1.** To look quickly: *to peek at the headlines.* —*n.* **2.** A quick look: *I took a peek at the headlines.*

- [Mime peeking through a small hole] Place the thumb side of the right *F hand,* palm facing left, around the right eye.

peek[2] *v., n.* (alternate sign)

- [Mime peeking around a partition] Beginning with the index-finger side of the right *B hand* in front of the nose, palm facing left, move the head to the right to look around the hand.

peek[3] *v.* See sign for NOSY[2].

peel[1] *v.* To strip the skin off (a fruit or vegetable): *to peel the potatoes before boiling them.* Same sign used for: **pare.**

peel

- [Mime peeling with a small knife]
Beginning with the knuckles of the right
10 hand against the extended left index
finger, both palms facing down, move
the right thumb open and closed with a
double movement.

peel[2] *v.* To strip away from something: *to peel the*
backing off the address label.

- [Demonstrates the action of peeling something
with the fingers] Beginning with the fingertips
of the right *9 hand* touching the back of the left
S hand, both palms facing down, move the
right hand upward and forward while twisting
the palm back.

peep *v.* To look out of a small opening: *to peep through*
the crack in the fence. Related form: **peeping** *n.*

- [Mime looking through a small hole] Beginning with
the fingertips of the right *flattened O hand* on the
back of the fingers of the left *flattened O hand*, both
palms facing down, move the right hand upward in
front of the face.

pee wee *n.* See sign for SMALL[1].

pelican *n.* A large bird with a huge expandable throat pouch: *The pelican caught the fish.*

- [**bird** + the shape of a pelican's throat] Close the
index finger and thumb of the right *G hand*, palm
facing forward, with a repeated movement in front
of the mouth. Then, beginning with the index-
finger side of the right *B hand* under the chin,
palm facing in and fingers pointing left, move the
hand downward and outward in a large arc while
turning the palm down in front of the chest.

pen *n.* See signs for WRITE[1,2].

penalize *v.* See sign for PUNISH.

penalty *n.* See sign for PUNISH.

pencil[1] *n.* A pointed tool with a graphite core to write or draw with:
to draw a picture with a pencil.

- [Indicates wetting the tip of a pencil and then writing with it] Touch
the fingertips of the right *modified X hand*, palm facing in, near the
mouth. Then move the right hand smoothly down and across
the upturned left *open hand* from the heel to off the fingertips.

pencil[2] *n.* See signs for WRITE[1,2].

pencil sharpener *n.* A device used to put a usable point on pencils: *sharpened all my pencils in the new pencil sharpener.*

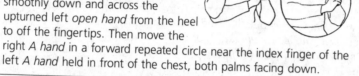

- ■ [**pencil** + mime sharpening a pencil] Touch the fingertips of the right *modified X hand*, palm facing in, near the mouth. Next move the right hand smoothly down and across the upturned left *open hand* from the heel to off the fingertips. Then move the right *A hand* in a forward repeated circle near the index finger of the left *A hand* held in front of the chest, both palms facing down.

pendant *n.* See sign for LOCKET[2].

pendulum *n.* A weight that is hung so that it swings freely by means of gravity and its own momentum: *The old clock was run by a pendulum that kept going for years.*

- ■ [Demonstrates the action of a pendulum swinging] With the left hand in the crook of the bent right arm, swing the right *5 hand*, palm facing in and fingers pointing down, in a large double arc in front of the body.

penetrate[1] *v.* To get into or through: *a light that will penetrate the darkness.* Same sign used for: **pierce, pierced.**

- ■ [Demonstrates something penetrating something else] Insert the extended right index finger, palm facing left and finger pointing forward, with a deliberate movement between the middle and ring fingers of the left *open hand* held in front of the chest, palm facing in and fingers angled right.

penetrate[2] *v.* (alternate sign) Same sign used for: **soak through.**

- ■ [Demonstrates something penetrating something else] Move the fingers of the right *5 hand*, palm facing in and fingers pointing down, downward to mesh with the fingers of the left *5 hand* held in front of the chest, palm facing up and fingers pointing right.

penetrate[3] *v.* To see into; come to understand: *to penetrate the mystery.*

- ■ [**think**[1] + a directional sign showing penetrating the mind] Move the extended right index finger from touching the right side of the forehead, palm facing down, forward in an arc and then back between the index and middle fingers of the left *5 hand* held in front of the chest, palm facing forward and fingers pointing up.

penguin *n.* A sea bird with wings reduced to flippers that lives in cold regions: *Its webbed feet help a penguin to swim.*

- [Mime the movements of a penguin when walking] With both *open hands* near each hip, palms facing down, and both arms held straight and tight against the sides of the body, shift the body weight from one foot to the other, causing the whole stiff body to shift from side to side with a double movement.

penis[1] *n.* The male organ of copulation and, in mammals, urinary excretion: *Urine leaves the man's body through the penis.* Same sign used for: **pee** (*slang, sometimes vulgar*), **phallus, urine.**

- [Initialized sign] Tap the middle finger of the right *P hand*, palm facing in, against the nose with a double movement.

penis[2] *n.* (alternate sign, considered vulgar) Same sign used for: **phallus, prick** (*vulgar slang*).

- [Indicates the movement of the penis] While holding the extended left index finger across the right wrist, move the extended right index finger, palm facing left and finger pointing forward, up and down with a double movement in front of the body.

penitent *adj.* See sign for SORRY. Related form: **penitence** *n.*

penitentiary *n.* See signs for JAIL[1,2].

penknife *n.* A small pocketknife: *I used a penknife to peel the orange.*

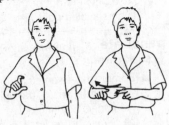

- [**small**[1] + **knife**] Hold the right *modified C hand* in front of the right side of the chest, palm facing forward. Then slide the bottom side of the extended right index finger, palm facing in, with a double movement at an angle across the length of the extended left index finger, palm facing in, turning the right palm down each time as it moves off the end of the left fingertip.

pennant *n.* A long, narrow, tapering flag: *hung the team pennant on the wall of their room in the dorm.*

- [The shape of a pennant] Beginning with the extended thumb and index finger of the right *L hand*, palm facing forward, touching the thumb and extended index finger of the left hand, palm facing forward, move the right hand to the right while closing the index finger to the thumb in front of the right side of the body.

penniless[1] *adj.* Very poor; without any money at all: *a penniless vagrant.*

■ [**none**[6] + **money**] Move the thumb side of the right *O hand,* palm facing left, back against the palm of the left *open hand* held in front of the chest, palm facing forward and fingers pointing up. Then tap the back of the right *flattened O hand,* palm facing up, with a double movement against the palm of the upturned left *open hand.*

penniless[2] *adj.* (alternate sign)

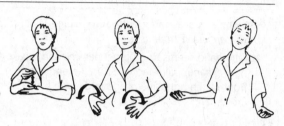

■ [**money** + **none**[4]] Tap the back of the right *flattened O hand,* palm facing up, with a double movement against the palm of the upturned left *open hand.* Then, beginning with both *5 hands* in front of each side of the body, palms facing in and fingers hanging down, bring the hands upward and forward while turning the palms up in front of each side of the body.

penniless[3] *adj.* (alternate sign) Same sign used for: **bankrupt, broke** (*informal*).

■ [Gesture indicates a broken neck to signify being broke] Bring the little-finger side of the right *bent hand,* palm facing down and fingers pointing back, against the right side of the neck with a deliberate movement while bending the head down to the left.

penny *n.* See sign for CENT.

pension *n.* A regular payment, other than wages, made to a person, especially for past services: *to receive a pension after retirement.* Same sign used for: **allowance, royalty, subscribe, welfare.**

■ With the right *curved hand* in front of the right shoulder, palm facing back, bring the hand downward and inward toward the right side of the chest with a double movement, closing the fingers to form an *A hand* each time.

pentagon *n.* **1.** A figure having five sides and five angles: *a box shaped like a pentagon.* **2. the Pentagon** A building in Arlington, Virginia, shaped like a pentagon and housing the offices of the U.S. Department of Defense: *works at the Pentagon on top-secret projects.*

■ [**five** + the shape of a pentagon] Hold the right *5 hand* in front of the right shoulder, palm facing in and fingers pointing up. Then, beginning with both extended index fingers touching in front of the chest, palms angled forward, move the hands outward to each side, then downward at an angle and then back together in front of the body, ending with the palms facing down.

people *n.* **1.** Men, women, and children collectively: *Only ten people visited the museum today.* **2.** Persons in general: *People don't want their intelligence insulted by their political leaders.* Same sign used for: **folk, public.**

- [Initialized sign] Move both *P hands,* palms facing down, in alternating forward circles in front of each side of the body.

pep *n.* See sign for INSPIRE.

pepper[1] *n.* A seasoning with a hot, spicy taste: *to put fresh pepper on the pasta.*

- [The hand seems to drop pepper on food] Shake the right *F hand,* palm facing down, up and down in front of the right side of the body with a repeated movement.

pepper[2] *n.* (alternate sign)

- [Initialized sign] Shake the right *P hand,* palm facing down, up and down in front of the right side of the body with a repeated movement.

Pepsi *n. Trademark.* See sign for ITALY.

per *prep.* See sign for EACH.

per annum See sign for ANNUAL.

percent *n.* A proportion expressed in parts or amounts of one hundred: *Ten percent of 1,000 is 100. The agent will want ten percent of your royalties.* Related form: **percentage** *n.*

- [Draw the shape of a percent sign in the air] Move the right *O hand* from near the right side of the face, palm facing forward, a short distance to the right, then down at an angle to in front of the right side of the chest.

perceive *v.* See signs for PREDICT[1,2], UNDERSTAND. Related form: **perception** *n.*

percolate *v.* **1.** (of a liquid) To drain through small holes or a porous substance: *to watch the chemical solution percolate through the filter.* **2.** To brew (coffee) in a percolator, in which boiling water is continuously forced up through a pipe and then filtered down through ground coffee: *They prefer to percolate the coffee rather than making it in a drip pot.* Related form: **percolator** *n.*

■ [**water** + shows the action of a percolator] Tap the index-finger side of the right *W hand*, palm facing left, against the chin with a double movement. Then, beginning with the right *flattened O hand* under the left *open hand* held across the chest, palm facing down and fingers pointing right, move the right hand upward while opening the fingers with a double movement.

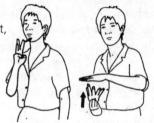

percussion instrument *n.* A musical instrument, as in a band or orchestra, played by striking: *The drum and the piano are percussion instruments.*

■ [Shows the action of a damper on a drum + **beat**[4]] Bring the palm of the right *curved 5 hand* downward with a double movement against the thumb side of the left *S hand* held in front of the chest. Then move the knuckles of the right *S hand*, palm facing in, with a double movement against the palm of the left *open hand* held in front of the chest, palm facing in and fingers pointing right.

perennial *adj.* **1.** Lasting for a long time: *a perennial leading lady.* **2.** (of plants) Having a life cycle of two or more years: *The climbing rose is a perennial flower.*

■ [**continue**[1] + **annual**] Beginning with the thumb of the right *10 hand* on the thumbnail of the left *10 hand*, both palms facing down in front of the chest, move the hands downward and forward in an arc. Then, beginning with the little-finger side of the right *S hand* on the index-finger side of the left *S hand*, palms facing in opposite directions, move the right hand upward and forward in an arc while extending the right index finger.

perfect *adj.* **1.** Without defect: *a beautiful, perfect face.* **2.** Conforming to or representing an ideal: *The children behaved like perfect ladies and gentlemen.* **3.** Correct and complete in every detail: *a perfect score.* Related form: **perfection** *n.* Same sign used for: **accurate, ideal.**

■ [Initialized sign showing things matching perfectly] Move the right *P hand*, palm facing left, in a small circle above the left *P hand*, palm facing up. Then move the right hand downward to touch both middle fingers together in front of the chest.

perform *v.* See signs for ACT[2], DO. Related form: **performance** *n.*

performer *n.* See signs for ACTOR[1,2].

perfume[1] *n.* A liquid or other substance having a fragrant, attractive smell: *puts on perfume before going out.*

- [Represents applying perfume to the neck] Touch the thumb of the right *Y hand,* palm facing left, to the throat. Then twist the hand slightly to the left and touch the thumb to the throat again.

perfume[2] *n.* (alternate sign)

- [Represents applying perfume to the neck] Touch the thumb of the right *A hand,* palm facing left, to the throat. Then twist the hand slightly to the left and touch the thumb to the throat again.

perfume[3] *n.* (alternate sign)

- [Represents applying perfume to the neck] Touch the bent middle finger of the right *5 hand,* palm facing in, to the throat. Then twist the hand slightly to the left and touch the bent middle finger to the throat again.

perhaps *adv.* See sign for MAYBE.

peril[1] *n.* Danger; grave risk: *You are in peril in this dark alley.*

- [Similar to sign for **awful** except sign moves upward] Beginning with both *8 hands* in front of each shoulder, palms facing each other, move the hands suddenly upward while flicking the fingers up to form *5 hands,* palms facing forward.

peril[2] *n.* See signs for DANGER, RISK[1,2].

period[1] *n.* A dot used to mark the end of a sentence or an abbreviation: *to put a period at the end of the sentence.* Same sign used for: **decimal point, dot, point.**

- [Draw a period in the air] With the right index finger and thumb pinched together, palm facing forward, in front of the right side of the chest, push the right hand forward a short distance.

period[2] *n.* A portion of time specified for some purpose: *to play the piano for a short period every afternoon.*

- [Initialized sign similar to sign for **time**[1]] Move the right *P hand,* palm facing left, in a small circle near the palm of the left *open hand,* palm angled forward, ending with the right palm against the left palm.

period[3] *n.* See signs for MENSTRUATION, TIME[1].

periodically *adv.* See signs for OCCASIONAL[1,2], SOMETIMES.

periodontist *n.* A dentist whose specialty is the
treatment of diseases and disorders of the
periodontium—that is, the gum and tissue
surrounding and supporting the teeth: *The
periodontist performed surgery on the gums.*

- ■ [**gums** + person marker] Touch the upper gums
  with the extended right index finger. Then move
  both *open hands,* palms facing each other,
  downward along the sides of the body.

peripheral[1] or **peripheral device** *n.* Any of the external auxiliary hardware units
of a computer: *The keyboard, monitor, and printer
are all peripherals.* Same sign used for: **periphery.**

- ■ [Initialized sign moving around something as if
  around the peripheral] Move the extended index
  finger of the right *P hand,* palm facing down, in a
  circle around the fingertips of the left *B hand,* palm
  facing in and fingers pointing up.

peripheral[2] or **peripheral device** *n.* (alternate sign)

- ■ [**belong**[1]-**belong**[1] + **equipment**[1,2]] Beginning with both
  curved 5 hands in front of the left side of the body, palms
  facing each other, bring the hands together with
  the thumb and index fingertips of each hand
  touching and intersecting with each other. Repeat
  in front of the right side of the body. Then move
  the right *E hand,* palm facing up, from in front of
  the middle of the body to the right in a double arc.

periscope *n.* An optical instrument that allows the crew of an underwater vessel to
view what is above the surface: *The submarine's periscope came into view.*

- ■ [**up** + the shape of a periscope moving around as if in surveillance] Move the
  extended right index finger upward in front of
  the right side of the chest, palm facing left,
  bending the index finger to form an *X hand.*
  Next move the thumb side of the right *X hand*
  to the left along the length of the bent left arm
  held across the chest. Then turn the right hand
  in the opposite direction near the left elbow
  and slide the little-finger side of the right *X
  hand* back toward the left fingers.

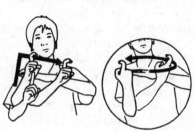

perish *v.* See signs for DIE[1], DISSOLVE.

perjury *n.* See signs for LIE[1,2].

permanent *adj.* See sign for CONTINUE[1].

permanent wave[1] *n.* A wave or curl set into the hair by a special chemical process so that it will last for several months: *It's obviously time for me to get another permanent wave.* Alternate form: **permanent.**

- [Represents the action of rollers crimping the hair] Beginning with both *C hands* near each side of the head, palms facing forward, bring the hands back toward the sides of the head while closing into *S hands*. Then move the hands downward and repeat the movement.

permanent wave[2] *n.* (alternate sign) Alternate form: **permanent.**

- [**hair** + abbreviation **p-w**] Hold a strand of hair with the fingers of the right *F hand*, palm facing left. Then form a *P* and a *W* with the right hand near the right side of the head.

permeate *v.* To soak through or into every part of: *The water permeated my coat.* Same sign used for: **soak through.**

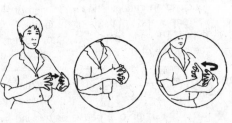

- [Demonstrates something penetrating something else] Beginning with both *5 hands* in front of each side of the chest, palms facing in and fingers pointing toward each other, bring the right hand forward, interlocking the left fingers. Then bring the right fingers back toward the chest, ending with the right palm facing right.

permit[1] *v.* To allow: *With a new baby, they don't want to permit smoking in the house.* Related form: **permission** *n.* Same sign used for: **privilege.**

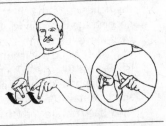

- [Initialized sign similar to sign for **try**[1]] Beginning with both *P hands* in front of the body, palms facing down, swing the wrists to move both hands forward and upward in small arcs.

permit[2] *v.* See sign for LET[1].

permit[3] *n.* See sign for LICENSE.

perpendicular *adj.* Straight up and down; vertical: *The shack doesn't have a single perpendicular wall.*

- [Demonstrates the angle created when one thing is perpendicular to another thing] Tap the extended right index finger, palm facing in and finger pointing down, with a double movement on the extended left index finger held across the chest, palm facing in and finger pointing right.

perpetual *adj.* Lasting forever: *a perpetual care cemetery.*

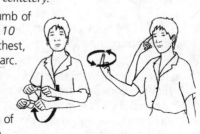

- [**continue**[1] + **forever**[2]] Beginning with the thumb of the right *10 hand* on the thumbnail of the left *10 hand,* both palms facing down in front of the chest, move the hands downward and forward in an arc. Then, beginning with the extended right index finger touching the right side of the forehead, palm angled down, move the hand downward and form a large circle in front of the right side of the body, palm facing in and finger pointing up.

perplexed *adj.* See sign for PUZZLED.

persecute *v.* See sign for TORTURE. Related form: **persecution** *n.*

persevere[1] *v.* To continue or persist in trying to do something in spite of obstacles: *We hope he will persevere in his studies.* Related form: **perseverance** *n.* Same sign used for: **persistence, persistent.**

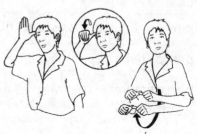

- [**stubborn** + **continue**[1]] With the extended thumb of the right *open hand* touching the right side of the forehead, palm facing forward, bend the fingers forward and downward with a double movement. Then, beginning with the thumb of the right *10 hand* on the thumbnail of the left *10 hand,* both palms facing down in front of the chest, move the hands downward and forward in an arc.

persevere[2] *v.* See signs for OBSESSION[1,2].

persist *v.* See sign for STUBBORN.

persistent *adj.* See signs for CONSTANT[3], OBSESSION[1,2], PERSEVERE[1], STUBBORN. Related form: **persistence** *n.*

person *n.* A man, woman, or child: *a remarkably nice person.*

- [Initialized sign following the shape of a person's body] Bring both *P hands,* palms facing each other, downward along the sides of the body with a parallel movement.

personal *adj.* Belonging to or concerning a particular person: *personal property.* Same sign used for: **personnel.**

- [Initialized sign] Move the right *P hand*, palm facing down, in a small double circle on the left side of the chest with a double movement.

personality *n.* **1.** The total of individual qualities that make a person different from others: *a personality that has developed over the years.* **2.** The visible characteristics that determine a person's social appeal: *a performer with a lot of personality and energy.*

- [Initialized sign similar to sign for **character**[1]] Move the right *P hand*, palm facing down, in a small circle in front of the left side of the chest. Then bring the thumb side of the right *P hand* back against the left side of the chest.

person marker *n.* A marker used as a suffix in sign language to denote a person.

- [The hands follow the shape of a person] Move both *open hands,* palms facing each other, downward along each side of the body.

personal digital assistant (PDA) *n.* See sign for TEXT MESSAGE.

personnel *n.* See sign for PERSONAL.

perspective[1] *n.* One's way of looking at people, facts, ideas, situations, etc., and understanding the relationships among them: *trying to see the situation in the proper perspective.* Same sign used for: **point of view, viewpoint.**

- [Represents eyes looking at something from different directions] Beginning with the index fingers of both *V hands* near each side of the face, palms facing down and fingers pointing toward each other, bring the hands outward in an arc and then forward toward each other in front of the chest.

perspective[2] *n.* (alternate sign) Same sign used for: **point of view, viewpoint.**

- [Represents the eyes looking at something] Move the right *V hand,* palm facing down and fingers pointing forward, from near the right eye toward the extended left index finger held in front of the chest, palm facing right and finger pointing up.

perspire *v.* See signs for SWEAT[1,2]. Related form: **perspiration** *n.*

persuade *v.* See signs for CONVINCE[1,2,3], ENCOURAGE, URGE. Related form: **persuasion** *n.*

pervade *v.* To spread throughout, especially in a subtle, lingering fashion: *The smell pervades the air.*

- [**continue**[1] + a gesture showing things intermingling] Beginning with the thumb of the right *10 hand* on the thumbnail of the left *10 hand,* both palms facing down in front of the chest, move the hands downward and forward in an arc. Then, beginning with the fingertips of both *flattened O hands* touching in front of the chest, palms facing in, open the hands and interlock the fingers.

pessimistic *adj.* Having or exhibiting a tendency to expect the worst: *a pessimistic view on life.*

- [**none**[6] + **hope**[1]] Beginning with both *O hands* in front of each side of the chest, palms facing each other, move the hands forward and downward in an arc. Then, beginning with the right *open hand* near the right side of the head, palm angled forward and fingers pointing up, and the left *open hand* in front of the chest, palm facing right and fingers pointing up, bend the fingers toward each other with a double movement.

pest *n.* See sign for PICK ON.

pester *v.* See sign for ANNOY[2].

pet[1] *v.* To stroke or pat gently: *to pet the kitten.* Same sign used for: **favor, spoil, tame.**

- [Demonstrates the action of petting something] Pull the fingertips of the right *open hand,* palm facing down, back toward the chest from the fingers to the wrist of the left *open hand,* palm facing down, with a long movement while bending the finger back into the palm. The noun is the same sign as the verb but made with a short double movement.

pet[2] *v. Slang.* To engage in amorous physical activity: *The boy and girl petted in the back seat of the car.* Same sign used for: **make love, neck.**

- [The fists represent two heads close together] Beginning with both *S hands* crossed at the wrists in front of the chest, palms facing in opposite directions, bend the hands downward with a short double movement.

petit *adj.* See sign for WORTHLESS.

petition[1] *n.* A formal request to some authority for a special privilege, a right, etc.: *a petition to the city for a new stoplight.*

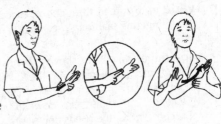

- ■ **[sign + paper]** Place the extended fingers of the right *H hand,* palm facing down, on the upturned palm of the left *open hand,* fingers pointing forward. Then brush the heel of the right *open hand,* palm facing down, on the heel of the left *open hand,* palm facing up, in front of the body with a double movement.

petition[2] *v.* See sign for SUGGEST.

petit jury *n.* See sign for JURY.

petty[1] *adj.* Having little importance: *a petty idea.*

- ■ **[tiny + not**[1] **+ important**[1,2]**]** With the right thumb tucked under the index finger of the right *X hand,* palm facing left, flick the thumb out. Next bring the extended thumb of the right *10 hand* from under the chin, palm facing left, forward with a deliberate movement. Then, beginning with the fingertips of both *F hands* touching in front of the chest, palms facing each other, bring the hands upward in a circular movement, ending with the index-finger sides of both *F hands* touching, palms facing down.

petty[2] *adj.* See sign for WORTHLESS.

petty cash *n.* A small cash fund for paying minor expenses: *paid for my taxi out of petty cash.*

- ■ **[fast**[1] **+ money]** Beginning with the thumbs of both *A hands* tucked under the index fingers, palms facing each other in front of each side of the chest, flick the thumbs out while twisting the wrists quickly forward. Then tap the back of the right *flattened O hand,* palm facing up, with a double movement against the palm of the left *open hand,* palm facing up.

pew *n.* See sign for COUCH.

phallus *n.* See signs for PENIS[1,2].

pharmacy *n.* A store that sells drugs and medicines and often toiletries, stationery, and other items; drugstore: *to buy the medicine at the pharmacy.*

■ [**medicine** + **store**[1,2]] With the bent middle finger of the right *5 hand,* palm facing down, in the upturned palm of the left *open hand,* rock the right hand from side to side with a double movement while keeping the middle finger in place. Then, beginning with both *flattened O hands* held in front of each side of the chest, palms facing down and fingers pointing down, swing the fingertips upward and back by twisting the wrists.

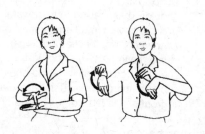

phase *n.* See sign for PART[1].

pheasant *n.* A game bird with a long tail: *They like to hunt wild pheasant.*

■ [Initialized sign] With the extended middle finger of the right *P hand* touching the right side of the neck, palm facing left, twist the hand forward, ending with the palm facing back.

phenomenon *n.* An extraordinary event or person: *an electrical phenomenon visible in the night sky; an artistic phenomenon who exhibited in galleries at the age of fourteen.*

■ [**wonderful**[1,2] + **always**] Push the palms of both *open hands,* palms facing forward and fingers pointing up, forward with a double movement in front of each shoulder. Then move the extended right index finger, palm facing in and finger pointing up, in a repeated circle in front of the right side of the chest.

phew *interj.* See sign for STINK[1].

Philadelphia *n.* A city in southeast Pennsylvania: *The Liberty Bell is in Philadelphia.*

■ [Initialized sign] Move the right *P hand,* palm facing forward, from near the right side of the head forward a short distance and then straight down to in front of the right side of the body.

philander *v.* See sign for FLIRT.

philanthropic *adj.* Concerned with and in aid of the needy; charitable: *They give generously to philanthropic causes.*

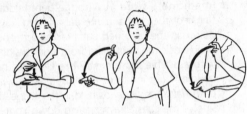

■ [**money** + **charity**] Tap the back of the right *flattened O hand,* palm facing up, with a double movement against the upturned palm of the left *open hand.* Next move the right *X hand* from in front of the right shoulder, palm facing left, forward and downward in a large arc in front of the right side of the body. Then move the left *X hand* from in front of the left shoulder, palm facing right, forward and downward in a large arc in front of the left side of the body.

philanthropist *n.* A person who gives frequently and generously to charity: *The philanthropist set up a foundation in aid of destitute children.*

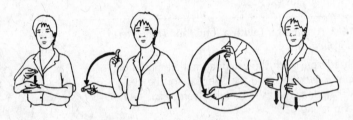

■ [**philanthropic** + **person marker**] Tap the back of the right *flattened O hand,* palm facing up, with a double movement against the upturned palm of the left *open hand.* Next move the right *X hand* from in front of the right side of the chest, palm facing left, forward and downward in a large arc in front of the body. Then move the left *X hand* from in front of the left side of the chest, palm facing right, forward and downward in a large arc in front of the left side of the body. Finally, move both *open hands,* palms facing each other, downward along each side of the body.

Philippines[1] *n.* A republic in southeast Asia consisting of more than 7,000 islands: *The capital of the Philippines is Manila.*

■ [Initialized sign similar to sign for **island**[1]] Move the extended index finger of the right *P hand,* palm facing down, in a circle on the back of the left *open hand* held across the chest, palm facing down and fingers pointing right.

Philippines[2] *n.* (alternate sign)

■ Move the thumb side of the right *9 hand,* palm facing left, in a circle in front of the face.

philosopher *n.* A person who expresses theories on questions in ethics, logic, metaphysics, and other such fields: *The philosopher explored questions of morality with his students.*

- ◾ **[philosophy + person marker]** Bring the right *P hand,* palm facing left, downward with a short double movement in front of the right side of the forehead. Then move both *open hands,* palms facing each other, downward along each side of the body.

philosophy *n.* **1.** The study and investigation of the general principles of existence, knowledge, ethics, etc.: *to study the philosophy of Plato.* **2.** A system of guiding principles, values, and beliefs for everyday living: *my philosophy about learning.*

- ◾ **[Initialized sign similar to sign for theory]** Bring the right *P hand,* palm facing left, downward with a short double movement in front of the right side of the forehead.

phlegm *n.* The thick mucus secreted in the respiratory passages, as during a cold: *He cleared the phlegm from his throat before speaking.*

- ◾ **[Indicates something coming up and being spit out]** Move the right *curved 5 hand,* palm facing in, upward in front of the chest to in front of the mouth. Then turn the hand over, bringing the palm side of the right *curved 5 hand* down into the palm of the left *open hand* held in front of the body, palm facing up and fingers pointing right.

Phoenix *n.* The capital of Arizona: *There are many resorts around Phoenix.*

- ◾ **[Abbreviation p-x]** Move the right *P hand* from in front of the right shoulder, palm facing down, in an arc forward and downward while changing into an *X hand.*

phone[1] *n., v.* See sign for CALL[2].

phone[2] *n.* See signs for TELEPHONE[1,2].

phonograph[1] *n.* A device that reproduces sound by playing records: *We like to listen to old records on the phonograph.* Same sign used for: **record.**

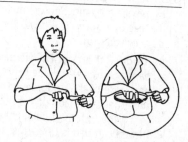

- ◾ **[Represents the needle on a phonograph moving around a record]** Move the index finger of the right *X hand,* palm facing down, in a flat circle near the palm of the left *C hand* held in front of the chest, palm facing right.

phonograph[2] *n.* See sign for RECORD PLAYER.

photo *n.* See sign for PICTURE. Alternate form: **photograph.**

photocopy *v.* See signs for COPY[2,3].

photograph *v.* See signs for TAKE PICTURES[1,2].

photographer[1] *n.* A person who takes photographs, especially professionally: *to have a picture taken at the photographer's.*

- [**picture** + **person marker**] Move the right *C hand*, palm facing forward, from near the right side of the face downward, ending with the index-finger side of the right *C hand* against the palm of the left *open hand*, palm facing right. Then move both *open hands*, palms facing each other, downward along each side of the body.

photographer[2] *n.* (alternate sign)

- [**camera**[1] + **person marker**] Beginning with both *modified C hands* near the outside of each eye, palms facing each other, bend the right index finger up and down with a repeated movement. Then move both *open hands*, palms facing each other, downward along each side of the body.

phrase *n.* See signs for MESSAGE[1,2], STORY[1,2].

physical *adj.* Of or pertaining to the body: *an annual physical examination.*

- [Initialized sign similar to sign for **body**] Touch the palm side of both *P hands*, palms facing in and fingers pointing toward each other, first on each side of the chest and then on each side of the waist.

physical examination *n.* See sign for LOOK FOR[3].

physical therapy *n. phrase.* Treatment of the bone, muscular, or nervous systems by physical or mechanical means with the goal of restoring normal function after disease or injury: *The doctor ordered six weeks of physical therapy.*

- [**body** + **therapy**] Pat the palm side of both *open hands* first on each side of the chest and then on each side of the abdomen. Then, beginning with the little-finger side of the right *T hand*, palm facing in, on the upturned palm of the left *open hand*, move both hands upward in front of the chest.

physician *n.* See sign for DOCTOR[1,2].

physicist *n.* A scientist specializing in physics: *The physicist researched the effects of the lack of gravity in space.*

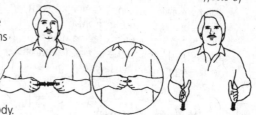

- ■ [**physics** + **person marker**] Tap the knuckles of both *bent V hands*, palms facing in, against each other in front of the chest with a double movement. Then move both *open hands*, palms facing each other, downward along each side of the body.

physics *n.* The science that deals with matter, energy, motion, and force: *to study physics in school.*

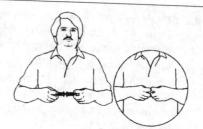

- ■ Tap the knuckles of both *bend V hands*, palms facing in, against each other in front of the chest with a double movement.

physique[1] *n.* The general appearance, shape, development, and condition of the body: *a muscular physique.*

- ■ [Shows the shape of one's figure + **hulk**] Beginning with both *curved hands* near each side of the chest, palms facing each other, move the hands downward along the sides of the body with a wiggly movement, twisting the wrists up and down as the hands move. Then, beginning with both *modified C hands* in front of each shoulder, palms facing each other, move the hands outward to each side with a large movement.

physique[2] *n.* See signs for SHAPE[1,2].

pianist *n.* A person who plays the piano, especially with professional expertise: *The pianist played a short Mozart piece.* Same sign used for: **organist.**

- ■ [**piano** + **person marker**] Beginning with both *curved 5 hands* in front of the right side of the body, palms facing down, move the hands to the left and then back to the right again while wiggling the fingers. Then move both *open hands*, palms facing each other, downward along each side of the body.

piano *n.* A large musical instrument played by striking keys on a keyboard: *learned to play the piano as a child.* Same sign used for: **organ.**

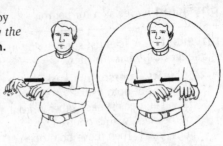

- [Mime playing a piano] Beginning with both *curved 5 hands* in front of the right side of the body, palms facing down, move the hands to the left and then back to the right again while wiggling the fingers.

pick *v.* See signs for CHOOSE[1,2,3], SELECT[1].

pick on *v. phrase.* To find fault with or tease persistently: *Why do they always pick on the little guy?* Same sign used for: **henpeck, nag, peck, pest.**

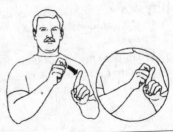

- [Indicates picking on someone] Tap the fingertips of the right *modified X hand*, palm facing left, against the extended left index finger, palm facing right and finger pointing up, in front of the chest with a double movement.

pick up *v. phrase.* See sign for FIND[2].

picket *v.* **1.** To protest company practices during a strike, especially by demonstrating in front of the entrance to obstruct it: *to picket the factory for unfair employment practices.* —*n.* **2.** A person who pickets during a strike: *The pickets marched in front of the factory carrying large placards.* Same sign used for: **protest.**

- [Mime holding a picket sign] With the little-finger side of the right *S hand* on top of the index-finger side of the left *S hand*, both palms facing in, move the hands forward in a short double movement.

pickle[1] *n.* A vegetable, especially a cucumber, preserved in brine or vinegar: *to eat a dill pickle with your hamburger.*

- [Similar to sign for **sour**] Twist the tip of the extended right index finger near the right corner of the mouth with a short double movement.

pickle[2] *n.* (alternate sign)

- [Initialized sign similar to sign for **sour**] With the middle finger of the right *P hand* touching near the right side of the mouth, palm facing left, twist the hand forward, ending with the palm facing back.

pickle³ *n.* (alternate sign)

- Move both *G hands,* palms facing each other, up and down past each other with an alternating double movement in front of the chest.

pickpocket *n.* A person who steals from other people's pockets, purses, etc.: *The pickpocket took my wallet.*

- [**steal¹** formed near a back pocket + **pocket**] Beginning with the fingertips of the right *V hand* touching the right hip, palm facing up, pull the hand outward while bending the fingers. Then slide the fingertips of the right *open hand* up and down a short distance on the right side of the body with a repeated movement.

picnic¹ *n.* A meal in the open air, as on a trip to the country: *went on a picnic.*

- Open and close the thumbs and index fingers of both *G hands* near each side of the face with a repeated movement, palms facing each other.

picnic² *n.* (alternate sign)

- [Represents eating a sandwich at a picnic] With the left *bent hand* over the back of the right *bent hand,* both palms facing down and fingers pointing toward the mouth, move the hands toward the mouth with a double movement.

picture *n.* A drawing, painting, or photograph: *a picture of my child.* Same sign used for: **image, photo, photograph.**

- [The hand seems to focus the eyes on an image and then record it on paper] Move the right *C hand,* palm facing forward, from near the right side of the face downward, ending with the index-finger side of the right *C hand* against the palm of the left *open hand,* palm facing right.

pie¹ *n.* A baked pastry crust with fruit, custard, meat, or other filling: *a piece of apple pie.* Same sign used for: **slice.**

- [Demonstrates cutting a pie into slices] Slide the fingertips of the right *open hand,* palm facing left, from the fingers to the heel of the upturned left hand, fingers pointing forward, and then perpendicularly across the left palm.

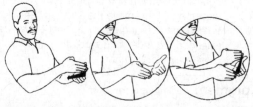

pie[2] *n.* (alternate sign)

■ [Initialized sign] Slide the extended middle finger of the right *P hand*, palm facing down, across the upturned palm of the left *open hand* held in front of the chest, fingers pointing forward, first perpendicularly across the left palm and then from the fingers to the heel.

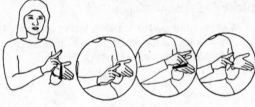

piece *n.* See signs for PART[1,2], SOME.

pierce *v.* See sign for PENETRATE[1]. Related form: **pierced** *adj.*

pierced ears *pl. n.* Ears with holes punctured through the lobes to allow the wearing of earrings: *to have pierced ears with more than one hole.*

■ [Shows where holes are pierced into ears] Move the extended index fingers of both hands, palms facing down, toward each ear.

pig *n.* A four-footed stout domestic animal with a short snout and short legs, usually raised as food: *pigs wallowing in the mud.* Same sign used for: **ham, hog, pork.**

■ [Similar to sign for **dirty**] With the back of the right *open hand* under the chin, palm facing down, bend the right fingers down and up again with a double movement.

pigeon *n.* A bird with a plump body and short legs: *There are many pigeons in the park.*

■ [Similar to sign for **pheasant**] With the extended right index finger touching the right side of the neck, palm facing forward, twist the hand forward, ending with the palm facing back.

piggy-back *adv.* On the back or shoulders: *to carry the child piggy-back.*

■ [**pig** + a gesture indicating a person on the back of another person] With the back of the right *open hand* under the chin, palm facing down, bend the right fingers down and up again with a double movement. Then move the fingers of the right *bent V hand*, palm facing down, against each side of the extended left index finger pointing up in front of the chest, palm facing right.

pigment *n.* See sign for RACE[3].

pile[1] *n.* **1.** A collection of things lying on top of one another: *a big pile of magazines on my floor.* **2.** A large number or amount: *made a pile of money in the stock market.* Same sign used for: **batch, bulk, load.**

- [The shape and size of a pile] Move the right *5 hand* from in front of the left side of the chest, palm facing right and fingers pointing forward, upward in an arc in front of the right shoulder, ending near the right side of the body, palm facing left.

pile[2] *n.* (alternate sign)

- [The shape and size of a pile] Beginning with both *5 hands* in front of the chest, palms facing down and fingers pointing forward, bring the hands outward and downward in large arcs, ending in front of each side of the body, palms facing each other.

pile[3] *n.* (alternate sign)

- [Shows the shape of a pile] With the bent arm of the left *open hand* across the chest, palm facing up, move the right *5 hand*, palm facing forward, from near the left elbow in an arc in front of the chest, ending with the palm facing left near the left fingers.

pile[4] *n.* See signs for AMOUNT[1,2], STACK.

Pilgrim *n.* One of the English Puritan settlers who founded Plymouth, Mass., in 1620: *The Pilgrims traveled on a ship.*

- [Initialized sign showing the shape of the traditional Pilgrim's collar] Beginning with both *P hands* in front of the chest, palms facing in and fingers pointing toward each other, bring the hands apart to each side of the chest and then upward to each shoulder.

pill[1] *n.* Medicine in tablet or capsule form made to be swallowed whole: *to take a vitamin pill.* Same sign used for: **capsule, take a pill.**

- [Represents flicking a pill into the mouth] Beginning with the index finger of the right *A hand* tucked under the thumb, palm facing in, flick the right index finger open toward the mouth with a double movement.

pill

pill² *n.* (alternate sign) Same sign used for: **capsule, take a pill.**

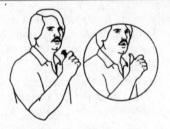

- [Represents flicking a pill into the mouth] Beginning with the thumb of the right *A hand* tucked under the right index finger, palm facing left, flick the thumb upward toward the mouth with a double movement.

pill³ *n.* (alternate sign) Same sign used for: **capsule, take a pill.**

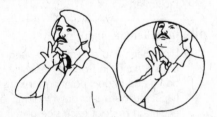

- [Shows the movement of a pill down the throat] Move the index-finger side of the right *F hand* from the chin downward along the throat, palm facing left.

pillage¹ *v.* To steal from with violence: *The robbers pillaged the town after the battle.*

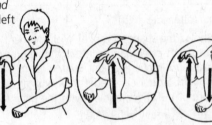

- [Similar to the sign for **capture**¹ but made with a repeated deliberate movement] Beginning with the right *curved 5 hand* in front of the right shoulder and the left *S hand* in front of the left side of the body, both palms facing down, move the right hand downward while closing into an *S hand* and the left hand upward while opening into a *curved 5 hand.* Repeat with an alternating double movement.

pillage² *v.* See sign for STEAL¹.

pillar *n.* A column or similarly shaped structure used as a building support or monument: *The house had eight pillars on the front porch.* Same sign used for: **column.**

- [The shape of a pillar] Rest the elbow of the extended bent right arm on the back of the left hand held across the chest, palm facing down. Then slide the left *C hand* from the elbow upward to the wrist of the bent right arm.

pillow¹ *n.* A case filled with soft material used to support the head while resting: *I like to sleep on a down pillow.*

- [The hands seem to squeeze a soft pillow] With the fingers of both *flattened C hands* pointing toward each other near the right ear, palms facing each other, close the fingers to the thumbs of each hand with a repeated movement.

pillow[2] *n.* (alternate sign)

- [**bed**[1,2] + **pillow**[1]] With the open left palm on top of the open right palm, rest the right cheek at an angle on the back of the left hand. Then with the fingers of both *flattened C hands* pointing toward each other near the right ear, palms facing each other, close the fingers to the thumbs of each hand with a repeated movement.

pilot *n.* A person who steers a ship or boat or who operates the controls of an aircraft in flight: *The pilot landed the plane on the runway.* Same sign used for: **aviator, flier.**

- [**airplane** + **person marker**] With thumb, index finger, and little finger of the right hand extended, palm angled forward, move the hand forward and upward in front of the right shoulder. Then move both *open ands,* palms facing each other, downward along each side of the body.

pimples[1] *pl. n.* **1.** A condition of the skin characterized by small inflamed swellings: *She developed pimples when she was sixteen.* **2.** These swellings: *an excellent medication for drying up pimples.*

- [Represents pimples popping out here and there on the skin] Beginning with the right *S hand* near the right side of the chin and the left *S hand* in front of the left side of the face, both palms facing forward, flick the right index finger forward while moving the right hand forward and moving the left hand back. Repeat the movement with the left hand from the left side of the chin.

pimples[2] *pl. n.* (alternate sign)

- [Represents a pimple popping out] Beginning with the right *S hand* against the right cheek, palm facing left, flick the right index finger upward with a double movement.

pin[1] *n.* An ornament with a pointed fastener: *to wear a cameo pin on a black dress.*

- [Represents clipping on a pin] Beginning with the thumb of the right *modified C hand* against the left side of the chest, palm facing left, pinch the right index finger to the thumb.

pin[2] *n.* A piece of metal, wood, or plastic used for
hanging one article from another: *Hang a note
on the bulletin board with a pin.* Same sign used
for: **pushpin, tack, thumbtack.**

- [Mime pushing a pushpin into a wall] Push the
right *F hand* forward, palm facing forward, a
short distance in front of the right shoulder.

pin[3] *n.* **1.** A slender piece of wire with a point on one end and a head on the other, used
for fastening things: *to use pins to attach the sewing pattern to the material.*
2. A similar pointed fastener with the wire bent back on itself to
form a spring and the point held in a guard: *I need a pin to fix my
torn hem.* —*v.* **3.** To fasten with a pin: *to pin the badge on at the
conference.* Same sign used for: **pushpin, safety pin, straight pin.**

- [Represents putting on a pin] Beginning with the thumb of the
right *G hand* against the left side of the chest, palm facing left,
pinch the right index finger to the thumb with a double
movement.

pin[4] *n., v.* (alternate sign for PIN[3], defs. 1 and 3)

- [Represents pinning something on] Brush the
fingertips of the right *F hand* downward on the
upper right side of the chest with a double
movement by twisting the wrist forward.

pinball machine *n.* A sloping table with a
mechanical device in which a ball is propelled by a
plunger to score points: *to play game after game on
the pinball machine.*

- [Mime pushing buttons to play a pinball machine]
Beginning with both *curved 5 hands* in front of each
side of the body, palms facing each other and finger
pointing forward, move the hands downward toward
each other with a double movement while bending
the middle finger of each hand.

pincers *pl. n.* **1.** The large claws of a
shellfish: *the crab's pincers.* **2.** A gripping
tool with pivoting limbs: *removing
nails from the wall with a pair of
pincers.*

- [Demonstrates the action of pincers]
Beginning with both *L hands* in front of
each side of the body, palms facing
forward, pinch the index finger and
thumb of each hand together with a
double movement.

pinch[1] *v.* **1.** To squeeze between the thumb and index finger: *to pinch the baby's cheek.* **2.** To press on or constrict painfully: *My shoes are pinching my toes.*

■ [Mime pinching] Move the curved index finger and thumb of the right hand downward in front of the chest, palm facing down, to pinch the back of the left *open hand,* palm facing down.

pinch[2] *v.* (alternate sign)

■ [Mime pinching] With the knuckle of the right *modified X hand* touching the back of the left *open hand* in front of the chest, both palms facing down, twist the right hand forward, ending with the palm facing back.

pinch[3] *v.* (alternate sign)

■ [Demonstrate the action of pinching] Beginning with the right *modified C hand* pointing forward in front of the right side of the body, palm facing forward, pinch the index finger and thumb together with a deliberate movement.

pincushion *n.* A small, soft pad for holding pins and needles: *to stick the pins in the pincushion.*

■ [pin[4] + mime putting pins into a pincushion] Brush the fingertips of the right *F hand,* palm facing down, downward on the upper right side of the chest with a double movement by twisting the wrist forward. Then touch the fingertips of the right *F hand* down in several places on the back of the left *S hand* held across the chest, palm facing down.

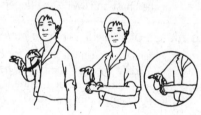

pineapple[1] *n.* A juicy tropical fruit with yellow, fibrous flesh: *Fresh pineapple tastes better than canned.*

■ [Initialized sign] Beginning with the middle finger of the right *P hand* touching the right cheek, palm facing left, twist the hand forward with a repeated movement, turning the palm back.

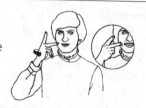

pineapple[2] *n.* (alternate sign)

■ [Slicing a pineapple] Move the right *open hand,* palm facing left and fingers pointing forward, downward past the fingertips of the left *B hand* held in front of the chest, palm facing in and fingers pointing right. Then move the right *open hand,* palm facing in, downward past the back of the left *B hand.*

Ping-Pong[1] *Trademark.* A table game
resembling tennis, played with a paddle and a
small hollow ball: *Play Ping-Pong with me.*
Same sign used for: **table tennis.**

- ■ [Initialized sign showing the action of
  swinging a Ping-Pong paddle] Beginning with
  the right *P hand* in front of the right side of
  the body, palm facing down, swing the hand
  to the left and back to the right.

Ping-Pong[2] *Trademark.* (alternate sign) Same
sign used for: **table tennis.**

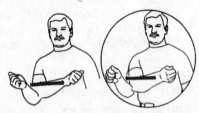

- ■ [Mime swinging a Ping-Pong paddle]
  Beginning with the right *A hand* in front of the
  right side of the body, palm facing up, swing
  the hand to the left while turning the palm
  down, and then back to the right again.

Ping-Pong[3] *Trademark.* (alternate sign) Same sign used
for: **table tennis.**

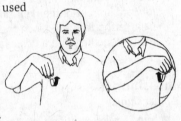

- ■ [Mime swinging a Ping-Pong paddle] Beginning
  with the right *flattened O hand* in front of the
  right shoulder, palm facing down and fingers
  pointing down, swing the fingertips forward.
  Then move the right hand in front of the left side
  of the chest and swing the fingers forward again.

pink *adj.* Of a pale red color: *a pink rose.*

- ■ [Initialized sign similar to sign for **red**[1]] Brush
  the middle finger of the right *P hand*, palm
  facing in, downward across the lips with a
  short repeated movement.

pinnacle *n.* **1.** The highest point, especially of a pointed, towering formation: *We
climbed to the pinnacle of the mountaintop.* **2.** The highest level that can be
achieved, as of power or fame: *to reach the pinnacle of success.*

- ■ [**high**[1] + **peak**] Move the right *H hand,* palm facing in and fingers pointing left, from
  in front of the right side of the chest
  upward to in front of the head. Then,
  beginning with both extended index
  fingers pointing up in front of each
  shoulder, palms facing each other, move
  the hands upward toward each other,
  ending with the index fingers touching in
  front of the head.

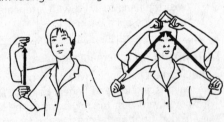

pinpoint *n.* See sign for POINT[3].

pipe[1] *n.* A tube with a bowl on one end used for smoking: *My professor smokes a pipe.*

■ [Represents smoking a pipe] Pat the thumb of the right *Y hand,* palm facing left, against the right side of the chin with a repeated movement.

pipe[2] *n.* (alternate sign)

■ With the fingertips of the right *bent hand* against the right side of the cheek, palm facing down, twist the wrist to move the hand up and down with a double movement.

pipe[3] *n.* A tube through which liquids flow: *a water pipe attached to the washing machine.* Same sign used for: **handle, lever, pole, rod, tube.**

■ [The shape of a pipe] Beginning with the index-finger sides of both *O hands* touching in front of the chest, palms facing forward, move the hands apart to in front of each side of the chest.

pipe[4] *n.* See sign for **stick**[2].

pipeline *n.* Lines of pipe for carrying gas and oil over great distances: *the oil company's pipelines.*

■ [**pipe**[3] + the shape of a pipeline in the ground] Beginning with the index-finger sides of both *O hands* touching in front of the chest, palms facing forward, move the hands apart to in front of each side of the chest. Then move the extended right index finger from on top of the back of the left *open hand* held across the chest, palm facing down and fingers pointing right, forward with a wavy movement to in front of the right side of the body, palm facing down and finger pointing forward.

piper *n.* A person who plays a flute or bagpipe: *The piper played some music and the children all followed him.*

■ [**music** + **play**[2]] Swing the little-finger side of the right *open hand,* palm facing in, back and forth across the length of the bent left forearm held in front of the chest. Then, beginning with the index-finger side of the left *curved hand* near the little-finger side of the right *curved hand,* palms facing in opposite directions, wiggle the fingers repeatedly.

pique *v.* **1.** To affect with resentment, annoyance, and wounded pride: *She was piqued that she wasn't invited.* —*n.* **2.** A feeling of such resentment and wounded pride: *filled with pique over the snub.* Same sign used for: **piss off** (*slang*).

■ [Initialized sign] Beginning with the extended index finger of the right *P hand* touching the nose, palm facing in, move the hand forward and downward with a quick movement by twisting the wrist, ending with the palm facing up.

pirate *n.* See sign for EYEPATCH.

pistol *n.* See sign for GUN.

pit *n.* A cavity in the ground: *The campers dug a pit to build a fire.*

■ [**hole**[1] + shape of a pit] Move the extended right index finger, palm facing in and finger pointing down, in a large circle near the palm side of the left *C hand,* palm facing right. Then move the right *B hand,* palm facing in and fingers pointing left, from the thumb of the left *C hand* in a downward arc while twisting the right wrist, ending with the right fingers, palm facing forward, near the little finger of the left hand.

pitch[1] *v.* To throw, as the ball to a batter in a baseball game: *learned to pitch the baseball in Little League.*

■ [Mime pitching a ball] Beginning with the right *curved 3 hand* near the right shoulder, palm facing left, bring the right hand downward and forward to the left with a quick double movement, ending with the palm facing up.

pitch[2] *v.* See signs for THROW[1,2,3].

pitchfork *n.* A long-handled tool, with curved tines at one end, used in pitching hay or grain: *to throw a pile of hay up into the hayloft with a pitchfork.*

■ [Shape of a pitchfork's tines + mime action of using a pitchfork] Slide the fingers of the right *V hand,* palm facing up, across the left *open hand,* palm facing up. Next push both *S hands* downward with a short deliberate movement near the left side of the waist, and then swing the hands upward and over the right shoulder.

pitcher[1] *n.* A container with a lip on one side and a handle on the other, used for pouring: *a pitcher of tea.*

- [Represents pouring from a pitcher into another container] Beginning with the left *C hand* in front of the left side of the body, palm facing right, and the right *S hand* in front of the right side of the body, palm facing in, bring the right hand upward in an arc while turning the palm down, and then back down again in the original position.

pitcher[2] *n.* (alternate sign)

- [Represents pouring from a pitcher] Beginning with the right *Y hand* in front of the right side of the body, palm facing left, tip the hand upward in an arc while turning the palm down, and then back down again in the original position.

pitcher[3] *n.* (alternate sign)

- [Represents pouring from a pitcher] Beginning with the right *A hand* in front of the right side of the chest, palm facing in, tip the thumb downward to the left and back up again.

pitcher[4] *n.* A player on a baseball team who throws the ball to the batter to hit: *The pitcher threw the ball again and struck the batter out.*

- [**pitch**[1] + **person marker**] Beginning with the right *curved 3 hand* in front of the right shoulder, palm facing left, bring the right hand downward and forward to the left with a quick double movement, ending with the palm facing up. Then move both *open hands,* palms facing each other, downward along each side of the body.

Pittsburgh *n.* A city in southwestern Pennsylvania: *Pittsburgh is a port on the Ohio River.* Same sign used for: **Maine.**

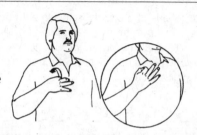

- Brush the fingertips of the right *F hand* upward and forward on the right side of the chest with a double movement.

pity *n.* See signs for MERCY[1,2,3,4]. Related form: **pitiful** *adj.*

pivot *n.* **1.** A pin, shaft, or the like, around which something revolves: *The wheel turns on a pivot.* **2.** The central issue, thing, or person on which something depends: *Economic opportunity was the pivot of the campaign. The director of the theater group is its pivot and guiding force.* —*v.* **3.** To turn on or as if on a pivot: *pivoted around quickly on one foot.*

■ [**important**¹ + twisting something in a hole] Beginning with the fingers of both *F hands* touching, palms facing each other, bring the hands upward with a circular movement, ending with the index-finger sides of both *F hands* touching in front of the chest. Then, with the fingertips of the right *R hand*, palm facing in and elbow extended, inserted in the opening of the left *S hand*, twist the right hand forward and back with a double movement.

pixel *n.* Short for *picture element.* A single point in a graphic image, or the basic unit of composition of an image on a television screen, computer monitor, or similar display. Pixels may have intensity and color.

■ [The dot pattern of pixels] With a small repeated movement, tap the fingertips of the right *curved 5 hand* from the fingers to the heel of the left *open hand* held in front of the chest, palm facing right and fingers pointing up.

pizza¹ *n.* An open pie made with tomato sauce, cheese, and other ingredients on a layer of dough: *to go out to an Italian restaurant for pizza.*

■ [**z** formed with *P hand*] Form a *Z* with the right *P hand*, palm facing left, in front of the right side of the chest.

pizza² *n.* (alternate sign)

■ [Shape of a pizza] Beginning with both *L hands* in front of each side of the chest, palms facing each other, turn the hands downward with a double movement.

placard *n.* A poster or similar printed or written public notice: *to hang a placard in the lobby announcing the meeting.*

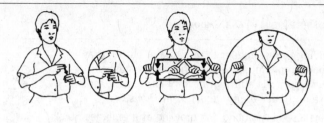

- [**name**[1] + **card**[1]] Tap the middle finger side of the right *H hand* across the index-finger side of the left *H hand* with a double movement. Then, beginning with the extended index fingers and thumbs of both *L hands* touching in front of the chest, palms facing forward, bring the hands apart, closing the fingers to the thumbs in front of each side of the chest.

place[1] *n.* A particular section of space, as for a designated purpose: *a place to play.* Same sign used for: **location, position, site, venue.**

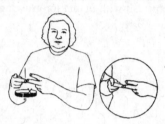

- [Initialized sign similar to sign for **area**[2]] Beginning with the middle finger of both *P hands* touching in front of the body, palms facing each other, move the hands apart in a circular movement back until they touch again near the chest.

place[2] *v.* See signs for AREA[1,2,3,4], PUT.

plague *n.* See sign for EPIDEMIC.

plaid *n.* See signs for SCOTLAND[1,2].

plain *adj.* Simple; without ornament or design: *a plain black dress.*

- [The hand seems to clean off something to make it plain] Beginning with the index-finger side of the right *open hand* against the chin, palm facing left, move the right hand down across the palm of the left *open hand* from the heel to the fingertips, palm facing up.

plan *n.* **1.** A program or procedure developed in advance for accomplishing something: *Our summer plans include a trip through the Rockies.* **2.** A design, arrangement, drawing, etc.: *a seating plan for the dinner.* —*v.* **3.** To make a plan: *to plan for the future.* Same sign used for: **arrange, arrangement, schedule.**

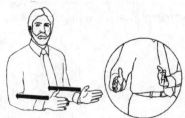

- [The hands show a smooth and orderly flow of events] Move both *open hands* from in front of the left side of the body, palms facing each other and fingers pointing forward, in a long smooth movement to in front of the right side of the body.

plane

plane *n.* See signs for AIRPLANE, SMOOTH[1].

plant[1] *n.* A living thing, smaller than a tree or shrub, that produces food from sunlight and inorganic substances through photosynthesis and that usually has leaves, roots, and a soft stem: *I have many plants in my house.*

■ [Represents a seed sprouting and growing as it emerges from the ground] Bring the right *flattened O hand,* palm facing in, with a repeated movement upward through the left *C hand,* palm facing in and fingers pointing right, while spreading the right fingers into a *5 hand* each time.

plant[2] *v.* **1.** To put in the ground to grow: *to plant tulip bulbs; to plant roses.* **2.** To furnish with plants for growing: *to plant your garden.* Same sign used for: **sow.**

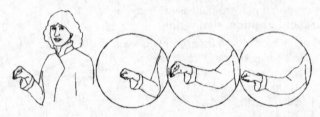

■ [Mime dropping seeds in a garden to plant them] Beginning with the right *flattened O hand* in front of the right side of the body, palm facing down, quickly close the fingers into an *A hand.* Repeat again somewhat forward from the body.

plant[3] *n.* See sign for MACHINE.

plasma *adj.* See sign for FLAT SCREEN DISPLAY.

plaster *n.* **1.** A soft mixture of lime, sand, and water that hardens as it dries: *We put plaster in the hole in the ceiling.* —*v.* **2.** To cover, fill, or spread with plaster: *to plaster the walls before we paint.*

■ [Mime spreading plaster on a wall] Beginning with the palm side of the right *S hand* on the open left palm, palms facing each other, move the right hand upward in an arc to the left.

plate *n.* See signs for DISH[1,2].

platform *n.* A raised horizontal surface, as flooring: *The speakers will sit on the platform.*

■ [**speak**[2] + **stand** + **table**[2]] Move the right *open hand,* palm angled up, in a repeated shaking movement forward and back in front of the right shoulder. Next place the fingertips of the right *V hand,* palm facing in and fingers pointing down, on the palm of the left *open hand* held in front of the chest, palm facing up and fingers pointing right. Then, beginning with the index-finger sides of both *B hands* touching in front of the chest, palms facing down and fingers pointing forward, move the hands apart to in front of each shoulder and then straight down while turning the palms toward each other.

platter *n.* A large shallow dish, sometimes oval in shape, for holding food to be served: *carving the turkey on a platter.*

■ [Similar to sign for **plate** except formed with a twisting movement] Beginning with both *modified C hands* in front of each side of the chest, palms facing each other, twist the wrists to move the hands downward with a double movement.

plausible *adj.* Apparently true; believable: *a plausible excuse.*

■ [**can**[2] + **true**] Move both *S hands,* palms facing down, downward simultaneously with a double movement in front of each side of the body. Then, beginning with the extended index finger of the right hand pointing up in front of the mouth, palm facing left, move the hand forward by twisting the wrist down.

play[1] *v.* **1.** To engage in recreational activity, as spontaneous frolicking or participating in a game: *to play in the park; to play football.* —*n.* **2.** Spontaneous recreational activity: *children at play.* Same sign used for: **romp.**

■ Swing both *Y hands* up and down by twisting the wrists in front of each side of the body with a repeated movement.

play[2] *v.* To perform music on (a reed or wind instrument): *to play a trumpet.*

■ [Mime fingering a clarinet] Beginning with the index-finger side of the left *curved 5 hand* near the little-finger side of the right *curved 5 hand* held near the chin, palms facing in opposite directions, wiggle the fingers repeatedly.

play[3] *n.* See sign for ACT[2].

play against *v. phrase.* See sign for CHALLENGE.

play cards *v. phrase.* See sign for CARDS.

player *n.* A person who plays, particularly on a team: *a baseball player.*

■ [**play**[1] + **person marker**] Swing both *Y hands* up and down by twisting the wrists in front of each side of the body with a repeated movement. Then move both *open hands,* palms facing each other, downward along each side of the body.

playground *n.* A place for outdoor play, often equipped with swings, slides, etc.: *a new playground for the neighborhood children.*

■ [**play**[1] + **land**[1]] Swing both *Y hands* up and down by twisting the wrists in front of each side of the body with a repeated movement. Next, beginning with both *flattened O hands* in front of each side of the body, palms facing up, move the thumbs of both hands smoothly across each fingertip, starting with the little fingers ending as *A hands.* Then, beginning with the thumbs of both *open hands* touching in front of the waist, palms facing down, move the hands forward and outward in circular movements, ending in front of each side of the body.

playhouse *n.* A small house intended for children to play in: *We made a little playhouse out of the carton the refrigerator came in.*

■ [**play**[1] + **house**] Swing both *Y hands* up and down by twisting the wrists in front of each side of the body with a repeated movement. Then, beginning with the fingertips of both *open hands* touching in front of the face, palms angled toward each other, bring the hands at a downward angle outward to in front of each shoulder and then straight down, ending with the fingers pointing up and the palms facing each other.

playwright[1] *n.* A person who writes plays: *written by a famous playwright.*

■ [**act**[2] + **author**] Bring the thumbs of both *A hands,* palms facing each other, downward on each side of the chest with an alternating circular movement. Next slide the palm side of the right *modified X hand* across the open left palm with a double movement. Then move both *open hands,* palms facing each other, downward along each side of the body.

playwright[2] *n.* See sign for AUTHOR.

plead *v.* See signs for BEG[1,2], ENTREAT.

pleasant *adj.* See signs for COOL, FRIENDLY.

please[1] *adv.* (Used to express politeness in a request, command, etc.): *Please open the window.*
- ■ Rub the palm of the right *open hand* in a large circle on the chest.

please[2] *v.* See sign for ENJOY. Related form: **pleasure** *n.*

please[3] *adv.* See sign for WORSHIP[1].

pleat *n.* **1.** A flat, well-defined fold made by doubling fabric back on itself and pressing, stitching, or the like: *The skirt had pleats all around.* —*v.* **2.** To arrange in pleats: *to pleat the front of the blouse.*
- ■ [Shows how fabric is folded over to form pleats, as in a skirt] Beginning with the left *B hand* in front of the right side of the body, palm facing in, and the right *B hand* near the index-finger side of the left hand, palm facing left, bring the right palm over to land on the back of the left *B hand*, both palms facing in and fingers pointing down. Repeat several places around the front of the waist.

pledge[1] *n.* **1.** A solemn promise or agreement: *He gave his pledge to stop smoking.* —*v.* **2.** To promise: *She pledged her loyalty.*
- ■ [Initialized sign similar to sign for **vow**[1]] With the bent right elbow on the back of the left hand held across the body, move the right *P hand* forward in front of the right shoulder, palm facing left.

pledge[2] *n.* See signs for OATH, PROMISE[1], VOW[1].

plentiful *adj.* More than enough: *a plentiful supply.* Same sign used for: **abundant, ample, bountiful.**
- ■ [Represents something being so full that it overflows] Push the palm side of the right *5 hand*, palm facing down, forward across the thumb side of the left *S hand*, palm facing in, moving the right hand forward in a large arc downward in front of the body.

pliable[1] *adj.* **1.** Easily bent: *a pliable piece of plastic.* **2.** Easily influenced; adaptable: *a pliable personality.* Same sign used for: **flexible.**

■ [**can**[2] + **bend**[2]] Move both *A hands* downward with a double movement in front of each side of the body. Then, with the fingers of the right *flattened O hand* grasping the fingers of the left *open hand*, both palms facing in, bend the left fingers forward and back with a double movement.

pliable[2] *adj.* (alternate sign) Same sign used for: **flexible.**

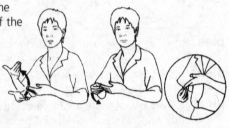

■ [**easy** + **bend**[2]] Brush the fingertips of the right *curved hand* upward on the back of the fingertips of the left *curved hand* with a double movement, both palms facing up. Then, with the fingers of the right *flattened O hand* grasping the fingers of the left *open hand*, both palms facing in, bend the left fingers forward and back with a double movement.

pliers *pl. n.* A tool with long jaws for bending, cutting, or gripping objects: *Tighten the bolt with a pair of pliers.*

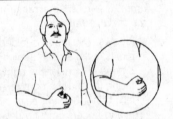

■ [Demonstrates the squeezing action used with pliers] Open and close the finger of the right *C hand* in front of the right side of the chest with a double movement, palm facing in.

plod *v.* To walk or move in a slow, dull way: *The horse plodded through the mud.* Same sign used for: **trudge.**

■ [Represents the movement of a horse's hoofs when walking slowly] Beginning with both *S hands* in front of each side of the chest, right hand higher than the left hand, move the hands up and down with an alternating double movement by bending the wrists.

plop *v.* **1.** To fall dully and with full force, as onto a flat object: *The orange plopped onto the sidewalk. We plopped backwards into the pool.* —*n.* **2.** An act or sound of plopping: *The eggs fell with a loud plop.* Same sign used for: **splat.**

■ [Demonstrates something falling and spreading out as it lands] Beginning with the palm side of the right *S hand* on the index-finger side of the left *S hand*, bring the right hand forward and downward in a large arc while opening into a *5 hand* in front of the body.

plot *n.* **1.** A secret plan or scheme: *a plot to kidnap the prime minister.* **2.** The main story in a book, play, etc.: *The plot of the movie was the same old "boy meets girl" story.* —*v.* **3.** To mark, as on a chart or diagram: *to plot the directions on a map.* **4.** To plan secretly: *The plotted to go on strike.*

■ [Initialized sign showing the lines on a graph] Move the extended middle finger of the right *P hand,* palm facing down, from the heel to off the fingertips of the upturned left *open hand,* fingers pointing forward.

plow[1] *n.* **1.** A large, bladed instrument, usually pulled by an animal or motorized, for turning over the soil to prepare it for planting: *Some farmers still use plows pulled by horses.* —*v.* **2.** To turn over (soil or the soil in) with a plow: *to plow the field.*

■ [Represents how a plow makes rows in the soil] Slide the little-finger side of the right *B hand,* palm facing left and fingers pointing forward, from the heel to off the fingertips of the upturned left *open hand,* fingers pointing forward.

plow[2] *v.* (alternate sign)

■ [Represents pushing dirt forward with a plow] Slide the little-finger side of the right *bent hand,* palm facing in and fingers pointing left, with a double movement from the wrist to off the fingertips of the left *open hand* held in front of the chest, palm facing down and fingers pointing forward.

plow[3] *n.* See sign for RAKE.

pluck *v.* (of a bird) To pull the feathers out of: *to pluck the chicken.*

■ [**bird** + a gesture representing pulling out feathers] Close the index finger and thumb of the right *G hand,* palm facing forward, with a repeated movement in front of the mouth. Then, beginning with the fingertips of the right *G hand,* palm facing down, touching the back of the left forearm held across the chest, pull the right hand upward while pinching the thumb to the fingertip. Repeat on several places on the back of the left hand.

plug *n.* **1.** A small multipronged device attached to one end of an electrical cord to fit into a socket to make an electrical connection: *Pull out the plug when you're finished ironing.* —*v.* **2.** To make an electrical connection for by inserting a plug into a socket: *Plug in the TV.*

■ [Represents inserting a plug into a socket] Move the right *V hand,* palm facing down, forward from in front of the right shoulder, ending with the fingers of the right *V hand* on either side of the extended left index finger held pointing up in front of the chest, palm facing right.

plumb

plumb *n.* A small weight suspended on the end of a line, used to check verticality: *to use a plumb to install the fence.*

■ [Shows the action of a plumb swinging on the end of a plumb line] With the extended right index finger pointing down in front of the right side of the chest, palm facing back and elbow extended, and the left *curved 5 hand* under the right index finger, palm facing up, swing both hands simultaneously from side to side in front of the body.

plumber *n.* A person who installs and repairs water pipes, fixtures, etc.: *If there's a leak, send for a plumber.* Same sign used for: **mechanic.**

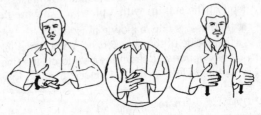

■ [**wrench + person marker**] With the extended left index finger inserted between the index finger and middle finger of the right *3 hand,* palm facing left, twist the right hand up and down with a double movement. Then move both *open hands,* palms facing each other, downward along each side of the body.

plump *adj.* See signs for FAT[1,2].

plunder *v.* To rob by force: *The marauders plundered the village.*

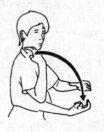

■ [A directional form of the sign for **steal**[1], used repeatedly] Beginning with both *V hands* in front of the body, right hand somewhat forward of the left hand, palms facing in opposite directions and fingers pointing forward, move the hands forward and back to each side of the chest with an alternating double movement, bending the fingers each time as the hands move.

plunge into *v. phrase.* To fling oneself or fall into (a body of water): *The boys plunged into the lake.* Same sign used for: **dive into, fall into.**

■ [Represents a person falling backwards a great distance] Move the bent fingers of the right *V hand* from near the right shoulder, palm facing back, downward in an arc past the palm side of the left *C hand,* palm facing right in front of the body, ending with the right palm facing up.

plus *prep.* **1.** Increased by: *Three plus two equals five.* **2.** In addition to: *She has brains plus beauty.* See also sign for ADD[1,2]. Same sign used for: **addition.**

■ [Shows the shape of a plus sign] Place the side of the extended right index finger, palm facing down and finger pointing left, against the extended left index finger, palm facing right and finger pointing up in front of the chest.

plush[1] *adj.* Having a pile fabric that is thick and soft: *a plush towel.*

■ [**fancy**[1] + **layer**[1,2]] Move the thumb of the right *5 hand,* palm facing left, upward and forward in a double circular movement in the center of the chest. Then slide the thumb of the right *modified C hand,* palm facing left, from the wrist to off the fingers of the back of the left *open hand* held in front of the chest, palm facing down and fingers pointing right.

plush[2] *adj.* See signs for LAYER[1,2].

P.M. or **p.m.** See sign for AFTERNOON.

pneumonia *n.* An infection of the lungs characterized by inflammation and congestion: *caught pneumonia during the freezing weather.*

■ [Initialized sign similar to sign for **lung**] Rub the middle fingers of both *P hands,* palms facing in and fingers pointing toward each other, up and down on each side of the chest with a double movement.

poach *v.* To cook in simmering hot liquid, as an egg: *poached salmon with dill sauce.*

■ [**flame**[1] + **with** + **water**] Beginning with both *curved 5 hands* in front of the chest, right hand higher than the left hand, palms facing in, and fingers pointing up, move the hands upward in large alternating repeated circles. Next bring the palm sides of both *A hands* together in front of the chest. Then tap the index-finger side of the right *W hand,* palm facing left, against the chin with a double movement.

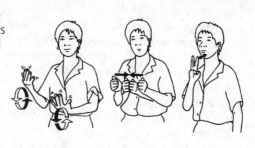

pocket *n.* **1.** A small opening sewn into clothing for carrying small articles: *Put the car keys in your pocket.* —*v.* **2.** To place in the pockets: *The thief pocketed the stolen wallet.*

■ [Mime putting the hand in one's pocket] Slide the fingertips of the right *open hand,* palm facing in, up and down a short distance on the right side of the body with a repeated movement.

pocketbook *n. Chiefly British.* A case with a notebook for carrying information in one's pocket: *to carry a pocketbook to the meeting.* See also signs for PURSE[1,2].

pocketknife

■ [**pocket** + **book**[1]] Slide the fingertips of the right *open hand,* palm facing in, up and down a short distance on the right side of the body with a repeated movement. Then, beginning with the palms of both *open hands* together in front of the chest, fingers angled forward, bring the hands apart at the top while keeping the little fingers together.

pocketknife *n.* A small knife with folding blades: *to carry a pocketknife.*

■ [**pocket** + **knife**] Slide the fingertips of the right *open hand,* palm facing in, up and down a short distance on the right side of the body with a repeated movement. Then slide the bottom side of the extended right index finger, palm facing in, with a double movement at an angle across the length of the extended left index finger, palm facing down, turning the right palm down each time as it moves off the end of the left index finger.

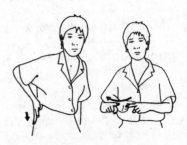

pod *n.* A long case, with side seams, in which the seeds of some plants, as peas, grow: *The seeds burst out of the pod when it ripened.*

■ [Shows the shape of a pod opening] Beginning with the heels and fingers of both *curved hands* together in front of the chest, open the fingers with a small double movement while keeping the heels together.

poem *n.* A composition in verse using imagery and rhythm: *Let's read the poem aloud.* Same sign used for: **poetry, Psalms.**

■ [Initialized sign similar to sign for **music**] Swing the middle finger of the right *P hand,* palm facing in, back and forth across the length of the bent left forearm.

point[1] *n.* The sharp or tapering end of something: *to sharpen the pencil point.* Same sign used for: **tip.**

■ [Indicates the top point of something] Tap the extended right index finger, palm facing down and finger pointing left, down on the tip of the extended left index finger, palm facing right and finger pointing up, with a double movement.

point[2] *n.* (alternate sign) Same sign used for: **tip.**

■ [Indicates the tapered end of something] Move the right *G hand* from holding the extended left index finger, both palms facing in, to the right while pinching the right thumb and index finger together.

point[3] *n.* **1.** A specific location: *at the point where the house used to stand.* **2.** The most important element or matter: *Get to the point of your story.* Same sign used for: **particular, pinpoint, specific, target.**

■ [Demonstrates pointing at a specific thing] Bring the right extended index finger from in front of the right shoulder, palm facing left and finger pointing up, downward to touch the left extended index finger held in front of the left side of the chest, palm facing right and finger pointing up.

point[4] *v.* See sign for THERE[2].

point[5] *n.* See sign for PERIOD[1].

point of view *n. phrase.* See signs for PERSPECTIVE[1,2].

poison[1] *n.* **1.** A drug or other substance that can destroy life or injure health: *searched for an antidote to the poison.* —*v.* **2.** To kill or attempt to kill with poison: *The victims were poisoned by arsenic.*

■ [Represents the crossbones from the skull and crossbones symbol on labels for poison] Cross the wrists of both *bent V hands,* palms facing the body, in front of the chest.

poison[2] *n.* See sign for MEDICINE.

Poland[1] *n.* A country in eastern Europe: *Poland is on the Baltic Sea.* Related form: **Polish** *adj., n.*

■ Touch the fingertips of the right *curved hand,* palm facing in, first on the left side of the chest and then on the right side of the chest.

Poland[2] *n.* (alternate sign, considered offensive) Related form: **Polish** *n., adj.*

■ Wipe the tip of the extended thumb of the right *10 hand,* palm facing left, upward on the nose with a double movement.

pole

pole *n.* See signs for PIPE[3], POST[1], STICK[2,3,4].

police[1] *n.* An organized civil force for maintaining order, preventing and detecting crime, and enforcing the law: *to report the robbery to the police.* Same sign used for: **badge, cop, marshal, security, sheriff.**

- [Shows the location of a police badge; also initialized form of **cop**] Tap the thumb side of the right *C hand*, palm facing left, against the left side of the chest with a double movement.

police[2] *n.* (alternate sign) Same sign used for: **badge, cop, marshal, officer, security, sheriff.**

- [Shows the location of a police badge] Tap the thumb side of the right *modified C hand*, palm facing left, against the left side of the chest with a double movement.

policeman *n.* A member of the police force: *asking for help from the policeman on the corner.*

- [**police**[1,2] + **man**[1,2,3]] Tap the thumb side of the right *modified C hand*, palm facing left, against the left side of the chest with a repeated movement. Then, beginning with the thumb of the right *10 hand* touching the right side of the forehead, palm facing left, bring the hand downward while opening into a *5 hand*, ending with the thumb touching the chest, palm facing left.

police officer *n.* A person serving on the police force: *The police officers raided the illegal gambling game.*

- [**police**[1,2] + **captain**] Touch the thumb side of the right *C hand*, palm facing left, against the left side of the chest. Then tap the fingertips of the right *curved 5 hand* on the right shoulder with a double movement.

policy *n.* See sign for PRINCIPLE.

polish[1] *v.* To make smooth and shiny, especially by rubbing: *to polish the silver.* Same sign used for: **rub, scrub.**

- [Demonstrates action of polishing something] Rub the knuckles of the right *A hand*, palm facing down, with a repeated movement on the back of the left *B hand*, palm facing down.

polish² *n.* **1.** A substance used to color or give shine to one's fingernails: *to use red fingernail polish.* —*v.* **2.** To apply polish to: *polish your fingernails.* Same sign used for: **fingernail polish.**

- [Mime painting one's fingernail] Move the fingertips of the right *U hand* with a double movement off the fingernail of the left index finger, palm facing down and finger pointing right.

polite¹ *adj.* Showing good manners; courteous: *a polite thank-you note.* Same sign used for: **courteous, courtesy, gentle, manners, prim.**

- Tap the thumb of the right *5 hand,* palm facing left, with a double movement against the center of the chest.

polite² *adj.* (alternate sign) Same sign used for: **courteous, courtesy, gentle, manners, prim.**

- Tap the thumb side of the right *open hand,* palm facing left, with a do

politics *n.* The science and art of conducting government and political affairs: *involved in politics before becoming a senator.* Related form: **political** *adj.*

- [Initialized sign similar to sign for **government**¹] Beginning with the right *P hand* near the right side of the head, palm facing forward, twist the wrist to turn the palm back and touch the middle finger of the right *P hand* against the right side of the forehead.

polka dots *pl. n.* See sign for SPOTS.

pollution *n.* See sign for DIRTY.

polo *n.* A game, similar to hockey, played on horseback between two teams who score points by hitting a ball into the opponent's goal with a long-handled mallet: *Polo is a popular sport in England.*

■ [**horseback riding**[1] + a gesture representing hitting with a polo stick] With the extended thumb of the right *U hand* against the right side of the forehead, palm facing forward, bend the fingers up and down with a double movement. Next, with the index finger and middle finger of the right *open hand*, palm facing in and fingers pointing down, straddling the index-finger side of the left *open hand*, palm facing right and fingers pointing forward, move the hands forward with a wiggly movement. Then, beginning with the right *modified X hand* in front of the right side of the body, palm facing left, swing the hand downward under the left *C hand* held in front of the chest, palm facing down, ending with the right palm facing up in front of the body.

pompom *n.* One of the ornamental tufts used by cheerleaders while leading cheers: *The cheerleader shook the pompoms from side to side.*

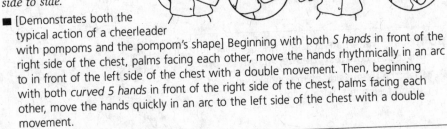

■ [Demonstrates both the typical action of a cheerleader with pompoms and the pompom's shape] Beginning with both *S hands* in front of the right side of the chest, palms facing each other, move the hands rhythmically in an arc to in front of the left side of the chest with a double movement. Then, beginning with both *curved 5 hands* in front of the right side of the chest, palms facing each other, move the hands quickly in an arc to the left side of the chest with a double movement.

poncho *n.* **1.** A rectangular or circular woolen cloak, originally from South America, with a slit or hole in the middle through which the wearer inserts the head: *brought back an authentic poncho from Mexico.* **2.** A similarly styled waterproof garment with a hood: *to wear a poncho in the rain.* Same sign used for: **hood.**

■ [Mime pulling up the hood of a poncho] Beginning with both *modified X hands* near each shoulder, palms facing down, bring the hands upward and forward in an arc, ending with the palms facing up near each side of the head.

pond *n.* See sign for PUDDLE.

ponder *v.* See sign for MULL.

ponderous *adj.* Dull; heavy-handed; labored: *a ponderous speech that seemed to go on forever.*

■ [**heavy** + **wonder**[2]] Beginning with both *5 hands* in front of each side of the chest, palms facing up, move the hands downward a short distance. Then move the extended right index finger, palm facing down, in a small circle near the right side of the forehead.

pontiff *n.* See sign for POPE.

pony *n.* One of a breed of small horses: *The child is waiting in line to ride a pony.* See also sign for COLT.

- [**horse** + **baby**[1]] With the extended thumb of the right *U hand* against the right side of the forehead, palm facing forward, bend the fingers up and down with a double movement. Then, with the right arm cradled on the bent left arm, both palms facing up, swing the arms from left to right in front of the body with a double movement.

poodle *n.* One of a breed of dogs with thick, curly hair: *a French poodle.*

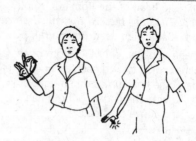

- [**France**[1,2] + **dog**[1,2,3]] Beginning with the right *F hand* in front of the right shoulder, palm facing forward, twist the hand quickly backward. Then pat the right thigh with a double movement with the open right palm, fingers pointing down.

pool[1] *n.* Any of various games played on a pool table by driving balls into pockets with a cue stick: *to play pool in the local pool hall.* Same sign used for: **billiards.**

- [Mime holding a pool cue] With the right elbow extended, move the right *A hand* forward a short distance near the right side of the body while holding the left *F hand* extended in front of the left side of the body.

pool[2] *v.* See sign for CHIP IN.

poor[1] *adj.* Having little or no money or goods: *sending food to poor people.* Same sign used for: **destitute, impoverished, pauper, poverty.**

- [Represents the tattered sleeves on the elbows of poor people] Beginning with the fingertips of the right *curved 5 hand,* palm facing up, touching the elbow of the bent left arm, pull the right hand downward while closing the fingers to the thumb with a double movement, forming a *flattened O hand* each time.

poor[2] *adj.* See signs for MERCY[1,2,3,4].

Poor baby! *Sarcasm.* See signs for MERCY[1,2,3,4].

poor thing *n. phrase.* See signs for MERCY[1,2,3,4].

pop up *v. phrase.* See sign for SHOW UP.

popcorn *n.* Kernels of corn that burst open and puff out when heated: *to eat buttered popcorn at the movies.*

■ [Shows action of popcorn popping] Beginning with both *S hands* in front of each side of the body, palms facing up, alternately move each hand upward while flicking out each index finger with a repeated movement.

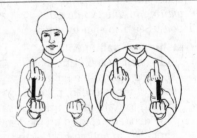

pope *n.* The head of the Roman Catholic Church: *The pope blessed the crowd at the Vatican.* Same sign used for: **papal, pontiff.**

■ [Shape of papal hat] Move both *open hands,* palms angled toward each other, from each side of the head upward in a double arc, ending with the fingers of both hands touching above the head.

Popsicle *n. Trademark.* See sign for LOLLIPOP.

popular *adj.* Liked and approved of by many people: *a popular song; a popular president.*

■ [Represents many people surrounding a popular person] With the extended left index finger against the palm of the right *5 hand,* twist the right hand around the index finger with a double movement.

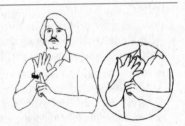

population *n.* The number of people in a city, country, district, or other defined area: *to keep track of the growing population in the suburbs.*

■ [Initialized sign similar to sign for **among**] Move the extended middle finger of the right *P hand,* palm facing in, in and out between the fingers of the left *5 hand,* palm facing in.

porch *n.* An appendage to a building, including a covered entrance: *to sit on the front porch in the early evening.*

■ Strike the index-finger side of the right *S hand,* palm facing in, first near the elbow and then on the forearm of the bent left arm held across the chest, palm of the left *open hand* facing down.

pork *n.* See sign for PIG.

porpoise *n.* Any member of one of the varieties of small whales with blunt snouts that travel in groups: *The porpoises were swimming ahead of the ship.* Same sign used for: **dolphin.**

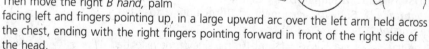

■ [**fish**[1,2] + diving movement] With the extended left index finger, palm facing in, touching the right wrist, move the right *B hand* from right to left with a double movement by bending the wrist. Then move the right *B hand,* palm facing left and fingers pointing up, in a large upward arc over the left arm held across the chest, ending with the right fingers pointing forward in front of the right side of the head.

porter *n.* **1.** A person who carries baggage at a railroad station or hotel: *Did you tip the porter for carrying your suitcase to the taxi?* **2.** *Chiefly British.* A person who guards the entrance to a building; doorman; gatekeeper: *The porter opened the door.*

■ [Shows the visor on a porter's hat + **person marker**] Slide the thumb side of the right *G hand,* palm facing left, across the forehead from left to right with a double movement. Then move both *open hands,* palms facing each other, downward along each side of the body.

portfolio *n.* **1.** A case for carrying papers or drawings: *I bought a leather portfolio.* **2.** The contents of a portfolio, especially paintings, drawings, or photographs representative of one's work: *Show me your portfolio.*

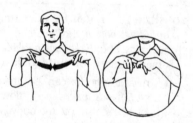

■ [Initialized sign similar to sign for **show**[1]] With the middle finger of the right *P hand,* palm facing in, on the palm of the left *open hand,* palm facing right and fingers pointing forward, move both hands forward in a small arc.

portion *n.* See signs for PART[1], SOME.

portray *v.* See sign for SHOW[1].

Portugal[1] *n.* A country on the west coast of Spain: *Portugal has mild, humid winters.* Related form: **Portuguese** *adj., n.*

■ [Initialized sign similar to sign for **Spain**[2]] Beginning with both *P hands* in front of each shoulder, palms facing in, move the hands toward each other, hooking the index fingers around each other in front of the chest.

Portugal[2] *n.* (alternate sign) Related form:
Portuguese *adj., n.*

- [Shows the profile of a person from Portugal]
Move the extended right index finger, palm
facing in, from the forehead to the chin,
following the facial profile.

position *n.* See sign for PLACE[1].

positive *adj.* **1.** Emphasizing what is hopeful: *a positive
attitude.* **2.** Showing agreement or affirmation: *a positive
reaction.*

- [Demonstrates a positive sign] Tap the side of the extended
right index finger, palm facing down and finger pointing left,
with a double movement against the thumb side of the
extended left index finger pointing up in front of the chest,
palm facing right.

posse *n.* A group of people legally authorized to aid the police in a particular matter:
The posse searched the forest for the lost child.

- [**police**[1,2] + **horde**] Tap the thumb side
of the right *C hand,* palm facing left,
against the left side of the chest with a
double movement. Then move both
curved 5 hands, palms facing down,
forward in front of each side of the
chest.

possess[1] *v.* To have: *possess an acre of land.* Related form: **possession** *n.*

- [**my** + **capture**[1]] Pat the palm side of the right *open
hand,* palm facing in and fingers pointing left,
against the center of the chest. Then, beginning
with both *curved 5 hands* in front of each side of
the chest, palms facing down and fingers pointing
forward, move the hands downward with a quick
movement while changing into *S hands.*

possess[2] *v.* See sign for CAPTURE[1].

possessive *adj.* See sign for GREEDY[1].

possible *adj.* **1.** Capable of existing, happening, or being achieved: *a possible
candidate; possible to finish on time.* **2.** Capable of being true: *The
prediction is unlikely but possible.* Related form: **possibly** *adv.*
Same sign used for: **potential.**

- [Similar to sign for **can**[2] but made with a double movement] Move
both *S hands,* palms facing down, downward simultaneously in
front of each side of the body with a double movement by
bending the wrists.

post[1] *n.* A column set upright to support something else: *attach the clothesline to the post.* Same sign used for: **pole.**

■ [The shape of a post] Beginning with the little-finger side of the right *C hand* on the index-finger side of the left *C hand,* palms facing in opposite directions, raise the right hand upward in front of the chest.

post[2] *v.* See signs for APPLY[1], BULLETIN BOARD[1].

post- *prefix.* Add: *postnatal.*

■ [Initialized sign similar to sign for **after**[1]] Beginning with the thumb side of the right *P hand,* palm facing down, touching the back of the left *open hand,* palm facing in and fingers pointing right, in front of the chest, move the right hand forward a short distance.

post a notice *v. phrase.* See sign for BULLETIN BOARD[1].

postage *n.* See sign for STAMP[1].

postage stamp *n.* See sign for STAMP[1].

poster *n.* See sign for BULLETIN BOARD[1].

postmark *n.* An official mark stamped on mail at a postal facility showing the facility's location and the date of handling the mail: *a New Jersey postmark.*

■ [**letter**[2,3] + **stamp**[2]] Touch the extended thumb of the right *10 hand* to the lips, palm facing in, and then move the thumb downward to touch the upturned palm of the left *open hand* held in front of the body, fingers pointing right. Then tap the little-finger side of the right *S hand,* palm facing in, with a double movement on the upturned palm of the left *open hand* held in front of the body, fingers pointing right.

postmortem *n.* The examination of a body to determine the cause of death: *They conducted a postmortem on the murder victim.*

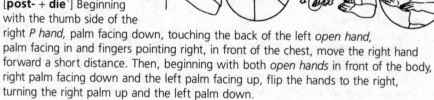

■ [**post-** + **die**[1]] Beginning with the thumb side of the right *P hand,* palm facing down, touching the back of the left *open hand,* palm facing in and fingers pointing right, in front of the chest, move the right hand forward a short distance. Then, beginning with both *open hands* in front of the body, right palm facing down and the left palm facing up, flip the hands to the right, turning the right palm up and the left palm down.

postpone *v.* To put off until a later time; defer: *to postpone the meeting.* Same sign used for: **continuance, defer, delay, put off.**

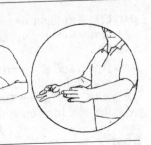

- ■ [Represents taking something and putting it off until the future] Beginning with both *F hands* in front of the body, palms facing each other and the left hand nearer to the body than the right hand, move both hands forward in a small arc.

postwar *adj.* Pertaining to, characteristic of, or occurring during a period following a war: *a nation coping with a postwar recession.*

- ■ [**battle**[1,2] + **after**[1]] Beginning with both *W hands* in front of each side of the chest, palms facing in and fingers pointing toward each other, move the hands with a swinging movement back and forth in front of the chest. Then, beginning with the palm of the right *bent hand* touching the back of the fingers of the left *open hand*, both palms facing in, move the right hand forward a short distance.

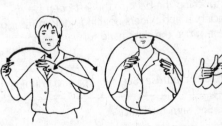

pot[1] *n. Slang.* See sign for MARIJUANA.

pot[2] *n.* See sign for BUCKET.

potato *n.* A hard, round edible tuber, cooked and eaten as a vegetable: *Potatoes are delicious baked, mashed, or fried.*

- ■ [Represents putting fork tines into a baked potato to see if it is done] Tap the fingertips of the right *bent V hand*, palm facing down, with a double movement on the back of the left *open hand*, palm facing down.

potent *adj.* See sign for POWER[1].

potential *adj.* See sign for POSSIBLE.

potter *n.* A person who makes pottery: *The potter used a celadon glaze on the vases.*

- ■ [**bowl** + **make**[1,2] + **person marker**] Beginning with the little fingers of both *C hands* touching in front of the body, palms facing up, bring the hands apart and upward, ending with the palms facing in front of each side of the chest. Next, beginning with the little-finger side of the right

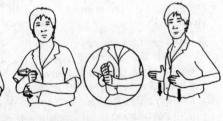

S hand on the index-finger side of the left *S hand,* both palms facing in, separate the hands slightly and twist the wrists in opposite directions and touch the hands together again, ending with the palms facing in opposite directions. Then move both *open hands,* palms facing each other, downward along each side of the body.

pouch *n.* **1.** A bag or sack: *carries the mail in a leather pouch.* **2.** A pouchlike anatomical structure: *A kangaroo has a pouch for carrying its young.*

■ [Demonstrates putting something down into a pouch] Slide the right *open hand,* palm facing in and fingers pointing down, downward behind the left *curved hand* held in front of the body, palm facing in and fingers pointing right.

poultry *n.* Domestic birds collectively, especially those raised for eggs or meat: *Turkeys, ducks, and chickens are kinds of poultry.*

■ [**bird** + **meat**] Open and close the extended fingers of the right *G hand,* palm facing forward, with a double movement in front of the mouth. Then, with the bent index finger and thumb of the right *5 hand,* palm facing down, grasp the fleshy part of the left *open hand,* palm facing down and fingers pointing right, and shake the hands forward and back with a double movement.

pound[1] *v.* To hit again and again: *pound the nail.*

■ [Mime pounding something] Strike the little-finger side of the right *S hand,* palm facing in, with a repeated movement on the upturned palm of the left *open hand* held in front of the waist, fingers pointing forward.

pound[2] *v.* See sign for BANG.

pound[3] *n.* See sign for WEIGH.

pour[1] *v.* To cause to flow in a steady stream: *Pour the milk into the pitcher.* Same sign used for: **fill.**

■ [Mime holding a large container and pouring from it] Beginning with both *C hands* in front of the body, palms facing each other, tip the hands so that the right hand is above the left hand, palm facing down, and the left hand is in front of the body, palm facing up.

pour[2] *v.* (alternate sign) Same sign used for: **fill.**

■ [Mime pouring from a pitcher] Beginning with the right *A hand,* palm facing in, in front of the right side of the chest, move the hand in a short downward arc to the left while raising the elbow to insert the right thumb in the thumb-side opening of the left *S hand.*

poverty *n.* See sign for POOR[1].

powder *n.* **1.** A fine, dusty substance pulverized from other matter by crushing, grinding, etc.: *ground the rocks into powder.* **2.** A preparation in this form: *Put medicated powder on the rash.* Same sign used for: **season, seasoning.**

■ [Mime shaking powder on something] Beginning with the right *C hand* in front of the right shoulder, palm facing forward, tip the hand downward with a double movement to the left, turning the palm outward to the right.

power[1] *n.* **1.** The ability to act or do with strength: *The wrestler has great power in his arms.* **2.** Command or control; authority: *the power to sign treaties.* Related form: **powerful** *adj.* Same sign used for: **mighty, potent, strength, sturdy.**

■ [Demonstrates power in one's arms] Move both *S hands,* palms facing in, forward with a short deliberate movement from in front of each shoulder.

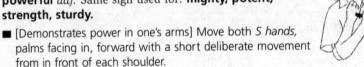

power[2] *n.* See sign for STRONG[1].

powerful *adj.* Having great power, strength, or force: *a powerful fighter; a powerful blow.* Same sign used for: **strong.**

■ [Shows the large muscles in the arms of a powerful person] Bring the fingertips and thumb of the right *C hand* down against the biceps of the bent left arm.

power surge *n.* A sudden increase in electric current, delivered through a power line, that may damage a computer or its memory: *The power surge shut down my computer.* Same sign used for: **spike, surge.**

■ [**electric** + **hit**[1]] Tap the knuckles of the index fingers of both *X hands* together with a double movement, palms facing in. Then strike the knuckles of the right *S hand,* palm facing in, against the extended left index finger held up in front of the chest, palm facing right.

practice *n.* **1.** Repetition of an activity to achieve or improve skill: *To do it well takes practice.* —*v.* **2.** To do repeatedly to improve skill: *to practice the piano every day.* Same sign used for: **drill, exercise, rehearse, training.**

■ [The repetitive action symbolizes doing something again and again] Rub the knuckles of the right *A hand,* palm facing down, back and forth on the extended left index finger held in front of the chest, palm facing down and finger pointing right, with a repeated movement.

praise¹ *v.* **1.** To speak well of: *to praise their efforts on the job.* —*n.* **2.** An expression of approval of something: *high praise for the team.* Same sign used for: **acclamation, compliment.**

■ [real + applaud] Bring the extended right index finger, palm facing left and finger pointing up, from in front of the mouth forward while changing into an *open hand.* Then clap the palms of both *open hands* together with a double movement in front of the body.

praise² *v.* See sign for APPLAUD.

prance *v.* **1.** To move in a sprightly manner; strut: *They pranced down the street as if they owned the world.* **2.** (of a horse) To walk lightly, springing from the hind legs: *The circus horses pranced around the ring.*

■ [Represents a horse's gait when prancing] Beginning with both *V hands* in front of each side of the body, palms facing down and fingers pointing forward, alternately bring the hands back toward the body by bending the wrists upward with an alternating movement while constricting the fingers each time.

prattle *v.* To talk in a foolish and childish way: *She prattled on about her operation.* See also sign for BLAB. Same sign used for: **babble, chat, chatter, gossip, talk, talkative.**

■ [Represents one's jaws going up and down when prattling at length] Beginning with the back of the right *open hand* in front of the face, palm facing forward and fingers pointing up, close the fingers to the thumb of the right hand with a rapid repeated movement, forming a *flattened O hand* each time.

pray¹ *v.* **1.** To petition God: *to pray for rain during a drought.* **2.** To offer praise or thanks to God: *to pray briefly before each meal.* Related form: **prayer** *n.*

■ [Natural gesture for praying] With the palms of both *open hands* together in front of the chest, fingers angled upward, move the hands forward with a double circular movement.

pray[2] *v.* See signs for AMEN[1], ASK, WORSHIP[1]. Related form: **prayer** *n.*

pre-[1] *prefix.* Before: *prenatal.* Same sign used for: **previous.**

- [Initialized sign similar to sign for **before**[3]] Beginning with the back of the right *P hand,* palm facing in, touching the palm of the left *open hand,* palm facing in and fingers pointing right in front of the chest, move the right hand in toward the chest a short distance.

pre-[2] *prefix.* See signs for BEFORE[2,3].

preach[1] *v.* To speak on a religious subject: *preach a sermon.* Same sign used for: **minister, nag.**

- Move the right *F hand,* palm facing forward, with a short double movement forward in front of the right shoulder.

preach[2] *v.* (alternate sign)

- [Initialized sign similar to sign for **preach**[1]] Move the right *P hand,* palm facing forward, downward with a short double movement in front of the right shoulder by bending the wrist.

preacher *n.* A person who preaches, especially one whose occupation is to preach the gospel: *the preacher at our church.* Same sign used for: **minister, pastor, reverend.**

- [**preach**[1,2] + **person marker**] Move the right *F hand,* palm facing forward, with a short double movement forward in front of the right shoulder. Then move both *open hands,* palms facing each other, downward along each side of the body.

preceding *adj.* See signs for BEFORE[2,3].

precious *adj.* **1.** Of great monetary value: *precious jewels.* **2.** Highly cherished: *My children are precious to me.* Same sign used for: **cherish, treasure.**

- [Holding something of value tightly in the hand] Beginning with the right *curved 5 hand* in front of the mouth, palm facing back, slowly close the fingers into an *S hand.*

precipice *n.* A steep or overhanging cliff: *climbed carefully onto the precipice.*

■ [**high**[1] + **place**[1] + showing the shape of a cliff] Move the right *H hand,* palm facing in and fingers pointing left, from in front of the chest upward in front of the head. Next, beginning with the middle fingers of both *P hands* touching in front of the body, palms facing each other, move the hands apart in a circular movement back until they touch again near the body. Then slide the fingers of the right *open hand,* palm facing down and fingers pointing forward, from the wrist to off the fingers of the left *open hand,* palm facing down and fingers pointing right, and then bring the right hand straight down while turning the palm left.

precise *adj.* Accurate; clear; definite: *the precise time of day.* Same sign used for: **accurate, concise, exact, just, specific.**

■ [Demonstrates something coming together precisely] Beginning with the right *modified X hand* over the left *modified X hand,* move the right hand in a small circle and then forward to touch the hands together in front of the chest.

predecessor *n.* A person who held an office, job, etc., before another: *The director's predecessor took all the files.* Same sign used for: **ancestor.**

■ [**my** + **ancestor**[1,2]] Pat the palm side of the right *open hand,* palm facing in and fingers pointing left, against the center of the chest. Then, beginning with both *open hands* in front of the right shoulder, palms facing in and right hand above the left hand, roll the hands over each other with an alternating movement while moving the hands back over the right shoulder.

predicament *n.* A difficult situation: *in a predicament I could not get out of.*

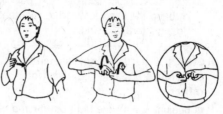

■ [**my** + **problem**[1]] Pat the palm of the right *open hand,* palm facing in and fingers pointing left, against the center of the chest. Then, beginning with the knuckles of both *bent V hands* touching in front of the chest, twist the hands in opposite directions with a deliberate movement, rubbing the knuckles against each other.

predict[1] *v.* To forecast: *predict the future.* Same sign used for: **forecast, foresee, foretell, perceive, perception, prophecy.**

■ [Represents the eyes looking forward into the future] Beginning with the fingers of the right *V hand* pointing to each eye, move the right hand forward under the palm of the left *open hand* while turning the fingers to point forward.

predict[2] *v.* (alternate sign) Same sign used for:
**forecast, foresee, foretell, perceive,
perception, prophecy.**

- [The sign **see** moving as if seeing into the future]
  Beginning with the fingers of the right *V hand*
  pointing to each eye, palm facing in, move the
  right hand forward under the palm of the
  downturned left *open hand* while turning the
  fingers to point forward.

predict[3] *v.* See sign for VISION[1]. Related form: **prediction** *n.*

preen *v.* To smooth or dress (feathers, fur, etc.) with the beak or tongue: *The bird preened itself.*

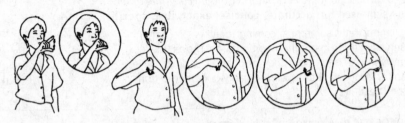

- [**bird** + a gesture representing a bird preening itself] Close the index finger and thumb
  of the right *G hand,* palm facing forward, with a repeated movement in front of the
  mouth. Then, with the index finger and thumb of the right hand pinched together,
  move the fingers downward with a double movement first on the right side of the
  chest and then on the left side of the chest.

prefer[1] *v.* To like better: *to prefer chocolate ice cream.* Related form: **preference** *n.* Same sign used for: **rather.**

- Beginning with the bent middle finger of the
  right *5 hand* touching the chin, palm facing
  in, bring the hand forward to the right while
  closing into a *10 hand.*

prefer[2] *v.* (alternate sign) Related form:
preference *n.* Same sign used for:
rather.

- Beginning with the right *open hand* on
  the chest, palm facing in and fingers
  pointing left, bring the hand upward to
  the right while changing into a *10 hand.*

prefer[3] *v.* See sign for FAVORITE[1]. Related form: **preference** *n.*

pregnant[1] *adj.* Having a baby developing in the womb: *After five years of marriage, she is pregnant.*

■ [The shape of a pregnant woman's stomach] Beginning with the right *5 hand* on the stomach, palm facing in and fingers pointing down, bring the hand forward while curving the fingers.

pregnant[2] *adj.* (alternate sign) Same sign used for: **conceive, breed.**

■ [The shape of a pregnant woman's stomach] Bring both *5 hands* from in front of each side of the body, palms facing in, toward each other, entwining the fingers in front of the stomach.

pregnant[3] *adj.* See sign for STUCK. This sign is used only when referring to an unwanted pregnancy.

prejudice[1] *n.* **1.** An unfavorable opinion or feeling formed without knowledge, thought, or reason.—*v.* **2.** To cause a person to pass judgment, favorably or unfavorably, based on unreasonable feelings or opinions: *Her fear of gaining weight prejudiced her against fat people.* Same sign used for: **bias, biased.**

■ [**mind + against**] With a double movement, tap the extended right index finger, palm facing in, against the right side of the forehead. Then hit the fingertips of the right *B hand* into the left *open hand,* palm facing right and fingers pointing forward.

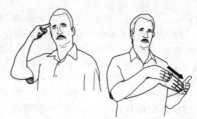

prejudice[2] *n.* See sign for AGAINST.

premeditate *v.* To plan beforehand: *The crime was premeditated.*

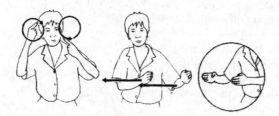

■ [**think**[3] + **plan**[1]] Move both extended index fingers in large alternating circles in front of each side of the forehead. Then move both *open hands* from in front of the left side of the body, palms facing each other and fingers pointing forward, in a long smooth movement to in front of the right side of the body.

preparatory *adj.* Designed to prepare: *a preparatory school.* Shortened form: **prep.**

■ Tap the extended right index finger, palm facing left and finger pointing up, with a double movement against the extended little finger of the left *I hand,* palm facing in.

prepare *v.* To make or get ready: *to prepare a meal; to prepare for the picnic.* Same sign used for: **arrange, in order, organize, sequence, sort.**

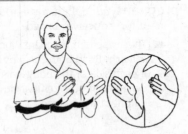

■ Beginning with both *open hands* in front of the left side of the body, palms facing each other and fingers pointing forward, move the hands in double downward arcs to in front of the right side of the body.

prepay *v.* To pay in advance: *We prepaid the shipment.*

■ [**finish**[1,2] + **pay**[1,2]] Beginning with both *5 hands* in front of each side of the chest, palms facing in and fingers pointing up, flip the hands over with a sudden movement, ending with both palms facing down and fingers pointing forward. Then, beginning with the extended right index finger touching the palm of the left *open hand* held in front of the body, palm facing up and fingers pointing right, move the right finger forward off the left fingertips while turning the right palm down, ending with the finger pointing forward.

Presbyterian *adj.* **1.** Designating, pertaining to, or belonging to a Protestant church governed by elders called presbyters: *The Presbyterian minister preaches and administers the sacraments.* —*n.* **2.** A member of a Presbyterian church: *There are Presbyterians throughout North America.*

■ [Initialized sign] Touch the middle finger of the right *P hand,* palm facing in, against the palm of the left *open hand,* palm facing right, with a double movement.

preschool *adj.* **1.** Of or designating children of an age between infancy and five: *preschool children.* —*n.* **2.** School intended for children younger than kindergarten age: *The toddlers attend preschool.*

■ [**pre-**[1] + **school**] Beginning with the left *open hand* in front of the chest, palm facing in and fingers pointing right, and the right *P hand* somewhat closer to the chest, palm facing in, bring the right *P hand* toward the chest. Then clap the palms of *both open hands* together with a double movement in front of the chest.

prescribe *v.* To order or direct a patient to use specific medication: *The doctor prescribed three aspirin per day.* Related form: **prescription** *n.*

■ [order[1] + medicine] Move the extended right index finger, palm facing forward and finger pointing up, forward and down from in front of the mouth, ending with the finger pointing forward and the palm facing down. Then, with the bent middle finger of the right *5 hand* in the palm of the left *open hand,* palms facing each other, rock the right hand from side to side with a double movement while keeping the middle finger in place.

prescription *n.* **1.** A written order by a physician for the preparation of a medicine: *Here is a prescription for an antibiotic that you can get filled at the drugstore.* **2.** Medicine so prepared: *Pick up your prescription from the pharmacy.*

■ [Initialized sign similar to sign for **medicine**] Move the middle finger of the right *P hand,* palm facing down, in a double circular movement in the palm of the left *open hand,* palm facing up.

presence *n.* See sign for FACE[3].

present[1] *n.* See signs for BOX, GIFT[1].

present[2] *adv.* See signs for HERE[1,2], NOW[1,2].

present[3] *v.* See signs for GIVE[1,2,3], GIVE ME[3], INTRODUCE, SUGGEST.

presentation *n.* See sign for SPEAK[2].

preserve *v.* See signs for SAVE[2,3,4]. Related form: **preservation** *n.*

preside over *v. phrase.* See sign for MANAGE.

president *n.* **1.** The chief of state of a republic: *president of the country.* **2.** The chief executive officer of an organization: *a quarterly report from the president of the company.* Same sign used for: **horns, superintendent.**

■ Beginning with the index-finger sides of both *C hands* near each side of the forehead, palms facing forward, move the hands outward to above each shoulder while closing into *S hands.*

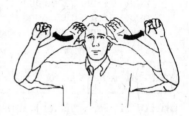

press *n.* See signs for NEWSPAPER, PRINT.

pressure *n.* **1.** Continued weight or force: *There is too much pressure on the shelf from all the books.* **2.** Stress; strain: *an executive job with a lot of pressure.* Same sign used for: **repress, repression, stress, suppress, suppression.**

■ [Demonstrates the action of applying pressure] Push the palm of the right *5 hand*, palm facing down, on the index-finger side of the left *S hand*, palm facing in, forcing the left hand downward.

presto *adv.* Quickly, as if by magic; suddenly; immediately: *Presto, the rabbit popped out of the hat.*

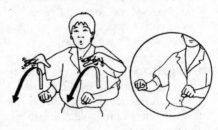

■ [The hands seem to cast a spell] Move both *S hands* from in front of each side of the body, palms facing down, upward while opening into *5 hands* and wiggling the fingers, and then quickly down again, forming *S hands* again in front of each side of the body.

presumptuous *adj.* Characterized by excessive boldness; taking too much for granted: *He was presumptuous to think I would give him half.*

■ [**excess** + **fake**[1,2]] Beginning with the fingers of the right *bent hand* on the back of the left *bent hand*, both palms facing down, bring the right hand upward. Then, beginning with the index finger of the right *4 hand* touching the right side of the forehead, palm facing left, move the hand forward in a circular movement.

pretend[1] *v.* **1.** To claim falsely: *Don't pretend that you're having fun when you're not.* **2.** To make believe: *Let's pretend we're in a spaceship.*

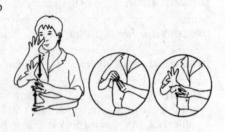

■ Beginning with the right *5 hand* in front of the face, palm facing down, and the left *curved 5 hand* in front of the body, palm facing up, bring the hands together in front of the chest while closing the fingers and then opening them again near each other.

pretend[2] *v.* See sign for FOOL[1].

pretty *adj.* See signs for BEAUTIFUL[1,2].

prevailing *adj.* See signs for NOW[1,2].

prevent *v.* To keep from happening: *a cream that helps to prevent sunburn.* Same sign used for: **ban, barrier, block, blockage, hinder, impair, obstruct.**

- [The hands seem to shield the body with a barrier] With the little-finger side of the right *B hand,* palm facing down, against the index-finger side of the left *B hand,* palm facing right, move the hands forward a short distance.

preview *v.* **1.** To view or show beforehand: *to preview the movie.* —*n.* **2.** An advance showing, as of scenes from a movie: *went to a preview of the new film.*

- [**see**[1] + **before**[1]] Bring the fingers of the right *V hand* from pointing at the eyes, palm facing in, forward a short distance. Then, beginning with the back of the right *open hand,* palm facing in and fingers pointing left, touching the palm of the left *open hand,* palm facing in and fingers pointing right, move the right hand back toward the right shoulder.

previous[1] *adj.* Occurring, existing, or coming before something else: *The previous owner has the key.*

- [The hand indicates a time in the past] Tap the fingertips of the right *bent hand* on the right shoulder with a double movement.

previous[2] *adj.* See signs for BEFORE[1], FORMER, PRE-[1].

price *n.* See signs for COST[1,2].

priceless *adj.* Having extremely high value; valued beyond a conceivable price: *a priceless piece of jewelry; priceless works of art.*

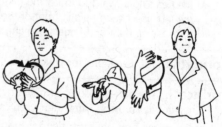

- [**important**[1,2] + **wow**[1,2]] Beginning with the fingertips of both *F hands* touching in front of the chest, palms facing each other, bring the hands upward in a circular movement, ending with the index-finger sides of the *F hands* touching. Then, beginning with the right *5 hand* in front of the right shoulder, palm facing in and fingers pointing left, shake the hand loosely up and down from the wrist with a double movement.

prick *n. Vulgar Slang.* See sign for PENIS[2].

prick up one's ears *v. phrase.* To pay attention; become alert: *He pricked up his ears when he heard his name mentioned.*

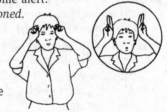

- ■ [Demonstrates a horse's ears standing erect, supposedly in order to hear better] With the thumbs holding down the index and middle fingers of both hands near each side of the forehead, palms facing forward, suddenly extend the index fingers and middle fingers of both hands upward.

pride *n.* See sign for PROUD.

priest[1] *n.* A member of the clergy of a Christian church: *a Catholic priest.*

- ■ [Shows the shape and location of a priest's collar] Move the index-finger side of the right *G hand*, palm facing left, from the left side of the neck around to the right side.

priest[2] *n.* A clergyman of an ancient church: *an Old Testament priest.* Same sign used for: **pastor.**

- ■ [Shows the shape of part of early priest's garments] Beginning with both extended index fingers touching near the middle of the chest, palms facing in, move the fingers to each side of the chest and, then, straight down.

prim *adj.* See signs for FANCY[1,2], POLITE[1,2], SOPHISTICATED.

prime *n.* The period of life when one has the combined advantages of vigor and experience: *She's in her 40s and in her prime.*

- ■ [**my** + **top**] Bring the palm of the right *open hand* against the chest, palm facing in and fingers pointing left. Then bring the palm of the right *open hand* from near the right side of the head downward to touch the fingertips of the left *open hand* held in front of the chest, palm facing right and fingers pointing up.

primitive *adj.* See signs for LONG AGO[1].

prince[1] *n.* The son of a king or queen: *The young prince will one day rule the country.* Same sign used for: **princess.**

- ■ [Initialized sign similar to sign for **king**] Beginning with the middle finger of the right *P hand* touching the upper left side of the chest, palm facing in, move the hand downward to touch the middle finger again near the right hip.

prince[2] *n.* (alternate sign)

- [**boy**[1] + **prince**[1]] Beginning with the thumb side of the right *flattened C hand* in front of the right side of the forehead, bring the hand forward while closing the fingers to the thumb. Then, beginning with the middle finger of the right *P hand* touching the upper left side of the chest, palm facing in, bring the hand down to touch the finger near the right hip.

princess[1] *n.* The daughter of a king or queen: *The young princess is well prepared to become queen.*

- [Initialized sign following the shape of bodice and sash worn by a princess] Beginning with the middle finger of the right *P hand* touching the upper left side of the chest, palm facing in, touch the finger again on the right side of the chest and then on the right hip.

princess[2] *n.* (alternate sign)

- [**girl**[1] + **prince**[1]] Move the thumb of the right *A hand,* palm facing left, downward on the right cheek to the right side of the chin. Then, beginning with the middle finger of the right *P hand* touching the upper left side of the chest, palm facing in, bring the hand down to touch the finger near the right hip.

princess[3] *n.* See sign for PRINCE[1].

principal *n.* The head of an elementary or secondary school: *Teachers report to the school principal.*

- [Initialized sign] Move the right *P hand,* palm facing down, in a small circle above the left *open hand,* palm facing down, ending with the middle finger of the right hand on the back of the left hand.

principle *n.* **1.** A fundamental truth: *Space travel is based on sound scientific principles.* **2.** A rule of conduct; standard for moral behavior: *We must live according to principles of decency.* Same sign used for: **policy.**

- [Initialized sign similar to sign for **law**] Touch the index-finger side of the right *P hand,* palm facing down, first against the fingers and then against the heel of the left *open hand,* palm facing forward and fingers pointing up.

print *v.* To reproduce on a printing press or equivalent device: *The journal plans to print the article.* See also sign for NEWSPAPER. Same sign used for: **press, publish.**

- [The fingers seem to set movable type for printing] Bring the thumb side of the right *G hand*, palm facing down, against the left *open hand*, palm facing up, while pinching the right index finger and thumb together as the hand moves toward the heel of the left hand. For the noun form, the sign is the same except made with a double movement.

printer *n.* A person whose profession is printing: *a printer who produces books using computer technology.* Same sign used for: **publisher.**

- [print + person marker] Bring the thumb side of the right *G hand*, palm facing down, against the left *open hand*, palm facing up, while pinching the right index finger and thumb together as the hand moves toward the heel of the left hand. Then move both hands, palms facing each other, downward along each side of the body.

printing press *n.* A machine for transferring ink to paper from type, plates, etc.: *We will have the book printed on a two-color rotary printing press.*

- [print + a gesture showing the action of a press opening and closing] Bring the thumb side of the right *G hand*, palm facing down, against the left *open hand*, palm facing up, and pinch the right thumb and index finger together with a double movement. Then, beginning with the palms of both *open hands* together in front of the body, fingers pointing in opposite directions, raise the right hand upward while turning the palm in with a double movement.

printout *n.* Computer output printed on paper: *He used the printout as a guide for his speech.*

- Beginning with the thumb of the right *G hand* on the heel of the left *open hand*, tap the right index finger down to the thumb with a double movement. Then, beginning with the right *flattened O hand* inserted in the palm side of the left *C hand*, bring the right hand upward.

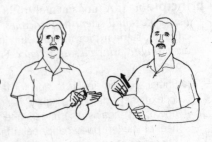

prior to *prep.* See signs for BEFORE[1,2,3]

priority *n.* Something given the right to precede other things in order of importance: *to keep your priorities in proper order.* Related form: **prioritize** *v.*

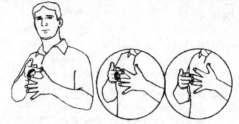

■ [Initialized sign touching each item on a list showing the order of priorities] Touch the middle finger of the right *P hand,* palm facing in, first to the thumb, then the index finger, and then the middle finger of the left *5 hand* held in front of the body, palm facing right and fingers pointing forward.

prison *n.* See signs for JAIL[1,2].

prisoner *n.* See sign for CONVICT[1].

private *adj.* See sign for SECRET. Related form: **privacy** *n.*

private eye *n. Informal.* See sign for DETECTIVE.

privilege *n.* See signs for PERMIT[1], RIGHT[2].

prize *n.* See sign for MEDAL.

probable *adj.* See sign for DOUBT[3]. Related form: **probability** *n.*

probably *adv.* See sign for MAYBE. Related forms: **probability** *n.,* **probable** *adj.*

probation *n.* See sign for TORTURE.

problem[1] *n.* Something that presents a difficulty and requires a solution: *a student having a problem with money.*

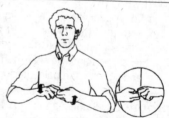

■ Beginning with the knuckles of both *bent V hands* touching in front of the chest, twist the hands in opposite directions with a deliberate movement, rubbing the knuckles against each other.

problem[2] *n.* See sign for DIFFICULT.

procedure *n.* A method or course of action: *Follow the procedure for submitting your expense report.* Related form: **procedural** *adj.* Same sign used for: **pace, process, progress, take steps.**

■ [Represents the progression of activities in a procedure] Beginning with both *open hands* in front of the body, palms facing in, left fingers pointing right and right fingers pointing left, and the right hand closer to the chest than the left hand, move the right over the left hand and then the left over the right hand in an alternating movement.

proceed

proceed *v.* See sign for GO ON¹.

procession¹ *n.* A body of persons, vehicles, etc., marching or moving forward in ceremonial order: *a wedding procession.*

- [Represents people marching in a procession] Beginning with both *4 hands* in front of the chest, left hand somewhat forward of the right hand, palms facing forward, and fingers pointing up, move the hands smoothly forward.

procession² *n.* See sign for MARCH.

proclaim *v.* See sign for ANNOUNCE. Related form: **proclamation** *n.*

procrastinate¹ *v.* To put off action until a later time; delay: *If a student procrastinates, it becomes more difficult to do the homework.*

- [The hand seems to put something off time and time again] Beginning with the fingertips of the right *F hand* touching the fingertips of the left *F hand,* palms facing each other, move the right hand forward in a series of small arcs.

procrastinate² *v.* See sign for DEFER¹.

produce *v.* **1.** To bring about; cause to exist: *Study will produce better grades.* **2.** To manufacture: *The factory produces cars.* **3.** To grow: *These farms produce wheat.*

- [Initialized sign similar to sign for **make**] Beginning with the little-finger side of the right *P hand* on the index-finger side of the left *P hand,* palms facing in, twist the hands so that the fingers point forward, ending with the palms facing in opposite directions.

product *n.* Same sign as for PRODUCE but made with a double movement. Related form: **production** *n.*

profession *n.* An occupation requiring special training: *to work in the legal profession.* Related form: **professional** *n., adj.*

- [Initialized sign similar to sign for **specialize**¹] Move the middle finger of the right *P hand,* palm facing down, from the base of the index finger of the left *B hand,* palm facing right and fingers pointing forward, to its tip.

professor *n.* See sign for TEACHER.

proficient *adj.* See signs for GOOD AT, SKILL.

profile *n.* A side view of the contour of a human face: *The actor was noted for his strong profile.*

- [The shape of a profile] Move the side of the extended right index finger, palm facing down and finger pointing left, from the forehead along the nose, mouth, and chin of the face.

profit *n.* The monetary gain made from a business or a particular transaction: *The business won't survive if it doesn't make a profit.* Same sign used for: **gain, gross.**

- [The hand seems to put a profit into one's pocket] Move the right *F hand*, palm facing down, downward with a double movement near the right side of the chest.

program[1] *n.* **1.** A plan of what is to be done or accomplished: *a new school program for gifted children.* **2.** A sequence of coded instructions for a computer: *wrote a program for sorting files by date.*

- [Initialized sign] Move the middle finger of the right *P hand*, palm facing left, from the fingertips to the base of the left *open hand*, palm facing right and fingers pointing up. Repeat the movement on the back side of the left hand.

program[2] *n.* (alternate sign)

- [Initialized sign] Move the middle finger of the right *P hand*, palm facing left, from the base to the fingertips of the palm of the left *open hand*, palm facing right and fingers pointing up, and then down the back of the left hand.

progress *n.* See sign for PROCEDURE.

prohibit *v.* See sign for FORBID.

project *n.* An undertaking: *plans to complete the project by March.*

- [Abbreviation **p-j** similar to sign for **program**[1]] Move the middle finger of the right *P hand*, palm facing left, from the fingertips to the base of the palm of the left *open hand*, palm facing right and fingers pointing up. Then move the right extended little finger from the fingertips to the base of the back of the left hand.

projection television *n.* A television with a large picture display produced by a beam of light that takes a small picture and displays it as a much larger size: *The family room had a projection TV.*

- **[T-V + wide + flash]** Form a *T* and a *V* with the right hand. Hold both *open hands* away from each shoulder, palms facing each other. Then, beginning with the right *flattened O hand* in front of the right shoulder, palm facing forward, flick the fingers open with a quick movement.

projector *n.* A machine for projecting an image on a screen: *a movie projector.*

- [Represents the light coming from a projector] Beginning with the index-finger side of the *flattened O hand*, palm facing left, against the palm of the left *open hand*, palm facing forward and finger pointing up, move the right hand forward while opening the fingers into a *curved hand.*

prolong *v.* See sign for EXAGGERATE.

prominent *adj.* See signs for ADVANCED, CHIEF[1].

promiscuous[1] *adj.* Characterized by or having casual sexual relations with many persons: *It is becoming increasingly dangerous to be promiscuous.*

- [Represents jumping from bed to bed] Move the right *bent V hand* from in front of the right side of the body, palm facing down, in an arc to in front of the body, and then to in front of the left side of the body.

promiscuous[2] *adj.* (alternate sign)

- [Represents going from one person to another] Move the right *bent V hand* in an arc from the thumb to the little fingers of the left *5 hand* held in front of the chest, palms facing each other.

promise[1] *n.* **1.** Something said or written that binds a person to do or not do something: *I hope you keep your promise to stay in touch.* —*v.* **2.** To pledge; give one's word: *Promise you'll come back.* See also sign for VOW[1]. Same sign used for: **affirm, commit, guarantee, obligate, obligation, pledge, warranty.**

- [**true** + a gesture seeming to seal a promise in the hand] Bring the extended right index finger, palm facing left and finger pointing up, from in front of the lips downward, changing into an *open hand* and placing the palm of the right hand on the index-finger side of the left *S hand* held in front of the body, palm facing right.

promise[2] *v.* See sign for SWEAR[1].

promote[1] *v.* To raise in importance; advance: *promoted to a new job.* Related form: **promotion** *n.* Same sign used for: **rank.**

- [**advanced** formed with a repeated movement to indicate levels of promotion] Move both *bent hands*, palms facing each other, from near each side of the head upward in a series of deliberate arcs.

promote[2] *v.* See sign for ADVANCED. Related form: **promotion** *n.*

prompt[1] *adj.* Quick or on time: *a prompt response.* Same sign used for: **punctual.**

- [**fast**[1] + **on** + **time**[2]] Beginning with the thumbs of both *A hands* tucked under the index fingers, palms facing each other in front of the body, flick the thumbs out while twisting the wrists quickly forward. Next bring the palm of the right *open hand* downward across the back of the left *open hand* held in front of the body, both palms facing down. Then tap the index finger of the right *X hand*, palm facing down, with a double movement on the wrist of the left *open hand* held across the body, palm facing down.

prompt[2] *n.* See sign for CURSOR.

promptly *adv.* See sign for REGULAR[1].

prone *adj.* See signs for CATCH[3], TEND.

pronounce[1] *v.* To articulate the sounds, words, sentences, etc., of speech: *Pronounce your words carefully.*

- [Initialized sign similar to sign for **say**[2]] Move the middle finger of the right *P hand*, palm facing in, upward in front of the lips in a double movement.

pronounce[2] *v.* See sign for SAY[2]. Related form: **pronunciation** *n.*

proof *n.* Evidence establishing the truth or believability of something: *to show some proof that they can do the job.* Related form: **prove** *v.* Same sign used for: **evidence.**

- [The hand seems to bring something forward to present to another as proof] Move the fingertips of the right *open hand*, palm facing in, from in front of the mouth downward, ending with the back of the right hand on the palm of the left *open hand*, both palms facing up in front of the chest.

propaganda *n.* See sign for ADVERTISE.

propeller[1] *n.* A device with motorized revolving blades: *the helicopter's propeller.* Related forms: **propel** *v.*, **propellant** *n.*

■ [**circle**[1] + **fan**[3]] Move the extended right index finger in a large circle in front of the right side of the body, palm facing left and finger pointing forward. Then, beginning with the extended left index finger, palm facing in and finger pointing right, touching the palm of the right *5 hand,* palm facing left, twist the right hand downward with a double movement.

propeller[2] *n.* (alternate sign) Related forms: **propel** *v.*, **propellant** *n.*

■ [Shows the action of twin propellers on a plane] Move both extended index fingers, palms facing down and fingers pointing forward, in large circles moving in opposite directions in front of each side of the body while puffing out the cheeks.

proper *adj.* See signs for APPROPRIATE, FANCY[1,2]. Related form: **properly** *adv.*

property[1] *n.* The body of things one owns: *That radio is my property!*

■ [Initialized sign similar to sign for **thing**[1]] Move the right *P hand,* palm facing down, from in front of the body in an arc to the right.

property[2] *n.* See sign for LAND[1].

prophecy *n.* See signs for FATE, PREDICT[1,2].

prophet *n.* One who speaks for God or by divine inspiration: *the Old Testament prophets.*

■ [**predict**[1,2] + **person marker**] Beginning with the fingers of the right *V hand* pointing to each eye, move the right hand forward under the palm of the left *open hand,* turning the right hand as it moves and ending with the right fingers pointing forward. Then move both *open hands,* palms facing each other, downward along the sides of the body.

proportion *n.* See sign for ACCORDING TO[1].

proposal[1] *n.* A formal plan or suggestion: *She presented her proposal to the board of directors.* Related form: **propose** *v.*

- [Initialized sign similar to sign for **suggest**] Beginning with both *P hands* in front of each side of the body, palms facing each other, move the hands upward and forward in simultaneous arcs.

proposal[2] *n.* See signs for NOMINATE[2], SUGGEST. Related form: **propose** *v.*

prose[1] *n.* Spoken or written language that is not poetry; discourse: *a reporter who writes excellent prose.*

- [**write**[1,2,3] + **long**] Slide the fingertips of the right *flattened O hand* from the heel off the fingertips of the open left palm with a double movement, palms facing each other. Then move the extended right index finger from the wrist up the length of the extended left arm to near the shoulder.

prose[2] *n.* See signs for STORY[1,2].

prosecute[1] *v.* To pursue a civil or criminal action against. Related form: **prosecution** *n.* Same sign used for: **suit.**

- Move the fingers of the right *V hand,* palm facing forward, downward on each side of the extended left index finger, pointing up in front of the chest. Then hit the fingertips of the right *B hand* into the left *open hand,* palm right and fingers pointing forward.

prosecute[2] *v.* See sign for TORTURE. Related form: **prosecution** *n.*

prospector *n.* A person who searches a region for valuable ore: *The prospector hunted for gold.*

- [**pry**[1] + **person marker**] Bring the extended right index finger, palm facing forward, from in front of the face downward in a large arc, changing into an *X hand* and touching the palm of the left *open hand* held in front of the body, palm facing up. Next scratch the index finger of the right *X hand* with a double movement from the fingers to the heel of the left palm with a double movement. Then move both *open hands,* palms facing each other, downward along each side of the body.

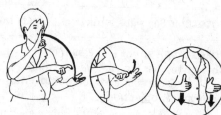

prosper[1] *v.* To be successful; thrive: *to prosper in business.* Related form: **prosperity** *n.*

■ [**grow** + **big**[1]] Bring the right *flattened O hand,* palm facing in and fingers pointing up, upward through the left *C hand,* palm facing right, while spreading the right fingers into a *curved 5 hand* in front of the chest. Then, beginning with both *modified C hands* together in front of the chest, palms facing each other, bring the hands apart, ending in front of each shoulder.

prosper[2] *v.* See sign for SUCCESSFUL.

prosperous *adj.* See sign for RICH.

prostitute *n.* A person who has sexual relations with others for money: *prostitutes loitering on the street corner.* Same sign used for: **whore.**

■ Twist the back of the fingers of the right *bent hand,* palm facing back, forward on the right side of the chin with a double movement, changing into an *open hand* each time.

prostrate *adj.* Being weak or helpless: *He was prostrate with illness.*

■ [**apathy** + **sick**[1,2]] Limply hold both *5 hands,* palms facing in and fingers dangling down, in front of each side of the body with the arms extended. Then touch the bent middle finger of the right *5 hand* to the forehead and the bent middle finger of the left *5 hand* to the lower chest, both palms facing in.

protect[1] *v.* To keep safe from harm or injury: *The car seat protected the baby during sudden stops.*

■ [The hands seem to block oneself from harm] With the wrists of both *open hands* crossed in front of the chest, palms facing in opposite directions, move the hands forward a short distance.

protect[2] *v.* See signs for DEFEND[1], GUARD, SHIELD[1]. Related form: **protection** *n.*

protest[1] *n.* A strong expression of objection, dissent, etc.: *He voiced his protest.* Same sign used for: **complaint, grievance, objection.**

■ Strike the fingertips of the right *curved 5 hand* against the center of the chest with a quick double movement.

protest² *n.* **1.** An organized public demonstration against a cause or policy: *Students staged antiwar protests.* —*v.* **2.** To engage in such protests: *to protest company rules.* Same sign used for: **rebel, rebellion, revolt, revolution, strike.**

- [Natural gesture indicating that a person is on strike] Beginning with the right *S hand* in front of the right shoulder, palm facing back, twist the hand sharply forward.

protest³ *v.* See signs for COMPLAIN, PICKET.

Protestant *n.* **1.** A member of any of certain Christian churches other than the Roman Catholic Church: *a group of Protestants at an ecumenical meeting.* —*adj.* **2.** Of or pertaining to the Protestant religion: *the Protestant faith.*

- [Represents a kneeling person] Bring the knuckles of the right bent fingers, palm facing in, with a double movement down on the palm of the left *open hand,* palm angled up.

proud *adj.* Feeling pleased about oneself, one's accomplishments, or the achievements of another: *I'm proud of your efforts.* Related form: **pride** *n.* Same sign used for: **arrogant.**

- Move the thumb of the right *10 hand,* palm facing down, from the center of the lower chest upward with a smooth movement.

prove *v.* See sign for PROOF.

provide *v.* See signs for GIVE¹,²,³, SUGGEST.

provoke *v.* To make angry: *She provoked her sister to anger.*

- [Represents twisting a knife and driving it in] Beginning with the extended right index finger, palm facing up, touching the palm of the left *open hand* held in front of the chest, palm facing right and fingers pointing forward, twist the right hand in toward the chest, turning the palm down. Then move both hands forward while keeping the index finger in place.

prowl *v.* To roam furtively, as to hunt for food or steal something: *The lion prowled through the jungle.*

prune

- [look for[1,2] + sneak[1]] Move the right *C hand*, palm facing left, with a double movement in a circle in front of the face. Then move the extended right index finger, palm facing down and finger pointing forward, in a wiggly forward movement under the palm of the left *curved hand* held across the body, palm facing down and fingers pointing right.

prune *v.* To cut off excess material from: *to prune the bushes.* Same sign used for: **trim.**

- [The left hand represents a tree and the right hand shows trimming it] With the bent left arm held up in front of the left side of the body, palm facing right, move the fingers of the right *V hand*, palm facing left, up the left arm while closing the fingers together with a repeated movement.

pry[1] *v.* To probe improperly; meddle: *to pry into someone's private papers.*

- [The sign represents one's nose extending down to dig in another's business] Bring the extended right index finger from in front of the face, palm facing forward, downward in a large arc, changing into an *X hand* and touching the left *open hand* held in front of the body, palm facing up. Then scratch the index finger of the right *X hand* from the fingers to the heel of the left palm with a double movement.

pry[2] *v.* See sign for NOSY[2].

Psalms *n.* See sign for POEM.

pseudo *adj.* See signs for FAKE[2,3].

psychiatrist[1] *n.* A doctor who diagnoses and treats mental disorders: *The psychiatrist prescribed a tranquilizer.*

- [psychiatry + person marker] Tap the middle finger of the right *P hand*, palm facing left, in the crook between the thumb and index finger of the left *open hand*, palm facing forward, with a double movement. Then move both *open hands*, palms facing each other, downward along each side of the body.

psychiatrist[2] *n.* (alternate sign)

- [Initialized sign similar to sign for **doctor**[2]] Tap the middle finger of the right *P hand* with a double movement on the wrist of the left *open hand*, palm facing up.

psychiatry *n.* The branch of medicine dealing with mental disorders: *to study psychiatry to help people with serious mental illnesses.*

- [Initialized sign similar to sign for **psychology**] Tap the middle finger of the right *P hand*, palm facing left, in the crook between the thumb and index finger of the left *open hand*, palm facing forward, with a double movement.

psychologist *n.* A specialist in psychology: *The psychologist administered a battery of intelligence tests.*

- [**psychology** + **person marker**] Tap the little-finger side of the right *open hand*, palm angled left, in the crook between the thumb and the index finger of the left *open hand*, palm facing forward, with a double movement. Then move both *open hands*, palms facing each other, downward along each side of the body.

psychology *n.* The science dealing with the mind and human behavior: *to study psychology and become a therapist.*

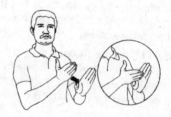

- Tap the little-finger side of the right *open hand*, palm angled left, in the crook between the thumb and the index finger of the left *open hand*, palm facing forward, with a double movement.

public[1] *n.* See signs for HEARING, PEOPLE.

public[2] *adj.* See sign for SAY[2]. Shared idea of public schools as placed where students characteristically can speak.

publication *n.* See sign for NEWSPAPER.

publicize[1] *v.* To give publicity to; advertise: *to publicize the fall dance.* Related form: **publicity** *n.*

- [**print** + **spread**[1]] Bring the thumb side of the right *G hand*, palm facing down, against the left *open hand*, palm facing up, while pinching the right index finger and thumb together with a double movement. Then, beginning with the fingers of both *flattened O hands* touching in front of the body, palms facing down, move the hands outward to each side while opening into *5 hands* in front of each side of the body.

publicize

publicize² *v.* See sign for ADVERTISE. Related form: **publicity** *n.*

publish *v.* See sign for PRINT.

publisher *n.* See sign for PRINTER.

puddle *n.* A small pool of water, especially rainwater: *Try to avoid stepping in a puddle.* Same sign used for: **pond.**

- [**water** + indicating the size of a puddle] Tap the index-finger side of the right *W hand*, palm facing left, against the chin with a double movement. Then move both *modified C hands*, palms facing each other, downward in front of the chest a short distance.

puff *n.* **1.** A short, quick blast of air, wind, smoke, etc.: *A puff of wind messed my hair.* —*v.* **2.** To send forth a short, quick blast of air: *He huffed and he puffed and he blew the house down.* **3.** To inflate with air: *to puff up your cheeks.* Related form: **puffy** *adj.* Same sign used for: **swollen.**

- [Indicates the shape of puffed cheeks] Beginning with both *O hands* near each side of the chin, palms facing each other, open the fingers into *curved 5 hands* near each cheek while puffing out the cheeks.

pug nose *n.* A short, turned-up nose: *The baby has a cute little pug nose.*

- [**nose** + pushing on the nose in order to form a pug] Touch the extended right index finger to the nose, palm facing in and fingers pointing up. Then quickly place the fingertips of the right *open hand* against the nose.

pull¹ *v.* To move something by grasping it and drawing it toward oneself: *to pull the wagon up the hill.* Same sign used for: **draw.**

- [Mime pulling something] Beginning with both *modified X hands* in front of the left side of the body, left palm facing up and right palm facing down, move the hands simultaneously to the right side of the body in a large arc, ending with both palms facing down.

pull² *v.* See signs for DRAG, HAUL¹.

pull someone's tooth *v. phrase.* To remove a tooth forcefully from someone's mouth: *The dentist pulled my broken tooth.*

■ [Mime pulling a tooth] Beginning with the right *S hand* near the right corner of the mouth, palm facing forward, pull the hand deliberately forward and outward a short distance.

pull the trigger *v. phrase.* See sign for TRIGGER[1].

pulse[1] *n.* The beating of the heart as reflected in the regular throbbing of the arteries: *a rapid pulse.* Related form: **pulsate** *v.* Same sign used for: **palpitate, throb.**

■ [heart[1] + demonstrate the pounding of a heartbeat] Tap the bent middle finger of the right *5 hand,* palm facing in, with a repeated movement on the left side of the chest. Then, beginning with the right *curved 5 hand* grasping the back of the left *S hand,* both palms facing in, move the right hand up and down with a short double movement.

pulse[2] *n.* (alternate sign) Same sign used for: **palpitate, throb.**

■ [Mime taking one's pulse] Place the fingertips of the right *flattened O hand,* palm facing down, on the unturned left wrist.

pulse[3] *n.* An abrupt change in voltage: *a negative pulse of electricity.*

■ [Shows the shape of a heartbeat on a graph] Move the extended right index finger from in front of the chest, palm facing down and finger pointing forward, straight outward to the right with a short movement upward and then straight outward again.

pumice *n.* An abrasive volcanic stone used for polishing: *Pumice is used to polish metal.* Same sign used for: **emery board, nail file.**

■ [Represents filing one's nails on pumice] Move the fingertips of the left *curved hand* downward with a repeated movement on the knuckles of the right *curved hand,* both palms facing in.

pump *n.* A machine used for forcing liquids or gases into or out of something: *a water pump.*

■ [Mime using a water pump] With the right elbow extended, move the right *A hand,* palm facing in, up and down in front of the right side of the body with a double movement.

pumpkin *n.* A large, round, edible, orange-colored fruit, the shell of which is traditionally carved into a jack-o'-lantern: *to carve a pumpkin at Halloween.* Same sign used for: **melon.**

- [Represents testing a pumpkin's ripeness by thumping it] With a double movement, flick the middle finger of the right *8 hand*, palm facing down, off the back of the left *S hand*, palm facing down, bouncing the right hand up slightly each time.

punch *n.* **1.** A hard, thrusting blow with the fists: *grew angry and gave the wall a resounding punch.* —*v.* **2.** To hit with the fists: *punched him in the eye.* Same sign used for: **hit.**

- [Mime giving a punch] Beginning with the right *S hand* in front of the right shoulder, palm facing forward, move the hand upward and forward in a large arc.

punctual *adj.* See sign for PROMPT[1].

punctuation *n.* **1.** The use of periods, commas, and other conventional symbols in printing or writing to clarify meanings and separate elements: *Artful punctuation is a sign of good writing.* **2.** The symbols used in punctuation; punctuation marks: *Use less punctuation in informal writing.* Related form: **punctuate** *v.* Same sign used for: **exclamation point.**

- [Draw an exclamation mark in the air] Move the right *modified X hand*, palm facing forward, from near the right side of the head downward to in front of the right shoulder and then forward a short distance.

punish *v.* To deal with severely, as by forcing to undergo pain, confinement, or death: *The justice system will punish the criminal.* Same sign used for: **penalize, penalty.**

- Strike the extended right index finger, palm facing left, downward across the elbow of the left bent arm.

puny *adj.* See signs for NOTHING[4], TINY[1,2].

pupil[1] *n.* A young student, as in school or learning under a private tutor: *The shorter pupils sat in the front row.*

- [Initialized sign similar to sign for **school**] Tap the index-finger side of the right *P hand*, palm facing down, with a double movement against the palm of the left *open hand* held in front of the left side of the chest, palm facing right and fingers pointing up.

pupil[2] *n.* The opening in the center of the iris of the eye, which expands and contracts to allow light to enter: *dilated pupils.*

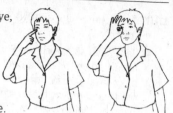

- ■ [**eye**[1] + the shape of one's pupil in the eye] Point the extended right index finger to the right eye, palm facing in. Then place the thumb side of the right *F hand,* palm facing left, in front of the right eye.

pupil[3] *n.* See sign for STUDENT.

puppet[1] *n.* A small movable doll manipulated by rods, wires, etc., to emulate a living creature: *to watch the puppets in the show.* Same sign used for: **marionette.**

- ■ [Mime the action of moving a puppet's strings] With the bent middle fingers of both *5 hands* pointing down in front of each side of the chest, palms facing down, move the hands up and down with an alternating movement in front of each side of the chest.

puppet[2] *n.* (alternate sign) Same sign used for: **marionette.**

- ■ [Mime pulling the strings of a marionette] Move both *F hands,* palms facing forward, up and down with a repeated alternating movement in front of each side of the chest.

puppy *n.* A young dog: *You may gently pet the puppy.*

- ■ [**baby**[1] + **dog**[1,2,3]] With the bent right arm cradled on the bent left arm, both palms facing up, swing the arms from left to right in front of the body with a double movement. Then, with a double movement, snap the right thumb gently off the right middle finger, palm facing up, in front of the right side of the chest.

purchase *v.* See sign for BUY.

pure[1] *adj.* **1.** Perfectly clean; free from contaminants: *pure water.* **2.** Free from adulterating matter: *pure platinum.* **3.** Innocent; wholesome; undefiled: *a pure mind.* Related forms: **purification** *n.,* **purify** *v.*

- ■ [Initialized sign similar to sign for **clean**] Move the middle finger of the right *P hand* from the heel to off the fingertips of the upturned left *open hand.*

pure[2] *adj.* (alternate sign) Related forms: **purification** *n.*, **purify** *v.*

- [Initialized sign + **clean**] Form a right *P hand*, palm facing down, near the heel of the left *open hand*, palm facing up in front of the chest. Then, as the right hand moves down, change to a right *open hand* and wipe it across the left palm from the heel to off the fingertips.

pure[3] *adj.* See sign for CLEAN.

purge *v.* **1.** To make clean; rid of undesirable elements: *to purge the chemical mixture of all impurities.* **2.** To free of difficult or troublesome people, activities, etc.: *to purge the office of petty thieves.* Same sign used for: **remove.**

- [Similar to sign for **remove**[1] except mime throwing whatever is removed over the shoulder] Bring the fingertips of the right *curved 5 hand*, palm facing down, downward to the palm of the left *open hand* held in front of the body, palm facing up, while closing the right hand into an *A hand* as it lands on the left palm. Then bring the right hand upward in a large arc while twisting the palm backward and opening the fingers into a *5 hand* as it goes over the right shoulder.

purify *v.* To make pure: *to purify the water.* Related form: **purification** *n.*

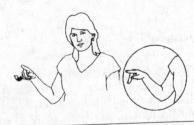

- [**water** + **dissolve**] Tap the index-finger side of the right *W hand* with a double movement against the chin, palm facing left and fingers pointing up. Then, beginning with both *curved 5 hands* in front of the chest, palms facing up, move the hands outward to in front of each side of the chest while smoothly moving the thumb of each hand across each fingertip, starting with the little fingers and ending as *flattened O hands* in front of each side of the body.

purple *n.* **1.** A dark color made by mixing red and blue: *You can tell from my outfit that I like purple.* —*adj.* **2.** Of a purple color: *a purple dress.*

- [Initialized sign] Shake the right *P hand*, palm facing down, back and forth in front of the right side of the body with a double movement.

purpose *n.* See signs for INTEND[1,2].

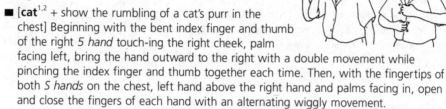

purr *n.* **1.** The low vibrating sound that a cat makes, as when pleased: *I love to listen to the cat's purr.* —*v.* **2.** To make this sound: *The cat sat on my lap and purred.*

■ [**cat**[1,2] + show the rumbling of a cat's purr in the chest] Beginning with the bent index finger and thumb of the right *5 hand* touch-ing the right cheek, palm facing left, bring the hand outward to the right with a double movement while pinching the index finger and thumb together each time. Then, with the fingertips of both *S hands* on the chest, left hand above the right hand and palms facing in, open and close the fingers of each hand with an alternating wiggly movement.

purse[1] *n.* A bag or rigid case, often with a handle or strap, for carrying personal articles, as a wallet or cosmetics; handbag: *to carry a purse.* See also sign for POCKETBOOK. Same sign used for: **luggage, suitcase.**

■ [Mime holding a purse] Shake the right *S hand,* palm facing left, up and down near the right side of the waist with the elbow bent.

purse[2] *n.* (alternate sign) See also sign for POCKETBOOK.

■ [Shows holding a purse under one's arm] Tap the fingertips of the right *bent hand,* palm facing back, under the right armpit with a double movement.

pursue *v.* See signs for APPROACH[1], CHASE.

pus[1] *n.* A thick yellowish fluid found in infected sores, abscesses, etc.: *The doctor cleaned the pus from the wound before applying the bandage.*

■ [**skin**[2] + a gesture indicating pus coming out of a boil] Pinch the right cheek with the index finger and thumb of the right *A hand* and shake slightly. Then, beginning with the index-finger side of the right *S hand* touching the right side of the chin, palm facing forward, thrust the fingers open.

pus[2] *n.* (alternate sign)

■ [**skin**[2] + a gesture indicating pus coming out of a boil] Pinch the right cheek with the index finger and thumb of the right *A hand* and shake lightly. Then, beginning with the fingertips of the right *O hand* touching the right side of the chin, bring the hand forward in a small arc, turning the palm up while opening the fingers into a *curved hand.*

push

push[1] *v.* **1.** To press against something in order to move it: *Push the stuck door harder.* **2.** To move something by pushing: *to push the cart.* See also signs for SHOVE[1,2].

- [Mime pushing something] Move the palms of both *open hands,* palms facing forward, with a deliberate movement forward in front of the chest.

push[2] *v.* See sign for NUDGE.

push down[1] *v. phrase.* To exert pressure to force something down: *to push down on the trash to compact it in the garbage bag.*

- [Demonstrates action of pushing down on something] With the palm of the right *open hand* on the thumb side of the left *S hand,* move both hands downward in front of the chest.

push down[2] *v. phrase.* (alternate sign)

- [Demonstrates action of pushing down] With the palm of the right *5 hand* on the palm of the left *open hand,* push the left hand downward.

pushpin *n.* See signs for PIN[2,3], THUMBTACK[1,2].

put *v.* To move into a particular location; place: *Put away the toys. Put down the package.* Same sign used for: **install, mount, place, set.**

- [The hands seem to take an object and put it in another location] Beginning with both *flattened O hands* in front of the body, palms facing down, move the hands upward and forward in a small arc.

put aside *v. phrase.* See signs for ASIDE[1,2].

put away *v. phrase.* See signs for ASIDE[1,2].

put clothes on *v. phrase.* See sign for SLIP[3].

put down[1] *v. phrase.* To write down: *Put down my address.* Same sign used for: **document, record.**

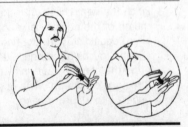

- [The hand seems to put something on a list] Touch the fingertips of the right *flattened O hand,* palm facing down, to the palm of the left *open hand,* palm facing up. Then slap the palm of the right *open hand* against the left palm.

put down[2] *v. phrase.* To pay as a deposit: *to put down some money on the car.*

- ■ [Represents putting a stack of money down as a deposit] Move the right *curved 3 hand,* palm facing forward, from in front of the chest in an arc over the back of the left *open hand,* palm facing down and fingers pointing right.

put down[3] *Slang.* See sign for INSULT[1].

put off *v. phrase.* See signs for DEFER[1], POSTPONE.

put on a ring *v. phrase.* To place a ring on one's finger: *She put on the engagement ring.*

- ■ [Mime putting on a ring] Push the bent thumb and middle finger of the right *5 hand* from in front of the right shoulder, palm facing left, down to the base of the ring finger of the left *5 hand* held in front of the chest, palm facing in.

put on a jacket, coat, etc. *v. phrase.*

- ■ [Represents putting on a jacket] Touch the fingertips of both *flattened O hands* to each side of the upper chest, palms facing in. Then bring them downward to touch again near each other at the waist.

putrid *adj.* See sign for STINK[1].

putt *v.* **1.** To strike a golf ball gently so as to make it roll on the green into the hole: *to practice putting on the green.* —*n.* **2.** A golf stroke made by putting: *an accurate putt.*

- ■ [Mime swinging a putter (golf club)] With both *A hands* held near each other in front of the waist, right arm extended, left arm bent slightly, and both palms facing in, swing the hands slightly to the left, miming a golf putt.

putter *n.* Same sign as for PUTT but made with a double movement.

put together *v. phrase.* See signs for ASSEMBLE[1,2].

putty *n.* A mixture used for fastening panes of glass in a window or filling small holes in plaster or woodwork: *to seal the hole with putty.*

■ [Mime pushing putty into a hole in the wall] With the thumb of the right *A hand* against the palm of the left *open hand*, palm facing right and fingers pointing up, twist the right hand forward and downward with a double movement.

put up with *v. phrase.* See signs for INSULT[1], PATIENT[1].

puzzle *n.* A problem or game to be solved, put together, filled in, etc.: *Put the pieces in the jigsaw puzzle. She does the Sunday crossword puzzle in ink.* Same sign used for: **jigsaw puzzle.**

■ [Represents fitting the pieces of a puzzle together] Beginning with the extended fingertips of both *H hands* touching in front of the chest, right palm facing forward and left palm facing in, twist the hands in opposite directions to reverse positions with a double movement.

puzzled *adj.* A condition of being confused or perplexed: *You look puzzled about what he said.* Same sign used for: **bewildered, paradox, perplexed, stymied.**

■ [Indicates a question in the mind] Beginning with the extended right index finger in front of the forehead, palm facing forward and finger angled up, bring the back of the right hand against the forehead while bending the finger into an *X hand*.

pyramid *n.* **1.** One of several large stonework structures with a square base and four steep triangular sides coming to a point on the top, as exemplified by the royal tombs of ancient Egypt: *Beautiful gold jewelry was found inside the Egyptian pyramids.* **2.** A solid form shaped like a pyramid: *a small pyramid worn as a charm.*

■ [Shows the shape of a pyramid from all directions] Move both *open hands* from in front of each side of the chest, palms angled toward each other, upward until the fingertips touch in front of the face. Then, beginning with the right *open hand* forward of the chest and the left *open hand* near the chest, palms facing each other, bring the hands upward again at an angle until the fingertips touch in front of the face.

quail *n.* A plump game bird: *to hunt for quail.*

- Move the fingertips of the right *V hand* against the right side of the neck with a double movement, palm facing down.

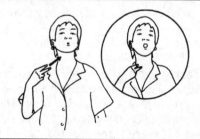

quaint *adj.* See sign for OLD.

quake *n.* See sign for THUNDER[2].

Quaker *n.* A member of the Society of Friends, a religious body that believes in direct inward understanding of God and is concerned with social reform: *Quakers hold meetings at which everyone may speak if led inwardly.*

- [Natural gesture used while waiting for inward spiritual guidance] With the fingers of both hands entwined in front of the waist, palms facing each other, twirl the thumbs around each other with a double movement.

qualification *n.* A characteristic or accomplishment that fits someone for a job, office, award, etc.: *The interviewee has good qualifications for the job.* Related form: **qualify** *v.*

- [Initialized sign similar to sign for **character**[1]] Move the right *Q hand* in a small circle and then back against the right side of the chest, palm facing down.

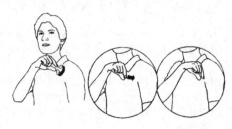

quarrel *v.* See signs for ARGUE[1,2].

quarter[1] *n.* **1.** One of the four equal periods of play in certain games: *losing by 12 after the third quarter.* **2.** One of four terms of instruction in a school year: *my grades for the first quarter.*

- [Initialized sign] Move the right *Q hand,* palm facing down, in a small downward circle in front of the right side of the body with a double movement.

quarter[2] *n.* A coin equal to one-fourth of a dollar: *change for a quarter.* Same sign used for: **twenty-five cents.**

■ **[cent + twenty-five]** Beginning with the extended right index finger touching the right side of the forehead, palm facing left and finger pointing up, twist the hand forward while changing into a *5 hand* and wiggle the bent middle finger, palm facing forward.

quarter[3] *n.* See signs for ONE FOURTH[1,2].

quarterly *adj.* **1.** Occurring at the end of each quarter of a year: *the quarterly business report.* —*adv.* **2.** Once each quarter: *The interest is calculated quarterly.* Same sign used for: **every three months.**

■ **[month** formed with a **three** handshape] Move the right *3 hand,* palm facing in, with a double movement down the thumbside of the extended left index finger pointing up in front of the chest, palm facing right.

quasi *adj.* See sign for SEEM.

queen *n.* **1.** A woman who rules a country; female sovereign: *the Queen of England.* **2.** The wife of a king: *The king asked her to become his queen.*

■ [Initialized sign similar to sign for **king**] Move the right *Q hand,* palm facing left, from touching the left side of the chest near the shoulder, downward to touch again near the right side of the waist.

queer[1] *adj.* See sign for STRANGE.

queer[2] *adj., n. Disparaging and offensive.* See signs for GAY[1], HOMOSEXUAL[1].

quell *v.* To suppress or subdue: *to quell the storm.*

■ **[silent + settle]** Beginning with both *open hands* in front of each side of the body, palms facing down, bring the hands upward toward each other, ending with both extended index fingers crossed in front of the upper chest. Then, beginning with both *5 hands* in front of each side of the body, palms facing down and fingers pointing forward, push the hands downward with a double movement.

quench *v.* To satisfy: *some iced tea to quench my thirst.*

- [**thirsty** + **drink**[1]] Bring the extended right index finger, palm facing in and finger pointing up, downward along the length of the neck. Then, beginning with the thumb of the right *C hand* near the chin, palm facing left, tip the hand upward toward the face.

query *v.* **1.** To inquire: *to query as to whether or not the class is available.* **2.** To ask questions of: *to query the witness.* See also sign for QUESTION.

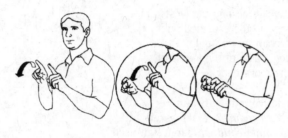

- [Form a question mark with each hand] Beginning with both extended index fingers pointing up in front of each side of the chest, palms facing forward, move the right hand down while bending into an *X hand* and then move the left hand down while bending into an *X hand,* ending with both *X hands* in front of the chest.

question *n.* **1.** Something asked in order to get information: *Ask your question before the teacher leaves.* —*v.* **2.** To ask questions of: *The policeman questioned the driver about the accident.* See also sign for QUERY. Same sign used for: **question mark.**

- [Draw a question mark in the air] Move the extended right index finger from pointing forward in front of the right shoulder, palm facing down, downward with a curving movement while retracting the index finger and then pointing it straight forward again at the bottom of the curve.

queue *v.* See sign for LINE UP.

quick *adj., adv.* See signs for ABRUPT[1,2], FAST[1,2,3]. Related form: **quickly** *adv.*

quicksand *n.* A deep bed of soft, wet sand that cannot support one's weight: *got caught in the quicksand and started to sink.*

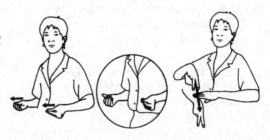

- [**dirt** + **sink**[1]] Beginning with both *flattened O hands* in front of each side of the body, palms facing up, move the thumb of each hand smoothly across each fingertip, starting with the little fingers and ending as *A hands*. Then, beginning with the fingers of the right *V hand*, palm facing in, protruding between the middle and ring fingers of the left *open hand*, palm facing down and fingers pointing right, bring the right hand straight down in front of the chest.

quick-witted *adj.* Having an alert mind; clever: *fun to be with such a quick-witted person.*

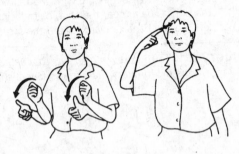

- [**fast**[1,3] + **think**[1]] Beginning with the thumbs of both *A hands* tucked under the index fingers, palms facing each other in front of the body, flick the thumbs out while twisting the wrists forward. Then tap the extended right index finger, palm facing down, against the right side of the forehead with a double movement.

quiet[1] *adj.* **1.** Relatively free of sound or movement: *a quiet room.* **2.** Making very little noise: *subdued, quiet children.* Same sign used for: **calm, passive, peaceful, serene, silent, still, tranquil.**

- [Natural gesture requesting others to be quiet] Beginning with both *B hands* crossed in front of the upper chest, palms angled outward in either direction, bring the hands downward and outward, ending with both *B hands* in front of each side of the waist, palms facing down.

quiet[2] *adj.* (alternate sign) Same sign used for: **Be quiet!, mute, silent.**

- [Natural gesture requesting others to be quiet] Place the extended right index finger in front of the pursed lips, palm facing left and finger pointing up.

quiet down *v. phrase.* See sign for SETTLE.

quill *n.* A pen made from a large feather, as from a goose: *People used to write with a quill.*

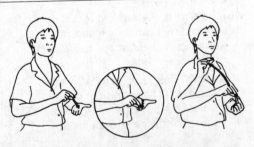

- [**write**[1,2,3] + shape of a feather] With the index finger and thumb of the right hand pinched together, slide the right fingers across the open left palm from the heel to the fingertips with a wiggly movement. Then, beginning with both *G hands* in front of the body, fingers touching, palms facing each other, and right hand above the left hand, pull the right hand upward toward the right shoulder while pinching the index finger and thumb of each hand together.

quit[1] *v.* To stop: *quit working.*

■ [Formed with the opposite movement as **join** and indicates withdrawing involvement with others] Beginning with the extended fingers of the right *H hand* inside the opening of the left *O hand* held in front of the body, palm facing right, bring the right hand upward, ending in front of the right shoulder, palm facing left and fingers pointing up.

quit[2] *v.* See signs for RESIGN, STOP[1].

quitter *n.* A person who gives up easily: *Don't be a quitter.*

■ [**quit**[1] + **person marker**] Beginning with the extended fingers of the right *H hand* inside the opening of the left *O hand* held in front of the body, palm facing right, bring the right hand upward, ending in front of the right shoulder, palm facing left and fingers angled up. Then move both *open hands,* palms facing each other, downward along each side of the body.

quiver *v., n.* See sign for SHIVER[1].

quiz *n., v.* See signs for TEST[1,2].

quota *n.* See sign for RESTRICT[1].

quotation[1] *n.* Someone else's spoken or written words, as from a book or speech, repeated exactly: *"To be or not to be" is a famous quotation.* Related form: **quote** *n., v.* Same sign used for: **idiom, subject, theme, title, topic.**

quotation

■ [Natural gesture forming quotation marks in the air] Beginning with both *V hands* held near each side of the head, palms facing each other and fingers pointing up, bend the fingers downward with a double movement.

quotation[2] *n.* See sign for EXCERPT. Related form: **quote** *n., v.*

quotes *pl. n.* See sign for TITLE[1].

rabbi[1] *n.* The spiritual leader of a Jewish congregation: *The rabbi is a scholar.*

- [Initialized sign tracing the location of a rabbi's prayer shawl] Beginning with the fingertips of both *R hands* touching each side of the upper chest, palms facing in, bring the hands straight down to each side of the waist.

rabbi[2] *n.* (alternate sign)

- [Initialized sign showing the location of Hasidic curls] Move the fingers of the right *R hand* from touching near the right ear, palm facing left, downward with a twisting movement to in front of the right shoulder. [This sign can be formed with two hands.]

rabbit[1] *n.* A small animal with soft fur and long ears: *fed their pet rabbit lettuce.* Same sign used for: **bunny, hare.**

- [Represents a rabbit's ears] With the *U hands* crossed above the wrists, palms facing in and thumbs extended, bend the fingers of both hands forward and back toward the chest with a double movement.

rabbit[2] *n.* (alternate sign) Same sign used for: **bunny, hare.**

- [Represents a rabbits ears] With the palms of both *U hands* against each side of the head, palms facing back, bend the fingers up and down with a double movement.

raccoon *n.* A small furry animal with a black, masklike band across the eyes and a bushy, ringed tail that lives in wooded areas and is active at night: *a raccoon in the tree.*

- [Indicates the distinctive coloring around the eyes of a raccoon] Beginning with the fingers of both *V hands* pointing toward each other around each eye, palms facing back, bring the hands outward with a double movement while closing the index and middle fingers of each hand each time.

race[1] *v.* To compete in a contest of speed: *to race against champions*. Same sign used for: **athletics, sports.**

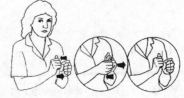

- [The hands move back and forth as if in contention with each other in a race] With an alternating movement, move both *A hands* forward and back past each other quickly by bending the wrists, palms facing each other in front of the body.

race[2] *n.* A contest of speed: *The car won the fifth race*. Same sign used for: **athletics, competition, contest, sports, track.**

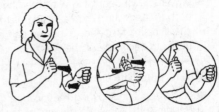

- [The hands move back and forth as if in contention with each other in a race] With the right *A hand* held near the right side of the chest and the left *A hand* held somewhat forward, palms facing each other, move the hands past each other with a deliberate alternating movement.

race[3] *n.* Any grouping of people based on ancestry or ethnicity: *member of the Caucasian race*. Same sign used for: **color, pigment.**

- [skin + color] Pinch the skin of the right cheek with the index finger and thumb of the right hand, palm facing left. Then wiggle the fingers of the right *5 hand* in front of the mouth, fingers pointing up and palm facing in.

race, harness *n.* See sign for HARNESS RACE.

radar *n.* An instrument using radio waves to determine distance and direction of an object: *The ship used radar to locate the approaching plane.*

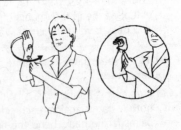

- [Represents the screening action of a radar dish] With the extended left index finger touching the wrist of the right *C hand*, palm facing forward, twist the right wrist to move the hand inward and around.

radiant *adj.* See signs for BEAM, BRIGHT.

radio[1] *n.* **1.** A device for sending and receiving sounds by electromagnetic waves without the use of wires: *broadcast a distress signal over the ship's radio.* **2.** A similar device that receives radio broadcasts: *carries around a portable radio to listen to music.* **3.** Commercial programs broadcast for reception by a radio: *listen to the radio.*

- [Represents radio headphones on the ears] With the fingers of the right *curved 5 hand* near the right ear, twist the hand forward with a double movement.

radio[2] *n.* (alternate sign)

- [The location of radio headphones on the ears] Tap the fingers of the right *curved 5 hand,* palm facing left, around the right ear with a double movement.

raft *n.* A floating platform, as of logs or inflatable rubber: *to cross the stream on a raft.*

- [**water** + gesture representing sitting on a rocking raft] Tap the index-finger side of the right *W hand,* palm facing left, against the chin with a double movement. Then, with the knuckles of the right *bent V hand* on the back of the left *open hand,* both palms facing down, twist the wrists to rock both hands from side to side with a double movement.

rage *n.* See sign for ANGER[1,2].

ragged *adj.* **1.** Having loose shreds or rough projections: *a ragged edge on the paper.* **2.** (of a column of type) Set with at least one side not justified: *Set the recipes in the cookbook ragged right.* Same sign used for: **crack, cracked, jagged.**

- [Shows the shape of a ragged crack] Beginning with the right *B hand* near the right side of the head, palm facing forward and fingers pointing up, move the hand in a large jagged movement down to in front of the right side of the body, ending with the palm facing left and the fingers pointing forward.

rah *interj.* See sign for RALLY.

raid[1] *n.* **1.** A sudden attack, as to seize contraband: *a police raid on a drug ring.*
—*v.* **2.** To make a raid on: *The police raided the house, searching for the criminals.*

- [**police**[1,2] + **enter** + **capture**[1]] Tap the thumb side of the right *C hand,* palm facing left, against the left side of the chest with a double movement. Next move the back of the right *open hand* forward in a downward arc under the palm of the left *open hand,* both palms facing down. Then, beginning with both *5 hands* in front of each side of the chest, palms facing down and fingers pointing forward, move the hands forward and down while closing into *S hands.*

raid[2] *v.* See signs for ROB[1,2].

rail

rail *n.* See sign for TRACK[1].

railroad *n.* See sign for TRAIN[1].

rain *n.* **1.** Water falling in drops from the clouds: *walking in the rain.* —*v.* **2.** To fall in drops of water from the clouds: *It rained all day and it's still raining.*

- [Represents raindrops falling] Bring both *curved 5 hands,* palms facing down, from near each side of the head downward to in front of each shoulder with a double movement.

rainbow *n.* An arch of the colors of the spectrum sometimes seen in the sky when the sun shines through mist: *to see a beautiful rainbow after the storm.*

- [The shape of a rainbow] Beginning with the right *4 hand* in front of the left shoulder, palm facing in and fingers pointing left, bring the hand upward in front of the face, ending in front of the right shoulder, palm facing in and fingers pointing up.

raincoat *n.* A waterproof coat worn for protection from the rain: *You'd better wear your raincoat and carry an umbrella.*

- [**rain** + **coat**] Bring both *curved 5 hands,* palms facing down, from near each side of the head downward to in front of each shoulder with a double movement. Then bring the thumbs of both *A hands* from near each shoulder, palms facing in, downward and toward each other, ending near the waist.

raindrop *n.* A drop of rain: *I felt the raindrops on my face.*

- [**rain** + showing drops falling] Bring both *curved 5 hands,* palms facing down, from near each side of the head downward to in front of each shoulder with a double movement. Then, beginning with both *S hands* near each side of the head, palms facing down, bring first the right hand and then the left hand downward to in front of each shoulder with an alternating movement, extending the index finger of each hand each time.

raise[1] *v.* To move to a higher position; lift up; *to raise the flag*. Same sign used for: **lift.**

■ [Natural gesture of raising something] Move the right *open hand*, palm facing up, upward from in front of the right side of the body to in front of the right shoulder.

raise[2] *v.* (alternatve sign) Same sign used for: **get up, lift, rise.**

■ [Natural gesture of raising something] Beginning with both *open hands* in front of each side of the body, palms facing up, lift the hands upward to in front of each shoulder.

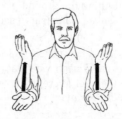

raise[3] *v.* (alternate sign, used for a window or windows)

■ [Mime raising a window] Move both hands, with the fingers curled toward the palms, from in front of each side of the waist, palms facing up, upward to in front of each side of the head, palms facing up.

raise[4] *v.* See sign for GROW UP.

raise[5] *n.* See sign for INCREASE[2].

raise one's hand *v. phrase.* To elevate one's hand with the arm outstretched to a position over one's head, so as to gain attention, as in a classroom: *Raise your hand if you know the answer.*

■ [Natural gesture] Move the right *open hand* from in front of the right shoulder, palm facing forward and fingers pointing up, upward to near the right side of the head.

raisin *n.* A sweet grape dried for food: *oatmeal and raisin cookies.*

■ [Initialized sign similar to sign for **grapes**] Touch the fingertips of the right *R hand*, palm facing down, down the back of the left hand held in front of the chest, palm facing down, from the wrist to the fingers.

rajah *n.* (formerly) A ruler in India: *His subjects had to obey the rajah.*

- [India[1,2] + **king**] Flick the extended right *10* thumb upward and forward on the middle of the forehead with a double movement. Then move the right *K hand*, palm facing in, from touching the left side of the chest near the shoulder downward to touch again near the right side of the waist.

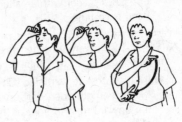

rake *n.* A long-handled agricultural tool with teeth on one end for smoothing the ground, gathering cut grass, etc.: *to rake the leaves.* Same sign used for: **hoe, plow, scratch.**

- [Demonstrate the action of raking] Move the fingertips of the right *curved 5 hand*, palm facing down, from the fingers to the heel of the upturned left *open hand* with a double movement.

rally *n.* A mass meeting, usually for a common purpose: *to attend the football rally.* Same sign used for: **hurrah, rah.**

- [Natural gesture used in leading a rally] Beginning with both *S hands* in front of each shoulder, palms facing each other, energetically move the hands upward with a double movement.

rampart *n.* A wall built around a fort to aid in its defense: *protected by the rampart.* Same sign used for: **fortress.**

- [Represents watching over a surface] Slide the palm side of the right *open hand* from the elbow to the fingers of the bent left arm held across the chest. Then slide the palm side of the right *V hand* from the elbow to the fingers of the bent left arm held across the chest.

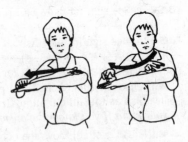

ramrod *n.* A rod used for inserting a charge in a muzzleloading firearm: *The Colonial soldier had to use a ramrod before firing his gun.*

- [Indicates the pressure exerted by a ramrod] Move the right *S hand* from in front of the right shoulder, palm facing down and elbow extended, forward and downward with a deliberate movement under the palm of the left *open hand* held in front of the body.

ranch *n.* See sign for FARM.

random[1] *adj.* Occurring without a plan or pattern: *a selection of random numbers.*

- [Initialized sign similar to sign for **variety**[1]] Beginning with the extended fingers of both *R hands* touching in front of the chest, palms facing down, move the hands apart to in front of each shoulder with a wavy movement.

random[2] *adj.* See signs for CIRCULATE[1], VARIETY[1].

range *n.* See sign for VARIETY[1].

rank *n.* See sign for PROMOTE[1].

ransack *v.* To search exhaustively through in order to plunder: *The thieves ransacked the house and threw things everywhere.*

- [Sign similar to **capture** except with an exaggerated movement] Beginning with the right *5 hand* somewhat forward of the right side of the body, palm facing down and fingers pointing forward, and the left *S hand* near the left side of the chest, palm facing down, bring the right hand back toward the chest while closing into an *S hand*, while extending the left hand forward and opening into a *5 hand*. Repeat with an alternating double movement.

rap[1] *v. Slang.* To talk freely; chat: *The father and son rapped for hours.*

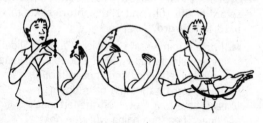

- [**blab** + **discuss**[2]] Beginning with both *flattened C hands* in front of the left side of the upper chest, left hand somewhat forward of the right hand and palms facing each other, close the fingers and thumbs of both hands together simultaneously with a repeated movement. Then tap the side of the extended right index finger, palm facing in, on the upturned open left palm with a repeated movement as the hands move from right to left in front of the body.

rap[2] *v.* See sign for KNOCK.

rape[1] *n.* **1.** The crime of forcing a person to submit to sexual intercourse against his or her will. —*v.* **2.** To commit such a crime: *She was raped by her captor.*

- [**intercourse**] Beginning with the right *C hand* in front of the right shoulder, palm forward, and the left arm bent across the body, move the right hand downward and forward, ending with the right wrist across the left wrist, both palms facing down. Then bring the right *V hand* downward in front of the chest to tap against the heel of the left *V hand* with a double movement, palms facing each other.

rape² *n., v.* (alternate sign)

- [Action of two bodies coming together] Beginning with both *curved 5 hands* in front of the chest, the right hand higher than the left, move the right hand down and the left hand up while changing to *S hands*.

rape³ *v.* See sign for STUCK.

rapid *adj.* See signs for FAST¹,²,³.

rapids *pl. n.* A part of a river where the water rushes swiftly, as over rocks: *to ride the rapids in a kayak.*

- [**water** + **flow¹** formed with a wiggling movement to represent moving water] Tap the index-finger side of the right *W hand*, palm facing left, against the chin with a double movement. Then, beginning with both *5 hands* in front of each side of the body, palms facing down and fingers pointing forward, move the hands forward while wiggling the fingers repeatedly.

rapier *n.* A long, narrow, 18th-century sword or a longer, heavier, double-edged sword of the 16th and 17th centuries: *knights who did battle with rapiers.* Same sign used for: **sword.**

- [**knife** + mime using a rapier in a duel] Slide the side of the extended right index finger, palm facing in, with a double movement at an angle across the length of the extended left index finger, palm facing down, turning the right palm down each time as it moves off the left index finger. Then, beginning with the right *A hand* in front of the right side of the body, palm facing left, move the hand in a circular movement and then straight forward while twisting the wrist slightly downward.

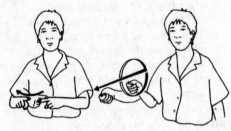

rapture *n.* Great joy; delight: *She was overcome with rapture.* Same sign used for: **absorb, evaporate, take up, vapor.**

- [Indicates something being absorbed] Beginning with both *5 hands* dangling down in front of each side of the body, palms facing in, bring the hands upward to in front of each shoulder while closing the fingers, forming *flattened O hands.*

rascal *n.* See sign for DEVIL.

rash *n.* A breaking out of spots on the skin: *The rash that erupted was only the first symptom.*

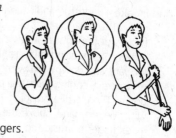

- [**red**[1,2,3] + a gesture showing the location of a rash on the arm] Bring the extended right index finger, palm facing in, from the lips downward while bending the index finger down toward the palm. Then move the fingertips of the right *curved 5 hand* upward on the left extended left arm with a double movement while repeatedly bending the fingers.

rasp *n.* A coarse file: *to shave the wood with a rasp.* Same sign used for: **file.**

- [Mime using a rasp to file] Slide the extended fingers of the right *U hand*, palm facing down and fingers pointing forward, with a repeated movement along the length of the extended left index finger held in front of the body, palm facing right and finger pointing forward.

rat[1] *n.* A long-tailed gnawing animal resembling a large mouse: *to see a rat scurrying around the garbage.*

- [Initialized sign similar to sign for **mouse**] Brush the index finger side of the right *R hand*, palm facing left, back and forth across the tip of the nose with a double movement.

rat[2] *v. Slang.* See sign for TATTLE.

rather *adv.* See signs for FAVORITE, PREFER[1,2].

ratify *v.* See sign for PASS[1]. Related form: **ratification** *n.*

ratio *n.* See sign for ACCORDING TO.

rational *adj.* See sign for REASON.

rationale *n.* See sign for REASON.

rattle *v.* **1.** To make repeated short, sharp sounds: *The window rattled from the wind.* —*n.* **2.** A toy or instrument that makes a rattling noise when shaken: *a baby's rattle.*

- [**hear** + mime shaking a rattle] Point the extended right index finger to the right ear. Then shake the right *modified X hand* with a short repeated movement in front of the right side of the body, palm facing left.

rattlesnake *n*. A poisonous snake with a rattle at the end of its tail: *bitten by a rattlesnake.*

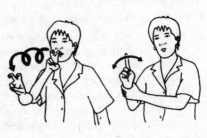

- [**snake** + a gesture indicating the movement of a rattlesnake's rattle] Beginning with the fingers of the right *bent V hand* in front of the mouth, palm facing forward, bring the hand forward and downward with a wavy movement, ending with the palm facing down. Then, while grasping the right wrist with the left hand, shake the extended right index finger from side to side in front of the right side of the body, palm facing forward.

rave *v*. To talk excitedly and enthusiastically: *He raved about the party.* Same sign used for: **crazy, wild.**

- [Indicates that the head is all mixed up] Move both *5 hands* from in front of each side of the head, one hand higher than the other, both palms facing down, in large repeated forward circles.

ravenous *adj*. See sign for HUNGRY.

ravine *n*. A steep, narrow valley formed by erosion: *a bridge that crosses the ravine.*

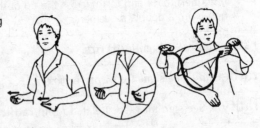

- [**dirt** + **valley**[1,2,3]] Beginning with both *flattened O hands* in front of each side of the body, palms facing up, move the thumb of each hand smoothly across each fingertip, starting with the little fingers and ending as *A hands*. Then, beginning with the index-finger sides of both *B hands* together at an angle in front of the left shoulder, fingers pointing forward, move the right hand downward to the right and back upward, ending in front of the right shoulder.

raw[1] *adj*. **1.** Not cooked: *slices of raw onion on the hamburger.* **2.** Uncooked or not fully cooked: *raw meat.*

- [**not**[1] + **finish**[1,2] + **cook**[1]] Bring the extended thumb of the right *10 hand* from under the chin, palm facing left, forward with a deliberate movement. Then, beginning with both *5 hands* in front of the chest, palms facing in and fingers pointing up, flip the hands over with a sudden movement, ending with both palms facing down and fingers pointing forward. Then, beginning with the fingers of the right *open hand,* palm facing down, across the palm of the left *open hand,* flip the right hand over, ending with the back of the right hand on the left palm.

raw[2] *adj.* (alternate sign)

- [**not** + **cook**[1]] Bring the extended thumb of the right *10 hand* from under the chin, palm facing left, forward with a deliberate movement. Then, beginning with the fingers of the right *open hand,* palm facing down, across the palm of the left *open hand,* flip the right hand over, ending with the back of the right hand on the left palm.

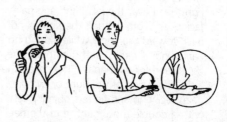

raw[3] *adj.* (alternate sign)

- [**yet**[1,2] + **cook**[1]] Bend the wrist of the right *open hand,* palm facing back and elbow held out, up and down with a double movement near the right side of the waist. Then, beginning with the fingers of the right *open hand,* palm facing down, across the palm of the left *open hand,* flip the right hand over, ending with the back of the right hand on the left palm.

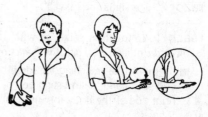

raw[4] *adj.* (alternate sign)

- [**never** + **cook**[1]] Move the right *B hand* from near the right side of the face, palm facing forward, downward with a large wavy movement to in front of the right side of the body, ending with the palm facing left..Then, beginning with the fingers of the right *open hand,* palm facing down, across the palm of the left *open hand,* flip the right hand over, ending with the back of the right hand on the left palm.

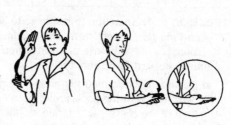

ray *n.* A narrow beam of light: *basking in the sun's rays.*

- [**light**[1] + a gesture showing light spreading] Beginning with the fingertips of the right *8 hand* near the chin, palm facing in, flip the middle finger upward and forward with a double movement while opening into a *5 hand* each time. Then move the fingertips of the right *flattened O hand* forward along the extended left index

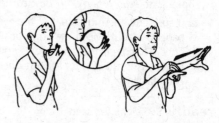

finger held in front of the chest, both palms facing down, opening the right hand into a *5 hand,* palm facing forward and fingers pointing up.

raze *v.* To tear down or level to the ground: *to raze the building.*

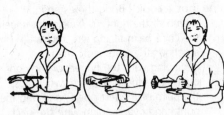

■ [**damage** + **plow**[1,2]] Beginning with both *curved 5 hands* in front of the chest, right hand over the left hand and palms facing each other, bring the right hand back toward the chest while closing both hands into *A hands,* and then bring the right hand forward again. Then slide the little-finger side of the right *open hand,* palm facing in and fingers pointing left, with a double movement from the heel to off the fingers of the left *open hand* held in front of the chest, palm facing up.

razor *n.* See signs for SHAVE[1,2].

reach[1] *v.* To touch or seize, as with an outstretched hand or other object: *to reach the books on the top shelf.*

■ [Demonstrates reaching for something] Move the right *curved 5 hand,* palm facing down, from in front of the right side of the body forward while changing into an *S hand.*

reach[2] *v.* See sign for ARRIVE.

react *v.* See signs for ANSWER, REPORT. Related form: **reaction** *n.*

reaction *n.* **1.** An action in response to some influence or event: *the staff's reaction to new regulations.* **2.** A physiological response, as to a disease or an irritation: *a bad reaction to smoke.* Related form: **react** *v.*

■ [Initialized sign formed similar to the sign for **opposite**] Beginning with the fingertips of both *R hands* touching in front of the chest, palms facing in, bring the hands apart to in front of each side of the chest.

read[1] *v.* To get meaning from print or writing by looking: *to read a book; off in a corner reading.*

■ [Represents the movement of the eyes down a page to read it] Move the fingertips of the right *V hand,* palm facing down, from the fingertips to the heel of the left *open hand,* palm facing right.

read[2] *v.* See signs for SCAN[1,2,3].

ready[1] *adj.* In a state of preparedness for action or use: *ready to go*. Related form: **readiness** *n*.

- [Initialized sign] Move both *R hands* from in front of the left side of the body, palms facing each other and fingers pointing forward, in a smooth movement to in front of the right side of the body.

ready[2] *adj.* (alternate sign)

- [Initialized sign] Beginning with both *R hands* crossed at the wrists in front of the chest, palms facing in opposite directions, twist the wrists to move the hands away from each other to in front of each side of the body, palms facing forward.

ready-made *adj.* Made ahead of time for general sale: *to buy a ready-made suit off the rack*.

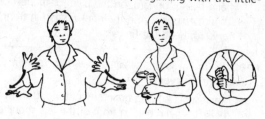

- [**finish**[1,2] + **make**[1]] Beginning with both *5 hands* in front of the chest, palms facing in and fingers pointing up, flip the hands over with a sudden movement, ending with both palms facing down and fingers pointing forward. Then, beginning with the little-finger side of the right *S hand* on the index-finger side of the left *S hand*, both palms facing in, separate the hands slightly, twist the wrists in opposite directions, and touch the hands again, ending with the palms facing in opposite directions.

real *adj.* **1.** Actually existing and not imaginary: *real life*. **2.** Not artificial; authentic: *real flowers*. Same sign used for: **actual, genuine.**

- [Movement emphasizes validity of one's statement] Move the side of the extended right index finger from in front of the mouth, palm facing left and finger pointing up, upward and forward in an arc.

realize *v.* See sign for REASON. Related form: **realization** *n*.

really *adv.* Actually; truly: *a really nice day*. Same sign used for: **actually.**

- Move the side of the extended right index finger from in front of the mouth, palm facing left and finger pointing up, forward with a double movement.

realm

realm *n.* Kingdom: *the queen's realm.*

■ [**real** + **land**[1]] Move the side of the extended right index finger from in front of the mouth, palm facing left and finger pointing up, upward and forward in an arc. Next, beginning with both *flattened O hands* in front of each side of the body, palms facing up, move the thumb of each hand smoothly across each fingertip, starting with the little fingers and ending as *A hands.* Then move the right *5 hand,* palm facing down and fingers pointing forward, from in front of the right side of the body in an arc to in front of the left side of the body.

ream *n.* A quantity of paper packaged in sheets of 500: *to purchase a ream of paper.*

■ [**paper** + **thick**[3,5] + **500**] Brush the heel of the right *open hand,* palm facing down, on the heel of the left *open hand,* palm facing up, with a double movement. Next place the thumb of the *modified C hand,* palm facing forward, on the palm of the left *open hand* held in front of the chest. Then, beginning with the right *5 hand* in front of the right shoulder, palm facing forward, bend the fingers.

reap[1] *v.* To cut grain, as for harvesting: *to reap wheat.* Same sign used for: **harvest.**

■ [Represents holding grain and cutting it off at the base] With the left *S hand* held in front of the left shoulder, palm facing in and elbow somewhat extended, slide the right *curved hand,* palm facing up, back and forth under the left hand with a double movement.

reap[2] *v.* See signs for COLLECT[1,2].

rear[1] *v.* See sign for GROW UP.

rear[2] *n.* See signs for BACK[1,2].

rearrange *v.* To arrange again, usually in a different way: *to rearrange the furniture.*

■ [**again** + **plan**[1]] Beginning with the right *bent hand* beside the left *open hand* in front of the chest, both palms facing up, bring the right hand up while turning it over, ending with the fingertips of the right hand touching the palm of the left hand. Then move both *open hands* from in front of the left side of the body, palms facing each other and fingers pointing forward, in a long smooth movement to in front of the right side of the body.

reason *n.* A cause or motive: *a good reason to be angry.* Related form: **reasonable** *adj.* Same sign used for: **rational, rationale, realization, realize.**

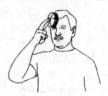

■ [Initialized sign similar to sign for **wonder**] Move the fingertips of the right *R hand*, palm facing in, in a circular movement in front of the right side of the forehead with a double movement.

reassure *v.* To encourage; restore to confidence: *The mother reassured the little boy.*

■ [**again** + **vow**[1,2]] Beginning with the right *bent hand* beside the left *curved hand*, both palms facing up, bring the right hand up while turning it over, ending with the fingertips of the right hand touching the palm of the left hand. Then, beginning with the right elbow resting on the back of the left bent arm, bring the extended right index finger, palm facing left and finger pointing up, from in front of the lips forward while changing into an *open hand*, palm facing forward and fingers pointing up.

rebel *v.* See signs for DISOBEY[2], PROTEST[2]. Related form: **rebellion** *n.*

rebirth *n.* **1.** A new or second birth, as with a spiritual revitalization or a religious conversion: *He had a rebirth in the church.* **2.** A revival: *The rebirth of democracy.* Same sign used for: **born-again.**

■ [**again** + **birth**[1,2]] Beginning with the right *bent hand* beside the left *curved hand*, both palms facing up, bring the right hand up while turning it over, ending with the fingertips of the right hand touching the palm of the left hand. Then, beginning with the back of the right *open hand*, palm facing in and fingers pointing left, touching the palm of the left *open hand*, palm facing in and fingers pointing right, bring the right hand down under the little-finger side of the left hand, ending with the right palm facing down.

rebound *v.* **1.** To spring back from an impact: *The ball rebounded from the fence.* **2.** To recover: *to rebound quickly from a disappointment.* —*n.* **3.** The act of rebounding: *an encouraging rebound from an illness.* **4. on the rebound** While still recovering emotionally, as from a broken romance: *She married him on the rebound.*

■ [Shows action of bouncing back] Move the right *V hand* from near the right side of the head, palm facing forward and fingers pointing up, downward while bending the fingers, and at the same time raising the left *bent V hand* and extending the fingers. Repeat with an alternating movement.

rebuild *v.* To build again: *to rebuild the house after the fire.*

■ [**again** + **build**[1,2]] Beginning with the right *bent hand* beside the left *open hand*, both palms facing up, bring the right hand up while turning it over, ending with the fingertips of the right hand touching the palm of the left hand. Then, beginning with the fingers of the right *H hand* overlapping the fingers of the left *H hand* in front of the chest, both palms facing down and fingers angled toward each other, reverse the position of the hands with a repeated movement as the hands move upward.

rebuke *v.* See signs for SCOLD, WARN.

recall[1] *v.* To call back into one's mind: *Try to recall the incident.* Same sign used for: **recollect, remind.**

■ [**call**[1] + **before**[1]] Slap the fingers of the right *open hand* on the back of the left *open hand*, both palms facing down, dragging the right fingers upward in front of the right shoulder. Then move the right *open hand*, palm facing in and fingers pointing up, from in front of the right side back back over the right shoulder.

recall[2] *v.* See signs for REMEMBER[1,2].

recapture *v.* **1.** To capture again: *to recapture the escaped convict.* **2.** To remember as if experiencing again: *To recapture the feeling of falling in love.*

■ [**again** + **capture**[1]] Beginning with the right *bent hand* beside the left *open hand*, both palms facing up, bring the right hand up while turning it over, ending with the fingertips of the right hand touching the palm of the left hand. Then, beginning with both *curved 5 hands* in front of each side of the chest, palms facing down and fingers pointing forward, move the hands downward while closing into *S hands*.

recede *v.* (of a hairline) To move back from the forehead and temples as hair ceases to grow: *a receding hairline.*

■ [Shows the location of a receding hairline] Move the index-finger side of the right *B hand*, palm facing down, from the right side of the forehead back along the side of the head, ending with the palm facing forward and fingers pointing up.

receive *v.* See sign for GET.

receiver[1] *n.* A person who receives the ball in a football game: *Pass the ball to the receiver.*

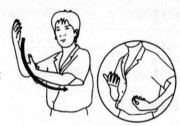

- [Mime catching a football in one's arms] Beginning with both *curved 5 hands* in front of the right shoulder, right hand higher than the left hand and both palms facing back, bring the hands downward in an arc to in front of the left side of the body.

receiver[2] *n.* (alternate sign)

- [**get** + **person marker**] Beginning with both *5 hands* in front of the chest, right hand above the left hand and palms facing in opposite directions, bring the hands back toward the chest while closing into *S hands*, ending with the little-finger side of the right *S hand* on the index-finger side of the left *S hand*. Then move both *open hands*, palms facing each other, downward along each side of the body.

recently[1] *adv.* At a time not long ago: *saw the movie recently.* Related form: **recent** *adj.* Same sign used for: **while ago, a**[2].

- [Represents the minute hand on a clock moving a short distance into the past] With the little-finger side of the right *1 hand*, palm facing in and finger pointing up, against the palm of the left *open hand*, palm facing right and fingers pointing up, bend the extended right index finger back toward the chest with a double movement.

recently[2] *adv.* (alternate sign) Same sign used for: **just, short time ago.**

- [Represents the minute hand on a clock moving a short distance into the past] With the little-finger side of the right *X hand* against the right cheek, palm facing back, bend the right index finger down with a small repeated movement.

receptacle *n.* See sign for SOCKET.

reception[1] *n.* A formal party where guests are received by the hosts: *to attend the wedding reception.*

- [Initialized sign similar to sign for **banquet**] Beginning with both *R hands* in front of the mouth, right hand somewhat nearer the mouth than the left hand, palms facing in and fingers pointing up, with an alternating movement bring the hands toward the mouth.

reception[2] *n.* See sign for BANQUET.

recess *n.* See signs for REST[1,2,3].

reckless *adj.* See signs for CARELESS[1,2].

recline *v.* See sign for LIE[3].

recliner *n.* A chair that extends to permit a person to recline: *to fall asleep while sitting in the recliner.*

- ■ [**sit** + showing the extended position of a person's legs when reclining] Beginning with the curved fingers of the right *H hand* hooked over the extended fingers of the left *H hand,* both palms facing down, slide the right hand forward while straightening the fingers.

recluse *n.* A person who lives alone, withdrawn from the outside world: *to live like a recluse for months at a time.* Same sign used for: **hermit.**

- ■ [**alone**[1] + **under**[1,2]] Move the extended right index finger in a small circle in front of the right shoulder, palm facing in and finger pointing up. Then move the thumb of the right *A hand,* palm facing left, in an arc under the left *curved hand* held in front of the chest, palm facing down.

recognize[1] *v.* To identify as someone or something known: *to recognize the man from his photo.*

- ■ [Initialized sign similar to sign for **notice**[1]] Bring the extended fingertips of the right *R hand* from touching the cheek near the right eye, palm facing left, downward to touch the palm of the left *open hand,* palm angled up, in front of the chest.

recognize[2] *v.* See sign for NOTICE[1].

recoil *v.* To draw back suddenly, as in fear: *to recoil from the snake.* Same sign used for: **back out, withdraw.**

- ■ [Mime recoiling from something] Beginning with both *5 hands* in front of each side of the body, palms facing down, fingers pointing forward, and elbows close to the body, bring the hands upward in front of each shoulder while bending the body back.

recollect *v.* See signs for HINDSIGHT, RECALL[1], REMEMBER[1,2]. Related form: **recollection** *n.*

recommend[1] *v.* To speak in favor of: *to recommend a restaurant.* Related form: **recommendation** *n.*

- [Initialized sign similar to sign for **suggest**] Bring both *R hands* from in front of the chest, palms facing up, forward in an upward arc.

recommend[2] *v.* See sign for SUGGEST. Related form: **recommendation** *n.*

reconcile[1] *v.* To become or cause to become friendly or compatible again: *The old friends reconciled after many years of enmity. We tried to reconcile the conflicting ideas.*

- [**friend**[1] + **belong**[1]] Hook the right bent index finger, palm facing down, over the left bent index finger, palm facing up. Next repeat, reversing the position of the hands. Then intersect the index fingers and thumbs of both *F hands* in front of the chest, palms facing each other, move the hands toward each other.

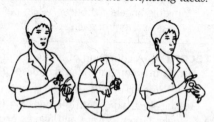

reconcile[2] *v.* (alternate sign)

- [**friend**[1] + **again** + **join**[1]] Hook the right bent index finger, palm facing down, over the left bent index finger, palm facing up. Next repeat, reversing the position of the hands. Then, beginning with the right *bent hand* beside the left *curved hand*, both palms facing up, bring the right hand up while turning it over, ending with the fingertips of the right hand touching the palm of the left hand. Finally, intersect the index fingers and thumbs of both *F hands* in front of the chest, palms facing each other.

record[1] *n.* **1.** Something on which sounds have been recorded for playback, as a grooved disc with music or words, used on a phonograph: *to listen to some classic LP records.* —*v.* **2.** To place (music, speech, etc.) on such a disc: *The band recorded two new songs.* Same sign used for: **LP.**

- [Represents the needle moving around a record revolving on a spindle] Move the bent middle finger of the right *5 hand*, palm and finger pointing down, in a flat circle around the bent middle finger of the left *5 hand*, palm and finger pointing up.

record

record² *n., v.* (alternate sign) Same sign used
for: **LP.**

- [Represents the needle moving around a record revolving on a spindle] With the bent middle finger and palm of the right *5 hand* pointing down and the bent middle finger and palm of the left *5 hand* pointing up, move the hands in opposite circles with a double movement.

record³ *n.* **1.** A tape on which sounds, as music or words, have been recorded for playback on a tape recorder or tape player: *to make a record of the speech on the tape recorder.* —*v.* **2.** To place (music, speech, etc.) on such a tape: *The band recorded another song and sent us the tape.* Same sign used for: **cassette tape, tape.**

- [Represents a double-reel tape recorder] Move the bent middle fingers of both *5 hands*, palms facing down, in small circles in front of each side of the body.

record⁴ *n.* A collection of related data fields treated as a unit in a computerized database: *There are ten fields in each record.*

- [Initialized sign] With the heel of the right *R hand*, palm facing forward and fingers pointing up, on the index-finger side of the left *4 hand*, palm facing in and fingers pointing right, rock the right hand from side to side with a double movement.

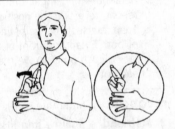

record⁵ *n., v.* See signs for LIST[1,2,3,4].

record⁶ *v.* See sign for PUT DOWN[1].

record⁷ *n.* See sign for PHONOGRAPH[1].

record player *n.* A machine used for playing records; phonograph: *to buy a new record player.* Same sign used for: **phonograph.**

- [record[1,2] + room[2]] Move the bent middle finger of the right *5 hand*, palm and finger pointing down, in a flat circle around the bent middle finger of the left *5 hand*, palm and finger pointing up. Then, beginning with both *open hands* in front of each side of the chest, palms facing each other and fingers pointing forward, move the hands deliberately in opposite directions ending with the left hand near the chest and the right hand several inches forward of the left hand, both palms facing in.

recorder *n.* See sign for AUTHOR.

recount *v.* **1.** To count again, as for verification: *to recount the members present.* —*n.* **2.** An additional count: *The vote was so close that we'll have to take a recount.*

■ [**again** + **count**] Beginning with the right *bent hand* beside the left *curved hand,* both palms facing up, bring the right hand up while turning it over, ending with the fingertips of the right hand touching the palm of the left hand. Then move the fingertips of the right *F hand,* palm facing down, across the upturned left palm from the heel to the fingertips with a double movement.

recover[1] *v.* To get back (something that was lost): *to recover the stolen goods.* Same sign used for: **founded, set up, undelete.**

■ [Formed with a movement opposite to that for **break down** showing a structure being set up again] Beginning with the fingertips of both *curved hands* entwined in front of the chest, palms facing down, bend the wrists to raise the fingers upward, ending with the palms angled toward each other.

recover[2] *v.* To get well again, as after an illness: *to recover quickly from the operation.*

■ [**again** + **well**[1]] Beginning with the right *bent hand* beside the left *curved hand,* both palms facing up, bring the right hand up while turning it over, ending with the fingertips of the right hand touching the palm of the left hand. Then, beginning with the fingertips of both *curved 5 hands* touching each shoulder, palms facing in, bring the hands forward with a deliberate movement while closing into *S hands.*

recreation *n.* See sign for FUN.

recruit[1] *v.* To hire, enroll, or enlist (new members or the like): *to recruit new students.*

■ [Natural gesture for beckoning someone] Beginning with the right *X hand* in front of the right shoulder, palm facing in, move the hand back and forth in front of the chest with a double movement, bending the finger as the hand moves.

recruit[2] *v.* (alternate sign)

■ [Initialized sign similar to sign for **come**[1]] Beginning with both *R hands* in front of the body, palms facing up and fingers pointing forward, bring the hands back toward the chest with a double movement.

recruit

recruit[3] *v.* (alternate sign)

■ [Natural gesture for beckoning someone] Bend the extended index fingers of both hands, palms facing up and fingers pointing forward, while bringing the hands in toward each side of the chest.

recruit[4] *v.* See sign for BECKON.

rectangle[1] *n.* A two-dimensional figure with four sides and four right angles: *A square is a rectangle with four equal sides.*

■ [Draw the shape of a rectangle in the air] Beginning with both extended index fingers side by side in front of the chest, palms angled forward and fingers pointing forward, bring the hands apart to in front of each shoulder, then straight down, and finally back together again in front of the lower chest.

rectangle[2] *n.* (alternate sign)

■ [Initialized sign showing the shape of a rectangle] Beginning with the fingertips of the index fingers and thumbs of both *R hands* touching in front of the chest, palms angled forward, bring the hands apart to in front of each side of the shoulders, then straight down, and finally back together again in front of the lower chest.

rectangle[3] *n.* See sign for SIGN[2].

rectory *n.* See sign for MONASTERY.

recur *v.* To happen again, as an event: *We're hoping his illness won't recur.*

■ [again + happen + happen] Beginning with the right *bent hand* beside the left *curved hand*, both palms facing up, bring the right hand up while turning it over, ending with the fingertips of the right hand touching the palm of the left hand. Then, beginning with both extended fingers in front of the right side of the body, palms facing in and fingers pointing up, flip the hands over toward each other, ending with the palms facing down and fingers pointing forward. Repeat in front of the left side of the body.

recursive *adj.* Of or being a procedure that can be used repeatedly: *a recursive routine in a computer program.* Related form: **recursively** *adv.*

■ [**call**[1] + **itself**] Slap the fingers of the right *open hand* on the back of the left *open hand,* both palms facing down, dragging the right fingers upward and closing them into an *A hand* in front of the right side of the chest. Then bring the knuckles of the right *10 hand,* palm facing in, firmly against the side of the extended left index finger, palm facing forward and finger pointing up in front of the chest.

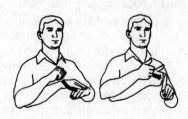

recuse *v.* See sign for RESIGN.

red[1] *adj.* Having the color of blood: *a red rose.*

■ [Shows the redness of the lips] Bring the extended right index finger, palm facing in, from the lips downward with a short double movement.

red[2] *adj.* (alternate sign)

■ [Initialized sign] Bring the fingertips of the right *R hand,* palm facing in, from the lips downward with a short double movement.

red[3] *adj.* (alternate sign)

■ [Shows the redness of the lips] Bring the extended right index finger, palm facing in, from the lips downward while bending the index finger down toward the palm.

Red Cross[1] *n.* An international organization that cares for people in times of calamity: *to give blood to the Red Cross.*

■ [**red**[1,2,3] + draw the shape of a cross in the air] Bring the extended right index finger, palm facing in, from the lips downward while bending the index finger down toward the palm. Then, beginning with the right *modified C hand* in front of the face, palm facing forward, bring the hand first downward and then from left to right in front of the chest.

Red Cross

Red Cross[2] *n.* (alternate sign)

- [**red**[1,2,3] + the shape of a cross on the uniform of a Red Cross worker] Bring the extended right index finger, palm facing in, from the lips downward while bend-ing the index finger down toward the palm. Then move the right *modified C hand* first downward and then from back to front on the left upper arm.

redeem[1] *v.* To set free, as from the consequences of sin: *redeemed from sin.* Same sign used for: **rescue.**

- [Initialized sign similar to sign for **save**[1]] Beginning with both *R hands* crossed at the wrists in front of the chest, palms facing in, twist the wrists to end with both hands in front of each shoulder, palms facing forward.

redeem[2] *v.* See sign for SAVE[1].

red-headed *adj.* Having red hair: *a red-headed baby.*

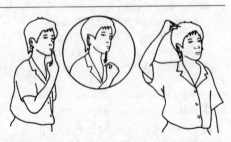

- [**red**[1,2,3] + **hair**] Bring the extended right index finger, palm facing in, from the lips downward while bending the index finger down toward the palm. Then grasp a small piece of hair with the index finger and thumb of the right hand.

reduce[1] *v.* To make less, smaller, etc.: *to reduce the price.* Related form: **reduction** *n.*

- [Initialized sign similar to sign for **less**[1]] Beginning with the right *R hand* in front of the chest, palm facing down and fingers pointing forward, and the left *R hand* in front of the waist, palm facing up and fingers pointing forward, bring the right hand downward to above the left hand.

reduce[2] *v.* See signs for BRIEF[1], DECREASE[1,2,3], LESS[1]. Related form: **reduction** *n.*

reel *n.* A spool on which thread, rope, film, etc., may be wound and from which it may be let out for use: *a movie reel.*

- [Initialized sign showing the action of winding something on a reel] Move the extended fingers of the right *R hand*, palm facing down and fingers pointing left, in a double forward circle near the thumb side of the left *S hand* held in front of the chest, palm facing forward.

reentry *n.* The act of entering again: *tracking the reentry of the spacecraft into the earth's atmosphere.* Related form: **reenter** *v.*

- [**repeat**[2] + **enter**] Beginning with the right *R hand* beside the left *open hand,* both palms facing up, bring the right hand up while turning it over, ending with the extended fingertips of the right hand touching the palm of the left hand. Then move the back of the right *open hand* forward and downward in an arc under the palm of the left *open hand,* both palms facing down.

refer *v.* To send or direct to a person or place for information or help: *They'll refer you to a good doctor.*

- [Initialized sign] Beginning with the fingers of the right *R hand,* palm facing in, on the back of the left *open hand,* palm facing in, twist the right hand forward, ending with the right palm facing down.

referee *n.* A person who judges the events of play according to the official rules of a game: *The referee blew the whistle to bring the action to a halt.* Same sign used for: **whistle.**

- [Natural gesture used to whistle between one's teeth] Tap the fingertips of the right *bent V hand,* palm facing in, against the lips with a double movement.

reference *n.* A statement about someone's character and abilities: *Your former employer will give you a good reference.*

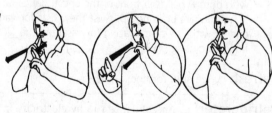

- [Initialized sign similar to sign for **communication**] Beginning with the right *R hand* in front of the mouth, palm facing left, and the left *R hand* somewhat forward, palm facing right, move the right hand forward and the left hand toward the mouth with an alternating double movement.

refill[1] *n.* **1.** A fresh supply of something that has been used up: *If you're out of ink, put a refill in the pen.* —*v.* **2.** To fill again: *Please refill my cup with coffee.*

- [**again** + **pour**[1,2]] Beginning with the right *bent hand* beside the left *open hand,* in front of the chest, both palms facing up, bring the right hand up while turning it over, ending with the fingertips of the right hand touching the palm of the left hand. Then bring the right *C hand* from in front of the right side of the body, palm facing left, upward in an arc while turning the hand over and forming a *10 hand,* ending with the extended thumb of the right *10 hand* in the opening of the left *S hand* held in front of the body, palm facing right.

refill[2] *n., v.* (alternate sign) Same sign used for:
fill up.

■ [Shows the level of something rising to the top] Beginning with the right *open hand* in front of the waist and the left *open hand* in front of the chest, both palms facing down and fingers pointing in opposite directions, move the right hand up against the left palm.

reflect[1] *v.* **1.** To cast back from a surface, as light or heat: *soft light reflected from the moon.* **2.** To give back an image: *looked at his face reflected in the mirror.* Related form: **reflection** *n.*

■ [Initialized sign similar to sign for **bounce**[1]] With a bouncing movement, bring the extended fingertips of the right *R hand* against the open left palm and off again.

reflect[2] *v.* See sign for BOUNCE[1].

reflect[3] *v.* See sign for WONDER.

Reform *adj.* Designating a branch of Judaism that stresses ethical behavior and simplifies some traditional religious practices to accommodate contemporary living: *The family belongs to a temple that practices Reform Judaism.*

■ [Initialized sign similar to sign for **free**[1]] Beginning with both *R hands* in front of the chest, palms facing in and fingers pointing up, twist the wrists forward, ending with the palms facing forward and the fingers pointing up.

refresh *v.* See sign for COOL.

refrigerator[1] *n.* An appliance run by electricity in which food is kept cool: *Put the butter in the refrigerator before it melts.*

■ [Initialized sign similar to sign for **door**] Beginning with both *R hands* in front of the chest, palms facing forward and fingers pointing up, bring the hands apart to in front of each side of the chest and twist the right wrist to face the palm back.

refrigerator[2] *n.* (alternate sign) Same sign used for: **icebox.**

■ [**cold**[2] + **table**[2]] Shake both *S hands* with a slight movement in front of each side of the chest, palms facing each other. Then, with the index-finger sides of both *open hands* touching in front of the chest, palms facing down and fingers pointing forward, bring the hands apart to in front of each shoulder, and then straight down, ending with the palms facing each other.

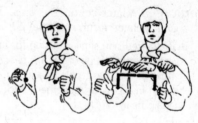

refrigerator[3] *n.* (alternate sign)

■ [Initialized sign similar to sign for **open**[2]] Beginning with the thumb side of the right *R hand*, palm facing forward and fingers pointing up, against the palm side of the left *open hand*, palm facing right and fingers pointing up, move the right hand to the right in an arc while twisting the palm back in front of the right side of the chest.

refund[1] *v.* **1.** To pay back: *The store refuses to refund my money.* —*n.* **2.** Return of money paid: *You'll receive the refund in the mail.* See also sign for RETURN[2]. Same sign used for: **come back.**

■ [Shows the direction that something takes in coming back to oneself] Beginning with both extended index fingers pointing up in front of the chest, palms facing in, bring the fingers back to point at each side of the chest, palms facing down.

refund[2] *v.* See sign for REPEAT[2].

refuse[1] *n.* Something discarded; waste; rubbish: *Put the refuse in the dumpster.*

■ [**dirty** + **pile**[1,2,3] + **throw**[1,2]] With the back of the right *curved 5 hand* under the chin, palm facing down, wiggle the fingers. Next, beginning with both *5 hands* in front of the chest, palms facing down and fingers pointing forward, bring the hands apart and down to in front of each side of the body, ending with the palms facing each other. Then, beginning with both *S hands* in front of each side of the chest, palms facing forward, move the hands quickly downward while opening into *5 hands*.

refuse[2] *v.* See signs for DECLINE[4], WON'T.

regarding

regarding *prep.* See sign for ABOUT¹.

region¹ *n.* A large continuous area: *a mountainous region.* Related form: **regional** *adj.*
- ■ [Initialized sign similar to sign for **area**²] Beginning with the fingertips of both *R hands* touching in front of the chest, palms facing in, move the hands apart in a circular movement back until they touch again near the chest.

region² *n.* See signs for AREA¹,²,³,⁴.

register¹ *v.* To enroll officially: *to register for school.* Related form: **registration** *n.* Same sign used for: **sign in, sign up.**
- ■ [Initialized sign similar to sign for **sign**³] Touch the fingertips of the right *R hand*, palm facing down, first to the heel and then to the fingertips of the palm of the left *open hand.*

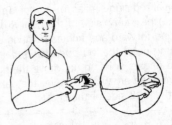

register² *v.* See sign for SIGN³.

registration *n.* See sign for CONTRACT.

regret *n.* See signs for REMORSE, SORRY.

regular¹ *adj.* Conforming to a habitual pattern, acceptable behavior, etc.: *a regular life.* Related form: **regularly** *adj.* Same sign used for: **ordinary, promptly, usual.**
- ■ With the right index finger extended, brush the little-finger side of the right hand, palm facing in, across the extended left index finger, palm facing in, as the right hand moves toward the chest in a double circular movement.

regular² *adj.* See sign for CONSISTENT¹.

regulate *v.* See sign for MANAGE.

regulation *n.* See sign for RULE¹.

rehabilitation *n.* Restoration to good condition or appropriate functionality: *The prisoner completed his rehabilitation and was released.* Related form: **rehabilitate** *v.*
- ■ [Initialized sign similar to sign for **help**] With the little finger side of the right *R hand* resting on the open left palm, raise the hands upward in front of the chest.

rehearse[1] *v.* To practice before performing: *rehearse the play.* Related form: **rehearsal** *n.*

■ [Initialized sign similar to sign for **practice**] Rub the heel of the right *R hand*, palm facing forward and fingers pointing up, back and forth on the back of the left *open hand* held in front of the chest, palm facing down and fingers pointing right, with a double movement.

rehearse[2] *v.* See sign for PRACTICE.

reign *v.* See sign for MANAGE.

rein *n.* See sign for HARNESS RACE.

reindeer[1] *n.* A large kind of deer with branching horns: *Reindeer live in arctic regions.*

■ [Initialized sign similar to sign for **deer**] Tap the thumbs of both *R hands*, palms facing forward, against each side of the forehead with a repeated movement.

reindeer[2] *n.* (alternate sign)

■ [Initialized sign showing the shape and location of antlers] Beginning with the thumbs of both *R hands* against each side of the forehead, palms facing forward, bring the hands upward and outward to each side in a small arc.

reindeer[3] *n.* See sign for DEER.

reinforce[1] *v.* To strengthen, as by adding support: *to reinforce the book's binding.* Same sign used for: **resource.**

■ [Initialized sign similar to sign for **help**] With the fingertips of the right *R hand*, palm facing in and fingers pointing up, touching the little-finger side of the left *S hand*, palm facing in, raise both hands upward in front of the chest.

reinforce[2] *v.* See signs for SUPPORT[1,2].

reiterate *v.* See signs for AGAIN, REPEAT[1].

reject[1] *v.* To refuse to accept, take, use, etc.: *rejected my help.* Same sign used for: **turn down, veto.**

■ [Natural gesture indicating turning down something] Beginning with the right *10 hand* in front of the right shoulder, elbow extended and palm facing down, twist

reject

the wrist downward, ending with the thumb pointing down and the palm facing right.

reject² *v.* To throw away: *to reject the bad copies.* See also sign for EXCLUDE. Same sign used for: **impeach.**

■ [The hand brushes away something that is not desired] Brush the fingertips of the right *open hand,* palm facing in, with a forward movement from the heel to the fingertips of the left *open hand,* palm facing up.

reject³ *v.* (alternate sign) See also sign for EXCLUDE.

■ [The hand brushes away something that is not desired] Brush the little-finger side of the right *open hand,* palm facing in, with a forward movement from the heel to the fingertips of the left *open hand,* palm facing up.

rejoice *v.* See sign for CELEBRATE.

relapse *n.* **1.** An act or instance of slipping back into a former state or an illness: *He had a relapse of the flu.* —*v.* **2.** To slip back into a former state or an illness: *to relapse into moody silence.*

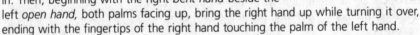

■ [sick¹,² + again] Touch the bent middle finger of the right *5 hand* to the forehead and the bent middle finger of the left *5 hand* to the lower chest, both palms facing in. Then, beginning with the right *bent hand* beside the left *open hand,* both palms facing up, bring the right hand up while turning it over, ending with the fingertips of the right hand touching the palm of the left hand.

relate *v.* See sign for COORDINATE.

relationship *n.* **1.** An association or involvement: *What is your relationship to this organization?* **2.** An emotional connection between people: *involved in a relationship that may lead to marriage.* Related form: **relate** *v.* Same sign used for: **ally, banded together, bond, connection, link, relevant, tie.**

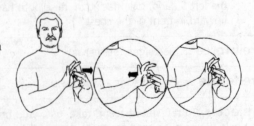

■ [Represents a link between two persons or things] With the thumbs and index fingers of both *F hands* intersecting, move the hands forward and back toward the chest with a double movement.

relative[1] *n.* A person who belongs to one's family by blood, adoption, or marriage: *My relatives live nearby.*

- ■ [Initialized sign similar to sign for **friend**[1]] Beginning with the extended fingers of the right *R hand,* palm facing down, across the extended fingers of the left *R hand,* palm facing up, twist the wrists in opposite directions to reverse positions.

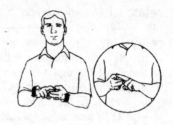

relative[2] *n.* (alternate sign)

- ■ [Initialized sign similar to sign for **family**] Beginning with the extended fingers of both *R hands* together in front of the chest, palms facing forward, bring the hands away from each other in outward arcs while turning the palms in, ending with the little fingers touching.

relative[3] *n.* (alternate sign)

- ■ [Initialized sign] Beginning with both *R hands* held in front of the body, both palms facing down and one hand somewhat forward of the other hand, slide the hands forward and back with a repeated alternating movement, brushing the index-finger sides of the hands as they move.

relative[4] *adj.* Considered in comparison with something else: *the relative advantages of moving or staying here.*

- ■ [Initialized sign similar to sign for **balance**] Beginning with both *R hands* in front of each side of the chest, palms facing down and fingers pointing forward, move the hands up and down with a double alternating movement.

relax[1] *v.* To become less tense: *She relaxed by the pool.*

- ■ [**rest**[1,2] + **tired**] With the arms crossed at the wrists, lay the palms of both *open hands* near the opposite shoulder. Then, beginning with the fingertips of both *bent hands* touching each side of the chest, palms facing in, drop the hands while keeping the fingers in place.

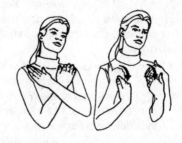

relax[2] *v.* See signs for REST[1,2,3], SETTLE.

---

relay *n.* **1.** A service allowing deaf and hearing people to communicate with each other by telephone through a trained intermediary, with the deaf person using a text telephone: *The deaf woman called her doctor using the relay.* —*v.* **2.** To pass along by means of a relay: *The operator relayed the message from the caller.*

■ [Initialized sign representing the passing of information back and forth] Beginning with both *R hands* in front of each shoulder, palms facing each other, move the hands past each other in front of the chest with a double movement, crossing the wrists each time.

---

release *v., n.* See signs for DISCONNECT, DISMISS, SPREAD[1].

---

relevant *adj.* See sign for RELATIONSHIP.

---

reliable *adj.* See sign for DEPENDABLE.

---

relic *n.* Something remaining from past ages: *archaeologists hunting for relics in the ruins.*

■ [**old** + **long time ago, a** + **thing**[1,2]] Move the right *C hand* from near the chin, palm facing left, downward a short distance while closing into an *S hand.* Next, beginning with both *5 hands* in front of the right shoulder, palms facing each other and left hand below the right hand, roll the hands over each other with an alternating movement while moving the hands back over the right shoulder. Then, beginning with the right *open hand* in front of the body, palm facing up and fingers pointing forward, move the hand in a large arc to the right.

---

relief *n.* An act or state of being freed from or experiencing reduction of pain or difficulty: *relief from the heat.* Related form: **relieved** *adj.* Same sign used for: **content, contentment, satisfy, satisfaction.**

■ [Shows feeling being calmed in the body] With the index-finger sides of both *B hands* against the chest, left hand above the right hand, move the hands downward simultaneously.

religion *n.* A system or set of beliefs and practices concerning faith in and worship of a superhuman agency, the nature of the universe, and what constitutes moral conduct: *the Christian religion.* Related form: **religious** *adj.*

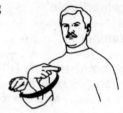

- [Initialized sign] Beginning with the fingertips of the right *R hand* touching the right side of the chest, palm facing down, twist the wrist outward, ending with the fingers pointing forward.

religious order *n.* A body of persons in a monastic community: *to belong to the Jesuit religious order.*

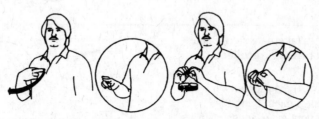

- [**religion** + **organization**] Beginning with the fingertips of the right *R hand* touching the right side of the chest, palm facing in, twist the hand outward, ending with the fingers pointing forward. Then, beginning with the fingertips of both *O hands* touching in front of the chest, palms angled forward, bring the hands away from each other in outward arcs while turning the palms in, ending with the little fingers touching.

relinquish *v.* See sign for GIVE UP.

relocate *v.* See signs for MOVE[1,2].

rely *v.* See sign for DEPEND.

rely on *v. phrase.* See sign for DEPENDABLE.

remain *v.* See signs for CONTINUE[1], STAY[2].

remark[1] *v.* **1.** To comment casually: *He remarked on the new decor.* —*n.* **2.** A casual or informal comment: *She was asked to make a few remarks at the annual dinner.*

- [**say**[1,2] + **something**[2]] Move the extended right index finger in a forward arc from in front of the chin, palm facing in and finger pointing left. Then move the extended right index finger back and forth in front of the right side of the body, palm facing in and finger pointing up.

remark[2] *v., n.* See signs for SAY[1,2].

remarkable

remarkable *adj.* See signs for WONDERFUL[1,2].

remarks *pl. n.* See signs for SAY[1,2], STORY[1,2].

remember[1] *v.* To call back to mind: *Remember how much we enjoyed our vacation.* Same sign used for: **recall, recollect, remind.**

- Move the thumb of the right *10 hand* from the right side of the forehead, palm facing left, smoothly down to touch the thumb of the left *10 hand* held in front of the body, palm facing down.

remember[2] *v.* (alternate sign) Same sign used for: **recall, recollect, remind.**

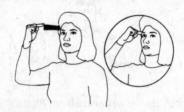

- [Represents finding something way back in one's mind] Bring the extended right index finger, palm facing in, deliberately against the right side of the forehead.

remember, Now I See sign for DISGUSTED[2].

remind[1] *v.* To cause (someone) to remember: *Remind me about the date of the party.* Related form: **reminder** *n.*

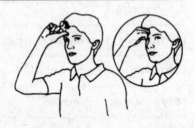

- [The thumb seems to push an idea into the brain] With the thumb of the right *10 hand* touching the middle of the forehead, palm facing up, twist the hand downward to the left.

remind[2] *v.* (alternate sign) Related form: **reminder** *n.*

- [Tapping someone as a reminder] Tap the fingertips of the right *bent hand*, palm facing down, with a double movement against the extended left index finger held up in front of the chest.

remind[3] *v.* See signs for RECALL[1], REMEMBER[1,2].

remodel *v.* See signs for IMPROVE[2], RENOVATE[1,2].

remorse *n.* A painful feeling of regret and guilt for having done something wrong: *The criminal showed no remorse.* Same sign used for: **regret.**

■ [**feel** + **sorry**] Move the bent middle finger of the right *5 hand*, palm facing in, upward on the chest with a repeated movement. Then rub the palm side of the right *10 hand* in a repeated circle on the left side of the chest.

---

remote *adj.* See signs for FAR[1,2].

---

remote control *n.* A device for controlling machines, appliances, etc., from a distance: *to change the channel on the TV with the remote control.*

■ [Mime operating a remote control with one's thumb] Bend the extended thumb of the right *10 hand*, palm facing in, up and down with a repeated movement in front of the right shoulder.

---

remove[1] *v.* To take away or move from a place or position: *Remove the things from the back seat of the car.* Related form: **removal** *n.* Same sign used for: **abolish, abort, abortion, deduct.**

■ [Demonstrates picking something up and tossing it away to remove it] Bring the fingertips of the right *curved hand* against the palm of the left *open hand* while changing into an *A hand*, palms facing each other. Then move the right hand downward off the left fingertips while opening into a *curved 5 hand* in front of the right side of the body.

---

remove[2] *v.* See signs for ELIMINATE[1,2], PURGE, TAKE OFF[2,3].

---

rendezvous *n.* **1.** An appointment to meet at a specified time and place: *arranging a rendezvous with someone new.* **2.** The meeting itself: *a rendezvous at the restaurant.*

■ [**we**[3] + **meet** + **time**[2]] Move the right *V hand* from near the right shoulder, palm facing in and fingers pointing up, from side to side with a double movement. Next, beginning with the extended fingers of both hands pointing up in front of each side of the chest, palms facing each other, bring the hands together in front of the chest. Then tap the bent index finger of the right *X hand*, palm facing down, with a double movement on the back of the left wrist.

renew *v.* **1.** To make new or as if new again: *to renew one's wedding vows.* **2.** To extend the period during which (a license, lease, etc.) is in force: *to renew the contract.*

- [**again** + **new**] Beginning with the right *bent hand* beside the left *open hand,* both palms facing up, bring the right hand up while turning it over, ending with the fingertips of the right hand touching the palm of the left hand. Then slide the back of the right *curved hand,* palm facing up, from the fingers to the heel of the upturned left *open hand* with a double movement.

renounce *v.* See sign for GIVE UP.

renovate[1] *v.* To restore to good condition: *to renovate the old house.* Same sign used for: **remodel, restore.** Related form: **renovation** *n.*

- [Sign similar to **improve** except with a repeated movement] Slide the little finger side of the right *open hand,* palm facing in, in a forward circular movement on the back of the left bent arm held in front of the body with a double movement.

renovate[2] *v.* (alternate sign) Related form: **renovation** *n.* Same sign used for: **remodel, restore.**

- [Initialized sign similar to sign for **change**[1]] With the heels of both *R hands* together in front of the chest, twist the wrists in opposite directions with a double movement. The sign may be made with a sequence of short movements to indicate on-going or a sequence of renovations.

renovate[3] *v.* See sign for IMPROVE[2].

rent *v.* **1.** To make regular payments for use of (property): *to rent an apartment from the landlord.* **2.** To allow the use of in return for a payment or regular payments: *They will rent you a car at the airport.* —*n.* **3.** Payment made for use of property, a residence, etc.: *How much rent do you pay?*

- [Initialized sign similar to sign for **monthly**] Move the middle-finger side of the right *R hand,* palm facing down and finger pointing left, downward with a double movement from the tip to the base of the extended left index finger, palm facing right and finger pointing up in front of the chest.

repair *v.* See signs for FIX[1,2].

repairman *n.* A person whose work is repairing equipment: *The repairman fixed the television.*

■ [**make**[2] + **man**[1]] Beginning with the little-finger side of the right *S hand* on the index-finger side of the left *S hand,* both palms facing in, twist the wrists in opposite directions with a quick repeated movement. Then, beginning with the thumb side of the right *flattened C hand* in front of the right side of the forehead, palm facing left, bring the hand straight forward while closing the fingers to the thumb.

repay *v.* To pay back: *to repay the loan.*

■ [**again** + **pay**[1,2]] Beginning with the right *bent hand* beside the left *open hand,* both palms facing up, bring the right hand up while turning it over, ending with the fingertips of the right hand touching the palm of the left hand. Then, beginning with the middle finger of the right *P hand* touching the palm of the left *open hand,* move the finger forward from the heel to off the fingertips of the left *open hand* held in front of the body.

repeat[1] *v.* To do or say again: *Please repeat what you just said.* Same sign used for: **reiterate.**

■ [**say**[1,2] + **again**] Move the extended right index finger in a forward arc in front of the chin, palm facing down and finger pointing left. Then, beginning with the right *bent hand* beside the left *open hand,* both palms facing up, bring the right hand up while turning it over, ending with the fingertips of the right hand touching the palm of the left hand.

repeat[2] *v.* (alternate sign) Same sign used for: **refund, return.**

■ [Initialized sign similar to sign for **again**] Beginning with the right *R hand* beside the left *open hand,* both palms facing up, bring the right hand up while turning it over, ending with the extended fingertips of the right hand touching the palm of the left hand.

repeat[3] *v.* See sign for AGAIN.

repel *v.* See signs for ELIMINATE[1,2].

repent

repent[1] *v.* To feel sorrow and regret for one's past conduct: *to repent one's sins.* Related form: **repentance** *n.*

■ [Initialized sign similar to sign for **change**[1]] With the palms of both *R hands* crossed in front of the chest, right hand closer to the body then the left, twist the hands to exchange places.

repent[2] *v.* See sign for SORRY.

replace[1] *v.* **1.** To take the place and assume the functions of: *The new person will replace the vice president.* **2.** To provide a substitute for: *to replace the light bulb.* Related form: **replacement** *n.*

■ [Initialized sign similar to sign for **trade**[2]] Beginning with both *R hands* in front of the chest, right hand somewhat higher than the left hand, palms facing in, and fingers pointing in opposite directions, move the hands in an arc around each other to reverse positions.

replace[2] *v.* See signs for TRADE[1,2,3].

reply *n., v.* See signs for ANSWER, REPORT.

report *n.* **1.** A detailed account, as of an event: *to submit a report about the conference.* —*v.* **2.** To give a detailed account: *to report on the meeting.* Same sign used for: **react, reaction, reply, respond, response.**

■ [Initialized sign similar to sign for **answer**] Beginning with fingers of both *R hands* pointing up, right hand closer to the mouth than the left hand and the palms facing each other, move the hands forward and downward with a deliberate movement, ending with the palms facing down and fingers pointing forward.

reporter[1] *n.* **1.** A person who reports: *The recording secretary will be our reporter.* **2.** A person who gathers and reports news, as for a newspaper or television program: *The reporter covered the story about the fire.*

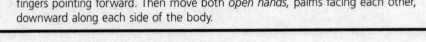

■ [**report** + **person marker**] Beginning with the fingers of both *R hands* pointing up, right hand closer to the mouth than the left and palms facing each other, move the hands forward and downward with a deliberate movement, ending with the palms facing down and the fingers pointing forward. Then move both *open hands,* palms facing each other, downward along each side of the body.

reporter[2] *n.* See sign for AUTHOR.

repossess *v.* See sign for CAPTURE[1].

represent *v.* To stand for, speak for, or express: *This letter represents my opinion.*

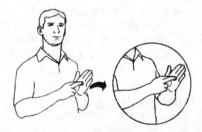

- ■ [Initialized sign similar to sign for **show**[1]] With the fingertips of the right *R hand,* palm facing down, against the left *open hand,* palm facing right and fingers pointing forward, move the hands forward together a short distance.

representative *n.* **1.** A person who represents another; agent: *She will be my representative during the negotiations.* **2.** A member of a legislative body who represents a constituency: *our representative to Congress.*

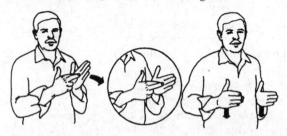

- ■ [**represent** + **person marker**] With the fingertips of the right *R hand,* palm facing down, against the left *open hand,* palm facing right and fingers pointing forward, move the hands forward together a short distance. Then move both *open hands,* palms facing each other, downward along each side of the body.

repress *v.* See sign for PRESSURE. Related form: **repression** *n.*

reprimand *v.* See signs for SCOLD, WARN.

reproduce *v.* **1.** To produce again: *scientists trying to reproduce the results of the experiment.* **2.** To make a copy of; duplicate: *reproducing the chart for the membership.* **3.** To undergo or cause to undergo a process that produces new individuals of the same kind of organism: *Ameba reproduce by fission.*

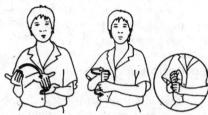

- ■ [**again** + **make**[1,2]] Beginning with the right *bent hand* beside the left *open hand,* both palms facing up, bring the right hand up while turning it over, ending with the fingertips of the right hand touching the palm of the left hand. Then, beginning with the little-finger side of the right *S hand* on the index-finger side of the left *S hand,* both palms facing in, twist the wrists in opposite directions with a quick repeated movement.

reptile *n.* Any of an air-breathing, cold-blooded class of vertebrates with a hard or scaly external covering: *Snakes and turtles are reptiles.* See also sign for SNAKE.

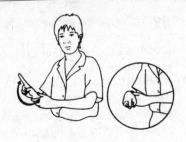

■ [Represents a reptile's tail moving] While holding the wrist of the right hand with the left hand, move the extended right index finger, palm facing forward, down and up with a double movement.

Republican *n.* A member of the Republican party: *The polls predict that a Republican will win the election.* Same sign used for: **republic.**

■ [Initialized sign] Shake the right *R hand,* palm facing forward, from side to side in front of the right shoulder with a double movement.

repudiate *v.* To refuse to accept; reject: *to repudiate the new rules.*

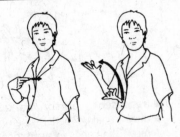

■ [**me + fuss**] Touch the extended right index finger against the center of the chest, palm facing right. Then, beginning with the thumb of the right *5 hand* touching the body, palm facing down, bring the right hand upward to in front of the chest while flipping the hand over, ending with the palm facing up.

repulse *v.* **1.** To refuse or reject: *repulsed his advances.* **2.** To fill with disgust: *Their behavior repulsed me.*

■ [**me + reject**[2,3]] Touch the extended right index finger the center of the chest, palm facing left. Then brush the fingertips of the right *open hand,* palm facing in, with a forward movement from the heel to off the fingertips of the left *open hand,* palm facing up.

reputation[1] *n.* **1.** The opinion of others regarding one's character, abilities, standing, etc.: *a bad reputation among his peers.* **2.** A favorable reputation; good name: *a reputation enhanced by good works.*

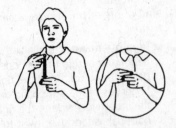

■ [Initialized sign similar to sign for **name**[1]] Tap the middle finger side of the right *R hand,* palm facing in, across the index finger side of the left *H hand,* palm angled right, with a double movement.

reputation[2] *n.* (alternate sign)

- [Initialized sign similar to sign for **character**[1]] Beginning with the right *R hand* in front of the chest, palm facing down, twist the wrist to bring the fingertips of the right *R hand* back against the left side of the chest.

reputation[3] *n.* (alternate sign, used to indicate a bad reputation)

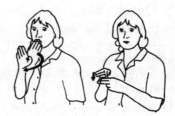

- [**bad** + **name**[1]] Move the fingertips of the right *open hand* from the mouth, palm facing in, downward while flipping the palm quickly down as the hand moves. Then tap the middle-finger side of the right *H hand* across the index-finger side of the left *H hand* with a double movement.

request *v.* See sign for ASK.

require[1] *v.* To need: *to require more time.*

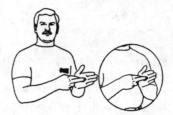

- [Initialized sign similar to sign for **demand**[2]] With the fingertips of the right *R hand*, palm facing in, touching the palm of the left *open hand,* palm facing right, bring both hands back toward the chest.

require[2] *v.* See sign for DEMAND[2].

rescue[1] *v.* **1.** To save from harm: *to rescue the drowning dog.* **2.** To free from a place of confinement: *stranded on an island and rescued after several weeks.*

- [**attend**[1] + **save**[1]] Beginning with both extended index fingers pointing up in front of the chest, right hand closer to the chest than the left hand and both palms facing forward, move the hands forward simultaneously while bending the wrists down. Then, beginning with both *S hands* crossed at the wrists in front of the chest, palms facing in, twist the wrists and move the hands apart, ending with hands in front of each side of the body, palms facing forward.

rescue[2] *v.* See signs for REDEEM, SAVE[1].

research *n.* **1.** Careful investigation to discover facts, revise theories, etc.: *engaged in medical research.* —*v.* **2.** To investigate carefully, as to discover facts: *to research the outbreak of the mysterious illness.*

■ [Initialized sign similar to sign for **investigate**] Move the fingertips of the right *R hand,* palm facing down, across the open left palm from the heel to the fingertips with a double movement.

resemblance *n.* See signs for APPEARANCE, LOOK ALIKE.

resent[1] *v.* To be provoked to anger by: *I resent your insulting remark.* Related form: **resentment** *n.*

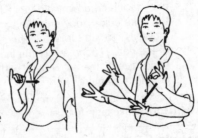

■ [I[1] + **hate**] Bring the thumb side of the right *I hand,* palm facing left, against the center of the chest. Then, beginning with both *8 hands* in front of each side of the chest, palms facing forward, flick the middle fingers forward while changing into *5 hands.*

resent[2] *v.* See sign for BOILING MAD.

reservation[1] *n.* An arrangement to reserve accommodations in advance: *a hotel reservation.* Related form: **reserve** *v.*

■ [Initialized sign similar to sign for **appointment**] Move the right *R hand,* palm facing forward and fingers pointing up, in a small circle and then down to the back of the left *R hand,* palm facing down and fingers pointing right.

reservation[2] *n.* See sign for APPOINTMENT.

reside[1] *v.* To dwell: *I reside on Fifth Avenue.* Related form: **residential** *adj.*

■ [Initialized sign similar to sign for **live**[1,2]] Move the extended fingers of both *R hands,* palms facing in and fingers angled down, upward to each side of the chest.

reside[2] *v.* See signs for ADDRESS[1], LIVE[2]. Related form: **residence** *n.*

residential school *n.* See sign for INSTITUTE[2].

residue *n.* Something that stays behind when the rest has been removed; remainder; remnant: *The soap left a scummy residue in the washing machine.*

- [**leave**[2] + **layer**[1,2]] Beginning with both *5 hands* in front of each side of the body, palms facing each other and fingers pointing down, thrust the fingers downward with a deliberate movement. Then slide the thumb of the right *G hand*, palm facing left, from the heel to off the fingers of the palm of the upturned left *open hand* held in front of the chest.

resign *v.* To give up a position, office, etc.: *to resign from his job; to resign his job.* Same sign used for: **back out, draw back, drop out, quit, recuse.**

- [Represents pulling one's legs out of a situation] Beginning with the fingers of the right *bent U hand*, palm facing down, in the opening of the left *O hand*, palm facing right, pull the right fingers out to the right.

resist *v.* To oppose; fight against; combat: *to resist a bad influence.* See also sign for DOUBT[2]. Same sign used for: **anti-, defensive, immune, uncertain.**

- [Natural gesture for resisting something] Move the right *S hand*, palm facing down, from in front of the right side of the body forward with a double movement.

resolve *v.* See sign for DISSOLVE.

resource[1] *n.* Material used to meet a need: *enough resources to teach the class.*

- [Initialized sign similar to sign for **thing**[2]] Beginning with the right *R hand* in front of the body, palm facing left, move the hand in a double arc to the right.

resource[2] *n.* See sign for REINFORCE.

respect *v.* **1.** To show honor or esteem for: *to respect your parents.* —*n.* **2.** Honor and esteem: *to show respect to older people.* Related form: **respectful** *adj.*

- [Initialized sign similar to sign for **honor**] Beginning with the index-finger side of the right *R hand*, palm facing left, near the right side of the forehead, bring the hand downward and forward.

respiration *n.* See sign for BREATH.

resplendent *adj.* Very splendid; radiant; brilliant: *an evening dress resplendent with sequins.*

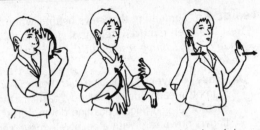

- ■ [**pretty** + **wow**[1,2] + **wonderful**[1,2]] Move the right *5 hand,* palm facing in, in a circular movement in front of the face, closing the fingers to the thumb in front of the chin to form a *flattened O hand.* Next, beginning with both *5 hands* in front of each side of the chest, palms facing in and fingers pointing toward each other, loosely drop the hands up and down with a double movement. Then, beginning with both *open hands* in front of each shoulder, palms facing forward and fingers pointing up, move the hands forward with a short double movement.

respond *v.* See sign for REPORT. Related form: **response** *n.*

response *n.* See sign for ANSWER.

responsible *adj.* See sign for BURDEN. Related form: **responsibility** *n.*

responsible, not See signs for NOT RESPONSIBLE[1,2].

responsibility *n.* **1.** The state or fact or an instance of being accountable: *The responsibility for the mistake is mine.* **2.** A burden or obligation: *Raising children is a big responsibility.* Related form: **responsible** *adj.*

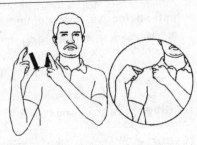

- ■ [Initialized sign indicating burden on one's shoulders] Tap the fingers of both *R hands,* palms facing in, on the right shoulder with a double movement.

rest[1] *v.* **1.** To be still or quiet or to sleep: *to rest after lunch.* —*n.* **2.** Repose, relaxation, or sleep: *Have a good rest.* Same sign used for: **idle, recess, relax.**

- ■ [Shows laying one's hands on one's chest as if in repose] With the arms crossed at the wrists, lay the palm of each *open hand* on the chest near the opposite shoulder.

rest[2] *v., n.* (alternate sign) Same sign used for: **recess, relax.**

- ■ [Natural gesture for relaxing] With the forearms crossed, lay each open palm down on the opposite arm near the elbow pushing the arms back against the chest.

rest[3] *v., n.* (alternate sign) Same sign used for: **recess, relax, retire.**

- [Initialized sign] With the arms crossed at the wrists, place the fingers of each *R hand* near the opposite shoulder.

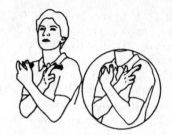

rest[4] *v.* See sign for LEAVE[2].

restaurant *n.* A place to buy and eat a meal: *to have a quiet dinner in a cozy restaurant.*

- [Initialized sign similar to sign for **cafeteria**] Wipe the fingertips of the right *R hand*, palm facing in, with a short movement first down the right side and then down the left side of the chin.

restless[1] *adj.* Characterized by an inability to rest: *to have a restless night; to be in a restless mood.* Same sign used for: **antsy.**

- [Represents one's legs turning over restlessly during a sleepless night] With the back of the right *bent V hand* laying across the open left palm, both palms facing up, turn the right hand over and back with a double movement.

restless[2] *adj.* Unable to sit still: *a restless child.* Same sign used for: **antsy.**

- [Represents one's legs shifting restlessly] Beginning with the heel of the right *bent V hand* on the extended fingers of the left *H hand*, both palms facing down, twist the right hand back and forth with a double movement.

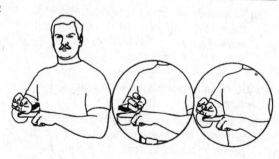

rest of See sign for AFTER[1].

restore *v.* See signs for RENOVATE[1], SAVE[3,4].

restrain *v.* See sign for CONTROL[1]. Related form: **restraint** *n.*

restrict

restrict[1] *v.* To keep within limits; confine: *Small cages at the zoo restrict the lions' movements.* Same sign used for: **limit, quota.**

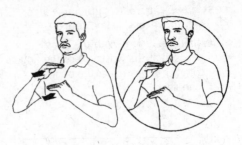

- [Shows the level of limit] Beginning with both *bent hands* in front of the chest, right hand above the left hand and both palms facing down, move both hands forward simultaneously.

restrict[2] *v.* (alternate sign)

- [Initialized sign showing the level or degree of a limit] Beginning with both *R hands* in front of the chest, right hand above the left hand and both palms facing down, move both hands forward simultaneously.

rest room[1] *n.* A room containing one or more sinks, toilets, counters, etc., as in a restaurant: *The rest rooms are one flight up.*

- [Abbreviation **r-r**] Tap the right *R hand*, palm facing down and the fingers pointing forward, downward first in front of the right side of body and then again slightly to the right.

rest room[2] *n.* See sign for TOILET.

result[1] *n.* Something that happens because of something else; outcome: *What was the result of your research?* Same sign used for: **outcome.**

- [Initialized sign similar to sign for **end**[2]] Move the fingertips of the right *R hand*, palm facing down, along the length of the index finger of the left *B hand*, palm facing in, and then down off the fingertips.

result[2] *n.* (alternate sign) Same sign used for: **outcome.**

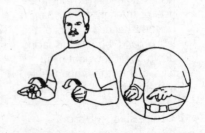

- [Initialized sign similar to sign for **happen**] Beginning with the fingers of both *R hands* pointing forward in front of the body, palms facing each other, flip the hands over toward each other, ending with the palms facing down.

resume or **résumé** *n.* A short summation of one's educational and professional qualifications: *a good idea to keep your resume up to date.*

■ [Initialized sign showing the shape of a typed resume] Beginning with the fingertips of both *R hands* touching in front of the chest, palms angled forward, bring the hands apart to in front of each shoulder, then straight down, and finally back together in front of the lower chest.

resurrection[1] *n.* The act of rising from the dead and coming to life again: *Many people hope for personal resurrection.* Same sign used for: **get up.**

■ [Represents getting up on one's legs] Beginning with the right *V hand* in front of the right side of the body, palm facing up, flip the hand over to the left to touch the fingers on the left *open hand,* palm facing up.

resurrection[2] *n.* (alternate sign) Same sign used for: **rise.**

■ [Represents one's legs rising into the air] Beginning with the extended fingertips of the right *V hand,* palm facing in, touching the palm of the left *open hand* held in front of the chest, palm facing up, bring the right hand upward to in front of the face.

retail *v.* See sign for SELL.

retain *v.* See signs for SAVE[2,3,4].

retainer *n.* See sign for BRACES.

retaliate[1] *v.* To return evil or injury with something similar or equivalent; get even: *The enemy retaliated with a bombing attack.* Related form: **retaliation** *n.*

■ Bring the right *modified X hand* upward from near the right hip to touch against the left *modified X hand* held in front of the body, palms facing each other.

retaliate[2] *v.* See sign for REVENGE.

retarded[1] *adj.* Characterized by limitations in intellectual development; developmentally slow: *mainstreaming retarded persons into the school system.* Same sign used for: **mentally retarded.**

■ [Initialized sign similar to sign for **mind**] Tap the extended fingers of the right *R hand* against the right side of the forehead with a double movement.

retarded[2] *adj.* (alternate sign) Same sign used for: **slow learner.**

■ [**mind + slow**] Touch the extended right index finger to the right side of the forehead. Then pull the fingertips of the right *5 hand*, palm facing down, from the fingers upward on the back of the left *5 hand*, palm facing down.

retire[1] *v.* To give up an occupation or career, as when one reaches retirement age: *retired from work at age 65.*

■ [Initialized sign similar to sign for **vacation**] Touch the extended thumbs of both *R hands*, palms facing each other, against each side of the chest.

retire[2] *v.* See sign for REST[3].

retirement *n.* Similar to sign for RETIRE[1] but made with a double movement.

retreat *n.* **1.** A quiet place of rest or refuge: *The cabin in the mountains is a lovely retreat.* **2.** A short period of retirement to a quiet place for religious meditation and spiritual renewal: *to go on a retreat organized by the church.*

■ [Initialized sign similar to sign for **run away**] Beginning with the extended fingers of the right *R hand*, palm facing forward, pointing up between the index finger and middle finger of the left *5 hand*, palm facing down, move the right hand outward to the right.

retrieve *v.* See signs for GET, OPEN[1].

retrospect *n.* See sign for HINDSIGHT.

return[1] *v.* **1.** To bring back: *to return the damaged item to the store.* **2.** To come or go back: *to return to my birthplace.*

■ [Initialized sign similar to sign for **come**[2]] Beginning with the extended fingers of both *R hands* pointing in opposite directions in front of the body, left hand closer to the body than the right hand and palms facing in, roll the hands over each other to exchange places until reaching the chest.

return[2] *v.* (alternate sign) See also sign for REFUND[1].

■ [Initialized sign similar to sign for **come**[1]] Bring the extended index fingers of both *R hands* from in front of the body, palms facing in and fingers pointing up, back to touch each side of the chest.

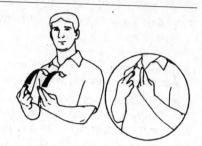

return[3] *v.* See signs for BRING, REPEAT[2].

Return key *n.* See sign for ENTER KEY.

reunion *n.* **1.** An act, state, or time of coming together again: *a reunion of the singers for a last concert.* **2.** A festive gathering, as of friends, relatives, or colleagues, after a period of separation: *a family reunion; a class reunion.*

■ [**again** + **belong**[1]] Beginning with the right *bent hand* beside the left *open hand*, both palms facing up, bring the right hand up while turning it over, ending with the fingertips of the right hand touching the palm of the left hand. Then, beginning with both *open F hands* in front of each side of the chest, palms facing each other, move the hands toward each other until they intersect and close.

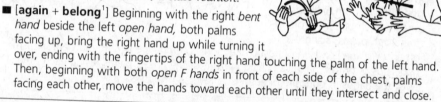

reveal *v.* See signs for ANNOUNCE, SHOW[1], TELL[1].

revenge *n.* An act of retaliation for an injury or wrong: *to take revenge on the people who hurt you.* Same sign used for: **avenge, get even, retaliate, vengance.**

■ Beginning with both *modified X hands* in front of the chest, left hand above the right hand and palms facing each other, bring the right hand upward until the knuckles of both the hands touch.

revenue *n.* See sign for INCOME[1].

reverberate *v.* See sign for BELL[1]. Related form: **reverberation** *n.*

reverend *n.* See sign for PREACHER.

reverse[1] *n.* **1.** The opposite of something: *When I moved left, you did the reverse.* **2.** The back of something: *The signature is on the reverse.* —*adj.* **3.** Opposite in position or direction: *the reverse side of the card.* —*v.* **4.** To turn in the opposite direction: *to reverse the ship's course.*

■ [Initialized sign similar to sign for **change**[1]] With the heels of both *R hands* against each other in front of the

chest, palms facing each other, twist the hands in opposite directions to exchange positions.

reverse[2] *n., adj., v.* (alternate sign) Same sign used for: **revert, swap, switch.**

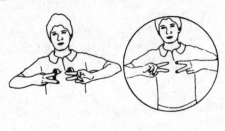

- [The fingers seem to reverse positions] Beginning with both *V hands* in front of the chest, right palm facing in and fingers pointing left, and left palm facing out and fingers pointing right, twist the hands in opposite directions to turn the palms the opposite way.

reverse interpret *v.* To translate sign language into speech: *They reverse interpreted the deaf actress's speech.*

- [**reverse**[1] + **interpret**] With the heels of both *R hands* against each other in front of the chest, palms facing each other, twist the hands in opposite directions to exchange positions. Then, with the fingertips of both *F hands* touching in front of the chest, palms facing each other, twist the hands in opposite directions to reverse positions.

revert *n.* See sign for REVERSE[2].

review *v.* To look at or study again: *to review your lessons.*

- [Initialized sign] With the little-finger side of the right *R hand*, palm facing left, on the open left palm, twist the right fingers back toward the chest.

revise *v.* See sign for REVONATE[2]. Related form: **revision** *n.*

revival *n.* A special, evangelistic religious service or event to encourage the renewal of faith: *to attend a revival.* Related form: **revive** *v.*

- [Initialized sign similar to sign for **excite**] Move the extended fingertips of both *R hands*, palms facing in, in repeated alternating circles on each side of the chest.

revive *v.* See signs for INSPIRE, LIVE[1].

revoke *v.* See signs for TEAR[1,2].

revolt *v.* See sign for PROTEST[2]. Related form: **revolution** *n.*

revolution *n.* A complete and usually forcible replacement of a government: *the American Revolution*. Related form: **revolt** *v., n.*

- [Initialized sign similar to sign for **protest**[2]] Beginning with the right *R hand* in front of the right shoulder, palm facing back, twist the hand forward, ending with the palm facing forward.

revolve *v.* See signs for AROUND[1,2].

revulsion *n.* See sign for DISGUSTED[1].

reward[1] *n., v.* See signs for CONTRIBUTION, GIFT[1,2].

reward[2] *v.* See sign for GIVE[1].

rewrite *v.* To write again or differently: *had to rewrite the letter several times.*

- [**write**[1,2,3] + **again**] Slide the fingertips of the right *flattened O hand* across the open left palm with a double movement. Then, beginning with the right *bent hand* beside the left *open hand,* both palms facing up, bring the right hand up while turning it over, ending with the fingertips of the right hand touching the palm of the left hand.

rhinoceros[1] *n.* A large, hoofed, thick-skinned mammal with one or two horns on the snout: *Many rhinoceroses are bad-tempered and will charge a human being.* Shortened form: **rhino.**

- [The shape of a rhinoceros's horn] Beginning with the index-finger side of the right *C hand* encircling the nose, palm facing left, bring the right hand upward in an arc while closing into an *S hand.*

rhinoceros[2] *n.* (alternate sign)

- [Shows the location of a rhinoceros's horn] Touch the thumb side of the right *I hand* against the nose, palm facing left.

rhyme *n.* **1.** Identity of sounds, particularly at the ends of words, as in nearby lines of verse: *The rhyme is not quite right in this poem.* **2.** A word having the same pattern of sounds at the end as another: *looking for a rhyme for "beautiful."* **3.** Poetry with rhyme; verse: *The girl read the rhyme aloud.* —*v.* **4.** To form a rhyme: *"Daisy" rhymes with "lazy."*

■ [**music** + an initialized form of **music**] Swing the little-finger side of the right *open hand,* palm facing left, back and forth across the length of the bent left forearm held in front of the chest. Then swing the extended fingers of the right *R hand,* palm facing down, back and forth across the length of the bent left forearm held in front of the chest.

rhythm *n.* A movement or pattern with regular repetition: *follow the rhythm.*

■ [Initialized sign indicating the movement of sound] Beginning with right *R hand* in front of the chest, palm facing left, move the hand in a wavy movement to the right.

ribbon[1] *n.* A strip of fabric used ornamentally, as for bows or belts: *to tie a ribbon in the girl's hair.*

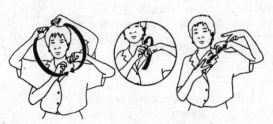

■ [Shows bringing a ribbon around one's head + **bow**[2]] Bring both *modified X hands* from the top of the head around each side of the head to under the chin and mime tying a bow. Then, beginning with the knuckles of both *bent V hands* together near the left side of the neck, palms facing in, bring the hands apart while straightening the fingers into *V hands.*

ribbon[2] *n.* See signs for BOW[2], MEDAL.

ribs *pl. n.* The curved bones, 12 pairs of which form the wall of the chest, in one's torso: *The football player broke two ribs in the game.*

■ [Location and shape of one's ribs] Beginning with both *curved 4 hands* on each side of the body, palms facing in, move both hands toward the center of the body with a double movement.

rice[1] *n.* The starchy seeds from an annual grass grown in wet areas for food: *a diet of rice.*

■ [Initialized sign similar to sign for **soup**] Move the right *R hand* from touching the open left palm held in front of the body, upward to the mouth.

rice[2] *n.* (alternate sign)

■ [Shape of a serving of rice] Beginning with the right *curved hand* over the left *curved hand* in front of the chest, palms facing each other, cup the hands together.

rich *adj.* Having much wealth, as money, possessions, and land: *A rich family bought the old mansion.* Same sign used for: **prosperous, wealth, wealthy.**

■ [Represents a pile of money in one's hand] Beginning with the little-finger side of the right *S hand*, palm facing left, in the open left palm held in front of the body, raise the right hand a short distance while opening into a *curved 5 hand*, palm facing down.

ricochet *v.* **1.** To bounce back after a glancing blow on a surface: *The bullet ricocheted off the wall and hit an innocent bystander.* —*n.* **2.** The rebound of an object in recocheting or the object itself: *I was struck by the ricochet of the bullet.* Same sign used for: **bounce.**

■ [Shows the movement of something ricocheting off another thing] Bounce the extended right index finger back against the open left palm and then forward again by twisting the wrist outward.

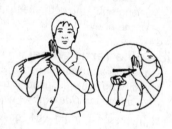

rid *v.* See signs for ELIMINATE[1,2].

riddle *n.* A puzzling question or statement requiring intricate thought to answer, unravel, or understand: *I had no answer to the riddle.*

■ [**funny** + an initialized sign] With a double movement, brush the nose with the fingertips of the right *U hand*, palm facing in, bending the fingers of the right *U hand* back to the palm each time. Then move both *R hands* back and forth with a short double movement in front of each shoulder, palms facing forward and fingers pointing up.

ride a bicycle[1] *v. phrase.* To sit astride a bicycle, causing it to move by pedaling: *rides a bicycle to work.*

- [Represents legs astride a bicycle] With the fingers of the right *V hand,* palm facing in and fingers pointing down, straddling the index-finger side of the left *open hand,* palm facing right, move the hands forward a short distance.

ride a bicycle[2] *v. phrase.* See sign for BICYCLE.

ride a horse *v. phrase.* To sit on and direct the motion of a horse: *learning to ride a horse.* Same sign used for: **horseback riding.**

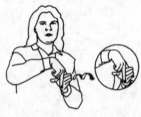

- [Represents straddling one's legs on a horse] With the index finger and the middle finger of the right *open hand,* palm facing in and fingers pointing down, straddling the index finger side of the left *open hand,* palm facing right, move the hands forward in a double arc.

ride a tricycle *v. phrase.* See sign for TRICYCLE.

ride in a car, truck, etc. *v. phrase.* To make a trip, as a passenger or driver, inside a car or similar vehicle: *There's room for you to ride in the car.*

- [Represents a person sitting in a vehicle] With the fingers of the right *bent U hand,* palm facing down, hooked over the thumb of the left *C hand,* palm facing right, move the hands forward from in front of the body.

ride on a ferris wheel *v. phrase.* To be carried on a ferris wheel, an amusement-park ride in the form of a large upright wheel with seats suspended from the rim: *You go up very high when you ride a ferris wheel.*

- [Represents sitting while going around a ferris wheel] With fingers of the right *bent U hand,* palm facing down, hooked over the thumb of the left *C hand,* palm facing right, move both hands upward and forward in a large circle in front of the chest.

rider *n.* See sign for PASSENGER.

ridicule *v.* See sign for TORTURE.

ridiculous *adj.* See signs for SILLY[1,2].

rifle *n.* A gun with a long barrel, usually fired from the shoulder: *Rifles can be fired with great accuracy at long range.*

■ [Mime pulling a trigger on a rifle] With the index fingers of both *L hands* pointing forward in front of the body, palms facing in opposite directions and right hand nearer the chest than the left hand, wiggle the thumb of the right hand up and down with a repeated movement.

right[1] *n.* **1.** The side that faces east when a person or thing is facing north: *Turn to your right.* —*adj.* **2.** Of, pertaining to, or located on or toward the right side: *the right side of the road.* —*adv.* **3.** On or toward the right side: *Turn right.*

■ [Initialized sign showing a right direction] Move the right *R hand,* palm facing forward, from in front of the right side of the body to the right a short distance.

right[2] *n.* Something that is legally or morally due someone: *As free people, we have a right to vote.* Same sign used for: **all right, okay, privilege.**

■ Slide the little-finger side of the right *open hand,* palm facing left, in an upward arc across the upturned left palm held in front of the body.

right[3] *adj.* Conforming to the truth; being correct: *the right answer.* Same sign used for: **accurate, correct.**

■ With the index fingers of both hands extended forward at right angles, palms angled in and right hand above left, bring the little-finger side of the right hand sharply down across the thumb side of the left hand.

right turn[1] *n.* A movement angling toward the right side: *to make a right turn.*

■ [Initialized sign indicating turning right] Beginning with the right *R hand* in front of the right shoulder, palm facing in and fingers pointing up, twist the hand forward, ending with the palm facing forward.

right turn[2] *n.* (alternate sign)

■ [Shows direction of a right turn] Move the right *open hand,* palm facing in and fingers pointing up, to the right by twisting the wrist, ending with the palm facing forward.

right-handed *adj.* **1.** More adept with the right hand than with the left: *Most people are right-handed.* **2.** Adapted for use with the right hand: *a right-handed pair of scissors.*

■ [**right**¹ + **hand**] Move the right *R hand*, palm facing forward, to the right in front of the right side of the chest. Then tap the palm of the right *curved hand* with a double movement on the back of the left *curved hand*, both palms facing down.

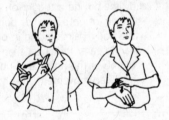

right-justify *v.* To align (text) on the right column: *to right-justify the copy.*

■ [**right**¹ + **side**²] Move the right *R hand*, palm facing down, from in front of the right side of the chest to the right. Then move the right *open hand*, palm facing left and fingers pointing forward, downward in front of the right side of the body.

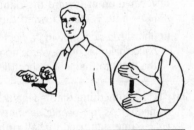

righteous¹ *adj.* Moral; virtuous: *a righteous man.*

■ [Shows the straight path a righteous person would take] Slide the little-finger side of the right *open hand*, palm facing left, from the heel to off the fingertips of the left *open hand*, palm facing up.

righteous² *adj.* (alternate sign)

■ [Initialized sign similar to sign for **clean**] Slide the little-finger side of the right *R hand*, palm facing left, from the heel to off the fingertips of the left *open hand*, palm facing up.

righteous³ *adj.* (alternate sign)

■ [Initialized sign similar to sign for **right**³] Tap the little-finger side of the right *R hand* on the index-finger side of the left *R hand* with a double movement, palms facing in opposite directions.

rigid *adj.* See sign for FREEZE.

rim[1] *n.* The border of a wheel: *the rim of the tire is bent.*

■ [**car**[1] + the shape of a tire rim] Beginning with both *S hands* in front of each side of the chest, palms facing in, move the hands up and down with a repeated alternating movement. Then move the extended right index finger, palm facing down and finger pointing left, around the curve made by the index finger and thumb of the left *modified C hand,* palm facing down and fingers pointing down.

rim[2] *n.* See sign for BRIM.

rind *n.* The outer covering of a citrus fruit: *an orange rind.*

■ [**skin**[2] + shape of a fruit and a gesture showing taking the rind off] Pinch the skin of the right cheek between the thumb and index finger of the right *A hand.* Then, beginning with the fingertips of both *curved 5 hands* together in front of the chest, palms facing each other, bend the right hand back from the wrist with a repeated movement in several directions.

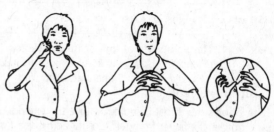

ring[1] *n.* A thin circle of metal worn on the finger: *a wedding ring.*

■ [The location of a ring on the ring finger] Move the bent thumb and index finger of the right *5 hand,* palm facing down, back and forth the length of the ring finger of the left *5 hand,* palm facing down, with a repeated movement.

ring[2] *v.* **1.** To cause a bell to sound: *to ring the church bells.* **2.** To give forth a sound: *The doorbell rang.* —*n.* **3.** The sound of a bell: *I heard the ring of the bells.*

■ [Initialized sign similar to sign for **bell**[1]] Quickly tap the index-finger side of the right *R fingers,* palm facing forward, against the open left palm with a repeated movement.

ring[3] *v., n.* See signs for BELL[1,2,3,4,5].

ringleader *n.* See sign for GUIDE[1].

ring tone *n.* On a mobile phone, the customized sound that indicates an incoming call.

- [**ring**[2] + **hear**] With a repeated movement, quickly tap the index-finger side of the right *R fingers*, palm facing left, against the open left palm. Then bring the extended right index finger to the right ear.

rinse *n., v.* See sign for DYE.

riot *v., n.* See signs for COMPLAIN, MESSY, MOB.

rip *v.* See signs for TEAR[1,2].

rise *v., n.* See signs for RAISE[2], RESURRECTION[2].

risk[1] *n.* **1.** The possibility of loss or injury: *He took a risk in the stock market.* —*v.* **2.** To expose to hazard or danger: *risked his life.* Same sign used for: **cutthroat, peril.**

- [Shows the throat being cut] Move the extended right index finger from left to right across the throat, palm facing down and finger pointing left, while grimacing.

risk[2] *n., v.* (alternate sign) Same sign used for: **peril.**

- [Initialized sign showing the throat being cut] Move the right *R hand* from left to right across the throat, palm facing down and fingers pointing left, while grimacing.

risk[3] *n.* See sign for DANGER.

rival *n.* See sign for ENEMY.

river[1] *n.* A large, natural stream of water flowing through a channel: *sailed down the river to the ocean.*

■ [**water** + initialized sign similar to **flow**[1] but formed with a wavy movement] Tap the index-finger side of the right *W hand*, palm facing left, against the chin with a double movement. Then move both *R hands*, palms facing down and fingers pointing forward, from in front of each side of the chest forward with a wavy up-and-down movement.

river[2] *n.* (alternate sign) Same sign used for: **creek, stream.**

■ [**water** + **flow**[1] formed with a wavy movement] Tap the index-finger side of the right *W hand*, palm facing left, against the chin with a double movement. Then move both *5 hands*, palms facing down, forward from in front of the chest with an up-and-down wavy movement.

rivet *n.* **1.** A metal bolt: *to hold the pieces together with a rivet.* —*v.* **2.** To fasten firmly: *to rivet the metal shelves together.*

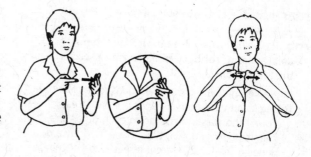

■ [**penetrate**[1] + **stretch**[1]] Insert the extended right index finger, palm facing left, between the middle finger and ring finger of the left *open hand*, palm facing in. Then hit the knuckles of both *S hands* together in front of the chest with a double movement, palms facing in.

road[1] *n.* A way between places for vehicles to travel on: *to take a different road.* Same sign used for: **avenue, boulevard, lane, path, route, street, trail, way.**

■ [Indicates the shape of a road] Move both *open hands* from in front of each side of the body, palms facing each other, forward with a parallel movement.

road[2] *n.* (alternate sign)

■ [Initialized sign showing the shape of a road] Move both *R hands* from in front of each side of the body, palms facing each other, forward with a parallel movement.

roam[1] *v.* To go about without a special plan: *roam around the city.* Same sign used for: **adrift, wander.**

■ [Represents the aimless movement of a roaming person] Beginning with the extended right index finger pointing up in front of the right shoulder, palm facing forward, move the hand to in front of the chest and then outward again in a large wavy motion.

roam[2] *v.* (alternate sign) Same sign used for: **adrift, wander.**

■ [Moving aimlessly alone] Beginning with the back of the extended right index finger, palm facing forward, near the back of the left *open hand* near the chest, palm facing in, move the right hand forward and to the right with a wavy movement.

roar *v., n.* See signs for SCREAM[1,2].

rob[1] *v.* To steal or steal from: *to rob a bank.* Related form: **robbery** *n.* Same sign used for: **burglary, hold up, raid.**

■ [Represents pulling out one's guns for a robbery] Beginning with both *H hands* in front of each side of the waist, palms facing each other and fingers pointing down, twist the wrists upward, bringing the hands in front of each side of the body, palms facing each other and fingers pointing forward.

rob[2] *v.* (alternate sign) Related form: **robbery** *n.* Same sign used for: **burglary, hold up, raid.**

■ [Represents aiming one's guns for a robbery] Beginning with both *L hands* in front of the chest, palms facing each other and index fingers angled upward move the hands downward with a double movement.

rob[3] *v.* See sign for STEAL[1]. Related form: **robbery** *n.*

robber[1] *n.* A person who robs: *The police will catch the robber.* Same sign used for: **bandit, burglar, crook, rustler, thief.**

■ Beginning with the fingertips of both *H hands* touching under the nose, palms facing down, bring the hands apart to in front of each shoulder.

robber[2] *n.* (alternate sign) Same sign used for: **bandit, burglar, crook, rustler, thief.**

- [A sign similar to sign for **robber**[1] + **person marker**] Beginning with the fingers of the right *H hand*, palm facing down, under the nose, bring the hand outward to the right. Then move both *open hands*, palms facing each other, downward along each side of the body.

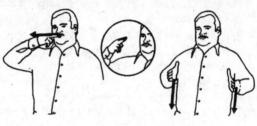

robe *n.* A long, loose garment: *to wear a robe over your pajamas.* Same sign used for: **bathrobe.**

- [Shows location of a robe on one's torso and then the way a robe overlaps] Touch the fingers of both *open hands*, palms facing in and fingers pointing toward each other, first to the upper chest and then near the waist. Then bring both *open hands*, palms facing in and fingers pointing down, across each other in front of the waist.

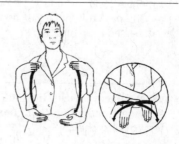

robin *n.* A small songbird with a reddish breast related to the thrush: *The robin made a nest.*

- [**red**[1,2,3] + **bird** + location of robin's red breast] Move the extended right index finger downward on the lips, bending the index finger down toward the palm as the hand moves. Next open and close the extended right index finger and thumb with a repeated movement in front of the mouth. Then, beginning with the index-finger side of the right *curved hand* against the chest, palm facing down, move the hand downward while turning the palm up, ending with the little-finger side of the right *curved hand* touching the body near the waist.

robot *n.* A mechanical form often shaped like a person, created to do routine tasks: *The robot walked across the room.*

- [Mime the traditional arm movements of a robot] Beginning with the right *open hand* in front of the right side of the body, palm facing left and fingers pointing forward, and the left *open hand* near the left hip, palm facing in and fingers pointing down, move the hands up and down with a deliberate alternating double movement.

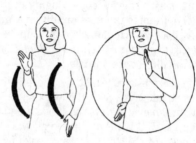

rock[1] *n.* **1.** A large mass of stone, as one forming a hill: *climbed the rock.* **2.** A stone of any size: *to throw a rock.* Same sign used for: **stone.**

- ■ [Indicates the hardness of a rock] Tap the back of the right *S hand,* palm facing up, on the back of the left *S hand* held in front of the chest, palm facing down, with a repeated movement.

rock[2] *n.* (alternate sign) Same sign used for: **stone.**

- ■ [Indicates the hardness of a rock] Tap the knuckles of the right *A hand,* palm facing down, on the back of the left *S hand* held in front of the chest, palm facing down, with a repeated movement.

rock[3] *v.* To move backward and forward with rhythm and a swaying motion: *to rock in a rocking chair.* Same sign used for: **rocking chair.**

- ■ [Shows movement of a rocking chair] Beginning with the thumbs of both *L hands* on each side of the chest, palms facing each other and index fingers pointing up, bring the hands forward and down to in front of each side of the waist, index fingers pointing forward, and then back up again with a double movement.

rock[4] *v.* (alternate sign)

- ■ [Shows movement of a rocking chair] Beginning with both *3 hands* in front of each side of the body, palms facing each other and fingers pointing forward, bring the hands up toward the shoulders and back down with a double movement, moving the body in rhythm with the hands and keeping the elbows close to the body.

rock[5] *n.* See sign for METAL.

rocket[1] *n.* **1.** A device consisting of a tube filled with explosives that burn very quickly to force the tube rapidly upward: *sent up rockets on the fourth of July.* **2.** A space vehicle launched or propelled by such a device: *to send a rocket to the moon.* Same sign used for: **missile, space shuttle.**

- ■ [Initialized sign showing the movement of a rocket being launched] Slide the index-finger side of the right *R hand,* palm facing forward and fingers pointing up, upward from the base to off the fingers of the left *open hand,* palm facing right and fingers pointing up.

rocket[2] *n.* (alternate sign) Same sign used for: **missile, space shuttle.**

- [Initialized sign showing the movement of a rocket being launched] Beginning with the heel of the right *R hand,* palm facing forward and fingers pointing up, on the back of the left *S hand* held in front of the chest, palm facing down, move the right hand upward in front of the face.

rocking chair *n.* See signs for ROCK[3,4].

rocking horse *n.* A toy horse on rockers: *to ride the rocking horse.*

- [**horse** + **rock**[4]] With the extended thumb of the right *U hand* against the right side of the forehead, palm facing forward, bend the fingers of the right *U hand* up and down with a double movement. Then, beginning with both *3 hands* in front of each side of the body, palms facing each other and fingers pointing forward, bring the hands up toward the shoulders and back down with a double movement, moving the body in rhythm with the hands and keeping the elbows close to the body.

rocky *adj.* Full of rocks: *a rocky road.*

- [**rock**[1,2] + a gesture showing the shape of boulders] Tap the palm side of the right *A hand,* palm facing down, on the back of the left *S hand* held in front of the chest, palm facing down, with a double movement. Then, with an alternating movement, bring first the right and then the left *5 hand* from in front of each shoulder, palms facing forward, downward to in front of the sides of the body, ending with the palms facing back and the fingers pointing down.

rod *n.* See signs for PIPE[3], STICK[2,3,4].

rodeo *n.* A competition of Western cowboy skills, as trick horseback riding and cattle roping: *There are men and women champions who ride in the rodeo.*

- [Represents a person bouncing while bronco riding] Bring the right *V* fingers downward with a repeated movement to straddle the index-finger side of the left *B hand* held in front of the chest, palm facing right.

role *n.* An actor's part in a play, movie, etc.: *an exciting role in the new TV drama.*

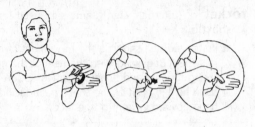

■ [Initialized sign similar to sign for **character**[2]] Move the fingers of the right *R hand* in a small circle near the open left palm, ending with the right fingertips touching the left palm.

roll *v.* To move along by turning over and over: *The ball rolled across the room; to roll a barrel.*

■ [Demonstrates the action of a rolling ball] Beginning with both extended index fingers pointing in opposite directions in front of the waist, palms facing in and right hand closer to the body than the left hand, move the index fingers over each other in large circles while moving the hands forward.

roller *n.* See sign for HAIR ROLLER[1].

roller skate *n., v.* See sign for SKATE[1].

rolling pin *n.* A cylinder used for rolling out dough: *to use a rolling pin to roll out the pie crust.*

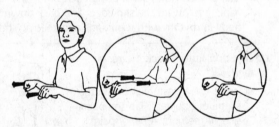

■ [Mime the action of using a rolling pin] Move both *S hands* from in front of the body, palms facing down, forward and back with a double movement.

roll one's hair *v. phrase.* To wrap one's hair on rollers to set it in curls or waves: *to roll my hair tonight.* Same sign used for: **hair roller, set one's hair.**

■ [Indicates the action of putting one's hair on rollers] Beginning with both extended fingers pointing in opposite directions near the right ear, palms facing down, move the fingers around each other in alternating circles with a repeated movement.

romance *n.* **1.** A love story: *likes to read romances.* **2.** A love affair: *the romance between a man and a woman.*

■ [Initialized sign] Bring the extended fingers of the right *R hand,* palm facing back, from touching the shoulder forward in a double arc.

Romania *n.* A republic in southeast Europe: *Bucharest is the capital of Romania.* Related form: **Romanian** *adj., n.*

■ Move the fingertips of the right *modified C hand* from the left side of the chest downward at an angle to the right side of the body.

Rome *n.* A city in Italy: *Rome is the capital of Italy.* Related form: **Roman** *n., adj.* Same sign used for: **Latin.**

■ [Initialized sign showing the shape of a Roman nose] Touch the fingertips of the right *R hand* first to the forehead and then to the nose.

romp *v., n.* See sign for PLAY[1].

roof[1] *n.* The external top covering of a building: *had to climb on the roof to fix it.*

■ [The shape of a roof] Beginning with the fingertips of both *B hands* touching in front of the head, palms angled down, bring the hands downward and outward at an angle to about shoulder width.

roof[2] *n.* (alternate sign)

■ [Initialized sign showing the shape of a roof] Beginning with the fingertips of both *R hands* touching in front of the forehead, palms angled down, bring the hands downward and outward at an angle to about shoulder width.

room[1] *n.* **1.** A space within a building enclosed by walls, a floor, and a ceiling: *The apartment has 6 rooms.* **2.** Such a space designed or available for a special purpose: *the living room.*

■ [Initialized sign similar to sign for **box**] Beginning with both *R hands* in front of each side of the body, palms facing each other, turn the hands sharply in opposite directions, ending with both palms facing in.

room[2] *n.* See sign for: BOX.

rooster *n.* A male fowl: *The rooster crowed.* Same sign used for: **cock.**

- ■ [Represents a rooster's comb] Tap the extended thumb of the right *3 hand*, palm facing left, against the forehead with a repeated movement.

root[1] *n.* The part of a plant that grows down into the soil and absorbs moisture and nutrients: *Water the plant so the roots are thoroughly moistened.*

- ■ [Represents roots growing beneath the soil] Beginning with the fingers of the right *flattened O hand,* palm facing down, inserted in the left *C hand,* palm facing right, push the right hand down while opening into a *5 hand* as it emerges.

root[2] *n.* (alternate sign)

- ■ [Initialized sign representing roots growing beneath the soil] Push the fingers of the right *R hand,* palm facing in, down through the opening of the left *C hand*, palm facing right, while opening the fingers into a *5 hand* as it emerges.

rope *n.* A thick cord made by twisting smaller cords together: *tied the bundle of newspapers with a rope.*

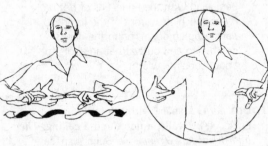

- ■ [Initialized sign showing the shape of a rope] Beginning with the fingertips of both *R hands* pointing toward each other and touching in front of the chest, palms facing in, bring the hands outward to in front of each shoulder while twisting the wrists as the hands move.

rosary *n.* **1.** A string of beads used in counting prayers, especially in the Roman Catholic Church: *cherishes her beautiful rosary.* **2.** These prayers recited as a private devotion: *to recite the rosary.*

- ■ [Initialized sign showing the shape of a rosary] Beginning with the fingers of both *R hands* touching in front of the chest, palms facing forward, move the hands outward and down to touch again in front of the waist, ending with the palms facing down and the fingers pointing forward.

rose *n.* A flower that grows on a thorny stem: *to smell the roses.*

■ [Initialized sign similar to sign for **flower**] Touch the extended fingertips of the right *R hand,* palm facing in, first to the right side of the nose and then to the left side.

rot[1] *v.* **1.** To decay: *The potato rotted.* —*n.* **2.** The state of being rotten, the process of rotting, or the decay itself: *The wood in the cellar was filled with rot.* Related form: **rotten** *adj.*

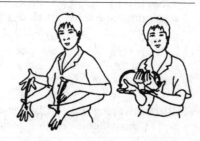

■ [**leave**[2] + **wear out**] Beginning with both *5 hands* in front of each side of the body, palms facing each other and fingers angled downward, thrust the hands downward with a deliberate movement. Then, beginning with both *flattened O hands* together in front of the chest, palms facing in and fingers pointing up, move the hands apart and downward while opening into *5 hands,* palms facing up.

rot[2] *v.* See sign for WEAR OUT. Related form: **rotten** *adj.*

rotary *adj.* See signs for AROUND[1,2].

rotate *v.* To turn around on an axis: *The earth rotates.* Related form: **rotation** *n.*

■ [Initialized sign showing the movement of something rotating around something else] Move the extended fingers of the right *R hand,* palm facing in and fingers pointing down, in a circle around the fingertips of the left *R hand,* palm facing in and fingers pointing up.

rotor *n.* The rotating part of a machine: *The rotor on the lawn mower is broken.*

■ [**machine** + **cycle**[1]] With the fingers of both *curved 5 hands* loosely meshed together, palms facing in, move the hands up and down in front of the chest with a repeated movement. Then move the extended right index finger, palm facing in and finger pointing left, in a circular movement around the thumb side of the left *modified C hand,* palm facing down.

rouge *n.* A red cosmetic used to color the cheeks or lips: *to put rouge on your cheeks.*

■ [**red**[1,2,3] + **make-up**[1,2]] Bring the extended right index finger, palm facing in, from the lips downward, bending the index finger down toward the palm as the hand moves. Then move the fingertips of the right *bent hand*, palm facing down, from touching the index-finger side of the left *S hand* held in front of the body, palm facing right, upward to rub on the right cheek with a circular double movement.

rough *adj.* **1.** Not smooth: *a rough surface.* **2.** Not finished or perfected; unpolished: *a rough draft of a composition.* **3.** Lacking gentleness or refinement: *a rough crowd.* **4.** Approximate: *a rough guess.* Same sign used for: **approximate, coarse, cruel, draft, estimate.**

■ [Indicates a rough, scratchy surface] Move the fingertips of the right *curved 5 hand*, palm facing down, from the heel to the fingertips of the upturned left *open hand* held in front of the body.

round[1] *adj.* Being shaped like a disc or a ball: *a round tire; to know that the earth is round.*

■ [Initialized sign similar to sign for **circle**[1]] Move the extended finger of the right *R hand* from pointing down in front of the body in a large flat circle in front of the body.

round[2] *adj.* See sign for CIRCLE[1].

roundup *n.* An act of guiding or driving cattle together, as to market: *It was time for the cowboys to ride in the roundup.*

■ [Indicates bringing scattered things together in a big circle] Beginning with both *curved 5 hands* held away from each side of the body, palms facing each other and fingers pointing forward, bring the hands around in large arcs until the fingers mesh in front of the body, palms facing in.

rouse *v.* To wake up: *to rouse the sleeping man.*

■ [**shake** + **raise**[1,2]] Move both *A hands*, palms facing down, back and forth with a repeated movement in front of each side of the body. Then move both *open hands* from in front of each side of the body, palms facing up, upward to in front of each shoulder.

route *n.* See sign for ROAD[1].

routine[1] *n.* A set of programmed instructions for a computer: *The programmer can use the same routine more than once in each program.* Same sign used for: **modules.**

■ [Initialized sign similar to sign for **program**²]
Move the fingers of the right *R hand,* palm
facing in and fingers pointing left, from the
palm side of the left *open hand* held in front of
the body, palm facing in, in an arc over to the
back side of the left hand.

routine² *n.* See sign for DAILY.

row¹ *v.* To use oars to move a boat: *to row the boat
across the lake.*

■ [Mime rowing a boat] Beginning with both *S
hands,* palms facing down, held in front of each
side of the body, bring the hands back to each side
of the body and forward in a repeated rhythmic
circular movement.

row² *n.* A line of adjacent chairs facing in the same
direction, as in a theater: *to sit in the front row.*

■ [Represents legs sitting in a row] Beginning with the
index-finger sides of both *bent V hands* touching in front
of the body, palms facing down, move the hands apart
to in front of each side of the body.

row³ *n.* (alternate sign)

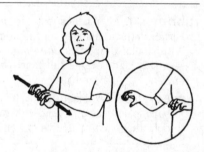

■ [Location of things in a row] Beginning with
the index-finger sides of both *C hands*
touching in front of the body, palms facing
down, bring the hands apart to in front of
each side of the body with a double
movement.

row⁴ *n.* **1.** The horizontal arrangement of
data in a spreadsheet or table: *Each row of
data represented one customer.* **2.** A line of
text in a word-processing document or a
line of text across a display screen: *She
moved the last sentence to the third row of
the paragraph.*

■ [Shows shape of a row] Move the right
G hand, palm forward, from in front of
the chest outward to the right.

row[5] *n.* See sign for LINE UP.

row[6] *v.* See sign for CANOE. Related form: **rowing** *n.*

royal *adj.* Of, pertaining to, or characteristic of kings and queens or other sovereigns and their families: *the royal family of England.*

■ [Initialized sign similar to sign for **king**] Move the right *R hand,* palm facing in, from touching the left side of the chest near the shoulder downward to touch again near the right side of the waist.

royalty *n.* See sign for PENSION.

rub[1] *v.* To move one thing back and forth against another: *to rub the cake of soap on the dirty cloth.*

■ [Mime rubbing ointment on something] Rub the fingers of the right *open hand,* palm facing down, back and forth across the palm of the left *open hand,* palm facing up, with a double movement.

rub[2] *v.* See signs for POLISH[1], WASH[1,3], WIPE[1].

rubber *n.* **1.** An elastic substance made from a certain tropical plant or a synthetic substance with similar properties: *tires made of rubber.* —*adj.* **2.** Made of this substance: *a rubber eraser.*

■ Bring the index-finger side of the right *X hand,* palm facing forward, downward on the right cheek with a double movement.

rubber band *n.* A circular band of rubber used to hold things together: *Put a rubber band around the index cards.*

■ [**rubber** + **stretch**[2]] Bring the index-finger side of the right *X hand,* palm facing forward, downward on the right cheek with a double movement. Then, beginning with the knuckles of both *modified X hands* touching in front of the chest, palms facing in, pull the hands apart to in front of each side of the chest with a double movement.

rubber stamp *n.* A block or die used for imprinting: *Use a rubber stamp to put the return address on all the envelopes.*

- ■ [**rubber** + **stamp**²] Bring the index-finger side of the right *X hand,* palm facing forward, downward on the right cheek with a double movement. Then hit the little-finger side of the right *S hand,* palm facing in, with a double movement on the upturned palm of the left *open hand* held in front of the chest.

rude¹ *adj.* Impolite: *to exhibit rude behavior.*

- ■ [Initialized sign] Brush the index-finger sides of both *R hands,* palms facing down, against each other with an alternating movement as the hands move forward and downward at an angle in front of the body.

rude² *adj.* See signs for MEAN¹, MEANNESS¹.

ruffle *n.* A gathered strip of cloth: *a ruffle on the drapes.*

- ■ [The shape of a ruffled flounce] Beginning with the index fingers of both *4 hands* touching in front of the body, palms facing down and fingers pointing forward, move the hands apart in large repeated wavy movements to each side.

ruin¹ *v.* To cause damage to: *Your muddy hands will ruin my picture.* Same sign used for: **spoil.**

- ■ Slide the little-finger side of the right *X hand,* palm facing left, across the index finger side of the left *X hand,* palm facing right.

ruin² *v.* See sign for DAMAGE.

rule¹ *n.* A statement outlining what can and cannot properly be done: *In this organization, we follow the rules.* Same sign used for: **regulation.**

- ■ [Initialized sign similar to sign for **law**] Touch the fingertips of the right *R hand* first on the fingers and then on the heel of the left *open hand,* palms facing each other.

rule² *v.* See sign for MANAGE.

ruler¹ *n.* A straight strip of wood or metal, marked off, as in inches, to be used for measuring: *Measure the size of the book with a ruler.*

- [The shape of a ruler + **measure**] Beginning with the index fingers and thumbs of both *G hands* touching in front of the chest, palms facing down, bring the hands apart to in front of each side of the chest. Then tap the thumbs of both *Y hands*, palms facing down, together in front of the chest with a double movement.

ruler² *n.* See sign for ADMINISTRATOR.

rumble *n.* A deep, continuous sound: *to hear the rumble of the train.*

- [**hear** + a gesture showing the movement of a rumble] Touch the extended right index finger to the right ear, palm angled down. Then move both *5 hands* up and down in front of each side of the body with a double movement by twisting the wrists.

rumor¹ *n.* An unverified statement: *I heard a rumor that you're leaving.*

- [Initialized sign showing information going back and forth] Beginning with both *R hands* held in front of the right side of the chest, palms facing forward and fingers pointing up, move the hands from side to side in front of the chest with a double movement.

rumor² *n.* See signs for GOSSIP¹, HEARSAY.

run¹ *v.* To go by moving the legs quickly so that at some moments both legs are off the ground at the same time: *Run faster.* Same sign used for: **jog, jogging.** Related form: **running** *n.*

- [Represents one's legs moving when running] With the index finger of the right

L hand, palm facing left and index finger pointing forward, hooked on the thumb of the left *L hand,* palm facing right and index finger pointing forward, move both hands forward.

run[2] *v.* (alternate sign) Same sign used for: **jog, jogging.** Related form: **running** *n.*

- With the thumbs of both *L hands* touching in front of the chest, palms facing forward and index fingers pointing up, move the hands forward while crooking both index fingers.

run[3] *v.* To flow: *The water is running.* Related form: **running** *n.*

- [Indicates a flow of liquid when leaking] Beginning with both *4 hands* in front of the chest, palms facing in and fingers pointing in opposite directions, bring the right hand downward with a double movement in front of the left hand.

run[4] *v.* (of a clock) To operate so as to tell the time: *The clock runs fast.*

- [Represents the hands on a clock moving] Beginning with the thumb side of the right *D hand* against the open left palm, twist the right hand to form a complete circle with the right index finger.

run[5] *v.* (of the nose) To discharge fluid, as during a respiratory illness: *My nose is running.* Same sign used for: **nosebleed.** Related form: **runny** *adj.*

- [Represents fluid dripping from the nose] Beginning with the index finger of the right *4 hand* touching the nose, palm facing in and fingers pointing left, bring the hand straight down with a double movement.

run[6] *v.* **1.** To operate or be responsible for the functioning of: *to run a business; to run the dishwasher.* **2.** To process by computer: *to run the program.* Same sign used for: **operate.**

- Brush the palm of the right *open hand* upward with a double movement across the left *open hand,* palms facing each other and fingers pointing forward.

run[7] *v.* See signs for EXECUTE, MACHINE, MANAGE.

run around[1] *v. phrase.* To go to many places: *to run around town.* Same sign used for: **fool around, tour, travel.**

■ With the left extended index finger pointing up in front of the body and the right extended index finger pointing down above it, both palms facing in, move both hands in alternate circles in front of the body.

run around[2] *v. phrase.* See signs for LAP[2,3].

run away *v. phrase.* To escape: *to run away from home.* See also sign for ESCAPE. Same sign used for: **escape, flee, get away, split** (*slang*).

■ [Represents one taking off quickly] Move the extended right index finger, palm facing left and finger pointing up, from between the index and middle fingers of the left *5 hand,* palm facing down in front of the chest, forward with a deliberate movement.

run out of[1] *v. phrase.* To use up: *to run out of eggs.* Same sign used for: **all gone, deplete, expire, used up.**

■ [Indicates grabbing everything so that nothing is left] Beginning with the little-finger side of the right *5 hand,* palm facing in, on the heel of the left *open hand,* palm facing up, bring the right hand forward to the left fingertips while changing into an *S hand.*

run out of[2] *v. phrase.* (alternate sign) Same sign used for: **all gone, deplete, expire, used up.**

■ Beginning with the little-finger side of the right *5 hand,* palm angled left, on the wrist of the downturned left *open hand,* bring the right hand across the back of the left hand while changing into an *S hand.*

run over *v. phrase.* See sign for OVERFLOW.

rung *n.* The rod used as a step on a ladder: *to climb up the first rung.*

■ [The shape and location of rungs on a ladder] Beginning with the index-finger sides of both *O hands* touching in front of the chest, palms facing down, bring the hands apart to in front of each side of the body. Repeat in front of the face.

runner-up *n.* A person who places second in a contest: *The runner-up won a red ribbon.*

■ [**second place**[1,2] + **place**[1]] Move the right *V hand* from in front of the right shoulder, palm facing left and fingers pointing forward, back toward the shoulder. Then, beginning with the middle fingers of both *P hands* touching in front of the body, palms facing each other, move the hands apart in a circular movement back until they touch again near the chest.

rush *v., n.* See signs for HURRY[1,2].

Russia[1] *n.* A country in eastern Europe and western and northern Asia: *The Volga River is in Russia.* Related form: **Russian** *adj., n.* Same sign used for: **Newfoundland, Soviet.**

■ [Location of the hands while doing a traditional Russian dance] Tap the index-finger sides of both *open hands,* palms facing down, against each side of the waist with a double movement.

Russia[2] *n.* (alternate sign) Related form: **Russian** *adj.*, *n.*

- Move the side of the extended right index finger, palm facing down and finger pointing left, across the chin from left to right with a double movement.

rustler *n.* See signs for ROBBER[1,2].

's *suffix.* (Used with nouns to form the possessive): *Tom's coat.*

■ [Initialized sign] Beginning with right *S hand* in front of the right shoulder, palm facing forward, twist the hand to face the palm back.

Sabbath *n.* The day of the week used for rest and worship: *Saturday is the Jewish Sabbath.* See also sign for Sunday.

■ [Initialized sign similar to sign for **Sunday**] Move both *S hands* in circles going in opposite directions in front of each shoulder, palms facing forward.

sac *n.* A small baglike structure that is part of an animal or plant: *The pupa stage of an insect forms in a sac.*

■ [The shape of a sac] Beginning with the little fingers of both *curved hands* touching in front of the chest, both palms facing in, bring the hands outward apart from each other in an arc toward the chest, ending with the thumbs of both hands touching, palms facing outward.

sack *n.* See sign for BAG.

sacrifice *n.* **1.** Someone or something surrendered, given up, or destroyed for the sake of preserving someone or something else: *sent their children to college at great financial sacrifice.* **2.** Something offered up to a deity, as in propitiation: *slew a calf upon the altar as a sacrifice.* —*v.* **3.** To make a sacrifice or offering of: *to sacrifice one's life.*

■ [Initialized sign similar to sign for **suggest**] Beginning with both *S hands* in front of each side of the body, move the hands quickly upward while opening into *5 hands*, palms facing in.

sad *adj.* Not happy; sorrowful: *I feel sad about your misfortune.* Same sign used for: **gloomy, grave, mournful, tragic, unhappy.**

■ [The hands seem to pull the face down to a sad expression] Move both *5 hands* from in front of each side of the face, palms facing in and fingers pointing up, downward a short distance.

safe[1] *n.* A place, as a steel box, for keeping valuables: *to put jewelry in the safe.*

■ [**table**[2] + mime turning the combination on a safe] Beginning with the index-finger sides of both *open hands* together in front of the body, palms facing down and fingers pointing forward, bring the hands apart and then straight down while turning the palms toward each other. Then turn the right *curved 5 hand*, palm facing forward, in a double movement in front of the right side of the body.

safe[2] *adj.* See sign for SAVE[1].

safety glasses *pl. n.* See sign for GOGGLES.

safety pin *n.* See sign for PIN[3].

sage *n.* A wise person: *asked the elderly sage for advice about the future.*

■ [**wise** + **story**[1,2]] Bring the thumb side of the right *X hand* downward in front of the forehead with a double movement, palm facing down. Then, beginning with the fingers of both *F hands* touching in front of the chest, palms facing each other, bring the hands apart while twisting the wrists downward with a double movement.

sail[1] *v.* To travel on water by the action of wind on sails: *to sail the boat on the lake.* Related form: **sailing** *n.*

■ [The right hand shape represents a boat moving forward on the water] With the little-finger side of the right *3 hand*, palm facing left, resting on the upturned palm of the left *open hand*, move both hands forward from in front of the chest.

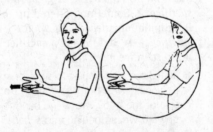

sail[2] *n.* See sign for BOAT. Related form: **sailing** *n.*

sailboat *n.* A boat that is moved by sails: *to skim over the water in a sleek sailboat.* Same sign used for: **ship.**

- [The right hands represents a boat's sail and the left hand represents a boat] Beginning with the little-finger side of the right *B hand,* palm facing in, against the palm side of the left *3 hand,* palm facing right, move both hands forward a short distance.

sailor[1] *n.* **1.** A person who sails or navigates a ship: *The sailor raised the sails on the mast.* **2.** A seaman or enlistee in a nation's Navy: *The sailor joined the Navy to see the world.* Same sign used for: **skipper.**

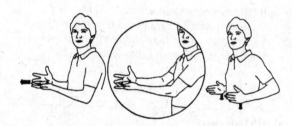

- [**sail**[1] + **person marker**] With the little-finger side of the right *3 hand,* palm facing left, resting on the upturned palm of the left *open hand,* move both hands forward from in front of the chest. Then move both *open hands,* palms facing each other, downward along each side of the body.

sailor[2] *n.* (alternate sign)

- [**Navy**[1] + **sail**[1] + **person marker**] Beginning with the index-finger sides of both *flattened O hands* touching, fingers pointing down, touch the fingers first to the right side and then to the left side of the waist. Then, with the little-finger side of the right *3 hand,* palm facing left, resting on the upturned palm of the left *open hand,* move both hands forward from in front of the chest. Then move both *open hands,* palms facing each other, downward along each side of the body.

saint *n.* **1.** A holy person formally recognized by the Christian church: *was canonized and made a saint.* **2.** A person who is humble and patient: *behaves like a saint in the face of trouble.*

- [Initialized sign similar to sign for **clean**] Move the heel of the right *S hand,* palm facing forward, from the heel to the fingertips of the left *open hand,* palm facing up.

salad[1] *n.* A cold dish of raw vegetables usually tossed together and served with a dressing: *made a salad with artichokes, tomato, and avocado.*

- ■ [Mime tossing a salad] Move both *curved hands,* palms facing up and fingers pointing toward each other, from in front of each side of the body toward each other with a double movement.

salad[2] *n.* (alternate sign)

- ■ [Mime tossing a salad with a fork] Move both *V hands,* palms facing up and fingers pointing toward each other, from in front of each side of the body toward each other with a double movement.

salad dressing *n.* See sign for SAUCE.

salary *n.* See signs for EARN, INCOME[1].

sale *n.* See sign for SELL.

salesperson *n.* See sign for DEALER.

saliva *n.* A liquid produced in the mouth, secreted by the salivary glands: *Saliva helps chewing.*

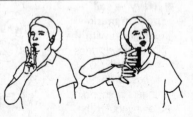

- ■ [water + drool] Tap the index-finger side of the right *W hand,* palm facing left, against the chin with a double move-ment. Then, beginning with the index finger of the right *4 hand* near the right side of the mouth, palm facing in and fingers pointing left, bring the hand downward in front of the chest.

saloon *n.* A place for buying and drinking liquor: *to go to the saloon for a drink after work.* Same sign used for: **bar.**

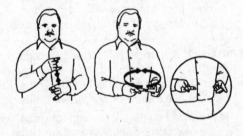

- ■ [whiskey + place[1]] With the index fingers and little fingers of both hands extended, tap the little-finger side of the right hand on the index-finger side of the left hand with a double movement, both palms facing in and fingers pointing in opposite directions. Then, beginning with the middle fingers of both *P hands* touching in front of the body, palms facing each other, move the hands apart in a circular movement and then back until they touch again near the chest.

salt[1] *n.* A white crystalline compound used as a seasoning and preservative: *to put salt on my egg.*

■ [Represents tapping out salt from a shaker on one's food] Alternately tap the fingers of the right *V hand* across the back of the fingers of the left *V hand,* both palms facing down.

salt[2] *n.* (alternate sign)

■ [Represents tapping out salt from a shaker on one's food] Tap the fingers of the right *V hand* with a double movement across the back of the fingers of the left *V hand,* both palms facing down.

salt[3] *n.* (alternate sign)

■ [**salt**[2] + **seasoning**] Tap the fingers of the right *V hand* with a double movement across the back of the fingers of the left *V hand,* both palms facing down. Then shake the right *C hand,* palm facing left, with a short movement in front of the right shoulder.

salt[4] *n.* (alternate sign)

■ [Initialized sign similar to sign for **seasoning**] Shake the right *S hand,* palm facing forward, with a short movement in front of the right shoulder.

salute[1] *v.* **1.** To raise the hand to the forehead as an act of respect: *to salute the officers in the army.* —*n.* **2.** A greeting made by raising the hand to the forehead: *He answered with a salute.*

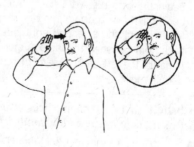

■ [Natural gesture for saluting] With a deliberate movement, bring the index-finger side of the right *B hand* against the right side of the forehead, palm angled left.

salute[2] *v.* See sign for HELLO.

salvation *n.* See sign for SAVE[1].

same *adj.* **1.** Not different; identical: *wearing the same dress I wore yesterday.* **2.** Similar or of the same kind: *I see you bought the same TV I did.* —*pron.* **3.** The same kind of thing: *She's having lasagna and I'll have the same.* —*adv.* **4. the same** In the same manner: *The twins walk and talk the same.* See also signs for ALIKE[1,2,3], LIKE[3]. Same sign used for: **mutual, similiar, such.**

■ [The fingers come together to show that they are the same] Beginning with both index fingers pointing forward in front of each side of the body, palms facing down, bring the hands together, ending with the index fingers together in front of the body.

sample[1] *n.* One part or specimen to show what the rest or others are like: *Here are some samples of her writing.* Same sign used for: **choice.**

■ [Picking various fingers as if to sample them] Beginning with the bent thumb and index finger of the right *5 hand,* palm facing down, touching the index finger of the left *5 hand,* palm facing in, pull the right hand upward while pinching the thumb to the index finger. Repeat off the middle finger of the left hand.

sample[2] *n.* See signs for SHOW[1], SYMBOL.

sandal *n.* A shoe made of a sole fastened to the foot by straps: *to wear sandals to the beach.* Same sign used for: **flip-flop.**

■ [Shows a thong coming between the toes] Beginning with the left *5 hand* in front of the body, palm facing down and fingers pointing forward, pull the extended right index finger back from between the index finger and middle finger of the left hand toward the chest with a double movement.

sandwich[1] *n.* Two or more slices of bread with filling between them: *to eat a ham sandwich.*

■ [Represents a sandwich being eaten] With the palms of both *open hands* together, right hand above left, bring the fingers back toward the mouth with a short double movement.

sandwich² *n.* (alternate sign)

- [Mime holding a sandwich in order to eat it] Bring the index-finger side of the right *flattened C hand*, palm facing down and fingers pointing left, against the mouth with a short double movement.

sandwich³ *n.* (alternate sign)

- [Represents sliding lunch meat between slices of bread to make a sandwich] Slide the back of the right *open hand*, palm facing up, across the fingers of the left *open hand*, palm facing up, into the crook of the left thumb and index finger with a double movement.

sandwich⁴ *n.* (alternate sign)

- [Represents putting two slices of bread together to make a sandwich and then eating it] Bring the palms of both *open hands* together in front of the chest, fingers pointing forward. Then tip the fingers back toward the mouth, ending with the fingers pointing up in front of the mouth.

sandwich⁵ *n.* (alternate sign)

- [Represents sliding meat between two slices of bread to make a sandwich] Slide the little-finger side of the right *open hand*, palm facing up, between the index finger and ring finger of the left *5 hand* held in front of the chest, palm facing in and fingers pointing right.

sane *adj.* Having a sound, healthy mind; rational: *The murderer was declared sane and had to stand trial.*

- [**think¹** + **specialize¹**] Touch the extended right index finger to the right side of the head, palm angled left. Then slide the little-finger side of the right *B hand*, palm facing left, forward along the index-finger side of the left *B hand*, palm facing right.

Santa Claus¹ *n.* The chubby, white-bearded man in a red suit who, according to folklore, brings gifts to children and represents Christmas giving: *Children believe in Santa Claus.*

- [Hand follows the shape of Santa Claus's beard] Beginning with the index-finger side of the right *curved hand* held on the chin, palm facing down, bring the hand forward and downward in an arc, ending with the little-finger side against the chest, palm facing up.

Santa Claus[2] *n.* (alternate sign)

- [Shows the shape of Santa Claus's beard] Beginning with the index-finger sides of both *C hands* against each side of the chin, palms facing each other, bring the hands in arcs down in front of the chest, ending with the little fingers touching, palms facing up.

sarcastic *adj.* See sign for IRONY[1].

sarcoma *n.* See sign for CANCER.

sash[1] *n.* An oblong strip of fabric typically worn around the waist or over one shoulder: *to tie the silk sash on over the uniform.* Same sign used for: **monsignor.**

- [Shows the shape and location of a sash] Beginning with right *curved hand* near the left side of the waist, palm facing in and fingers pointing down, move the hand across the waist to the right side.

sash[2] *n.* See sign for BELT[2].

Satan *n.* See sign for DEVIL.

satchel *n.* A small bag, as of leather, for carrying books, equipment, etc.: *to carry a book satchel.*

- [**basket** + **purse**[1]] Move the index-finger side of the right *B hand*, palm facing down, from the wrist to near the elbow of the bent left arm while turning the palm up. Then move the right *S hand*, palm facing in, up and down with a double movement near the right side of the body by bending the elbow.

sated *adj.* See sign for FULL[1].

satellite *n.* **1.** A natural body orbiting around a planet: *The moon is a satellite of the earth.* **2.** A device launched into orbit, as for broadcasting scientific information: *information beamed back to earth by satellite.*

- [Indicates the movement of a satellite over the earth] Beginning with the right *curved 5 hand*, palm facing down and fingers pointing down, near the extended left index finger held in front of the chest, palm facing in and finger pointing up, move the right hand to in front of the left side of the chest and then back to in front of the right shoulder.

satellite dish *n.* See sign for DISH³.

satellite radio *n.* A digital radio signal broadcast by a communications satellite allowing a subscriber to roam across the country and listen to radio programming with uninterrupted reception: *The truck driver had satellite radio in his truck.*

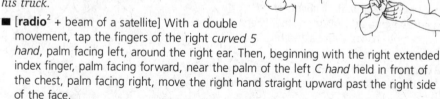

■ [**radio**² + beam of a satellite] With a double movement, tap the fingers of the right *curved 5 hand*, palm facing left, around the right ear. Then, beginning with the right extended index finger, palm facing forward, near the palm of the left *C hand* held in front of the chest, palm facing right, move the right hand straight upward past the right side of the face.

satellite television¹ *n.* A television system in which subscribers receive digital signals directly from satellites, as contrasted with signals transmitted through cables: *The Johnsons have satellite television.* Same sign used for: **Direct Broadcast Satellite (DBS), DirecTV.**

■ [**direct** + **T-V**] Beginning with the right *B hand* in front of the right side of the chest, palm facing in and fingers pointing left, and with the left index finger pointing up somewhat forward in front of the left side of the chest, move the right hand to touch the fingers against the left index finger. Then form a *T* and a *V* in front of the chest.

satellite television² *n.* (alternate sign) Same sign used for: **Direct Broadcast Satellite (DBS), DirecTV.**

■ [**satellite** + **T-V**] Beginning with the right extended index finger, palm facing forward, near the palm of the left *C hand* held in front of the chest, palm facing right, move the right hand straight upward past the right side of the face. Then form a *T* and a *V* in front of the chest.

satisfy¹ *v.* To fulfill the desires or needs of: *A snack will satisfy my hunger.* Related form: **satisfaction** *n.* Same sign used for: **appease, content.**

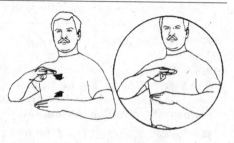

■ Beginning with both *B hands* in front of the chest, right hand above the left hand and both palms facing down, bring the index-finger sides of both hands against the chest.

satisfy² *v.* See sign for RELIEF. Related forms: **satisfaction** *n.*, **satisfied** *adj.*

saturate *v.* To soak with liquid: *to saturate the cloth.*

■ [**water** + **penetrate**[2]] Tap the index-finger side of the right *W hand,* palm facing left, against the chin with a double movement. Then move the fingers of both *5 hands,* palms facing each other and fingers pointing forward, deliberately forward to entwine with the fingers of both hands with each other.

Saturday *n.* The seventh day of the week, following Friday: *She often has to work on Saturday.*

■ [Initialized sign] Move the right *S hand,* palm facing back, in a small circle in front of the right shoulder.

sauce *n.* A liquid served over food as seasoning: *to put a sauce on the ham.* Same sign used for: **salad dressing, syrup.**

■ [Represents pouring sauce over food] Move the extended thumb of the right *10 hand,* palm angled down, in a circle over the palm of the left *open hand,* palm facing up in front of the body.

saucer *n.* See signs for DISH[1,2].

sausage *n.* Chopped meats stuffed into a thin tubelike casing: *likes to eat sausage with eggs.* Same sign used for: **wiener.**

■ [Shows the shape of sausage] Beginning with the index-finger sides of both *C hands* touching in front of the chest, palms facing forward, bring the hands apart while squeezing them open and closed from *C* to *S hands,* ending with *S hands* outside the sides of the body.

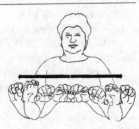

savage *adj.* See sign for FIERCE[1].

save[1] *v.* **1.** To rescue from harm or loss: *saved the dog's life by rushing it to the vet.* **2.** To set free from sin: *a belief that Christ saved the world.* Same sign used for: **free, freedom, liberate, liberty, redeem, rescue, safe, salvation, secure, security.**

■ [Initialized sign similar to sign for **free**[1]] Beginning with both *S hands* crossed at the wrists in front of the chest, palms facing in opposite directions, twist the wrists and move the hands apart, ending with the hands in front of each shoulder, palms facing forward.

save[2] *v.* To set aside for future use: *to save money in the bank.* Same sign used for: **keep, preservation, preserve, retain, storage, store.**

- Tap the fingers of the right *V hand* with a double movement on the back of the left *V hand,* both palms facing in.

save[3] *v.* (alternate sign) Related form: **savings** *pl. n.* Same sign used for: **keep, preservation, preserve, restore, retain, store, stuff.**

- Tap the fingers of the right *V hand* with a double movement on the back of the fingers of the left *S hand,* both palms facing in.

save[4] *v.* (alternate sign) Related form: **savings** *pl. n.* Same sign used for: **keep, preservation, preserve, restore, retain, store, stuff.**

- Tap the fingers of the right *V hand,* palm facing up, with a double movement on the little-finger side of the left *S hand* held in front of the chest, palm facing in.

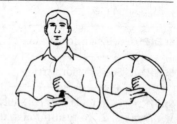

save[5] *v.* See sign for INVEST[2]. Related form: **savings** *pl. n.*

saw[1] *n.* **1.** A tool with a series of sharp teeth used for cutting: *to cut the log with a saw.* —*v.* **2.** To cut with a saw: *to saw the board in half.*

- [Demonstrates the action of sawing] Beginning with the right *S hand* near the right side of the chest and the left *S hand* forward of the body, palms facing in opposite directions, swing the hands forward with a double movement.

saw[2] *v.* See signs for WOOD[1,2].

sawdust *n.* The fine particles of wood made from sawing: *there is sawdust on the floor.*

- [**wood**[1,2] + **leak**[1]] Slide the little-finger side of the right *open hand,* palm facing left and fingers pointing forward, forward and back with a repeated movement on the index-finger side of the left *B hand* held in front of the chest, palm facing in and fingers pointing right. Then move the right *5 hand,* palm facing in and fingers pointing left, downward

say

from the left *open hand* held in front of the chest, palm facing down and fingers pointing right, while wiggling the right fingers as the hand moves downward.

say[1] *v.* To speak or speak about: *to say what you mean.* Same sign used for: **comment, comments, remark, remarks, state.**

- ■ [Points to where words are said] Tap the extended right index finger, palm facing in, on the chin with a double movement.

say[2] *v.* (alternate sign) Same sign used for: **comment, comments, pronounce, pronunciation, public, remark, remarks, state.**

- ■ [Represents words coming from the mouth] Move the extended right index finger in a repeated upward circular movement in front of the chin, palm facing in and finger pointing left.

scale *n.* See sign for WEIGH.

scalp *n.* See sign for BALD.

scan[1] *v.* **1.** To look over carefully: *He scanned the book for mistakes.* **2.** To read through quickly: *to scan the newspaper headlines.* Same sign used for: **browse, look over, read.**

- ■ [**read** formed with a quick repeated movement] Move the extended fingers of the right *V hand,* palm facing down and fingers pointing forward, downward with a double movement near the palm of the left *open hand* held in front of the chest, palm facing in and fingers pointing right.

scan[2] *v.* (alternate sign) Same sign used for: **browse, look over, read.**

- ■ [Represents the movement of the eyes when scanning a page] Move the fingertips of the right *U hand,* palm facing down, from the fingertips to the heel of the left *open hand,* palm facing up.

scan[3] *v.* (alternate sign) Same sign used for: **browse, look over, read.**

- ■ [Represents reading a book so fast that it just passes before the nose] Bring the palm of the right *open hand,* palm angled toward the face, from in front of the chest upward at an angle past the face.

scant *adj.* See signs for TINY[1,2].

---

scared *adj.* See signs for AFRAID, FEAR[1]. Related form: **scare** *v.*

---

scarf *n.* A piece of cloth worn on the head or around the neck: *to tie the scarf around her hair.* Same sign used for: **Mennonite.**

- Beginning with both *modified X hands* touching each side of the head, palms facing each other, bring the hands downward around the face, ending near each other under the chin.

---

scatter *v.* To throw about in several directions: *to scatter the seeds.*

- [Mime scattering something] Beginning with both *S hands* in front of each side of the chest, palms facing forward, move the hands alternately forward while opening into *5 hands*.

---

scenic *adj.* Having the beauty typical of a natural landscape: *a scenic view of snowcapped mountains.*

- [**pretty** + **view**] Beginning with the right *5 hand* in front of the face, palm facing in, move the hand in a circular movement, closing the fingers to the thumb in front of the chin to form a *flattened O hand*. Then, beginning with both *V hands* in front of the right side of the body, palms facing down and fingers angled toward the right, move the hands from right to left in front of the body, while following the movement with the head and eyes.

---

scent *n., v.* See sign for SMELL[1].

---

schedule[1] *n.* A written statement of detailed procedure: *to follow the schedule set up for the project.* Same sign used for: **chart, graph.**

- [Shows the rows and columns on a schedule] Beginning with the left *open hand* held in front of the left shoulder, palm facing right and fingers pointing forward, bring the fingers of the right *4 hand*, palm facing left, down the heel of the left hand, and then drag the back of the right fingers across the length of the left palm from the heel to the fingertips.

schedule[2] *n.* See signs for PLAN[1,2].

scholarly *adj.* **1.** Concerned with research and knowledge: *spent a lifetime engaged in scholarly pursuits.* **2.** Of or befitting a scholar: *to have scholarly habits.* Same sign used for: **genius.**

■ Touch the thumb of the right *C hand,* palm facing left, against the forehead.

school *n.* An institution for teaching and learning: *old enough to go to school.*

■ Tap the fingers of right *open hand,* palm facing down, with a double movement on the upturned palm of left *open hand.*

science *n.* A branch of knowledge based on observed facts and tested truths: *Physics and chemistry are branches of science.* Same sign used for: **chemical, chemistry, laboratory.**

■ [Represents mixing chemicals in a scientific experiment] Beginning with the right *10 hand* in front of the right shoulder and the left *10 hand* in front of the left side of the chest, both palms facing forward, move the hands in large alternating circles toward each other.

scientist *n.* A person who is specially trained in some branch of science: *The noted scientist has studied both biology and mathematics.*

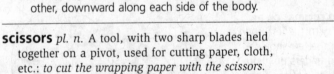

■ [**science** + **person marker**] Beginning with the right *10 hand* in front of the right shoulder and the left *10 hand* in front of the left side of the chest, both palms facing forward, move the hands in large alternating circles toward each other. Then move both *open hands,* palms facing each other, downward along each side of the body.

scissors *pl. n.* A tool, with two sharp blades held together on a pivot, used for cutting paper, cloth, etc.: *to cut the wrapping paper with the scissors.* Same sign used for: **clippers, shears.**

■ [Mime cutting with scissors] Open and close the index and middle fingers of the right *V hand,* palm facing in and fingers pointing left, with a repeated movement.

scold *v.* To blame and reprimand with angry words: *to scold the naughty child.* Same sign used for: **admonish, rebuke, reprimand.**

- [Natural gesture for scolding someone] Move the extended right index finger from in front of the right shoulder, palm facing left and finger pointing up, forward with a double movement.

scoop[1] *v.* To pick up with a swooping motion: *to scoop up a handful of snow.*

- [Mime the action of scooping] Move the right *curved hand,* palm facing left, to the left while twisting the palm up in front of the right side of the body.

scoop[2] *n.* A rounded amount or portion: *a scoop of ice cream.*

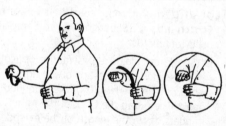

- [Mime scooping an serving something] Move the right *curved hand,* palm facing left, to the left while twisting the palm up in front of the right side of the body. Then turn the right *curved hand* over above the left *C hand,* palm facing right, in front of the left side of the body.

score *n., v.* See signs for LIST[1,2,3,4].

scorn[1] *v.* **1.** To feel contempt for: *We're not afraid of the bullies, we scorn them.* —*n.* **2.** A feeling of contempt: *to feel scorn for the bullies.*

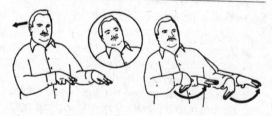

- [**look at** + **away** formed with both hands] With both *V hands* in front of each side of the chest, palms facing down and fingers pointing forward, move the head and chest backward. Then, beginning with both *bent hands* in front of each side of the body, palms facing in and fingers pointing down, flip the hands outward, ending with the palms facing down and the fingers pointing forward.

scorn[2] *n.* See sign for CONTEMPT.

scorpion *n.* A small insect with a poisonous stinger on its tail: *A scorpion lives in the woodpile.*

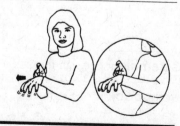

- [Represents a scorpion crawling] With the heel of the right *X hand,* palm facing forward, on the back of the left *curved 5 hand* held in front of the chest, palm facing down, move the hands forward while wiggling moving the left fingers.

Scotland[1] *n.* A division of the United Kingdom in the northern part of Great Britain: *bought a handknit wool sweater in Scotland.* Related forms: **Scotch** *adj., n.* **Scottish** *adj., n.* Same sign used for: **plaid.**

■ [Shows the plaids representative of Scottish kilts] Bring the fingertips of the right *4 hand* from back to front on the left upper arm. Then drag the back of the right fingers downward on the left upper arm.

Scotland[2] *n.* (alternate sign) Related forms: **Scotch** *adj., n.,* **Scottish** *adj., n.* Same sign used for: **plaid.**

■ [Shows the plaids representative of Scottish kilts] Bring the fingertips of the right *4 hand* down the length of the extended left arm. Then drag the back of the right fingers down the length of the extended left arm.

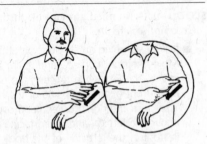

scour *v.* See signs for LOOK FOR[1,2,3].

Scout[1] *n.* A person belonging to the Boy Scouts or Girl Scouts: *earned merit badges as a Scout.*

■ [Mime giving a Scout salute] Beginning with the index, middle, and ring fingers of the right hand together in front of the right side of the forehead, palm angled left and fingers angled upward, tap the index finger against the right side of the forehead with a double movement.

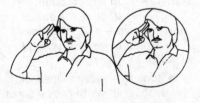

Scout[2] *n.* (alternate sign)

■ [The hand shape used while taking the Scout's oath] Hold the extended index finger, middle finger, and ring finger of the right hand upward in front of the right shoulder, palm facing forward.

scramble *v.* See sign for MIX[1].

scrapbook *n.* See sign for ALBUM.

scrape *v.* To rub with something sharp, as to clean it: *to scrape the paint off the window.*

■ [Demonstrates the action of scraping something] Slide the little-finger side of the right *open hand,* palm facing in and fingers pointing left, with a double movement from the heel to the fingers of the left *open hand* held in front of the chest, palm facing up and fingers angled right.

scratch[1] *v.* **1.** To mark with a rough object: *to scratch the floor with heavy shoes.* **2.** To rub with the fingernails, as to relieve an itch: *Would you scratch my back?*

■ [Shows the action of scratching] Pull the curved extended right index finger with a short double movement downward on the palm of the left *open hand,* palm facing right and fingers pointing forward.

scratch[2] *v.* (alternate sign)

■ [Shows the action of scratching] Beginning with the fingertips of the right *curved 5 hand* on the open left palm, bend the right fingers back toward the right palm with a double movement, changing into an *A hand* each time.

scratch[3] *v., n.* See signs for CUT[1], RAKE.

scream[1] *v.* **1.** To make a loud, sharp, piercing cry: *to scream for help.* —*n.* **2.** A loud, sharp, piercing cry: *I heard a terrible scream!* Same sign used for: **call out, cry, roar, shout, yell.**

■ [The hand seems to take a loud sound from the mouth and direct it outward] Beginning with the fingers of the right *C hand* close to the mouth, palm facing in, bring the hand forward and upward in an arc.

scream[2] *v., n.* (alternate sign) Same sign used for: **call out, cry, roar, shout, yell.**

■ [The hands seem to take a loud sound and direct it outward] Beginning with the fingertips of both *curved 5 hands* close to the mouth, palms facing in, bring the hands upward and outward in a double arc.

screen[1] *n.* **1.** A wire, mesh, or solid movable partition used to protect or hide: *the window screen; a tall screen with three tapestry panels.* —*v.* **2.** To protect or conceal with a screen: *to screen the alcove from view.* **3.** To examine systematically with some criteria in order to separate into groups, consider, or select: *to screen the candidates for the job.*

■ [Shows the wire mesh in a screen] Beginning with the fingers of both *4 hands* crossed in front of the chest, palms facing in, bring the hands downward and outward with a double movement.

screen[2] *n.* See sign for NET[1].

screw[1] *v.* Same sign as for SCREWDRIVER but formed with a single movement.

screw[2] *n.* See sign for SCREWDRIVER.

screwdriver *n.* A tool for turning screws: *to use a screwdriver to put the bookcase together.* Same sign used for: **screw.**

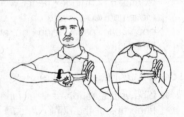

■ [Shows the action of using a screwdriver] Twist the fingertips of the right *H hand* in the palm of the left *open hand,* palm facing right, with a double forward movement.

scribble *n.* See signs for DIARY, WRITE[1,2,3].

scrimmage *n.* A practice football game: *a preseason scrimmage.*

■ [Represents two teams coming together to scrimmage] Beginning with both *flattened O hands* in front of each shoulder, palms facing each other, bring the hands together while opening into *5 hands,* ending with the palms touching in front of the chest, fingers pointing up.

script *n.* The written text of a play: *to study the script before the first rehearsal.*

■ [Initialized sign similar to sign for **article**] Move the right *S hand,* palm facing left, downward across the palm of the left *5 hand* held in front of the chest, palm facing right and fingers angled forward.

scroll *v.* To move through copy line by line on a computer display screen: *to scroll through the data.* Related form: **scrolling** *n.*

■ [Shows how information moves up a screen when scrolling] Beginning with the little finger of the right *4 hand* on the index finger of the left *4 hand,* both palms facing in and fingers pointing in opposite directions in front of the chest, move the hands upward in front of the chest with a double movement.

scrounge *v.* See sign for ADVANTAGE[1].

scrub *v.* See sign for POLISH[1].

sculpture[1] *n.* A work of art in three dimensions made by carving, modeling, or casting: *a sculpture of an angel.* Related form: **sculpt** *v.*

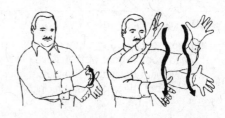

■ [**carve** + showing the shape of a sculpture] Flick the thumb of the right *10 hand* upward with a double movement off the palm of the left *open hand* held in front of the chest. Then, beginning with both *5 hands* in front of each side of the chest, palms facing each other and fingers pointing forward, move the hands downward with a wavy movement, twisting the wrists up and down as the hands move.

sculpture[2] *n.* See sign for CARVE.

scurry *v.* To scamper: *The mouse scurried across the floor.*

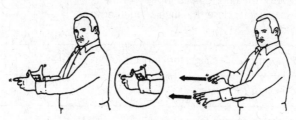

■ [**run**[1,2] + a gesture indicating many things running around quickly] With the index finger of the left *modified C hand* hooked on the thumb of the right *modified C hand*, palms facing in opposite directions, move the hands forward while bending both index fingers up and down. Then, beginning with both *5 hands* in front of the body, palms facing down and fingers pointing forward, move the hands forward simultaneously while wiggling the fingers.

seal[1] *n.* A sea animal with large flippers, living in cold regions: *The seal swims in cold water.*

■ [Shows a clapping movement often made by seals with their flippers] Beginning with both *open hands* in front of the waist, palms facing each other and fingers pointing forward, bring the palms together with a double movement.

seal[2] *n.* (alternate sign)

- [Shows a clapping movement often made by seals with their flippers] With the backs of both *open hands* together in front of the chest, palms facing in opposite directions and fingers pointing down, bend the fingers with a repeated movement.

seal[3] *v.* To close tightly: *to seal the jar.*

- [Represents putting a stopper on a jar] Bring the right *curved 5 hand* from in front of the chest, palm facing down, deliberately downward to land on the index-finger side of the left *S hand* held in front of the body, palm facing in.

seal[4] *v.* See sign for STAMP[2].

seal one's lips[1] *v. phrase.* To keep a secret: *My lips are sealed, and I promise not to tell.* Same sign used for: **airtight, keep quiet, keep secret.**

- [Represents sealing one's mouth] Beginning with the index-finger side of the right *C hand* in front of the mouth, palm facing left, close the fingers together to form an *S hand.*

seal one's lips[2] *v. phrase.* See sign for SHUT UP.

seamstress *n.* See sign for TAILOR.

search for *v. phrase.* See signs for LOOK FOR[1,2,3].

searchlight *n.* A powerful light that can be beamed in any direction: *The police car had a searchlight.*

- [**look for**[1] + **light**[1] + move the hand around as if searching for something] Move the right *C hand,* palm facing left, in a circular movement in front of the face. Next, beginning with the fingertips of the right *8 hand* near the chin, palm facing in, flick the middle finger upward and forward with a double movement, opening into a *5 hand* each time. Then, with the elbow of the right bent arm resting on the left *open hand* held across the body, move the right *5 hand* in a large arc from in front of the left side of the body to the right side of the body.

season *v.* See sign for POWDER.

seasoning[1] *n.* Something, as salt, an herb, or a spice that enhances the flavor of food: *to put some seasoning in the bland food.*

- [Mime shaking seasoning on food] Shake the right *curved hand,* palm facing forward and fingers pointing left, downward in front of the chest with a double movement.

seasoning[2] *n.* See sign for POWDER.

seat *n.* See sign for CHAIR.

seat belt[1] *n.* A belt or set of straps designed to keep an occupant secure in a vehicle: *Fasten your seat belt.*

- [**sit** + a gesture showing pulling a seatbelt across oneself and fastening] Place the fingers of the right *H hand,* palm facing down, across the extended fingers of the left *H hand* held in front of the chest, palm facing down and fingers pointing right. Then move the right both *H hand* from near the right shoulder downward toward the left *H hand* held in front of the waist until the fingers overlap, both palms facing in.

seat belt[2] *n.* See sign for BUCKLE.

secluded *adj.* See sign for HIDE.

second[1] *n.* **1.** One of the 60 equal periods of time that make up a minute: *a watch that marks the hours, minutes, and seconds.* **2.** A moment: *Wait a second.*

- [Shows the movement of the second hand on a clock] With the palm side of the right *1 hand* against the left open palm, fingers pointing up, twist the extended right finger forward a very short distance.

second[2] *adj.* **1.** Next after the first: *the second time you've done that.* —*n.* **2.** The one after the first in a series of two or more: *the second in command.* —*adv.* **3.** In the second place: *always comes in second in contests.* Same sign used for: **two dollars.**

- [**two** + a twisting movement used to indicate ordinals] Beginning with the right *2 hand* in front of the right shoulder, palm facing forward and fingers pointing up, twist the wrist, ending with the palm facing in.

second³ *adj.* (alternate sign)

- [Indicates the second finger] Touch the extended right index finger, palm facing left, to the index finger of the left *L hand* held in front of the body, palm facing right.

second⁴ *adj.* (alternate sign)

- [Uses second finger of the *2 hand* to indicate second finger] Touch the middle finger of the right *2 hand*, palm facing down, to the extended index finger of the left *L hand* held in front of the body, palm facing right.

second-hand *adj.* Previously owned: *to buy a second-hand car.* Same sign used for: **used.**

- Beginning with the right *L hand* in front of the right side of the chest, palm facing down and index finger pointing forward, twist the wrist with a double movement.

second place¹ *n.* The next place after the first: *The contestant came in second place.*

- Move the right *2 hand*, palm facing in and fingers pointing left, from in front of the left side of the chest across to in front of the right side of the chest.

second place² *n.* (alternate sign)

- Beginning with the right *2 hand* in front of the right shoulder, palm facing left and fingers pointing forward, bring the hand back toward the right shoulder.

second the motion *v. phrase.* To offer support to a motion, as to allow further discussion or an official vote, during a parliamentary procedure: *I second that motion.*

- Beginning with the right *L hand* in front of the right side of the head, palm facing left and index finger pointing up, move the hand deliberately forward while tipping the hand downward, ending with the index finger pointing forward.

secrecy *n.* The state or condition of keeping things secret: *secrecy around the office.*

■ [Similar to sign for **secret** except formed with a repeated movement made with two hands] Bring the thumbs of both *A hands,* palms facing each other, back against the mouth with an alternating double movement.

secret *adj.* **1.** Hidden from the knowledge of others: *a secret hiding place.* —*n.* **2.** A piece of hidden information: *It's difficult to keep a secret.* Same sign used for: **classified, confidential, privacy, private.**

■ [The movement seems to silence the lips to keep a secret] Tap the thumb side of the right *A hand,* palm facing left, against the mouth with a repeated movement.

secretively *adv.* See sign for SNEAK[1].

secretary[1] *n.* **1.** A person who keeps records, as for a company or committee meetings: *The secretary will send out the minutes of the meeting.* **2.** A person who does correspondence, typing, filing, and other support work in an office: *to work as a secretary.*

■ [The hand seems to take words from the mouth and record them on paper] Bring the right *P hand,* index finger near the mouth, from the chin downward, wiping the middle finger of the right *P hand* across the palm of the left *open hand* from the heel to off the fingertips.

secretary[2] *n.* (alternate sign)

■ [The hand seems to take words from the mouth and record them on paper] Bring the index-finger side of the right *H hand* from the right side of the chin downward, wiping the fingers of the right *H hand* across the palm of the left *open hand* from the heel off the fingertips.

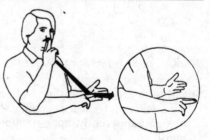

secretary[3] *n.* (alternate sign)

■ [The hand seems to take words from the mouth and write them on paper] Bring the right *modified X hand* from near the right side of the chin downward across the palm of the left *open hand* from the heel to off the fingertips.

section *n.* See signs for CLASS, PARAGRAPH, PART[1], SOME.

secure *v.* See sign for SAVE[1]. Related form: **security** *n.*

security *n.* See signs for DEFEND[1], POLICE[1,2].

sediment *n.* Material left at the
bottom of a liquid; dregs: *sediment
left at the bottom of the bucket.*

- ■ [Showing a layer of something +
  leave[2]] Slide the thumb of the
  right *G hand,* palm facing
  forward, from the wrist to off the
  fingers of the index-finger side of
  the left *B hand* held in front of the chest, palm facing in and fingers pointing right.
  Then, beginning with both *5 hands* in front of each side of the body, palms facing
  each other and fingers angled forward, thrust the fingers downward with a deliberate
  movement.

see[1] *v.* To perceive with the eyes: *I didn't see you come into the
room.* Same sign used for: **eyesight, sight, vision, visualize.**

- ■ [The fingers follow the direction of vision from the eyes] Bring
  the fingers of the right *V hand* from pointing at the eyes, palm
  facing in, forward a short distance.

see[2] *v.* (alternate sign)

- ■ [The fingers follow the direction of vision from the eyes]
  Beginning with the fingers of the right *V hand* pointing at the
  eyes, palm facing in, twist the wrist to point the fingers
  forward.

seek *v., n.* See signs for LOOK FOR[1,2,3].

seem *v.* To appear to be, do, feel, etc.: *The natives of
the small town seemed to be friendly.* Same sign
used for: **apparently, appear, imply, look like,
quasi.**
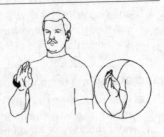
- ■ [Looking in a mirror] Beginning with the right *open
  hand* near the right shoulder, palm facing forward
  and fingers pointing up, turn the hand so the palm
  faces back.

seesaw *n.* A plank, balanced in the middle on a fulcrum, that allows people sitting
on the two ends to go up and down with an alternating motion: *played on the
seesaw in the playground.*

■ [Represents two people, sitting on each end of a seesaw, going up and down] Beginning with the right *bent V hand* in front of the right shoulder and the left *bent V hand* in front of the left shoulder, both palms facing down, move the hands up and down with a repeated alternating movement.

seethe *v., n.* See sign for BOILING MAD.

see-through *adj.* See sign for VISIBLE.

segment *n.* See sign for PART[1].

seize *v.* See signs for CAPTURE[1,2].

seizure *n.* A sudden attack, as experienced by people with epilepsy: *His seizure caused him to fall to the ground.* Same sign used for: **epilepsy.**

■ [Represents a body lying with feet up] Wiggle the right *bent V hand,* palm facing up, around on the palm of the left *open hand,* while repeatedly bending the right index and middle fingers.

seldom *adv.* Not often; infrequently: *He is seldom home.*

■ [**once** formed with a rhythmic repeated movement] Bring the extended right index finger, palm facing in, downward against the upturned palm of the left *open hand* and then swing it upward in a slow upward arc with a double movement.

select[1] *v.* To choose from among others: *to select the best apples.* Related forms: **selection** *n.,* **selective** *adj.* Same sign used for: **pick.**

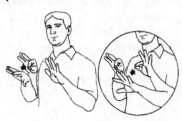

■ [**pick**[1] formed with a repeated movement] Beginning with the bent thumb and index finger of the right *5 hand* pointing forward in front of the right shoulder, palm facing forward, bring the right hand back toward the right shoulder while pinching the thumb and index finger together. Repeat with the left hand in front of the left shoulder.

select[2] *v.* See signs for APPOINT[1], CHOOSE[1,2,3].

self *n.* See signs for OWN[1,2].

self-addressed *adj.* Addressed to the sender: *Enclose a self-addressed envelope with your inquiry.*

- ■ [**own**[1,2] + **address**[1]] Bring the thumb side of the right *A hand*, palm facing left, back against the center of the chest. Then move both *A hands*, palms facing in, upward on each side of the chest with a double movement.

self-confidence *n.* Faith in one's own ability: *She has plenty of self-confidence.*

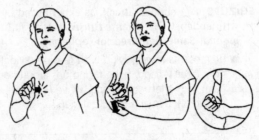

- ■ [**own**[1,2] + **confident**] Bring the thumb side of the right *A hand*, palm facing left, back against the center of the chest. Then, beginning with both *curved 5 hands* in front of the chest, right hand above the left hand and palms facing in, bring both hands forward a short distance with a deliberate movement while closing into *S hands*.

self-conscious *adj.* Awkward or fearful about being noticed by others: *I felt self-conscious giving the speech.*

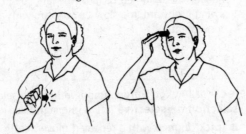

- ■ [**own**[1,2] + **aware**[1]] Bring the thumb side of the right *A hand*, palm facing left, back against the center of the chest. Then tap the fingertips of the right *bent hand*, palm facing in, against the right side of the forehead with a double movement.

self-defense *n.* An act or instance of defending oneself, one's property, etc.: *He was justified in using self-defense to guard his possessions.*

- ■ [**own**[1,2] + **defend**[1,2]] Bring the thumb side of the right *A hand*, palm facing left, back against the center of the chest. Then, with the wrists of both *S*

hands crossed in front of the chest, palms facing in opposite directions, move the hands forward with a double movement.

---

self-employed *adj.* Earning a living from one's own business or profession: *a self-employed artist.*

■ [**own**[1,2] + **work**[1,2]] Bring the thumb side of the right *A hand*, palm facing left, back against the center of the chest. Then tap the wrist of the right *S hand* on the wrist of the left *S hand* with a double movement, both palms facing down.

---

self-government[1] *n.*

Government, as of a country or community, by its own people: *The country achieved self-government after the revolution.*

■ [**own**[1,2] + **government**[1,2]] Bring the thumb side of the right *A hand*, palm facing left, back against the center of the chest. Then, beginning with the right index finger near the right side of the head, palm facing forward, twist the wrist to touch the fingers to the right temple, palm facing back.

---

self-government[2] *n.* (alternate sign)

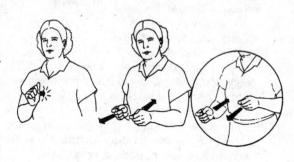

■ [**own**[1,2] + **manage**] Bring the thumb side of the right *A hand*, palm facing left, back against the center of the chest. Then move both *modified X hands*, palms facing each other, in an alternating double movement forward and back in front of each side of the chest.

---

self-respect *n.* Pride in one's own character, appearance, etc.: *To wear neat clothes shows self-respect.*

■ [**own**[1,2] + **respect**] Bring the thumb side of the right *A hand*, palm facing left, back against the center of the chest. Then, beginning with the index-finger side of the right *R hand*, palm facing left, near the right side of the forehead, bring the hand downward and forward in an arc.

---

selfish *adj.* **1.** Caring too much for or concerned only with one's own interests: *an utterly selfish person.* **2.** Manifesting excessive concern for oneself: *selfish reasons for lending the money.* Same sign used for: **stingy.**

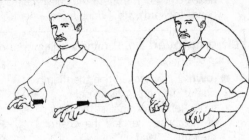

■ Beginning with both *3 hands* in front of each side of the body, palms facing down, bring the hands back toward the body while bending the fingers in toward the palms.

self-restraint *n.* Restraint imposed on one's own feelings and behavior; self-control: *He shows remarkable self-restraint in difficult situations.*

■ [**own**[1,2] + **control**[1]] Bring the thumb side of the right *A hand,* palm facing left, back against the center of the chest. Then, beginning with both *curved 5 hands* in front of each side of the chest, palms facing in, bring the hands downward while closing into *S hands.*

self-satisfied *adj.* Pleased, often to the point of smugness, with oneself, one's accomplishments, etc.: *acting a little too self-satisfied.*

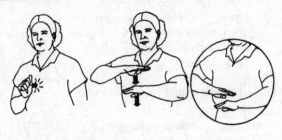

■ [**own**[1,2] + **relief**] Bring the thumb side of the right *A hand,* palm facing left, back against the center of the chest. Then, beginning with both *B hands* in front of the chest, right hand over the left hand, both palms facing down and fingers pointing in opposite directions, bring the index-finger sides of both hands against the chest.

sell *v.* To exchange something for payment: *to sell my house.* Same sign used for: **distribute, export, merchandise, pawn, peddle, retail, sale.**

■ [The hands seem to hold something out for inspection in order to sell it] Beginning with both *flattened O hands* held in front of each side of the chest, palms facing down and fingers pointing down, swing the fingertips forward and back by twisting the wrists upward with a double movement.

seller *n.* See sign for DEALER.

sell to me *v. phrase.* See sign for IMPORT.

sell to us *v. phrase.* See sign for IMPORT.

semen *n.* Male reproductive cells manufactured in the testicles and ejaculated during sexual intercourse. Same sign used for: **seminal fluid, sperm.**

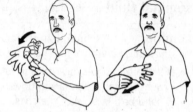

- [**ejaculate + white**] While touching the wrist of the right *S hand* with the left extended index finger, palms facing in opposite directions, move the right hand forward while opening into a *4 hand*, ending with the right palm facing left and fingers pointing forward. Then, beginning with the fingertips of the right *curved 5 hand* on the chest, pull the hand forward while closing the fingers into a *flattened O hand*.

semester *n.* A portion, usually half, of a school year: *started French during the first semester.*

- [Initialized sign] Move the right *S hand* from in front of the right shoulder, palm facing forward, a short distance to the right and then straight down in front of the chest.

semiannual *adj.* See sign for BIANNUAL.

semiannually *adv.* Same sign as for BIANNUAL but made with a double movement to indicate repetition.

semicircle *n.* Half of a circle or anything arranged in an arc the shape of a half circle: *The class will sit in a semicircle.*

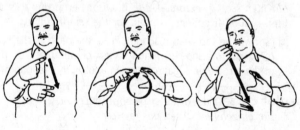

- [**onehalf**[1,2,3] + **cycle**[1] + a gesture showing cutting a circle in half]
Beginning with the extended right index finger angled upward in front of the chest, palm facing in, bring the hand downward while changing into a *2 hand*. Next, move the extended right index finger in a large circle around the shape formed by the left *C hand*, palm facing right. Then bring the right *B hand*, palm facing in and fingers angled up, downward at an angle past the palm side of the left *C hand*.

semicolon *n.* A punctuation mark (;) indicating the separation of ideas within a sentence: *Use a semicolon rather than a comma between two related clauses.*

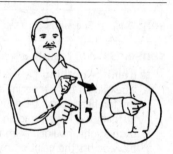

- [Draw a semicolon in the air] With the index finger and thumb of the right hand pinched together, palm angled forward, push the hand forward a short distance in front of the chest. Then lower the hand slightly and twist the wrist, turning the palm up.

seminal fluid *n.* See sign for SEMEN.

seminary *n.* A school that prepares students for the clergy: *to study at a seminary to be a minister.*

- [Initialized sign similar to sign for **college**[1]] Beginning with the right *S hand*, palm facing down, on the palm of the left *open hand* held in front of the chest, palm facing up, move the right hand upward in an arc.

senate *n.* A powerful lawmaking assembly in a government: *a member of the senate.* Same sign used for: **staff.**

- [Initialized sign similar to sign for **Congress**] Move the index-finger side of the right *S hand*, palm facing left, from the left side of the chest to the right side of the chest in a small arc.

send *v.* See signs for MAIL[1,2].

send out *v. phrase.* See signs for MAIL[1,2].

senior *n.* **1.** A student who is a member of the graduating class of a high school or college: *a scholarship to college for one of our high school seniors.* —*adj.* **2.** Of or pertaining to seniors in high school or college: *a prom for the senior class.*

- [Shows the top year in school] Place the palm of the right *5 hand*, palm facing down and fingers pointing left, on the thumb of the left *5 hand*, palm facing in and fingers pointing right.

senior citizen *n.* An older person; retiree: *The senior citizens are given bus passes.*

- [Abbreviation **s-c** formed in the same location as the sign for **old**] With the right hand, form an *S* and then a *C* in front of the chin, palm facing left.

sensation *n.* See sign for FEEL.

sense *v., n.* See signs for FEEL, MIND.

senseless[1] *adj.* Foolish: *a senseless deed.*

- [**think**[1] + **nothing**[5]] Move the extended right index finger from touching the right side of the forehead, palm facing in, forward while opening the fingers into an *open hand* in front of the right shoulder, palm facing up. Then blow across the palm of the right *open hand.*

senseless[2] *adj.* (alternate sign)

- **[think**[1] + **tiny**[1]**]** Bring the extended right index finger from touching the right side of the forehead, palm facing in, forward and downward while changing into a *6 hand* in front of the right side of the chest, palm facing up. Then flick the thumb quickly off the little finger of the right hand.

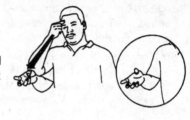

sensitive *adj.* **1.** Easily affected: *sensitive feelings.* **2.** Easily offended: *Don't be so sensitive.* **3.** Responsive and sympathetic to the feelings of others: *looking for a relationship with a sensitive person.*

- [Formed with the finger used for feelings] Beginning with the bent middle finger of the right *5 hand* touching the right side of the chest, flick the wrist forward, ending with the palm facing down.

sentence *n.* A group of words that express a complete thought, as a statement, question, or command, having an overt or understood subject and a predicate with a finite verb: *They never learned how to write a complete sentence.* Same sign used for: **declaration, statement.**

- [Represents stretching out words into a sentence] Beginning with the thumbs and index fingers of both *F hands* touching in front of the chest, palms facing each other, pull the hands apart with a wiggly movement, ending in front of each side of the chest.

separate[1] *v.* **1.** To bring, force, or keep apart: *The cashier separated the coins from the bills.* —*adj.* **2.** Detached; not shared: *They sat at separate tables.* Related form: **separation** *n.* Same sign used for: **apart.**

- [The hands pull apart as if to separate] Beginning with the knuckles of both *A hands* touching in front of the chest, palms facing in, bring the hands apart.

separate[2] *v.* See sign for PART[3].

sequel *n.* See sign for UPDATE.

sequence *n.* See sign for PLAN[2], PREPARE.

serene *adj.* See sign for QUIET[1].

sergeant *n.* A noncommissioned officer in the armed services: *The sergeant marched his men around the field.*

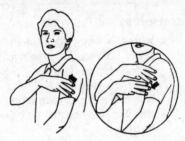

■ [The shape of three stripes on a sergeant's sleeve] Pull the fingers of the right *W hand* forward across the left upper arm, first at an upward angle and then at a downward angle.

series *n.* See sign for CLASS.

serious *adj.* **1.** Thoughtful; requiring thought: *a serious book.* **2.** Important; significant: *Quitting school is a serious matter.* **3.** Threatening: *a serious illness.* Same sign used for: **severe.**

■ With the extended right index finger touching the chin, palm facing left, twist the right hand, ending with the palm facing back

sermon *n.* See sign for SPEAK[2].

serpent *n.* See sign for SNAKE.

servant *n.* See sign for WAITER.

serve *v.* **1.** To give service to, as by providing with food and drink: *to serve the customers at the restaurant.* **2.** To provide assistance to: *How may I serve you?* Related form: **service** *n.* Same sign used for: **host, minister, wait on.**

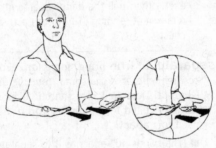

■ [The hands seem to carry something to serve it] Beginning with both *open hands* in front of each side of the body, palms facing up and right hand closer to the body than the left, move the hands forward and back with an alternating movement.

server *n.* A high-capacity computer with resources such as a hard disk and printer that are available to other terminals in a computer network: *The office was hooked up to a central server.*

■ [**center** + **spread**] Move the right *open hand*, palm facing down, in a circular movement over the upturned left *open hand*, bending the fingers as the hand moves and ending with the fingertips of the right *bent hand* touching the middle of the left palm. Then, beginning with the fingertips of both *flattened O hands* touching in front of the chest, palms facing down, move the hands forward and away from each other while opening into *5 hands* in front of each side of the body, palms facing down.

session *n.* See sign for MEETING.

set[1] *n.* (*as in computer programming*) See sign for SOCIETY. Shared idea of a group of instructions combined to perform certain functions.

set[2] *v.* See sign for PUT.

set off *v. phrase.* See sign for ZOOM[1].

set up[1] *v. phrase.* **1.** To raise into place: *to set up the tent.* **2.** To get ready for something by putting things into place: *to set up for the luncheon.* Same sign used for: **erect.**

■ [The movement represents setting up something] Beginning with the fingertips of both *curved hands* touching in front of the chest, palms facing down, bend the fingers upward, ending with the fingers angled upward and touching each other.

set up[2] *v. phrase.* See signs for ESTABLISH, RECOVER[1].

set one's hair *v. phrase.* See sign for ROLL ONE'S HAIR.

settle *v.* **1.** To quiet down; make calm: *medicine to settle the stomach.* **2.** To come to rest: *to settle in a comfortable position.* **3.** To place in order: *to settle their business affairs.* Same sign used for: **calm, calm down, quiet down, relax, settle down.**

■ [Natural gesture for calming someone down] Beginning with both *5 hands* in front of each side of the chest, palms facing down, move the hands slowly down to in front of each side of the waist.

seventh *adj.* **1.** Next after the sixth: *rested on the seventh day.* —*n.* **2.** The one after the sixth in a series of seven or more: *seventh in line.* —*adv.* **3.** In the seventh place: *placed seventh in the graduating class.* Same sign used for: **seven dollars.**

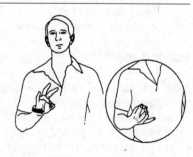

■ [**seven** formed with a twisting movement used to indicate ordinals] Beginning with the right *7 hand* in front of the right side of the chest, palm facing forward, twist the hand to the left, ending with the palm facing back.

several *adj.* See sign for FEW.

severe *adj.* See sign for SERIOUS.

---

sew¹ *v.* **1.** To fasten with stitches by hand using a needle and thread: *to sew a button on.* **2.** To make or fix with stitches in this way: *to sew and embroider a dress.* Related form: **sewing** *n.* See also sign for STITCH.

- [Mime sewing with a needle] With the thumbs and index fingers of both *F hands* touching in front of the chest, palms facing each other, move the right hand in a double circular movement upward in front of the right shoulder, meeting the fingertips of the left hand each time it passes.

---

sew² *v.* To make or fix by working with needle and thread on a sewing machine: *They sew all their children's clothes.* Related form: **sewing** *n.* See also sign for STITCH. Same sign used for: **sewing machine.**

- [Represents the action of a sewing machine needle moving across fabric] Move the bent index finger of the right *X hand,* palm facing down, with a double movement from the base to off the fingertip of the extended left index finger, palm facing down and finger angled to the right.

---

sew³ *v.* See sign for NEEDLEWORK.

---

sewage *n.* Waste that goes through the sewage system: *The sewage went down the drain.*

- [**water** + **dirty** + **absent**] Tap the index-finger side of the right *W hand,* palm facing left, against the chin with a double movement. Next with the back of the right *curved 5 hand* under the chin, palm facing down, wiggle the fingers. Then, beginning with the right *curved hand* in front of the upper chest, palm facing in and fingers pointing up, bring the hand downward through the opening formed by the left *C hand* held in front of the chest, palm facing in, closing the right fingertips as the hand emerges, forming a *flattened O hand.*

---

sewing machine *n.* See sign for SEW².

---

sex *n.* **1.** Either of the two divisions, male and female, of human beings and some other species, as distinguished by their reproductive functions: *Mammals of the female sex bear the young.* **2.** Human sexual attraction and fulfillment: *a movie showing a bit of tasteful sex.* Related form: **sexual** *adj.* Same sign used for: **gender.**

- Touch the index-finger side of the right *X hand,* first to near the right eye and then to the lower chin, palm facing forward.

Shabbat *n. Hebrew.* The Jewish sabbath holiday: *to celebrate Shabbat.* Same sign used for: **sundown, sunset.**

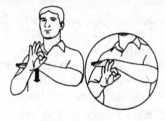

- ■ [Represents the sun going down at sunset] Move the thumb side of the right *F hand,* palm facing left, downward past the little-finger side of the left *open hand* held across the chest, palm facing down and fingers pointing right.

shadow[1] *n.* A shaped area of shade cast by an object: *in the shadow of the tree.*

- ■ [**black** + **shape**[1]] Draw the side of the extended right index finger, palm facing down and finger pointing left, from left to right across the forehead. Then, beginning with both *10 hands* in front of each side of the chest, palms angled forward, bring the hands downward with a wavy movement, ending in front of each side of the waist, palms facing down.

shadow[2] *n.* See sign for DARK.

shake *v.* **1.** To move or cause to move in a jerky manner: *My knees were shaking. The baby shook the rattle.* **2.** To move violently or dislodge with violent movements: *to shake the rug; to shake the dirt out of the rug.*

- ■ [Mime shaking something] With both *A hands* in front of each side of the body, palms facing down, move the hands from side to side with a repeated movement.

shake hands *v.* See sign for HANDSHAKE.

sham *n.* See signs for FAKE[3,4].

shame[1] *n.* A painful feeling of having done something improper: *to blush with shame.* Related form: **shameful** *adj.*

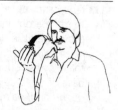

- ■ Beginning with the backs of the fingers of the right *bent hand* against the right side of the chin, palm facing down, twist the hand upward and forward, ending with the right *bent hand* in front of the right side of the chest, palm facing up.

shame[2] *v.* To cause to feel shame: *They shamed me into doing the right thing.* Same sign used for: **shame on you.**

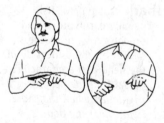

- ■ [Natural gesture for shaming someone] Slide the bottom of the extended right index finger from the base to off the fingertip of the extended left index finger, both palms facing down, with a double movement.

shame³ *n.* See sign for ASHAMED¹. Related form: **shameful** *adj.*

shampoo *n.* **1.** A cleansing preparation for washing the hair: *My shampoo has conditioner added.* —*v.* **2.** To wash one's hair with shampoo: *to shampoo my hair every day.* Same sign used for: **wash hair.**

■ [Mime shampooing one's hair] Move both *curved 5 hands*, palms facing each other, in and out near each side of the head with a repeated movement.

shape¹ *n.* The form of the outer surface or an outline of an object: *a round shape.* See also sign for FIGURE¹. Same sign used for: **figure, form, image, physique.**

■ [The hands outline the image of a shape] Beginning with both *10 hands* in front of each side of the chest, palms facing forward, bring the hands downward with a wavy movement, ending in front of each side of the waist.

shape² *n.* (alternate sign) Same sign used for: **figure, form, image, physique.**

■ [Shows a shapely figure] Beginning with both *curved hands* near each side of the chest, palms facing each other, move the hands downward along the sides of the body with a wavy movement, twisting the wrists up and down as the hands move.

shape³ *n.* See sign for STATUE.

share *v.* To use or participate in together: *to share the same room.* Same sign used for: **change.**

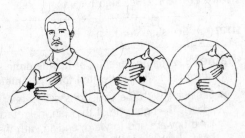

■ [The hand moves back and forth as if to share a portion of something] Move the little-finger side of the right *open hand*, palm facing in, back and forth with a double movement at the base of the index finger of the left *open hand*, palm facing in.

shark *n.* A type of fish, usually carnivorous and predatory, with a wide mouth on the underside of the head and a characteristic dorsal fin: *The people were frightened when the shark swam near the boat.*

- [**fish**[1,2] + a gesture representing the shape and movement of a shark's fin] Beginning with the extended left index finger touching the wrist of the right *B hand,* palm facing forward, wave the right fingers back and forth with a double movement. Then, with the wrist of the right *B hand,* palm facing forward, against the index-finger side of the left *B hand,* arm bent across the chest and palm facing down, move the hands forward with a wavy movement.

sharp *adj.* Having a thin cutting edge or fine point: *a sharp knife.* Same sign used for: **keen.**

- Flick the bent middle finger of the right *5 hand,* palm facing down, forward off the back of the left *open hand* held in front of the body.

sharpen a pencil *v. phrase.* To make the point of a pencil sharp or sharper: *to sharpen the pencil by hand.* Related form: **pencil sharpener** *n.*

- [Mime turning a manual pencil sharpener in order to sharpen a pencil] Move the right *A hand,* palm facing down, in a circular movement near the index-finger side of the left *S hand* held in front of the chest, palm facing down.

shave[1] *v.* To remove a beard or excess hair growth with an electric razor: *to shave every day.* Same sign used for: **razor.**

- [Represents holding an electric razor to shave] Move the fingertips of the right *flattened C hand* up and down on the right cheek with a repeated movement.

shave[2] *v.* To remove a beard or excess hair growth with a hand-held razor: *to shave every morning.* Same sign used for: **razor.**

- [Represents holding a hand razor to shave] Move the knuckles of the right *Y hand,* palm facing left, downward on the right cheek with a repeated movement.

she[1] *pron.* The female person or animal specified, under discussion, or last mentioned: *She had her house painted.*

- [Initialized sign using e formed near the female part of the head] Move the right *E hand* forward from the right side of the chin, palm angled forward.

she[2] *pron.* See sign for HE[1].

shears *pl. n.* See sign for SCISSORS.

sheath *n.* A close-fitting case for the blade of a sword, often worn at the waist: *Put the sword in the sheath.*

- [Mime putting a sword in a sheath] Bring the fingers of the right *H hand*, palm facing in, downward into the opening formed by the left *O hand* held near the left side of the waist, palm facing in.

sheep *n.* A cud-chewing mammal, closely related to the goat, often bred for its coat of wool: *a flock of sheep.*

- [Represents cutting the wool from sheep] Slide the back of the fingers of the right *K hand*, palm facing up, from the wrist up the inside forearm of the left bent arm with a short repeated movement.

sheepish *adj.* Timid; bashful: *He felt sheepish in front of girls.*

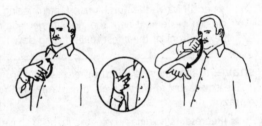

- [**feel** + **silly**[1,2]] Move the bent middle finger of the right *5 hand*, palm facing in, upward on the chest with a double movement. Then, beginning with the right *Y hand* in front of the face, palm facing in, twist the wrist outward with a double movement, brushing the right thumb across the nose with each movement.

shelf *n.* A flat, slablike surface fastened horizontally to the wall or in a frame to hold things: *to put books on the shelf.* Same sign used for: **mantel.**

- [The shape of a shelf] Beginning with the index-finger sides of both *B hands* touching in front of the chest, palms facing down and fingers pointing forward, bring the hands apart to in front of each side of the chest.

shelter *n.* See sign for SHIELD[1].

shepherd *n.* A person who herds, tends, and guards sheep: *The shepherd watched the flock graze in the meadow.*

- [**sheep** + **care**[1] + **person marker**] Slide the back of the fingers of the right *K hand*, palm facing up, from the wrist up the inside forearm of the left bent arm with a short repeated movement. Next, with the little-finger side of the right *K hand* on the thumb side of the left *K hand*, palms facing in opposite directions, move the hands in a flat circle in front of the body. Then move both *open hands* downward along each side of the body, palms facing each other.

sheriff *n.* See signs for POLICE[1,2].

shield[1] *n.* **1.** Anything, as a barrier, used to protect: *The fence provides a shield from the wind.* —*v.* **2.** To protect: *to shield them from harm.* Same sign used for: **protect, shelter.**

■ [Represents holding a shield in front of the body] With the left *open hand* held in front of the chest, palm facing in and fingers pointing up, move the right *open hand* in a repeated circle in front of the left hand, palm facing forward.

shield[2] *v.* See sign for DEFEND[1].

shift[1] *n.* A scheduled period of time for work at a place where separate groups of employees cover portions of a lengthy or continuous workday: *hired to work the first shift at the factory.*

■ [**work** + a gesture indicating the two things are trading places] Tap the heel of the right *S hand* on the back of the left *S hand* with a double movement, both palms facing down. Then, beginning with both *C hands* in front of the chest, palms facing in opposite directions and the right hand closer to the chest than the left hand, move the right hand forward in a large circular movement while moving the left hand back toward the chest, exchanging positions.

shift[2] *n.* See sign for STICK SHIFT.

shift[3] *v.* See sign for CHANGE[1].

shine *v.* See sign for LIGHT[2].

shingle *n.* A thin piece of wood, asbestos, etc., laid in overlapping rows as a covering on exterior walls and roofs: *to put new shingles on the house.*

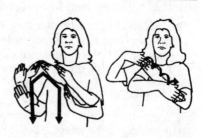

■ [**house** + the shape of shingles on a roof] Beginning with the fingertips of both *open hands* touching in front of the chest, palms angled toward each other, bring the hands at an downward angle outward to in front of

shiny

each shoulder and then straight down, ending with the fingers pointing up and the palms facing each other. Then, beginning with the palm of the right *open hand* on the back of the left *open hand,* both palms angled right and fingers pointing in opposite directions in front of the right shoulder, move the right hand in a series of small arcs down the left arm.

shiny[1] *adj.* Reflecting light; bright; glossy: *a shiny penny.* Related form: **shine** *n., v.* Same sign used for: **glitter, glossy, glow, luminous, sparkle.**

■ [Indicates the glare reflecting off something shiny] Beginning with the bent middle finger of the right *5 hand,* palm facing down, touching the back of the left *open hand,* palm facing down, bring the right hand upward in front of the chest with a wiggly movement.

shiny[2] *adj.* See sign for BEAM.

ship[1] *n.* A large sailing vessel: *to go to the Caribbean by ship.* Same sign used for: **cruise, sailboat.**

■ [The right hand represents a ship moving on waves] With the little-finger side of the right *3 hand,* palm facing left, resting on the palm of the left *open hand,* palm facing up, move both hands forward in a series of small arcs.

ship[2] *n.* See signs for BOAT.

shirk *v.* See sign for AVOID[1].

shirt[1] *n.* A lightweight garment, usually with sleeves, worn on the upper part of the body: *a new shirt with a tailored collar.* Same sign used for: **top.**

■ [Indicates the location of a shirt] Pull a small portion of clothing from the upper right chest forward with the fingers of the right *F hand,* palm facing in, with a double movement. [This sign can be formed using two hands.]

shirt[2] *n.* (alternate sign) Same sign used for: **top.**

■ [Indicates the location of a shirt] Pull a small portion of clothing from the upper right chest forward with the fingertips of the right hand, palm facing in, with a double movement.

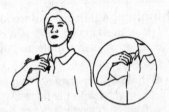

shit *n.* Vulgar. See sign for FECES.

shiver[1] *v.* **1.** To shake with cold or fear: *to shiver with fright.* —*n.* **2.** An act, instance, or attack of shivering: *to feel a shiver down my back.* Same sign used for: **quiver.**

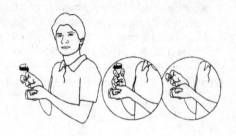

- [Represents teeth rattling together when shivering] Beginning with the heels of both *bent V hands* touching in front of the chest, twist the right hand with a double movement.

shiver[2] *v., n.* See sign for COLD[2].

shock[1] *n.* **1.** A sudden feeling of surprise or horror: *It was a shock to learn of his illness.* —*v.* **2.** To feel a sudden sensation of surprise or horror: *shocked by what I saw.* Related form: **shocking** *adj.* Same sign used for: **astounded, dumbfounded, startled.**

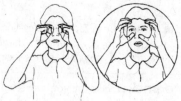

- [Represents one's eyes bulging open when shocked] Beginning with the index-finger sides of both *S hands* in front of each eye, palms facing each other, open the hands simultaneously into *C hands.*

shock[2] *v.* (alternate sign) Related form: **shocking** *adj.* Same sign used for: **dazed, dumbfounded, jolt, panic, stunned.**

- [Indicates the mind fainting when shocked] Beginning with both extended index fingers touching each temple, palms facing forward, move the hands forward simultaneously while opening into *curved 5 hands* in front of each side of the chest, palms angled forward.

shoe *n.* An outer covering for the foot, often of leather: *Time to polish your shoes.*

- [Represents clicking the heels of shoes together] Tap the index-finger sides of both *S hands* together in front of the chest with a double movement, palms facing down.

shoelace[1] *n.* A strip of cloth or leather for fastening a shoe: *to tie your shoelaces.* Alternate form: **shoestring.**

shoelace

■ [**shoe** + **tie**[2]] Tap the index-finger sides of both *S hands* together in front of the chest with a double movement, palms facing down. Then, beginning with the bent index fingers and thumbs of both *modified X hands* touching in front of the body, palms facing down, mime tying a bow.

shoelace[2] *n.* (alternate sign) Alternate form: **shoestring.**

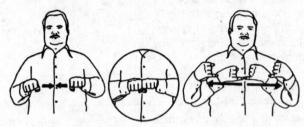

■ [**shoe** + **line**] Tap the index-finger sides of both *S hands* together in front of the chest with a double movement. Then, with the extended fingers of both *I hands* touching in front of the chest, palms facing in, bring the hands apart.

shoemaker *n.* A person wose work is mending shoes: *Take your worn-out shoes to the shoemaker.* Same sign used for: **cobbler.**

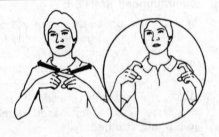

■ [Represents stitches] Beginning with both extended index fingers crossed in front of the chest, both palms facing down, bring the hands apart to in front of each shoulder with a double movement, forming *X hands* each time.

shoot[1] *v.* **1.** To send forth a bullet or other missile from a gun: *to shoot a gun.* **2.** To hit, wound, kill, etc., with a bullet: *The storekeeper was shot by a burglar.* Same sign used for: **fire.**

■ [Mime pulling back the hammer on a gun] With the index finger of the right *L hand* pointing forward in front of the right side of the chest, palm facing left, bend the thumb up and down while moving the hand forward by bending the wrist down.

shoot[2] *v.* (alternate sign) Same sign used for: **fire.**

■ [The hands represent a pair of guns] With the index fingers of both *L hands* pointing forward in front of each side of the chest, palms facing each other, bend both thumbs up and down with a repeated movement.

shoot[3] *interj.* See sign for ALAS.

shoot[4] *v.* See signs for MOVIE CAMERA, TAKE PICTURES[1,2].

shoot[5] *v.* See sign for INJECT.

shoot up *v. phrase.* To grow taller and develop rapidly: *The girl has shot up over the last six months and is now as tall as her mother.* Same sign used for: **become successful, skyrocket, zoom.**

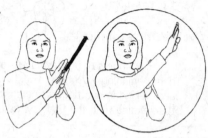

- [An upward movement] Slide the index-finger side of the right *B hand,* palm angled forward, upward from the heel to off the fingertips of the left *open hand* held in front of the chest, palm facing right and fingers pointing up.

shop[1] *v.* To visit stores to look at or buy goods: *to go shopping on Saturday.* Related form: **shopping** *n.*

- [The hand takes money and gives it in payment] Beginning with the back of the right *flattened O hand,* palm facing up, across the palm of the left *open hand,* palm facing up, move the right hand forward and slightly upward with a double movement.

shop[2] *n.* See signs for STORE[1,2].

shoplift *v.* To steal from a store while pretending to be a customer: *arrested for shoplifting in a department store.* Same sign used for: **burglary, steal, theft.**

- [The hands spread out to grab things] Beginning with the fingers of both *5 hands* pointing toward each other in front of the body, palms facing down, bring the hands outward and away from each other in arcs, ending with the hands in front of each side of the body. Then close the fingers into *A hands.*

short[1] *adj.* Having little length; not long: *a short time.* Related form: **shortage** *n.* See also sign for BRIEF[2]. Same sign used for: **soon, temporary.**

- [The fingers measure off a short distance] Rub the middle-finger side of the right *H hand,* palm angled left, back and forth with a repeated movement on the index-finger side of the left *H hand,* palm angled right.

short

short² *adj.* See signs for LITTLE², THIN¹.

short circuit *n.* A flow of excess electrical current, as caused by wires touching: *The short circuit blew a fuse.*

- **[electric + conflict¹]** Tap the knuckles of the index fingers of both *X hands* together, palms facing in, with a double movement. Then, beginning with both extended index fingers in front of each side of the chest, palms facing in and fingers angled toward each other, move the hands toward each other, ending with the fingers crossed.

shortcut¹ *n.* A short or quick way of doing something or getting somewhere: *to take a shortcut home.*

- **[short¹ + truncate]** Rub the middle-finger side of the right *H hand*, palm angled left, back and forth with a repeated movement on the index-finger side of the left *H hand*, palm angled right. Then move the right *V hand*, palm facing left, across the fingertips of the left *open hand*, palm facing down, with a deliberate movement while closing both fingers of the *V hand* together.

shortcut² *n.* (alternate sign)

- **[brief² + brief¹]** Brush the middle-finger side of the right *H hand*, palm angled left, with a sweeping movement across the index-finger side of the left *H hand*, palm angled right. Then, beginning with both *curved 5 hands* in front of the chest, right hand higher than the left hand and fingers pointing in opposite directions, bring the hands toward each other while squeezing the fingers together, ending with the little-finger side of the right *S hand* on top of the thumb side of the left *S hand*.

short hair *n.* Hair that is cut and styled to be short or that is shorter than usual or expected: *The boy now has short hair.*

- **[The hands show the length of short hair]** Move both *bent hands*, palms facing down and fingers pointing back, from each side of the head upward simultaneously a short distance.

shorthand *n.* A method of writing rapidly in short strokes, symbols, and abbreviations that represent letters, words, and phrases: *to take dictation in shorthand.*

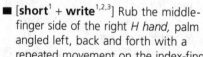
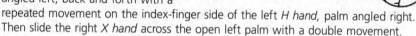

■ [**short**[1] + **write**[1,2,3]] Rub the middle-finger side of the right *H hand,* palm angled left, back and forth with a repeated movement on the index-finger side of the left *H hand,* palm angled right. Then slide the right *X hand* across the open left palm with a double movement.

shortly *adv.* See signs for SOON[1,2].

shorts *pl. n.* Loose trousers reaching to above the knees: *to wear shorts in summer.*

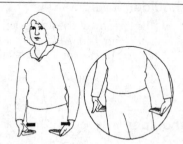

■ [Shows the length of shorts] Slide the little-finger sides of both *bent hands,* palms facing up, with a double movement from in front of each thigh around to each side ending with the fingertips touching the sides of each thigh.

short-sleeved *adj.* Having sleeves that end above the elbows: *a short-sleeved shirt.*

■ [Shows the length of short sleeves] Touch the little-finger side of the right *open hand,* first near the left shoulder and then near the left elbow, palm facing up. The right hand can indicate any length of sleeve depending on where it touches—long sleeves, three-quarter-length sleeves, etc.

short time ago, a See sign for RECENTLY[2].

shot *n.* An injection, as of a vaccine, a drug, or vitamins: *a shot against polio.* Same sign used for: **hypodermic, injection, innoculate, vaccination, vaccine.**

■ [Mime pushing the plunger on a hypodermic syringe] With the index finger of the right *L hand* touching the left upper arm, bend the right thumb down.

shotgun *n.* A gun with a long barrel that fires small pellets: *to hunt for geese with a shotgun.*

■ [Mime holding a shotgun and pulling the trigger] With the index finger of the right *L hand* pointing forward in front of the chest, palm facing left, and the left *curved hand* somewhat forward of the left side of the chest, palm facing up, move the hands back toward the chest while bending the right thumb and pulling the torso back.

should *auxiliary v.* See sign for MUST.

shoulder[1] *n.* The part of the human body to which the arm is attached: *He put his hand on my shoulder.*

■ [The location of one's shoulder] Pat the palm of the right *curved hand,* palm facing down, with a single movement on the left shoulder.

shoulder[2] *n.* (alternate sign)

■ [The location of one's shoulder] Tap the fingertips of the right *bent hand,* palm facing down, on the right shoulder with a double movement.

shoulder[3] *n.* A border along the side of a road: *Drive onto the shoulder and stop.*

■ [**highway** + **shoulder**[1,2]] Beginning with the right *H hand* in front of the chest and the left *H hand* near the left shoulder, palms facing down and fingers pointing toward each other, move the hands past each other in opposite directions with a repeated movement. Then tap the fingers of the right *bent hand,* palm facing down, on the right shoulder with a double movement.

shoulder pad *n.* A mass of stuffing shaped to be worn on the shoulder for protection or design: *The shoulder pads made her shoulders look broader.*

■ [Mime placing shoulder pads on each shoulder] Bring the fingertips of the right *curved 5 hand* downward on the left shoulder and then the fingertips of the left *curved 5 hand* downward on the right shoulder.

shout *v.* See signs for SCREAM[1,2].

shove[1] *v.* To push: *shove the box out of the way.* See also sign for PUSH.

- [Mime shoving someone or something] Move the right *5 hand,* palm facing forward, from the chest forward with a deliberate movement.

shove[2] *v.* (alternate sign, used to indicate that another is shoving the speaker) See also sign for PUSH.

- [Directional sign indicating that someone shoves you] Move the right *5 hand,* palm facing in, back against the chest, forcing the body backward, and then bounce the hand forward.

shovel *v.* See sign for DIG[1].

show[1] *v.* To display to or cause to be seen by another: *I want to show you this student's term paper.* Same sign used for: **demonstrate, example, expose, indicate, indication, portray, reveal, sample.**

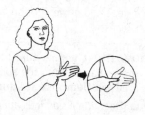

- [The finger points to something in the hand and moves it to show it to someone else] With the extended right index finger, palm facing in, touching the open left palm, move both hands forward a short distance.

show[2] *v.* (alternate sign, used when something is shown to many people) Same sign used for: **exhibit.**

- [Represents showing something around to many people] With the extended right index finger, palm facing in, touching the open left palm, move both hands in a flat circle in front of the body.

show[3] *v.* See sign for ACT[2].

show[4] *n.* See sign for FILM[1].

show off *v. phrase.* See signs for BRAG[1,2].

show up *v. phrase.* To put in an appearance; arrive: *to show up at the party.* Same sign used for: **appear, come up, incident, materialize, occur, pop up, surface, turn up.**

- [Represents something popping up into sight] Push the extended right index finger, palm angled left, upward between the index finger and middle finger of the left *open hand,* palm facing down.

shower[1] *n.* **1.** A bath in which water pours down on the body from an overhead nozzle: *to take a shower every morning.* —*v.* **2.** To take a shower: *I'd rather shower than take a bath.*

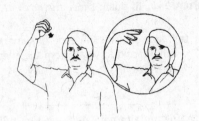

- [Represents water coming down from a shower head] Beginning with the right *O hand* above the right side of the head, palm facing down, open the fingers into a *5 hand* with a double movement.

shower[2] *n.* (alternate sign)

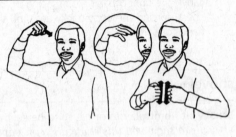

- [**shower**[1] + **bath**] Beginning with the right *O hand* above the right side of the head, palm facing down, open the fingers into a *5 hand* with a double movement. Then rub the palm sides of both *A hands* up and down with a repeated movement on each side of the chest.

show me *v. phrase.* (used to request another to show something to the speaker) Same sign used for: **demonstrate, indicate.**

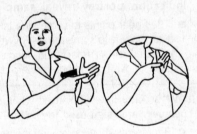

- [Directional sign indicating that another person is to show something to you] With the extended right index finger, palm facing in, touching the open left palm, move both hands in toward the chest.

shred[1] *v.* To tear into small pieces: *to shred the documents.*

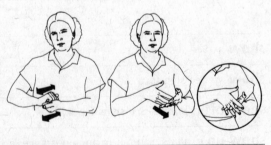

- [The movement of a shredder + **penetrate**[2]] Rub the palm sides of both *S hands* together with a repeated movement in front of the chest. Then move the fingers of the right *5 hand* downward to intersect the fingers of the left *5 hand* held in front of the chest, palms facing each other.

shred[2] *v.* (alternate sign) Related form: **shredder** *n.*

- [Action of paper going through a shredder] With a double movement, move the fingers of the right *4 hand* downward to intersect with the fingers of the left *4 hand* held in front of the chest, both palms facing down.

shrimp *n.* A small, long-tailed shellfish, some species of which are used for food: *to eat shrimp at a seafood restaurant.*

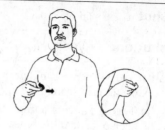

■ [Represents a shrimp's tail] Beginning with the extended right index finger pointing left in front of the right side of the chest, palm facing in, bend the finger into an *X hand* with a double movement.

shrink *v.* See signs for DECREASE[2], DIET.

shroud *n.* **1.** A cloth in which a corpse is wrapped for burial: *an ancient shroud discovered by archaeologists.* **2.** Something that conceals: *a shroud of fog over London.* —*v.* **3.** To wrap in a shroud for burial: *to shroud the body.* **4.** To conceal: *to shroud the statue until the unveiling.*

■ [Shows a shroud wrapped around a body] Move the fingers of the right *open hand,* palm facing in and fingers pointing down, in a repeated circle around the fingers of the left *flattened O hand* held up in front of the chest, palm facing in.

shrug[1] *v.* **1.** To raise the shoulders, as to express disinterest: *She shrugged at the idea of going out.* —*n.* **2.** The raising of one's shoulders in indifference: *He walked away with a shrug.*

■ [Natural gesture for shrugging] Raise the shoulders upward with a natural gesture.

shrug[2] *v., n.* See sign for WELL[3].

shudder *v.* To tremble, as in fear or horror: *We shuddered when we walked into the dark room.*

■ [Natural gesture showing a shudder] With both *5 hands* in front of each side of the chest, palms facing forward and fingers pointing up, shake the hands back and forth with a repeated movement.

shuffle *v.* To intermix cards to put them in random order: *to shuffle the deck before dealing the cards.*

■ [Mime mixing up a deck of cards + mime cutting a deck of cards] With the little-finger side of the right *C hand* on the index-finger side of the left *C hand* in front of the chest, palms facing in opposite directions, raise the right *C hand* upward a short distance at an angle to the right with a double movement.

shut

shut *v.* See sign for CLOSE[3].

shut one's eyes *v. phrase.* See sign for CLOSE ONE'S EYES.

shut out *v. phrase.* To defeat an opposing team without allowing it to score: *shut out the opponent.*
- ■ [Indicates a score of zero] Move the right *O hand,* palm angled forward, from near the right eye forward with a deliberate movement.

shut the door *v. phrase.* See signs for CLOSE THE DOOR[1,2].

shut the window *v. phrase.* See sign for CLOSE THE WINDOW.

shutter[1] *n.* An outside cover for a window: *Close the shutters.*
- ■ [**window** + representing shutters being closed] Bring the little-finger side of the right *open hand* downward with a double movement to hit the index-finger side of the left *open hand,* both palms facing in and fingers pointing in opposite directions. Then, beginning with both *open hands* in front of the body, palms facing forward and fingers angled outward, twist the wrists to move the hands toward each other, ending with the fingers touching in front of the chest, palms facing in.

shutter[2] *n.* The device in a camera that opens and closes to expose film to light for an appropriate amount of time: *a fast shutter.*

- ■ [**camera**[1] + showing a shutter closing and opening] Beginning with the right *modified C hand* near the right eye and the left *C hand* near the left eye, palms facing each other, bend the right index finger up and down with a double movement. Then, beginning with both *C hands* in front of the chest, palms facing each other, move the hands toward each other while closing into *A hands,* ending with the little-finger side of the left hand on the index-finger side of the right hand. Finally, bring the hand apart again while opening into *C hands.*

shut up[1] *v. phrase.* To stop talking; become silent: *Shut up and listen.* Same sign used for: **keep quiet, seal one's lips.**

- [Represents closing one's mouth to shut it up] Beginning with the thumb of the *flattened C hand* touching the chin, palm facing in, close the fingers to the thumb, forming a *flattened O hand.*

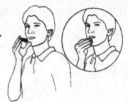

shut up[2] *v. phrase.* (alternate sign) Same sign used for: **didn't mean that, didn't say that.**

- [The finger quiets the mouth] Bring the extended right index finger sharply against the mouth, palm facing left and finger pointing up, while shaking the head negatively.

shy[1] *adj.* Uncomfortable or timid in company: *a shy child.* Same sign used for: **bashful.**

- Beginning with the palm side of the right *A hand* against the lower right cheek, twist the hand forward, ending with the palm facing back.

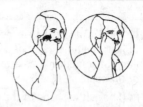

shy[2] *adj.* See sign for ASHAMED[1].

sick[1] *adj.* In poor health or afflicted with a disease: *I feel sick from this cold.* Related form: **sickness** *n.* Same sign used for: **ill, illness, malady.**

- [The finger used to indicate feeling touches the forehead to show that a person doesn't feel well] Touch the bent middle finger of the right *5 hand,* palm facing in, to the forehead.

sick[2] *adj.* (alternate sign) Related form: **sickness** *n.* Same sign used for: **ill, illness, malady.**

- [The finger used to indicate feeling touches the forehead and stomach to show that a person doesn't feel well] Touch the bent middle finger of the right *5 hand* to the forehead and the bent middle finger of the left *5 hand* to the lower chest, both palms facing in.

sick of[1] *Informal.* Weary of; exasperated with: *sick of your excuses.*

- [**sick**[1] formed with a deliberate movement] With the bent middle finger of the right *5 hand* touching the forehead, twist the hand to the left with a deliberate movement.

sick of² *Informal.* (alternate sign)

- ■ Beginning with the bent middle finger of the right *5 hand* pointing forward in front of the right side of the head, twist the hand sharply back, turning the palm in.

side¹ *n.* Either the right or the left half of the body: *my left side.* Same sign used for: **beside.**

- ■ [Location of the side of the body] Bring the right *open hand*, palm facing left and fingers pointing forward, from under the armpit downward along the side of the body.

side² *n.* **1.** One of the surfaces forming the outside of an object: *the north side of a building.* **2.** An area at the edge of something, as a room: *Everyone move to the side of the road.*

- ■ [Shows the shape of the side of a wall] Bring the right *open hand,* palm facing left and fingers pointing forward, downward in front of the right side of the body.

sideburns *pl. n.* Facial hair growing in front of the ears: *He has long sideburns.*

- ■ [Location of sideburns] Beginning with the fingers of both *G hands* touching each side of the face, palms facing each other, move the hands downward on each cheek.

sidestep *v.* To avoid (an issue): *to sidestep the problem.*

- ■ [Represents a person's legs moving off to the side] Move the fingers of the right *bent V hand,* palm facing down, from the extended left index finger held in front of the left side of the chest, palm facing right, in a downward arc to the right.

sidetracked *adj.* See sign for ASTRAY.

sift *v.* To put through a sieve: *to sift the flour.*

- [Shows action of sifting + **leak**[1]] Rub the little-finger side of the right *S hand,* palm facing left, with a repeated movement across the open left palm. Then bring the right *4 hand,* palm facing in and fingers pointing left, downward with a double movement under the left *open hand,* palm facing in and fingers pointing right.

sigh *v.* **1.** To let out a long, deep breath: *He sighed because he was tired.* —*n.* **2.** A long, deep breath: *I heard her tired sigh.*

- [Shows the heaving of the chest when sighing] With the fingers of the left *5 hand* over the fingers of the right *5 hand,* both palms facing in and fingers pointing in opposite directions, move the hands forward and back from the chest while raising the shoulders.

sight *n.* See sign for SEE[1].

sighting *n.* See signs for VIEW[1], VISION[2].

sightseeing *n.* The act of going around to see places of interest: *to go sightseeing in Washington.*

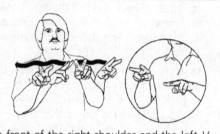

- [Represents the movement of one's eyes when sightseeing] Beginning with the right *V hand* in front of the chest and the left *V hand* in front of the left shoulder, move both hands to the right with a wavy movement, ending with the right *V hand* in front of the right shoulder and the left *V hand* in front of the chest, both palms facing down.

sign[1] *v.* **1.** To communicate in sign language: *Watch how well they sign to each other.* —*n.* **2.** A grammatical unit within sign language: *speak in signs.*

- [Represents one's hands moving when using sign language] Beginning with both extended index fingers pointing up in front of each side of the chest, palms facing forward and the left hand higher than the right hand, move the hands in large alternating circles toward the chest.

sign[2] *n.* A posted notice: *read the sign.* See also sign for SQUARE[1]. Same sign used for: **billboard, rectangle.**

- [The shape of a sign] Beginning with the index fingers and thumbs of both *L hands* touching in front of the chest, palms facing forward, bring the hands apart to in front of each shoulder, palms facing forward, and then close the index fingers to the thumbs of each hand.

sign[3] *v.* To affix one's name in writing: *to sign the check.* Same sign used for: **endorse, register.**

- ■ [Represents placing one's name on a paper] Place the extended fingers of the right *H hand,* palm facing down, firmly down on the upturned palm of the left *open hand* held in front of the chest.

sign[4] *n.* See signs for SQUARE[1], SYMBOL.

signature *n.* See sign for CONTRACT.

significant *adj., n.* See signs for IMPORTANT[1,2]. Related form: **significance** *n.*

sign in *v. phrase.* See sign for REGISTER[1].

sign language *n.* The language of deaf people in which motions, especially of the hands, stand for ideas: *learned to communicate in sign language.* See also signs for AMERICAN SIGN LANGUAGE[1,2].

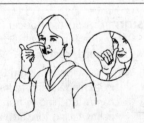

- ■ [**sign**[1] + **language**] Beginning with both extended index fingers pointing up in front of each side of the chest, palms facing forward and the left hand higher than the right hand, move the hands in large alternating circles toward the chest. Then move both *L hands* from in front of the center of the chest, palms angled down, away from each other to in front of each shoulder with a wavy movement.

sign off *adj. v. phrase.* See sign for LOG OFF.

sign up *v. phrase.* See sign for REGISTER[1].

silent *adj.* See signs for QUIET[1,2]. Related form: **silence** *n.*

sill *n.* See sign for WINDOWSILL.

silly[1] *adj.* Without sense or reason: *a silly thing to do.* Same sign used for: **absurd, foolish, ridiculous.**

- ■ Beginning with the right *Y hand* in front of the face, palm facing in, twist the wrist outward with a double movement, brushing the right thumb across the nose with each movement.

silly[2] *adj.* (alternate sign) Same sign used for: **absurd, foolish, ridiculous.**

- ■ Beginning with the right *Y hand* in front of the nose, palm facing left, twist the hand back and forth with a double movement.

silky *adj.* See signs for SMOOTH[2], SMOOTHLY.

silver[1] *n.* **1.** A white precious metal used to make coins, jewelry, tableware, etc.: *a necklace made of silver.* —*adj.* **2.** Made of silver: *a silver spoon.*

- ■ [Initialized sign similar to sign for **gold**[2]] Bring the extended right index finger, palm facing in, from pointing to the right ear downward and turning forward while changing into an *S hand* and shaking it in front of the right shoulder, palm facing forward.

silver[2] *n.* (alternate sign)

- ■ [Movement is similar to the sign for **shiny**[1]] Beginning with the bent middle finger of the right *5 hand* touching the right side of the head, palm facing in, move the hand outward with a wavy movement.

similar *adj.* See signs for ALIKE[1,2,3], SAME.

simple[1] *adj.* **1.** Easy to understand: *simple directions.* **2.** Uncomplicated: *a simple design.* **3.** Unadorned: *She chose a simple suit for her wedding dress.*

- ■ Beginning with both *F hands* in front of the body, the right hand higher than the left hand and palms facing in opposite directions, bring the right hand down, striking the fingertips of the left hand as it passes.

simple[2] *adj.* See sign for EASY.

simulate *v.* To imitate: *to simulate flight on the computer.* Related form: **simulation** *n.*

- ■ [**do** + **same**[1]] Move both *C hands*, palms facing down, from side to side with a repeated movement in front of the body. Then, beginning with both index fingers pointing forward in front of each side of the body, palms facing down, bring the hands together, ending with the index fingers side by side in front of the body.

simultaneous communication *n.* A method of talking and using sign language at the same time: *He uses simultaneous communication as his preferred method to communicate.*

- [Abbreviation **s-c** formed similar to the sign for **communication**] Beginning with the index-finger side of the right *S hand* near the right side of the chin, palm facing left, and the left *C hand* somewhat forward, palm facing right, move the right hand forward and the left hand back to reverse positions with an alternating double movement.

sin[1] *n.* **1.** An act of breaking divine laws: *Stealing is a sin.* —*v.* **2.** To commit a sin: *sinned by envying others.* Same sign used for: **trespass.**

- Beginning with both extended index fingers angled upward in front of each side of the chest, palms facing in, move the hands toward each other in a double circular movement.

sin[2] *n., v.* (alternate sign) Same sign used for: **trespass.**

- Beginning with both *X hands* in front of each side of the body, palms facing in, move the hands toward each other in a double circular movement.

since[1] *prep.* From a past time until now: *since we moved here.* Same sign used for: **all along, been, ever since, lately, since then, so far, up to now.**

- [Shows passage of time from the past to the present] Move the extended index fingers of both hands from touching the upper right chest, palms facing in, forward in an arc, ending with the index fingers angled forward and the palms angled up.

since[2] *conj.* See signs for BECAUSE[1,2].

sing *v.* See sign for MUSIC.

Singapore *n.* A small island country in southeast Asia: *The capital of Singapore is Singapore.*

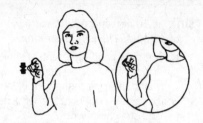

■ Pinch the curved index finger and thumb of the right hand together with a double movement in front of the right shoulder, palm facing forward.

singer *n.* A person who sings, especially one who is trained professionally: *The singer is a soprano.* Same sign used for: **musician.**

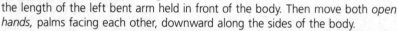

■ [**music** + **person marker**] Swing the little-finger side of the right *open hand* with a double movement back and forth along the length of the left bent arm held in front of the body. Then move both *open hands,* palms facing each other, downward along the sides of the body.

single[1] *adj.* Only one in number: *the single child in a room full of adults.* Same sign used for: **alone, swinging single.**

■ [Shows a person moving around alone] Beginning with the extended right index finger pointing up in front of the right side of chest, palm facing in, move the hand in to the middle of the chest and then back to the right again.

single[2] *adj.* (alternate sign)

■ [Initialized sign similar to sign for **twin**] Bring the index-finger side of the right *S hand* downward, first on the right side of the chin and then on the left side of the chin.

single file *n.* An arrangement of persons or things one behind the other: *to march in single file.*

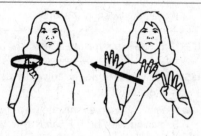

■ [**alone**[1] + **line up**] Move the extended right index finger in a small circle in front of the right shoulder, palm facing in and finger pointing up. Then, beginning with the little finger of the right *4 hand,* palm facing in, touching the index finger of the left *4 hand,* palm facing forward, move the right hand toward the right shoulder.

sink[1] *v.* To descend to a lower level; slip beneath the surface of a liquid: *The ship is sinking.*

- [The right hand represents a vehicle sinking under the surface of the water] Beginning with the thumb of the right *3 hand*, palm facing left, pointing upward between the index and middle fingers of the left *open hand*, bring the right hand straight down.

sink[2] *v.* (alternate sign)

- [Represents a person's legs sinking under the surface of the water] Insert the extended fingers of the right *V hand*, palm facing in and fingers pointing down, downward between the fingers of the left *open hand* held in front of the body, palm facing down and fingers pointing right.

sinner *n.* A person who sins: *God forgives repentant sinners.*

- [**sin**[1,2] + **person marker**] Beginning with both extended index fingers angled upward in front of each side of the chest, palms facing in, move the hands toward each other in a double circular movement. Then move both *open hands,* palms facing each other, downward along each side of the body.

siren[1] *n.* A loud, piercing, prolonged noise used as a signal or warning: *an ambulance siren.*

- [**hear** + **ambulance**[1,2]] Touch the extended right index finger to the right ear, palm facing in. Then move the right *5 hand,* palm facing up, in a circular movement near the right side of the head by repeatedly twisting the wrist.

siren[2] *n.* See signs for AMBULANCE[1,2].

sissy *n.* A weak, timid, or cowardly person: *acts like a sissy.*

- [Hands show an effeminate way of walking] Beginning with both *F hands* in front of each side of the body, palms facing down, move the right hand down and the left hand up with an alternating double movement.

sister[1] *n.* A female with the same parents as another person: *My sister is two years older than I am.*

- [A combination of the signs for **girl**[1] and **same**[1] indicating siblings] Move the thumb of the right *A hand*, palm facing left, downward on the right cheek. Then move the right hand smoothly down while changing into a *1 hand*, ending in front of the body touching the extended forefinger of the left *1 hand*, both palms facing down and fingers pointing forward.

sister[2] *n.* (alternate sign)

- Beginning with the thumb of the right *L hand* touching the right side of the chin, palm facing left, move the right hand downward, landing the little-finger side of the right *L hand* across the thumb side of the left *L hand*, palm facing right.

sister[3] *n.* (alternate sign)

- Beginning with the thumb of the right *A hand* touching the right side of the chin, palm facing left, move the right hand downward while changing into an *L hand*, ending with the little-finger side of the right *L hand* across the thumb side of the left *L hand* held in front of the chest, palms facing right.

sister-in-law *n.* The sister of one's husband or wife or the wife of one's brother or the wife of the brother of one's husband or wife: *going to visit my new sister-in-law.*

- [A combination of a sign similar to the sign for **sister**[2] + **law**] Beginning the thumb of the right *L hand* touching the right side of the chin, palm facing left, move the right hand downward, landing on the upturned palm of the left *open hand*. Then move the right *L hand* to touch again near the heel of the left *open hand*, palm facing up and fingers pointing forward.

sit *v.* To rest with the knees bent and the lower part of the body supported on the buttocks and thighs: *to sit on a comfortable chair.*

- [The bent fingers represent one's legs dangling from the edge of a seat] Hook the fingers of the right *curved U hand*, palm facing down, perpendicularly across the fingers of the left *U hand* held in front of the chest, palm facing down and fingers pointing right.

site *n.* See sign for PLACE[1].

situation *n.* Condition; state of affairs; set of circumstances: *got himself into a bad situation with his boss.* Same sign used for: **surround.**

■ [Initialized sign similar to sign for **atmosphere**] Move the right *S hand* in a circle around the extended left index finger, palm facing right in front of the chest, by twisting the right wrist.

six months *pl. n.* See sign for BIANNUAL.

sixth *adj.* **1.** Next after fifth: *my sixth cup of coffee today.* —*n.* **2.** The one after the fifth in a series of six or more: *She's the sixth in line.* —*adv.* **3.** In the sixth place: *placed sixth in the competition.* Same sign used for: **six dollars.**

■ [**six** formed with a twisting movement that is used to indicate ordinals] Beginning with the right *6 hand* in front of the right side of the chest, palm facing forward, twist the hand to the left, ending with the palm facing up.

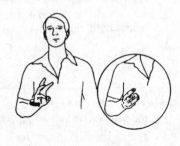

size[1] *n.* The proportions, dimensions, or extent of something: *What is your shoe size?*

■ [The hands seem to measure out a size] Beginning with the thumbs of both *Y hands* touching in front of the chest, palms facing down, bring the hands apart to in front of each side of the chest.

size[2] *n.* See sign for MEASURE.

sizzle *v.* To make a hissing sound when cooking: *The bacon sizzled enticingly.*

■ [**hot** + **burn**[1]] Beginning with the right *curved 5 hand* in front of the mouth, palm facing in, twist the wrist forward with a deliberate movement while moving the hand downward a short distance. Then wiggle the fingers of both *curved 5 hands* in front of the chest, palms facing up and fingers pointing up.

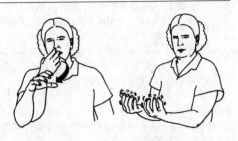

skate[1] *n.* **1.** A shoe fitted with rollers so that a person can glide on a surface: *to try those new in-line roller skates.* —*v.* **2.** To glide along on roller skates: *to skate down the street with my friends.* Same sign used for: **roller skate.**

■ [Shows the action of a person roller skating] With both *bent V hands* in front of each side of the chest, palms facing up, move the hands forward and back with a repeated alternating swinging movement.

skate[2] *n.* **1.** A shoe fitted with a blade so that a person can glide on ice: *ice skates with newly sharpened blades.* —*v.* **2.** To glide along on ice skates: *She skates so well she can do spins and triple jumps on the ice.* Same sign used for: **ice skate.**

■ [Shows the action of a person who is ice skating] With both *X hands* in front of each side of the chest, palms facing up, move the hands forward and back with a repeated alternating swinging movement.

skeleton *n.* The framework of bones in the body: *to study the bones in the skeleton.* Same sign used for: **bone.**

■ [Resembles the skull and crossbones symbol on poisons] With the arms crossed at the wrists, lay the palms of both *V hands* on the chest near the opposite shoulder and bend the fingers up and down with a repeated movement.

skeptic *n.* See sign for DOUBT[1].

skeptical[1] *adj.* **1.** Failing to believe or trust; uncertain: *I'm skeptical about her motivations for giving me a present.* Related form: **skeptic** *n.* Same sign used for: **unsure.**

■ [As if one is blind to what is doubted] Beginning with the right bent V fingers in front of the eyes, palm facing in, constrict the fingers with a short repeated movement.

skeptical[2] *adj.* See sign for DOUBT[3].

sketch[1] *v.* **1.** To draw quickly and roughly: *sketched a map of the neighborhood showing the bus stop.* —*n.* **2.** A quickly done drawing: *did a sketch of my house.* Same sign used for: **draft, drawing, illustration.**

■ [The finger moves as if sketching something] Move the extended little finger of the right *I hand*, palm facing left, with a repeated movement near the left *open hand* held in front of the chest, palm facing right and fingers pointing forward.

sketch

sketch² *n.* See sign for ART.

sketch³ *v.* See sign for DRAW¹.

ski *n.* **1.** One of a pair of long, slender pieces of hard wood fastened to the feet to enable a person to glide on snow: *to put on a pair of skis.* —*v.* **2.** To glide over snow on skis: *to ski down the mountain.* Related form: **skiing** *n.*

- [Represents the movement of skis on snow] Beginning with both *X hands* in front of the chest, palms facing up and right hand closer to the chest than the left hand, move the hands forward.

skid *v.* (of a vehicle) To slide unexpectedly and without the driver's control, especially sideways: *skidding off the road during a rainstorm.*

- [The right hand represents a vehicle moving sideways out of control] Move the right *3 hand,* palm facing left and fingers pointing forward, from the back of the left *open hand,* held in front of the chest, in an arc forward and to the left back toward the chest.

skill *n.* Ability to do something well, gained from talent, training, or practice: *skill in playing the piano.* Related form: **skilled** *adj.* Same sign used for: **ability, able, agile, capable, efficient, enable, expert, good at, handy, proficient, talent.**

- Grasp the little-finger side of the left *open hand* with the curved right fingers. Then pull the right hand forward while closing the fingers into the palm.

skillful *adj.* See signs for ADROIT, NEAT².

skin¹ *n.* The outer layer of tissue on the body: *soft, smooth skin.* Same sign used for: **flesh.**

- [The location of skin on one's hand] Pinch and shake the loose skin on the back of the left *open hand,* palm facing down, with the bent thumb and index finger of the right *5 hand.*

skin² *n.* (alternate sign) Same sign used for: **flesh.**

- [The location of skin on the cheek] Pinch and shake the skin of the right cheek with the index finger and thumb of the right hand, palm facing left.

skin diver *n.* A person skilled in skin diving: *The skin diver found an underwater cave.*

- ■ [**skin diving** + **person marker**] Tap the index-finger side of the right *W hand,* palm facing left, against the chin with a double movement. Then, beginning with the fingers of the right *V hand,* palm facing in and fingers pointing down, on the back of the left *open hand* held in front of the chest, palm facing down and fingers pointing right, flip the right hand forward and over while bending the fingers, ending with the right *bent V hand* in front of the chest, palm facing in and fingers pointing up. Then move both *open hands,* palms facing each other, downward along each side of the body.

skin diving *n.* Swimming underwater with flippers, a mask, and sometimes air breathing equipment: *to go skin diving in the Pacific Ocean.*

- ■ [**water** + a gesture demonstrating the action of diving] Tap the index-finger side of the right *W hand,* palm facing left, against the chin with a double movement. Then, beginning with the fingers of the right *V hand,* palm facing in and fingers pointing down, on the back of the left *open hand* held in front of the chest, palm facing down and fingers pointing right, flip the right hand forward and over while bending the fingers, ending with the right *bent V hand* in front of the chest, palm facing in and fingers pointing up.

skinny *adj.* Very thin; emaciated: *She has skinny legs.* See also sign for THIN[2].

- ■ [Indicates the shape of a skinny person] Move the right *I hand,* palm facing in and finger pointing up, downward in front of the right side of the chest.

skip[1] *v.* To avoid attending; be absent from: *to skip class.* See also sign for ABSENT. Same sign used for: **cut class, lack, miss.**

- ■ Beginning with the left *5 hand* held across the chest, middle finger bent downward, move the extended right index finger, palm facing left and finger pointing forward, from right to left in front of the chest, hitting the bent left middle finger as it passes.

skip[2] *n.* **1.** A light jump, especially in a series alternating from one foot to another: *moved along with a lighthearted skip.* —*v.* **2.** To move along with a series of skips: *skipped all the way home.*

■ [Shows the action of skipping] Touch the middle finger of the right *P hand,* palm facing down, on the palm of the left *open hand,* first near the base and then near the fingertips.

skip[3] *v.* To pass over or omit: *I skipped one of the questions on the test.*

■ [The right fingers represent a person's legs skipping on to the next item] Tap the palm side of the right *bent V hand,* palm facing forward, first on the index finger and then the middle finger of the left *5 hand* held in front of the chest, palm facing in.

skipper *n.* See sign for SAILOR[1].

skirt *n.* **1.** A woman's garment, not joined between the legs, that hangs from the waist: *to wear a plaid skirt.* **2.** The lower part of a dress: *The buttons go from the collar to halfway down the skirt.*

■ [The location of a skirt] Brush the thumbs of both *5 hands,* palms facing in and fingers pointing down, from the waist downward and outward with a repeated movement

skunk *n.* A small black, bushy-tailed mammal with white markings that defends itself by spraying a fluid with a strong odor: *It smells as if a skunk has been here.*

■ [The location of the markings that start on a skunk's head] Bring the thumb side of the right *K hand,* palm facing left, from near the forehead back over the top of the head, ending with the palm facing forward.

sky *n.* The region of the upper air: *clouds in the sky.*

■ [The location of the sky] Bring the right *curved hand* from over the left side of the head, palm facing down, in a large arc to the right, ending above the right shoulder.

skyrocket *v.* See sign for SHOOT UP.

slacks *pl. n.* See sign for PANTS.

slam the door See signs for CLOSE THE DOOR[1,2].

slam the window See sign for CLOSE THE WINDOW.

slap *v.* To strike with the open hand: *to slap someone's face.*
- ■ [Demonstrates the action of slapping something] Bring the fingers of the right *open hand* from in front of the right side of the chest, palm facing left and fingers pointing forward, with a deliberate movement to in front of the left side of the chest, hitting the extended left index finger held in front of the chest, palm facing forward and finger pointing up, as the right hand moves.

slash[1] *v.* To cut with a sweeping stroke: *slashed the curtains in a fit of rage.*
- ■ [Demonstrates the action of slashing something with a knife] Beginning with the right *A hand* in front of the right shoulder, palm facing left, move the hand downward across the body in a large arc while twisting the wrist, ending with the right hand in front of the left side of the body, palm facing in.

slash[2] *n.* **1.** A symbol (/) used in text to separate items: *He/she will put on his/her shoes.* **2.** A keyboard key that inserts this character or symbol: *Enter slash and then the Enter key.* Same sign used for: **forward slash.**
- ■ [Shape of a slash] With a deliberate movement, bring the right *B hand*, palm facing left, from in front of the right shoulder downward to the left.

slaughter *v.* See sign for KILL[1].

slavery *n.* The condition of being the property of another and being forced to work without proper compensation: *sold people into slavery.* Related form: **slave** *n.*
- ■ [Represents a person's wrists been bound in slavery formed with a continuing movement] With the wrists of both *S hands* crossed in front of the body, palms facing down, move the arms in a large, flat circle in front of the body with a double movement.

slay[1] *v.* To kill with violence: *several people slain in the train wreck.*
- ■ [Demonstrates slaying something with a knife] Bring the little-finger side of the right *S hand* from in front of the right shoulder, palm facing back, with a deliberate

movement against the palm of the left *open hand* held in front of the left side of the chest, palm facing right and fingers pointing up.

slay² *v.* See sign for KILL¹.

sled¹ *n.* A vehicle mounted on runners for use on ice or snow: *to pull the sled over the snow.*

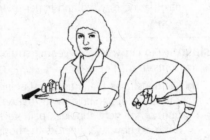

■ [Represents the runners on a sled moving across the snow] Beginning with the back of the right *bent V hand,* palm facing up, across the back of the left *open hand,* palm facing down, push the right hand forward.

sled² *n.* (alternate sign)

■ [**snow** + a movement representing sliding down a hill on a sled] Move both *5 hands,* palms facing down and fingers pointing forward, from above each shoulder forward and downward in large arcs, wiggling the fingers as the hands move. Then, beginning with the right *open hand* across the back of the left *open hand,* both palms facing down, move the right hand downward and forward in an arc in front of the chest.

sleep¹ *v.* **1.** To rest with consciousness suspended: *to sleep for eight hours a night.* —*n.* **2.** The condition or state of sleeping: *Go to sleep. Did you have a good sleep?* Same sign used for: **doze, nap, slumber.**

■ [Laying one's head against a pillow to sleep] Bring the right *open hand,* palm facing left and fingers pointing up, in against the right cheek.

sleep² *v., n.* (alternate sign) Same sign used for: **doze, nap, slumber.**

■ [The hand brings the eyes down into a sleeping position] Beginning with the fingers of the right *curved 5 hand* pointing toward the face, move the hand forward and down while drawing the fingertips and thumb together.

sleep together *v. phrase.* See sign for GO TO BED TOGETHER.

sleepy *adj.* Feeling inclined to sleep: *I get sleepy after lunch.* Same sign used for: **drowsy.**

- ■ [The hand brings the face down as if nodding] Beginning with the right *curved 5 hand* in front of the face, palm facing in and fingers pointing up, bring the fingertips downward to in front of the chin with a double movement.

sleeveless *adj.* Without sleeves: *a sleeveless dress.*

- ■ [Shows that the sleeves are cut off] Move the little-finger side of the right *bent hand,* palm facing right, from on top of the left shoulder downward to in front of the left shoulder.

sleigh *n.* A horse-drawn carriage on runners for use on snow: *to ride in a sleigh.*

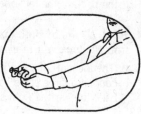

- ■ [Represents the movement of a sleigh on runners on the snow] Beginning with both *bent V hands* in front of the shoulders, palms facing in, move the hands downward in a large arc in front of the chest, ending with the palms facing up, and push the hands forward.

slice[1] *v.* **1.** To cut into thin pieces: *Slice the meat for our dinner.* —*n.* **2.** A thin, broad cut of something: *a slice of bread.*

- ■ [Demonstrates the action of slicing off the end of something] Bring the palm side of the right *open hand,* palm facing left and fingers pointing forward, from in front of the chest straight down near the thumb side of the left *S hand* held in front of the body, palm facing down.

slice[2] *v., n.* (alternate sign)

- ■ [Demonstrates the action of slicing off the end of something] Bring the extended right index finger from in front of the right side of the chest, palm facing left and finger pointing forward, downward with a deliberate movement past the thumb side of the left *1 hand,* palm facing down and finger pointing right, striking the extended left index finger as it passes.

slice

slice[3] *n.* See sign for PIE[1].

---

slide *v.* See signs for SLIP[1,2].

---

slides *pl. n.* Small transparent photographs, framed for use in a projector to be shown on a screen: *to look at slides.*
- ■ Beginning with both *H hands* in front of the chest, palms facing in, left fingers pointing right, and right fingers pointing left, move the right fingers to the left across the back of the left fingers with a double movement.

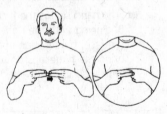

---

slim *adj.* See signs for DIET, THIN[2,3].

---

slime *n.* A soft, sticky substance: *The floor was smeared with slime.* Related form: **slimy** *adj.*
- ■ [**wet**[2] + **surface**[1]] Beginning with both *curved 5 hands* in front of each side of the chest, palms facing up, bring the hands down with a double movement while closing the fingers to the thumbs of each hand. Then rub the fingers of the right *open hand* in a circular movement on the back of the left *open hand* held in front of the chest, both palms facing down.

---

sling *n.* A loop of cloth fastened around the neck to support a hurt arm: *His broken arm was in a sling.*
- ■ [The location of a sling around one's arm] Move the right *open hand* in a large circle completely around the bent left forearm and back to near the right shoulder.

---

slingshot *n.* A rubber band fastened to a Y-shaped stick, used to shoot pebbles or other small objects: *broke the window with a slingshot.*
- ■ [Mime pulling on a slingshot] Beginning with the right *9 hand*, palm facing forward, near the left *V hand*, palm facing in and fingers pointing up, bring the right hand back toward the face, changing into a *5 hand* as the hand moves.

---

slink *v.* To move in a guilty, furtive manner: *slinked out of the meeting.*
- ■ [The right hand represents a person's head moving downward to hide in shame] Move the right *S hand*, palm facing forward, downward through the palm side of the left *C hand* held in front of the body, palm facing right.

slip[1] *v.* To slide suddenly and accidentally: *I slipped on the ice. The glass slipped from my fingers.* Same sign used for: **slide.**

■ [Represents a person's legs slipping] Beginning with the fingertips of the right *V hand* touching the upturned palm of the left *open hand,* push the right fingers forward, ending with the right palm on the left palm.

slip[2] *v.* (alternate sign) Same sign used for: **slide.**

■ [Represents a person's legs slipping] Move the middle finger of the right *P hand,* palm facing down, across the upturned palm of the left *open hand* from the base to off the fingertips, ending with the right palm on the left palm.

slip[3] *v.* To put on or take off easily: *slip into some dry clothes.* Same sign used for: **put clothes on.**

■ [Represents pulling clothes down over one's body] Move the palm side of the right *C hand* from in front of the right shoulder, palm facing left, downward around the extended left index finger, palm facing right and finger pointing up.

slipper *n.* A light shoe that is slipped on easily: *Put on your slippers and rest.*

■ [Represents sliding one's foot into a slipper] Slide the right *open hand,* palm facing down, forward across the palm of the left *curved hand,* palm facing up, while closing the left fingers around the right fingers.

slit *v.* **1.** To make a long, straight cut in: *to slit the envelope open.* —*n.* **2.** A long, straight cut or opening: *left a slit open when he closed the door.*

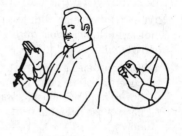

■ [The right hand slits the left hand open] Bring the little-finger side of the right *B hand,* palm facing left, downward with a deliberate movement between the extended fingers of the left *V hand* held in front of the chest, palm angled in and fingers pointing up.

sliver *n.* A long, thin, sharp piece of wood: *got a sliver in her finger.*

■ [**wood**[1,2] + a gesture indicating a sliver going into the skin] Slide the little-finger side of the right *B hand,* palm facing left, forward and back with a repeated movement on the index-finger side of the left *B hand* held in front of the chest, palm facing in. Then slide the middle-finger side of the extended right index finger, palm facing in, down the middle finger of the left *B hand* held in front of the chest, palm facing down. Note that the sign for a sliver made of something other than wood, such as glass, would use the sign for that substance.

slope[1] *n.* An area of ground with a natural incline: *to ski down the slope.*

- [The shape of a slope] Beginning with both *open hands* held in front of the left shoulder, both palms facing down and fingers pointing forward, bring the right hand down to the right in a large arc.

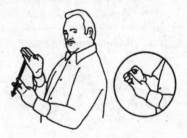

slope[2] *n.* See sign for GRADE.

sloppy *adj.* See sign for FARM.

slothful *adj.* See sign for LAZY.

slouch *v.* **1.** To sit or stand with a drooping posture: *Don't slouch when you sit at the piano.* **2.** To move with a drooping posture and a shuffling gait: *He slouched down the street.* —*n.* **3.** A drooping posture: *He sits with a slouch.*

- [**back**[1] + shows shape of a bent body] Tap the fingertips of the right *open hand,* palm facing down, against the right shoulder. Then move the right *X hand,* palm facing left, in an arc from the right shoulder forward, ending with the palm facing down.

slow *adj.* Proceeding with less speed than usual; not fast or quick: *slow traffic.* Related form: **slowly** *adv.*

- [Demonstrates a slow movement] Pull the fingertips of the right *5 hand,* palm facing down, from the fingers toward the wrist of the back of the left *open hand,* palm facing down.

slow learner *n.* See sign for RETARDED[2].

slumber *v.* See signs for SLEEP[1,2].

slump *v.* **1.** To fall or collapse suddenly: *He slumped over in his chair.* —*n.* **2.** A decline in health, business, or efficiency: *a slump in the economy.*

■ [Shows a downward slump] Move the right *open hand,* palm facing left and fingers pointing up, in an arc from in front of the right shoulder and then downward at an angle to the left in front of the body.

sly *adj.* See sign for SNEAK[1].

smack[1] *v.* **1.** To kiss loudly: *He smacked her on the lips.* —*n.* **2.** The sound made by a kiss: *The baby kissed me with a loud smack.* **3.** A loud kiss: *She gave him a smack right on the lips.*

■ [Represents two people kissing] Bring the fingertips of both *flattened O hands* from in front of each side of the chest, palms facing in, together to touch in front of the chest. Then quickly pull the hands apart, opening into *5 hands,* ending with the palms facing each other in front of each side of the chest.

smack[2] *v., n.* (alternate sign)

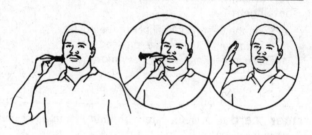

■ [Represents a big kiss on the cheek] Bring the fingertips of the right *flattened O hand,* palm facing left, against the right cheek. Then bring the hand quickly outward to the right while opening into a *curved hand.*

small[1] *adj.* Not great in amount or extent; limited in size: *a small amount.* See also signs for LITTLE[1,2]. Same sign used for: **mini, pee wee.**

■ [Shows a small size] Hold the right *G hand* beside the right side of the face, palm angled forward.

small[2] *adj.* (alternate sign) See also signs for LITTLE[1,2]. Same sign used for: **meager, mini, tiny.**

■ [Shows a small size] Beginning with both *open hands* in front of each side of the chest, palms facing each other and fingers pointing forward, bring the palms close to each other in front of the chest.

small

small[3] *adj.* See sign for CROWDED[1].

smart[1] *adj.* Showing a quick intelligence; clever: *We need a smart person to run the department.* Same sign used for: **brilliant, clever, intelligence, intelligent.**

- [Represents that one is thinking straight] Beginning with the extended right forefinger against the forehead, palm facing left and finger pointing up, bring the hand forward a few inches.

smart[2] *adj.* (alternate sign) Same sign used for: **bright, brilliant, clever, intelligence, intelligent, sharp.**

- [Indicates brightness coming from the brain] Bring the bent middle finger of the right *5 hand* from touching the forehead, palm facing in, forward in an arc while twisting the wrist, ending with the palm facing forward.

smart[3] *adj.* (alternate sign) Same sign used for: **brilliant, clever, genius, intelligence, intelligent.**

- Bring the bent middle finger of the right *5 hand* from touching the forehead, palm facing in, forward with a wavy movement.

smart card *n.* A credit card with built-in computer memory: *She used a smart card to buy souvenirs.*

- [smart[1,2] + card[1,2]] Bring the bent middle finger of the right *5 hand* forward from touching the forehead, palm facing in, while turning the palm forward. Then, beginning with the fingertips of both *L hands* touching in front of the chest, palms facing forward, bring the hands apart to in front of each shoulder, and then pinch each thumb and index finger together.

smart media card *n.* See signs for MEDIA CARD[1,2].

smash *v.* See signs for MASH[1,2].

smear *v.* To spread a wet, oily, or sticky substance over something: *to smear the windows with fingerprints.*

- [Represents something spreading and smearing] Beginning with the right *A hand* in front of the right side of the chest, palm facing left, and the left *A hand* in front of the left side of the chest, palm facing right, move the right hand to the left in an arc while opening both hands into *5 hands* and rubbing the right hand across the palm of the left.

smell[1] *v.* **1.** To detect by breathing in through the nose: *to smell the food cooking.* —*n.* **2.** An odor: *the smell of roses.* Same sign used for: **fragrance, fume, odor, scent.**

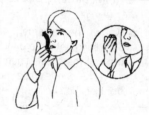

- [Represents bringing something from in front of the nose to smell it] Brush the fingers of the right *open hand*, palm facing in, upward in front of the nose with a double movement.

smell[2] *v.* See sign for SNIFF.

smelly *adj.* See sign for STINK[1].

smile[1] *v.* **1.** To show pleasure, amusement, etc., on the face with an upward curve of the mouth: *He smiled when I told him how handsome he looked.* **2.** To look with favor on: *The fates smiled on the wedding.* —*n.* **3.** An act or instance of smiling: *She reacted with a big smile.* Same sign used for: **grin.**

- [The shape of the mouth when smiling] Beginning with both extended index fingers at the corners of the mouth, palms facing down and fingers pointing toward each other, pull the fingers back to each cheek while forming a smile with the mouth.

smile[2] *v., n.* (alternate sign) Same sign used for: **grin.**

- [The shape of the mouth when smiling] Beginning with both *flattened C hands* near each side of the mouth, palms facing each other, pull the fingers back and upward to each cheek in the shape of a smile while pinching the fingers together, forming *flattened O hands* near each side of the head, palms facing down.

smoke

smoke[1] *v.* To draw the smoke from a pipe, cigar, or cigarette into the mouth and puff it out again: *to smoke a cigarette; to smoke after meals.* Related form: **smoking** *n.*

- [Mime smoking a cigarette] Beginning with the fingers of the right *V hand* touching the right side of the mouth, palm facing in and fingers pointing up, bring the hand forward with a double movement.

smoke[2] *n.* A visible mixture of gases that rise from anything burning: *Smoke from the campfire told us where they were.*

- [Shows the movement of smoke upward from a fire] Beginning with the palms of both *A hands* together in front of the chest, open the fingers of both hands into *curved 5 hands* while moving the right hand upward in front of the chest in a repeated circular movement.

smoke[3] *n.* (alternate sign)

- [Shows the movement of smoke upward from a fire] Beginning with the right *curved 5 hand* above the left *curved 5 hand,* palms facing each other in front of the chest, move the hands in repeated flat circles in opposite directions.

smolder *v.* See sign for BOILING MAD.

smooth[1] *adj.* Having an even surface: *smooth boards.* Same sign used for: **membrane, plane.**

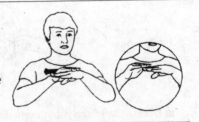

- [Demonstrates a smooth flat surface] Move the fingers of the right *open hand,* palm facing down, from the wrist to the fingertips across the top of the left *open hand* held in front of the body, palm facing down.

smooth[2] *adj.* Free from unevenness; allowing an uninterrupted flow of movement: *a smooth ride.* Same sign used for: **fluent, fluently, go smoothly, silky.**

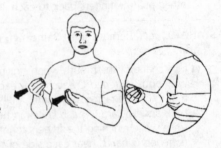

- [The fingers seem to feel something smooth in the fingertips] Beginning with both *flattened O hands* in front of each side of the chest, palms facing up, slide the thumb of each hand across the fingertips from the little fingers to the index fingers with a smooth movement, ending with *A hands.*

smoothly *adv.* In a smooth manner: *The party was run smoothly.* Same sign used for: **fluent, fluently, go smoothly, silky.**

- ■ [Demonstrates a quick movement indicating that something went quickly] Beginning with both *8 hands* in front of each side of the chest, palms facing up, flick the thumbs off the middle fingers while bringing the hands quickly forward and down.

smother *v.* To suffocate or stifle: *to smother the cough.*

- ■ [The hand covers the mouth as if to smother a person] Bring the palm side of the right *curved hand* firmly back across the mouth.

snack *v.* **1.** To eat lightly, especially between regular meals: *We snacked before bedtime.* —*n.* **2.** A light meal or small portion of food or drink: *eat a snack after school.*

- ■ [Demonstrates picking up a snack to eat it] Move the fingertips of the right *F hand* from touching the open left palm held in front of the chest, palms facing each other, upward to the mouth with a double movement.

snag *n.* **1.** A hole or tear in fabric caused by a sharp, rough projection: *a snag in my pantyhose.* **2.** An unexpected obstacle: *We ran into a snag trying to set up the project.* —*v.* **3.** To catch on a sharp, rough projection: *He snagged his coat on the fence.* **4.** To become hindered by an impediment or obstacle: *The campaign was snagged for months on the opponent's dirty tricks.*

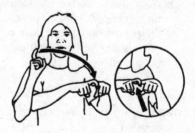

- ■ [Represents something moving until it hooks or snags on something] Beginning with the right *X hand* pointing up in front of the right shoulder, palm facing left, bring the hand downward to hook the bent right index finger over and pull up the extended left index finger held in front of the chest, palm facing down and finger pointing right.

snake *n.* A long, slender, flexible, limbless reptile, some species of which are venomous: *The snake slithered across the lawn.* See also sign for REPTILE. Same sign used for: **serpent, viper.**

- ■ [Represents a snake striking with its fangs] Beginning with the back of the right *bent V hand* in front of the mouth, palm facing forward, move the hand forward in a double spiral movement.

snap

snap¹ *v.* **1.** To make a sudden, sharp sound: *the awful sound of the whip snapping.* **2.** To break with a sudden, sharp sound: *The limb snapped off the tree.* —*n.* **3.** A sudden, sharp sound: *The snap of twigs under foot.* **4.** Something that is done quickly and easily: *Solving the problem was a snap.*

■ Bring the little-finger side of the right *X hand*, palm facing left, with a deliberate movement against the index-finger side of the left *X hand*, palm facing right.

snap² *v., n., adj.* See sign for ABRUPT¹.

snapshot *n.* An informal photograph taken with a handheld camera: *to look at snapshots of my vacation.*

■ [**picture** + **take pictures²**] Move the right *C hand* from near the right side of the face, palm facing forward, downward, ending with the index-finger side of the right *C hand* against the palm of the left *open hand*, palm facing right. Then open and close the right hand with a repeated movement.

sneak¹ *v.* To move in a stealthy, furtive way: *to sneak in by the back door.* Related form: **sneaky** *adj.* Same sign used for: **secretively, sly, stealthy.**

■ [Represents a person sneaking around] With the right index finger extended, move the right hand, palm facing down and finger pointing forward, in a wavy movement under the left *open hand*, sliding the left palm up the right forearm as the right hand moves forward.

sneak² *v.* See sign for ADULTERY³. Shared idea of sneaking around to cheat on one's spouse.

sneakers *pl. n.* High or low canvas shoes with rubber soles: *Please wear sneakers in the gym so you don't damage the floor.*

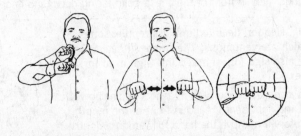

■ [**rubber** + **shoe**] Bring the index-finger side of the right *X hand,* palm facing forward, downward on the right cheek with a double movement. Then tap the index-finger sides of both *S hands* together in front of the chest with a double movement, palms facing down.

sneer *v.* **1.** To show contempt, as by acting or looking scornful: *He sneered at the weak explanation.* —*n.* **2.** A look expressing contempt: *She had a sneer on her face.*

■ [Sign similar to sign for **pry**[1] except made with a double movement] Bring the bent index finger of the right *X hand,* palm facing forward, with a double movement into the opening formed by the left *flattened O hand* held in front of the chest, palm facing in.

sneeze *v.* To expel air suddenly and spasmodically through the mouth and nose: *An allergy makes her sneeze.*

■ [Natural gesture used in trying to stop a sneeze] With the extended right index finger under the nose, palm facing down and finger pointing left, bend the head downward a short distance.

sniff *v.* To draw air through the nose in short breaths: *He sniffed the cold air.* Same sign used for: **smell.**

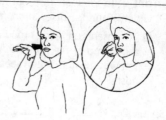

■ [Represents pulling air into the nostrils when sniffing] Bring the back of the *curved 5 hand,* palm facing forward and fingers pointing forward, back against the nose while closing into a *flattened O hand.*

snip *v.* To cut with quick, small strokes: *to snip the thread.* Same sign used for: **trim.**

■ [Indicates quickly cutting on the surface of something] Move the right *V hand,* palm facing down and fingers pointing forward, with a double movement across the extended left index finger held in front of the chest, palm facing down and finger pointing right, opening and closing the extended fingers of the right hand as the hand moves.

snob *n.* A person who is condescending to those he or she considers inferior socially, professionally, or intellectually: *Aloof and patronizing, they were behaving like snobs.* Same sign used for: **snub.**

■ [Indicates one's nose up in the air] Push the extended right index finger, palm facing left, upward and forward in front of the nose.

snoop *v.* See sign for NOSY[2].

snooze *v.* To take a nap: *He snoozed all afternoon.*

- [Represents snoring coming from a person who is snoozing] Move the right *5 hand*, palm facing down, forward with a double movement from the mouth.

snore *v.* To breathe during sleep with hoarse, rasping, whistling, or snorting sounds: *She claims he snores, but he denies it.*

- [**sleep**[1,2] + represents snoring coming from a person who is sleeping] Beginning with the fingers of the right *curved hand* near the forehead, move the hand forward and downward while closing the fingertips and thumbs together, forming a *flattened O hand* in front of the nose, palm facing in. Then move the right *5 hand*, palm facing left, forward with a double movement from the mouth while wiggling the fingers up and down.

snort *v.* To force air through the nose with a violent sound: *Horses snort frequently.*

- [Represents sniffing through each nostril] Push the thumb of the right *10 hand* upward under the right nostril. Then repeat with the left nostril.

snot *n. Vulgar.* A thick discharge from the nose, as during a cold: *"Wipe the snot off your face,"* said the older brother angrily.

- [Mime picking one's nose and discarding the mucus] Beginning with the index finger of the right *X hand* touching the right nostril, palm facing back, turn the wrist forward and thrust the hand downward with a deliberate movement, ending with the palm facing down.

snow[1] *n.* **1.** Ice crystals that fall to earth in the form of soft, white flakes that frequently stick together to form a layer on the ground: *A pile of snow covered the car.* —*v.* **2.** (of snow) To fall from the sky: *It snowed all day.*

- [Represents snow on one's shoulders + the movement of snow falling] Beginning with the fingers of both *5 hands* touching each shoulder, palms facing down, turn the hands forward and bring the hands slowly down to in front of each side of the body while wiggling the fingers as the hands move.

snow[2] *n., v.* (alternate sign)

■ [Shows the movement of snow falling] Beginning with the fingers of both *5 hands* in front of each side of the chest, palms facing down, bring the hands slowly down in front of the body, wiggling the fingers as the hands move.

snowball *n.* A ball made of snow pressed together: *to throw snowballs.*

■ [**snow**[1,2] + **ball**[1]] Beginning with the fingers of both *5 hands* touching each shoulder, palms facing down, turn the fingers forward and bring the hands slowly down to in front of each side of the body. Then tap the fingertips of both *C hands*, palms facing each other, together in front of the chest with a repeated movement.

snowmobile *n.* See sign for MOTORCYCLE.

snowplow *n.* A machine for clearing snow from the streets: *The snowplow came through and cleared the main streets.*

■ [**snow**[1,2] + **plow**[1,2]] Beginning with both *5 hands* near each side of the head, palms facing forward, bring the hands slowly down in front of the body, wiggling the fingers as the hands move. Then slide the little-finger side of the right *curved hand,* palm facing in and fingers pointing left, with a double movement from the heel to off the fingertips of the palm of the left *open hand* held in front of the chest, palm facing up and fingers pointing forward.

snub *v.* See sign for SNOB.

snug *adj.* Warmly comfortable; cozy: *reading quietly in a snug corner of the room.*

■ Bring the index-finger side of the right *B hand,* palm facing down, back against the chest with a deliberate movement.

so *interj.* See sign for WELL[3].

soak through *v. phrase.* See signs for PENETRATE[2], PERMEATE.

soap *n.* A substance made from treated fat, used for washing: *Wash your hands with soap.*

- [Represents rubbing soap on one's hands] Wipe the fingers of the right *bent hand* on the palm of the left *open hand* from the fingers to the heel with a double movement, bending the right fingers back into the palm each time.

soap suds *pl. n.* Frothy bubbles made with soap and water: *to fill the bathtub with soap suds.*

- [**soap** + **bubble**[1]] Wipe the fingers of the right *bent hand* on the palm of the left *open hand* from the fingers to the heel with a double movement, bending the right fingers back into the palm each time. Then, with puffed cheeks and beginning with both *flattened O hands* in front of the body, palms facing down, open the hands into *curved 5 hands* as they move upward to in front of each shoulder, wiggling the fingers repeatedly as the hands move.

so-called *adj.* See sign for TITLE.

soccer[1] *n.* A form of football played between two teams using their feet or other parts of the body except the hands and arms to propel a round ball to the opponent's goal: *to play soccer on Saturday.*

- [Represents kicking a soccer ball] Twist the wrist of the right *S hand* upward with a double movement to hit against the little-finger side of the left *open hand,* palm facing in and fingers pointing right.

soccer[2] *n.* (alternate sign)

- [Formed similar to **kick**[2] but with a double movement] Move the right *B hand* upward in front of the body to hit the index-finger side of the right hand against the little-finger side of the left *B hand* with a double movement, both palms facing in at angles.

socialize *v.* See sign for ASSOCIATE.

social work *n.* An occupation focused on improving social conditions and helping troubled families: *Her profession is social work.*

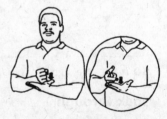

- [Abbreviation **s-w**] Hit the little-finger side of the right *S hand,* palm facing left, on the heel of the left open palm held in front of the body, followed by hitting the little-finger side of the right *W hand* near the left fingertips.

social worker *n.* A person who performs social work: *The social worker who helps the underprivileged children in our neighborhood has a very large caseload.*

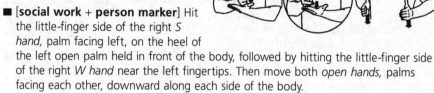

- [**social work** + **person marker**] Hit the little-finger side of the right *S hand,* palm facing left, on the heel of the left open palm held in front of the body, followed by hitting the little-finger side of the right *W hand* near the left fingertips. Then move both *open hands,* palms facing each other, downward along each side of the body.

society *n.* A group of persons joined together by a common purpose: *a society of computer buffs.* Related form: **social** *n.* Same sign used for: **set** (*computer*), **sorority.**

- [Initialized sign similar to sign for **class**] Beginning with the index finger of both *S hands* touching in front of the chest, palms facing forward, move the hands away from each other and in outward arcs until the little fingers meet again in front of the chest.

sock *n.* Short covering for the foot and ankle, sometimes calf-length: *to wear a pair of argyle socks.*

- Rub the sides of both extended index fingers back and forth with an alternating movement, palms facing down and fingers pointing forward in front of the body.

socket[1] *n.* An electrical outlet: *to plug the toaster into the socket.* Same sign used for: **receptacle.**

- [**electric** + **plug** + **square**[1]] Tap the knuckles of the index fingers of both *X hands* together, palms facing in, with a double movement. Next move the right *V hand,* palm facing down, forward from in front of the right side of the chest, ending with the fingers of the right *V hand* on either side of the index finger of the left *V hand,* held up in front of the chest, palm facing in. Then, beginning with both extended index fingers touching in front of the chest, palms angled forward, bring the hands apart to in front of each shoulder, then straight down, and finally back together again in front of the lower chest, palms facing down.

socket[2] *n.* See sign for JOINT[1].

soda pop *n.* A nonalcoholic, carbonated drink: *to drink a soda pop with lunch.* Alternate forms: **soda, pop.** Same sign used for: **soft drink.**

■ [Represents re-capping a soda pop bottle] Insert the bent middle finger of the right *5 hand*, palm facing down, into the hole formed by the left *O hand*, palm facing right. Then slap the right *open hand*, palm facing down, sharply on the thumb side of the left *O hand*.

sodomy *n.* A term referring to any type of sex act disapproved of by the legislature.

■ Insert the little finger of the right *I hand* into the index-finger side of the left *S hand* held in front of the chest, palm down.

sofa *n.* See sign for COUCH.

so far *adv.* See sign for SINCE[1].

soft *adj.* Yielding or smooth to the touch; not hard or stiff: *a soft pillow; a soft silk dress.* Same sign used for: **gentle, mellow, tender.**

■ [The hands seem to feel something soft] Beginning with both *curved 5 hands* in front of each side of the chest, palms facing up, bring the hands down with a double movement while closing the fingers to the thumbs each time.

softball *n.* See sign for BASEBALL.

soft drink *n.* See sign for SODA POP.

soft-hearted *adj.* Sympathetic: *a bonus from our soft-hearted boss.* Alternate form: **big-hearted.** Same sign used for: **kind, tender.**

■ [**soft** formed near the heart] Beginning with the right *curved 5 hand* near the left side of the chest and the left *curved 5 hand* somewhat lower in front of the left side of the body, bring the hands downward, with a double movement, while closing the fingers to the thumbs each time.

soil *n.* See sign for DIRT.

soiled *adj.* See sign for DIRTY.

solder *v.* See sign for WELD.

soldier *n.* A person who serves in an army: *trained as a soldier.* Same sign used for: **military.**

■ [**army** + **person marker**] With both *10 hands* on the right side of the chest, the right hand above the left hand and palms facing in, pat the hands, with a double movement, against the chest. Then move both *open hands,* palms facing each other, downward along each side of the body.

solely *adv.* See signs for ALONE[1,2].

solicit *v.* To try to obtain, as by petition or entreaty: *to solicit new business through the mail.* Same sign used for: **intercept, nab.**

■ [The fingers seem to nab one who has been solicited] Move the fingers of the right *V hand* from in front of the right side of the chest in an arc forward around to hook on the extended left index finger, palm facing forward and finger pointing up, pulling the left index finger back toward the chest.

solid *adj.* See signs for HARD[1,2], STRONG[2,3], STURDY[1].

solidify *v.* See sign for FREEZE.

solution *n.* See sign for DISSOLVE.

solve *v.* See sign for DISSOLVE.

some *adj.* A quantity of: *Drink some milk.* Same sign used for: **part, piece, portion, section.**

■ [The hand seems to divide an object] Pull the little-finger side of the right *bent hand,* palm facing left, across the palm of the left *open hand,* palm facing up and fingers pointing forward.

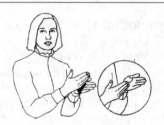

someday *adv.* See sign for FUTURE[2].

someone[1] *pron.* Some person: *Someone took my wallet.* Alternate form: **somebody.** Same sign used for: **something.**

■ [Indicates one person] With the right extended index finger pointing up in front of the right side of the chest, palm facing in, move the right hand in a circle with a repeated movement.

someone[2] *pron.* (alternate sign) Alternate form: **somebody.**

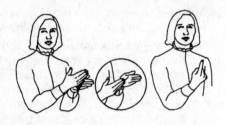

- ■ **[some + one]** Pull the little-finger side of the right *bent hand,* palm facing left, across the palm of the left *open hand,* palm facing up and fingers pointing forward. Then hold the extended right index finger up in front of the chest, palm facing in.

something[1] *n.* An indeterminate thing not known or specified: *I think I forgot something.*

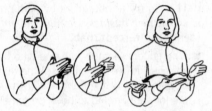

- ■ **[some + thing**[1,2]**]** Pull the little-finger side of the right *bent hand,* palm facing left, across the palm of the left *open hand,* palm facing up and fingers pointing forward. Then, beginning with *open hands* in front of the body, palms facing up, move the right hand to the right in a double arc.

something[2] *n.* (alternate sign)

- ■ With the right extended index finger pointing up in front of the right side of the chest, palm facing in, move the right hand from side to side with a repeated movement.

something[3] *n.* See sign for SOMEONE[1].

sometimes *adv.* Now and then; on some occasions: *Sometimes I forget my keys and get locked out.* Same sign used for: **ever so often, occasional, once in a while, periodically.**

- ■ [Similar to sign for **once** except repeated to indicate reoccurrence] Bring the extended right index finger, palm facing in, downward against the upturned palm of the left *open hand* and up again in a rhythmic repeated circular movement.

somewhere *adv.* In, at, or to an unknown or unspecified place: *If you're tired of the city, go somewhere else.*

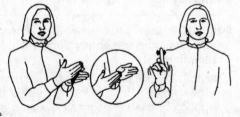

- ■ **[some + where]** Pull the little-finger side of the right *bent hand,* palm facing left, across the palm of the left *open hand,* palm facing up and fingers pointing forward. Then move the extended right index finger, palm facing forward and finger pointing up, with a wiggly movement from side to side in front of the right shoulder.

son¹ *n.* A male child in relation to his father and mother: *a younger son.*

■ [A combination of the signs for **boy**¹ and **baby**¹] Beginning with the index-finger side of the right *flattened C hand* near the right side of the forehead, palm facing left, close the fingers to the thumb. Then bring the right hand down while opening into an *open hand,* ending with the bent right arm cradled on the bent left arm held across the body, both palms facing up.

son² *n.* (alternate sign)

■ [Begins at the male area of the head + **baby**¹] Beginning with the fingertips of the right *B hand* against the forehead, palm facing left, bring the right hand downward, ending with the bent right arm cradled in the bent left arm held across the body, both palms facing up.

song *n.* See sign for MUSIC.

son-in-law *n.* The husband of one's daughter: *My son-in-law is a computer programmer.*

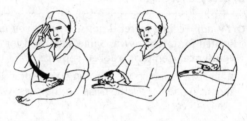

■ [**son**² + **law**] Beginning with the fingertips of the right *open hand* against the forehead, palm facing left, bring the right hand downward, ending with the bent right arm cradled in the bent left arm held across the body, both palms facing up. Then move the right *L hand* from touching first on the palm of the upturned left *open hand* to touching on the left wrist.

soon¹ *adv.* Within a short time: *Soon it will be time to go.* Same sign used for: **near future, in the; shortly.**

■ Touch the fingertips of the right *F hand,* palm facing in, to the middle of the chin.

soon² *adv.* (alternate sign) Same sign used for: **near future, in the; shortly.**

■ With the thumb of the right *curved 3 hand,* palm facing left, touching the right side of the chin, twist the hand back.

soon[3] *adv.* See sign for SHORT[1].

sophisticated *adj.* Worldly-wise: *a sophisticated, well-traveled woman.* Same sign used for: **prim.**

■ With the thumb, index finger, and little finger of the right hand extended, push the right index finger upward and forward under the chin, palm facing left.

sophomore *n.* A student in the second year of high school or college: *a college sophomore.*

■ [Indicates a middle year in school] Touch the middle finger of the left *5 hand* with the extended right index finger, both palms facing in.

sordid *adj.* See sign for AWFUL.

sore *adj.* See signs for PAIN[1], SUFFER[2], HURT[1,2].

sorority *n.* See sign for SOCIETY.

sorry *adj.* Feeling regret: *I am sorry that you have to leave so soon.* Related form: **sorrow** *n.* Same sign used for: **apologize, apology, penitence, penitent, regret, repent.**

■ [Indicates rubbing the chest in sorrow] Rub the palm side of the right *A hand* in a large circle on the chest with a repeated movement.

sort *v.* See signs for FILE[1,2,3], KIND[3,4], PLAN[2], PREPARE.

sort of *adj.* See sign for FAIR[3].

so-so *adj.* See sign for FAIR[3].

soul[1] *n.* **1.** The spiritual part of humans as distinct from the physical: *The souls of the children are pure.* **2.** The seat of human personality and emotions: *He had a good feeling in his soul.*

■ Move the right *bent hand* from in front of the right shoulder, palm facing forward, back to touch the fingertips against the chest.

soul[2] *n.* See signs for SPIRIT[1,2].

sound[1] *n.* What can be heard when the organs of hearing are stimulated, as noises, voices, or music: *I heard a sound coming from the next room.*

- [Initialized sign formed near the ear] Move the right *S hand,* palm facing forward, from near the right ear outward to the right.

sound[2] *n.* See signs for HEAR, NOISE.

soundproof *adj.* **1.** Not allowing sound in or out: *a soundproof room.* —*v.* **2.** To make soundproof: *We had to soundproof the music studio.*

- [**noise + none**[1]] Point the extended index fingers of both hands, palms facing down, to each ear. Then move both *5 hands* up and down with a double movement near each ear, palms facing back and fingers pointing toward each other. Then move the hands downward and outward in an arc while forming *O hands* in front of each side of the body, palms facing forward.

soup *n.* A liquid food usually made by boiling a combination of seasonings, vegetables, fish, or meat in water: *to make vegetable soup from leftovers.*

- [Mime eating soup with a spoon] Move the fingers of the right *U hand* from touching the palm of the left *open hand* upward to the mouth, both palms facing up.

sour *adj.* Having a sharp, acidic, biting taste, like lemon or vinegar: *The milk has turned sour.* Same sign used for: **bitter, tart.**

- [Points to puckered lips from eating something sour] With the tip of the extended right index finger on the chin near the mouth, palm facing left, twist the hand, ending with the palm facing back.

source *n.* See sign for START[1].

south[1] *n.* **1.** The general direction opposite of north: *The new buildings face the south.* —*adj.* **2.** Lying toward, located in, or coming from the south: *a south wind.*

—*adv.* **3.** To, toward, or in the south: *The birds travel south for the winter.* Related form: **southern** *adj.*

■ [Initialized sign indicating a southern direction on a map] Move the right *S hand*, palm facing in, downward in front of the right side of the chest.

south[2] *n., adj.* (alternate sign) Related form: **southern** *adj.*

■ [Initialized sign indicating a southern direction on a map] Move the right *S hand*, palm facing forward, downward in front of the right side of the chest.

South America *n.* A continent in the southern part of the western hemisphere: *Spanish and Portuguese are spoken in South America.*

■ [**south**[1,2] + **America**] Move the right *S hand*, palm facing in, downward in front of the right side of the chest. Then, with the fingers of the both hands loosely entwined, palms facing in, move the hands in a circle in front of the chest.

southeast *n.* **1.** The general direction midway between south and east: *They're moving somewhere in the southeast.* —*adj.* **2.** Lying toward or facing the southeast: *a southeast window.* **3.** Coming from the southeast: *a blustery southeast wind.* —*adv.* **4.** Toward the southeast: *Go southeast until you come to the light.*

■ [**south**[1,2] + **east**] Move the right *S hand*, palm facing forward, downward in front of the right side of the chest. Then move the right *E hand*, palm facing forward, a short distance to the right.

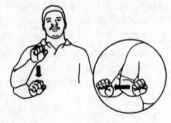

southwest *n.* **1.** The general direction midway between south and west: *I'm pointing toward the southwest.* —*adj.* **2.** Lying toward or facing the southwest: *The road is southwest of here.* **3.** Coming from the southwest: *a hot, dry southwest wind.* —*adv.* **4.** Toward the southwest: *The storm is turning southwest.*

■ [**south**[1,2] + **west**[1,2]] Move the right *S hand*, palm facing forward, downward in front of the right side of the chest. Then move the right *W hand*, palm facing forward, a short distance to the left in front of the chest.

Soviet *n., adj.* See sign for RUSSIA[1].

sow *v.* See sign for PLANT[2].

so what! *interj.* See sign for TOUGH[2].

space[1] *n.* **1.** An extent or area in three dimensions: *not enough space in my office.* **2.** An extent or area in two dimensions: *left too much space between words on this page.* **3.** An area designated for a particular purpose: *a parking space for my car.* **4.** Alternate form: **outer space** The vast area beyond the atmosphere of the earth: *The ship hurtled into space, destined to go beyond the solar system.*

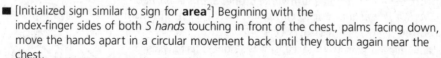

- ■ [Initialized sign similar to sign for **area**[2]] Beginning with the index-finger sides of both *S hands* touching in front of the chest, palms facing down, move the hands apart in a circular movement back until they touch again near the chest.

space[2] *n.* See signs for AREA[1,2,3,4].

space[3] *n.* See sign for EMPTY. Shared idea of a vacant space.

spaceship[1] *n.* A vehicle for traveling in outer space: *The astronauts were in the spaceship, getting ready for the launch.* Same sign used for: **spacecraft.**

- ■ [The hand shape represents a spaceship moving through space] Move the right *curved 3 hand,* palm facing in and fingers pointing left, from in front of the head to the right.

spaceship[2] *n.* (alternate sign) Same sign used for: **spacecraft.**

- ■ [The sign represents an **airplane** encircling the globe] With the thumb, index finger, and little finger of the right hand extended, palm angled forward, move the hand in a large forward circle around the left *flattened O hand* held in front of the chest, palm facing down.

space shuttle *n.* See signs for ROCKET[1,2].

spade *n.* See sign for SPATULA.

spaghetti[1] *n.* Long, slender strings of pasta, cooked by boiling and often served with tomato sauce: *serving the classic dish of spaghetti and meatballs.*

- ■ [The shape of spaghetti] Beginning with both extended little fingers touching in front of the chest, palms facing in, bring the hands apart in small arcs, ending in front of each shoulder.

spaghetti[2] *n.* (alternate sign)

- [Represents tossing spaghetti] Beginning with both extended index fingers angled upward near each other in front of the chest, palms facing in, bring the hands downward and outward in either alternating or simultaneous circular movements.

Spain[1] *n.* A country in southwest Europe: *Spain is on the Iberian Peninsula, next to Portugal.* Related form: **Spanish** *n., adj.* Same sign used for: **Hispanic.**

- Beginning with the fingertips of the right *C hand,* palm facing in, touching the right side of the body, bring the right hand up to the left shoulder while opening into an *open hand,* palm facing forward.

Spain[2] *n.* (alternate sign) Related form: **Spanish** *n., adj.* Same sign used for: **Hispanic, Mexico.**

- [Represents the mantilla worn by Spanish women] Beginning with the index fingers of both *X hands* touching each side of the chest, palms facing in, twist the wrists to bring the hands downward and toward each other, ending with the index fingers hooked in front of the chest, palms facing in opposite directions.

Spain[3] *n.* (alternate sign) Related form: **Spanish** *n., adj.* Same sign used for: **Mexico.**

- Beginning with the index fingers of both *X hands* touching each side of the chest, palms facing in, bring the hands downward and forward ending in front of each side of the body.

spangle *n.* A small, round, shiny piece of metal or similar material, used as decoration on fabric: *The dress was covered with spangles.*

- [As though pouring spangles on an object + **shiny**[1]] Shake the index-finger side of the right *C hand,* palm facing forward, with a double movement over the back of the left *open hand* held in front of the chest, palm facing down and fingers pointing right. Then, beginning with the bent middle finger of the right *5 hand,* palm facing down, touching the back of the left *open hand,* palm facing down, bring the right hand upward in front of the chest with a wiggly movement.

spank[1] *v.* To strike as punishment with an open hand or a flat object, especially on the buttocks: *to spank the naughty child.* Related form: **spanking** *n.* Same sign used for: **whack, whip, whipping.**

- [Demonstrates the action of spanking] Bring the palm of the right *open hand* downward from in front of the right side of the chest to strike against the palm of the left *open hand,* palm facing up, with a repeated movement.

spank[2] *v.* See sign for PADDLE.

spark[1] *n.* A flash of electrical light or fire: *A spark came from the wires.*

- Beginning with the right *modified X hand* touching the extended left index finger in front of the chest, both palms facing forward, flick the right index finger upward with a double movement.

spark[2] *v.* See sign for START[2].

sparkle *v.* See sign for SHINY[1].

spasm[1] *n.* An uncontrollable contraction of muscles: *A sudden stomach spasm took her by surprise.*

- [**abdomen** + shows a tightening of muscles in the abdominal area.] Tap the palm of the right *open hand* against the abdomen with a double movement. Then close the fingers of both *curved 5 hands,* palms facing in, with a tight movement in front of the abdomen, forming *S hands.*

spasm[2] *n.* See sign for CRAMP[2].

spatula *n.* A tool with a flat, flexible blade, used in preparing food, spreading plaster, and the like: *Turn the pancakes with a spatula.* Same sign used for: **dig, spade.**

- [Shows action of turning food over with a spatula] Push the fingertips of the right *open hand,* palm facing up and fingers pointing forward, with a short movement forward on the fingers of the left *open hand* held in front of the chest, palm facing up. Then flip the right hand over in an arc, ending with the palm facing down.

speak[1] *v.* To say words, especially to communicate: *Speak softly.* Same sign used for: **talk.**

- [Represents words coming from the mouth] Beginning with the index-finger side of the right *4 hand* touching the chin, palm facing left, move the hand forward with a repeated movement.

speak

speak[2] *v.* To express ideas in front of a group of people, as in delivering a speech: *She spoke on the broad topic of international unrest.* Same sign used for: **address, lecture, presentation, sermon, speech, talk.**

■ Beginning with the right *open hand* near the right side of the head, palm facing left and fingers pointing up, twist the wrist to move the fingers forward and back with a repeated movement.

speakerphone *n.* The feature on a telephone that allows the reception and transmission of speech through a microphone and loudspeaker instead of through a handset, making it possible for more than one person to participate in a conversation at one time: *The meeting was conducted using a speakerphone.*

■ [Mime setting down a phone + **listen**[3]] Move the right *Y hand* down a short distance, palm facing down, in front of the right side of the body. Then touch the thumb of the right *curved 5 hand,* palm facing left, near the right ear.

special[1] *adj.* Distinguished from the ordinary; distinctive; unusual: *a special dessert just for you.* Same sign used for: **especially, except, exceptional, unique.**

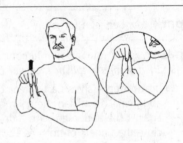

■ [Demonstrates pulling one thing out that is special] Grasp the extended left index finger, palm facing in and finger pointing up, with the fingers of the right *G hand* and pull upward in front of the chest.

special[2] *adj.* (alternate sign) Same sign used for: **especially, except, exceptional, unique.**

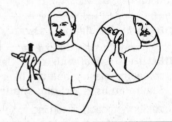

■ [Demonstrates pulling one thing out that is special] Grasp the extended left index finger, palm facing in, with the bent thumb and index finger of the right *5 hand,* and pull upward.

specialize[1] *v.* To select a field to pursue professionally or for study: *to specialize in economics.* Related form: **specialty** *n.* Same sign used for: **field, main, major, straight.**

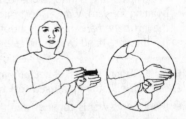

■ Slide the little-finger side of the right *B hand,* palm facing left and fingers pointing forward, along the index-finger side of the left *B hand* held in front of the chest, palm facing right and fingers pointing forward.

specialize[2] *v.* (alternate sign) Related form: **specialty** *n.* Same sign used for: **direct.**

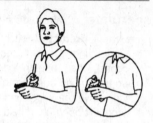

- Slide the extended right index finger, palm facing in, from the base to the fingertip of the extended left index finger, palm facing right.

specific *adj.* See signs for POINT[3], PRECISE.

specifications *pl. n.* A detailed description of materials needed, workmanship required, etc., for the construction, renovation, or performance of something: *a list of the specifications for the new building.*

- [Formed similar to **precise** except with a double movement] With the right *modified X hand* closer to the face than the left *modified X hand* and palms facing each other in front of the chest, bring the hands to touch each other with a short double movement.

speck *n.* A small spot: *a speck of dirt on the window.*

- [**tiny**[1,2] + **dirty** + a gesture showing a speck reflecting into the eye] With the right thumb tucked under the right little finger, palm facing in, flick the thumb upward with a small double movement. Next, with the back of the right *curved 5 hand* under the chin, palm facing down, wiggle the fingers. Then bring the bent index finger of the right *X hand*, palm facing forward, downward to touch the palm of the left *open hand*, palm facing up, and then upward again in front of the chest.

spectacles *pl. n.* See sign for GLASSES.

speculate[1] *v.* To think carefully, express one's thoughts, or guess: *to speculate about the outcome of the campaign.* Related form: **speculation** *n.*

- [**me** + **feel**] Touch the extended right index finger, palm facing in, to the center of the chest. Then move the bent middle finger of the right *5 hand*, palm facing in, upward with a double movement on the chest.

speculate[2] *v.* (alternate sign) Related form: **speculation** *n.*

■ [me + predict[1,2]] Touch the extended right index finger, palm facing in, to the center of the chest. Then, beginning with the fingers of the right *V hand* pointing to each eye, palm facing in, move the right hand forward in an arc under the left *open hand* held across the body, palm facing down, turning the right hand as it moves, ending with the right fingers pointing forward.

speculate[3] *v.* See sign for LET'S SEE. Related form: **speculation** *n.*

speech[1] *n.* The ability to speak, an act of speaking, or an utterance spoken with the mouth, vocal cords, and other organs of speech: *trained to use good, understandable speech.*

■ [Shows the movement of the lips when speaking] Move the bent fingers of the right *V hand,* palm facing in, in a small repeated circle in front of the mouth.

speech[2] *n.* See sign for SPEAK[2].

speechread *v.* See sign for LIPREAD.

speed *n.* **1.** Rapid movement, as of a vehicle: *a driver who loves speed.* **2.** Relative rate of motion or activity: *works at a fast speed.* —*v.* **3.** to go or move quickly: *The boat sped across the lake.*

■ Beginning with both extended index fingers pointing forward in front of each side of the chest, palms facing in opposite directions and right hand forward of the left hand, bend the fingers with a double movement.

speedy *adj.* See signs for FAST[1,2,3].

speedometer *n.* An instrument for measuring the speed of a vehicle: *The speedometer reads sixty miles per hour.*

■ [Represents the movement of the dial on a speedometer] With the right wrist against the index-finger side of the left *open hand* held in front of the chest, palm facing down, move the extended right index finger, palm facing forward, with a double movement from side to side in front of the chest.

spell *v.* See sign for FINGERSPELL. Related form: **fingerspelling** *n.*

spend¹ *v.* To pay out: *to spend some money.*

- ■ [Represents taking money from the pockets and distributing it] Beginning with both *S hands* in front of each side of the body, palms facing up, move the hands forward while opening the fingers slowly into *curved hands.*

spend² *v.* To pay out money wastefully: *to spend a fortune at the carnival.*

- ■ [Represents money slipping through one's hands] Beginning with both *curved hands* in front of each side of the chest, right hand nearer the chest than the left hand and both palms facing up, move the hands forward while moving the thumbs across the fingers, ending with *10 hands.*

spend³ *v.* To pass time in a particular manner or place: *spend your vacation on a cruise.*

- ■ [Represents time flitting away] Beginning with the index fingers and thumbs of both hands pinched together, palms facing up in front of the body, move the hands upward while flicking the index fingers forward.

sperm *n.* See sign for SEMEN.

sphere *n.* See sign for BALL².

spider *n.* A small wingless creature with eight legs, known for spinning webs that trap insects for food: *The black widow spider is poisonous.*

- ■ [Represents a spider's legs] With the wrists of both *curved 4 hands* crossed in front of the body, palms facing down and right wrist over the left wrist, wiggle the fingers with a repeated movement.

spike¹ *n.* A pointed metal projection: *Golf shoes have spikes on the soles.*

- ■ [The shape of spikes] Move the right *4 hand,* palm facing left, in a circle around the left *open hand* held across the body, palm facing down and fingers pointing right.

spike

spike[2] *n.* See sign for POWER SURGE.

spill *v.* **1.** To cause or allow (liquid or other loose material) to run or fall from a container, especially accidentally: *to spill the milk.* **2.** To run out of or fall from a container, as onto a surface: *The milk spilled.*

■ [Represents something spreading out when it is spilled] Beginning with both *flattened O hands* touching in front of the body, palms facing down and fingers pointing down, move the hands forward and apart while opening the fingers into *5 hands*, palms facing down.

spin *v.* **1.** To turn around or cause to turn around rapidly: *The ice skater spun so quickly that she looked like a blur. You may spin the top on the rug.* —*n.* **2.** A spinning movement: *The dancer did a perfect spin on stage.*

■ [Demonstrates the action of something spinning] With the extended right index finger pointing down and the extended left index finger pointing up in front of the chest, right hand above left and both palms facing in, move both hands in circles with an alternating movement while the fingers move forward and outward to the right in a circular movement.

spindle *n.* A rod on which thread is wound, as on a spinning wheel or other machine: *Put the spindle back on the sewing machine.*

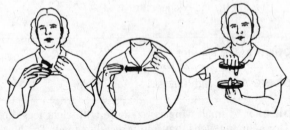

■ [**thread**[1] + winding thread around a spindle] Beginning with the right *curved hand*, palm facing left, around the extended little finger of the left *I hand*, palm facing in and finger pointing right, pull the right hand outward to the right with a double movement, closing into a *flattened O hand* each time. Then, with the extended right index finger pointing down and the extended left index finger pointing up in front of the chest, both palms facing in, move the fingers in circles around each other going in opposite directions.

spine *n.* The series of disclike bones forming the axis of the skeleton: *A chill went up and down my spine.* Related form: **spinal** *adj.* Same sign used for: **backbone**.

■ [Point to the spine + the shape of the spinal column] Touch the extended right index finger to the right side of the body near the spine, palm facing up. Then, beginning with the left *modified C hand* above the right *modified C hand* in front of the face, bring the right hand straight down in front of the body.

spiral *n.* **1.** A winding coil: *The tornado was shaped like a spiral.* —*adj.* **2.** Having a coiled shape: *a spiral staircase.*

- [The shape of a spiral] With the extended right index finger pointing down in front of the head, and the extended left index finger pointing up in front of the chest, both palm facing in and fingers pointing toward each other, move the hands in repeated circular movements as the hands pull away from each other.

spirit[1] *n.* **1.** The intangible animating essence of human life: *Though they're gone, their spirits will live on.* **2.** One's fundamental emotional nature; temperament: *She has a bright, happy spirit.* **3.** An attitude of courage and optimism: *The soldiers in the field had amazing spirit.* **4.** A supernatural being: *God is a spirit.* Related form: **spiritual** *adj.* Same sign used for: **ghost, soul.**

- [The hand seems to pull a spirit out of the other hand] Beginning with the fingertips of the right *9 hand* inside the opening formed by the left *O hand,* pull the right hand upward in front of the chest, palm facing down.

spirit[2] *n.* (alternate sign) Related form: **spiritual** *adj.* Same sign used for: **ghost, soul.**

- [Shows a wispy form representing a spirit] Beginning with the bent index finger and thumb of the right *5 hand* pointing down above the bent index finger and thumb of the left *5 hand,* palms facing each other, close the index fingers and thumbs of both hands together, touching each other. Then pull the hands apart, moving the right hand upward in front of the chest.

spit[1] *v.* **1.** To eject saliva from the mouth: *The dentist said to spit into the sink.* —*n.* **2.** Saliva ejected from the mouth: *There was spit on the sidewalk.*

- [Indicates the movement of spitting] Beginning with the thumb holding down the bent index finger of the right hand in front of the mouth, palm facing forward, move the hand forward while flicking the index finger forward.

spit[2] *v., n.* (alternate sign)

- [Shows the direction of spit coming from the mouth] Beginning with the index-finger side of the right *4 hand* on the chin, palm facing left, move the hand forward with a deliberate movement while twisting the fingers downward.

splash

splash *v.* To dash or shower, as with liquid or mud: *to splash dirty water on the sidewalk.* Same sign used for: **splatter.**

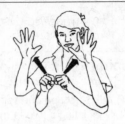

- [Represents the movement of a liquid splashing] Beginning with both *S hands* near each other in front of the chest, palms facing forward, move the hands upward and apart while opening quickly into *5 hands,* ending in front of each shoulder, palms facing forward and fingers pointing up.

splat *n.* See sign for PLOP.

splendid *adj.* See sign for WONDERFUL[1].

splice *v.* **1.** To join two pieces together: *to splice the film.* —*n.* **2.** A place where two things are joined together: *a weak splice.*

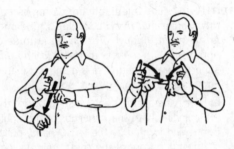

- [slice[2] + a gesture that shows how two things are overlapped to splice them] Bring the extended right index finger, palm facing left, downward in front of the chest with a deliberate movement past the thumb side of the left *1 hand,* hitting the extended left index finger, palm facing down and finger pointing right, as it passes. Then bring both extended index fingers from in front of each shoulder, palms facing each other, downward toward each other, landing the extended right index finger on the fingertip of the extended left index finger, both palms facing down.

splint[1] *n.* Wood or other supporting material arranged to hold a broken bone in place: *a splint on his arm.*

- [wood[1,2] + mime wrapping tape around a splint] Slide the little-finger side of the right *B hand,* palm facing left, forward and back on the index-finger side of the left *B hand* held in front of the chest, palm facing in and fingers pointing right. Then move the right *B hand* in a circular movement around the bent left arm held across the chest, both palms facing in.

splint[2] *n.* (alternate sign)

■ [**sliver** + mime wrapping a splint around the arm] Slide the little-finger side of the right *B hand*, palm facing left, forward and back with a double movement across the index-finger side of the left *B hand* held in front of the chest, palm facing in and fingers pointing right. Then slide the middle-finger side of the extended right index finger, palm facing in, down the middle finger of the left *B hand* held in front of the chest, palm facing down. Then move the right *B hand* in a circular movement around the bent left arm held in front of the chest, both palms facing in.

---

split[1] *n., v.* See signs for CRACK[1], DIVIDE[2].

---

split[2] *v. Slang.* See signs for RUN AWAY, ZOOM[1].

---

split up *v. phrase.* See sign for DIVIDE[2].

---

spoil *v.* See signs for PET[1], RUIN[1].

---

sponge *n.* A piece of absorbent porous material used for soaking up liquid: *to wipe up the spill with a sponge.*

■ [Mime squeezing a sponge + rub the arm as if bathing] Beginning with both *curved 5 hands* in front of the chest, left hand slightly above the right hand and palms facing each other, squeeze the fingers in and out with a double movement. Then rub the knuckles of the right *A hand* up and down the extended left arm.

---

sponsor[1] *n.* A person who is responsible for, vouches for, or supports something or someone: *My sponsor sent me to college.*

■ [**support**[1,2] + **person marker**] Bring the knuckles of the right *S hand* up under the little-finger side of the left *S hand*, both palms facing in, to push both hands upward a short distance in front of the chest. Then move both *open hands*, palms facing each other, downward along each side of the body.

---

sponsor[2] *v.* See signs for SUPPORT[1,2].

---

spontaneous *adj.* See signs for FAST[1,2,3].

---

spooky *adj.* See sign for MONSTER.

---

spool *n.* **1.** A reel or other cylinder, as for magnetic tape, around which something may be wound: *a spool of tape.* —*v.* **2.** To wind on a spool: *to spool the loose tape.* Related form: **spooling** *n.*

■ [Shows the location of tape around a spool] Move the extended right index finger, palm facing in and finger pointing left, in a forward circle with a repeated movement near the index-finger side of the left *S hand* held in front of the chest, palm facing down.

spoon *n.* A utensil with a shallow bowl at one end of a handle, used for eating, stirring, serving, etc.: *ate my soup with a large, round spoon.*

- [The fingers represent a spoon scooping up food] Wipe the backs of the fingers of the right *U hand*, palm facing up and thumb extended, across the upturned palm of the left *open hand* from the fingers to the heel with a double movement.

sports *n.* See sign for RACE[2].

spot[1] *v.* To locate, notice, or recognize: *spotted my friend in the crowd.*

- [Indicates a person's eyes directed at whatever is spotted] Beginning with the right *S hand* near the right cheek, palm facing forward, move the hand forward while flicking the thumb and index finger open to form a *G hand.*

spot[2] *n.* **1.** A rounded mark, as a stain: *I have a spot on my blouse.* **2.** A blemish on the skin: *The sun is causing spots to come out on my hands.* Same sign used for: **stain.**

- [Shape and location of a spot] Touch the thumb side of the right *F hand* to the left side of the chest, palm facing left.

spots *pl. n.* **1.** Marks, stains, or elements of design, as on a surface: *I have ink spots on this jacket.* **2.** Blemishes on the skin, as from acne: *spots on the face.* Related form: **spotted** *adj.* Same sign used for: **dots, polka dots.**

- [Shows the shape and location of spots on someone or something] Move the index-finger sides of both *F hands*, palms facing each other, with an alternating movement, touching against the body randomly in several locations.

spotty *adj.* Having or marked with spots: *He has a spotty complexion. The wallpaper has an oddly spotty design.*

- [**red**[1,2] + showing the location of spots on the hand] Bring the extended right index finger, palm facing in, from the lips downward with a short double movement, bending the finger each time. Then bring the fingertips of the right *curved 5 hand*, palm facing left, downward, touching in several locations on the palm of the left *open hand* held in front of the chest, palm facing right.

spousal support *n.* See sign for ALIMONY.

sprain[1] *v.* **1.** To injure the ligaments around a joint without a fracture: *sprained my wrist.* —*n.* **2.** An injury to the ligaments around a joint: *an ankle with a bad sprain.*

- [Shows a twist causing a sprain] Beginning with both *bent V hands* in front of the chest, right palm facing out and left palm facing in, twist the hands in opposite directions, reversing the direction of the palms.

sprain[2] *v.* See sign for TWIST[1].

spray *v.* To sprinkle through the air in small drops: *to spray the bushes with insecticide.*

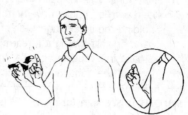

- [Mime pushing down on an aerosol can] Beginning with the extended right index finger pointing up in front of the right shoulder, palm facing forward, bend the finger down to form an *X hand* and move the hand from side to side with a double movement.

spread[1] *v.* To distribute or expand over a large area: *They want to spread the news. The news will spread.* Same sign used for: **disseminate, distribute, outbreak, release.**

- [Demonstrates something spreading outward] Beginning with the fingertips of both *flattened O hands* touching in front of the chest, palms facing down, move the hands forward and away from each other while opening into *5 hands* in front of each side of the body, palms facing down.

spread[2] *v.* (alternate sign)

- [Shows movement of something spreading] Beginning with the fingertips of the right *flattened O hand*, palm facing down, on the extended left index finger held in front of the chest, palm facing down and finger pointing forward, slide the right hand forward while opening into a *5 hand*.

spring *n.* The season between winter and summer: *to plant a garden in the spring.*

- [Similar to sign for **grow** except made with a double movement] Beginning with the right *flattened O hand*, palm facing up, being held by the left *C hand*, palm facing in, move the right hand upward with a double movement, opening into a *5 hand* each time.

sprinkle

sprinkle *v.* To scatter drops or little pieces: *to sprinkle nuts on the cake.* Related form: **sprinkles** *pl. n.*

- [Mime sprinkling something] Move the right *curved hand* forward in front of the chest while wiggling the fingers with a repeated movement.

sprinkler *n.* A sprinkling device: *Turn on the sprinkler in the yard.*

- [**water** + a gesture representing the movement of a lawn sprinkler] Tap the index-finger side of the right *W hand*, palm facing left, against the chin with a double movement. Then, while holding the index-finger side of the left *open hand* against the right forearm, move the right *5 hand* in a repeated circular movement in front of the right shoulder, palm facing in.

sprout *v.* See sign for GROW.

spunk *n.* Spirit; pluck; courage: *The child has a lot of spunk.*

- [**zeal** + **wow**[1,2]] Rub the palms of both *open hands*, palms facing each other, back and forth against each other with an alternating double movement. Then shake both *5 hands*, palms facing in, up and down with a repeated movement in front of each side of the chest.

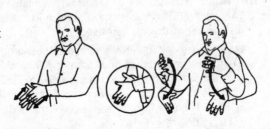

spurt *v.* **1.** To gush out: *Water spurted out of the hole.* —*n.* **2.** A sudden, forceful gushing: *The sudden spurt of water through the wall frightened all of us.*

- [Represents the movement of a liquid spurting out] Beginning with the left *C hand* holding the right *S hand*, palms facing each other, bring the right hand upward and forward in a large arc while opening the fingers into a *5 hand*, ending with the right hand in front of the body, palm facing in and fingers pointing down.

spy *n.* **1.** A person who obtains secret information, as for a government or corporation: *The spies from the two countries traded secrets.* **2.** A person who watches others secretly: *Some spy in the office has been reading my mail!* —*v.* **3.** To watch secretly: *He spied on the neighbors.* **4.** To act as a spy for a government or corporation: *They were caught spying for a rival software company.*

■ [Represents eyes peeking around a corner to spy] Bring the right *V hand,* palm facing down, from behind the bent left arm held up in front of the left shoulder, in an arc forward and to the left around the left arm.

spyglass[1] *n.* A small telescope: *using a spyglass to see the dancers on stage.*

■ [Mime looking through binoculars] With the *flattened C hands* around each eye, palms facing each other, turn the head and hands from side to side with a double movement.

spyglass[2] *n.* (alternate sign)

■ [Mime holding and looking through a spyglass] With the index-finger side of the left *F hand* around the right eye and the right *F hand* somewhat forward, move the head and hands in a double movement from side to side.

squabble *v.* See signs for ARGUE[1,2].

squander *v.* To spend or use wastefully: *He squandered his entire fortune.*

■ [Represents throwing money away] Beginning with both *A hands* near each side of the body, palms facing in, thrust the hands upward with a double movement while changing into *5 hands* in front each shoulder, palms facing in.

square[1] *n.* **1.** A two-dimensional figure with four equal sides and four equal angles: *to draw a square measuring four inches by four inches.* —*adj.* **2.** Having a square shape: *a square box.* See also sign for SIGN[2].

■ [Draw a square in the air] Beginning with both extended index fingers touching in front of the upper chest, palms angled down and fingers pointing forward, bring the hands straight out to in front of each shoulder then straight down, and finally back together in front of the waist.

square[2] *adj.* Slang. See sign for MORON[1].

squeal *v.* Slang. See sign for TATTLE.

squeeze[1] *v.* To force together by pressing from more than one direction: *Squeeze the sponge to get all the water out.*

squeeze

- [Mime squeezing a tube with both hands] Beginning with the little-finger side of the right *C hand*, palm facing left, above the index-finger side of the left *C hand*, palm facing right, twist the hands in opposite directions while closing into *S hands*. Repeat if desired.

squeeze[2] *n.* See sign for BRIEF[1].

squint *v.* To look through partially closed eyes: *He squinted at the sun.*

- [Shows the size of the eyes when squinting] Place the thumb sides of both *G hands* near the outside of each eye, palms facing each other, while squinting the eyes.

squirrel[1] *n.* A bushy-tailed rodent that lives in trees: *saw black squirrels in Canada.*

- [Represents the gnawing action of a squirrel's teeth] With the heels of both hands together in front of the chest, palms facing each other, tap the fingertips of both *bent V hands* together with a double movement.

squirrel[2] *n.* (alternate sign)

- [Represents the gnawing action of a squirrel's teeth] With the heels of both hands together in front of the chest, right hand on top of the left hand and palms facing each other, tap the fingertips of both *bent V hands* together with a double movement.

squirrel[3] *n.* (alternate sign)

- [Represents the gnawing action of a squirrel's teeth] Move the right *bent V hand* from in front of the nose, palm facing left, downward to touch the left *bent V hand*. Then, with the heels of both hands together in front of the chest, palms facing each other, tap the fingertips of both *bent V hands* together with a double movement.

squirt *v.* **1.** To force fluid in a jet, as through a small hole: *to squirt water from the water gun.* —*n.* **2.** A narrow stream of fluid from a small opening: *hit me with a squirt of water.*

■ [Demonstrates the action of a liquid squirting out of an opening] Beginning with the little-finger side of the right *S hand* on the index-finger side of the left *S hand* in front of the chest, palms facing in, move the right hand upward and forward in an arc while opening into a *5 hand,* palm facing left and fingers pointing down.

stab¹ *v.* To pierce with or as if with a pointed weapon: *to stab the meat with a knife; stabbed at me with his finger.*

■ [Mime stabbing something with a knife] Bring the right *S hand* from in front of the right shoulder downward with a deliberate movement in front of the right side of the chest in a large arc.

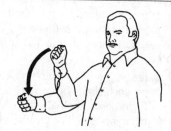

stab² *v.* (alternate sign)

■ [Mime stabbing something with a knife] Bring the right *S hand* in a large arc from in front of the right shoulder forward to hit against the open left palm held in front of the chest, with a deliberate movement.

stab³ *v.* (alternate sign)

■ [Mime stabbing something with a knife] Bring the right *S hand* from in front of the right shoulder forward in an arc to hit against the back of the left *open hand* held in front of the chest, palm angled forward.

stack *n.* **1.** A relatively orderly pile of things, one on top of another: *a stack of books.* —*v.* **2.** To pile in a stack: *Stack the books in the corner.* Same sign used for: **pile.**

■ [Shows a pile of things stacked on top of other things] With an alternating movement, bring each *open hand* upward over the other hand in a small arc as the hands raise in front of the chest, both palms facing down and fingers angled in opposite directions.

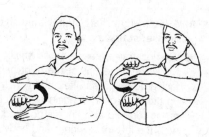

staff *n.* See sign for SENATE.

stage *n.* The platform in a theater on which the actors perform: *to walk across the stage and turn toward the audience.*

■ [Initialized sign representing the stage floor] Move the right *S hand,* palm facing forward, across the back of the left *open hand,* palm facing down, from the wrist to off the fingers.

stain[1] *n.* **1.** A discoloration or spot, as on fabric, produced by soil, food, or other foreign matter: *a stain on my dress.* —*v.* **2.** To spot or soil: *The coffee stained the rug.*

■ [**eat** + a gesture indicating food spilling on one's clothes + **spot**[2]] Bring the fingertips of the right *flattened O hand,* palm facing in, back to the mouth with a double movement. Next move the palm side of the right *5 hand* against the chest with a sudden movement. Then place the index-finger side of the right *F hand,* palm facing left, against the chest.

stain[2] *n.* See sign for SPOT[2].

stairs[1] *pl. n.* A series of steps for going from one level or floor to another: *to climb the stairs.* Same sign used for: **staircase, stairway.**

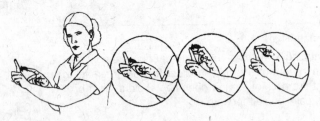

■ [Demonstrates the action of walking up stairs] Move the fingertips of the right *bent V hand,* palm facing forward, in an alternating crawling movement up the extended left index finger, palm facing forward.

stairs[2] *pl. n.* (alternate sign) Same sign used for: **staircase, stairway.**

■ [Demonstrates the action of walking up stairs] Move the fingertips of the right *bent V hand,* palm facing down, in an alternating crawling movement up the back of the fingers of the left *4 hand,* palm facing forward and fingers pointing right, beginning with the left index finger and ending with the little finger.

stairs[3] *pl. n.* (alternate sign) Same sign used for: **staircase, stairway, steps.**

■ [Demonstrates the action of walking up stairs] Beginning with both *open hands* in front of each side of the body, move the hands upward with a repeated alternating movement.

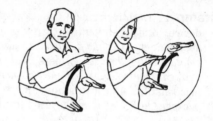

stale *adj.* No longer fresh and interesting: *a stale idea for a movie.* Same sign used for: **bored, boring.**

■ [Formed in the same location as the sign for **dry**] Beginning with the right *C hand* in front of the left side of the chin, palm facing left, bring the hand across the chin to the right while closing into an *S hand.*

stalk[1] *n.* The main stem or any other slender supporting part of a plant: *a celery stalk.*

■ [**stem**[2] + **stick**[3]] Move the extended right index finger, palm facing left, upward in front of the chest past the thumb side of the left *B hand* held across the chest, palm facing down. Then, beginning with the sides of the index fingers of both *F hands* touching in front of the chest, palms facing in opposite directions, move the right hand upward in front of the face.

stalk[2] *v.* To follow a person about in a way that instills fear of bodily harm: *The fan stalked the movie star wherever she went.*

■ [Represents two people moving in tandem] With the palm side of the right *1 hand* on the index-finger side of the left *1 hand,* both palms facing forward, move both hands forward in a random movement.

stall *v.* See sign for SUSPEND.

stamp[1] *n.* **1.** A small label with a sticky back, issued by postal authorities in various denominations, to place on items for mailing as evidence that postal charges have been paid: *to lick the stamp.* —*v.* **2.** To affix a postage stamp to: *to stamp the letters.* Same sign used for: **postage, postage stamp.**

■ [The fingers seem to lick a stamp and place it on an envelope] Move the fingers of the right *H hand* from the mouth, palm facing in, down to land on the fingers of the left *open hand,* palm facing up, in front of the body.

stamp[2] *n.* **1.** An instrument, as a block with a raised imprinting device, to mark an item with an instruction, an official seal of approval, etc.: *Use the department stamp to mark all the bills before mailing them.* **2.** A mark made with such an instrument: *marked the invoice with the department's stamp.* —*v.* **3.** To place an official or instructional mark on an item: *Stamp the package "RUSH."* Same sign used for: **brand, guarantee, seal.**

- ■ [Mime stamping something with a rubber stamp] Move the right *S hand,* palm facing left, from in front of the chest downward, ending with the little-finger side of the right *S hand* on the upturned palm of the left *open hand.*

stampede *n.* **1.** A headlong, frenzied flight of a group of frightened animals: *a stampede of buffalo on the prairie.* **2.** A flight or rush of people: *He avoided the rush-hour stampede by leaving early.* —*v.* **3.** To flee in a large, frenzied group: *The crowd stampeded through the doors to escape the fire.*

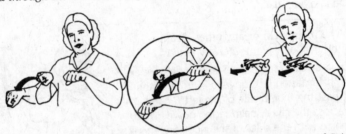

- ■ [**plod** + a gesture representing a large group moving forward en masse] Bring both *S hands* downward in front of each side of the chest with an alternating double movement. Then move both *5 hands,* palms facing down, forward from in front of each side of the chest with a double movement while wiggling the fingers.

stand *v.* To be in or rise to an upright position on one's feet: *The teacher stood in front of the classroom.*

- ■ [The fingers represent erect legs] Place the fingertips of the right *V hand,* palm facing in and fingers pointing down, on the upturned palm of the left *open hand* held in front of the body.

stand for *v. phrase.* See signs for INTEND[1,2].

standard[1] *n.* **1.** Something considered usual and normal or accepted as a basis for comparison: *a student whose behavior provides an exemplary standard.* —*adj.* **2.** Generally recognized as usual or normal: *standard-size 8½ by 11 paper.* Related form: **standardized** *adj.* Same sign used for: **common, uniform.**

- ■ [**same**[1] formed with a circular movement to indicate everything is the same] Beginning with both *Y hands* in front of the body, palms facing down, move the hands in a large flat circle.

standard[2] *n., adj.* (alternate sign) Related form: **standardized** *adj.* Same sign used for: **common, uniform.**

- [**same**[1] formed back and forth to indicate similarity] With the thumbs of both *Y hands* together in front of the left side of the body, palms facing down, move the hands to the right with a double movement.

stanza *n.* A group of usually four or more lines of poetry: *Read the first stanza of the poem aloud.*

- [**paragraph** signed downward as if to measure out each stanza] Move the fingertips of the right *flattened C hand,* palm facing left, from the fingertips of the left *open hand* held in front of the chest, palm facing right and fingers pointing up, downward in small arcs, touching the left bent arm in several places as the hand moves toward the elbow.

staple *v.* Same sign as for STAPLER but formed with a single movement.

stapler *n.* A machine used for fastening with staples, short pieces of wire bent to hold things together: *Use a stapler, not a paper clip, to fasten the receipts to the expense report.* Related form: **staple** *n.*

- [Mime pushing down on a stapler] Press the heel of the right *curved 5 hand,* palm facing down, on the heel of the left *open hand,* palm facing up, with a double movement.

star *n.* A hot, gaseous heavenly body that shines by its own light: *stars in the sky.* Same sign used for: **asterisk, wild card.**

- Brush the sides of both extended index fingers against each other, palms facing forward, with an alternating movement as the hands move upward in front of the face.

stare[1] *v.* To gaze intently and directly: *Don't stare at me like that.*

- [Directional sign indicating that all eyes turn to look at you] Beginning with both *4 hands* in front of each side of the chest, palms facing down and fingers pointing forward, twist the wrists toward each other to point the fingers back toward the face.

stare[2] *v.* (alternate sign)

- [Directional sign indicating that eyes turn to look at you] Beginning with both *V hands* in front of each side of the chest, palms facing down and fingers pointing forward, twist the wrists toward each other to point the fingers back toward the face.

stare[3] *v.* (alternate sign)

- [Directional sign indicating that eyes turn to look at you] Beginning with both *4 hands* in front of each side of the chest, palms facing down and fingers pointing back, move the fingers back toward the face with a deliberate movement.

stare[4] *v.* (alternate sign)

- [Directional sign indicating that eyes are looking intently at something] Gaze steadily along the extended fingertips of both *V hands* held in front of the left side of the body, palms facing down and fingers pointing forward. [This sign can be formed with one hand.]

stare[5] *v.* (alternate sign)

- [Directional sign indicating that someone's eyes are looking at you] Point the extended fingers of the right *V hand*, palm facing down, toward the right side of the face.

stare[6] *v.* (alternate sign)

- [**me** + **look at**] Touch the extended right index finger to the center of the chest. Then gaze steadily along the extended fingers of the right *V hand* held in front of the right side of the body, palm facing down and fingers pointing forward.

starry[1] *adj.* **1.** Abounding with stars: *a starry night.* **2.** Shining like stars: *starry eyes.*

- [Indicates shiny eyes] Bring the bent middle finger of both *5 hands*, palms facing in, from each eye forward with a wiggly movement.

starry[2] *adj.* (alternate sign)

- ■ [star + a gesture showing the location of the stars in the sky] Brush the sides of both extended index fingers against each other in front of the chest, palms facing forward and fingers angled up, with an alternating double movement. Then move both *5 hands,* palms facing forward and fingers pointing up, forward above the head while wiggling the fingers.

start[1] *n.* A beginning: *a good start for the project.* Same sign used for: **beginning, origin, origination, source.**

- ■ [Represents turning a key to start ignition] Beginning with the extended right index finger, palm facing down, inserted between the index and middle fingers of the left *open hand,* palm facing right and fingers pointing forward, twist the right hand back, ending with the palm facing in.

start[2] *v.* **1.** To begin or set out: *to start working; to start on a journey.* **2.** To put into action: *to start the engine.* Same sign used for: **begin, commence, ignite, initiate, originate, spark.**

- ■ [Represents turning a key to start an ignition] Beginning with the extended right index finger, palm facing in, inserted between the index and middle fingers of the left *open hand,* palm facing right and fingers pointing forward, twist the right hand down, ending with the palm angled forward.

start[3] *v.* To cause the motor of to go into action: *to start the car.*

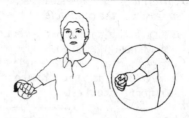

- ■ [Mime turning a key to start an ignition] Beginning with the right *A hand* in front of the right side of the body, palm facing forward, twist the wrist to turn the palm to the left.

starter *n.* Same sign as for START[3] but formed with a double movement. Same sign used for: **ignition.**

startle *v.* See signs for FLABBERGAST[1,2], SURPRISE.

startled *adj.* See sign for SHOCK[1].

starved *adj.* See sign for HUNGRY.

state[1] *n.* A politically unified territory within a nation: *the state of Texas.*

- [Initialized sign similar to sign for **law**] Move the index-finger side of the right *S hand*, palm facing forward, down from the fingers to the heel of the left *open hand*, palm facing right and fingers pointing up, in front of the chest.

state[2] *v.* See signs for SAY[1,2].

statement *n.* See sign for SENTENCE.

statistics *n.* A branch of mathematics that deals with collecting and analyzing numerical data: *used statistics to determine the probability of increased sales.*

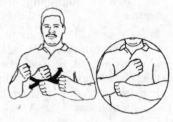

- [Initialized sign similar to sign for **mathematics**] Beginning with both *S hands* in front of each side of the chest, palms facing in, move the hands past each other with a double movement while rubbing the little-finger side of the right hand over the index-finger side of the left hand.

statue *n.* A carved or molded three-dimensional image: *a statue of a famous person.* Same sign used for: **shape.**

- [Initialialized sign similar to sign for **shape**[1]] Beginning with both *S hands* near each other in front of the face, palms facing forward, bring the hands downward and apart in a wavy movement.

staunch *adj.* Firm and steadfast, as in loyalty: *a staunch supporter of the candidate.*

- [Sign similar to **support**[1] except made with a deliberate movement] With the knuckles of the right *S hand*, palm facing forward, under the little-finger side of the left *S hand*, palm facing in, push the hands upward to the left in front of the chest.

stay[1] *v.* To remain: *Stay here.*

- [Indicates a location where one is to stay] Move the right *Y hand*, palm facing down, downward in front of the right side of the body with a deliberate movement.

stay[2] *v.* (alternate sign used to show duration) Same sign used for: **remain.**

- With the thumb of the right *10 hand* on the thumbnail of the left *10 hand,* both palms facing down in front of the chest, move the hands forward and down a short distance.

stay away *v. phrase.* To remain far or apart from a given place, person, or thing; not come or go near: *You'd better stay away from the edge.*

- Beginning with the thumb of the right *Y hand* touching the thumb of the left *Y hand* in front of the chest, both palms angled down, move the right hand forward and to the right in a small arc.

steadfast *adj.* See sign for CONSTANT[3].

steady[1] *Informal.* —*n.* **1.** One's exclusive sweetheart; boyfriend or girlfriend: *He is my steady.* —*adj.* **2.** Constant; regular; habitual: *my steady date.* Same sign used for: **companion, go steady.**

- [**with** signed with a repeated movement] Beginning with the palm sides of both *A hands* together in front of the chest, move the hands forward with a repeated movement.

steady[2] *adj.* See signs for CONSTANT[2,3].

steak *n.* See sign for MEAT.

steal[1] *v.* To take from the rightful owner without permission: *stole the jewelry from the store.* Same sign used for: **burglary, pillage, rob, robbery, theft.**

- [The fingers seem to snatch something] Beginning with the index-finger side of the right *V hand,* palm facing down, on the elbow of the bent left arm, held at an upward angle across the chest, pull the right hand upward toward the left wrist while bending the fingers in tightly.

steal[2] *v.* See sign for SHOPLIFT.

stealthy *adj.* See sign for SNEAK[1]. Related form: **stealthily** *adv.*

steel[1] *n.* An alloy of iron and carbon: *beams made of steel.*

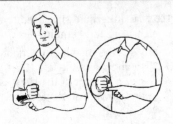

■ Move the little-finger side of the right *S hand,* palm facing left, forward from the base to the tip of the extended left index finger, palm facing in and finger pointing right, with a double movement.

steel[2] *n., adj.* See sign for METAL.

steer *v.* See signs for LEAD[1,2].

stem[1] *n.* The long, slender part of a plant that ascends above the ground: *Cut the stems of the roses with the shears.*

■ [The shape of a long stem] Beginning with the thumb and index finger of the right *G hand,* palm facing left, holding the base of the extended left index finger, palm facing right and finger pointing up, pull the right hand upward along the length of the index finger and off its tip a short distance, while pinching the thumb and index finger together.

stem[2] *n.* (alternate sign)

■ [Indicates a stem growing up from the earth] Move the extended right index finger of the right hand, palm facing left, upward in front of the chest past the thumb side of the left *B hand* held across the chest, palm facing down.

step[1] *n.* **1.** A movement made by lifting the foot and putting it down again: *Take a big step.* —*v.* **2.** To move the legs in steps, as in walking: *Step forward.* Same sign used for: **pace.**

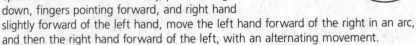

■ [Demonstrates the action of stepping with one foot and then the other] Beginning with both *open hands* in front of the body, palms facing down, fingers pointing forward, and right hand slightly forward of the left hand, move the left hand forward of the right in an arc, and then the right hand forward of the left, with an alternating movement.

step[2] *n., v.* (alternate sign) Same sign used for: **pace.**

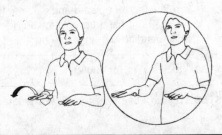

■ [Demonstrates the action of stepping forward] Beginning with both *open hands* in front of the body, palms facing down and fingers pointing forward, move the right hand upward and forward in an arc.

stepbrother *n.* A son of one's stepparent by a former marriage: *He is my older stepbrother.*

- ■ [**second-hand** + **brother**[2]] Beginning with the right *L hand* in front of the right side of the chest, palm facing down, twist the wrist forward with a deliberate movement. Then bring the right *L hand,* palm facing left, from the forehead down while closing the thumb to the hand, ending with the index fingers of both *1 hands* together in front of the chest.

stepdaughter *n.* A daughter of one's husband or wife by a former marriage: *My stepdaughter and I are very close.*

- ■ [**second-hand** + **daughter**[2]] Beginning with the right *L hand* in front of the right side of the chest, palm facing down, twist the wrist forward with a deliberate movement. Then bring the right *B hand,* palm facing left, from the chin downward while opening into an *open hand,* ending with the bent right arm cradled on the bent left arm held across the body, both palms facing up.

stepfather[1] *n.* The husband of one's mother by a subsequent marriage: *We live with my stepfather.*

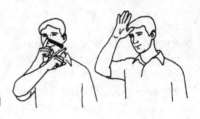

- ■ [**false** + **father**[1,2]] Brush the extended right index finger, palm facing left, across the tip of the nose from right to left. Then place the thumb of the right *5 hand,* palm facing left and fingers pointing up, against the middle of the forehead.

stepfather[2] *n.* (alternate sign)

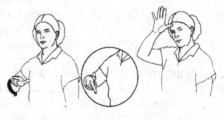

- ■ [**second-hand** + **father**[1,2]] Beginning with the right *L hand* in front of the right side of the chest, palm facing down, twist the wrist forward with a deliberate movement. Then, with the thumb of the right *5 hand* touching the forehead, palm facing left and fingers pointing up, wiggle the fingers.

stepmother[1] *n.* The wife of one's father by a subsequent marriage: *The children now get along well with their stepmother.*

- ■ [**false** + **mother**[1,2]] Brush the extended right index finger, palm facing left, across the tip of the nose from right to left. Then place the thumb of the right *5 hand,* palm facing left and fingers pointing up, against the center of the chin.

stepmother[2] *n.* (alternate sign)

■ **[second-hand + mother**[1,2]**]** Beginning with the right *L hand* in front of the right side of the chest, palm facing down, twist the wrist forward with a deliberate movement. Then, with the thumb of the right *5 hand* touching the chin, palm facing left and fingers pointing up, wiggle the fingers.

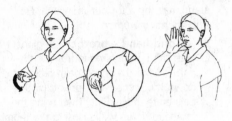

steps *pl. n.* See sign for STAIRS[3].

stepsister *n.* A daughter of one's stepparent by a former marriage: *The two stepsisters look amazingly alike.*

■ **[second-hand + sister**[2]**]** Beginning with the right *L hand* in front of the right side of the chest, palm facing down, twist the wrist forward with a deliberate movement. Then bring the thumb of the right *L hand,* palm facing left, from the chin smoothly down while closing the thumb to the hand, ending with the index fingers of both *1 hands* together in front of the chest.

stepson *n.* A son of one's husband or wife by a former marriage: *getting to know my stepson.*

■ **[second-hand + son**[2]**]** Beginning with the right *L hand* in front of the right side of the chest, palm facing down, twist the wrist forward with a deliberate movement. Then bring the fingers of the right *B hand* from touching the right side of the forehead downward while opening into an *open hand,* ending with the bent right arm cradled on the bent left arm held across the body, both palms facing up.

sterilization *n.* The tying of a woman's fallopian tubes to render her infertile: *chose sterilization to prevent further pregnancies.* Related form: **sterilize** *v.* Same sign used for: **tubal ligation, vasectomy.**

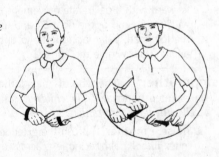

■ [Mime tying to represent tying one's tubes for sterilization] Beginning with both *modified X hands* touching in front of the waist, right palm facing down and left palm facing in, pull the hands deliberately apart to each side of the waist.

stern *adj.* See sign for STRICT.

stethoscope *n.* A medical instrument with earpieces and a long tube for listening to internal sounds in the body, as the heartbeat and quality of breathing: *The doctor used a stethoscope to listen to the patient's heart.*

■ [Mime holding a stethoscope to the ear and to the chest] Place the palm side of the left *flattened O hand* near the right ear while touching the fingertips of the right *flattened O hand* to several places on the chest.

stick[1] *v.* To fasten or attach, as with glue: *to stick a stamp on the envelope.* Same sign used for: **adhere, adhesive, expose, fasten.**

■ [Demonstrates something sticky causing the finger and thumb to stick together] With the thumb of the right *5 hand,* palm facing down, touching the palm of the left *open hand,* palm facing up, close the right middle finger down to the thumb.

stick[2] *n.* A relatively long and slender piece of wood: *to knock down a beehive with a stick.* Same sign used for: **pipe, pole, rod.**

■ [Shape of a stick] Beginning with the thumb sides of both *F hands* touching in front of the chest, palms facing forward, move the hands apart.

stick[3] *n.* (alternate sign) Same sign used for: **pole, rod.**

■ [Shape of a stick] Beginning with the sides of the index fingers of both *F hands* touching in front of the chest, palms facing in opposite directions, move the right hand upward in front of the face.

stick[4] *n.* (alternate sign) Same sign used for: **pole, rod.**

■ Beginning with the little-finger side of the right *C hand* on the index-finger side of the left *C hand,* both palms facing in, raise the right hand upward to in front of the face.

sticker *n.* A gummed label: *The manufacturer put a sticker on the cardboard box.*

■ [Mime peeling off a sticker from a paper] Beginning with the thumb and index finger of the right *F hand,* palm facing down, touching the upturned palm of the left *open hand* in front of the body, raise the right hand upward in an arc to the right.

stick shift *n.* A manual transmission for putting a motor vehicle into gear: *learned to drive with a stick shift.* Same sign used for: **shift.**

- ■ [Mime moving a stick shift] Beginning with the right *S hand* in front of the right side of the body, palm facing left, move the hand in a jagged deliberate movement forward as if miming shifting gears.

sticky[1] *adj.* Apt to stick: *sticky gum.*

- ■ [Demonstrates something sticky causing the finger and thumb to stick together] With a repeated movement, tap the middle finger of each hand to the thumb of each hand, forming an *8 hand* in front of each side of the body, palms facing up.

sticky[2] *adj.* Same sign as for STICK[1] but formed with a double movement.

still[1] *adv.* As previously: *still at home.* Same sign used for: **yet.**

- ■ [**stay**[1] formed with a continuing movement to show passage of time] Move the right *Y hand,* palm facing down, from in front of the right side of the body forward and upward in an arc.

still[2] *adv.* (alternate sign) Same sign used for: **yet.**

- ■ Beginning with both *Y hands* in front of each side of the chest, palms facing down, move the hands downward and forward with simultaneous movements.

still[3] *adj.* See signs for QUIET[1,2].

sting *v.* **1.** To prick and wound with a sharp, pointed organ, as on a bee or wasp: *A bee stung me!* —*n.* **2.** An act or instance of stinging: *Stings are more dangerous for the bees than for us.* **3.** A wound caused by stinging: *medicines to sooth a bee sting.*

- ■ [Represents the stinger of an insect penetrating to wound] Beginning with the right *X hand* held in front of the right side of the chest, palm facing left, bring the bent index finger down deliberately against the back of the left *S hand,* palm facing down, and then back upward quickly.

stingy[1] *adj.* Unwilling or reluctant to spend money or to give in other ways: *difficult to get a donation from a stingy person.* Same sign used for: **miserly, niggardly, thrifty, tight, tightwad** (informal).

- [Represents scraping] Beginning with the fingertips of the right *curved 5 hand* on the fingers of the left *open hand,* palm facing up, bring the right hand back toward the heel of the left hand with a double movement while closing into an *A hand* each time.

stingy[2] *adj.* See sign for SELFISH.

stink[1] *v.* **1.** To give off a strong, offensive smell: *Rotting fish really stink.* —*n.* **2.** A strong, offensive smell: *a terrible stink in the room.* Related form: **stinky** *adj.* Same sign used for: **phew, putrid, smelly.**

- [Natural gesture for holding the nose when something smells bad] Pinch the nose with the bent index finger and thumb of the right *5 hand,* palm facing in.

stink[2] *v., n.* Related form: **stinky** *adj.*

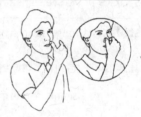

- [Natural gesture for holding the nose when something smells bad] Bring the thumb and index finger of the right *G hand,* palm facing in, back to pinch the nose.

stir *v.* See signs for BEAT[1,2], MESSY, MIX[1].

stitch *n.* **1.** A single loop of thread, in a connected series of such loops, put into fabric with a needle: *One more stitch and the hem will be finished.* —*v.* **2.** To fasten with stitches: *to stitch the rip in the jacket.* See also signs for SEW[1,2].

- [Mime sewing with a needle] Beginning with the fingers of the right *F hand,* palm facing down, touching the back of the left *open hand,* palm facing down, pull the right hand upward and back toward the chest by twisting the wrist. Repeat the movement from a different place on the back of the left hand.

St. Louis *n.* A city in eastern Missouri: *St. Louis is a port on the Mississippi River.*

- ■ [Abbreviation **s-l** formed in the shape of the St. Louis arch, a famous landmark in the city] Beginning with the right *S hand*, palm facing down, near the elbow of the bent left arm held across the body, move the right hand upward in an arc while changing into an *L hand*, palm facing forward, ending with the heel of the of the right *L hand* on the back of the left *open hand*, palm facing down.

stocking *n.* A knitted covering for the foot and leg: *likes to wear nylon stockings instead of pantyhose.* Same sign used for: **hose.**

- ■ [Represents pulling on a long stocking] Bring the fingers of the right *5 hand*, palm facing in, from the wrist up the forearm of the extended left arm with a smooth movement.

stocks *pl. n.* See signs for INVEST[1,2].

stole *n.* A long, narrow band of fabric worn over the shoulders: *the bishop's stole.*

- ■ [Location and shape of a stole] Bring the fingertips of both *C hands*, palms facing in, downward on each side of the chest with a simultaneous movement.

stomach *n.* See signs for ABDOMEN[1,2].

stomachache[1] *n.* A pain in the stomach area: *I have a stomachache from eating green apples.*

- ■ [**hurt** formed near the stomach] Beginning with both extended index fingers pointing toward each other in front of the body, palms facing up, jab the fingers toward each other with a short double movement.

stomachache[2] *n.* See sign for DISGUSTED[1].

stone *n.* See signs for ROCK[1,2].

stoop *v.* To bend forward and downward from an erect position: *stooped to pick up the trash.*

■ [Finger represents a body stooping over] Beginning with the wrist of the right hand, index finger extended and palm facing forward in front of the right shoulder, resting on the index-finger side of the left *open hand* in front of the chest, palm down, bring the right wrist forward while bending the finger into an *X hand*.

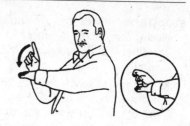

stop[1] *v.* To cease from moving or doing: *to stop work at three o'clock.* Same sign used for: **abate, cease, enjoin, halt, quit.**

■ [Demonstrates an abrupt stopping movement] Bring the little-finger side of the right *open hand*, palm facing left and fingers pointing up, sharply down on the upturned palm of the left *open hand* held in front of the body.

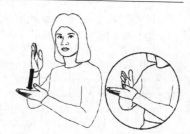

stop[2] *v.* See signs for DESIST.

stoplight[1] *n.* A set of electric signal lights used to control the flow of traffic at an intersection: *The stoplight turned red.* Same sign used for: **traffic light.**

■ [**stop**[1] + **light**[1]] Bring the little-finger side of the right *open hand*, palm facing left, sharply against the upturned palm of the left *open hand* held in front of the body. Then, beginning with the fingertips of the right *8 hand* near the chin, palm facing in, flick the middle finger upward and forward with a double movement while opening into a *5 hand* each time.

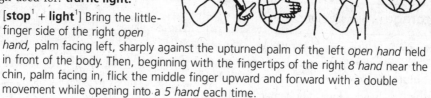

stoplight[2] *n.* (alternate sign)

■ [**stop**[1] + **light**[1] + a gesture indicating the flashing of a stoplight] Bring the little-finger side of the right *open hand*, palm facing left, sharply against the upturned palm of the left *open hand* held in front of the body. Next, beginning with the fingertips of the right *8 hand* near the chin, palm facing in, flick the middle finger upward and forward with a double movement while opening into a *5 hand* each time. Then, with the fingers of the left *open hand* on the elbow of the bent right arm held up in front of the right side of the body, open and close the fingers, forming a *flattened O hand* and opening into a *5 hand* with a double movement near the right side of the head, palm facing back.

stopper *n.* A plug, cork, or similar closing for a bottle or other container: *Put the stopper in the thermos.*

- [**water** + **absent** + **lid**[1]] Tap the index-finger side of the right *W hand*, palm facing left, against the chin with a double movement. Next move the right *curved 5 hand*, palm facing in, downward through the palm side of the left *C hand* held in front of the chest, palm facing right, closing the fingers of the right hand to form a *flattened O hand* as it emerges below the left hand. Then bring the palm of the right *curved hand* firmly down on the index-finger side of the left *S hand* held in front of the body.

stopwatch *n.* A watch that can be stopped or started instantly for precisely timing events: *According to the stopwatch, you won by two seconds.*

- [**time**[2] + mime clicking a stopwatch] Tap the bent index finger of the right *X hand*, palm facing down, with a double movement on the back of the left wrist. Then, with the right *10 hand* in front of the right shoulder, palm facing back, bend the extended thumb up and down with a double movement.

storage *n.* See sign for SAVE[2].

store[1] *n.* A place where goods are sold: *Go to the grocery store.* Same sign used for: **market, mart, shop.**

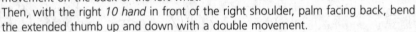

- [The hands seem to hold merchandise out for inspection and sale] Beginning with both *flattened O hands* in front of each side of the body, palms facing down and fingers pointing down, swing the fingers forward and back from the wrists with a repeated movement.

store[2] *n.* (alternate sign) Same sign used for: **market, mart, shop.**

- Beginning with both *modified X hands* in front of each side of the body, palms angled in, swing the hands forward and back from the wrists with a repeated movement.

store[3] *v.* See signs for SAVE[2,3,4].

storm *n.* See signs for MESSY, WIND[1].

story[1] *n.* A narrative account of some true or fictitious happening: *to tell a long story.* Same sign used for: **fable, narrative, novel, parable, phrase, prose, remarks, tale.**

■ [**sentence** formed with a repeated movement to indicate many sentences] Bring the thumb and index finger of each *5 hand* to intersect with the other hand, palms facing each other, forming *F hands.* Then pull the hands apart to in front of each side of the chest. Repeat.

story[2] *n.* (alternate sign) Same sign used for: **fable, narrative, novel, parable, phrase, prose, remarks, tale.**

■ [The hands seem to pull out sentences to form a story] Beginning with both *flattened C hands* in front of the chest, palms facing each other and the right hand slightly over the left hand, close the fingertips to the thumbs of each hand and then pull the hands straight apart in front of each shoulder with a double movement.

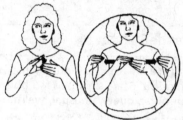

storyteller *n.* See sign for NARRATOR.

straight[1] *adj.* **1.** Without a curve: *a straight line.* —*adv.* **2.** In a straight line: *Walk straight to the corner.* Same sign used for: **direct.**

■ [Indicates a straight direction] Beginning with the index-finger side of the right *B hand* against the right shoulder, palm facing left and fingers pointing up, move the hand straight forward by bending the wrist down.

straight[2] *adj., adv.* See sign for SPECIALIZE[1].

straight[3] *adj.* **1.** Correct and direct, as in character: *straight thinking.* —*adv.* **2.** Honestly: *to live straight.*

■ [Indicates a straight direction] Beginning with the index-finger side of the right *B hand* against the right eye, palm facing left and fingers pointing up, move the hand straight forward by bending the wrist slightly down.

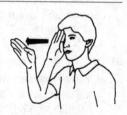

straight hair *n.* Hair without curl: *I like the look of sleek, straight hair.*

■ [Shows straight hair falling down to the shoulders] Beginning with both *S hands* near each side of the head, palms facing down, drop the hands to near each shoulder while opening the hands into *curved hands,* fingers pointing down.

straight pin

straight pin *n.* See sign for PIN³.

strainer *n.* A filter or sieve that strains: *Put the spaghetti in the strainer to get the water out.*

- [**bowl** + **leak**¹] Beginning with the little-finger sides of both *curved hands* together in front of the chest, palms facing up, bring the hands apart from each other and upward, ending with the palms facing each other. Then bring the right *4 hand* downward, palm facing left and fingers pointing forward, with a double movement below the little-finger side of the left *open hand*.

stranded *adj.* See sign for STUCK.

strange *adj.* Unusual; extraordinary: *a strange incident.* Same sign used for: **bizarre, freak, odd, peculiar, queer, unusual, weird.**

- Move the right *C hand* from near the right side of the face, palm facing left, downward in an arc in front of the face, ending near the left side of the chin, palm facing down.

stranger¹ *n.* **1.** A person who is not known to one: *A perfect stranger entered the room.* **2.** Newcomer: *a stranger in town.*

- [**strange** + **person marker**] Move the right *C hand* from near the right side of the face, palm facing left, downward in an arc in front of the face, ending near the left side of the chin, palm facing down. Then move both *open hands,* palms facing each other, downward along each side of the body.

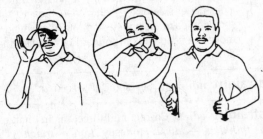

stranger² *n.* (alternate sign)

- [**new** + **person marker**] Slide the back of the right *curved hand,* palm facing up, from the fingers to the heel of the left *open hand,* palm facing up, with a double movement. Then move both *open hands,* palms facing each other, downward along each side of the body.

strangle *v.* To kill by squeezing the throat: *The murderer had strangled the victim.*

- [Mime shaking someone and then trying to strangle that person] With the fingertips of both *curved hands* touching in front of the chest, palms facing each other, shake the hands forward and back with a repeated movement. Then, with the *curved hands* crossed at the wrists, place each hand on either side of the neck and shake the head.

strategy *n.* Planning for achieving a goal: *If we follow the strategy as outlined, the office will be computerized by May.*

- [Initialized sign] Beginning with both *S hands* in front of each side of the chest, palms facing forward, move the hands downward with a wavy movement.

straw[1] *n.* A slender hollow tube used for sipping: *to drink the soda with a straw.*

- [The right hand represents a straw leading from a liquid to the mouth] Beginning with both *F hands* together in front of the body, palms facing each other and right hand closer to the lips than the left hand, move the right hand upward to touch the mouth with a short double movement.

straw[2] *n.* (alternate sign)

- [The right hand represents a straw leading from a liquid to the mouth] Beginning with both *G hands* together in front of the body, palms facing each other and right hand closer to the lips than the left hand, move the right hand upward to touch the mouth with a short double movement.

strawberry[1] *n.* A small, red, fleshy fruit from a vine: *to eat strawberries and cream.*

- Wipe the right extended index finger, palm facing in, downward on the lips. Then wipe the thumb of the right *10 hand,* palm facing in, downward on the lips.

strawberry[2] *n.* (alternate sign)

- [As if eating a strawberry and pulling away the hull] Beginning with the fingertips of the right *G hand* pointing toward the mouth, bring the hand forward while pinching the index finger and thumb together, palm facing in.

---

stray *v.* See sign for ASTRAY.

---

stream[1] *n.* **1.** A technique for transferring data such that it can be processed as a steady and continuous stream. **2.** A steady flow. —*v.* **3.** To transfer data using such a technique: *The multimedia file was downloaded from the Internet by streaming.* Related form: **streaming** *n.* Same sign used for: **flow.**

- [Action of steady flow of information or liquid] Beginning with both *B hands* in front of the right side of the chest, right palm facing up and left palm facing down, move the hands downward to the left with a double movement.

---

stream[2] *n.* See sign for RIVER[2].

---

street[1] *n.* A usually paved public road in a city or town, often including sidewalks: *to walk down the street.*

- [Initialized sign formed similar to **road**[1]] Move both *S hands* from in front of the body, palms facing each other, forward with a parallel movement.

---

street[2] *n.* See sign for ROAD[1].

---

strength *n.* See signs for POWER[1], STRONG[2,3], WELL[1].

---

stress[1] *v.* See sign for IMPRESS.

---

stress[2] *n.* See signs for EMPHASIS, PRESSURE.

---

stretch[1] *v.* To draw out to greater size: *to stretch the elastic band.* Same sign used for: **elastic.**

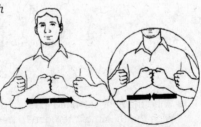

- [Mime stretching out some elastic] Beginning with the knuckles of both *S hands* touching in front of the chest, palms facing in, bring the hands apart to in front of each side of the chest with a double movement.

stretch[2] *v.* (alternate sign) Same sign used for: **elastic.**

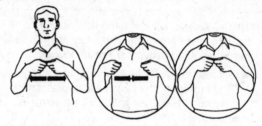

- [Mime stretching out some elastic] Beginning with both *modified X hands* touching in front of the chest, palms facing in, pull the hands apart to in front of each side of the chest with a double movement.

stretch[3] *v.* See sign for EXAGGERATE.

strict *adj.* Conforming to regulations, principles, and rules: *strict discipline.* Same sign used for: **bold, firm, stern.**

- Strike the index-finger side of the right *bent V hand* against the nose with a deliberate movement, palm facing left.

strike *v.* See signs for BEAT[4], BEAT UP, COMPLAIN, HIT[1], PROTEST[2].

strike a match[1] *v. phrase.* To cause a match to ignite by friction: *to strike a match on the sole of your shoe.* Same sign used for: **light a match.**

- [Mime striking a match] With the palm side of the right *modified X hand* touching the palm of the left *open hand,* palm facing right, in front of the chest, move the right hand upward with a quick movement.

strike a match[2] *v. phrase.* See sign for IGNITE[1].

string *n.* See sign for LINE.

strip[1] *n.* A long, narrow piece of anything: *a strip of paper.*

- [The shape of strips of something] Beginning with the thumbs and index fingers of both *G hands* touching, left hand over the right hand and palms facing each other, move the right hand straight down with a double movement in front of the chest.

strip[2] *v.* **1.** To remove, as covering: *to strip the wrapping from the package.* **2.** To remove the covering of: *to strip the orange of its rind.*

- [The fingers seem to scrape or strip something] Beginning with the fingertips of the right *curved 5 hand* touching the open left palm, palms facing each other, bring the right hand downward with a double movement, scraping the fingernails across the left palm each time.

strip[3] *v.* See signs for TEAR[1,2].

stripe *n.* A long, narrow band differing in color, texture, etc., from adjacent parts: *red and white stripes.* Same sign used for: **barcode, UPC (Universal Product Code).**

■ [Represents the shape of stripes] Beginning with the right *4 hand* in front of the left shoulder, palm facing in and fingers pointing left, pull the hand straight across the chest to in front of the right shoulder.

strive *v.* See sign for TRY[1].

stroke *n.* A sudden attack of illness caused by injury to or blockage in a blood vessel leading to the brain: *paralysis of one side as a result of a stroke.*

■ [**think**[1] + a gesture that represents an attack on the heart] Tap the index finger of the right hand to the right side of the head. Then bring the right *S hand,* palm facing forward, upward to strike the palm of the left *open hand* held in front of the chest, palm facing down and fingers pointing right.

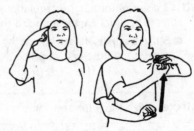

stroll *v.* See signs for WALK[1,2].

strong[1] *adj.* Having much power or strength: *a strong personality.* Same sign used for: **mighty, power.**

■ [Initialized sign showing someone flexing muscles] Beginning with both *S hands* near each shoulder, palms facing in, move the hands forward with a deliberate movement.

strong[2] *adj.* (alternate sign) Same sign used for: **brawny, solid, strength.**

■ [Shows the shape of a bulging muscle] Beginning with the index-finger side of the right *B hand,* palm angled forward, touching the extended left arm near the shoulder, move the right hand down in an arc, ending with the little-finger side touching near the crook of the left arm, right palm facing up.

strong[3] *adj.* (alternate sign) Same sign used for: **solid, strength.**

■ [Initialized sign formed similar to **power**] Beginning with the index-finger side of the right *S hand* near the left shoulder, palm facing left, move the right hand down in an arc, ending with the little-finger side of the right *S hand* touching near the crook of the left arm, palm facing up.

strong[4] *adj.* See signs for POWERFUL, WELL[1].

structure *n.* **1.** Something composed of parts arranged together: *the structure of the novel.* **2.** A building: *a tall structure going up on the next street.*

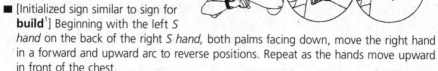

- [Initialized sign similar to sign for **build**[1]] Beginning with the left *S hand* on the back of the right *S hand,* both palms facing down, move the right hand in a forward and upward arc to reverse positions. Repeat as the hands move upward in front of the chest.

struggle *v.* **1.** To contend vigorously, as with an adversary: *to struggle with the robber.* **2.** To make great efforts or perform hard work: *to struggle with a problem.* —*n.* **3.** Great effort or hard work: *a great struggle.* Same sign used for: **antagonism, at odds, banter, conflict, controversy, opposition.**

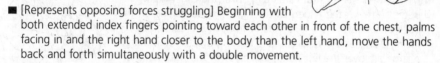

- [Represents opposing forces struggling] Beginning with both extended index fingers pointing toward each other in front of the chest, palms facing in and the right hand closer to the body than the left hand, move the hands back and forth simultaneously with a double movement.

stubborn *adj.* Having fixed opinions and an unyielding nature or attitude: *a stubborn person who won't listen to opposing arguments.* Same sign used for: **determined, obstinate, persist, persistence, persistent.**

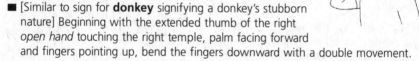

- [Similar to sign for **donkey** signifying a donkey's stubborn nature] Beginning with the extended thumb of the right *open hand* touching the right temple, palm facing forward and fingers pointing up, bend the fingers downward with a double movement.

stuck *adj.* Fixed in position; unable to proceed or escape: *stuck in the mud.* Same sign used for: **blocked, caught, confined, deadlock, pregnant, rape, stranded, trapped.**

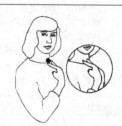

- [Indicates where food gets stuck in the throat] Move the fingertips of the right *V hand,* palm facing down, against the throat with a deliberate movement.

student *n.* A person enrolled and studying in a school or college: *a high school student.* Same sign used for: **pupil**[3].

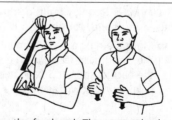

- [**learn + person marker**] Beginning with the fingertips of the right *flattened C hand,* palm facing down, on the upturned palm of the left *open hand,* bring the right hand up while closing the fingers and thumb into a *flattened O hand* near the forehead. Then move both *open hands,* palms facing each other, downward along each side of the body.

study *v.* **1.** To apply oneself to the acquisition of knowledge: *to study for an examination.* —*n.* **2.** The application of one's mind to the acquisition of knowledge: *You won't get decent grades without study.* **3. studies** A student's work at school or college: *He found the answer in his studies about ecology.*

■ While wiggling the fingers, move the right *5 hand*, palm facing down, with a double movement toward the left *open hand* held in front of the chest, palm facing up.

stuff *n.* See sign for SAVE[4].

stuffed *adj.* See sign for FULL[1].

stuffing *n.* See sign for INSIDE.

stumble *v.* To stagger or fall from striking the foot against something: *He stumbled on a rock.* Same sign used for: **trip.**

■ [The fingers demonstrate stumbling over the other hand] Beginning with the fingers of the right *V hand* resting on the back of the left *open hand* held in front of the chest, palm facing down and fingers pointing right, move the right hand in a large arc over the left hand, ending with the right hand in front of the body, fingers pointing in.

stump *n.* The lower part of a tree left in the ground when the top part is cut off: *hired someone to dig out a tree stump from the front yard.*

■ [The left arm represents a tree + mime cutting the tree off at the stump + showing that only a small amount remains] Bring the palm of the right *open hand*, palm facing up and fingers pointing forward, to hit above the elbow of the bent left arm held in front of the left side of the body. Then place the right *modified C hand* on the left forearm near the elbow.

stunned *adj.* See signs for INCREDIBLE[1], SHOCK[2].

stupid *adj.* See signs for DUMB, IGNORANT[1].

sturdy[1] *adj.* Strongly built: *a sturdy chair.* Same sign used for: **solid, tough.**

■ Move the right *S hand* from in front of the right side of the chest, palm facing in, in a downward arc across the back of the left *S hand* held in front of the chest, palm facing down, and back again.

sturdy[2] *adj.* See sign for POWER[1].

style *n.* See sign for FASHION[2].

---

stymied *adj.* See sign for PUZZLED.

---

sub- *prefix.* Under; beneath; less than: *subway; subbasement; subnormal.*

- [Initialized sign formed similar to sign for **base**] Move the right *S hand,* palm facing forward, in a double circular movement under the left *open hand* held across the chest, palm facing down and fingers pointing right.

---

subdue *v.* See sign for DEFEAT[1].

---

subject *n.* See signs for QUOTATION[1], TITLE.

---

submarine *n.* An ship that can be navigated under water: *The submarine dived below the surface.*

- [The right hand represents a ship moving down under water and then moving forward] With the index-finger side of the right *H hand,* palm facing left and thumb extended, under the left *open hand* held in front of the chest, palm facing down and fingers pointing right, move the right hand downward and then straight forward under the left hand.

---

submit *v.* See signs for ADMIT[1,2], SUGGEST. Related form: **submission** *n.*

---

subroutine *n.* A part of a computer program that can be used in a routine: *The program will then perform the subroutine.*

- [Abbreviation **s-r** similar to sign for **program**[2]] Beginning with the index-finger side of the right *S hand* near the heel of the left *open hand,* palm facing right and fingers pointing up, move the right hand up the left palm while changing into an *R hand* and then down the back of the left hand.

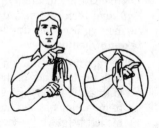

---

subscribe *v.* See sign for PENSION.

---

subscriber *n.* A person who subscribes to magazines, newspapers, concert series, cable TV, etc.: *The newspaper made a list of its subscribers.*

- [**pension** + **person marker**] With the right *curved hand* in front of the right shoulder, palm facing back, bring the hand downward and in toward the right side of the chest with a double movement while closing into an *A hand.* Then move both *open hands,* palms facing each other, downward along each side of the body.

subsidiary *n.* A company controlled by another company, which owns more than 50 percent of its voting stock.

- ■ [Abbreviation **C-O** + **business** + **under**] Fingerspell *C-O*. Then brush the base of the right *B hand*, palm facing forward, with a repeated rocking movement on the back of the left *open hand*, palm facing down. Then move the right *10 hand* from in front of the chest downward and forward under the left *open hand* held in front of the chest, palm facing down and fingers pointing right.

substance[1] *n.* The physical material of which something is made: *Cement is a rough substance.*

- ■ [Represents feeling a substance] Grasp the left *open hand* with the fingers of the right *flattened C hand*, both palms facing down. Then move the hands forward and back with a double movement.

substance[2] *n.* See sign for MEAT.

substitute *v.* See signs for TRADE[1,2,3]. Related form: **substitution** *n.*

subtitle *n.* See sign for CAPTION.

subtract *v.* **1.** To take away, as a part from a whole: *Subtract four from seven.* **2.** To perform the mathematical operation of substraction (on): *First multiply, then subtract; to subtract the numbers.* Same sign used for: **deduct, discount, eliminate, exempt, minus.**

- ■ [Demonstrates removing something] Beginning with the fingertips of the right *curved 5 hand* touching the palm of the left *open hand* held in front of the left side of the chest, palm facing right and fingers pointing up, bring the right hand down off the base of the left hand while changing into an *S hand*.

subway *n.* An electric railroad running under the streets of a city: *to ride the subway.*

- ■ [Initialized sign formed under the left hand representing moving under street level] Move the right *S hand*, palm facing left, forward and back under the palm of the left *open hand* held across the chest, palm facing down and fingers pointing right.

subwoofer *n.* A loudspeaker dedicated to the reproduction of bass audio frequencies: *The subwoofer sat on the floor by the sound system.*

- ■ [**music** + **hear** + **flash**[2] directed toward the ear] Swing the little-finger side of the right *open hand*, palm facing in, back and forth with a double movement across the

length of the bent left forearm held in front of the chest. Then point to the right ear with the extended right index finger. Then, beginning with the right *flattened O hand* near the right side of the head, fingers pointing toward the right ear, flick the fingers open with a quick movement.

succeed *v.* See sign for FINALLY[1].

success *n.* See sign for ACHIEVE[1].

successful *adj.* **1.** Having or manifesting a favorable result: *a successful event.* **2.** Possessing wealth, honors, professional position, etc. Related forms: **succeed** *v.,* **success** *n.* See also sign for ACHIEVE[1]. Same sign used for: **accomplish, accomplishment, achievement, prosper, triumph.**

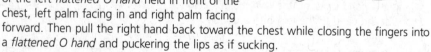

■ Beginning with both extended index fingers pointing up in front of each shoulder, palms facing back, move the hands in double arcs upward and back, ending near each side of the head.

such *adj., adv.* See sign for SAME[1].

suck[1] *v.* To draw something into the mouth by creating a partial vacuum: *to suck through a straw.*

■ [Represents the mouth when sucking] Open and close the fingers of the right *flattened C hand* with a double movement around the fingertips of the left *flattened O hand* held in front of the chest, left palm facing in and right palm facing forward. Then pull the right hand back toward the chest while closing the fingers into a *flattened O hand* and puckering the lips as if sucking.

suck[2] *v.* (alternate sign)

■ [Demonstrates a sucking action] Beginning with the fingertips of the right *curved 5 hand* on the back of the left *open hand*, both palms facing down, bring the right hand upward with a double movement, closing into a *flattened O hand* each time and puckering the lips as if sucking.

suck

suck[3] *v.* (alternate sign)

- [Demonstrates putting something in the mouth to suck on it] Move the extended right index finger, palm facing in, back toward the mouth with a double movement.

suck[4] *v.* (alternate sign)

- [Demonstrates a sucking action] Bring the fingertips of the right *curved 5 hand*, palm facing left, with a repeated movement to clasp around the extended left index finger held in front of the chest, palm facing down.

sucker *n.* See sign for LOLLIPOP.

sudden *adj., adv.* See signs for FAST[1,2,3].

suddenly *adv.* See sign for SURPRISE.

sue[1] *v.* To take legal action (against): *to sue for damages; to sue the driver after an accident.*

- Beginning with the right *B hand* in front of the right shoulder, palm facing left and fingers angled forward, bring the hand down to sharply touch the fingertips against the palm of the left *open hand*, palm facing in and fingers angled to the right.

sue[2] *v.* See sign for PROSECUTE.

suffer[1] *v.* To have pain or grief: *to suffer from headaches.* Same sign used for: **grief.**

- [Similar to sign for **hurt** except with a double movement] Beginning with the thumb of the right *A hand* touching the chin, palm facing left, twist the hand to the left with a double movement.

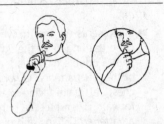

suffer[2] *v.* (alternate sign) Same sign used for: **agony, grief, sore, wound.**

- Beginning with the thumb of the right *A hand* touching the chin, palm facing left, move the right hand downward and over the left hand held in front of the body, palm facing in, as the left *A hand* moves over the right hand.

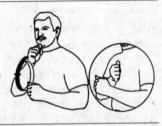

sufficient *adj.* See sign for ENOUGH.

sugar *n.* See sign for CANDY.

suggest *v.* To mention or put forward, as an idea: *I suggest we go swimming.* Related form: **suggestion** *n.* Same sign used for: **appeal, bid, motion, offer, petition, present, proposal, propose, provide, recommend, submission, submit.**

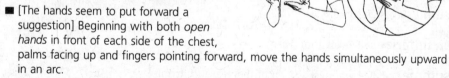

- ◾ [The hands seem to put forward a suggestion] Beginning with both *open hands* in front of each side of the chest, palms facing up and fingers pointing forward, move the hands simultaneously upward in an arc.

suicide[1] *n.* The taking of one's own life: *to commit suicide.*

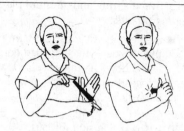

- ◾ [**kill**[1,2] + **myself**[1,2]] Push the side of the extended right index finger, palm facing down, across the palm of the left *open hand,* palm facing right, with a deliberate movement. Then tap the thumb side of the right *10 hand,* palm facing left, against the chest with a double movement.

suicide[2] *n.* (alternate sign)

- ◾ [Initialized sign similar to sign for **kill**[1]] Push the index-finger side of the right *S hand,* palm facing down, across the palm of the left *open hand,* palm facing right, with a deliberate movement.

suicide[3] *n.* (alternate sign)

- ◾ [Mime shooting oneself in the head + **myself**[1,2]] With the index finger of the right *L hand* touching the right side of the head, palm facing back, bend the right thumb up and down. Then tap the thumb side of the right *10 hand,* palm facing left, against the chest with a double movement.

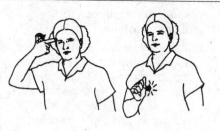

suit[1] *n.* A set of matching clothing, as a jacket and pants or a skirt, to be worn together: *a woman's tweed suit.*

- ◾ [The hands follow the shape of a suit's lapels] Beginning with the thumbs of both *A hands* on each side of the chest, palms facing each other, pull the hands downward and toward each other to about the middle of the chest.

suit[2] *v.* See signs for FIT[1], MATCH[1].

suit[3] *n.* See signs for CLOTHES, PROSECUTION.

suitable *adj.* See sign for APPROPRIATE.

suitcase *n.* See signs for BASKET, PURSE[1].

sum *v.* See sign for ADD[1].

summarize *v.* See sign for BRIEF[1].

summer *n.* The warmest season of the year, occurring between spring and autumn: *plans to go on vacation this summer.*

- ■ [Represents wiping sweat from the brow] Bring the thumb side of the extended right index finger, palm facing down and finger pointing left, across the forehead with a double movement while bending the index finger into an *X hand* each time.

summon *v.* See sign for CALL[1].

sun[1] *n.* The star around which the earth and other planets of the solar system revolve and from which they receive light and heat: *the bright sun shining in the sky.*

- ■ [Represents shielding one's eyes from the sun] Tap the thumb and index finger of the right *C hand*, palm facing forward, against the right side of the head with a double movement.

sun[2] *n.* (alternate sign) Same sign used for: **grace, sunbeam, sunlight, sunshine.**

- ■ [Represents the sun's rays shining down on a person] Beginning with the right *flattened O hand* near the right side of the head, palm facing forward, twist the wrist to turn the palm down and flick the fingers open into a *5 hand.*

sun[3] *n.* (alternate sign) Same sign used for: **sunbeam, sunlight, sunshine.**

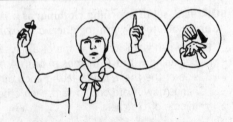

- ■ [Point to the sun + **sun**[2]] Beginning with the extended right index finger pointing up near the right side of the head, palm facing forward, twist the wrist, ending with the palm facing back. Then, beginning with the right *flattened O hand* near the right side of the head, palm facing down, flick the fingers open into a *5 hand*.

sun[4] *n.* A ray or rays of sunlight: *The sun came through the window.* Same sign used for: **sunbeam, sun ray, sunshine.**

■ [**sun**[1] + **sun**[2]] Tap the thumb and index finger of the right *C hand*, palm facing forward, against the right side of the head with a double movement. Then, beginning with the right *flattened O hand* near the right side of the head, palm facing forward, bring the hand downward and forward while opening into a *5 hand*.

sunburn *n.* A skin inflammation caused by overexposure to sunlight: *The girl got a sunburn at the pool.*

■ [**sun + burn**] Beginning with the right *flattened O hand* above the right shoulder, palm facing down, bring the right hand downward toward the face while opening into a *curved 5 hand*. Then, beginning with the right *S hand*, palm facing up on the back of the left wrist, open the right hand to a *curved 5 hand* and slide the back of the right hand toward the crook of the left arm while wiggling the right fingers with a repeated movement.

Sunday *n.* The first day of the week, the Sabbath of most Christian denominations: *to go to church on Sunday.* See also sign for SABBATH.

■ Beginning with both *open hands* in front of each shoulder, palms facing forward and fingers pointing up, move the hands toward each other in small arcs with a double movement.

sundown *n.* See signs for SHABBAT, SUNSET[1].

sunglasses *pl. n.*
Eyeglasses used to protect the eyes from sunlight: *to wear sunglasses at the beach.*

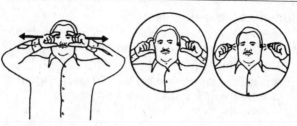

■ [The shape of sunglasses] Place the index-finger sides of both *modified C hands,* palms facing each other, around the outside of each eye and bring the hands outward with a double movement, pinching the index fingers and thumbs together each time.

sunlight *n.* See signs for SUN[2,3].

sun ray *n.* See sign for SUN[4].

sunrise[1] *n.* **1.** The first appearance of the sun above the horizon in the morning: *to wake up at sunset.* **2.** The colorful scenic phenomena in the atmosphere accompanying this: *a beautiful sunrise.*

■ [**sun**[1] + showing the sun coming up over the horizon] Tap the thumb and index finger of the right *C hand,* palm facing left, near the outside of the right eye. Then move the right *C hand,* palm facing left, from the waist upward past the bent left arm held across the chest.

sunrise[2] *n.* (alternate sign)

■ [Represents the sun coming up over the horizon] Bring the index-finger side of the right *F hand,* palm facing left, upward past the little-finger side of the left *open hand,* palm facing down and fingers pointing right, held across the chest, ending with the right *F hand* in front of the face.

sunset[1] *n.* **1.** The descent of the sun below the horizon in the evening: *a walk by the river at sunset.* **2.** The colorful scenic phenomena in the atmosphere accompanying this: *to watch a beautiful sunset through multicolored clouds.* Same sign used for: **sundown.**

■ [**sun**[1] + showing the sun going down below the horizon] Tap the thumb and index finger of the right *C hand,* palm facing left, near the outside of the right eye. Then move the right *C hand,* palm facing left, downward past the bent left arm held across the chest.

sunset[2] *n.* See sign for SHABBAT.

sunshine *n.* See signs for SUN[2,3,4].

super *adj.* Very good: *a super person.* Same sign used for: **Superman.**

■ [Initialized sign formed like the "S" on Superman's shirt] Move the right *S hand,* palm facing in, in an "S" shape down the chest.

superb *adj.* Excellent: *a superb day with the sun shining.* Same sign used for: **excellent, fantastic, okay.**

■ [Natural gesture to indicate something is superb] Move the right *F hand*, palm facing left, forward with a short double movement in front of the right shoulder.

superhighway *n.* A highway with multiple lanes designed for high-speed travel: *A superhighway connects the two cities.* Same sign used for: **expressway, freeway, thruway.**

■ [**fancy**[1,2] + **highway**] Move the thumbs of both *5 hands,* palms facing each other, upward in double alternating circular movements on each side of the chest. Then, beginning with both *H hands* held in front of the chest, palms facing down, fingers pointing toward each other, and right hand closer to the chest than the left hand, move the hands past each other with a double movement.

superintendent *n.* See sign for PRESIDENT.

superior *n., adj.* See sign for CHIEF[1].

Superman *n.* See sign for SUPER.

superstition *n.* See sign for IMAGINATION. Related form: **superstitious** *adj.*

superstitious *adj.* Having irrational fears that certain objects or occurrences can bring about unknown effects: *a superstitious person who believes that black cats bring bad luck.* Related form: **superstition** *n.*

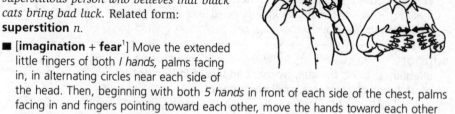

■ [**imagination** + **fear**[1]] Move the extended little fingers of both *I hands,* palms facing in, in alternating circles near each side of the head. Then, beginning with both *5 hands* in front of each side of the chest, palms facing in and fingers pointing toward each other, move the hands toward each other with a short double movement.

supervise *v.* See sign for CARE[1].

supervisor *n.* A person who watches over and directs the work of others: *The supervisor called a meeting of the customer service personnel.*

supper

- [**care**[1] + **person marker**] With the little-finger side of the right *K hand* on the thumb side of the left *K hand,* palms facing in opposite directions, move the hands in a flat circle in front of the body. Then move both *open hands* downward along each side of the body, palms facing each other.

supper[1] *n.* The evening meal: *We eat supper at six o'clock.*

- [Initialized sign similar to sign for **eat**] Tap the index-finger side of the right *S hand,* palm facing left, against the chin with a double movement.

supper[2] *n.* See sign for DINNER[3].

supplement *v.* See sign for ADD[2].

supply *v.* See signs for FEED[1,2].

support[1] *v.* **1.** To give help, sustenance, money, or comfort to: *to support one's family.* **2.** To advocate: *to support the cause.* —*n.* **3.** An act or instance of supporting: *Your support is appreciated.* **4.** Help; backup: *He brought extra support with him when he took over the fund raising.* Same sign used for: **advocate, allegiance, back, backup, boost, endorse, fund, in behalf of, in favor of, reinforce, sponsor, uphold.**

- [Initialized sign similar to sign for **help**] Push the knuckles of the right *S hand,* palm facing in, upward under the little-finger side of the left *S hand,* palm facing in, pushing the left hand upward a short distance in front of the chest.

support[2] *v.* (alternate sign) Same sign used for: **advocate, allegiance, back, backup, boost, endorse, fund, in behalf of, in favor of, reinforce, sponsor, uphold.**

- [Initialized sign similar to sign for **help**] Push the knuckles of the right *S hand,* palm facing left, upward under the little-finger side of the left *S hand,* palm facing in, pushing the left hand upward a short distance in front of the chest.

suppose *v.* To consider as a possibility: *Suppose it rains this afternoon.* Same sign used for: **if, in case of.**

■ [Indicates a thought coming from the mind] Move the extended little finger of the right *I hand*, palm facing in, forward from the right side of the forehead with a short double movement.

---

supposed to *v. phrase.* See sign for NEED.

---

suppress *v.* See signs for CONTROL[1], PRESSURE. Related form: **suppression** *n.*

---

supreme *adj.* See sign for ADVANCED.

---

sure[1] *adj.* Free from doubt: *Are you sure?* Same sign used for: **certain.**

■ [Indicates that true facts are coming straight from the mouth] Move the extended right index finger from in front of the mouth, palm facing left and finger pointing up, forward with a deliberate movement.

---

sure[2] *adj.* See sign for HONEST.

---

surf[1] *n.* **1.** The swell of the ocean on the shore: *The surf is high.* —*v.* **2.** To ride the crest of a wave on a surfboard: *young people who surf at California beaches.*

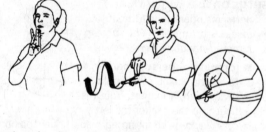

■ [**water** + **surfboard** moving up and down on the waves] Tap the index-finger side of the right *W hand*, palm facing left, against the chin with a double movement. Then, beginning with the fingertips of the right *H hand*, palm facing down, on the back of the left *open hand* held in front of the chest, palm facing down, move both hands up and down in a wavy movement as the hands move forward.

---

surf[2] or **surf the Net** *v.* To explore the Internet, especially casually or recreationally: *I surfed the Net looking for good airline prices.* Related form: **surfer** *n.*

■ [**look for**[1] + **sneak**[1]] Move the right *C hand*, palm facing left, with a double circular movement in front of the face. Then, with the right index finger extended, move the right hand, palm facing down and finger pointing forward, in a wavy movement under the left *open hand*, sliding the left palm up the right forearm as the right hand moves forward.

surface[1] *n.* The outside of something: *Rub the surface of the roast with garlic.*

- ■ [Indicates the surface of something] Move the palm side of the right *open hand* in a circle on the back of the left *open hand,* both palms facing down in front of the chest.

surface[2] *v.* See sign for SHOW UP.

surfboard *n.* A long, narrow board used for riding the crest of waves in the surf: *to float in to shore on a surfboard.* Same sign used for: **surfing.**

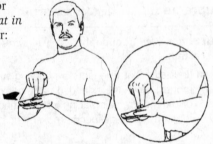

- ■ [Represents a person standing on a surfboard] With the fingertips of the right *H hand,* palm facing down, on the back of the left *open hand,* palm facing down in front of the chest, move both hands forward.

surge *n.* See sign for POWER SURGE.

surgeon *n.* A doctor who performs operations to treat diseases or injuries: *The surgeon removed my appendix.*

- ■ [**operate**[1] + **person marker**] Move the thumb of the right *A hand,* palm facing left, from the fingers to the heel of the left *open hand,* palm facing right and fingers pointing forward. Then move both *open hands,* palms facing each other, downward along each side of the body.

surgery *n.* See signs for OPERATE[1,2].

surprise *n.* **1.** A feeling of wonder from encountering something unexpected; astonishment: *The party was a pleasant surprise.* —*v.* **2.** To strike with surprise: *I was surprised to find out how much the bill was.* Related form: **surprised** *adj.* Same sign used for: **amaze, amazement, astonish, astonishment, astound, bewilder, startle, suddenly.**

- ■ [Represents the eyes widening in surprise] Beginning with the index fingers and thumbs of both hands pinched together near the outside of each eye, palms facing each other, flick the fingers apart, forming *L hands* near each side of the head.

surrender[1] *v.* To give up or yield to the demand or power of another: *to surrender one's passport at customs.*

- [Initialized sign similar to the sign for **give up**] Beginning with both *S hands* in front of the body, palms facing down, flip the hands upward in large arcs while opening into *5 hands,* ending in front of each shoulder, palms facing forward.

surrender[2] *v.* See sign for GIVE UP.

surround *v.* See sign for SITUATION.

surrounding *adj.* See signs for AROUND[1,2].

surround sound *n. phrase.* Multichannel audio created by expanding the sound of audio playback and by recording additional sound channels that can be reproduced using additional speakers placed around the listener: *install surround sound in the room.*

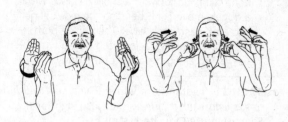

- [Location of sound around face + **hear** + **flash**[2] directed toward both ears] Beginning with both *curved hands* in front of each side of the head, palms facing in and fingers pointing up, move the hands back to the sides of the head, turning the palms forward near each ear. Then point the extended index fingers to each ear. Then, beginning with both *flattened O hands* near each side of the head, fingers pointing in, flick the fingers open with a quick movement.

surveillance[1] *n.* Covert monitoring of a person's movements and activities, especially by law enforcement authorities: *The cops had him under surveillance.*

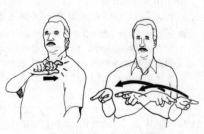

- [**police** + **watch**] With a double movement, tap the thumb side of the right *modified C hand,* palm facing left, against the left side of the chest. Then, beginning with both *V hands* in front of the left side of the body, palms facing down and fingers pointing forward, swing the hands in large simultaneous arcs to the right.

surveillance[2] *n.* See sign for WATCH[5].

survive *v.* See signs for LIVE[1,2]. Related form: **survival** *n.*

suspect[1] *v.* **1.** To think something is likely: *I suspect that it will snow.* **2.** To doubt or mistrust: *Don't suspect my motives.* **3.** To believe to be guilty: *The detective suspects*

suspect

the butler. Related forms: **suspicion** *n.*, **suspicious** *adj.*

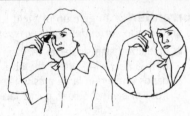

■ Beginning with the extended right index finger touching the right side of the forehead, palm facing down, bring the hand forward a short distance with a double movement, bending the index finger into an *X hand* each time.

suspect[2] *n.* A person under suspicion of having committed a crime or other offense.

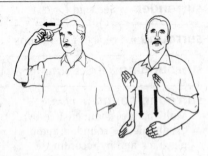

■ [**suspect + person marker**] Beginning with the extended right index finger touching the right side of the forehead, palm facing down, bring the hand forward a short distance with a double movement, bending the index finger into an *X hand* each time. Then move both *open hands*, palms facing each other, downward along the sides of the body.

suspend *v.* To stop for a while: *The school will have to suspend your privileges.* See also sign for HOLD[3]. Same sign used for: **halt, stall.**

■ [Demonstrates something suspending from another thing] With the index fingers of both *X hands* hooked around each other in front of the body, move both hands upward in front of the chest.

swallow[1] *v.* To take into the stomach through the mouth and throat: *so nervous I can't swallow a bite of food.* Same sign used for: **gulp.**

■ [Shows the path food follows when swallowed] Move the extended right index finger, palm facing left and finger angled upward, in an arc from in front of the chin down the length of the neck.

swallow[2] *v.* (alternate sign) Same sign used for: **gulp, humiliate, humiliation.**

■ [Represents the movement of food being swallowed] Move the extended right index finger, palm facing left and finger pointing forward, downward behind the left *open hand* held in front of the chest, palm facing in and fingers pointing right.

swap *v.* See signs for REVERSE[2], TRADE[1,2,3].

swap places *v.* See sign for TRADE PLACES.

swear[1] *v.* To make a solemn declaration or oath: *Swear you'll tell the truth.* Same sign used for: **cross your heart, promise.**

- ■ [Draw a cross on one's heart] Move the extended right index finger, palm facing in and finger pointing left, first downward and then from left to right on the left side of the chest.

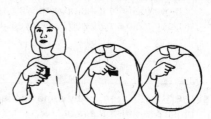

swear[2] *v.* See signs for CURSE[1,2], VOW[1].

sweat[1] *v.* **1.** To emit moisture from one's pores: *tends to sweat in summer.* —*n.* **2.** The moisture so emitted: *drenched with sweat.* Same sign used for: **perspire, perspiration, toil.**

- ■ [Represents sweat coming from one's brow] Beginning with both *S hands* in front of each side of the forehead, move the hands forward while opening into *curved hands,* palms facing down and fingers pointing toward each other.

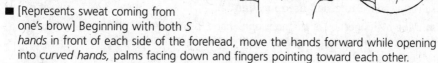

sweat[2] *v., n.* (alternate sign) Same sign used for: **humid, perspire, perspiration.**

- ■ [Represents sweat coming from one's brow] Move the right *4 hand,* palm angled forward and fingers pointing left, from right to left across the forehead while wiggling the fingers.

sweat[3] *v., n.* See sign for WHEW[2].

sweater *n.* A knitted covering, as a cardigan or pullover, for the upper torso: *to wear a sweater in the fall.*

- ■ [Demonstrates pulling on a sweater] Beginning with the thumb sides of both *A hands* on each side of the chest, palms facing in, bring the hands straight downward.

Sweden *n.* A country in northern Europe: *Sweden is on the Scandinavian Peninsula.* Related forms: **Swede** *n.,* **Swedish** *adj., n.*

sweep

■ Beginning with the fingertips of the right *flattened C hand* on the back of the left *open hand*, both palms facing down, move the right hand upward with a double movement, closing into a *flattened O hand* each time.

sweep[1] *v.* To clean, as by removing loose dust and dirt, with a broom: *to sweep the floor.*

■ [Demonstrates a sweeping movement] Brush the little-finger side of the right *open hand,* palm facing in, from the fingers toward the heel of the left *open hand* held in front of the chest, palm facing up.

sweep[2] *v.* See sign for BROOM[1].

sweet *adj.* Pleasant and agreeable; amiable and kind: *a genuinely sweet person.* Same sign used for: **gentle.**

■ Wipe the fingertips of the right *open hand,* palm facing in and fingers pointing up, downward off the chin while bending the fingers.

sweetheart *n.* Someone with whom one shares a love relationship: *My sweetheart sent me a valentine.* Same sign used for: **beau, honey, lover.**

■ With the knuckles of both *10 hands* together in front of the chest, palms facing in and thumbs pointing up, bend the thumbs downward toward each other with a double movement.

swell *v.* See sign for EXPAND[1].

swift *adj., adv.* See signs for FAST[1,2].

swim *v.* To move through the water by moving the arms, legs, tail, or fins: *Fish swim in the ocean.* Related form: **swimming** *n.*

■ [Demonstrates the movement of the hands when swimming] Beginning with the fingers of both *open hands* crossed in front of the chest, palms facing down, move the hands apart to each side with a double movement.

swindle *v.* See sign for BETRAY[1].

swindler *n.* A person who cheats others out of money: *The swindler tricked me into investing in some undeveloped land.* Same sign used for: **con artist.**

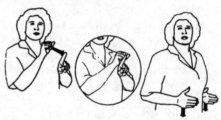

■ [**trick** + **person marker**] Tap the palm of the right *A hand,* palm facing forward, with a double movement against the extended left index finger held up in front of the body, palm facing forward. Then move both *open hands,* palms facing each other, downward along each side of the body.

swing[1] *v.* **1.** To move back and forth with a regular movement: *to swing on the open gate.* —*n.* **2.** A suspended seat hung from a support as by ropes: *to sit in the swing.* Related form: **swinging** *n.*

■ [Represents a person's legs over a swing seat while swinging] With the curved fingers of the right *H hand,* palm facing down, across the extended fingers of the left *H hand,* palm facing down, swing both hands forward and back in arcs with a double movement.

swing[2] *v., n.* (alternate sign) Related form: **swinging** *n.*

■ [Mime holding on to the ropes of a swing] Beginning with both *S hands* in front of each side of the chest, palms facing each other, swing the hands forward and back in arcs with a double movement.

swinging single *n.* See sign for SINGLE[1].

switch *v.* See signs for CHANGE[1], REVERSE[2], TRADE[1,2,3].

switch places *v.* See sign for TRADE PLACES.

Switzerland[1] *n.* A country in central Europe: *The people of Switzerland speak German, French, and Italian.* Related form: **Swiss** *n., adj.*

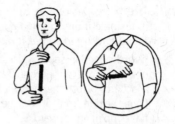

■ [The shape of a cross on the Swiss flag] Move the fingertips of the right *C hand,* palm facing in, first downward and then from left to right across the chest.

Switzerland[2] *n.* (alternate sign) Related form: **Swiss** *n., adj.*

■ [Shows the cross on a Swiss military uniform] With the extended right index finger, draw a cross on the left side of the chest by first going across from left to right and then moving downward.

swollen[1] *adj.* Enlarged abnormally, as by injury: *Her wrist is swollen from the bump on the bookcase.*

- ■ [Indicates the shape of a swelling on the wrist] Beginning with the right *curved 5 hand* on the back of the left *open hand* held in front of the chest, both palms facing down, raise the right hand a short distance.

swollen[2] *adj.* See sign for PUFF.

sword[1] *n.* A weapon with a long, sharp, narrow blade attached to a handle or hilt: *He pulled his sword out of the sheath.*

- ■ [Mime taking a sword from its sheath] With the little-finger side of the left *C hand* near the right side of the waist, palm facing in, move the right *A hand*, palm facing back, upward in an arc while twisting the wrist, ending with the palm facing left in front of the right side of the body.

sword[2] *n.* See sign for RAPIER.

swordfish *n.* A large fish with a long, bladelike bone extending from its upper jaw: *The swordfish swam in the ocean.*

- ■ [**fish**[1,2] + the shape and movement of the fin on a shark] With the index finger of the left *B hand* touching the wrist of the right *B hand*, palm facing left and fingers pointing forward, move the right fingers back and forth with a double movement. Then move the extended right index finger, palm facing left and finger pointing forward, from side to side in front of the nose with a double movement.

sworn *adj.* See sign for VOW[1].

syllable[1] *n.* A part of a word that can be pronounced with a single uninterrupted sound: *Break the word into syllables and try to sound it out.*

- ■ [**word** signed in several places to show the small parts of a word] Move the right *G hand*, palm facing left, in short arcs across the length of the extended left index finger held in front of the chest, palm facing right and finger pointing forward.

syllable[2] *n.* (alternate sign)

- ■ [**syllable**[1] + a slashing movement indicating the word being cut into syllables] Move the right *G hand*, palm facing left, in a series of small arcs across the length of the extended left index finger, palm facing right and finger pointing forward. Then move the right *open hand,* palm facing left and fingers pointing up, in a series of slashes near the right side of the head, downward toward the left.

symbol *n.* Something that represents something else: *The flag is a symbol of our country.* Same sign used for: **sample, sign, symptom.**

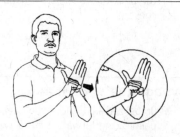

- [Initialized sign similar to sign for **show**[1]] With the index-finger side of the right *S hand,* palm facing forward, against the palm of the left *open hand* held in front of the chest, palm facing right and fingers pointing up, move both hands forward a short distance.

sympathy *n.* See signs for MERCY[1,2,3,4].

symphony[1] *n.* An elaborate musical composition written for a large orchestra: *listening to a symphony by Mozart.*

- [Initialized sign similar to sign for **music**] With the left *open hand* held across the chest, palm facing up and fingers pointing right, swing the right *S hand* back and forth along the left arm with a double movement while twisting the right wrist.

symphony[2] *n.* (alternate sign)

- [**music** + a movement as if conducting a symphony orchestra] Swing the little-finger side of the right *open hand,* palm facing in, back and forth along the length of the left bent forearm held in front of the chest. Then move both *open hands* from in front of each side of the body forward and upward in a large arc.

symptom *n.* See sign for SYMBOL.

synagogue[1] *n.* A Jewish house of worship, often used as well for religious instruction: *goes to the synagogue on Friday nights.*

- [Initialized sign similar to sign for **church**] Tap the heel of the right *S hand,* palm facing forward, downward with a double movement on the back of the left *open hand* held in front of the chest.

synagogue[2] *n.* (alternate sign)

- [**Jew** + **synagogue**[1]] Drag the fingertips of the right *curved 5 hand* from touching the chin, palm facing in and fingers pointing up, downward with a double movement while closing into a *flattened O hand* each time. Then tap the heel of the right *S hand*, palm facing forward, downward with a double movement on the back of the left *open hand* held in front of the chest.

synagogue[3] *n.* (alternate sign)

- [Initialized sign] Move the heel of the right *S hand*, palm facing forward, with a swinging movement back and forth on the back of the left *S hand* held across the chest.

syntax *n.* See sign for GRAMMAR.

synthetic *adj.* See signs for FAKE[3,4].

syrup[1] *n.* A thick, sweet liquid prepared for table use: *to put syrup on pancakes.*

- Wipe the extended right index finger, palm facing down, from under the nose across the right cheek.

syrup[2] *n.* See signs for GRAVY, SAUCE.

system[1] *n.* An orderly combination of things, methods, or other parts that fit together to make a coherent whole: *an order-processing system.*

- [Initialized sign] Beginning with the index-finger sides of both *S hands* touching in front of the chest, palms angled down, move the hands apart to in front of each shoulder, then downward toward each other, and then outward, ending with the hands in front of the sides of the body.

system[2] *n.* (alternate sign)

- [Initialized sign] Beginning with the index-finger sides of both *S hands* touching in front of the chest, palms angled down, move the hands outward to in front of each shoulder and then straight down a short distance.

tabernacle *n.* See sign for TEMPLE.

table[1] *n.* A piece of furniture with a flat, horizontal top on legs, a pedestal, or other support: *to eat at the table.* Same sign used for: **desk.**

- [Represents the flat surface of a table top] Beginning with the bent arms of both *open hands* across the chest, right arm above the left arm, move the right arm down with a short double movement.

table[2] *n.* (alternate sign)

- [The shape of a table] Beginning with the index-finger sides of both *B hands* touching in front of the chest, palms facing down and fingers pointing forward, bring the hands apart to in front of each side of the body and then downward while turning the palms toward each other.

table[3] *n.* See sign for DESK[2].

tablecloth *n.* A cloth for covering the top of a table, as during a meal: *a lace tablecloth for the special dinner.*

- [**table**[1,2] + shows rubbing the mouth with a napkin] Beginning with the index-finger sides of both *B hands* touching in front of the chest, palms facing down and fingers pointing forward, bring the hands apart to in front of each side of the body and then downward while turning the palms toward each other. Then rub the knuckles of the right *A hand*, palm facing in, with a double movement back and forth across the mouth.

table tennis *n.* See signs for PING-PONG[1,2,3].

tack[1] *n.* **1.** A short, sharp nail with a broad, flat head: *He hung the picture with a tack.* —*v.* **2.** To attach with a tack: *to tack the poster to the wall.*

- [Represents a tack being inserted] Insert the extended index finger of the right hand into the opening formed by the left *O hand* held in front of the body, palm facing down.

tack

tack[2] *n.* See signs for PIN[3], THUMBTACK[1,2].

tackle *v.* To seize or throw down (another player), especially in sports: *The guard tackled the quarterback.*

■ [Represents someone tackling another person's legs] Move the right *curved 5 hand*, palm facing left, to the left in front of the chest to close around the extended fingers of the left *H hand* pointing down in front of the left side of the body, palm facing left and elbow extended.

tag[1] *n.* A card, piece of plastic, or the like attached to something to label or identify it: *Put a tag on the suitcase.*

■ [The shape of a tag] Beginning with the curved index fingers and thumbs of both *modified C hands* touching in front of the body, palms facing each other, bring the hands apart and close the index fingers to the thumbs.

tag[2] *n.* (alternate sign)

■ [Shows putting a tag on something] With the palm side of the right *H hand* on the bent left arm near the elbow, bend the fingers of the right hand downward to the arm with a double movement.

tag[3] *n.* (alternate sign)

■ [**name** + **label**] Tap the middle-finger side of the right *H hand* across the index-finger side of the left *H hand* with a double movement. Then wipe the extended fingers of the right *H hand*, palm facing forward, from the heel to the fingers of the left *open hand*, palm facing in and fingers pointing right.

tag[4] *n.* (alternate sign)

■ [Shows where a label is located on clothing] Tap the fingers of the right *U hand*, palm facing down, with a double movement on the left shoulder near the neck.

tag[5] *n., v.* See sign for LABEL.

tail *n.* The rear part of an animal's body forming a distinct, usually flexible, appendage that sticks out past the trunk: *The dog wagged its tail.*

- [Shows action of a tail wagging] With the extended left index finger touching the right wrist, palms facing in opposite directions, wave the extended right index finger from side to side with a double movement.

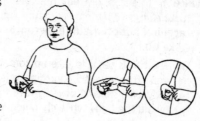

tailor *n.* A person whose business is making or altering clothes: *The tailor shortened the skirt.* Same sign used for: **seamstress.**

- [**sew**¹ + **person marker**] With the thumb and index fingers of both *F hands* touching in front of the chest, palms facing each other, move the right hand upward in a double circular movement in front of the chest, meeting the fingertips of the left hand each time it passes. Then move both *open hands*, palms facing each other, downward along each side of the body.

tailspin *n.* The downward spiraling movement of an airplane in a nosedive: *The plane was in a tailspin.*

- [The hand shape represents an airplane spinning downward] With the thumb, index finger, and little finger of the right hand extended, palm facing down and fingers pointing forward, move the hand from in front of the chest downward in a spiral movement.

Taiwan *n.* An island near the southeastern coast of China, the governmental seat of the Republic of China: *Taiwan was once a Japanese territory.*

- Beginning with the heel of the right *S hand* touching the chin, palm facing in, twist the hand with a double movement, turning the palm forward each time.

take¹ *v.* To seize or grasp with the hands to get possession of: *to take the package.*

- [Mime taking something] Bring the right *curved 5 hand* from in front of the right side of the body, palm facing down and fingers pointing forward, a short distance to the left in front of the body while changing into an *S hand*.

take² *v.* To accept or undertake, as an obligation: *to take charge of the project.* Same sign used for: **acquire, adopt, assume, assumption, takeover, take up.**

- [The hands seem to take up something] Beginning with both *curved 5 hands* in front of each side of the body, palms facing down, move the hands upward toward the body while changing into *S hands.*

take a chance *v. phrase.* See sign for GRAB².

take advantage of *v. phrase.* See signs for ADVANTAGE¹, LEECH.

take a hike *v. phrase. Slang.* See sign for GET OUT.

take a pill *v. phrase.* See signs for PILL¹,²,³.

take away *v. phrase.* To remove from the present location; convey: *Take these old magazines away.*

- [The hand seems to take something away from one place] Bring the right *curved 5 hand* from in front of the right side of the body, palm facing down and fingers pointing forward, to the left across the body while changing into an *S hand.*

take care *v. phrase.* See sign for CAREFUL.

take care of *v. phrase.* See sign for CARE¹.

take me *v. phrase.* To transport, conduct, or escort me: *Please take me with you.*

- [Directional sign of another taking oneself] Beginning with the fingers of the right *curved 5 hand* on the chest, palm facing in, bring the hand forward while closing into an *S hand.*

take off¹ *v. phrase.* To begin flight: *The plane took off.*

- [The hand shape represents an airplane taking off] With the thumb, index finger, and little finger of the right hand extended, move the right hand from resting on the left *open hand* held in front of the body, palm facing up, upward in a large arc, ending with the palm facing forward.

take off² *v. phrase.* To remove: *take off your clothes.* Same sign used for: **remove, undress.**

■ [Mime taking off one's clothes] Beginning with the fingers of both *curved hands* on each side of the chest, palms facing in, bring the hands outward to in front of each shoulder while closing into *S hands,* palms facing each other.

take off[3] *v. phrase.* (alternate sign) Same sign used for: **remove, undress.**

■ [Mime taking off one's clothes and putting them down] Beginning with the palms of both *S hands* on each side of the chest, move the hands downward while opening into *5 hands,* ending with the palms facing down and fingers pointing forward.

takeover *n.* See signs for CAPTURE[1], TAKE[2].

take pictures[1] *v. phrase. Take pictures of the wedding.* Same sign used for: **photograph, shoot.**

■ [Represents the shutter on a camera opening and closing] Beginning with both *modified C hands* near the outside of each eye, palms facing each other, bend the right index finger downward.

take pictures[2] *v. phrase.* (alternate sign) Same sign used for: **flash, photograph, shoot.**

■ [Mime holding a camera and snapping a picture] Beginning with the index-finger side of the right *flattened O hand,* palm facing left, touching the left *open hand,* palm facing forward and fingers pointing up, open and close the right fingers.

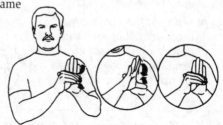

take steps *v. phrase.* See sign for PROCEDURE.

take turns *v. phrase.* See sign for TURN[2].

take up *v. phrase.* See signs for RAPTURE, TAKE[2].

tale *n.* See signs for STORY[1,2].

talent *n.* See sign for SKILL.

talk[1] *v.* To exchange ideas by using words: *to talk on the phone.* Same sign used for: **dialogue, mediate, mediation.**

talk

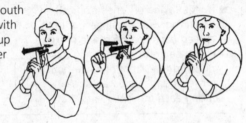

- [Represents words coming from the mouth and from another person] Beginning with both extended index fingers pointing up in front of the mouth, right hand closer to the mouth than the left hand and palms facing in opposite directions, move the hands forward and back with an alternating movement.

talk[2] *v.* (alternate sign)

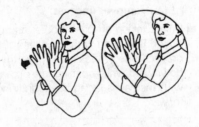

- [Represents words coming from the mouth] Beginning with the index finger of the right *4 hand* in front of the mouth and the index finger of the left *4 hand* touching the right little finger, palms facing in opposite directions, move the hands forward with a double movement.

talk[3] *v.* (alternate sign)

- [Shows words coming from the mouth] Beginning with the index-finger side of the right *4 hand* in front of the mouth, palm facing left and fingers pointing up, move the hand forward with a double movement.

talk[4] *v.* To communicate using sign language: *The two friends are talking in sign language.* See sign for: **chat.**

- Beginning with both *curved 5 hands* in front of each shoulder, palms facing forward, move the hands up and down with an alternating double movement in front of each side of the chest.

talk[5] *v.* To spread information around to various people; gossip: *to talk around the neighborhood.*

- [Represents talk coming and going from different directions] Beginning with both extended index fingers pointing up in front of the chest, palms facing in opposite directions and right hand closer to the chest than the left hand, move the hands forward and back with an alternating movement. Repeat in front of the right side of the chest.

talk[6] *v.* See signs for BLAB, CHAT[1], PRATTLE, SPEAK[1,2]. Related form: **talkative** *adj.*

talk with *v. phrase.* To have a conversation with: *to talk with a friend.*

- [Represents the action of two mouths talking to each other] Beginning with the right *flattened C hand* in front of the chin and the left *flattened C hand* somewhat forward, palms facing each other, close the fingers and thumbs of both hands together simultaneously with a double movement.

tall[1] *adj.* A thing having a relatively great height: *a tall building.*

- [Indicates the height of a tall thing] Move the extended right index finger, palm facing forward and finger pointing up, from the heel upward to off the fingertips of the left *open hand,* palm facing right and fingers pointing up, ending with the right hand in front of the head.

tall[2] *adj.* (alternate sign used to refer to a person) Same sign used for: **height.**

- [Shows height of a tall person] Raise the right *open hand,* palm facing down, upward from in front of the right shoulder.

tame *v.* See sign for PET[1].

tan *adj.* **1.** Light brown in color: *a tan sweater.* —*n.* **2.** A light brown color: *The color scheme is tan and blue.* **3.** A brown color acquired by the skin from exposure to the sun: *She has a nice tan.*

- [Initialized sign similar to sign for **brown**] Slide the index-finger side of the right *T hand,* palm facing left, downward on the right cheek.

tangle *v.* **1.** To twist together in confused, interlaced strands: *to tangle the wires.* —*n.* **2.** A confused mass or snarl: *The ropes were in a hopeless tangle.*

- [Shows the shape of things all tangled up] With the curved index finger of the right *X hand* hooked over the curved index finger of the left *X hand,* both palms facing down, twist the wrists in a repeated movement, twisting the right wrist in a circle to wrap the right finger around the left.

tank

tank[1] *n.* An armored combat vehicle: *The enemy tanks came down the road, guns blazing.*

- ■ [The extended index finger represents the gun on a tank moving up and down when moving over rough terrain] With the right index finger extended, place the right little finger on the thumb of the left *3 hand*, palms facing in opposite directions, and move the hands forward in a wavy movement.

tank[2] *n.* A large container for holding liquid: *a fish tank.*

- ■ [**water** + the shape of a tank] Tap the index-finger side of the right *W hand*, palm facing left, against the chin with a double movement. Then, beginning with the little fingers of both *open hands* together in front of the body, palms facing up and fingers pointing forward, bring the hands apart and then upward in front of each side of the body, turning the palms toward each other.

tantrum *n.* A fit of bad temper, especially a violent rage: *The boy threw a tantrum, rolling around on the floor and screaming.*

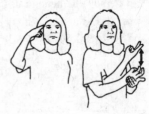

- ■ [**think**[1] + a gesture showing a person jumping up and down on the floor throwing a tantrum] Tap the index finger of the right hand against the right side of the forehead. Then bring the back of the right *bent V hand* downward with a double movement on the palm of the left *open hand,* both palms facing up, straightening the right fingers each time.

tape[1] *n.* **1.** A long strip of magnetic plastic, usually on a reel, for recording audio or visual signals: *to listen to the cassette tape through the earphones.* —*v.* **2.** To make a recording on a magnetic tape: *tape the music.*

- ■ [Initialized sign represents dual tape recorder reels] Beginning with both *T hands* in front of each side of the chest, palms facing forward, move the hands in simultaneous double circles.

tape[2] *n.* A long, narrow strip of sticky material, used for sealing, binding, etc.: *Put some tape on the package before you send it.* Same sign used for: **adhesive tape.**

- ■ [Demonstrates applying tape on something] Beginning with the fingers of the right *H hand* over the fingers of the left *H hand*, palms facing each other, move the right hand to the right while bending the fingers.

tape[3] *n.* See signs for BANDAGE, RECORD[3].

tape measure *n.* A long, flexible, ribbonlike length of fabric or metal marked off to be used for measuring: *to measure the room with a tape measure.*

■ [**measure** + a gesture showing stretching out a tape measure] Tap the thumbs of both *Y hands*, palms facing forward, together in front of the chest with a double movement. Then, beginning with both *modified X hands* together in front of the chest, palms facing down, move the right hand smoothly outward to the right.

tardy *adj.* See sign for LATE.

target *n.* See signs for GOAL[1], POINT[3].

task *n.* See signs for WORK[1,2].

tassel *n.* A tuft of threads bound at one end and cut evenly at the other, especially that traditionally hanging from the top of a graduation cap: *a green and gold tassel.*

■ [**graduate** + showing a tassel swinging] Beginning with the right *G hand* in front of the right side of the chest, palm facing left, move the hand in a small circular movement and then straight down, ending with the little-finger side of the right hand on the upturned open left palm. Then hold the extended right index finger down in front of the right shoulder, palm facing back, and swing the right finger from side to side with a double movement.

taste *n.* **1.** Flavor: *a spicy taste.* **2.** The sense by which flavor is perceived in the mouth: *enjoying food through the senses of taste and smell* —*v.* **3.** To sample the flavor of: *to taste the soup.*

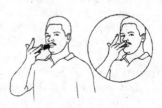

■ [The finger used for feeling points toward the sense of taste] Touch the bent middle finger of the right *5 hand*, palm facing in, to the lips.

tasty *adj.* See signs for DELICIOUS[1,2,3].

tattle *v.* To tell something secret about another: *The boy tattled on the girl who threw the paper airplane.* Same sign used for: **rat** (*slang*), **squeal, tattletale.**

■ [Shows words coming from the mouth when talking directly about another] Beginning with the index-finger side of the right *S hand* in front of the mouth, palm facing left, move the hand forward with a double movement, extending the right index finger each time.

taut *adj.* See sign for THIN[3]. Shared idea of something tightly drawn.

tax *n., v.* See sign for COST[1].

taxi *n.* See sign for CAB.

tea *n.* A drink made by pouring hot water over specially dried and prepared tea leaves: *to drink a cup of tea.*

- ■ [Mime dipping a tea bag in hot water] With the fingertips of the right *F hand*, palm facing down, inserted in the hole formed by the left *O hand* held in front of the chest, palm facing in, move the right hand in a small circle.

teach *v.* **1.** To help to pass on knowledge to: *to teach the class.* **2.** To help to pass on knowledge of: *to teach music.* Same sign used for: **educate, education, indoctrinate, indoctrination, instruct, instruction.**

- ■ [The hands seem to take information from the head and direct it toward another person] Move both *flattened O hands,* palms facing each other, forward with a small double movement in front of each side of the head.

teacher *n.* A person who teaches: *The teacher needs new textbooks for the class.* Same sign used for: **educator, instructor, professor.**

- ■ [**teach** + **person marker**] Move both *flattened O hands,* palms facing each other, forward with a small double movement in front of each side of the head. Then move both *open hands,* palms facing each other, downward along each side of the body.

team *n.* **1.** A number of people forming one of the sides in a game: *a football team.* **2.** A number of people working together, as on a project: *a software development team of top programmers.*

- ■ [Initialized sign similar to sign for **class**] Beginning with the index-finger sides of both *T hands* touching in front of the chest, palms angled forward, bring the hands away from each other in outward arcs while turning the palms in, ending with the little fingers touching.

teamwork *n.* The coordinated, cooperative action of people working together: *We will accomplish the task with good teamwork.*

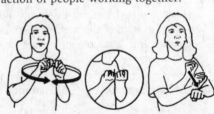

- ■ [**team** + **work**[1,2]] Beginning with the index fingers of both *T hands* touching in front of the chest, palms angled forward, bring the hands away from each other in outward arcs while turning the palms in, ending with the little fingers touching. Then tap the heel of the right *S hand* on the back of the left *S hand* with a double movement, both palms facing down.

tear[1] *v.* To pull apart by force: *to tear the paper.* Same sign used for: **revoke, rip, strip, torn.**

- [Mime tearing something] Beginning with the index-finger sides of both *modified X hands* touching in front of the chest, palms facing down, pull the right hand back toward the body with a deliberate movement.

tear[2] *v.* (alternate sign) Same sign used for: **revoke, rip, strip, torn.**

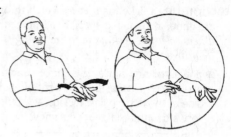

- [Mime ripping a piece of paper] Beginning with the index-finger sides of both *F hands* touching in front of the chest, palms facing down, move the right hand back toward the body with a deliberate movement while moving the left hand forward.

tear apart *v. phrase.* See sign for BREAK.

tear down *v. phrase.* See sign for BREAK DOWN.

tears[1] *pl. n.* Drops of salty water coming from the eyes when crying: *His face was covered with tears.* Same sign used for: **teardrop.**

- [Represents tears flowing from the eye] Beginning with the index finger of the right *4 hand* touching the cheek near the right eye, palm facing in and fingers pointing left, bring the hand downward a short distance.

tears[2] *pl. n.* (alternate sign) Same sign used for: **teardrop.**

- [The fingers follow the path of tears rolling down the cheeks] Bring both extended index fingers, palms facing in and fingers pointing up, downward on each cheek from each eye with a simultaneous movement.

tease *v.* To irritate or annoy, as with persistent taunts or playful mockery: *The grownups kept teasing the child about his shyness.* Related form: **teasing** *n.* Same sign used for: **jest, joke, joking, kid, kidding.**

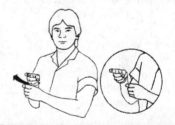

- [The hand seems to direct jabbing remarks at someone] Push the little-finger side of the right

technical

X hand, palm facing left, forward with a repeated movement across the index-finger side of the left *X hand*, palm facing right.

technical *adj.* Pertaining to specialized facts and techniques of science, the arts, professions, and trades: *delivered a technical paper at the conference.* Same sign used for: **technique, technology.**

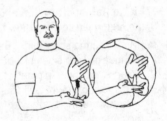

- Tap the bent middle finger of the right *5 hand*, palm facing up, upward on the little-finger side of the left *open hand*, palm facing right and fingers pointing forward, with a double movement.

technique[1] *n.* The manner in which things are done, as by using specialized procedures: *a new scientific technique for restoring paintings.*

- [Initialized sign similar to sign for **road**[1]] Move both *T hands* from in front of each side of the body, palms facing each other, forward with a simultaneous movement.

technique[2] *n.* See sign for TECHNICAL.

technology *n.* See sign for TECHNICAL.

tedious *adj.* See sign for BORING[1].

teenager *n.* A person between the years thirteen to nineteen: *She is looking forward to being a teenager.* Alternate form: **teen.**

- [Initialized sign similar to sign for **adult**] Touch the index-finger side of the right *T hand*, palm facing forward, first to the right side of the forehead and then to the right side of the chin.

teeny *adj.* See signs for TINY[1,2].

tee-shirt *n.* A lightweight, usually short-sleeved, pullover shirt: *allowed to wear a tee-shirt to work on Fridays.*

- [Form a T shape with the fingers + **shirt**[1,2]] Tap the extended right index finger, palm facing down, across the top of the left extended index finger with a double movement. Then grasp a small piece of fabric from the right side of the chest with the right fingers and shake with a double movement.

teeth *pl. n.* **1.** Plural of TOOTH: *The six-year-old lost two teeth this week.* **2.** The set of hard bodies attached in a row to each jaw, used for chewing: *Brush your teeth.*

■ [Location of the teeth] Move the curved index finger of the right *X hand* from right to left across the top front teeth, palm facing in.

telegraph *n.* **1.** A system or apparatus for sending coded messages between two electrical devices connected by wire: *She received a message sent by telegraph.* —*v.* **2.** To send a coded message through this apparatus: *Telegraph me in case of an emergency.* Related form: **telegram** *n.*

■ [Demonstrates the action of tapping out a message in code on a telegraph] Touch the bent middle finger of the right *5 hand,* palm facing down, to several places on the left *open hand,* moving from the palm to the fingers.

telephone[1] *n.* An instrument or system for sending speech over distances electrically: *She used the telephone to call us from the airport.* Same sign used for: **call, phone.**

■ [Represents holding a telephone receiver to the ear] Tap the knuckles of the right *Y hand,* palm facing in, with a double movement on the lower right cheek, holding the right thumb near the right ear and the little finger in front of the mouth. The same sign is used for the verb, *to telephone,* but made with a single movement.

telephone[2] *n.* (alternate sign) Same sign used for: **call, phone.**

■ [Represents talking on an old-fashioned telephone] Move the right *S hand,* palm facing forward, toward the right ear and the left *S hand,* palm facing right, toward the mouth.

telescope *n.* An optical instrument with lenses for making distant things appear larger and therefore closer, showing greater detail than is visible through the naked eye: *to look at the stars through a telescope.*

■ [Mime looking through a telescope] Beginning with the right *C hand* in front of the left eye, palm facing left, and the left *C hand* somewhat forward, palm facing right, move the left hand forward and upward.

teletypewriter *n.* A device for sending typed messages over electrical wires to a similar instrument: *Send the letter to me on the teletypewriter.* Abbreviation: **TTY.**

- ■ [**telephone**[1] + **typewriter**] Tap the knuckles of the right *Y hand* palm facing in, with 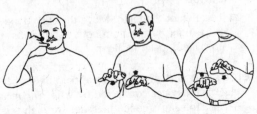 a double movement on the lower right cheek, holding the right thumb near the right ear and the little finger in front of the mouth. Then move both *curved 5 hands,* palms facing down, up and down with a short double alternating movement in front of the chest.

television or **TV** *n.* A device that transmits transient images by converting light and sound into electrical waves and then reconverting them into visible light rays and audible sound.

- ■ [Abbreviation **T-V**] Form a *T* and then a *V* in front  of the right shoulder with the right hand, palm facing forward.

tell[1] *v.* To say or make known (to): *Tell me about the party. Tell the truth.* Same sign used for: **reveal.**

- ■ [Represents words coming from the mouth toward  another person] Beginning with the extended right index finger near the chin, palm facing in and finger pointing up, move the finger forward in an arc by bending the wrist, ending with the finger angled forward.

tell[2] *v.* See sign for ANNOUNCE.

tell off *v. phrase.* See sign for BAWL OUT.

temper[1] *n.* **1.** An outburst of anger or displeasure or general irritability: *I don't like your temper.* **2.** Disposition: *a bad temper.*

- ■ [**hot** + **mind**] Beginning with the right *curved*  *5 hand* in front of the mouth, palm facing in, flip the hand quickly forward, ending with the palm facing forward. Then tap the curved index finger of the right hand against the right side of the forehead with a double movement.

temper[2] *n.* See sign for BLOWUP.

temperature *n.* **1.** A measure of the warmth or coldness of an object, the atmosphere, etc.: *What is the temperature today?* **2.** The degree of heat of the human body: *He has the flu, with a high temperature and a sore throat.* Same sign used for: **fever.**

■ [Symbolizes the mercury in a thermometer rising and falling] Slide the back of the extended right index finger, palm facing in and finger pointing left, up and down with a repeated movement on the extended index finger of the left hand, palm facing right and finger pointing up.

temple *n.* A building used for worship: *The family goes to the temple for religious services.* Same sign used for: **tabernacle, tomb.**

■ [Initialized sign similar to sign for **church**] Tap the heel of the right *T hand,* palm facing forward, with a double movement on the back of the left *S hand* held in front of the chest, palm facing down.

temporary *adj.* See sign for SHORT[1].

tempt *v.* To appeal to (someone), as to do something immoral or ill-advised: *Don't tempt me to eat that dessert.* Related form: **temptation** *n.* Same sign used for: **entice.**

■ [Shows tapping someone in order to tempt] Tap the curved right index finger, palm facing in, with a double movement on the elbow of the bent left arm.

ten cents *pl. n.* See sign for DIME.

tend *v.* To be inclined or disposed toward: *We tend to stay home on weekends.* Related form: **tendency** *n.* Same sign used for: **inclined to, prone.**

■ [The fingers used for feeling move from the heart] Beginning with the bent middle fingers of both *5 hands* touching each side of the chest, palms facing in, move both hands forward in small arcs.

tender *adj.* See signs for PAIN[1], SOFT, SOFT-HEARTED.

ten dollars *pl. n.* See sign for TENTH.

tennis *n.* A game played by two players or two pairs of players in which a ball is hit back and forth over a low net with rackets: *They play tennis on public courts.*

■ [Mime swinging a tennis racket] With the right *modified X hand* in front of the left shoulder,

palm angled down, swing the hand downward to the right. Then repeat in front of the right shoulder, moving downward to the left.

tense *adj.* See sign for TIGHT².

tent¹ *n.* A portable shelter made of canvas and supported by poles: *The scouts slept in tents when they went camping.*

- [Shows the shape of a tent] Beginning with the fingertips of both *V hands* touching in front of the chest, palms angled toward each other, bring the hands apart at an angle.

tent² *n.* See sign for CAMP.

tenth *adj.* **1.** Next after the ninth: *waiting for the tenth person.* —*n.* **2.** The one after the ninth in a series of ten or more: *the tenth in line.* —*adv.* **3.** In the tenth place: *graduated tenth in the senior class.* Same sign used for: **ten dollars.**

- [**ten** formed with a twisting movement used for ordinals] Beginning with the right *10 hand* in front of the right side of the chest, palm facing left, twist the hand to the left, ending with the palm facing back.

tepid *adj.* Moderately warm; lukewarm: *tepid water.*

- [**warm** + **water**] Beginning with the right *E hand* in front of the mouth, palm facing in, move the hand upward and forward while opening into a *curved 5 hand.* Then tap the index-finger side of the right *W hand,* palm facing left, against the chin with a double movement.

term *n.* A specific, finite period of time during which an agreement is operative or an interest rate remains good, or at the end of which an obligation matures: *The guarantee was good for a term of one year.*

- [**time** + a sign indicating limit] With a double movement, tap the bent index finger of the right *X hand,* palm facing down, on the wrist of the downturned left hand. Then, beginning with both *bent hands* in front of the chest, right hand above the left hand and both palms facing down, move both hands forward simultaneously.

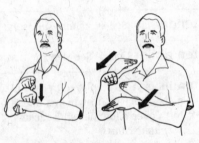

terminal[1] *n.* A device for entering information into a central computer: *The staff were given computer terminals instead of individual PCs.* Same sign used for: **monitor.**

■ [Initialized sign showing the shape of a terminal] Beginning with the index-finger sides of both *T hands* together in front of the chest, palms facing forward, bring the hands apart to in front of each shoulder and then straight down.

terminal[2] *adj.* Occurring at the end of a sequence or event: *to have terminal cancer.* Related form: **terminate** *v.*

■ [Initialized sign similar to sign for **end**[2]] Slide the heel of the right *T hand*, palm facing forward, along the index-finger side of the left *B hand* held in front of the chest, palm facing in and fingers pointing right, and then straight downward in front of the right side of the body.

terminate *v.* See signs for ELIMINATE[1,2], FIRE[3].

terrible *adj.* See signs for AWFUL, HORROR.

terrific *adj.* See signs for FINEST, WONDERFUL[1].

terrify *v.* See sign for AFRAID. Related form: **terrified** *adj.*

terror[1] *n.* Intense, overwhelming fear: *I have a terror of airplanes.*

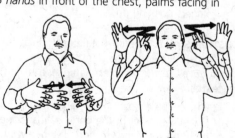

■ [**fear**[1] + **awful**] Beginning with both *5 hands* in front of the chest, palms facing in and fingers pointing toward each other, move the hands toward each other with a deliberate movement. Then, beginning with both *8 hands* in front of each shoulder, palms facing forward, move the hands forward with a double movement while flicking out the fingers, forming *5 hands* each time.

terror[2] *n.* See sign for HORROR.

test[1] *n.* **1.** A means for evaluating knowledge, abilities, performance, etc.; examination: *studying to pass the test.* —*v.* **2.** To examine by subjecting to a test: *We tested the children in mathematical skills.* Same sign used for: **inquire, quiz, testify.**

■ [**question** formed with both hands to indicate the questions on a test] Beginning with both extended index fingers pointing up in front of each side of the head, palms facing forward, bring the hands down while bending the index fingers into *X hands* in front of the chest, ending with the palms facing down.

---

test[2] *n., v.* (alternate sign) Same sign used for: **inquire, quiz, testify.**

■ [Draw question marks in the air + a gesture representing distributing the test to a group] Beginning with both extended index fingers pointing up in front of the head, palms facing forward, bring the hands in arcs to the side and then downward while bending the index fingers into *X hands* and continuing down while throwing the fingers open into *5 hands* in front of the body, palms facing down and fingers pointing forward.

---

test[3] *n., v.* (alternate sign) Same sign used for: **exam, examination.**

■ [**check**[1] + **test**[1,2]] Move the extended right index finger from a position near the nose downward to strike the palm of the left *open hand* and then outward to the right. Then, beginning with both *modified C hands* in front of each shoulder, palms facing forward, drop the hands while opening into *5 hands*, ending with the palms facing down.

Testament *n.* One of the two main divisions of the Bible: *the New Testament and the Old Testament.*

■ [Initialized sign similar to sign for **law**] Touch the index-finger side of the right *T hand,* palm angled forward, first to the fingers and then to the heel of the left *open hand* held in front of the chest, palm facing right and fingers pointing up.

---

testicles *pl. n.* The two male reproductive glands, located in the scrotum: *Sperm are produced in the testicles.* Same sign used for: **testes.**

■ [The shape of testicles] Beginning with both *C hands* in front of the body, palms facing up, drop the hands a short distance with a double movement.

---

testify *v.* See signs for OATH, TEST[1,2]. Shared idea of disclosing information. Related form: **testimony** *n.*

---

testimony[1] *n.* A statement given under oath, used in evidence: *gave his testimony at the trial.* Related form: **testify** *v.*

■ [Sign **talk**[3] while holding the hand up as if giving testimony in court] While holding the left *open hand* in front of the left shoulder, palm facing forward and fingers pointing up, move the fingers of the right *4 hand* forward a short distance in front of the mouth with a double movement, palm facing left and fingers pointing up.

---

testimony[2] *n.* (alternate sign) Related form: **testify** *v.*

■ [Initialized sign similar to sign for **preach**[1]] Move the right *T hand,* palm facing left, in a short double movement forward in front of the right side of the head.

Texas *n.* A southwestern state in the United States: *The capital of Texas is Austin.* Related form: **Texan** *n., adj.*

■ [Initialized sign with **x** hand shape] Move the right *X hand,* palm facing forward, a short distance to the right and then straight down in front of the right side of the body.

text *n.* See sign for WORD.

textbook *n.* See sign for BOOK.

text message *n.* A message consisting of words that are typed or entered on a keypad and sent electronically to a cell phone, especially from another cell phone: *She received a text message about the meeting.* Related form: **text** *v.* Same sign used for: **personal digital assistant (PDA).**

■ [Mime action of thumbs when text-messaging] Bend the extended thumbs of both *curved hands* with a random up-and-down movement.

texture *n.* The structure that gives something, especially a surface, its characteristic feel: *the rough texture of the tweed coat.*

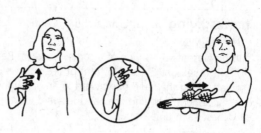

■ [**feel** + a gesture feeling the texture of fabric] Move the bent middle finger of the right hand upward on the chest with a double movement. Then rub the fingers of the right *open hand,* palm facing down, with a double movement on the left forearm held across the chest.

Thailand *n.* A country in southeast Asia: *Thailand used to be called Siam.*

■ Beginning with the extended right index finger touching the top of the nose, palm facing down and finger pointing left, move the finger downward and forward in an arc.

than *conj.* (Used after comparatives to introduce the second item being compared): *taller than I.*

■ Move the fingers of the right *open hand,* palm angled left, downward by bending the right wrist, hitting the fingers of the left *bent hand* held in front of the chest, palm and fingers angled forward, as it passes.

thank *v.* To express gratitude to: *Thank the guests for coming.* Same sign used for: **thank you.** Related form: **thanks** *n.*

■ [The hand takes gratitude from the mouth and presents it to another] Move the fingertips of the right *open hand,* palm facing in and fingers pointing up, from the mouth forward and down, ending with the palm angled up in front of the chest.

thankful *adj.* See sign for GRATEFUL.

Thanksgiving[1] *n.* A national holiday of the United States and Canada set aside for giving thanks to God: *Thanksgiving is celebrated in November in the United States.* See also sign for THANKSGIVING DAY.

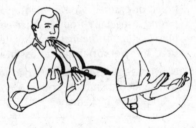

■ [**thank** formed with both hands and a movement similar to **present**[1]] Beginning with the fingertips of both *open hands* near the mouth, palms angled in, move the hands downward and then forward in front of the chest, ending with the palms facing up and fingers pointing forward.

Thanksgiving[2] *n.* (alternate sign) See also sign for THANKSGIVING DAY.

■ [Represents the shape of a turkey's wattle] Beginning with the right *G hand* in front of the nose, palm facing left, bring the hand downward in an arc with a double movement, bringing the hand forward in front of the chest each time.

Thanksgiving[3] *n.* (alternate sign) See also sign for THANKSGIVING DAY.

■ [Represents the shape of a turkey's wattle] Move the right *G hand* from in front of the nose, palm facing left, forward and downward in an arc, bringing the index-finger side of the right *G hand* back against the chest.

Thanksgiving[4] *n.* (alternate sign) See also sign for Thanksgiving Day.

- Beginning with the fingers of both *open hands* near the mouth, palms facing in and fingers pointing up, bring the hands downward while closing into *A hands* in front of the chest and then upward in forward arcs while opening into *5 hands,* ending with the palms facing up.

Thanksgiving Day *n.* A national holiday of the United States and Canada set aside for giving thanks to God: *We go to church on Thanksgiving Day.* See also signs for Thanksgiving[1,2,3,4].

- [**Thanksgiving**[1,2,3,4] + **day**] Move the right *G hand* from in front of the nose, palm facing left, forward and downward in an arc, bringing the index-finger side of the right *G hand* back against the chest. Then, beginning with the bent right elbow resting on the back of the left hand held across the body, palm facing down, bring the extended right index finger from pointing up in front of the right shoulder, palm facing left, downward toward the left elbow.

thank you See sign for THANK.

that[1] *pron.* **1.** (Used to indicate a specific person, idea, or thing, as one previously mentioned): *I didn't know that.* —*adj.* **2.** Being the one spoken of: *that girl.*

- Bring the palm side of the right *Y hand* with a deliberate movement down to land on the palm of the left *open hand* held in front of the chest, palm facing up.

that[2] *pron., adj.* (alternate sign)

- Move the right *Y hand,* palm facing down, from in front of the right shoulder downward.

the *definite article.* (Used before a noun, as to specify it as particular or to indicate that it is well-known): *the boy with the hat; the Rocky Mountains.*

- [Initialized sign] Beginning with the right *T hand* in front of the right shoulder, palm facing in, twist the wrist to turn the palm forward.

theater[1] or **theatre** *n.* **1.** A building or other place to view movies or plays: *a season ticket to the local theater.* **2. the theater** Dramatic performances; the drama: *We often go to the theater.*

- [Initialized sign similar to sign for **act**] Bring the thumbs of both *T hands,* palms facing each other, down each side of the chest with alternating circular movements.

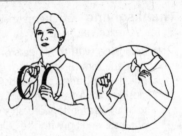

theater[2] *n.* See sign for ACT[2].

theft *n.* See signs for SHOPLIFT, STEAL[1].

their *pron.* A form of the possessive case of THEY, used as an adjective before a noun: *It's their idea, not mine.* Related form: **theirs** *pron.*

- [Gestures toward the referents being discussed] Move the right *open hand,* palm facing forward and fingers pointing up, from in front of the right side of the body outward to the right.

them[1] *pron.* The objective case of THEY, used as a direct or indirect object: *I like them. Give them the money.* Same sign used for: **these, they.**

- [Points toward the referents being discussed] Move the extended right index finger, palm facing down and finger pointing forward, from in front of the right side of the body outward to the right.

them[2] *pron.* (alternate sign) Same sign used for: **these, they.**

- [Gestures toward the referents being discussed] Move the right *open hand,* palm facing up and fingers pointing forward, from in front of the right side of the body outward to the right.

theme *n.* See signs for QUOTATION[1], TITLE.

themselves *pl. pron.* A reflexive form of THEM, used to refer back to the persons last mentioned: *They did it themselves.*

- [This hand shape is used for reflexive pronouns and is directed toward the referents being discussed] Move the right *10 hand* from in front of the right side of the body, palm facing left, outward to the right.

then *adv.* See signs for FINISH[1,2], OR[1].

theology *n.* The study of religion and divinity: *to study theology in order to become a minister.*

■ [Initialized sign similar to sign to **religion**] Beginning with the palm side of the right *T hand* against the left side of the chest, twist the wrist while moving the hand forward and outward, ending with the palm facing forward in front of the right shoulder.

theory *n.* **1.** A coherent group of principles: *Einstein's theory of relativity.* **2.** A proposed explanation: *My theory is that the key is lost.*

■ [Initialized sign similar to sign for **wonder**] Move the right *T hand,* palm facing forward, in a double circle near the right side of the forehead.

therapist *n.* **1.** A person trained to use methods of treatment and rehabilitation: *The therapist worked with the invalid.* **2.** A person trained to use psychological methods for the treatment of mental or emotional problems: *The client told the therapist about early childhood memories.*

■ [**therapy** + **person marker**] Beginning with the little-finger side of the right *T hand,* palm facing in, on the palm of the left *open hand* held in front of the body, palm facing up, move both hands upward in front of the chest. Then move both *open hands,* palms facing each other, downward along each side of the body.

therapy *n.* A rehabilitation program, as for treating mental or physical disorders: *to place a student in speech therapy.*

■ [Initialized sign similar to sign for **help**] Beginning with the little-finger side of the right *T hand,* palm facing in, on the palm of the left *open hand* held in front of the body, palm facing up, move both hands upward in front of the chest.

there[1] *adv.* In that place: *go over there.*

■ [Indicates a place away from the body] Move the right *open hand* from in front of the right side of the chest, palm facing up and fingers pointing forward, forward a short distance.

there[2] *adv.* (alternate sign) Same sign used for: **point.**

■ [Points to a specific place away from the body] Push the extended right index finger from in front of the right shoulder forward a short distance, palm facing forward and finger pointing forward.

therefore *adv.* For that reason: *It rained; therefore we couldn't go.*

■ Move the right *modified X hand,* palm facing forward in front of the right shoulder, outward to the right and then downward in an angle to the left in front of the body.

thermometer[1] *n.* An instrument for measuring temperature: *the thermometer shows it is ninety degrees outside.*

■ [Initialized sign similar to sign for **temperature**] Slide the little-finger side of the right *T hand,* palm facing left, up and down with a double movement on the extended left index finger held in front of the chest, palm facing right and finger pointing up.

thermometer[2] *n.* (alternate sign used when taking one's temperature orally)

■ [Represents a thermometer in the mouth] Touch the extended right index finger, palm facing down and finger pointing down, to the right side of the mouth.

these *pron.* See signs for THEM[1,2].

they *pron.* The plural of *he, she,* and *it,* used as the subject of a sentence. See signs for THEM[1,2].

thick[1] *adj.* Fat, broad, or deep; not thin: *a thick coat of paint.*

■ [Similar to the sign for **layer** except indicating a thicker layer] Slide the thumb side of the right *modified C hand,* palm facing forward, from the wrist across the back of the left *open hand* held in front of the chest, palm facing down.

thick[2] *adj.* (alternate sign)

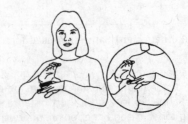

■ [Shows the thickness of a thick layer] Slide the thumb side of the right *C hand,* palm facing forward, from the wrist across the back of the left *open hand* held in front of the chest, palm facing down.

thick³ *adj.* (alternate sign)

■ [Shows the thickness of something] Place the thumb side of the right *modified C hand,* palm facing forward, on the left *open hand* held in front of the chest, palm facing up.

thick⁴ *adj.* (alternate sign) Same sign used for: **bold.**

■ Move the right *modified C hand* from in front of the mouth, palm facing in, forward in a large arc.

thick⁵ *adj.* (alternate sign) Same sign used for: **bold.**

■ [Shows the thickness of something] Hold the right *modified C hand* in front of the right shoulder, palm facing forward.

thief *n.* See signs for ROBBER¹,².

thimble *n.* A small cap worn on the finger to protect it when pushing a needle through cloth while sewing: *My grandmother used a thimble.*

■ [**sew**¹ + mime putting a thimble on the thumb] With the fingertips of both *F hands* touching in front of the chest, move the right hand to the left with a double movement. Then slide the fingers of the right *flattened C hand* over the extended thumb of the left *10 hand* held in front of the body, palm facing right.

thin¹ *adj.* Narrow; not thick: *a thin coat of paint.* Same sign used for: **short.**

■ [Shows the thickness of a thin layer] Slide the thumb side of the right *G hand,* palm facing forward, from the wrist to the fingers of the left *open hand* held in front of the chest, palm facing down.

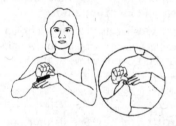

thin[2] *adj.* Not well fleshed; slender: *She was too thin for her height.* See also sign for SKINNY. Same sign used for: **lean, slim.**

- ■ [Indicates something or someone that is very thin] Beginning with the extended little fingers of both *I hands* touching in front of the chest, right hand above the left hand and palms facing in, bring the right hand upward and the left hand downward.

thin[3] *adj.* (alternate sign) Same sign used for: **gaunt, lean, slim, taut.**

- ■ [Shows the hollow cheeks of a thin person] Beginning with the extended fingers of the right *G hand* in front of the mouth, palm facing in, bring the hand downward a short distance.

thin[4] *adj.* See sign for DIET.

thing[1] *n.* **1.** An inanimate object: *What is that strange-looking thing on your desk?* **2.** One of someone's personal possessions: *Pick up your things.*

- ■ Bring the right *open hand,* palm facing up and fingers pointing forward, from in front of the body in a large arc to the right.

thing[2] *n.* (alternate sign)

- ■ Move the right *open hand,* palm facing up and fingers pointing forward, from in front of the right side of the body to the right in a double arc.

think[1] *v.* **1.** To use one's mind, as in analyzing and evaluating: *It's too noisy in here for me to think clearly.* **2.** To have as the subject of one's thoughts: *Think about what you're going to do next.* Related form: **thought** *n.*

- ■ [Indicates the location of the mind] Tap the extended right index finger, palm facing in, to the right side of the forehead with a short double movement.

think[2] *v.* See signs for CONCERN[1], WONDER.

think about *v. phrase.* See sign for WONDER.

think for yourself *v. phrase.*

■ [**think**¹ + **yourself**] Beginning with the extended right index finger, palm facing in, touching the right side of the forehead, move the hand forward while changing into a *10 hand*, palm facing left.

---

thinking *n.* See sign for WONDER.

---

third¹ *adj.* **1.** Next after the second: *She's the third candidate for the position.* —*n.* **2.** The one after the second in a series of three or more: *the third in line for the throne.* —*adv.* **3.** In the third place: *came in third in the competition and took the bronze medal.* Same sign used for: **three dollars.**

■ [**three** formed with a twisting movement used for ordinals] Beginning with the right *3 hand* in front of the right side of the chest, palm facing forward, twist the wrist to turn the palm back.

---

third² *adj., n.* (alternate sign)

■ [Points to the third finger] Touch the extended right index finger, palm facing left, to the middle finger of the left *3 hand* held in front of the body, palm facing right.

---

third³ *adj., n.* (alternate sign)

■ Move the right *3 hand,* palm facing in near the left shoulder, from left to right in front of the chest.

---

third⁴ *n.* See sign for ONE THIRD.

---

thirsty *adj.* Having a thirst; craving liquid: *After spicy food I am always thirsty.* Related form: **thirst** *n.* Same sign used for: **dry, parched.**

■ [Indicates a dry throat] Move the extended right index finger, palm facing in and finger pointing up, downward on the length of the neck, bending the finger down as it moves.

---

this¹ *pron.* **1.** (Used to indicate a person or thing that is nearby or a person, thing, or idea just mentioned or under discussion): *Why do you want to keep this?*

this

—*adj.* **2.** (Used before a noun to indicate that the person or thing is close by, specified, or under discussion): *I like this idea on page twenty.*

- [Points to a specific thing held in the hand] Move the extended right index finger, palm facing down and finger pointing down, from in front of the chest in a circular movement and then down to touch the left *open hand* held in front of the body, palm facing up.

this[2] *adj.* (alternate sign)

- [Points to a specific thing nearby] Move the extended right index finger, palm facing down and finger pointing forward, toward the thing being referred to.

thorax *n.* The upper part of the human body below the neck and above the abdomen: *The heart and lungs are in one's thorax.* Same sign used for: **torso.**

- [The location of one's thorax] Slide the little-finger side of the right *open hand*, palm facing up, from right to left with a double movement across the lower neck, and the left *open hand*, palm facing up, with a double movement from left to right across the waist.

thorough *adj.* See sign for THROUGHOUT. Related form: **thoroughly** *adv.*

those[1] *pron., adj.* The plural of THAT: *Those are mine. Those books go back to the library.*

- [Points to several referents] Move the extended right index finger, palm facing down and finger pointing forward, from in front of the right side of the body in a large arc to in front of the left side of the body.

those[2] *pron., adj.* (alternate sign)

- [Indicates several referents] Move the right *Y hand*, palm facing down, from in front of the body in a series of arcs to the right.

thought *v.* (Used when referring to one's own actions or mistakes, as in) **I should have thought of it before.** See sign for DISGUSTED[2].

thoughtless[1] *adj.* **1.** Revealing lack of consideration for others; inconsiderate: *Going out after inviting them over was thoughtless.* **2.** Done without proper thought; careless: *Driving so quickly was thoughtless behavior.* Related form: **thoughtlessly** *adv.*

- [**wonder**[1] + **reject**[3]] Move the extended right index finger, palm facing in, in a small circle near the right side of the forehead. Then move the little-finger side of the right *open hand,* palm facing in, from the heel to off the fingertips of the left *open hand* held in front of the body, palm facing up.

thoughtless[2] *adj.* (alternate sign)

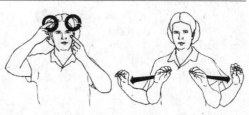

- [**concern**[1] + **none**[1,2,3]] Beginning with both extended index fingers in front of each side of the forehead, palms facing in and fingers angled up, move the fingers in repeated alternating circular movements toward each other in front of the face. Then move both *O hands,* palms facing forward in front of the body, apart to the sides, past the shoulders.

thousand *n.* **1.** A number equal to ten times one hundred: *Count to a thousand.* **2.** This number of persons or things: *If you have paper clips in stock, I'll take two thousand.* —*adj.* **3.** Amounting to one thousand in number: *A thousand people attended.*

- Bring the fingertips of the right *bent hand,* palm facing in, downward against the palm of the left *open hand* held in front of the body, palm facing up and fingers pointing forward.

thread[1] *n.* A fine cord: *Roll the thread on the spool.* Same sign used for: **yarn.**

- [Represents pulling a thread from a spool] Beginning with the right *curved 5 hand,* palm facing left, around the extended little finger of the left *I hand,* palm facing in and finger pointing right, pull the right hand outward to the right with a double movement, closing into a *flattened O hand* each time.

thread[2] *n.* See signs for CORD[1], LINE.

threat *n.* See sign for DANGER.

three dollars *pl. n.* See sign for THIRD[1].

three of us *n. phrase.* See sign for WE[5].

three times See sign for TRIPLE.

threshold[1] *n.* **1.** An entrance or doorway to a room or building: *standing at the threshold.* **2.** The sill, or horizontal piece of wood, at the base of a doorway: *to walk over the threshold.*

■ [**door** + a gesture showing the shape of a threshold + **stand**] Beginning with the index-finger sides of both *B hands* together in front of the chest, palms facing forward and fingers pointing up, swing the right hand in to the right by twisting the wrist and turning the palm left. Then, with the index-finger sides of both *modified C hands* touching in front of the chest, palms facing down and fingers pointing down, move the hands apart. Then place the fingertips of the right *V hand,* fingers pointing down, on the back of the left *open hand,* palm facing down and fingers pointing right.

threshold[2] *n.* The point at which a stimulus begins to produce an effect: *to have a low threshold for pain.*

■ [**maximum** + a gesture showing something being level with the top] Move the right *open hand,* palm facing down, upward in front of the chest to touch the palm of the left *open hand* held in front of the neck, palm facing down and fingers pointing right. Then move the right hand outward to the right until the fingertips of both hands touch.

thrice *adv.* See sign for TRIPLE.

thrifty *adj.* See sign for STINGY[1].

thrill *n.* See sign for EXCITE. Related form: **thrilling** *adj.*

throat *n.* **1.** The front of the neck: *wore a pendant on a chain at her throat.* **2.** The upper part of the passageway to the lungs and stomach, extending from the back of the mouth to below the larynx: *to have a sore throat.* Same sign used for: **larynx.**

■ [Location of the throat] Move the extended fingers of the right *G hand,* palm facing in, downward along the length of the neck.

throb *v., n.* See signs for PULSE[1,2].

through[1] *prep.* From one end or side of to another, between the parts of, or across the extent of: *to go through a tunnel; made their way through the crowd; drove through the countryside.* Same sign used for: **by way of, via.**

■ [Demonstrates movement through something] Slide the little-finger side of the right *open hand*, palm facing in and fingers angled to the left, between the middle finger and ring finger of the left *open hand* held in front of the chest, palm facing right and fingers pointing up.

through[2] *adj.* See sign for FINISH[1].

throughout *prep.* In or every part of: *throughout the land.* Same sign used for: **thorough, thoroughly.**

■ [Sign similar to **through** except the hand moves between the fingers in two directions] Slide the little-finger side of the right *open hand,* palm facing left and fingers pointing forward, forward between the middle finger and ring finger of the left *bent hand* held in front of the chest, palm facing up and fingers pointing up. Then turn the right hand and slide the little-finger side back toward the chest between the index finger and middle finger of the left hand.

throw[1] *v.* **1.** To cast away or dispose of: *to throw the trash into the trash can.* **2.** To propel with the hand by hurling or tossing: *Throw the stick to the dog.* Same sign used for: **cast, dump, pitch, throw away, toss.**

■ [Mime throwing something] Beginning with the right *S hand* in front of the right shoulder, palm facing forward, move the hand forward and downward while opening into a *5 hand,* palm facing down.

throw[2] *v.* (alternate sign) Same sign used for: **cast, dump, pitch, throw away, toss.**

■ [Mime throwing something held in each hand] Beginning with both *S hands* in front of each side of the chest, palms facing forward, move the hands quickly forward and downward while opening into *5 hands,* palms facing down.

throw[3] *v.* To pitch: *to throw the baseball.* Same sign used for: **pitch.**

■ [Mime holding and throwing a baseball] Bring the right *curved 3 hand* from in front of the right shoulder, palm facing forward, forward and downward while turning the palm downward.

throw out *v. phrase.* See sign for ABANDON[2].

throw up *v. phrase.* See sign for VOMIT.

thrust *v.* **1.** To push with force: *He thrust the sword at his opponent.* —*n.* **2.** An act or instance of thrusting: *the thrust of a spear.*

■ [Demonstrates a thrust upward] Beginning with the right *S hand* in front of the right side of the body, palm facing left, move the hand forward past the left *bent hand* held in front of the body, palm facing in and fingers pointing right.

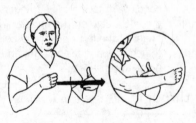

thruway *n.* See sign for SUPERHIGHWAY.

thumb *n.* The short, thick, innermost finger of the hand: *The thumb of the human hand is opposable, which aids in grasping.*

■ [Location of the thumb] Rub the extended right index finger, palm facing down and finger pointing forward, back and forth with a short double movement on the extended thumb of the left *10 hand* held in front of the body, palm facing in.

thumbtack[1] *n.* A small tack with a broad, flat head: *Put the note on the bulletin board with a thumbtack.* Same sign used for: **pushpin, tack.**

■ [Mime pushing a thumbtack into a wall] Push the extended thumb of the right *10 hand,* palm angled left, first against the fingers and then the heel of the left *open hand* held in front of the left side of the chest, palm facing right and fingers pointing up.

thumbtack[2] *n.* (alternate sign) Same sign used for: **pushpin, tack.**

■ [Mime pushing in a tack held with other hand] With the left *flattened O hand* in front of the left side of the chest, palm facing right, bring the right *10 hand,* palm facing left, toward the left fingers and touch the left thumb.

thumbtack[3] *n.* See sign for PIN[2].

thunder[1] *n.* **1.** The loud, explosive, reverberating sound caused by the expansion of air that is heated by lightning: *I heard the thunder all during the storm.* —*v.* **2.** To emit thunder: *It thundered all evening.* **3.** To make a noise like thunder: *We heard the cannons thundering during the battle.*

■ [**hear** + a movement that represents the vibration of a loud sound] Touch both extended index fingers to each ear, palms angled toward each other. Then move the hands forward while changing into *S hands,* and shake both *S hands* from side to side with a repeated movement in front of each shoulder, palms facing forward.

thunder[2] *n., v.* (alternate sign) Same sign used for: **quake.**

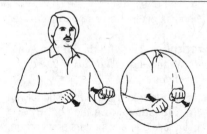

■ [Represents the vibration of a loud sound] Beginning with both *S hands* in front of each side of the body, palms facing down, move the hands forward and back with an alternating double movement.

thunder[3] *n.* (alternate sign)

■ [**hear** + a movement that represents the vibration of a loud sound. Touch the extended right index finger to the right ear, palm facing left. Then shake both *S hands* from side to side with a repeated movement in front of each shoulder, palms facing forward.

thunderbolt[1] *n.* A flash of lightning and the crash of thunder that follows it: *The sudden thunderbolt terrified us.* Same sign used for: **thunderclap.**

■ [Shows the movement of lightening + **thunder**[1,2]] Beginning with the extended right index finger, palm facing forward and finger pointing up, by the right side of the head, move the right hand downward near the right side of the body with a large jagged movement. Next touch the extended index fingers to the ears, palms angled toward each other. Then shake both *S hands* from side to side with a repeated movement in front of each shoulder, palms facing forward.

thunderbolt[2] *n.* See signs for LIGHTNING[1,2].

thunderstorm[1] *n.* A storm with thunder and lightning: *waited through the thunderstorm.*

■ [Shows lightning occurring during a thunderstorm] Move both extended index fingers from pointing up near each side of the head, palms facing forward, downward with jagged movements in front of each side of the chest, ending with the fingers pointing forward and palms facing down.

thunderstorm[2] *n.* (alternate sign)

- [Initialized sign showing the movement of lightning] Move both *T hands,* palms facing forward near each side of the head, downward with jagged movements in front of each side of the chest, ending with the fingers pointing forward and palms facing down.

Thursday[1] *n.* The fifth day of the week, after Wednesday: *Thursday is the day before Friday.*

- [Initialized sign using **h** to distinguish it from **Tuesday**] Move the right *H hand,* palm facing in and fingers pointing up, in a circle in front of the right shoulder.

Thursday[2] *n.* (alternate sign)

- With the extended right index finger pointing up in front of the right side of the body, palm facing up, and the bent right thumb at the base of the index finger, palm facing up, flick the middle finger up and down with a double movement.

Thursday[3] *n.* (alternate sign)

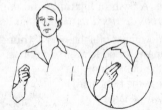

- [Abbreviation **t-h**] Beginning with the right *T hand* in front of the right shoulder, palm facing left, flick the index and middle fingers forward, forming an *H hand.*

Thy *adj.* Belonging to or associated with *thee* or *you* (traditionally used when addressing or referring to God, as in prayer): *Hallowed be Thy name.*

- [Gestures toward the traditional location of God in heaven] Push the right *open hand,* palm facing forward, forward and upward near the right side of the head.

ticket *n.* A piece of paper or cardboard that officially entitles the holder to a privilege, service, etc.: *to buy two tickets for the train to Washington.* Same sign used for: **citation.**

- [Represents punching a ticket to show it has been used] Insert the bent fingers of the right *V hand,* palm facing down, with a repeated movement around the little-finger side of the left *open hand* held in front of the chest, palm facing in and fingers pointing up.

tidy *adj.* See sign for CLEAN.

tie[1] *v.* **1.** To fasten with a cord or the like: *to tie one's shoelaces.* **2.** To form by looping and lacing together ends or pieces of cord or the like: *to tie a knot or a bow.* Same sign used for: **knot.**

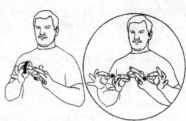

- [Mime tying a bow] Beginning with the fingers of both *F hands* together in front of the chest, move the fingers around each other and then apart, miming tying a bow.

tie[2] *v.* (alternate sign) Same sign used for: **knot.**

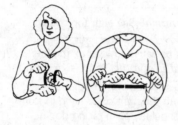

- [Mime tying a bow] Beginning with both *modified X hands* together in front of the chest, move the fingers around each other and then apart, miming tying a bow.

tie[3] *n.* See signs for EQUAL, NECKTIE, RELATIONSHIP.

tie up *v. phrase.* See sign for BIND.

tiger *n.* A large, fierce cat of jungles and forests with tawny gold and black stripes: *Tigers are native to Asia.*

- [Indicates a tiger's whiskers] Beginning with the fingertips of both *curved 5 hands* near each side of the face, palms facing in, move the hands outward to each side with a double movement while bending the fingers toward the palms each time.

tight[1] *adj.* **1.** Firmly fixed into place: *a tight door.* —*adv.* **2.** In a secure manner: *The screw held tight no matter how hard he tried to turn it.*

- [Shows shaking something that is tight] With the little-finger side of the right *S hand,* palm facing left, on the index-finger side of the left *S hand,* palm facing right, shake the hands.

tight[2] *adj., adv.* (alternate sign) Same sign used for: **tense.**

- [Shows shaking something that is tight] Shake both *S hands,* palms facing in, in front of each side of the chest.

tight

tight³ *adj.* See sign for STINGY.

tightrope *n.* A tightly stretched horizontal rope on which acrobats perform feats of balance: *to walk a tightrope.*

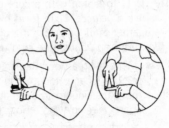

- ■ [Represents a person's legs walking on a tightrope] With an alternating movement, move the extended index finger and middle finger of the right hand, palm facing in and fingers pointing down, from the base to the tip of the extended left index finger held in front of the body, palm facing down.

tightwad *n. Informal.* See sign for STINGY.

tilt¹ *v.* **1.** To lean or cause to lean or incline: *a tilting desk; to tilt the board.* —*n.* **2.** A slant: *the board is at a tilt.* Same sign used for: **unbalanced.**

- ■ [Demonstrates something off balance] Beginning with the right *open hand* in front of the right shoulder, palm facing down, and the left *open hand* in front of the left side of the body, palm facing down, move the right hand upward and the left hand downward while bending the body to the left side.

tilt² *n.* An act of tilting a pinball machine in an attempt to control the direction of the balls: *The pinball machine showed a tilt and the game stopped.*

- ■ [**pinball machine** + a gesture showing that the machine is off-balance] Move the bent middle fingers of both *5 hands,* palms facing each other, toward each other with a short double movement near each side of the body. Then, beginning with the right *curved 5 hand* in front of the right shoulder and the left *curved 5 hand* in front of the left side of the chest, palms facing each other, twist the hands quickly, reversing positions.

time¹ *n.* A period during which something occurs or a period between given events: *at that time in history.* Same sign used for: **epoch, era, period.**

- ■ [Initialized sign showing the movement of the minute hand around a clock face] Move the right *T hand,* palm facing left, in a circle around the left *open hand* held in front of the chest, palm facing right, ending with the right hand on the left heel.

time[2] *n.* A specific point in time as measured, usually in hours and minutes, in a given time zone of the earth: *What time is it?*

- [Indicates the location of a person's watch] Tap the bent index finger of the right *X hand,* palm facing down, with a double movement on the wrist of the left *open hand* held in front of the chest, palm facing down.

time-out *n.* A brief suspension of activity: *The naughty child went to his room for a time-out.*

- [This is the signal used in sport to indicate a time-out] With a double movement, tap the palm of the right *open hand* held in front of the chest, palm facing down, downward on the fingertips of the left *open hand,* palm facing right.

timepiece *n.* See signs for WATCH[1,2].

timid *adj.* See sign for AFRAID.

tint *n., v.* See signs for DIM[1,2].

tiny[1] *adj.* Very small: *a tiny flower.* Same sign used for: **bit, little bit, puny, scant, teeny.**

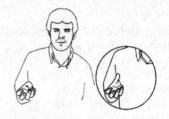

- Beginning with the right *6 hand* in front of the right side of the chest, palm facing up, flick the thumb off the little finger with a quick movement.

tiny[2] *adj.* (alternate sign) Same sign used for: **bit, little bit, puny, scant, teeny.**

- [Natural gesture used to indicate a little bit] Beginning with the right *modified X hand,* palm facing back, in front of the right side of the chest, flick the thumb upward.

tiny[3] *adj.* See sign for SMALL[2].

tip[1] *n.* **1.** A piece of secret information: *Give me a tip on who will win the race.* **2.** A useful hint: *tips on gourmet cooking.*

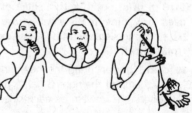

- [**secret** + **inform**[1]] Tap the thumb of the right *A hand,* palm facing left, against the mouth with a double movement. Then, beginning with the fingers of the right *flattened O hand* near the forehead and the left *flattened O hand* in front of the chest, palms facing in, move the hands downward while opening into *5 hands*, palms facing up.

---

tip[2] *n.* A small token of money given for services rendered: *to leave a tip for the waitress.*

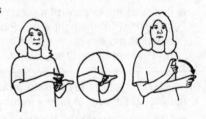

- ■ [**money** + **give**[1]] Pat the back of the right *flattened O hand,* palm facing up, with a double movement on the palm of the left *open hand* held in front of the chest. Then move the right *X hand,* palm facing left, in a forward arc.

---

tip[3] *n.* See signs for POINT[1,2].

---

tiptoe[1] *v.* **1.** To walk quietly on one's toes: *tiptoe through the room.* —*n.* **2.** The tips of one's toes: *walk on tiptoe.*

- ■ [A movement that represents a person moving on tiptoes] Beginning with both extended index fingers pointing down in front of the body, palms facing in and right hand higher than the left hand, move the hands forward in alternating double arcs.

---

tiptoe[2] *v., n.* (alternate sign)

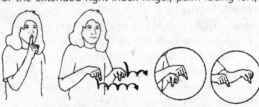

- ■ [**quiet**[2] + **tiptoe**[1]] Bring the side of the extended right index finger, palm facing left, to the mouth. Then, beginning with both extended index fingers pointing down in front of the body, palms facing in and fingers pointing down, move the hands forward in a series of alternating arcs.

---

tired *adj.* Weary; fatigued: *I am tired at the end of the day.* Same sign used for: **exhausted, fatigue, weary.**

- ■ [The hands show that energy has dropped in the body] Beginning with the fingertips of both *bent hands* on each side of the chest, palms facing outward in opposite directions, roll the hands downward on the fingertips, ending with the little-finger sides of both hands touching the chest.

---

tissue[1] *n.* A disposable, thin sheet of paper used for wiping: *to blow one's nose in a tissue.* Same sign used for: **Kleenex** (*trademark*).

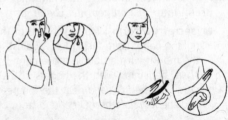

- ■ [**cold** + **paper**] Bring the index finger and thumb of the right *G hand,* palm facing in, downward on each side of the nose with a double movement, pinching the fingers together each time. Then brush the heel of the right *open hand,* palm facing down and fingers pointing left, with a double movement on the heel of the left *open hand* held in front of the body, palm facing up and fingers pointing right.

tissue[2] *n.* (alternate sign)

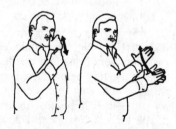

■ [**handkerchief** + **paper**] Squeeze the nose with the thumb and bent index finger of the right *A hand* while pulling the hand slightly forward with a double movement. Then brush the heel of the right *open hand,* palm facing down, on the heel of the left *open hand,* palm facing up in front of the body, with a double movement.

tissue[3] *n.* See sign for HANDKERCHIEF.

tithe *n.* **1.** A contribution equaling one-tenth of one's income, paid as support to the church: *to give a tithe.* —*v.* **2.** To pledge and give a tithe of or from: *to tithe $2,000; to tithe one's income.* Same sign used for: **one-tenth.**

■ [**one** + **ten** formed above each other like a fraction] Beginning with the extended finger of the right *1 hand* held up in front of the right shoulder, palm facing in, bring the hand downward while changing into a *10 hand.*

title[1] *n.* The distinguishing name of something, as a creative work: *the title of the book.* Same sign used for: **entitle, quotes, so-called, subject, theme, topic.**

■ [Represents quotation marks around a title] Beginning with both *bent V hands* near each side of the head, palms facing forward, twist the hands while bending the fingers down, ending with the palms facing back.

title[2] *n.* See sign for QUOTATION[1].

to *prep.* (Used to express direction toward a destination approached or reached): *on the way to the store; to go to church.*

■ [Shows a movement to another person] Move the extended right index finger, palm facing down and finger pointing forward, a short distance forward to meet the extended left index finger held up in front of the chest, palm facing in.

toast[1] *n.* **1.** Sliced bread browned by exposure to dry heat: *to put jelly on the toast.* —*v.* **2.** To expose to dry heat: *toasted the rolls.*

toast

■ [Represents the prongs of the toaster holding the bread in place] Touch the fingertips of the right *bent V hand*, palm facing left, first on the palm and then on the back of the left *open hand* held in front of the chest, palm facing right and fingers pointing up.

toast² *n.* **1.** A welcome, tribute, etc., proposed in someone's honor to accompany a congratulatory drink and traditionally marked by the participants clicking their glasses together before drinking: *to propose a toast to the new director.* **2.** An act or instance of having such a congratulatory drink: *to drink a toast to the future of the project.* —*v.* **3.** To propose or drink such a toast in honor of: *We toast the bride and groom.*

■ [Represents clicking two glasses together in a toast] Beginning with both *C hands* in front of each side of the chest, palms facing in, bring the hands upward and toward each other in a large arc, ending with the knuckles of both hands touching in front of the face, palms facing in.

toast³ *v., n.* (alternate sign)

■ [Represents clicking two glasses together in a toast] Beginning with both *Y hands* in front of each side of the chest, palms facing in, bring the hands upward toward each other in large arcs, ending with the little fingers of both hands near each other.

tobacco *n.* Leaves of certain plants of the nightshade family prepared for recreational chewing: *to chew tobacco.* Same sign used for: **chewing tobacco.**

■ [Shows tobacco in the cheek] Rotate the fingertips of the right *curved hand*, palm facing forward, against the right side of the chin while turning the palm down.

toboggan *n.* **1.** A long, narrow, flat-bottomed sled: *to ride a toboggan down the snow-covered hill.* —*v.* **2.** To slide downhill on such a sled: *to toboggan downhill.*

■ [Shows the shape of a toboggan and its movement down a hill] Move the right *curved hand* from near the right side of the head, palm facing back, forward to rest the right wrist in the palm of the left *curved hand*, palm facing up. Then slide the right arm forward, ending with the left hand near the right elbow.

today¹ *n.* **1.** This day: *Today is Monday.* **2.** This present age: *today's powerful computers.* —*adv.* **3.** During or on this day: *What are you doing today?*

■ [**now**[1,2] + **day**] Bring both *Y hands,* palms facing up, downward a short distance in front of each side of the body. Then, beginning with the elbow of the bent right arm resting on the back of the left hand held across the body, palm facing down, bring the extended right index finger from pointing up in front of the right shoulder, palm facing left, downward toward the left elbow.

today[2] *n., adv.* (alternate sign used also to express the sense 'at the present time; these days')

■ [Sign similar to **now**[2] except with a double movement] Bring both *Y hands,* palms facing up, in front of each side of the body, downward with a short double movement.

today[3] *n., adv.* (alternate sign)

■ [Sign similar to **now**[3] except with a double movement] Bring both *bent hands,* palms facing up, downward in front of each side of the body with a short double movement.

toe *n.* Any of the articulated digits of the foot: *It hurt when I stubbed my toe on the door.*

■ [Initialized sign] Place the index-finger side of the right *T hand,* palm facing forward, near the fingertips of the left *open hand* held in front of the body, palm facing down and fingers pointing right.

together *adv.* With each other: *to go shopping together.*

■ [Sign similar to **with** except with a circular movement indicating duration] With the palm sides of both *A hands* together in front of the body, move the hands in a flat circle.

toggle *v.* To switch from one setting to another when there are only two possible settings: *toggle the Caps lock key on.* Related form: **toggle switch** *n.* Same sign used for: **DIP switch, flip-flop.**

■ [Action of switching back and forth] With the palm sides of both *L hands* together in front of the chest, palms facing each other, flip the hands over, exchanging places.

toil

---

toil *v.* See signs for SWEAT[1], WORKAHOLIC.

toilet *n.* **1.** Same sign used for: **bathroom, lavatory, rest room, washroom.** A bathroom or washroom: *looking for the toilets at the restaurant.* **2.** A bathroom or washroom fixture with a bowl and a device for flushing with water, used for urination and defecation: *Remember to flush the toilet and close the lid.*

- [Initialized sign] Move the right *T hand*, palm facing forward, from side to side in front of the right shoulder with a repeated shaking movement.

---

toilet paper *n.* Lightweight, absorbent paper used for personal cleansing after urination or defecation and usually packaged in a roll of perforated square sheets: *Don't forget to take toilet paper on the camping trip.*

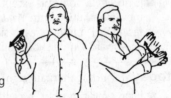

- [**toilet** + **paper**] Move the right *T hand*, palm facing forward, from side to side in front of the right shoulder with a repeated shaking movement. Then brush the heel of the right *open hand*, palm facing down, on the heel of the left *open hand*, palm facing up in front of the body, with a double movement.

---

tolerate[1] *v.* To endure or permit: *The teacher tolerated the noisy classroom.* Related forms: **tolerance** *n.*, **tolerant** *adj.*

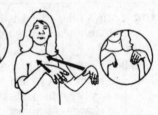

- [An exaggerated form of **suffer**[1] + **accept**] Beginning with the thumb of the right *A hand* touching the chin, palm facing left, bring the hand down toward the chin with a wiggly movement. Then, beginning with both *5 hands* in front of the body, palms facing down and fingers pointing forward, bring both hands back toward the chest while pulling the fingertips and thumbs together, forming *flattened O hands.*

---

tolerate[2] *v.* (alternate sign) Related form: **tolerant** *adj.*

- [The sign for **accept** is repeated to indicate tolerance] Beginning with both *flattened C hands* in front of the chest, fingers pointing down, bring both hands back toward the chest while closing the fingertips and thumb of each hand together.

---

tolerate[3] *v.* See signs for CONTROL[1], PATIENT[1]. Related form: **tolerant** *adj.*

---

tomato *n.* A large juicy berry, usually red, eaten raw or cooked as a vegetable: *Put a tomato in the salad.*

- [**red**[1] + **slice**[1]] Bring the extended right index finger from the lips, palm facing in, downward with a deliberate movement across the thumb-side of the left *O hand* held in front of the chest, palm facing down, ending with the right palm facing down in front of the body.

---

tomb *n.* See sign for TEMPLE.

tomorrow *n.* **1.** The day after today: *They predict snow for tomorrow.* **2.** A future period: *Tomorrow will be the age of electronics.* —*adv.* **3.** On or during the day after today: *The new movie opens tomorrow.* **4.** At a future time: *Will there be passenger spaceflight tomorrow?*

■ [The sign moves forward into the future] Move the palm side of the right *10 hand*, palm facing left, from the right side of the chin forward while twisting the wrist forward.

tongs *pl. n.* A tool with two attached movable arms, used for grabbing and picking up: *to pick up spaghetti with tongs.*

■ [Shows the action of tongs + demonstrates the action of opening and closing tongs] With the right extended index finger above the left extended index finger in front of the body, palms facing each other, move the fingers up and down toward each other and then apart. Then, with the right *S hand* above the left *S hand*, palms facing each other in front of the body, move the hands together and apart with a double movement.

tongue[1] *n.* A movable muscle growing out of the floor of the mouth, an organ of speech and taste: *to taste the lollipop with your tongue.*

■ [Location of the tongue] Touch the extended right index finger to the tongue.

tongue[2] *n.* See sign for LANGUAGE.

tonight[1] *n.* **1.** This night or this coming night: *Tonight is unusually cold.* —*adv.* **2.** During this night or this coming night: *Will there be a full moon tonight?*

■ [**now**[1,2] + **night**] Bring both *Y hands*, palms facing up, downward in front of each side of the body. Then tap the heel of the right *bent hand*, palm facing down, with a double movement on the back of the left *open hand* held across the chest, palm facing down.

tonight[2] *n.* See sign for NIGHT.

tonsillectomy *n.* An operation to remove one or both tonsils: *I had a tonsillectomy when I was a child.*

tonsils

- [Represents pulling the tonsils out] Beginning with the fingers of the right *V hand* touching the upper neck, palm facing down, bring the hand forward and upward while bending the fingers.

tonsils *pl. n.* The mass of tissue on each side of the throat at the back of the mouth: *She had her tonsils removed when she was five.*

- [Location of tonsils] Place the thumb sides of both *F hands*, palms facing each other and fingers pointing up, near each other on the upper neck.

too *adv.* See signs for AS[1,2].

too much *adj.* See signs for EXCESS, OVER[1].

tooth *n.* One of the hard bodies attached in a row to each jaw, used for chewing: *to see the dentist about a broken tooth.*

- [Location of a tooth] Touch a front tooth with the extended right index finger, palm facing down.

toothache *n.* Pain in or around a tooth: *a toothache in a molar.*

- [**pain** formed near the location] With both extended index fingers pointing toward each other in front of the mouth, palms facing down, jab the fingers toward each other with a short double movement.

toothbrush *n.* A small brush with a long handle for cleaning the teeth: *The dentist recommends brushing with a softer toothbrush.*

- [Mime the action of brushing one's teeth] Move the extended right index finger, palm facing down and finger pointing left, back and forth with a repeated movement in front of the front teeth.

toothless *adj.* Without teeth: *a toothless man.*

- [**tooth** + **blank**[1] formed in front of the teeth to indicate that the teeth are gone] Touch a front tooth with the extended right index finger, palm facing down. Bring the bent middle finger of the right *5 hand*, palm facing in, from left to right in front of the open mouth.

toothpaste *n.* A pastelike substance used to clean teeth: *Put toothpaste on your toothbrush.*

■ [Mime squeezing out toothpaste on the bristles of a toothbrush] Push the thumb of the right *10 hand,* palm facing in, downward on the base of the extended left index finger held in front of the body, palm facing in and finger pointing right. Then slide the right thumb along the length of the left extended index finger.

toothpick[1] *n.* A pointed piece of wood used for removing particles of food from between the teeth: *Try to use your toothpick discreetly.*

■ [Mime using a toothpick] Wiggle the right *modified X hand,* palm facing in, up and down with a small movement in front of the mouth.

toothpick[2] *n.* (alternate sign)

■ [Represents picking food from the teeth] Beginning with the fingertip of the extended right index finger pointing toward the mouth, palm facing in, move the hand forward in a small arc with a double movement.

top[1] *n.* **1.** The highest point: *the top of the hill.* **2.** The upper surface: *the top of the table.* —*adj.* **3.** Located at or forming the top: *the top shelf.* Same sign used for: **become successful, peak, top performer.**

■ [The location on the top of something] Bring the palm of the right *open hand,* palm facing down and fingers pointing left, downward on the fingertips of the left *open hand* held in front of the chest, palm facing right and fingers pointing up.

top[2] *n.* See signs for LID[1,2], SHIRT[1,2].

top-down *adj.* Of or pertaining to a method of software programming that starts with a general statement about the program's purpose from which appropriate subfunctions are derived, each of which is expressed through an independently coded program module: *Structured programming languages, like C++, lend themselves well to top-down programming.*

■ [Points to the top of something and then points down] Bring the extended right index finger, palm facing forward and finger pointing up, upward to touch the palm of the left *open hand* held in front of the chest, palm facing down and fingers pointing right. Then turn the right hand to point the index finger down and move the hand down again.

topic *n.* See signs for QUOTATION[1], TITLE.

top performer *Business.* See sign for TOP[1].

topple[1] *v.* To fall down, as from weakness or top-heaviness: *The chimney suddenly toppled.*

- ■ [Shows the movement of something toppling] With the side of the extended left index finger, palm facing right, against the palm of the right *open hand* held in front of the head, palm facing forward and fingers pointing up, move both hands downward in front of the body by turning the wrists, ending with the right palm facing down and the left palm facing right.

topple[2] *v.* (alternate sign)

- ■ [Shows the movement of something toppling] Beginning with the elbow of the right *A hand* on the fingers of the left *open hand* held across the body, palm facing down, move the right *A hand* from near the head, palm facing left, downward to land on the left arm near the elbow.

Torah[1] *n.* The scrolls on which the Hebrew Scriptures, the Five Books of Moses, are written: *to read the Torah in the synagogue.*

- ■ [Represents unrolling the Torah] Beginning with both *S hands* in front of the body, palms facing each other, twist the wrists to move the palms up while moving the hands outward to in front of each side of the body.

Torah[2] *n.* (alternate sign)

- ■ [Initialized sign representing unrolling the Torah] Beginning with both *T hands* in front of the body, palms facing down, twist the wrists to turn the palms up while moving the hands outward toward each side of the body.

torn *v.* Past participle of TEAR. See signs for TEAR[1,2].

tornado[1] *n.* A violent, destructive windstorm characterized by a large funnel-shaped cloud causing extreme damage as it moves along the ground: *You can tell from the utter destruction of the buildings that a tornado hit the town.*

- ■ [Initialized sign showing the circular winds during a tornado] Beginning with the right *T hand*, palm facing down, over the left *T hand*, palm facing up in front of the chest, move the hands in large alternating repeated circles.

tornado[2] *n.* (alternate sign)

■ [Shows the circular winds occurring during a tornado] Beginning with the right *B hand* in front of the chest, palm facing in and fingers pointing down, and the left *B hand* lower than the right hand, palm facing in and fingers pointing up, move the hands in large alternating repeated circles.

tornado[3] *n.* (alternate sign)

■ [Shows the circular winds occurring during a tornado] Beginning with the thumbs of both *modified C hands* touching in front of the chest, right hand above the left hand, right palm facing forward and left palm facing in, bend the index fingers up and down with a repeated movement as the hands move to the left in an arc in front of the chest.

tornado[4] *n.* (alternate sign)

■ [Shows the circular winds occurring during a tornado] Beginning with the extended right index finger pointing down in front of the right side of the chest, palm facing in, and the extended left index finger pointing up in front of the chest, palm facing in, move the hands in small alternating circles around each other as the hands move in an arc to the left in front of the chest.

tornado[5] *n.* (alternate sign)

■ [Shows the circular winds occurring during a tornado] Move the extended right index finger, palm facing in and finger pointing down, in a repeated circle over the left *open hand* held in front of the chest, palm facing up.

torso *n.* See sign for THORAX.

tortoise *n.* See sign for TURTLE.

torture *n.* **1.** The act of inflicting severe pain, as to coerce someone into revealing information: *The spy suffered extreme torture before confessing.* **2.** Agony or the cause of agony: *These tight shoes are pure torture.* —*v.* **3.** To subject to torture: *tortured the prisoner.* Same sign used for: **abuse, haze, maltreatment, mutilate, persecute, persecution, probation, prosecute, prosecution, ridicule.**

■ Shove the little-finger side of the right *X hand,* palm facing left, forward across the index-finger side of the left *X hand,* palm facing right, while moving the left hand upward to repeat the movement with the left hand over the right hand.

toss *v.* See signs for THROW[1,2].

total[1] *adj.* See sign for ALL THE TIME[2].

total[2] *v.* See sign for ADD[1].

total[3] *n.* See sign for ALL[1].

Total Communication *n.* A philosophy in which all forms of communication—including sign language, speech, and writing—are used with deaf and hard-of-hearing people: *The school for deaf students uses Total Communication in the classroom.*

- [Initialized sign using **t-c** similar to sign for **communication**] Move the right *T hand* and left *C hand*, palms facing each other, forward and back from the chin with an alternating movement.

touch[1] *v.* **1.** To cause a part of the body, as the hand or finger, or something held with or on a part of the body, to come in contact with: *to touch the hot pan; to touch the step with your shoe.* —*n.* **2.** The sense by which one perceives the texture, temperature, and other qualities of things around one by feeling, as with the hand: *I felt your touch on my shoulder.*

- [Demonstrates touching something with the middle finger, used frequently to indicate feelings] Bring the bent middle finger of the right hand, palm facing down, downward to touch the back of the left *open hand* held in front of the body, palm facing down.

touch[2] *v.* To affect with some feeling, as tenderness: *Her story touched my heart.*

- [Represents touching one's heart with the finger used frequently to indicate feelings] Bring the bent middle finger of the right *5 hand*, palm facing in, toward the body to touch on the left side of the chest.

touchdown *n.* An act or instance of scoring six points in football: *The running back made a touchdown.*

- [Natural gesture used by referees to indicate a touchdown] Beginning with both *B hands* in front of the body, palms facing each other and fingers pointing forward, bring both hands upward in simultaneous arcs to in front of each side of the head, palms facing each other and fingers pointing up.

touch football *n.* A kind of football in which the act of tackling is replaced by touching to stop the ball carrier on the opposing team: *Touch football was played on the White House lawn.*

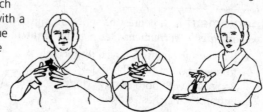

■ [**football** + **touch**[1]] Beginning with both *5 hands* in front of the chest, palms facing in and fingers pointing toward each other, bring the hands together with a double movement, interlocking the fingers each time. Then touch the bent middle finger of the right hand, palm facing down, against the back of the left *open hand* held across the body.

touching *adj.* Causing tender feelings; moving; affecting: *a touching movie.* Related forms: **touched** *adj.*, **touchy** *adj.*

■ [**touch**[1] + a gesture used for the suffix **-ing**] Bring the bent middle finger of the right *5 hand*, palm facing down, from in front of the right shoulder downward to land on the back of the left *open hand* held in front of the chest, palm facing down. Then move the right hand outward to the right while changing into an *I hand*, palm facing forward.

tough[1] *adj.* Difficult to do or deal with: *a tough problem.*

■ Slide the little-finger side of the right *bent V hand*, palm facing in, in an arc to the right off the back of the left *S hand* held in front of the body, palm facing down.

tough[2] *adj. Slang.* Difficult to bear (used sarcastically to indicate that the speaker thinks the listener will have to continue to endure whatever circumstances are involved): *So they've moved you to a smaller office. That's tough!* Same sign used for: **so what!**

■ Beginning with the knuckles of the right *bent hand* under the chin, palm facing in, move the hand forward in an arc, ending with the palm facing up in front of the chest.

tough[3] *adj.* See sign for GANG[1].

tough[4] *adj.* See sign for STURDY[1].

tour[1] *n.* **1.** A trip to visit a number of places: *We will take a tour of Europe.* **2.** A short guided visit: *The foreman gave us a tour of the plant.* —*v.* **3.** To travel from place to place: *to tour the eastern Asia.* **4.** To go through a place: *We toured the cookie factory.* **5.** To give performances at different locations: *The choir toured the East coast.* Same sign used for: **adventure, field trip, travel.**

■ Move the right *bent V hand* from in front of the right side of the chest, palm facing down, upward and forward with a wavy movement.

tour[2] *n.* See signs for RUN AROUND[1], TRIP[2].

---

tournament *n.* A contest or series of contests between many competitors in some sport: *a golf tournament.* See sign for: **match.**

- [Represents opposing teams responding to the action of the other side] Beginning with both *bent V hands* in front of the chest, right hand higher than the left hand and both palms facing forward, move the hands up and down in front of each side of the chest with an alternating double movement.

---

tow *v.* See signs for DRAG, HAUL[1].

---

toward *prep.* In the direction of: *Drive toward town.*

- [Demonstrates a movement toward something] Beginning with the extended right index finger in front of the right shoulder, palm facing left, move the hand in an arc to the left, ending with the right extended index finger touching the left extended index finger pointing up in front of the left side of the body, palm facing right.

---

towel *n.* **1.** A piece of absorbent cloth or paper used for drying something wet: *to dry the dishes with a towel.* —*v.* **2.** To dry with a towel: *to towel the baby after its bath.*

- [Mime drying one's back with a towel] Beginning with the right *S hand* above the right shoulder, palm facing forward, and the left *S hand* near the left hip, palm facing back, move the hand simultaneously upward and downward at an angle with a repeated movement.

---

tower *n.* A high structure: *You can see for miles from the top of the Eiffel Tower in Paris.* Same sign used for: **Paris.**

- [The shape of the Eiffel Tower] Beginning with both *V hands* in front of each side of the chest, fingers angled toward each other, move the hands upward toward each other, ending with the extended fingers touching in front of the head.

---

town *n.* A populated area, usually smaller than a city, with recognized boundaries and a local government: *always wanted to live in a small town.* Same sign used for: **community, village.**

- [Represents the rooftops in a town] Tap the fingertips of both *open hands* together in front of the chest with a double movement, palms facing each other at an angle.

---

toy *n.* Something made to be played with: *to buy a toy for my child.*

■ [Initialized sign similar to sign for **play**[1]] Beginning with both *T hands* in front of each side of the chest, palms facing in, twist the hands forward with a repeated movement.

trace *v.* To copy by following a previous outline: *to trace the picture.*

■ [Initialized sign similar to sign for **write**[1]] Slide the right *T hand,* palm facing left, from the heel to the fingers of the left *open hand* held in front of the body, palm angled right.

track[1] *n.* A pair of parallel lines of metal rails for railroad cars to run on: *The train is running on the southbound track.* Same sign used for: **rail.**

■ [**train**[1] + the shape of railroad tracks] Rub the fingers of the right *H hand* back and forth with a repeated movement on the fingers of the left *H hand* held in front of the body, both palms facing down. Then move both *G hands,* palms facing down, from each side of the body forward in a parallel movement.

track[2] *n.* A path on the surface of a recording medium, as a disk or tape, along which electronic data can be recorded: *an eight-track tape.*

■ [Initialized sign similar to sign for **record**[1]] Move the right *T hand,* palm facing down, in a repeated flat circle over the left *open hand* held in front of the body, palm facing up.

track[3] *n.* See sign for RACE[2].

track down *v. phrase.* See sign for FOLLOW.

traction *n.* See sign for WHEEL.

trade[1] *v.* To exchange: *traded books with each other.* Same sign used for: **budget, exchange, instead, replace, substitute, substitution, swap, switch.**

■ [Demonstrates moving something into another thing's place] With both *modified X hands* in front of the body, right hand forward of the left hand and palms facing each other, move the right hand

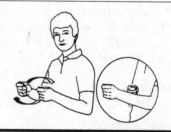

back toward the body in an upward arc while moving the left hand forward in a downward arc.

---

trade² *v.* (alternate sign) Same sign used for: **budget, exchange, replace, substitute, substitution, swap, switch.**

■ [Demonstrates moving something into another thing's place] Beginning with both *F hands* in front of the body, palms facing each other and right hand somewhat forward of the left hand, move the right hand back toward the body in an upward arc while moving the left hand forward in a downward arc.

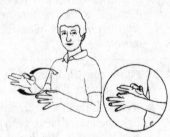

trade³ *v.* (alternate sign) Same sign used for: **budget, exchange, replace, substitute, substitution, swap, switch.**

■ [Demonstrates moving something into another thing's place] Beginning with both *flattened O hands* in front of the chest, palms facing in and right hand closer to the chest than the left hand, move the hands in arcs around each other, reversing positions.

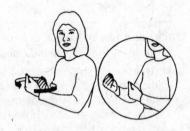

---

trade in¹ *v. phrase.* To give (a used article) as partial payment toward a purchase: *I wish I could trade in my old computer.* Related form: **trade-in** *n.*

■ [Demonstrates two things being exchanged with each other] Beginning with both *L hands* in front of the chest, right hand closer to the chest than the left hand and both palms facing in, move the right hand forward in an arc under the left hand while the left hand moves back in an arc to exchange places.

trade in² *v. phrase.* To exchange a used car as partial payment on a new car: *to trade in my old car for the newest model.* Related form: **trade-in** *n.*

■ [Demonstrates two cars being exchanged with each other] Beginning with both *3 hands* in front of the chest, right hand closer to the chest than the left hand and both palms facing in, move the right hand forward in an arc under left hand while the left hand moves back in an arc to exchange places.

---

trade places *v.* To exchange locations: *The two girls traded places in the classroom.* Same sign used for: **change places, swap places, switch places.**

■ [Directional sign representing a person trading places with the referent toward whom the sign is formed] Beginning with the right *V hand* near the right side of the waist, palm facing down and fingers pointing forward, flip the hand over, ending with the palm facing up.

tradition[1] *n.* **1.** The handing down of beliefs and customs from generation to generation, especially by word of mouth: *to preserve tradition and welcome innovation.* **2.** Something so handed down: *Birthday dinners at a restaurant are a tradition in our family.* Related form: **traditional** *adj.*

■ [Initialized sign similar to sign for **habit**] With the heel of the right *T hand,* palm facing forward, on the back of the left *S hand,* palm facing down, move both hands downward in front of the chest.

tradition[2] *n.* (alternate sign) Related form: **traditional** *adj.*

■ [Initialized sign similar to sign for **generation**] Beginning with both *T hands* in front of the right shoulder, palms facing in opposite directions and right hand above the left hand, roll the hands over each other with an alternating movement while moving the hands forward.

traffic *n.* The movement of vehicles and people coming and going along a route: *heavy traffic on Main Street during the rush hour.*

■ [Represents many vehicles moving quickly past each other in both directions] With both *5 hands* in front of the chest, palms facing each other and fingers pointing up, move the right hand forward and the left hand back with a repeated alternating movement, brushing palms as they pass each time.

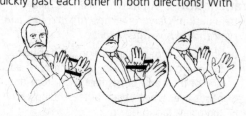

traffic light *n.* See sign for STOPLIGHT[1].

tragedy *n.* A dreadful or catastrophic event, especially one in which one or more people die: *The accident was a tragedy.* Related form: **tragic** *adj.*

■ [Initialized sign similar to sign for **tears**[2]] Beginning with both *T hands* near each cheek, palms facing each other, bring the hands downward simultaneously.

tragic *adj.* See sign for SAD.

trail[1] *v.* See sign for FOLLOW.

trail[2] *n.* See sign for ROAD[1].

trailer *n.* See sign for TRUCK.

train[1] *n.* A connected line of railroad cars: *to ride the train across the country.* Same sign used for: **go by train, railroad, travel by train.**

■ [Represents the crossties on a railroad track] Rub the fingers of the right *H hand* back and forth with a repeated movement on the fingers of the left *H hand* held in front of the body, both palms facing down.

train[2] *v.* To teach or guide; help form the disciplined habits of: *to train the new employees.*

■ [Initialized sign similar to sign for **practice**] Slide the heel of the right *T hand,* palm facing forward, back and forth with a double movement along the index-finger side of the left *B hand* held in front of the chest, palm facing down.

training[1] *n.* Initialized sign similar to sign for TRAIN[2] except made with a larger movement.

training[2] *n.* See sign for PRACTICE.

tranquil *adj.* See signs for QUIET[1,2].

transaction *n.* A piece of business or a negotiation: *Opening a checking account is a typical banking transaction.*

■ [Initialized sign similar to sign for **happen**] Beginning with both *T hands* in front of each side of the body, palms facing up, turn the hands over toward each other, ending with the palms facing down.

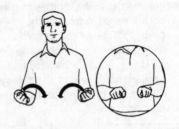

transfer[1] *v.* **1.** To remove from one place, person, or position to another: *to transfer the property to the new owner.* —*n.* **2.** A person who has transferred, as from one school to another: *She is a transfer from the junior college.*

■ [Represents a person's legs moving to another place] Swing the right *bent V hand* from in front of the chest, palm facing in, to the right in an arc, ending with the palm facing down.

transfer[2] *v., n.* (alternate sign)

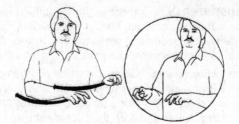

- [Represents a person's legs moving to another place] Beginning with both *bent V hands* in front of the left side of the body, palms facing down, swing the hands to the right.

---

transform *v.* See sign for TRANSLATE.

---

transient *adj.* Not permanent; lasting for a short time; fleeting: *a transient laborer.*

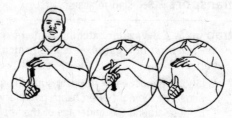

- [**show up** + **disappear**[1]] Insert the extended right index finger, palm facing forward and finger pointing up, upward between the middle finger and ring finger of the left hand held across the chest, palm facing down and fingers pointing right. Then pull the right hand down again.

---

translate *v.* To convert (text or speech) from one language to another: *to translate the French poems into Spanish.* Related form: **translation** *n.* Same sign used for: **transform.**

- [Initialized sign similar to sign for **change**[1]] Beginning with the palms of both *I hands* together in front of the chest, right hand over the left hand, twist the wrists to exchange positions.

---

transmitter *n.* An electronic device that generates and amplifies a carrier wave, modulates it with a signal derived from speech or other sources, and radiates the resulting signal from an antenna: *The transmitter is in the antenna tower outside of town.*

- [**chip** + insert chip + **flow**[2]] Beginning with the fingers of both *G hands* touching in front of the chest, palms facing each other, bring the hands apart a short distance and pinch each thumb and index finger together. Then place the fingertips of the right *G hand* into the upturned palm of the left *open hand*. Then, beginning with both *open hands* in front of the right side of the body, right palm facing up and left palm facing down, swing the hands to the left with a double movement.

transparency *n.* A piece of photographic film, usually mounted in a frame, containing textual information, diagrams, etc., and viewed by means of a projector that throws the enlarged lighted image onto a screen: *Put another transparency on the projector.*

- [Initialized sign showing the shape of a transparency] Beginning with the index-finger sides of both *I hands* touching in front of the chest, palms facing forward, bring the hands apart to in front of each shoulder, then downward, and then back together in front of the chest.

transparent *adj.* See sign for VISIBLE.

transport *v.* See sign for BRING.

trap¹ *n.* **1.** A device for catching game or other animals: *to catch a rat in the trap.* —*v.* **2.** To catch in a trap: *to trap a rabbit.*

- [Shows the action of trapping something] Bring the fingers of the right *open hand,* palm facing left, down to close around the fingertips of the left *bent hand* held in front of the chest, palm angled down and fingers pointing right.

trap² *n., v.* (alternate sign)

- [Represents trapping something by cornering it] Push the fingers of the right *V hand,* palm facing down, forward on each side of the extended left index pointing up in front of the chest, palm facing right.

trapeze *n.* A short horizontal bar attached to the ends of two suspended pieces of rope, used by acrobats as a swing on which to perform: *to swing on the trapeze and do a somersault in midair.*

- [Represents the action of a trapeze swinging] With the extended left index finger in front of the chest, palm facing in and finger pointing right, swing the fingers of the right *bent V hand,* palm facing in and fingers pointing down, forward and back with a repeated movement under the left hand.

trapped *adj.* See sign for STUCK.

trash¹ *n.* Worthless material or items; garbage: *Take out the trash.* Same sign used for: **litter.**

- [**dirty** + **throw**¹] With the back of the right *curved 5 hand* under the chin, palm facing down, wiggle the fingers. Then, with the right *S hand* in front of the right shoulder, palm facing forward, thrust the hand downward while opening into a *5 hand,* palm facing down.

trash[2] *n.* See sign for GARBAGE.

travel *v.* See signs for RUN AROUND[1], TOUR[1], TRIP[2].

travel by train *v. phrase.* See sign for TRAIN[1].

tray[1] *n.* A flat, shallow container with a rim for carrying things: *To carry the tray with the coffee cups into the cafeteria.*

- [Mime holding a tray] With both *modified X hands* in front of each side of the body, palms facing each other, move the hands forward simultaneously.

tray[2] *n.* (alternate sign)

- [Intitialized sign showing the shape of a tray] Beginning with both *T hands* in front of the body, palms facing each other, move the hands apart to in front of each side of the body, then back toward the chest, and then back together in front of the chest.

treacherous *adj.* Not to be trusted; unreliable or ready to betray: *a treacherous road with many hills and curves; a treacherous person whose smile masks a vicious nature.*

- [**awful** + **danger**] Beginning with both *8 hands* near each shoulder, palms facing forward, move the hands forward with a double movement while flicking out the fingers, forming *5 hands* each time. Then move the thumb of the right *10 hand,* palm facing left, upward and inward on the back of the left *open hand,* palm facing down, with a double movement.

treasure *v., n.* See sign for PRECIOUS.

treasurer *n.* A person, as a governmental or corporate officer, in charge of money: *the company treasurer.*

- [**money** + **collect**[2] + **person marker**] Tap the back of the right *flattened O hand,* palm facing up, with a double movement against the palm of the left *open hand,* palm facing up. Next slide the little-finger side of the right *curved hand,* palm facing in, in an arc across the palm of the left *open hand,* palm facing up, from the fingers to the heel of the hand. Then move both *open hands,* palms facing each other, downward along each side of the body.

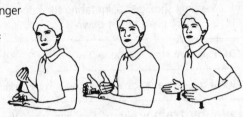

treat[1] *n.* **1.** A gift from the speaker, especially of entertainment or food: *This evening's dinner out is my treat.* —*v.* **2.** To provide with food or amusement at one's own expense, especially as a gesture of friendship or regard: *to treat the visiting colleagues to dinner.*

■ **[my + feed**[1]**]** Bring the palm of the right *open hand* back against the chest. Then rub the thumbs of both *flattened O hands* across the fingers with a repeated movement as the hands move forward in front of the chest.

treat[2] *n., v.* (alternate sign)

■ **[my + pet**[1]**,** in the sense of 'favor'] Bring the palm of the right *open hand* against the chest. Then wipe the fingers of the right *bent hand* upward with a double movement on the back of the left *open hand* held in front of the chest, bending the right fingers toward the palm each time.

treat[3] *n., v.* (alternate sign)

■ **[my + gift**[1]**]** Bring the palm of the right *open hand* against the chest. Then, beginning with both *X hands* touching, palms facing each other in front of the chest, move the hands upward and forward in an arc, ending with the hands apart slightly.

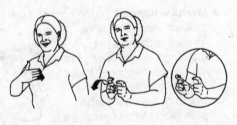

tree *n.* A usually tall plant with a thick woody trunk and branches that emerge at some distance from the ground: *to stand in the shade of the old tree.*

■ [Represents a tree trunk and branches at the top] Beginning with the elbow of the bent right arm resting on the back of the left *open hand* held across the body, twist the right *5 hand* forward and back with a small repeated movement.

tremble[1] *v.* To shake involuntarily, as from fear or excitement: *They trembled with fear when the tornado was about to strike.*

■ [Represents one's legs trembling] With both extended index fingers pointing down in front of the chest, move the fingers from side to side with a short repeated movement.

tremble[2] *v.* (alternate sign)

■ [Represents one's hands trembling with nervousness] With both *open hands* dangling from the wrists in front of each side of the chest, palms facing in, shake the fingers from side to side with a short repeated movement.

tremble[3] *v.* (alternate sign)

■ [Represents a person's body trembling with nervousness] With both *5 hands* in front of each side of the body, palms facing down and fingers pointing forward, shake the hands from side to side with a short repeated movement.

tremble[4] *v.* See sign for EARTHQUAKE.

tremor *n.* Involuntary trembling of the body: *A hand tremor made it difficult for her to sew.* Same sign used for: **Parkinson's disease.**

■ [Action of a tremor] While holding the wrist of the right *open hand,* palm facing down, with the left hand, shake the right hand slightly from side to side.

trespass *n., v.* See signs for SIN[1,2].

trial *n.* See sign for JUDGE[1].

triangle[1] *n.* A two-dimensional figure having three sides and three angles: *Draw a triangle with three unequal sides on the blackboard.*

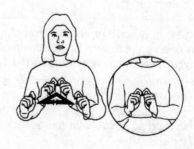

■ [Initialized sign showing the shape of a triangle] Beginning with the index-finger sides of both *T hands* touching in front of the chest, palms facing forward, bring the hands apart and downward at an angle and then back together in front of the chest.

triangle

triangle[2] *n.* (alternate sign)

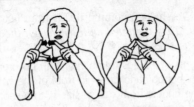

- [The shape of a triangle] Bring the thumbs and index fingers of both *L hands* together in front of the chest to form a triangle, palms facing each other.

tribute *n.* See signs for GIFT[1,2].

trick *n.* **1.** Something done cleverly, maliciously, or playfully to deceive: *The class played a trick on the teacher by hiding the chalk.* —*v.* **2.** To deceive by using tricks: *We tricked the boss into closing the office early.* Same sign used for: **con, fool.**

- Tap the knuckles of the right *A hand*, palm facing forward, with a double movement against the extended left index finger held up in front of the body, palm facing right.

trickle *n.* **1.** A small flow of water or other liquid: *A trickle of water came through the window.* —*v.* **2.** To flow in a small stream: *The water trickled down the wall.*

- [**water** + a gesture showing liquid coming down + **leak**[1]] Tap the index-finger side of the right *W hand*, palm facing left, against the chin with a double movement. Next, beginning with both *5 hands* in front of the right side of the head, move the hands downward while wiggling the fingers, palms facing each other. Then move the left *5 hand*, palm facing in, downward from the little-finger side of the right *open hand* held in front of the chest, palm facing in, while wiggling the right fingers as the hand moves.

tricycle *n.* A three-wheeled vehicle moved by pedaling: *The children rode their tricycles around the block.* Same sign used for: **ride a tricycle.**

- [Initialized sign similar to sign for **bicycle**] Beginning with both *T hands* in front of the chest, palms facing down, move the hands in alternating double circles.

trigger[1] *n.* A small projecting lever that fires a gun when pressed by the finger: *The cowboy took aim and pulled the trigger.* Same sign used for: **pull the trigger.**

- [Mime pulling a trigger] Beginning with the extended index finger of the right *L hand* pointing forward in front of the body, palm facing left, bend the index finger, forming an *X hand* as it moves back toward the chest.

trigger[2] *v.* To set off: *The burglar triggered the alarm.*

■ [**start**[2] + **something**[2]] With the extended right index finger, palm facing down, inserted between the middle finger and ring finger of the left *open hand* held in front of the chest, palm facing in and fingers pointing right, twist the right hand, turning the palm to the left. Then move the extended right index finger, palm facing in and finger pointing up, in a small circle in front of the right shoulder.

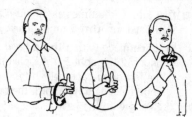

trigonometry *n.* The branch of mathematics concerned with the study of angles and their applications: *In our trigonometry class, we're learning to measure the ratio of one side of an angle to another.*

■ [Initialized sign similar to sign for **mathematics**] Beginning with both *T hands* in front of each side of the chest, palms facing each other, move the hands past each other with a double movement, brushing the little-finger side of the right hand across the index-finger side of the left hand as the hands pass each other.

trim[1] *v.* To make neat by cutting away excess: *trim the hedges.*

■ [Shows cutting a thin layer from the top of something] Slide the extended fingers of the right *V hand*, palm facing down, with a double movement down the length of the left *open hand* held in front of the chest, palm facing down and fingers pointing forward.

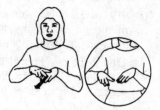

trim[2] *v.* See signs for PRUNE, SNIP.

trio *n.* See sign for WE[5].

trip[1] *v.* To stumble: *to trip over the rock.*

■ [Represents legs walking and then tripping over an obstacle] Beginning with the middle finger of the right *P hand*, palm facing down, touching the index finger of the left *B hand* held in front of the chest, palm facing in and fingers pointing right, move the right hand forward in an arc down the back of the left hand, ending with the right palm facing in.

trip[2] *n.* A journey: *preparing to go on a trip.* Same sign used for: **journey, mobilize, tour, travel.**

■ [Represents legs moving as if on a trip] Move the right *bent V hand*, palm facing down, from in front of the right side of the body upward and forward in an arc, ending with the palm facing forward.

trip³ *v.* See sign for STUMBLE.

triple *adj.* Three times as much: *a triple-dip ice cream cone.* Same sign used for: **three times, thrice.**

■ [once made with a **three** hand shape] Beginning with the middle finger of the right *3 hand,* palm facing down, touching the palm of the left *open hand* held in front of the chest, palm facing up and fingers pointing right, flick the right hand upward to the right, ending with the palm facing left in front of the right shoulder.

triumph *n.* See sign for SUCCESSFUL.

trivial *adj.* See sign for NOTHING⁴.

trombone *n.* A large musical wind instrument with a metal tube ending in a bell-shaped opening and a slide used for varying the tone: *plays a trombone in the school band.*

■ [Mime playing a trombone] With the index-finger side of the right *S hand* in front of the mouth, palm facing left, and the left *S hand* somewhat forward, palm facing right, move the left hand forward and back with a double movement.

trophy¹ *n.* An object won as a prize and symbolizing victory or achievement: *to win an athletic trophy.* Same sign used for: **award.**

■ [The shape of a trophy] Tap the thumbs and little fingers of both *Y hands,* palms facing in, together in front of the body with a double movement.

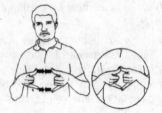

trophy² *n.* See sign for CHAMPION.

trouble¹ *n.* Difficulty or annoyance: *This situation is bound to cause trouble.* Same sign used for: **anxious, care, concern, worry.**

■ [Represents problems coming from all directions] Beginning with both *B hands* near each side of the head, palms facing each other, bring the hands toward each other with a repeated alternating movement, crossing the hands in front of the face each time.

trouble² *n.* (alternate sign) See also signs for WORRY¹,². Same sign used for: **anxious, care, concern, worry.**

■ [The hands seem to ward off problems coming from all directions] Beginning with the right *B hand* near the right side of the head and the left *B hand* in front of the left shoulder, palms facing each other, move the hands in repeated alternating circles toward each other in front of the face.

trouble³ *n.* See sign for DIFFICULT.

troubleshoot *v.* To locate an error through a process of elimination: *The technician used a computer program to troubleshoot the problem.*

■ [**analyze + problem**[1]] With both *V hands* pointing toward each other in front of the chest, palms facing down, move the fingers down and apart with a double movement, bending the fingers each time. Then, beginning with the knuckles of both *bent V hands* touching in front of the chest, twist the hands in opposite directions with a deliberate movement, rubbing the knuckles against each other.

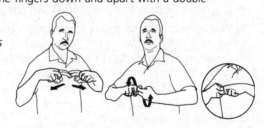

trousers *pl. n.* See sign for PANTS.

truant *n.* A student who is absent from school without permission: *The child was a constant truant during sixth grade.*

■ [**school + skip**[1]] Tap the fingers of the right *open hand,* palm facing down, with a double movement on the upturned palm of the left *open hand.* Then, beginning with the left *5 hand* held across the chest, little finger bent downward, move the extended right index finger, palm facing left and finger pointing forward, from right to left with a double movement in front of the chest, striking the bent left middle finger as it passes each time.

truck *n.* A vehicle with an elongated back used for hauling: *The store delivered the furniture in a large truck.* Same sign used for: **trailer.**

■ [Initialized sign similar to sign for **bus**[1]] Beginning with the little-finger side of the right *T hand,* palm facing left, touching the index-finger side of the left *T hand,* palm facing right, move the right hand back toward the chest while the left hand moves forward.

trudge *v.* See sign for PLOD.

true *adj.* In accordance with fact and reality; not false: *a true story.* Related form: **truly** *adv.* Same sign used for: **actual, actually, certain, certainly, truly.**

■ [Represents words coming from the mouth] Move the side of the extended right index finger from in front of the mouth, palm facing left and finger pointing up, forward in an arc.

truly *adv.* See sign for ABSOLUTE.

truly yours See sign for BELONG[2].

truncate *v.* To shorten by cutting off a part: *We had to truncate the copy to fit the space allotted in the "name" field of the database.* Same sign used for: **cut off.**

- [Mime cutting off the end of something] Move the right *V hand,* palm facing left, forward across the fingertips of the left *open hand,* palm facing in and fingers pointing right, with a deliberate movement while closing the right fingers together.

trust *n.* See sign for CONFIDENT.

trustee *n.* A person legally responsible for administering another's property: *The trustee managed the child's inheritance.*

- [Initialized sign similar to sign for **member**[2]] Touch the thumb side of the right *T hand,* palm facing left, first to the left side of the chest and then to the right side of the chest.

truth[1] *n.* That which is true: *swore to tell the truth.* Same sign used for: **fact.**

- [Represents the truth coming straight from the mouth] Move the extended right index finger from pointing up in front of the mouth, palm facing left, forward with a deliberate movement.

truth[2] *n.* (alternate sign) Same sign used for: **fact.**

- [**truth**[1] + **honest**] Beginning with the extended right index finger pointing up in front of the mouth, palm facing left, move the right hand downward while changing into an *H hand.* Then slide the extended fingers of the right *H hand,* palm facing left, forward from the heel to the fingers of the left *open hand,* palm facing up.

truth[3] *n.* See sign for HONEST.

try[1] *v.* To make an effort to do or accomplish: *Please try to be home on time.* Same sign used for: **attempt, strive.**

- [The hands push forward indicating effort] Move both *S hands* from in front of each side of the body, palms facing each other, downward and forward in simultaneous arcs.

try[2] *v.* (alternate sign)

- [Initialized sign pushing forward to indicate effort] Move both *T hands* from in front of each side of the body, palms facing each other, downward and forward in simultaneous arcs.

TTY *Abbreviation.* See sign for TELETYPEWRITER.

tubal ligation *n.* See sign for STERILIZATION.

tube[1] *n.* A long, hollow cylinder: *The water rushed through the tube.*

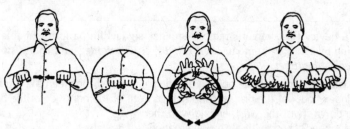

- [Shows putting together + **stick**[2]] Beginning with both *S hands,* palms facing down, in front of the sides of the body, bring the hands together in front of the chest. Then, beginning with the index-finger sides of both *F hands* together in front of the body, palms facing forward, bring the hands downward in a circular movement while turning the hands over, ending with the little-finger sides together, palms facing up. Next, beginning with the index-finger sides of both *F hands* near each other, palms facing down, bring the hands apart.

tube[2] *n.* See sign for PIPE[3].

tuberculosis or **TB** *n.* An infectious disease affecting particularly the lungs: *an outbreak of tuberculosis among people who are homeless.*

- [Abbreviation **t-b** + **lung**] With the right hand, palm facing forward, form a *T hand* and then a *B hand* in front of the right shoulder while moving the hand slightly to the right. Then rub the fingertips of both *bent hands,* palms facing in, up and down with a repeated movement on each side of the chest.

tuck *v.* To stick the edge of into place: *to tuck the sheets around the mattress.*

- [**bed**[1,2] + **blanket** + shows tucking a blanket under a mattress] Place the right *open hand* against the right cheek

while bending the head slightly to the right. Next move both *B hands* from in front of the chest, palms facing down and fingers pointing toward each other, toward the body, ending with the index fingers against the chest. Then, beginning with both *bent hands* on each side of the body, palms facing down, jab the fingers inward toward each side of the body with a double movement, ending with the fingers pointing toward each other and palms facing each other.

Tuesday *n.* The third day of the week, following Monday: *If today is Tuesday, there will be a science article in the newspaper.*

- [Initialized sign] Move the right *T hand*, palm facing in, in a circle in front of the right shoulder.

tuner *n.* A device that converts radio frequency signals into a form suitable for processing by other equipment: *His VCR, TV, DVD recorder, and sound system are all connected to the tuner.*

- [**turn on + balance**] While holding an imaginary switch between the thumb and bent index finger of the right *X hand* held in front of the right side of the body, palm facing down, twist the wrist, ending with the palm facing in. Then, with a small alternating movement, bring the right *bent hand* and the left *bent hand*, both palms facing down, up and down in front of each side of the chest, shifting the entire torso slightly with each movement.

tuning fork *n.* A steel instrument that produces a definite, constant musical sound when struck; used to provide a standard for tuning a musical instrument: *tuned the piano using a tuning fork.*

- [**hear** + hitting the tines of a tuning fork against a surface] Touch the extended right index finger to the right ear, palm facing in. Then bring the middle finger of the right *V hand*, palm facing forward, to the left to strike the left *open hand* held in front of the left shoulder, palm facing right, and then back to the right again.

turban *n.* **1.** A man's headdress worn in parts of Asia, made with a length of cloth wound around the head: *The man always wears a turban in public.* **2.** A woman's hat resembling this: *a South American actress who wore elaborately decorated turbans.*

- [Shows holding the end of a turban in place while wrapping it around one's head + shows the height of the turban] While holding the palm of the left *open hand* against the side of the head, move the right *curved hand* around the head in a circular movement, fingers pointing down. Then, beginning with both *open hands* on each side of the head, palms angled down, move the hands upward toward the top of the head.

Turkey *n.* A republic in Asia Minor and southeastern Europe: *a native of Turkey.* Related form: **Turk** *n.*

■ Move the right *modified C hand,* palm facing left, back with a double movement against the forehead.

turkey *n.* A large, pheasantlike North American bird: *The turkey has a wattle, a fleshy lobe hanging down from the throat.*

■ [Represents the action of a turkey's wattle] With the thumb side of the right *G hand* under the chin, palm and fingers pointing down, wiggle the fingers from side to side with a repeated movement.

turn[1] *v.* To move part way around: *Turn left at the corner.*

■ [Demonstrates moving to a location around a corner] Beginning with both index fingers pointing up in front of the chest, palms facing in opposite directions and right hand nearer the chest than the left hand, move the right hand forward around the left finger, turning the palm as the hand moves and ending with the palm facing in.

turn[2] *n.* A chance or requirement to do something in an agreed-upon order: *It's your turn to drive.* Same sign used for: **alternate, next, take turns.**

■ [Indicates alternating positions in order to take turns] Move the right *L hand* from in front of the body, palm angled left, to the right by flipping the hand over, ending with the palm facing up.

turn[3] *v.* See sign for CHANGE[1].

turn around[1] *v. phrase.* To reverse direction or change the direction of so as to face in the opposite direction: *Turn around so I can see your face. Turn the chair around.*

■ [Natural gesture used to tell someone to turn around] Move the extended right index finger, palm facing in and finger pointing down, in a small circular movement in front of the right shoulder.

turn around[2] *v. phrase.* (alternate sign)

■ [Indicates the movement of turning around] Beginning with the right extended index finger pointing down in front of the left side of the chest, palm facing in, and the left extended index finger pointing up in front of the body, palm facing in, move the right hand across the chest from left to right and then forward in an arc around the left finger.

turn down *v. phrase.* See signs for DECLINE[4], REJECT[1].

turn down the lights *v. phrase.* See signs for DIM[1,2].

turning point *n.* See sign for CRISIS.

turn into *v. phrase.* See sign for BECOME.

turn off *v. phrase.* See signs for TURN ON.

turn on *v. phrase.* **1.** To allow something to flow through: *to turn on the faucet.* **2.** To switch on or activate: *to turn on the radio.* Same sign used for: **turn off.**

- [Mime turning a knob so as to turn something on or off] While holding an imaginary switch between the thumb and bent index finger of the right *X hand* held in front of the right side of the body, palm facing up, twist the wrist, ending with the palm facing down.

turn over *v. phrase.* See sign for COOK[1].

turn up *v. phrase.* See sign for SHOW UP.

turtle *n.* A reptile with the trunk enclosed in a hard shell, inside which the animal can hide its head and appendages: *The turtle lived in the creek.* Same sign used for: **tortoise.**

- [Represents a turtle's head coming from under the shell] Cup the left palm over the right *A hand,* palm facing left, and wiggle the right thumb with a repeated movement.

tutor *n.* **1.** A private teacher: *The tutor worked with the boy on his math.* —*v.* **2.** To act as a private teacher to: *tutored the girl in English grammar.*

- [Initialized sign similar to sign for **teacher**] Beginning with both *T hands* in front of each side of the head, palms facing each other, move the hands forward with a short double movement. Then move both *open hands,* palms facing each other, downward along each side of the body.

twentieth century *n.* The next after the nineteenth century: *We live in the twentieth century.*

- [**twenty** + **hundred** + **year**] Pinch the index finger and thumb of the right *G hand,* palm facing forward, together with a double movement. Next form a

C hand and move it back toward the right side of the body. Then, beginning with the right *S hand*, palm facing left, over the left *S hand*, palm facing right, move the right hand forward in a complete circle around the left hand, ending with the little-finger side of the right hand on the thumb side of the left hand.

twenty-five cents *pl. n.* See sign for QUARTER².

twice *adv.* Two times: *We already read the story twice.* Same sign used for: **double, two times.**

■ [**once** formed with a **two** hand shape] Strike the middle finger of the right *V hand*, palm facing down, upward on the left *open hand*, palm facing up, by twisting the wrist, ending with the right palm facing up.

twin *n.* One of two children born at the same time from the same mother: *They seem to be identical twins.*

■ [Initialized sign] Touch the index-finger side of the right *T hand*, palm facing left, first to the right side of the chin and then to the left side of the chin.

twist¹ *v.* To wring: *to twist the rope.* Same sign used for: **sprain.**

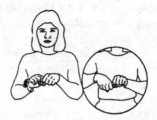

■ [Mime twisting something] Beginning with the index-finger sides of both *S hands* together, right palm facing forward and left palm facing in, twist the wrists to turn the right palm in and the left palm forward.

twist² *v.* See sign for WRING.

twitch *v.* **1.** To move the eye with a jerky movement: *My eye twitches when I'm really tired.* —*n.* **2.** A jerky movement: *I have a twitch in my eye.*

■ [A movement showing the eye twitching] Beginning with the extended right index finger pointing left in front of the right eye, palm facing down, bend the finger with a short double movement, forming an *X hand* each time.

twitter *v.* To utter tremulous chirping sounds: *We could hear the tiny birds twittering in the garden.*

■ [**feel** + **bird**] Move the bent middle finger of the right *5 hand*, palm facing in, upward on the chest with a double movement. Then, beginning with the right *G hand* in front of the mouth, palm facing forward, open and close the index finger and thumb with a double movement.

two dollars *pl. n.* See sign for SECOND[2].

two of us *n. phrase.* See sign for WE[4].

two of you *n. phrase.* See sign for YOU[3].

twosome *adj., n.* See sign for YOU[3].

two months *pl. n.* See sign for BIMONTHLY.

two times See sign for TWICE.

two weeks *pl. n.* See sign for BIWEEKLY.

type[1] *v.* To write with a typewriter or typewriterlike keyboard: *to type a letter on the electric typewriter; learned to type using a software tutorial.* Related form: **typing** *v.*

- [Mime typing] Beginning with both *curved 5 hands* in front of the body, palms facing down, wiggle the fingers with a repeated movement.

type[2] *n.* See sign for FAVORITE. Related form: **typical** *adj.*

type[3] *n.* See signs for KIND[3,4].

typeset *v.* To set text in type: *finding a compositor to typeset the book.*

- [**type** + **establish**] Beginning with both *curved 5 hands* in front of the body, palms facing down, wiggle the fingers with a repeated movement. Then bring the little-finger side of the right *10 hand,* palm facing in, downward on the back of the left hand held in front of the body, palm facing down.

typewriter *n.* A machine used for writing characters by manually pressing the keys on a keyboard: *to type a letter on the typewriter.*

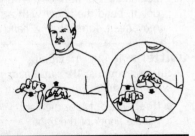

- [Shows the action of the hands when typing] Beginning with both *curved 5 hands* in front of the body, palms facing down, move the hands up and down with a short alternating double movement.

---

ugly *adj.* Unpleasant in appearance; very unattractive: *an ugly color.*

■ Beginning with the extended right index finger in front of the left side of the face, palm facing left and finger pointing left, move the hand to the right side of the face while bending the index finger to form an *X hand.* [This sign can be formed with two hands.]

---

umbilicus *n.* See sign for NAVEL.

---

umbrella *n.* A portable circular cover of waterproof fabric on folding ribs attached to a long handle, used as protection from rain or snow: *to carry an umbrella in case it rains.*

■ [Mime raising an umbrella] Beginning with the little-finger side of the right *S hand* on the index-finger side of the left *S hand* in front of the chest, palms facing in opposite directions, raise the right hand upward in front of the head.

---

unable *adj.* See sign for INCAPABLE.

---

unaccustomed *adj.* Not familiarized with through custom or use: *unaccustomed to eating breakfast at such an early hour.*

■ [not[1] + custom] Bring the extended thumb of the right *10 hand* from under the chin, palm facing left, forward with a deliberate movement. Then bring the right *C hand* from in front of the chest, palm facing left, downward to land on the back of the left *curved hand* in front of the chest, palm facing down, while closing both hands into *S hands* and bringing them downward a short distance.

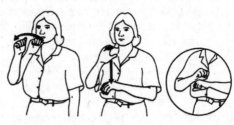

---

unaided *adj.* Without help: *The new pilot was able to land the plane unaided.*

■ [none[2,3] + help] Move both *flattened O hands,* palms facing forward, from in front of the chest apart to in front of each shoulder with a deliberate movement. Then bring the palm of the right *open hand* upward with a double movement against the little-finger side of the left *S hand* held in front of the chest.

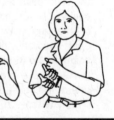

---

unanimous[1] *adj.* **1.** Being in complete agreement: *The committee was unanimous in voting to disband.* **2.** Showing complete agreement: *a unanimous vote.*

■ [**only**[1] + **one**] Move the extended right index finger, palm facing forward and finger pointing up, in a circle in front of the right shoulder. Then twist the wrist to bring the finger back toward the chest, ending with the palm facing in and the finger pointing up.

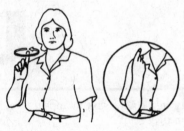

unanimous[2] *adj.* (alternate sign)

■ [**vote** + **defeat**[1]] Insert the fingertips of the right *F hand*, palm facing down, into the opening formed by the left *O hand* held in front of the chest, palm facing fight. Then move the right *S hand* from in front of the right shoulder, palm facing forward, downward and forward, ending with the right wrist across the wrist of the left *S hand*, both palms facing down.

unavoidable *adj.* Unable to be avoided: *an unavoidable delay at the airport.*

■ [**can't** + **avoid**[1]] Bring the extended right index finger downward in front of the chest, striking the extended left index finger as it moves, both palms facing down. Then, beginning with the knuckles of the right *A hand*, palm facing left, near the base of the thumb of the left *A hand*, palm facing right, bring the right hand back with a wavy movement toward the body.

unaware *adj.* See sign for DON'T KNOW.

unbalanced[1] *adj.* Lacking the proper balance: *The table is a bit unbalanced.*

■ [**not**[1] + **balance**] Bring the extended thumb of the right *10 hand* from under the chin, palm facing left, forward with a deliberate movement. Then, with an alternating movement, bring the right *open hand* and the left *open hand*, both palms facing down and fingers pointing forward, up and down in front of each side of the chest, shifting the torso slightly with each movement.

unbalanced[2] *adj.* See sign for TILT[1].

---

unbeaten[1] *adj.* Not defeated or never defeated: *Our team remains unbeaten.* Same sign used for: **undefeated.**

■ [**yet**[1,2] + **defeat**[2]] Bend the wrist of the right *open hand,* palm facing back and fingers pointing down, back with a double movement near the right side of the waist. Then, beginning with the right *S hand* somewhat forward of the body, palm facing in, and the left *S hand* held across the chest, move the right hand back toward the right side of the chest by bending the elbow.

---

unbeaten[2] *adj.* (alternate sign used when referring to another, another's team, etc.) Same sign used for: **undefeated.**

■ [**yet**[1,2] + **defeat**[1]] Bend the wrist of the right *open hand,* palm facing back and fingers pointing down, back with a double movement near the right side of the waist. Then move the right *S hand* from in front of the right shoulder, palm facing forward, downward and forward, ending with the right wrist across the wrist of the left *S hand,* both palms facing down.

---

unbeaten[3] *adj.* (alternate sign) Same sign used for: **undefeated.**

■ [**yet**[1,2] + **lose**[2]] Bend the wrist of the right *open hand,* palm facing back and fingers pointing down, back with a double movement near the right side of the waist. Then bring the palm side of the right *V hand* downward with a deliberate movement on the left *open hand* held in front of the body, palm facing up.

---

unbelievable *adj.* **1.** Beyond belief; improbable: *He told us an unbelievable story about being kidnapped.* **2.** Very impressive; extraordinary: *This apple pie is unbelievable.*

■ [**not**[1] + **believe**] Bring the extended thumb of the right *10 hand* from under the chin, palm facing left, forward with a deliberate movement. Then bring the right *curved hand,* palm facing down, downward in front of the chest to clasp the left *curved hand* held in front of the chest, palm facing up.

unbreakable *adj.* Not breakable:
unbreakable glass in the windows.

■ [**can't** + **break**] Bring the extended right index finger downward in front of the chest, striking the extended left index finger as it moves, both palms facing down. Then, beginning with both *S hands* in front of the body, index fingers touching and palms facing down, move the hands away from each other while twisting the wrists with a deliberate movement, ending with the palms facing each other.

unbuckle *v.* To unfasten the buckle of:
You may unbuckle your seatbelt now.

■ [**belt**[1] + **disconnect**] Beginning with both *H hands* in front of the waist, palms facing in and fingers angled toward each other, move the right hand to the left to overlap the left fingers. Then, beginning with the thumbs and index fingers of both hands intersecting, palms facing each other, release the fingers and pull the hands apart.

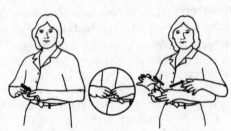

uncertain[1] *adj.* 1. Not clearly known: *The word is of uncertain origin.* 2. Not confident: *has an uncertain manner.*

■ [**not**[1] + **sure**[1]] Bring the extended thumb of the right *10 hand* from under the chin, palm facing left, forward with a deliberate movement. Then, beginning with the extended right index finger pointing up in front of the mouth, palm facing left, move the right hand forward in an arc.

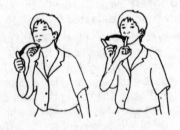

uncertain[2] *adj.* See signs for INDECISION, RESIST.

uncle *n.* 1. A brother of one's father or mother: *My uncle still teases my father.* 2. The husband of one's aunt: *He's friendlier since becoming my uncle.*

■ [Initialized sign formed near the male area of the head] Shake the right *U hand*, palm facing forward and fingers pointing up, back and forth near the right side of the forehead.

unclean *adj.* **1.** Not clean; dirty: *The old house seemed musty and unclean.* **2.** Impure: *In some religions, certain foods are considered unclean.*

■ [**not**[1] + **clean**] Bring the extended thumb of the right *10 hand* from under the chin, palm facing left, forward with a deliberate movement. Then slide the palm of the right *open hand* from the heel to off the fingertips of the left *open hand* held in front of the body, palm facing up.

unclear *adj.* See sign for VAGUE.

uncomfortable *adj.* **1.** Experiencing discomfort; not comfortable: *I am uncomfortable in the new chair.* **2.** Causing discomfort: *This chair is uncomfortable.*

■ [**not**[1] + **comfortable**] Bring the extended thumb of the right *10 hand* from under the chin, palm facing left, forward with a deliberate movement. Then wipe the right *curved hand* down the back of the left *curved hand* and then repeat with the left *curved hand* on the back of the right *curved hand*, both palms facing down.

unconcerned *adj.* Lacking in feeling or concern; indifferent: *Unconcerned about the weather, they booked a transatlantic flight.*

■ [**concern**[2] + **none**[2,3]] Touch the bent middle fingers of both *5 hands* against each side of the chest with an alternating double movement. Then move both *flattened O hands*, palms facing forward, from in front of the chest apart to in front of each shoulder with a deliberate movement.

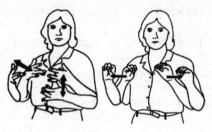

unconscious[1] *adj.* Not conscious; lacking awareness, especially temporarily: *He was knocked unconscious.*

■ [**not**[1] + **know**] Bring the extended thumb of the right *10 hand* from under the chin, palm facing left, forward with a deliberate movement. Then tap the fingertips of the right *bent hand*, palm facing down, against the right side of the forehead.

unconscious[2] *adj.* See signs for DON'T KNOW, FAINT.

unconstitutional *adj.* Contrary to or unauthorized by the U.S. Constitution: *The lower-court decision was declared unconstitutional.*

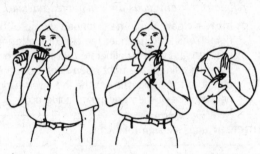

- ■ [**not**[1] + **Commandment**] Bring the extended thumb of the right *10 hand* from under the chin, palm facing left, forward with a deliberate movement. Then move the right *C hand*, palm facing forward, from touching first the fingers and then the heel of the left *open hand*, fingers pointing up and palm facing right.

undecided[1] *adj.* Having failed as yet to make up one's mind: *undecided about how to vote.*

- ■ [**yet**[2] + **decide**[1,2]] Bend the wrists of both *open hands*, palms facing back and fingers pointing down, back with a double movement near each side of the waist. Then, beginning with both *D hands* in front of each side of the chest, palms facing each other and index fingers pointing up, move the hands downward, ending with the index fingers pointing forward.

undecided[2] *adj.* See sign for INDECISION.

undefeated *adj.* See signs for UNBEATEN[1,2,3].

undelete *v.* See sign for RECOVER[1].

undependable *adj.* See sign for UNRELIABLE.

under[1] *prep.* Below; beneath: *shoes under the living room couch.*

- ■ [Shows a location under something else] Move the right *10 hand*, palm facing left, from in front of the chest downward and forward under the left *open hand* held in front of the chest, palm facing down and fingers pointing right.

under[2] *prep.* (alternate sign)

- ■ [Initialized sign showing a location under something else] Move the right *U hand*, palm facing left and fingers angled up, from in front of the chest downward under the left *open hand* held in front of the chest, palm facing down and fingers pointing right.

underage *adj.* Below the legal, required, or appropriate age: *They want to get married, but they're underage.*

- ■ [**under**[1,2] + **age**] Move the right *U hand,* palm facing left and fingers angled up, from in front of the chest downward and forward under the left *open hand* held in front of the chest, palm facing down and fingers pointing right. Then, beginning with the right *C hand* in front of the chin, palm facing left, move the hand downward while closing into an *S hand.*

underclothes *pl. n.* See sign for UNDERWEAR[1].

underline *v.* In word processing, to create a line under characters in the text: *The author underlined words that should appear in italics.* Related form: **underlined** *adj.* Same sign used for: **underscore.**

- ■ [**under**[1] + **line**] Move the right *10 hand,* palm facing left, from in front of the chest downward and forward under the left *open hand* held in front of the chest, palm facing down and fingers pointing right. Then, beginning with the extended little fingers of both *I hands* touching in front of the chest, palms facing in, move both hands outward.

underlying *adj.* See sign for BASEMENT.

underscore *v.* See sign for UNDERLINE.

understand *v.* To grasp the meaning of: *I understand your question.* Same sign used for: **apprehend, comprehend, perceive.**

- ■ [Comprehension seems to pop into one's head] Beginning with the right *S hand* near the right side of the forehead, palm facing left, flick the right index finger upward with a sudden movement.

understandable *adj.* Same sign as for UNDERSTAND but made with a double movement.

underwater *adj.* **1.** Being or occurring below the surface of the water: *underwater excavations for oil.* —*adv.* **2.** Below the surface of the water: *He swam underwater.*

- ■ [**under**[1,2] + **water**] Move the right *U hand,* palm facing left and fingers angled up, from in front of the chest downward and forward under the left *open hand* held in front of the chest, palm facing down and fingers pointing right. Then tap the index-finger side of the right *W hand,* palm facing left, against the chin with a double movement.

underwear

underwear[1] *n.* Clothing worn next to the skin underneath one's outer clothing: *to put on fancy new underwear.* Same sign used for: **underclothes.**

- ■ [Location of underwear worn on the body] Beginning with the fingertips of both *bent hands* touching each side of the abdomen, palms facing in, twist the wrists upward, ending with both *open hands* in front of each side of the waist, palms facing down and fingers pointing forward.

underwear[2] *n.* (alternate sign)

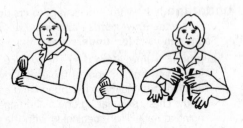

- ■ [**inside** + **clothes**] Insert the fingertips of the right *flattened O hand,* palm facing down, inside the opening formed by the left *O hand* held in front of the chest, palm facing right. Then brush the fingertips of both *5 hands,* palms facing in and fingers pointing toward each other, downward on each side of the chest with a double movement.

underweight *adj.* Weighing less than the required weight or the weight optimal for health: *The boxer is underweight for his class.*

- ■ [**light**[3] + **weigh**] Beginning with both *5 hands* with bent middle fingers in front of the body, palms angled forward, twist the wrists to raise the hands quickly toward each other and upward, ending with the hands in front of each side of the chest, palms facing in. Then, beginning with the extended fingers of the right *H hand* across the extended index-finger side of the left *H hand,* palms angled toward each other, rock the right hand back and forth with a double movement.

undress[1] *v.* To take off one's clothes: *to undress and change clothing in the rest room.*

- ■ [**take-off**[1,2] + **clothes**] Beginning with the palm sides of both *S hands* against each side of the chest, bring the hands forward and downward while opening into *5 hands,* palms facing down and fingers pointing forward. Then brush the fingertips of both *5 hands,* palms facing in and fingers pointing toward each other, downward on each side of the chest with a double movement.

undress[2] *v.* See signs for TAKE OFF[2,3].

unemployed *adj.* Not having a job: *The number of unemployed persons has increased.*

- [none[2,3] + work[1,2]] Move both *flattened O hands,* palms facing forward, from in front of the chest apart to in front of each shoulder with a deliberate movement. Then tap the heel of the right *S hand,* palm facing forward, on the back of the left *S hand* held in front of the chest, palm facing down, with a double movement.

unfair *adj.* Not fair; unjust: *an unfair decision.*

- Bring the fingertips of the right *F hand,* palm facing left, downward, striking the fingertips of the left *F hand,* palm facing right, as it passes.

unfaithful *adj.* Not faithful, as to a spouse or lover: *She divorced him when she discovered he had been unfaithful.* Related form: **unfaithfulness** *n.*

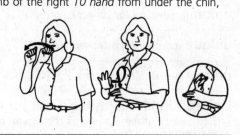

- [not[1] + faith[3]] Bring the extended thumb of the right *10 hand* from under the chin, palm facing left, forward with a deliberate movement. Then move the right *F hand,* palm facing forward, in a circular movement above the left *F hand* while turning the right wrist, ending with the little-finger side of the right *F hand* across the index-finger side of the left *F hand.*

unfinished *adj.* Not finished; incomplete: *My paper is unfinished, so I can't hand it in.*

- [not[1] + finish[1,2]] Bring the extended thumb of the right *10 hand* from under the chin, palm facing left, forward with a deliberate movement. Then, beginning with both *5 hands* in front of the chest, palms facing in and fingers pointing up, flip the hands over with a sudden movement, ending with both palms facing down and fingers pointing forward.

unhappy[1] *adj.* Sad; miserable: *I am unhappy about the decision.*

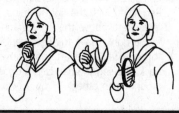

- [not[1] + happy] Bring the extended thumb of the right *10 hand* from under the chin, palm facing left, forward with a deliberate movement. Then brush the fingers of the right *open hand,* palm facing in and fingers pointing left, upward in a repeated circular movement on the chest.

unhappy[2] *adj.* See sign for SAD.

unheard-of *adj.* **1.** Unknown: *The winner was unheard-of until the awards were given out.* **2.** Outrageous; shameful: *unheard-of prices.*

■ [**hear** + **never**] Touch the extended right index finger, palm facing in, to the right ear. Then move the right *open hand* from near the right side of the face, palm facing left, downward with a large wavy movement to in front of the right side of the body.

uniform *adj.* See signs for ALIKE[3], STANDARD[1,2].

unintelligible *adj.* Not intelligible; not able to be understood: *an unintelligible statement.*

■ [**not**[1] + **understand**] Bring the extended thumb of the right *10 hand* from under the chin, palm facing left, forward with a deliberate movement. Then, beginning with the right *S hand* near the right side of the forehead, palm facing left, flick the right index finger upward with a sudden movement.

union *n.* See sign for COOPERATION.

unique *adj.* See signs for SPECIAL[1,2].

unite *v.* See sign for BELONG[1].

United Kingdom *n.* A kingdom in northwest Europe: *London is the capital of the United Kingdom.* Same sign used for: **Great Britain.**

■ Place the curved index finger and thumb of the right *modified C hand*, palm facing in, on each side of the chin.

unity *n.* See sign for COOPERATION.

universal *adj.* See sign for COOPERATION.

universe *n.* Everything there is; the entire world throughout space: *all planets in the universe.* Related form: **universal** *adj.*

■ [Initialized sign similar to sign for **world**] Beginning with the right *U hand*, palm facing left, above the left *U hand*, palm facing right, move the right hand forward while the left hand moves back, moving the hands in a circle around each other.

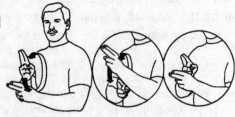

university *n.* An institution of higher learning, offering undergraduate and graduate studies: *left a junior college to attend the university.*

- [Initialized sign similar to sign for **college**] Beginning with the palm side of the right *U hand* on the left *open hand* in front of the chest, palm facing up, move the right hand in a circular movement upward and forward.

unkind *adj.* See sign for MEAN[1].

unknown *adj.* See sign for DON'T KNOW.

unlawful *adj.* See signs for CRIME[1,2].

unlike *adj.* See sign for BUT.

unnatural *adj.* See sign for ABNORMAL.

unnecessary *adj.* See sign for NEEDLESS.

unnumbered *adj.* Not numbered; having no numbers: *The pages are unnumbered.*

- [**none**[2,3] + **number**] Move both *flattened O hands,* palms facing forward, from in front of the chest apart in front of each shoulder with a deliberate movement. Then, with the fingertips of both *flattened O hands* touching, left palm facing up and right palm facing down, twist the wrists in opposite directions and touch the fingertips again, ending with the left palm facing down and the right palm facing up.

unreliable *adj.* Not reliable: *an unreliable worker.* Same sign used for: **undependable.**

- [**not**[1] + **depend**] Bring the extended thumb of the right *10 hand* from under the chin, palm facing left, forward with a deliberate movement. Then, with the extended right index finger across the extended left index finger at an angle, palms facing down, move both fingers down slightly with a double movement.

unsafe *adj.* See sign for DANGER.

unshaven *adj.* Not shaved; having a beard or stubble on one's face: *The hitchhiker was unshaven and scruffy looking.*

- [Shows the location of one's unshaved whiskers] Beginning with the back of the right *C hand* on the left cheek, palm facing left, pull the hand around the chin, ending with the back of the right *C hand* on the right cheek, palm facing right.

unskilled *adj.* Lacking in required skills: *a need to provide jobs for unskilled workers.* Same sign used for: **clumsy, inexperienced.**

■ While grasping the thumb of the right *5 hand,* palm facing in and fingers pointing down, with the left *S hand,* palm facing down, twist the right wrist to move the right fingers upward, ending with the palm facing forward.

unsure *adj.* See sign for SKEPTICAL[1].

until *prep.* **1.** Up to the time of: *The cafeteria is open until eleven o'clock.* —*conj.* **2.** Up to the time when: *I will wait until you come.*

■ [Uses a movement indicating the passage of time] Move the extended right index finger, palm facing left, in an arc to meet the extended left index finger in front of the left side of the chest, palm facing right and finger pointing up.

unusual *adj.* See sign for STRANGE.

unwanted *adj.* See sign for DON'T WANT.

unwilling *adj.* See sign for LOATH.

unwind *v.* To remove from a spool or undo from a coiled condition: *to unwind the thread.*

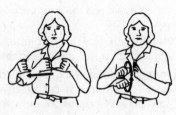

■ [line + wind[1,2]] Beginning with the extended little fingers of both *I hands* touching in front of the chest, palms facing in, move the right hand to the right. Then move the right *modified X hand,* palm facing down, in a repeated circle near the palm of the left *open hand* held in front of the chest, palm facing right and fingers pointing forward.

up *adv.* **1.** In or to a higher place: *The airplane went up.* —*prep.* **2.** To or at a higher place on or in: *to go up the mountain.* Same sign used for: **upward.**

■ [Points up] With the right extended index finger pointing up in front of the right shoulder, palm facing forward, move the right hand upward a short distance.

UPC or Universal Product Code *n.* See sign for STRIPE.

update *v.* **1.** To make current: *to update the files.* —*n.* **2.** New, up-to-date information: *Give me an update on the situation.* **3.** A new, updated account, version, etc.: *selling an update of the textbook.* Same sign used for: **conversion, sequel.**

■ Beginning with the right *10 hand* in front of the right side of the chest, palm facing down, and the left *10 hand* in front of the left side of the chest, palm facing right, twist the right wrist to the right to turn the palm left. Then bring the knuckles of the right hand against the heel of the left hand, pushing it forward.

upgrade *v.* See sign for IMPROVE[2].

uphold *v.* See sign for SUPPORT[1,2].

upload *v.* To transmit a file from one computer to another: *upload my files to the Internet.* Same sign used for: **export.**

■ [Action of information flowing up] Beginning with both *bent V hands* in front of the body, palms facing each other and fingers pointing up, move the hands in and then upward to the right while straightening the fingers to form *V hands.*

upon *prep.* See sign for ON.

ups and downs *pl. n.* High and low points; good and bad times: *This job has its ups and downs.*

■ [Natural gesture showing an up-and-down movement] Beginning with the right *B hand* in front of the right side of the body, palm facing forward and fingers pointing up, move the hand upward and then bend the fingers to go downward and upward again with a double movement in front of the right side of the body.

upset[1] *v.* **1.** To disturb or distress physically or emotionally: *His actions upset me somewhat.* —*adj.* **2.** Physically or emotionally disturbed or distressed: *an upset stomach.* —*n.* **3.** A disturbance: *a general upset over the fire downtown.*

■ [The stomach seems to turn over as when upset] Beginning with the right *P hand* in front of the abdomen, palm facing down, twist the wrist forward, ending with the palm facing up.

upset[2] *v., adj., n.* (alternate sign)

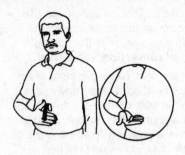

- [The stomach seems to turn over as when upset] Beginning with the right *open hand,* fingers pointing left, against the abdomen, flip the hand forward, ending with the palm facing up.

upset[3] *v.* See sign for DISGUSTED[1].

upstairs *adv.* Same sign as for UP but made with a double movement.

up to *prep.* See sign for MAXIMUM.

up to now See sign for SINCE[1].

upward *adv.* See sign for UP.

urge *v.* To encourage earnestly: *I urged him to go to college.* Same sign used for: **persuade.**

- [The hands seem to hold reins and use them to urge a horse forward] With both *modified X hands* in front of each side of the chest, palms facing in opposite directions and right hand closer to the chest than the left hand, move the hands forward with a short double movement.

urgent *adj.* See signs for HURRY[1,2], NOW[1,2].

urine *n.* See sign for PENIS[1].

us[1] *pron.* The objective case of WE, used as a direct or indirect object; used in referring to the person speaking plus one or more others: *Take us with you. They gave us new office furniture.*

- [Initialized sign similar to sign for **we**[1,2]] Touch the index-finger side of the right *U hand,* palm facing left and fingers pointing up, to the right side of the chest. Then twist the wrist and move the hand around to touch the little-finger side of the right *U hand* to the left side of the chest, palm facing right.

us[2] *pron.* See signs for WE[2,3].

usage *n.* See signs for USE[1,2,3].

use[1] *v.* To put into service; employ for some purpose: *Use a pen to write the check.* Same sign used for: **usage, useful, utilize.**

- [Initialized sign] Move the right *U hand,* palm facing forward and fingers pointing up, in a repeated circle over the back of the left *S hand* held in front of the chest, palm facing down, hitting the heel of the right hand on the left hand each time as it passes.

use[2] *v.* (alternate sign) Same sign used for: **usage, useful, utilize.**

- [Initialized sign] Move the right *U hand,* palm facing forward and fingers pointing up, in a repeated circle over the back of the left *U hand* held in front of the chest, palm facing down and fingers pointing right, hitting the back of the left hand with the heel of the right hand each time as it passes.

use[3] *v.* (alternate sign) Same sign used for: **usage, useful, utilize.**

- Move the right *U hand,* palm facing forward and fingers pointing up, in a circle in front of the right shoulder.

use[4] *v.* See sign for APPLY[1].

used *adj.* See sign for SECOND-HAND.

used to[1] Accustomed to: *The students got used to going home at three o'clock.* Same sign used for: **usual, usually.**

- [Initialized sign similar to sign for **custom**] With the heel of the right *U hand,* palm facing forward and fingers pointing up, on the back of the left *S hand* held in front of the chest, palm facing down, move both hands downward.

used to[2] See signs for LONG AGO[1].

used up *v. phrase.* See signs for RUN OUT OF[1,2].

useful *adj.* See signs for USE[1,2,3].

usual *adj.* See signs for DAILY, REGULAR, USED TO. Related form: **usually** *adv.*

usurp *v.* To seize and hold by force: *The revolutionaries usurped the government's power.*

■ Bring the right *C hand* from in front of the body, palm facing down, upward past the index-finger side of the left *S hand* held in front of the chest, palm facing down, while changing the right hand into an *S hand*, palm facing in, and then continuing up in front of the right shoulder while opening the fingers into a *5 hand*, palm facing back and fingers pointing up.

utilize *v.* See signs for USE[1,2,3].

vacant *adj.* See sign for EMPTY. Related form: **vacancy** *n.*

vacation *n.* A free time away from one's usual duties, as for rest or travel: *to go on vacation.*

- With the thumbs of both *5 hands* near each armpit, palms facing in and fingers pointing toward each other, wiggle the fingers with a repeated movement.

vaccinate[1] *v.* To inoculate with a vaccine, a preparation for producing immunity to a specific disease: *to vaccinate the city's population against smallpox.* Related form: **innoculate, vaccination** *n.*

- [Shows the traditional location on the upper arm for vaccinations] Rub the fingertips of the right *modified X hand* downward with a double movement on the left upper arm.

vaccinate[2] *v.* See sign for INJECT.

vaccine *n.* See sign for SHOT.

vacuum[1] *v.* To clean with a vacuum cleaner: *to vacuum the carpet.*

- [Demonstrates the action of dirt being sucked into a vacuum hose] With the left *C hand* around the right wrist, bring the fingers of the right *5 hand,* palm facing down and fingers pointing forward, back into the palm of the left hand with a double movement, closing the fingers of the right hand into a *flattened O hand* each time.

vacuum[2] *v.* (alternate sign)

- [Demonstrates the action of a vacuum drawing in dirt] Open and close the fingertips of the right *flattened O hand* with a short repeated movement on the palm of the left *open hand* held in front of the chest, palm facing up and fingers pointing forward.

vacuum³ *v.* (alternate sign)

■ [Shows the action of a vacuum cleaner] With the fingertips of the right *flattened C hand* on the palm of the left *open hand* held in front of the chest, palm facing up and fingers pointing forward, move the right fingers forward toward the fingers of the left hand with a short wiggling movement.

vacuum cleaner *n.* An electrical appliance used for cleaning carpets, floors, furniture, etc., by suction: *to clean the living room walls with a vacuum cleaner.*

■ [**vacuum**¹,²,³ + **clean**] Move the fingertips of the right *flattened O hand* with a short repeated movement on palm of the left *open hand* held in front of the chest, palm facing up and fingers pointing forward. Then, beginning with the right *open hand* on the heel of the left *open hand,* palms facing each other, slide the right palm off the fingers of the left hand.

vagina *n.* A canal between the vulva and the uterus in female mammals: *a woman's vagina.*

■ [The shape of one's vagina] Tap the index fingers and thumbs of both *L hands,* palms facing in and index fingers pointing down, together with a double movement in front of the body.

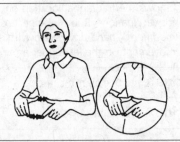

vague *adj.* Not clear; indefinite; indistinct: *offered only a vague explanation that told us nothing.* Same sign used for: **ambiguous, blurry, fade, hazy, illegible, unclear.**

■ [Represents a blurring of the facts] With the palms of both *5 hands* together at an angle in front of the chest, right palm facing forward and left palm facing in, move both hands in circular movements going in opposite directions, rubbing the palms against each other.

vain *adj.* Having too much pride in or concern with one's appearance or achievements: *Vain people can be tiresome, always thinking about themselves.* Same sign used for: **vanity.**

■ [Initialized sign] Beginning with both *V hands* in front of each shoulder, palms facing in and fingers pointing up, move the fingers backward over each shoulder with a double movement.

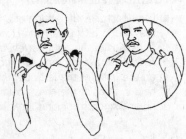

valentine[1] *n.* A greeting card sent on St. Valentine's Day as a token of affection: *She always gets a valentine from her boyfriend.*

■ [The shape of a valentine heart on the area of the heart] Beginning with the bent middle finger of both *5 hands* near each other on the left side of the chest, palms facing in, move the hands in a heart shape downward on the left side of the chest.

valentine[2] *n.* See signs for HEART[2,3].

valley[1] *n.* An elongated area of low land between hills or mountains: *The stream runs through the valley.*

■ [Shows the shape of a valley] Beginning with the index-finger sides of both *B hands* held up in front of both shoulders, palms facing down and fingers pointing forward, bring the right hand downward and then upward again, ending with the index-finger sides of both hands touching in front of the left shoulder.

valley[2] *n.* (alternate sign)

■ [Shows the shape of a valley] Beginning with both *B hands* in front of each side of the head, palms facing down and fingers pointing forward, move the hands downward toward each other, ending with the index-finger sides of both hands touching in front of the body.

valley[3] *n.* (alternate sign)

■ [Initialized sign showing the shape of a valley] Beginning with both *V hands* in front of each side of the head, palms facing down and fingers pointing forward, move the hands downward toward each other, ending with the index-finger sides of both *U hands* touching in front of the body, palms facing down and fingers pointing forward.

valuable *adj.* Having material worth, merit, esteem, importance, etc.: *a valuable document.* Related form: **value** *n.*

■ [Represents bringing something valuable to the top of the pile] Beginning with both *V hands* in front of the body, palms facing up, move the hands outward and upward in arcs, ending with the index-finger sides of both *V hands* touching in front of the chest, palms facing down.

value *n.* See signs for COST[2], IMPORTANT[1,2].

valve *n.* A moveable part of a device that opens
and closes to control the flow of something:
the gas valve.

- ■ [Shows the action of a valve] Beginning with
  the palm of the right *open hand* on the
  index-finger side of the left *S hand,* raise the
  right fingers up and down with a double
  movement while keeping the heel of the
  hand in place.

vampire *n.* (in European folklore and
literature) A corpse that becomes
reanimated at night and rises from its coffin
to suck blood from its victims: *There have
been several movies about vampires.*

- ■ [Represents a vampire's teeth biting a
  person's neck] Bring the fingertips of the
  right *bent V hand,* palm facing left, in
  against the right side of the neck.

vanilla *n.* **1.** A flavoring: *to put vanilla in
the cake. —adj.* **2.** Flavored with vanilla:
vanilla ice cream. Same sign used for:
vitamin.

- ■ [Initialized sign] Shake the right *V hand,*
  palm facing forward and fingers pointing
  up, from side to side with a small double
  movement in front of the right shoulder.

vanish *v.* See sign for DISAPPEAR[1].

vanity *n.* See sign for VAIN.

vanquish *v.* See sign for DEFEAT[1].

vapor *n.* See sign for RAPTURE.

variable *adj.* Changeable, as in quality or
size: *looking for a database program that
allows variable-length records for storing
text.* Same sign used for: **different.**

- ■ [Initialized sign indicating unevenness]
  Beginning with both *V hands* in front of
  the chest, palms facing down and
  fingers pointing forward, move the
  hands apart in a large wavy movement
  to in front of each shoulder.

variety[1] *n.* **1.** The state of being diverse: *Your writing lacks variety.* **2.** A collection of different forms of things in the same general category: *a variety of answers to the same question.* Same sign used for: **and so forth, et cetera, random, range.**

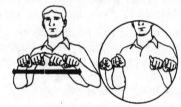

- Beginning with the extended index fingers of both hands touching in front of the chest, palms facing down, move the hands apart to in front of each side of the chest while bending the index fingers downward, forming *X hands* with a double movement.

variety[2] *n.* (alternate sign) Same sign used for: **different.**

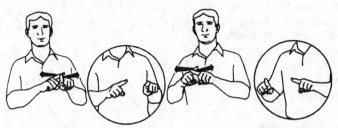

- [**different-different**] Beginning with the extended index fingers of both hands crossed in front of the left side of the chest, palms facing down, move the hands apart with a quick movement. Repeat in front of the right side of the chest.

vary *v.* **1.** To be different or to change periodically: *The data varies from record to record.* **2.** To alter: *to vary your response in different circumstances.* Related form: **variable** *adj.* Same sign used for: **diverse.**

- Beginning with both extended index fingers pointing forward in front of the chest, palms facing down, move the right hand up and the left hand down with an alternating repeated movement as the hands move outward.

vasectomy *n.* See sign for STERILIZATION.

vegetable *n.* Any plant, one or more parts of which, as the leaves, flowers, stems, or roots, is eaten as food: *Vegetables are part of a balanced diet.*

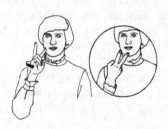

- [Initialized sign] Beginning with the index finger of the right *V hand*, palm facing forward, touching the right side of the chin, twist the wrist to turn the palm back and touch the middle finger to the right side of the chin.

---

vehicle *n.* See signs for CAR[1].

---

vending machine *n.* A machine from which food or drink or other small items can be obtained by inserting coins: *to get a soda from the vending machine.*

- ■ [**machine** + mime putting money in a vending machine and pulling a knob for one's selection] With the fingers of both *curved 5 hands* loosely meshed together, palms facing in, move the hands up and down in front of the chest with a repeated movement. Next, with the right thumb holding down the bent left index finger in front of the right shoulder, palm facing left, quickly flick the index finger up. Then, with the right thumb tucked under the bent right index finger, palm facing left, pull the right hand back toward the right side of the body.

---

venetian blinds *n.* See sign for BLINDS.

---

vengeance *n.* See sign for REVENGE.

---

venison *n.* Deer meat: *to make stew from venison.*

- ■ [**deer** + **meat**] Touch the thumbs of both *5 hands* to each side of the head, palms facing forward and fingers pointing up. Then, with the bent index finger and thumb of the right *5 hand*, palm facing down, grasp the fleshy part of the left *open hand*, palm facing in and fingers pointing right, and shake the hands forward and back with a double movement.

---

venue *n.* See sign for PLACE[1].

---

verb *n.* A word that can function in a sentence as the main element in the predicate, expressing action, state, or relation, and can often be inflected for tense, mood, agreement with the subject, etc.: *A complete declarative sentence has a subject and a verb.*

- ■ [Initialized sign] Move the right *V hand*, palm facing in and fingers pointing left, from left to right in front of the chin.

verse¹ *n.* **1.** A poem: *wrote a verse in your honor.*
2. Poetry, especially metrical poetry: *writes verse rather than fiction.* **3.** A group of lines of poetry; stanza: *Read the first verse silently before the class discussion.*

- [Shows the size of a verse on paper] Slide the fingertips of the right *G hand,* palm angled left, from the heel to the fingers of the left *open hand* held in front of the body, palm facing right and fingers pointing forward.

verse² *n.* (alternate sign)

- [Initialized sign showing the size of a verse on paper] Move the fingertips of the right *V hand,* palm facing in and fingers pointing left, from the heel to the fingers of the left *open hand,* palm facing right and fingers pointing forward.

versus¹ *prep.* Against (used especially to join names of parties in a legal case or competing teams in a sports contest): *the Bears versus the Lions.* Same sign used for: **match.**

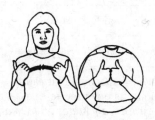

- [Represents two opponents meeting] Beginning with both *10 hands* in front of each side of the chest, palms facing in, bring the knuckles together in front of the chest.

versus² *prep.* See sign for CHALLENGE.

vertical *adj.* Straight up and down; upright: *Draw a vertical line on the blackboard.*

- [Demonstrates a vertical position] Beginning with the side of the extended right index finger across the index-finger side of the left *B hand* in front of the body, palm facing in and fingers pointing right, raise the right finger upward in front of the chest. Then, beginning with the little-finger side of the right *B hand,* palm facing left and fingers pointing forward, across the index-finger side of the left *B hand,* raise the right hand in front of the chest.

very *adv.* In or to a high degree; extremely: *a very good job.*

- [Initialized sign similar to sign for **much**] Beginning with the fingertips of both *V hands* touching in front of the chest, palms facing each other, bring the hands apart to in front of each shoulder.

veterinarian *n.* A doctor who deals with the prevention and treatment of diseases and injuries in animals: *We have to take the dog to the veterinarian for immunization shots.*

■ [**animal** + **doctor**[1,2]] With the fingertips of both *bent hands* touching the chest, palms facing in opposite directions, rock the hands with a repeated movement from side to side while keeping the fingertips in place. Then tap the fingertips of the right *M hand,* palm facing down, with a double movement on the wrist of the left *open hand* held in front of the body, palm facing up.

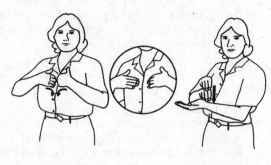

veto *n.* See sign for REJECT[1].

via *prep.* See sign for THROUGH.

vibrate *v.* See sign for BEAT[3]. Related form: **vibration** *n.*

vibrator *n.* A machine that causes vibrations, as one used for massage: *The therapist used a vibrator on my bad back.*

■ [**machine** + a gesture showing a vibrating movement] With the fingers of both *curved 5 hands* loosely meshed together, palms facing in, move the hands up and down in front of the chest with a repeated movement. Then, with the right *curved hand* grasping the back of the left *curved hand,* both palms facing down, shake the hands with a short repeated movement.

vice-president *n.* The officer next in rank to the president: *The vice-president called the meeting to order.*

■ [Abbreviation **v-p**] Beginning with the right *V hand* in front of the right side of the forehead, palm facing forward and fingers pointing up, move the hand downward by twisting the wrist, forming a *P hand* in front of the right shoulder.

vicinity[1] *n.* A region near a place: *set up a drug-free zone in the vicinity of the schoolyard.*

■ [**close**[1,2] + **here**[1] + **area**[1,3,4]] Bring the fingers of the right *open hand,* palm facing in and fingers pointing left, back toward the left *open hand* held in front of the chest, palm facing in and fingers pointing right. Next move both *open hands,* palms facing up and fingers pointing forward, in circles in front of each side of the body, going in opposite directions. Then move the right *open hand,* palm facing down and fingers pointing forward, in a large circle in front of the right side of the body.

vicinity[2] *n.* See signs for AREA[1,2,3,4].

victim *n.* A person who has been badly taken advantage of or who suffers loss, injury, or death because of the action of others or some agency: *She was the victim of fraud.*

■ [Initialized sign similar to sign for **body**] Beginning with the extended fingers of both *V hands* touching each side of the chest, palms facing in and fingers pointing toward each other, move the hands downward on each side of the body.

victory[1] *n.* **1.** The defeat of an opponent: *The candidate declared a victory.* **2.** A triumph or success: *achieved a victory over the illness.*

■ [Initialized sign similar to sign for **celebrate**] Beginning with both *V hands* near each side of the head, palms facing forward and fingers pointing up, move the hands in small circles going in opposite directions.

victory[2] *n.* See sign for CELEBRATE.

video camera *n.* See sign for MOVIE CAMERA.

videotape[1] *n.* **1.** A magnetic tape on which images, often with accompanying audio, can be recorded: *to watch a videotape.* —*v.* **2.** To make a recording of, as a television program, on magnetic tape: *videotaped the movie that was broadcast at midnight.*

■ [Abbreviation **v-t**] Beginning with the index finger side of the right *V hand,* palm facing forward and fingers pointing up, against open left palm held up in front of the chest, palm facing right, move the right hand forward in a circular movement while changing into a *T hand* as the hand moves.

videotape[2] *v., n.* (alternate sign)

■ [Represents the fluttering pictures on a videotape] With the index-finger side of the right *C hand* against the palm of the left *open hand* held in front of the chest, palm facing right and fingers pointing up, close the right fingers and thumb toward each other with a quick repeated movement.

videotape[3] *n., v.* See sign for MOVIE CAMERA.

Vietnam or **Viet Nam** *n.* A far-eastern country: *a war fought in Vietnam.* Related form: **Vietnamese** *n., adj.*

■ [Initialized sign] Beginning with the index finger of the right *V hand* near the outside of the right eye, palm facing forward and fingers pointing up, twist the wrist forward with a double movement, turning the palm left.

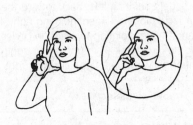

view[1] *v.* To survey: *view the problem.* Same sign used for: **sighting.**

■ [Represents the movement of one's eyes when scanning a view] Beginning with both *V hands* in front of the left side of the chest, palms facing down and fingers pointing forward, swing the hands slowly to the right in large arcs.

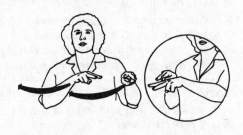

view[2] *v.* See signs for LOOK OVER[2], OVERLOOK[2].

viewpoint *n.* See signs for PERSPECTIVE[1,2].

vigilance *n.* See sign for WATCH[5].

village *n.* See sign for TOWN.

vinegar *n.* A sour, acidic liquid used as a condiment or preservative: *Put either vinegar or lemon juice in the salad dressing.*

■ [Initialized sign similar to sign for **water**] Beginning with the index finger of the right *V hand* touching the chin, palm facing left and fingers pointing up, move the hand forward with a short double movement.

violate *v.* To break (a law, promise, etc.): *to violate the rules.*

- [Initialized sign similar to sign for **but**] Beginning with the index fingers of both *V hands* touching in front of the body, palms facing down and fingers angled forward, bring the hands quickly apart and upward while turning the wrists, ending with the palms facing each other and the fingers pointing up in front of each shoulder.

violation *n.* See signs for CRIME[1,2].

violin *n.* A musical instrument, the treble member of the modern stringed instruments, held in one arm and played with a bow drawn across the strings by the other hand: *listening to a master play the violin.* Same sign used for: **fiddle.**

- [Mime playing a violin] While holding the left *curved hand* in front of the left shoulder, palm facing in, move the right *F hand* forward and back toward the left side of the chest with a swinging movement, palm facing down.

VIP *n. Short for very important person.* See sign for CHIEF[1].

viper *n.* See sign for SNAKE.

virgin *n.* A person who has not had sexual intercourse, as a maiden: *The virgin was modest and innocent.*

- [Initialized sign] Slide the index-finger side of the right *V hand,* palm facing forward, downward on the right cheek toward the right side of the chin.

virtual[1] *adj.* **1.** Having the effect of although not actually being such: *Because she had not seen him for years, he was a virtual strange.* **2.** Simulated by computer software; functionally behaving like: *a virtual disk in RAM.*

- [Initialized sign similar to sign for **dream**] Beginning with the index-finger side of the right *V hand* touching the right side of the forehead, palm facing left, move the hand forward in a double arc.

virtual[2] *adj.* See sign for FAKE[1].

visibility *n.* **1.** The condition of being able to be seen or noticed: *a politician with national visibility.* **2.** The distance one can see in given weather conditions: *The plane was able to land although the visibility was poor.* Related form: **visibly** *adv.*

■ [**see**[1,2] + **look at** + **can**[2]] Beginning with the extended fingers of the right *V hand* pointing toward the eyes, palm facing in, twist the wrist to point the fingers forward. Next, beginning with the right *V hand* in front of the right side of the face, palm facing down and fingers pointing forward, push the hand forward a short distance. Then, beginning with both *S hands* in front of each side of the chest, palms facing down, move the hands downward with a short double movement.

visible *adj.* Able to be seen: *The trees were visible through the fog.* Same sign used for: **see-through, transparent.**

■ [**see**[1] + **through**] Move the fingers of the right *V hand,* palm facing down and fingers pointing forward, from near the right side of the face forward between the index finger and middle finger of the left *5 hand* held in front of the face, palm facing in and fingers pointing right.

vision[1] *n.* The power of seeing or predicting the future: *I saw a vision of a world without war.* Same sign used for: **envision, foresee, predict, prediction.**

■ [Represents one's eyes seeing past the present into the future] Beginning with the right *V hand* in front of the face, palm facing in and fingers pointing up, move the hand forward in an arc under the left *open hand* held in front of the face, palm facing down and fingers pointing right.

vision[2] *n.* (alternate sign) Same sign used for: **sighting.**

■ [Represents one's view being enlarged] Beginning with both *S hands* in front of the face, palms facing in opposite directions and the right hand closer to the face than the left hand, bring the hands apart while opening into *curved hands* in front of each side of the face.

vision[3] *n.* See sign for SEE[1].

visit *v.* **1.** To go and stay with or at for a short time: *to visit a friend in the hospital; to visit Vermont.* —*n.* **2.** An act or instance of visiting: *looking forward to a long visit with you.*

■ [Initialized sign] Beginning with both *V hands* in front of each side of the chest, palms facing in and fingers pointing up, move the hands in repeated alternating circles.

visitor *n.* A person who visits: *A visitor from abroad came to our house.* Same sign used for: **guest.**

■ [**visit** + **person marker**] Beginning with both *V hands* in front of each side of the chest, palms facing in and fingers pointing up, move the hands in repeated alternating circles. Then move both *open hands*, palms facing each other, downward along each side of the body.

visual aid *n.* An instructional device, as a graph or chart, to help clarify information: *The teacher uses effective visual aids in the social studies classes.*

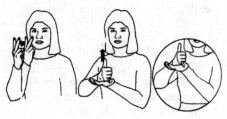

■ [**see**[1] + **help**] Beginning with the right *V hand* in front of the right side of the face, palm facing in and fingers pointing up, move the hand forward a short distance. Then, with the little-finger side of the right *10 hand* on the upturned curved left palm, move both hands upward in front of the chest.

visualize *adj.* See sign for SEE[1].

vitamin *n.* See sign for VANILLA.

vocabulary[1] *n.* **1.** The words in a language: *studying vocabulary in Russian.* **2.** The stock of words known by a person or group: *The baby has a big vocabulary for her age.*

■ [Initialized sign similar to sign for **word**] Tap the fingertips of the right *V hand*, palm facing down, with a double movement on the extended left index finger held in front of the body, palm facing in and finger pointing right.

vocabulary[2] *n.* (alternate sign)

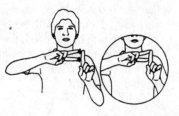

■ [Initialized sign similar to sign for **letter**[1]] Tap the fingertips of the right *V hand*, palm facing forward and fingers pointing left, with a double movement against the extended left index finger pointing up in front of the left side of the body, palm facing forward.

vocabulary

vocabulary[3] *n.* See sign for WORD.

vocal *adj.* See sign for VOICE. Related form: **vocalize** *v.*

voice *n.* The sound made through the mouth, as by human beings in speaking or singing, especially the type of sound unique to a given individual: *a high-pitched voice.* Same sign used for: **vocal, vocalize.**

■ [Initialized sign showing the location of one's voice] Move the fingertips of the right *V hand*, palm facing down, upward on the throat with a double movement.

void *adj.* See sign for EMPTY.

volcano *n.* A mountain having an opening formed around a vent in the earth's crust through which steam and lava are or have been forced out: *an active volcano.*

■ [Shape of a hill + **erupt**[1]] Beginning with both *C hands* in front of the chest, palms facing each other, move the hands apart and downward in arcs. Then, beginning with the right *S hand* cupped in the left *C hand*, both palms facing in, bring the right hand suddenly upward while opening into a *5 hand* in front of the face, palm facing in and fingers pointing up.

volleyball[1] *n.* **1.** A game played by two teams using a large ball kept in motion by the hands hitting it back and forth over a net: *to play a game of volleyball.* **2.** The ball used in this game: *to hit the volleyball over the net.*

■ [Mime hitting a volleyball] Beginning with both *open hands* near each side of the head, palms facing forward and fingers pointing up, push the hands upward and forward with a double movement.

volleyball[2] *n.* (alternate sign)

■ [Initialized sign showing hitting a volleyball] Beginning with both *V hands* near each side of the head, palms facing forward and fingers pointing up, push the hands forward with a short double movement.

volume[1] *n.* **1.** The amount of space that an object occupies, as measured in cubic units: *The volume of air in tires is about 32 pounds.* **2.** The physical unit of storage available on an electronic storage medium, as a hard or floppy disk: *It's a good idea to name the volume when you format the floppy disk.*

■ [Initialized sign similar to sign for **area**[2]] Beginning with the index fingers of both *V hands* touching in front of the chest, palms facing forward and fingers pointing up, move the hands in outward arcs until the middle fingers of both *V hands* touch again in front of the body.

---

volume[2] *n.* See sign for DISK.

---

voluntary *adj.* See sign for APPLY[2].

---

volunteer *v.* See sign for APPLY[2].

---

vomit *v.* **1.** To eject the contents of the stomach through the mouth; throw up: *vomited because of food poisoning.* —*n.* **2.** The substance ejected from the stomach: *had to clean up the vomit.* Same sign used for: **throw up.**

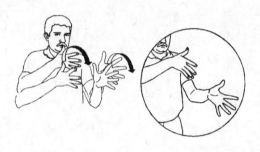

■ [Represents food being expelled from the mouth] Beginning with the right *5 hand* near the mouth, palm facing left and fingers pointing forward, and the left *5 hand* forward of the right hand, palm facing right and fingers pointing forward, move both hands upward and forward in large arcs.

---

vote *n.* **1.** A formal choice made by an individual or body of individuals: *The vote was in favor of the proposition.* **2.** A ballot or equivalent mechanism for making such a choice: *to count the votes.* —*v.* **3.** To express such a choice officially, as by casting a ballot: *to vote for your favorite candidate.* Same sign used for: **elect, election.**

■ [Represents putting one's vote into a ballot box] Insert the fingertips of the right *F hand*, palm facing down, with a double movement in the hole formed by the left *O hand* held in front of the chest, palm facing right.

VOW[1] *n.* **1.** A solemn promise: *He gave his vow.* —*v.* **2.** To make a promise: *I vow not to smoke again.* See also sign for PROMISE[1]. Same sign used for: **assurance, assure, commit, commitment, obligate, pledge, swear, sworn.**

■ [Natural gesture for making a pledge] Beginning with the extended right index finger in front of the mouth, palm facing left and finger pointing up, move the right hand forward with a deliberate movement while opening into an *open hand,* palm facing forward and fingers pointing up, and hitting the right forearm against the index-finger side of the left *open hand* held across the body, palm facing down and fingers pointing right.

VOW[2] *n., v.* (alternate sign)

■ [Initialized sign] Beginning with the extended right index finger in front of the mouth, palm facing left and finger pointing up, move the right hand forward while opening into a *V hand,* ending with the heel of the right *V hand* against the index-finger side of the left *open hand* held in front of the chest, palm facing down and fingers pointing right.

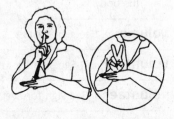

wacky *adj. Slang.* See signs for CRAZY[1,2], WILD[1].

wade *v.* To walk through shallow water: *to wade in the puddles.*

- [**water** + **walk**[1,2]] Tap the index-finger side of the right *W hand,* palm facing left, with a double movement against the chin. Then, beginning with both *open hands* in front of each side of the body, right palm angled forward and left palm angled down, move the hands up and down with an alternating movement by bending the wrists.

wag *v.* To move or be moved from side to side: *The dog wagged its tail. The dog's tail wagged.*

- [Represents a dog's tail wagging] Beginning with the extended right index finger pointing left, palm facing in, and the extended left index finger touching the right wrist, palm facing down, move the right index finger in an arc from side to side with a long, slow double movement.

wager *n., v.* See sign for BET.

wages *pl. n.* See signs for EARN, INCOME[1].

wagon[1] *n.* Any of various kinds of four-wheeled vehicles used to carry loads, ranging from small, open carts pulled by children to motor-driven trucks: *The toddler has learned to pull the little red wagon.*

- [Mime pulling a child's wagon] Move the right *modified X hand,* palm facing up, from behind the right side of the body forward to near the right hip.

wagon[2] *n.* (alternate sign)

- [Initialized sign similar to sign for **car**[2]] Beginning with the ring-finger side of the right *W hand* touching the index-finger side of the left *W hand,* palms facing in opposite directions, move the right hand back toward the chin.

wagon

wagon[3] *n.* See sign for HARNESS RACE. This sign is used only when referring to a horse-drawn wagon.

waistband *n.* See sign for BELT[2].

wait *v.* **1.** To remain inactive or in readiness, as until something expected happens: *to wait for the bus.* —*n.* **2.** An act, instance, or state of waiting: *It was a long wait.*

■ [Seems to indicate twiddling the finger while waiting impatiently] Beginning with both *curved 5 hands* in front of the body, palms facing up, wiggle the fingers with a repeated movement.

waiter or **waitress** *n.* A person who waits on tables in a restaurant: *The waiter (or waitress) brought the food.* Same sign used for: **servant.**

■ [**serve + person marker**] Beginning with both *open hands* in front of each side of the body, palms facing up and right hand closer to the body than the left hand, move the hands forward and back with an alternating movement. Then move both *open hands,* palms facing each other, downward along each side of the body.

wait on *v. phrase.* See sign for SERVE.

waive *v.* See signs for DISMISS, GIVE UP.

wake up *v. phrase.* See sign for AWAKE[1].

walk[1] *v.* To go or travel on foot at a moderate speed: *to walk down the hall.* Same sign used for: **stroll, wander.**

■ [Represents a person's legs moving when walking] Beginning with both *3 hands* in front of the body, palms facing down and fingers pointing forward, move the hands forward and back with an alternating double movement.

walk[2] *v.* (alternate sign) Same sign used for: **stroll, wander.**

■ [Represents a person's legs moving when walking] Beginning with both *open hands* in front of each side of the body, left palm facing in and fingers pointing down and right palm facing down and fingers pointing forward, move the fingers of both hands upward and downward with an alternating movement by bending the wrists.

wall[1] *n.* An upright side of a room or other structure: *a ten-foot wall.*

- [The shape of a wall] Beginning with both *open hands* together in front of the chest, palms facing forward and fingers pointing up, bring the hands apart to in front of each shoulder.

wall[2] *n.* (alternate sign)

- [The shape of a wall] Beginning with both *open hands* in front of each side of the chest, palms facing in and fingers pointing toward each other, bring the hands straight down.

wall[3] *n.* See sign for BOARD[1].

wallet *n.* A flat folded case with compartments for carrying paper money and other items, as credit cards or identification: *put your money in your wallet.* Same sign used for: **billfold.**

- [Represents opening a folded wallet] Beginning with the palms of both *open hands* together in front of the chest, bring the heels apart with a double movement while keeping the fingertips together.

wallpaper *n.* **1.** Paper printed with a pattern used for covering walls: *to put waterproof wallpaper in the bathroom.* —*v.* **2.** To paste wallpaper on or in: *to wallpaper the room.*

- [**wall**[1,2] + **paper**] Beginning with both *open hands* in front of the chest, palms facing forward and fingers pointing up, move the hands apart to in front of each shoulder. Then brush the heel of the right *open hand,* palm facing down, on the heel of the left *open hand,* palm facing up in front of the body, with a double movement.

walrus *n.* A large mammal that lives in the Arctic seas: *The walrus has large ivory tusks and a wrinkled hide.*

- [The location of a walrus's tusks] Beginning with the index-finger sides of both *O hands* near each side of the mouth, palms facing each other, bring the hands outward and forward in arcs, ending near each other in front of the chest.

wan

wan[1] *adj.* **1.** Unnaturally pale; pallid and sickly looking: *a wan complexion.* **2.** Showing illness, weakness, or fatigue: *a wan smile.*

■ [**feel** + **weak**] Move the bent middle finger of the right *5 hand,* palm facing in, upward with a double movement on the chest. Then bring the fingers of the right *5 hand,* palm facing in and fingers pointing down, downward with a double movement on the open left palm, bending the right fingers each time.

wan[2] *adj.* See sign for PALE.

wander *v.* See signs for ROAM[1,2], WALK[1,2].

want *v.* To wish for: *I want to eat dinner.* Same sign used for: **desire, passion.**

■ [Represents bringing a wanted thing toward oneself] Beginning with both *curved 5 hands* in front of the body, palms facing up and fingers pointing forward, bring the hands back toward the chest while constricting the fingers toward the palms.

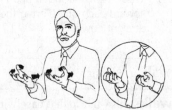

war *n.* See signs for BATTLE[1,2].

wardrobe *n.* A collection of clothes or costumes: *She has a large wardrobe, with clothing for every occasion.*

■ [**clothes** + a gesture indicating a row of clothes in a closet] Brush the fingertips of the right *5 hands,* palms facing in and fingers pointing toward each other, downward on each side of the chest with a double movement. Then, beginning with the left *5 hand* near the little finger of the right *5 hand,* palms facing in opposite directions and fingers angled up, move the left hand downward.

warm *adj.* Having or giving out a feeling of heat: *a warm room.* Related form: **warmth** *n.*

■ Beginning with the fingers of the right *E hand* near the mouth, palm facing in, move the hand forward in a small arc while opening the fingers into a *C hand,* ending with the palm facing up.

warn *v.* To give notice or advice to, as of impending danger: *They warned us about the impending snowstorm.* Related form: **warning** *n.* Same sign used for: **admonish, alert, beware, caution, rebuke, reprimand.**

■ [Indicates tapping someone on the hand as a warning] Tap the palm of the right *open hand* with a double movement on the back of the left *open hand* held in front of the chest, both palms facing down.

warp[1] *v.* **1.** To twist out of shape, as from a flat form: *The board was warped from the dampness.* —*n.* **2.** A bend or twist: *a warp in the wood.*

■ [**wood** + a gesture showing things are not aligned] Slide the little-finger side of the right *open hand,* palm facing left and fingers pointing forward, forward and back across the index-finger side of the left *open hand* held in front of the chest, palm facing in and fingers pointing right. Then, beginning with both *open hands* in front of the chest, palms facing down and fingers pointing toward each other, twist the hands in opposite directions, ending with the right palm facing in and the left palm facing forward.

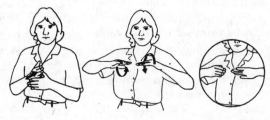

warp[2] *v.* See sign for BEND[3].

warranty *n.* See sign for PROMISE[1].

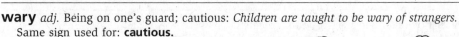

warship *n.* A ship built or armed for war: *The country sent warships to the area as a warning.*

■ [**ship** + a gesture representing four guns on a warship] Beginning with the left *3 hand* in front of the chest, palm facing in and fingers pointing right, bring the fingers of the right *4 hand,* palm facing forward and fingers pointing up, upward with a double movement from behind the left hand to expose the fingers each time.

wary *adj.* Being on one's guard; cautious: *Children are taught to be wary of strangers.* Same sign used for: **cautious.**

■ [**not**[1] + **confident**] Bring the extended thumb of the right *10 hand* from under the chin, palm facing left, forward with a deliberate movement. Then, beginning with both *C hands* in front of the chest, palms facing in and right hand above the left hand, bring the hands downward and in toward the body while closing into *S hands.*

was[1] *v.* First and third person singular past tense of BE: *He was here yesterday.* Same sign used for: **past, were.**

■ [The hand gestures toward the past] Bring the fingertips of the right *bent hand,* palm facing back, down on the right shoulder.

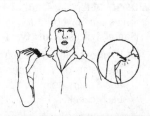

was[2] *v.* (alternate sign)

- [Abbreviation **w-s**] Beginning with the right *W hand* near the right side of the face, palm facing left and fingers pointing up, bring the hand back while changing into an *S hand.*

was[3] *v.* See signs for AGO[1], BE[2].

wash[1] *v.* To clean with water or another liquid, as by dipping and rubbing: *to wash the sweater by hand.* Same sign used for: **rub, wipe.**

- [Demonstrates the action of rubbing something to wash it] Rub the palm side of the right *A hand* with a repeated movement across the upturned palm of the left *A hand.*

wash[2] *v.* (alternate sign, used for washing something flat held in the hand, like a dish) Same sign used for: **wipe.**

- [Demonstrates the action of rubbing something to wash it] Rub the palm side of the right *open hand* in a circular movement on the upturned palm of the left *open hand.*

wash[3] *v.* (alternate sign, used for washing something in front of you, as a window or a car) Same sign used for: **rub.**

- [Demonstrates the action of washing windows or a car] Beginning with both *A hands* in front of each side of the chest, palms facing forward, move the hands in large alternating circles.

wash[4] *v.* (alternate sign, used to indicate cleaning the face)

- [Demonstrates the action of washing one's face] Move both *A hands,* palms facing each other, in alternating circles on each cheek.

wash[5] *v.* See sign for WASHING MACHINE.

washcloth *n.* A small piece of fabric used for washing one's face or body: *to wash your face with a washcloth.* Same sign used for: **wash face, washrag.**

- [Demonstrates the action of washing one's face] Move the palms of both *open hands,* palms facing each other and fingers pointing up, in simultaneous circles near each cheek.

washer *n.* See sign for WASHING MACHINE.

wash face *v.* See sign for WASHCLOTH.

wash hair *v.* See sign for SHAMPOO.

washing machine *n.* An appliance for washing clothes, linens, towels, etc.: *put the dirty laundry in the washing machine.* Same sign used for: **washer, wash laundry.**

■ [Indicates the action of a washing machine's agitator] Beginning with the right *curved 5 hand* over the left *curved 5 hand* in front of the chest, palms facing each other, twist the hands with a repeated movement in opposite directions.

Washington[1] **(D.C.** or **state)** *n.* **1.** The capital of the United States; the District of Columbia: *A new administration brings new faces to Washington.* **2.** A state in the northwest United States: *We plan to visit the outdoor market in Seattle, Washington.*

■ [Initialized sign made near the location used for **capital**[2]] Beginning with the right *W hand* in front of the right shoulder, palm facing left, move the hand forward in a double arc.

Washington[2] (alterate sign)

■ [Initialized sign made near the location used for **capital**[2]] Beginning with the right *W hand* in front of the right shoulder, palm facing left, move the hand forward in a circular movement.

wash laundry *v.* See sign for WASHING MACHINE.

washrag *n.* See sign for WASHCLOTH.

washroom *n.* See sign for TOILET.

waste *n.* **1.** Useless material: *The waste in the bin is to be thrown out.* **2.** Useless consumption or expenditure: *This is a total waste of my time.* —*v.* **3.** To put to poor use or to squander: *Don't waste my time with excuses.*

■ [The hand seems to toss waste away] Beginning with the back of the right *S hand,* palm facing up, in the upturned palm of the left *open hand* held in front of the chest, move the right hand forward while opening into a *5 hand.*

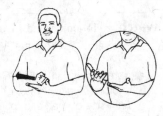

watch

watch[1] *n.* A small, portable device for telling time, as a wristwatch: *She refuses to wear a watch.* Same sign used for: **timepiece, wristwatch.**

- ■ [Location of a person's wristwatch] Slip the bent index finger and thumb of the right hand, palm facing down, downward with a double movement around the left wrist.

watch[2] *n.* (alternate sign) Same sign used for: **timepiece, wristwatch.**

- ■ [The shape of a watch's face] Place the palm side of the right *F hand* on the back of the left wrist.

watch[3] *v.* To look at carefully and attentively: *to watch the children play.*

- ■ [Represents the eyes looking at something] Beginning with both *V hands* in front of the right shoulder, palms facing down and fingers pointing forward, move the hands forward with a short double movement.

watch[4] *v.* (alternate sign)

- ■ [Represents the eyes looking at something] Beginning with the right *V hand* in front of the right side of the face, palm facing down and fingers pointing forward, move the hand forward.

watch[5] *v.* (alternate sign) Same sign used for: **patrol, surveillance, vigilance.**

- ■ [Represents the eyes looking in all directions] Beginning with the palm side of the right *V hand* on the back of the left *V hand*, both palms facing down, move the hands in a flat circle in front of the body.

watch[6] *v.* To look at me (used to indicate that someone is to look at or is looking at the speaker): *Watch me while I do this.*

- ■ [Directional sign indicting that one is being watched by another] Beginning with the right *V hand* in front of the right side of the head, palm facing in and fingers pointing toward the face, move the hand inward toward the face.

watch[7] *v.* See signs for ATTENTION, OBSERVE[1].

watch out *v. phrase.* See signs for CAREFUL, LOOK OUT.

water *n.* The transparent, odorless, tasteless liquid that falls from the sky as rain and is found in impure form in oceans, lakes, underground springs, etc.: *a bucket of water.*

- [Initialized sign] Tap the index-finger side of the right *W hand,* palm facing left, against the chin with a double movement.

watercolor *n.* **1.** Water-soluble pigment that produces a transparent stain: *He paints lovely landscapes in watercolor.* **2.** A picture painted using watercolors: *got out the paints and the brushes to paint a watercolor.*

- [**water** + **paint**[1,2,3]] Tap the index-finger side of the right *W hand,* palm facing left, with a double movement against the chin. Then, with the right thumb extended, swing the right *U hand,* palm facing left, forward and back near the left *open hand* held in front of the chest, palm facing up and fingers pointing forward.

watermelon *n.* A large, oval, edible melon with a hard green rind and juicy red or pink pulp: *Watermelon is a refreshing summer dessert.*

- [**water** + **melon**] Tap the index-finger side of the right *W hand,* palm facing left, against the chin with a double movement. Then, with a double movement, flick the middle finger of the right *8 hand,* palm facing down, off the back of the left *S hand,* palm facing down, bouncing the right hand up slightly each time.

waterproof *adj.* Not able to be penetrated by water: *a waterproof coat.*

- [**water** + **can't** + **penetrate**[2]] Tap the index-finger side of the right *W hand,* palm facing left, against the chin with a double movement. Next bring the extended right index finger downward in front of the chest, striking the extended left index finger as it moves, both palms facing down. Then move the fingers of the right *5 hand,* palm facing left and fingers pointing down, downward to mesh with the fingers of the left *5 hand* held in front of the chest, palm facing up and fingers pointing right.

wave[1] *n.* A moving ridge or swell of water in the ocean: *A high wave overturned the little boat.*

- [The shape of a wave] Beginning with both *5 hands* in front of each side of the body, palms facing down, move the hands upward and down again in a large wavy movement.

wave[2] *v.* **1.** To signal or greet by moving the hand back and forth or up and down: *to wave your hand; to wave to the crowd.* —*n.* **2.** An act or instance of waving the hand: *I saw your frantic wave and came running.*

- [Natural gesture for waving at someone] Move the right *5 hand,* palm facing forward and fingers pointing up, from side to side with a repeated movement in front of the right shoulder.

wavy *adj.* Full of waves; abounding in curves: *drew a wavy line to represent the surface of the ocean.*

- [Indicates a wavy shape] With the left *open hand* extended across the body, palm facing down and fingers pointing right, move the right *open hand,* palm facing down and fingers pointing forward, forward with an up-and-down wavy movement.

wavy hair[1] *n.* Hair that falls in curves: *Some people want to straighten their wavy hair.*

- [**hair** + a gesture showing wavy hair] With the right index finger and thumb, grasp a piece of hair. Then move the right *open hand,* palm facing left and fingers pointing up, from near the top of the head downward with a wavy movement.

wavy hair[2] *n.* (alternate sign)

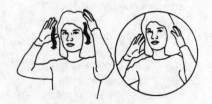

- [Shows the shape of wavy hair] Move both *open hands* from near the top of the head, palms facing each other and fingers pointing up, downward along the head in a wavy movement.

way[1] *n.* **1.** Manner: *I like the way he treats the children.* **2.** A method or plan: *We came up with a way to finish sooner.* **3.** A passage on a path or course: *Can you find your way to her office?*

- [Initialized sign similar to sign for **road**[1]] Beginning with both *W hands* in front of each side of the body, palms facing each other, move the hands straight forward.

way[2] *n.* (alternate sign)

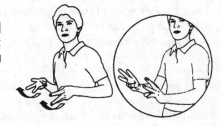

- [Initialized sign similar to sign for **try**[1]] Beginning with both *W hands* in front of each side of the body, palms facing each other, move the hands forward and upward in an arc.

way[3] *n.* See sign for ROAD[1].

we[1] *pron.* The nominative plural of I, used as a subject; used in referring to the person speaking plus one or more others: *We will go together.*

- [Initialized sign similar to sign for **our**] Beginning with the index-finger side of the right *W hand* near the right side of the chest, palm facing left and fingers pointing up, move the hand in an arc across the front of the chest while turning the palm, ending with the palm facing right.

we[2] *pron.* (alternate sign) Same sign used for: **us.**

- Touch the extended right index finger, palm facing down, first to the right side of the chest and then to the left side of the chest.

we[3] *pron.* (alternate sign, used to refer to the speaker plus one other) Same sign used for: **both of us, us.**

- [The fingers point to the referent and oneself] Move the right *2 hand,* palm facing in and fingers pointing up, forward and back with a double movement in front of the right shoulder by bending the wrist.

we[4] *pron.* (alternate sign) Same sign used for: **two of us.**

■ [The fingers point to the referent and oneself] Beginning with the right *2 hand* in front of the right shoulder, palm facing in and fingers pointing up, shake the hand back and forth with a rapid repeated movement.

we[5] *pron.* (alternate sign) Same sign used for: **three of us, trio.**

■ [The fingers point to two others plus oneself] Beginning with the right *3 hand* in front of the right side of the body, palm facing up, move the hand in a double circular movement.

weak *adj.* Lacking in strength, vigor, or force: *feeling weak in the knees; a weak personality.* Related form: **weakness** *n.* Same sign used for: **fatigue, feeble, frail.**

■ [The fingers collapse as if weak] Beginning with the fingertips of the right *5 hand*, palm facing in, touching the palm of the left *open hand* held in front of the chest, move the right hand downward with a double movement, bending the fingers each time.

weak-minded *adj.* See sign for MORON[2].

wealth *n.* See sign for RICH.

wealthy *adj.* See sign for RICH.

wean *v.* To cause (a human baby or other baby mammal) to stop nursing from the breast or a bottle: *tried to wean the baby too early.*

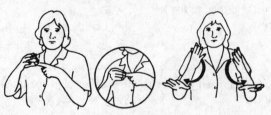

■ [**suck**[4] + **finish**[1,2]] Open and close the fingertips of the right *curved 5 hand*, palm facing left, around the extended left index finger held in front of the chest, palm facing in and finger pointing right. Then, beginning with both *5 hands* in front of the chest, palm facing in and fingers pointing up, flip the hands over with a sudden movement, ending with both palms facing down and fingers pointing forward.

wear *v.* To carry or have on the body as a covering or ornament: *to wear a coat; to wear jewelry.*

■ Move the right *U hand,* palm facing forward and fingers pointing up, in a circle in front of the right side of the body with a double movement.

wear out *v. phrase.* To use until damaged, unfit, or useless: *to wear out your shoes.* Same sign used for: **decay, rot, rotten.**

■ Beginning with both *S hands* together in front of the chest, palms facing up, move the hands forward with a sudden movement while opening into *5 hands,* palms facing up.

weary *adj.* See sign for TIRED.

weather[1] *n.* The state or condition of the atmosphere regarding temperature, moisture, winds, etc.: *good weather expected this week.* Same sign used for: **climate.**

■ [Initialized sign] With the fingertips of both *W hands* together in front of the chest, palms facing each other, twist the hands in opposite directions with a double movement.

weather[2] *n.* (alternate sign) Same sign used for: **climate.**

■ [Initialized sign following the direction of falling rain or snow] Beginning with both *W hands* in front of each shoulder, palms facing forward and fingers pointing up, move the hands downward in front of each side of the chest with a wavy movement.

weave *v.* **1.** To interlace threads in a pattern to form a fabric or something made of such fabric: *to weave a blanket.* —*n.* **2.** A pattern of interlaced threads in a fabric: *a coarse weave.* Related form: **weaving** *n.* Same sign used for: **web, webbing.**

■ [Represents threads woven together] Beginning with the fingers of both *5 hands* loosely entwined in front of the body, palms facing down, push the fingers forward with a double movement, twisting the fingers between each other.

wedding

wedding *n.* A marriage ceremony: *a beautiful wedding.* Related form: **wed** *v.*

- [Represents bringing the bride's and groom's hands together during a wedding] Beginning with both *open hands* hanging down in front of each side of the chest, palms facing in and fingers pointing down, bring the fingers upward toward each other, meeting in front of the chest.

Wednesday *n.* The fourth day of the week, after Tuesday: *a class trip planned for Wednesday.*

- [Initialized sign] Move the right *W hand,* palm facing in and fingers pointing up, in a circle in front of the right shoulder.

week *n.* **1.** A period of seven successive days starting on Sunday and ending with Saturday: *the second week of the month.* **2.** A period of seven successive days starting on a specified day: *She'll be away for a week, starting Thursday.* **3.** The work week, normally thought of as a five-day period starting on Monday and going through Friday: *You can take next week off from work.* Same sign used for: **one week.**

- [The finger moves along the days of one week on an imaginary calendar] Slide the palm side of the right *1 hand* from the heel to the fingertips of the left *open hand* held in front of the chest, palm facing right.

weekend[1] *n.* The end of a week, usually including Friday evening, Saturday, and Sunday: *plans to go fishing this weekend.*

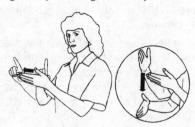

- [**week** + a shortened form of **end**[2]] Slide the palm side of the right *1 hand* from the heel to the fingertips of the left *open hand* held in front of the chest, palm facing right. Then move the palm side of the right *open hand* downward along the fingertips of the left *open hand* held in front of the chest, palm facing right.

weekend[2] *n.* (alternate sign)

- [An initialized form of **week** + an initialized form of **end**[2]] Slide the palm side of the right *W hand* from the heel to the fingertips of the left *open hand,* palm facing right. Then move the right *E hand,* palm facing forward, downward along the fingertips of the left *open hand* held in front of the chest, palm facing right and fingers angled forward.

weekly *adj.* **1.** Done, occurring, appearing, etc., every week: *a weekly meeting.* —*adv.* **2.** Once a week: *The newspaper is published weekly.*

- ■ [**week** formed with a repeated movement] Move the palm side of the right *1 hand* with a double movement in an arc across the left *open hand* held in front of the body, palm facing right.

weep[1] *v.* To cry; shed tears: *She wept when her dog died.* Same sign used for: **cry.**

- ■ [Represents tears pouring from one's eyes] Beginning with the index fingers of both *4 hands* touching each cheek, palms facing in and fingers pointing toward each other, move both hands downward with a repeated movement.

weep[2] *v.* See signs for CRY[1,2].

weigh *v.* To measure how heavy something is: *to weigh the package.* Related form: **weight** *n.* Same sign used for: **pound, scale.**

- ■ [The fingers seem to balance something as if on a scale] With the middle-finger side of the right *H hand* across the index-finger side of the left *H hand,* palms angled toward each other, tip the right hand up and down with a repeated movement.

weird[1] *adj.* Strange or unearthly: *a weird sound.*

- ■ [Initialized sign similar to sign for **strange**] Move the right *W hand,* palm facing down and fingers pointing left, across the front of the face, bending the fingers as the hand moves.

weird[2] *adj.* See sign for STRANGE.

welcome[1] *v.* **1.** To greet cordially: *to welcome the visitors.* —*n.* **2.** An act or instance of welcoming: *Let's give the president a kind welcome.* —*adj.* **3.** Gladly received: *a welcome phone call.* —*interj.* **4.** (Used as a friendly greeting): *"Welcome to the club!"*

- ■ [Initialized sign similar to sign for **hire**] Beginning with the right *W hand* in front of the right side of the body, palm facing up and fingers pointing forward, swing the hand to the left and in toward the body.

welcome

welcome[2] *v., n., adj., interj.* (alternate sign)

- ■ [Initialized sign] Beginning with the index-finger side of the right *W hand,* palm facing forward, touching the right side of the forehead, swing the hand downward to the center of the chest, ending with the palm facing up.

welcome[3] *v.* See sign for INVITE[1].

welcome me *v. phrase.* See sign for INVITE[2].

weld *v.* To join by heating and hammering together, as pieces of metal or plastic: *to weld the pipes, forming a permanent seal.* Same sign used for: **solder.**

- ■ [The finger represents a soldering iron] Move the index finger of the right *L hand,* palm facing in and finger pointing left, in a repeated circle near the palm of the left *open hand* held in front of the left side of the chest, palm facing right and fingers pointing up.

welfare *n.* See sign for PENSION.

well[1] *adj.* **1.** In good health: *Sorry you don't feel well.* —*adv.* **2.** In a satisfactory manner: *doing well in school.* Same sign used for: **bold, cure, heal, healthy, strength, strong.**

- ■ [The hands seem to pull health from the body] Beginning with the fingertips of both *5 hands* on each side of the chest, palms facing in and fingers pointing up, bring the hands forward with a deliberate movement while closing into *S hands.*

well[2] *n.* A deep hole drilled into the earth to obtain water: *Without indoor plumbing, they have to get water from the well.*

- ■ [**water** + a gesture pointing down into a well] Tap the index-finger side of the right *W hand,* palm facing left, against the chin with a double movement. Then push the extended right index finger, palm facing in and finger pointing down, downward from in front of the right shoulder through the palm side of the left *C hand* held in front of the chest, ending in front of the waist.

well³ *interj.* (Used to express acceptance or lack of concern, to introduce a new thought, or to resume a conversation): *"Oh, well, I didn't want that anyway." Well, what do you think?* Same sign used for: **shrug, so.**

- [Natural gesture for shrugging] Beginning with both *open hands* in front of each side of the body, palms facing in and fingers angled down, flip the hands over and outward while shrugging the shoulders, ending with the palms facing up.

well⁴ *adj., adv.* See signs for FINE, GOOD.

were¹ *v.* **1.** First, second, and third person plural past tense of BE: *We were late for church.* **2.** Second person singular past tense of BE: *You and your brother were not at the game.*

- [Abbreviation **w-r**] Beginning with the right *W hand* near the right side of the chin, palm facing left, move the hand back while changing into an *R hand.*

were² *v.* See signs for AGO¹, BE², WAS¹.

west¹ *n.* **1.** The general direction 90 degrees to the left of north: *The coast is to the west of the mountains.* **2.** (*sometimes cap.*) The western states of the United States: *likes to read novels about cowboys in the old West.* —*adj.* **3.** Lying toward or located in the west: *the west side of the street.* —*adv.* **4.** To, toward, or in the west: *Go west, young man.* Related form: **western** *adj.*

- [Initialized sign showing a western direction on a map] Beginning with the right *W hand* in front of the right shoulder, palm facing forward and fingers pointing up, move the hand to the left in front of the right side of the chest.

west² *n., adj., adv.* (alternate sign) Related form: **western** *adj.*

- [Initialized sign showing direction as on a map] Move the right *W hand,* palm facing forward, a short distance to the right in front of the right shoulder.

wet¹ *adj.* Covered or soaked with water or some other liquid: *a wet towel.* Same sign used for: **damp, dew, humid, misty, moist, moisten, moisture.**

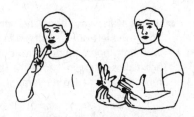

- [**water** + a gesture as if feeling something wet] Tap the index-finger side of the right *W hand,* palm facing left, against the chin with a double movement. Then, beginning with both *5 hands* in front of the body, palms facing up, bring the hands downward while closing the fingers into *O hands* with a double movement.

wet² *adj.* (alternate sign) Same sign used for: **damp, dew, humid, misty, moist, moisten, moisture.**

- [The hands seem to feel something wet] Beginning with the right *5 hand* near the right side of the chin, palm facing left, and the left *5 hand* in front of the left side of the chest, palm facing up, bring the hands downward while closing the fingers to the thumbs of each hand.

whack *v.* See sign for SPANK¹.

whale *n.* A huge mammal that lives in the ocean, breathes through a blowhole in the top of the head, and has a fishlike body and flippers: *The whale we saw must have weighed 100 tons.*

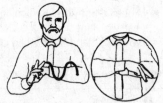

- [Initialized sign demonstrating the action of a whale swimming] Move the index-finger side of the right *W hand*, palm facing left, with a wavy up-and-down movement from the wrist to the elbow of the bent left arm held across the chest.

what *pron.* (Used interrogatively to request information): *What is your name?*

- Bring the extended right index finger, palm facing left, downward across the left *open hand* held in front of the chest, palm facing up.

whatever¹ *pron.* **1.** No matter what: *Whatever happens, you can count on me.* **2.** Anything that: *Say whatever comes to mind.*

- [**what** + **anyway**] Bring the right extended index finger, palm facing left, downward across the left *open hand* held in front of the chest, palm facing up. Then, beginning with both *open hands* in front of the body, fingers pointing toward each other and palms facing in, move the hands forward and back from the body with a repeated alternating movement, striking and bending the fingers of each hand as they pass.

whatever[2] *pron.* See sign for ANYWAY.

what for? Why: *What are you fixing that old thing for?*

- ■ [**for** formed with a repeated movement] Beginning with the extended right index finger touching the right side of the forehead, palm facing down, twist the hand forward with a double movement, pointing the index finger forward each time.

what happened?

- ■ [**what** + **happen**] Bring the extended right index finger, palm facing left, downward across the left *open hand* held in front of the chest, palm facing up. Then, beginning with both extended fingers in front of each side of the chest, palms facing up and fingers pointing forward, flip the hands over toward each other, ending with the palms facing down.

what's happening?[1] Same sign used for: **what's up?**

- ■ [Fingerspell **d-o**] Beginning with both *D hands* in front of each side of the chest, palms facing each other, bend the extended index fingers down with a double movement, closing into *flattened O hands* each time.

what's happening?[2] Same sign used for: **what's up?**

- ■ Beginning with the bent middle fingers of both *5 hands* touching the chest, palms facing in, bring the hands upward and forward with a quick double movement.

what's the matter? Same sign used for: **what's wrong?**

- ■ [Similar to sign for **wrong**] Bring the knuckles of the right *Y hand,* palm facing in, against the chin with a deliberate movement while showing a questioning look on the face.

what's wrong? See sign for WHAT'S THE MATTER?

wheel *n.* A round frame or disk mounted on a central shaft around which it turns, as in a machine or on a vehicle: *The cart is pulled along on two wheels.* Same sign used for: **traction.**

■ [Indicates the action of wheels turning] Move both extended index fingers in forward repeated circles in front of each side of the body, palms facing in and fingers pointing toward each other.

when *adv.* At what time: *When will you go?*

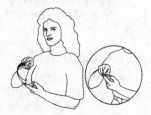

■ Beginning with the extended right index finger in front of the chest, palm facing down and finger pointing forward, and the left extended index finger in front of the lower chest, palm facing up and finger pointing forward, move the right index finger in a circular movement down to land on the left index finger.

where *adv.* At what place: *Where do you live?*

■ Move the extended right index finger, palm facing forward and finger pointing up, with a short double movement from side to side in front of the right shoulder.

wherever *conj.* In whatever place: *Sit wherever you like.*

■ [**where** + **anyway**] Move the extended right index finger, palm facing forward and finger pointing up, with a short movement from side to side in front of the right shoulder. Then, beginning with both *open hands* in front of the body, fingers pointing toward each other and palms facing in, move the hands forward and back from the body with a repeated alternating movement, striking and bending the fingers of each hand as they pass.

whether *pron.* See sign for WHICH.

whew[1] *interj.* (Used to express surprise, dismay, relief, etc.): *Whew! It's hot in here. Whew! We're finished!*

■ Bring the fingertips of the right *F hand*, palm facing left, back against the chin with a deliberate movement.

whew[2] *interj.* (alternate sign) Same sign used for: **sweat.**

■ [Natural gesture used to wipe sweat from the forehead] Wipe the index-finger side of the right *B hand,* palm facing down, from left to right across the forehead and then throw the right hand downward in front of the right shoulder, ending with the palm facing in and fingers pointing down.

whew[3] *interj.* See sign for FINEST.

whew[4] *interj.* See sign for WOW[2]. Shared idea of amazement.

which *pron.* **1.** What one: *Which do you want?* —*adj.* **2.** What one, out of a number or group mentioned or implied: *Which book is yours?* Same sign used for: **either, either-or, whether.**

■ [The movement indicates indecision] Beginning with both *10 hands* in front of each side of the chest, palms facing in and right hand higher than the left hand, move the hands up and down with an alternating movement.

while *conj.* See sign for DURING.

while ago, a[1] A span of time in the past: *a short while ago.* Same sign used for: **few seconds ago, a.**

■ [The finger moves only slightly into the past] Beginning with the little-finger side of the right *1 hand,* palm facing left, on the left *open hand* in front of the chest, palm facing up, move the right index finger back toward the chest by pivoting on the left hand.

while ago, a[2] See sign for RECENTLY[1].

whimper *v.* **1.** To cry quietly and sadly: *The sick baby whimpered for hours.* —*n.* **2.** A low whimpering sound: *I heard a whimper in the next room.*

■ [Indicates tiny tears coming from the eyes] Brush both extended index fingers, palms facing in, downward on each cheek with a short double movement bending the fingers each time.

whip[1] *v.* **1.** To beat with a thin, flexible object, as a strap or stick: *The jockey whipped the horse as they took the final turn.* —*n.* **2.** An implement used for beating, typically a lash attached to a long, rigid handle: *We were shocked to see them use the whip on their animals.*

■ [Mime hitting with a whip] Move the right *modified X hand,* palm facing left, downward and then upward again with a quick movement in front of the right shoulder.

whip[2] *n., v.* See signs for BEAT[1,2], PADDLE, SPANK[1]. Related form: **whipping** *n.*

whisk broom *n.* A small, hand-held broom for brushing clothes: *to clean the cat hairs from the coat with a whisk broom.* Same sign used for: **brush, whisk.**

■ [Represents using a whisk broom to brush lint off oneself] Brush the back of the fingers of the right *curved hand,* palm facing right, back with a double movement on the left upper arm, spreading the fingers into a *5 hand* each time.

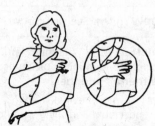

whiskey *n.* **1.** A strong intoxicating drink made from fermented grain: *to drink whiskey and water.* **2.** A drink of whiskey: *I'll have a whiskey and soda.* Same sign used for: **alcohol, brandy, liquor.**

■ With the index fingers and little fingers of both hands extended, tap the little-finger side of the right hand with a double movement on the index-finger side of the left hand, palms facing in opposite directions.

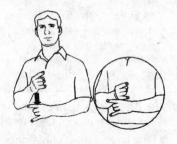

whisper[1] *v.* **1.** To speak softly using the breath, but without vibration of the vocal cords: *to whisper a secret in someone's ear.* —*n.* **2.** A whispered sound: *They spoke in a whisper.* **3.** Something uttered softly or discreetly, as a rumor: *I haven't heard a whisper about his new job.*

■ [Represents shielding one's mouth in order to whisper privately] Hold the index-finger side of the right *B hand,* palm facing left and fingers pointing up, against the left corner of the mouth.

whisper[2] *v., n.* (alternate sign, used to indicate private communication in sign language)

■ [Represents fingerspelling secretly as if sharing private information] With the index-finger side of the right *flattened C hand,* palm facing forward, against the open left palm held in front of the chest, palm facing right and fingers pointing up, wiggle the right fingers.

whistle[1] *n.* **1.** A device or instrument through which air is blown to produce a high, clear whistling sound: *The police use a whistle to direct traffic.* —*v.* **2.** To produce high, clear whistling sounds by forcing air through the teeth or a whistling device: *He whistled for a cab.*

■ Tap the bent fingers of the right *V hand*, palm facing down, with a double movement against the lips.

whistle[2] *n., v.* See sign for REFEREE.

whistleblower *n.* An employee who reports dangerous or illegal conduct of an employer to the authorities: *The whistleblower reported the misused funds.*

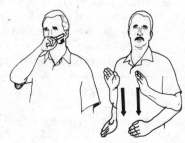

■ [**tattle + person marker**] Beginning with the thumb side of the right *S hand* near the right side of the mouth, palm facing forward, flick the index finger upward with a deliberate movement. Then move both *open hands*, palms facing each other, downward along the sides of the body.

white *adj.* Having the color of snow: *a white flower.*

■ Beginning with the fingertips of the right *curved 5 hand* on the chest, palm facing in, pull the hand forward while closing the fingers into a *flattened O hand*.

white person *n.* See sign for PALE.

whiz *n.* See sign for ADROIT.

who[1] *pron.* What person or persons: *Who is that?* Same sign used for: **whom.**

■ [The finger follows the circular shape of the pursed lips forming the word "who."] Move the extended right index finger, palm facing in, in a small circle around the pursed lips.

who[2] *pron.* (alternate sign) Same sign used for: **whom.**

■ With the thumb of the right *modified C hand* touching the chin, palm facing left, bend the index finger up and down with a double movement.

whoever *pron.* Whatever person: *Whoever wants to come is invited.*

■ [**who**[1,2] + **anyway**] Move the extended right index finger, palm facing in, in a small circle around the pursed lips. Then, beginning with both *open hands* in front of the body, fingers pointing toward each other and palms facing in, move the hands forward and back from the body with a repeated alternating movement, striking and bending the fingers of each hand as they pass.

whole *adj., n.* See sign for ALL[1].

whom *pron.* See signs for WHO[1,2].

whore *n.* See sign for PROSTITUTE.

whose *pron.* **1.** The possessive case of *who* used as an adjective: *I can't tell whose writing this is.* **2.** Belonging to what person or persons: *Whose coat is this? Whose is that one?*

■ [**who**[1,2] + suffix **-'s**] Move the extended right index finger, palm facing in, in a small circle around the pursed lips. Then, beginning with the right *S hand* in front of the right shoulder, palm facing forward, twist the wrist to turn the palm back.

why[1] *adv.* For what reason: *Why did you do that?*

■ Beginning with the fingertips of the right *bent hand* touching the right side of the forehead, palm facing down, move the hand forward with a deliberate movement while changing into a *Y hand.*

why[2] *adv.* (alternate sign)

■ With the right index finger, little finger, and thumb extended, palm facing in, wiggle the bent middle fingers with a small repeated movement in front of the forehead.

wicked[1] *adj.* Evil; sinful; morally bad: *a wicked deed.*

- [Initialized sign similar to sign for **bad**] Beginning with the index-finger side of the right *W hand* near the mouth, palm facing left, bring the hand downward and forward at an angle and then straight down to land palm down on the left *open hand* held in front of the body, palm facing up.

wicked[2] *adj.* See signs for BAD, DEVIL.

wide *adj.* Of great extent from side to side: *a wide street.* Same sign used for: **broad, general.** Related form: **width** *n.*

- [Indicates a wide space] Beginning with both *open hands* in front of each side of the body, palms facing each other and fingers pointing forward, move the hands apart to the sides of the body, palms facing forward.

widescreen *adj.* Refers to a film, computer, or television image that has a wider aspect ratio than the traditional Academy frame used in older movie theaters: *She chose a widescreen video to play on their new LED widescreen television.*

- [**wide** + **full**[2]] Beginning with both *open hands* in front of each side of the body, palms facing each other and fingers pointing up, move the hands apart to the sides of the body. Then slide the palm of the right *open hand*, palm facing down, from right to left across the index-finger side of the left *S hand*, palm facing right.

wiener *n.* See sign for SAUSAGE.

wife *n.* A married woman: *the doctor's wife.*

- [The hand moves from near the female area of the head + **marry**] Move the right *curved hand* from near the right side of the chin, palm facing forward, downward to clasp the left *curved hand* held in front of the body.

wild[1] *adj.* Unrestrained, frantic, unruly, or irrational: *a wild idea.* Same sign used for: **wacky** (*slang*).

- [Initialized sign similar to sign for **fake**[1]] Beginning with the index finger of the right *W hand,* palm facing left, touching the right side of the forehead, move the hand forward in a double arc.

wild

wild² *adj.* See signs for CRAZY², RAVE.

wildcard *n.* See sign for STAR. Shared idea that an asterisk, which is a symbol for wildcard, is star-shaped.

will¹ *n.* **1.** Purpose and determination, as carried out by, affecting, or required of others: *It is God's will.* **2.** The power to choose one's own actions consciously and deliberately: *I took on that job of my own free will.*

- [Initialized sign similar to sign for **law**] Touch the index-finger side of the right *W hand,* palm facing forward, first on the fingers and then on the heel of the left *open hand* held in front of the chest, palm facing right and fingers pointing up.

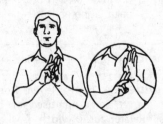

will² *n.* (alternate sign)

- [Initialized sign similar to sign for **against**] Hit the index-finger side of the right *W hand,* palm facing forward, against the left *open hand* held in front of the chest, palm facing right and fingers pointing up.

will³ *v.* (Used preceding another verb to express the future tense): *We will win tomorrow.*

- [The hand moves into the future] Move the right *open hand,* palm facing left and fingers pointing up, from the right side of the chin forward while turning the fingers forward.

will⁴ *v.* (alternate sign)

- [Initialized sign representing moving into the future] Move the right *W hand* from near the right side of the chin, palm facing left, forward while turning the fingers forward.

will⁵ *v.* (alternate sign)

- [Abbreviation **w-l**] Beginning with the right *W hand* near the right side of the chin, palm facing left, move the hand forward while changing into an *L hand.*

willing *adj.* See signs for ADMIT¹,².

will not See sign for WON'T.

wilt[1] *v.* To droop and become limp (used only for plants): *The flower wilted.*

■ [**flower** + a gesture indicating a plant falling when wilting] Touch the fingers of the right *flattened O hand* first to the right side of the nose and then the left side of the nose. Then, beginning with the right *open hand* held up near the right side of the face, palm facing forward and fingers pointing up, bend the hand downward over the extended left index finger held across the body, palm facing in, ending with the right fingers pointing down and palm facing in.

wilt[2] *v.* (alternate sign, used to indicate limp hair) Same sign used for: **droop.**

■ [**hair** formed with two hands + a gesture indicating that one's hair is wilting] Grasp hair on each side of the head with the bent index fingers and thumbs of both hands. Then, with the thumbs of both *open hands* touching each side of the head, palms facing forward and fingers pointing up, drop the fingers forward with a deliberate movement.

win[1] *v.* **1.** To be successful over others in (a game, competition, battle, etc.): *to win the contest.* —*n.* **2.** A victory: *It was a big win.*

■ Beginning with the right *5 hand* in front of the right shoulder, palm facing forward and fingers pointing up, and the left *5 hand* in front of the body, palm facing right and fingers pointing forward, sweep the right hand downward in an arc across the index-finger side of the left hand while changing both hands into *S hands.* Then bring the right hand upward in front of the chest, palm facing in.

win[2] *v.* (alternate sign)

■ Beginning with the right *5 hand* in front of the right shoulder, palm facing forward and fingers pointing up, and the left *5 hand* in front of the body, palm facing right and fingers pointing forward, sweep the right hand downward in an arc to hit on the index-finger side of the left hand while changing both hands into *S hands.* Then bring the right hand upward, changing to an *X hand* in front of the face.

win[3] *v.* (alternate sign)

■ [Waving a flag in victory] Move the right *modified X hand*, palm facing left, in a repeated circular movement near the right side of the head.

wind

wind[1] *n.* Moving air: *a strong wind.* Related form: **windy** *adj.* Same sign used for: **storm.**

■ [Represents the action of wind blowing] Beginning with both *5 hands* in front of the left side of the body, palms facing each other and fingers pointing forward, move the hands back and forth in front of the chest with a repeated movement. Use a more rapid movement for stronger wind or a storm.

wind[2] *v.* To roll around a spool: *wind the thread.* Same sign used for: **winch.**

■ [Demonstrates the action of winding thread on a spool] Move the right *S hand,* palm facing down, in a forward circle near the palm of the left *open hand* held in front of the chest, palm facing right and fingers pointing forward.

wind[3] *v.* (alternate sign) Same sign used for: **winch.**

■ [Demonstrates the action of winding thread on a spool] Move the right *modified X hand* in a forward circle, palm facing in, around the fingertips of the left *flattened O hand* held in front of the chest, palm facing in and fingers pointing right.

wind[4] *v.* To enable to operate by tightening the springs on, as a watch, especially by turning a knob: *to wind your watch.*

■ [Mime winding a watch] Rub the thumb on the index finger of the right *A hand,* palm facing left, with a repeated movement on the back of the left wrist held in front of the chest.

wind up *v. phrase.* See sign for END[2].

window *n.* **1.** An opening in a wall to let in light or air, usually fitted with one or more frames containing panes of glass: *The window is broken.* **2.** An area on a computer display screen that displays data, programs, or other information: *The address list was open in one window and the letter was open in another window.* Same sign used for: **Windows** or **Microsoft Windows.**

■ [Represents closing a window] Bring the little-finger side of the right *open hand* down sharply with a double movement on the index-finger side of the left *open hand,* both palms facing in and fingers pointing in opposite directions.

Windows *n. Trademark.* Short for *Microsoft Windows.* See sign for WINDOW.

windowsill *n.* The piece of wood at the base of a window: *The cat sat on the windowsill.* Same sign used for: **sill.**

- [**window** + **shelf**] Bring the little-finger side of the right *B hand* down with a double movement to hit the index-finger side of the left *B hand,* both palms facing in and fingers pointing in opposite directions. Then, beginning with the index fingers of both *B hands,* palms facing down and fingers pointing forward, touching in front of the chest, bring the hands apart to each side of the chest.

wine *n.* An alcoholic drink made by fermenting the juice of grapes or other fruit: *a glass of wine.*

- [Initialized sign] Move the right *W hand,* palm facing left, in a small forward circle near the right side of the chin.

wings *pl. n.* See signs for ANGEL, FLY[1].

wink *v.* To blink one eye once, as to signal humorous or flirtatious intent: *winked at us to let us know it was only a joke.* Same sign used for: **blink.**

- [Shows the action of winking one's eyelid] Beginning with the thumb side of the right *G hand* near the right eye, palm facing left, close the index finger and thumb together and open again.

winter[1] *n.* The season between fall and spring: *It was a cold winter.*

- [Initialized sign similar to sign for **cold**] Beginning with both *W hands* in front of the body, palms facing each other, move the hands toward each with a repeated shaking movement.

winter[2] *n.* See sign for COLD[2].

wipe[1] *v.* To rub in order to dry or clean: *It's your turn to wipe the dishes.* Same sign used for: **rub.**

- [Demonstrates the action of wiping something] Wipe the palm side of the right *A hand* with a repeated movement back and forth on the left *open hand* held in front of the body, palm facing up.

wipe[2] *v.* See signs for DUST, WASH[1,2].

wire[1] *n.* A pliable metallic strand sometimes clad or electrically insulated, used chiefly for structural support or to conduct electricity: *The gardener tied up the tomato plants with a wire.* Same sign used for: **cable.**

- [Shape of a wire] Beginning with both extended little fingers pointing toward each other in front of the chest, palms facing in, move the hands apart from each other.

wire[2] *n.* See signs for CORD[1,2].

wireless *adj.* Having no wires: *use a wireless telephone.*

- [**none**[2] + **wire**[1]] Beginning with both *flattened O hands,* palms facing forward, in front of the chest, move the hands apart to each side. Then, beginning with both extended little fingers pointing toward each other in front of the chest, palms facing in, move the hands apart from each other.

wise *adj.* **1.** Having the power to judge what is true, right, beneficial, etc.: *a wise person.* **2.** Revealing or benefiting from such power: *a wise decision.* Related form: **wisdom** *n.*

- Move the right *X hand,* palm facing left, up and down with a double movement in front of the right side of the forehead.

wish *v.* **1.** To desire: *to wish for a new car; to wish to leave the city.* —*n.* **2.** The expression or formation of a desire: *I made a wish.* **3.** Something one wishes for: *I hope you get your wish.* Same sign used for: **desire.**

- Move the fingers of the right *C hand,* palm facing in, downward on the chest a short distance.

witch[1] *n.* A person, especially a woman, who professes or is believed to have magic power: *The witch cast a spell.*

- [Represents the traditional hooked nose of a witch] Move the bent index finger of the right *X hand* from near the right side of the nose, palm facing left, in front of the nose and downward, ending with the palm facing down.

witch[2] *n.* (alternate sign)

- Beginning with the back of the right *X hand* against the nose, palm facing forward, bring the right hand down in an arc to touch the bent right index finger to the bent index finger of the left *X hand* held in front of the chest, palm facing up.

with *prep.* **1.** Accompanied by: *to serve gravy with the potatoes.* **2.** Using or showing: *to slice it with a knife; to eat with gusto.*

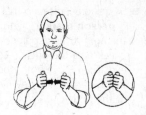

■ [Indicates two things coming together so they are with one another] Beginning with both *A hands* in front of the chest, palms facing each other, bring the hands together.

withdraw[1] *v.* **1.** To take or pull back: *Kindly withdraw your hand from my shoulder.* **2.** To remove oneself, as from an activity: *to withdraw from class.*

■ [Abbreviation **w-d**] Beginning with the right *W hand* in front of the right shoulder, palm facing forward, bring the hand back toward the right shoulder while changing into a *D hand.*

withdraw[2] *v.* See signs for DISCONNECT, FORSAKE[1], LEAVE[1], RECOIL.

within *prep.* See sign for INCLUDE.

without *prep.* Not having, lacking, or free from: *to go outside without a coat; a world without poverty.*

■ [**with** + releasing the hands to indicate the opposite meaning] Beginning with the palm sides of both *A hands* together in front of the chest, bring the hands apart while opening into *5 hands,* fingers pointing forward.

witness[1] *n.* **1.** Testimony: *to give witness in court.* **2.** A person who is present at and can give an accurate account of an event: *a witness to the murder.* —*v.* **3.** To be present at or know about personally: *They witnessed the landing of the space shuttle.* **4.** To testify; give evidence: *to witness in court regarding the accident.*

■ [Initialized sign similar to sign for **proof**] Beginning with the index finger of the right *W hand* near the right eye, palm facing left, bring the hand down while turning the palm up, ending with the back of the right *W hand* on the left *open hand* held in front of the chest, palm facing up.

witness[2] *n.* A person who has seen or heard something relevant to a case or an investigation: *The witness testified against the defendant.* Same sign used for: **eyewitness.**

wolf

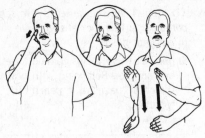

- [A gesture indicating that one saw something + **person marker**] With the index finger of the right *X hand*, pull down slightly on the cheek near the outside corner of the right eye. Then move both *open hands*, palms facing each other, downward along the sides of the body.

wolf *n.* A wild, carnivorous mammal of the dog family: *Wolves tend to run in packs.*

- [The shape of a wolf's nose] Beginning with the fingertips of the right *curved hand* around the nose, palm facing in, bring the hand forward with a double movement while closing the fingers and thumb into a *flattened O hand* each time.

woman *n.* An adult human female: *a woman of many accomplishments.* Same sign used for: **female.**

- [A gesture beginning near the female area of the head + **polite**] Beginning with the extended thumb of the right *open hand* touching the right side of the chin, palm facing left, bring the hand downward to touch the thumb again in the center of the chest.

wonder *v.* To think or speculate with curiosity: *I wonder what happened.* Same sign used for: **consider, contemplate, meditate, ponder, reflect, think, think about, thinking.**

- [Represents thoughts going around in one's head] Move the extended right index finger, palm facing in, in a small circle near the right side of the forehead with a repeated movement.

wonderful[1] *adj.* Remarkably good; excellent; marvelous: *a wonderful movie.* Same sign used for: **amaze, excellent, fantastic, great, incredible, marvel, marvelous, remarkable, splendid, terrific.**

- Move both *5 hands*, palms facing forward and fingers pointing up, from in front of each side of the head forward with a short double movement.

wonderful[2] *adj.* (alternate sign) Same sign used for: **amaze, excellent, fantastic, great, incredible, marvel, marvelous, remarkable.**

- Move both *5 hands,* palms facing forward and fingers pointing up, in a smallcircular movement near each side of the head.

won't Contraction of *will not: I won't go.* Same sign used for: **refuse, will not.**

- [Natural gesture for refusing to do something] Beginning with the right *10 hand* in front of the right shoulder, palm facing left, move the hand deliberately back toward the shoulder while twisting the wrist up.

wood[1] *n.* **1.** The hard fibrous substance composing the trunk and branches of a tree: *a piece of wood.* —*adj.* **2.** Made of wood: *a wood box.* Same sign used for: **lumber, saw.**

- [Shows action of sawing wood] Move the little-finger side of the right *B hand,* palm facing left and fingers pointing forward, forward and back with a double movement on the back of the left *open hand* held in front of the body, palm facing down.

wood[2] *n., adj.* (alternate sign) Same sign used for: **lumber, saw.**

- [Shows action of sawing wood] Slide the little-finger side of the right *open hand,* palm facing left and fingers pointing forward, forward and back with a double movement on the index-finger side of the left *open hand* held in front of the chest, palm facing in and fingers pointing right.

woods *pl. n.* See signs for FOREST[1,2].

woodworker *n.* See signs for CARPENTER[2].

word *n.* An independent unit of language that carries meaning, usually separated from other words in running text: *New words are constantly added to the vocabulary.* Same sign used for: **text, vocabulary.**

- Tap the extended fingers of the right *G hand,* palm facing left, with a double movement against the extended left index finger pointing up in front of the left side of the chest, palm facing right.

word processing *n. phrase.* A type of program that enables a computer to create, edit, proofread, format, and print documents: *use the computer for word processing.*

work

■ [**word + procedure**] Touch the extended fingers of the right *G hand,* palm facing out, against the extended left index finger pointing up in front of the chest, palm facing right. Then, beginning with both *open hands* in front of the body, palms facing in, left fingers pointing right and right fingers pointing left, and with the left hand closer to the chest than the right hand, move the left hand over the right hand, then the right hand over the left hand, in an alternating movement.

work[1] *n.* **1.** Mental or physical effort: *This project takes a lot of work.* **2.** One's occupation: *to go to work.* —*v.* **3.** To labor: *to work hard all day.* **4.** To be employed: *He works in management.* **5.** To function; be in operation: *The toaster doesn't work.* Same sign used for: **employment, job, labor, occupation, task.**

■ Tap the heel of the right *S hand,* palm facing forward, with a double movement on the back of the left *S hand* held in front of the body, palm facing down.

work[2] *n., v.* (alternate sign) Same sign used for: **employ, employment, job, labor, occupation, task.**

■ Tap the heel of the right *S hand,* palm angled left, with a double movement on the wrist of the left *S hand,* palm facing up.

work[3] *n., v.* See sign for ACTIVE[1].

workaholic *n.* A person who works long hours, especially obsessively: *The boss is a workaholic—at the job till past midnight.* Same sign used for: **overwork, toil, work hard, working.**

■ [**work**[1] formed with a repeated circular movement] Bring the heel of the right *A hand,* palm facing forward, in a double circular movement down across the back of the left *S hand* held in front of the chest.

work hard *v. phrase.* See sign for WORKAHOLIC.

working *adj.* See sign for WORKAHOLIC.

work out *v. phrase.* See sign for EXERCISE[2].

workshop *n.* A small group of people that meets to study, learn skills, or work together: *to attend a workshop in advanced ASL.*

■ [Abbreviation **w-s**] Beginning with the thumbs of both *W hands* together in front of the chest, palms facing each other, move the hands outward in arcs while closing into *S hands,* ending with the little fingers of both *S hands* touching in front of the body, palms facing in.

world *n.* **1.** The planet earth: *traveled around the world.* **2.** All or most of the people on the earth; the public: *The world will hear of your accomplishments.* **3.** The universe: *The world is vast.*

■ [Initialized sign indicating the movement of the earth around the sun] Beginning with both *W hands* in front of the body, palms facing each other, move the hands in alternating forward circles, ending with the little-finger side of the right hand on the index-finger side of the left hand.

worm *n.* A small, slender, legless, crawling animal with no backbone: *I'm collecting worms from the garden so I can go fishing with my friends.*

■ [Demonstrates the movement of a crawling worm] Beginning with the right index finger pointing forward against the heel of the left *open hand* held in front of the chest, palm facing right and fingers pointing forward, move the right hand, palm facing down, forward to the left fingertips, bending the index finger up and down as the hand moves.

worry[1] *v.* To be anxious or uneasy: *Don't worry about the speech—you'll do fine.*

■ [Initialized sign similar to sign for **trouble**[2]] Beginning with both *W hands* in front of the head, right hand higher than the left hand and fingers angled in opposite directions, move the hands in repeated alternating circles toward each other in front of the face.

worry[2] *v.* See sign for TROUBLE[1,2].

worse[1] *adj.* Bad or ill to a greater degree than others: *a worse cold than ever before.* Related form: **worsen** *v.*

■ Beginning with both *V hands* in front of each shoulder, palms facing in, push the hands past each other in front of the chest, brushing the little-finger side of the right hand across the index-finger side of the left hand.

worse[2] *adj.* See sign for LOUSY.

worship

worship[1] *n.* **1.** A ceremony of reverent homage to God: *to attend worship every Sunday.* —*v.* **2.** To pay homage to God: *The family worshiped together regularly.* Same sign used for: **adore, beg, please, pray.**

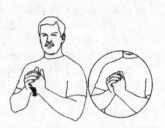

- ■ [Similar to sign for **amen**[2] except with a double movement] With the right fingers cupped over the left *A hand,* bring the hands downward and in toward the chest with a double movement.

worship[2] *v.* See signs for HAIL[2], IDOL[1].

worth *n., prep.* See signs for COST[2], IMPORTANT[1,2].

worthless *adj.* Having no worth, use, importance, etc.: *a worthless idea.* Related form: **worthlessness** *n.* Same sign used for: **frivolous, hopeless, invisible, petit, petty.**

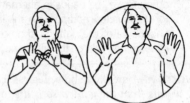

- ■ [Begins as similar to sign for **important**[1] and then releases to indicate an opposite meaning] Beginning with the fingertips of both *F hands* touching in front of the chest, palms facing forward, bring the hands apart while opening into *5 hands* in front of each shoulder, palms facing forward and fingers pointing up.

wound *v., n.* See signs for HURT[1,2], SUFFER[2].

wow[1] *interj.* (Used to indicate surprise, wonder, amazement, etc.)

- ■ [Natural gesture] Swing the right *5 hand,* palm facing in and fingers pointing left, limply down in front of the right side of the body with a double movement.

wow[2] *interj.* (alternate sign) Same sign used for: **whew.**

- ■ [Natural gesture] Limply swing both *5 hands,* palms facing in, up and down with a repeated movement in front of each side of the body.

wrap *v.* To cover: *wrap the gift.*

- ■ [Represents wrapping paper around a package] Beginning with both *B hands* in front of the body, palms facing in, fingers pointing toward each other, and left hand closer to the body than the right hand, move the hands in alternate circles around each other.

wreath *n.* A ringlike form made of leaves, flowers, ornaments, etc.: *a Christmas wreath.*

- [**flower** + shape of a wreath] Touch the fingers of the right *flattened O hand* first to the right side of the nose and then the left side of the nose. Then, beginning with both *C hands* in front of the face, palms facing forward, move the hands outward and down in arcs, ending in front of each side of the chest.

wrench *n.* A tool used for twisting a pipe, nut, etc.: *The plumber used a pipe wrench to fix the leak.* Same sign used for: **maintenance.**

- [Shows twisting action of a wrench] With the extended left index finger inserted between the index finger and middle finger of the right *3 hand,* both palms angled in, twist the right hand up and down with a double movement.

wrestling[1] *n.* A sport in which two opponents force each other to the mat or the ground, as by throwing or pinning according to authorized rules: *There are various kinds of wrestling, including freestyle and Sumo.*

- [Represents the legs of two wrestlers struggling] Beginning with the bent fingers of both *curved 5 hands* together in front of the chest, right palm facing forward and left palm facing in, twist the hands in opposite directions to reverse positions.

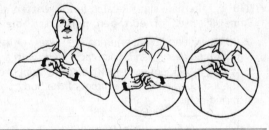

wrestling[2] *n.* (alternate sign)
- Beginning with the fingers of both *5 hands* enmeshed in front of the chest, palms angled toward each other, move the hands downward with a double movement.

wring *v.* **1.** To twist forcibly, as or as if to squeeze liquid out of: *to wring the washcloth out; to wring the neck of the chicken.* **2.** To force out by squeezing: *Wring all the soapy water out of the dish cloth.* Same sign used for: **twist.**

- [Mime wringing out something] Beginning with the right *C hand* in front of the right side of the chest, palm facing forward, and the left *C hand* in front of the left side of the chest, palm facing in, twist the hands in opposite directions while closing into *S hands.*

wrist

wrist *n.* The joint between the hand and the forearm: *a sweater with sleeves down to the wrist.*

- [Location of one's wrist] With the bent middle finger and thumb of the right *5 hand*, palm facing down, grasping each side of the left wrist, bend the left *S hand* up and down with a double movement.

wristwatch *n.* See signs for WATCH[1,2].

write[1] *v.* **1.** To make letters, words, etc., as on paper: *to write your name.* **2.** To communicate with in writing: *wrote me a postcard from London.* **3.** To be the author of: *wrote a wonderful short story.* Related form: **written** *adj.* Same sign used for: **edit, pen, pencil, scribble.**

- [Mime holding a pen to write] Slide the palm of the right *modified X hand*, palm facing left, from the heel to the fingertips of the left *open hand* held in front of the body, palm facing right.

write[2] *v.* (alternate sign) Related form: **written** *adj.* Same sign used for: **edit, pen, pencil, scribble.**

- [Mime writing on paper] Bring the fingers of the right *modified X hand*, palm facing left, with a wiggly movement from the heel to the fingers of the left *open hand* held in front of the body, palm facing right.

write[3] *v.* (alternate sign) Related form: **written** *adj.* Same sign used for: **edit, scribble.**

- [Indicates writing on paper] Slide the fingertips of the right *flattened O hand*, palm facing down, with a double movement from the heel to the fingertips of the left *open hand* held in front of the body, palm facing up.

writer *n.* See sign for AUTHOR.

wrong *adj.* Not correct; in error: *the wrong answer.* Same sign used for: **incorrect.**

- Place the middle fingers of the right *Y hand*, palm facing in, against the chin with a deliberate movement.

xerography *n.* See sign for COPY[3].

Xerox (*Trademark.*) See sign for COPY[3].

xylophone *n.* A musical instrument consisting of a series of wooden bars of graduated lengths played by striking with wooden hammers held in each hand: *You usually play the xylophone standing up.*

■ [Mime playing a xylophone] Beginning with the palms of both *modified X hands* facing each other in front of each side of the body, move the hands up and down with an alternating movement.

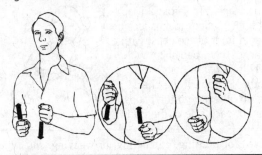

yank *v.* **1.** To pull suddenly and quickly; tug: *The boy kept yanking her hair. We yanked on the rope.* —*n.* **2.** A sudden, sharp pull: *Give the cord a yank.*

■ [Mime yanking something back toward the body] Beginning with the right *5 hand* in front of the right side of the body, palm facing left and fingers pointing forward, bring the hand suddenly back toward the chest while closing into an *S hand.*

yardstick *n.* A rulerlike stick thirty-six inches long, used as a measuring instrument: *to measure the amount of fabric you want with a yardstick.*

■ [**measure** + the shape of a yardstick] Tap the thumbs of both *Y hands,* palms facing down, together in front of the chest with a double movement. Then, beginning with the fingers of both *G hands* pointing toward each other in front of the chest, palms facing each other, bring the hands apart to in front of each side of the body.

yarn[1] *n.* Thread used for knitting, crocheting, or weaving: *soft, thick yarn.*

■ [**thread**[1] + **wind**[2,3]] Beginning with the fingers of the right *curved 5 hand,* palm facing left, around the extended little finger of the left *I hand* held in front of the chest, palm facing in, bring the right hand outward to the right while closing into a *flattened O hand.* Then move the right *modified X hand* in a forward circle, palm facing down, around the fingertips of the left *flattened O hand* held in front of the chest, palm facing in and fingers pointing right.

yarn[2] *n.* See sign for THREAD[1].

yawn *v.* **1.** To open the mouth wide, especially involuntarily, as because of tiredness or boredom: *He yawned during the sermon.* —*n.* **2.** An act or instance of yawning: *He stifled a yawn.*

■ [Natural gesture used to cover the mouth when yawning] Bring the fingers of the right *open hand,* palm facing in and fingers pointing up, back against the mouth with a double movement.

yeah *adv. Informal.* See sign for YES.

---

year *n.* **1.** A period of twelve months, especially as calculated from January through December: *I will buy a car sometime next year.* **2.** Such a twelve-month period calculated from some other point: *The next conference will be held in a year.* **3.** A period of a year or less established for some specified purpose: *the fiscal year; the academic year.*

- ■ [Represents the movement of the earth around the sun] Beginning with the right *S hand,* palm facing left, over the left *S hand,* palm facing right, move the right hand forward in a complete circle around the left hand while the left hand moves in a smaller circle around the right hand, ending with the little-finger side of the right hand on the thumb side of the left hand.

---

yearly *adj.* Same sign as for YEAR-ROUND but made with a double movement.

---

yearn *v.* See sign for HUNGRY.

---

year-round *adj.* **1.** Available for use throughout the year: *a year-round resort.* —*adv.* **2.** Throughout the year: *travels year-round.* Same sign used for: **cycle, orbit, year-long.**

- ■ [Represents the movement of the earth around the sun] Beginning with both extended index fingers pointing toward each other in front of the chest, right hand slightly higher than the left hand and both palms facing down, move the right index finger in a complete circle around the left index finger.

---

yell *v.* See signs for CALL[4], SCREAM[1,2].

---

yell at *v. phrase.* See sign for BAWL OUT.

---

yellow *adj.* Having the color of the sun: *a yellow flower.*

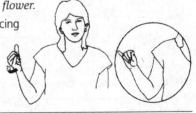

- ■ [Initialized sign] Move the right *Y hand,* palm facing left, with a twisting double movement in front of the right shoulder.

---

yes *adv.* (Used to show consent, affirmation, agreement, etc.): *Yes, I will go.* Same sign used for: **yeah** (*informal*).

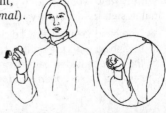

- ■ [Represents a person's head nodding in approval] Move the right *S hand,* palm facing forward, up and down in front of the right shoulder by bending the wrist with a repeated movement.

yesterday

yesterday[1] *n.* **1.** The day before today: *Yesterday was a cold day.* **2.** A period of time in the immediate past: *It seems like yesterday that we were young.* —*adv.* **3.** On the day before today: *I tried to call you yesterday.* **4.** In the immediate past: *Yesterday, things were less expensive.*

- ■ [The hand moves back into the past] Move the thumb of the right *10 hand,* palm facing forward, from the right side of the chin upward to the right cheek.

yesterday[2] *n.* (alternate sign)

- ■ [Initialized sign moving back into the past] Move the thumb of the right *Y hand,* palm facing forward, from the right side of the chin upward to the right cheek.

yet[1] *adv.* **1.** So far: *The package hasn't arrived yet.* **2.** At the present time; now: *Are we there yet?* Same sign used for: **not yet.**

- ■ [The hand gestures back into the past] Bend the wrist of the right *open hand,* palm facing back and fingers pointing down, back with a double movement near the right side of the waist.

yet[2] *adv.* (alternate sign) Same sign used for: **not yet.**

- ■ [The hands gesture back into the past] Bend the wrists of both *open hands,* palms facing back and fingers pointing down, back with a double movement near each side of the waist.

yet[3] *adv.* See signs for STILL[1,2].

yield *v.* See signs for GIVE UP, LOOK OUT.

yonder *adv.* At or to that distant place, usually within view: *Look yonder, just past those trees.* Same sign used for: **beyond.**

- ■ [The hand gestures toward the distance] Beginning with the right *curved hand* in front of the right shoulder, palm facing up, raise the hand while opening into an *open hand.*

you[1] *pron.* (Used to designate a single person being addressed): *I want you to handle this problem alone.*

- [Point toward the referent] Point the extended right index finger, palm facing down, toward the person being talked to.

you[2] *pron.* (Used to designate two or more persons being addressed): *All of you have done well.*

- [Point toward the referents] Point the extended right index finger, palm facing down, forward and then move the finger outward to the right in an arc.

you[3] *pron.* (Used to designate two persons being addressed): *You both had the same idea.* Same sign used for: **both of them, two of you, twosome.**

- [Gestures back and forth between the referents] Move the right *2 hand*, palm facing up and fingers pointing forward, from side to side with a double movement in front of the right side of the body.

young *adj.* Being in the early part of life or growth; not old: *a young boy and his older brother.* Same sign used for: **youth.**

- [Represents bringing up youthful feelings in the body] Beginning with the fingers of both *bent hands* on each side of the chest, palms facing outward, brush the fingers upward with a double movement.

your[1] *pron.* The possessive form of YOU used as an adjective: *your home.* Related form: **yours** *pron.*

- [The hand moves toward the referent] Push the palm of the right *open hand*, palm facing forward and fingers pointing up, toward the person being talked to.

your[2] *pron.* (alternate sign) Related form: **yours** *pron.*

- [The hand moves toward the referents] Move the right *open hand,* palm facing forward and fingers pointing up, from in front of the body in an arc to the right.

You're too late See sign for MISS[2].

yourself *pron.* **1.** A reflexive form of *you,* used as an object: *Ask yourself if you really want to resign.* **2.** (Used as an intensifier): *You said it yourself!* **3.** Oneself: *Do it yourself.*

- [This hand shape is used for reflexive pronouns and moves toward the referent] Push the extended thumb of the right *10 hand,* palm facing left, forward with a double movement toward the person being talked to.

yourselves *pron.* The plural form of *yourself: You should be ashamed of yourselves.*

- [The hand shape is used for reflexive pronouns and moves toward the referents] Move the extended thumb of the right *10 hand,* palm facing left, from in front of the body in an arc to the right.

youth *n.* See signs for ADOLESCENT, YOUNG.

zap *v. Informal.* **1.** To destroy with sudden speed: *The insect spray zapped the bugs.*—*n.* **2.** A forceful, sudden, and destructive attack: *With one zap, the older boy knocked the little one over.* Same sign used for: **got you!** or **gotcha!**

- ■ [The fingers mime zapping something] Beginning with the right *H hand* in front of the chest, palm facing forward and fingers pointing up, move the fingers forward and then back again with a quick movement.

zeal *n.* Enthusiastic fervor: *The team approached basketball practice with zeal.* Same sign used for: **ambitious, anxious, aspiration, aspire, eager, earnest, enthusiastic, motivation, motive, zealous.**

- ■ [Rubbing the hands together in eagerness] Rub the palms of both *open hands,* palms facing each other, back and forth against each other with a double alternating movement.

zebra *n.* A wild, hoofed mammal related to the horse with a coat characterized by black or dark brown stripes on a light background: *Zebras live in Africa.*

- ■ [Indicates a zebra's stripes] Beginning with the fingertips of both *4 hands* pointing toward each other in front of the chest, palms facing in, pull the hands apart to each side of the chest. Repeat in front of the waist.

zero[1] *n.* The symbol or numeral 0 indicating an absence of any quantity; nothing: *Just remember that zero times any number is still zero.* Same sign used for: **none.**

- ■ [The hand forms a zero to indicate the concept of nothing] Move the right *O hand,* palm facing left, from in front of the chin forward.

zero[2] *n.* See sign for NONE[6].

zigzag

zigzag *n.* **1.** A line or course characterized by a series of sharp turns first to one side and then to another: *ran across the battlefield in a zigzag.* —*v.* **2.** To move on or along a zigzag course: *The car zigzagged down the street.* —*adj.* **3.** Having short, sharp turns: *a zigzag pattern.*

- [Draw a zigzag in the air] Move the extended right index finger, palm facing left and finger pointing forward, back and forth while moving downward in front of the right side of the body.

zip[1] *v.* Same sign as for ZIPPER[1] but formed with a single movement.

zip[2] *v.* Same sign as for ZIPPER[2] but formed with a single movement.

zipper[1] *n.* A fastener for clothing, luggage, etc., consisting of two flexible tracks of teeth or coils that can be interlocked or separated by a slide: *This zipper opens easily.*

- [Mime pulling a zipper up and down] Move the right *modified X hand* up and down with a double movement in front of the chest, palm facing in.

zipper[2] *n.* (alternate sign)

- [Shows the movement of a zipper] Move the palm side of the right *modified X hand* up and down with a double movement on the left *open hand* held in front of the chest, palm facing right and fingers pointing up.

zoom[1] *v.* To move quickly, especially away: *The airplane zoomed off beyond the clouds.* Same sign used for: **abscond, set off, split.**

- [Represents something getting smaller as it goes off into the distance] Beginning with the thumb of the right *G hand,* palm facing forward, at the base of the extended left index finger held in front of the chest, palm facing down and finger pointing right, move the right thumb across the length of the left index finger, closing the right index finger and thumb together as the hand moves to the right.

zoom[2] *v.* See signs for FOCUS[4], SHOOT UP.

American Manual Alphabet

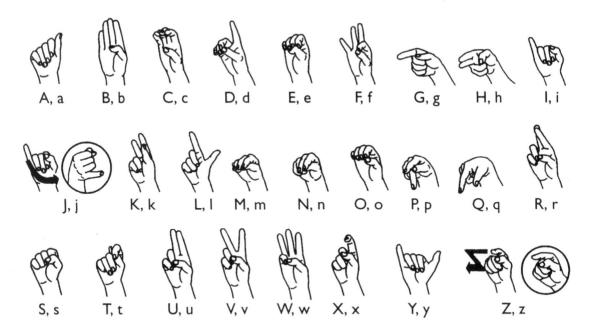

A, a B, b C, c D, d E, e F, f G, g H, h I, i

J, j K, k L, l M, m N, n O, o P, p Q, q R, r

S, s T, t U, u V, v W, w X, x Y, y Z, z

Handshapes

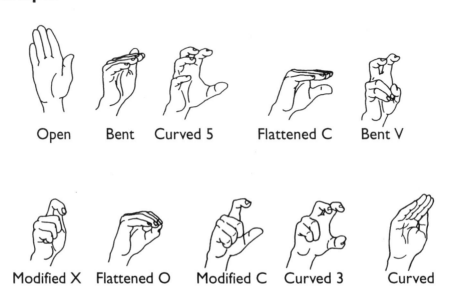

Open Bent Curved 5 Flattened C Bent V

Modified X Flattened O Modified C Curved 3 Curved